GLAMOUR

GLAMOUR

— A HISTORY —

STEPHEN GUNDLE

OXFORD
UNIVERSITY PRESS

OXFORD

UNIVERSITY PRESS

Great Clarendon Street, Oxford OX2 6DP

Oxford University Press is a department of the University of Oxford.
It furthers the University's objective of excellence in research, scholarship,
and education by publishing worldwide in

Oxford New York

Auckland Cape Town Dar es Salaam Hong Kong Karachi
Kuala Lumpur Madrid Melbourne Mexico City Nairobi
New Delhi Shanghai Taipei Toronto

With offices in

Argentina Austria Brazil Chile Czech Republic France Greece
Guatemala Hungary Italy Japan Poland Portugal Singapore
South Korea Switzerland Thailand Turkey Ukraine Vietnam

Oxford is a registered trade mark of Oxford University Press
in the UK and in certain other countries

Published in the United States
by Oxford University Press Inc., New York

© Stephen Gundle 2008

British Library Cataloguing in Publication Data

Data available

Library of Congress Cataloging in Publication Data

Gundle, Stephen, 1956–
Glamour: a history / Stephen Gundle.
p. cm.
Includes bibliographical references and index.
ISBN 978–0–19–921098–5
1. Beauty, Personal—France—History. 2. Beauty, Personal—England—History
3. Beauty, Personal—Social aspects. 4. Fashion—France—History.
5. Fashion—England—History. 6. Fashion—Social aspects. I. Title.
GT499.G86 2008
646.7′2—dc22 2008009772

Typeset by SPI Publisher Services, Pondicherry, India
Printed in Great Britain
on acid-free paper by
Clays Ltd, St Ives plc

ISBN 978–0–19–921098–5

1 3 5 7 9 10 8 6 4 2

For Simona

ACKNOWLEDGEMENTS

I have lost count of the number of conversations I have had about glamour since I first started to reflect on this most elusive yet most obvious of phenomena. Over a good many years, I discussed glamour with friends, colleagues, relatives, and students. At first at least, nearly everyone was happy to talk to me about it and to give me their personal impressions and interpretations. Only occasionally did I meet someone who declared themselves completely uninterested in the topic and immune to its charms. I was glad to encounter such robust rejections of glamour's seductions. They reminded me that it was not impossible to resist the sparkle and dazzle of illusion. But for most people, including myself, glamour was not just make-believe, it was also a source of visual excitement and pleasure. My first discussions about glamour were with Robert Gordon and Nicholas White. I am grateful to both of them for pushing me towards the nine-teenth-century and high-cultural aspects of a phenomenon that, at the time, I was sure was a feature solely of contemporary mass culture. Richard Barraclough, Guido Bonsaver, Rebecca Bonsaver, Stella Bruzzi, Tom Buchanan, Martin Conway, Barbara Corsi, Denise Cripps, Fabrice d'Almeida, Anek Dürig, David Forgacs, Sophie Gilmartin, Paul Ginsborg, Caroline Hollinrake, Claire Honess, Newton Key, Jordan Lancaster, Robert

Lumley, the late Patrick McCarthy, Franco Minganti, Elizabeth Morris, Jonathan Morris, Penny Morris, Anne Mullen, Daniele Nannini, Giuliana Pieri, Katia Pizzi, Veronica Pye, Chris Rigden, Vanessa Roghi, Nina Rothenberg, Sita Trini Castelli, Nicola White, Nikola White, and Susanna Zinato all gave me the benefit of their views or kindly gave reactions to mine. I am grateful to Giulio Lepschy for alerting me at an early stage to the matter of the origins of the word glamour. My sister, Alison Gundle, supplied some important background information and numerous references to mythological and mystical sources. Réka Buckley provided me with helpful advice on the interrelationship of glamour, fashion, and film stardom. Peter Kramer and NoëlleAnne O'Sullivan kindly gave constructive comments on some of my first writings on the theme, while David Ellwood read and provided detailed commentary on an early version of the text. Lucy Riall read part of the manuscript at a later stage and provided me with just the sort of critical stimulus I needed to refine it one final time. Some of the ideas contained here flow from an earlier collaborative project on glamour that I undertook with Clino Castelli, that was in turn partly inspired by Nanni Strada's work with colours and material effects. Pierre Sorlin's observations on the volume that resulted from that collaboration informed my approach in the present work. Simona Storchi was always happy to act as a sounding board during the writing of this volume. She helped me clarify my approach to some issues and also gave me the benefit of her reflections on several issues and personalities. Thanks are also due to the staff of the British Library in London, the Bibliothèque Nationale in Paris, and the Biblioteca Nazionale in Rome, and of the libraries of my former institution, Royal Holloway—University of London, and the Getty Research Institute in Los Angeles. Without the rich resources of these institutions, it would have been impossible to write this book. The patient encouragement of Luciana O'Flaherty and Matthew Cotton at Oxford University Press has ensured that it has been carried through to conclusion.

S.G.

London 2007

CONTENTS

LIST OF PLATES

INTRODUCTION

When he was killed in July 1997, Gianni Versace was hailed worldwide as the master of glitz and glamour. The fashion designer from the tip of the Italian peninsula who had conquered Milan and then the world was one of the best-known names in contemporary fashion. Thanks to eye-catching dresses worn by some of the world's most beautiful women, he had also become a household name. His murder outside his lavishly refurbished villa on Ocean Drive in South Beach, Miami was headline news. News reports and obituaries referred to the brashness and ostentation of his creations, to his love of celebrities and his taste for publicity. It was said that he had established a huge fashion empire by following Oscar Wilde's dictum that nothing succeeds like excess. It was he more than anyone else who turned Claudia Schiffer, Cindy Crawford, Naomi Campbell, and a handful of other fashion models into 'supermodels' and stars. When Elizabeth Hurley, then an unknown minor actress, wore a daring Versace creation to accompany her boyfriend Hugh Grant to the London premiere of *Four Weddings and a Funeral* in 1994, the show-stopping black gown, slashed all the way down the side and joined with gold Medusa-headed safety pins, she attracted front-page coverage in several leading newspapers. For observers worldwide, Versace was the king of glitz, the man who combined beauty with vulgarity. His style catered to those who desired to flaunt their wealth or sex appeal. The press commented on the designer's penchant for opulent beauty, the dramatic, showy nature of his creations, the mingling in his work of street style and high fashion, the heavily sexual element, his flamboyant lifestyle, and professional and personal relationships with the famous. Glamour was the word that recurred most frequently.

In the contemporary media, glamour is a buzzword with a special resonance. *Vogue*, *Elle*, celebrity and women's magazines, not to mention glossy newspaper supplements, all employ the term on a regular basis to underline the allure of an occasion, a dwelling, a product, a place, or a person: 'Hollywood: The Power and the Glamour' (*Vanity Fair*, April 1995); 'Glamour! The people who live it—the clothes that scream it—the make-up that makes it' (*Elle*, December 1996); 'The new glamour burns bright' (*Interview*, March 1997); 'What's glamorous now—the cars, the bags, the shoes, cool cocktails, sexy getaways' (*In Style*, August 2001). Many magazines routinely use the word on their covers while one monthly belonging to the Condé Nast stable published in numerous national editions has it as its title.

As a word, glamour carries talismanic qualities. It has a sparkle and glow about it that enhance the people, objects, and places to which it is attached. Yet, despite the ubiquity of the term, glamour is notoriously difficult to define. Everyone has an idea of what they think it means but few know where it comes from and why it is so tantalizing to so many. Even those who are professionally concerned with its evocation and perpetuation often seem nonplussed when invited to provide more than a throwaway comment about it. When fashion periodicals and women's magazines enquire into the meaning of glamour, seeking a range of opinions from experts and celebrities, the results rarely seem to produce any consensus. When in November 1994 *She* magazine questioned a selection of British male personalities known for having 'a touch of glamour themselves', it received responses that included the following: 'A sense of glamour is something you are born with' (John Fashanu, footballer), 'Glamour is something that comes from within—you've either got it or you haven't' (Marco Pierre White, chef), 'My idea of glamour is someone who is chic, well-groomed, cool, not wearing too much make-up and just an understated elegance' (Robert Kilroy-Silk, television presenter), 'Glamour to me is slightly flashy and sometimes bold' (Paul Costelloe, fashion designer), 'Glamour is not about glitz, red lips and big breasts. It is about being quietly sensuous, knowing your face and figure can make a statement with the rest of your look played down. It's not just about figure-hugging dresses, more the way you wear them' (Nicky Clarke, hairdresser). According to these views, glamour can be showy or understated, a purely exterior phenomenon or a fact of personality. The only point of which all agree is that it is a quality attaching to persons that is instantly perceptible to those who encounter it.

Glamour is often presented as a quality mainly attaching to women. Whether it can apply to all women or only to a select few is, however, a moot point. For some, glamour is an aesthetic cloak ready for every woman who is willing to dress up in a uniform of high heels, coiffed hair, bold red lipstick, strong make-up, and vibrant colours, regardless of her age or position. For others it is a personal attribute of more limited application, something that accrues over a period of time to women who gradually acquire the personal characteristics and aesthetic traits of the recognized figure of glamour. This dichotomy is constantly played out in the press and other media. On the one hand film stars, models, millionaires' wives, pop music performers, and many other people basking in the glow of wealth and success are held up as examples of a fabulously exciting and irresistibly envious lifestyle. Glossy magazines featuring spreads on the glamorous homes and glamorous wardrobes of beautiful people who have glamorous jobs and lives conjure up a world that is familiar as fantasy but utterly removed from the daily lives of average people. The realm of glamour is a universe inhabited by the very wealthy, the talented, the beautiful, the famous, and the lucky. On the other hand, magazine articles, books, and television programmes continually spell out how every woman can glamorize herself. The winter 1997 issue of the house magazine of the British department store chain Debenhams promised readers 'top-to-toe glamour in minutes' by illustrating 'the look—the style—the difference'. These were conveniently divided on the basis of the time required for their assembly: 15 minutes, 30 minutes, and 60 minutes.

Guides of this type are nothing new. In 1938, *Glamour and How to Achieve It* by a now forgotten actress called Sali Löbel claimed that 'glamour is not the elusive pimpernel attainable only through the god of riches.... It is easy to attain at least *some* of it, if not all of it, and half a loaf is better than none.'[1] The author distinguished between what she called 'photographic glamour', that was the achievement of cinema, and 'the glamour of reality' that was available to all women if they followed her regime of exercise and diet, dressed and made up in a way that highlighted their best features and disguised their worst, and adopted the right determined and positive attitude to life. Of course, the more prosaic glamour of reality was informed and driven by the dazzling images of photographic glamour.

Recipes like this show that glamour is uniquely appealing as a source of self-definition and even empowerment. The trappings of glamour—make-up, clothes, accessories, etc.—give everyone a chance in theory of defying the effects of age and the limitations of the physical body. Through them, a dream version of the self can be forged. Glamour is a weapon and a protective coating, a screen on which an exterior personality can be built to deceive, delight, and bewitch. It is apparently egalitarian; more than any notion of natural beauty, it is an ideal that almost anyone can share.[2] In an effort to pin down glamour, the editor-in-chief of *Interview* magazine asked a drag artist for a description of this elusive effect. In reply, he said: 'On a gray day, the view from my window is ugly, so I turn and face my closet, which is full of makeup and clothes. I see my feather fans, all my jewelry, and I either put some of it on or pretend it's already on.... You know, you have to make your own glamour, but that's what's so great about it—you can.'[3]

The element of pretend or make-believe is a crucial part of the illusion of glamour. Sali Löbel urged her readers always to retain the power to dream. 'Dreaming is good—it beautifies,' she declared.[4] Dreams provide the bridge between everyday reality and the fabulous world of the magazines. They embody commonplace yearnings and our hopes. These may be individual and specific to each of us in the form they take. However, this does not mean that glamour is the product of individual taste or personality. Rather it is a visual effect that is most commonly created by costume or fashion designers, hairdressers, press agents, and photographers. The same designers and hairdressers who create the looks of the stars lend their names to products that are advertised on television, in the press, and on billboards. Indeed it is often the desire to sell to a mass public that leads a designer to seek the endorsement of a star and it is why such endorsements or testimonials are often paid at fabulous rates. As such, they are powerful mediators of the collective imagination. Our fantasies and dreams of escape are part and parcel of the commercial world; they sustain it and are continually stimulated by it.

The fascination with a man like Gianni Versace was related to his mastery of the mysterious and magical arts of glamorous transformation. He was a modern Merlin with the power to make dreams come true. The unstated promise of every Versace catwalk show and of every multi-page Versace advertising spread was that the man who had created the supermodels and who, by the loan of one dress, turned Elizabeth Hurley from an unknown actress into one of the sexiest and best-known women in the United Kingdom, could do the same for any woman and, even, since the label also did menswear, any man too. The lavish window displays of Versace stores on London's Bond Street, Rodeo Drive in Los Angeles, and Via Montenapoleone in Milan confirmed that the brashest and sexiest garments in the world could be bought by anyone. The only stumbling blocks were cost and also, perhaps, a fear of not being equal to the physical ideal the designer propagated in his advertisements. The price tags on Versace's ready-to-wear clothes were eye-wateringly steep and the models stunningly attractive. For most, therefore, his creations remained tantalizingly out of reach. But this too was part of the glamour. What was accessible and ostensibly available was also exclusive. Conveniently, there were also ranges of products that, while still premium-priced, came more within the realm of possibilities of the average shopper, including diffusion-line garments, fragrances, eyewear, shoes, watches, scarves, and umbrellas. Löbel's 'half a loaf' could also be achieved—people were induced to believe—by buying commodities such as these, which were endowed with a diluted form of the magic.

In my view, glamour is best seen as an alluring image that is closely related to consumption. It is an enticing and seductive vision that is designed to draw the eye of an audience. It consists of a retouched or perfected representation of someone or something whose purpose it is to dazzle and seduce whoever gazes on it. While a certain confidence and an extrovert personality may assist the elaboration of a glamorous personal image, glamour derives from something other than those qualities. More important is the social or professional milieu with which someone is associated. People are selected and groomed to be glamorous, but usually their glamour derives in large part from the role they or their image plays in the strategy of seduction and persuasion of an industry, a medium, or an institution. The subjects of glamour are very varied. They may be people, things, places, events, or environments, any of which can capture the imagination by association with a range of qualities, including several or all of the following: beauty, sexuality, theatricality, wealth, dynamism, notoriety, movement, and leisure. The more of these that are present, the more glamorous the result and the more successful the image is likely to be in arousing wonder and envy among those who see it.[5]

I have written this book to try and get to the heart of what glamour is and what it has meant to women and to men. My decision to write a history of glamour is justified by the fact that the history of this phenomenon is one of its least understood aspects. In preparing this book, I came across references to the glamour of ancient Egyptian pharaohs and to Nefertiti, the glamour of the princely courts of the Renaissance and royal courts, especially that of the Sun King, Louis XIV. References to the glamour of the aristocracy of all periods were commonplace, as were modern complaints about the glamorization of crime, prostitution, and drug addiction.[6] I even found a reference to the glamour of monastic life, although quite what was meant by this I do not know.

It is often assumed that glamour is regal or high class in origin. By contrast, I argue that neither monarchy nor the aristocracy was the principal originator or social bearer of glamour. Although monarchs, courts, and aristocrats offered examples of luxurious living and high style, it was the fabrication of these by the emergent men and women of the bourgeois era, by the new rich and commercial establishments and the world of entertainment that was glamorous. In my view, glamour is a quintessentially modern phenomenon. Important inputs came from the lower reaches of society as well as the top. The elite of capitalist society acquired glamour because it was self-created; its exclusivity was relative, not absolute. In the context of an expanding commercial culture, a shared language of allure consisting of materialism, beauty, and theatricality was forged with contributions from various actors from the higher and the lower echelons of society. Its polyvalent appeals meant that it captured the imagination in an age when deference was giving way to democracy. Glamour contained the promise of a mobile and commercial society that anyone could be transformed into a better, more attractive, and wealthier version of themselves.

As a word, it was first given prominence in English in 1805 when Walter Scott employed it in his poem *The Lay of the Last Minstrel* to mean a magical power capable of making ordinary people, dwellings, and places seem like magnificent versions of themselves. That the term should have been coined by a solicitor's son was not casual. It was precisely this power that the men and women of the middle ranks sought as they acquired wealth and social influence. If glamour could turn frogs into princes then it could surely turn a bourgeois into a stylish gentleman, a provincial writer into a splendid figure of romance, a woman of dubious virtue into a society beauty. Glamour involved a mixture of qualities, some of which had been at one time the near exclusive prerogative of the aristocracy. Others were born from the market, from the particular cultural configuration of the bourgeoisie, from the new patterns of consensus and social integration that, with difficulty, were taking shape in urban environments, and from the world of entertainment. Glamour was a function not of aristocratic social influence but of the dreams of commercial society. It was not a property of the well-born or well-bred and there was no such thing as pure or off-the-market glamour. It had no prior existence before becoming commodified and commercialized.[7] The dreams of consumers included, of course, fantasies of social promotion and of self-aggrandizement. But the advent of bourgeois society did not result simply in the aura of aristocracy passing intact to the new class or even to selected members of it. Glamour was a result of the release on to the market of the possessions, heritage, prerogatives, styles, and practices of the aristocracy and of the appropriation and manipulation of these by commercial forces and other actors in the urban environment.

The conversion of royal and aristocratic magnificence into modern glamour occurred as a result of the spread of manufactured commodities, the growth of large cities dominated by widespread anonymous socialization, the replacement of hereditary privileges by meritocracy, the transformation of the urban mob into a modern public, and the development of the press and advertising. It is clear that these developments all were the result of larger processes of economic and political change. These included the end of absolutism and rise of popular sovereignty, the Industrial Revolution and the birth of modern consumption, a transformation of sexual mores, and the emergence of a dominant system of values in which deferred gratification rather than the immediate satisfaction of wants was the norm.[8] The last change is important because it fuelled a process of yearning that sustained an entire culture of dreams. Cultural enterprises sprang up to supply material in the form of novels, periodicals, illustrations, plays, and public entertainments that both provided vicarious satisfactions and channelled desires towards consumption. Consumption and entertainment invariably flourished in areas close to centres of wealth and power and from the early nineteenth century they acquired an allure as tourist sights, places of style and opulence, and homes to all that was modern and fashionable. Such areas became places of fleeting impressions, of encounters with people of unknown provenance. They were labyrinths, or places of riddle, which created forms of social interaction and of fame and celebrity in their own right. In such places, seductive appearances had great currency.[9] As the middle class asserted its influence, its members desired to establish their pre-eminent status and communicate it to their fellow men. One way of doing this was through the assertion of virtue and through differentiated gender roles that consigned women to the home. Another way was by establishing status markers by means of material display. Mostly, this was modulated in such a way as to conform to bourgeois values. For example, the domestic environment was often given priority in the construction of luxury.[10] Attention was also paid to the reform of public places and to the development of the public good. However, in contexts in which the aristocracy conserved social pre-eminence or in which an earlier generation of bourgeois had established its pseudo-aristocratic domination, the main way in which a bid for entry was made was through material competition. The new elite appropriated the cultural heritage of the past through collection and imitation and publicized the fruits of its pecuniary power. Although aristocrats offered examples of luxurious living and high style, it was the fabrication of these by the new rich and by stores and the theatre that was properly glamorous. Popular theatre and spectacle appropriated and re-elaborated signs of exterior success and allure. In the nineteenth century public opinion came to be dominated by the press and publishing, which were increasingly commercialized and permeated by advertising. Public debate was accompanied by forms of consensus that privileged acclamation and applause while publicity created imitation forms of prestige and of staged display of 'showy pomp'.[11] It offered excitement and distraction to build an atmosphere of consent.

The key to the processes whereby glamour took shape as a language of allure and seduction in capitalist society lies in the radically different set of views and values that the bourgeoisie held with respect to the aristocracy. In its formative phase, bourgeois culture developed a moral critique of the aristocracy that was directed not only at its undeserved privileges but at its debauchery, artificiality, and wastage. This was informed by a distinctive set of attitudes and beliefs. The bourgeois was not a man of grand appetites, seigneurial arrogance, or flamboyant dress. He worked for his living and—before the mid-nineteenth century—did not display his material wealth ostentatiously. He was serious and puritanical. His wife and family similarly adopted an ethic of modesty and deferred gratification. In contrast to the refinements of courtly dress and self-presentation, naturalness and simplicity were preferred in matters of appearance.

The bourgeois ethic of deferred gratification was related to its attitude towards sexuality. The aristocratic custom of discreet sexual freedom for both men and women after the production of children was rejected in favour of sexual abstinence before marriage and fidelity during it. This produced two effects: first a rigid distinction between respectable and non-respectable that was mainly but by no means exclusively applied to women and, second, a series of desires and yearnings that were deflected on to consumption and entertainment. Commercial establishments attracted attention and persuaded through suggestions of sex and excess. Merchants and retail pioneers drew heavily on showmanship, magic, and religion. Although many goods were sold on the basis of their practical utility, luxury goods relied heavily on the ideas that were associated with them, in particular the promise of magical transformation or instant escape from the constraints of everyday life. Theatres too offered dazzling spectacles of colour, excess, and excitement. These provided sensory delights and moments of imaginative transport. They also created platforms for actresses to act out dramatic transgressions of bourgeois norms. By abrogating to themselves regal prerogatives in matters of morality, they occupied a terrain that served as a safety valve for societal impulses. Thus a parallel culture existed of sensuous pleasure, of noise, excess, distraction. Publicity campaigns and store displays offered scenarios of social promotion, escape, and pleasure. These appeals provoked some hostile reactions, especially in countries of Protestant religion. However, sex appeal was often knowing, ironic, or self-referential. It signalled the appeal of the performer and her need to be desired by, and available to, a paying audience.

In several ways, the culture of the bourgeois era was a culture of image-making, of masks and appearances. Creating and maintaining appearances was essential to the bolstering of status, to selling goods, and to providing entertainment. The impact of theatricality on social life, and the consequent importance of the theatre itself, provided unique opportunities for self-invention. Theatres were the site of a visual interplay between performers—who drew their status from their beauty, extravagance, and notoriety—privileged spectators in the boxes, and the mass of playgoers. Audiences looked to the theatre for imaginative stimulus and guides to modern patterns of conduct. They took fashion cues from the stage and followed the exciting personal narratives that performers wove from their roles on and off the stage.

Glamorous people belonged to the world of representation, where play-acting and fakery were commonplace. The political sphere provided a platform for some colourful and unconventional personalities who seemed to make their own rules. The British Conservative Benjamin Disraeli wove a personal mythology around himself that found expression in his dandyism and mastery of language.[12] The Italian adventurer Giuseppe Garibaldi had a huge impact on the public, especially outside his native land; his striking physical appearance, dramatic life, and exotic costumes exercised a sensual persuasion on the crowds who saw or read about him.[13] However, the human bearers of glamour are most frequently women. Courtesans were among the first fully glamorous personalities. In their playful appropriation of the characteristics of the lady, these flamboyant and luxurious sex objects set themselves up as society figures and pioneers of consumption. In contrast to respectable women, they were rarely tastefully attired or restrained. They were showy and eye-catching in an obvious and sexual way. Glamour is excessive and abundant and it strikes the imagination by bypassing the commonly accepted bourgeois sense of moderation and measure. It is not elaborate style so much as a popularization of style that everyone can understand. It mixes the appeals of class and sleaze in a way that produces unsettling effects that, for its audiences, are predominantly pleasurable.

Glamour took shape as a series of attractions deriving from a variety of sources. It was driven by personalities, both real and fictional, who broke the bounds of convention and configured themselves as exceptional, unusual, and compelling. It was also sustained by lifestyles of great material wealth. Among the qualities that contributed to its functioning were some that were powerful on their own. For example, beauty was a critical feature that would retain over time its centrality in all elaborations of glamour. Beauty of men and especially of women has historically been prized and it possesses intrinsic powers of attraction and persuasion.[14] In commercial society, beauty became an accepted channel of social mobility for women and the selection and presentation of beauty soon became a business. This was not the only catalyst of interest. As its economic and political power declined, the men of the aristocracy competed with those of the bourgeoisie to secure the most beautiful women as wives and lovers. Indeed, there was a triangular competition involving aristocracy, the bourgeoisie, and the world of entertainment. Feminine beauty was an example of a quality that was not limited by social class either in its supply or in its appreciation. Although different classes, regions, and ethnic groups established preferred ideal qualities that varied slightly over time, in essence beauty crosses barriers and draws the eye of all. Beauty was often blended with specific values of commercial society such as fashionableness, expensiveness, and fame. The glamorous woman was not usually drawn from the upper ranks but from humble or unidentified milieux. Indeed, two patterns of mobility may be identified as typical: vertical mobility involving ascent from the lower reaches of society by means of talent, luck, or sexual favours, and horizontal mobility or geographical displacement. The woman of glamour was often a foreigner who was seen to encapsulate some particular spirit like French eroticism, Latin passion, or Eastern exoticism. In both cases, there was ample opportunity for the construction of dream-inducing narratives about the subject's rise from poverty, her mysterious origins, or her varied life experiences.

The physical body has always been a factor in glamour. It is a project or canvas on which a variety of socially significant meanings may be inscribed. The female body carried special connotations for societies that practised sexual repression. It was a source of fantasies that could be deployed to excite interest, sell goods, and provide entertainment. The male body was not a tool in the same way, although, appropriately costumed and represented, it could nonetheless act as a vehicle for fantasies and dreams. The sexualization of clothes, furnishings, and interiors was one of the central features of consumer culture as it took shape in the nineteenth century. Although the shopper, even at that time, was most likely to be a woman, the particular functions of allegory, metaphor, and desirability conventionally ascribed to the female sex ensured that femininity rather than masculinity supplied the visual imagery of commodity culture. The feminine image aroused particular desires that suited it well to associations with commodities and advertising.[15] The growing visibility of alluring women provided a resource for store display, the periodical market, and the theatre as well as painters, photographers, and the nascent advertising industry. All of these participated in the bringing together of commodities and the erotic.

The use of female allure to tease and to tempt, at once offering and withholding gratification, points to the oxymoronic qualities of glamour. Sleazy elegance, accessible exclusivity, democratic elitism: these are just three of the ostensibly incompatible pairings that lie at its core. The logical incongruity of these helped fuel illusions and deceive people about the hierarchical reality of social relations. In this way, glamour played an important role in the creation and maintenance of a given pattern of power. Its function was bound up with the expansion of publicity and the press. The newspapers and magazines were vital in fuelling interest in the activities and appearances of an elite that aroused envy and did not disdain the flashbulb and the narrative of the printed page. The alluring image became increasingly important as the mass media developed. Illustrated magazines and, later, cinema and radio provided opportunities for staging, representing, and inventing people, events, and commodities. For this reason they were seized on by the new retail and cultural industries. The media lifted glamour out of specific contexts and made it into a generalized, everyday experience parallel to regular life.[16]

Glamorous people are not rooted but rather are constantly on the move. Images and suggestions from remote periods and places have often informed glamour and the specific imagery of movement and travel has also been important. To be on the move, almost nomadic, is often a feature of the person of glamour. The mode of transport is not in itself always significant, although the shorter the distance and the more familiar the place to be reached, the more important other values are to render the movement interesting or enviable. Travelling in style, in rare or luxurious means of transport, was suggestive both before and after the advent of mass tourism. But the allure of glamorous travel derives mostly from two things. First, from travel that is more frequent than average, indicating leisure and means; second, from the tension between recognition and unfamiliarity. That is to say, in order to resonate, places should have been heard of but should not have been widely visited;[17] they should carry a narrative deriving from suggestions that have entered the popular consciousness. The speed of travel is not particularly important, but a fast pace of movement, whether or not in a competitive environment, often arouses interest and envy.

The representation of travel is often related to fame. At least three dynamics of the social and economic system fuelled a culture of fame that became extensive in modern society. First, there was the dynamic of social mobility. With an established hierarchical order having been smashed open, various channels were opened for the elevation of outsiders to one or more elites. Second, there was the dynamic of novelty. A fluid and constantly evolving economy needed novelty; new personalities were as necessary as new fashions. The thrust of renewal constantly demanded new objects, styles, faces, and stories. Third, competition between forms of entertainment

13

and, within a sector like theatre, between different companies, fuelled publicity campaigns. All three were sustained by the press and by travel, that with the development of communications and technology became one of the key features of the glamorous personality. Glamorous people 'arrived', they 'made entrances', and they were careful not to tire the public by remaining on view for too long at a time.

Distance is a necessary factor in the maintenance of glamour.[18] It serves to conceal or disguise the aspects of a person's being that are not glamorous. We generally see the glamorous personality they way they want us to see them. At most, we may be allowed glimpses of a process of glamorous transformation; almost never of de-glamorization. For this reason, no one we know intimately can be glamorous for us. Some form of separation or stage is required to stimulate interest. Modern society created all manner of such separations, from the theatrical stage or the bar to delineations between private and public. Glamour is experienced at one remove and sometimes, in the age of the media, at several removes, through magazine articles, photographs, performances, and films. It belongs to the realm of representation not knowledge.

The relationship between fashion and glamour is a complex one. One enduring feature of glamour is its identification with fashion, but it is not always clear which aspects of 'fashion' are glamorous. Is it the latest designer collections, the presentation of those collections, or the representation of that presentation in the media? Or is it something else entirely, such as the perceived lifestyle of designers and models or particular garments or types of garment? If it is all of these things then the two terms are synonymous, but parts even of the visible universe of fashion are distinct from, and perhaps are above, glamour. In an analysis of fashion photography, one author found that in the fashion press 'glamour' was contrasted with 'sophistication'. While the latter was poised, controlled, and upmarket, the former was extrovert, youthful, dynamic, pleasure-seeking, voluble, gregarious, short-term, uncultured, volatile, public, and downmarket.[19] Such a sharp distinction can be questioned, but it highlights how the qualities associated with glamour can simultaneously be 'out of fashion' (if, say, a sophisticated style is in vogue) and at the same time refer to the key structural aspects of the fashion industry milieu. In any event, glamour is often about excess. It is always *more* than average: more showy, more visible, more beautiful, more sexy, more rich.[20] In consequence, a varied wardrobe, preferably comprised of expensive and fashionable garments, is a sure way to capture interest. However, the role of dress can be overemphasized in glamour. More significant is the general context or the way in which a particular garment or style is worn and publicized, the people these are associated with, and the fantasies with which publicity invests them. Outside of this framework, clothes are often of even more ephemeral interest than the glamorous effects to whose realization they contribute.

Despite their prominence, members of the glamorous elite do not normally hold any political power or institutional role. The fact that they are mostly women also serves to distance them from the formal structures of power. But in economic terms they are significant and influential. They are vehicles of dreams who communicate with the public. Unlike some of the stylish upper-class and artistic figures of the past, who were interested only in impressing a small coterie, the glamorous personality is always performing for an audience, without whose envy or admiration he or she would not exist. Such people live for the publicity that turns them into objects of mass curiosity and individual fantasy. Glamour simply cannot exist without mass involvement. Not even the most interesting, sexy, and fashionable person can be glamorous without venturing into the public realm and winning attention.

The professionally glamorous are often seen to embody the sort of personal qualities that are identified with glamour itself—particularly by those who see it as an adjunct of personality. They are regal, self-centred, confident, polished, and poised. If they have accumulated experience and acquired the patina of a narrative, then they are also configured as survivors. 'Joan Collins has stood the test of time better than all her contemporaries, deftly side-stepping those familiar showbiz levellers such as substance abuse, weight problems and a fickle public, and fairly routing the worst foe of all—age,' reported the magazine *Live Wire* in August–September 1996:

She has beaten Hollywood and emerged radiant from courtroom dramas and ill-fated romances. She is the last true pre-Sixties revolution diva who walks it like she talks it, the sole survivor of a generation of studio-bred actresses for whom opulence and ostentation were not only a right, but a duty to their public. Big jewels, big furs and big hair were the hallmarks of stardom then, and, in a world where glamour is sorely lacking, today's public wants Joan more than ever.[21]

The survivor, who is almost always a big star, is one bearer of glamour. However, for every survivor there are legions of the once-glamorous who have learned the hard way that the quality is not a permanent attribute linked to personality. It can be lost or simply fade as those who have it get old, hit hard times, or lose favour with the public. For example, few occupations are as glamorous as those of model or film actor. Yet all models and many actors are launched with what may be described as inbuilt obsolescence. Their glamour derives almost solely from the publicity in which the industries of fashion and cinema are drenched and from their commercial power. To some extent, the very anonymity of routine performers allows the glamorous image of their contexts to shine through unchallenged. It was no different a century ago. The showgirls of the popular theatre of the late nineteenth and early twentieth century were anonymous, rootless young women who inhabited symbolic spaces with special connotations. Only by donning feathers, sequins, and furs to seduce and enchant their audience did they become glamorous. Dazzled by their gloss and sparkle, the public did not realize that the image of the showgirl was an artificial contrivance behind which there was hard work, regimentation, and humiliation. While the processes of recruitment to such roles was often publicized, little or nothing was said about the process of selection that weeded out those deemed too old or ill to continue. It took the occasional personal tragedy for people to see that glamour was a system rather than a personal attribute and to reassure ordinary people that maybe it is better to dream about it than actually to live it. Such events show that there is a price to be paid for being blessed with the good fortune to enter the magic realm of the rich and beautiful.

The history presented here is not limited to any specific country. Because the nature of glamour is international, its history needs to be examined in relation to a range of countries and situations. I have chosen to focus on

Britain, France, the United States, and, to a lesser extent, Italy. Although it would certainly be possible to consider the role of glamour in other countries, the privileged place occupied in my investigation of these countries is justified by the decisive contribution they have made to the history of glamour since at least the nineteenth century. The sources I have employed are numerous and varied. They include novels, memoirs, films, photographs, paintings and portraits, biographies and autobiographies, and the press. I have also made ample use of many excellent studies that treat single aspects of the complex phenomenon under examination. To a large extent, this book is a work of synthesis. It maps the origins of glamour and investigates the forms that it took in the nineteenth and twentieth centuries. Attention is paid to the men and, mainly, the women who have embodied glamour, from Napoleon and Lord Byron to the fictional creations of Walter Scott, from the Paris courtesans to Marlene Dietrich, Marilyn Monroe, Jacqueline Kennedy, Princess Diana, and Paris Hilton. The role of writers, journalists, artists, photographers, film-makers, and fashion designers is explored as well as occupations like the model and the air stewardess, cities and resorts such as Paris, New York, and Monte Carlo, and products including planes and luxury cars that have been associated in the public mind with the magical aura of glamour. The book captures the excitement and sex appeal of glamour while exposing its mechanisms and exploring its sleazy and sometimes tragic underside. Its purpose is to provide a first full-length account of something that all too often is considered to have the consistency and significance of candyfloss but which I believe to be significant enough to merit analysis.

Glamour is not to everyone's taste. Even the diehard devotee can find that, like chocolate or heavy perfume, a surfeit is nauseating. For some, the large dose of glamour served up in this volume may provoke a similar reaction. By contrast, it is my hope that readers will be intrigued by my investigation of the extraordinary mixture of themes, periods, personalities, places, and events that make up the history of this evanescent and seductive phenomenon.

CHAPTER 1

GLAMOUR AND MODERNITY

B etween the 1770s and 1830s, the American and French revolutions, combined with the ideas they championed of liberty and equality, heralded the birth of the modern age. The triumph and collapse of the Napoleonic Empire, together with the spread of industrialization, the development of the commodity culture, and the growth of public opinion, all contributed to far-reaching innovations in patterns of rule and of consent. In an age of turbulence and change, many old certainties were shaken, the position of social classes was redefined, and a variety of new men drawn not from the aristocracy but from the minor nobility and the middle ranks came to the fore. In culture, Romanticism captured the contradictory impulses of the period through highly imaginative works that expressed yearnings for some remote and rich past or escape into alluring alternatives from a world that was increasingly seen as mundane and bourgeois.

Among the many novelties of the period was the birth of glamour, understood as an imaginative synthesis of wealth, beauty, and notoriety that was enviable and imitable rather than a hereditary prerogative. Glamour was not, as has sometimes been argued or more often casually assumed, a timeless phenomenon. While many different rulers from ancient Egypt to Louis XIV, as well as wider elite groups, had made splendour and aesthetic refinement their vocation, the particular configuration of qualities that are associated with glamour had not existed before and nor had the pattern of social relations that underpinned it and gave it meaning. Glamour was not only about magnificence, which the politician and theorist Edmund Burke referred to in his treatise on the sublime and the beautiful as 'a great profusion of things which are splendid or valuable in themselves'.[1] Rather it involved the superb injection of fantasy into public rituals and consumption practices, and arose from the opportunities that these supplied for possible or imaginary transformations of the self. It was the market and industrial production on the one hand, and equality and the erosion of structured deference on the other, that formed the basis of the diffusion of glamour.

Glamour was born in a context in which the bourgeoisie was contesting many of the hereditary privileges of the aristocracy and in which society was becoming more open than before. However, even though it was losing power, the traditional aristocracy still defined many features of the desirable lifestyle. It had for centuries enjoyed a near monopoly over style, beauty, fashion, luxury, and even fame. Even after the French Revolution and the rise and fall of Napoleon, and beyond the period of the restoration well into the twentieth century, some members of the aristocracy preserved their wealth and status. As a class it conserved social and cultural influence by offering a template for the new men and women who now came to the fore, made fortunes, or occupied the public limelight. Glamour was about the way in which the most visually striking manifestations of aristocratic privilege were taken over and reinvented by newly emergent people, groups, and institutions. This occurred in several realms including the political sphere, the modern city, consumption and lifestyles, and theatre. Commodity culture provided a key channel for this process of appropriation which did not simply take the form of imitation. Rather it occurred in ways that reflected the system of values and culture of the bourgeoisie and its particular imaginative world. This caused problems for rulers and the manner in which they were accustomed to appear to the public, but it also presented them with some challenges. For figures from the cultural sphere and the commercial world, by contrast, these developments only opened up glittering opportunities.

Glamour did not emerge suddenly as an identifiable phenomenon. In fact the word itself, although it entered the English language in the early nineteenth century, was not widely used until the early twentieth century. Its origins are bound up with the complex process whereby the transition occurred from aristocratic to bourgeois society. In this chapter, these origins will be explored with particular reference to France and Great Britain. The former is important for two reasons: first, because the Revolution and the rise and fall of Napoleon were the great events of the age that profoundly shaped politics and culture across the Continent and beyond. Second, because France retained, with only a brief interruption, the international pre-eminence it had established under Louis XIV in matters of luxury and style. Britain is significant for other reasons. The aristocracy was still the dominant class but, because the country had experienced a revolution of its own a century and a half previously, merchants, business people, and professionals already had a certain role that, with the Industrial Revolution, was expanding rapidly. It also gave rise to the specific imaginative forms that came to be identified with glamour. Walter Scott, one of the key architects of the fabulous dream world that was to establish itself in this period as a feature of bourgeois culture, and the man who brought the word 'glamour' into the English language, was convinced that, in the new world taking shape after the revolutionary upheavals, English literature would have a unique imaginative role to play in Europe.[2]

Glamour required a certain dynamism and flexibility in the economy and social system that were not present in pre-revolutionary France. Rather a static system of privilege combined with economic mismanagement exacerbated the institutionalized gulf between the most stylish court in Europe and a working population that was starving for lack of bread. The royal residence at Versailles had been built by Louis XIV after the Frondist protests had left him feeling unsafe in Paris. He had pursued a policy of magnificence and style to affirm a status gap between royalty and the court on the one hand and the rest of the population on the other.[3] He tied a fractious and

20

disputatious nobility to the throne by demanding their presence at court, a demand which forced them to spend lavishly and reinforced their dependency on royal favour. The development of luxury also served to establish the pre-eminence of the French court in Europe and to promote French fine goods abroad.

Historians have not hesitated to describe some courts as glamorous. Reference has been made to the desire of nobles in seventeenth-century Vienna and London to match 'the glamour of the monarch's residence'.[4] Renaissance princes have been described as making their courts 'more inviting and glamorous' and the court of Louis XIV has been seen as having 'exclusive glamor'.[5] Indeed, the Sun King has been said to have had a 'program for redefining France as the land of luxury and glamour'.[6] The use of this term communicates to readers something of the fabulous and dazzling facade projected by the courts, and especially that of Versailles and its creator. Yet none of them was glamorous. The French court did not seek to cultivate a dynamic of imitation within France or draw in the bourgeoisie. Everything about Louis XIV's court was stylized and governed by protocol but any desire to impress or set a trend was either directed inwards (Louis began a fashion for wearing red heels, for example, that was widely copied by courtiers) or was aimed at the king's fellow sovereigns and their diplomatic representatives at court.[7] No self-respecting monarch would have made the impact on public opinion a priority, although pomp may have had the incidental effect of provoking awe or admiration in crowds.[8] One of the flashiest courts in history, that of the Medici in Florence, used magnificence precisely to disguise the ruling family's bourgeois origins and assert its sovereignty.[9] In general, it was the liturgical element at the heart of theatrical ceremonials which gave them meaning and that was far more important than the display of material opulence.[10] In short, courts became centres of wealth, style, and display in order to communicate grandeur and magnificence or to establish legitimacy. Their luxury could be refined and sophisticated; but it was not systematically displayed to the people and still less was it intended to arouse their envy. But there were contradictions in the adoption of material splendour, for this practice shifted the emphasis in monarchy towards wealth and things that could be obtained for money.

Unlike glamour, which was about image, magnificence involved the massive accumulation of treasures and luxuries as a right. It fuelled business and sometimes exports, but it had drawbacks. By the end of the Sun King's reign, a huge national debt was undermining the economy and fuelling resentment at the splendid style of the court. His great-grandson and successor, Louis XV, did little to promote reform or correct systematic abuses. The neglect of agriculture, which was one consequence of the absenteeism of French nobility from their estates and their confinement within the glittering cage of Versailles, persisted. With his notorious indecisiveness and timidity in policy matters, Louis XV has been labelled 'the least estimable of the Bourbon kings' and the 'chief gravedigger of the ancien regime'.[11] He played the part of an imperial king but, unlike the great showman who preceded him, he was not fond of his public duties and hated making public appearances. Some brushes with the discontent of his people, including an assassination attempt in 1757, led him to bury himself further in the cocoon of Versailles. Over time, life in this splendid palace isolated the king from public opinion in ways that would prove fatal to the Bourbon dynasty.

By the late eighteenth century, the conventional pattern of deference was fast crumbling and the material emphasis of the Bourbons was a contributory factor. No French king had to face more public dissent than Louis XVI. Thousands came to present petitions and angry marches to Versailles brought the king and queen into brusque contact with popular discontent. A particular victim of the growing disenchantment with the monarchy was the king's Austrian-born wife, Marie Antoinette, who was made the scapegoat of the situation. When the Revolution exploded in 1789 it was the high point of a long process of change to ideas, customs, and institutions that touched the entire social, moral, and cultural order of society. Such was the force of popular anger that the royals were forced to flee those who held them responsible for the economic disaster into which the country had fallen. The lavish lifestyle of the court was forcefully targeted by the mob. Far from being a seductive means of binding people to the monarchy, it fuelled bitter resentment at embedded and extreme privilege. Although it may have been apocryphal, the claim that Marie Antoinette dismissed protest about the lack of bread with the injunction to 'Let them eat cake' seemed a plausible reflection of a situation in which the court lived in an utterly different way from the bulk of the French people.[12]

In fact, some modern ideas penetrated court society. Versailles in the 1780s was still a dazzling centre of luxury and cultish ritual, but Louis XIV's successors were less keen on presenting a dazzling mask to the world. They lacked his taste for the ostentatious display of power and they were less personally interested in asserting the divine right of kings through magnificence and obsessive ritualization of all the king's daily acts and bodily functions. The court remained a huge structure that was larger and more costly to run than the government, but court ceremonials were in decline before the Bourbon monarchy was toppled and some prevailing ideas about personal privacy were gaining currency. Louis XV carved out a private space for himself away from the court surrounded only by a small circle. His grandson and heir, too, was a man of quite simple tastes who had little of the grand manner of a monarch.[13] Even Marie Antoinette, who was castigated for her extravagance and wasteful luxury, indulged in the eighteenth-century taste for pastoral simplicity. Royalty no longer seemed like a race apart as some forms of exclusivity relating especially to material goods and celebrity became more available and circulated more freely. Indeed they increasingly came to be seen and ordinary and subject to criticism. These views found an echo well over a century later in the writings of the Austrian author Stefan Zweig, who suggested in a biography written in the 1930s that his compatriot Marie Antoinette was a mediocre woman who merely play-acted at being queen. She was, he argued, 'a tepid creature, an average woman' and 'nothing more than a lay-figure decked out in queen's robes'.[14] One of his reasons for making this claim was the keen interest that the queen took in the frivolities of fashion. Like Louis XV's mistress Madame de Pompadour, who was a bourgeois outsider with a marked taste for material objects, interiors, and decor,[15] the queen did not disdain the influences of the city of Paris, which had a life of its own that produced personalities, novelties, and trends that on occasion permeated the court. Far from being regal and remote, she enjoyed gossip and the excitement of novelty. Yet this still does not mean that there was a fruitful exchange between court and city at this time. Although the queen was drawn to fun and ostentation, access to the French court was very restricted. While 30 per cent of the 558 individuals who were presented between 1783 and 1788 came from families who had not been there before, most of the newer nobles and all the bourgeoisie were excluded.[16] The court's highly formal procedures and rigid rules of etiquette were not even written down since the vast majority of those who lived by them knew them through long-standing familiarity. When Marie Antoinette granted regular audiences to her couturière Rose Bertin, it was regarded as a scandalous breach of protocol.[17]

For the queen's biographer Antonia Fraser, 'The glamour of Marie Antoinette—to use a twentieth-century word which nonetheless seems appropriate—appeared to fit her admirably for the position of Queen of France.'[18] The use of this term in this context does not seem justifiable. Fraser's hesitation is due to the fact that glamour is a concept which—while not in fact of twentieth-century origin—postdates the feudal court. She substantiates her decision to employ it by reference to the queen's beauty 'or the illusion of beauty she gave', citing 'the radiance of the Queen's smile', 'the brilliance of her complexion', and 'the graceful whole' that made such an impression on those who met her.[19] 'Of course the physical charms of royalty are seldom cried down, the lustre of a crown enhancing even the most mediocre appearance in the eyes of the public,' she adds; 'yet in the case of Marie Antoinette there is such unanimity of report from so many sources, including foreign visitors as well as her intimates, that it is difficult to doubt the truth of the picture.'[20] Such testimonies are indeed plentiful. The painter Elisabeth Vigée Le Brun, seeing her outdoors at Fontainebleau with her ladies, 'thought that the dazzling Queen, her diamonds sparkling in the sunlight, might have been a goddess surrounded by nymphs'.[21] In the main, these were conventional tributes to a female royal personage. Within her circle, Marie Antoinette was constantly 'surrounded by the incense fumes of extravagant idolisation'.[22] For Zweig, 'to be near her was to be in the sunshine for this vainglorious, ambitious crowd; for her to glance at them was the bestowal of a gift; her laugh entranced them; her coming was a festival.'[23] As dauphine, she was popular. Although, following the custom of French royalty, she did not often submit herself to the public gaze, she was acclaimed in the street by crowds in the early 1770s and the audience rose to applaud her at the theatre. At this time she seemed to have the love of all the people. She became, Fraser says, 'an ideal and idealized French princess'.[24] In his *Reflections on the Revolution in France* (1790), Edmund Burke, a Whig Member of Parliament who had previously supported the American colonies' battle for independence, offered his own personal recollection of the queen. 'It is now sixteen or seventeen years since I saw the Queen of France, then the dauphiness, at Versailles, and surely never lighted on this orb, which she hardly seemed to touch, a more delightful vision,' he wrote.[25] She was, he recalled, 'glittering like a morning star, full of life, and splendour, and joy'.

The enthusiasm Marie Antoinette engendered and her visual allure mean that, to contemporary eyes, she has some features of the glamorous personality. This is how she was portrayed, for example, in Sofia Coppola's 2006 film *Marie Antoinette*, in which she was played by the American actress Kirsten Dunst. Despite a haughty profile, the queen was blonde and alluring and she endeavoured to please people. Frivolous and materialistic, she spent much time gambling, shopping, and having her hair done by her faithful coiffeur, Monsieur Léonard. She also surrounded herself with a riotous, fun-loving coterie and was acquainted with some celebrated English beauties of her day, including the notorious Georgiana, Duchess of Devonshire, but also the actress, author, and courtesan Mary Robinson, who introduced to London some fashions she had pioneered.[26] Yet there was little or nothing about her personally that was geared to the conquest of wide popularity. Fundamentally, her sphere was a narrow one that did not extend beyond the nobility. Despite her grasp of the potential of clothes to capture attention and communicate status, she repeatedly misjudged what the responses would be among her subjects.[27] As a result, she rapidly alienated their sympathies. Used to dazzling courtiers with her mastery of the Versailles glide— a technique for skimming over floors apparently without taking steps—she merely antagonized commoners who saw her as utterly removed from the real world. The pamphleteers of her time did not engage in flattering descriptions of her style and beauty; rather they were ferocious in their criticism. The key medium of public opinion that was the press thus did nothing to enhance her appeal or build potential glamour. Goodwill towards her, such as it was, had so evaporated by the time of the Revolution that the crowds were baying for her blood; her execution in October 1793 was greeted with general delight. Her allure was not of a type that involved the population in a relationship of admiration and emulation; rather it was a feature of an absolutist society in which the monarchy was supported by a special system of image-building sustained by patronage. As that system crumbled, so the queen's highly institutionalized allure evaporated, leaving only her personal admirers to cultivate fond memories of her kindness and beauty.

Nevertheless, Marie Antoinette is an interesting figure in the history of glamour because she was caught up in the contradictions of a period of transition. She loved both simplicity and material goods, the pastoral idyll of the mock village of the Petit Trianon and the pomp and splendour of Versailles; she was drawn to theatricals and to fashion yet lived in a world of the utmost formality and etiquette. She was highly frivolous, yet, especially during the most difficult phase of the Revolution, behaved with regal dignity. She was mostly a figure of the *Ancien Régime*, yet the connection she established to the commercial styles of the city brought her into contact with the social and cultural humus from which glamour would emerge. In that urban milieu, alongside luxury trades that lived in symbiosis with the court, new ideas about politics, society, and morality gained ground and fuelled the pressures that led to revolution. Critics of the government engaged in a moral critique of the aristocracy and presented themselves as defenders of virtue. Inspired by ideas of ethical rigour and civic passion deriving from Rousseau, their outlook was also conditioned by specific attitudes towards public and private, spending and consumption, work and leisure, luxury and utility, and sex. Far from giving rise to admiration, this sparked a campaign of denigration of Marie Antoinette on the basis of spurious charges of lesbianism, debauchery, and corruption of her children.[28] As would also occur two centuries later, the press pilloried a prominent woman by peddling questionable tales of illicit sex and bad motherhood.

All these currents served to undermine the elaborate system of illusions that surrounded the monarchy. The anti-revolutionary Burke argued that the rise of rationalism and the demise of a natural order of power would inevitably lead to the destruction not only of long-established arrangements but also of the magical aura that surrounded and legitimated them. 'All the pleasing illusions, which made power gentle, and obedience liberal, which harmonized the different shades of life, and which, by a bland assimilation, incorporated into politics the sentiments which beautify and soften private society, are to be dissolved by this new conquering empire of light and reason,' he predicted: 'All the decent drapery of life is to be rudely torn off. All the superadded ideas, furnished from the wardrobe of a moral imagination, which the heart owns, and understanding ratifies, as necessary to cover the defects of our naked shivering nature, and to raise it to dignify in our estimation, are to be exploded as ridiculous, absurd, and antiquated fashion.'[29]

Burke feared that in the emerging order plainness, boredom, and uniformity would reign and that there would be no place for image-making and visual seductions. In fact, this would not prove to be the case. A complex process of social change would see the rise of a coalition of aristocratic and bourgeois forces. The new ruling elite took over and refashioned many of the attributes of the old regime. No matter how different the basic system of values of the bourgeoisie was, the members of this class admired and envied aspects of the aristocratic lifestyle. They rejected the morals of the aristocracy but did not disdain material manifestations of status. The bourgeois phenomenon of glamour began precisely as a refashioning for new times and new purposes of the exterior glitter that the nobility had sought to reserve to itself to affirm its social and economic superiority. In contrast to splendour and magnificence, it was a flexible attribute that bolstered relative rather than absolute exclusivity.

The political and social transition of which this process of reconfiguration was a part can be read in relation to the rise of a set of interests and ambitions centred on Paris. In this fluid context, Napoleon Bonaparte muscled his way to the fore. The Corsican corporal who rose to become emperor of the French was the key figure in the transition from magnificence to glamour. Napoleon fascinated his contemporaries. His many ambiguities, and especially his mixing of elements of old and new, captured public attention and contributed to his becoming the dominant personality of his age. He was widely seen as a product of the Revolution, yet he also had a certain appeal for conservatives because he found a new way of organizing the state in which firm authority was exercised in the public good and in the name of the people. In an age in which religious and paternal symbols of royal authority had crumbled, and deference had ceased to act as a basis for political obedience, egalitarian ideas could not be dismissed. The symbols and representations of power therefore had to pass through different routes and take account of different emotional, psychological, and political needs. Some observers saw Napoleon's elevation to emperor as a recrudescence of regal splendour and a betrayal of the egalitarian values of the Revolution. But the style and ritual of the Napoleonic Empire, despite some superficial similarities, were profoundly different to those of the Bourbons.

As a product of the minor Corsican nobility, Napoleon was precisely the sort of man who would never have been presented at court or won preferment under the *Ancien Régime*. He was a new man, a product of the times, whose very rise signalled that there had been a change of era. From the time he established himself as the saviour of Paris by firing on the mob, he plotted his rise to power, making his mark through the largest war the Continent had ever seen. His destiny, as he saw it, was to guide the French out of the instability of the post-revolutionary era and save the country in its hour of need.[30] He dramatically undermined the old order across Europe by replacing established hereditary rulers with his own appointees, leading to the foundation of a new empire on a scale not seen since the time of the Roman Empire. Napoleon was a fabricator of his own myth who forged a system of authority that served his purposes. He was a supreme propagandist who had a strong sense of history. Also significant is the broader cultural impact he and his actions had on the imaginative realm of his time. He repeatedly transformed himself, constructing a life narrative that aroused awe and inspired authors. His coronation as Emperor of the French in 1804—a title, like that of consul, which owed more to Rome than to the *Ancien Régime*—was a sign that nothing could ever be the same again. The lavish ceremony was indicative of a monarchical ambition and a determination to harness grandeur and luxury to the national purpose. A sumptuous spectacle that was hailed as the greatest public entertainment since the time of Louis XIV, it was partly inspired by the rituals of the Bourbon kings although, in contrast to royal coronations at Reims, it took place at Notre-Dame in Paris. Eight thousand outriders accompanied the emperor's coach, which was pulled by eight horses, the very number that the Bourbons had established as a royal prerogative. In fact, it was Charlemagne, the medieval warrior-king who had been crowned in Rome in 800, who was Napoleon's model. He used the recently signed Concordat to force the Pope to attend the ceremony and then placed the crown on his head himself. It was an eclectic pageant that owed more to theatre than to history. Having transformed himself from general to emperor, after conquering much of Europe, he felt at liberty to bolster his position by raiding the past. 'At that time, very little was known about the early Middle Ages; so it was a romantic and wholly inaccurate notion which prevailed instead,' commented the Duchesse d'Abrantès in her posthumously published memoirs.[31]

Napoleon consolidated his power on the social plane by re-establishing the court. Already some courtly practices had returned under the Directory, which had held receptions for officials and overseen a certain return of pomp. These were formalized and extended by Napoleon, who was sensitive to the view that a splendid court was necessary to France.[32] On becoming first consul of the French Republic in a *coup d'état* in 1799, he had set about establishing a new pattern of rule. Balls, receptions, dinners were held to anchor individuals to the new regime and provide them with the social recognition for which many of them yearned. The court had always shaped manners and customs; it had played a role in national prestige, and it had sustained the economy by promoting luxury trades. Napoleon was most interested in the way that features of the court had their uses as political weapons.[33] He realized that the weakness of modern institutions was precisely their inability to speak to the imagination and he set about using the tools at his disposal to correct this.[34] Visual splendour was a vital way of communicating with the people and capturing their attention.[35] Fundamentally, he was a rationalizer, a reformer, and modernizer of the state and the institutions who saw himself as the embodiment of the best spirit of the Revolution. The recourse that he made to past ceremonials and patterns of power showed the difficulty of finding new ways of representing authority in a context in which its conventional forms had been disrupted and thrown into question.[36] The irrational appeals of spectacle and magnificence were annexed to secular authority to lend it an imaginative dimension.

Napoleon's court was a public structure rather than a largely domestic one. It was not a product of consolidated traditions and rights but rather the conscious invention of a ruler. It was the emperor's position that was glorified rather than his physical person. Napoleon had been happy to be painted posing in his study by Jacques-Louis David and even as emperor he dressed simply in private. There was none of the ritualized attention to daily acts and bodily functions that had bound senior courtiers to the monarchy. Napoleon was essentially a private figure who cultivated a public dimension; he had many fewer personal attendants than the Bourbon kings. There was also a new distance between ruler and populace. Versailles had been surprisingly open, with visitors able to wander at will not only into the gardens but also into the royal apartments. Despite the growing popular unrest, this had still been the case under Louis XVI since the king was assumed to occupy a position at the top of a natural hierarchy in which people knew their place. Now that such notions had been swept aside, the curious were excluded while formal access was granted to far wider groups. The imperial court was the first where non-nobles held senior posts. Etiquette did not remain unwritten, as in Louis XVI's time, but was set out so that newcomers could study it. The tone was more egalitarian and the emperor mixed with his guests at balls and paid attention to them. Although not well mannered—he was given to shoving and tweaking his collaborators—he exercised some personal charm.

Napoleon behaved clannishly and granted all the members of his family important titles and posts. But in most respects, his court was open to the real configuration of society; both minor nobles and non-nobles gained admission and many more foreigners than in the past were presented.[37] The elite he forged was quite different from the *Ancien Régime* aristocracy; it was not predicated on inherited rights and it was organized and calibrated in a novel way. Its fundamental principles were bourgeois and meritocratic. Valiant generals, civil servants, and bankers were all awarded titles in a drive to manufacture an aristocracy that, unlike the pre-revolutionary one, was expected to command the respect of a country in which, despite the growing apparatus of censorship, public opinion counted. Napoleon was acutely aware of this and kept a tight grip on the press. He did not intend to allow it to deflect from or undermine the general image of material opulence. Napoleon constructed a system of personal rule that was fantastically opulent and drenched in magnificence. This recalled the cultivation of luxury by Louis XIV. However, Napoleonic splendour was an exterior appropriation, a parvenu emulation, rather than a return to the past.[38] Opulence was not purely viewed as a prerogative. Rather it was used to win the respect of domestic and foreign elites and seduce wider public opinion; magnificence was to offset lack of heritage.[39] It was a means of capturing the imagination of France and the world.

Nevertheless, the sheer scale of this was extraordinary. Royal palaces were decorated with supreme opulence; new furniture of superb quality was installed, and N emblems as well as bee and eagle symbols were affixed everywhere. The bee had been Charlemagne's symbol and evoked immortality and resurrection, while the eagle, the symbol of imperial Rome, was associated with military victory. Napoleon demanded that his dukes, counts, and barons occupy splendid palaces and live in luxury. Their carriages were to be gorgeous and their hospitality lavish. All this with the intention of giving the court the most fabulous visual impact. 'He wanted his court to be the most splendid ever seen,' wrote the Duchesse d' Abrantès; 'he ceaselessly exhorted his dignitaries to live lavishly in splendid houses; he often gave them large sums of money, usually taken from the contributions paid by defeated enemies, and expected them to spend every penny, on the assumption that there would always be more where that came from.'[40] Napoleon's attitude was that the new aristocracy should assert its social prominence through the programmatic display of luxury. This was not wastage; the use of material magnificence was functional. As one French historian has noted, 'he was happy, if necessary, to pay millions for the receptions of the court, *but he did so counting them*'.[41]

There were elements of restoration to the imperial court. Some officials and servants from the past were given new appointments. However, Napoleon's court was not a structure apart, but part of the city. It was not established at Versailles, which remained unused until the Bourbon restoration (it was eventually turned into a museum by the citizen-king Louis-Philippe after he came to power in 1830). Rather it was installed at the Tuileries, the royal palace in the city of Paris. In the course of the Revolution, the city, with its salons, festivals, and celebrities, had replaced the court as the social centre. Napoleon knew that, despite his accomplishments on the battlefield, his power was contingent and that it needed to be consolidated through public display and ceremonial. His mother had written to him, 'You know how much external splendour add to that of rank or even personal qualities in the eyes of public opinion.'[42]

One marked novelty of Napoleon's court was an unusually high quotient of female beauty. Courtiers were no longer drawn from the narrow stratum of the high aristocracy but from far wider social backgrounds. In contrast to the strange-looking physical specimens thrown up by the hereditary order of the *Ancien Régime*, youth and beauty were very much in evidence. The women who enjoyed especial prominence were striking for their beauty or allure. They included Napoleon's wife Empress Josephine, his sexy sister Pauline, and the young banker's wife and salon hostess Juliette Récamier. These women were not shrinking violets; they had risen to prominence by becoming key social players with power bases in the city and its centres of wealth and hospitality. They were glamorous figures with chequered histories. Josephine herself was the widow of an aristocrat who had thrown his lot in with the Revolution and gone to the scaffold in 1794.[43] She had survived the Terror to reinvent herself as a hostess and a mistress to the rich during the Directory. Although not conventionally beautiful, she was pretty, languorous, and erotically alluring. Born on the Caribbean island of Martinique, she incarnated, along with a handful of other women, the fluid and hedonistic spirit of the times; she shopped, socialized, and spent hours on her appearance. She was an integral part of the fashionable life of Paris. She was linked at once to the old order and the louche salons of financial intriguers and speculators.[44] As such, she was an ideal trophy for the rising Bonaparte who courted and married her in 1796.

Although she was a very different figure from the late queen, Napoleon gave Josephine the task of organizing a court that would be no less brilliant than that of Marie Antoinette. It was expected, though, that she would overcome the contradictions that had damned the queen and render social splendour attractive. Her talents were deployed to bring together different elite groups and create a single focus for social life, infusing it with brilliance and beauty. The links she maintained to the city distinguished her from Marie Antoinette but also from Louis XV's influential mistress Madame de Pompadour, who, in her time, had been a significant city socialite. On becoming the royal mistress, she was brusquely removed from the urban scene and transplanted at court. She was only sent back after her death for burial. The women of the new era, by contrast, bridged the court and the city and belonged equally to both. The emperor paid great attention to their appearance and had no qualms about telling a lady that she was overdressed, underdressed, or that she did not look sufficiently youthful and radiant.[45]

Despite his attention to feminine beauty, to bolster legitimacy Napoleon insisted on a certain decorum. He acted to suppress risqué fashions and marginalize libertinism. In the new era, rulers could not openly disregard the general morality of the people. Like Rousseau and many revolutionaries including Robespierre, he considered women's role to be subordinate.[46] Burke had noted that the new order desacralized monarchy and produced a new pattern of gender relations. 'On this scheme of things,' he argued, 'a king is but a man; a queen is but a woman; a woman is but an animal; and an animal not of the highest order. All homage paid to the sex in general as such, and without distinct views, is to be regarded as romance and folly.'[47] This was a more accurate prediction than some of Burke's others, for the post-revolutionary order was a decidedly masculine one. Despite the role of the empress and some society hostesses, women were seen mainly in relation to reproduction. That this was more important than decorativeness was illustrated when Napoleon's ambition to found a dynasty led him to divorce Josephine in 1809 following her failure to produce an heir. To confirm his own royal status and embellish his imperial crown, he subsequently married the Austrian princess Marie Louise in a ceremony that, despite its not being recognized by the Pope, was marked in Paris with fabulous public celebrations. Although Josephine was allowed to keep the title of empress, her open-tap spending after her dismissal from court was deeply resented since it was no longer functional but entirely self-serving.

The Napoleonic regime was the first in history than can accurately be described as glamorous. Its image of magnificence was not bolstered by history or divine right. Rather it worked autonomously to seduce the French public and foreign rulers. It was brash and eye-catching, it was colourful and theatrical. It revelled in new money and in the worldly beauty of the women who rose to the top of a heterogeneous urban society. Napoleon himself, for all his narcissism, always knew that he was an upstart. He had transformed himself from a nobody into a magnificent emperor and reshaped his country in his own image. This extraordinary achievement had enormous resonance and communicated a wide-ranging lesson about the decline of hereditary authority and the opportunities that existed for self-invention and affirmation.

Napoleon had a far-reaching impact on the political and cultural landscape in Britain, although he would for many years be a bogeyman. The fact that Britain was drawn into a war with France that lasted on and off from 1793 to 1815 had something to do with this. The Corsican corporal who became a general, then a dictator, and finally became an emperor, before falling from grace and rising again before encountering final defeat and exile, was the man of the age who profoundly influenced the way his contemporaries felt about their time. For many, he was a complex figure of numerous sides who announced the arrival on the scene in many spheres of new men. With his personal odyssey he showed that glory and splendour were attributes that, in the modern era, were likely to be temporary. He and Josephine were utterly different from any other type of contemporary ruling family.

In England, wealth was spread more widely than in France and there were many from middle-class and non-noble backgrounds who were eager for more influence. The public sphere was no longer narrow and there was an awareness of new figures and possibilities for social mobility. Because the country had essentially been a constitutional monarchy for some time, the shift in values and norms was not marked by any dramatic political events. But fear of violence and revolution and the mobilization against Napoleon had the effect of creating a social glue in the form of patriotism combined with an attitude of seriousness and strong support for the dominant moral code that steadily infiltrated even the higher classes.[48]

Because Britain experienced industrial development earlier, modernity manifested itself more on the commercial plane and in the field of culture than in terms of political agitation. The massive disruptions of the era fuelled the Romantic movement, whose members were committed to the development of the imagination as a realm of experience. They were the prime cultural interpreters of the feelings of anxiety and nostalgia that arose in a period of change. It was among the Romantics that the richest and most interesting responses to Napoleon's symbolism emerged. For the Lake poets, Wordsworth, Coleridge, and Southey, as well as Hazlitt, Scott and Byron, he was a remarkable stimulus to their creative work. He was crucial to the way they thought about themselves and their roles.[49] Most of them were hostile, yet they were fascinated by Napoleon. Wordsworth and Coleridge compared him to Milton's Satan, while other authors compiled a fantastic list of historical precursors that included Alexander the Great, Augustus, Julius Caesar, Cromwell, Rob Roy, Macbeth, Moloch, Moses, Genghis Khan, Belshazzar, and Nebuchadnezzar.[50] As hero or villain, he seemed far larger than life. The English Romantics easily grasped the glamour of Napoleon. Coleridge saw that he fascinated, bewitched, and enchanted his contemporaries and pronounced himself utterly averse to 'the great Giant-fiend'.[51] He argued in essays published in the *Morning Post* that, from the time of his Egyptian expedition, Napoleon had become an 'object of superstition and enthusiasm'. His 'splendour' and 'brilliance' had 'dazzled' and 'blinded' observers. As a despot, he had embraced 'splendid robes and gaudy trappings' that were tantamount to a 'miserable masquerade' to disguise his tyranny. Wordsworth too noted the optical seduction of his 'splendour' and 'glory', that he pronounced false, while Hazlitt, who was more positive in his attitude—and who wrote a four-volume biography of Napoleon—argued that his exploits had a 'dazzling appearance' that produced a 'dazzling glare'.[52]

Few British writers of the period enjoyed the great popularity at home and abroad of the poet Lord Byron and the poet and historical novelist Walter Scott. A creative artist of extraordinary range and industry, Scott has been hailed as the greatest single popular imaginative inspiration of the nineteenth century.[53] For his part, Byron effected a uniquely powerful synthesis of art and life that profoundly influenced his contemporaries. Both were well aware of the susceptibility of the men of their time to glittering facades and to imaginative and alluring descriptions of places and people. They engaged with the Napoleonic cult and drew inspiration from it to develop glamour as an alluring imaginative realm connected to lived reality. Like others operating in the cultural realm, they exercised more flexibility and freedom in this respect than those who occupied the spheres of politics and the state. They were able to exploit to the full the opportunities for fame and profit that the commercial sphere offered.

Both writers skilfully combined elements of the past and present. Scott contributed to the development of the medieval vogue that took hold in the first decades of the century. He was not the founder of this genre of historical fiction. Horace Walpole's *Castle of Otranto* and the Gothic novels of the late eighteenth century had fuelled interest, as had Coleridge with his poem *Christabel*.[54] However, Scott's poems and novels were huge successes and his best-known novel, *Ivanhoe*, sold more copies than any previous literary work.[55] The whole of European culture was influenced by his evocations of medieval and Renaissance chivalry and adventure. He was the first novelist in Britain to become a public figure and to arouse enthusiasms that went beyond the confines of the established reading public. His literary creation of a world of adventure and heroism greatly appealed in a time of uncertainty and change. In his many works, the imaginative realm is stimulated and manipulated with repeated use of picturesque settings, dramatic encounters, beautiful characters, meticulously described material environments and objects, and passionate emotions. The massive quantity of his production (numerous lengthy poems and short stories as well as twenty-seven major novels between 1814 and 1832, plus a long series of historical works) was such that he more than met the demand of readers for exciting and engaging historical fiction. Like few others, Scott caught the mood of his generation. Kings and queens, great aristocrats and minor nobles, squires, businessmen, educated women, and artisans all thrilled to his fabulous tales of a glorious past. Although Carlyle argued that his popularity was 'of a select sort . . . not a popularity of the populace', it extended further than that of any living author.[56] Right across Europe, men and women imagined themselves drawn into the drama and romance of his works. Many of them belonged to a new reading public that was just taking shape. Byron was, if anything, even more of a celebrity. His title and dark good looks, combined with a prodigious poetic talent, quickly made him into a widely admired figure who attracted devoted followers.

Scott had a deep knowledge of Scottish folklore, ballads, and myths and he often employed picturesque language to supply local colour and a sense of antiquity.[57] Some of the words he employed were antiquated and were merely being reintroduced. Others were of Scottish derivation.[58] Among these was 'glamour'. The word was an Anglicized version of 'glamer' which had been in use in Low Scotch for around a century.[59] 'Glamer' referred to 'the supposed influence of a charm on the eye, causing it to see objects differently from what they really are'.[60] *The Etymological Dictionary of the Scottish Language*, published in 1879, traces the term's origins to two possible Scottish sources: 'glimbr' (meaning splendour) or 'glam-skygn' (meaning squint-eyed).[61] Scott may have had one or both sources in mind when he coined a term that would come to have applications well beyond the usage it had previously had in Scottish. He used the word 'glamour' in his first major success, *The Lay of the Last Minstrel* published in 1805, a long prose poem that pulsated with magic and adventure.[62] The fictional narrator-minstrel, who is reputed to be the last of a race of people who inhabited the Scottish borders, recounts the customs of his partly pastoral and partly warlike fellows. The poem tells of a border feud that takes place in the sixteenth century in which sorcery is employed by a noblewoman to obstruct a marriage of which she does not approve. The convoluted story is permeated with the supernatural. A dwarf page with the appearance of a goblin is charged with procuring for his master a magic book of spells. When he finds it and opens it, he reads one short spell, of which he says:

> It had much of glamour might,
> Could make a ladye seem a knight;
> The cobwebs on a dungeon wall
> Seem tapestry in lordly hall;
> A nut-shell seem a gilded barge,

A sheeling seem a palace large,
And youth seem age, and age seem youth —
All was delusion, nought was truth.[63]

Glamour was used here to convey a capacity to transform, to delude through illusion. Through glamour, something could be made to seem what it is not (the word 'seem' recurs five times in the space of a few lines), and especially something better, more alluring and splendid. It was a transformative force conjured by magic that could make things appear far better than they really were. Although Scott insisted on the Scottish orgin of the word,[64] Such a power alluded, no matter how indirectly, to the extraordinary rise of the Corsican corporal and the fantastic quasi-fictional character of his deeds. The odyssey of Napoleon, whose coronation occurred just one year before the publication of *The Lay of the Last Minstrel*, profoundly shaped perceptions of what men could achieve. His acts of self-transformation were the greatest of an age that was itself marked by far-reaching change.

Scott had had no sympathy with the French Revolution, yet he was powerfully influenced by the legend of Napoleon. He wrote a significant poem *The Field of Waterloo* in 1815 and even composed a lengthy biography in 1827 that was only mildly hostile towards its subject.[65] Bonaparte impressed him because he was a 'new man' who had emerged from nothing, rather like himself. He was also a man of order who willingly drew on the symbols and imagery of the age of chivalry. Of course, Scott's works operated in a very different sphere, but there were strong connections and they had something of the same eclectic quality. Napoleon created a peculiar mix of old and new that the Scottish author identified with.

Napoleon was a compelling and intensely controversial figure and he would remain so long after his time.[66] His concern with image-building and his manipulation of the tools of communication of his time led some to see him as a confidence trickster. Thomas Carlyle, the great champion of heroes and great men, considered him not to be the genuine article but rather a fraud. While he possessed some of the qualities of the charismatic hero, 'outer manoeuvrings and quackeries' prospered until, in Carlyle's view, 'the fatal charlatan-element got the upper hand'.[67]

Others viewed him as a mystery man or sphinx. Writing over a century later, at the end of the Second World War, the Italian historian Luigi Salvatorelli dubbed him 'an unknown'. 'The mystery of Napoleon is to be seen as a spiritual emptiness,' he wrote. 'The "pure activist", the professional hero is empty: at the conclusion of the unleashing of his actions, behind the façade of his gestures, there is nothing.'[68] From the point of view of glamour, precisely this focus on exterior appearances and their effects is significant. The imagination was the realm in which Napoleon built his most enduring empire.

Byron was not merely influenced by Napoleon; he was an admirer. In *Don Juan*, he made explicit his identification with him, referring to himself as 'the grand Napoleon of the realms of rhyme'.[69] Napoleon loomed large in his life and he regarded him as an inspiration, perhaps because, more than any other man, he had won the attention of his contemporaries and expanded the very sense of fame and glory. Byron composed an 'Ode to Napoleon Bonaparte' which, unlike Scott's poem, contained praise and he referred to him in his *Childe Harold's Pilgrimage* as 'the greatest . . . of men'.[70] Byron saw the Frenchman as an outsider of great energy and stamina who, like himself, triumphed over mediocrity and achieved great things. Carlyle and Keats saw the two men as both being histrionic and theatrical. 'In the collective visual imagination they stood fixed in alliance, stocky powerful Napoleon, exquisitely handsome Byron, the superlative odd couple of their time,' writes the poet's most recent biographer.[71]

Like Scott, Byron was part of an emerging world of mass publishing.[72] His early triumph, *Childe Harold's Pilgrimage*, published in 1812, turned him into a contemporary idol. A poem of discovery written in exhilarating language, its questioning of established values led to it being seen as a blast for freedom and a product of the post-French Revolution era.[73] The 'Childe' of the title was part Byron and part modern man. It was subversive in tone and reflected the erosion of deference. Reviewers noted a similarity with Scott's *The Lady in the Lake*, published the previous year, which featured a similar wanderer (in that case a knight) of mysterious origins.[74] The rival authors both catered to a public hunger for escapist romantic narratives unfolding in enticing contexts. Byron fashioned a dream world of his own that was equal in power to Scott's and which would in similar ways combine the fabulous and the faraway with the particular themes and impulses of the modern era. The difference was that Byron worked in an exotic key.[75] His poetry was infused with images of remote places and unusual experiences that had an authentic ring on account of his extensive travels in Albania, Greece, and Turkey. Through these, he developed an Oriental persona of his own. He cultivated his own image and encouraged an identification between himself and the alluring heroes of his writing. One of the best-known portraits of Byron, by Thomas Phillips, shows him as a dashing adventurer in full Albanian costume.

No more than the medieval vogue was exoticism a true novelty and it also gained new force in the early years of the century. The Orient appealed especially as a place of illusion and transformation in which everything could turn into its opposite.[76] For over a century luxury goods had been imported from the East but the connections increased with the expansion of trade and colonialism.[77] In Egypt, Napoleon had revelled in Oriental magnificence and admired the limitless power of the region's despots. Some of Byron's backdrops were borrowed, others—particularly those of *The Hebrew Melodies*—were largely taken from the Old Testament.[78] Despite this, he was able to provide a plausible rendition of the East and find a winning formula by combining exotic heroes and mysterious, suggestive settings.[79] In his poems *The Gaiour, The Bride of Abydos, The Corsair,* and *Lara* he fashioned a world of adventure and marvel that proved extremely popular. *The Corsair,* for example, sold 10,000 copies on the first day of publication in 1814.[80]

Byron's celebrity was so instant that it was almost as if there had been a yearning for such a figure in English society. He was at the heart of a bustling scene and, through the mediation of several of his female admirers, including Lady Caroline Lamb and Lady Melbourne, he was propelled into the highest spheres of society. This connection, and the title 'Lord', were key elements of the way Byron was packaged and sold to a reading public that 'still clung to the paraphernalia of aristocracy' and was 'avid for glamour'.[81] He was an unusual sort of aristocrat who cared little for tradition or for his landed possessions. He showed himself quite willing to sell off both his ancestral estates of Rochdale and Newstead for ready cash. In consequence, he possessed deracinated aristocratic attributes that were turned to commercial ends by the publisher John Murray and which lent allure to his nomadic persona.[82]

Byron seemed to be both embedded in high society and rootless, two ostensibly antithetical qualities that rendered him alluring and saleable to his readers. Byron and Murray showed by their actions that they were well aware that, as the odyssey of Napoleon proved, image-making was a fundamental part of modern society and of commercial society in particular. The poet's biographer claims he had a need for exposure that was his lifeblood.[83] An isolated child who had struggled with disability, he offset feelings of inadequacy by fashioning the image of himself as a romantic idol. There was a strong visual dimension to this. Byron was darkly handsome with a certain androgynous—some said, feminine—appearance. His impact on women—both those he knew and his fans—is well known. The audience for his writings was to be found especially among the increasing numbers of women of the middle class who in the industrial era were left with leisure time as the tasks of breadwinning were monopolized by their menfolk.[84]

Byron not only carefully cultivated his appearance by disguising his club foot (curiously, Scott too was lame), undertaking frequent diets, and choosing his portraits and poses carefully; he also styled his entrances and exits, as well as his costumes and the locations in which he appeared. Always theatrical, his poetry too relied for its effects on showing, looking, and seeing.[85] Murray underlined this by publishing his works in sumptuous editions containing illustrations, drawings, and engravings.

Scott and Byron both produced fabulously imaginative texts and were seen as masters of enchantment. On account of his unrivalled inventiveness, Scott was dubbed 'the Wizard of the North'. Even his son-in-law and biographer, J. G. Lockhart, refers to him as a magician on two or three occasions.[86] The ease with which he produced verse of vigour and energy marked with clear, picturesque scenes struck all readers. In the ten years following *The Lay of the Last Minstrel*, he published many poems inspired by Scottish history. He created an appetite for historical evocations and fictions that flourished during the Napoleonic era. Subsequently, he turned his prodigious energies to prose fiction and produced *Waverley*, a novel of the Jacobite rising of 1745, that was rapidly followed by a sequence of other titles.

In 1819, the still anonymous 'author of *Waverley*' produced his first English novel, *Ivanhoe*, a historical romance set in the twelfth century. The novel is considered to be his finest work and it is certainly today his best-known title. In terms of colour, drama, and brilliance, this tale of chivalry and love is unequalled in Scott's canon.

The mood the novel caught was a quintessentially modern one in which elements of yearning for nobility and grace mixed with materialism, nationalism, and fantasy. The critic A. N. Wilson has referred to the 'spell' of *Ivanhoe* and has sought to uncover the secret of its enchanting effects. Among Scott's tricks, he identifies an atmosphere of excitement, twists and turns of plot, a variety of colourful and contrasting characters, and a sharp dichotomy between good and evil.[87] To this list might be added a love story and some dramatic set-piece scenes including a tournament and a siege.[88] More broadly, the novel offered a fabulous fantasy that was infused with the materialism of modern commercial society. The pageantry is glittering and splendid, and the settings richly described. Garments are detailed in such a way as to throw their magnificence into sharp relief. A Saxon chief's fur-trimmed tunic, golden-clasped sandals, gold bracelets and collar, and richly embroidered cap are minutely itemized, as are the gold rings, precious gems, fine-leather sandals and embroidered cope of a religious elder. Interiors are evoked with a mass of detail and occasional comments connect these to the experiences of readers. Ancient dinner tables, it is said, 'may be still seen in the antique colleges of Oxford or Cambridge', while a mantle of black serge is 'in the shape of something like the cloak of a modern hussar'.[89] Wilson draws attention to numerous improbable details (the Norman nobleman Brian de Bois-Guilbert has black slaves, for example) that merely serve the need for effect. As 'romances', Scott's novels offered images of a fantasy world that was largely unreal even though it seemed to be grounded in history.[90] His writings reflected the sturdy sobriety of the middle classes, from which he came. Unlike the aristocracy, the bourgeoisie did not believe that it had a God-given right to satisfy all its wants and needs; it practised economy, restraint, and measure in matters concerning money, personal consumption, and sex. Yearnings and imaginative pleasures were a key characteristic of its specific mentality.[91]

The decorative focus of Scott's writings was noted by some of his contemporaries. William Hazlitt believed that the author reflected surrounding
objects, and that, like Napoleon in reality, he borrowed his imagined scenery
and costumes 'from comparatively obvious and mechanical sources'.[92] He
noted that Scott's backgrounds were the most attractive feature of his
novels.[93] These were precisely the part that could most readily be assembled
by means of compilation and imitation. This eclectic quality was the typical
taste of a materially based society. Like the Scottish novels, *Ivanhoe* gave rise
to a slew of works with English themes and settings that formed the basis for
the extraordinary influence that he exercised over European culture in the
nineteenth century.

Byron and Scott adopted different approaches towards their heroes, a fact
which reflected their different values. While some of Scott's were notoriously
bland and upright (Rob Roy was one exception), Byron's were compelling
and unfathomable. Ambivalent in the way that Coleridge and Wordsworth
had found Napoleon, they were not moral examples but fascinating traps for
the fantasies of readers. According to one critic, 'they gain their power from
a quasi-magical ability to attract and retain attention, even though they do
nothing to solicit it'.[94] Yet their subversive potential was contained because
their adventures were located far from Britain in remote exotic locations.
The heroes of *Lara* and *The Corsair* were outsiders and adventurers, men
who were modelled on Napoleon or a mixture of Napoleon and Byron
himself. By functioning just beyond the realm of the permissible without
directly challenging the model of contained, untheatrical masculinity that
was fast becoming dominant in Britain,[95] they were vehicles of glamour.
Scott's middle-class conservatism prevented him from toying with his
readers' values in this way. Instead, he concentrated on detail and backdrop.
However, although the right and the moral always won out in the end,
alternatives to bourgeois ideals and values were amply explored. His most
compelling male figures tended to be villains, who he made more rounded
and intriguing than his heroes. In a letter of July 1814, he wrote: 'I am a bad
hand at depicting a hero, properly so called, and have an unfortunate
propensity for the dubious characters of the Borderers, buccaneers, Highland robbers, and all others of a Robin Hood description. I do not know

what it should be, as I am myself, like Hamlet, indifferent honest, but I suppose the blood of the old cattle-drivers of Teviotdale continues to stir in my veins.'[96] Despite, or perhaps because of, his moralism, it was glamorous rebels who grabbed his interest and fired his imagination.

By the same token, his most seductive female characters were not his heroines, but outsiders. The Whig historian G. M. Trevelyan claimed—not without a touch of sexism—that there was a link between both authors' depictions of women and increasing female leisure. 'Scott's pseudo-medieval ideals of the "lady" worshipped by the enamoured hero, and Byron's sultanic vision of woman as odalisque,' he argued, 'helped to inspire the artificial uselessness of the would-be fashionable sisterhood.'[97] But, in fact, some of Scott's secondary female characters are no less compelling than Byron's ambiguous heroes. The heroine of *Ivanhoe*, the Saxon princess Rowena is blandness made flesh. The novelist Thackeray dismissed her as 'that vapid, flaxen-haired creature' and deemed her 'unworthy of Ivanhoe and unworthy of her place as a heroine'.[98] However, the novel features a much richer and more intriguing female figure in the person of the dark-haired and olive-skinned Jewess Rebecca. Even the wounded knight Ivanhoe, who is promised to Rowena, cannot resist gazing on her 'beautiful features and fine form, and lustrous eyes'. Eyes, Scott adds, 'whose brilliancy was shaded, and, as it were, mellowed, by the fringe of her long silken eyelashes, and which a minstrel would have compared to the evening star darting its rays through a bower of jessamine'.[99] Unlike the Saxon princess, Rebecca is a fascinating outsider. She is exotic and unusual; her appearance is showy and eye-catching. To have a sense of her allure, it is probably best to think of her as the young Elizabeth Taylor, who played her in the 1952 film version of the novel. Rebecca has a sex appeal that the virginal Rowena lacks and which is emphasized by allusions to her physical charms. Scott uses Rebecca's outsider status to construct her as alluring, different, and glamorous. It is the combination of her beauty with her remote, mysterious background and her unconventional dress and priceless jewellery that makes her intriguing and tantalizing.[100] Such a juxtaposition of effects was not new. In eighteenth-century works of fiction, including Daniel Defoe's *Roxana*, in which the eponymous heroine performs at court a Turkish dance in a richly coloured gown and a headdress studded with precious jewels,[101] the Oriental woman was often deployed as an icon of luxury. Luxury had been associated with the East since ancient times and this was reinforced by a burgeoning trade in luxury goods. By the early nineteenth century, such trade was an integral part of a growing consumer culture. In Byron, such exotic female figures abound. The slave girl Leila in *The Gaiour* was the type of languid, dark female he preferred. The erotic Zuleika in *The Bride of Aydos* was a highly sexualized, if ultimately pure, figure.

Byron and Scott offered two of the staple variants of glamour: one specialized in remote places and compelling people, the other opted for distant times and colourful scenes. The two writers also reflected the ideological ambiguity of glamour as a subversive and alluring power and as a force easily annexed by authority. Byron was the rebel and wanderer, the morally questionable renegade who was compelled to leave England under the cloud of a sexual scandal in 1816. The disintegration of his marriage and allegations of homosexuality led to his banishment from society and turned him into a rootless nomad. Later, with his customary theatricality, he took up the nationalist cause in Italy and Greece, participating in the latter until his death in 1824. Scott, by contrast, became ever more respectable and institutionalized. He was made a baronet and he built an eclectic baronial home at Abbotsford that became a personal medieval fantasy world: his 'romance in lime and stone', as Lockhart called it.[102] It was a flight from features of the modern world he disliked, a revelling in the ancient trappings of feudal nobility and distinction. Scott did in fact embrace technological innovations with some enthusiasm. He installed gas lighting and water closets at Abbotsford, as well as a complex system of air-bells. He would also welcome steamships and the railways. In politics though, he sided with the forces of conservatism.

'When the eldest son of George the Third assumed the Regency, England was in a state of political transition,' Captain Gronow noted in his reminiscences on the period.[103] 'The convulsions of the Continent were felt amongst us; the very foundations of European society were shaking, and the social relations of men were rapidly changing.' This increased after the end of the Napoleonic wars, when agricultural prices suddenly rose with the result that the poor were driven to near starvation while the rich, aided by the Corn Laws, got richer. The campaign for the repeal of these laws took on a mass character that alarmed the authorities. When one mass protest was violently repressed in August 1919, Scott voiced his backing.[104] He also threw his support behind the monarchy in the person of George IV. Born in 1762, Prince George became regent in 1811 in place of his mentally unstable father. He inherited the throne in 1820 and reigned until his death in 1830.

George was a very different figure from his father George III. While the latter was a simple, easygoing monarch who cared little for pomp, his son loved luxury, pleasure, and colour. The prince regent was another ruler who was caught up in the contradictions of an era in which deference was giving way to citizenship and in which the allure of material goods was coming within the purview of ever wider groups. The few triumphs and many tragedies of his reign show how difficult it was, and perhaps the impossibility of any attempt, to hitch magnificence to the emerging dynamic of glamour. George was a man who indulged in a taste for exteriors. He spent vast sums of money forever seeking to improve his residence, Carlton House (dubbed by one observer, 'one of the meanest and most ugly edifices to disfigure London' and later demolished),[105] he cultivated the most elaborate and excessive exterior appearance and he amply indulged his tastes for wine, food, and women. He personally designed the sumptuous, eye-catching uniforms of his personal regiment, the Tenth Hussars. Taking his cue from the elaborate, fur-trimmed, gold-buttoned, and buckled uniforms of central and Eastern Europe, with their various bells, belts, and epaulettes, he aimed to make this privileged corps into the most visually impressive in the army. The Prince Regent was not an ignorant man. He had a developed interest in the arts and followed all the novelties in literature. He loved Scott's works and was not immune to the delights of Byron's Oriental fantasies. Both the vogue for the Gothic that Scott fuelled and the taste for things Oriental captured his imagination and informed his building projects. In the course of the eighteenth century, Brighton had emerged as a fashionable resort, in part due to the patronage of the prince and his high-living coterie. In their wake would come many middle-class holiday-makers, turning the town into a sort of adjunct of a growing London.[106] The prince's most eye-catching contribution to Brighton was the Pavilion. The original scheme, by Henry Holland, envisaged French decor with the addition of brighter colours. However, the prince changed ideas as frequently as he did architects and the resulting building was an eclectic Oriental palace in which the outside was Indian-inspired and the interiors informed by a mixture of Chinese and Japanese motifs. It was a fabulous building that was no less informed by dreams and masquerade than Byron's writings on the Orient. Windsor Castle was another of his projects. As a result of extensive rebuilding, it was turned into a Walter Scott-style Gothic fantasy.

The prince did not only seek personally to harness the most popular fantasy worlds, he also wanted to outdo Napoleon in the matter of magnificence. He saw the French emperor as a rival, but only in terms of his opulence, not as a man who had emerged from a political process that dramatically overturned patterns of rule and consent. George repeatedly staged celebrations and festivities and also sought to win popular favour. When he became Regent, Carlton House was thrown open to the public for three days and this rare chance to see the lifestyle of royalty drew 30,000 people on the last day alone. On several occasions, firework displays for the public were held in parks. Not without reason, the historian Steven Parissien has dubbed his reign 'the grand entertainment'.[107] George's coronation in July 1821, when he was 59 and no longer the dashing prince, was a magnificent ceremony for which he persuaded Parliament to vote no less a sum than £243,000. He envied Napoleon's fabulous coronation and sent a tailor to Paris to inspect the robes he had worn in order to ensure that his own would be no less impressive.[108] The splendid descriptions in Scott's Elizabethan novel *Kenilworth* no doubt informed the Elizabethan theme of the coronation.[109] Despite the legitimacy of his position, George's coronation was no less a piece of historical pastiche than his rival's.[110] Such was the sumptuousness of his clothes and coronation robes (over £24,000 had been spent on his robes, £855 on the ermine alone) that one observer suggested that he looked like 'some gorgeous bird of the East'.[111] However, the whole affair nearly turned to farce when the George's estranged wife, Queen Caroline, sought gain admission to Westminster Abbey and had to be barred.

Walter Scott was present at the coronation and he acted as choreographer-in-chief on the occasion of the royal visit to Scotland in 1822.[112] The month-long sojourn was the high-point of George's reign and possibly the moment of his greatest popularity. The king arrived with a fabulous array of costumes made especially for the visit including Highland attire and numerous Scottish accessories. Crowds cheered as he rode through the highly decorated streets of Edinburgh. Streamers and thistles, feathered hats, and displays of crowns and stars marked an occasion that was seen as having consolidated support for the monarchy north of the border. In the course of his visit, the king attended a command performance of *Rob Roy*, merely one of several of Scott's works that were adapted for the stage.

Despite these moments of celebration, George had not been popular as Prince of Wales or as Regent and he was not a popular king. For all his preoccupation with visual effects and appearances, his role was above and separate from the hurly-burly of the commercial realm, even if he chose to immerse himself in it. Like all established royalty, he was on a higher plane. He was not a new man of the modern era and there was no mystique about him since that normally pertaining to a monarch had dissolved in ridicule. In some respects, he was a throwback. He embodied a model of eighteenth-century indulgence and excess at a time when this was ever less tolerated. Although the political sphere was still largely dominated by the aristocracy, public opinion was in the hands of the middle class. In England as in France, the bourgeoisie sustained a polemic against the aristocratic mode of living, its luxury, effeminacy, high living, dissoluteness, and wastage, which were often depicted as feminine.[113] In the aftermath of the Napoleonic wars, this view gained the ascendancy. For many critics, George was the personification of indulgence and excess. As such, he was mercilessly lampooned in magazines like *Satirist* and *Scourge* and was frequently the target of caricaturists.[114] The novelist Jane Austen, whose works he admired, subtly mocked him in her third novel, *Mansfield Park*. A prime exponent of the respectable provincial middle class, she drew in Tom Bertram a character who runs the affairs of his father while the latter is in the West Indies. Like the Regent, on whom he is modelled, Tom lives well, gambles, runs up debts, and loves ceremonial.[115] Although the press was not as vicious in its attacks on George IV as regent and king as pamphleteers had been about Marie Antoinette, it was still firmly hostile. The attitude of public opinion to both royal persons shows how pomp and luxury could very easily, if deprived of the necessary legitimation deriving from the practices of bourgeois society, become manifestations of undeserved privilege and lead to a dramatic loss of approval. Glamour in this respect was an articulation of qualities that passed through the market and public opinion rather than through a hereditary hierarchy.

Napoleon and George IV both tried to convey an image of magnificence to impress their countrymen and other rulers. As a result, they were flashy, colourful, and theatrical. However, Napoleon, the new man who trans- formed Europe, gave rise to a legend that would persist long after his death. The dominant image of George, despite his magnificent garb and some superbly flattering portraits of him by Sir Thomas Lawrence, was of an idle wastrel who was merely a burden on the public purse. Writing thirty years after his death, Thackeray itemized the millions of pounds that the king consumed during the course of his existence and his limitless expend- itures on luxury.[116] 'The handsomest prince in the whole world' in his youth, he became a portly, bloated monstrosity by maturity. The novelist deemed his invention of a particular type of shoe-buckle to be one of his most significant achievements.[117] He was also held to have been self-delu- sional. 'I believe it is certain about George IV', Thackeray continued, 'that he had heard so much of the war, knighted so many people, and worn such a prodigious quantity of marshal's uniforms, cocked-hats, cock's feathers, scarlet and bullion in general, that he actually fancied he had been present in some campaigns...and led a tremendous charge at Waterloo.'[118] From the standpoint of the mid-Victorian era, the lavish spectacles that were associated with him were deplorable indulgences. 'He is dead thirty years, and one asks how a great society could have tolerated him?', Thackeray asked.[119] If Napoleon was, for Carlyle, a charlatan, then George was 'a great simulacrum'. 'After reading of him in scores of volumes,' Thackeray commented, 'you find you have nothing—nothing but a coat and a wig and a mask smiling below it.' The sense of void that commentators found in Napoleon was testimony to the fact that he had risen from nowhere. He was, in a way, any man. George's lack of substance arose from the fact that he was seen as a type of monarch who had no place in the present age.

English men and women were by no means insensitive to the fabulous seductions of bright colours, precious fabrics, lavish spectacles, and alluring images. But, like their French counterparts, they were not attracted to exhibitions of personal excess on the part of royal persons who openly disdained the egalitarian values that were ever more shared. Much more suggestive were the forms of glamour that were associated with the new personalities that the age of political and industrial revolution created. These shook up the long-standing association of material rewards with the hereditary elite and offered examples of self-creation that appealed directly to the imagination of everyone. This development caused intense problems to royalty and the great contradictions into which two fashionable royal persons such as Marie Antoinette and the Prince Regent fell amply illustrated this. In the sphere of the state, only Napoleon succeeded in developing a combination of appeals and behavioural patterns that resolved these contradictions and harnessed glamour to his purpose. But even he was obliged to impose censorship on the press and the theatre to avoid the perils of critical public opinion. Cultural figures were more fortunate, since they could weave narratives on their own terms and even use negative public opinion to cultivate an alluring image. They were able to employ the market and manipulate the media with strategies that were not conditioned by the requirements of statecraft. More than anywhere else, it was the modern city and its institutions that supplied the stage on which such personalities could flourish. As we shall see in the next chapter, the magic of glamour was inseparable from the hurly-burly of the metropolitan life.

CHAPTER 2

URBAN ENCHANTMENTS

C ities grew exponentially from the mid-eighteenth century and fashion, consumption, and entertainment became increasingly centred on them. Although royal courts continued to be a focus of elite social life for the rest of the nineteenth century, cities were more open to novelty and change and less formal in their rituals and institutions. In France, the court of Louis XIV and Louis XV had had a profound impact on the development of the luxury trades, theatre, and urban development of Paris. But it was always the court that, as the main focus of power and privilege, dominated. It was important in providing a platform for personalities and in forming the social calendar, as well as establishing the extremely refined forms of living, hospitality, and entertainment that bolstered monarchical authority. However, while Paris lost out to Versailles in the seventeenth and during most of the eighteenth century, it continued to expand and increasingly it acted as an alternative pole of attraction. The city offered a social milieu that drew in far more people and was less selective; it was brash, money-centred, and exciting. Its heroes and heroines did not always have much in the way of noble patina but instead they were rich, colourful, varied, eye-catching, good-looking, and stylish.

In London too, the stodgy and dull court of George III was eclipsed by urban events, scenes, and spectacles. In the late eighteenth century, the English capital was the largest city in Europe and around one-tenth of the country's population lived there. It was a city of work and of trade, but also a city of pleasure and display. Social life took place in coffee houses, taverns, parks, theatres, and brothels, and in the streets. London was also a city of shops. Already at the start of the nineteenth century, Oxford Street had over one hundred and fifty. Stores and theatres contributed to the culture of display that characterized the visual experience of metropolitan life and lent it variety and vibrancy. The fantastic range of goods testified to the wide reach of the British Empire and the variety of products that the Industrial Revolution had brought. Foodstuffs, beverages, confectionery, and spices tempted with their smells, while jewellers, silk mercers, drapers, tailors, milliners, and shoemakers offered everything the smart man or woman could desire. All of them aimed to attract the passer-by and customer with eye-catching displays. Meanwhile book and print shops, and newspaper vendors, brought the public events, novelties, and personalities.

The metropolis shaped the customs of the whole country and most especially the urban centres. While Paris emerged as a Mecca of style and luxury not only in France but in Europe and beyond, London established a special dominance in England as the Industrial Revolution undermined village life and fuelled interest in fashionable consumer goods. As early as 1771, the writer and economist Arthur Young noted that, with improvements in travel and communication, young men and women were increasingly drifting towards the capital.[1] Neither city developed in a way that was balanced. The grandeur and glitter of the nobility and the rich existed in sharp contrast to the poverty and degradation of the poor. But there was a mobile and democratic spirit to cities that was completely different from a countryside where the aristocracy still ruled in conventional fashion.[2] London, the actress and writer Mary Robinson observed in 1800,[3] was 'the centre of attraction for the full exercise of talents, and the liberal display of all that can embellish the arts and sciences'.[4] Many cities had some luminaries of national importance, but only in the capital, 'the lustre of these accumulates and collects itself into a focus of dazzling light'. 'The customs, opinions, amusements, and propensities of the community at large,' she added, 'may be said to derive their leading features from the pursuits and pleasures which are practised in the metropolis of a kingdom.' In other words, the city was alluring and glamorous. Spectacle and display in the life of the metropolis served to unify rather than divide the classes through the common pursuit of certain customs and aesthetic effects. The city's '*spectacles* [are] well attended by nearly all ranks of persons', Robinson observed; 'and even the lower orders of society enjoy the humorous scenes of Sadler's Wells, the wonderful horsemanship of Astley, and the pantomime pageants of similar theatres'.[5] The promenade, especially on Sundays, was also an institution of note that was not exclusive and drew wide participation. The roads 'are thronged with pedestrians of all classes, and the different ranks of people are scarcely distinguishable either by their dress or their manners'. 'Refinement is ... visible in the exterior ornaments of all ranks of people,' she claimed;[6] decorative accessories were adopted even by those whose general dress was not very elegant. This was not yet the mass age, and Robinson certainly exaggerated, but there was a certain democratization of the life of the capital that was driven by ideas and economic change. It manifested itself in the rough and tumble of low life as well as high life, the wide interest in theatre and fashion, the variety of personalities and their mixed origins, and in the primacy of money, merit, and beauty over birth.

Public opinion in the early nineteenth century was not fully formed but it did have, in embryonic form, some of the features that would mark it in later decades. While Paris, due to the dramatic political events, witnessed setbacks in the development of a free press as well as economic progress, London witnessed steady development on both fronts. In the last decade of the eighteenth century, there were some sixteen daily papers in the capital, while two were published twice a week and a further seven three times per week.[7] In addition to serious papers, there were many others that provided a ready diet of gossip, scandalmongering, satire, titillating sketches. 'The monthly miscellanies are read by the middling orders of society, by the literati, and sometimes by the loftiest of our nobility,' Robinson noted.[8] By contrast, 'the daily prints fall into the hands of all classes: they display the temper of the times'. The press played a crucial role in creating a shared pattern of metropolitan life. Robinson only churlishly acknowledged its significance, like some celebrities today. 'The press is the mirror where folly may see its own likeness, and vice contemplate the magnitude of its deformity,' she observed, before accepting that 'it also presents a tablet of manners; a transcript of the temper of mankind'.[9] Papers and magazines provided something that was part mirror, part stage, and part social barometer. By recording and commenting on events and personalities, and channelling information, they created the image of metropolitan life. In this era the press was by no means the most important mediator of social relations; it was merely a factor in a complex equation in which personal observation and acquaintance with people, places, and events was more important. But it had a special purchase on the perceptions of those who were not able, for reasons of geographical or, sometimes, social distance to see things first-hand. Even in the 1790s, some 8.6 million copies of London newspapers were sent every year to readers in the rest of the country.[10]

In the history of glamour, cities are always important. The very idea of the modern city is bound up with wealth, power, beauty, and publicity. They are sprawling conurbations where very heterogeneous populations mix and thrive; they are a permanent laboratory of practices and lifestyles, personalities and situations. The press and other media constantly present pictures of fashionable people, events, occasions, places, openings, launches, and ceremonies to a public that is far broader than it was two centuries ago. Yet, even then, many of the characteristics of contemporary metropolitan life were present. Glamour was the aspect of the urban scene that captured and seduced ordinary people. To exist, it requires a high degree of urbanization, the social and physical mobility of capitalist society, some sense of equality and citizenship, and a distinctive bourgeois mentality. All of these were present in cities which increasingly presented numerous visual delights and pathways to self-transformation.

For the critic William Hazlitt, metropolitan life was 'an endless phantasmagoria'; 'even the eye of childhood', he continued, 'is dazzled and delighted with the polished splendour of the jewellers' shops, the neatness of the turnery-ware, the festoons of artificial flowers, the confectionary, the chemists' shops, the lamps, the horses, the carriages, the sedan-chairs'.[11] This visual inclusiveness constituted a vital condition of glamour. The spectacle was not created solely by or solely for the social and political elite, although its contribution was important. Prominent people were keen to impress each other, but their practices of self-advertisement and display were absorbed into the more general visual festival. Colour, finery, and beauty could be glimpsed in many quarters; fame could spring from any number of public events and commercial institutions; desirability derived not from official sanction but rather from a combination of elements including the place a given personality occupied in the public realm, their physical appearance, and the narrative that was created around them. The buzz of the present, the clamour of novelty, the irresistible beauty of places, people, and events, were all features that arose out of the dynamism of the metropolis itself. This is not to say, of course, that the city was somehow instrinsically democratic, although its inhabitants were likely to have wider experience, more choice and more sense of themselves as individuals than their country cousins. 'In London there is a public; and each man is part of it,' Hazlitt noted.[12] Cities were centres of money and commerce, while also being the setting of a broader culture of leisure and pleasure.

For most of the period between the late eighteenth and the early twentieth centuries, London and Paris were rivals. Rivalry was primarily political; each country wished to have an impressive modern capital that testified to its might and glory. Napoleon wanted to make Paris the greatest and most beautiful city in the world and the leading city in Europe.[13] To this end, various improvements were introduced, new bridges and a new ceremonial route were built, all with the aim of creating new spaces. Monumental building took the form of the Arc de Triomphe and Les Invalides, but there were few demolitions, which were limited to one of the most dangerous districts.[14] Although Paris became a vast building site, few projects were fully completed. At the end of his rule, there were still virtually no pavements, very little illumination, and streets were still used as sewers.[15]

The Prince Regent admired Napoleon's vision and promoted reforms of his own to London. The royal parks were opened to the people on certain occasions and there was some attention paid to the beauty of squares, public buildings, and bridges. He commissioned the visionary architect John Nash to formulate solutions to the problems of communication in central London and design a processional avenue, with precisely the aim of eclipsing the splendours of Napoleon's Paris.[16] In London too there were new public spaces and institutions. London was a larger and richer city than Paris; by the late century, it was over twice the size. But it was the French who constantly seized the initiative in developing a paradigm of the modern city. This was not only because of the imperial ambitions of the Napoleonic era. After Louis XVI was compelled to leave Versailles and return to Paris in 1789, the previous split between court and city was abolished and the latter became the sole focus of social and political power. Already a vibrant centre, it flourished after the Terror as a glamorous stage. Fashion businesses, jewellers, architects, and decorators turned towards the city and its emerging ruling elite. When war was not on, wealthy Britons used to regarding Paris as the capital of style visited regularly and marvelled at the way beauty and wealth combined. Luxury trades revived and restaurants founded by former chefs to the aristocracy flourished. The institutions of the state held lavish balls and celebrations while a rapidly rising bourgeoisie took over aristocratic palaces, tastes, and luxuries. The new class of nouveaux riches which rose very quickly during the Revolution was louche and ostentatious. Mores were relaxed and some of the sexiest fashions ever seen prospered until the emperor banished them from his court. Although the frenzied social life of the Directory was short-lived, glitz and ostentation continued to flourish under Napoleon. Unlike Marie Antoinette, Empress Josephine, who lived in the former queen's royal apartments,[17] was part of the sprawling texture of the city's visible social life. Every day she selected new goods from the retailers and manufacturers who sought the patronage of the most fashionable woman in Paris.

In terms of glamour, fashionable milieux were crucial because they were the channel through which social privilege was blended with the life of the metropolis as a whole. Certain areas acquired an aura of desirability through the presence of the rich, their patterns of competition and display, and the institutions of consumption and entertainment. It was precisely in such locations that the contradiction of exclusivity and accessibility was played out because the display of privilege was part of the visual experience of the metropolis as a whole. Elite areas were not merely enclaves of privilege; they were central to the new image of the city as a whole. The city image came to be shaped by the most beautiful and prestigious roads with their ostentation, dynamism, aspirations, and illusions. The commercial and entertainment establishments that sprang up within these areas were crucial tools of reinforcement and diffusion of this image. With the rapid development of the commercial sector, shops and stores came to occupy an increasingly important place in the visual and sensory experience of metropolitan life.

In London, the area of fashion was remarkably small. The so-called *beau monde* or *haut ton* in the early nineteenth century was restricted to the streets and squares of Mayfair.[18] Pall Mall, St James's Street, Piccadilly, and Bond Street were the main thoroughfares. The clubs, restaurants, and shops that catered to the needs of wealthy aristocrats and the men of fashion were all located there. The first luxury hotels were established in the same area during the Napoleonic wars to provide high-class accomodation to army and navy officers on leave.[19] The urban scene was one in which the rich and fashionable were constantly seeking to establish exclusivity in a context in which public places and commercial institutions, to some degree, were open. Pleasure gardens provided one of the more popular entertainments. Ranelagh Gardens in Chelsea enjoyed a heyday in the late eighteenth century before being eclipsed by Vauxhall Gardens, which, later in the century, would in turn be displaced by Cremorne Gardens. These were the amusement parks of their day; they featured theatres, labyrinths, artificial groves, refreshments, bandstands, dance arenas, lighting effects, and other diversions. Respectable during the day, they were more raucous and sexy at night. There was little social selection in such settings. The upper and lower classes mingled as they did at sports grounds. In general, the rich generally preferred a type of rendezvous that, while not private, was less accessible to others. Hyde Park, and especially the area known as Rotten Row, became just this sort of semi-exclusive place. At five o'clock in the afternoon, horses and carriages of striking beauty and expense were flaunted by fashionable gentlemen and ladies, just as they were at the Bois de Boulogne in Paris. However, even with such a cost discriminator, exclusivity was difficult to maintain. 'In the early years of the century,' the social observer Captain Gronow moaned, 'the equipages were generally much more gorgeous than at a later period, when democracy invaded the parks, and introduced what may be termed a "Brummagem society", with shabby genteel carriages and servants.'[20] In those earlier days, you never saw, he remarked, 'any of the lower or middle classes of London intruding themselves in regions which, with a sort of tacit understanding, were then given up exclusively to persons of rank and fashion'.

Women were generally less prominent than in France except for those who were drawn to or were products of the world of celebrity, fashion, and entertainment. At the interface between this world and high society there was considerable confusion between the grand and the faux-grand since everyone was egocentric, theatrical, visible, and controversial. The portrait painter Sir Thomas Lawrence, whose works were important in fixing the public images of many famous people, could make little distinction between the ultra-fashionable Georgiana, Duchess of Devonshire, and the prominent actress Mrs Siddons. While the former was naturally theatrical, it was said, the latter was naturally aristocratic.[21] In France in the same period, many society women had themselves painted wearing opulent jewels and fashionable dress just like actresses.[22] Glamorous women were not those who conformed to conventional morality and remained confined to approved spaces. They were those who were part of the glitter of fashionable life. They paraded their beauty, they shopped, and they pioneered fashions. They were the objects of a continuous narrative about their lives, loves, and whims.

The *haut ton* seized opportunities for public display. Indeed, it only assembled, Gronow added, 'to see and be seen'.[23] London thrived on the personalities and the doings of the upper classes. Gossip arose out of intimacy; that is to say out of a context in which aristocratic people knew each other.[24] But the press made the circle far wider. In contrast to France, where censorship was heavy and, under Napoleon's rule, the newspapers published were reduced from seventy to thirteen (he personally thought that there should be only one), the press flourished. People enjoyed learning of the pleasures and peccadilloes of the famous, which were conveyed with glee by chroniclers. Newspaper accounts encouraged a certain posturing. 'Men are tempted to make themselves notorious in England by the ease with which they succeed,' noted the poet Robert Southey who, under the pseudonym of Don Manuel Alvarez Espriella, published in 1807 a volume of *Letters from England*:

The Newspapers in the dearth of matter for filling their daily columns, are glad to insert any thing,—when one lady comes to town, when another leaves it, when a third expects her accouchement; the grand dinner of one gentlemen, and the grand supper of another are announced before they take place; the particulars are given after the action, a list of the company inserted, the parties who danced together exhibited like the characters of a drama in an English bill of the play, and the public are informed what dances were called for, and by whom.[25]

The middle classes were fascinated by their social superiors. While they criticized wastage and excess, they enjoyed vicarious escape into glittering high society. This taste inspired an entire literary genre from the 1820s that made a significant contribution to the development of glamour. Appearing after the successes of Scott and Byron, the so-called 'silver fork' novels acquired their name on account of the great prominence that one of their authors, Theodore Hook, gave to grand dinners that he described in great detail right down to the nature of the cutlery used. The creation of an enterprising publisher called Henry Colburn, they were set in the fashionable world of London's West End which was rendered as a fast, refined, materialistic, and eminently desirable milieu.[26] Colburn marketed the novels (which were mostly published anonymously) as though they were the work of authentic members of high society. In several cases this was true, but in others authors were aspirational fantasists with vivid imaginations. The novels appealed to several different constituencies. They entertained the upper classes, who read them as *romans à clef*; they were also eagerly devoured by the wealthy bourgeoisie who gleaned information from them about such things as the rituals of the social season, where to rent a house, which shops to patronize, what was the correct time to take a ride in the park, and so on. In addition, they were consumed by middle-class subscribers to circulating libraries who gained from them fascinating glimpses into the life of the *beau monde*.[27]

The novels always featured balls, dinners, duels, dandies, country houses, ruinous gambling, beautiful ladies, and charming villains, usually drawn from the lower ranks of the aristocracy.[28] They were liberally sprinkled with noble-sounding names and descriptions of material objects and environments.

There was a particular attention to public or semi-public establishments that most readers would have heard of and to which even vicarious access would have seemed more plausible than entry to private houses. These included Almanack's, the exclusive dance club run by women, and Crockford's gambling club. Publishers quickly learned that glamorous elements to captivate the public were best woven into works that dealt with high life, low life, ancient life, and exotic life. All provided fantasies of transformation away from the mundane and the everyday.[29]

Published between the 1820s and 1840s, the novels of Catherine Gore, Benjamin Disraeli, and others were in fact often set during the Regency.[30] Authors used the glitter and style of the period to fascinate audiences for whom its hedonism and excesses were no more than a memory. The exciting age of the Regency was not one that the stolid middle classes of the era of William IV and Queen Victoria wanted to restore. Rather they despised its self-serving indulgence and immorality, but they were drawn to it as imaginative escape, as a beautiful but flawed age.[31] The 'silver fork' genre had first been called the 'Dandy School' and among the real-life personalities who was evoked directly or indirectly in the novels was one of the most notable figures of the Regency era, the celebrated dandy George 'Beau' Brummell, who came to have a significant impact on the dynamics of metropolitan life.

In the past, social leaders had established their superior status by means of refined clothing and accessories. The sheer cost of the clothing of noblemen and women had acted as an insurmountable obstacle to parvenus and social climbers. However, not only was such excess ever less convenient in the prevailing climate but excess had been carried to almost satirical extremes by the eccentrically dressed Macaroni who flourished in the 1760s and 1770s. Flamboyance and foppery were the main hallmarks of young men who mimicked courtly clothing and current French and Italian fashions, which they had picked up while away on the Grand Tour. These men took more interest in themselves and each other than in women and may have been homosexuals.[32] They were certainly labelled as effeminate. They celebrated artifice and self-fashioning but their excesses made extravagance seem ridiculous and vulgar,[33] even when embraced by members of royalty. In the years that followed, consumption became more discreet and subtle.

The pioneer of what would become the dress style of the English gentleman, Brummell favoured an emphasis on understatement and precision. He
disdained the colour and visual flair of flamboyant dandies for a limited
palette of black, white, and subdued tones. This was more in line with the
sort of clothes that were worn by rough-house Regency bucks, high-spirited
aristocratic men who indulged fully in the pleasures of both town and
country. But Brummell was less interested in sports than in style. He set
great store by scrupulously white, country-laundered shirts and perfectly
tied neckties. He was a polished and impeccably groomed man who was
perfectly in tune with—and who indeed contributed to create—the fashion
culture of the metropolis. For Brummell, fashionable primacy had to be
asserted on a terrain where competition was inevitable. For this reason, his
most recent biographer, Ian Kelly, sees him as a transitional figure who
symbolized important changes in what he describes as 'the semiotics of
peacockery'.[34]

Brummell was born into a family that was close to the elite (his father had
been secretary to the prime minister Lord North) but he was not socially
distinguished and he owed his emergence to a stroke of luck. After studies at
Eton and Oxford, he met and impressed the Prince of Wales to the extent
that he was granted a commission in the Tenth Hussars, his personal
regiment for which he had even designed the uniforms. Brummell allegedly
resigned his commission when the regiment was to be transferred to Manchester. However, this experience placed him at the centre of the London
scene and provided him with the platform from which he launched his social
career. If glamour is taken to be a melange of bright and not always tastefully
arranged materials and effects, then Prince George was a far more glamorous
figure than Brummell. At his father's birthday in June 1791, when he was still
Prince of Wales, he arrived wearing a striped silk coat and breeches in deep
red and bottle green and a silver waistcoat studded with gems. There were
even diamond buttons on his coat and waistcoat, a custom started by none
other than Louis XIV.[35] But in other, more important, respects, Brummell
was at the centre of the social and cultural transformations that brought
glamour as a system of relations and effects into being. Although he owed
his initial rise to the prince, Brummell's influence was due to a new pattern

of male dressing that did not distinguish so overtly between the rich man and the poor man or the noble and the commoner. A hierarchy of beauty and taste emerged that was distinct from, and, in the context of the metropolis, more important than, lineage or even—to rather lesser an extent—money.[36] Brummell was the first product of this system just as related breaks in the social and political order had permitted the rise of Napoleon and Byron. A man of middle-class origins who mixed in the most exclusive social set, he performed a masquerade of superiority that was admired by contemporaries and seemed to be eminently copiable.[37] He was desirable and desired, imitable and imitated. Moreover, he was at the core of the publicity machine of his day.

In the context of the metropolis, appearances took on a special importance because people were constantly encountering others whom they did not know.[38] This provided opportunities for those who invested time and effort in cultivating a front. The dandy was a figure who was not distinguished by the nature of his clothes so much as by the importance he attached to them. 'A dandy', Thomas Carlyle declared in his satire *Sartor Resartus*, 'is a Clothes-wearing Man, a Man whose trade, office and existence consists in the wearing of Clothes.'[39] 'Appearing at the top of the mode no longer depended on the power of purchasing certain expensive articles of dress, or in the right of wearing them,' Hazlitt observed. Rather, he continued, 'any one who [chooses] might cut as coxcombical figure as the best.... A lord is hardly to be distinguished in the street from an attorney's clerk; and a plume of feathers is no longer mistaken for the highest distinction in the land!' 'Clothes and social confidence will set anybody up in the trade of modish accomplishment.'[40] Hazlitt proclaimed this to be a modern achievement: 'The idea of natural equality and the Manchester steam-engines together, have, like a double-battery, levelled the high towers and artificial structures of fashion in dress, and a white muslin gown is now the common costume of the mistress and the maid, instead of one wearing, as heretofore, rich silks and satins, and the other coarse linsey-wolsey.'[41]

By the early nineteenth century, manufacturing had brought fashion and consumer goods within the reach of far wider strata. Fashion was no longer largely a courtly interest but part of the texture of metropolitan life that thanks to fashion plates and improvements in roads and communications reached even village-dwellers and shops.[42] The duchess and her chambermaid, Mary Robinson argued, albeit with some exaggeration, 'are dressed exactly alike'. She observed that 'the nobleman and his groom are equally ambitious of displaying the neat boot, the cropped head, and the external decorations, as well as the quaint language, of the stable-boy'. These insights point to the existence of metropolitan fashions that were not purely related to the class system; even though status was still and would remain important, there were some modes and manners that were intrinsically metropolitan. 'Refinement is . . . visible in the exterior ornaments of all ranks of people,' Robinson claimed;[43] decorative accessories were adopted even by those whose general dress was not very elegant. No one was under any illusion that the great cities were places of equality. London was still highly class-conscious and differences of wealth were very marked. The great novelty was that distinctions were no longer seen to be fixed.

Mary Robinson was not the only one to comment on the strangely inclusive nature of the metropolitan parade. Hazlitt, a near contemporary, mused on the way cockneys (by which he meant all Londoners who had never lived outside London) identified with the most desirable environments and pastimes, even those they were practically excluded from. The typical cockney, he observed, 'sees everything near, superficial, little, in hasty succession':

The world turns round, and his head with it, like a roundabout at a fair, till he becomes stunned and giddy with motion. Figures glide by as in a *camera obscura*. There is a glare, a perpetual hubbub, a noise, a crowd about him; he sees and hears a vast number of things, and knows nothing. He is pert, raw, ignorant, conceited, ridiculous, shallow, contemptible. His senses keep him alive; and he knows, inquires, and cares for nothing further. He meets the Lord Mayor's coach, and without ceremony treats himself to an imaginary ride in it. He notices the people going to court or to a city-feast, and is quite satisfied with the show. He takes the wall of a lord, and fancies himself as good as he. He sees an infinite quantity of people pass along the street, and thinks there is no such thing as life or a knowledge of character to be found out of London.[44]

Processes of social selection and exclusion no longer occurred solely on the basis of position or birth.[45] Rather there was a series of institutions and rituals where practices of exclusion obtained, from gentlemen's clubs to the

Hyde Park promenade, from dress style to language. This meant that even some of the well-born could find themselves marginalized on some level, or subject to the capricious judgement of a parvenu like Brummell, on account of their physical or social awkwardness, or lack of wit and style. Through this means, a fashionable coterie was forged that, while not exactly meritocratic, was defined on the basis of the life of the metropolis rather than the aristocratic principle of the land and birth. Exhibitionist and fun-loving aristocrats were fully part of this, but so too were attention-seekers, ambitious creative types, and beauties. They figured prominently in the press and the scandal sheets that reported on them and glorified them. It was this world, where it was ultimately not birth but money that was king, that Thackeray captured in *Vanity Fair*. From his viewpoint the fashionable world was a fair of vanities, a notion that by itself conveyed the idea of noise, crowds, competition, and display.

Brummell was a snob and a social climber who was sometimes seen as a new man like Napoleon. He was a self-aware model for the ambitious. As Captain Gronow put it, 'all the world watched Brummell to imitate him, and ordered their clothes of the tradesman who dressed that sublime dandy'.[46] The man himself spent his days on a round of pleasures that included walking, riding, shopping, gambling, dining, and hanging out with courtesans. According to his biographer, he 'was always drawn to glamour'.[47] He shared with the courtesans a reliance on image in maintaining position. His aloof attitude and position as an *arbiter elegantarium* inevitably made him intriguing and fascinating.[48] He enjoyed widespread fame and a general desire to imitate his mastery of style spread among men of all classes. By seeking to be 'inimitable', he automatically established a relationship with emulative practices and aspirations. He was the first embodiment of the glamorous paradox of accessible exclusivity.

The dandy phenomenon was one that was widely regarded as intriguing and this ensured that it was continually debated. The author of one satire, entitled *Dandymania*, noted that there were 'Dandy Lawyers, Dandy Parsons, Dandy Physicians, Dandy Shopkeepers, Dandy Clerks, Dandy Authors, Dandy Beggars, and Dandy Pickpockets'.[49] Robert Southey found that in 'the famous Bond-street' there is a 'professor... who, in lessons at half a guinea, instructs gentlemen in the art of tying their neckerchiefs in the newest and most approved style'.[50] The cult also crossed the Channel as Parisians began to copy English dress styles and 'dandies in black dress coats and shiny riding boots made their appearance on the boulevards'.[51] As a Lakeland poet, Southey had little time for the fashionables. 'These gentlemen stand highest in the scale of folly, and lowest in that of intellect, of any in the country', he thundered.[52] 'It is impossible to describe them, because no idea can be formed of infinite littleness; you might as reasonably attempt to dissect a bubble or to bottle moonshine, as to investigate their characters.' Brummell himself would be ridiculed in several 'silver fork' novels some time after his stiff collars and high cravats had passed out of fashion. Yet he was difficult to pigeonhole. On the one hand, he adapted to the personal reserve and rejection of theatricality that marked the emerging model of masculinity; on the other, he subverted it by making a display of his sartorial and grooming practices.[53] His highly ritualized five-hour morning toilette drew spectators, among whom there was, on a few select occasions, even Prince George.

Like many later arbiters of style who were not an organic part of the social elite, Brummell probably suspected that his position was not exactly unassailable. But the manner in which the prince studied him, adopted the fashion for snuff-taking, and sought tips on male elegance, in addition providing him with frequent hospitality, bolstered his confidence. Brummell often indulged in witty banter but his encounters with the prince lost some of their cordiality. After receiving a snub, Brummell and his friends organized a reception to which they deliberately failed to invite the prince. The ensuing fuss obliged them to back down and issue an invitation. When the prince arrived, he conversed with some of the hosts but turned his back on Brummell. The dandy responded by loudly asking one fellow, 'Alvanley, who is your fat friend?' Brummell owed his entry into high society to the favour he enjoyed with the prince; this insult caused it to evaporate.[54] Soon after, he fled to northern France, where he would spend the rest of his days.

The loss of royal patronage was damaging but Brummell's downfall was not in fact solely due to his falling-out with his one-time patron. He was the architect of his own demise in so far as he, a man without extensive resources, had been seduced by the ruinous Regency vogue for heavy gambling. Like duelling, the indifference to loss it entailed showed the gentlemanly sangfroid of its practitioners and distinguished them from social upstarts. Ultimately, it was the imminent threat of ending up in prison for debt that led Brummell to abandon the scene and flee to France. His rise and fall was the typical trajectory of the glamorous personality, as the cases of his contemporaries Byron and Napoleon showed. His downfall marked the end of the social career of the man but not the phenomenon in which he had been a catalyst.

A society that attributed importance to front and performance needed mirrors to hold up to itself. In the social relations of the metropolis, theatre won new importance. It was a realm unto itself, a sphere that was both special and separate with respect to society, while also being an integral part of it. It was one of the prime locations for the formation and perpetuation of a common metropolitan culture. It acted as a codifier of behaviour in an impersonal society in which appearances and rituals were important and the deference that was still commonplace in the countryside was lacking. It attracted all classes and was an essential element of daily pleasure.[55] It was the one place where everyone was on display at once.[56] To this extent, theatres had a pedagogical function. For Mary Robinson, 'the open schools of public manners, which exhibit at all times the touchstone of the public mind, are the theatres'. Hazlitt concurred, noting that 'a playhouse alone is a school of humanity'.[57] This was so despite a constant recycling of Shakespeare, as well as of certain standards such as Sheridan's brilliant comedy of manners and social types *School for Scandal*, which remained a favourite for several decades after its debut with an all-star cast in 1777. With its sparkling dialogue and mocking of aristocratic pretensions, the play was one of the channels through which a sense of the new fluidity in social relations took shape. In cities there was a sense of belonging and citizenship and indirect social relations prevailed. Hazlitt added that only in big cities such as London, 'there is a public; and each man is part of it'.[58]

It was through theatre that a special grammar of composed behaviour was forged that was a feature of metropolitan life.[59] A man like Byron, for example, cannot be understood without reference to it. A regular habitué of theatreland and an admirer of Edmund Kean, he loved the world of professional illusion and the possibilities it offered for the displacement of conventional morality.[60] Brummell's sense of composure and performance derived from personal experience of the stage, including acting during his school days at Eton. The theatre offered him an understanding of how he could occupy a role in London society and use wit and style as arms of combat.

Theatre was part of the fabric of leisure of the city. Plays were performed at fairs and in pleasure gardens as well as taverns. It was not just what was seen and heard on stage that mattered, but the whole experience. People went to look at the audience as much as the stage and to be seen by others. Select theatres such as the King's Theatre in the Haymarket, the home of the Italian opera and the ballet, offered box subscriptions for sale that were eye-wateringly expensive. For the fashionable elite, men like Brummell and his friends, the theatre was another opportunity for social performance of their own. While the middle classes and out-of-towners came for the play, the *haut ton* distinguished itself by arriving halfway through the performance of plays that, for it, were usually very familiar. Its members typically made a great deal of noise as they occupied the boxes that served as a means to establish visibility and social prominence. However, theatre audiences were made up of a cross-section of society and were often rowdy and vocal. Far from being deferential towards their betters, they often subjected the occupants of the boxes to positive or negative responses according to whim.

In the early eighteenth century, theatres were closely regulated. In Paris, Louis XIV had established state theatres and given them a monopoly of certain types of entertainment. Only two theatres in London were licensed for prose productions and the repertoire of plays was very limited. A century later, the same two theatres dominated the scene, but, after they were burned down in fires, Covent Garden was rebuilt to hold 2,500 people and Drury Lane 3,600.[61] When Southey visited the latter, he wrote: 'I had heard much of this theatre, and was prepared for wonder; still the size, the height, the beauty, the splendour, astonished me.'[62] To attend them was seen as a right and any rise in ticket prices provoked protests. Paris was well behind London in the development of larger theatres, although commercial theatre developed from the 1760s bringing plays to the poorer classes, who previously had only encountered performance at fairs. In the following decades, the theatre became a forum of public opinion, with apparently innocuous plays being loudly applauded when a phrase of some possible wider application was pronounced.[63] During the 1790s, royal theatres were stripped of their privileges and restrictions on new establishments were lifted. Professional actors played to a public that often indulged in amateur theatricals and which was said to be gripped by *théâtromanie*.[64] The city had no large theatres under the Empire but a large quantity of small stages. There were so many in fact that Napoleon, who was suspicious of their subversive potential, closed down three-quarters of them by decree, leaving only the four official theatres and four privately owned ones. 'Is it not disgraceful that Paris does not have a sole French theatre or opera worthy of the city that hosts it?', he exclaimed.[65] In consequence, discussions began that would eventually lead to construction of the Opéra Garnier under the Second Empire.

The idea was forged during this period of the metropolis as a place where things happened and where life was lived more intensely. As such, it lent itself to narratives of a fictional and semi-fictional nature. One of the earliest and most successful examples of the way the metropolis bred narratives of itself was provided by Pierce Egan's characters Tom and Jerry (the historical antecedents of the cartoon cat and mouse). First published as monthly instalments in 1821, Egan's 'Life in London' was originally intended to exploit a possible market in the provinces for tales of London life. Its premiss was that 'if Londoners [were] keen on books about country and outdoor pursuits why should not provincials and even Cockneys be anxious to learn about life in London[?]'[66] In the stories, Corinthian Tom, a town dandy, and his country cousin Jerry Hawthorne are Regency bucks who cavort in the canonical locations of Mayfair and go cruising in the Burlington Arcade. They get into scrapes with roughnecks and are drawn irresistibly to gambling clubs. The serial, illustrated by Cruikshank, was a huge success and even reached the attention of George IV, to whom it was dedicated. Tom and Jerry were men about town whose adventures were full of identifiable characters, streets, and gin-shops. The opening song of the stage version celebrated London as 'a dashing place . . . where novelty is all the rage—from high to low degree'.[67] As with all metropolitan dramas, much emphasis was given to appearances. 'A man must have the look of a gentleman, if nothing else,' Tom declared; 'We must assume a style if we have it not.'[68] The stage show was so successful that it gave rise to numerous pirated versions. Other authors imitated the structure of Egan's work, including Bernard Black-mantle, whose *The English Spy* catered to a 'silver fork' public by including more and better-observed high society episodes.[69] Such successes confirmed that London was as much an imaginary place as a real one and that fantasies of London life often provided people with keys to interpret the city as a site of adventure and excitement where fashionable places and people, as well as low-life haunts, were accessible to everyone.

Gossip about the socially prominent that had been the bread and butter of the scandal sheets gave way to more acceptable coverage of performers and theatrical events. The rise of respectability resulted in the world of perform-ance taking on the burden of society's fantasies of transgession. Writing in 1839, Charles Dickens noted how 'theatrical converse' had become common currency in a London that was filled with people aspirant above their social station.[70] Theatre was a key platform in many a launch to fame and notoriety. For example, a prominent figure like Mary Robinson, who enjoyed celebrity status following a brief liaison with the Prince of Wales, appeared on stage, was a fashionable icon who introduced the latest French modes, a professional beauty, a royal mistress, and wrote novels.[71] For someone such as her who, like Brummell, owed some of her celebrity to a royal connection, the metropolis was a great stage; its pleasure gardens, theatres, salons, and social gatherings were all places to be seen. Robinson was a master manipulator of public opinion who regularly reinvented herself. She was a glamorous, much-admired, personality who was regularly to be seen in her superb carriages. For the press, the ongoing narrative of her love life was public property. She was one of the first people to appreciate and exploit the commercial value of celebrity.

The buzz of theatrical novelty did not derive from the established playhouses so much as the new theatres that produced musical entertainments, shows, and dancing. Patrons of theatrical entertainments, regardless of their social class, were fond of variety, colour, and spectacle. Establishments such as Astley's amphitheatre provided a mishmash of drama, circus, horsemanship, and pantomime that reflected a love of novelty and brightness that characterized metropolitan life in general.[72] Pictorial extravaganzas and visual sensations became more important as the century progressed. In this way theatre provided the regular outlet for the demand for display that modern society generated. Audiences whose lives were marked by routine found an escape in the colourful dramas and personalities of the theatre.

While printed material and books remained important, visual novelties provided a more direct stimulus to the common imagination. Projected images and limelight were deployed in extravagant shows and pantomimes. Giant productions, with huge crowd scenes and spectacular effects were a stock-in-trade at Astley's, which re-enacted great world events such as the fall of the Bastille or the battle of Waterloo, often within days of them occurring.[73] Costumes, 'pictorial splendours', and the pursuit of illusion were feared by some contemporary observers to be displacing the ability to treat human feeling and behaviour.[74] None the less, workers and the middle classes especially found in entertainment a welcome relief from the daily grind. The development of electricity in the last decade of the nineteenth century led to further stress on the brash and garish. So 'profuse and glaring' was the light bathing the stage that, according to one journalistic observer, 'all distance and mystery is lost, while the scene painters are compelled, in self-defence, to make their colours as fiery as possible'. Their attempts were not entirely successful. 'The glare of light in which our stages are bathed is fatal to all illusion,' noted the same observer; 'it reveals everything, the rifts in the boards, the texture and creases in the canvas, the streaks of paint. The light, playing on the edges of the side scenes, would show us that they were mere screens.' However there was a way forward. Once its use could be properly modulated and controlled, electric light could assist rather than undermine illusion: 'with subdued lighting, and low, rich tones and colours, the edges would be softened away, and all made into one whole'.[75]

In his disguise as a foreign visitor to London, Southey found himself 'astonished at the opulence and splendour of the shops.... Nothing which I had seen in the country prepared me for such a display of splendour'.[76] As the city grew as a centre of entertainment, so it expanded as a retail centre. With the early nineteenth-century rebuilding of the West End, which gave social prominence to new shopping areas, such as Regent Street and Oxford Street, that were near to the fashionable elite and the theatres, more shops sprang up. Even though men like Brummell notoriously ran up huge debts on their accounts, the dandy was a great boon to shopkeepers. The great attention these men gave to their appearance and the extensive publicity they received ensured that tradesmen were able to profit from their custom on a grand scale and benefit from the influence they had on others. Shirt-makers, silversmiths, cobblers, tailors, hatters, glovers, and perfumers took advantage and played on the allure of sophisticated lifestyles to win converts to consumption. In the wake of the dandy craze, many tailors and shops set up in the vicinity of St James's Street and Jermyn Street, which functioned as a sort of open-air salon for men of fashion.[77]

Shopping was already a leisure activity and a pastime in the 1750s. Dr Johnson remarked on the proliferation of fashionable shops in exclusive areas in London, although his distrust of any activity that required new clothes did not make him an ideal customer.[78] The phenomenon was not limited to the rich. The expansion of shops and shopping was driven by the desires and the habits of ordinary people and especially the burgeoning middle class.[79] Business people, professionals, and clerks embraced con-sumer goods on account of the values of politeness, modernity, respectabil-ity, and independence that they conveyed. They were not associated with aristocratic excess but with civility, taste, and moderation. At a time when land was difficult to obtain, even for the rich, or was beyond reach, goods tended to become adopted as the main symbols of distinction. Although British consumption in the eighteenth century was fuelled by the global trade in Eastern luxuries, most new goods were made with modern methods and materials. The process of manufacture created a 'semi-luxury' that lacked the uniqueness of upper-class luxury, even if some of the pleasures provided by sight, smell, and taste were shared.[80] Techniques of selling and presentation developed in tandem as shopkeepers decorated their exteriors with coloured paints and adornments and furnished their interiors to make them inviting. Because of these innovations, the historian Maxine Berg has argued that 'the eighteenth century is the defining moment in the history of consumer culture in the west'.[81] On the one hand consumption was about lifestyles, on the other it was about dreams and desires. Yearning and longing, phenomena of the imagination largely unknown to the feudal aristocracy, were central to middle-class consumption.[82] In between these poles, there was an intermediate realm of sensorial pleasure that was both stimulated by, and which in turn further stimulated, imaginings and longings. Exoticism was one of the key ways in which these various elements were held together.[83] The success of Byron's Eastern poems and the curiosity his adventures aroused were fuelled by this nascent consumer culture.

The development of a national market and national advertising for manufactured goods began as early as the 1760s. Josiah Wedgwood pioneered mass-produced pottery and developed original ways to sell it.[84] He used press advertising, smart showrooms, and astute self-promotion. An innovative manufacturer, he was also a publicity genius who realized that by attaching an aristocratic or even royal patina to his products he could sell them for higher prices. He went to great lengths to secure customers among the nobility, even to the extent of sending them unordered items for which they were later billed. He then advertised this patronage to promote his wares among the broader public. His greatest coup came in 1773, when Catherine the Great of Russia commissioned a thousand-piece dinner service for state occasions. Before it was shipped, Wedgwood put the service on display and even charged admission to view it. The exhibition drew a massive audience that included even some royals and many nobles. The aristocracy may no longer have dominated consumption but it preserved a role as tastemaker and example that carried great cachet.[85] The street culture of the modern metropolis was populated by the would-be aristocrats, swaggering apprentices, shabby-genteel people, theatrical young gentlemen, and bragging imposters that Dickens observed in his notes on London.[86] Many of these approximated to Baudelaire's Parisian *flâneurs* as observers of the city's novelties and curiosities. They were ostensibly looking up at their betters, but imitation was not, in this instance, the most sincere form of flattery. Consumption was never only about social climbing. It also involved fantasies about individual identity and material gratifications.

Glamour was the seductive and captivating surface aspect of the urban scene. Scintillating occasions caught their attention and provided them with spectacle and amusement. For Hazlitt, the London dweller was a man who 'comes so often in contact with fine persons and things, that he rubs off a little of the gilding, and is surcharged with a sort of secondhand, vapid, tingling, troublesome self-importance'.[87] He is 'dazzled with noise, show, and appearances' and in consequence 'lives in a world of romances—a fairyland of his own'.[88] Baudelaire, more famously, observed similar phenomena in the Paris of the 1840s. His *flâneur*, like Hazlitt's Londoner, was a male figure who delighted in the sights that the city offered, glittering displays, shop windows, pretty women, fine carriages, and so on. But whereas the Frenchman concentrated on the visual surface of modern life, the English critic captured the way urban visual sensations have a remarkable capacity to distort social relations and create a common experience. Fleeting sensations were curiously sticky and memorable. Hazlitt's subject was not the well-to-do idler (or Bond Street lounger, in the London language of the 1820s) but rather a worker: a footman, a tailor, a barker, or a slopseller. It was men like these who were drawn into the milieu of the metropolis and its 'gorgeous, glowing scene'.[89] Glamour was a blend of desirable and opulent lifestyles, spectacle, and sex appeal that became a feature of modern urban society. All classes were susceptible to this, although they each related to it in different ways. The appropriation of elite style and cachet and the remaking of these qualities by the commercial sector contributed vitally to the formation of a common language of allure. Style was only glamorous to the extent that it was perceived as such by the lower urban classes.

Although many people were drawn to shops and fashion, there were cultural obstacles to continuous acquisition. This meant that strategies of enticement were required to manipulate wants and needs, to attract interest, to promote aspirations and create rituals that made consumption satisfying. Merchants and pioneers of retailing drew heavily on showmanship, magic, and religion. Great attention was dedicated to where and how goods were shown and sold, advertising developed as a medium, and technology was harnessed to maximum effect. These efforts served to create contexts that endowed commodities with an aura, a mystery, or an appeal that went beyond their basic essence.[90] The daydreaming to which novelists had become so expert in catering to was sustained and further stimulated in the arcades and stores that became the new retail outlets of the age of consumption.

While abstraction, rationality, and money became the guiding principles of the economic system, irrational impulses, romantic currents, and illusions prospered. Magic, trickery, and illusion were annexed to the commercial imperative to camouflage it and render banal things desirable, beautiful, enviable, and intriguing. Corridors of iron and glass forming arcades of small shops were the first edifices specifically to be erected as centres of consumption. As enclosed multi-unit environments, they were the forerunners of the shopping malls of the late twentieth century. Specializing in luxury goods and situated in fashionable areas, they drew both the wealthy and curious browsers. The Marxist critic Walter Benjamin, writing in the 1930s, identified commercial arcades of the type that were built in London in the 1810s and in Paris a little later as the prototypical setting of the consumerist dream world. In them, he wrote, 'commodities are suspended and shoved together in such boundless confusion, that [they appear] like images out of the most incoherent dreams'.[91]

As the century progressed, the dreams seemed less incoherent due to the increasing sophistication and scale of work of image-makers. Photographers, graphic artists, industrial designers, architects, and lighting specialists all contributed to the building of arcades, panoramas, winter gardens, theatres, public spas, stores, stations, as well as the great exhibitions. All these institutions distorted reality or created alternative realities. 'All collective architecture of the nineteenth century provides housing for the dreaming collective,' Benjamin argued,[92] although he also found dream material in middle-class interiors. The heavy objects, dark colours, and overworked furniture of the late Victorian era created an aesthetic of excess that was itself dream-inducing.[93] Consumers wanted to be something different from what they were and they shaped their material environments in line with their dreams.[94]

The great exhibitions, which became a hallmark of the industrial age, were ephemeral monuments to the new material civilization. They were huge encampments into which all could gain access and experience the wonders and the abundance of the age of industry. Although the first great exhibition was held in London in 1851, Paris took over the idea and made it its own. The gigantic spectacles of the great exhibitions that were held in Paris in 1855, 1867, 1889, and 1900 were central to the French bid to establish their capital as the centre of European civilization. Napoleon III presided over a massive increase in French industrial production and promoted prosperity as a diversion from dictatorship. All forms of spectacle, excitement, and display were harnessed to this end. Even after the fall of the Second Empire in 1870, the connections between consumerism and entertainment were especially close in France.

The exhibitions admitted people of all classes and took them into a realm of possibilities that previously could not have been imagined. They brought together art and commerce, and technology and entertainment. Whereas the London exhibition displayed no prices, with the result that the abundance of goods provoked awe rather than covetousness, the Paris exhibition of 1855 displayed goods in a sumptuous fashion with price tags on view, giving people the opportunity to 'browse, explore and dream of potential ownership'.[95] As spectacles, the exhibitions were unrivalled. They were huge in scale, highly innovative in their architecture, and at the forefront of developments in applied technology. At first elites were wary of dropping the entry price low enough to admit the masses. But experience showed that workers were no less fascinated than others by the display of wonder and plenty.

However, they were soon joined and eventually eclipsed by department stores. Outside very large cities, such stores today struggle to survive but, in the middle of the nineteenth century, they were the monuments to the grandeur and wealth of the cities which hosted them. The big stores sold huge quantities of goods to vast numbers of people at prices that were lower than ever before. They contributed to the new function of the city as a pleasure zone by offering the shopper a range of sights, seductions, and services.[96] They also added to the brightness and magical atmosphere that marked districts characterized by wealth, power, entertainment, and consumption.

The Oriental imagery that became increasingly important was informed by France's imperial involvements. The expositions of 1867 and 1889, for example, included reproductions of Egyptian temples and streets, and Moroccan tents. In North America, Eastern enchantments were part of the pedlar tradition in rural communities. Pedlars who sold clothes, perfume, or jewellery were reputed to deal in glamour and magic because their focus was personal image and transformation.[97] Oriental motifs were employed by New York retail magnate A. T. Stewart in store interiors in 1863 and they would find regular deployment in other large-scale temples of consumption on both sides of the Atlantic. By this means, the link between the market and exotic Oriental goods was firmly established in the minds of female customers in particular.[98] Displays were not, however, accurate reproductions of distant cultures.[99] The journalist Maurice Talmeyr, writing for a high-profile weekly, remarked that the exhibits at one of the great Paris exhibitions were a gaudy and incoherent jumble of 'Hindu temples, savage huts, pagodas, souks, Algerian alleys, Chinese, Japanese, Sudanese, Senegalese, Siamese, Cambodian quarters . . . a bazaar of climates, architectural styles, smells, colors, cuisine, music'.[100] Animals from different locations were mixed up, with stuffed wild boars and elephants filling the Indian exhibit and camels the Andalusian one. Talmeyr cited examples of the 'nullity, buffoonery, gross alteration, or absolute falsity' that abounded, before concluding that behind the mad 'ornamental delirium' and numerous deceptions lay a consistent principle.[101] The aim of commercial exhibitors was not to inform visitors but to amuse and excite consumers. Talmeyr denounced the systematic falsification that was involved. Visitors were drawn into a full-blown substitution of subjective images for external reality. Ultimately they were duped: 'Seeking a pleasurable escape from the workaday world, they find it in a deceptive dream world which is no dream at all but a sales pitch in disguise.'[102]

The flamboyance and eclecticism of the exhibitions were repeated in department stores. Zola's well-documented *Au bonheur des dames* (Ladies' Paradise) contains abundant Oriental decor. 'The counters of the department store present a disconnected assortment of "exhibits," a sort of "universe in a garden" of merchandise. The sheer variety, the assault of disassociated stimuli, is one cause of the numbed fascination of the customers . . . It is a style which may without undue flippancy be called the chaotic-exotic.'[103] Within single exhibits repetition was often employed 'to numb the spectator further'. Rugs, umbrellas, and all manner of other articles were lifted into a festive dimension. The lavish and the foreign, the jumble of striking and unusual images, all served to fuel desire for escape from the ordinary and the everyday. Their purpose was simply to attract and hold the spectator's attention. Thus questions of taste were irrelevant. Although the stores—in a marked difference to some of the arcades—courted mainly women customers, exotic decor was seductive rather than ladylike.[104] Exotic decor occupied a limbo between art and commerce. It had the stylistic traits of art, yet it had no uplifting aim; artistic trappings served merely to wrap up commercial purpose and lend it a supposed dignity.[105]

The Parisian Bon Marché store, which Zola took as the model for his novel, pioneered the revolution in marketing.[106] Aristide Boucicaut, the store's founder, was a showman who turned it into a permanent happening. He went about this by tantalizing and seducing his customers with special events, fantasies, and promotions. To visit the store was an exciting event that made the act of purchase into an experience. Scale was an important part of this. Unlike the exquisite charm of the gaslit fairyland of the arcades, the store was a monster, a massive structure that made abundance and variety the key to its basic identity. With its enormous open displays of commodities, it became a permanent fair and a spectacle on a grand scale that added to the lustre and image of the city.[107]

Stores could be brash and lurid, but they also embraced pomp and ceremony, mixing stately rituals with baser passions and longings. These were employed to suggest a this-worldly paradise that was stress-free and happy.[108] As part of this, sexual suggestions and appeals were crucial in attracting the attention of the public and stimulating its desires. In consequence, courtesans played a central part in fuelling the development of modern consumption. As professionals of make-believe and living luxury objects, they occupied a special place in the imagination of the nineteenth-century public. The fact that they also hailed, in most instances, from very ordinary or foreign backgrounds made them ideal vehicles for fantasies of social mobility and vicarious pleasure.

CHAPTER 3

THE BIRTH OF SEX APPEAL

C ourtesans were the glamour queens of the nineteenth century. They were flamboyant women who, through determination and luck, rose to become icons of beauty and leaders of fashion. They occupied an important place in the social and commercial life of several capitals and they loom large in the art and literature of the period. They were figures of luxury who led extraordinarily opulent lifestyles. Typically, they were young women of lowly or foreign origins who possessed charm, beauty, and steely determination. At one level, they were high-class prostitutes, but they were also much more than this. They were a category with specific features and functions that mediated the complex social and cultural passage from aristocratic to bourgeois society. The courtesans were all distinctive individuals with particular histories and influences. In some instances they were versatile figures, like the actress and writer Mary Robinson, who enjoyed a number of high-profile liaisons from which she drew profit; in others, like the most famous courtesan of the Regency, Harriet Wilson, they were commodities available to the men who frequented the Rotten Row promenade, the theatre and the opera, and Brighton. After the Regency, courtesans played a limited role in London life, but they prospered elsewhere, and most especially in Paris, where they became part of the city's attractions. They were a feature of the developing consumer economy and of the dream world that it fuelled. As professionals of performance and masquerade, they pioneered the modern idea of sex appeal as an organized tease. By this means, they reinforced the role of sex in glamour and established a connection that would never be broken.

In the late eighteenth and early nineteenth century several women, like the wayward duchess Georgiana and Mary Robinson in London, and Josephine de Beauharnais and Pauline Bonaparte in Paris, occupied a blurred area between aristocratic society and the world of fashion and pleasure. The courtesans, as a category with a fairly precise identity and social role, were a product of the new sexual hierarchy of the bourgeois era. Modern cities, as they developed in the early nineteenth century, were male-dominated and were largely geared to male requirements and pleasures. Respectable women could not be seen on the street and were not welcome in the areas of men's clubs, shops, and restaurants. They were confined to specific realms and institutions that were reserved for them. Their social power was exercised in the private sphere, where they determined the rules of entry to high society and ran the marriage market. Men preferred to choose their wives from among the blushing virgins who were presented to them at heavily chaperoned balls, but for fun and frolics they opted for the company of women of few scruples. Prostitution was a commonplace feature of every large city, but the favours of the courtesans could not simply be bought. They were polished up to near respectability and acted the part of ladies of leisure. Choice was one of their prerogatives. They were adept at using their sexual allure to exploit the desires and opportunities that arranged mar-riages and extensive leisure brought to aristocratic and rich men. Moreover, they were public figures who were vital to the buzz and dash of the modern metropolis. The courtesans simultaneously satisfied the demands of rich men for sexual pleasure and for kudos. The conditions for their existence and their public visibility were twofold: first, a dominant morality which permitted licence to men while denying it to women; second, an attitude towards money that was informed by the aristocratic refusal to be limited by

economy and self-restraint. These practices survived the onset of the industrial era, and indeed, like gambling, flourished within it, as nobles wasted
money on a grand scale to distinguish themselves from bankers and speculators. They were followed by some bourgeois men who could not resist
aping the aristocratic example.

The courtesans were celebrities, although the degree to which they were
socially acceptable varied greatly. In Regency London, the 'demi-reps' or
'Cyprians', as they were colloquially known, conquered a place at the centre
of the fashionable world. In the Victorian era, by contrast, they largely
disappeared as prostitution in all forms was relegated to the social margins.
In Paris, they flourished under Napoleon and the restoration, maintained
their place under Louis-Philippe and then enjoyed an unprecedented heyday
in the Second Empire. Whereas Great Britain in the Victorian era privileged
respectability, France's Napoleon III encouraged a climate of excess and
distraction that extended to the sexual arena. The allure of the women of
Paris became a calling-card of the city, a key indicator of its legendary 'gaiety'.

Even if not all of them were held to be beautiful, the courtesans were
intensely glamorous figures who knew how to make themselves desirable.
They were always expensively attired and wore their jewellery as a general
would wear his medals, as proof of battles fought and won. They were highly
visible figures who pioneered new fashions and whose example was often
followed by the women of respectable high society. They thrived on publicity;
to feature in the news or to be gossiped about was a way of increasing their
notoriety and exchange value. Each of them created a narrative that was made
up of her famous liaisons and the celebrated stunts or incidents she had been
involved in. The knowledge we have of them derives mostly from the press and
the memoirs of those who knew them. Like other figures of fashion whose
main concern was with appearances, they invested in surfaces and lived for the
moment. Few of them left any testimony behind. They cared little for reflection
or self-examination, so they remain mysterious for us, enigmas who will never
reveal all their secrets. Moreover, very few of them were painted by the artists of
their day, with the result that, for those who were famous before the age of
photography, we are forced to rely on the accounts of witnesses to have any idea
of what they looked like. One first-person account that we do have is provided

by the memoirs of Harriet Wilson.[1] Written at a time when her fortunes were low, she conceived them as a money-spinner, not so much because she hoped to reap the rewards of a best-selling book, but because she aimed to secure pay-offs from former lovers in return for leaving them out. The Duke of Welling-ton's famous exhortation, 'Publish and be damned!' was his abrupt response to Wilson's request for such a payment.[2] The image that transpires from her prose is that of a woman with a strong sexual appetite who was a master of the sort of faux-respectable appearance and manners that the well-to-do men of her era appreciated. She expected to be courted and to be treated with civility; blunt approaches were regarded as insulting. Wilson grew up in a humble family who lived in close proximity to Mayfair; her education in the ways of rich men thus began early.

The courtesan was a euphemistic figure who disguised her true identity. She was a product of the advance of gentility that affected all areas of society from the later eighteenth century. The slow rise of respectability brought an end to the custom of providing explicit guides to the sexual attractions of London's prostitutes. Crude and to the point, guides such as *Harris's List* did not romanticize or skate over the ugliness, coarseness, and physical attributes of some women of the town. Descriptions of 'squat, swarthy, round-faced wenches' and 'tolerably well-made' plump girls with 'eyes [that look] both ways at once' were provided along with the beauties and all were listed by name and address.[3] In 1795, however, the guides came to an end following a trial for obscenity which resulted in the editors receiving a £100 fine and twelve months in prison. In the period that followed, higher class prostitutes took on the external appearance of respectable women. The colours they wore may have been brighter and their engagement with foreign-inspired fashions more enthusiastic, but in many respects they were not readily distinguishable from high society women. As fake ladies, they were excluded from formal society but were an integral part of the public sphere.

Thackeray's anti-heroine Becky Sharp in *Vanity Fair* has many of the traits of the ambitious Regency courtesan. Unscrupulous and calculating, but possessed of a veneer of refinement due to her half-French background, she worms her way into the affections of several men, marries one, and is mistress to another before a downward spiral leads her to the lower rungs of prostitution. She reaches the outer edges of high society and mingles with nobility—notably the rake Lord Steyne—but fundamentally she is a sexual opportunist on the make. However, she is presented to the readers of *Vanity Fair* in a way that conceals her true behaviour; she is glossed to make her acceptable to those who preferred not to see vice called by its name. In one of his customary authorial interventions in the text, Thackeray challenges anyone to deny that she has been presented in 'a perfectly genteel and inoffensive manner'.[4] He proudly asserts that everything he has included has been 'proper, agreeable and decorous' and that 'the monster's hideous tail' has remained below water. Only those who 'may peep down under waves that are pretty transparent . . . see it writhing and twirling, diabolically hideous and slimy, flapping among bones, or curling around corpses,' he concluded chillingly. His concern not to offend was shared, curiously, by Harriet Wilson whose memoirs offer curious vignettes of the men of her day in the boudoir, but only the vaguest allusions to sex. Courtesans always carried an aura of scandal about them, but, outside their immediate circle, their bedroom practices were often the least well-known aspect of their lives. Wilson even wrote to Byron to upbraid him for the lewdness of *Don Juan*.[5] Euphemism was the dominant ethos in representation and glamour was inflected with this. It employed dazzle to ward off scandal.

In nineteenth-century London, scarcely less than in Paris, fashionable public rituals presented prostitutes with opportunities to insinuate themselves. The theatres and smart shopping districts were favourite haunts. Among the horsewomen to be seen taking rides in Hyde Park were elegant women who might have been taken for ladies had it not been for the fact that they were generally more beautiful and even, it was said, more graceful than their respectable counterparts. The pleasure gardens, arcades, and promenades were their natural habitat. In early nineteenth-century London, the Cyprians (as high-class prostitutes were then called) even staged their own balls and were sometimes invited to the masked balls that Brummell and his friends organized. It greatly amused these men that the device of the mask allowed them to draw the courtesans into a respectable context without fear of detection. Their real status was not readily visible except in their more daring manners as well as their studied fashionableness.

The theatre was often the setting that provided a courtesan with the best opportunity to get noticed or to increase her cachet. For most of the nineteenth century, no sharp distinction was drawn between the actress or performer and the prostitute. All women who put themselves on view or embraced different guises were considered to be beyond the bounds of respectability. Actresses were outsiders, at once highly visible and lacking any specific place in the social hierarchy. Often the pay of female stage performers was so low that they were obliged to seek financial support from their admirers. Yet courtesans were not necessarily stage performers, even though several began their careers as actresses. They used the theatre as a place where their social cachet could be asserted. By placing themselves on open view in expensive settings, such as elegant boxes, they advertised their availability and gave a rough indication of their market value. In the meantime, common prostitutes milled in the bars, corridors, and social areas of theatres, or in the street outside. Such practices persisted in some form over a long period. In Victorian London, prostitutes promenaded outside the Empire Theatre in Leicester Square—not far from the vice district of Soho—until the 1890s.[6] In Paris, subscription holders at the Palais Garnier opera house were only excluded from going behind the scenes to pick up dancers in 1927.[7]

As objects of desire endowed with public visibility, courtesans had a special fascination. Due to their wealthy sponsors, the women exercised a power in the field of consumption that was reflected first of all in their wardrobes. This in turn made them trendsetters and taste-makers for others. Mary Robinson noted that the influence of foreign fashion—by which she meant French influence—had led to an improvement in the general standard of dress and that a more natural elegance had displaced 'unmeaning flounces of many coloured frippery'.[8] In 1800 she proclaimed that 'The females of England are considerably indebted to our most celebrated actresses for the revolution in dress. Accustomed of late years to behold the costume of various nations gracefully displayed at our theatres, women of rank, who lead the capricious idol FASHION, through all the mazes of polite society, speedily adopted what they considered as advantageous to beauty.'[9] She might well have been speaking of herself since periodicals gave as much attention to her toilettes as to her beauty and, unusually for a woman in her position, her wit.

Comments such as Robinson's show that female glamour was the product of very specific processes that defined the industrial age and the modern city. Consumerism placed systematic emphasis on spectacle and display and fostered a commercialization of femininity. Patterns of communication and transmission of ideas about appearance, dress, and self-presentation emerged that did not follow the established social hierarchy but accorded prominence to outsider figures. A process of self-fashioning, and in some cases, of self-invention, developed that relied on clothes, cosmetics, and so on. These developments provided some women with opportunities to take on prominent roles, but at the same time they stereotyped them in ways that fitted in with the requirements of a male-dominated society.

The prominence or otherwise of courtesans in the social life of capital cities depended greatly on the ethos that was transmitted from the top. The sexual licence that characterized the upper realms of society during the Regency gave way to the primness of the Victorian era. By contrast, the modest, respectable rule of King Louis-Philippe, who ruled France during the so-called July Monarchy of 1830–48 and who had no court and even took strolls in the street with his wife,[10] was replaced by the rampant hedonism of the Second Empire. Thus, while courtesans exited the scene in London, they maintained a key place in the social system in Paris. With its emphasis on money, pleasure, and distraction, Napoleon III's regime produced an atmosphere that accorded unusual prominence to a category that consisted in total of perhaps a hundred women. The ceaseless round of entertainments in Paris influenced the attitude towards pleasure at the upper levels of society. Rapid social and economic change and a parvenu elite enabled the two dozen or so most prominent high-class prostitutes to live the most lavish and ostentatious of lifestyles.

The Second Empire used entertainment and consumption as a diversion from dictatorship and widespread poverty. The brash magnificence of the regime was incarnated only to a limited degree by Louis-Napoleon—the self-styled Napoleon III—himself. A man significantly less impressive in his achievements than his uncle, he did not seek monarchical legitimacy but instead set himself in the context of the Revolution and Bonapartism. Embracing popular sovereignty, he refused a dynastic marriage. On announcing that he would marry for love, he frankly proclaimed himself to be a parvenu, which he asserted was 'a glorious title when one succeeds to it by the free suffrage of a great nation'.[11] He allowed his Spanish-born wife Eugénie to dominate a court in which luxury and excess were the order of the day. The visual splendour of the formal festivities was fashioned by three men: Baron Georges-Eugène Haussmann, the influential prefect of the Seine, who acted as ringmaster-in-chief at the four official balls that were held each year; Charles Frederick Worth, the couturier who was chiefly responsible for the astonishing crinoline dresses that grew ever wider as the atmosphere of excess became more rarefied; Franz Xavier Winterhalter, the German painter who became chief portraitist of the imperial family and of the court. Worth, an Englishman, was a key figure in the commercial fashion of the period and his clients included many courtesans as well as the empress and ladies of the court.[12] Unlike Marie Antoinette's couturière, Rose Bertin, who created new styles in complicity with the queen and acted as guardian of the exclusivity of her patroness's gowns, while treating other clients haughtily,[13] Worth had a more pragmatic approach that made money the sole discriminator. His prestigious fashion house, founded in 1858, developed significant foreign sales, although the association with Paris was now more important than the connection with the court. Worth's most significant innovation in the history of couture was to bring the creative design of dresses and their fabrication together under one roof for the first time.[14] Winterhalter painted separately both the emperor, in a sumptuous dress uniform of vivid colours and with much surface dash, and the empress. His works were in the prevailing style of court painting and were more about status than individual character. Their vivid colours and uncomplicated surface appeal gave them a brash quality that matched the materialism of the age.

The Second Empire desperately sought to present a respectable and composed image to the world. Napoleon and Eugénie were on good terms with European royal families and they aimed to put themselves on a par with them. They developed their own equivalent of Brighton in the fishing village of Biarritz on the Atlantic coast of south-west France. After Eugénie built a palace on the beach, it became a fashionable resort that attracted British and

Spanish royals as well as noble and wealthy visitors. Yet the regime has been said to have been driven on purely by 'the phantasmagoria of money'.[15] The cultivated magnificence of the royal household, with its brightly uniformed and multifarious functionaries and its ostentatious general style, 'made the whole thing even more *parvenu*-like'.[16] Although the courtesans were kept rigorously separate from court society, the latter was regarded by some as the chief focus of louche behaviour and money-driven ostentation. Napoleon's 'carnival empire' had a strongly theatrical dimension which struck foreign aristocratic visitors as fabricated and imitative.[17] Not by chance, opulence, beauty, sensory excitement, and the dream of sudden wealth constituted the stock in trade of operetta, the entertainment form that most characterized theatre in an era of tight censorship. All the courts depicted in the many works of the leading composer of operetta, Jacques Offenbach, were modelled on Napoleon's own.[18] The era was not without its hypocrisies. While sex was widely commercialized, both Flaubert's *Madame Bovary* and Manet's *Déjeuner sur l'herbe* were the subject of prosecutions for offending morals.

Napoleon III harked back, like his more celebrated uncle, to some of the courtly rituals and practices of the Bourbons although, after several changes of regime there was no longer any easy distinction between the Bonapartist and the Bourbon styles. Louis XVIII had remained in Paris most of the time and kept many of Napoleon's ostentatious rituals and furniture, including even some emblems and his throne.[19] More than any of his predecessors, Louis-Napoleon systematically set about transforming Paris into great modern city. He continued Napoleon I's work but on a much larger scale and with the destruction of many buildings. Between the 1850s and the 1870s, old structures that dated in some instances from the Middle Ages were demolished and replaced with modern road systems and more standardized housing and public buildings. Expansions of population and the changing nature of work posed problems of order and integration that necessitated urban reform. The innovations that were carried out in Paris by Baron Haussmann, in his capacity as prefect of the Seine, were far-reaching. The reforms of the Haussmann era saw the blossoming of the image of Paris as a centre of display and distraction. However, the French capital was not alone. Major cities throughout the industrial world witnessed the development of zones dedicated to consumption and entertainment and Haussmann drew inspiration from changes that were already underway in London and in American cities like Chicago and Philadelphia. Despite a notional sense of equality, the pattern of urban reform catered mainly to the requirements of the wealthy. Public spaces were geared to private display and private enterprise was given free reign. In Paris, the wide boulevards opened out the city and imposed a long perspective that rendered it easier to occupy militarily as well as better geared to ceremonial and display. Reform also involved the relocation of the poor away from emerging areas of prestige. The west, as in London, was turned into a residential area for the rich and a site of social display. It was here that monuments, squares, parks, boulevards, and palaces made Paris a showcase within which political power asserted itself and the wealthy and stylish flaunted their social superiority.[20] Although class and other demarcations remained in force, the new image of the city was the homogenized one of the boulevards, with their ostentation, dynamism, aspirations, and illusions.[21]

Under the Second Empire, social life was endlessly displayed. The play-acting, the pantomime aristocracy, the facade of elegance and refinement which had at its core the courtesan and the racy crowd of *viveurs* who joined her in making over the image of the city had a vibrant and exciting effect.[22] Few notions conjure up mid-nineteenth-century Paris more than the *demi-monde*. Women belonging to it were celebrities who were constantly to be seen at theatres, restaurants, spas, taking rides in the park, celebrating winners at the races, and visiting couturiers. They systematically attracted attention and conferred the buzz of sex appeal on places and events in a way that truly upper-class women could not. The women of the *demi-monde* were not all identical; some were refined or artistic while others were ill-mannered and coarse. But all shared a cult of the self and of the material that made them ideal figures of modern fashion and celebrity. Some figures of a distinctly non-respectable stamp were received at court, such as the Italian beauty the Contessa di Castiglione who set about seducing the emperor with a well-rehearsed repertoire of tricks. Lacking the freshness of youth or an attractive personality, she planned her appearances to ensure that she always suggested a tantalizing aura of mystery.[23] However, it was mainly in public opinion that the court and the vibrant festivities of the city were confused.

The term *demi-monde* derived from the title of a play by Alexandre Dumas *fils* first performed in 1852. It gained more widespread recognition following publication of the novel *La Dame aux camélias*, Dumas's fictionalized account of his liaison with the consumptive courtesan Marie Duplessis. The novel became an international success and inspired Verdi's opera *La traviata*. These works highlighted the existence of a social milieu that was akin to Thackeray's *Vanity Fair*. It was made up of wealthy men and a range of déclassé women who joined it on the basis of their beauty and notoriety.[24] In the eyes of the ordinary public, there was little difference between the *demi-monde* and the *grand-monde*, or at least the two were not mutually exclusive. In every metropolis, high-class prostitutes haunted the most fashionable districts, placing their goods and promises of pleasure on display together with those of the stores. In keeping with the high tone of the modern city, they had turned themselves into mock-ladies by learning how to ride, speak, and comport themselves.[25] The top stratum of Paris courtesans formed a sort of international star system and several of them were of foreign origin. Cora Pearl was from England, Giulia Barucci from Italy, and La Païva (Therèse Lachmann) from Russia. Others, like the senior member of the group, Adèle Courtois, or Anna Deslions, Blanche D'Antingny, and Margherite Bellanger—who became Napoleon III's lover in 1863—were of humble French background. Each of them attracted men by developing individual qualities of charm, beauty, and erotic appeal.[26] They all catered to an international clientele that was defined by its leisured lifestyle and disdain for bourgeois convention. Such was the interest in these women among the wealthy visitors to the great exhibitions that the Goncourt brothers lamented that Paris had become a 'foreigner's bordello'.[27]

Due to Dumas's romantic portrayal, Marie Duplessis became, in the guise of her fictional alter ego Marguerite Gautier, the epitome of the courtesan. For film-goers of the middle decades of the twentieth century, Greta Garbo memorably brought her once more to life in the 1936 film *Camille*. The consumptive heroine who sacrifices her personal happiness to save the honour of her lover's family was a noble ideal. She was, however, an exception in her simplicity and also in the love she shows for Armand. Gautier is constantly described as being pale and wearing white clothing, in reference to her tuberculosis and the purity of her sentiments. But if there was one colour that was most associated with the *cocottes*, it was red. Scarlet carried connotations of the passion of Spain, of the Gypsies, and the Orient. Through these places and cultures—real but also imagined—red's association with sex and the unrespectable was codified in art, literature, and social behaviour. The interiors of theatres were usually plush red as were the bordellos from which they were not clearly distinguished before the twentieth century. In nineteenth-century Paris, red came to be identified as the modern colour of sex. As such it was employed by actresses and prostitutes, and only sparingly by respectable women, unless they were explicitly flirting with the subculture of sleaze. To win the love of a courtesan is exceptionally difficult, Dumas observed, since their bodies have used up their spirits, the senses have burned their hearts, and debauchery has cauterized their feelings. As a result 'they are better protected by their calculations than a virgin by her mother and her convent'.[28] All their efforts were geared to winning and keeping at least one prestigious and well-heeled lover. Like Gautier before she chooses love, the goal of them all was to have a duke at their beck and call. Typically, two or three protectors, usually known to each other, would befriend them simultaneously.

The most famous courtesan of the Second Empire conformed to this pattern. La Païva was the grandest example of the courtesan as a performer who plays at being a lady before public opinion and at being a devoted lover with her protector.[29] In a culture that celebrated wealth and money more than anything else, her avariciousness symbolized the period. Despite acquiring a noble Portuguese title through marriage, La Païva never won official recognition; yet she enjoyed pecuniary prestige and was able to establish a salon that was frequented by leading artists and writers.[30] La Païva's splendid mansion has been described as the most complete example of Second Empire style. Positioned on the most prestigious of the new boulevards, her palace (which was open to the public in the early years of the twentieth century; today it is occupied by the Touring Club) was an insolent affirmation of personal glory.[31] All the interiors, including the

89

furnishings, were new, and talented, sometimes undiscovered, artists were employed to fashion them. Some would make their reputations through it, even though the styles were drawn from an eclectic range of places and periods. The sculpted yellow onyx bathtub that would occupy pride of place in the bathroom received an award at the 1867 universal exposition. The ceiling of the salon was executed by Paul Baudry, who would later decorate the foyer of the Palais Garnier opera house—the edifice that is commonly seen as the symbol of Napoleon III's regime, even though it was not inaugurated until 1875. Positioned in the heart of the new Haussmann-reformed Paris of the boulevards and the stores, it was a triumph of the eclecticism that the period fostered.

Louis-Napoleon had no personal taste in matters of art or architecture; he merely encouraged others by public commissions and competitions. The style of the period has been described as bourgeois on account of its overt and eclectic materialism.[32] Appropriation and imitation were prevalent practices as the newly rich sought to bolster their position and self-perception by seizing hold of all the previous artistic products of aristocratic society. By the mid-nineteenth century, they were no longer outsiders seeking acceptance but a new elite in the process of consolidation. Convinced that the creations of the past could be refashioned and remade in a more cost-effective way by means of modern manufacturing methods, the new upper class born of speculation and industrial prosperity preferred new versions of the styles it ransacked. Appearances and comfort were what it was concerned with, not authenticity. This extended right up to the imperial family itself.

Louis-Napoleon had sought to compare his wife to his grandmother Josephine, whom he idealized. Eugénie, for her part, was strangely fascinated by Marie Antoinette and often introduced eighteenth-century motifs into her furnishings. However, the colours she chose were the brash ones of the Second Empire and chairs were tufted in the manner of the furniture of a bourgeois household.[33] Winterhalter was such a popular painter with the empress and the new rich of the time because he depicted his sitters as they wished to be presented, or rather, as they dreamed of themselves. His bold and alluring portraits are lifelike, yet elegant and idealized. He placed his subjects in compositions that often had a theatrical quality. The texture of fabrics, furs, and jewellery is almost tangible. His celebrated portrait of Eugénie surrounded by her ladies-in-waiting is a sumptuous feast of colour and beauty that underscored the primacy of female imagery in the articulation of the public face of the regime. The painting did not succeed in disguising the upstart nature of the imperial court, but it successfully presented the short and dumpy Eugénie as a woman of grace and style.[34]

The courtesans were a dependent category; they existed for men and were reliant on the latter's finances. But although they had often risen from nothing, some of them resented their exclusion from official society and did everything possible to compensate for it. By establishing her name and gaining wealth, the courtesan could mitigate her inferiority complex and mask the source of her success. Yet, for all her luxury, the bawdy aspect of the life of the courtesan was intrinsic and constant. Derided and notorious, it was said that La Païva 'would have given herself to a miner for a nugget'.[35] To her guests, she offered the finest dishes accompanied by vulgar and scatological conversation of the most salacious kind. The social activities of the courtesans were always occasions for the fabulous display of diamonds, pearls, and other precious stones. In 1860, *Le Figaro* announced a fancy-dress ball at which the goddesses of Olympus were to be represented by the Parisian courtesans. La Païva had, it was said, arranged to come as Juno; the treasures of diamonds, pearls, and precious stones she scattered over her dazzling tunic were valued at no less than 1,250,000 francs. For her part, Anna Deslions went as Venus, with 300,000 francs' worth of gems.[36] The courtesans were distinguished by the fabulous price tags that they indirectly expressed in their glittering jewellery, extravagant toilettes, sumptuous dwellings, and general lifestyle. The display of wealth and luxury made it apparent that a man had paid an exorbitant price for her favours. Social prestige within male circles derived from an individual establishing that he had the massive spending power to be able to waste vast sums on a woman who was not even his wife. The more lavish a courtesan's lifestyle, the more she was desirable as a vehicle of status to very rich men. The publicity that they attracted further enhanced their standing and rubbed off on the men who associated with them. Within the *demi-monde* at least, the courtesans were celebrities. The two dozen most famous were ostentatious to an extraordinary degree, dressing and furnishing their residences with every manner of luxury and costly ornamentation.[37] Although their activities were cloaked in the language of love, there was no category on earth that was more calculating. Ambition and money were the twin principles that drove them.

In return for their financial support and gifts, men did not only gain intimate access to a woman celebrated for her desirability. Merely sexual favours, even of the most refined kind, could be had for far less, and for far less trouble since the category of the courtesan was known for its paradoxical frigidity. Rather they acquired a reputation for high living, style, and fashionableness. The prominent aristocrats whose friendship was necessary to win the courtesan her fame were often happy to assert in this way a class difference with respect to the straight-laced bourgeoisie. The pursuit of pleasure for no end other than itself and a disdain for respectability and virtue were the hallmarks of these noblemen. To maintain a courtesan, like fighting a duel, was a futile gesture that showed a certain carelessness about practical matters such as one's fortune and self-preservation. The benefits also appealed to some wealthy bourgeois, who were much less inclined to sacrifice all for a courtesan but who appreciated the indirect advantages that association with one of them brought. For them, it was simply a matter of conspicuous consumption. Wealthy men could and did spend money on their wives but of necessity such expenditures were official, restricted by respectability, and were 'off the market'.[38] Since pecuniary power was typically established through non-productive forms of spending that were visible and acknowledged, the utility of such domesticated forms of expense was limited. To parade as a mistress one of the most visible and notoriously costly women of the day was a true luxury, entirely disassociated from necessity and achieved by beating the financial offers of rivals. In contexts where the values of respectability were not totally dominant, it therefore had greater value. The courtesans functioned as luxury objects and status symbols that appealed to bourgeois men who could procure them temporarily without having to violate bourgeois norms by personally displaying the outward signs of wastage and indulgence. They were emblems of success that were sought after by all those who wanted to establish their fashionable aloofness from all matters of budget.[39]

It was precisely their ostentatious lifestyles that made the courtesans so uniquely desirable. In *La Dame aux camélias*, Gautier confesses to Armand Duval that if a courtesan were to reduce her standard of living all her admirers would disappear: 'It is not, alas, our qualities that they appreciate but rather our faults and our extravagances. It is our luxury that attracts them, like the light draws butterflies.'[40] The courtesans were elaborate, fashionable objects who existed not because of their own will but because they performed a function in the social economy. At the best of times, they provided gaiety, pleasure, and fashionable company. Frequently, however, the feverish hedonism of the fast life into which their friends were drawn led to ruin, since the inevitable complement to a relationship with a courtesan was a taste for other forms of heroic luxury, such as those associated with a big gambling loss or the spectacular blowing of a sudden gain.[41] A courtesan's market value was only enhanced when she caused a lover to suffer a loss of a fortune and reputation. Especially sought after in a time of feverish speculation, they were the most desirable and dangerous of commodities.

Although they presented themselves as the natural companion of aristocracy, the costly novelties preferred by the courtesans owed much to the sort of seductive aesthetic that was associated with the arcades and the stores. The complex bourgeois attitude to sex produced repressions and displacements that were exploited in the commercial sphere. The impulse towards sexual pleasure was employed to attract and hold the attention of consumers.[42] Even more than the new rich, it was the *demi-mondaines* who lived a department-store lifestyle. While the most prestigious craftsmen and tradespeople still sought the patronage of court ladies, high-class prostitutes were often 'launched' by local dressmakers and even laundresses who would lend magnificent garments belonging to well-to-do customers. Various tradespeople including upholsterers and furniture makers set up courtesans in luxurious apartments at exorbitant rents and arranged repayment on instalment plans.[43] In *La Dame aux camélias*, when word spreads that Gautier no longer enjoys the protection of her duke, all her suppliers are quick to demand settlement of their accounts. These women represented the deluxe modern commodity and were packaged and displayed for maximum impact on potential customers and the wider public.[44]

Under the Second Empire, the courtesan dictated fashion trends and was sometimes imitated by the society lady. Some of the latter went so far in their use of rouge, false hair, and so on, that they were nicknamed *cocodettes*.[45] This appellative was not applied to the Empress Eugénie, who some have seen as the last ruling monarch to exercise any direct personal influence over fashion. However, it was not by virtue of her regal status that she was regarded as a model; rather it was a consequence of the 'inevitable element of *parvenu* about the Empress'. As she had 'no royal birth to fall back upon she was compelled in some sort to win estimation by being in the forefront of fashion'.[46] This inevitably brought her into a realm that was also occupied by leading courtesans. Eugénie's ostentation can be compared to the idiosyncratic behaviour of another empress who was even more obsessed by matters of appearance, Empress Elizabeth of Austria ('Sissi'). After her marriage to Franz Joseph in 1854, she was largely absent from court and led a nomadic existence travelling restlessly through resorts in Europe and the Mediterranean. She abhorred protocol and followed her whims while cultivating her beauty and her famously slim physique. Elizabeth had the beauty to win attention and, by stepping out of the court, she gave rise to interest that owed more to popular culture than to deference. Her dislike of photography only served to stimulate curiosity about her appearance. In royal terms, both women were highly unusual and it was these unconventional aspects that made them glamorous. Despite their positions, they were mainly identified with spheres independent of power like fashion and beauty.

Critics of the courtesans and their prominence were legion. Sometimes these directed their disapproval at individuals. The Goncourt brothers wrote that La Païva had a face that 'at moments...takes on some terrible likeness to a rouged corpse'.[47] Her over-use of cosmetics made her seem completely artificial. Cora Pearl was said to behave like a beauty, when in fact she had a plain face.[48] She achieved the illusion by enveloping her body in clouds of fabric and decorating herself with jewels and metal adornments. The prominent novelist Émile Zola offered a more thorough critique. If Dumas provided the most romanticized image of a courtesan, then the most striking negative representation was Zola's powerful literary creation, Nana. Nana first appeared as an adolescent in *L'Assommoir* in 1877 and was then portrayed in a celebrated painting by Manet before Zola dedicated a whole novel to her rise and fall in 1880. Written several years after the end of the Second Empire but set during it, the novel's heroine incorporates elements of several well-known courtesans.[49] She also draws for some of her features on lower level theatrical entertainers and common prostitutes. Nana is exactly the sort of woman of pleasure who became a celebrity. Before her tragic decline, she is the toast of Paris and 'the queen of first class tarts'. 'Her photo was on display in every shop window; her name featured in the newspapers,' Zola writes.[50] When her landau arrives at the race course, there is 'a stir amongst the spectators as if it was royalty going by'.[51]

To denounce the putrefaction of society as well as the parasitic nature of the cult of commercial sex, Zola likened his heroine to a fly on a dung-hill. She is a gutter Venus whose youthful plebeian beauty is unredeemed by any moral quality. She cackles like a hen, torments her lovers, flaunts her success, and leaves a trail of destruction in her wake. This mix of vulgarity and social prominence revealed the corruption of the Second Empire; its worthlessness was shown by the sort of person to whom it accorded high status. But in fact Nana was not the freak product of a particular moment; her successors would enjoy scarcely less prominence under the democratic Third Republic. Sex and celebrity would remain united in the persons first of courtesan-performers and then of stars of the stage and the silver screen.

Zola deplored the rise of the *demi-monde* and put the blame largely on an established society that had failed to erect proper barriers to maintain decorum. The *demi-monde*, in his view, had spilled over into the main-stream. He describes the ball given by the Comtesse de Muffat, the wife of Nana's protector, to celebrate the renovation of her house and simultan-eously mark the signing of her daughter's marriage contract. The party was not exclusive, the author observes; rather five hundred invitations had been issued to all levels of polite society. 'In this smart, permissive society dedicated purely to pleasure, full of people whom a society hostess would pick up in the course of some short-lived intimacy,' Zola wrote, the sanctity of the family was destroyed and the primacy of the fashionable crowd asserted.[52] Dukes mixed with crooks and 'girls in low-cut dresses flaunting their bare shoulders', while one woman 'was in such a skin-tight skirt that people were following her progress with amused smiles'. Only the sheer magnificence of the occasion and the setting disguised the 'decline of the ruling classes brought about by their shameful compromises with the debauchery of modern life'.[53]

The glitter that was a trademark of the upper class was appropriated by the new mixed environments that the period spawned. Zola refers to a splendid drawing room chez Muffat in which 'the chandeliers and crystal sconces lit up a luxurious array of mirrors and fine furniture',[54] providing an ideal frame for a 'dazzling, crowded evening'. As the dancing began on one such occasion, 'women in light-coloured dresses were going past, mingling with the dark patches of the men's tail-coats, while the large chandelier gleamed down over the surging heads below with their sparkling jewels and the rustle of white feathers, a whole flower garden of lilacs and roses'.[55]

Zola describes Nana's environments meticulously. It is striking how similar the jumble of periods and colours is to his evocation two years later of the Oriental decor of the department store. The Renaissance–style mansion she inhabits, purchased for her complete with all furnishings by the Comte de Muffat, contains 'a ragbag of knick-knacks, of wonderful Oriental hangings, antique sideboards, and huge Louis XIII armchairs'. Nana found herself surrounded by 'a mass of expertly chosen artistic furniture, a jumble of various periods'.[56] The small drawing room that leads off her bedroom is 'an amusing hotch-potch of exquisitely crafted objects of every style and every country'; wide armchairs and deep sofas set the mood for 'the drowsy existence of the harem'. Such eclecticism perfectly matched bourgeois taste and confirms the view that maintaining a courtesan was quite literally like buying a building and furnishing it. The tastes of Nana herself, the former flower-girl 'who once used to stand day-dreaming in front of the shops of the arcade', was apparent in touches of 'gaudy magnificence', although nothing was 'too conspicuously tartish'.[57] As her extravagance mounts and luxury is piled on luxury, this relative restraint is submerged in an orgy of excess and glitz.

A typical juxtaposition of the Second Empire, that would persist afterwards as the sign of the courtesan, was that of jewels and naked flesh. On the stage of Bordenave's theatre, at the start of her rapid career, Nana appears naked before the silent gaze of a male audience. Protected only by a simple veil, her whole body can be glimpsed through the transparent gauze. Her red hair, firm breasts, sturdy thighs, broad hips, and well-rounded shoulders bewitch her many admirers. Although established courtesans normally masked their physical appearance to a greater extent, titillating appearances remained their stock in trade. 'The men who buy love like to inspect the merchandise before taking it,' Gautier writes to Duval.[58] In 1864 Cora Pearl made her entrance to the Jockey Club ball clothed in nothing other than her long red hair. La Barucci is reported to have excused herself for arriving one hour late for a meeting with the Prince of Wales by turning round and exposing her bare buttocks—a free view of her best feature, she said. Alice Ozy appeared almost naked in one play—save for a tiara worth 200,000 francs. These women were scandalous figures who challenged and parodied respectability and whose celebrity relied on occasional exhibitions of just this sexuality.

Throughout this period the issue of nudity was controversial. The controversy caused by Manet's paintings *Le Déjeuner sur l'herbe* and *Olympia* in 1863–4 derived from the realism of the female subjects. In place of highly idealized goddesses and nymphs that featured in academic painting, he offered striking depictions of ordinary prostitutes—in the first case in an open-air location and in the second in a boudoir. The shock value and complexity of these pictures turned them into founding statements of modern art.[59] His paintings were at one level the opposite of glamorous; they were unsettling rather than pleasurable. They did not gloss reality or seduce through visual tricks. But by situating the naked female body (rather than the academic nude) at the centre of modern culture, Manet created a premiss that would be widely imitated in art but also in entertainment. Revealing glimpses of flesh and nudity became less abstract and more a feature of urban popular entertainment in general. However, nudity was only glamorous as a suggestion or lure since the sex in glamour was never explicit. Glamour was often scandalous and transgressive but, since it was generated by the hierarchies and boundaries of bourgeois society not by their denial, it was rarely outrageous.

The fall of Napoleon III in the wake of the Franco-Prussian War of 1870 signalled the end of the frenetic hedonism that had characterized his rule. Yet the courtesans did not disappear as they had done in England with the onset of the Victorian era. Rather they were absorbed by an expanding entertainment industry that placed great emphasis on female spectacle. The sensual ideal of Paris and the Parisian woman emerged as a distinctive trait of French national identity in the aftermath of the war because it was seen as a civilized characteristic that was utterly alien to the Prussian mentality. What was termed *galanterie* (which the boulevard newspaper *Gil Blas* defined as a light-hearted, uninvolved attitude towards love and sex that was refractory to routine and uniformity)[60] was originally a feature of the aristocratic milieu of the pre-revolutionary era. In a context in which the French required consolation and pride, it was recuperated by nouveau riche, middle-class, and even lower-class milieux.[61] Here it served not merely to justify adultery but create a mood that served the cause of entertainment. Theatre managers and impresarios realized that the huge popular interest in the great *demi-mondaines* of the Second Empire could be exploited as entertainment for mass audiences. The last two decades of the nineteenth century witnessed the development of a star system that was sustained less by a dependent *demi-monde* and more by popular theatre, the press, and photographic studios. Carolina Otero, Liane de Pougy, Émilienne d'Alençon, and Cléo de Mérode all achieved international celebrity in the period between 1890 and 1900 and would retain it until at least 1914. Otero, de Mérode, and de Pougy were dancers while d'Alençon was primarily a variety artiste. Views differ as to their talents. None can truly be said to have a left a mark by her art that outlived her time. It was the physical appearances and reputations of these women that served as the main attraction.

The Folies Bergère provided them with their most celebrated platform. This theatre was a veritable forging ground of stars. Founded in 1869, on the model of London's Alhambra Theatre, a Leicester Square institution that resembled an enormous Oriental palace, it was the first Parisian music hall. Relaunched under new management in 1886, it provided a forum for every kind of famous performer from France and abroad. It was a sort of cabaret that was a *café-chantant* writ large. The principal stars of the 1890s were the *grandes cocottes* who offered themselves as female spectacles refined into a sort of art form. People came not to see a show but to see them, their legendary bodies, their fabulous costumes, and their priceless jewels. If the belle époque was in large part a celebration of female sexuality and beauty, as has been claimed,[62] then the Folies Bergère was the main temple in which the cult was celebrated. It provided spectacular shows while also featuring a *promenoir* that was frequented by the most notorious prostitutes of the district.[63] The theatre drew vast numbers of foreigners for whom the combination of erotic spectacle and sexual commerce was irresistible. Manet's celebrated painting *The Bar at the Folies Bergère* captures the surface glitter and gaiety of the Folies, while the unsmiling face of the barmaid at the centre of the picture alludes to the joyless resignation of at least some of the women who in one capacity or another worked there.

Carolina Otero was already well known when she made her debut there in 1893. A fiery Spaniard, she became the symbol of the Folies for ten years. She had acquired an international reputation on a series of engagements abroad beginning with a triumphal visit to New York in 1890.[64] Every spring she embarked on a series of foreign engagements, appearing in London, Vienna, Berlin, Rome, Zurich, St Petersburg, Budapest, and other cities. On each occasion, she seduced her audiences in an utterly self-aware manner. Otero impressed observers with her Andalusian features and colouring and her captivating dancing. The combination of richly coloured costumes, jewels, and erotic dance, led some to see her as exotic. 'She has all the spells of the Orient in her hips,' exclaimed Hugues Le Roux.[65] One of her specialities was the tango, while many images show her holding castanets. All her performances evoked the passion and colour of Spain or Latin America. Her movements were said to be agile and seductive. She could switch from fast dramatic steps to slow rotations on an axis that tantalized audiences already transfixed by the close-fitting costume and black stockings that outlined the curves of her figure once her bejewelled outer garments were removed. Her performances consisted of a physical spectacle in which each part of her body in turn was used as a lure. The male spectator was in this way teased and induced to imagine himself having sex with her. As she would later muse in her memoirs: 'Isn't the true sense of dance a pantomime of love?'[66] The writer Colette, who was a friend and admirer, and who refers to Otero in *Mes apprentissages*, commented on her greedy appetite for food and the way she loved, even in later life, to dance into the early hours of the morning.[67] Responses to her shows were enthusiastic and impassioned wherever she went. Otero was hailed as the best and most seductive dancer, the most beautiful and luminous of women. Honours and gifts flowed and invitations multiplied. She was initially contracted to the Folies Bergère for 5,000 francs per month but this figure increased to 35,000 francs in the course of her ten-year winter residency at the theatre.

Liane de Pougy was Otero's greatest rival. As a French national, she aroused special interest at home and even became a sort of national symbol.[68] Looking back from the 1950s, Jean Cocteau memorably described all these women as 'the geishas of France', but only de Pougy was singled out for inclusion in his book on female icons, *Reines de la France*.[69] In contrast to the tempestuous Otero, she was cultivated and ethereal. Her reputation rested largely on her amorous adventures with both sexes and her exploitation of these in a series of *romans à clef*. De Pougy took acting lessons from Sarah Bernhardt, who had built her reputation by playing a series of decadent femmes fatales including Cleopatra, Tosca, Phaedra, and Fedora, all of which, in her hand, became creatures reminiscent of the Parisian *demimonde*. But it was in the domain of self-publicity that she most closely resembled the great actress.[70] De Pougy was a master of the publicity stunt who was highly adept at drawing the press into her triumphs and tribulations. She ensured the success of her debut performance at the Folies Bergère in 1884 by writing to the Prince of Wales, inviting him to attend—an invitation he accepted. On another occasion, she shocked newspaper readers when she claimed that her celebrated jewellery collection had been stolen, thereby initiating a trick to secure news coverage that would still be practised by press agents fifty years later.[71] She endorsed a fragrance that was named 'Liane' after her and appeared in fashion advertisements. Her greatest moment of notoriety came when she reacted to her abandonment by her lesbian lover, the American heiress Natalie Barney, by publishing the thinly disguised story of their affair in a novel entitled *Idylle sapphique*. The following year a spoof marriage announcement appeared linking her name to the notoriously camp writer Jean Lorrain.[72] Even carefully staged suicide attempts were geared to ensuring press coverage. As her career drew to a close, she married the Romanian prince Georges Ghika. When, fifteen years later, he deserted her for a younger woman, she withdrew to a convent. She inspired Proust and some have seen her as the model for the character of Odette de Crécy, the courtesan whom Swann falls for and marries.[73]

This group of women was not particularly good on stage. De Pougy was probably the least effective as a performer, although Émilienne d'Alençon too had something of Max Beerbohm's beautiful but untalented Zuleika Dobson about her.[74] While the fictional Dobson performed magic tricks, d'Alençon showed pink-dyed performing rabbits. Otero was said to transfix audiences with her dramatic fandangos, although she had had no training and, some said, no technique. In her memoirs, she breezily admitted: 'I never learned to dance; I dance as naturally as a bird sings.'[75] By contrast, Cléo de Mérode began her career in the ballet of the Paris Opéra before she was lured into a more lucrative, if less cultivated, sphere by the manager of the Folies Bergère. It was in the realm of publicity that they made their true mark.

The highly public rivalry between Otero and de Pougy was encapsulated in an episode that, in different versions, is recounted in a host of memoirs and biographies. In an uncertain location that might have been the chic restaurant Maxim's or, more plausibly, a Riviera hotel, the two women were struggling to outdo each other in the matter of jewellery display. Like her courtesan predecessors, Otero exhibited ostentatious jewellery on- and offstage as proof of her amorous conquests. Commenting on one performance, *Le Figaro* wrote: 'Her bosom is more covered with jewels than a Chief of Protocol's chest is with medals and crosses. . . . They are in her hair, on her shoulders, arms wrists, hands and legs, and dangle from her ears, and when she ends the dance, the boards continue to glitter as if a crystal chandelier had been pulverised on them.'[76] The Spaniard thought she had triumphed when, one evening at dinner, she made a dazzling entrance covered in jewels, necklaces, bracelets, rings for every finger, and even a tiara. However, she was humiliated when de Pougy responded by arriving in a black dress devoid of adornment. The gasps of surprise from other diners gave way to delighted applause when she stood back to reveal her maid, who was wearing a servant's cap and a dress with diamonds sewn all over it.[77] As a cultivated courtesan who, unlike the fiery Otero, surrounded herself with artists and writers, de Pougy could allow herself the luxury of dressing down. Yet even she later went on a tour organized by an impresario who exhibited her under the slogan: 'Liane de Pougy will appear on stage in a million francs' worth of jewels.'[78]

Material performance and competition were the public dimensions of the materialism and self-gratification that Simone de Beauvoir argued were the key characteristics of the courtesan. In contrast to the artist, the courtesan does not reveal herself to the world or in any way question the social order. Rather she exploits the world as it is for her own benefit. She places herself before the judgement of men and in so doing confirms a passive idea of femininity. However, 'she endows it with a magical power that enables her to catch the men in the snare of her presence and batten off them; she engulfs them along with her in immanence.'[79] De Beauvoir's forthright condemnation rings true on one level, but ignores the fact that these women were part of a burgeoning commercial sphere. There was a complex industry that staged them and whipped up interest in them. Prestigious lovers and admirers brought wealth and notoriety that in turn generated publicity for their shows. The magical power they exercised was born in the nexus of femininity, commercialism, theatre, and publicity. They offered a phantasmagoria of glamour as a commercial aesthetic of illusion and fascination.

The courtesan-performers of the belle époque were figures whose lives were a constant parade. They lived like modern celebrities in the public eye and their various activities were eagerly covered by a press that was happy to weave around them legends and stories that were often exaggerated. They were manna to publications like *Gil Blas*, *L'Echo de Paris*, *Le Figaro*, and *La Vie parisienne* that thrived on their activities and conveyed them to a mass readership. As women on the make, they counted on a good measure of popular sympathy in France, as well as curiosity. Although several of them performed on stage in London, it was only in Paris that their erotic life was a matter of continuous press interest and comment. Otero, de Pougy, and company were true stars whose images were reproduced on thousands of postcards as well as in magazines and posters. The Reutlinger studio specialized in images that captured their specialized sex appeal. Founded in 1850 by Charles Reutlinger, his studio on the Boulevard Montmartre produced magazine illustrations, postcards, and sumptuously bound volumes of women in a variety of sensual and leisure-oriented settings including the beach, the boudoir, the theatre, and the bustling boulevard. Women were sometimes featured singly and at other times in groups, but men were rigorously absent. As a result, there was 'a distillation of the image of femininity to a subject in and of itself'.[80] The human bearers of this image were self-aware performers engaging in allusive but unquestionably sexualized display.[81] They included the most famous courtesans but also some professional female performers and many anonymous young women.

Although they were often grouped together with Otero and d'Alençon, and featured on numerous Reutlinger studio postcards, both Cléo de Mérode and the Italian singer Lina Cavalieri enjoyed an artistic reputation. De Mérode came from an aristocratic background (her 'de' was genuine, not a pseudo-aristocratic affectation) and accounts suggest that she was a highly accomplished dancer. Even after she left the opera for more profitable work in the popular theatres of Paris, London, New York, and St Petersburg, her shows were typically of classical inspiration. She also worked in an exotic idiom; at the 1900 universal exposition, she appeared in a cycle of Cambodian-inspired dances. Cavalieri first appeared on the Paris stage at the Folies Bergère in 1895, when she substituted for de Pougy in a production of Jean Lorrain's pantomime *L'Araignée d'or*. In her later career she emerged as one of the first women to become a star in a contemporary way, using several media and all her attributes to promote herself incessantly. In an Italian book of interviews with most of the famous figures mentioned here, published *c*.1903, Cavalieri showed an awareness of what she termed 'the psychology of the public'.[82] About to make her debut in *Manon Lescaut*, Puccini's adaptation of Abbé Prevost's tale of a young beauty lured into a life of wealth and immorality, she was alert to the need to appear serious and avoided responding to the interviewer's frivolous questions about her shoe size or the number of gloves she possessed. None the less, the male author indulged his readers at length with considerations on her eyes, her skin, her neck, her hair, and her hands.[83]

The courtesans displayed their jewels, not as a badge of their husbands' worth like respectable women (since, with just one or two exceptions, they did not marry), but as an indication of the devotion they had inspired in admirers. Cocteau said that maintaining one of these women was as complex as buying a house and furnishing it room by room. However, they had a magpie's eye for diamonds. Ever since Louis XIV studded his garments with them, diamonds had been a mark of status. In the course of the nineteenth century, they became a female prerogative. More jewellery indicated more generous and richer suitors and therefore higher status. The courtesan-performers were the first to insure their bodies and announce the fact—as Otero did when she rejected an assessment of the value of her legs at $10,000 and insured them for $80,000 each. Even if the particular conjuncture of the belle époque favoured the public emergence of women whose every gesture was designed to attract publicity and further their notoriety, the heritage of the old-style *demi-monde* was constantly evoked. Sarah Bernhardt frequently appeared in plays such as *La Dame aux camélias* and *Salomé*. In the variety theatres, a singer like Yvette Guilbert happily made reference to a variety of sensual characters and experiences in her 'Chansons Pompadour' and 'Chansons Crinoline'. The Folies Bergère ran a number entitled *Une soirée chez la Païva*. But in time their own legends overtook these in the public imagination. Otero's popularity reached such a pitch that the Théâtre des Mathurins in Paris even put on an entire musical comedy entitled *Otero chez elle*, starring Otero herself, in which she re-enacted episodes from her life and colourful professional and amorous career.

Although the courtesan-performers, and also actresses, were often experts at self-fashioning and publicity, their individual images always required some assistance from professionals. In the Regency era, Sir Thomas Lawrence had played a crucial role in forging a language of allure for actresses like Mrs Siddons and Elizabeth Farren. His outdoor portrait of the latter was a masterpiece of coquettishness; smiling and sexy, her head turned flirtatiously, she was at once an object of desire and a free spirit.[84] In the second half of the century, the couturier Charles Frederick Worth and his successors, Paquin, Doucet, and Poiret; painters including Boldini, Helleu, and Sargent; and subsequently photographers, all created image techniques that did not rely on specific subjects. Such men helped forge glamour as a structure and as a system. Occasionally working in cooperation (the artists often borrowed gowns from the couturiers), they combined material seductions with poses, attitudes, and looks that could be conferred on any subject to create panache and arouse desire. Boldini often painted anonymous prostitutes and his pictorial sexiness was informed by his familiarity with the world of commercial sex.[85] Typically, all performers chose a style marked by flamboyant excess, with more eye-catching jewellry, stronger perfume, brighter colours, and more revealing gowns than were worn by upper-class women. They also made ample use of cosmetics to enhance their beauty, something that was forbidden to respectable ladies for whom modesty and understatement in public were de rigueur.

The courtesan-performers boasted of their liaisons with royalty. Among Otero's many suitors, she counted some of the most prominent members of Europe's royal families who, no less than more ordinary men, were bewitched by the aura of glamorous sin that surrounded her. These included at least five present or future monarchs: Kaiser Wilhelm II; Edward, Prince of Wales; Grand Duke Nicholas of Russia, Alfonso XIII of Spain; and Prince Albert of Monaco. Some of these encountered Otero when she was on tour in their capitals; others benefited from a Parisian rendezvous. Needless to say, news of these royal liaisons travelled far and wide and added greatly to her fame and to the legend of her beauty. Such tales fuelled the public's imagination and wove around the leading figures of the belle époque a legend of transgression, beauty, and fearlessness.

De Mérode owed a considerable part of her fame to the attention she received from an infatuated Leopold II of Belgium. Unlike d'Alençon, who had accepted both his lavish gifts and his amorous overtures, she accepted the former while rejecting the latter. Despite this, his attentions became public knowledge and the unfortunate monarch was irreverently nicknamed Cléopold. The brouhaha that ensued permanently tainted her with the brush of the *cocotte*. In later years de Mérode repeatedly denied that she had conducted liaisons for gain, even suing Simone de Beauvoir (and winning symbolic damages of 1 franc) when the latter referred to her as a great *hetaera* in *The Second Sex*.[86] In her support, she could have cited de Pougy's *roman à clef* entitled *Mademoiselle de la Bringue,* that featured a certain 'Mademoiselle Méo de la Clef' who 'personifies *Love* WITHOUT MAKING IT'.[87] Yet few believed that de Mérode was not a courtesan, for all her understated delicacy and background in classical ballet. People preferred to imagine her as erotically available. She indulged moreover in gestures that were reminiscent of the courtesan. When the sculptor J. A. J. Falguière exhibited a magnificent statue of a nude dancer in 1896 that closely resembled de Mérode, the dancer asserted to general disbelief that she had posed only for the head.[88]

Liaisons with royalty were good publicity but increasingly it was relations with the super-rich bourgeois of their day that sustained these women. Otero boasted of the necklaces she received from the wealthy Viennese banker Baron Ollstreder that had once belonged to Empress Elizabeth ('Sissi') of Austria. The new rich also competed for the mercenary affections of the most fashionable women of Paris as they took over the social position and exterior lifestyle of the aristocracy. The wealthy of the United States, Britain, and Europe needed such women in the way they needed a yacht, a stable, or a hunting estate. According to the writer and journalist Octave Uzanne, 'what they want from her is neither love nor erotic pleasure but the consecration of their renown as men-about-town (*viveurs*)'. In a passionless contract, she is annexed by the bourgeois as 'the friend, the representative of his elegance, the mascot of his chic'.[89] For intimate business, Otero's price in 1897 was said to be 25,000 francs for fifteen minutes.[90] However, for a woman as instinctive and passionate as Otero, purely instrumental deals were unsatisfactory. She left Ollstreder because all he wanted was to be with a famous *demi-mondaine* whose luxury would bring him honour.[91] She perceived that this embourgeoisement of *galanterie* eliminated its spontaneously gay character. It reflected a luxury that had become predictable and systematic. Instead of receiving gifts of champagne, performers like Otero were invited to appear in branded champagne advertisements.

Otero's special resonance derived from her identification with Spain. As Mario Praz showed in his magisterial study *The Romantic Agony,* the powerful misogynistic trope of the femme fatale was born in Spain, albeit the imaginary Spain of Prosper Merimée's *Carmen.* She then moved to Russia, before Théophile Gautier and Flaubert located her definitively in 'an atmosphere of barbaric and Oriental antiquity, where all the most unbridled desires can be indulged and the cruellest fantasies can take on concrete form'.[92] Many of the character traits or costume features of the femme fatale were drawn from an Oriental repertoire. Her morbid associations with death, the natural, and the supernatural fitted the image of the East as a place of cruelty, superstition, and danger. But Spain carried strong associations of female fire, passion, and sex. Otero comfortably fitted the stereotype. A force of nature, who was renowned for her fiery spirit, in February 1892 she was even said to have fought a duel against an actress who had joked at her expense. This incident was rendered even more scandalous by the rumour that both parties had fought topless.[93]

Whatever their imaginary associations, the stamping grounds of the courtesan-performers were the institutions of the commercial public sphere that, formed in the mid-nineteenth century, blossomed in the 1890s. These included hotels like the Ritz, the racetracks, restaurants, theatre premieres, and the Bois de Boulogne as well as some salons and the artistic community.[94] Especially popular was Maxim's, the legendary establishment that was frequented by all the rich and beautiful people of the period and which was immortalized in several plays and books including Georges Feydeau's comedy *La Dame de chez Maxim*. The Rue Royale restaurant was notorious for its clientele of courtesans, including a quota who did not yet have a permanent protector. In his memoirs, the one-time *maître d'hôtel* of this unique establishment did not hesitate to reveal the contents of a notebook he kept listing available smart women.[95]

The distinction between respectable society and the world of spectacle and seduction was supposed to be rigid. But in an age of publicity, the emergence of theatre to social prominence, fashion, and the internationalization of the season, the barriers between *monde* and *demi-monde* were not what they had once been. The most socially heterogeneous locations were those spas and resorts that were developed especially by the British, including Biarritz, Deauville, Dinard, Cabourg, Monte Carlo, and the Riviera. Monte Carlo thrived on its racy reputation, to which the casino and its clients greatly contributed. Kings, princes, nobles, bankers, rentiers, artists, writers, actresses, and many others arrived in the resort in early summer, retreating once it became too hot. The courtesans were always on the move, either touring or looking out for new patrons. Such an appetizing place attracted them like magnets. Otero was a regular visitor and her legendary wins, and especially losses, at the gaming tables contributed to its image as a 'dazzling center for chance and caprice'.[96] The Riviera was a place where, it seemed, anything could happen and quite often did. The simple fishing villages that marked the highly picturesque coastline developed into a stage for the public and private rituals of a heterogeneous international elite that, because it was constituted temporarily away from conventional expectations and power structures, was relatively unrestricted by responsibility, decorum and social distinctions. The Riviera was a place of imagination that produced a powerful mythology.[97] The social mix of royals, the rich, courtesans and gold-diggers, gigolos, writers, exiles, newspapermen, and publicists fuelled the dreams and aspirations of magazine readers who thrived on gossip and sensation. This mix was often not spontaneous but the deliberate strategy of publicists who invented events, invited celebrities and wove legends around them. The queens of the *demi-monde* were vital in adding a pinch of high-class sleaze. Although they frequented all the Riviera resorts, they left their mark especially on the environment of Cannes and Monte Carlo. The Salle Blanche at the Casino de Monte Carlo is dominated by a large-scale 1903 painting that depicts La Belle Otero, Liane de Pougy, and Émilienne d'Alençon as the three graces,[98] while Otero's opulent breasts served as the model for the twin cupolas of the Carlton Hotel in Cannes.

In what was seen of the fashionable life, the courtesans were prominent and they had precisely the attributes of beauty, desirability, wealth, and immorality that were associated in the popular mind with the upper class. Their backgrounds endeared them to the masses while their stunts kept everyone interested. But the fascination with the upper class never went away. Indeed, in bourgeois society, it increased not as deference but as curiosity and envy. Due to economic development and the spread of democracy, people felt themselves to be part of a collectivity that included the rich and famous. The glamorization of the upper class of the turn of the century is the subject of the next chapter.

CHAPTER 4

WEALTH, STYLE, AND SPECTACLE

B efore the last few decades of the nineteenth century, the new rich were rarely richer than those who had inherited land and wealth. The expansion of industry in the late nineteenth century and the growth of the American economy created for the first time new fortunes without parallel. The men who accumulated them saw themselves as an emergent new elite and they craved acknowledgement. Because they had neither heritage nor breeding to draw on, they set about winning this by fashioning a lifestyle of great ostentation. Massive palaces, ultra-refined interiors, enormous yachts, grand summer houses, glittering parties, elegant weddings, and international travel became the key markers of status of the super-rich. A correlative of such ostentation was publicity. Much of this was deliberately sought, since one sure way to attract the attention of the established holders of social power was to occupy the social pages and set new standards of luxury and elegance. At this time, New York was already the Mecca of American high society. To win recognition there was a guarantee that one had truly arrived. Needless to say, there were risks in attracting attention in such a highly competitive location, since the press was not subservient or particularly deferential. The American rich who flocked to the city found that several publications were pleased to cultivate the curiosity of their readers for every aspect of their domestic and private lives. The press was a product of a fast-developing urban society and, by its gleeful intrusions, it turned the doings of the wealthy into a source of diversion and mass entertainment.

Much of the public interest in the new rich derived from their highly publicized battles to gain access to high society. They found that gaining admittance was by no means straightforward. The established elite, which was made up of families whose wealth had been accumulated two generations previously, modelled itself on European court society and granted itself prerogatives that were hereditary. The forms taken by upper-class life were developed precisely in order to guarantee the pre-eminence of this restricted group that was commonly referred to as the 'Four Hundred': the number of people who supposedly could fit into the ballroom of Caroline Astor, wife of William Astor, who occupied the pinnacle of New York high society between the 1870s and the 1890s. It was she who, with the aid of her social ringmaster Ward McAllister, determined who got in and who did not.[1] The Vanderbilts, for example, whose fortune was based on railroad expansion, were long regarded as too uncouth to be admitted, even though Cornelius ('the Commodore') Vanderbilt, at the time of his death in 1877, was the richest man in America. The exclusion of the new millionaires from the inner sanctum of high society compounded an outsider image that won them sympathy. Everyone could identify with their battle against snobbery and prejudice.

The wealthy families of the American 'gilded age'—an expression coined by Mark Twain—mesmerized their contemporaries with their enormous and recently acquired wealth. People of all classes were riveted by the ever-spiralling luxury of elite life that was recounted in great detail in the newspapers and magazines. The families seemed to many to be living the American rags-to-riches dream. The beauty and style of some of the women also enhanced their glamour. People identified with them and their rites of passage were treated from the 1880s as public festivities in which everyone had the right to participate at some level.

The case of the Vanderbilts shows that social progress was a complex matter. Even after the Commodore's demise, his handsome and more polished son William K. (Willie) Vanderbilt faced obstacles. Despite installing themselves in a huge and dazzling house on Fifth Avenue, and winning invitations to some events, he and his wife Alva remained outside the core elite. To rectify this, Alva waged a concerted campaign that culminated in March 1883 with what would become known as the Vanderbilt ball. By inviting 1,600 members of the elite and succeeding in making this house-warming event the social occasion of the season, she created the necessary pressure to cause Mrs Astor's resistance to crumble.[2] Such public assaults on the citadel of the elite inevitably meant that the new rich lived in a goldfish bowl. Messy divorces, adultery, and other scandals all received ample coverage and, while they brought condemnation from some quarters, enhanced the soap-opera quality of the lives of the protagonists. The mass public was fascinated by their extravagances and followed them as it did the actresses and courtesans.

The sudden rise of new industrial fortunes had a significant impact beyond the United States. In their search for embellishment and recognition, the rich travelled to Europe, notably France and Great Britain, countries in which wealth was blended with institutionalized social privilege. American millionaires found in the France of Napoleon III that new money was not disdained at the very top of society.[3] Their lavish spending contributed to the festive elegance and ostentation of social life that was the means whereby a parvenu court secured its pre-eminence. It was also welcomed in England, especially in the late Victorian and Edwardian years. Edward, Prince of Wales cared little for the stuffy formalities of court society and happily mixed with what the American novelist Edith Wharton called 'gentlemen with short pedigrees and long purses'.[4] A variety of bankers and millionaires who would previously never have come near the royal family were inducted into high society, which at this time had two of its major centres in Edward's London and country homes, Marlborough House and Sandringham.[5] Some came because they had been shunned by the American elite, others because they admired England's 'true aristocracy'. William Waldorf Astor turned his back on 'vulgar' America in 1890 and set up home in England, buying Cliveden, a Restoration baroque mansion that was one of the most beautiful houses in the country.[6] He filled it with treasures accumulated on his travels in Europe. The prince shared the plutocrats' love of luxury and he appreciated their willingness to support his costly lifestyle.[7] He also found that the men often shared his passion for theatre and its female performers.

The first American arrivals were surprised by the sheer cost of taking part in London life, with its many rituals and social occasions. The highest standards of hospitality were obligatory and the women especially were expected to dress to impress at all times. However, the newcomers were not easily deterred. American millionaires were wealthier and more materialistic than most Europeans. Their acquisitiveness contrasted with the English nobility's conventional (if sometimes feigned) disinterest in material objects.[8] Unless they were recent inventions, new things were generally not of much interest to the aristocracy and old ones only had value if they were inherited. As Vita Sackville-West wrote in *The Edwardians*, typically 'they thought more of a small old family than a large new fortune'.[9] The emphasis shifted as the plutocrats introduced a sharpened element of competitiveness into upper-class lifestyles as they used luxury to overcome social barriers.[10] The 'intrusion of money' was seen as a characteristic of both the Americans and of the Edwardian years, the period of their greatest ascendancy in British high society.[11] One contemporary observer denounced the 'insane competition' that accompanied the rising standard of living. 'Where one house sufficed, now two are demanded; where a dinner of a certain quality, now a dinner of superior quality; where clothes or dresses or flowers, now more clothes, more dresses, more flowers.'[12] For the English landed aristocracy, all this was alarming, not least because agricultural rents were falling. With wealth becoming the key factor in determining status, their ability to remain pre-eminent was threatened.[13] The influx of wealth, and in particular of American wealth into British high society, had the added disadvantage of intensifying competition within the aristocratic marriage market. The naked ostentation of wealth led to denunciations of 'cash power' and 'money-dominance', with particular hostility being reserved for the displacement of older standards by vulgar ostentation and greed.[14]

Although the outlay of capital was a means of winning recognition and prestige, pecuniary strength alone was never enough. To win social recognition, the money values of Wall Street needed to be translated into the cachet of Fifth Avenue or, failing that, a European title. The new rich were intrigued by the example of the courts and the aristocracies of the past. In an effort to mitigate or camouflage the novelty of their wealth, they sought to acquire the attributes of taste and culture by appropriating historical styles and objects.[15] Art and architecture of the classical and Renaissance periods were especially favoured by those with aristocratic pretensions. But the borrowing of taste was rarely tasteful. The extraordinary competition to build European-style stately homes on Fifth Avenue in New York and in the summer resort of Newport led to a proliferation of 'great gawdy palaces' in Italian, Gothic, and Oriental styles.[16] These were not private residences in the strict sense, but material manifestations of wealth and theatres of status.[17] The Vanderbilts' Marble House on Ocean Drive in Newport reflected its owner's obsession with Louis XIV. The house not only had a gold ballroom, portraits of the Sun King, and period bronze furniture in the dining room, it also featured a copy of Bernini's bust of Louis XIV on the first-floor landing. A portrait of the house's architect was placed next to one of an architect of Versailles.[18] In the USA, no less than in Britain, writers and cartoonists lampooned the eclecticism of the new rich and their pretensions. Negative comment, however, was mainly confined to an elite of taste; others found the display awe-inspiring and utterly admirable.

The heiress was the figure who, in the public imagination, embodied the millionaires' aspirations for recognition and acknowledgement. Her efforts to net a suitably prestigious husband received much coverage. There were several reasons for this. In the first place, women played a symbolic role for the rich. According to the eclectic American academic Thorstein Veblen, who in 1896 wrote a tongue-in-cheek account of the American 'leisure class' that remains widely cited, wealth and leisure were displayed in order to establish gentility and civilization.[19] Women were the prime vehicle of this since the duties of vicarious leisure and consumption had devolved to them. Thus a daughter who conformed to prevailing ladylike standards of appearance and deportment was a valuable asset.[20] In addition, the press found that its readers, who were used to seeing news and pictures of actresses and performers, could relate to heiresses, who were more appealing and picturesque than crusty millionaires. Some heiresses were of more interest than others. The extraordinary fame of the five

Langthorne sisters of Virginia in the 1890s was due to their beauty, spirit, and elegibility.[21] The marriage of each attracted frenzied publicity. A new dimension was added to the narrative when some heiresses headed for Europe in search of a titled husband. These young women, whom Edith Wharton memorably labelled 'buccaneers' in her last, unfinished, novel, were not on the whole treated with respect or deference abroad. Outside their native context, they were detached from 'certain signs of social position' and were regarded as fair game by the press and others.[22] The nobility was lured by their lucre and it was this that propelled some of them into matrimonial alliances with families whose gentility they doubted. For the same reason, the press latched on to them and turned them into personalities.

No single young woman embodied the role of the golden heiress more than Consuelo Vanderbilt, the daughter of Willie and Alva, who, at the age of 18, married the ninth Duke of Marlborough in New York in November 1895. The wedding was one of the most spectacular that the city had ever seen and curiosity about every aspect of it was intense. Consuelo herself was a refined and educated young woman whose long neck and graceful figure marked her out as a physical embodiment of what Veblen called pecuniary beauty.[23] The couple's engagement was presented to New Yorkers as an all-American tale that confirmed the ascendancy and vitality of the new world. The most eligible peer in England had chosen for his bride the most sought-after heiress in America. In fact, this alliance was more or less a simple trade between money and titled distinction in which the bride was little more than a pawn in her mother's schemes for social aggrandizement.[24]

The celebrations, which began with the announcement of the engagement in September, sparked a wave of publicity. This was fed by Alva Vanderbilt, who released full information about the wedding dress (made of cream and white satin, with a 15-foot train, it cost $6,720), the bridesmaids, and the guest list. Samples of her daughter's trousseau were even delivered to the offices of *Vogue* magazine.[25] Many years later, Consuelo disingenuously gave the impression that she was a victim of press intrusiveness. She wrote that while 'reporters called incessantly, anxious to secure every particle of news...little news was given out'.[26] This, she claimed, led them to fabricate information to pander to readers' appetites. 'I read to my stupefaction that my garters had gold clasps studded with diamonds, and wondered how I should live down such vulgarities,' she wrote. It is not clear which she regarded as more vulgar: the publicity given to her undergarments or the implication that she indulged in such jaw-dropping refinements. On the day, thousands of enthusiastic on-lookers thronged the streets waving handkerchiefs and cheering loudly. The bride, however, recalled that, as the couple exited the church, 'the crowd surged towards us and women tried to snatch flowers from my bouquet. There were spasmodic cheers and less friendly sallies.'[27] Although the American rich were viewed with more sympathy than those of other countries, there was always some envious resentment of their lives of privilege.

Unlike high society in the United States or France, in England it had always been an adjunct of politics. Its existence was based on the assumption that those who were politically pre-eminent were also socially pre-eminent; high society and political society were coterminous.[28] The rationale of the social season, with court functions, Royal Ascot, the Cowes yachting events, and so on, lay in its connection to the parliamentary calendar. Its more frivolous aspects were not ends in themselves, but a balance to serious work, that had the added advantage of providing a forum in which the marriage market could function. In the 1890s, however, the two worlds grew apart as other factors, including consumption, the press, and social competition as an end in itself, took the place of politics as leading dynamics of high society.[29]

In this context, there was a marked increase in what, some years earlier, Walter Bagehot called 'the theatrical show of society'.[30] In place of stuffy private rituals, more glittering events were staged that gratified not only the participants but also the wider society's demand for spectacle. These pro-vided a stage for the rich and famous, on which the titled and the powerful had influential but not necessarily leading parts. 'A fine dress was no longer something to be worn at court or at selected private assemblies; it was something to be worn in the most public manner possible,' the fashion historian James Laver observed.[31] 'Strange hocus pocus, that juggles certain figures into prominence, so that their aspect is familiar to the wife of the bank-clerk, and their doings a source of envy to the daughter of the chemist in South Kensington!', a character muses in The Edwardians;[32] 'With what glamour this scheme is invested, insolent imposture!'

115

In New York, the theatrical turn of high society is regarded as the achievement of Mrs Astor's lieutenant, Ward McAllister. A born courtier, who had acquired on his travels in Europe a veneer of taste and style, he persuaded Mrs Astor that he could produce a show in which she would be the leading lady.[33] As a Southerner from Georgia who had reinvented himself as a social grandee, McAllister played on the myth of antebellum Southern courtesy and grace. Northerners viewed the old South in a manner similar to the Napoleonic bourgeoisie's outlook on the *Ancien Régime*, as a world of courtly manners and style to be annexed or drawn on in their own pursuit of refinement.[34] Thus the Virginian Irene Langthorne, who had already won some attention in the New York papers as a Southern Belle, found herself personally invited by him to lead the grand march at the super-prestigious Patriarch's Ball in 1893. Paradoxically, the exclusivity of such events added to their appeal as spectacle. 'The 400 are in the social business,' commented the magazine *Town Topics* in 1896. 'They do not spare pains, expense or advertising for the sake of maintaining a brilliant and refined series of continuous social performances. They are the actors, the rest of us are the spectators; but there is this difference between their show and all other shows, that they not only give the performance, but they do not charge anything for the privilege of looking at it.'[35] At this time, it became common to refer to high society as a circus and to social events as theatrical displays,[36] a perception that gave rise to criticism. 'We protest against . . . the tendency manifest in some quarters to hold such a class of frivolous drones up to the public gaze as "society",' commented the *Los Angeles Times*, adding that 'the rising generation . . . are too apt to be impressed by the glamor of wealth'.[37]

Society journalism emerged at just the moment that competition for high status was growing. Publicity became a weapon in this competition. By the early years of the twentieth century, the interiors of the millionaires' homes had become the subject of photographic features in illustrated magazines.[38] This showed that new members of high society were happy to play to the gallery.[39] The press won readers by offering them the spectacle of the lives of the wealthy and fashionable, while the latter enhanced their status and kudos by acquiring a broader stage. Old elite members often considered publicity to be vulgar or intrusive, but it soon became a crucial tool not only in mediating relations between elite and mass in modern society but also in determining the rhythms of elite life itself. 'The signature of pecuniary strength should be written in characters which he who runs may read,' observed Veblen.[40]

Magazines like the *World* in London or *Town Topics* in New York served high society while also providing information for the curious and the ambitious. Edith Wharton's upwardly mobile character Undine Spragg in *The Custom of the Country* has been 'nurtured on Fifth Avenue'; she 'knew all of New York's golden aristocracy by name, and the lineaments of its most distinguished scions had been made familiar by passionate poring over the daily press'.[41] Specialist reporters were employed to gather news, gossip, and pictures, and to describe events and romanticize them. Apart from cases of divorce, murder, or suicide, high society material did not feature in the news pages. It was a self-contained realm that provided readers with a tantalizing escapist dream.

The press was not the only institution that afforded a public stage to the rich and famous. The increasing numbers of rich people, and their tendency to congregate in the capitals, fuelled the development of luxurious commercially run establishments. Grand hotels, expensive restaurants, theatres, and nightclubs were founded to cater for the wealthy elite. The Paris Ritz opened in 1898 and its London sister hotel in 1906. When the Waldorf-Astoria opened in New York the 1890s (the two constituent hotels were respectively opened in 1893 and 1897), on the site of the present-day Empire State Building,[42] it immediately became synonymous with the Four Hundred who stood at the apex of New York society. The *maître d'hôtel*, Oscar Tschirky (known to all simply as 'Oscar'), was expected to greet each member of the leading families by name. It was also his task to bar non-members from the Palm Garden dining room and divert them to secondary rooms. The management sought to attract middle-class custom by means of its elite connections (which were also exploited in advertising material) while keeping the two categories of guests separate.[43] All parts of the hotel and even the staff were organized on a rigidly hierarchical basis. But this sort of practice was difficult to maintain in the long term. Exclusionary mechanisms could only be partial in establishments that were by definition within the reach of anyone with money and which seemed to invite everyone else to aspire one day to be a guest. The Waldorf-Astoria's lavish charity balls were themselves significantly more open than Mrs Astor's since its Marie Antoinette drawing room, which was a reproduction of the queen's private apartments at Versailles, could accommodate 1,500 people. Oscar, moreover, also offered advice to businesses, national organizations, alumni groups, and regular guests on how to entertain.[44] It was this very mix of the exclusive and the accessible that made such places glamorous to the wider public. They helped render elite lifestyles and personalities intriguing, exemplary, and imitable.

Specialist publications aimed to cater to the elite by making themselves into indispensable aspects of the wealthy lifestyle. In this way publishers could provide advertisers of luxury goods with a select audience who would be interested in their wares. *Vogue* was the pioneer publication of this type. Everything about the magazine was designed to appeal exclusively to the cultivated and the moneyed. It was not, in those days, primarily a fashion journal. It ran many articles on the arts, on domestic interiors, gardens, and even sport. It featured a wide range of personalities drawn from established families and theatre and it ran short stories as well as bringing news of new trends. The latest fashion information from Paris was just one feature, albeit an important one, in a complete package.[45] Under Condé Nast, a Midwesterner who bought it in 1909, *Vogue* was a magazine that recounted 'society, fashion and the ceremonial side of life' to the social elite of America's East coast.[46] Nast had no interest in reaching a mass readership and instead aimed to make the publication essential reading for the celebrated top Four Hundred people. In his aim, he certainly succeeded; he once claimed that every single member of the Four Hundred was a subscriber.

Needless to say, the magazine was also read by the Undine Spraggs of this world, who combed it for tips on elegant living. Stories of the lives, houses, wardrobes, and travels of the rich were fascinating and helped fuel interest in consumer goods. Commerce prospered on the back of the appetites of the rich for ever more refined goods, services, and entertainments.[47] Newspaper coverage of their activities was punctuated by advertisements for furnishings, alcoholic beverages, holiday resorts, and other goods. Through a variety of associations between places, images, and people, glamorous images were created. Entrepreneurs around the world saw the value of these attributes both as a guarantee for upper-class clients and an allure for aspiring ones. Stores, in particular, traded on this. An editorial writer for a British trade magazine called *Modern Business* observed in 1908 that 'People shop in the magic West End because in some mysterious way they believe they get better goods there.... By years of suggestion [it] has created a special atmosphere.'[48]

Atmospheres and suggestions permeated the whole of commercial culture, often mixing motifs of class and spectacle. *Vogue* portrayed socialites in ways that highlighted their elegance, grace, and mystery. The magazine featured elegant cover illustrations of women in fantastic hats with generous plumes; the subjects reclined on chaises longues or were depicted gliding over carpets made of stars of the Milky Way.[49] The American upper-class female ideal was encapsulated in Charles Dana Gibson's graphic creation, the Gibson Girl. After first appearing in *Collier's* magazine in 1890, Gibson's line drawings grew so much in popularity that they had become, by the early 1900s, 'the foremost image of female perfection for Americans'.[50] Every young woman in America envied her slim waist, long neck, regal bearing, and air of remote self-satisfaction. 'The Gibson girl was the first great American glamour girl long before there were movie stars,' wrote the legendary fashion editor Diana Vreeland in 1975; 'Every girl in America wanted to be her... Every man in America wanted to win her.'[51] As an angular, elongated figure, of the Consuelo Vanderbilt type, the Gibson Girl symbolized confident grace. She was often depicted in motion. Her tall, slim body, and swan neck automatically signalled the woman of fashion and, by implication, the woman of high status. She always had poise and a certain composure that together indicated refinement and leisure.[52] Her flowing skirts and dreamy eyes were regarded as sexually alluring.[53] Although more wholesome than decadent, in keeping with the American emphasis on health and pioneer endeavour, she was later seen as a New World counterpart to the femme fatales of nineteenth-century European decadent literature.[54] As the first American dream girl, she served various decorative or status-related purposes in the applied arts and advertising.[55] The original models were

New York high society girls who Gibson, the charming scion of a respectable Boston family, personally knew. One was Irene Langthorne, who married the illustrator in 1895. Their wedding, which was seen as one of several symbolic reconciliations of North and South, turned Irene into 'the' Gibson Girl. In this way, her family's biographer asserts, she 'turned the vanishing Southern Belle into a modern media fantasy'.[56]

These innovations bore directly on the manner in which the women of the new rich were represented in other media. To depict socialites as simultaneously fashionable and noble, alluring and virtuous was not an easy task. Upper-class women always had to be respectable. Unmarried women were expected to be pure and married women to maintain a good reputation. The strong emphasis on female modesty was an important feature of bourgeois morality that was applied rigidly. Anyone who flouted social convention was subject to swift censorship or, in extreme cases, ostracism. This meant that any reference to sexuality, a key element of glamour, was controversial. Even *Vogue* only featured hints of sexiness; the drawn female subjects of its covers have been described as 'a little perverse, given to aloof pursuits and secret smiles'.[57] The problem was exacerbated by the fact that Parisian associations were employed to confer values of fashionableness, worldliness, and desirability on both women and goods. As the world's most dynamic and alluring capital and a city that had made luxury production a key hallmark, Paris offered a variety of attractions to the American rich. Wealthy and upperclass women were eager to appear fashionable, and this could not be achieved without some suggestion of the spirit of gaiety and hedonism that was associated with the French capital. The very richest regularly visited Paris and did their shopping there. In New York fashionable dressmakers and hairdressers affected French names and manners in the knowledge that this would appeal to the vanity and aspirations of their clients and enable them to charge more.[58] Images of the Paris courtesans were also used to promote some luxury goods.

Painters like John Singer Sargent and Giovanni Boldini were kept very busy producing portraits of the richest and most ambitious men and, especially, women of their day. The Italian-born American Sargent, in particular, eventually became expert in conferring an air of relaxed superiority and comfortable composure on subjects who had elbowed their way to the front of the social pack. However, both artists struggled to forge a style that was simultaneously sexy and classy, candid and alluring, dignified and attention-grabbing. Both men ran into trouble in the course of their careers for erring too far towards the sexy. The young Sargent's promising career in Paris ground to a halt after his daring portrait of the eccentric young American-born French Creole socialite Virginie Gautreau (in which the subject was only identified as 'Madame X') was greeted with derision when it was shown at the salon in 1884. The 23-year-old Madame Gautreau was depicted wearing a simple, but exceptionally low-cut, black gown with a shoulder strap hanging down over one arm. Her skin tone was bluish and her attitude, underscored by a head turned in profile, at once immodest and haughty.[59] This louche depiction, which was taken to suggest that its subject was either about to have—or had just had—sex, produced a horrified reaction.[60] Not even the capital of sex appeal was ready for a society portrait that presented its female subject as a debauched woman of pleasure. Sargent's commissions dried up over night and he was forced to leave Paris. An Italian who took over Sargent's rooms after the latter's departure, Boldini found several prominent women refused to sit for him, while the husbands of others demanded that portraits be retouched to restore them to respectability. Italy's Queen Margherita, for example, declined his offer to paint her and his sensual portrait of the Sicilian industrialist's wife Donna Franca Florio so enraged her husband that the artist was obliged to make modifications.[61]

It was often the menfolk who were most protective of their wives' reputations. The former Consuelo Vanderbilt recalled a stopover at the Hôtel de Paris in Monte Carlo shortly after her marriage in the course of which she ate her meals 'among a lively crowd of beautiful women and elegant men, many of whom were acquaintances of my husband. When I asked him who they all were I was surprised by his evasive answers and still more startled when informed that I must not look at the women whose beauty I admired.' 'It was only after repeated questioning', she continued, 'that I learned that these were ladies of easy virtue whose beauty and charm had their price.'[62] She was also instructed not to acknowledge the men who were accompanying the courtesans even if she knew them personally. These exclusions did not apply universally and they were sometimes broken by the courtesan performers on their tours abroad. Otero won acclaim in New York and was temporarily accepted by sections of high society. She even attended a ball at Consuelo's parents' Newport residence Marble House.[63] However, while women were drawn to Parisian gaiety, they had to be careful not to become contaminated by it.

Both Boldini and Sargent later painted Consuelo as Duchess of Marlborough, although not in isolation. Sargent painted the Marlborough family group (the Duke, Duchess, and their two children) at Blenheim Palace, producing a large-scale work that was graceful and stylish, if a little over-composed. For his part, Boldini created a more intimate and beautiful picture of Consuelo, seated in a reception room at Blenheim Palace with her young son Ivor. The painting, which was deemed superior to Sargent's, was both elegant and domestic. It managed to show its female subject as both maternal and fashionable. On the whole, Boldini ably managed to balance the different demands of his clients. Unlike the well-bred Sargent, he developed a system of representation that drew on his own low-life experiences. Throughout his career he frequented the *demi-monde* and he counted the great actress-courtesans among his friends. He happened to work at just the time when the fashionable society beauty was being challenged and to some extent replaced by the professional beauty who had risen through the *café-concert* or the theatre.[64] This process was caught and possibly accelerated by the artist, who derived a technique of representation from the entertainment world that he then transferred to new rich and aristocratic subjects in a diluted form. Boldini conferred on the wives of financiers and industrialists, as well as society figures keen to show off their status, a fashionably elongated physique complete with small head, delicate features, a long neck, and trailing arms. He twisted and turned the female form into the serpentine poses that had come to be identified with the femme fatale.[65] In brief, he turned them into Parisian-style Gibson girls. Boldini did not derive his model—save in small part—from the tradition of aristocratic portraiture; rather he forged a new one that merged and catered to the tastes of the new rich and the show-business elite. His trademark style blended sensuality—in the form of twisting figures, swagged gowns, and uncovered flesh—with a theatricality that was evident in bright colours and a subdued exoticism. His female portraits were always elegant but at the same time he conferred on his subjects a certain daring attitude that was drawn from the *demi-monde*.[66] To arrive at this model, Boldini drew on his long experience of painting small-time actresses and prostitutes.

Boldini was especially good at portraying strong and daring women. His most striking portrait is a magnificent full-length painting of the Italian aristocrat the Marchesa Luisa Casati, in which the subject is swathed in black and accompanied by greyhounds, all rendered with the artist's customary bold diagonal brushstrokes. It is the perfect blend of high style and eye-catching visual effects. Casati was an eccentric noblewoman who was interested only in establishing her striking originality. She was painted and photographed by many leading artists who considered her to be something of an art object. A wealthy divorcee who lived mainly in Venice, where she kept a menagerie in her palace and staged magnificent parties in St Mark's Square, she was the embodiment of the sort of high society femme fatale that the Italian writer Gabriele d'Annunzio depicted in his racy novels. Like Benjamin Disraeli, the author of several imaginative 'silver fork' novels in the 1820s and 1830s before he entered Parliament, d'Annunzio was a poet and novelist who gave readers the impression that his highly refined and often perverse depictions of elite society were a mirror image of the real thing. He conducted a rich and refined lifestyle, mostly on credit, that was fed to his readers as 'unimitable'. In fact, he had a wide impact on fashion, interior decoration, the applied arts, and literature, above all in his native Italy.[67] Like Disraeli, he was a trendsetter of relatively undistinguished origins who, by sheer force of talent and self-invention, turned himself into one of the most prominent men of his time. His elegance, love affairs, fine living, and series of triumphs and setbacks made him a beacon of glamour. On the model of Byron, he crowned his career by throwing himself into nationalist politics. Adopting the mantle of the man of action, he made himself into a symbol of the Italian cause during and after the First World War.[68]

A Boldini of the pen, d'Annunzio contributed to the styling and mystique of the Marchesa Casati and formed a unique creative and sexual bond with the great naturalistic actress Eleonora Duse. Prominent, exhibitionist figures such as these, who moved at will between major European (and, in the case of Duse, American) cities were part of the current of new wealth, glamour, and social ambition that was taking shape in partial opposition to exclusive, hidebound, aristocratic rituals. They were important in eroding the barriers dividing the worlds of theatre and high society.[69] This was ocurring in a number of ways. The uprooting and relocation of tradition and material artefacts by the new rich created a precedent for imitation and appropriation. The elite lifestyle was no longer the organic expression of a way of life developed over time, but a superficial pastiche that was vulgar in taste and easy in its impact on the senses. It was an artificial facade, a fashioned image that was part of a newly dominant commercial aesthetic. Remoulded in this way, upper-class lives gave a recognizable shape to dreams of wealth and social elevation.

By the 1880s, theatre was fully exploiting links with display, fashion, and shopping. It conveyed the visual impression of class and exclusivity with the specific end of cultivating interest, desire, envy, and emulation. Much to the dismay of some critics, it 'mimetically produced the spaces and commodities of an ideal bourgeois material world'.[70] In London in 1893, Gilbert and Sullivan's *Utopia (Limited)* featured a drawing-room scene that, according to the advertising, was an exact replica of one of Queen Victoria's reception rooms. Such re-creations simultaneously stimulated curiosity in the lifestyles of the upper stratum of society and satisfied it.[71] Retailers contributed by filling store windows (which, after Selfridges pioneered the practice, would even be illuminated after dark) with scenes from life, with shop dummies dressed and posed in a way that permitted the best display of goods as objects of desire. The realistic element in such scenes was intended to induce onlookers to project themselves imaginatively into them.[72] Thus high society dinner parties, drawing rooms, and weddings were all represented in a variety of contexts: the press, theatre, and shop window tableaux. Such practices brought theatre and high society closer as manifestations of a society that encouraged the quest for status, comfort, and happiness through display and consumption.

At one time, it would have been inconceivable for actors and actresses to be presented at court or even received in society. Even afterwards it was rare, but by the end of the century, due to the material opulence of theatre, the theatricalization of high society and the role of the press in projecting personalities, the two worlds were in some ways linked. While the press reported elite events and lifestyles, sometimes embellishing or injecting fiction into them, theatre actually manufactured them. English actresses on the whole were modest and rather domestic. Madge Kendall's genteel ladies and Ellen Terry's romantic heroines were anything but disturbing figures. However, they remained on the margins. Only male actors could simultaneously enjoy all the honours of official acceptance while continuing in the profession. For women, acting was not seen as an art, or a way of earning a living, so much as a vocation for those who rejected the usual rules and norms of society. The public at large perceived actresses as mysterious and even dangerous. According to the *Englishwoman's Review*, 'the life of an actress is to the world at large a curious *terra incognita* peopled by forbidding phantoms of evil or seductive visions of pleasure and success'.[73] This perception was magnified where continental European actresses were concerned. French and Italian actresses exploited fully the opportunities that arose for tantalizing audiences obsessed with respectability. The London appearances of such Continental exotics as Ristori, Réjane, Bernhardt, and Duse provided a fabulous gallery of queens, empresses, courtesans, and freedom-loving women that contrasted with more modest home-grown products.[74] These actresses were often powerful personalities whose offstage reputations and activities added value to their performances. No less than courtesans, they traded in transparent make-believe; their art involved the construction of a personality in which distance from reality was an accepted norm.[75] It was Théophile Gautier, 'the true founder of exotic aestheticism',[76] who turned Cleopatra into 'a sort of oriental Lady Macbeth' and made her a prototype of the femme fatale.[77] This figure was the product of a profoundly misogynist culture.[78] She encapsulated and played out all the fears of the feminine, the irrational, the degenerate, and the racially impure which permeated Victorian culture. As such it mesmerized and fascinated. Although some examples, notably Salomé and Salammbò, the heroine of Flaubert's novel of the same name, were colourless, the opposition the femme fatale offered to the standard image of virtuous womanhood lay rather in the way she combined 'authority and vigor with intense sexual power' and 'imperiously [expressed] her disdain for the world and values of men'.[79] For this reason, she appealed to some women; certainly the great actresses of the period revelled in such roles. Their costumes bore exterior witness to prevailing ideas about the eternal animal in woman.[80] Feathers, elaborate headgear, animal skins, capes, an abundance of jewellery, and make-up testified to the role of woman as nature and as the chief artificer of civilization.[81]

The leading actress of the age, Bernhardt thrilled audiences with a passionate emotional style in which actress and character were seen as indistinguishable. She built her reputation by playing a series of decadent femmes fatales including Cleopatra, Tosca, Phaedra, Théodora, and Fedora, in many roles written especially for her by Victorien Sardou. Sardou's repetitive and historically inaccurate melodramas all showcased Bernhardt's talents and confused the Oriental and the modern. In *Théodora*, for example, Bernhardt played a whorish dancing girl who rises from a life of debauchery to become the glorious empress of Byzantium.[82] A tortuous plot allowed the actress to display a wide variety of attitudes and costumes. Her unique stage presence stemmed from the way in which she used her whole body to establish a style consisting of a hypnotic tone of voice, majestic and daring poses, spasmodic bodily movements, and piercing eyes.[83] Tears could be summoned up at will. However, more than an actress, Bernhardt was a modern celebrity who practised conspicuous self-display and deliberately sought sensation. She was self-consciously artificial and made ample use of cosmetics and jewellery. Exoticism and eccentricity were her hallmarks, and were reinforced by stage cross-dressing and tales of her unusual diet, a menagerie of pets including monkeys, a cheetah, and jewel-encrusted snakes, and her custom of sleeping in a coffin lined in pink silk. Her performances and offstage publicity stunts blended seamlessly in a continuous effort at startling and dazzling her audiences. She was seen as the Sphinx of Paris, a symbol and ideal more than a woman.

Bernhardt tapped into a new and fast developing culture of spectacle that linked theatres, metropolitan newspapers, print and billboard advertising, international exhibitions, travelling entertainments, as well as stores, dance halls, and other sites of amusement and pleasure.[84] She knew that one function of the actress was that of populating the fantasy world of the people. Her constructed femininity provided a resource for store display and the periodical market photographers and the nascent advertising industry. All of these participated in the process whereby commodities and manufactured eroticism were blended. In this way, she helped attach glamour to these means of communication. Whenever she travelled abroad, Bernhardt's reputation preceded her and massive crowds turned out to see the world's most famous and most scandalous actress.[85] She undertook regular London engagements between 1879 and 1913 and nine American tours between 1880 and 1918. On her eleven-week tour of Australia in 1891, her carriage was mobbed, her hotels besieged, and theatres overrun with unprecedented demand for tickets.[86] Churchmen railed against her immorality, little realizing that in so doing they only increased the public's fascination. She was the exact antithesis of Victorian puritanism and bourgeois gender values and was seen as a real-life femme fatale. As such, she was irresistibly glamorous. The glamour of the actress derived from her fame and her lifestyle but also from her capacity to merge her personality with the roles she played.[87] Details of her lavish and costly dresses were extensively reported in the press. Such was the quantity and variety of garments and accessories deployed by the actress on- and offstage that newspapers were able to talk about them for the duration of a tour.[88] She favoured soft and floating fabrics, richly embroidered and beaded, that were draped around her body in a way that suggested freedom. Press articles speculated about their value and discoursed at length on the way she wore them. In the United States, her Parisian provenance meant that women scrutinized her wardrobe for fashion tips. In this way, she contributed to the constitution of the feminine self as desirable, and desiring became a key feature of the new publicly focused female culture of the second half of the nineteenth century.

Theatregoers were spellbound by such actresses. The romantic novelist Elinor Glyn felt that her whole imaginative world opened up when, at age 16, in 1880, she was taken to see Bernhardt perform *Théodora*.[89] Marcel Proust offered a fascinating account of the processes whereby a young man was drawn into the fascinations of theatre by the image of the great actress 'Berma' (a composite of Bernhardt and Réjane, according to Proust's recent biographers).[90] Every morning he goes to view the Morris column near his house to see the announcements of new plays—an experience that nourished his imagination with daydreams. Stimulated by strange titles and bright colours, he conjures up 'vivid and compelling pictures' of plays of different types that he equates to desserts presented at the dinner table.[91] In contrast to Glyn, when finally he is taken to see Berma, he is initially disappointed. Faced with the inconveniences of spectatorship in a real-life theatre and a mannered performance, he finds the work of his imagination superior.[92] But the enthusiasm of others highlights for him the interrelationships between stage performance, imaginative hedonism, fashion, and femininity. The glamour of a great actress is revealed to be less distinctive than was widely supposed: far from being the personalized, unique experience that the young narrator had expected, it was imaginative, sensual, absorbable, and ostensibly available for appropriation through consumption. The enticing image of the actress was a constructed one that the spectator could partially reconstruct in private fantasies, but most especially in relation to collectively sustained imaginings.

Actresses were bearers of collective sexual fantasy who occupied the public scene in a hundred ways. Where most upper-class women held back, they appeared on the stage, frequented hotels and restaurants, appeared in magazines and the newspapers, and circulated widely as images on picture postcards. On- and offstage, they attracted interest and gave rise to exploits that the press followed with glee, finding the theatre to be a source of excitement and interest for its readers. A performer like Lillie Langtry, a clergyman's daughter from Jersey who became a society beauty, artists' muse, and actress, as well as the lover of several royal men, was intensely fascinating. Guided by Oscar Wilde, in whose *She Stoops to Conquer* she made her stage debut in 1881, she appealed to different sections of the public by developing a persona expressed through poses, performances, and adventures.[93] Her image was widely reproduced and she also provided celebrity endorsements of cosmetics and soaps. While print culture offered men new opportunities to acquire titillating images of compliant femininity and indulge in fantasies of possession,[94] magazines and shop windows exercised a special fascination for women.[95]

The lower-class origins of stage performers gave every girl the hope that she too, one day, might bask in celebrity and enjoy a life of charm and luxury.[96] The growth of the service sector brought thousands of young women to big cities to work in shops, bars, restaurants, and other places of leisure and entertainment. Such women were caught up in the metropolitan culture of images, dreams, fashion, and aspiration. The very arrangement of their places of work, such as the introduction of the public bar in the late Victorian period, which separated the female server from male customers, provided them with a simple staging. Although their class and regional origins were rarely mysterious, the fact of their being on display and the distance separating them from consumers endowed them with a residual form of the glamour that attached to professional image-makers.[97] For these women, as well as young female magazine readers of all classes, actresses were an ideal projection of themselves.

The lure of the theatre was so strong that many young and not so young women, even from comfortable families, were willing to throw caution to the wind and pursue a career on the stage. 'The glare, glitter and glamor of the dramatic stage, it seems, never ceases [sic] to attract giddy heads, notwithstanding the trials, hardships and reverses that are daily experienced by theatrical people,' commented an American newspaper.[98] Very often, stage-struck youngsters saw theatre purely in terms of fame and their own ability to achieve it by achieving the right visual effects. One young woman who replied to an advertisement seeking an amateur actress for a new drama told a theatre manager:

I should not have answered that advertisement, for I have never been on the stage, and I know nothing about theatricals. No, I have never even taken part in amateur theatricals. But I am just dying to be an actress; I just know I would succeed. My friends and relatives would seriously object to my adopting the profession; but I would just do it anyhow; and after I became a great star it would be all right, I guess. Now I know that to be a success on the stage one must wear fine dresses, and I have got any number of them. . . . Do they compel you to wear rouge when acting? If so, I would have to, I suppose. You see I have almond-shaped eyes, and can make them appear a little larger by painting under the eyebrows[99]

The theatre was a channel of dreams through which an ordinary life could be transformed into an extraordinary one. Any girl could dream of achieving a magical makeover that appeared to require little or no talent or work. Such beliefs were mostly delusional but the theatre did in fact offer opportunities to some young women of little talent, so long as they had a pleasing manner and an attractive appearance. The development of female spectacle did not rely solely on the great actresses. Rather theatres increasingly specialized in entertainments that were systematic rather than dependent on individuals. A particularly influential model was provided by the 'Gaiety Girls', who were world-renowned for their refined beauty and decorative elegance. Invented by George Edwardes, the manager of the Gaiety Theatre on London's The Strand, they were the world's first branded showgirl. These women sometimes sang and danced, while some were required merely to decorate the stage and respond with individual mannerisms to what was going on around them. They looked like ladies, except they were widely held to be prettier. Within a strict paradigm, each one cultivated a different stage identity.

The Gaiety Girl phenomenon was closely linked to the rise of musical comedy which began in 1886 when Edwardes took over the Gaiety and launched a highly successful musical show entitled *Dorothy*. It offered some sort of story, tuneful music, witty lyrics, sumptuous and varied sets, exquisite costumes, and pretty girls. This show did better business than any Gilbert and Sullivan operetta and inaugurated a new genre. Many of the shows at Edwardes's theatre featured the word 'girl' in the title (*The Shop Girl, The Circus Girl, The Quaker Girl*, etc.) and the girls were often the biggest attraction. He carefully selected, groomed, and glorified them, providing lessons in elocution, singing, dancing, and fencing. Their costumes were always in the latest fashions and their elegance was much celebrated. Tanning was forbidden in order to preserve an aristocratic whiteness of complexion and make-up was never worn offstage. The girls were reputedly always polite and very well behaved. Selected from hundreds of young women who came each week for chorus auditions, they became a British female ideal of the 1890s. They can be compared at some level to the Gibson Girl, but they lacked the American's outdoor qualities and their frame was show business. Edwardes encouraged them to go out and be seen in elegant places, since this would drum up business for the theatre. They were generally treated respectfully by the admirers who pleaded to take them to supper at the Savoy Grill after a show. They could be spotted dining at the best restaurants, enjoying Henley and Ascot, and other society occasions.

The Gaiety Girls were extremely popular with young men about town. They were mock-aristocrats who were sometimes more genteel that the originals. Their fame was compounded when Gertie Millar became Countess of Dudley and Rosie Boote Marchioness of Headfort. For traditionalists, the phenomenon of stage girls marrying into the aristocracy was confirmation that the established order of society had gone into irreversible decline. The scale of it, however, was less than that of transatlantic marriages. It has been estimated that there were 102 marriages between American women and English peers (or sons of peers) between 1870 and 1914, while there were 21 marriages between peers and stage players between 1879 and 1914.[100] In a contest between money and beauty, the former was most likely to win. 'A lovely face is very attractive, and men pay much attention to its happy possessor,' argued an article in the *Los Angeles Times*, 'but there is a wonderful glamour surrounding a woman who is popularly supposed to curl her hair with banknotes, which no amount of personal charm can ever supercede.'[101] In the popular imagination, though, debutantes and chorus girls were rivals. Not by chance, money and the desire for it was one of the stock themes of popular entertainment. The rags-to-riches theme was often present. In *The Shop Girl*, for example, a good-hearted millionaire, who has struck it rich in Colorado, comes to London to find and bestow riches on the daughter of his old, but now deceased, friend from the mining camps. The daughter of course, is none other than the eponymous shop girl.

The Gaiety Girls were manufactured as socialites, but there was a strong showgirl element to them that inevitably entailed sex appeal. For all his insistence on respectability, Edwardes never failed to ask his scouts, when they were recommending a girl discovered in the provinces, 'Would you want to sleep with her?'[102] Sexual desirability was a key attribute for a theatrical performer, and especially if she was a young woman. Male theatregoers, including the fashionably attired and socially polished, were enchanted by the girls of the chorus. 'The chorus girl is sometimes pretty and always interesting to the young man who haunts the front row and lingers after the [show] is over,' commented one newspaper. The reason why they were 'bewitched by ladies of the chorus', however, had more to do with their own fantasies than the talent of the women or the success of a show. While many companies went out of their way to assert the good behaviour of their employees, 'there seems to be a very general impression among young men that the girls in a comic opera company, or any other theatrical company, will readily surrender to their advances, and are not restrained by the ideas of propriety of conduct generally recognized by girls in good social standing'.[103] Such beliefs did not stem only from established perceptions but were actively encouraged by leading performers.

For all the developments in popular theatre and extravaganza in London and in the United States, only Paris was capable of forging original forms of spectacle that harnessed the energy of the metropolis to fantasy and eroticism. France led the world in entertainment and it proved this by supplying an endless series of personalities, performing types, dances, visual motifs, and artistic expressions. After the Folies Bergère, the Moulin Rouge was the second most famous burlesque theatre in Paris. An architectural oddity designed by the artist Willette, the Moulin Rouge featured on the outside a windmill and—from 1890—a lifesize model elephant, while the interior was extravagant in the eclectic, Oriental style. Far more even than the department stores, it was gaudy and confusing. 'The architecture is full of surprises', remarked one observer; it 'is transformed by its arches and brightened by its mysterious vaults. It is Granada, it's Spain. Here it's a cottage which reminds me of Normandy. There it's a windmill which makes me think of Holland . . . it's surprising, it's charming, it's mad.'[104] The memorable, bold posters of Toulouse-Lautrec further enhanced the lurid, vivid appeal of the place and its performers. The poster image of the Moulin Rouge, bright red and redolent with sexuality and personality, was so powerful that the journalist Maurice Talmeyr exclaimed that 'the wall poster . . . is the natural language of the lowest excitements'. Prostitution and exhibitionism were its sources of inspiration, he argued, and as a consequence of its influence 'each resident of Paris carries within himself a sort of perpetual interior "Moulin Rouge" '.[105]

Established to capitalize on the large crowds that flocked to Paris for the exposition of 1889, it turned the frenetic dancing of the nightclubs of the artists' district of Montmartre into a world-renowned spectacle. In the 1890s the club became bound up with the image of Paris. It drew many celebrated visitors including, inevitably, the Prince of Wales (among whose mistresses were Lillie Langtry and Sarah Bernhardt). In its first incarnation, the theatre retained the mark of the street. The coarseness of the performers undiluted by any sprinkling of refinement. La Goulue (Louise Weber), the most famous dancer of the quadrille, who was immortalized by Lautrec, was renowned for her blatant exhibitionism, her sexual excesses, and a refusal to mask her vulgarity. It has been said that her accessibility—she danced topless at street parties and posed for photographs with her legs open as she held a glass of champagne in one hand and a pipe in the other—was a direct emanation of the brothel.[106] The Moulin Rouge did not specialize in star performers (most of the dancers were just known by nicknames). Rather its forte was the marketing of overt female sexuality for entertainment. The leading cancan dancers usually began as amateurs before being picked out for the stage because they were popular with audiences. They mingled freely with customers and were sexually available to them.

In the early years of the twentieth century, the theatre's overt sexual exhibitionism was moulded into something less explicit and more polished.[107] Image and spectacle took the place of semi-spontaneous euphoria and erotic commerce. At the Moulin Rouge itself, fully fledged shows were staged that were produced by Jacques-Charles in company with a Briton, Earl Leslie. These revues employed two categories of female performer, the chorus girl and the showgirl. The former was an invention of the 1890s and she has been compared to other new figures such as the shop girl, the barmaid, and the typist.[108] All of these were roles that were seen as typical of the evolving nature of work and of leisure. They were urban jobs that were typically performed by young women. In the public imagination, chorus girls summed them all up. They were breezy, cheerful, and carefree girls on the make whose dancing and singing reflected a modern, vital spirit. By contrast, showgirls were purely icons of visual pleasure and fantasy. They did not really perform but, like the Gaiety Girls, posed, adopted attitudes and presented themselves as constructed ideals of femininity and consumption.[109] However, the two were often blended and the public usually made little distinction between them.

While the British showgirl was generally a mock aristocrat, the Parisian showgirl had a more democratic image. She was seen by no less a figure than Edward VII as 'both a great lady and a woman of the people', able to switch between the manners of a society hostess and an actress. 'Only in Paris does one meet with anything so complete,' he is reported to have said.[110] One of the most remarkable stars of the period was a French performer whose stage name was Gaby Deslys. An extremely seductive stage presence, who has been described as an Edwardian Marilyn Monroe, she was a bridge between courtesan-performers like Otero and the highly professional showgirls of the interwar years. She was also one of the first to enjoy equal fame in France, England, and the United States and to offer audiences cultural novelties imported from each of these countries. After being spotted in France, she made her first appearance in London at the Gaiety, which had a long history of staging French plays.[111] She featured in a musical comedy as 'the charm of Paris', who appeared as if by magic out of an enormous basket of flowers, like the genie from Aladdin's lamp. Dressed in the full regalia of the Paris music hall, complete with fluffed-out skirt and a fabulous hat, she flashed her smile at the audience and winked at them with her pale blue eyes. In this show she sang a couple of numbers but such was her reception that in all her future appearances she would top the bill.

Gaby Deslys was an utterly theatrical phenomenon who also created a sensation by scandalous dalliances with a number of prominent men. Her admirers were legion and were utterly smitten by a figure who appeared frivolous, excessive, and artificial. Publicity was like oxygen to her; 'her life had the aura of a fireworks display, a series of breathtaking explosions of light and colour', her biographer claims.[112] She lived in the glare of publicity and seemed to have no existence outside it; certainly she revealed very little of herself. Physically, she was fresh-faced and curvaceous. According to the choreographer Jacques-Charles, when he first saw her, she struck him as 'of compact build, with rounded breasts, hips and rump; her pins were imprisoned in high boots. She had a mountain of fake blonde curly hair that was covered with an amazing mixture of flowers, tulle, bird's feathers and sequins.'[113] Her personal style was hyperbolic; ostrich feathers and giant hats were her calling cards. In London, she embodied 'le chic parisien'. She communicated youth, *joie de vivre*, and hedonism.

Deslys was a commercial icon who was paid to be seen wearing the clothes of designers including Doucet and Paquin. Indeed, her eye-popping stage costumes were always exaggerations of the most current modes. Deslys's sets included such scenes as a luxurious boudoir and the deck of an ocean liner, while wide staircases allowed her to make protracted entrances. Her collection of jewellery, which she wore constantly in public and only removed for her performances, was astonishing. She understood perfectly that 'men have more respect for my jewels and my beauty than for my talent'.[114] She also knew that as long as she had her mansion, car, and pearls, she could 'hold [her] head high'. 'No-one will dare insult me,' she asserted. By her wealth she could pass over rumours that she could be had by the quarter-hour.[115] Gordon Selfridge, of department store fame, lavished vast sums on her upkeep, turning her into a brilliant instance of conspicuous consumption.[116] When she returned to Paris in 1917 to inaugurate the Casino, her notoriety had been embellished by a notorious affair with young king Manöel of Portugal (a liaison that allegedly contributed to his overthrow). She had also acquired the patent of Gaiety Girl and a slight English accent and she brought with her a jazz band. Before her early death in 1920, at age 36, she had become the stuff of legend.

The writer and photographer Cecil Beaton offered a memorable posthumous portrait of Deslys. 'She was a marvellous creature, of brillantine and brilliance, and Christmas-tree tinsel—madly artificial and so gaily irresponsible, the epitome of self-consciousness and at the same time utterly childish; a little ragamuffin playing on the sands with pearls, but she knew the value of the pearls!', he wrote.[117] 'She had the incessant vitality of an over-excited child, and oh! what sex appeal, oh! what glamour! It was impossible to look at anyone else while she was on the stage: not one of the glorious chorus behind her would be noticed, for Gaby riveted all attention with her fantastic affectations.' 'After every performance,' he continued, 'the entrance to the stage door of the theatre at which she happened to be playing was surging with a crowd of feverishly excited hoboes, Guardsmen, aesthetes and filberts, who cheered while Gaby made her way to her huge black-and-white motor-car, that had many more than the usual number of large windows, and her initials blazing on its doors.' Her influence, Beaton asserted, was far-reaching: 'How well she realised the value of overdoing everything: the feathers soared to the ceiling! She is entirely responsible for Mistinguett's head-dresses, for the glut of spangles at the Casino de Paris, and for the window displays at Selfridge's store.'[118]

Money was always a key theme for showgirls. Deslys's successor, Mistinguett, made explicit and repetitive reference to money and the love of money.[119] These also provided her with many of her themes—most notably her signature song 'Je cherche un millionaire'. Just as the courtesan-performers exploited and helped create popular perceptions of the female entertainer as femme fatale and gold-digger, so Mistinguett, in her many performances and songs that irrevocably linked love and money, reinforced the myth.[120] Mistinguett was an original type whose rootlessness enabled her to forge a personality that was a reflection of mass desires for material well-being and happiness. She was aware of the need to put on a good show and be upbeat at all times in order to please her working-class admirers ('twenty-four hours a day I wore a gay smile clamped on my features like a carnival mask', she wrote in her memoirs).[121]

The embodiment of Parisian glamour for a generation, Mistinguett was similar in many respects to the courtesan-performers. She was on intimate terms with kings and she gambled on the house at casinos to stimulate clients. Like Otero, she insured her legs, for 500,000 francs in 1919. She endorsed beauty products in the United States, and she played various mistresses of the past, including Louis XV's Madame Du Barry. However, she saw herself as being on a lower rung of the ladder than the courtesan-performers. As the star attraction at the Casino de Paris, she was located more firmly within the world of theatre and for this reason she was seen, like Bernhardt, as embodying the theatre and a particular version of theatrical Parisian-ness. She was devoted to maintaining a relationship with the public—which she called 'the most demanding of lovers'.[122] Her life was not a comedy of front stage and backstage; everything was subordinated to the parade. 'I knew how to run my private life so that I should be talked about,' she recalled. 'I knew how to rub shoulders with the crowd—but just enough to intrigue them without making a nuisance of myself. I could be seen everywhere; at the races, in restaurants, at charity balls and midnight matinées. I displayed, for the public's delectation, my pearls, my dresses, my pet dogs and my leading man.'[123]

Critics saw the rise of an organized show-business dreamworld as the Americanization of a Parisian idiom.[124] The influences that Deslys brought to the Casino de Paris were certainly American and so too was the emergence of the new role of producer. But other changes were more due to the need to address a different and wider clientele that was taking on mass characteristics. In an era of motor transport and sport, the public demanded from entertainment the same sort of movement and variety that it experienced in life.[125] The professionalization of the performer led to observations that Paris was witnessing the application of mass production methods to entertainment and that the theatres were becoming factories of pleasure. To go to a show became the ordinary man's equivalent of the rich man's ostentatious maintenance of a wasteful mistress. It was a luxury expenditure that was utterly unproductive save for the status it brought and the temporary gaiety it afforded. Accordingly, the shows offered sensual pleasure in the form of the decor, the costumes, the female bodies, and the brash comfort of the theatres themselves. They offered not merely escapism on a par with alcohol (*l'oubli*), but a systematic dreamworld informed by eclectic appropriations from other cultures and eras. By the 1910s, performers were definitively distanced from audiences and prostitutes were banished from the environs of most theatres.

However, France remained a crucial reference point. The American producer Florenz Ziegfeld specialized in the appropriation and reinterpretation of French qualities for an American audience. Initially, Ziegfeld employed European exoticism, importing and presenting Anna Held, a young musical performer who, despite a friendship with Liane de Pougy, traded on her innocence. Held had been born in Poland but was seen as a French music-hall star who was qualified to represent Parisian fashion and style. Ziegfeld married Held and invested great efforts in promoting her as a desirable role model for American women.[126] She became the most publicized woman in America thanks to a series of stunts that included buying and refurbishing Lillie Langtry's old rail carriage to take her on tour around the country.[127] However, the showman's main contribution was in evolving a brand name chorus girl on the George Edwardes model: the 'Ziegfeld Girl'. A key figure in the French-inspired Ziegfeld Follies, which in various versions ran from 1908 until 1931, the girl was a standardized patriotic product for whose authenticity and quality Ziegfeld personally vouched. Like their European counterparts, his chorus girls were generally lower class in social extraction and they were trained in the British way to walk and to dress offstage like ladies. As decorative ornaments they were packaged as high class and expensive. The 'work' element of their performance was always concealed beneath their visual effects. Ziegfeld Girls were always posited as first-class products in the genre of female spectacle. Although the shows and the girls' costumes were extravagant, they enjoyed a reputation for good taste. At a time when divisions between high and low entertainment were quite rigid, the Ziegfeld Follies occupied a curious median position. A key element was the blending of high- and low-class codes that is essential to glamour. Even his moulding of Anna Held originated in a desire to replace the coarse atmosphere of vaudeville with glamour, taste, and charm.[128] At a time when fashion was coming within the purview of wider social groups, beautiful costumes were a way of attracting a female audience and holding its interest. The performers also taught women that, in the words of a contemporary newspaper, 'the little air of conscious beauty, which is not vanity, but assurance of a stable fact, throws a glamour over its wearer's appearance that is marvelously flattering. Indeed it is far more effective in establishing her reputation for being beautiful than regularity of feature or harmony of coloring.'[129]

The showgirl became a national institution in the United States, where the Folies Bergère manager Paul Derval noted acidly that she was 'mass pro-duced like a Chevrolet or a tin of ham'.[130] Lacking the means to train vast numbers of girls, Derval aimed for diversity rather than uniformity. 'A firm believer in the French maxim that uniformity breeds boredom,' he selected dancers 'in the hope that each one will claim the attention of a certain number of spectators'.[131] Champions of the primacy of French charm believed that it was Paris itself that produced and shaped a special type of seductive femininity that was unrivalled. 'At every step of the social ladder, a woman is a hundred times more woman in Paris than in any other city of the universe,' commented the writer and journalist Octave Uzanne.[132] The city inculcated special smiles, glances, ways of walking, and a seductive charm that turned the *Parisiennes* into 'an aristocracy among the women of the globe'.[133] The appeal of this special quality also derived from the sense that it was a fragile one that would not last much longer. 'Every year the city becomes more Americanised and loses, under the ugly thrust of progress, one of the attractions that were its glory and its charm,' lamented Uzanne.[134] Yet mass entertainment was not a purely American phenomenon. An average 500,000 people went to the theatre every week in Paris between the 1880s and 1910; in 1900, 274 *cafés-concerts* operated in the city.[135] In such a context, rationalization was unavoidable. In practice, ideas and techniques were regularly exchanged between the USA and France. However, the American custom of thinking of markets in terms of masses of consumers rather than sectoral interests and tastes was the way of the future. In the years following the First World War, the American impact on glamour would be even more pronounced than it was in the gilded age.

CHAPTER 5

CAFÉ SOCIETY AND PUBLICITY

I n the years after the First World War, a series of changes occurred in the relationship between the upper classes and the press, between the older and younger generations, and between the mass public and the communications media. The conflict had a major impact on social relations because women had been drawn into the workplace to an unprecedented degree and millions of men had been killed. Moreover, the classes had been thrown together somewhat, lessening the distinctions between them.[1] On account of the 'democracy of suffering', a more widespread democratic ethos permeated society. For the first time, ordinary soldiers and not just the generals were commemorated and their names inscribed on monuments. The sense of the masses, and indeed use of the word 'mass' to describe the lower classes, was a feature of the age. The masses were not passive but turbulent and demanding. The rise of left-wing parties and movements demonstrated that discontent was widespread. Although the political consequences of this varied from country to country, everywhere there was a widening of public opinion that was formed increasingly through the press. The emergence of a new type of middlebrow newspaper catered to the demands of its readers for excitement, novelty, and escapism by creating an image of upper-class life that high-lighted the activities of the young and especially young women. Young men and women of privileged backgrounds participated fully in this scene-making and even on occasion worked for the press. Their unconventional antics provoked much criticism but their high visibility and ready superficial embrace of styles and fads originating in the United States and in the movies turned them into figures of glamour. Their taste for fun, fashion, and adventure made them desirable and enviable to those whose lives were more restricted and whose income did not allow them to hop every night from club to restaurant by taxi or to own one of the superbly stylish sports cars that were so beloved of the fast set.

In America first, and then Britain, newspapers pioneered a more popular type of journalism that was heavily illustrated, personality-oriented, and sensational. Tabloid papers like the New York *Evening Graphic* and *Illustrated Daily News* abandoned the formality of the established newspapers for short stories, personal details, lurid crime reports, and scandal. In England, the old-style provincial press that privileged liberal opinion and rational debate was gradually superseded by new, mass-circulation, London-based papers like the *Daily Sketch* and the *Daily Express* that were brash and xenophobic.[2] In the early twentieth century, newspapers had served less as a connecting tissue of society than as a means of conveying facts and articulating opinion, mainly within the educated elite. After the war, the popular press began to cater more to mass audiences. It aimed to shape events as much as to report them.[3] Entrepreneurs like Lord Beaverbrook, the founder of the *Express*, grasped that there was a widespread desire for heroes and celebrities. He understood that the curiosity about high society was an aspect of this and sought to exploit it.[4] The public took an interest in society figures for several reasons. Their doings provided a narrative that amused and titillated, while also giving rise to puritanical disapproval. They were unusual, privileged, and yet not immune from setbacks and disappointments including heartbreaks and other personal tragedies. At a time of economic hardship, they offered an image of a gilded existence that was intensely enviable. They also functioned as a channel whereby novelties and fashions were imported and presented. For these reasons, interest in them was almost obsessive and focused on the minutiae of upper-class homes, opinions, dress styles, and language.[5]

Beaverbrook and other proprietors began to take on well-connected people to write their social news, with the result that social columns became more vibrant and well informed, something that caused indignation in some quarters.[6] The better information and livelier reporting turned them from a minority interest into a mass recreation. They featured prominently in the morning papers and were read by a huge middle- and working-class public. For the first time, members of high society were permanently on view, a fact that was noted by Patrick Balfour, a British aristocratic commentator who experienced these changes first-hand. 'The public that in the past had stood on chairs to see Lily Langtry in the Park and had blocked Bond Street as it gazed at the Society beauties in the photographers' windows, could henceforward gratify all its curiosity about all the Lily Langtrys without stirring from its breakfast table,' he observed.[7]

Debutantes were one of the main subjects of this type of reporting. Margaret Whigham (who subsequently became the Duchess of Argyll and is today best remembered for her involvement in a scandalous divorce case in 1963)[8] was the most striking example of a new breed of debutante. Born into a Scottish aristocratic family, she had spent her childhood in the United States and came to England in 1926, aged 13. When she came out in 1930, she was hailed as the most beautiful girl of the year. Unlike the debutantes of an earlier generation, she did not solely inhabit a world of private houses and balls; she dined out in restaurants, attended functions in hotels, and was a constant presence in the press. Formally, she was still chaperoned. In reality, it was left to the family chauffeur to ensure she got home after a series of dates for dinner, dancing, and late night club-hopping. The only rule imposed by her parents was that, whatever time she went to bed, she had to be dressed for breakfast at nine. With her unusually hectic social life and distinctive beauty, Whigham was the centre of attention. Gossip columns detailed her numerous social engagements and her varied wardrobe in a way that at once delighted and horrified readers. She was said to have invented almost single-handedly what was known as the 'deb-ballyhoo industry'.[9] She was regarded as a trendsetter after she became the first girl to wear pearl-coloured nail varnish that was luminous at night. For charity, she once appeared on stage in a production entitled 'A Day in the Life of a Debutante'. With her square face, sunken eyes, and elongated neck, she became an easy subject for cartoonists. Whigham was treated like a star and became as well known as one.[10] Suddenly, young women still in their teens had to cope not only with the judgement of the adult members of their own restricted circle but with the scrutiny of the social columns.[11] They became public figures and bearers of glamour.

The debutantes undoubtedly appealed to the press and the public because they were upper class. The sheer unusualness and privilege of their lives lent them mystery and made them fascinating to readers of the press. However, it was never debutantes in general who won coverage but bold and daring individuals who broke with some established upper-class patterns of behaviour. A few controversial or original gestures turned young women like Whigham into attention magnets who aroused curiosity whenever they dined out, attended a public event, or were spotted in the company of a suitor. These girls were treated not with the deference of a hierarchical order but with the curiosity of a fast-moving, mass society. The cult of the debutante was a result of the popular newspapers' search for colourful personalities around whom a narrative could be built. It was part of a trend whereby the most beautiful or privileged women and men were singled out for extended coverage and turned into front-page news together with royalty, politicians, and actresses. Alongside the sporting hero, the actress, and the great criminal, there was a place in the papers for an eye-catching debutante.

The transformation of a select group of debutantes from gauche girls into savvy celebrities was part of a wider process that saw high society become ever more completely penetrated and remoulded by publicity. Whigham emerged at a time when sections of the press were beginning to treat socialites as celebrities and gossip about them. The English aristocrats who wrote social columns, like Balfour in the *Sketch* and the larger-than-life Valentine Charles Browne—Viscount Castlerosse—in the *Sunday Express*, were anomalous figures with a feet in two spheres. In some ways, they were not dissimilar to the men satirized by Evelyn Waugh in his memorable novel

Vile Bodies, published in 1930. But whereas Waugh's impoverished aristo-cratic gossip hunters were desperate men who begged invitations to this or that occasion, the best-known columnists were quite powerful since their coverage could determine the significance and success of a social event. They could make, and even break, some would-be celebrities. A good deal of the attention Whigham and a handful of other debutantes received, she later revealed, was due to their friendship with popular social columnists.[12] These men attended many parties and balls and they referred in their columns to the comings and goings of the most high profile and ubiquitous of the debutantes. They wrote them up in a hyperbolic way because they liked the girls and they assumed readers would be charmed by them too.

The frenzy around debutantes was not an exclusively British phenomenon. The American press pursued one or two debutantes each year with no less enthusiasm. A girl was selected not on the basis of the importance of her family but because she was good copy, someone who fitted the need of the press for a photogenic, emblematic figure who could act as an ornament for its col-umns.[13] Brenda Duff Frazier, who made her debut in 1938, fitted the bill to perfection. The daughter of the twice-married heir to a grain-broking dynasty and an ambitious but unconventional Canadian, she had striking blue-black hair, deep-set eyes, and full, round cheeks. Her features were described as doll-like and ample use of heavy red lipstick made it look as though her lips were painted on. She was described as beautiful and composed, although a photo-graph of her used by *Life* on its cover made her look like a 17-year-old ingénue. Frazier became a star of the press, a girl about whom five thousand articles were written and whose every act seemed to result in a photograph. She was called, in a term invented by a prominent New York columnist, Maury Paul, 'Glamour Girl No. 1'.[14] According to Paul, the girl who received this unofficial title should be monied and mysterious, exotic in appearance, and daring in her gestures—in brief, she should have the potential to be glamorous. Although no one could explain quite why it was Frazier and not someone else who attracted so many headlines, she received hundreds of fan letters, some of which were simply addressed to 'Brenda Frazier No. 1 Glamour Girl' or 'Brenda Duff Frazier, The World's Prettiest Debutante'. Even more than Whigham, Frazier was drawn into a realm that had more to do with showbusiness than elite living. She mingled with film actors and sportsmen, a perfume was named in her honour, and her likeness was borrowed by department stores for fashion illustrations.[15] She was even photographed dunking a doughnut. When she went to the Metropolitan Opera, the special arena of bejewelled high society matrons, she was applauded to her seat. All this led to negative reactions from upper-class traditionalists but helped foster her popularity among those for whom she was a fad and a celebrity.

Although deference was declining in favour of an emphasis on the amusing, the curious, or the extravagant, the temptation of irreverence, in England at least, was tempered by the fact that the aristocracy was tied to the monarchy, an institution that commanded near universal respect. In America, a more abrasive style of reporting was developed by the sharp-tongued print—and later radio—journalist Walter Winchell, who pioneered a variety of journalistic voyeurism. Such was his influence that he is said to have acted as midwife to the creation of a mass culture that was fixated with personalities.[16] With his familiar tone and focus on individuals, he judged society figures according to the criteria of the street. Winchell was a tough New Yorker who had little time for upper-class frivolity or debutantes, whom he called by their first names and disparaged as 'debutramps'.[17]

Such practices were part of the process whereby following elite events became a mass spectator activity. This was a double-edged development as far as the social elite was concerned. On the one hand its social prominence appeared to be confirmed but at the same time its members were turned into creatures of publicity. As high society was opened up and made more visible than ever before, it was exposed to popular judgement and brought into competition with an expanding entertainment industry. This was just one of the changes that the 1920s brought. Communications and transportation improved as automobiles and public transport made travel easier and the telephone entered more common usage. Photography and the movies altered perception by expanding the realm of the visible. In the large cities, advertising hoardings, neon signs, and places of entertainment including dance halls and cinema all aimed at an undifferentiated audience. Radio and spectator sports further contributed to the emergence of a unified mass audience.

After 1945, those who participated in high society in the 1930s liked to remember it as a world of grace and refinement. It was an era in which the aristocracy still commanded substantial public attention and its rituals, from debutante balls and grand society weddings to visits to the opera and theatrical premieres, continued to affirm its social superiority. 'Looking back now on the glamour of it all, the first summer season seems like a dream,' Whigham wrote. 'It belongs to another world—a world of manners and elegance that has now vanished.'[18] However, while the particular grace and style of the upper-class world of the 1930s may have disappeared after the Second World War, the developments of the period in terms of publicity and glamour would remain. As a young woman in 1930, Whigham perhaps did not realize how far upper-class life had already evolved. Although the aristocracy formally maintained its historic position at the top of the social hierarchy, the way some of its members became well known and which of them were most popular was changing fast. The socially prominent were ubiquitous—the British newspapers were full of the doings of society beauty Lady Diana Cooper and eccentric heiress Nancy Cunard—but a great deal progressed in the society around them and this affected the way they were viewed. The upper classes were mainly of interest when they met certain criteria of newsworthiness or gave rise to sensations. Some were even employed in advertisements.

All this served to create a different sort of relationship between the social elite and the broad mass of people. When Whigham used 'glamour' to evoke the whirlwind events of her debut year, she did so as though it were synonymous with upper-class living. In fact, in 1930 the term was more widely understood as a quality of excitement and magnetism that was associated with some famous men and women regardless of their background. Not by chance, the word 'glamour' entered common usage at precisely this time, a fact that by itself shows how images of wealth, luxury, and beauty were more widely deployed than ever before and were consumed by an eager audience. How far people took these images seriously or how they affected their views of the upper classes remains unclear, although it has been argued that they functioned to promote the interests of the social elite if only by perpetuating the idea of high society as a necessary institution.[19]

In May 1930, Cecil Beaton wrote an article in the London *Sunday Dispatch* in which he described glamour as the attribute of those who were 'surrounded perpetually by a roseate aura of excitement and thrill'.[20] He did not regard this as a modern quality; indeed, he wrote that it was striking that there should be 'a chosen few who stand out as radiant favourites and figures of mysticism and interest in these frank days of Christian names, dial telephones and skyscrapers'. But in his evaluation of various people whom he considered to be glamorous, Beaton did not solely consider the high-born and the privileged. Royalty by definition was glamorous, he argued, but otherwise it depended on a person's profession or personal qualities. Movie stars, some artists and writers, actresses, and sportsmen were just as likely to be alluring as a beautiful socialite. Glamour, in short, was random. 'There is hope for everyone,' Beaton concluded, since there was no way of knowing who or what would emerge as the next phenomenon.

Beaton adored both aristocracy and the theatre and it was probably this that led him to insist that glamour was inimitable and to discourage the efforts of the unworthy to appropriate it. 'By being under the impression that you have it and by giving yourself airs and graces,' he cautioned, 'you will most likely become uncontemporary and result in being a crashing bore.' Beaton was right to argue that glamour could not be possessed by everyone. What he did not fully grasp was that awkward attempts to do so were not a result of misplaced ambition. They were triggered by the nature of glamour itself as an effect arousing envy and desire. Precisely because glamour could almost never be obtained, it led to an unquenched yearning. At the time he was writing, professional stylists, publicists, decorators, couturiers, social organizers, and the luxury trades in general were all learning how to fashion images and confer an allure that the mass public would find intriguing and enviable. The paradox of magical allure in an age of increasing homogenization and declining individuality lay in the fact that it was constructed and moulded in a systematic way and sold to people on the basis that it was indeed imitable. Even when it was applied to members of the titled aristocracy, as it sometimes was, glamour referred not to their inherited qualities or natural leadership but to their newsworthiness, physical beauty, material ease, and leisure.

Many of those involved with commercializing style and luxury were impoverished aristocrats. Members of the elite were lured towards commerce because, after the war, inflation and tax increases reduced both the ranks of the established wealthy and the quantity of the income of those who retained their wealth.[21] Even for those without money problems, the increasing appeal of factory jobs made it difficult to recruit domestic servants. Not even in its new form, blended with the new blood of international plutocracy, could aristocracy continue as before. As a result, ostentation and privilege on the scale of the Edwardian years declined. At the same time, many fortunes were made quickly in the boom period of the 1920s, some of them legitimately by industrialists and entrepreneurs, others less legitimately by war profiteers, financial speculators, and bootleggers. Most of those who came to the fore were outsiders with no claim to social distinction yet, like the new rich of earlier generations, they paraded their new-found wealth and sought recognition from other sectors of society. In this they sought assistance from the male and female members of high society who entered the world of business. Some ran boutiques and gift shops, while others took positions in department stores or went into the theatre. Yet others worked for the press or became public relations advisers and consultants. More aggressively and systematically than ever before, the symbols of the wealthy lifestyle were appropriated by outsiders and newcomers. This in turn aroused the interest of the mass of ordinary people.

The sense of glamour was related to these changes in the way the social elite was formed and in the distribution of wealth. The wealthy lifestyle was no longer something that was seen as remote and hidebound. Tableaux of upper-class life were often employed in the advertisements of the time as advertisers and publicists, sensing a widespread interest in it, sought to evoke such milieux, if possible using authentic exponents to market goods.[22] American manufacturers above all did their best to win endorsements from aristocratic beauties and wealthy women. Royalty was normally exempt from this but, among others, Queen Marie of Romania lent her name to a great many products, including Pond's face cream. At one level, this trend was the inevitable consequence of the publicity that illuminated the lives of the privileged, for publicity heralded commercialization. As the poster artist Cassandre expressed it, 'publicity is not a medium for self-expression, it is a means of communication between the seller and his public'.[23] At another, it was an indication of the way exclusivity acquired a market value and upper-class lifestyles became part of the imaginative realm of wide groups of people. This was facilitated by the way the life of the privileged was blended with modern innovations and entertainments. Through this change, it became more widely desirable and, in theory at least, imitable.

Of all the novelties of the period, none was more far-reaching than the movies. From 1918, the American film industry began the conquest of world markets that would give it an unrivalled purchase on the popular imagination in the twentieth century. Film would make a huge contribution to the development and diffusion of glamour because it was a medium that provided a unique connecting tissue between classes and nations and because it was infused with images of heroism, luxury, and beauty. The first generation of movie stars enjoyed unprecedented fame and financial rewards. Charlie Chaplin, Mary Pickford, and Douglas Fairbanks achieved worldwide prominence and held a power in the industry that virtually no subsequent star would obtain. Pickford and Fairbanks were seen as the 'royal couple' of Hollywood. Each was a major star who drew people in their millions to the cinema. For audiences, Pickford was the 'Girl with the Golden Curls', the little girl who could do no wrong, while Doug, the star of the swashbuckling epics *The Mark of Zorro* and *The Thief of Baghdad*, was the ever-smiling, ever-cheerful athletic adventurer. Together they lived in a luxurious twenty-two-room mansion (the first in Los Angeles to have a private swimming pool which, in the sort of excess people would come to expect of Hollywood, was set in a formal garden) which they dubbed Pickfair. They conducted two major European tours in 1920 and 1924 and impressed everyone by their combination of showmanship and charm.

In conventional terms, the stars were not socially distinguished. Typically, in fact, they hailed from humble and sometimes troubled backgrounds. Fairbanks, for example, was born Douglas Elton Ulman in Denver, Colorado to an alcoholic father of Russian Jewish background, who abandoned his wife a few years after his son was born. But this was of no significance at all

149

compared to the personality he had become. Visiting movie stars were welcomed into salons and private palaces everywhere they went. They were regarded as trophies to be exhibited by upper-class hostesses who competed with each other in staging the most glittering social events. Those who had once sought to secure the presence of the most noble and distinguished of guests now also pursued athletes, entertainers, speed kings, aviators, fashion designers, as well as film stars. No longer was it necessary to be bound into the upper class by close family ties to secure invitations to dinners and soirées. Money or celebrity were often sufficient qualifications to find a way in.

In the interwar years, high society was more fluid and less exclusive than its pre-1914 predecessor. It was increasingly evolving into a stage for the rich, the famous, and the beautiful, in which the titled and the powerful had influential but largely background roles. There were still grand hostesses like the London-based Americans Lady Astor, Emerald Cunard, and Laura Corrigan, but they conserved their role by offering co-optation to a wider range of people than ever before. In London above all, high society acquired a unique ability to bring together the worlds of fashion, learning, power, and sport, which in continental European countries scarcely met at all. As its political role declined, London high society presented what historian Ross McKibbin describes as 'a picture of metropolitan glamour'.[24] Its exponents were no less eager to maintain their prominence and role at the peak of the social order but to achieve this they had to seek celebrity guests and sensations more than ever before. This sharply undercut the continuity of family and tradition that had held the old upper class together and placed it at the mercy of trends and innovations that started elsewhere.

Although the movies were a phenomenon that aimed at, and attracted, a mass audience, they were intensely fashionable as a novelty. As such, the youthful vanguard of high society embraced them with fervour. 'By 1921 everyone had gone "movie-mad" and *The Glorious Adventure*, which was the first British film in colour, had a society cast which reads like a page from *Debrett*,' gushed Barbara Cartland in her memoir of the period.[25] In America, the upper class was more staid but F. Scott Fitzgerald's 1922 portrait of young New York café society, *The Beautiful and Damned*, revealed an upper-class obsession with glamour, performance, and movie styles. When the Hollywood actress Gloria Swanson visited Europe in 1925, she noted that 'snobbish Parisians' were not above asking her discreetly 'what people did at parties at Pickfair and what kind of pomade Rudolph Valentino wore on his gorgeous hair'.[26] The upper classes were genuinely curious about the people they saw on the screen but they also marvelled at Hollywood's ability to arouse the enthusiasm and adoration of the masses.

Even a few core members of the British elite were not exempt from movie-star gestures. The honeymoon sojourn in 1922 of Queen Victoria's great-grandson Lord Mountbatten and his wife Lady Edwina at Pickfair shocked members of high society on both sides of the Atlantic, but the couple evidently revelled in the Hollywood environment. They toured film sets, appeared in a Charlie Chaplin film, and posed for photographs in the Grand Canyon dressed in Wild West outfits. Other young English high society figures followed and found diversion in the not quite real houses and fabulous luxury of the stars. Any reader of newspapers and magazines in the interwar years would have been accustomed to seeing pictures of Lord Mountbatten in remote places, in modern poses, or dressed stylishly. He acquired a debonair, 'American' veneer that lent him a 'dashing style and easy charm as he sailed through life without dropping anchor'.[27] He and Lady Mountbatten were probably the only prominent members of the British Establishment to have a penthouse flat in Park Lane designed entirely in the modernist idiom that had the advantage of being fitted with the most up-to-date conveniences. They showed that, to distinguish itself, the upper class did not have to be stuffy.

Edward, Prince of Wales, the future Edward VIII, was also influenced by American movies and modern fashion. He was the leading example of a young man who stood out against those who regarded conservatism and continuity as always best. The first heir to the throne of the era of publicity, Edward adopted an affected accent, used American slang, and displayed a taste for ostentatious leisure wear that led him to be seen as the world's fashion plate.[28] He helped popularize skiing and, later, air travel, showing an open-mindedness that led the hostess and heiress Emerald Cunard to tell him that he was 'the most modernistic man in England'. Edward seemed to know instinctively that his every gesture was a matter of interest. He was especially alert to questions of image, cleverly giving up polo when he realized that the public regarded the players of that elitist sport as no more than playboys. He wore generously cut suits in colourful tweeds and was amused at the anger of courtiers and the king when he was photographed walking in the street with an open umbrella. The prince enjoyed the spotlight and he mixed mainly with people, including entertainers and film stars, who shared his tastes. He preferred informality to the ceremonial aspects of royalty and cultivated a taste for showbusiness, jazz, and interesting foreigners. Much to the displeasure of the establishment, Edward's colourful inner circle resembled that of his grandfather Edward VII.[29] By contrast, Edward's father, King George V, was the very embodiment of instinctive conservatism. Among the many things he viewed with distaste were 'Soviet Russia, painted fingernails, women who smoked in public, cocktails, frivolous hats, American jazz, and the growing habit of going away for weekends'.[30] He even had to ask his son to stop whistling at Sandringham a melody he had picked up at the Ziegfeld Follies in New York.

Like his younger friend Louis Mountbatten, Edward was an example of upper-crust glamour. He was a good-looking public figure who had a modern buzz about him. He was widely thought to be a trendsetter, but this was mainly because, as a royal, his departures from tradition seemed more striking than they really were and his sartorial choices received more coverage. In fact, most of the novelties that emerged at this time, and which he embraced, hailed from the United States as the leading industrial nation. The spirit of the Roaring Twenties, or what F. Scott Fitzgerald called the Jazz Age, crossed class lines. For Fitzgerald, who knew little about jazz music, this term was used to denote a state of permanent nervous stimulation to which sex, music, and dancing all, in their own ways, contributed.[31] Dance fads, cocktails, sportswear, and movie palaces were among the most evident features of an extraordinary influx of American ideas and novelties. New fashions, tastes, and customs were eagerly absorbed by youth, with the result that a gap soon opened up between the old generation and those who reached adulthood in the post-war years. The young upper classes were by no means the only section of society to enjoy novelties or be attracted by them. Indeed, the chief departure was precisely this, that the privileged were appropriating products aimed at a mass market of ordinary consumers. By indulging in the vogue for jazz and other recorded music, they renounced for the first time a leadership in the consumption of culture that had once been unquestioned.

Neither Edward nor Mountbatten belonged strictly speaking to the so-called 'Bright Young Things', but there were connections. This term was widely used in the press to describe the colourful antics and attitudes of a variable and multi-tiered group of young people who seemed possessed of a particular generational ethos. With millions of men wiped out by the First World War, the gap between the generations was stark. The young fashion-able set found conventional rituals tedious and they resented the funereal atmosphere that followed the conflict. They were animated by a ceaseless pursuit of fun and novelty.[32] Cocktails, dancing, and all-night parties were among their passions, although a bohemian element also brought a taste for theatre and art.[33] London socialites held treasure hunts and fancy dress parties so frequently that some feared ideas for them might dry up. A Baby Party was once held, for which old nannies were reluctantly brought out and obliged to lead their fully grown charges on donkeys round Rutland Gate. Fashion designer Norman Hartnell organized a Circus Party, complete with performing animals and acrobats. A particularly shocking event, widely reported in the press, was a Bath and Bottle Party, held in July 1928 at a London swimming bath. Guests arrived in outlandish bathing dresses and danced to a band composed of black musicians, while rubber horses and flowers floated in the pool. The whole thing was illuminated with coloured lighting. In this instance, the high jinks reached such a level that the police arrived to break up the party and send everyone home.[34]

Such parties were all about ventilating stuffiness and throwing off inhib-itions. The atmosphere was not that of a private gathering but rather that of a nightclub. For this reason, it seemed natural to those involved to invade public spaces with their frivolity. In consequence, uninvited guests made their appearance at parties. The festivities of the Bright Young Things were often drunken, hedonistic affairs with few holds barred. 'Sexy was not a word we threw about much in the twenties,' Barbara Cartland recalled, 'but that is what the parties became, orgies which shocked and disgusted not only the newspapers and the older generation, but also ourselves.'[35] Some put the blame for the spread of vice and degeneracy not on the young members of high society but on the social climbers and hangers-on who easily gained access by donning a costume or otherwise looking the part. However, this was to ignore the fact that carefree manners were endorsed as fashionable and were reasonably widespread.

The young bloods who belonged to the Bright Young Things were a mixture of hedonists, trendies, artistic types, and fools. The principal figures were intensely committed to modernity but without ever renouncing the privileges of their coterie. Their love of fancy dress was a sign of refusal of the regular world. They may have been envied by some, but they were also regarded with distaste. Pictures that show them laughing and joking as they 'borrow' the tools of workmen repairing roads do not show smiles on the faces of the workers. They were widely despised for their antics and their careless display of privilege without responsibility. Their stunts caused shock and outrage among the older generation, the Church, and sections of the press. After a Wild West party in which the emphasis was on the 'wild', Harold Acton recalled that servants handed in their notice and he and his friends were warned that they had done untold harm to the Conservative Party in the local parliamentary constituency.[36]

The emphasis on fun was not itself new. Members of the upper class had notoriously short attention spans and, because conventional rituals were repetitive, they lived in fear of boredom. Like Mrs Stuyvesant Fish in New York in the 1890s, the London-based American hostess Laura Corrigan amused her guests with tombolas, in which the most costly prizes were always won by the most noble guests. Once, she let it be known that if Edward's brother, Prince George, were to turn up at one of her soirées, she would mark the occasion by standing on her head. He heard about the promise and duly arrived; without a single qualm, Mrs Corrigan performed the anticipated headstand. The difference between the 1890s and the 1920s was that, whereas many of the innovations of the earlier period occurred in private (even if they were then reported), the events of the latter spilled over into the public realm and attracted widespread attention. Responses were complex and by no means always positive. Upper-class frivolity and eccentricity often appeared clownish or pointless when depicted in the press. Moreover, they aroused antipathy that on occasion extended more widely. When debutantes queued in chauffeur-driven limousines down The Mall as they waited to be presented to the king, they often had to bear abuse and derision from a disrespectful crowd. At best, the interwar years were an Indian summer for an aristocracy that was no longer sure of its role.

Through the 1920s and 1930s, hotels, restaurants, and clubs in fashionable districts became meeting places of the elite. Although some of the great houses continued to function, many others gradually closed. In London, only one or two Park Lane mansions remained while others were demolished.[37] A similar fate befell the Fifth Avenue palaces built by the Astors, the Vanderbilts, and others. The first of ten Vanderbilt mansions on Fifth Avenue had been completed in 1883. The first was demolished in 1914 and by 1947 the last had gone.[38] Instead, the economic and social changes of the period gave a big impulse to the expansion of costly and elegant commercial establishments. In itself this was not a new development. From the late nineteenth century, socializing became less domestic and more public. After the war there was a significant development of this trend. Habitués of high-class commercial establishments found themselves dubbed members of a new 'café society'. The precise origins of this term are unclear. In London it was assumed that it was inspired by the Mayfair club, the Café.[39] In New York, it was attributed to the gossip columnist Maury Paul, who one night in February 1919 noticed how many members of high society were dining at the Old Ritz.[40] This was taken as a sign that high society was going out and that barriers of exclusion were coming down. In many establishments dancing took place and old assumptions that dance clubs were not suitable places for respectable married women, let alone the unmarried, fell by the wayside.[41] In addition to men, respectable women occupied these public-private places and not just the courtesans and prostitutes of the past. At the London Savoy, it was acceptable for women to dine in public, even unescorted, from 1907.[42] Formal entertaining at home lost a good part of its appeal as the 'restaurant habit' took hold.[43]

Café society was most significant and identifiable as a phenomenon in those countries where high society remained insular. It existed in London too, even if in that city it was not so easy to distinguish where high society finished and café society started. It was a development that followed from the expansion of the commercial sector and the growing heterogeneity of the social elite. Once, barriers of exclusion had been constructed largely on the basis of personal familiarity within the elite. Now the widening of the environment of socializing undermined this barrier. Three other factors served to bring upper-class privilege under pressure. First, the international nature of wealthy socializing meant that processes of selection and filtering based on conventional criteria no longer functioned so effectively. Second, criteria of distinction such as fashionableness, good looks, and creativity, that were related to the new configuration of modern society, led to the emergence of new figures of influence. Third, new money clamoured for admission and could easily find it in the commercial sphere and in resorts.

Secret codes and rules of taste and behaviour were the traditional way the socially prominent wrapped an aura round themselves and barred, or at least significantly delayed, the access of the bearers of recent or dubious fortunes into high society. By this method they drew a line between correct form and vulgar efforts at imitation. Fitzgerald's celebrated novel *The Great Gatsby* drew a portrait of one man who built an illicit fortune in the Prohibition era and set about building a social career. Fitzgerald cloaked his hero in romance and tragedy to turn him into one of the great figures of American fiction. Jay Gatsby has vitality and drive but his inexperience leads him to wear pink suits and to choose a car of monstrous length and 'so bright with nickel' that it is described as 'being terraced with a labyrinth of wind-shields that mirrored a dozen suns'.[44] His parties are held for the sole purpose of attracting attention and are filled with people of dubious background who he does not know. Gatsby is a fake, an 'Oxford man' purely because he once followed a short course for former servicemen at Merton College. But he is treated sympathetically by the novel's narrator and, through him, by the author. He is not just an ambitious individual but a man who has a dream, a dream that can be seen as the American dream of success and personal happiness. He is a New Man who represents his age.

The emphasis that was increasingly accorded to publicity undermined the balance between ostentation and restraint that was the hallmark of the established rich. Publicity fuelled vulgarity or at least did nothing to discourage it since the grand gesture, the gaudy house, and the surfeit of display were all effective as a strategy of communication. They were readily understandable even to the least sophisticated of audiences and therefore became the common currency of the press and the movies. A man like Gatsby was certainly glamorous (a point that was magnified by the 1974 film of the novel which starred Robert Redford in the title role) even if gauche. In time he would have evolved into something smoother and more polished. Social promiscuity, restaurants, and the movies all contributed to a change in customs. In place of the aristocratic principle, a new standard of behaviour was emerging that was cosmopolitan and standardized. Patrick Balfour described this as a norm that members of the elite conformed to and sometimes embodied in the eyes of the public, but which they did not invent.

In shaping this, it was not individual social arbiters who played a crucial role but guides and style bibles. Condé Nast had turned *Vogue* into vital reading matter for the American elite. He repeated the trick with the arts-based magazine *Vanity Fair*. In the twenties, Nast ceased to be an outsider who serviced the needs of the rich. He became a major player himself and was indeed the first major ringmaster of café society. The heterogeneous content of his magazine—features juxtaposed socialites and artists, debutantes and playwrights, models and singers, sporting figures and politicians—led him to foster the real-life equivalent in the regular parties that he held in his magnificent Manhattan apartment.[45] After successfully inviting Alva Vanderbilt and composer George Gershwin (whose 'Rhapsody in Blue' was a sort of soundtrack to the period) to the same party, he created a social cocktail that was novel above all in its breadth. *Vogue* reached beyond the top of society and ultimately assisted its expansion and transformation. The journalist Cleveland Amory later argued that, through *Vogue* and *Vanity Fair*, 'high society was redefined, no longer as the "Four Hundred" but as a complex entity embracing the arts, theatre and later cinema'.[46] Nast was able to achieve this in part because the times were changing, but his personal role was important.

Vogue was a pioneer in the use of photography. This medium was a vital factor in the affirmation of appearances over breeding and money. Initially, photography was not prestigious and there was resistance to it on the part of prominent subjects. These were overcome largely due to the photography of Baron de Meyer, who worked exclusively for *Vogue* and *Vanity Fair*. His characteristic soft-focus settings and lighting came to decorate every issue of the magazines. It became a mark of elegance for a New England aristocrat or a musical star to have her portrait, signed by de Meyer, in *Vogue*. It was said that the photographer gave them all an aura of elegance derived from English chic, Slavic charm, and Parisian dressmakers.[47] After he was lured away by *Harper's Bazaar*, the baron's place was taken by others who built on his artistic style. Edoard Steichen, Hoyningen-Huëne, and Cecil Beaton all brought to the magazine individual trademarks that mixed elements of the classical and the fashionable. They also flattered their subjects. Beaton in particular extensively retouched his portraits of society women in order to rejuvenate and slim down subjects.

The creation of a distinctive elite look in photography was a true example of glamour, in that a mode of representation took shape that was merely conferred on the socially prominent while not being exclusive to them. By virtue of its easy reproducibility and capacity for making the false seem true, photography was the medium that was most becoming to glamour. It allowed for the secret weaving of myths and enticements that caught spectators unawares, enchanting them under the guise of a true representation. It was also a medium of mass society, profoundly linked to modernity and to the emphasis on visual wonders and effects that had marked commercial promotion since the early nineteenth century. Even more than the text of Nast's publications, photographs of the privileged and the prominent entranced aspirant middle-class readers and unleashed the dynamic of envy that was central to glamour. In keeping with the general tone of the magazine, its photographs were always evocative and flattering. *Vogue* never criticized or ridiculed the rich and famous. It never dedicated any space to scandal or gave anything other than a brilliant portrayal of them.

Vogue was also significant because it was part of a growing internationalism among the arts and in high society. One of the keys to its success with the American elite lay in its regular accurate reports of Paris fashion. Fashion was already highly international and Nast's magazine played a part in bringing American clients into contact with Parisian designers and thereby in reinforcing the mythology of Paris as the centre of all that was fashionable. English and French editions of the magazine (that were promptly nicknamed *Brogue* and *Frog* in the New York office) were created in 1916 and 1921 respectively, and these further underlined its importance as a style bible. *Vogue* was by no means the only factor in the emergence of what would become known as the 'international set', but it played a key part in depicting a smart world that was perennially in motion, leisured, stylish, and beautiful.[48] This set was composed of chic transatlantic travellers who were seemingly on permanent vacation. Numerous articles and photographs about Americans abroad, Europeans in New York, and the fashionable world in general were printed.[49] They also appeared in the daily press and became a key component of the dreamscape of the period. The magazine always aimed to be at the forefront of fashionable life and it came to dedicate far more space to the wealthy, the talented, and the good-looking than to stately aristocrats.

More than any other group, it was young women who were at the forefront of the new era. Even high-born young women rejected the ideal of the aloof and reserved aristocratic woman. 'We didn't want to be ladylike in 1920,' recalled Cartland. 'We wanted to be dashing, we wanted to be gay, and most of all we wanted to be romantic.'[50] In the 1920s, modernity was defined through women who quite literally made spectacles of themselves, in the sense that they became, and often sought to become, the objects of the collective gaze. This phenomenon extended to all those who were engaged in activities that were seen as new or controversial. Women still had decorative and ornamental functions, but they were much less static or statuesque than before. Bright young women like Brenda Dean Paul and Elizabeth Pononsby, as well as certain debutantes, seemed to live wholly in public. Their visibility and their engagement with all the novelties of the urban environment served as a codifier of modernity, a visual representation of everything that the modern age had to offer.

The modern female was given a variety of labels by observers, including the New Woman, the Modern Girl, and the *garçonne*. However, the flapper was the figure who first embodied in the public realm a desire for personal freedom and self-definition. The term flapper had once been used to refer to very young prostitutes and sexuality was central to the popular image of the girls of the 1920s. They were slim, angular, energetic, and sexually charged.

An American invention, the flapper was moulded by fashion influences from Paris and modern advertising. Flappers were by no means always upper class; in fact their class origins were usually disguised by the fact that they behaved and dressed in a boldly unconventional manner. In the modern city, class was blurred rather than immediately legible. In the fast-paced life of the metropolis, it helped to be rich and privileged, but it was more important to have an up-to-date wardrobe and an athletic body, and to be always on the move. The flappers wore short, bobbed hair, lipstick, cloche hats, and dresses that only came down to the knee. They were enthusiasts of fashion and they loved novelty in music and dance (the Charleston was indelibly associated with them). Depicted as flighty and déclassé, they were all young and were avid consumers of the popular media. Flappers gave rise to narratives and stylized representations in advertising. The press on both sides of the Atlantic was full of their doings, and novels, plays, and films perpetuated and elaborated their image.

The elements of glamour that were associated with the new women of the 1920s included being at the centre of a public discourse sustained by publicity, being associated with fashion, movement, and modern ways, and deliberately stepping over the boundaries of conventional, respectable behaviour. Their beauty was not natural but unusual and artificial while their lean bodies suggested a modern dynamism. The fact that several film stars, including Clara Bow, Louise Brooks, and Greta Garbo, took the part of flappers on screen added glamour to every fashionable young woman by making her part of a larger modern narrative. Bow and company embodied the 'fast' and stylish women of the age and were the first film stars to define a look that impressed the fashionable social elite.[51] There were even a few London debutantes who, taking their cue from Bow, cut their hair short, dyed it red, and wore make-up.

Who invented the flapper? Scott Fitzgerald is often credited with creating the type in his first novel *This Side of Paradise*, although Zelda Sayre, whom he married in 1920, not only personified the phenomenon but wrote about it in her short stories.[52] On the other side of the Atlantic, the dress designer Gabrielle 'Coco' Chanel claimed some credit since the simple, practical clothes, youthfulness, and slimness of the flapper were her invention.

The flapper soon evolved in the popular imagination into a new type, the sophisticated metropolitan woman. The mass media, patterns of consumption, and sexual emancipation eroded the once rigid distinctions between the high society woman, the actress, and the young city girl and created a fascinating new blend. Even upper-class young women, who previously had been chaperoned everywhere, went out alone and did what they pleased. 'The blushing débutante is as dead as the English breakfast in Mayfair,' concluded the gossip columnist Patrick Balfour.[53] The London-based writer Michael Arlen's hit novel *The Green Hat* contributed to this phenomenon in that it presented a stylish and restless heroine, Iris Storm, who drove a yellow Hispano-Suiza car, had nicotine-stained fingers, and whose sexuality was unabashed. It was the first best-selling novel to describe a female libertine without depicting her as a victim or a fallen woman.[54] Various socialites claimed that they had been Arlen's inspiration, although two had a better claim that most. Nancy Cunard, daughter of Emerald, heiress to the shipping company of the same name, had shocked by her eccentric ways, that included taking a black man, the jazz musician Henry Crowder, as a lover. For Harold Acton, she was a woman with an 'electro-magnetic' personality who was 'the Gioconda of the age'.[55] Another real-life equivalent who made a special mark, not least because of her utter disregard for convention, was Tallulah Bankhead, an American senator's daughter who illuminated the London stage in the 22-year-old Noel Coward's comedy of lust and memory, *Fallen Angels*, and the theatrical adaptation of *The Green Hat*, before being talent-spotted and tempted to Hollywood by Paramount Pictures. Her smouldering sexuality and uninhibited ways marked her out from even the most daring of modern English women.[56] Her female following was extensive. She was a trendsetter whose appeal was such that she produced a female mob hysteria in London that was unprecedented.[57] Arlen's success was capped when Metro-Goldwyn-Mayer decided to film *The Green Hat* and cast Greta Garbo as Iris Storm. Even though the resulting film was not very good, it gave his novel a resonance it might not otherwise have had.

Arlen's fortunes would eventually decline, but while he bathed in public recognition he was generous with younger writers. He financially supported the first production of Coward's sex and drug abuse drama *The Vortex* in

Hamsptead, unaware that the actor-author would soon take his place as the most fashionable literary figure. The themes of decadence and affluence that he had introduced would be elaborated to a higher pitch by Coward in a series of controversial plays including *Fallen Angels*, the nervous and indolent country house comedy *Easy Virtue*, and the louche *Semi-Monde* (that was so controversial that it did not receive its premiere until 1977). His plays were set in hotels, country houses, and drawing rooms but instead of light banter between the players there was razor wit, drug-taking, and depravity. The plays were usually brilliantly designed using contemporary props and fashionable costumes. At a time when theatre was fashionable, and was seen as a central vehicle of society's reflection on itself, they produced a picture that was at once sophisticated and sleazy.

In the early 1920s, a great premium was placed, especially by women, on being 'original'. In an era when it was fashionable to be fast and bold, daring gestures were crucial attention-grabbers. By the second half of the decade, originality was displaced by commercialized stylishness. In an age when appearances counted for much, clothes were primarily statements of attitude and status. Sophistication and elegance in day- as well as eveningwear were at a premium and this was expressed through streamlining and bias-cut garments. Fur of every type was used although silver fox epitomized stylish luxury. However, the fast-changing fashions and improved technology made it difficult for wealthy women to keep pace and avoid confusion with the less well-off. Instead of relying on their own taste and initiative, wealthy women were obliged to seek guidance from a source such as *Vogue*. A new breed of fashion designers also created exclusive couture and ready-to-wear garments that provided a short cut to stylishness. Whereas society women had once sought to establish individual wardrobes that matched their means, personality, and age, now they tended to conform to trends determined by professionals. The theatre and the movies were important factors in this new mix that tended to be international.

The greater openness of society and the prominence of women helped a designer like Coco Chanel become the glamorous embodiment of her own creations. Couturiers like Worth in the mid-nineteenth century, or Paul Poiret in the early twentieth century, had embraced creativity and adopted the guise of the artist. They were not themselves part of the high society to which their customers belonged. Chanel, by contrast, did not just dress women. She emerged as a public personality who was the best testimonial for the products that her company produced. The quicker pace of life saw a throwing-off of the fussy and the complex in favour of simple, practical solutions. Women's fashions were the first to reflect this change while even buildings were designed on more sleek and functional lines, without the ornamentation and intricate exterior styling of the pre-war era. Chanel sold a new casual look made of jerseys, blouses, sports dresses, and low-heeled shoes that fell between sportswear and formal afternoon attire. Her clothes were youthful and simple and ideal for a range of new leisure pursuits including motoring, sailing, tennis, and sunbathing. She opened her first store in the aristocratic resort of Deauville in 1913, with the help of the wealthy polo player Arthur 'Boy' Capel, and steadily built an empire that was to embody the understated essence of modern fashion. Chanel benefited from the interest of the press in fashion and the development of international high society. She was friends with many Paris-based artists and members of café society and was welcomed into English high society. She enjoyed a long friendship with the super-rich but unconventional Duke of Westminster, whom it was even thought she might marry.

Chanel had worked in a cabaret in her youth and was sophisticated and worldly. She understood that modern style only worked if it was subtlely infused with sexual suggestiveness and that this infusion was what made the style photogenic and glamorous. This use of sexuality had been a trait of the Paris courtesans. Even though the age of the courtesan was now over, sex appeal still had a place in fashion. Chanel's designs may have looked simple 'in the flesh' but in photographs they were highly seductive. Chanel was a favourite with *Vogue* and other fashion magazines and her garments appealed well beyond the rich clientele who frequented her boutiques. One of her friends was the American socialite Wallis Simpson, who would become the Duchess of Windsor. Mrs Simpson was an eye-catching, ambitious woman who was precisely the sort of hybrid figure the age produced. Slim and hard-faced, neither beautiful nor pretty, even by her own reckoning, the twice-married Wallis had a strong personality and an undeniable sexual allure. Her magnetism derived from this combined with other characteristics that British upper-class observers found distasteful, such as her blatant social climbing and the garish colour of her lipstick.[58] Even Lady Diana Cooper, a beauty who had acted on stage and screen, commented on her 'commonness and Becky Sharpishness'.[59]

Although she was mentioned in the social columns and was regarded by *Vogue* as an authority on finger food, Mrs Simpson was not well known enough in the early 1930s to be glamorous. To be stylish or chic was a help but it was not sufficient in order to be glamorous. With the rise of the press and the entertainment media, it was also necessary to be available to the public and to be committed to the development of a theatrical public image. The type of personality who was glamorous was generally available to the public and, for commercial or professional reasons, regarded this availability as an important part of their being. This included royalty and some aristocrats but Mrs Simpson, for example, had little interest in cultivating a public image even though she had some of the qualities to become a personality. Increasingly, it was professionals who performed this task. In the end, it was not debutantes or wealthy socialites who were the best examples of glamorous personalities but people from commonplace backgrounds who by chance or talent had blossomed in the public eye.

Women like the aviators Amy Johnson and Amelia Earheart, and the French racing driver Hellé Nice, were glamorous because they were good-looking and were directly associated with modern technological advancements. Each belonged to an exciting realm since travel, in its various forms, was one of the great innovations of the age. Each, moreover, knew how to exploit the situation to personal advantage through the adoption of a carefree attitude, fashionable dress, studied gestures, personal magnetism, and planned stunts. Their prime audience was not high society but the social body as a whole.

Aviation was a great mania of the second half of the 1920s. People of all classes and nations were enthralled by the adventure of the skies. The press gave great attention to daredevils and record-breakers of all types, even putting up prizes for some achievements. There were air weddings, air christenings, acrobatics, and even air-related songs. Intense public interest led newspapers to build up aviators into stars, a phenomenon that reached an extraordinary zenith after Charles Lindbergh single-handedly crossed the Atlantic in a mono-plane in 1927.[60] Titled adventurers were keen to get in on the act and pioneer airmen were joined by a series of smart rich women who took advantage of the drive for female emancipation. These amateurs were supplanted by women of a more professional outlook, of whom Johnson was one. The popular press latched on to the fact that she was not titled but an ordinary girl trying to fulfil her dreams.[61] Dubbed the 'flapper ace' in the press,[62] she was referred to, somewhat romantically, as a 'penniless nobody' or 'the little typist', although in fact she had been to university.

A photogenic young woman with a good figure, 'Johnnie'—as she liked to be called—was given full celebrity treatment by the *Daily Mail* in particular. Each of her long-distance flights was heralded as a triumph and she was greeted with frenzy when she returned. In 1930 a song composed in her honour, 'Amy', which proclaimed the nation's love for her, was a popular hit. After she became a public figure, she underwent a notable makeover. She did not go as far as her American colleague Earhart, who created her own signature line of clothing but, with the aid of the Irish-born dress designer Captain Molyneux, she learned how to wear fashionable clothes, furs, and diamonds. She found her celebrity value and newly polished look aroused the interest of managers of luxury hotels, jewellers, vendors of fast cars and *maîtres d'hôtel* of smart restaurants, all of whom were keen to win her patronage.[63] After she had her hair set in waves, streamlined her eyebrows, and adopted discreet make-up, she took on the appearance of a Mayfair socialite. Johnson was briefly welcomed into society salons, but she retained her northern English accent and her unhappy personal life won her widespread sympathy.

Like aviation, automobiles had a special romantic allure and motor racing was a field in which rich men dominated. Race tracks lacked the other-worldly appeal of the skies, but speed had a special fascination and thrill of its own. As a spectacle, racing offered many promotional opportunities that were exploited by advertisers and publicity-seekers. Competitive events offered an exciting spectacle and there were even championships for actors. Moreover, the personal risk involved was, if anything, greater than with flying since there was a high rate of racing fatalities. Hellé Nice had been a dancer at the Casino de

Paris, an experience that prepared her for the publicity she received when she won several major mixed and all-female races in her gleaming blue Bugatti.[64] Manufacturers were keen on female drivers because of the modern allure they added to vehicles that were already crafted like beautiful mechanical beasts. Photographs show Nice sitting in her vehicle applying her make-up before a race, wearing striking white overalls and flashing a 100-watt smile at cameras. She also did handstands on the bonnet of her car. Whenever she won, she was careful to slip out of her overalls and into an elegant gown in order to receive her prize. Even more than Johnson, she lived extravagantly, revelling in the trappings of wealth, and mixed with noblemen, several of whom became her lovers. While Johnson endorsed Castrol Oil and Shell petrol, Nice advertised Lux soap and Lucky Strike cigarettes as well as Esso petrol.

In the mind of the public, figures like Michael Arlen and Noel Coward were the epitome of male glamour. Unlike upper-class moderns like Mountbatten, who used contemporary fads and fashions to update the public image of the privileged elite, they took contemporary style and moulded it into something enviable and imitable. They created a lifestyle that was entirely publicity-oriented, in the sense that they were constantly in the press and delighted in presenting their homes, wardrobes, travel plans, and tastes to the public. They were men who had propelled themselves upwards socially by means of their talent, their nose for controversy and novelty, and their personal self-fashioning. Both of them moved easily between London, New York, and the French Riviera. After the success of *The Green Hat*, Arlen became a figure of the moment who, for a short period, was the highest-paid short-story writer on either side of the Atlantic. He adopted a public persona to match the extensive newspaper coverage he received. 'Young, full of dash, and neither quite a gentleman, and neither not,' as his son would later describe him,[65] he dressed impeccably, lunched at the Ritz, drove around London in a yellow Rolls Royce, and established his main residence in Cannes.

If Arlen was a Romanian refugee who invented a glamorous identity for himself, Coward was scarcely less an outsider. Born in unfashionable Teddington, it was said that his mother had been a charwoman. In fact his family was middle class but impoverished. His daring plays, in which he usually acted himself, brought much publicity and connected Coward in the public mind with cocktails and decadence.[66] He embraced an appropriately elegant and urbane lifestyle complete with luxurious trappings including new suits, silk shirts, a car, and large quantities of pyjamas and dressing gowns (which became his trademark garment). For Cecil Beaton, he embodied 'the glamour of success'.[67] He was photographed everywhere: in public places, in his dressing room, at the piano, and even sitting up in bed in a Chinese dressing gown, while making a breakfast telephone call supported by an ample cushion. The latter image, reproduced on the cover of *The Sketch*,[68] brought accusations of degeneracy.

Coward knew that publicity and controversy were good for business. For the world he acted the part of a symbol of the Jazz Age. More than any other English writer he seemed to understand the turbulent era of which he was a part.[69] He was also versatile. After a sequence of topical and controversial plays, he decided to go for pure style and to try his hand at a revue, to which he gave the title *London Calling*. A hugely popular entertainment form of the 1920s, revues were pure escapism. They were opulent stage shows that transported their mainly middle-class audiences into improbable worlds of glamour and romance. They depended for their success on a skilful combination of well-known performers, sumptuous costumes, lavish scenery, catchy songs, and brisk, well-timed choreography.

The king of the London revue was another middle-class man who constructed for himself a theatrical persona. One of the most popular stage figures of the period, Ivor Novello was a Welshman who had been born David Ivor Davies. He was a handsome songwriter and performer who was always thought of in association with revues like *Careless Rapture* and *Glamorous Night* (the latter was sold to the directors of the Drury Lane theatre purely on the basis of the combination of the two words that made up the title—a fact which by itself perhaps offers an insight into the 1920s mind).[70] For audiences, the stars of revues were magic people who had no real existence outside the romantic make-believe world of the stage. According to Novello's biographer, the public was not wrong in its assumption in his case since he was only ever fully at ease in the illusory world of the footlights.[71]

Arlen, Coward, and Novello were all manufactured, self-made men who impersonated the upper class. They looked and sounded like gentlemen and they always situated themselves in contexts that were polished and worldly. At the same time, they offered the wider public an image of upper-class life that was more stylized and appealing than the reality. This work of fabrication heightened surface appeal and contributed to the process whereby 'class' was turned into a question of style, pose, and performance. This rendered it both interesting and accessible. Coward and Novello did not always enjoy an easy relationship with those who assumed that no one could be more stylish than themselves, and who knew that they were impostors. As a personality and acknowledged trendsetter, Coward was welcomed into salons as an equal, but found himself cut dead by the Prince of Wales on at least one occasion. Nevertheless, he became a major influence in fashionable society and had a broader impact on customs. He gave rise to a clipped, wise-cracking manner of speaking that was adopted by upper- and middle-class men throughout the English-speaking world.[72]

Beaton, who went to Harrow and Oxford, was not a social upstart to the extent of Arlen and Coward, although his family was more upper-middle than upper class. At a young age, he learned the advantages of publicity and even succeeded in propelling his mother into the social columns of *The Times*.[73] He devoured magazines and learned to identify well-known faces in Hyde Park on Sundays. His infatuation with high society persisted through his time as a student, little of which was spent studying. He regularly sent pictures of himself to magazines and made sure that all his work on the costumes and sets of student production won recognition. He loved the fancy dress parties that were so much in vogue and his taste for all things theatrical made him a natural soulmate of the Bright Young Things. His sketches of the fashionable provided his first work for *Vogue*, although he was soon also supplying photographs. Beaton set himself up as an authority on matters of beauty and style and wrote regularly for fashionable magazines and for the press. Before long, he became a key figure in the stylish world that he so admired. In the late 1930s he became the official court photographer.

The stylish facades constructed by these men not only camouflaged their social origins, it also concealed their sexual orientation. This element of concealment added a touch of danger and mystery to their personae and, as such, it was a component of their glamour, albeit a less obvious one than their aura of sophistication. Coward and Novello were both homosexuals who, in intolerant times, went to some lengths to disguise their sexual preferences. Their highly aestheticized exteriors were part of the disguise, although there was always the risk, as Coward's bed photograph showed, that an ill-judged pose might give the game away. The playwright once gave a lesson to Beaton on how to build a personal facade composed of speech, gestures, and dress that would make him acceptable in heterosexual company. 'You should appraise yourself,' he advised. 'Your sleeves are too tight, your voice is too high and too precise. You mustn't do it. It closes so many doors... It's hard, I know. One would like to indulge one's own taste. I myself dearly love a good match, yet I know it is overdoing it to wear tie, socks and handkerchief of the same colour. I take ruthless stock of myself in the mirror before going out. A polo jumper or unfortunate tie exposes one to danger.'[74]

Behind the scenes a large number of professionals played a vital role in creating and sustaining the contexts, events, and individuals that basked in the aura of glamour. These were not just impoverished aristocrats but salaried experts, men and women who were masters of techniques including photography, dress design, fashion illustration, journalism, and popular literature. In the past many of them would have been regarded as little more than tradesmen, background figures who would rarely if ever have commanded public attention. This was still the case with some, such as the American *Vogue* editor Edna Woolman Chase, who had no special social connections and avoided events.[75] Others, like the legendary networker and party organizer Elsa Maxwell, occupied a median position. An American lesbian who was anything but personally glamorous, Maxwell was not known to the public before the 1950s. Yet she was friends with Coward, Laura Corrigan, and many other key figures in the arts, commerce, and high society in the United States, Britain, and continental Europe. Neither stylish nor young, she was so ugly that she quite plausibly dressed up as US President Harding or German President Hindenburg at the fancy dress balls she adored. However, she was a publicity genius who single-handedly bestowed a magical allure on places, people, and events. More than anyone else, she was the *éminence grise* behind the 'international set'.

Maxwell launched the career of the fashion designer Edward Molyneux, by bringing him into contact with an international clientele. It was her idea that he should found and run the smartest nightclub in Paris. She also played a key role in creating a high-living image for Jean Patou. The Parisian designer is today remembered mainly for the perfume Joy, that is still on sale. In the 1920s, he was a highly fashionable figure whose modern sports and leisure wear perfectly suited the androgynous woman of the time. Like his rival Chanel, he forged a public image that complemented the universal appeal of his modern women's clothes and fragrances. Many of his clients were Americans and he fashioned an elegant facade to appeal to them. Maxwell helped him to see the publicity value of having famous clients, such as the film star Gloria Swanson, who embodied his idea of modern luxury.[76] Perhaps his most famous client was French tennis star Suzanne Lenglen, who pioneered his pleated tennis skirts and sleeveless dresses. In reality, Patou was a family man but, with Maxwell's help, he used his business to sustain a social world around himself. He became a leading figure in international café society known for his extravagance and cultivated an image based on the allure of the Riviera, fast cars, and legendary gambling.

The authorities of the Venice Lido commissioned Maxwell to promote it as a fashionable summer resort. Using her ample address book and her organizing skills, she lured numerous wealthy and prominent people with the promise of fun and hedonism. The parties that Maxwell organized on behalf of her wealthy friends were usually fast and colourful affairs that gave the idle rich ample opportunity to show off. They were also notorious for their debauchery. Distant from the social controls of the capital cities, guests were able to indulge themselves as they wished. In Venice, she could rely on the support of the singer and songwriter Cole Porter, whose circle practised a relaxed hedonism that appealed to Coward. He delighted in the heavy drinking, cocaine, and indiscriminate sexual experimentation that were commonplace among members of the Lido set.[77] Like the Riviera and other watering holes, Venice was a great scene of social mixing. It was a place where American heiresses, British aristocrats, and elegant French women mingled with writers and artists on an equal basis.

Maxwell understood the importance of entertainment and surprise in socializing and she also knew how important it was to calibrate press coverage. It was, she later wrote, 'the life-blood of fame. It spells the difference between legend and oblivion.'[78] She sought coverage for the events and people she staged but, at the same time, she knew that privacy was necessary if celebrities were not to be always 'on guard'. Oddly, for such a key figure in several of the developments in modern glamour, Maxwell was a snob who had little time for the mass public. She lived entirely in a world of rich people, grand houses, and fabulous hotels, where she could always be sure of free hospitality. Although she could not have existed without the development of travel, the emergence of the mass media, and social practices such as popular fashion and dance music, that all brought people of different classes and nations into an unprecedented set of relations with each other, she resented the social climbing and ambition that they brought.

In the 1920s, the general public was fascinated by technical innovations, record-breaking, gossip, and style. It loved reading about the rich and famous. The rise of the movie star, the record-breaker, the sports hero, the pioneer aviator and racing driver signalled the arrival of a society based on publicity and entertainment. From the moment it first came into being in the early nineteenth century, glamour had functioned as a visual repertoire of seduction that drew on a plurality of ostensibly incompatible sources. It evolved as a quality forged through the reciprocal influence of commerce, popular spectacle, and social prestige. Now it was refined into a structure that was sustained principally by modern communications and the commercial public sphere. This both gave members of high society a new platform and undermined the special access to public attention that they had previously commanded. This led to a transformation of the role of the aristocracy and ultimately contributed to its decline. In the years of the Depression, the cinema offered the public all the glamour and romance it needed.

CHAPTER 6

THE HOLLYWOOD
STAR SYSTEM

T he most complete embodiment of glamour that there has ever been is the Hollywood film star. In the period in which the major studios established their dominance over the leisure of the entire industrial world, no one was more highly polished, packaged, and presented than the men and women who became the majors' main lure in their efforts to captivate the public. Suspended between the ordinary and the extraordinary, the real and the ideal, the stars were the gods and goddesses of a modern Olympus. To the man or woman in the street, it did not seem as if they worked at all for a living. Their fabulous lives were choreographed, pictured, described, and evoked by publicity departments that drip-fed the world's press with news and information. For audiences worldwide, these alluring personalities were the stuff of fantasy. A fantasy, however, that was somehow accessible. Although several early stars were packaged as extreme or unusual personalities, the star as a fabulous everyman or everywoman emerged fully in the 1930s. Among the many and varied appeals that Hollywood cinema developed in its golden age, one key one was the premiss that anyone, potentially, could be a star.

The greatest Hollywood star of all was a mixture of the mysterious and exotic elements that marked the star system before the advent of sound film and the more general characteristics that emerged later. She was a woman whose legendary self-containment made her a compelling player of a wide variety of historical and contemporary roles. When she arrived in Los Angeles in 1925, the future Greta Garbo still bore the surname Gustaffson, she was just short of 20 and looked like what she was, an unsophisticated girl from the backwaters of Sweden. Her front teeth were crooked, her hair was frizzy, and there was a hint of a double chin. She was taller than average and she had a boyish frame. But there was something about her, some hidden potential was waiting to be discovered.[1] However, bringing out her star quality on screen was no easy task. Garbo did not photograph well under strong lights and initially had developed a nervous tic in her cheek when filmed in close-up. Her first MGM screen test had not made a good impression due to poor lighting. Only when the master of soft-focus effects, cinematographer Henrik Sartov, was brought in was her potential fully revealed. According to her biographer, Sartov's lens and its magical ability to 'clean out' the face through spot lighting finally brought out her beauty.[2]

For some twelve years, Garbo reigned supreme as the queen of the largest and most prestigious of Hollywood studios. Her films were always the most costly and fabulously confectioned products of a studio that specialized in total perfection. She was almost always cast in European roles of a marked erotic connotation. She repeatedly played performers, courtesans, or fallen women in films including the title role in the biopic of the ill-fated dancer and spy *Mata Hari*, a seductive opera singer in *Romance*, a cabaret singer in *As You Desire Me*, a kept woman in *The Fall and Rise of Susan Lennox*, a tormented actress in *Grand Hotel*, and Marguerite Gautier in *Camille*. In perhaps her greatest part, she played the title role in *Queen Christina*, a film biography of the androgynous seventeenth-century Swedish queen. Close-up shots established the iconic status of her extraordinary face and presented it as the most intriguing blank canvas in cinema. She offered to the viewer's gaze 'a sort of Platonic Idea of the human creature', the critic Roland Barthes later wrote.[3] Garbo's erotic appeal was always underlined by the most extraordinary and imaginative screen costumes, which were designed for her at MGM by Gilbert Adrian.

Although she could neither sing nor dance convincingly (a fact glaringly demonstrated in *Mata Hari*), she was packaged as a rare luxury object and presented as a supremely sexual woman. She had a world-weary, melancholy air and a distinctive style. Her films were adult and were shot through with a decadent, sensual atmosphere. In the 1920s, her screen partnership with John Gilbert, her off-screen lover, held audiences entranced. Their long horizontal kisses were among the most suggestive ever seen on film. Unlike Gilbert, whose squeaky voice ensured that his career declined sharply with the end of the silent era, Garbo had a timbre that seemed entirely to match her enigmatic image. Her husky tone, European accent, and slow, drawn-out enunciation added to her allure and brought her new fans. Her long reign at MGM only came to an end when the closure of overseas markets weakened her position at the studio and she refused to make films that were not equal to her particular talents. Wartime audiences, her biographer has observed, preferred Betty Grable's great legs to Garbo's great art.[4]

The key to Garbo's personality was mystery. She was never the most pliable or cooperative of stars. Even at the peak of her success, she often threatened to return home to Sweden and she refused, famously, to allow her private life to be exploited for publicity purposes. Instead of putting audiences off, this aloofness would drive them into a frenzy of curiosity. The celebrated sentence, delivered in the 1932 film *Grand Hôtel*, 'I want to be let alone' (in which 'want' was pronounced with a Germanic 'w'), became her trademark. Garbo at times infuriated studio head Louis B. Mayer, but her stubbornness taught the studios that star images were complex and that sometimes an appeal could be enhanced by holding back, by not being everything to everyone. Film-goers wanted to know everything about their idols but it was the maintenance of this yearning, rather than its satisfaction, that was the necessary condition for a star's continued box-office success.

Hollywood was an American industry that was founded, run, and largely peopled by immigrants. For at least the first twenty years of its existence, it was dominated by men who had been born in Europe and who had fled to America to escape war, tyranny, racial prejudice, and economic crisis. The creators of Hollywood glamour were émigrés and exiles from Germany, Hungary, Russia, France, and Britain.[5] American cinema was all the more powerful because the men who built the film industry were themselves refugees who gave rise to an imagined America as a land of freedom, tolerance, wealth, and personal realization. There were connections between cinematic fascinations and the earlier techniques of salesmanship.[6] Nineteenth-century pedlars were often German or East European Jews too and this was a factor in their marginality and their association with the mysterious East, as well as sorcery and magic. Like the pedlars, the movie moguls offered dazzling images that promised instant personal transformation and provided rich material for daydreams. The difference was that these images were no longer conjured up by the oral and presentational skills of individual salesmen operating in face-to-face situations. They were embedded in a new second-order reality that overlay daily life and was experienced purely through the media.[7]

Hollywood films, produced by companies that had a firm stake in the exhibition and distribution sectors, conformed largely to the escapist imperative. They offered a range of options for audiences to choose from, including European-style decadence, American aristocracy, theatrical opulence, showgirl glitz, and youthful beauty as well as city savvy, down-home Americanism, and pioneer virtues. But above all Hollywood created a unique blend of the aristocratic, fashionable, sexual, theatrical, and consumerist appeals that had emerged and uneasily coalesced in Europe and America in the preceding period. This blend, which emerged as the American motion picture industry's signature style from the 1920s, exercised an unprecedented influence over global aspirations, desires, and lifestyles. The strong traces of European decadence and exoticism that were apparent in the films of one of the five major studios, Paramount, were balanced by the predominant emphasis on optimism and democracy in the output of others. Because it was located in California, far from the main centres of privilege and style, the film industry reinvented glamour as an enticing image that relied solely on technique, artifice, and imagination and was remote from specific social referents.

The consolidation of the industrial structure of Hollywood in the second half of the 1920s ensured that production strategies were stronger than any individual performer and that corporate power was the determinant factor in the industry. The arrival of sound and the impact of the Depression in the early 1930s reinforced the near monopoly of the five major film studios. In a situation in which the mass-production methods of Fordism were finding application in the film industry no less than the rest of the American economy, the production of star figures also became an assembly-line matter subject to precise codes, procedures, and practices. The American film industry in the 1930s and 1940s was widely known as 'the dream factory' or 'the glamour factory'. Like the automobile industry, it furnished products in large numbers for mass consumption. The only difference between the motor cars, household products, and clothing produced by American manufacturers and the movies furnished by the motion picture industry was the fact that the latter catered not to practical needs and situations but precisely to the imagination. Of course, more practical goods were often sold in alluring settings (stores, catalogues, etc.) and modern advertising, which developed from the 1920s, weaved spells of aspiration and desire around even those that were not. The movie star was a standardized product that came in a limited number of varieties and was subject to continuous revision and modification. What distinguished Hollywood stardom from that of other cinemas was precisely the systematic nature of star production and distribution.

More than any other studio, MGM turned glamour into a corporate product. It was the largest and most successful studio of the sound era; in 1932 *Fortune* described its list of stars as 'vastly the most imposing' in the industry.[8] Paramount was its only serious rival in the matter of star production. The other studios, 20th Century Fox, Warner Brothers, and RKO plus the minor companies Columbia, Universal, and United Artists placed less emphasis on stars. Fox, for example, had under contract only four top-ranking stars between the mid-1930s and the late 1940s: Shirley Temple, Betty Grable, Tyrone Power, and Gregory Peck; Warners relied on James Cagney, Bette Davis, and Humphrey Bogart.[9] The point, ultimately, was one of cost. 'There are only two kinds of merchandise that can be made profitably in this business—either the very cheap pictures or the expensive pictures,' wrote David O. Selznick to his treasurer when he left MGM to found his own company. This was as true in the 1930s and 1940s as it had been in the 1920s.[10] Companies like Warners which did not share MGM's commitment to 'general finish and glossiness',[11] or smaller companies which could not afford the luxury of high cost production values, did not develop promising actors or invest in lavish sets, but instead concentrated on familiar genres, characters, or settings. Although some performers went over with audiences without any particular preparation, the heavy investment that was normally required to mould and successfully launch a star persona could only be made by the big studios. Stars alone could not bring success to a film, but they could account for around a 15-per-cent variation in box office.[12]

Hollywood acquired a distinctive style leadership in the 1930s. The films themselves were the most important factor in giving the movie capital a design edge. Although art directors do not normally receive anything like the attention accorded to producers and directors, the house style of the major studios, as well as the particular appearance of given films, was largely their work. While the Oriental imagery of the early 1920s testified to cinema's reliance on the stage, the clean deco lines of the 1930s were products of a process that saw moves towards an independent concept of set design. The most prominent art director was MGM's Cedric Gibbons, an influential figure who took overall responsibility for the look of every single film produced by the studio between 1924 and 1956. He personally designed the sets for several of MGM's most luxurious film vehicles. Gibbons was responsible more than anyone else for linking the manufacture of glamour to contemporary aesthetic trends. He maintained a simple approach to designing for film, abandoning cluttered grandeur for art deco and turning this modern style into a potent symbol of transatlantic glamour.[13] Starting from 1925, the year Gibbons undertook a visit to the Paris Exposition of Decorative Arts that pioneered what, at the time, was known as the *moderne* style, art deco furnishings and geometric interior designs were used to frame and locate screen characters who were associated with jazz music, 'fast' behaviour, and a generally decadent lifestyle.[14] Cecil B. De Mille was the first director to use upper-class settings and MGM in particular persisted with the upscale image; the studio boss Louis B. Mayer thought that wealth would automatically be assumed to be moral. Whereas 'good' women in films were placed in traditionally decorated contexts, sexually promiscuous, independent, modern women were often associated with architectural modernism as well as the exterior trappings of wealth: furs, jewels, fashionable attire, cars.[15] Although, with hindsight, the Hollywood deco style looks spare and elegant in its emphasis on streamline and two-tone effects, it was in fact a promiscuously eclectic style that drew on the art of many cultures, countries, and periods.[16] In this sense it tied in well with the eclectic jumble of sensations and effects that marked mass culture.

'The glamour of MGM personalities is part of a general finish and glossiness which characterizes MGM pictures and in which they excel,' wrote *Fortune* magazine: 'Irving Thalberg subscribes heartily to what the perfume trade might call the law of packaging—that a mediocre scent in a sleek flacon is a better commodity than the perfumes of India in a tin can. MGM pictures are always superlatively well-packaged—both the scenes and personalities which enclose the drama have a high sheen. So high a sheen that it sometimes constitutes their major box-office appeal.'[17] Mary Astor wrote in her memoirs that, at Metro, 'all automobiles were shiny. A picture never hung crooked, a door never squeaked, stocking seams were always straight, and no actress ever had a shiny nose.' If an actor or actress was spattered with mud in one scene, somehow the mud had disappeared by the next.[18] More than at other studios, actresses looked at all times as if they had just come from the beauty parlour. 'You practically had to go to the front office if you wanted something as real as having your hair mussed,' Astor recalled. This improbable perfection was a crucial aspect of Hollywood glamour.

As human commodities, movie stars were the main object of Hollywood fantasy. In the 1930s and 1940s vast amounts of effort and money were invested in their creation. The construction of a star was no less a process of transformation than the turning of a bare set into a fantasy environment. In contrast to the theatrical impresario Florenz Ziegfeld, who concentrated on transforming raw young women into one-dimensional stage icons who neither spoke nor emerged as individuals, the studios took Broadway actors, foreign starlets, athletes, beauty pageant winners, and others and moulded them into fully fledged screen personalities. The sort of beauty that showed up well on screen featured good bone structure, an oval or square-shaped face with a high forehead, expressive eyes, generous lips, possibly of an interesting shape, and a winning smile. Personality had to shine through on screen. Stars had to have magnetism and a talent for holding attention.

'I always looked for the actor with personality first,' talent scout Al Trescony said; 'I've found that a person with a fantastic personality will attract the attention of everyone in a room, not unlike a beautiful young woman. But people will look at the beauty and after a moment return to their conversation. The one with personality will hold their attention.'[19] A performer had to be able to make people believe him or her and this too was perceivable mainly through the eyes. 'The eyes show everything a person is thinking. It comes through the celluloid right out to the audience,' Trescony continued.

The initial material was not always promising. When she arrived from Berlin, Marlene Dietrich was plump by American standards; she had a wide nose and a strong, square face. Her manners are said to have been coarse and Teutonic. Joan Crawford was a brassy and unsophisticated working-class girl. She was shorter than most, had wide eyes, flared nostrils, and freckles. Even as a chorus girl, she had not demonstrated any great talent. Carole Lombard's curvaceous figure and athletic ability seemingly suited her to be one of Mack Sennett's swimsuited Bathing Beauties but nothing more. There was little to suggest that any of these women had star potential. Yet each had some special quality that persuaded studio bosses that she could be transformed into a magical, alluring figure who would exercise a magnetic influence over film-goers. In addition to some acting ability, youth was important as a criterion for star-building and so was beauty, but more significant were two more elusive attributes: a photogenic quality and personality.

To enhance audience interest in them, stars were wrapped in a romantic aura; biographies were falsified or invented, and names were often changed (just as Greta Gustaffson became Greta Garbo, so Joan Crawford had originally been Lucille LeSueur, while Carole Lombard and Cary Grant had been respectively baptized Jane Peters and Archie Leach). Often the humble origins of American stars were played up while aristocratic or well-to-do backgrounds were developed for Europeans. Stars were portrayed as confident, seductive, exotic, debonair, paternal, or funny in accordance with the type of roles they played. The intention was to mingle reality with illusion and fantasy to make quite ordinary people into fascinating ciphers of individual dreams and aspirations.

The special allure of Hollywood cinema derived from a combination of factors including the genre system and screenplays, as well as the great investment in the overall look of films. But the importance of the stars was such that every aspect of their being was subject to meticulous grooming and manufacture. Hollywood moguls had precise ideas about the way a star should look and they remodelled their new talent accordingly.[20] Women were usually put on a rigid diet and subjected to intensive massage treatment to lose excess pounds that would look unflattering on the screen. In this way cheekbones showed through and the face acquired an angular quality that the light could capture and the body took on a sleeker look. Teeth were fixed, corrective plastic surgery was applied if necessary, hair was smoothed out.

After this, the make-up department went to work, thinning out and redesigning eyebrows, lengthening eyelashes, enlarging eyes, reducing noses, removing beauty spots, and covering freckles. The intention was not to make the stars more pronounced as individuals but rather less. Make-up depersonalized the face in order to turn it into something artificial and alluring. This did not, contrary to popular opinion, turn stars into godlike beings. In the view of the French sociologist Edgar Morin, who in the late 1950s wrote a penetrating analysis of stardom, 'make-up in cinema does not counterpose a sacred face to a profane, everyday face; it raises everyday beauty to the level of superior, radiant, incontrovertible beauty. The natural beauty of the actress and the artificial beauty of the make-up join in a unique synthesis.'[21] Perhaps the most obvious point of synthesis was in hairstyling. Mary Pickford's curls, Jean Harlow's platinum blonde tresses, Claudette Colbert's bangs, and Veronica Lake's 'peek-a-boo' style were all influential.

Stars were presented to the public primarily as objects of sexual desire. To achieve this effect, film companies seized hold of the culture of sexual representation that had developed in the theatres of Europe and the United States. Writing in 1932, Gertrude Aretz argued that 'the chosen beauties of the film world' had become the bearers of the erotic femininity that was previously the preserve of the *Parisienne*. There was a continuity, she argued, between their tastes and 'the luxurious *demi-monde* of the Old World'.[22] However, the 'sex appeal' that was a vital quality for every star was not the same as the commodified sexual appeal of the courtesan and showgirl.[23] Indeed, it was regarded by some European observers in the 1930s as a mysterious quality.[24] French journalist Blaise Cendrars found that in

Hollywood great emphasis was placed on symmetry and harmony of the face and body in achieving the 'flash', the 'magnetic attraction' that was central to sex appeal; the contribution of the artifice of hairstyling was also deemed of central importance.[25] Perplexity arose because there was no immediately recognizable connection between the calculated strategies of the professional seductresses of a previous generation and the less explicit, subdued fascination of the stars. The latter combined class and sleaze no less than the Parisian courtesans but, instead of holding the two qualities in precarious equilibrium, they blended them in a fascinating original synthesis.

The inventor of 'sex appeal' in cinema was in fact Elinor Glyn, the English aristocratic author of a scandalous novel entitled *Three Weeks* that portrayed the passionate seduction of a young British aristocrat by a Balkan princess.[26] Glyn taught the popular actress Gloria Swanson and other protégées how to project 'star quality', that is 'a kind of ever-warm but slightly aloof benevolence when seen socially or at public functions'.[27] Crucially, she also taught film-makers how to encode sexuality, first coining the term *It* (the title of one of her stories, which gave rise to a 1927 film of the same title featuring Clara Bow—the 'It' girl) which evolved into sex appeal.[28] The point was to make sex secondary to magnetism. Women, Glyn advised, 'ought to remain mysterious and elusive in order to keep their men interested, even after marriage' and the same applied to movie stars and their audiences.[29] This view reflected the background of Glyn, who was basically a romantic conservative, but her usefulness lay in providing a bridge between turn-of-the-century innocence and modern customs that saw men and women regard each other as friends, work colleagues, and potential sexual partners.[30] One of Glyn's favourite motifs was the exotic. One way in which sex appeal was generated was through contrasts between light and shade; these were usually mapped on to the cultural differences that were highlighted through the use of light and shadows. The light skin of white actresses was deployed to express purity, cleanliness, godliness, nobility, and the generality of humankind against supposed lower orders of humanity who were distinguished by darker complexions. This presumed cultural supremacy made itself felt forcefully in early cinema. In D. W. Griffith's 1915 racist extravaganza *The Birth of a Nation*, Lillian Gish was bathed in light as the embodiment of the myth of a racially pure American South.[31] However, there was also room for diversity, and ethnic difference was turned into an exotic spectacle. In keeping with a view of the swarthy foreigner, whether of Southern or Eastern extraction, as a source of sexual danger, and therefore sexual excitement, Rudolph Valentino, a dark-haired Italian, donned the exotic persona of an Arab in *The Sheik* and *Son of the Sheik*. Chinese, Hispanic, and Arabic motifs were also employed to add mystery, sultriness, and allure.[32]

As Glyn and others conceived it, sex appeal was primarily a feminine matter. In this sense its cinematic application opened a new chapter in the culture of woman as spectacle. The development of cinema allowed male producers and artists new possibilities for moulding women and creating figures of fantasy, even to the point of reconstructing ideals of femininity. The practical aspects of stardom, with its attention to beauty, artifice, display, fashion, luxury were considered by many to be exquisitely female. However, American audiences and fans were largely female and several male stars were also packaged and costumed in a similar way to their female colleagues.[33] Such stars could find themselves under attack for effeminacy. Valentino's masculinity was questioned because women fawned over him, he was a skilful dancer, and wore a bracelet given to him by his wife. A notorious attack by the Chicago *Tribune*, in which he was dubbed a 'pink powder puff', was said to have contributed to his final illness and death.[34] In general, the acting profession, in particular when this involved a male setting himself up as an object of desire, was deemed an inappropriate activity for a man. Men did not pose and costume themselves; they performed real physical work or took part in sport.

Hollywood offered its audiences a wide variety of entertainments and glamour was present in several popular genres. However, it was especially present in contemporary films which breathed some of the modern spirit of the period. Clara Bow, Louise Brooks, and Joan Crawford were American girls from humble backgrounds who conferred their own distinctive traits on the flapper phenomenon. They all played socialites even though they did not physically resemble conventional upper-class girls. Indeed, in their films, their vibrancy and energy are explicitly contrasted with the colourless, respectable young women who are presented as typical of the stuffiness of formal high society. Bow was the biggest idol of the mid-1920s. A Brooklyn girl who won a fan-magazine contest and did a successful screen test, she found herself catapulted to stardom in the 1926 film *Dancing Mothers*, an adaptation of a Broadway play in which she played the part of Kittens, the flapper daughter of a high-society matron. She injected such vitality into her playing that Paramount gave her a cameo appearance as herself, Clara Bow, movie star, in the film *Fascinating Youth*. The interplay between biography, personality, and fiction was strong in the case of an actress who had red hair, drove a red open-top sports car, and owned a dyed-red dog. The opening sequence of her film *Red Hair* was even shot in colour at exorbitant cost to show audiences her flaming tresses.

In one of her first major films, *Our Dancing Daughters*, Crawford—who would become one of the biggest stars in the 1930s—plays a freewheeling socialite who loves jazz and takes off her skirt at a formal event to dance the Charleston more easily. This too was a biographical reference since the actress had first come to public attention as the winner of a Charleston competition. Like her fellow flappers, Crawford's character still lives with her parents, yet she shocks and alienates the man she loves with her carefree mores. She eventually wins back her beau, but she remains modern and sexy in a way that marks her out from more conventional members of her circle. In the film, she seems just like she was, a brash working-class girl who had risen beyond her station. Films like this created the illusion for audiences that fashion and novelty created patterns of shared experience that did not just blur but actually erased class boundaries. This reflected and magnified the extent to which invention or self-invention were common features of an age in which appearances were important for all modern women.

The star image was also shaped by a variety of extra-filmic elements. The off-screen lifestyles and personalities of prominent film actors were not simply part of the paraphernalia of movie marketing but an integral part of what made an actor a star. The aura of stardom was generated as much by magazines, photographs, advertising, and audience perceptions as screen performance.[35] The public image of movie people was derived from the super-rich, although its main purpose was not to establish status within the group so much as to impress the public. Large houses, private swimming pools, limousines, fine clothes, and an exciting social life were the recurrent features of the Hollywood lifestyle. The producer Thomas Ince was the first movie figure to take up a way of life that in California had been adopted by oil magnates. He built a Spanish-style villa and developed a leisure-oriented way of life based on outdoor sports pursuits, large automobiles, and weekend entertaining.[36] Others followed with dream castles and lavish mansions above Hollywood and in Bel Air and Brentwood. Although the homes of the stars were featured more regularly in the press in the 1930s, even the first mansions were regularly photographed, with the result that tourists and autograph hunters descended on Hollywood.

From the point of view of established social elites, Hollywood was a vulgar and ostentatious place, characterized by excess and idiosyncracy. In an industry peopled by newcomers, nobodies, and the deracinated, social life was marked by the sort of hedonism that exploded with the Fatty Arbuckle trials, in which the corpulent actor was accused—and eventually acquitted—of causing the death of a young actress by rupturing her bladder during a sex game. With the help of aristocratic advisers such as Elinor Glyn, more accurate imitations of elite customs were developed on- and off-screen. Glyn wrote screenplays, acted as a consultant on several films, and tried to introduce criteria of taste to Hollywood living—dispensing judgements on dining rooms, gardens, fashions, colours, food, and anything else that caught her eye—although the results often fell short of her intentions. The larger-than-life image of the star involved, typically, exaggeration and attention-grabbing at the expense of taste. But for the masses, the Hollywood version of high society was more comprehensible and accessible than the closed world of the established rich, based as this was on family line and tradition, more than money and success. Mary Pickford and Douglas Fairbanks were the first stars to introduce an element of sobriety and dignity into a community that was typified by parvenu excess. Richer, more powerful, and better-known than those that followed, they had seen how the European upper class lived on their travels abroad during the early 1920s and aimed to create their own version of a courtly social elite. Under their influence, the film community set about creating a replica high society in Los Angeles. This involved a hierarchy based on earning power that also prescribed a certain decorum. There was a rigid process of selection that marginalized those who failed to match up in terms of acceptability. This was not based on social origins of course, but on the success or otherwise of a given person's efforts to transcend their background. Clara Bow found herself ostracized not because she grew up in a slum community but because she had dreadful manners and retained her Brooklyn accent. At a time when formal dress was de rigueur, she once turned up for a dinner at the Beverly Hills Hotel in a belted bathing suit.[37] By contrast, Crawford (who married Douglas Fairbanks junior in 1929) made a point of studying etiquette manuals. To cultivate a glamorous appearance, it was crucial to strike the right balance between old and new, and high and low. The absorption of elements drawn from the upper classes had to blend seamlessly with the modernity, good looks, and the commonplace characteristics of the star.

Although status anxiety was pronounced, several stars laboured under the illusion that Hollywood society was the *ne plus ultra* until they came face to face with the European nobility. One of Glynn's protégées, Gloria Swanson, was the most photographed woman in America in the 1920s, yet she was not at all worldly. The embodiment of what one commentator dubbed 'the shopgirl's dream of glamour', she travelled to Paris in 1924 to star in the first Franco-American co-production, *Madame sans Gêne*. Appearing in a Napoleonic-era drama and mixing in Parisian society provided her with her first encounter with art, culture, and history. From this, Swanson, who many years later would play a forgotten silent-era diva in Billy Wilder's *Sunset Boulevard*, drew the conclusion that 'The glamour of Hollywood illusion dimmed to nothing beside the real glamour of the European rich, whether they were heading for Ascot or driving through the Bois de Boulogne in a Hispano-Suiza'.[38] The elitist lifestyle appealed to her greatly and she embraced it with the enthusiasm of a novice, spending a fortune in the fashionable boutiques of Patou and Chanel. In true gold-digger fashion, she set about integrating herself in a more stable way. When she returned to Los Angeles after a two-year absence, having married a minor French nobleman in Paris she was feted on a grand scale like the new rich of an earlier generation. In fact, what she had seen was not glamour but rather the lifestyle of a wealthy hereditary elite. For the world, it was the stars of Hollywood who were the epitome of glamour.

The stars travelled far and wide; as ambassadors of the movie industry they were an invaluable marketing tool. When Pickford and Fairbanks undertook world tours in the early 1920s, they were mobbed wherever they went. Photographs of movie actors in stylish coats and furs, standing by trains, planes, and luxury automobiles, with quantities of leather luggage, convey something of the identification with modernity and mobility that they embodied. The audiences never saw their promotional tours as work. Like the upper classes, they seemed to live a magical, leisure-oriented *vie sans frontières*. A few stars with well-to-do backgrounds possessed enough taste and self-confidence to assert their own style. The producer Irving Thalberg's actress wife Norma Shearer was known for her understated allure. Although she put on the movie star look for parties and premieres, informal publicity shots show her as the epitome of casual style. Together with Thalberg, she provided a patrician image that was closer to East Coast elegance than Hollywood glitz.[39] Claudette Colbert also offered a well-bred, fashionable look that derived in part from her upbringing in Paris. The public appears to have been fascinated by stars like Constance Bennett and Katherine Hepburn whose very physiques expressed their upper-crust backgrounds. However, behind most of Hollywood's refined appearances were English aristocratic advisers like Glyn or Richard Gully, an illegitimate son of the second Viscount Selby, who was an important figure on the Hollywood social scene between the 1930s and the 1960s.[40]

Hollywood did not have much confidence in the early years in its own potential to create fashion. It copied European theatrical uses of costume and fashion for publicity and made ample recourse to Parisian haute couture. This appropriation, like that of French deco, was a transitional phase to a context in which Hollywood acquired the resources and know-how to assert itself as the primary source of glamour. However, collaborations with French fashion designers like Coco Chanel, who, at the behest of Samuel Goldwyn, worked on two MGM productions in the early 1930s, were not very successful. No resource was spared, but Chanel's pared-down approach did not translate well into the exaggerated idiom of film costume. Although Paris never ceased to be a reference point, the film companies found ways of their own to produce garments and accessories that were effective on screen. The wardrobe departments of major studios were small factories employing hundreds of workers and it was the job of chief designers (Adrian at MGM, Travis Banton and Edith Head at Paramount, Orry-Kelly at Warner's) to provide costumes for the stars and to develop detailed wardrobe plots showing the sequence of ensembles a star was to wear in the scenes shot.[41] The designer had to conceal defects—often using special undergarments—and stress good points in order to create an illusion of physical perfection. Stars like Garbo, Dietrich, or Crawford could have as many as twenty costumes for a film, each requiring up to six fittings.[42] The costliest materials were used and clothes were designed cinematically, that is in an exaggerated manner and using textures, colours, and effects that would achieve the greatest impact on screen.

The moguls, several of whom had begun their working lives in the garment trade, attached great importance to costume. For millions of women film-goers, star personas were associated with fashion and there was intense interest in what new costumes actresses would wear in a film. Film publicity agents promoted the idea that every woman should draw inspiration from a star personality whose face, figure, or temperament broadly resembled her own. To assist the process, fashion and beauty advice ostensibly dispensed by stars appeared regularly in magazines and stores, and pattern companies made garments seen on film commercially available.[43] These of course were cheap adapted versions, for actual star looks were extremely costly and incorporated the fantastic as well as the realistic. Adrian added greatly to Garbo's allure with his elaborate work on *Queen Christina*, *Mata Hari*, and *Camille* and Travis Banton's exquisite costumes for Dietrich helped turn her into the orchid of Paramount. Stars like Joan Crawford, Kay Francis, Rosalind Russell, Constance Bennett, and a few others were little more than elegant clothes horses. Although she was Adrian's greatest challenge owing to her broad shoulders and imperfect figure, Crawford made fashion news when she wore a sensational ruffled gown in the 1932 success *Letty Lynton* which was widely copied.[44] In the late 1930s Adrian developed the wide-shouldered, narrow-hipped silhouette that became her fashion trademark. In a market in which there was as yet little interest in labels and brands, the stars were vital to the launch of new fashions.[45]

As fashion icons, stars exercised a new and highly important role. They introduced a marked element of fantasy that spoke directly to the dreams of the masses. Expensive materials, creative designs, original gowns, and furs, all of which had connotations of high society, European 'taste', and exclusiveness,[46] were now deployed to dazzle an audience. In essence, stars dressed to excite attention, their look was sumptuous and theatrical; 'Dietrich's things were more than fashion—they were superfashion,' Head once said.[47] They suited Dietrich's own definition of glamour as 'something indefinite, something inaccessible to normal women—an unreal paradise, desirable but basically out of reach'.[48] On account of their enormous following, the stars inevitably invaded the fashion magazines that had once been the preserve of the social elite. For example, Horst P. Horst photographed Dietrich and many others for *Vogue*. It was a measure of Hollywood's growing confidence and autonomy in this sphere that in the late 1930s designers like Orry-Kelly and Head were releasing their own retail collections. Although the European associations of fashion were never eliminated, the presentation was distinctively American.

The stars were often dressed in dramatic or unusual ways. Both Garbo and Dietrich cross-dressed and sought to confound conventional expectations of elegant clothing.[49] At a time when independent women still aroused curiosity, the androgynous aspects of these stars aroused widespread fears and aspirations. By contrast, Luise Rainer, who won an Oscar two years in a row in 1936 and 1937, completely rejected movie-star fashions in favour of simple beige dresses and shoes. Whatever form it took, the display of fashion became a key element of many movies as well as of the public images of stars and was sometimes incorporated formally as part of the overall spectacle. Many films either featured fashion shows or were little more than a sequence of episodes linking display set pieces. *Roberta*, *The Bride Walks Out*, *Artists and Models*, *Vogues of 1938*, and *Mannequin* all relied on fashion as spectacle and took advantage of the opportunities for luxurious display that the fashion show offered. Several of these films were musicals and the fashion parade blended with revue sets and musical performance.[50] These elements of film glamour drew on the carnivalesque traditions of popular theatre. They were playful and deliberately exaggerated, stimulating the imagination by stressing the entertainment value of luxury and style.[51] It is this reliance on vaudeville that reveals the populism of Hollywood fashion. It was not on the whole deferential towards established style hierarchies or the class images associated with them. Haute couture was often parodied and demystified, its elitism and eccentricity becoming an object of mirth. In this way elite forms were appropriated and rendered accessible. Hollywood effected a major shift in the way fashion worked by creating a glamorous blend of high fashion, popular spectacle, and street style that was both theatrical and reproducible. Such was the impact of this blend that Paris itself was forced to take notice. In the 1930s designers took inspiration from costume dramas and Elsa Schiaparelli even based a whole collection on the 'Mae West look'.[52]

During the Depression years, the image of celebrity in popular magazines was domesticated and turned into an exaggerated version of the typical. This coincided with glamour's becoming became fully Americanized and democratized. Previously, there were those who had considered it to be a foreign import. In the 1930s it was standard in the United States to spell the word with a 'u', a usage that would return fully only in the 1990s. 'Why is the English form of "our" preserved in this word? The u could be left out without hurting the pronunciation, as in labor, honor etc.,' wrote one newspaper correspondent.[53]

More than anything else, it was the Depression that was directly responsible for the emergence of glamour as Hollywood's most marketable commodity.[54] At a time of widespread poverty and hardship, the masses lived vicariously through stars who knew that they were offering a fabulous escape from everyday worries. A special role in turning them into an image of a sexual and material heaven for poor and hungry people who needed a dream of perfection was played by the studio photographers. These professionals were past masters at making the stars into Hollywood icons. George Hurrell, Clarence Sinclair Bell, and others worked in studio photographic galleries and sometimes in their own studios. The stars who came to them, usually at the end of a long day of filming, were not always appreciative of their efforts. But their work appeared very widely, above all in fan magazines, and was crucial in making them into desirable images. In contrast to photographs of royalty or other important personages, the shots of stars lingered on their physical perfection and communicated seductive appeal. Highly retouched, the stills revelled in artificiality; indeed precisely their abstract, constructed character made them 'consumable' by the viewer. The aim of the photographers was to create a mood through the use of light and props. They emphasized sensuous surfaces of skin and hair; dwelt on furs, silks, and satins; they alluded to sex by having actresses lie on rugs or wear loose gowns or a negligee. Hurrell found that some of his subjects had a natural aptitude for projecting themselves. Even when they entered a room, 'they had internal trumpets that blew for them just as the door [opened]'.[55]

The 'glamour look', in Hurrell's view, was quite simply a 'bedroom look'.[56] 'You know, glamour to me was nothing more than just an excuse for [taking] sexy pictures,' he told John Kobal. 'In other words, my interpretation was entirely one of saying "Come on, we're going to take some sexy pictures."' 'You can create glamour totally, I think. But a woman in our business generally has some quality of it,' he added. By this, he meant that they were often exhibitionists or professionally seductive. Another photographer, Paul Hesse agreed. It was important to capture 'that look', he claimed; without it 'you won't get much of a picture. The beautiful exterior is not what I am after. I want that inner person who speaks through her eyes.'[57] However, this quality was something that some at least were able to learn and to turn on at whim. Hesse's idea of a sexy and provocative face was Lana Turner's, but her full, parted lips and invitational eyes were composed in an instant. 'Lana is so busy that whenever I have photographed her I have had the feeling of catching a bird on a wing,' Hesse said.

On occasion still photographers like Hurrell and Sinclair Bull were engaged on the set to shoot close-ups, but there were some directors who had a great technical grasp of the camera's possibilties. First among these was Josef von Sternberg, the man who discovered Marlene Dietrich. The actress had earned just $5,000 for her debut film in Berlin *The Blue Angel*, while the film's star Emil Jannings had been paid $200,000.[58] But after its triumphant release, she eclipsed him. Her role in the 1930 film *Morocco* turned her into a Hollywood star. She was, by her own account, largely created as a screen persona by von Sternberg. Although his decorative style was often considered to be trashy and kitsch, he found a way to illuminate her bone structure, emphasize her deep-set eyes, and achieve a halo effect that made her hair glisten. By bathing her in light, he created a moody, seductive effect.[59] 'In my case the face was *created*,' Dietrich affirmed, remarking that she became the vehicle of the director's aspiration to bring to life on the screen 'the dream of the little man'.[60] After they parted, following the making of the Spanish drama *The Devil is a Woman*—a title that was imposed on the director—von Sternberg looked back at what he had achieved with her and mischievously repeated, 'I am Marlene Dietrich'.[61] In her memoirs, the actress seemed to concur. 'Before von Sternberg took me in hand, I was utterly helpless. I was not even aware of the task awaiting me,' she wrote. 'I was a "nobody", and the mysterious energies of the creator breathed life into this nothingness. I'm not entitled to the least recognition for the roles I played in his films. I was nothing but pliable material on the infinitely rich palette of his ideas and imaginative faculties.'[62] Far from regarding such comments as flattering to his genius, von Sternberg responded with great irritation. He perceived that, by this means, Dietrich was seeking to highlight the tyrannical moulding to which she had been subjected and win the sympathy of audiences for her courage and capacity for survival.[63] Nevertheless, the actress learned a lot from her Pygmalion—according to Hurrell, she knew everything there was to know about photography and lighting—and developed a sharp sense of herself as a glamorous star. Off-screen, she exercised a high degree of control over her public image. As she put it, an actress is 'a woman who must always appear impeccable'.[64] 'I find all that pretty stupid,' she added. 'Of course, we're beautiful in the photos and also in life; but we were never as extraordinary as the image that was drawn of us. We clung to this image because the studio demanded that we do so. But none of us enjoyed it. To us, it was just a routine job and we just did it well.'[65] People only very rarely saw the discipline and sacrifices that the stars made in order to shine for the public.

One of the closest relationships that stars had was with studio publicity departments, which played a crucial part in building their careers and forging their images. Together with the advertising and 'exploitation' departments, these were vital institutions that employed at their height between sixty and one hundred people per studio.[66] As MGM publicity chief, Howard Strickling was responsible for constructing and maintaining star images. In his accounts actresses did not drink or smoke, they did not even have babies; each of their usually many romances was made in heaven. They were presented and photographed only in the most ideal circumstances. Metro staff were instructed never to mention what stars earned, as quoting money placed commerce ahead of glamour. Moreover everything was puffed-up.[67] 'If you had a farm, it was an estate. If you had a field it was full of horses,' said Warner Brothers' Celeste Holm.[68] By these means, stars were turned into larger-than-life figures who everyone, including even the publicists themselves, believed were special.

The stars were commodities and the way they interacted with their fans was conditioned by the developing object world. Stars shone, glittered, and enchanted as they took on the personalization of novelty and the appearance of wealth. Because they were commercial and available, they spoke directly to the dreams and aspirations of the masses. Watching films in the dark on a big screen, people projected on to the protagonists their own interior lives and aspirations.[69] 'On the plane of daily emotions', Edgar Morin argued, the class struggle 'translated itself into new aspirations, new forms of individual participation'. Improvements in material conditions combined with new leisure practices to produce a situation in which workers and salaried employees 'join the spiritual civilisation of the bourgeoisie'. Alongside material demands, they made a new 'basic demand: the desire to live one's life, that is to say to live one's dreams and to dream one's life'.[70]

The movies were both product and spell and this latter aspect was underscored by the environments in which they were shown. First-run movie theatres were often situated in the immediate proximity of stores and a mutual dependency soon developed.[71] While stores advertised films and featured still pictures of stars in their window displays, films and related publicity directed the material desires of the public towards given products. For their part movie theatres offered opportunities for commercial enterprises to exhibit their goods. Through the 1920s and 1930s, picture palaces grew larger and ever more elaborate, taking styles from all manner of places and periods. Each contained an elegant, plush lobby area resembling that of a grand hotel, while uniformed staff attended customers and guided them to their seats. Only the inevitable queues for tickets undermined the sensation that film-goers were experiencing some luxuries once reserved for the rich. The most famous movie theatre in the world was Grauman's Chinese Theater on Hollywood Boulevard in Los Angeles. Opened in 1927, five years after the nearby Egyptian Theater, it was built to a Chinese-inspired design and was decorated with authentic objects including pagodas and Fu dogs. The theatre seated 1,500 and was the location of the Academy Awards ceremony in the mid-1940s. Unlike many movie theatres of that period, it is still in regular use and often hosts film premieres. It is famous as the site of the many hand prints left in wet concrete by film stars dating back to Norma Talmadge and Tom Mix. Grauman's was special but every large city in the Western world had its own dream palaces, and even more modest establishments rejoiced in opulent-sounding names like Roxy, Rialto, Rex, Alhambra, Palace, Majestic, Coronet, Grand. Even in provincial towns, Moorish domes, marble columns, Oriental decor, plush interiors, and American-style streamlining flourished.

The press was a crucial mediator between the studios and the public. It provided information, explanations, and advice relating to readers' everyday lives. The most influential fan magazine, *Photoplay*, treated Hollywood as a dream capital, a place full of glamour, adventure, and excitement.[72] The magazines promoted youth, beauty, love, and leisure rather than work, family, routine duties, and limitations. This was first because they were mainly read by young people, and young women in particular, but also to provide a world of desire in contrast to the humdrum. 'The place to study glamour today is the fan magazines,' wrote the author Margaret Thorp:

Fan magazines are distilled stimulants of the most exhilarating kind. Everything is superlative, suprising, exciting...Nothing ever stands still, nothing ever rests, least of all the sentences...Clothes of course are endlessly pictured and described usually with marble fountains, private swimming pools or limousines in the background...Every aspect of life, trivial and important, should be bathed in the purple glow of luxury.... However thick the luxury in which a star is lapped, she takes care today to make it known that she is really a person of simple wholesome tastes, submitting to elegance as part of her job but escaping from it as often as possible. It soothes the fans to hear that luxury is fundamentally a burden.[73]

Writing in 1939, she defined the principal characteristics of glamour as 'sex appeal plus luxury plus elegance plus romance'. In the same year, Condé

Nast founded a new magazine: *Glamour of Hollywood*. The aim was to make available to ordinary women the knowledge about how to maximize the appeal and attractiveness that movie designers, costume departments, and make-up artists had developed for the stars. The magazine exploited the sex-and-style publicity power of the film industry and signalled this by publishing the picture of a film star on most covers.

The promise was that anyone could benefit from the application of the techniques of the glamour factory. Beauty had become more a product of modern science than a God-given endowment. 'Why do the glamour girls of Hollywood usually look like ordinary women when you run into them on the boulevard, while on the screen they are alluring, mysterious and beautiful?', asked the *Los Angeles Times*.[74] The answer was simple. At their service they have beauty specialists, hairdressers, dress designers, and photographers. To prove that any woman, given the same advantages, could become glamorous, the newspaper took a local typist of average appearance named Nina Peron and put her step by step through the process by which the studios created glamour. The final result, it claimed, put her on the same level as Norma Shearer, Garbo, and many other stars.

The impact of the movies on everyday life was far-reaching. By drawing attention to appearance, clothing, and self-presentation in general, they stressed the fact that maintaining a good appearance was an important part of the performance of daily life. Women in particular were encouraged to see parallels between the studios' struggle to maximize their stars' glamour value and popular appeal and their own efforts to make the best of themselves.[75] Cosmetics companies led by Max Factor highlighted the artifice of Hollywood make-up, celebrating the artificiality of the made-up face as proof of the democratization of beauty.[76] Although cosmetics were still widely regarded as not respectable, especially for young women, the years between 1909 and 1929 witnessed a doubling in the United States of perfume and cosmetics manufacturers and a tenfold increase in the volume of sales.[77] After the First World War, they became more widespread and entered the repertoire of middle- and working-class women.

Like mannequins, stars showed clothes, cosmetics, and other products to excellent effect. The movies helped people to dream and the apparatus of consumerism assisted them in partially turning those dreams into lived experience. Commercial tie-ups were a central part of movie promotion; some involved national deals between studios and manufacturers over specific films, while others were left to the local initiative of exhibitors. However, some stars and some producers were uneasy about practices that undermined the element of mystery that was essential to glamour. Mary Pickford turned down a potentially lucrative advertising contract on the grounds that it would be undignified and risky to have her name 'bandied about in all sorts of good, bad, and indifferent commercial projects' and other top stars followed suit.[78] *Gone With the Wind* producer David O. Selznick even expressed reservations about the free endorsements that stars very regularly offered to Max Factor and which appeared in magazines throughout the world.

The magical transformative power of the glamour factory helped promote the clothing industry. The sale of women's apparel brought $1,205,000 to Los Angeles County in 1914, while by 1935 it was $28,104,000. 'It is the proximity of the movie stars which lends an enchantment to products from California,' reported the *Los Angeles Times*.[79] 'Hundreds of millions of women see Hollywood's motion pictures and all of them are subtly but gently persuaded into the ways of cinema glamour, into the art of wearing their hair down as it's more flattering to their faces, into the technique of adorning the figure in sleek, streamlined clothes because they set off to perfection the feminine form.' Bathing suits, made in Hollywood and photographed in Palm Springs, had a special allure. The extra push from a massive quantity of publicity 'emanating from the movie capital to cities all over the world...gives Los Angeles merchandise a colourful promotional quality to stores over America and other sister countries,' the paper commented, adding that 'the rest of the world wants Hollywood glamour and is willing to pay for it'.[80]

Throughout the world, young women were finding ways of integrating elements of Hollywood glamour into their everyday lives. Young men were often equally dazzled, but it was the 'movie-struck girl' who summed up the phenomenon of the fan. Unlike young men, girls took their cue not only from the movies but from numerous related magazines and advice manuals.

The author of one of these, the actress Sali Löbel, told her readers: 'Glamour is not the elusive pimpernel attainable only through the god of riches.... It is easy to obtain at least *some* of it, if not all of it, and half a loaf is better than none.'[81] 'It is unfortunate', she added, 'that the very word has such an expensively euphonious atmosphere. It must be the "Gl" at its commencement—those two consonants close together are sound-dangerous!' In her view, health, determination, hard work, and an ability to laugh and love were important elements of the glamorous personality, but so too was the power to dream. 'It is this aesthetic quality'—which could be stimulated by a few moments spent looking at a shop window—'which will create around you that atmosphere of beauty and glamour which is for ever green.'[82]

Such advice encountered a great deal of success because it keyed into real changes in aspirations. Young women in the interwar years wanted to live their lives differently from their mothers and, if education had failed them, this feeling derived enormous impetus from the cinema.[83] 'Via the high street or the sewing machine,' one British historian argues, 'the mantle of glamour passed from the aristocrat and courtesan to the shop, the office, or factory girl via the film star.'[84] The advantage of the American film stars was that they were unlike either women of the older generation or actual aristocrats. Far more than the courtesans of the nineteenth century, the glamorous screen heroine offered the fantasy that she was little more than the girl next door who was her fan. Although the abundant, elaborate femininity of the stars was unattainable for most British women, fans enjoyed the fantasy and were 'full of envy and admiration' for their looks and lifestyles.[85] Even in Fascist Italy, girls embraced commercial culture and its pleasures as a way of defining themselves as modern and asserting some independence not only with respect to their families but also to the regime.[86] Mussolini's followers loathed the made-up, fashionable look that they associated with Paris and Hollywood, but their efforts to suppress it proved ineffectual.[87] Shop girls, typists, students, and even factory workers found rare avenues of self-definition through the movies.

In the 1930s, glamour was ubiquitous. The phenomenon became so widespread that it was freely attached to the most diverse people and roles. Appearances suddenly counted for more than ever before. In the United

States, the phenomenon of the 'glamour boy' was widely noted. The top 'glamour boys' of course were the good-looking young men who appeared in the movies, but they could be found in a variety of service industries where a handsome and charming man was deemed a boon to business.[88] He was a recognized feature at soda fountains, at service stations, on the staff of estate agents, and even in politics. Always he was to be found in urban contexts. Because there was 'no glamour on the farm', young men were leaving the land in droves, it was claimed, with the result that the whole system of food production was at risk. 'What the farm needs today is some glamour,' the American House of Representatives Agriculture Committee was reported to have demanded in 1942.[89] However, even this unlikely field was not entirely devoid of the magical brush of glamour, at least so long as it was not too far from Los Angeles. The Guernsey cows to be shown at the western states breeders' cooperative show at the Los Angeles Union Stock Yards were dubbed 'Guernsey Glamour Girls' in the local press.[90] Root vegetables had for several years been considered ripe for glamorization and the *Los Angeles Times* cookery columnist advised readers that 'It's easy to put carrots in the glamour class when you use a can of cream of mushroom soup for the sauce'.[91]

Inevitably, such an overdose of glamour produced some negative reactions. The phenomenon that most distilled glamour was the 'glamour girl'. These were 'the most artificial creations of an artificial-loving business'.[92] Some, it was claimed, were 'little more than animated mannequins day-dreaming through movies', store-window dummies whose individuality was entirely overridden by the professional grooming and image-making to which they had voluntarily submitted. 'Hollywood's de-natured dream girls are, of necessity, spiritually static, with no more "soul" than a geisha,' wrote B. R. Crisler in the *New York Times*.[93] 'With the make-up man constantly standing by to pat the perspiration from her face and with "wardrobe" dancing attendance to guard her gown (specially designed to minimize anatomical defects) from wrinkles, she is as far above the plane of mortal infirmities, and consequently is as uninteresting, psychologically, as a statue in a museum.' Glamour was a quality in which the whole of Hollywood was wrapped, but there were particular film genres, actors, and studios where it was present at a much higher pitch than elsewhere. When Universal

Studios tried to dub its wholesome teenage singing star Deanna Durbin 'glamorous' there were protests from those who disagreed. 'Glamour indeed! as if it had not been her very freedom from glamour, Hollywood style, that has endeared her to millions! Glamour! as if that word were more precious than the freshness, the gay vitality, the artful artlessness and the youthful radiance she has brought to the screen!' exclaimed Frank Nugent.[94] Praise was heaped on the actress Helen Hayes, who starred opposite Gary Cooper in the 1932 version of *Farewell to Arms*, since she was deemed 'a girl without glamour' because 'she has never needed any'.[95] Her talent alone was held to be sufficient box-office attraction.

By the mid 1930s, even independent producer Samuel Goldwyn claimed that the public was tired of glamour. 'Overdressing the movies is going to cease. The audiences are fed up with too luxuriant costumes and sets; they want what is simple,' he argued.[96] With the exception of musicals, where exaggeration and spectacle were obligatory, films needed to be closer to reality. Producers, he continued, should not 'thrust expensiveness into [the] face' of audiences by means of 'overdone backgrounds', 'too much flashiness in dress', and 'the made-up look of many of the stars'. The recognized expert on feminine beauty Cecil Beaton caused a stir when he announced that 'the glamour girl is as dead as mutton'. 'There is a swing back to naturalness,' he claimed, 'a girl today must show signs of being human and real—she must have a sense of humor and a spirit of camaraderie.'[97] In fact there was no real swing back, but there were some important shifts of emphasis. Although it was far from true that glamour was coming to an end, its production would never again be concentrated so powerfully in the hands of relatively few men. The Second World War produced a widespread demand for glamour and created new conditions for its becoming once more a phenomenon with a strong European inflection, albeit a phenomenon that the whole world by now identified as American.

CHAPTER 7

PARIS, ROME, AND
THE RIVIERA

W hen Christian Dior unveiled his debut couture collection in February 1947, he was aware that his opulent fabric-rich dresses and coats would cause a stir. By presenting garments that flouted the prevailing climate of post-war austerity, he made a statement that inevitably provoked a reaction. All the dresses belonging to the collection were long and were constructed using many metres of material. The most famous one consisted of a jacket nipped in at the waist that then opened over a wide pleated skirt. Immediately dubbed the 'New Look' by the American journalist Carmel Snow,[1] the collection was widely perceived as a bold rejection of economy and privation at a time when rationing and hardship were still widespread. Although Dior himself insisted that it was not revolutionary, his collection proclaimed the desirability of conspicuous extravagance.[2] Reactions, it would be fair to say, were mixed. Official opinion everywhere in Europe at this time favoured restraint and low consumption to help stabilize war-torn and debt-burdened economies. Moreover, those who had promoted the reforms that had brought women the vote for the first time in France and Italy were suspicious of the return of conventional elegance. In the United

States, women's organizations expressed strong disapproval of the return of long skirts. One British Member of Parliament, Mabel Ridealgh, pronounced the new look to be 'too reminiscent of the "caged bird" attitude' and urged women to reject attempts to curtail their freedom.[3] For the left, which was politically influential in the years after the war, it smacked of a restoration. When models were sent to Montmartre for a photographic session, where they were to display Dior's clothes against the backdrop of a street market, they were insulted, pelted with vegetables, and physically assaulted by class-conscious stallholders.[4]

The New Look quickly became a talking point throughout the world. As the most ready vehicle through which people could change their appearance and adopt a new persona, clothes occupied a special place in the hopes for material improvement that had blossomed amid the privations of the war years. Especially among women, many of whom had been drawn into the war effort, there was a strong desire for feminine garments that were not utilitarian. They had been deprived of cosmetics and fashion for too long for a collection like Dior's not to attract massive interest. The French fashion houses discovered the potential of fashion to capture the imagination when, in March 1945, before the war had ended in much of Europe, a reduced–scale fashion exhibition had opened at the Pavilion Marsan of the Louvre. Keen to show that they were still in existence, the houses had presented their latest designs in miniature on specially made artistic dolls. The exhibition was an unexpected triumph. It was not only visited by industry insiders, clients, and well-wishers, but by tens of thousands of ordinary men and women. Within a few weeks, over 100,000 people had visited it.[5]

Dior did not seek popular appeal, yet within weeks of its presentation, the New Look was seen widely on the streets of Paris. Although the designer had mainly been concerned to attract an established clientele of elegant women,[6] his idea was widely imitated, albeit without the complex and elegant construction that marked the original. For the first time haute couture had an impact on the mass imagination. Only in fiction could a Battersea cleaning woman like Paul Gallico's character Mrs Harris not only crave beauty and colour but actually save up and go to Paris to fulfil a lifelong ambition to buy a Dior dress.[7] However, thanks to the presence in many households of a sewing machine, imagination could be turned surprisingly quickly into reality. Billowing skirts, narrow shoulders, and curves suddenly abounded. 'It was as if all [women] had ever dreamed of, no matter what their social standing, was to play the femme fatale or the grand lady,' remarks Marie-France Pochna.[8] Dior's backer, textile manufacturer Marcel Boussac, was keenly aware of the knock-on effects that the designer's innovative styles would have at all levels of the industry. Not by chance is he said to have encouraged Dior to put even more fabric into his skirts, knowing that this would stimulate ordinary women to think more about appearances and want to buy more clothes.[9] Even in Britain, where the fiscal policies of austerity chancellor Sir Stafford Cripps kept taxes high and reduced surplus spending to a minimum, the ready-to-wear industry quickly latched on to the demand. Shorn of Parisian extravagance and modified to meet the needs of working women who travelled on buses and the Underground, the new look became an expression of the democratic luxury of the post-war years.[10]

The success of the collection re-established the pre-eminence of Paris in matters of fashion. Given the disruptions of the war years, this was by no means a foregone conclusion. It also turned Dior into a fashion authority with more influence even than Charles Frederick Worth a century previously. Until his untimely death in 1957, Dior had an unrivalled ability to determine what women wore and what they desired. He was seen as a dictator of hemlines who could, apparently by whim, fix the precise length of the skirts that the women of the world would wear in a given year. Because he sanctioned the return of wealthy ostentation, some saw in his influence evidence of a broader social restoration. Following years of mass privation and what Dior called 'the coarse feasts' of black marketeers,[11] the rich gradually re-emerged and displayed their stylish cars and huge yachts at resorts, regattas, polo matches, and race meetings. The Paris season re-established traditional elegance and the balls of the aristocracy provided old and new rich alike with opportunities to dress up and show off.[12] Dior's special prominence meant that his showroom was taken by storm as hordes of wealthy French women demanded fittings. American and British socialites also converged on Paris.

One of the great novelties of the post-war years was the presence in Europe of large numbers of wealthy Americans. Dior was not slow to appreciate that the prestige of Paris fashion depended on a close relationship with the American market. He curried favour with American buyers and with the press (a *Life* article about him prior to the unveiling of the New Look was a crucial factor in its success). He struck deals with leading American stores and even licensed name brand stockings which were manufactured directly in the United States. Subsequently, he established a branch of his house in New York and designed separate, simplified collections for the wider American market.[13] He also developed a series of deals whereby manufacturers and retailers could sell an 'original Christian Dior copy' and clothes made from paper patterns licensed by Dior.[14] While the Americans were most advanced in understanding how fashion could be sold to a broader public, the wartime streamlining of the ready-to-wear industry in France meant that Parisian couture was not a separate sphere but the prestigious tip of a whole system of production. As a result, high fashion styles, which were always highly publicized and featured heavily in the press, had an influence on the entire market. While houses were always concerned about pirated versions of their creations, their models were legitimately disseminated through official copies, approved modifications, sketches, and patterns. Dior also lent his name to a fragrance and a variety of accessories.

Hollywood stars were crucial to Dior's success and they were among his most notable clients, with Olivia de Havilland buying a 'Passe-Partout' suit priced at 30,000 francs and Rita Hayworth opting for an evening gown with two tiers of blue taffeta pleats to wear to the premiere of the movie *Gilda*. Margot Fonteyn chose a suit, while Marlene Dietrich and Ava Gardner also placed orders. Their patronage brought Paris fashion to the attention of Americans of all classes and added to its desirability. British theatrical couple Vivien Leigh and Laurence Olivier viewed Dior's 1947 collection at his house's headquarters in the Rue de la Paix and were struck by the number of American accents they heard among the customers.[15] In bridging the gap between the once-closed world of haute couture and the dreams of the masses, the stars played a critical role. Figures of glamour par excellence, they were aware of the importance of fashion to their image. By embracing the New Look, they brought it within the realm of the desires of ordinary women. Elegance no longer seemed like a source of distinction but rather a realistic aspiration for people in all social classes.

Hollywood stars enjoyed great cachet in a post-war Europe that had seen several monarchies toppled and the aristocracy lose influence. Their arrival in significant numbers was greeted with massive public curiosity. Dreams had been woven around them before the war and now they seemed, by their presence in Europe, to be holding out a promise of prosperity for all. They brought a practical demonstration of wealth and style that was more appealing and democratic than that offered by local elites.

Although female stars were usually the focus of most interest, it was a male actor who was one of the first to spend time in Europe. Tyrone Power was a leading heart-throb of the silver screen and the star of the hugely successful bull-fighting drama *Blood and Sand*. A dark-haired man of charm and fine features, he was mobbed wherever he went. The announcement that he would marry in Rome in January 1949 mobilized newsreel companies, photographers, and the press of two continents. For months they talked of the forthcoming 'wedding of the century'. The event was a great attraction but there was also a political aspect to it. Rome was the centre of the Catholic Church and a capital that, after the left-leaning coalitions of the immediate post-war years, now had a centrist pro-Western government. Since Italy no longer had a monarchy, the marriage of a Hollywood star was the nearest it was likely to get to a royal wedding. As such, it was a quasi-high society matter. However, in contrast to royal rituals, the entire event was conceived and staged for public consumption. Power was at the height of his fame and an enormously popular figure in Italy, which he had visited several times. His bride was a European-educated American starlet named Linda Christian whom he had fallen for when she asked him for his autograph in Rome's Hotel Excelsior. At that time, Power was still married to the French actress Annabella, whom he had married in 1939 in a civil ceremony. On the assumption that divorce would be straightforward, the couple were soon planning their nuptials. The preparations were highly publicized, and Christian's visits to the Fontana sisters' fashion house for her dress received ample magazine coverage. She also appeared on the cover of magazines in the company of Italy's Christian Democrat prime minister, Alcide De Gasperi. Cameras filmed Power's six stag nights and the hen night of his bride.

Newspaper accounts of the wedding spoke of the huge crowd which filled the pavements along the Via dei Fori Imperiali, from the Piazza Venezia to the Colosseum. It was bigger than any of those mustered by Italy's large Communist Party and its leader Palmiro Togliatti. 'For once the crowd did not gather to protest and the police did not have to protect ministries or politicians,' wrote one journalist.[16] He observed that he could not remember seeing a gathering of similar size in Rome since before the war—'it had what might be termed an "oceanic" character. One could say that Tyrone Power has beaten Togliatti.' The crowd was composed of 'gossiping girls and mop-headed adolescents', 'hundreds of youth who wear their hair like Power and who gesticulate and walk in a manner copied from his films. . . . hundreds of girls who had bunked school or slipped out of offices . . . elderly ladies, women of the people, and old folk, modern girls, hysterical widows, and young dandies covered in brillantine right down to their toe-nails', 'groups of young girls carrying books under their arms', 'smart young guys wearing sky blue ties, striped nylon socks, scruffy hair and suede moccasins', and 'distinguished ladies in furs'.[17] It was a lively gathering which 'hundreds of Carabinieri, policemen, and police on horseback struggled to keep in check'. Comments and appreciations were shouted, especially by 'youths with grease-backed hair' at the arrival of Linda Christian, although cries of 'Come on Tyro' were heard from the girls. But it was also a gathering that had its commercial side. While many of the young people present had clearly abandoned the classroom in order to attend, others had merely taken time out from shopping ('the halls of the big stores were rather empty yesterday morning, like during the flu epidemic', wrote one daily).[18] Newsvendors waved copies of a one-off paper bearing the enormous headline 'Ty e Linda sposi' (Ty and Linda Are Married) while tradesmen sold coloured balloons, almond bars, and other confectionery.

The wedding itself was an event conceived and executed as one to be consumed by a mass, worldwide audience. Italian and foreign broadcasting companies won unprecedented permission for radio equipment to be installed in the church of Santa Francesca Romana and photographers took shots during the ceremony; the films were then rushed by motorcycle to the central telegraph office from where they were wired to newspapers around the globe. Indiscreet photographers emerged from bushes and hedges around the church as soon as the couple appeared and made towards a waiting limousine. Christian later recounted that she and Tyrone 'pushed slowly forward through the almost impenetrable mass around us. Smiling, cheering faces pressed against the car windows. People jumped on the moving car—on the front and back, even on the roof—and it rocked under their weight.... When we arrived we discovered a torn coat-sleeve caught on one of the door handles.'[19]

For many Italian commentators the jamboree was reminiscent of an American B-film, vulgar and commercial, and marked by unseemly enthusiasm. The fact that Power's divorce from Annabella only became legally effective hours after the ceremony added to these feelings. The event was described by Rome daily *Il messaggero* as 'more picturesque than a technicolor film'.[20] The 'wedding of the century' was seen as a modern fairy tale, particularly by older women and young girls. The romance and marriage of the handsome actor and his beautiful starlet bride was a distraction from prevailing problems. That the dream was an eminently material one was evident, however, in the extraordinary publicity machine that surrounded it. The wedding was a mock high society event attended by a mixed bag of publicity-hungry aristocrats and celebrities that provided newspapers and magazines with glamorous copy. Special attention was reserved for Christian's dress, which was described in minute detail; according to one newspaper, 'pearls were distributed like constellations along the Milky Way of the silver embroidery; here and there, golden touches highlighted the embroidery'.[21] The wedding offered Romans a rare chance to see Hollywood aristocracy with their own eyes. Although the crowd soon broke up, leaving the road and pavements clear once more, it was a significant, if temporary, public coming-together of film fans, magazine readers, shoppers, and cultivators of celebrity.

After the war and the disruption it brought, the stars were very prominent. They were untainted by any connection with recently fallen regimes and they were alluring. Of course, they were not perfect, and several of them made controversial choices in their personal lives. Yet the desire for modern fairy tales was so strong that sometimes it even eclipsed the scandal that surrounded any illicit liaison. One of the most shocking scandals of the period involved Rita Hayworth, who began an affair with Prince Aly Khan while she was separated, but not yet divorced, from the actor-director Orson Welles. Her adultery provoked outrage throughout the Western world.[22] Khan was heir to the Aga Khan's throne of gold as well as a legendary playboy, of whom the social organizer Elsa Maxwell said that his 'animal magnetism...shaped his celebrity'.[23] For her part, Hayworth had become one of the top Hollywood stars during the war years and had also been a popular wartime pin-up. In some ways she was the epitome of the studio-manufactured star. Originally a dancer of Mexican origin named Margarita Cansino, she had been physically transformed by Columbia Studios into the ideal all-American girl. The star of wartime Technicolor extravaganzas including the musical *Cover Girl* and *Blood and Sand*, in which she was Power's co-star, she had consolidated her popularity throughout the world with *Gilda*, which upped the erotic content of Hollywood-style sex appeal. A beauty whose signature features were her legs, smile, and luxuriant auburn hair, she was seen abroad virtually as the embodiment of the United States. Her likeness was even placed on the first nuclear bomb to be tested after the Second World War, which was dropped by the Americans on the Atoll Bikini in the Marshall Islands in 1946. This fact earned Hayworth the enmity of Europe's Communists, who were already suspicious of American foreign policy intentions. But even some left-wing activists could not resist the fabulous allure of Gilda, as French film director Vera Belmont would reveal several decades later in her screen evocation of her Communist adolescence, *Rouge baiser* (1985).

When Hayworth and Prince Aly announced their intention to wed, she was redeemed. Her period of disgrace ended and she was recuperated and repackaged for the public as a Cinderella princess. Before they came together, the two couple's two worlds had been largely separate. For Hayworth, Khan was a virile and charming man who also had the allure of royalty. For him, the actress was a completely novel prospect, a trophy movie star, who provided an introduction into 'an unexplored sphere of glamour'.[24] The couple had sought privacy, but their notoriety precluded that. Despite its remote location, the civil ceremony at the town hall of Villauris on the Côte d'Azur was anything but low-key. Much to the chagrin of the bride and groom, the Communist mayor of the village refused to conduct the ceremony behind closed doors and ordered that they be literally thrown open to 'let the peasants in'.[25] The ceremony became a media event with reporters and photographers struggling to see and speak to the bride and groom. The next day a further ceremony took place according to the rite of the Shia Ismaili branch of Islam, of which the Aga Khan was the hereditary leader. This was followed by what had been called 'one of the biggest, gaudiest wedding receptions ever held on the Riviera'.[26] Hayworth had invited over five hundred guests, among them representatives of every major American and European press organization. These managed to consume six hundred bottles of champagne and fifty pounds of caviar as well as other delicacies. Aly Khan, who was not unused to publicity, seems to have been dazed by the whole experience. In his memoirs, he recollected, 'This was a fantastic semi-royal, semi-Hollywood affair; my wife and I played our part in the ceremony, much as we disapproved of the atmosphere with which it was surrounded.'[27]

The enthusiasm and interest that surrounded these celebrity weddings revealed that, despite the prevailing austerity, people clamoured for glamour and spectacle. They also showed a strong attachment to the institution of marriage after the wartime disruption to family life and sexual mores. Governments, like Britain's avowedly egalitarian Labour administration, had little idea how to respond to this. The Attlee government was more concerned with social justice and the collective project of economic recovery than it was with the aspirations of individuals. The way it dealt with popular demand for a tonic and a signal that a better future reflected this. Held in 1951 on the South Bank of the Thames, near Waterloo station, and in smaller versions around the country, the Festival of Britain carried the mark of the age of the welfare state, the commitment to planning and paternalism. The Conservative administration which succeeded Labour was not enthusiastic about the festival and instead decided to make the monarchy the focus of patriotism and spectacle.

The royal family enjoyed great popularity after the war and much attention was focused on the young Princess Elizabeth, whose marriage to Philip Mountbatten in 1947 was a great public event that attracted massive press coverage.[28] When the health of her father, King George VI, began to fail four years later, she stood in for him on several public occasions. After he died, in February 1952, *Time* magazine selected the 27-year-old English princess as the world personality who most embodied the hope of the times. She captured on an international scale, the magazine asserted, the mysterious power of ancient monarchs 'to represent, express and effect the aspirations of the collective subconscious'.[29] In fact, the era had seen the overthrow of more than one monarchy and it was the youth and beauty of Elizabeth that appealed most.

The coronation on 2 June 1953 was a grand affair in which pomp and established ritual combined with modern techniques of mass communication. Despite the continuing atmosphere of austerity, the celebration created a new sense of enthusiasm and optimism. Faultlessly planned and executed as a ceremonial ritual by the Duke of Norfolk in his capacity as the Earl Marshal, the coronation was both a national communion and an injection of lavish display into the dingy world of post-war Britain. Hundreds of thousands of people took to the streets of London to glimpse the procession. Many more took part in street parties up and down the land. International interest was high and the Queen's diamond tiara, sash, and Garter star captured wide attention. The first significant public event to be televised, it was viewed by some twenty million people in the United Kingdom and many more abroad. Only the sacred moment of the anointment was concealed from the cameras. The merchandising of the ceremonial was extensive. Mugs, plates, flags, booklets, special newspaper editions, magazines, badges abounded while street parties and church services turned the event into a community celebration. A lavish Technicolor documentary film of the day, narrated by Sir Laurence Olivier, was released in record time to capitalize on the enormous interest the coronation aroused. For royal biographer Robert Lacey, 'the house records which the film *A Queen is Crowned* broke in New York, Boston and Detroit confirmed the global glamour Elizabeth II possessed'.[30]

The success of the event showed that colour and spectacle did not necessarily have to be surrounded by the disorderly hullabaloo that often accompanied the stars. On the contrary, the lavish spectacle of the coronation and images of a happy young queen elevated the monarch to the status of star of stars. At a time when Britain's influence in the world was fast declining, she provided glittering proof that there was nothing more dazzling than a queen. To foreigners, the British royals possessed considerable appeal as celebrities. Magazines like *Paris-Match* in France, *Stern* in Germany, and *Oggi* and *Epoca* in Italy, all of which imitated the highly visual recipe of the American illustrated weekly *Life*, mixed the Windsors into an upbeat diet of leisure and consumption, liberally sprinkled with personalities, gossip, and images of faraway places.[31] Even in Britain newspaper and magazine editors created a soap opera around the royal family and elected the Queen as its star.[32] They regarded the Queen and the royal family as the sole element of hereditary power to be worthy of intense media coverage. For one social historian, 'the monarch was processed into a super personality in whom . . . the audience naturally possessed proprietary rights'.[33] As a newsworthy phenomenon, the monarchy underwent a change that the Queen's consort, Prince Philip, later acknowledged. 'I think the thing, the Monarchy, is part of the kind of fabric of the country. And as the fabric alters, so the Monarchy and its people's relation to it alters,' he reflected.[34] By the late 1960s, he felt, 'I would have thought we were entering probably the least interesting period of the kind of glamorous existence,' whereas fifteen to twenty years earlier 'young people, a young Queen, and a young family [were] infinitely more newsworthy and amusing'.

Royalty encouraged and collaborated in the processes that turned them into star-like figures. In various concealed ways, members of the royal family benefited from the techniques of Hollywood glamour. They were often photographed, for example, by photographers like Cecil Beaton and Dorothy Wilding who had refined their craft on the stars and who knew how to create flattering likenesses, also with the aid of props and retouching techniques.[35] The Queen's official dress designer Hardy Amies confessed that he sometimes drew inspiration from cinema and that one royal gown was modelled on one of Marlene Dietrich's outfits.[36] Yet there was still a significant difference between even an attractive young queen and a film star, whose great appeal lay, first, in being of the people and, second, in being groomed and presented solely for public consumption. In 1957 the author Martin Green argued that one distinction between royal and Hollywood glamour was that the former 'remains essentially well-bred and, as it were, unconscious of the public, so that the latter gets a rather snubby lesson in good behaviour as well as the thrill it came for'.[37] The respectful, not to say submissive, attitude that persisted at least among the British press testified to the continuing prerogatives of the monarchy within a traditional power structure and to the limited nature of pageantry as necessary concession. The hereditary nature of monarchy contrasted with the availability and imitable qualities of the stars. Moreover, even the young and better than averagely good-looking Queen Elizabeth and Prince Philip were deprived of sex appeal by their utter respectability,[38] which had been grasped as a core part of royalty's pact with the nation after the abdication crisis of 1937.

Within a flamboyant ceremonial like the coronation, royal conduct was marked by an element of restraint and inhibition. This expressed a detachment from a public composed not only of spectators but also of subjects from whom deference was expected. The Queen's own view of her role was infused with mysticism.[39] She had prepared for the occasion not by receiving coaching in public relations but by undertaking daily readings from the Scriptures and meditations prepared for her by the Archbishop of Canterbury. In his account of the coronation, the fashion designer Norman Hartnell, who created the coronation dress, stressed the magnificence of the procession, which, he wrote, was 'as though a jewel box has become unloosed and the precious jewels of myriad colours spill upon the velvet floor'.[40] Evoking the fabulous costumes of foreign guests, he described 'an Eastern Imperial Highness [who] gleams in silver and violet tissue, with strange feathers curling from a headgear of purple and amethyst' while 'peacock glory' was offered by another prince, who was adorned with 'brocade of lapis and malachite and ornaments of sapphire and emerald'. However, his tone was far more measured when he referred to the Queen. 'A slight and gentle figure, graceful in her glistering gown, her hands clasped and her eyes cast down,' she advanced 'in beauty and solemnity, most slowly... to her great and lonely station.'[41]

The great and the good of the aristocracy were present in large numbers at the coronation but they counted for even less. The milieu the Queen mixed in seemed to magazine readers to be one largely populated by political figures and celebrities. One of the most notable events in the royal calendar from this point of view was the annual Royal Film Performance. This institution had a long history dating back to 1896. Up until 1948, it was known as the Royal Command

Film Performance. The removal of the imperious 'Command' from the title marked the more democratic atmosphere of the post-war years. Nonetheless, it was clear for whom the event was supposed to be an honour. The arrival of the royal couple was greeted with the national anthem and, at the conclusion of the screening, world-renowned actors lined up to receive the privilege of being presented to Their Royal Highnesses. The Queen, in short, was special and different. The place of movie glamour in the official British scheme of things was decidedly secondary.

Royalty was not so much unglamorous as more than glamorous; precisely because it was something even more magnificent, it exercised a huge appeal. The coronation was widely seen as having consecrated the success of the medium of television not only in Britain but in several continental European countries. The extraordinary interest that had built up around the British monarchy was something that the commercial fabricators of glamour could not ignore. In particular, Hollywood cinema saw in the allure of royalty a repertoire of suggestive associations that could be appropriated or reproduced. After the fall of several monarchies in the aftermath of the First World War, more countries, including Italy, Romania, Bulgaria, and Hungary, and slightly later Egypt, became republics, while others reduced their royal families to the level of state functionaries. This created a gap that the dream merchants were not slow to exploit. At a time when the major film studios, for political and economic reasons, were beginning systematically to make movies on location in Europe, regal elements provided a way of reconfiguring glamour as a blend of upmarket themes. From the American point of view, royalty was a phenomenon of the European past that only made sense when conceived through the prism of glamour. This cultural project fitted very well with the United States' broader aim to remodel West European economies and promote consumerism. The partial absorption of the British royals into a celebrity culture suggested that there was a market for more accessible versions of the royal mystique. Spectacle, beauty, theatricality, and publicity were best organized by the movie studios on a professional basis rather than being left to institutions inherited from the past.

The film that first harnessed the allure of royalty to the practical dreams of the movies was the Paramount light comedy *Roman Holiday*, starring

Gregory Peck and, in her American debut, Audrey Hepburn.[42] Released in the USA in September 1953, the film was an utterly charming story of a princess who briefly escapes from her royal duties while on an official trip to Rome and enjoys a series of incognito pleasures in the company of an American journalist. Hepburn was a completely new type of star. Slender and waif-like, she had the physique of a ballet dancer and the elegance of a fashion model. *Roman Holiday* offered up to film-goers a new and entirely plausible princess figure who, as chance would have it, was descended on her mother's side from the Dutch aristocracy. The film absorbed the public's fascination with monarchy, presenting the female lead as a contemporary version of royalty, and proposed the filmic spectacle itself in the place of rare, time-honoured ritual.[43] By implication, the film declared that from now on it was Hollywood's role to identify and present the new European royalty and to carry out the largely symbolic duties of monarchy. Its task was to transcend national boundaries, create a common cultural currency, and help to imagine and to bring about a future Europe that was peaceful and integrated.[44] The film benefited from an unexpected tie-in when, immediately prior to its release, a scandal exploded over the relationship of England's Princess Margaret with a divorced man, Group Captain Peter Townsend. Both the real and the fictional princess renounced love for duty and appeared to be condemned to sadness.

European cinema did not allow Hollywood a free run in the field of imagined royalty. But it made more use of history to capture the attention of its audience. An actress whose screen persona was endowed with royal elements from the start was Romy Schneider, the Viennese daughter of actors who made her screen debut at the age of 15 in 1953. In a trilogy of lavish German-made colour films about the early years of the beautiful Empress Elizabeth of Austria, which employed the empress's familiar name Sissi in their titles, she provided a charming and nostalgic picture of nineteenth-century Austrian court society. Released between 1955 and 1957,[45] the movies were huge hits with audiences across Western Europe. In consequence a significant fusion occurred between Schneider and Sissi, with the actress being referred to in the German press as 'our "Sissi"' and the 'Crown Princess of German Cinema'.[46] It was assumed that the virginal and girlish qualities attributed to Sissi in the romantic portrait of the films were also attributes of the young actress.

Unusually for an American star, albeit of Dutch–British origins, Hepburn cultivated her own image on screen. By rejecting studio costumes for haute couture, she established herself as a fusion of European and American allure. From the Billy Wilder film *Sabrina*, yet another modern Cinderella tale which was released in the USA a year after *Roman Holiday*, she insisted that her costumes for every contemporary film be designed by the couturier Hubert de Givenchy.[47] As Sabrina, a gardener's daughter who is transformed into a sophisticated young woman by her stay in Paris, Hepburn confirmed her status as an icon of taste and dignity. This began with the scene in *Sabrina* when she makes her appearance in her father's employers' house for her first dance with the debonair playboy David Larrabee, played by William Holden. 'Her dress is sumptuous, her movements aristocratic, her essence fragile. This image was to reverberate like a drum roll,' one commentator noted.[48] Not by accident, some of her most successful films were made with Cary Grant, another actor who personally fostered a highly polished, groomed image that appeared to blend with his personality.[49] More than any other actress, she proved that it was possible simultaneously to be a major star and a fashion leader. It was she who enhanced the clothes she wore rather than vice versa.

In an age when fashion was central to dreams of self-improvement, female fans liked their favourites to be elegant. Following her marriage to Aly Khan, Hayworth became a familiar figure on the European scene. She was often spotted at the racecourses where her husband's thoroughbreds were a prominent fixture, and at fashionable nightclubs. She was also a regular visitor to Paris fashion houses, although, according to the model Bettina, who saw her view the creations of designer Jacques Fath, she was generally bored and irritable on such occasions.[50] Typically, it was the sophisticated Khan who chose the dresses for her. Like many playboys, he had a great knowledge of women's fashions and prided himself on his taste. The refined image that Hayworth acquired enhanced her appeal to fans like Renée Arter, a British film-goer, who years later wrote: 'Although I wished to look like a different star each week depending on what film I saw, I think my favourite was

Rita Hayworth, I always imagined if I could look like her I could toss my red hair into the wind . . . and meet the man of my dreams.'[51] Other stars followed in her wake. Like Hayworth, Ava Gardner came from a very humble background, in her case in North Carolina. A sultry, dark-haired actress who was regarded as one of the world's most beautiful women, she developed an interest in couture clothes while she was filming *The Barefoot Contessa* in Rome. The film told the story of a poor Cinderella who rose to be a star and a countess. It seemed to have been based on a mixture of her own and Hayworth's life stories. During the shoot, Gardner, who at the time was still married to Frank Sinatra, forged a collaboration with the Fontana sisters, who had made Linda Christian's wedding dress. Thanks to Gardner's patronage, the house achieved unprecedented visibility and its creations became the envy of women throughout the world. Few of the couturiers of the post-war years were society figures. Dior was a private man who knew publicity was important but did not enjoy it. Several of his colleagues were remote figures. Only Jacques Fath, whose matinée idol good looks and showy personality made him the darling of the magazines until his untimely death in 1954, followed Jean Patou in mixing with the famous and living ostentatiously.

In a continent that was ravaged by the experiences of dictatorship, war, and foreign occupation, and in which economic hardship and political unrest persisted well into the 1950s, the stars of Hollywood were an ideal and an inspiration. They offered a spectacle of luxury and glamour that was associated with the glamorous impression of America itself as the land of prosperity, sex appeal, and excitement. For the public, the stars were enviable role models who appeared to be living the dreams of millions. They served as a focus not of deference or resentment but of imitation and aspiration. The formation of a new, more attractive, and more public aristocracy of beauty and talent created new centres of prestige and exclusivity, new rituals which drew in younger traditional aristocrats, creating a new more visible, open hierarchy of status that was style imbued with elements of heritage. The old scenarios and palaces continued to serve a role, but mainly as backdrops to an elite that was more open and accessible.

The stars seemed to be independent and free; only one or two voices queried the nature of their position. Simone de Beauvoir, the feminist author of *The Second Sex*, a book which had a wide impact following its publication in 1949, saw Hayworth as a totally dependent figure who, even after she had left her film career, required the constant support of a man 'for her weapons are magical and magic is capricious'.[52] She owed her fame to her face and figure and these were not her property so much as that of Columbia Pictures, which had moulded and polished them for public presentation. Even where they were not tied firmly to a studio, female stars often remained the protégées of a given producer or director. 'The industrialist or producer who offers pearls and furs to his friend affirms through her his fortune and power,' de Beauvoir asserted; 'whether the woman is a means for earning money or a pretext for spending it is immaterial; the servitude is the same. The gifts with which she is weighed down are her chains.'[53] De Beauvoir viewed the female star as a new version of the courtesan adapted to the age of publicity and the mass media. In a context in which the *demi-monde* had become the *monde*, 'the latest incarnation of the *haetera* is the star', she observed. Like the prostitute or courtesan of the past, the star was the modern embodiment of a type of fantasy female that men adored and to which they offered fortune and glory.

By claiming that the *demi-monde* had become the *monde*, de Beauvoir meant that, in the era of mass civilization and publicity, stars had taken over from the established elite in what was dubbed 'the monkey cage of Society'.[54] No longer economically or politically powerful, aristocrats were fast losing their residual social pre-eminence. The historian David Cannadine argues that they were 'inadequately glittering in the age of Hollywood film stars . . . their bright day was done'.[55] In the United States, Britain, and France, the post-war years witnessed significant changes in high society rituals and practices. In Britain the period saw 'the almost total disintegration of patrician high society', while in the United States the world of celebrity eclipsed café society the way this had, in the 1920s, displaced the old elite.[56] In New York, the social commentator Cleveland Amory noted the rise of 'Publi-ciety'. This, he wrote, was 'a combination of publicity and what people used to think of, in happier days, as Society. . . . [It] is the actual ogre under which, whether we like it or not, we all live today. It is a world in which the arbiter is the gossip columnist or, outside of the gossip areas, the

Society columnist. He or she alone, decides who, socially speaking, is who.'[57] In the old days, the high society fixer Elsa Maxwell observed, 'the "old guard" stuck together, saw only each other, talked only about each other. They were the "right people" and they knew it. They were thoroughly satisfied with themselves and the *status quo*. . . . Today all that has changed. Society is mobile, flexible, changing.'[58] It was now common for members of the upper class to work and for debutantes to do things other than wait for a marriage proposal. Social climbers were less concerned to win the accept-ance of the socially prominent than to get their name in the papers. 'It's my firm belief that today, everybody—or nearly everybody—dreams of a star-ring role in the celebrity circus,' Maxwell argued; 'deep down in some secret heart, almost everyone wants to make the headlines.'[59]

The merger of Old World tradition and New World glamour was an irresistible combination. It was one that was constantly evoked in movies, including Grace Kelly's last film, *The Swan*, that eerily foreshadowed her future romance and marriage. Directed by Charles Vidor, the film told the story of a prince, played by Alec Guinness, who is combing Europe in search of a bride. When he is on the point of giving up, he falls for Kelly's Princess Alexandra, leading to a fairy-tale wedding. Kelly was a star whose subtle sex appeal was evident just beneath the surface of her icy exterior.[60] With her fair hair, porcelain complexion, and poise, she had the bearing and appearance of an East Coast debutante. When he first met her, the director Fred Zinne-man 'was astonished and delighted by her demure appearance'. 'She was', he said, 'the first actress I ever interviewed who wore white gloves.'[61] She was of monied Irish stock from Philadelphia and had played socialites in hugely popular films including the musical *High Society* and the Riviera adventure *To Catch A Thief*, for which Edith Head pulled out all the stops to make the actress's costumes among the most elegant ever seen on screen. This image served to mask the director Hitchcock's overtly sexual presentation of the actress in the film. So refined and poised was she that, when her engagement was announced to Prince Rainier of Monaco, it was widely believed in America that she was marrying beneath her. To those Americans who had heard of Monaco, it was a fading resort city best-known for its financial scandals. 'He's Not Good Enough For a Kelly,' headlined the *Chicago*

Tribune, in reference to Prince Rainier, adding boldly: 'She is too well bred a girl to marry the silent partner in a gambling parlour.'[62] It was public knowledge that the controversial Greek shipping magnate Aristotle Onassis had bought a controlling share in the Société des Bains de Mer which owned Monaco's casino, leading hotel, and various other facilities.

The marriage of Grace Kelly and Prince Rainier in April 1956 constituted the acme of the process of appropriation that began with *Roman Holiday*. Although, as in the early twentieth century, there were several weddings in the period between aristocrats and actresses, nothing staged subsequently would eclipse this event. The evolution of Grace Kelly into Princess Grace of Monaco offered a vindication of the dream factory's ability to invent social types. It also showed that the language of glamour of Hollywood could absorb older images of luxury and splendour.[63] The ceremony was orchestrated by the Metro-Goldwyn-Mayer studio. In return for suspending Kelly's film contract indefinitely, the studio exercised considerable control over the organization of the nuptials. It made a gift to the bride of all the clothes she had worn in *High Society* and it also paid the Oscar-winning costume designer Helen Rose to create a magnificent wedding dress. The making of this stunning gown required six weeks' work by no fewer than three dozen seamstresses. The designer claimed that it was the most expensive she ever made.[64] Rainier also dressed up, designing himself a sky blue, black, and gold uniform based on those worn by Napoleon's marshals. Metro owned the exclusive film rights to the ceremony and installed its lights and cameras, alongside television cameras, for both the civil and religious ceremony. The civil ceremony was staged a second time purely for the benefit of the studio, which made a documentary, *The Wedding of the Century*, that was later shown in cinemas throughout the world. The religious service in Monaco's cathedral was viewed on television by thirty million people in nine European countries. Among the six hundred guests were many royals and several film stars. A handful of reporters sneaked in disguised as cassocked priests while one of the most notorious Riviera jewel thieves was a chauffeur in the wedding party.[65] 'In the mid-Twentieth Century, somehow it was extremely fitting, in the general picture of Society, that the crowning climax to the long history of America's title search should be delivered by an American movie star,' Amory reflected. The marriage was also a landmark event in another way for, in contrast to the respectful treatment of Queen Elizabeth's coronation, it fixed a new benchmark in the power, prestige, and pushiness of the press.[66] According to celebrity social organizer Elsa Maxwell, 'the ceremony itself, a beautiful old-world extravaganza, was reduced in newsprint to a large and rather gaudy carnival.'[67]

The wedding consolidated the popular passion for fashion and elevated aristocratic-type stars and models to a central position in its diffusion. The mania that the event unleashed in the United States created an appetite for a certain type of sophisticated woman. One figure who catered to this was a journalist called Eugenia Sheppard, who wrote a fashion column for the New York *Herald Tribune*. Like the gossip columnists of the 1920s, who chased after the chic and the stylish women of their time, she elevated a category of women into heroines of her reports. In contrast to the interwar years, her 'fashion-society celebrities' were solely heroines of consumption. What they did and who they mixed with was of much less interest than what they wore. Sheppard began her column immediately after Grace Kelly's wedding and became a cheerleader for the fashion industry, 'one of fashion's go-go girls' as she was once dubbed.[68] She became an indispensable fixture on New York's party lists and was soon the darling of wealthy women who relished the chance to join the envied realm of publicity. Her rise marked a peculiar kind of inversion. Whereas, before the Kelly wedding, female stars had aspired to marry into aristocracy or even royalty, achievement of this objective heralded a new phenomenon according to which society women became as hungry for publicity and as eager and desperate starlets.[69] In earlier decades they had sought recognition in the press of their pre-eminent status. Now they wanted acknowledgement of their pre-eminent stylishness. In Sheppard's writing, clothes were always central. They were the vehicle through which women gained citizenship in the realm of publicity and acquired a position of dependency on the garment industry.

The style leaders included women like C. Z. Guest, the Duchess of Windsor, and Princess Grace. Barbara 'Babe' Paley, Gloria Guinness, Slim Keith, Marella Agnelli, and other trophy wives were women who had married men so rich that they had the freedom to pursue an aesthetic quality in life.

Sophisticated, beautiful, and stylish, they set the standards of chic in their time. In Europe and America they were regarded as 'high priestesses of the social arts, avatars with a secret knowledge of beauty, fashion, decorating and entertaining'.[70] The press fawned over them and they attracted some notable flatterers, including the writer Truman Capote, who became the confidant of several of them. A gossipy charmer, he idolized the wealth and style of women he saw as elegant swans. It was striking that almost none of them was in fact high-born. What appealed to Capote about them, beyond their wealth and style, which invoked in him—and many others—feelings of awe and envy, was the fact that 'they all had stories to tell': 'Few of them had been born to wealth or position; they had not always glided on serene and silvery waters; they had struggled, schemed and fought to be where they were,' his biographer commented. 'They had created themselves, as he himself had done. Each was an artist, he said, "whose sole creation was her perishable self".'[71]

Like Jacqueline Bouvier, who, as the wife of President John F. Kennedy, would be credited with restoring aristocratic taste to the White House, these women presented a version of upper-class manners that was appealing and comprehensible to a broader public. To adopt the historian Paul Fussell's classification of the American class system, they belonged not to the 'top out-of-sight' class but to the more visible 'upper' or 'upper middle' brackets.[72] Even Babe Paley who, between her marriages to two of America's richest men, had been a fashion editor of *Vogue*, was essentially a figure in this category. She and her second husband, CBS chief William Paley, lived in a suite at the St Regis Hotel in New York during the week and on a huge estate on Long Island. Although they preferred to socialize privately, Babe was a public figure who was regarded as an icon of elegance.[73] She regularly appeared on best-dressed lists and was always immaculately turned-out. As one of the first 'fashion-society celebrities',[74] she provided American women with an example of a picture-perfect glamorous lifestyle. No-one guessed that behind the image there was the heartbreak of a marriage that was based more on ambition than love.[75]

By contrast to the pre-war era, socialites were fully immersed in the commercial sector. For companies engaged in the various branches of the luxury trade, they had immense promotional value. The great cosmetics houses traded on ideas of exclusivity and refinement and they required the validation of great names. For example, Elizabeth Arden aimed to 'capture the aura of the drawing rooms of the great mansions that lined upper Fifth Avenue'.[76] At her New York beauty salon, consultations were held in the white-and-gold Oval Room, while treatment rooms were decorated in subdued pastels. Touches of gold and silver, a combination signalling wealth and taste,[77] were also regularly used on Arden packaging. Revlon's salons were no less striking. Clients were dazzled by the extravagant gold-and-white decor and the innovative lighting design.[78]

Estée Lauder also sought to capture the mystery and glamour of elegant society and market it to a wider public. She associated with Princess Grace, the Duchess of Windsor, and others. Lauder herself was the result of a feat of self-creation. Born in New York in 1908 to a humble Jewish family, she completely erased her origins in order to turn her name into a signifier of glamour, exclusivity, and social cachet.[79] She sold not just fragrances or cosmetics, but dreams, fantasies, and ideals of beauty.[80] The Lauder name signified domestic luxury and gracious living. Her aspiration, she claimed in her memoirs, was to use elegance and class rather than sex appeal to sell her products. The Lauder woman was 'classic', 'a sophisticated woman with charm and éclat, as well as beauty' who was 'sensual rather than sexy'. She was 'successful' and 'had that certain, indefinable air known as class'.[81] In particular she pursued good taste, which meant 'classic design for image and packaging'. To this end, Lauder even marketed solid perfume in elegant porcelain eggs, trimmed in gold and etched in enamel, which looked in every way like Fabergé eggs. She also incorporated aristocratic resonances into the advice she offered on elegant living, for example on table decoration. For fifteen years a single model of unmistakable WASP appearance, Karen Graham, was the face of Estée Lauder.

There was undoubtedly a conservative aspect to the preoccupation with style and status. Right-wing writers seized the opportunity to turn aristocracy into an aesthetic curiosity bathed in nostalgia and near-extinct beauty. For example, in his 1944 novel, *Brideshead Revisited*, English Catholic Evelyn Waugh offered an alluring portrait of the 1920s world of the aristocratic

Flyte family. The novel was narrated from the point of view of an outsider who meets the golden boy Sebastian Flyte at Oxford and is drawn into a magical world whose existence he had barely dreamed existed. Far from being a careful evocation of a bygone world, this was a false picture for the consumption of middle-class readers. Informed observers noticed that, in his fawning passion for the upper classes, Waugh had 'overdrawn the aristocratic glamour'.[82] Like the 'silver fork' novelists of one hundred years earlier, he conveyed his own enthusiasm for a partly imagined aristocracy to eager middle-class readers.

At precisely the moment when conventional high society ceased to be the aristocratic ideal prospered as a deracinated mood or look. The reworking of refinement that marked the 1950s was accompanied by a flowering of feminine images shot through with aloofness and elitist chic. The idea of class, breeding, taste, refinement, and style enjoyed widespread currency. Indeed, as qualities detached from any direct and structured social referent, refinement and sophistication were appropriated by a wide variety of commercial activities and professions. In this sense, the Paris couturiers were the handmaidens of a new sort of aristocracy. The tall, slim, angular woman, perfectly groomed and cool, proliferated in magazines and advertisements. Although these images were unapproachable for some women, they were not as far removed from the average as might be thought. They often showed women acting in a confident and sophisticated way in public places, unencumbered by family and domestic duties.[83] Others, in particular those of Richard Avedon, whose photographs for *Harper's Bazaar* in these years established him as the world's leading fashion photographer, were passionate, adventurous, and imaginative. His models were not static; they laughed, smiled, and held the stage. His famous picture of the model Dovima in a Dior evening gown standing arms aloft between two elephants seemed to say that couture could astonish even in the jungle.[84] Images of models like Lisa Fonssagrives and Bettina, and by extension those of other models of their type and some sophisticated film stars, actually seemed accessible to all women. In contrast to the indistinct debutantes that Cecil Beaton continued to photograph, they offered grace, balance, and reserve, combined with a certain energy.[85] Such women appeared to be in control and true to themselves.

Fonssagrives's background in dance gave her a sense of theatre so that her outfits never looked mannered or awkward. Rather she appeared to be engaged in a comfortable masquerade that could be copied by anyone.[86] In fact, the models of the post-war years sometimes only had the appearance of refined women. The most celebrated French model was Praline, who for Ginette Spanier of the Balmain fashion house was 'the last of the great French mannequins—the Mistinguett of the Haute Couture'.[87] As a working-class girl who joined the elite caste of haute couture models, she became a popular figure who embodied French beauty and chic. In addition to her fashion work, she won several competitions including Miss Cinémonde. In an autobiographical book published in 1951, she described how her life changed as she became the first 'mannequin volant'.[88] Dior and other designers had begun the custom of sending French models abroad to promote their creations and Praline was among the pioneers. She recounted at length her travels, especially a trip to Hollywood during which she met many stars, offering a picture of a lifestyle that to readers will have seemed highly glamorous. Thus the rise of the pedigreed woman blended with a popularization of elite images. It did not amount to any sort of social restoration. In fact, the last English debutantes were presented at court in 1958.

Due to commercial air travel and faster communications, international society developed a genuinely cosmopolitan flavour. Newport, Nassau, and Montego Bay, together with old elite centres such as Cannes, Nice, Monte Carlo, Capri, Ischia, and Portofino, became the playgrounds of a cosmopolitan coterie of wealthy nomads. Paris too, with its unrivalled night life and high style, and Rome, with its cafés, restaurants, grand hotels, and expanding film industry, attracted fun-seekers. Monaco developed into a glamorous Mecca for film stars and celebrities. The principality had languished since Elsa Maxwell had been hired in the 1920s to update the Casino and the Hôtel de Paris and to stage events that would draw the cream of international café society. Despite the influence of Aristotle Onassis, it now acquired an unfamiliar air of respectability that was heightened by the presence of Princess Grace. She was a fairytale princess who in an instant brushed away Monte Carlo's louche and declining image and made it once more a focus of international society. Due to her influence, traditional customs, such as the annual pigeon shoot, were done away with and replaced by grand charitable fund-raising events at which Frank Sinatra, David Niven, and Cary Grant were regular guests.[89] Thanks to an injection of Hollywood glamour, the royal family acquired celebrity value. By blending the mythology of the princess with the allure of the star, Grace became something uniquely appealing, a modern hybrid of class and style. Although some observers in the early 1960s still found that 'Monaco in those days was something out of Central Casting. Dowager Russian princesses and out-of-work Balkan kings....a very stodgy watering spot for European millionaires and down-at-heel aristocrats,' things soon changed.[90] A building boom reflected the new aura that the principality acquired. With its white buildings and palm trees and its fairytale princess, it took on a new Ruritanian charm.[91] Hotels were revitalized, races and rallies sponsored, and artistic events held. By inviting actors and celebrities in her capacity as president of the Monaco Red Cross, Grace provided the magic touch that Monaco had lacked since the belle époque.[92] Other resorts, notably Capri, retained the hedonistic reputation that they gained earlier. Invaded by movie stars and wealthy Americans, the island became the synonym of money, extravagance, and excess. With its numerous famous, wealthy, and artistic visitors, it became a breeding ground of casual fashions, images of relaxed pleasure, and legends of sexual indulgence.[93] All this gave it the glamour of a modern paradise.

Grace and Rainier became central figures in the glittering Mediterranean social carousel. They were joined by several deposed and exiled former rulers who congregated in capital cities and watering holes. The Duke and Duchess of Windsor were one of the most prominent couples in international café society. Ever since the Duke's abdication from the British throne in 1937, they had moved between Paris, New York, Biarritz, Cap d'Antibes, and the Bahamas, where they were welcomed with open arms. Edward had never liked solemnity or ritual but, in exile, he and Wallis sought perfection in their immediate environment and in the construction of a ritualized lifestyle. Wallis became a fashion icon who endlessly pursued style, obsessively attending fashion shows and beauty salons, going shopping, and attending parties. She became an expert on interior decoration and jewellery, of which she had a most extensive collection. They were a king and queen of café society, who were sustained by rich friends who derived social cachet from their association with them. They became the epitome of the international jet set, a glamorous couple who lived in the same realm as movie stars.

The increasing internationalization of social life was accompanied by the expansion of American business abroad. Hotelier Conrad Hilton emerged in this period as the proprietor of a chain of luxury hotels that extended from the United States to Western Europe and beyond. He regarded his foreign hotels as outposts of American civilization and he sought to attract to them the same mixture of crowned heads, celebrities, prime ministers, diamond millionaires, and admirals that patronized the Waldorf-Astoria in New York, which he had bought in 1945. 'Rome and Madrid interested me mightily from the standpoint of building hotels,' he wrote. 'An integral part of my dream was to show the countries most exposed to Communism the other side of the coin—the fruits of the free world.' In Rome he found much support among the ruling Christian Democrats for his project of a new hotel, but considerable opposition from Communists, who were a significant opposition force on the city council. Hilton understood luxury but lacked extensive experience of women. 'My first five years as an innkeeper in Texas involved me in . . . a series of romances in which girls played little part,' he later wrote.[94] 'I found myself developing a real crush on each potential hotel. . . . Romance blossomed the minute I could see through a frowsy facade to potential glamour—the inherent ability to make money.'

On one occasion that he would come to regret, he succumbed to the lure of glamour instead of deploying it to entrap others. His short marriage to the Hungarian actress Zsa Zsa Gabor, who in total would marry eight times, taught him that glamour could also be costly. With hindsight, he regarded her as a luxury too far. 'Glamour, I found, is expensive, and Zsa Zsa was glamour raised to the last degree,' he wailed.[95] 'She also knew more days on which gifts could be given than appear on any holiday calendar. And then, of course, you could always give gifts because it was no special day at all and thereby transform it. Zsa Zsa was not always on the receiving end by any manner of means. She herself loved to give. She showered presents and attentions on my mother . . . and for me there were custom shirts and solid gold cuff links, most of which showed up mysteriously on my charge accounts.'

Foreign cities and resorts resonated with tradition and style, but they also, in some instances, had strong bohemian associations. They provided opportunities not so much for formal socializing, with all its protocol and stiffness, but for the rich and famous to let their hair down. The rapid transformation of Italy from a Fascist dictatorship and backward economy into a dynamic centre of style and beauty saw the capital, and the country's most beautiful coastal resorts, develop into elite playgrounds. Thanks to the presence of the American film studios and the expansion of the local film industry into one of the largest in the world, Rome became a magnet for a heterogeneous mixture of deposed monarchs, displaced aristocrats, gold-diggers and playboys, artists, and actors. When the Swedish starlet Anita Ekberg, who had arrived in Italy in 1955 to take a supporting role in *War and Peace*, married the English actor Anthony Steel in Florence six weeks after the Monaco extravaganza, the event was deliberately low-key and informal. A woman whose curves were so generous that one journalist observed, after her arrival in the Italian capital, that the hills of Rome were no longer seven but nine, Ekberg acquired a reputation for refusing to cooperate with the press. American reporters dubbed her 'Anita Iceberg'. Her civil wedding was intended to be simple and definitely not grand 'à la Kelly'. However, Steel gave her an engagement ring that was proclaimed as the biggest in the world and press curiosity was intense. She chose as a wedding dress a daring off-the-shoulder gown that provoked condemnation in the British press. For some observers, it was more suited to Tarzan's companion Jane than a bride.[96] The couple were followed everywhere by photographers, who even broke into the apartment they had rented to snap their bedroom and living room. Despite these and other difficulties with the press, Steel and Ekberg smiled and waved endlessly for the curious public who stopped to applaud them as they drove through the streets in an open horse-drawn carriage.

No star was less associated with formality than Brigitte Bardot and no star was more adept at making her off-screen life just as newsworthy, and sometimes as remunerative, as screen performance. Bardot became famous above all for her look—the pouting lips and tousled, apparently sun-bleached hair—and for her amorous liaisons. The latter were publicized more heavily than her films. She rejected many aspects of the official imagery of the star in favour of a more apparently natural manner. From the 1956 film *Et Dieu créa la femme,* which turned her into a star, she was associated with St Tropez, a small fishing village that in time would become no less exclusive than Monte Carlo while preserving a casual feel. Thanks in part to Bardot, the Côte d'Azur was reinvented in the 1950s as a paradise where the sun always shone and the beautiful people were at play.[97] The consequences of the association of star and place were perceived by the celebrity photographer Edward Quinn, who spent the 1950s looking for opportunities for unlicensed snaps outside the Riviera's great hotels and at gala evenings in Monte Carlo—places that had once been the stamping grounds of La Belle Otero and Liane de Pougy: 'The worldwide fame of St Tropez, on the extreme west of the Côte d'Azur, dates from the Fifties, thanks partly to that new vehicle of liberty, the motor car, partly, of course, to Brigitte Bardot,' he observed. 'Until then only a few artists and aristocrats had heard of the place and it was visited by a small elite. It was very hard to get to then...but after popular tourism reached it in the Fifties, St Tropez was invaded. It became overcrowded, especially during the summer, and it lost its former charm.... The Côte d'Azur during the "Golden Fifties" was one of the largest and most beautiful stages in the world. Its actors were magnificent and glamorous. And though the curtain has gone down, the memories remain.'[98]

Bardot struck a blow against some of the traditional canons of movie star glamour. She rejected the costly gowns and rigid formality of previous French stars and instead proposed a casual, yet sexy and glamorous, alternative that consisted of gingham dresses, Capri pants, and striped tops, that were left cheekily unbuttoned.[99] Her imperfect, bottle blonde mane symbolized her casual, carefree manner. In an era in which stiffness reigned, she offered a dream of emancipation and an image of unlimited desire. Bardot was hugely successful abroad but highly controversial at home. French women in particular disliked her, but so too did some critics. 'Paul Reboux said of me that I had the physique of a servant girl and the way of speaking of the functionally illiterate,' Bardot later wrote.[100] For over a decade, Bardot would attract the photographers at the Cannes film festival like nobody else. 'She was so world-renowned by 1957 that when she hosted her own "BB" festival party,' the festival's historians write, 'the Hollywood trades reported it had to be held in nearby Nice to accommodate the four hundred police-men necessary to guard the event. Other papers concentrated on the fact that the hostess was clearly without underwear beneath her T-shirt and jeans.'[101] Bardot herself acutely perceived the nature of her rebellion: 'Sophia Loren and Gina Lollobrigida, the big stars of the festival that year would only appear in public with their bosoms and diamonds on show, in costly fur coats, sumptuous gowns and Rolls ... in other words in all the indispensable finery of cinematic *noblesse oblige*. I was not part of the system and this was the original and worrying thing.'[102]

Bardot's men included some of the many playboys who made the Medi-terranean their special stage. These were men like David Larrabee (William Holden), the charmer who, in *Sabrina*, woos the eponymous heroine before she opts for his dour, but safe, brother Linus, played by Humphrey Bogart. Like birds of prey, they gravitated around upwardly mobile women, whether they were film stars, heiresses, or beautiful ingénues. Both Prince Rainier and Aly Khan were men of this type. Like other men who led lives of privilege, they were attracted to the stars like bees to a honey-pot. At a time when male screen actors did not necessarily have to be likeable, rather they were expected to reveal a troubled side, a malaise, or a concern, the playboys caught the public's imagination. Stars like Yves Montand or Marcello Mastroianni combined physical authority with a certain authenti-city. For each of them, acting seemed like an extension of a persona forged through real experience. According to French author Pierre Cendrars, post-war films 'no longer offered perfect heroes or shop dummies. To please, the leading man, he had for better or worse to be sincere ... To last, a young actor had to make people forget that he was handsome.'[103] No such stric-tures applied to the heroes of the gossip pages. Fiat heir Gianni Agnelli, Brazilian entrepreneur Francisco 'Baby' Pignatari, Dominican diplomat Porfirio Rubirosa, and others avoided steady work and instead devoted themselves to life's pleasures. They loved fast cars, dangerous sports, luxury yachts, air travel, gambling, fine tailoring, nightlife, and the pursuit of women.[104] Like the *viveurs* and devotees of *galanterie* in the belle époque, they were engaged in a constant competition with each other and with themselves. They were rarely in one place for more than a short time and set great store by whim. With his marriages to Flora, the daughter of the Dominican dictator Trujillo, French actress Danielle Darrieux, and the heiresses Doris Duke and Barbara Hutton, the handsome gold-digger Rubirosa was a gift to the news media. With his legendary virility and range of questionable diplomatic and financial dealings, he was a regular hero of the celebrity gossip features that replaced the old society pages in the press.

The playboys usually saw their women as temporary appendages or transient passions, but there were a few who figured more prominently. These included Anita Ekberg after the failure of her marriage, Linda Christian after her separation from Tyrone Power—and the latter's sudden death from a heart attack—and the English socialite Pamela Churchill, who was linked to Agnelli and who was with him when he suffered a car crash that nearly cost his life. Rome became their preferred destination as the city's once tame nightlife came to life with the opening of numerous bars and nightclubs in the vicinity of the glittering Via Veneto. However, they found themselves at risk from packs of young freelance photographers who hung around on street corners or on Vespa scooters ready to snap the illicit behaviour of celebrities who were away from home. Even playboys like Baby Pignatari—who enjoyed a turbulent on-off relationship with Linda Christian—found themselves caught in their lenses. Gianni Agnelli escaped his liaison with Ekberg from being exposed by paying off reporters and editors. The birth of the 'paparazzi' phenomenon in Rome signalled a change in the nature of modern celebrity. Stars were no longer aloof figures to be placed on a pedestal and worshipped, but ordinary mortals who succumbed easily to the temptations of the flesh. In the eyes of readers of Rome's *Lo Specchio*, or of the *Paris-Match* or the London *Evening Standard*, the film colony in Rome provided a continuous feast of scandals including adultery, attempted suicides, orgies, and drugs. The New York gossip magazine *Confidential* and other scandal sheets with names like *Hush-Hush, Whisper, Wink,* and *Inside Story* supplied the salacious details and speculation that even these publications shied away from.

Scandals did not damage the glamour of Rome, but rather lent it a dark but compelling hue that director Federico Fellini would exploit in his masterful depiction of the cosmopolitan Rome, *La dolce vita*. This was a film that both absorbed all the movie glamour that had assembled in the Italian capital, and presented it in concentrated form, and explored the disintegration of this in a series of set piece scenes that registered the decline of the intellectuals, the break between generations, the meaninglessness of contemporary religion, the hypocrisy of the famous, the irrelevance of the aristocracy, and the worship of the worthless. Through all this, Marcello Mastroianni as a press agent and the bored socialite Maddalena, played by French actress Anouk Aimée, cruise as two stylish black-clad nightowls who glide over the surface of the human debris that surrounds them.

La dolce vita consecrated the eternal city's reputation for sex and sensation. It became, in the public imagination, a place where the dominant moral values of society were routinely transgressed. For public opinion, the most scandalous event of the period was the flagrant adultery that was committed by Elizabeth Taylor and her co-star Richard Burton during the filming in Rome of Joseph Mankiewicz's blockbuster *Cleopatra*. Taylor was already a legend and was by far the bigger star in 1962. Burton impressed her with his theatrical credentials. Despite the fact that both actors were in Rome with their respective spouses, they were drawn irresistibly to each other. When they were snapped kissing on set, the press and the public assumed that their playing of two of history's greatest lovers had spilled over into reality. Immediately their liaison—which was not yet admitted by either party—became a matter of speculation on the part of columnists. For months, they dominated the headlines and when their adultery was incontrovertible, they were sternly condemned by the Church and sectors of the press. However, in contrast to the early 1950s, the scandal did not lead to disgrace. Neither actor cared much for public opinion or for convention and they revelled in being at the centre of press attention. Their messy and drawn-out separations from their spouses and emergence as a couple transfixed the public. The fact that the tryst had begun in Rome made it all seem understandable and even forgivable.[105] Moreover, there was a great rush to cash in on the part of 20th Century Fox and the press, while Burton found that his link to Taylor had turned him into a superstar. Offers of work poured in provided that both of them were in the cast. The second film they made together, a Terence Rattigan-scripted drama set largely in the VIP lounge at London's Heathrow airport, was released with the title *The VIPs*. The parts they played seemed not unlike their real selves, a fact that was not accidental since Rattigan had more or less written them directly into his screenplay. It was released not long after *Cleopatra* and was a hit, even eclipsing the notorious blockbuster in box office revenues. For several years, Taylor and Burton defined the meaning of glamour as their disregard for conventional mores made them seem larger than life and their lavish lifestyle caught the public imagination. In an age in which movement and international travel were coming within the reach of middle-class families, they were pioneer members of the 'jet set'. By breaking the rules of respectability and getting away with it, they showed that celebrities were no longer subject to the same moral judgements as everyone else. Their glamour lifted them into a realm that was beyond the reach of the guardians of social order.

CHAPTER 8

GLAMOUR AND MASS CONSUMPTION

A merica in the 1950s was a land of optimism and plenty, a land where all the problems of man seemed to have been solved and where prosperity was no longer a dream but a lived experience. Scarcity was gone for ever and the healthiest and wealthiest generation in history was living a life that was projected towards a future of ever greater opportunities and comforts. Despite the Korean War and fears, in the early part of the decade, that the cold war would lead to another major conflict, the period was America's golden age. It enjoyed a far higher average standard of living than anywhere else in the world. More than at any other time, the world looked at the United States with wonderment at the abundance of its goods, the dynamism of its entertainment, and the lavishness and ease of its citizens' lives. For hard-pressed Britons and French people, many of whom were still living in wartime conditions of scarcity, America was nothing short of a dreamland. However, unlike in the interwar years, when Hollywood's images of American life were experienced as pure fantasy, after 1945, these were connected to a realizable future. For the first time, the lifestyle of a whole country appeared to resonate with glamour. In its involvement in European reconstruction and development, the United States made great play of its success in combining democracy and prosperity. It promised, through the Marshall Plan, to help convert economies to the mass production systems that it had pioneered in the 1920s. Europeans were led to believe that, if they voted for pro-Western parties and worked hard, then they too would be able to live in the American way and sample the fruits of prosperity. The propaganda effort that was developed to support the Marshall Plan told Europeans 'You Too Can Be Like Us'. Through trains, exhibitions, talks, slide shows, posters, magazine articles, and many other means, the way ahead from economic recovery to modernity and progress was indicated by means of economic know-how, modern techniques, fashions, personalities, and lifestyles.[1] The plan's cheerleaders did not just seek to persuade governments and business organizations, they also reached out to ordinary people and sought to influence their dreams and aspirations.

The post-war United States was an imperium with the outlook of an emporium, the historian Victoria de Grazia has written.[2] It made use not just of economic power and political leverage but 'soft power' to persuade Europeans towards its model of mass consumption for all. It did not just wield a stick to make its allies fall into line, it offered a carrot in the form of movies, stars, and a stream of new products and lifestyle suggestions. One of the features of this soft power was glamour. There was a feminine sensibility to the way American consumerism presented itself as the housewife's friend and promoter of familial domesticity. But there was also a systematic use of female imagery to sell products including motor cars, hotels, vacations, grooming aids, and fragrances to men. The tensions between domesticated and eroticized female appeals was played out not only in the mass media and the leisure industries but also in the new dialectic that the American-led consumer revolution created between the United States and Western Europe.[3] Although the United States was far ahead of Europe in its experience of mass consumption, this could not evolve without constant new stimuli. While Europeans were exposed to far more American and American-inspired images than vice versa, Americans were drawn to European ideas of sophistication, class, taste, and sex and to the products that somehow embodied them. Air travel boomed, facilitating tourism, while magazines, continental movies, Hollywood runaway productions, and imported goods

232

fuelled regular encounters and exchanges. Although American-style glamour was dominant in the post-war decades, it incorporated a significant European component that was made up of national elements that on occasion took on the form of variants on the dominant model.

Various facets of the American lifestyle were dressed with glamour, but none was more immediately attractive than the motor car. The mass production motor car had been a phenomenon of the 1920s and it remained, through the 1950s and beyond, the cornerstone of the American economy. It drove the American consumer society and it was also what would propel European economies towards growth and development. In the projection of the United States, cars were not merely useful appliances that Americans owned, but fabulous wonder vehicles that seemed like a mixture of a warplane and a living room. The American car, on the basis of size alone, kick-started the imagination. The fact that it was also styled in the most impossibly alluring of ways gave a potent symbolism to mass motorization. It was inconceivable that anyone driving such a triumphant blend of fact and fantasy was not filled with optimism and confidence.

As early as the late 1920s, American manufacturers realized that customers did not just see cars solely as utilitarian tools but as objects of status and desire. Ford's strategy of cutting the price on his model T and making cars as basic as possible was replaced by a new emphasis on styling which ensured that cars first, and then many other material objects, became associated with images and ideas that were highly symbolic. The development of styling came to a halt during the war years only to be resumed from the late 1940s. The form it took was the tail fin, a design touch that at first provoked perplexity and then became associated with prestige. Due to wartime advances in electronics and moulded plastics, as well as assembly-line production, the hugely productive American economy was transformed into a consumer economy on a scale without precedent. Every manufactured artefact—from the motor car and the refrigerator to the toaster and the teapot—was redesigned to include a quotient of fantasy and style. Colour and shape were the twin tools of this reconfiguration of the object world.

The first suggestion of tail fins appeared on the 1948 Cadillac, but for the most part goods conserved a streamlined appearance until the mid-1950s, when the end of the first, tense years of the cold war gave way to a more optimistic mood. The 1955 Chevrolet has been seen as the turning point. This was not a luxury brand like the Cadillac, but a routine one that hitherto had been associated with basic transportation needs. This affordable model marked the first of a series that looked exciting; it had a mildly futuristic appearance, was available in lively colours, and gave its driver a sense of prosperity. Not only had the one-time luxury become a necessity; it had done so without losing the air of luxury that made it desirable in the first place. In the following years a whole repertoire of motifs and decorative features were incorporated into cars that grew larger and larger. From the bottom of the range Chevrolet to the top of the range Cadillac, every car became in some measure a dream car. The man who is credited with having turned styling into a key part of the design, manufacture, and selling of automobiles, Harley Earl, headed the Art and Colour department at the General Motors (GM) Corporation from 1927 until 1959. He had been born in Hollywood and began his career as a customizer of cars for the stars. His main task at GM was to invent dream cars that would present new ideas and test public taste.[4] Visual ideas were meant to stimulate aspirations and build the market for the models of the future. The first dream cars were large in size and had a sculpted look to them. The bends and curves of their chassis reflected the fact that they were first modelled in clay rather than the conventional wood. Earl himself would often use test vehicles for his personal transport, delighting in astonishing the members of the golf and country clubs he frequented. His aim was not to come up with the perfect design but rather to offer a variety of different ones that would appeal to different fantasies.

Optimism and opulence were not just moods of the time but qualities that were incorporated into generously styled vehicles available in a range of colours and models. Fabulous and enormous American cars were the product of a series of developments whereby objects took on a special exaggerated quality that expressed confidence, excitement, and even joy.[5] The fantasy element in the American automobiles of the 1950s came from two sources. The first of these was aviation. Earl was fascinated by planes, especially military fighter planes such as the Lockheed P-38 Lightning.[6] He took the impression of sleekness and speed that they had and used it to create cars that were longer and lower than before. He named his first post-war dream car the Le Sabre XP-8 after the F86 Sabre jet of the US airforce. Later he took inspiration from the delta-wing, needle-nosed Douglas F-4D Skyray, whose spectacular appearance would influence the entire automotive industry.[7] Several companies manufactured cars with aviation features; one of the earliest being the bullet-nosed 1950 Studebaker. Cars often incorporated aviation imagery into their advertising or directly into their names, such as the Thunderbird, launched by Ford in 1953. Earl's second source of inspiration was Hollywood. In his view, design was about entertainment and he wrote in numerous magazine articles that he particularly admired Cecil B. De Mille, from whom he learned large-scale theatricality, and Al Jolson, who taught him how to understand and respond to an audience. He connected with the public by providing it with emotionally satisfying signs of stylishness and prestige.

In the age of Earl, the presentation of cars itself became a branch of show business. At the Motorama shows that were held in various cities, new ideas and prototypes were presented in a theatrical fashion. Placed on stages and illuminated to maximize their dramatic presence and gleaming allure, they dazzled a public that was alert to visual novelty. The aim was to stimulate its desires by holding out the prospect of something new and better that was two or three years away. The unveiling of new models each year, a novelty of this period that reflected the development of planned obsolescence, was treated in a manner akin to the exploitation of a new film. The public had to be wowed and persuaded to buy in large numbers while the item still had the appeal of newness. The epitome of what Chrysler called the 'Forward Look' was its slogan for 1957: 'Suddenly it's 1960!'[8]

Even though American cars were unashamedly mass manufactured, few standard models were sold. Optional extras, customized details, and colours chosen from an ample range, including two-tones, meant that each vehicle had something different. Cars became fashion statements and were dispensed with as soon as their shape or colour was no longer the mode. A vehicle's appearance gave some indication of the taste and attitudes of the person who drove it. This applied even to the more economical makes and models. Styling was not for the privileged few, like the stars whose cars Earl had once customized. Everyone was willing to pay a little extra for some additional non-functional mark of luxury.[9] The car designs of this period were not tasteful. Nor, despite their jet-plane echoes, were they particularly fast. They were eye-catching celebrations of individuality and status, expressions of 'rampant vulgarity and joy'.[10] The car that more than any other exemplified the exuberant design excesses of the decade was the 1959 Cadillac Coupe de Ville. This enormous vehicle was the motoring equivalent of an all-singing, all-dancing stage-show. Fantastically long and wide, its hyperbolic tail fins and bullet lights gave it the appearance of a vehicle more geared to space travel that cruising along freeways. Adorned with acres of chrome on its front and rear, it screamed luxury and limitless opulence.

For the Canadian Marshall McLuhan, one of the most attentive observers of the impact of mass communications in the age of high mass consumption, the car was a great unifier that had reduced social distance as well as physical space. It bypassed all differences of class and race, uniting motorists and making pedestrians into second-class citizens. The car 'more than any horse . . . is an extension of man that turns the rider into a superman', he declared, observing that 'an American is a creature on four wheels'.[11] By labelling it a 'mechanical bride', he alluded to the powerful sexual symbolism of the car. For men, ownership of a vehicle became a sign of virility and sex appeal as well as status. While sports models functioned as a means of peacock display to attract women, the softer curves and friendlier grille designs that in mid-decade substituted the aggressiveness of models like the Plymouth Fury turned the car itself into a woman who had already been captured and tamed. The connection between cars and sex was deliberately exploited by advertisers and marketers following the discovery, by pioneer advertiser Ernest Dichter, that glamorous convertibles in a showroom had the appeal of a mistress to men who came looking for a wifely family vehicle.[12] The theory was that, if they could be induced to fantasize about the former, they would end up being seduced into buying one of the middle-of-the-road saloons on offer.

In the USA, the automobile was fully integrated into the routine pattern of everyday life where it fulfilled practical functions. 'The automobile is part of domestic life and is an extension of it—a means to connect the home to the shopping center, a sort of modern equivalent of a wind-tunnel connecting

1. George IV, as Prince Regent, encouraged the creation of the Royal Pavilion in Brighton as a fabulous building of dreams and desires. The outside was Indian-inspired, while the interiors were Chinese and Japanese.

2. Rebecca, the fascinating and beautiful Jewess from *Ivanhoe* whose elaborate dress and ornate jewellery broke the rules of good taste.

3. Winterhalter's sumptuous portrait of Empress Eugénie surrounded by her maids of honour depicted a dumpy royal consort as an icon of grace and style and furnished the parvenu imperial court of Napoleon III with a seductive élan.

4. The Moulin Rouge music hall was marked by an eclectic jumble of styles and artefacts (the model elephant came from the 1890 international exposition) where overt female sexuality was marketed as entertainment to wealthy customers.

5. 'Si j'étais reine': Parisian courtesans and showgirls lived out popular fantasies of wealth and upward social mobility; as such, they were dazzling role models for thousands of ordinary women.

6. 'Sur le Boulevard': The Paris boulevard in the evening was a place of glittering commercial enchantments where smart men and women promenaded and engaged in flirtatious exchanges.

LIANE DE POUGY

7. Émilienne d'Alençon, Liane de Pougy and Caroline Otero were the top three courtesan-performers of the Belle Époque. Arch rivals, they competed over the size of their jewellery collections and for space in the gossip columns.

8. Paris in the nineteenth century was the capital of eroticism where photographic sex appeal was first developed as a subtle tease for male consumers.

9. Italian painter Giovanni Boldini developed a uniquely potent pictorial style based on high fashion and sex appeal that he drew on to depict numerous wealthy female subjects as stylish seductresses.

10. (*Above*) Brenda Frazier, American 'Glamour Girl No.1' of 1938, was a popular debutante who became a publicity-magnet and a press personality.

11. (*Left*) New York café society in the 1920s met at clubs like El Morocco where photographers were on hand to ensure socialites and celebrities were always pictured for the papers.

12. The shopgirls' idol, film actress Gloria Swanson was the most photographed woman of the post-World War One era. Groomed for stardom by British aristocrat Elinor Glyn, she married a minor French nobleman in 1925.

13. Marlene Dietrich was turned by Josef von Sternberg into a dazzling photographic illusion but her screen image owed much to Paramount's costume designers and her own steely professionalism.

14. MGM's glamour queen Greta Garbo tantalised film audiences by projecting a sumptuously-costumed, world-weary sexual allure while refusing to pander to intrusive publicity.

15. In films like *Flying Down to Rio*, starring Fred Astaire and Ginger Rogers, Hollywood studios supplied Depression-era audiences with superlative spectacles blending luxury, excess, optimism and mass enchantment.

16. The bullet-nosed 1950 Studebaker seduced suburban American consumers with fantasy-laden design features which advertisers combined with sophisticated suggestions of the urban nightscape.

17. Rome's Via Veneto, as depicted in *La Dolce Vita*, was a nocturnal meeting point of international café society and a hunting ground for scandal-mongering Paparazzi.

18. In her early career at Rank, where she was promoted as 'the British Ava Gardner' Joan Collins mastered a repertoire of seductive poses and calculated sex appeal that she later deployed in her role as Alexis Carrington in *Dynasty*.

19. (*Right*) In the 1960s, companies like Southwest Airlines turned stewardesses into brand images and replaced the traditional emphasis on their efficiency with explicit sex appeal and the buzz of showbiz.

20. (*Below*) Beauty contests like Miss World 1970 offered a mixture of glamour and show-manship in which grooming and deportment were as important as physical perfection.

21. The fashion designer Gianni Versace, shown with models Carla Bruni and Naomi Campbell, was labelled on his death as a master of glitz and glamour who glorified sex and excess.

22. The supermodels Linda Evangelista, Cindy Crawford, Naomi Campbell and Christy Turlington were latter-day silent stars whose glamour concealed the sleazy underside of the model industry.

23. *(Left)* Diana, Princess of Wales stepped out of the frame of royalty to develop a powerful personal allure based on beauty, style, sex appeal and individual charm.

24. *(Below)* Paris Hilton (right), shown here with Nicole Richie, her partner on the TV reality show 'The Simple Life 2', marketed herself as the embodiment of the Beverly Hills heiress and party girl.

two wood huts,' observed one American author.[13] The fantasy factor in automobile design derived precisely from a desire to offset this humdrum dimension. For Europeans, by contrast, cars were not so quotidian. They were objects of a certain rarity and fascination that were often contemplated more than they were used, even by some of those who were fortunate enough to own one.[14] The pictures of cars that adorned Marshall propaganda posters and that were seen in Hollywood movies and occasionally at motor shows, testified to the great gulf that separated the old continent from the new. Even in 1961 only one in eight French people owned a car, as opposed to one in three Americans.[15] The cheapest Fiat 600 model, launched in 1953, had a cost equivalent to a year's wages for a worker at the company and half the annual salary of a white-collar worker.[16] In Europe, the glamour of cars derived not from the fantasies that were built into them by astute designers and manufacturers but rather from the suggestions of writers and film-makers, the popularity of motor racing, and their associations with celebrities. This gave European sports cars and some other vehicles a special allure for wealthy Americans for whom they were external to the pre-packaged dreams they were accustomed to. They had the same appeal as Continental movies that were exhibited not in mainstream movie theatres but in specially designated art houses.

One of the most innovative inventions of the post-war years were the Italian Vespa and Lambretta scooters. Designed in 1946 by Corrado d'Ascanio, who adapted it from a simple transport vehicle used for moving goods on military airfields, the Vespa would prove to be much more than simply the precursor of the motor car in a country where few could afford them. With its smooth curves and practical allure, it would prove to be a design classic and a market hit throughout Europe.[17] Piaggio, the producer of the scooter, cleverly wrapped glamorous imagery around it, employing pin-up art and female film stars to give the Vespa sex appeal.[18] Although most purchasers would be men, who often used Vespas to get to work, it was sold as a tool of freedom and leisure. To own a Vespa was to belong to a new universe of weekend travel, trips to the seaside, and courtship away from prying eyes. After Audrey Hepburn and Gregory Peck rode a Vespa in *Roman Holiday*, it was associated by foreigners with fun, tourism, and Italy itself.

European manufacturers had been making prestige and sports vehicles for decades. Motor racing had been a prestigious, if highly dangerous, sport in the interwar years. After 1945, it flourished once more as some competitions of the pre-war years, such as the Italian Mille Miglia rally and the Le Mans 24-hour race resumed. From 1950 the Formula One World Championship was introduced and immediately caught the imagination of the public with exciting races that, through the first decade of competition, were dominated by the ace Argentine driver Juan Manuel Fangio. His great rival, Stirling Moss, was never able to win a single championship. The period largely featured teams run by car manufacturers including Mercedes, Alfa Romeo, Ferrari, and Maserati. All of these manufacturers, and others too, also produced road vehicles. The challenge for most companies was to produce stylish vehicles for the masses that were not simply pared-down imitations of more costly models. The resulting automobiles, perhaps not surprisingly, took inspiration from the United States. Even the shark-like Citroën DS, first introduced in 1955, owed something to the streamlining of American designer Raymond Loewy. With its futuristic shape, long body, and colour options it clearly had an American inspiration, even if a series of technical innovations including front-wheel drive and hydro-pneumatic suspension gave it a profoundly original character. Its unveiling at the Salon de l'automobile in Paris inspired the critic Roland Barthes to his famous observation that cars were the modern equivalent of medieval cathedrals in that they were the highest expression of the civilization that created them.[19]

The excitement that cars like the Citroën aroused could be measured by the extraordinary coverage they received in the press and magazines. Cars also featured frequently in the novels and films of the period where the thrill of speed and the power of narration endowed them with near-mythical status, even if the sense of independence driving afforded, especially when the vehicle in question was an open-top sports car, often combined with the horror of a fatal accident.[20] The intense depiction of cars in the period before they became a commonplace fact of European life testified to the differences between the two continents. In Britain, motor cars remained outside the reach of the majority of the population until 1958 when the last restrictions on hire purchase were abolished and instalment buying suddenly widened the market for larger consumer goods. The mass cars that captured the attention were no longer the staid vehicles produced by Austin and Morris with fuddy-duddy names like Oxford and Cambridge, but popular dilutions of the styles that proved popular across the Atlantic. The Ford Zephyr and the more expensive Zodiac were chrome-decorated six-cylinder cars that had touches of American glitz. Indeed, it was Ford USA that initially determined their look. They were fresh and bold in their styling and incorporated transatlantic optimism into their front and rear design, while remaining comparatively modest in their overall proportions. Produced by Ford's Dagenham factory, they were affordable symbols of status and modernity. They were the automotive equivalents of local crooners and pop stars. These cars lacked conventional taste but they had panache and a certain swagger, qualities that were enhanced by Ford's practice of using them in rallies and their regular appearance in the popular BBC television police drama *Z Cars*. The screen police officers who drove them were not old-style 'bobbies' on the beat but tough and gritty US-style cops with attitude. The fact that the series was set in a nondescript 'new town' lent it a certain glamorous rootless-ness, even though the north-western English accents of the protagonists added a regional flavour. Although this depiction offended some senior figures in the police, it influenced the manner of some policemen who imagined themselves to be protagonists of a real-life version of the TV show.[21]

The car was the protagonist of a society on the move, that was increasingly mobile and in which people travelled more, also to foreign countries. Travel became big business in the 1950s as it came within reach of many Americans and smaller numbers of Europeans. Around one and a half million Americans were going abroad every year by the end of the decade. Passenger airlines had appeared in the 1930s, but only after the war did they flourish. The introduction of commercial jet travel at the end of the 1950s reduced the length of the journey between New York and Paris to six hours. During this period, aviation lost little of the glamour that it had acquired during and after the First World War. However, travel was no longer glamorous because it was heroic, but rather because it was practised by the rich and the well-known, and because it opened up the possibility of reaching exotic and unfamiliar places. Its allure was no longer associated with the dashing personas of the pioneer aviators. What Barthes called 'the glamorous singularity of an inhuman condition' was replaced by a new breed of jet pilots who belonged to 'a new race in aviation, nearer to the robot than to the hero'.[22] The increasing enclosure of travel in the contained units of the motor car and the aeroplane isolated the passenger and reduced the experience of movement to one that could be largely controlled and managed. Daniel Boorstin, whose powerful book *The Image*, published in 1961, aimed to identify the ills of modern man, lamented this tendency to homogenize life. 'If we go by air,' he commented, 'then we are encompassed in music, and enjoy our cocktail in a lounge with the décor of the best resort hotel.'[23] In-flight movies were introduced by TWA in 1961, while the German company Lufthansa promised in its promotional material that every flight was 'a charming, informal Continental supper party, eight jet-smooth miles over the Atlantic'. When they arrived at their chosen destination, tourists were often accommodated in hotels that replicated the same conveniences that they were used to at home. The expansion of international hotel chains facilitated this process. The great pioneer was Conrad Hilton, who opened hotels in Puerto Rico in 1947, Madrid in 1953, and Istanbul in 1955, and then in Rome, West Berlin, Montreal, and many other world cities. Each opening saw Hilton fly American celebrities to the city concerned, both to secure publicity and create a glamorous buzz around the new hotel.

Although travel to Europe boomed, for many Americans, the high life was associated with resorts that were closer to home and which skilfully developed irresistible appeals to the middle-income vacationer. Las Vegas had developed as a gambling paradise in the interwar years and witnessed the development of a rash of new hotels and casinos in the 1940s. The emblematic resort of Miami Beach was born in the same period as a man-made getaway for wealthy winter holiday-makers. Its numerous art deco hotels lent it a festive and contemporary air. During the war, thousands of servicemen were stationed there and the appeals of its warm climate became more widely known. In the years that followed, it used its elite associations to promote itself to middle-class Americans. As garish and enormous new hotels including the Fountainbleu, the Eden Roc, and the Deauville, opened on the North Beach, publicity promised visitors variously Hollywood-by-the-sea or an American-style Riviera experience.[24] The eclectic mix of styles, themes, and inspirations of the architecture of the hotels recalled department stores of the nineteenth century, a model that they did not disdain. They offered 'packaged happiness' and flattered people by serving them, entertaining them, and making them feel they were indulging in the glamorous life of the rich.[25] Casinos and nightclubs provided a buzz that, while not as brashly vulgar as Las Vegas's 'sin city' reputation, mixed strong doses of luxury, sex appeal, and spectacle. Between 1949 and 1964, Miami Beach grew into the biggest single resort in the United States thanks to packaged air tours and regular shots of glamour in the form of the Miss America and Miss Universe pageants and super-shows drawing on the top show-business and sports stars of the day. Resort advertising always featured beautiful girls cavorting on the magnificent beaches.

Feminine imagery and mass consumption seem to go together hand in glove. As tourism became a feature of the American lifestyle, the air hostess replaced the pilot as the emblematic figure of air travel. United Airlines had hired the first stewardesses in 1930, recruiting 'attractive, personable young women who were not pilots'.[26] Women were preferred to men because they would better allay passengers' anxieties and make air travel seem safe and comfortable. The hostess quickly became a popular cultural icon. Even in the interwar period, there were movies such as *Air Hostess*, released in 1937, and romantic novels featuring stewardesses. Feature articles on some of their number outlined their daily lives, stressed their practical, no-nonsense approach, even when dealing with celebrity passengers, and their eminent marriageability.[27] They confirmed that immaculate appearance, movement, and the contemporary spirit were not necessarily antithetical. According to Boorstin, the airline stewardess, 'a breed first developed in the United States and now found on all major international air-lines', was 'a new sub-species of womankind. With her standardized impersonal charm she offers us, anywhere in the world, the same kind of pillow for our head and the latest issue of *Look* or *Reader's Digest*. She is the Madonna of the Airways, a pretty symbol of the new homogenized blandness of the tourist's world.'[28]

In the fifties the air stewardess emerged as a glamorous figure who embodied many of the dreams of the moment. It was more realistic for girls to aspire to be a stewardess than a fashion model, yet they were no less likely to travel to exotic locations or meet the rich and famous. Stewardesses were usually trained nurses acting as waitresses and hostesses, women whose jobs were rendered alluring by the mystique of air travel, stylish uniforms, and their public visibility. One of the first post-war British hostesses, Joyce Tait, who was an object of such curiosity that she wrote a book about her experiences, stressed the many practical aspects of a job that continually presented new challenges. She did this because the drudgery and discipline required of the stewardesses was normally entirely concealed from the public.[29] Any dream Tait and her colleagues may have had about becoming 'glamorous queens of the air' were cancelled even before the end of their training by the discovery of discomforts and innumerable rules. 'Only one thing could restore it,' she acknowledged, 'and the glorious day actually came at last when we were sent to be fitted for our uniforms.'[30] As with several European carriers, these were designed with a keen fashion sense (the uniforms of the stewardesses of the Italian company Alitalia, for example, were designed by the Fontana sisters, who had made Linda Christian's wedding dress and Ava Gardner's costumes for *The Barefoot Countess*). Great emphasis was placed by airlines on the image of the hostesses. 'Appearance was a great thing. "Neat but not gaudy" was the rule,' Tait asserted. Style and status were the rewards for women who were seen almost to be as glamorous as Hollywood stars.[31]

Achieving the right balance of efficiency and sex appeal was not always straightforward. Stewardesses were selected from single, girl-next-door types but they had to be sufficiently polished to blend easily with wealthy passengers. In addition, they had to be cool, competent, and sympathetic in manner. Brought up in Lisbon, Tait found that her way of walking was deemed by her instructor to be too obviously sexy. It gave her a provocative air that an initial make-up trial did nothing to dispel. 'It was bad enough having a Continental wiggle; with that *and* the sort of face that had been painted on me no one in London would have had any doubts about my origin—or my profession,' she wrote.[32] Tait soon adopted a modest, pared-down look that left space only for the regulation matching lips and nails. Differently to their European counterparts, for whom para-aristocratic manners were important, American stewardesses aimed to please like the stars and 'learned to *smile!*' 'On the Continental airlines like Air France, Alitalia, Lufthansa, and SAS, it was the norm for flight attendants...to behave most haughtily or at least cooler than their American counterparts,' Pan-Am stewardess Aimée Bratt observed. 'It was unacceptable on the American carriers in the cabins...In America, you have to smile or at least give the appearance of friendliness.' 'Nevertheless, in Pan-Am we still acted a bit "superior", or call it sophisticated, which was simply a result of flying the world for years.'[33]

At a time when mass air travel was starting and the romance of the skies seemed like a mixture of the adventure of the aviation pioneers and Hollywood, the stewardess embodied an ideal type who in her smiling, unruffled perfection seemed like nothing so much as a uniformed Ziegfeld Girl. Bratt recalled that she and her colleagues were rigorously moulded to a standard pattern: 'I don't know how it is possible, but we were glorified and humbled at the same time. We were molded into perfect stewardesses. Like soldiers in an army we had to cut our hair (it could not touch the collar), lipstick and nail polish had to be red or coral, make-up applied according to regulation, uniform skirt not too tight or too loose, and undergarments were mandatory—full slip, nylon hose, full bra, panties, and girdle—and we were checked periodically.'[34] Airlines gave their stewardesses a look whose maintenance required an ongoing performance in testing conditions. Like Tait, she gained some compensation from wearing the uniform. 'The Pan-Am uniform was actually great-looking,' she acknowledged; 'blue-grey gabardine, a pillbox hat (the fashion of the sixties), black high-heeled shoes, leather over-the-shoulder handbag, and white, white gloves! Some people thought of it as oppressive, but one has to admit—we had *style!*'[35]

Stewardesses were always associated at some level with sex. Even in the 1950s, when they were pictured as the perfect bride, their cordial smiles lured passengers to the companies. In his contribution to the collective film *Rogopag*, an episode entitled 'Illibatezza' (Purity), the director Roberto Rossellini explored a demure Italian stewardess's efforts to shake off the attentions of an amorous American businessman.[36] 'Something about plane rides gives some men the irresistible temptation to slap a stewardess' backside as she walks by,' *Life* had reported in 1941.[37] In the sixties, the airlines ceased combating this image and worked explicitly to turn hostesses into flying sex objects, 'the carefree envy of women, the sexual fantasy for men'.[38] As competition for custom hotted up in the United States and advertising spending increased, they became the official face of airlines which turned them into the main attraction of air travel.[39] For Paula Kane, a stewardess of the 1960s who would revolt against being regarded as a 'sex object in the sky', 'the airlines...cleverly constructed the airborne fantasy world'.[40] Safety matters took second place in their recruitment and training to appearance and grooming. 'I don't know exactly what I expected in flight training school, but it was certainly not what I got,' she later wrote: 'the school was more like a crash course for the Miss America pageant. We were forced into a total, narcissistic self-absorption. Girdles, fingernail polish, false eyelashes, ratted hair, make-up, how to walk and sit down and climb stairs—these were our obsessions for the next six weeks.'[41] From the blonde bombshells of Pacific Southwest to the girls-next-door of United, 'We are supposed to be the fresh, wholesome girls who love men, the quiet concubines of the pilots, and the submissive partners to male sexual fantasies,' Kane lamented.[42]

The stewardess fantasy became embedded in the popular psyche at precisely the time when travel was separating work and domicile, loosening the bonds of family life and turning even next-door neighbours into strangers. For the public, hostesses led glamorous lives. They dated sportsmen and movie stars, they visited far-flung locations and were at home in cocktail bars, with which commercial planes were fitted in the 1950s. They were not imprisoned in a pattern of fixed obligations and social controls and were seen as sexually available. They went skiing in Switzerland, shopping in Hong Kong, and nightclubbing in Las Vegas. The glamour image was not entirely false and determined why some women joined the airlines and how passengers perceived them. 'Men dream of escaping their families for a few days of romantic freedom to another city, perhaps picking up a stewardess on the way,' Kane observed.

The male fantasy of quick and obligation-free sex was a product of the sensory environment of the American suburban dweller. Mass surburbia was a phenomenon of these years into which many middle-class Americans were willingly integrated. New towns and residential communities were based on a pattern of standardized living that matched the domination of the economy by large corporations and the development of the mass consumer economy. They also met the strong post-war desire to settle down that fuelled the trend towards early marriage and the baby boom. In the suburbs, families lived the lifestyle of the modern home, family motor car, and stylish furniture, while continually being solicited to yearn for improvements. The range of goods and the choices they were presented with were astonishing. Surburban dwellers were not traditionalists; they were mobile, both socially and geographically, and their attitudes towards goods were similarly provisional. Only a minority of Americans in fact lived in the new suburbs, but these set the tone for modern lifestyles in the way that cities had done in earlier decades. In advertisements, television comedies, and even school textbooks, the average American had left the city for the practical paradise of suburbia.

Commentators and sociologists were intrigued by the new lifestyles and the sort of culture that was taking shape in an era of standardized prosperity. The suburban dwellers were participants in what the British writer and commentator J. B. Priestley called 'Admass', that is 'the whole system of an increasing productivity, plus inflation, plus a rising standard of material living, plus high-pressure advertising and salesmanship, plus mass communications, plus cultural democracy and the creation of the mass mind, the mass man'.[43] The journalist William H. Whyte, in his classic text *The Organization Man*, was the first to highlight the extreme conformity of the white collar workers who were the typical suburban dwellers. Although McLuhan would insist that the car had levelled Americans up towards the aristocratic idea rather than down, since it 'gave to the democratic cavalier his horse and armor and haughty insolence in one package',[44] Whyte found that suburbanites did not struggle to keep up with the Joneses but *down* with them. *Inconspicuous* rather than conspicuous consumption was the rule in settings where houses and lifestyles were broadly identical. 'When they see a neighbor vaunting worldly goods, they can see this as an offence—not to them individually, mind you, but to the community,' Whyte noted.[45] However, he added that, while people passed negative comment on conspicuous display, they were always careful to add that they themselves saw nothing wrong with it; it was *other people* who might object. In other words, the downward pressure arose from fears of being left behind, but a leap ahead for oneself was not disdained as a prospect. The conspicuous display of the celebrities fed such dreams; their glamour provided a vicarious outlet for the secret aspirations of the masses.

The nervy concern with what others were doing and consuming, that Whyte highlighted, derived from a phenomenon that had been noted a little earlier by a prominent sociologist. David Riesman stimulated a wide-ranging debate with his idea that there had been a shift in the structure of human behaviour from what he called 'inner-direction' to 'other-direction'.[46] Other-directed behaviour was not reliant on values assimilated at an early age and held to be positive in themselves. It was, on the contrary, a behaviour pattern in which the individual was moulded by external pressures and suggestions. The sort of 'other-directed' personalities that Riesman saw as the new American character-type emerging with consumer society were typically young working women in their late teens or early twenties who were particularly reliant on their contemporaries and the mass media for their sources of orientation.[47] They were less 'inner-directed' than the older generation and placed more importance on exterior self-fashioning and personal relationships. Even in the workplace, they were less likely to think of themselves as loyal and efficient assistants than as 'glamor-exuding personalities'.[48]

The 1950s were the great heyday of American sociology and social psychology. New forms of living and working presented scholars with opportunities for all manner of inquiries. Glamour never emerged as an independent topic for the sociologists who studied American society. However, it can be glimpsed here and there in the interstices of their writings. Riesman mentions it a handful of times. In his view, glamour had been democratized along with consumption and as such had lost much of its capacity to enchant: 'Whereas the deprived inner-directed person often lusted for possessions as a goal whose glamour a wealthy adulthood could not dim, the other-directed person can scarcely conceive of a consumer good that can maintain for any length of time undisputed dominance over his imagination.'[49] Yet glamour remained a key tool to stimulate interest in goods. Glamour, he asserted, was 'one sovereign remedy... to combat the danger of indifference and apathy'.[50] In packaging and the advertising of products, it substituted price competition and in politics it took the place of self-interest. In each case, it involved the use of psychological and aesthetic appeals attractive to the customer or voter.

In the era of high mass consumption, the home was a crucial counterpart to the new emphasis on mobility and travel. The British cultural critic Raymond Williams coined the term 'mobile privatisation',[51] to describe the transformation of the motor car into a travelling living room and the living room into a miniature cinema. The domestic environment had been a site of the reproduction of the bourgeois dream world since the mid-nineteenth century. Now this function was confirmed. The declining female presence in the labour market in the 1950s, coupled with the growth in the United States of the suburban ideal, heralded a renewed emphasis on the feminine in marking the visual appeal of the object world. In mass consumer society, the suburb—and the consumption in Europe of its idealized representation in advertising, film and television shows—stood for status, perfection, and domestication. Lacking the chaos of the street and the flux of the city, it offered an enclosed, privatized world that excluded the natural and took the place of the spontaneity of earlier versions of modernity. Competition over status and appearances centred on the home, especially the kitchen, the motor car, and the personal presentation of the housewife and mother. The primary mirror of this new world was no longer cinema but television. Visual broadcasting brought new faces into living rooms and added a new layer to family life. The television set replaced the hearth as the focal point of the home and its output provided a second-order experience of company.

If, in Europe, television was a powerful means of integrating rural and peripheral populations into urban ways, in the USA it was rather suburbia that triumphed. What defined television was its low intensity and its small size. This meant that the sort of environments that were best depicted on the small screen were either small and contained or varied in surface texture. Westerns seemed to work particularly well, whereas slick and glamorous metropolitan environments, such as stylish nightclubs and other places of entertainment, were better suited to the movie camera.[52] Presenters, entertainers, and situation comedy families were cordial familiar presences in an imaginary world.

Unlike cinema the medium did not provide detailed information concerning objects and the close-up was not the exception but the norm. As McLuhan observed, 'the audience participates in the inner life of the TV actor as in the outer life of the movie star'.[53] In contrast to the movie star, the television actor had a quality of ordinariness that blended in with everyday life; people seeing him on the street often could not place him or remember his name.

Despite its domestic focus and the important role of women in managing the home environment, television was a predominantly masculine medium in which women were severely underrepresented.[54] Newsreading, announcing, presenting, and even entertaining were exclusively or largely performed by men. Women, by contrast, played supporting or decorative roles. The women of the small screen were always polished and groomed, young or youthful, and smiling. In the gendering of roles, glamour was their prerogative. A striking number of quiz shows in the US and Western Europe deployed entirely mute hostesses who merely adorned the screen and provided a visual foil for male presenters. In the US, Marie Wilson and the curvaceous blonde Dagmar (born Virginia Egnor) provided the small screen with pin-up appeal while in Britain, the curvaceous blonde Sabrina, who appeared alongside comedian Arthur Askey in *Before Your Very Eyes* in 1955, offered a highly artificial, hyperbolic female image. Every time she was about to say something, the band, in a running gag, struck up to silence her. After becoming one of the most talked about and depicted people in the country, the former waitress moved on to more varied work in films and the theatre.

The few women who performed more serious roles often faced difficulties. These problems are exemplified by the case of Faye Emerson, who was a more complex figure of American television. A former B-film actor, Broadway performer, radio host, and newspaper columnist who presented a series of interview programmes in the early 1950s, Emerson was dubbed 'the first lady of television'.[55] With her famous décolletage, she presented a 'visual image of vivacious beauty' while also enjoying a reputation for intelligence. She initially presented a fashion programme on local television in New York before hosting late evening and prime time talk shows for CBS in which she would converse with guests on topics ranging from current stage shows to the Korean War. Emerson's shapely figure and groomed appearance were always presented as being natural and genuine, in accordance with the medium's preference for the everyday. However, her unrehearsed braininess was less easily absorbable. Despite her sexualized persona, she was deemed an emasculating presence who did not fit in with television's emerging pattern of comfortable and passive female stereotypes. In Italian television, the only female presenter, Enza Sampò, was always paired on screen with a man. She was not permitted to undertake external broadcasts without the presence of a chaperone whose task was to protect her physical and moral integrity.[56]

The domestic ideology of television was not readily compatible with the highly constructed image of the film performer. Indeed, one commentator in the early 1950s argued that 'television, by bringing celebrities into every home has murdered glamour'.[57] 'Old fashioned glamour and mystery', Mary Margaret McBride asserted, had been eroded by greater accessibility. Others felt that even the movie stars of the 1950s 'have sex appeal but they don't have that old-time mystery'.[58] Too much was known about their lives for them to be intriguing. They no longer even received the sort of build-up that was usual in the past, largely because the studios did not have the same degree of ownership over them and control over their careers. Nevertheless, there were stars who had been forged a little earlier whose larger-than-life images were not compatible with television. For McLuhan, this was because television was a 'cool' medium and the movies a 'hot' one. Television made fame look banal and challenged the premiss that notoriety and success were absolute values.[59] The exceptional qualities ascribed to the big stars clashed with the commercial and domestic nature of the medium.[60] Thus it was mostly second- or third-rank film stars, like the redhead Lucille Ball, whose domestic situation comedy *I Love Lucy* was a worldwide hit, who migrated to the new medium. After her big-screen role as dancer Jane Avril in John Huston's *Moulin Rouge* and her headline-grabbing marriages and affair with Porfirio Rubirosa, Zsa Zsa Gabor found that there was a more ready audience for her glamorous mixture of gold-digging tips and European sophistication on television. In dramas and talk-show appearances, she translated a real world of international café society into suburban commercial terms and became the fantasy alter ego of every housewife. She appeared regularly on *The Jack Paar Show* and told audiences of the three telephones she had at her bedside in Bel Air (to receive regular calls from London, Paris, and New York, she said) and her liking for wearing three perfumes at once. She sponsored so many products and spent so much time on her public presentation that, she claimed, she became 'Zsa Zsa Incorporated'.[61]

The sort of female image that television conveyed to housewives was a man-made one that was accessible to everyone so long as they bought the right products. The mass media of the period demanded of women a continuous self-scrutiny that was crucial to the selling of cosmetics, clothes, and domestic accessories. Quizzes and magazine articles compartmentalized women in terms of acceptable traits, creating pigeonholes for them to slot in to.[62] In American society, cosmetics companies like Max Factor put all their discoveries immediately at the disposal of everyone and took on the task of spreading the word about beauty.[63] The Revlon company reached a huge market by sponsoring the popular television programme *The $64,000 Question*, but in the process lost much of its class appeal. One of the most striking features of the beauty industry at this time was the diffusion of hair dye.[64] Companies like Clairol and L'Oréal vied to tie their products to evolving feminine ideals. They promised customers that by going blonde they would fully enter the world of glamorous modernity even while staying within their own homes. The perfect tableau of domestic life was completed by a housewife who resembled a star. The genius of L'Oréal lay in its tying domesticity to self-confidence with its 'Because I'm worth it' slogan.

Goods were packaged in the 1950s in ways that blended artificial femininity and glamorized objects. This practice had a number of precedents. Cellophane, originally invented in France, was a perfect example of a man-made product that became the epitome of glamour and elegance in a society that had displaced the natural. Even when no protective wrapping was needed, when visibility was of no obvious value, cellophane's shimmering presence provided ordinary, everyday products with a strong dose of what retailers coyly referred to as 'eye appeal'.[65] It lent a touch of glamour and gloss to the most mundane objects, lifting their appeal by enhancing the context in which they were sold. It had something alluring, even cinematic, about it. In Cole Porter's song 'You're the Top', the line 'Your Garbo's secretary' was immediately followed by 'You're cellophane'. In the exuberant style of the Busby Berkeley musicals, it encased mundane reality in a shiny new outfit and made it look like a Christmas gift.[66] This effect of cellophane packaging was similar to striptease, which achieved its effect by constantly making the unveiled body more remote. Products were available but untouchable and therefore inaccessible. Ostensibly, everything was there to be seen but their packaging associated them with an icy indifference, a haughty distance from the grubby fingers of the masses.[67]

Glamour, in its American application, implied a democratic making available of the discoveries that scientists had made. It was infused with novelty and mass appeal. This notion was especially pronounced in beauty advertising but it also transferred to domestic goods. A product of applied technology, plastic was a great innovation that somehow encapsulated the pliant femininity of the period.[68] This aesthetic lives on in the Barbie doll. A product of the late 1950s, it offered an image of perfect, constructed femininity in moulded plastic form. As a toy, it provided girls with a consumption ideal; as an exaggerated, inorganic feminine image, devoted to waste and self-fashioning, it also offered a new version of the artificial female model of the late nineteenth century. Like a film star, Barbie offered a face full of nothing that demanded that she be transformed into something.[69] Barbie was the ultimate conformist, a truly malleable woman, and her willingness to please led her to adopt every new style.[70] Her 'availability' was intrinsically linked to her being made of plastic.

Plastic came in a variety of forms, some of which carried upmarket associations while preserving the mass appeal of a manufactured product. They added a fantasy dimension to daily life, taking sex appeal into the home. The new plastics, many of which had been developed during the war years, reshaped the domestic landscape. Their inorganic allure came to be associated with the explosion of synthetic colour and pinks that was bound up with technological development and the extension of consumerism to wider sections of the population.[71] In the form of small kitchen accessories and items of tableware, they performed the role of units of pure colour which could be arranged in the interior like paint marks on a canvas.[72] In this way, they matched the garish Technicolor movies of the fifties. 'Plastic is wholly swallowed up in the fact of being used: ultimately, objects will be invented for the sole pleasure of using them,' Barthes predicted in 1957. 'The hierarchy of substances is abolished: a single one replaces them all: the whole world *can* be plasticized, and even life itself since, we are told, they are beginning to make plastic aortas.'[73]

Tupperware was the emblematic American plastic product of the 1950s, the epitome of the attempt to glamorize the domestic environment. Invented by an entrepreneur named Earl Tupper, it was tough, mouldable, and frosted translucent. Unlike the hard, monochrome, and masculine Bakelite, it was soft and sensual and available in a wide range of pastel hues. Through the innovative selling device of house parties, Tupperware became a central part of domestic feminine culture. Plastic containers for preserving food may seem far from glamour, but Tupper's world has been seen by some observers as one that oozed sexuality and kinkiness. It was a fantasy world of garish colours and girly goodies dispensed by a big daddy who understood all the fetishes and obsessions of his female customers.[74] Colour mania was ultimately the sign of a definitive cultural shift away from the natural. Barthes noted that the spread of 'chemical-looking' colours derived from plastic's inability to retain any other type; 'of yellow, red and green,' he wrote, 'it keeps only the aggressive quality and names, being able to display only concepts of colours'.[75]

Brash pastels subsequently became linked with what was seen as the vulgarity of 1950s consumerism and its particular manifestation in the appearance, homes, and possessions of the Hollywood film stars of that period.[76] In fifties' America, Beverly Hills was not so much a dreamland as an exaggerated version of suburbia. If, as has been claimed, glamour is 'the ugly stepsister to elegance',[77] then it was exemplified by the lifestyles of stars like Kim Novak, who lived in a house in the Bel Air district of Los Angeles that had colour-themed rooms. When press agent Bill Davidson visited her, he was offered a breakfast that consisted of caviar, pickled green tomatoes, French toast, Roquefort cheese, and champagne.[78] The star herself was wearing a skintight black leotard. 'You can't just have a plain old Rolls-Royce in Hollywood,' he wrote; 'it must be a custom-made Rolls-Royce fitted with liquor bar, make-up bar, reclining seats and two telephones.'[79] Quantity and novelty were just as important as quality in a society that was dominated by the newly rich.

In the 1950s, Hollywood glamour presented itself with at least two faces. On the one hand, there was the lady, on the other there was the sex goddess. Although the golden age of the studios was coming to an end and film-going was in decline, the majors responded energetically and in various ways to the challenge of television and consumerism. Colour film and the widescreen Cinemascope were two strategies employed to differentiate the experience of film-going from that of television. Another was a greater emphasis on sex. Marilyn Monroe provided 1950s audiences with an unrivalled body-spectacle. Instead of the porcelain-hard artifice of a figure like Jean Harlow, she offered a pliable, vulnerable humanity that was trusting and available. In keeping with her origins as a pin-up, she was a persona created for male pleasure and male consumption. Monroe was the emblematic star of the 1950s, the last and most perfect product of the studio system. With her trademark blonde hair, perfect white complexion, and shiny red lips, the sensual curves of her body, and her infantile manner, she was the star par excellence, the figure who most completely represented the concept of Hollywood glamour for the world public. Modelled by 20th Century Fox as the stereotypical blonde, the physical incarnation of the idealized pin-ups that soldiers had known during the war, she became the ideal woman and the embodiment of America at the time of that country's ascendancy. She was neither the first sex symbol nor the first dumb blonde, but somehow she managed to combine these qualities and dress them with an air of healthy innocence.

Monroe was highly sexualized as a star figure. Her breasts, the famous wiggle of her hips as she walked, and her parted lips all signalled availability. In contrast to stars like Joan Crawford and even Rita Hayworth, whose elaborate wardrobes and grooming signalled their particular relationship with female audiences, Monroe relied to an unprecedented degree on her body for her appeal to men. Although the sexualization of star figures dovetailed with the central importance that sexuality was assuming in the dynamics of individual identity in consumer society, Monroe's compliant availability was far more restrictive a view of femininity than had been offered by any previous major star.[80] Her full-colour nude calendar shot published in the first issue of *Playboy*, but taken several years earlier, opened the way to a narrow but persistent definition of glamour as soft pornography. Her image was not a total invention. Whereas Grace Kelly's wealthy, genteel background was used to cultivate her image as 'elegant' 'lady-like', 'patrician', Monroe's youthful waywardness and early marriage were used to bolster a more sexually connoted and vulnerable image.[81]

Monroe's success in films including *Niagara, Gentlemen Prefer Blondes, How to Marry a Millionaire,* and *Some Like It Hot,* served as an example to other studios. In the era of high mass consumption, production took place in series and this applied no less to stars than to automobiles. Hollywood had cloned copies of successful originals from the 1920s and this was even more the case in the 1950s. Indeed production and reproduction occurred simultaneously. Mamie van Doren, Sheree North, and the British Diana Dors were all Monroe imitations, while Jayne Mansfield and Anita Ekberg, with their outsize breasts, seemed more like parodies. Mansfield was the type of star who believed that it was her duty to bring the public into her life. Groomed explicitly as a rival to Monroe, of whom she imitated the giggly 'the girl can't help it' screen persona, she lived with her muscle-builder husband Mickey Hargitay in a pink palace with a heart-shaped pink swimming pool. She represented the same opulently synthetic aesthetic that produced the monstrously kitsch 1959 Cadillac Coupe de Ville.

Dors was one of the products of the British studio Rank who lived out the dream of the ordinary girl who wants to be a film star. Although she was trained by the studio's famous charm school to speak properly, dress well, and behave with good manners, she had an earthy quality that made her ideal for promotion as a home-grown sex goddess.[82] Her success was based on her being, according to the film critic Raymond Durgnat, 'a happy rendezvous of old vulgarity and new affluence'.[83] She was the highest-paid film star in Britain in 1956 and she cheerfully embraced every aspect of the materialism of the age. She was a bottle blonde, exuberant, and vocal; she made no secret of her ambition for celebrity and wealth. She even exceeded Mansfield in her numerous publicity stunts, which included wearing a mink bikini in a gondola at the Venice film festival and arriving at the Cannes festival in a pink Cadillac. Sex and glamour were what the public expected from her and they were what it got. Although she was lured to the United States by the offer of a contract with the minor studio RKO, she became better known for her personality and appearance than her films. A brassy East End girl made not quite good but at least an eye-catching phenomenon, she filled magazines with the soap opera of her personal life. She had a strong American veneer, but her British fans related to her real-life struggles against adversity.

In an era in which publicity was as omnipresent as plastic, the stars were no less subject to planned obsolescence than the electrical appliance. They were disposable figures for whom publicity was a lifeblood that spelled 'the difference between legend and oblivion'.[84] Because, beneath the image, there was a human being, this process produced tragedies. To bear the burden of constant scrutiny and figure as a cipher for all collective aspirations and preoccupations—from beauty and fashion, to love and sex, and leisure and lifestyle—was too much for several stars. The intolerable pressure on the apparently carefree Bardot was fearlessly scrutinized by Louis Malle in the film *Vie privée* (A Very Private Affair), which was closely modelled on real life. Marilyn Monroe was the last seductive image produced by the studio system before its final demise. The ending of the old studios' domination of distribution and exhibition, as well as declining audiences, brought a whole phase to a close. Her death in August 1962 signalled the end of an era. It revealed that tragedy lay behind the polished image of the wonderful, rich, happy life of the stars. For Edgar Morin, 'the death marks the end of the star system. It is the natural demythologising element, the dam through which the truth flows: there no longer exists a star-model, there no longer exists a happy Olympus.'[85] After her death, stars were no longer seen as perfect or even necessarily as happy.

The desire to be famous, to step up into the limelight, was none the less widespread and was encouraged in various ways. The role that had been occupied in the press of the interwar years by the debutante was taken over by the beauty queen. The formation of national communities through the media and the egalitarianism of the age led to mechanisms of selection of candidates for fame that were more open and transparent. Beauty contests had existed since the early years of the twentieth century but in the 1950s and 1960s they developed into national spectacles and big business. Originally devised to promote holiday resorts by lengthening the season, they evolved from beachside amusements into glitzy spectacles that provided work for numerous organizers, choreographers, beauticians, consultants, sponsors, journalists, and broadcasting executives.[86]

The Miss America pageant, which had been established in 1921, was brought to the centre of the mainstream in 1935 when the its image was recast as one of respectability by Lenora Slaughter. It was due to her influence that Miss America became 'the ultimate celebration of the girl-next-door'.[87] The wide coverage of the contest in newsreels and the press and the proliferation of local contests turned hundreds of thousands of young women into potential contestants. While spreading the dream of a glamorous new life, the pageant demanded that the winner be an icon of virtue, innocence, family values, and patriotism. Contestants were chaperoned to ensure respectability and a clean moral image. It required ordinariness and a commitment to self-improvement and rewarded the chosen few with a car, a glamorous wardrobe, jewellery, scholarship funds, and an exciting life for a year. The contest was broadcast live on American television from 1954. Miss Italia attracted national attention from its creation in 1946 and Miss France from its resumption in 1947. The first Miss World competition took place within the Festival of Britain in 1951. All these events were covered in newsreels and on television from the 1960s.

Although the contests were strangely unmemorable, efforts were made to turn the finale into something that seemed substantial. The investment of money in evening dress parades, 'personality' competitions, and the crowning ceremony itself all contributed to the artificial creation of a fantasy event. The illusion of substance rested on all concerned, organizers, spectators, press, and contestants, taking it seriously.[88] The choreography of the contest was pioneered in the United States and then widely adopted elsewhere. Eric Morley, the creator of the British-based Miss World, availed himself of American expertise in the field of showmanship to bring glamour to the occasion.[89] By staging a lavish final in the style of a musical show, that was broadcast on television, he introduced what he called 'the charms of the surface' and '*professional* glamour'.[90] For many contestants, the pageant final was the concluding stage of a long process of competing in local and regional competitions, gaining experience, and honing their presentational skills.

While most of the audience viewed pageants as the lightest of light enter-tainment, they required of participants determination, self-confidence, con-geniality, poise, beauty, and polish.

Each contest followed the same basic format although the criteria of selection were variable. Following parades in swimsuits and evening gowns, the final five contestants were summoned forward to hear the announcement of the winners.[91] Finally, the ecstatic winner, unable to control her emotions, was crowned with a tiara and adorned with a sash that proclaimed her title. Winners received many lavish prizes and they travelled the world on jets, visiting far-flung places, meeting celebrities, heads of state, and religious leaders. They were accorded extensive media exposure. As queens of the people, they were given royal treatment. 'Who isn't jealous of Miss World?', asked one journalist. 'Millions of ordinary hard-working girls would like to exchange positions with her, to taste the nectar of her exotic life even just for a day. It would make a pleasurable reprieve from the office or factory, where they are incarcerated.'[92]

The beauty contest turned the everyday practices of feminine grooming into a spectacle to be scrutinized and assessed by all. They existed in a context in which the feminine ideal was constantly being redefined and they became televised spectacles that were followed by everyone.[93] News-papers and magazines found that coverage increased sales massively. The fashion element made them fascinating to women and girls. The winner was expected to behave with a majestic mixture of cordiality and reserve; she had to be friendly but elegant, forever smiling but spontaneous. As Miss Great Britain 1960 later said, 'I had to be immaculately turned out, but not flashy, look like a film star, but act and walk like a lady and talk well.'[94]

'Beauty contests on TV were a magic mirror that, willy-nilly, made every girl and woman into a participant . . . and recalcitrant tomboys like me were not exempt' recalled the author of a book about the contests.[95] 'In our dizzy identification with winners and losers alike,' she added, 'a whole generation of women and girls in the fifties and sixties tumbled in a narcissistic dream of our own potential perfection.' Those who took part in the contests found that they were an ideal way to reinforce their fantastical, secretly glamorous self-image by arousing the admiration and envy of others. Wearing elegant evening dresses made them 'feel marvellous', 'glamorous', and 'dreamy'.[96] As one British contestant later recalled, 'Dressing up always makes you look and feel good.'[97] While the custom of high grooming and costly outfits aroused the hostility of some left-wingers, many former contestants recalled that their self-confidence was boosted by the experience. 'The only negative thing is that everyone expects me to look 22–24 for ever, [which is] an awful strain,' commented one.[98]

The driving aim, however, was commercial. It was to find girls who went over well with the public, who created something akin to a sales atmosphere. They could then be used to market any product or cause. Contests were a huge industry that helped sell newspapers, promote resorts, advertise products, and maintain interest in beauty products. Sponsors were an important feature of the American competition from the earliest days and they became increasingly important in Europe in the 1950s. It was this commercial exploitation of beauty that provoked the first feminist critiques of beauty contests and the first revolts against them in the late 1960s. Winners were generally expected to conform to standardized ideals and when they did not, like Bess Myerson, the only Jewish Miss America, who won the contest in 1945, they were ignored.[99] Many contestants dreamed of becoming film stars and they were comforted in this by the knowledge that some of the most famous stars had first emerged in the pageants. Diana Dors, for example, had first been spotted at a beauty contest in 1945 and in Italy, Gina Lollobrigida, Sophia Loren, and many other post-war actresses had reached the finals of the national Miss Italia competition. The opportunities available to finalists in the beauty contest heyday of the 1960s were numerous. Television rather than cinema offered numerous possibilities for ornamental femininity: hostesses, link announcers, and game-show assistants were all recruited from the pageants.

The wide use of 'the sexual sell' in mass consumption was a phenomenon that feminist Betty Friedan related to the increasing depersonalization of social relations and the focus on suburban domesticity.[100] A society that relied on the mass media and consumer goods for its connecting texture transferred human instincts to the vicarious realm, she argued. This was a more complex position to that of the author of *The Lonely Crowd*. For David

Riesman, sex was important in modern society as a response to apathy. Because it was a biological impulse that could not be ignored, sex provided 'a kind of defense against the threat of total apathy'.[101] The other-directed person gave prominence to sex because 'he looks to it for reassurance that he is alive'. Curiosity about—and envy of—the sex lives of others was enhanced because 'sexual glamour' had been democratized: due to 'the mass production of good-looking, well-groomed youth' it was available to all. As such, sex manuals had become 'matter of fact, toneless and hygienic'.[102] By contrast, he argued, cookery books had, in the era of other-direction, become more glamorous. They privileged visual effects to attract readers and help them embellish their tables with eye-catching dishes. 'The sphere of pleasure and consumption is only a side show in the era of inner-direction, work of course being the main show. This is truer for men than for women,' he noted.[103] For outer-directed people, this sphere was absolutely central. While Riesman assumed that improvements in health and standards of living meant that sex was more widespread, Friedan argued that commercial fantasies in the form of 'sex-glutted novels, magazines, plays and films' were the corollary of the disappearance of sex from suburban marriages.[104] The 'spurious senselessness of our sexual preoccupation' stemmed from this paradox.

While women were not supplied with many fantasies, there was an extraordinary variety and sophistication of the forms of female spectacle that were available to men. These accustomed them to think of women in terms of their conformity to a standardized model. The leading sociologist C. Wright Mills drew a striking picture of a feminine type, which he called 'The All-American Girl', who had absorbed all the lessons of female spectacle of the previous half-century. This category included both professionals and young housewives:

In any New York night club on a big night at the time of the two o'clock show her current model can be found: with the doll face and the swank body starved down for the camera, a rather thin, ganted girl with the wan smile, the bored gaze, and often the slightly opened mouth, over which the tongue occasionally slides to insure the highlights. She seems, in fact, always to be practising for those high, nervous moments when the lens is actually there. The terms of her competition are quite clear: her professional stance is the stance of the woman for whom a haughty kind of unconquerable eroticism has become a way of life. It is the expensive look of an expensive woman who feels herself to be expensive. She has the look of a girl who knows her fate rests quite fully—even exclusively—upon the effect of her look on a certain type of man.

This is the queen—the all-American girl—who, whether she be debutante or fashion model or professional entertainer, sets the images of appearance and conduct which are imitated down the national hierarchy of glamour, to the girls carefully trained and selected for the commercial display of erotic promise, as well as to the young housewife in the kitchen.[105]

If modern society indeed organized women in terms of a hierarchy of glamour, and housewives were at the bottom of it, then even the most domesticated of men were systematically led to explore higher levels, or at least were being tempted by them. There had been major developments in erotic display since the war. During the conflict, men had got used to vicarious sexual satisfaction in the form of idealized pin-ups. Stars like Rita Hayworth and Betty Grable, or the fantasy illustrations of artists like Alberto Vargas ('Varga') and Gil Evgren, presented soldiers with pictures of healthy, optimistic, and erotically desirable women. As the conflict receded and organized leisure developed on a new scale, the pin-up girl also moved closer to the mainstream in the advertising culture of post-war consumerism. Having burgeoned in a subcultural milieu of men without women, she became the embodiment of the male-dominated American dream ('To a Frenchman, a pretty girl drinking from a Coca-Cola bottle is a gangster's moll or a hippie or some other out-of-the-ordinary personage. To an American, she is simply thirsty,' remarked one observer of the phenomenon).[106] At the same time, fantasies of eroticized femininity prospered in live entertainment. Burlesque stage-shows were offered by dedicated theatres, vaudeville houses, and nightclubs. These varied greatly in quality and sophistication from down-at-heel 'bump and grind' acts to lavish and ritzy striptease shows. On account of local censorship, performers seldom offered the sort of nude show that had been honed into a fine art in Paris. Instead, they developed elaborate stage personalities and used props and gimmicks to signal

260

individuality. The top performers became part of integrated programmes of entertainment in upmarket supper clubs and the large hotels of Las Vegas and Miami Beach. The flame-haired artiste Tempest Storm, who was widely seen as the queen of burlesque, matched the period's taste for the outsize. Her curvaceous figure suggested an 'excessive sexual appetite and the fantasy of sexual appetite'.[107] A larger-than-life figure, she owned Cadillacs, dressed in Cassini and Dior, and had a diamond collection to rival those of the Paris courtesans of yore. Like them she numbered some of the most celebrated men of her time among her lovers.[108] Her films of the mid-1950s included such masturbatory delights as *Hollywood Peepshow* and *Teaserama*.

Burlesque performers were sometimes launched by photographers who eagerly supplied a whole market of clandestine and semi-clandestine magazines for male consumption. Often short-lived, due to both the threat and reality of prosecution, titles like *Gent, Frolic, Show, Vue,* and *Escapade* featured nude or semi-nude models in a variety of standardized erotic poses and costumes. In Hollywood, nude photography was a commercial milieu parallel to cinema in which both aspirant and downward-sliding women found a role. There was a whole clandestine photographic market in the United States. Some of this operated on the basis of private commissions. Even the studio photographers occasionally took naked shots of female subjects for private use. George Hurrell claimed that he personally 'was never asked to do any private shots of stars for any of the executives in the studios' but he implied that other photographers were.[109] To avoid prosecution, photographers claimed that their work was pro-health or art-related. The most common camouflage, however, was glamour. Since glamour and sex appeal were so closely related, the term was widely used from the 1950s as a synonym—and sometimes as a euphemism—for erotic or soft-pornographic photography. A glamour photographer was a specialist in the polished presentation of female nudes.

Bruno Bernard was one of the more legitimate practitioners of this applied art. A German Jewish exile who set up in Los Angeles in 1940, he traded off the Hollywood name. 'Bernard of Hollywood' was one of the major signatures of pin-up photography. His aim was to 'sell' actors to the studios and, reputedly, he was expert at transforming 'nice-looking' women into larger-than-life illusionary beauties. One aspiring actress who entrusted herself to him was the future Marilyn Monroe. She was convinced that a portfolio of sex pictures would get her work. Bernard disagreed and told her that she should counterbalance her curvy figure with a look of complete innocence. 'Blend waif with Venus and you'll create combustion in photos,' he affirmed.[110] Under his tutoring, 'she changed the French baby-whore look into a variety of child-woman expressions'.[111] Sexuality remained her platform but it was moulded and contained by the criteria of the time. The result was a fabricated identity that would shortly evolve into 'Marilyn' the sex goddess.

A photographer who pursued a more specific erotic agenda was Russ Meyer, who would make his name in the 1960s with a series of low-budget erotic adventure films featuring large-breasted women. Meyer had no time for pseudo-artistic pretension. 'I am clearly in the business of producing glamor pictures for magazines for the express purpose of making money. I won't go as far as to say this is the only reason, but I will say it is the primary one,' he admitted.[112] He based his whole approach on the conviction that full-figured actresses like Marilyn, Anita Ekberg, Jayne Mansfield, and Sophia Loren succeeded at the box office due to their physique: 'if I may draw a parallel, my own production of glamor photographs has been greatly affected by my choice of full-bodied subjects,' he declared.[113] He made his base in Hollywood because of its marketing appeal but also because he found that there was no shortage of suitable subjects to be encountered even on the streets of the movie capital. Meyer began by photographing burlesque artistes, chorus girls, dancers, and so on. He claimed to have discovered Tempest Storm, who he photographed on several occasions.

With his forthright appreciation of the shapely female figure and adolescent references to what he called 'tittyboom',[114] Meyer exemplified the organized lechery that characterized this sector. However, the lucrative nature of the market and the opportunities it offered for female exhibitionism appealed to some women. Bunny Yeager established herself as one of very few all-round female protagonists of the art of male entertainment. A blonde beauty with a tanned body who loved southern California's beaches, she was a pageant winner who became a pin-up cover girl. Then she took up designing swimwear and turned her hand to photography. Yeager quickly established herself as a leading 'photographer of female pulchritude', to use her own description.[115] Several of her typical scenarios were reminiscent of movie scenes and she played herself as a photographer commissioned to capture Las Vegas showgirls in the film *Bunny Yeager's Nude Las Vegas*. Compared to Meyer's preference for the outsize, Yeager's models were lithe and she photographed them with a certain grace. However, both favoured movement in their models and preferred to shoot in the open air. Meyer talked of 'outdoor glamour', that is to say a natural look where nature contributed to the overall effect, while Yeager often used jungle settings and went for beach and swimsuit shots.

Both of them recognized the importance of a model having the right sort of face. 'Attractive facial characteristics' were vital both to delight the consumer and create a mood reminiscent of the pin-up. Yeager shot hundreds of models in the course of her career. Her most significant discovery was Bettie Page, the one erotic model who became well known not only because of her popularity but also because she was called before a Senate committee investigating obscenity. Page was not the most beautiful or striking of models. Nor, with her long, dark hair and averagely proportioned but toned physique, was she a product of the prevailing taste for artifice and excess. She established a huge following among men, it has been argued, because she was able to cover in a convincing way a wide range of niche tastes, from the beach shot to the sinister darkness of fetish wear, through the exoticism of jungle settings. Her 'on-tiptoes' poses and looks of innocent surprise meant that glamour pictures featuring her were always closer to tease than sleaze.

Yeager made Bettie Page famous by sending her pictures to *Playboy* founder Hugh Hefner who made her 'playmate of the month' in January 1955. Yeager had appeared in *Playboy* herself and was aware that the magazine, founded in 1953, was qualitatively different from the small-time publications that dominated the sex market. By virtue of its status as a class publication, it gave glamour photography legitimacy. It presented a curious mixture of luxury goods, conspicuous consumption, and airbrushed sex appeal. It was ostensibly aimed not at the furtive reader of men's magazines, but at the affluent, sexually attractive bachelor who was stylish and uninhibited. Hefner himself lived a lifestyle that was footloose and swinging. Perennially attired in pyjamas and dressing gown, he gave the impression that his main business was conducted at night, in strip joints, clubs, and casinos. Packed with upmarket advertising, *Playboy* deployed its centrefolds to guarantee the heterosexuality of its consuming male readers. At first, it employed professional models like Page, but then Hefner hit on the idea of recruiting girls-next-door such as contestants in the Miss America pageant.[116] This decision propelled the magazine to the centre of mainstream culture.[117] Several of the centrefolds were photographed by Meyer, including one featuring his wife Eve. As his profile grew, he also did portraits of female stars including Anita Ekberg, who, he said, was the most beautiful of all his subjects.[118]

Europeans often found it difficult to understand the whole business of pin-ups and centrefolds. 'Examine a group of modern pinups: at first they look extremely suggestive and in some ways they are,' wrote Richard Hoggart in his analysis of post-war British working-class culture.[119] 'And yet they are strangely ersatz, the sex has been machined out of them; at least all has gone except a strange kind of sex. They inhabit regions so stylized, so pasteurized, that the real physical quality has left them. But they have an unreal and remote perfection in their own kind of "sexiness". Everything has been stripped to a limited range of visual suggestions—can one imagine a mushy body-smell, un-artificially disordered hair, an uneven texture to the skin, hair on the arms and legs, beads of perspiration on the upper-lip, on one of these neatly-packaged creatures?', he wondered. During his journey through the United States in the mid-1950s, English writer J. B. Priestley noted many 'good-looking girls who have slender and almost boyish figures, with no pelvis to suggest maternity... yet carrying breasts that are exceptional among young white women, [yet which] are now the favourite erotic symbols of *Admass* men'.[120] He argued that the ubiquity of breasts showed the domination of the masculine principle; they did not suggest any true feeling for Woman but rather revealed a perversion of femininity at the hands of men with the appetites of a 'famished and frustrated baby, never finally weaned, still eager and hungry for the breast'.

European photographic eroticism had a different feel. In France, the traditional supplier of erotic images and ideas to the world, the market was dominated by the magazine *Folies de Paris et de Hollywood*, which began publishing in 1947 and sold 80,000 copies per fortnight. It presented scantily clad models and starlets cavorting in boudoirs, cabarets, or in the open air. Models posed directly on film sets or in saucily connotated Parisian cabarets. The culture of Parisian striptease was employed to turn the model into a sophisticated package that was distinguished from 'its sassy, bare-all, occasionally bargain basement American counterpart'.[121] In fact there was some cross-fertilization between the two countries, as the magazine title itself suggests. American artistes sometimes affected French attitudes, while some leading French performers, like Rita Cadillac and Dodo d'Homberg, spoofed American excess and glitz. In Britain, semi-clandestine suppliers of erotic material mostly imported their wares from France, although some was home-made. The 'Argyle Studios' in suburban Ealing peddled black-and-white and colour booklets of models with exotic names like Candita, Venecia, or even Nudita. Professional temptresses in various guises of semi-nudity flashed cheeky smiles and offered their untoned bodily charms in a range of kitsch settings and poses. Themed issues bore titles like 'Nude Charm', 'Nudes in Focus', 'Tropical Eves', or 'Modern Eves'.

Not by chance did the improbable, exotic names of the models in pornographic or glamour magazines belong to the same realm as the sequence of disposable nymphets that figure in Ian Fleming's spy novels featuring his character James Bond. Pussy Galore, Honey Rider, Kissy Suzuki, and Vesper Lynd are not real women but glamorized figments of a pornographic imagination. They are luxuries to be surveyed and enjoyed for recreational purposes.[122] In conception, they were elaborations of all the female figures of glamour modern men knew, from models to the air stewardesses whose charms were so blatantly plugged by the companies they worked for. Fleming's fantasy world would find a grand cinematic projection in the James Bond films from the first of the series, *Dr No*, in 1962. Like the novels, the films were riddled with the atmosphere of the cold war. But they were also glamorous fantasies of consumerism and hedonism.[123] The screen Bond was less of an establishment figure and more of a mongrel than he was in the novels. Sean Connery, for all his earthy authenticity, assembled agent 007's screen persona from elements taken from several older stars, including Clark Gable and Cary Grant. The former provided a template for the character's macho attitudes and the latter for his style and sophisticated tastes.

Grant was one of the most bankable stars of the 1950s and early 1960s and, despite the fact that he was well into middle age (he was born in 1904), he was among those considered for the Bond role. He was the ideal star of the age of affluence. His unique synthesis of British reserve, American optimism, urbane *savoir faire*, and fine tailoring created an irresistible hybrid that was lower class in conception. Grant, like Jay Gatsby—to whom his persona has been likened—was a common man who was living a dream of fulfilment that was exhibited for all to see.[124] He was a walking manual of how a modern gentleman should look and behave that was available for anyone to consult. A product of the big city, he had a holiday aura and was always 'triumphantly suntanned'.[125] Although Connery projected a more violent and carnal profile than Grant, the constructed nature of the Bond persona allowed male spectators to project themselves on to him.

Glamour in the 1950s was all about the attachment of dazzle and enchantment to mundane goods and routine lives. It was about the corporate orchestration of dreams and desires along scientifically programmed lines. The most common ciphers of these were feminine. In some quarters, glamour came to be defined as little more than the presentation of female beauty for the camera. The surrounding material environment was, however, always important. The fantasies of the era of mass consumerism were shaped by the product world. Yet the forms of living that took shape in the post-war years did not lead to universal acceptance of packaged lives and predictable temptations. Innovations in travel and communications, the demise of high society, and the rise of youth all brought new innovations in patterns of visual appeal. In consequence glamour, as a language of allure and desirability specific to capitalist society, also underwent changes. One consequence of these was that the focus on photography and female imagery expanded further. The photographic image became the mirror of a society in which glamour was a routine feature.

CHAPTER 9

PHOTOGRAPHY AND THE FEMALE IMAGE

Jacqueline Kennedy Onassis was the most photographed woman in the world in the 1960s. An ostensibly shy woman of semi-aristocratic American background, she became the most famous face of a decade that witnessed radical changes in politics, society, and culture. As the wife of President Kennedy, she redefined the image of the first lady; as his widow, she held a special place in the imagination of the nation and the world; later, as the wife of the Greek shipping millionaire Aristotle Onassis, she became a queen of café society—no longer a saint, she became a super-celebrity. 'Jackie' was the informal sobriquet by which everyone knew her. Most people, of course, 'knew' her only through the press, where she was not a person so much as a series of images. The most memorable of these were etched on the consciousness of the world because they were associated with the assassination of her first husband in Dallas on 22 November 1963. The pictures of her climbing over the back of the open-top limousine following Kennedy's shooting; the images, taken hours later, of her standing, mouth open in shock, in the same blood-spattered coat next to Lyndon Johnson on Air Force One as he was sworn in as president; her veiled face full of dignified sadness at her husband's interment at Arlington Cemetery—all of these contributed to her beatification. Her 'baptism by gunfire', to borrow Camille Paglia's expression,[1] situated her in a special place in the collective imagination. Not by chance, these were the images that Andy Warhol chose to incorporate into his celebrated silk screen portrait 'Sixteen Jackies', which was in fact just one of many single and multi-image depictions of her that the artist made using colours including red and gold.

By the time of the assassination, Jackie Kennedy was already a figure with a very precise image. She had married John F. Kennedy, the junior senator from Massachusetts and one of the most eligible bachelors in the United States, in September 1953, when she was 24, and she achieved nationwide fame during his election campaign in 1960. As first lady, she embarked on the highly publicized project of redecorating the White House. Moreover, she brought a particular fashion dimension to her role. *Women's Wear Daily* cheekily dubbed her 'Her Elegance' and she quickly rose to the top of best-dressed lists worldwide.[2] Her appointed couturier, Oleg Cassini, a naturalized American of Russian stock who had been raised in Florence, provided her with garments of a refined elegance. Her aim was to avoid sensationalist fashion stories or charges of extravagance. She did not wish to be 'the Marie Antoinette or Empress Josephine of the 1960s', she told Cassini.[3] Instead she informed him that she wanted to dress as if her husband were the president of France. She demanded approval of any publicity that he should issue and also instructed him to ensure that her dresses were unique. Her inauguration wardrobe marked the beginning of what would become known as 'the Jackie look'. While the department store Bergdorf's made her dress for the swearing-in ceremony and Cassini created a fawn-coloured coat with sable collar and muff to wear with it, it was the fur-trimmed pillbox hat created by the couturier Halston (the professional name of Roy Halston Fowick) that captured most attention. It was youthful and playful and, although not a novelty, it became identified with her more than anyone else.

Together Jack and Jackie Kennedy were one of the most glamorous couples in world. They created a special dynamic with the public that sprang from their youth and good looks as well as their wealth and style. Jack had become the Democratic Party's poster boy soon after he was elected to the

Senate in 1952 at age 32. He was aware of the political utility of his handsome looks and used to send signed 'glossy glamour-boy photographs' of himself to constituents.[4] When the party leadership opted for a political figure rather than an actor to narrate a Metro-Goldwyn-Mayer produced documentary on its history, he was an obvious choice for the role.[5] A female dimension to his image was added when, at his father Joe's instigation, Jack's presidential campaign mobilized the women in the family clan as cheerleaders. With their strong looks and fine heads of hair, they aroused the curiosity of the electorate. None, however, had more impact than Jackie. Some supporters feared that, as a couple, they would be too polished and glitzy for the voters in the Democratic primaries. According to Charles Peters, editor of *Washington Monthly* and one of JFK's Democratic nomination campaign organizers in West Virginia, the effect was in fact the reverse. 'What amazed me most, I think, was the way people reacted to Jackie,' he later recalled. 'I first got the sense through Jackie's emerging popularity, of what was happening in American society. There was no question that instead of identifying with the woman who was like them—Muriel Humphrey [wife of Kennedy's rival for the nomination, Senator Hubert Humphrey]—they identified with the Princess. You could just tell they wanted Jackie. They had a wondrous look in their eyes when they saw her. After the dowdiness of Eleanor Roosevelt, Bess Truman and Mamie Eisenhower, they were looking for an aristocratic image. And the Kennedys did a superlative job of merchandising that image.'[6]

What was meant in the America of the late fifties and early sixties by 'an aristocratic image'? No return to the extreme inequalities of the gilded age was desired, nor was there any appetite for the hauteur of the mid-nineteenth-century social elite. The idea of aristocracy still implied some element of breeding and taste, but in the era of mass consumption and rising living standards this was conceived as a template rather than an inherited attribute. In the age of Audrey Hepburn and Grace Kelly, the idea of aristocracy evolved into an image of accessible class that combined elements of glamour, taste, and manners. This was not quite the 'more than glamour' of royalty since it was moulded for public consumption and lacked the bolster of history. Something akin to Grace Kelly's 'sexual elegance' was regarded as the modern equivalent of female aristocratic style and Jackie supplied this.[7] She was contemporary, steeped in French culture, and was highly photogenic. Although, as the first lady, she occupied a terrain removed from the hurly-burly of celebrity, she was drawn by events into the realm of glamour.

Over the decade, the nature of Jackie's image changed significantly in ways that were related to the broader changes that the decade brought. While the 1950s had been marked by a return to family, authority, and religion in the aftermath of war, the 1960s saw the emergence of youth culture and protest, changes in personal relationships and behaviour, freer expression in literature, the arts and the mass media, and attitudes towards life and life goals.[8] A loosening of conventions and standards occurred in a context that witnessed the affirmation of television as the dominant medium and a sudden multiplication of theatres, nightclubs, discotheques, photographic and model agencies, film companies, and magazines.[9] With mass communications taking such a central role, it was not without reason that the French situationist Guy Debord formulated the idea of the 'society of spectacle'.[10] The commercialism of the era and the development of electronic media broke down barriers and facilitated mobility and exchange between continents, classes, and cultural forms. All public acts entered the realm of the media, thanks to the complex interaction of the press, public opinion, and commercial interests.[11] These innovations had the effect of sidelining conventional high society—which no longer attracted the intense curiosity of earlier decades—in favour of metropolitan elites of youth, beauty, talent, and creativity. The consequence of this was a new informal focus on glamour. Jackie's personal trajectory after the assassination of her husband made her into a symbol and conduit of some of these transformations.

Jackie's background prepared her well for the type of sympathetic, attractive upper-class image that went over well in the media. She did not in fact belong to the upper crust of American society. Her stepfather, Hugh Auchinloss, belonged to one of the oldest families in America but her own father, John 'Black Jack' Bouvier, was a disreputable rake. He had been born into a rich Long Island family and made money in the stock market, but he was best known for his movie-star good looks, fastidious dressing, and womanizing.[12] Jackie's mother's social background was less exalted and she was seen as a social climber. Jackie's sophistication came from having grown up in New York, attending the best schools, and taking vacations in Europe.[13] She studied at Vassar and the Sorbonne; she had also been debutante of the year, and had won the *Vogue* Prix de Paris contest for college seniors, although she had not taken up the prize of a year-long *stage* in Paris. She could speak reasonable French, Spanish, and Italian.

The first to realize the potential of Jackie's curriculum was Joe Kennedy, who thought that her Frenchness could balance and correct the Kennedys' Irishness. She was the ideal mate for his son because, while also being Catholic, she brought the possibility of upward social mobility. Joe had made his money bootlegging and producing B movies and had no social cachet. The Kennedys, moreover, were not an accepted part of the Boston social scene.[14] He decided to put his sons into politics by way of compensation. He was sure that the American public would be no less wowed by Jackie's poise and manner than he was, precisely because her patrician image was more stylized than real.[15] Despite appearances, she was neither rich nor possessing lineage. Indeed, she behaved like a social climber. She liked to meet the rich and famous and had aimed to marry well. Although the Kennedys lacked the refinement to which she was accustomed, they had money.

A core aspect of the glamour of both Jack and Jackie was that they offered an image of accessible class. They were not wrapped up in the aloof remoteness of the long-established rich; rather they had a touch of vulgarity that made them understandable and popular. They revelled in the public realm and they were public property.[16] As the president's wife, Jackie was inevitably forced to live in a way that was less than private. She struggled to make her life in the White House and that of her children as much of a normal domestic environment as possible. However, the frenzy that surrounded her went well beyond that accorded to previous first ladies. She was charming, refined, and fashionable. Her ability to fascinate was the product of the training she received from her father in how to keep herself intriguing and slightly aloof.[17] Even in the smallest gatherings, her magic was not dimmed. She delighted numerous political figures by becoming, according to one observer, 'a bewitching lighthouse beacon of charm'.[18] In the popular imagination, Jackie was often treated like a star, but, like Grace Kelly, one with a difference. American celebrity magazines happily placed her on their covers alongside TV and movie stars. *Photoplay* and other magazines paired her with Elizabeth Taylor. In the early 1960s, with Liz's affair with Richard Burton at its height, the two women were contrasted: 'Marriage and Taste' marked Jackie's life, while Liz's was mired by 'Passion and Waste'.[19]

Jackie, it was said, made Washington a brighter and gayer place to be. She ensured that the style of entertaining became grander and more formal. She raised the quality of cuisine and introduced French chefs and menus. Her favourite historical figure was Madame Récamier, the beautiful *saloniste* of Napoleonic France.[20] The presidential couple were bathed in an unprecedented glow of publicity and their every move was recounted and scrutinized. What surprised some was that the first lady received more of the limelight than the president. Whole swathes of the press found her female glamour more interesting than his male charm. Nowhere was this truer than during the presidential visit to Paris in May 1961. Relations between France and the United States were not very good at that time, and for that reason much attention was fixed on the president's Francophile wife, who was identified as a bearer of goodwill between the two countries. Eyes were trained on her to such an extent that Jack quipped during a speech at the gala dinner at Versailles: 'I do not think it entirely inappropriate for me to introduce myself. I am the man who accompanied Jacqueline Kennedy to Paris,' adding, lest anyone think he was resentful, 'and I have enjoyed it'.[21] Her styling for the occasion was in expert hands. Her hair, worn down rather than up on formal occasions, was entrusted to Alexandre, hairdresser to Greta Garbo and Elizabeth Taylor, while Hubert de Givenchy, Audrey Hepburn's favourite designer, designed the gown she wore to the state banquet at Versailles. Her make-up for that occasion was executed by the well-known artiste Nathalie.

Photographic images of Jackie are very numerous. She was probably the most photographed woman of the 1960s and at least some of her appeal derived from the fact that she was also 'the most photogenic woman in the world', to quote Cecil Beaton.[22] In this sense she was a highly emblematic figure of the period and a part of pop culture. Not only was she prominent and glamorous, she was also a founding member of a new community of famous people whose fame derived partly or wholly from their relationship with the camera. These were people who inhabited the post-war world of the illustrated magazines. Photography was a feature of Jackie's existence right from her engagement in June 1953. After the announcement, she and Jack spent three days posing for a *Life* magazine photographer for a cover story about their romance. Her wedding too was a media event. Jackie's mother had intended a small, exclusive ceremony in Newport without pictures or crowds but was informed by Joe Kennedy that publicity was inevitable so it might as well be harnessed from the start. As he saw it, the aim was not to hide Jackie but to show her to best advantage.[23] Her magazine life continued with a fashion shoot with her sister Lee for the *Ladies' Home Journal* in December 1957 and beyond. Jackie always expected to be photographed in a flattering way and to exercise control over her image. As a woman whose smile lit up a thousand magazine covers and who was perpetually on 'best-dressed' lists, she was a publicity magnet.

Jackie's appeal cannot be separated from her physical being. Young, and slightly taller than average at 5' 7", she had high cheekbones, sensuous lips, wide-set eyes, and a sleek athletic figure. She had a wild, earthy beauty, one observer noted, that seemed fragile in photographs.[24] She had the grace of a ballet dancer and was seen to have the same refined brunette appeal as Audrey Hepburn. Totally different from the buxom blondes who were regarded as the embodiment of post-war America, she was distinct from the erotic ideal of consumer society. Her sex appeal was contained and subtle rather than up for grabs. She was imagined by Cassini as 'an ancient Egyptian princess'. 'There was her sphinxlike quality and her eyes, which were classically, very beautifully set. When I thought of Jackie, I saw a hieroglyphic figure: the head in profile, broad shoulders, slim torso, narrow hips, long legs, and good carriage,' he later wrote.[25] Her fascination was enhanced by the fact that she did not give interviews; she was an icon and a cipher whose silence betrayed an emptiness into which everyone could project themselves. Not by chance, she was drawn to Greta Garbo, who, long after her sudden retirement from the screen, was still an object of curiosity.[26]

Jackie's initial image as first lady was bound up with her restoration of formality, fine dining, and high taste to public life. She was keen on history and was very sensitive to it in the project of redecoration she undertook on the White House. However, her close association with the world of fashion meant that she was alert to trends that would undercut the continuity of social rituals and radically shake up relations between the old and young generations as well as between rich and poor and black and white. As photography acquired a special role in creating as well as recording and spreading fame on the international level, youth and beauty won out over power or pedigree. Changes followed in relations between the rich and powerful, the fashion world and the press. These were not peculiar to the United States; they occurred with equal force on both sides of the Atlantic.

A key figure in the process of rejuvenation was the fashion editor Diana Vreeland, first of *Harper's Bazaar* then—from 1962—of *Vogue*. Vreeland was a key mover and shaker of the decade. She had the appearance of a high priestess; she loved gold jewellery and adored vivid styles and artifice. She invented the role of the contemporary fashion editor, not as a society figure but as a mediator and innovator. In this capacity, she made connections between high fashion and the social currents of the period. She mixed celebrities, political figures, and artists with coverage of new trends and the Third World. She glorified influential individuals and made them current through make-up and fashion.[27] To assist her in her revolution, Vreeland mobilized a variety of talents. She turned first to one of the most long-established figures in the world of fashion. Cecil Beaton had been a royal favourite since the 1930s and was responsible for the official portraits at the 1953 British coronation. He had photographed the exiled royals of Italy and Romania and the Hollywood elite; he worked for leading fashion magazines on both sides of the Atlantic, often featured on lists of best-dressed men, holidayed with socialites and millionaires in the Mediterranean, was the house guest of British aristocrats, and designed films and stage shows including a highly successful *My Fair Lady* in London. He often commentated on beauty and glamour and published a first volume of memoirs, *The Wandering Years*, in 1961.[28]

Despite his long experience, Beaton was always keen to remain at the head of the pack. By virtue of his position, he was drawn into the reconfiguration of glamour that began to take shape in the early 1960s. Even though he was

274

still photographing debutantes, Vreeland told him in 1961 that high society was no longer interesting; 'today only personality counts, with very few exceptions unless it is a "new beauty",' she wrote.[29] He was asked to get 'some very young, raky types that would be amusing for us also etc. Youth is the best thing we can get.' One of the key developments of the 1960s was the emergence of beauty as a quality equivalent to material success.[30] Vreeland was quick to see this and coined the expression 'the beautiful people'. By this she simply meant 'people who are beautiful to look at'.[31] 'It's been taken up to mean people who are rich,' she later clarified; 'we mean the charmers but there is no harm to be rich.' The members of this new estate were able to bypass the social thresholds of the 1950s because they had qualities of youth, health, and sexiness. A few years later, in May 1965, Vreeland was on the prowl for more beauties and new stars and told Beaton: 'only you can give the super duper quality and make the choices'.[32] By this time, the photographer was 61 and had recently completed what would remain his best-known work—designing the Edwardian sets and costumes for the film version of *My Fair Lady*. He was happy to immerse himself in the new culture of the day. It has been said that Vreeland's 'greatest contribution is to have understood the 1960s immediately'.[33] She saw that the dramatic changes in taste of the period were liberating to style. She made the most of the explosion of energy in art, pop, and society and was open to alternatives to Western beauty and style. Democratic in attitude, she 'stood for the accessible ideal'.[34] In glamour this is crucial and would become ever more so in the age of youth culture and mass consumption.

As an older generation photographer who conserved a notable influence, Beaton was not alone. Norman Parkinson was another eccentric gentleman photographer who had begun work in the 1930s but who remained active into the 1960s and 1970s. Like Beaton, he was a man of middle-class origins who reinvented himself as a quasi-aristocratic personality and who maintained a theatrical public image throughout his career—complete with trademark dress style and quirky touches (notably, the invention of the Porkinson sausage).[35] Born Ronald Smith, he had grown up in the comfortable London suburb of Putney and attended Westminster school. However, his aristocratic stature (he was 6′ 5″ tall) and right-wing views somewhat offset his middle-class origins (his father had been a shopkeeper). In stark contrast to Beaton's highly artificial compositions, he preferred the dynamism and energy of the modern world. Even in the 1930s, he shot in the street, embracing the freedom of the open-air. The invention by Leica in 1935 of a new camera with a shutter speed of 1/1000 second allowed fashion photography to take to the streets. New York news photographer Martin Munkacsi first photographed clothes in real life situations where they might actually be worn. Then Edward Steichen synchronized the new shutter speed with flashbulbs permitting faster movement in a wider range of contexts to be captured. Parkinson learned from their work even as he continued with society portraiture and conventional fashion pictures. In the 1940s and 1950s, he worked for *Vogue*, for which he shot many pictures of fashionable women on stations, in public houses, and in ordinary places. The effect was twofold: the models looked extraordinary in contrast to their inelegant surroundings, while they and their sumptuously styled garments were made to look part of the real world.

The press was an important innovator of the period and, while some established magazines were swift to change, important headway was made by new titles or new editorial directions. *The Queen* was a house magazine of the British landed and moneyed classes that was bought in 1957 by Jocelyn Stevens. Nephew of Edward Hulton, the publisher of Britain's post-war illustrated weekly, *Picture Post*, Stevens gradually reinvented the magazine.[36] In the mid-1950s, the British press regarded debutantes as good copy and their activities as ideal fodder for the mass of newspaper readers. 'What the papers really wanted was debs, hundreds of them, preferably photographed having a jolly nice time dancing the night away at some high-society party,' recalled upper-class photographer Patrick Lichfield.[37] By sacking the fashion editor and clearing out the former debutantes who staffed the magazine, Stevens opened the way for the unconventional. Steadily, he turned it into one of the conduits of the new energy that would shake up society and its rituals. He hired Cartier-Bresson to provide the pictorials of Queen Charlotte's ball, the traditional first engagement of the debutante season, while his Cambridge contemporary Antony Armstrong-Jones was allowed to inject irony into his pictures of the Chelsea Flower Show and the Trooping of the Colour. Cruft's was similarly subjected to mild lampooning. This did not win him any credit with Beaton who only ever worked for the most prestigious publications. He took the view that, by working for magazines and newspapers, the younger man had sullied himself.[38] In Beaton's aloof view, this was second-rate drudgery. Nevertheless, Armstrong-Jones was vital and charming and was much in demand. His witty and informal pictures were unusual and started a trend that would prove influential. In the sixties, Parkinson left *Vogue* for *Queen* (Stevens dropped 'The' from its title) and brought his trademark fluency and sense of movement to the magazine. He engaged with the artistic trends of the time, for example translating the geometrism of op art into his work. The magazine also accepted early photographs of Chelsea designer Mary Quant's boutique wear and published Helmut Newton pictures that had been rejected by *Vogue* on the grounds that they were indecent.[39]

Vreeland and Stevens were very different individuals but they were on the same wavelength in seeking to move their magazines towards a new way of relating to society. Before, no one had got into *Queen* who was not a member of high society. Now new talents were emerging and youth culture was making its presence felt as the post-war baby boomers took on the con-figuration of a new generation. Like Vreeland, Stevens took 'the view that society was dead', and 'began to promote the alternatives'.[40] Although neither of them completely bypassed debutantes, they only selected the most interesting or modern for coverage.[41] Together with their collaborators they contributed to the transformation and opening-out of high society.[42] Photography provided a key channel through which the feel of these and other publications was updated. While the writing was also given an ad-renalin shot, in *Queen*'s case with gossipy reviews and features, photographs were crucial in widening the visual horizons of a publication and bringing new people into the mix. They did not attack the existing structures of society but cut coverage of the aristocratic and wealthy elite and published pictures that reflected the real world. The new visual horizon of fashion and high society magazines was increasingly international. Models were photo-graphed in Kenya and nearly a whole issue of *Queen* was devoted to Cartier-Bresson's photographs taken in Communist China. In consequence, the doings of debutante Charlotte or baronet Sir Charles seemed small and uninteresting. *Queen* boldly declared in 1964 that haute couture, which in the late 1940s had seemed on the verge of a renaissance, was dead. Although several new houses had opened at that time, the overall number dropped in the years that followed as fewer women had the time or resources to devote to its demanding perfection and the occasions on which formal dresses might be worn diminished.

One consequence of the shake-up in society was a larger role for the press and for photographers in particular. They found themselves performing a crucial role of social mediation in the more fluid social context that was taking shape. With just a handful of exceptions, photographers were still background figures. Former Eton pupil and Cambridge graduate Armstrong-Jones first covered debutantes' parties for *Queen* magazine while he was apprenticed to a society photographer. Despite his well-to-do background, he found that upper-class hostesses treated him as a workman and more or less showed him to the tradesman's entrance when he arrived.[43] Even Beaton was sometimes given brusque treatment by the royal family.[44] Armstrong-Jones's courtship of, and marriage in 1960 to, the Queen's playgirl sister Princess Margaret instantly transformed the position of the photographer. Although some old fogies wondered if the Princess's home of Clarence House would soon be invaded by beatniks demanding all-night bottle-parties, most of the establishment did not openly question his suitability.[45] As the Earl of Snowden, Armstrong-Jones brought kudos to his profession and lent it social visibility. No more would the photographer be seen as little better than a glorified hairdresser or plumber. 'Almost overnight', Jonathan Aitken wrote, 'lensmen became invested with glamour and prestige.' [46] Advertisers, newspapers and magazines, and fashion companies suddenly realized their power and influence and their earnings went up dramatically.

The collapse of interest in debutantes did not mean that there was a lack of curiosity about young beauty. If the debutante was a dying breed, then the world of the media found a replacement in the form of the fashion model. Models had become better known as individuals in the post-war years. Magazines liked them because they helped simplify and humanize fashion by creating clear and identifiable 'looks'. Young, beautiful, and photogenic, models provided the bridge between the remote realm of haute couture and the real horizons of their readers.[47] Their status was further enhanced by a series of feature films based on their worlds, including the 1957 Audrey Hepburn vehicle *Funny Face*. For Ginette Spanier, director of the Balmain fashion house, this elevation was an effect of publicity that was especially marked in the English-speaking world. 'In England and America mannequins are regarded with awe-struck fascination as though they were a new part of the aristocracy,' she lamented. 'Just like the Gaiety Girls and the chorus girls of the 1890s, they are capable of escaping from their environment. But this means they usually create a furore in their own right: as the "Most Beautiful Deb" of the year might do... as Miss World usually does.'[48] However, even in France models were taking on new functions distinct from their specific roles in fashion houses. The mannequin Bettina was one of the first to leave her employer, Jacques Fath, to embark on a new career as a photographic model or 'cover-girl'. 'In those days, being a cover-girl was something new in France,' she recalled. 'It involved quite different techniques from those used by a mannequin and required altogether different qualities.... Just as the mannequin collaborates with the couturier. So the model collaborates with the photographer. A good cover-girl takes up her stance immediately, and is paid more because she saves time and money.'[49] Even more than mannequins, the photographic models had to convey an idea that met the needs of the moment. 'When I was at the height of my career,' Bettina noted, 'fashion decreed very sophisticated photographs. Models never smiled, but stood with half-open lips in stiff, dramatic poses, and were represented as impersonal creatures, unreal things.'[50] She found that in New York the spontaneity of Paris was replaced by 'factory-like discipline': improvisation and good humour had no place in a system that privileged speed, uniformity, and efficiency. There was less difference in the results, though, since American cosmetics companies preferred elitist aloofness like the French.

Models were mostly photographed in studios where they worked with photographers to create sophisticated and elaborately artificial images. However, although the posed, highly artificial studio shot created by photographers like Horst P. Horst, Beaton, and Hoyningen-Huené persisted well into the post-war years, street photography of the type favoured by Parkinson became more popular. Despite the debacle of the attempt to shoot Dior models in the working-class district of Montmartre, Russian exile Alexander Liberman imported the unposed realism of news photography into Paris fashion coverage. The aim was to overcome the mannered exercises of the past and allow fashion to breathe the air of contemporary life.[51] The new style generated some classic images of fashion photography such as Lisa Fonssagrives modelling dresses on the Eiffel Tower, while many other models were posed with scenes of everyday life as their backdrop. Although he became the most famous couturier in the world after he took over the mantle of Christian Dior, the man who stood for Paris fashion more than any other in the world's eyes, Yves Saint Laurent, was far from being a defender of tradition. He boldly challenged expectations by presenting in 1960 a 'Beat' collection, consisting of black turtleneck sweaters in cashmere, shiny crocodile-skin jackets, and leather boots, that was inspired by the Left Bank beatniks. Although high artistry and exquisite quality were not lacking, it was the first time that street styles had been seen on a couture catwalk.[52]

Although Beaton and Parkinson contributed to the process of rejuvenation, there were limits to their powers of adaptation. In 1963, Parkinson was 50 and Beaton well into his sixties; inevitably some of the energy of the 1960s passed them by. It was the younger photographers who captured the urban street buzz of the moment and who moved beyond the old styles of fashion and portrait photography. David Bailey served his apprenticeship as an assistant to John French, a prominent British fashion photographer of the 1950s who stole a march on his contemporaries by perfecting a crisp and clear black-and-white photography that worked well in newspapers. French was a photographer of the old school who saw himself as a composer of works of art. He dressed formally and spoke in a clipped manner. Bailey, by contrast, was an unrefined and uneducated East Ender who made no attempt to disguise his origins. He was good-looking and cocky, but not too arrogant to realize that he could gain much from his boss. While French composed his models into marvels of poise and static elegance in his studio,

Bailey's job was to arrange the props and carry out what was regarded as the menial task of clicking the camera.

French's connections with the daily press would be crucial in allowing Bailey to build a career of his own. At the start of the 1960s, he had the great advantage of being in the right place at the right time. The press was discovering youth, old rituals were being shaken up by wider access to education and the spread of consumer society, and there was a more casual atmosphere. British *Vogue* was aware of being a bit stuffy and looked to him to provide some rejuvenation. His work was featured in a rubric called 'Young Idea'. Bailey was the first new man of the sixties, a good-looking charmer who forced his way into a glamorous world without in any way reinventing himself as faux-posh. He was an East Ender who spoke with a cockney accent and revelled in his street credentials. Soon, totally new photographers like Bailey and his working-class colleagues Terence Donovan and Brian Duffy were everywhere. They forced their way into a profession that was the preserve of men of a different stripe by capturing a mood and a moment in a new way. They were almost all young men who had a healthy disrespect for the conventions of their trade and for social hierarchy. With their carefree manner and unique way of turning their trade into a lifestyle, they situated themselves at the heart of a cultural transformation that deposed conventional glamorous imagery and replaced it with something younger, more casual, and breezy. The photographers did not offer real or simulated images of grand style but instead captured the spirit of their times and of the cities they worked in.

The young photographers had a number of things in common with the Roman photographers of the *dolce vita*. Both were young men from outside the establishment; they were of working-class origin and they would play a part in shifting public attention away from the social elite towards the casually famous. However, although some of the paparazzi, including Tazio Secchiaroli, the most prominent of their number, would become set photographers working closely with film directors, none of them would ever enter the inner circle of Italian fashion. The Londoners by contrast stormed the citadel and revolutionized the way in which fashion was narrated and

281

depicted in specialist magazines and the daily press. They achieved this by bringing in a breath of fresh air and introducing excitement and sex appeal. Using youth as their calling card, they pioneered a whole new way of picturing fashion that restored its connection with the buzz of the city and its personalities. They did not use statuesque ladylike models but girls they found on the street, ordinary young women who became at their hands contemporary icons.

Bailey and his protégée and lover Jean Shrimpton were at the forefront of a transformation in the relationship between fashion and society. They were able to seize centre stage because the cult of the fashion model was not a new phenomenon but one that had been taking shape for several years. In Britain, informal, accessible pictures came into their own in the 1960s. While John French insisted on white gloves, pearls, and stud earrings as props to an idea of femininity, Shrimpton was always more down-to-earth. Although her difference from earlier models can be exaggerated, as she had poise and some class, she struck her contemporaries as a new type. Duffy used her at the start of her career for a Kellogg's cornflakes advertisement because they wanted 'an ordinary girl who looked as if she might come from the country'; 'Duffy had chosen me because I was the epitome of ordinariness,' she later claimed.[53] In fact, she was privately educated and was not at all 'working class', despite her own claims to this effect; but she was certainly not upper class or rich. Shrimpton always made a point of being a scruff. 'In those early days, at a time when model girls and young actresses were bandbox perfect, I had little flair for fashion. . . . I have always been a bit of a mess. Yet somehow there are people who seem to warm to this messiness,' she self-deprecatingly recalled in her autobiography.[54] She had acquired poise and confidence on a Lucie Clayton modelling course but, despite some assignments for *Vogue*, had little idea about cosmetics, grooming, or clothes. Bailey spotted in her some waifish, coltish quality that he could mould into what became the Jean Shrimpton look, a look that required little hairdressing or make-up.[55] One of the first English models not to have a cut-glass accent, she had an ironical, detached view of fashion.

Shrimpton became, in Bailey's hands, the first model in England to become famous solely on the strength of her photographic work. Prior to her, the models in the magazines had been anonymous. With only one or two exceptions, no one beyond the cognoscenti knew who they were. Shrimpton was immediately distinctive. She had blue eyes, exotic eyebrows, a perfect squareish face, generous lips, and a pointed nose. Stiff and gawky, she looked like a cross between Vivien Leigh and Brigitte Bardot, a look that also applied to the actress Suzy Kendall. Bailey groomed her and arranged for her to be photographed by Beaton and other established names. However, his own pictures were what made Shrimpton into 'The Shrimp', a face and name everyone knew. He did not focus on the clothes in his fashion pictures but rather on the model. 'The girl is always the most important, then the dress,' he declared. 'If she's not looking stunning, then I figure the dress doesn't, either. The girl is the catalyst that brings it all together.'[56] Diana Vreeland, the then newly appointed editor of American *Vogue*, was receptive to the novelty Bailey represented. He had worked in the United States before and had sent shock waves through the magazine world by turning up in jeans and leather jacket. Vreeland, however, took to him immediately and hailed his and Shrimpton's arrival in her office with a peremptory, 'Stop! They are adorable! The English have arrived!'[57] Bailey's shots of Shrimpton on the streets of New York for an April 1962 *Vogue* feature entitled 'Young Idea Goes West' were striking for the originality of the urban compositions and the mood of reality that permeated them. Shrimpton was shot in Harlem, Chinatown, and Greenwich Village with passers-by included.

Between 1962 and 1964, Bailey photographed Shrimpton almost exclusively, turning her into the most famous model in the world. The one-time country girl became a girl-about-town and she was drawn into Bailey's mainly low-life milieu. Although he was earning a lot of money, was constantly travelling abroad for work, and even drove a Rolls Royce, he preferred to relax on his own territory. He had a wide network of acquaintances but always preferred to hang out with photographers, models, and musicians in the informal offbeat cafés, pubs, and dives of the East End. After Shrimpton left him for the actor Terence Stamp, her lifestyle changed. Although Stamp was also an East End boy, he had undergone a metropolitan makeover and he was aspirational. Unlike Bailey, he had a taste for the high life. He and Shrimpton were hailed as the two most beautiful people in London and they enjoyed lavish living that was no longer the preserve of the established rich. 'No more driving down to Chang's in the East End for chow mein,' recalled Shrimpton:

night after night we went to the White Elephant Club in Curzon Street or the Caprice in Arlington Place just down the road from the Ritz. In these watering-holes for the rich and famous we sat in pink satin and red plush surroundings while the waiters fussed over us. Everyone watched us as we sat at our usual table eating off fine china set on pink linen tablecloths and, equally curious, we watched back. The clientele was mostly celebrities—people like Richard Attenborough and his wife, John Mills and his wife, and Elizabeth Taylor when she was in town. In those days film people lived grander lives than they do today. We made our appearances in these obligatory restaurants with clockwork regularity. Terry and I were the young glamorous couple around town, on display each night with whoever he had invited to join us.[58]

The East End photographers propelled their discoveries into the public eye and made them into emblems of the moment. In this, they were assisted by a press that was fascinated by beautiful models of run-of-the-mill origins. Celia Hammond, originally discovered by Norman Parkinson, was taken up by Terence Donovan, while Brian Duffy made Paulene Stone into a household face. The 'model makers' themselves achieved almost as much coverage and they were equated with the pop singers who were giving the period its soundtrack. Although they did not consider themselves to be an organic part of the fashion industry, they became the new gatekeepers of a world that more disposable income had turned into a central arena of contemporary culture. Pop music, television, advertising, art, design, and architecture were all new or rapidly changing spheres generating new money and new faces. Soon a new elite had emerged of pop bands, actors, models, and new-style entrepreneurs, plus a few privileged and moneyed types who were hip enough to fit in.[59] Pop music proved to be an instant launch pad and *Queen* itself helped turn pop stars into celebrities. In 1964, for example, it published a Parkinson photographic feature under the title 'How to Kill 5 Stones With 1 Bird' that juxtaposed a female model with the Rolling Stones.[60] New acts could be conjured up out of almost nothing. To take one example, Marianne

Faithfull was a former convent girl with long fair hair and a husky voice, who was spotted by record producer Andrew Loog Oldham at a Rolling Stones launch party in 1964 and signed up on the spot. Her record 'As Tears Go By', penned by Oldham with Mick Jagger and Keith Richard, was a hit and she was photographed by Bailey. Soon she was a part of the metropolitan milieu and enjoyed a much-publicized relationship with Jagger.

A 1965 *Queen* article on 'The New Class' argued that the 'pop revolution' had heralded the emergence of a new publicity-hungry class based on income not capital. It featured, among others, Andy Warhol, the Beatles, the Rolling Stones, designer Terence Conran, and Princess Margaret.[61] Such people, it was claimed, 'were bred from the Affluent Arts out of the Consumer State. The Arts have blossomed into Entertainment. They have swallowed up Media and Communication. They are now swallowing up the World.'[62] Bailey added his contribution with the publication in December of the same year of his *Box of Pin-Ups*.[63] This was a collection of thirty-six stark black-and-white portraits of the famous faces of the day and included top models and pop stars as well as Stamp, Michael Caine, David Hockney, Vidal Sassoon, and, most notoriously, the East End gangsters the Kray twins. In his introduction to the collection, Francis Wyndham argued, 'Glamour dates fast, and it is its ephemeral nature which both attracts Bailey and challenges him.'[64] By glamour, Wyndham did not simply mean 'fame', but rather a type of celebrity aura in which novelty, youth, beauty, and controversy were all important elements. The people pictured knew that it was this quality that was being photographed and this was reflected in their insouciant or arrogant attitudes. The fact that Bailey also included the image-makers Brian Epstein, manager of the Beatles, and Andrew Loog Oldham showed that he was keenly aware that glamour was closely related to the manipulation of the image of fame. The makers of fame became in the process famous themselves.

The in-crowd of the sixties bore some resemblance to café society and its publicity-driven successor—'publi-ciety'.[65] It was visible and public, it was reasonably accessible, it was mixed and exciting; in addition, it included the best-looking people and those who were currently most famous. It relied heavily on publicity and indeed was dominated by it. But whereas café society and publi-ciety were subordinates or emanations of high society, the new in-crowds were born outside and were distinct from the social elite. However, like Hollywood in the 1920s, rarely were they entirely separate for long. The excitement they offered drew young and déclassé aristocrats, who bonded by virtue of youth with the new talents and drew them towards the places and manners of the elite. Some pop stars, perhaps most strikingly Mick Jagger, eagerly socialized with the upper class and a number of them would later follow the American millionaires of the nineteenth century in buying up aristocratic piles and living in the country like landed gentry. In the process, the image of formal, dressed-up elegance that had been the sign of aristo-cratic good taste lost influence. The formal elegance of debutantes' balls, which persisted even after palace presentations were discontinued, simply crumbled under the impact of high jinks and simple disaffection. Upper-class young people took their lead from others. 'People stopped wearing white ties and stumped around in dinner jackets...they just arrived in whatever they were wearing,' Philippa Pullar lamented: 'there was a new class image and pop stars were the new elite, the whole of society was mostly made up of restless rootless people with no connection to the soil, spending most of their time in cities.'[66] The new milieu often first took shape outside established zones of prestige and wealth, for example in Chelsea not Mayfair in London, on the Left rather than the Right Bank in Paris and in Greenwich Village rather than Fifth Avenue in New York. But the input of new money often brought a new atmosphere to nightlife in or near the most prestigious zones. In London, pop stars, models, hairdressers, sportsmen, actors, and others gathered in clubs like the Bag o'Nails in Soho or the Ad Lib in Leicester Square.[67] The newly famous cheerfully marked their success by appropriating established symbols of wealth such as the Rolls Royce, sports cars, jewellery, champagne, and exotic travel, often stripping them in the process of their class connotations.

One of the most important features of all the new industries of the 1960s was that they connected with mass audiences and evolved in close relation with their tastes and preferences. The old trickle-down model whereby innovations in fashion, style, and entertainment started at the top of society and then gradually worked their way down to the lower levels, provoking—as it became diffuse—a differentiating action from the elite that produced innovation and a new cycle, no longer applied.[68] The channels of transmission and innovation were quite different, as Yves Saint Laurent's appropriations of youth themes and reworking of African and Oriental motifs showed. Moreover, it was not necessary even to have wealth to be able to live the desirable lifestyle. Youth, and especially girls and young women, took up ideas that had a contemporary feel and that matched the greater independence and sexual freedom that marked the age. Energy, vitality, and pleasure were more desirable than the virginal glow that, save for its brief eclipse in the 1920s, had conventionally distinguished young upper-class feminine beauty. In the fashioning of a new glamour, informality, sex appeal, and movement were central. Girls were active and on the go.[69] Mary Quant, whose boutique fashions were defining the contemporary youthful look, championed them and often acted as their spokesperson. The miniskirt was in fact invented by the Parisian designer Courrèges but it was adopted and democratized in London and became forever associated with Quant. She achieved prominence when *Queen* ran some pictures of her creations after other magazines rejected them. Her 'Chelsea set' had a vibrant contemporary feel that contrasted with the official quasi-high society world of fashion everywhere. The new modes were often intensely controversial and provoked much disapproval. When Shrimpton wore a miniskirt and no hat, gloves, or stocking to Derby Day at Flemington racecourse in Melbourne, Australia in 1965, sartorial choices that in her environment would have seemed natural, it caused outrage among those who thought the world's highest-paid model was cocking a snoop at polite convention.[70]

Both within Britain and in international popular culture, London established an enviable primacy. It was seen as the heart of a loosening of social and cultural hierarchies and of a cultural renaissance. Mass fashion, pop music, and style all seemed to emanate from the British capital. The American magazine *Time*, which devoted its cover to 'Swinging London' on 15 April 1966, also commented on the 'new and surprising leadership community' that was taking shape.[71] It was, the magazine declared, a classless phenomenon, 'a swinging meritocracy'. Needless to say, this was the ideology of sixties' London rather than the reality but it was not without significance that 'everyone looks at England, London has become the target, the beacon, the "city of youth" '.[72] Although New York had its heterodox star-like 'fashion-society celebrities',[73] and Paris had its own subcultures and a pop culture with its own young female stars in Françoise Hardy and Sylvie Vartan,[74] it was London that constantly generated novelties.

The most striking novelty of 1966 was Twiggy. The young model was not a protégée of any newly established image-maker or the creation of a cultural industry. Her emergence was a phenomenon that would have been un-imaginable elsewhere. It showed both a receptiveness to novelty and the importance of the interaction of different facets of London's media. Aged just 16, Lesley Hornby—to give Twiggy her real name—was an ordinary girl from Neasden working in a hairdressing salon when she was spotted by Nigel Davies, who, as Justin de Villeneuve, would become her Pygmalion.[75] Like all girls of her age she was outer-directed; she loved shopping, fashion, and pop music. She was truly everygirl and much of her popularity derived from her ingenuous reactions to being suddenly elevated into the glamorous world of modelling, magazines, jet travel, celebrities, fashion, and money. Her path to fame was brief. Given a new twenties-style haircut by Leonard of Mayfair, her picture was taken by Barry Lategan and seen by Deidre McSharry, fashion editor of the *Daily Express*. As soon as the journalist caught sight of her, she dubbed her 'the face of 1966', a label that made her famous overnight. 'I was an instant celebrity,' Twiggy later wrote.[76] Unlike all previous models, she was invented through public opinion and owed noth-ing either to a fashion house or a photographer. While *Vogue* ignored her and Bailey briefly boycotted her, the daily press could not get enough of her. She was not just a face but the cheeky, unvarnished voice of modern youth. The *Daily Sketch* sent her to Paris to watch the fashion shows; predictably, she declared them middle-aged and old-fashioned, a comment that led to her being banned. With her stick-thin figure and large eyes, she seemed half-orphan and half-Martian but, as a teenager who liked to dance and loved music, Twiggy was a product of sixties' London. She was a lower middle-class girl who had grown up with post-war suburban consumerism: 'the suburban influence was important because it meant that all my tastes were suburban, and that meant I liked all modern things,' she recalled. 'Anything modern was wonderful, and anything old was terrible. It has a lot to do with the middle-class, suburban way of thinking, to revere new things, everything up to date, up to the minute, brand new and streamlined and contemporary— that's what everything has to be—houses, home décor, ornaments, clothes!'[77] Within a year, she was not only voted one of the most influential people in the United Kingdom, but was granted her own waxwork at Madame Tussaud's.

Reactions to Twiggy in some quarters of the fashion world were horrified. Compared even to the unconventional style of Shrimpton, she was novel and unrefined. However, because her capacity to sell clothes was remarkable and her own-label merchandise was a sell-out, the fashion establishment could not long ignore her. US *Vogue* selected her to model the Paris collections, photographed by Bert Stern, and she was also shot by Richard Avedon. When she arrived in New York, she unleashed a pandemonium. Stern was commissioned by the ABC network to make a series of television films of the whole US trip: *Twiggy in New York, Twiggy in California*, and *Twiggy Who?* The 'Twiggy look' proved hugely popular and was copied throughout the world. Two features were important: the legs, that were encased in coloured tights and composed in knock-kneed fashion at a gawky angle; and the face, to which a boy's haircut and big eyelashes gave a doll-like quality. Twiggy was a constant presence in the press. She was youth, androgyny, lower-class aspiration, outspokenness, pop music, and image all rolled into one. Unlike previous models who seemed like still-life compositions, Twiggy moved; she had great sense of rhythm and many of her best-known poses were the result of her body's responses to pop music.

Twiggy and Shrimpton were the consecration of youth and beauty. They had perfectly proportioned faces and were intensely photogenic. Both seemed quite natural, although their appearance was, however, only natural up to a point since they used eyeliner, lipstick, and mascara to create individual looks. 'Makeup old-style is out,' declared Mary Quant; 'it is used as expertly as ever, but it is not designed to show, the ideal now is to look as if you have a baby skin untouched by cosmetics.'[78] Suddenly, the ideal body was young and adolescent beauty was discovered to possess a selling power that exceeded all the classic appeals of class, tradition, luxury, and fantasy. Twiggy was even dubbed, by one observer, an 'elongated matchstick'. However, there was still a 'right' way to do hair and make-up, a 'right' way to wear clothes, and 'right' fashions to adopt. Style was no longer bound up with breeding and was presented as a disposable quality whose content at a given moment was determined by professionals with their finger on the contemporary pulse. It was a widespread, shared phenomenon that came from a variety of places and which was diffused by recognized stars.

According to older definitions of glamour, Twiggy was not glamorous at all. She was not rich or sexy and she had had no time to build a personal narrative. The term was still widely taken to apply most accurately to a star like Elizabeth Taylor or a fashion leader like Jackie Kennedy, that is to say women who were somehow associated with luxury, movement, and high style. By contrast, Twiggy's authentic personality and cockney accent lent her the quality of *My Fair Lady*'s Eliza Doolittle before Professor Higgins begins his experiment of transformation. Everything about her domestic, familiar, and teenage persona contradicted established ideas of glamour. She had raw charm but no obvious sex appeal. The teenage 'dolly birds' in any case were neither prey nor honeytrap; their sexuality was provocative in an assertive way that suggested self-determination.[79] Yet there were three ways in which Twiggy mobilized the magical aura of enviability for her contemporaries. In the first place, she was down-to-earth and accessible; she seemed to be acting the part of a successful model in a way that unleashed a 'me too' response from her contemporaries. Secondly, she was a photographic personality. Hornby herself was well aware of this and worked to enhance her visual appeal. She took as her example American model Penny Moffat, whom she happened to see at the start of her modelling career. Moffat moved her head and arms, creating designs with her body, turning it into an artistic construct. 'She's one of those who looks better in pictures than in life, because she really works at presenting herself to the camera,' Twiggy declared.[80] Although there was a sultry aspect to Moffat's persona that did not carry over to the young model, Twiggy nevertheless established a uniquely imitable visual presence. As photography theorist Clive Scott argues, the fashion photograph must not present its image as reality but rather negotiate between the image's origin in false reality and its future in real possibility.[81] Thus there is always a falsity to the model who has this element of unreality built into her. This is the part that determines her image for the viewer and in which her glamour is largely invested. 'Twiggy''s pictures, in this sense, carried a high quotient of glamour.

Thirdly, Twiggy's lifestyle became intensely glamorous. She recounted her experiences in the press and her first-hand accounts preserve the wonder of the ordinary girl at the sudden change in her existence. Instead of tending to customers at the hairdresser's, she received red-carpet treatment wherever she went. 'Whenever I appeared in town I was big news and there were private Lear jets and Cadillacs to pick me up and whisk me to some reception or other,' she wrote of her experiences in the United States.[82] In California, she stayed in the Bel Air Hotel and, at her request, met singers Sonny and Cher, who held a party for her at which the guests included Eve Marie Saint, Tony Curtis, Robert Mitchum, and Steve McQueen. Being so new to fame, she experienced the life of limousines, aeroplanes, and hotel rooms as an outsider. 'It sounds so glamorous, but would you like it?', she asked her readers rhetorically. 'Even my short experience of it was enough for me.'[83] However, the pose of detachment was not consistently maintained, not surprisingly considering that perks not normally available to Neasden girls were involved. 'Life was pretty glamorous for us,' she wrote, referring to her life with Villeneuve. 'For our holidays, we used to rent a whole island— Five Star Island, off Bermuda. Six acres to ourselves, and two landing jetties. We almost bought the island at one point.'[84]

Part of Twiggy's appeal, especially abroad (in Italy, she and Shrimpton were affectionately dubbed 'Grissino' and 'Gamberetto', the former being the Italian word for a bread stick and the latter for a shrimp), was due to the emerging awareness of Swinging London. There was a coming together of a variety of currents in the English capital that, according to Quant, 'grew out of something in the air which developed into a serious effort to break away from the Establishment'.[85] The outsider status of people like Bailey and Twiggy, and Quant herself, was a crucial catalyst in overturning established social and cultural preconceptions and propelling painters, photographers, architects, musicians, writers, socialites, actors, racing drivers, sportsmen, television producers, and advertising men to the centre of national culture. Creativity and originality were the driving impulses of a whole variety of cultural industries. Quant's Chelsea coterie, with its stress on vibrant youth, coffee bars, and Italian restaurants gave an alternative feel to the new London, but the media, fashion, pop music, sport, and publishing were powerful industries that very quickly shaped the image of the country. They all offered a premiss that was ostensibly democratic: anyone of talent or beauty could be suddenly transformed into a celebrity.

Similar patterns were emerging everywhere in the Western world although not always so vigorously. In Paris, boutiques were opening by the dozen on the Left Bank and even couturiers were getting in on the act.[86] Yves Saint Laurent more than anyone else was responsible for challenging the traditional exclusivity of couture and shifting the focus of fashion from couture to prêt-à-porter. He opened his Rive Gauche boutique in 1966, which was followed by branches in London and New York.[87] It sold casual creations to fashionable customers at prices that were not cheap by normal standards but which were lower than those of couture. The Left Bank hosted a thriving milieu of artists, intellectuals, jazz and pop musicians, and media professionals.

Beaton played a key role in fashioning the elite of the new age of the photographic image. He ranged over periods, classes, and countries and could photograph Queen Elizabeth just as he could Mick Jagger, Twiggy like Princess Alice, Countess of Athlone, or the elderly dancer Cléo de Merode. His worlds included royalty and aristocracy, fashion, the theatre and films, plus the rich and famous of at least three continents. Beaton was accepted by the young talents as a figure who had knowledge and experience and was open to new things. He was never ridiculed and was able to mix at the interface of young talent and young aristocracy. Among the few who turned him down was the French photographer Henri Cartier-Bresson, the father of modern photojournalism who was just four years younger than himself. Rejecting Beaton's overtures, he declared: 'there are three categories of people who should never be photographed—prostitutes, private detectives and photographers'.[88]

Beaton saw that the end of a certain way of dressing among women and the unusual physicality of some pop musicians had brought the sexes together and made a new form of male glamour possible. It was not just youth but also gender that was being redefined. Mick Jagger, for example, intrigued him; he had a mystery about him. His face, Beaton confided to his diary, reminded him of the ballet dancer Nijinsky. When he eventually photographed him in Morocco, he found him to be a compliant yet unsettling subject: 'He was a Tarzan of Piero di Cosimo. Lips of a fantastic roundness, body white and almost hairless. He is sexy, yet completely sexless. He could nearly be a eunuch. As a model he is a natural,' he noted.[89] Vreeland was fascinated by Jagger's generous lips which she saw as a pop cultural phenomenon rather than a feature of the man. They simply could not have existed, she believed, without the precedent of Bardot's pout.[90]

The sexual ambiguity that Beaton and Vreeland saw in some male stars was in part a matter of costume. Many pop performers had been to art school or, despite their regional or affected working-class accents, came from creative middle-class backgrounds. Dressing up in vibrant colours and dandyish outfits and wearing long hair was part of their rebellion against arid normality. It was also a deliberate challenge to established gender codes. Compelling and ambiguous men came to the fore in several fields. Rudolf Nureyev, the Kirov ballet dancer who defected to the West in 1961, was one of the most prominent. His unfamiliar physical beauty, technical mastery, arrogance, and personal flamboyance turned him into an icon of the decade. He was the first male ballet dancer of the second half of the century to take ballet to a wider audience. His talent, exoticism, and voracious bisexuality made him into a something of a Byronic figure and the dancer played up to this image explicitly in his public image and his later work.[91]

Despite the importance of pop musicians, models, and hairdressers in giving a recognizable sound and shape to London in the mid-sixties, the photographer was the crucial figure in shaping the impact of almost every personality and cultural phenomenon. It was his ingenuity, flair, and imagination that moulded the natural attributes of his subjects into fashionable images. Thus it was entirely natural that the Italian film director Michelangelo Antonioni should have made a fashion photographer the protagonist of *Blow Up*, a film that would stand as one of the most representative films of the era. Despite his early background in Italian neorealism, Antonioni was a director who preferred to explore modernity and in particular the alienation of modern life. His desire to make a film about the fashion world led him to consider Rome and then Paris and New York before he opted for London.

He arrived in the city in 1965 to begin research for his film.[92] He had already shown a special interest in fashion in his work, notably in the films *Cronaca di un amore* (Chronicle of a Love) and *Le amiche* (The Girlfriends). He had also made by then the trilogy of *L'avventura* (The Adventure), *La notte* (The Night), and *L'eclisse* (The Eclipse) that would later be regarded as his best work. His 1961 film *La notte* was a sort of *La dolce vita* remake set in Milan, in which Marcello Mastroianni (the star of both films) exchanged the decadence of the aristocracy and the film world for the thrusting ambition of the bourgeoisie and the publishing industry of the Italian economic boom. *Blow Up* can be read as yet another take on Fellini's film, this time set in the British capital. His decision to shoot the film there says much about the way London was seen abroad.

Antonioni had wanted to cast many people as themselves, including Bailey and Twiggy. In the end, after rejecting Stamp—who had allegedly paid too much attention to the director's lover Monica Vitti—he cast Bailey lookalike David Hemmings as the photographer, while the real-life models who took part in the film included the German Amazon Verushka and Jill Kennington. *Blow Up* reinforced the idea of Swinging London and was widely seen as a celebration of a city in vibrant transition. In fact it offered a penetrating critique of a civilization that had exchanged surface for substance. The preoccupation with image is so strong in the film that no one is at all interested in the possible murder that the photographer uncovers in the blown-up detail of one of his photographs. The concluding scenes of a tennis match being mimed without balls, while the sound of them being struck features quite normally in the soundtrack, exemplifies the emptiness of a world in which the attention was being focused on nothing.

In contrast to *La dolce vita*, *Blow Up* did not arouse any political controversy since the critique it offered did not touch the ruling elite.[93] Instead it was controversial for its fleeting nudity and sex scenes. The film's protagonist is not a modern lothario; rather he has a wife and children off screen. But a scene of an orgy at the end of a photo session, in which the photographer engages in a tumble with a couple of models, nonetheless confirmed the idea that the contemporary fashion world was imbued with sex. In the mid-1960s, the representation of sex was still a delicate matter and nowhere more than in England where the trial for obscenity of the English publisher of D. H. Lawrence's 1928 novel *Lady Chatterley's Lover* (which had initially been published in Italy) in 1960 was still recent, and the unseemly revelations of upper-class depravity at the Duke and Duchess of Argyll's divorce trial and the Profumo scandal in 1963 had received sensational coverage. One of the key impulses of the sixties was towards liberation of sexual mores and the practical behaviour of the protagonists of Swinging London exemplified this. But in the matter of representation, artists and film-makers were bound to encounter prevailing values and brush up against legal restrictions as well as shape emerging standards.

For Susan Sontag, the photographer had become a modern hero by the 1920s.[94] The capacity of practitioners of this art to expand visual horizons brought them a crucial role in capitalist society, which by its very nature required a culture based on images. However, in sixties' London a new socially and geographically mobile group of photographers were active public figures who were often as well known as their subjects. *Blow Up* consecrated the photographer as the hero par excellence of the decade. It also put paid to the residual idea that photographers, like hairdressers, were mainly homosexual. It highlighted the fact that the new fashion photographers were heterosexuals who often enjoyed relationships with their models. In this they differed from the earlier generation whose imagery was as desexualized as their personal relations with their models were platonic. In contrast to the stiffness and formality of the recent past, photographs were sexed-up; they were infused with the new atmosphere breathed in the studios. As Shrimpton confessed, 'Photographers do have a lure for models, and a photographic session can be a very seductive time.' Locked together in the studio, they experienced a sexual buzz that, she was keen to stress, normally ended when a session ended.[95] But there is no question that both the relationships between models and photographers and, more particularly, the public presentation of them in the media, brought the allure of sex to the way in which the whole work of photography and fashion marketing was seen.[96] Helmut Newton noted that the sexy image made photography irresistible as a profession. In Paris, he said that,

after *Blow Up*, 'the young people, everybody, wanted to be a fashion photographer. It became a big cult.'[97]

The sexual revolution was about the loosening of mores but it entailed
numerous contradictions since it was as much about the representation of
sex and the sexually titillating as about changes in sexual behaviour. More
relaxed censorship opened opportunities to film-makers and publishers to
cater to demands for explicit material. The sexy image of the fashion world
provided a cover for an expansion of a different type of modelling related
purely to the gratification of male sexual appetites. Sontag argues that the
main effect of photography is 'to convert the world into a department store
or a museum-without-walls in which every subject is depreciated into an
article of consumption, promoted into an item for aesthetic appreciation'.[98] The term 'depreciated' is only appropriate here because Sontag
was discussing human beings; in terms of commercial aesthetics what was
being referred to was an enhancement—or the formation—of an image. In
his examination of British working-class culture, Hoggart noted that many
working-class sex magazines were marked by 'a pseudo-sophisticated and
knowing urban coarseness'.[99] The models had vulgar faces and 'a large-
mouthed and brassy vulgarity of expression'. They were close to the reality
of street prostitution: the images were not erotic or psychological but 'real'
and immediately sexual. The debut in 1965 of a new men's magazine,
Mayfair, heralded a change that was informed by, but not reducible to,
the example of *Playboy*. Like Bob Guccione's *Penthouse*, which was founded
in the same year, *Mayfair*'s title suggested wealth, sophistication, and
pleasure. Semi-nude models were inserted into a dream world of exotic
leisure and turned them into component parts of consumer culture.
The glamour photography of the 1960s differed from the film studio
portraits of the heyday of the Hollywood studio system. The demand for
that sort of highly artificial photography evaporated in the sixties and
instead 'glamour' was taken to be a genre of photography that was solely
concerned with the heightened presentation of female beauty for male
consumption. Its techniques were applied not to create a complete illusion but to emphasize the sex appeal of the model. Thus, while George

Hurrell claimed to be able to glamorize anyone, even if some subjects were more suited to the task than others, later more stress was laid on the physical characteristics of exclusively female models. A 'glamour model' was a woman whose physical attributes suited her to representation for the pleasure of heterosexual men. Most often, she was a teenager or in her early twenties, with a fresh, natural look and a slim body, unlike some of the older professional models who appeared in the erotic magazines of the 1950s. While beefcake magazines catered to male homosexual tastes, the models were not presented according to the same visual language. Body-building and sport were the main inspirations.

The 1960s witnessed a boom of 'glamour photography'. This involved the 'deliberate effort to create visual pleasure and heightened femininity'.[100] It was a contrived idealization that used both truth and fiction to create a new synthetic quality to feminine allure. The label signified at once a link with Hollywood sex appeal and a differentiation from cruder products. There was enormous interest in glamour photography among amateurs and this was demonstrated by the number of manuals that were published for their benefit by professionals. The best models were deemed to be the women who were able to communicate without too much artifice a sense of refined sex appeal. One Italian guide suggested that any items of clothing should not be too luxurious as they would take attention away from the model.[101] Much better were either specialist sexy garments, or modish youth clothes. A minimum of props in the form of a bed, divan, cushions, plants, mirrors, or a fireplace was necessary to contextualize the model's body, for 'nudity alone does not constitute glamour; photography must induce the imagination to develop nudity but it must not present it totally'.[102] The photographer Rayment Kirby (Ray) argued that glamour 'consists of using every technical trick and artifice to create an effect; to turn an ordinary human being into an illusion of complete fantasy'.[103] However, the results should be ostensibly natural. 'The word glamour, as applied to photography today, is in simple terms making women look their best,' he asserted. 'The glamour photographer, whether male or female, is in much the same position as that of the model's hairdresser or mirror.' It was all about imagination; the subject was simply a prop for erotic fantasies. He advised eager amateurs that 'healthy looking girls with good figures are what you need for your pictures'.[104] A cheerful attitude was also important. Closed or pessimistic characters were unsuited to the work in the view of one author, for 'they will never be able to produce good glamour photography because they cannot sense the atmosphere and therefore will be unable either to stimulate or capture in the model the necessary sex appeal'.[105]

Modern glamour girls, more natural and no longer groomed, polished, and bleached to within an inch of their humanity, were widely employed in movies and television programmes. In the James Bond films, including *Dr No* and *From Russia With Love*, they were impersonated by Continental actresses, in these cases the Swiss Ursula Andress and the Italian Daniela Bianchi, who were packaged and presented as the objects of male fantasy. They were beautiful, rootless women of a certain spirit and independence who were available to the male protagonist and, as filmic images, to the film-goer. Similarly refined, but home-grown sex symbols populated British-produced, Bond-inspired television shows like *The Saint*, *The Avengers*, and *Department S*, which featured precisely the sort of exotic locations and alluring places like nightclubs, grand hotels, and casinos that filled upmarket magazines. Although they attracted sizeable audiences, the shows were dismissed in some quarters as 'glossy British rubbish' with characters taken from advertisements for hair shampoo.[106] Roger Moore, who took the lead role in *The Saint* and would later replace Sean Connery as James Bond, was the perfect vehicle for upwardly mobile dreams. His character's smooth bachelor manner and transatlantic accent made him a small-screen Cary Grant, whose suburban polish and flawless modern wardrobe matched his taste for pretty girls, cocktails, and Continental sports cars. Even more than his model, his screen image was that of a glamorous persona from nowhere who had kicked away the ladder on which he had climbed up from nothing.

Movement and travel were crucial to the new glamour of the 1960s. The most suggestive source of ideas of glamour and travel were supplied by members of the jet set. Elizabeth Taylor commanded more attention than most. She was, wrote Francis Wyndham of *Queen*, who visited her on the set of the airport drama *The VIPs*, 'the most film-starry film star in the world'.[107] She was 'the one film star who can still impose her whims on any producer and get away with it because she has the box office solidly behind her'. Bardot was another globetrotter, who married her playboy lover Gunther Sachs in Las Vegas in 1966. She consistently rejected the conventional idea of the star and drew criticism from the French and international press for her bad taste and bohemian ways. The casual allure of her simple dress style, however, made her a model for thousands of French girls.[108] High living and consumerism were bound into notions of travel at precisely the moment that foreign tourism took on mass proportions. Airlines traded shamelessly on this in their advertising. The cordial and caring presentations of stewardesses that had been used in the previous decade were replaced by highly sexualized images that portrayed them as swingers and playmates. Southern airways even swopped traditional uniforms for miniskirts while Southwest adopted hot pants and boots. Such blatant exploitation of women who were workers rather than airborne party-goers gave rise to an increase in instances of harassment which contributed to an unexpected growth of militancy on the part of stewardesses.[109] Protest invested numerous spheres towards the end of the decade and even the Miss World contest was disrupted by feminists in 1969. Television stations, however, continued to make ample use of decorative femininity and several Miss World winners and finalists, including Austria's Eva von Ruber-Staier, who won the title in 1969, found employment on game shows.

The relaxed spirit of the age and the greater informality can be seen in the field of 'How To' books about glamour written by women for women. These were no less popular in the 1960s than they had been in previous decades, but they placed less importance on exterior artificiality. Two popular manuals of the fifties, *Anita Colby's Beauty Book* and *Glamour School*, stressed the need to mould the figure and personality by working on clothes, make-up, hair, posture, and social skills.[110] Disguising a woman's worst points was no less important than dramatizing her best ones. Later works tended to stress personal discipline as the basis of glamour. 'Makeup, hairstyle and chic can add the dazzle that makes you a striking beauty, but their effects are transient unless they are sustained by stringent living habits,' observed the lean-figured sportswear designer and Roman aristocrat Princess Luciana Pignatelli in one guide.[111] In the cultural flux of the period, 'casual glamour' in the form of sports clothes and loose hair was contemporary, but good hair and bone structure and a candid outlook on life were required to carry it off.[112] 'There is no longer a fashion center that can dictate,' Pignatelli argued. 'You have to think out your own style, your own brand of glamour. Anything goes so long as it goes together with you.'[113] The end of the option of simply conforming to the prevailing fashion template presented a considerable challenge.

The international celebrity circuit was a mixture of playground and publicity stunt for a select group of people. At its centre was the shipping magnate Aristotle Onassis. Unlike many international businessmen, he did not disdain publicity but actively sought it with the aid of a public relations adviser whose task was to enhance his glamorous image. Onassis was not a good-looking man but he had charisma and was associated with glamorous places and activities. This gave him leverage over public opinion and concealed the sordid or questionable aspects of his business dealings.[114] Celebrities including the Kennedys, the Earl of Snowden and Princess Margaret, Elizabeth Taylor and Richard Burton, Cary Grant, and Margot Fonteyn, as well of course as his lover Maria Callas, accepted invitations to join him on his cruise ship *Christina*. They enjoyed his hospitality while he, in turn, used them as decorations for his various activities.

Jackie Kennedy first travelled on the *Christina* while she was still first lady and was recovering from a miscarriage. After the interlude of her mourning period, she entered the realm of the jet set, becoming a regular social presence on both sides of the Atlantic. In 1964 she moved back to New York and, when she was in Europe, she mingled with the beautiful people in resorts like Gstaad, Capri, and Rome. Like any young widow, she found that with time the circle that she had frequented with her husband dwindled. She was obliged to seek new pastures and forge new friendships, which she found in the ranks of the flotsam and jetsam that comprised the international jet set. She had got used to the high life and became accustomed to private planes, yachts, and the lifestyle of the super-rich. This milieu provided her with a form of protection. Jackie craved privacy but everywhere she went there was excess attention. Even in moments that she regarded as private, away from Washington, she was tailed by photographers and reporters. She had a special draw that turned her into a prisoner. She was a dazzling celebrity who could not live normally even in New York.

At this time her fashion influence reached its height. Travel was crucial to her glamorous image and, like Empress Sissi a century before, she always seemed to be in the most desirable and evocative places. 'To be in fashion means to be on the go,' remarked journalist Marilyn Bender; 'the important thing is to keep moving, to arrive after everyone has heard of the place but before everyone has been there. Acapulco, Antigua, Gstaad, Hawaii, the Greek islands have all had their moment of glory.'[115] American women in the sixties did not find models they could emulate in the movies which had lost some appeal and were producing more male than female stars. Consequently, the fashion industry elected Jackie as its patron saint. Once removed from the White House, she seemed to get younger, at least in terms of her personal style, which reflected the youth-orientation of the era.[116] According to Cassini, she did not want to be regarded as a trendsetter, but rather as stylish in her own right. She was fascinated by facades and appearances of all types: furnishing, decorating, and staging events were her favourite pastimes. She was attentive to her personal style and kept faith with it. Her high visibility and distinctive beauty made her more influence than influenced. Her basic look consisted of Chanel-style suits, bright colours, and low-heeled shoes. It was sufficiently casual and youthful to amount to a contribution to the fashion trends of the 1960s. However, little or nothing was left to chance. Jackie was a poseur in a literal sense; there was a premeditated, quasi-theatrical quality to her actions. She cultivated her image and choreographed her life. In the autumn of 1966, she shortened her skirts to near-mini length, a move that immediately legitimated the mini and turned it into mainstream fashion. This is just one example of how fashion influence no longer trickled down but instead was diffused in different ways through the media and key mediators. A mass audience eagerly studied the details of Jackie's wardrobe as well as the broader style choices she made.[117] Her trademark huge dark glasses and her wide smile were unmistakable. Jackie spent prodigiously, forever changing outfits and accessories, sometimes idiosyncratically, a fact that caught the attention of consumer-oriented and upwardly aspiring women in the United States.[118]

Jackie offered a walking style lesson. Her life, moreover, appeared to be choreographed; nothing was casual, it was like the unfolding of a play; every action had significance. However, a significant shift occurred when she took up with the Greek shipping magnate Aristotle Onassis. For the American people, the announcement of the couple's engagement broke the spell. It was as if the queen had abdicated. It was felt that she was betraying her husband's memory and demeaning herself. Onassis was widely seen as a Greek pirate, a vulgar tycoon and a figure of the jet set, a nightclubber and womanizer who compulsively pursued beautiful and famous women.[119] Like the *viveurs* of the belle époque, he frequented Maxim's in Paris and vulgarly exhibited the symbols of his wealth. Jackie was the ultimate trophy wife and by winning her he scored a huge publicity coup. He showered her with jewels and indulged the spending splurges for which she had become known even before entering the White House. Like the Duke and Duchess of Windsor, with her wedding in 1968, she came down from Olympus and joined café society, where she 'migrated from taste to waste and joined Liz'.[120] She was depicted as a pleasure seeker and big spender whose love life was of no less interest than a movie star's. She was snapped dancing the Twist, in bathing costumes, and even while sunbathing nude on Onassis's private Greek island of Skorpios.

The paparazzi were forever on the lookout for revealing shots of celebrities in the Mediterranean. In Jackie's case her fame ensured that her image always had value and the attention did not stop when she returned home. Between 1967 and 1973, the year she went to court to end his alleged harassment of her, she was assiduously pursued by the paparazzo photographer Ron Galella. The first photographers to fashion new images of celebrity were the freelance snappers who pursued the celebrities in Rome and on the Côte d'Azur. The paparazzi were insolent and aggressive towards many of their subjects. They were concerned simply to exploit the fame of the latter to maximize their earnings. But their photographs had a striking immediacy. When they caught illicit couples in a furtive embrace, snapped an inebriated celebrity husband or his wife in a dishevelled state, they gave the public an insight into the disorderly hurly-burly that characterized the leisure of the rich and famous. Famous punch-ups on the Via Veneto between paparazzi and their victims only served to enhance the public's fascination with the lives of its favourites.

Galella, by contrast, was in fact one of her greatest fans, who saw her as 'the perfect model of wife, mother, woman—someone whose ways of being should exist as instruction to all wives, all mothers, all women'.[121] 'I admit', he later wrote, 'to being obsessed with tearing after every reasonable and fair opportunity to photograph this splendid woman—to make a lasting record of her infinite moods and endlessly varied comings and goings.' In his many disguises, Galella succeeded in capturing his idol in numerous instances when her guard was down. His portraits were none the less very different to the snaps taken of celebrities by the Roman paparazzi because they never showed Jackie in an unflattering light. On the contrary, the celebrated picture he took of her near the intersection of Madison Avenue and 88th Street in Manhattan is the most iconic picture of her post-White House period. Striding confidently forward with sunglasses in hand, her hair blowing in her face as she turns towards the photographer, she is dressed simply in faded jeans and a ribbed woollen top. Shot from a taxi, the picture, for Galella, said something like 'see the thoroughbred striding'.[122] The photograph has a sense of the instant, of real time, of the trivial made eternal. It is the exemplification of critic Susan Sontag's observation that photography 'offers instant romanticism about the present'.[123] Its very ordinariness disguises what is extraordinary about it: although her clothing is merely functional, Jackie appears as a fit, trim woman in complete charge of her body and its movements; she is unencumbered by any excess baggage; even the wind contrives to blow her hair in such a way as to enhance her mystery.[124] It posits its subject as supremely enviable and naturally impeccable.

Jackie remained a figure of the imagination and a woman of great popularity despite her brushes with public opinion. As others rose and fell—even Bailey fell from grace and Twiggy retired at 19—she was a continuous presence. She had many fans, one of whom was the popular author Jacqueline Susann, whose best-selling potboiler *Valley of the Dolls* explored the perils and tragedies of misplaced ambitions. Susann strongly identified with her namesake's elegance and beauty, even though, with her big hair, sequins, hard-living, and high heels, she always looked like show business on legs.[125] She even wrote a quasi-*roman à clef*, *Dolores*, her last novel, in which she dated her heroine's transition from ornament to personality from her visit to Paris as the wife of the American president. In that moment, 'Dolores had come into her own as a full-fledged glamorous personality.'[126] The novel can only be termed a quasi-*roman à clef* because Jacqueline Kennedy Onassis also appears briefly in the text. Dolores is a sort of meta-projection of her alter ego: 'Jacqueline Onassis was already established "news" like Elizabeth Taylor. Now *she*, Dolores Ryan, was the new glamour girl of the world.'[127] The former first lady's transformation was that which Dolores's sister Nita spells out to her several years after the assassination of her husband: 'the real society is gone. Finished. Except for a few seventy-year-old dowagers. You take a good look at today's society, gay Princes and Lords, rock stars, plus any beast from the States with over a million. Even movie stars make it! And you, my dear, you're not social anymore, you're a celebrity. You are on all the magazine covers.'[128]

Jackie's glamour was the result of the interaction of factors: her borrowed auras and superficial similarities to Princess Grace and to the screen princess Audrey Hepburn, combined with the constancy of her visual appearance to make her an icon of popular culture. She was also a factor in the political sphere; through her role she brought a new attention to surface, to the feminine, and to style. 'Her political role is mostly visual,' *Time* noted; a statement that one acute observer remarks could be reversed.[129] Her visual image was her armour, her defence against a hostile world and a weapon against her neglectful husband. She was remote and one-dimensional in the public mind but this absence enhanced rather than diminished her allure. In this sense, perhaps it is right to say that 'Jackie is glamorous because she seems not thoroughly here'.[130] However, she could electrify places and spheres by association; for example, by becoming an editor at Viking after the death of Onassis in 1975, she single-handedly glamorized the world of New York publishing.

The modern glamour of the 1960s was different from that of the past. It was more youthful and dynamic, as well as pleasure-seeking. It was separated from sophistication and freer of the social hierarchy that had born on it up to that point.[131] It was no longer mock-upper class but instead was imbued with a sense of the current moment, of nowness. Youth and beauty were the key dynamics, although material attributes continued to exercise a far-reaching appeal. In the interrelation of wealth, sex appeal, and beauty, the balance shifted in favour of beauty. In the past, only monarchs, members of the fashionable elite, and professional performers of various types had been interested in the cultivation of a saleable exterior. In the 1960s, this became a widespread phenomenon. Image was a matter of fashion and fashion was widely communicated. Everyone wanted to be part of it, to feel as though they were not merely spectators at someone else's party but that they were participants. As a consequence, the backroom boys and girls of glamour emerged into the daylight and became key players. Photographers, models, hairdressers, make-up artists, boutique and club owners, and designers became as famous as the objects of their ministrations. They lost their previous anonymity and became the principal artificers of their own images, which were also important factors in their commercial success. The new creative elite did not hail from conventional metropolitan or upper-class backgrounds. Consequently, they did not style themselves on the social elite but rather maintained a distinctive and sometimes overtly lower-class profile.

CHAPTER 10

STYLE, PASTICHE, AND EXCESS

G lamour, for Andy Warhol, was a passion. Throughout his career as photographer, film-maker, artist, publisher (of *Interview* magazine), author, cultural commentator, personality, and social gadfly, he was fascinated by appearances and images, especially those that were resonant of fame, mass consumption, popular culture, and style. He was not a detached observer of the surface phenomena of contemporary life but an active participant in the cultivation of celebrity and image. He was eclectic in approach, collecting images and inspirations from the most varied of sources, high and low, which he then interrogated and deconstructed before reinventing and reproposing them in new ways. His best-known work consists of his repeated screen prints of the movie stars Marilyn Monroe and Elizabeth Taylor. Dating from the 1960s, these works took emblematic images of the most famous and glamorous people of the era and subjected them to repetition, with minor variations of colour and shade. Like his celebrated prints of multiple cans of Campbell's soup, these images acknowledged the special resonance of the mass-produced object in contemporary culture. Many of his creations explored the particular artificial aura that was associated with these objects and indulged in the possibilities it offered for further reproduction. Although Warhol was intrigued by many everyday products, it was the stars that fascinated him most. Growing up in industrial Pittsburgh during the Depression, he was drawn irresistibly to the larger-than-life personalities who populated the movies of the period. Hollywood glamour was a fabulous confection that entranced and seduced him, shaping his whole subsequent outlook on art, film, fashion, and advertising. The aura of beauty, wealth, desire, and scandal that celebrities emanated was something that Warhol experienced mainly through magazines and tabloid newspapers.[1] Like many fans, he collected press and publicity photographs and kept old magazines and memorabilia. Mostly, it was female stars like Greta Garbo and Jean Harlow, as well as later actresses including Monroe, Kim Novak, or Brigitte Bardot, who grabbed his attention, but he also owned a pair of shoes that had reputedly once been worn by Clark Gable.

Glamour became a constant theme of all Warhol's work. 'He had one motivating idea. Absolutely central.... He was interested in the idea of glamour. Glamour fascinated him,' declared the art critic Robin Pincus-Witten.[2] Unlike most observers, he believed that it was not just a property of the stars he adored. Rather it was an effect that emerged also through the admiration and involvement of ordinary mortals. Glamour did not hinge on deferential awe but an attitude of participation and appropriation. In other words, it was something that could be taken over and refashioned by its consumers. Most especially, the stars of the recent past, whose images had been widely diffused by the media, were public property. Since Hollywood no longer forged stars in the manner of old, Warhol's screen prints did not merely record the aura of Marilyn or Liz; by elaborating and manipulating it, they had the effect of underlining the iconic status of these stars in the collective consciousness.

Inspired by the example of the great studios, Warhol fashioned his own stars in his famous sixties' studio, the Factory. In this industrial loft space in New York, he painted and, with his colourful entourage, created films, rock music, and happenings. Acolytes including the socialite Edie Sedgwick, the handsome hustler Joe Dallesandro, and the transvestites Candy Darling and Holly Woodlawn, were turned into 'superstars' by the Factory publicity machine. Warhol invented a series of star vehicles, such as 'The Thirteen Most Beautiful Women', 'Fifty Fantastics', and 'Fifty Personalities' into which a changing selection of people were placed.[3] He presided over a hip milieu that drew in artists, models, poets, fashion designers, as well as musicians including John Cale and Lou Reed, whose Velvet Underground became the Factory's house band. Warhol revelled in his power to shape and mould his discoveries. By forging his own stars, and blurring the boundaries between art, film, fashion, and publicity, he was able to grasp and reproduce in his own way the elusive aura of glamour that had intrigued him since his youth.[4] The Factory was a marginal, underground experience even though the news media by no means ignored its doings. The scene it represented was also documented by such luminaries as Richard Avedon and Cecil Beaton as well as house photographers. The pictures, featuring artfully composed groups of outlandish personalities in various playful and frivolous poses, captured a certain mood that was later seen to embody the spirit of the sixties. Warhol's own look changed in accordance with his new status as an avant-garde artist. The bow-tied and besuited appearance of the commercial artist of the 1950s gave way to a more 'artistic' look that reflected his growing interest for painting, film, and music. In his guise as director of the Factory, he wore leather jackets, striped smock shirts, polo neck sweaters, dark glasses, jeans, and a silver wig.

Warhol was tantalized by glamour's capacity to transform a commonplace individual into a dream-being. With the aid of its magic, a nobody could be somebody, a boy could be a girl, and anyone, in theory, could be a star. In the lights-and-cameras playground of the Factory, everybody could invent themselves and have their close-up. Warhol's superstars had theatrical standout names that disguised their prosaic origins. His best-known pro-tégé, Candy Darling, was a pre-operative transsexual who shared his love of old Hollywood films and who had learned to imitate stars like Joan Bennett and Kim Novak. An elegant blonde with a pallid skin and large, sad eyes, she appeared in the Factory film *Flesh* in 1968 and took a central role as a Long Island socialite who joins a women's liberation group in *Sex* (later retitled *Women in Revolt*) in 1971. Her arch, actressy, and emotional acting style reflected her make-believe persona and derivative femininity. Born James

308

Slattery, she subordinated her whole existence to the project of being Candy Darling. Her blonde hair, pale face, unsmiling mouth with strong red lips, and Monroe-esque beauty spot featured in movie-star style portraits of her by Bill King and David Bailey, as well as by Warhol himself. One of the best-known images of Darling appeared on a mock-up of a *Cosmopolitan* cover by the magazine's regular cover photographer, Francesco Scavullo. Her commitment to artifice and self-invention led her to take hormone pills that caused her tragically early death aged 29 in 1974 from cancer. Behind the construction of her glamorous persona was a mixture of discipline and suffering. Few images are more poignant than the claustrophobic black-and-white studio-style photographs that show her wrapped in shiny black sheets, reclining on what she knew would shortly be her deathbed.

Darling was a female impersonator who donned a 'real disguise' to conceal her residual masculinity and turn herself into a fully feminine figure. She was more subtle than the drag queens whose 'fake disguise' meant that they always looked like men dressed as women.[5] Both were drawn to the stars, but it was the latter who were most committed to recreating film-star personae. This aroused Warhol's interest in them. 'Drag queens are living testimony to the way women used to want to be, the way some people still want them to be, and the way some women still actually want to be,' he wrote.[6] 'Drags are ambulatory archives of ideal moviestar womanhood. They perform a documentary service, usually con-secrating their lives to keeping the glittering alternative alive and available for (not-too-close) inspection.' 'It's hard work to look like the complete opposite of what nature made you and then to be an imitation woman of what was only a fantasy woman in the first place,' he continued. 'When they took the movie stars and stuck them in the kitchen, they weren't stars any more—they were just like you and me. Drag queens are reminders that some stars still aren't just like you and me.'[7] For Warhol, the only unequivocal beauties were to be found in the movies, 'and then when you meet them, they're not really beauties either, so your standards don't even really exist'.[8] In his view, for example, Monroe's lipstick lips were not kissable—rather they were 'very photographable'.[9] Drag queens worked off the photographic and movie representations of beauty. These had an unreal, quasi-fantastical allure that seemed like a neat dose of vintage glamour in an era in which there were no more old-style, studio-groomed stars. Warhol was not averse to personally embracing a glamorous feminine persona when it suited him.[10] A closet homosexual who was obsessed with his appearance,[11] he posed for a series of head-and-shoulders self-portraits from 1981 that show him being made-up and trying out a series of female wigs. The poses reeked of wannabe movie star glamour. Warhol's ageing, pock-marked face is transformed by artifice into a series of grotesque drag portraits that make a play of femininity and of glamour's man-made beauty.

In the Warhol persona there was something of the blandness and repetitiveness of modern consumerism. His film *Kitchen* (1965), a minimalist plotless work that mimicked the humdrum everyday ordinariness of domestic America, reflected this, as did his famous Campbell's soup cans. In *The Philosophy of Andy Warhol*, he indicated airports as having his favourite kind of atmosphere, his ideal city as being completely new (Rome, he said, was an example of a city whose buildings had lasted too long),[12] and declared his love of American standardization. The most beautiful things in Tokyo, Stockholm, and Florence, he provocatively affirmed, were the branches of the McDonalds hamburger chain.[13] He was aware that mass-produced plastics shaped a new man-made environment that carried connotations of sameness and repetition.[14] Unlike many, he celebrated the fact that it was banal and disposable as well as synthetic. 'I love plastic idols,' he proclaimed.[15] He has even been seen as a 'plastic celebrity' who personally evoked artificiality.[16] Yet, at the same time, he preferred what he called 'properly-made clothes' and expressed the opinion that man-made fibres looked awful. He loved stars as they used to be and yearned for the time when 'things didn't change so fast' and it was possible to hope to realize a fantasy image before it was swept away by the next trend. Nostalgia and regret informed many of his insights. He noted that whereas once people used to idolize a whole star, following one and loving everything about them, modern-day fans were more fickle and picked and chose the bits they liked.[17] Stardom was also becoming less rare as new categories of people were put up as stars, such as sports personalities and pop performers. His celebrated 1968 statement, 'In the future everybody will be world-famous for

15 minutes' had actually come true, he noted in 1979.[18] Despite some reservations about the end of select fame, Warhol approved the fact that glamour was not unattainable but obtainable and available to all. If he had a dream, it was of a world in which the magical and the commonplace merged; in which people became the artificial surfaces they embraced. 'I don't know anybody who doesn't have a fantasy. Everybody must have a fantasy,' he noted,[19] adding 'I've never met a person I couldn't describe as a beauty.'[20]

Warhol was an avant-garde artist with very close links to the commercial mainstream, in which he began his career. Many of his artistic practices worked off cultural currents that in some instances he helped render visible. In the history of glamour he was an innovator who followed a well-established pattern by mixing elements of nostalgia with an attitude that was informed by the more democratic and egalitarian climate of his time. In the Napoleonic era and after, the rising bourgeoisie had appropriated and refashioned aristocratic styles. In the gilded age, new millionaires had endeavoured to harness and replicate these to bolster their self-image as a new aristocracy. Hollywood cinema in the interwar years had in turn remoulded the lifestyles of the wealthy elite and presented them for mass consumption. Warhol too looked back at the past and drew on it to fashion a popular allure. In his case the template was provided by Hollywood cinema and its applications in mass consumption. The stars, in his outlook, were a meritocracy whose fascination could be recaptured by anyone who took over and re-enacted their way of being. There were, however, significant differences with respect to the past. First, Warhol was not a socio-economic force but an artist, albeit one who devised practices that mobilized the energies of a range of people. Second, the source of his remixes was not a societal elite but a collection of images supplied by an industry. In consequence, his appropriations were doubly derivative. The strong sense of the superficial in his work derives precisely from this. However, his originality lay in showing that surfaces, paradoxically, were not always superficial or at least that superficiality had potential and a strange depth of its own. Without in any way undermining the specific historical qualities of glamour's original bearers, he at once demystified their aura and re-enchanted it. The allure of glamour could never be fully appropriated, but he rendered it more available than before and showed how it could be made into a repertoire for everyone. It could even become, if one wished it, an aspect of the self. This had a special appeal for those like transvestites and homosexuals who felt marginalized from mainstream life.

Warhol's DIY approach to fame was unusual in the early 1960s but it was much less so in the 1970s, when the innovations of the previous decade spread among the wider population. His work anticipated but was not in contrast with a major trend of the period towards individual expression. A cultural revolution had undermined conventional structures of authority and legitimated lifestyle experimentation, permitting women's liberation and gay pride to emerge as vehicles for further change. These processes were politicized but they were also fostered by forms of small-scale entrepreneurialism that evolved into rampant commercialism as the utopian impulses of the late 1960s receded. The long hair and vibrant colours worn by the hippies were turned into mass fashions that broke the clear visual and sartorial language separating men and women. The fashion industry and the mass media helped make what had initially been marks of distinction with respect to the mainstream into modish trends available even to people of middle age living far away from metropolitan or other cultural centres. In this way they contributed to a change in the nature of glamour, that ceased to be the exclusive prerogative of a mainly female metropolitan elite and was turned into a repertoire of props and hints also available to provincial young men.

The desire to throw off sartorial conventions, dress up, and create a fantasy persona fed into 'glam' or glitter rock, a circumscribed phenomenon that exploded in Britain in the early 1970s and which also found a limited following in the United States, especially in New York. Between 1971 and 1973, a range of musical performers including Marc Bolan of T. Rex and David Bowie, as well as Roxy Music and the less artful Gary Glitter, Sweet and Slade, championed an aesthetic of glitter and slap. Although the music could be raunchy and rock-driven, the lyrics of these bands explored various responses to sexual or teenage angst and feelings of displacement. None of the leading exponents of glam rock was openly homosexual—although some minor ones, including Jobriath and Wayne County (who had been part of the Factory fringe),[21] were—but it was a product of a distinct conjuncture in which rigidly gendered behavioural models were being questioned and challenged by innovations in dress, hairstyles, and sexual mores. Recent reforms to the law on homosexuality (which was effectively decriminalized in England and Wales in 1967) and open protest against police discrimination, symbolized by the Stonewall action in New York, led to a more visible gay milieu in large cities and in nightlife, and to distinctly gay fashions. Bowie was one of several artists to proclaim his bisexuality (in *Melody Maker* in January 1972). In his Ziggy Stardust and Aladdin Sane periods, his groomed, long hair, gaunt figure, and androgynous, made-up face were set off by a range of costumes. His glittery Ziggy outfit and the elegant white satin Aladdin skirt and boots were widely copied by his legions of fans. Although astronauts never enjoyed the glamour in the 1960s and 1970s that pilots had in the 1910s and 1920s, Bowie played on a certain popular fascination with space travel. His alien guises suggested that he belonged to another realm. Dandified, effeminate appearances evoked at turns Hollywood glamour, Las Vegas glitz, and voguish sci-fi. Warhol's drag queen superstars, especially Jackie Curtis, whose glitter-surrounded eyes, frizzy hair, and torn dresses first came to public attention in the New York nightclub Max's Kansas City, inspired a riot of cosmetics, glitter-covered costumes, platform boots, gold trousers, leopard skin jackets, capes, and elaborately styled hair.[22] Extravagant costumes and cosmetics made all the glam bands, some of whom hailed from the deeply unglamorous 'black country' in the English Midlands, look flamboyant and out of the ordinary.

In contrast to the United States, dressing up and camping it up were not very controversial in Britain, where cross-dressing was a staple element of popular entertainment.[23] One exuberant drag performer, Danny La Rue, regularly featured on prime-time television. Resplendent in his trademark figure-hugging sequined gowns and magnificent wig, he offered a visually exhilarating parade of middle-of-the-road songs and mild comedy. His act, it has been said, was 'the epitome of glamour in a glamour-starved country and a final gasp of British music hall and variety'.[24] Thus working-class bands like Sweet and Slade seemed just to be having fun and indulging in a spot of pantomime. For others, the theatrical turn was more programmatic.

David Bowie declared, 'I think rock should be tarted up, made into a prostitute, a parody of itself. It should be a clown, the Pierrot medium.' While the counter-culture of the late 1960s despised glamour as symbolizing affluence, capitalism, and show business,[25] art school rockers like Bowie saw artifice as a way of rendering musical performance more visual and complex and, through this, of blurring gender boundaries. Glam rockers mostly did not have the sophistication of Warhol but they drew inspiration from his example. In the USA, the New York Dolls offered a shambolic form of dandified rock that seemed inspired by a drawing-board cross of Bowie with the lace blouse-wearing Mick Jagger of the late sixties. Theatrical American singers and bands like Alice Cooper and Kiss pushed the idea even further, the latter even performing in full-face make-up.

Glam rock became a channel whereby show-business razzamatazz of the type embraced by Elvis Presley in his Las Vegas shows was reconciled with pop and rock.[26] With his gold lamé and white, stone-encrusted costumes, Elvis entered what the critic Karal Ann Marling terms his Byzantine period.[27] For rock and pop bands, the influences were mostly more prosaic. Television and more ambitious stage shows fuelled interest in the visual imagery of music on the part of musicians and their fans, a development which itself showed that rock was fast evolving into mass entertainment. Sparkle and glitter became a way of inventing a new more radiant persona and the contrived singing voices of many performers, including Bolan and Bowie, highlighted the extent to which they had transformed themselves. Paradoxically, this artifice made it easy for fans to imitate their style and manner, something that was difficult if not impossible with artists who only highlighted their musical brilliance. In this way, the more innovative glam rockers established a community of feeling with their followers. At a time of economic recession, following the oil crisis of 1973, glitz and glamour offered a glorious escape.

More than any other band, Roxy Music toyed with meanings of glamour. Formed in 1972, most of the group's five original members were art school graduates from the provinces who looked as though they had travelled to earth from another planet.[28] 'Our costumes were quite deliberately takes on those Fifties visions of space nobility—the masters of the galactic parliament and so on,' declared keyboard player Brian Eno later.[29] 'We were looking to the past in a kitsch way, and imagining the future as it might be—but perhaps in an equally kitsch way.'[30] While the band's members had the swagger of futuristic dandies, their songs had a wistful, nostalgic air. The group's very name was evocative of the picture houses of the golden age of cinema. Names like Gaumont, Rialto, and Locarno had been considered before the decision was taken to opt for Roxy.[31] The band's first album cover featured a model posing in Betty Grable's wartime pin-up style, while the sleeve of the second album 'For Your Pleasure' was a fabulously glossy confection featuring a model in stiletto heels that was redolent of the allure of metropolitan nights. Subsequent sleeves all featured models and drew on the repertoire of pin-up photography. Singer Bryan Ferry cultivated the manner of a lounge lizard and appeared in a variety of costumes including a GI uniform and a tuxedo. 'I don't really have a fixed notion of glamour; I love the glamour of Las Vegas, for instance—the extravagance of showgirls with long false eyelashes, masses of hair and high heels. I think that's fabulous, even though it's completely tacky,' he declared.[32] The band found a rich visual and thematic vein in the history of glamour that its members turned through sophisticated art direction into a contemporary blend of style, fashion, and image. Antony Price, the fashion designer who styled the band, always regretted that he had been born 'too late for the glamorous Hollywood period'.[33] With Roxy, the look was always paramount. The band, one journalist has said, 'represented a world of glamorous fantasy which brought the avant-garde to the British High Street by way of the catwalk'.[34] Roxy fans were mostly ordinary young men whose aspirations had been lifted from the level of the High Street by the movies and the getaway world of glossy magazines.

The vogue for masquerade represented a new stage of the other-directed personality type that David Riesman had identified in *The Lonely Crowd* in 1950.[35] He had argued that peer groups and the media were replacing conventional institutions as the main influences on modern behaviour. The result was a more malleable personality that needed external validation. A focus on exterior appearance and personal self-fashioning was an unavoidable consequence and the sources of inspiration were precisely the mass media. This idea was further elaborated by Christopher Lasch, one of the leading social critics of the period, who deplored the development as an impoverishment of the human condition. 'To the performing self,' he wrote, 'the only reality is the identity he can construct out of materials furnished by advertising and mass culture, themes of popular film and fiction, and fragments drawn from a vast range of cultural traditions, all of them equally contemporaneous to the contemporary mind.'[36] In his view, 'the disparity between romance and reality, the world of beautiful people and the workaday world gives rise to an ironic detachment that dulls pain but also cripples the will to change social conditions, to make even modest improvements in work and play, and to restore meaning and dignity to everyday life.'[37] He noted that the erosion of meaningful projects of social and political change had brought a new focus on individualism and pleasure. With social life less structured around social institutions following the cultural revolutions of the 1960s, and the concomitant displacement of collective sensibilities, what the writer Tom Wolfe referred to as the 'Me Decade' had heralded a widespread turn to self-expression and personal gratification.[38] One of the prime examples Lasch gave of the type of the 'new Narcissus' was, perhaps not surprisingly, Andy Warhol. His detached and pseudo-self-aware persona embodied exactly the shallow sense of self that the critic deplored. Yet, in another perspective, it was precisely the importance attached to surface that made Warhol's glamour recipe so seemingly empowering for those who preferred to create a glittering exterior persona rather than face the mundanity of their everyday lives.[39] The subjugation of the individual to a media panorama in place of the institutions of family, religion, and community authority freed him or her to construct an individual story or identity, albeit within the range of possibilities suggested by media that were organically part of the consumer economy. Warhol's focus on 'deep surfaces' perfectly fitted this atmosphere.[40]

Bands like Roxy Music created dream worlds that consisted of images and suggestions taken from films, magazines, and television. They evoked the privileged world of the beautiful people, the nomadic lives of the jet set, exotic paradises, and stylish romance. In their songs, the Riviera, Palm Beach, and Hollywood, the past, the present, and the future, all merged into one portmanteau fantasy. In this way, they promoted a cult of pop glamour that fuelled their fans' desire to live glamorously and act out their dreams. This imaginary uplift from banal quotidian experience was not new but in the 1970s it took on a new significance as it coincided with the disappearance of a distinctive elite of style, taste, and privilege. Whereas, in the not so remote past, women like Babe Paley or Mona Bismarck had belonged to a tiny international elite of style, now the rich had multiplied and the special grace that had once touched the fashionable few had evaporated. According to Truman Capote's biographer, Gerald Clarke, 'a new kind of glamour, based solely on publicity, had taken its place'.[41] In this vacuum, pop offered an alluring pastiche of sophistication. Roxy Music brought an intoxicating air of louche elegance to Britain's high streets and precincts, launching an epidemic of copycat haircuts and attitudes.[42] In this, they were a major influence on later bands, and notably on the champions of 1980s' New Romantic glamour, Duran Duran. As the band's fortunes increased, Bryan Ferry's lifestyle came to resemble his fantasies. He had set his sights on turning himself by means of his art, clothes, and music into a modern aristocrat. He stepped out with the Texan model Jerry Hall and then married the daughter of a well-connected Lloyd's broker. The couple were fixtures of the London party scene and occasionally joined the international jet set.[43]

Once, picture houses had been the theatres of dreams, vehicles of fantasies, and sensory stimulations. In the 1970s, discotheques and nightclubs brought a whiff of excitement to the lives of young people living in provincial towns and cities. They were tempting and alluring places where the workaday world receded and everyone could indulge in escapes from the everyday. Various currents brought about a situation in which the nightlife of leading cities began to sparkle and sizzle with unprecedented intensity. After the 1960s, more people had surplus income and demanded leisure opportunities that provided an alternative to the regimentation of the workplace. This contrasted with earlier leisure, which had been predominantly collective and often voluntary, in the form for example of working men's clubs and organized outings, with only cinema and dance being mainly organized through the market. A general enthusiasm for dressing-up and exhibitionism combined with the burgeoning gay subculture and the mood of escape to generate an atmosphere of hedonism.

Discotheques had begun in France in the 1960s as a type of nightclub where, instead of there being a live band, recorded music was played through a sound system. They had quickly spread to London where drinking and dancing clubs in Piccadilly and Soho adopted the name. These were often hybrid establishments, however, that still featured some live music and occasionally even included a casino. Their clientele was more moneyed than young and stylish.[44] In fashionable clubs in Paris and on the Riviera, disc jockeys created sequences of sounds, blending one disc into another to ensure that dancing was uninterrupted. Paris clubs such as Flamingo and Club Sept, which opened in 1968, created a semi-clandestine scene that was distinct from conventional social life. There was an openly gay element that was disguised by the general emphasis on dressing-up and escapism.[45] Light systems coordinated with sounds and glass dance floors with coloured lights added to the experience. Discotheques soon spread to major cities through-out the Western world and then to smaller towns and the provinces. But the impulses that came to bear on the industry of after-hours entertainment were most evident in locations in which the mix of money, creativity, and beautiful people was most intense, that is to say in New York, Paris, Los Angeles, Miami, and on the Riviera. The music that able producers created for disco dancing contributed to the atmosphere. They mixed soaring vocal sounds with a steady beat and a pulsating bass line. Forsaking the guitar-dominated sound of rock, they made recourse to horns, strings, and electric pianos and guitars to create a powerful, swirling rush of sound capable of rousing even the most reluctant dancers to their feet. Donna Summer, Barry White, Chic, and the Jackson Five were the leading exponents of a musical genre that would dominate the hit parades between the mid- and late 1970s. Rooted in the Tamla Motown sounds of the 1960s, disco evolved into a distinct musical style through the soul sounds of Philadelphia and New York contaminated with pop and funk. It was loathed by rock fans who clung to the counter-culture's unglamorous masculine aesthetics and insistence on the authenticity of live music.

The disco music boom brought to the fore a series of behavioural tropes that were further codified and amplified by the movie *Saturday Night Fever*, which was released in the United States in December 1977. Tony Manero's sharp white suits and black shirts (which were in fact inspired by Marcello Mastroianni's costume in some later scenes of *La dolce vita*), his strutting his stuff with physical self-confidence, his living for the night as a sphere of self-realization opposed to the banality of his daytime life, and the syrupy ecstasy of the Bee Gees soundtrack all turned disco from a subculture into into a social and cultural phenomenon. Played by John Travolta, Manero was an example of a young working-class man who was a king while he was in the discotheque. With his sharp suits and dance-floor magnetism, he was untouchable; outside that context he was hemmed in by drudgery, squabbling parents, deadbeat friends, and community tensions. The discotheque provided him with a platform to realize his dream self. There he was the supreme dancer, the sexual magnet, the fashion leader, and the master of all he surveyed.

No club would mark the disco experience more than New York's Studio 54. It only had a brief heyday (from April 1977 to February 1980), but during that time it enjoyed an unrivalled reputation. It was flamboyant and excessive, decadent and debauched, and desirable in the extreme.[46] Situated on West 54th street in Manhattan in an old CBS television studio from which many popular live television shows had been broadcast, it boasted a 5,400-square-foot dance floor and stunning lighting effects. Created by nightclub promoters Steve Rubell and Ian Schrager, it was a concentration of disco, glitter, celebrity, libertinism, and gay culture. Studio 54 was quite unlike old-established New York clubs like El Morocco and Le Club that were reserved for the rich. Its sheer scale distinguished it from clubs in London and Paris that had brought together heterogeneous groups of celebrities, arts and fashion, socialites, and beautiful people but which were small. Studio 54 brought a new dimension to New York nightlife that was seductive, hedonistic, exuberant, and wild. It flourished at a time when the city had one of the highest crime rates in the world and was on the verge of bankruptcy. It was a counter to stagnation and a diffuse sense of decline. It was also the tip of an iceberg of semi-clandestine entertainments geared to every type of hetero- and homosexual taste.

The club was located far away from the fashionable parts of Manhattan in a rundown area known for its pornographic cinemas and gay brothels. Despite this, it was launched with a bang. Gossip columnists built expectations and 5,000 famous people drawn from fashion, film, music, and the jet

319

set were personally invited to the opening. Shortly after, a birthday party was held for Mick Jagger's Nicaraguan socialite wife Bianca (the couple married in St Tropez in 1971) that propelled the club on to the front pages as a place of glorious excess. Her sensational entry into the disco on a white horse instantly made Studio 54 the most famous nightclub in the world. 'Bianca's party was the catalyst,' observed the club's doorman Marc Benecke, 'it just snowballed from there.'[47] It was busy every night of the week and became the preferred hang-out for celebrities including Liza Minelli, Truman Capote, Elizabeth Taylor, Elton John, Cher, Andy Warhol, Margaux Hemingway, Brooke Shields, Rudolph Nureyev, Sylvester Stallone, Diana Ross, Grace Jones, Gloria Vander-bilt, Donald and Ivana Trump, the fashion designers Calvin Klein and Roy Halston, and Diana Vreeland and former first lady Betty Ford, who was a more suprising guest than another former first lady, Jackie Onassis. Everyone wanted to be there. From one day to the next, it seemed, the tabloids became obsessed with the personalities, eccentricities, sensations, and gossip of Rubell and Schrager's glamorous hothouse. At the centre, the ringmaster was the highly visible and charismatic Rubell. He directed an ever-changing show that relied on lots of theme nights, including evocations of the Folies Bergère and a Shanghai street as well as novelties like the 1-foot-deep gold glitter that was spread over the dance floor on New Year's Eve in 1978. In a bold endorse-ment of drug culture, a sculpted figure of the man in the moon snorting cocaine from a spoon hung from the ceiling. A huge circular bar was staffed by bare-chested bartenders in tight jeans.

In keeping with the conventions of glamour, Studio 54 was at once accessible and exclusive. Rubell attributed great importance to getting the right mix of people in his club. A strict door policy ensured that undesirables were excluded. This did not mean, however, that the habitués consisted solely of the rich and famous. This was simply not possible given the club's great size. Every night, under a black marquee with a silver art-deco-style logo bearing the club's name, hundreds pushed to gain admittance. Many queued and clamoured and never got in. Having the right look was crucial, as Rubell liked an unpredictable assortment of people. Drag queens, gays, and preppy types were favoured, and a sprinkling of roller skaters, mafioso types, hookers in hot pants, and disco fans welcomed, while ethnic minorities were heavily filtered, and provincial lotharios and star-watchers excluded. While John Travolta gained admittance with no difficulty, his character Tony Manero might have struggled to receive the nod from the door staff. As Rubell once said, 'if you let in too many people who look as if they come from the outer boroughs, no one will be interested in coming next week.'[48] 'The grey people' therefore had to be kept at arm's length. Getting the mix right, he asserted, was like casting a play or 'tossing a salad'.[49] While around 150 friends and celebrities had free entrance, as well as access to the balcony and a reserved VIP room, everyone else faced the challenge of the velvet rope on the street. One of the appeals of Studio 54 was that it was impossible to buy one's way in. Notoriously, some celebrities were barred or ejected.

The elect of Studio 54 became, through the press, an elite based on appearance and style. This was extremely exciting for men like Warhol, who had never previously enjoyed tabloid fame and gossip column status, or like Capote who, following publication of chapters from his unfinished confessional novel *Answered Prayers* by *Esquire* magazine, was no longer persona grata in the homes of the rich.[50] For them, the club was both a recreation ground and a showcase that turned them into fully fledged celebrities. The club's reputation for glorious excess, drug-fuelled hedonism, men dancing with men, and casual sex even on the premises made it seem like a fantasyland for adults. Above all, it was a place of transformation where dreams and desires found an immediate realization. A handful of journalists freely gathered stories while photographers took innumerable pictures of wild abandon and groups of inebriated guests. Warhol's posthumously published diaries show the extent to which his social world was defined by a seamless sequence of celebrity parties, dinners, and soirées and Studio 54. On Saturday, 21 January 1978, despite a blizzard, he 'cabbed it' over to the club with a female companion and found Rubell turning people away as usual. Among the dancers, he spotted former heavyweight boxing champion Ken Norton. 'Then we wanted to go down to a place called Christy's restaurant on West 11th Street where there was a *Saturday Night Live* party for Steve Martin,' he wrote:

We went outside to try and get a cab but we couldn't. Then along came a white guy and a black girl in a car who offered us a ride anywhere we wanted to go and we took it. They said that Stevie wouldn't let them in to Studio 54 because they didn't look right, but they looked okay to me—I mean, he looked like a fairy and she looked like a drag queen, it was the Studio 54 look. As we were going along Catherine looked out the window and said wasn't that Lou Reed on the street, and it was. He was with a Chinese chick, and they got in and he was very friendly. When we got to Christy's, Steve Martin was great, he seemed thrilled to meet me.[51]

This entry shows the transformation that occurred in Warhol's life. By the mid-1970s he preferred to frequent the rich and famous instead of the motley gaggle he had hung out with previously. In the past, only Edie Sedgwick had connected him vicariously with the uptown social world. After he was shot and badly wounded in 1969 by a woman who had appeared in some of his underground movies, he avoided former cronies and became friends with people like Bianca Jagger. With her dark hair and full lips, she bore a curious resemblance to her husband. For fashion writer Kennedy Fraser, the Nicaraguan socialite had a grace and style that came from her wealthy background; she was 'like a jungle orchid . . . both fragile and luscious'.[52] She wore white satin trouser suits and wielded a dandyish Regency cane that testified to her artistic conception of her persona. Bianca was already an activist for women's rights and humanitarian issues, but she was also exceptionally photogenic and glamorous. Unlike most Studio 54 regulars, she did not use drugs, Warhol noted.[53] For this reason, she was able to skate over the surface of the human wreckage of the night world and always appear fragrant and fresh. She made the crossover smoothly from international high society to modern celebrity thanks to her looks, connections, poise, and ubiquity.

The press was a crucial factor in turning Studio 54 from an important but circumscribed phenomenon into a focus of mass dreams and aspirations. The club did not just attract enthusiastic coverage; it also gave rise to strong criticism from social conservatives. Most significantly, it was a factor in the birth of a new type of reportage in which the doings of celebrities took the place of hard news. As a continuous feast of familiar and not so familiar faces, the club provided almost limitless opportunities for new photographs of the beautiful and the famous, and for gossip, profiles, and style pieces.

Many of the new ideas came from *Interview*, the magazine that Warhol founded in 1969. This was the vital platform that enabled him to move from the margins and from experimental art to the mainstream of contemporary celebrity. Having the power to grant magazine space to individuals suddenly made him a highly desirable friend or guest. The monthly was a mixture of fan magazine, film bulletin, art journal, and style glossy that covered all areas of popular culture. It anticipated a contemporary preoccupation with celebrity and style at the expense of traditional cultural products such as film and music. Its most original contribution was the featured celebrity interview, in which the famous were interviewed by their peers in a relaxed, conversational manner that was neither inquisitorial nor fawning. An air of intimacy permeated the magazine, giving readers the sense that they were part of the elect community of the stylish and famous. Celebrity was explored from the inside with young photographers being given early opportunities for exposure and encouragement to experiment. *Interview*'s stars were not perfect confections, just beautiful people with individual profiles playing at glamour. Instead of established high society, Warhol and his editor Bob Colacello ran features on social climbers, heiresses, and young and beautiful wannabes. The visual design was bold and unconventional, with the covers featuring tacky yet alluring coloured paintings of famous faces made from photographs that mimicked Warhol's own silk screens in an outsize, simplified way.[54] Although the connection was not direct, it can been seen as the inspiration for British magazines like *The Face* and *Blitz* that were less interested in the socially visible than in music but which shared the passion for style and surface. In the British context, they turned style culture from a clandestine pursuit into a pervasive cultural phenomenon of which they proposed themselves as leaders and guides.[55]

One of *Interview*'s most significant contributions was to draw fashion into the mainstream by pioneering a certain type of coverage that treated designers, models, make-up artists, and anyone who looked good in clothes as a celebrity. This type of coverage came at a time when fashion was undergoing a series of changes. Haute couture had declined dramatically since the 1950s as society had evolved and formal rituals had dissolved. Instead, boutique fashion, pioneered in London by Mary Quant and Biba, and in

Paris by Sonia Rykiel, prospered because its focus on the casual was more suited to changing lifestyles.[56] Between 1971 and 1973, no Saint Laurent couture collections were presented, as the designer preferred to concentrate on his more casual and leisure-oriented line. He also branched out into menswear. He became the idol of the young and fashionable, grabbing the headlines with his de luxe hippy styles, velvet jackets, kaftans, printed silk shirts, chain belts, and safari suits. He developed new styles every season that reflected the contemporary mood and set trends which reverberated through the mass market. He also helped redefine perceptions of beauty by becoming the first couturier to work with models from a wide variety of ethnic backgrounds, including Africa and Asia. Saint Laurent was himself a glamorous figure whose friends included Rudolph Nureyev, Andy Warhol, and Paul and Talitha Getty, at whose Marrakesh house he started experimenting with drugs. In 1971, he consolidated his personal reputation for daring, iconoclastic stances when he posed for Jeanloup Sieff cross-legged on a leather cushion, naked save for his trademark rectangular spectacles.[57]

Saint Laurent's image was that of an aloof genius. However, his partner in life and in business, Pierre Bergé, was always attuned to new ways of taking the label to the wider market. Through his endeavours, a new business model for fashion houses was pioneered. Without losing the association with luxury and elite style that was fundamental to whipping up the glamour that was needed to be able to sell goods at premium prices, he developed strategies to raise profits through licensing agreements. These put the house's name on goods including fragrances that created brand awareness and thereby reinforced the status value of the core collections. These in turn gave licensed goods their glamorous desirability. In a context in which the desire to look alluring and sexy was not unusual or restricted to a select few but widespread, fashion houses began to see that there were opportunities to reach wider strata of potential customers by deploying glitz and glamour. This led to changes in presentation and a more marked accent on mass culture and show business.[58]

Like many designers of his generation, Saint Laurent's imagination was fired by iconic stars like Greta Garbo, Joan Crawford, and Marlene Dietrich, whose mannish costumes inspired his celebrated trouser suits. He admired strong women and always selected models with a determined attitude. There was a lot in common between his vision and that of the photographer Helmut Newton and the two men inspired each other reciprocally. They were both thoroughly imbued with bourgeois culture while being sceptical of its values and critical of its hypocrisies. As a refugee from Nazism, Newton knew only too well that corruption, authoritarianism, and sexual perversion were never far from the centre of the bourgeois subconscious,[59] while Saint Laurent, as a homosexual born in Oran, Algeria, then a French colony, had seen racism at work and had personally experienced discrimination on account of his orientation. The cultural climate of the seventies allowed them to bring their convictions about the bourgeoisie into the commercial and artistic mainstream.

Fashion photography had always had a fantasy function. For decades, its ideal had been the imaginary lady. In the 1960s, this was displaced by the girl. In the 1970s, the imagination of fashion was increasingly shaped by a loose concoction of decadent themes including sex, money, and luxury that often merged in a sleazy melange. In Newton's work, these themes were brought boldly to the fore. No one more than him stamped his mark so fully on the image of glamour at the time. In his editorial work for French *Vogue*, he developed a highly material fantasy world that caught the sexual climate of the period and blurred the boundaries between fashion, the movies, sadomasochism, soft pornography, and travel advertising. The world he created from his base in Monte Carlo resonated with jet-set values and glossy high consumption.[60] It was not artistic but brashly materialistic. In its suggestions of adventure, it was, according to one journalist, 'a bit James Bond and, sometimes, even a bit Milk Tray'.[61] His work had a stylized, hyperreal quality to it that was striking especially for its overt sexualization of his female models, who were always Amazonian. His vision, he declared, 'was of a highly sexual woman, in all respects Western, whose native habitat was Paris, Milan, and maybe New York'.[62] Newton's photographs were widely criticized for their relentless objectification of women and the overt voyeurism of the point of view.[63] None was more controversial than the shot he took for the French luxury company Hermès of a model in riding gear on all fours on a bed with a saddle on her back. His photographs had a shiny, glossy appeal that highlighted their production values: his preferred settings were luxury hotels, millionaires' villas, penthouse apartments, swimming pools, and beaches, preferably in Paris, New York, Los Angeles, or on the Mediterranean. Models were made-up, oiled, dressed in PVC, stiletto heels, or items of lingerie, or were posed totally or partially nude, with their pubic hair often on full view. Rarely well-known, they were treated as mannequins or props in scenarios that reeked of money and/or perversion. Many of Newton's photographs, while indisputably luxurious, exude menace and even an atmosphere of impending doom.

Born in Berlin in 1920, Newton (his real surname was Neustädter) was a German Jew who, as a boy, was in thrall to the movies and stars like Marlene Dietrich. After leaving Germany in 1938, he lived in Singapore and, for nearly twenty years, in Australia before moving to Paris to work for French *Vogue* in the mid-1950s. The influence of old films was clear in his work, as was a whole tradition of open-air and real-life fashion and news photography that blended artificiality with everyday life. Although he disdained the studio and special effects, his images always had a strong fantasy element that he claimed was completely personal.[64] In the 1970s, they were erotic and kinky, sophisticated in atmosphere, and utterly frigid in tone. Like Guy Bourdin, his rival and colleague on French *Vogue*, whose imagery was no less sexualized and glossy but darker and tendentially macabre, he had a strong vision that had nothing to do with conventional good taste. Indeed, he frequently spoke in favour of vulgarity, as he did of artificiality. The great theme of his artwork was the female nude. Two of his most famous pictures show the same group of four models walking in formation with an air of insouciance and self-possession. In the first black-and-white picture, they are wearing fashionable street clothes; in the second, they are naked, save for—a typical Newtonian touch—high-heeled shoes. In the 1930s and 1940s, Hollywood studio photographers sometimes used the time at the end of photo sessions to take nude pictures of female stars and starlets for clandestine sale or private use. Newton similarly took his nude shots at the conclusion of commercial shoots, but his work was in all but a handful of cases destined for galleries and books.[65] He also took portraits of many of the leading figures of his day from the worlds of fashion, the arts, and politics.

Saint Laurent and Newton were both drawn to the actress Catherine Deneuve, who had played perverse bourgeois women in *Belle de Jour* and *Tristana*, two art house films made, respectively in 1967 and 1970, by the iconoclastic surrealist director Luis Buñuel. Newton took her as a subject, Saint Laurent as a muse. A cool blonde of great poise and personal elegance who made her film debut at the age of 13 in 1956, Deneuve was widely regarded from the 1970s as a symbol of the cultivated but unconventional bourgeois Frenchwoman. Aloof both to gossip and petty exhibitionism, she lived her life freely, marrying photographer David Bailey and having children out of wedlock with Roger Vadim and Marcello Mastroianni.[66] Men found in her an irresistible mix of detachment, self-control, ambiguity, and transgression. For Newton, as for Saint Laurent and Buñuel, she was at once an 'official' bourgeois icon, an embodiment of France (she would be chosen by French mayors to be the model for a bust of the national symbol Marianne in 1985), a model of elegance (for many years she was the face of Chanel No. 5),[67] a sex symbol, and a glamorous film star. These multiple identities gave them the opportunity to highlight one or more over others, or even to play one off against another to suggest an air of sinfulness and decadence. She was the perfect vehicle for increasing the sexual element in glamour while maintaining class and a high-end commercial appeal. Deneuve's ultimate appeal was her mystery; she was a modern sphinx into which directors, designers, photographers, and the public read what they wanted.

It would not be the French, but rather the Americans and the Italians, who would most clearly see that the interest in glamour and appearances opened the possibility of reorganizing the fashion industry on new bases. The large American stores had always been keen promoters of fashion and they had long bought Paris couture designs and had them remade for sale under their own labels. When Jacqueline Kennedy was in the White House, fashion became of much wider interest. Her stylish appearance mesmerized millions. The press and American women more generally started to pay attention to the names of designers she patronized. This began a trend that led to the designer's name becoming more prominent on ready-to-wear garments. By the mid-1960s, designer labels were already beginning to displace those of the stores as indicators of quality and style.

New York was host to a garment industry at least as large, if not as prestigious, as Paris. There was a top echelon of couture designers like James Galanos and Pauline Trigère who dressed the famous. Below them was a tier of less well-known designers, including Bill Blass, Oscar della Renta, and Geoffrey Beene, who not only catered to rich clients but also designed for the stores. These men were the troupers of American high fashion who travelled the country doing trunk shows for wealthy local matrons. None of them could hope to replicate the unique allure of Yves Saint Laurent or other Parisian designers, who exercised an irresistible appeal for the wealthiest and most cosmopolitan American women. American and Italian fashion producers had always been poor relations who, lacking the immense prestige and historic pre-eminence of Paris, had aimed to sell on price and quality. Despite this, established names were not generally well equipped, on account of their close links to the social elite, to reach out to a fluid and heterogeneous market. New names were called for who were in touch with contemporary culture and who could therefore interpret social trends and respond flexibly to changing demands.

In the 1970s, there was a thirst for prestige and originality that stretched well beyond the upper tier of the market to the middle and lower levels. There were also significant middle-level markets for two types of clothing. These reflected the 'disparity between romance and reality, the world of beautiful people and the workaday world' that Christopher Lasch identified.[68] On the one hand, practical clothes were required for the 'workaday world'. However, these were likely to be more appealing if they incorporated some suggestion of romance, permitting the wearers to lift themselves on the imaginary level out of the quagmire of banality. Glamour, as David Riesman had shown, was likely to enter the workplace when that was the main arena of an individual's social interaction.[69] This was important because changes in women's education as well as the expansion of the tertiary sector brought radical changes in the structure of the labour market. Many women were mobile professionals who needed wardrobes to match their new-found status. They did not want conventional seasonal styles but practical designs that could be worn over more than one season. They were especially drawn to garments that combined this necessity with romance. The latter also

fuelled a demand for leisure wear that allowed those who wore it to vicariously join the beautiful people. The attitude of ironic detachment that Lasch
saw as the key trait of the contemporary personality was assembled with the
support of suggestions taken from advertising, popular music, and films and
fiction. In this context, elegance diminished as a value, while seduction and sex
appeal became central. The distinctions of the past between formal and
informal gave way to a more fluid style in which the body was the starting
point. As people saw themselves increasingly as sexual beings, it became a locus
of fantasies and a project of self-construction. It was not a given but a modifi-
able reality that was as much imagined as it was experienced.

The rise of designer ready-to-wear is an important chapter in the history of
glamour. In the decade from 1978 the fashion business witnessed a revolution
as prêt-à-porter ceased to be a poor relation of couture and emerged as the
neo-couture of mass society. The Americans and the Italians were quicker to
seize the potential than the French. Firms like GFT (Gruppo Finanziario
Tessile), which produced ready-to-wear in Turin, did not back haute couture,
as Marcel Boussac had done when he supported Dior in the 1940s;[70] rather
they showed that fashion stars could be created in a short time if there was
heavy investment in production and advertising. All the new designers were to
some degree or other trend-spotters and style magpies. Typically, they were
also outsiders as far as the conventional elite was concerned. A striking
number of them were drawn to Studio 54 because it was a world unto itself
that created legends and myths. It generated forms of glamour that were no
longer related to, or derived from, the social hierarchy. The American designers Halston and Calvin Klein were regulars, while Yves Saint Laurent and the
Paris-based German Karl Lagerfeld were occasional visitors. The latter was less
interested in the jet set than Saint Laurent; an early convert to ready-to-wear,
it was the trends that fascinated him.[71]

The first new fashion star was not in fact an outsider. Although he had
been born in Des Moines, Iowa, Halston was a milliner by training who
worked for the Bergdorf Goodman luxury goods department store and was
admired by such prominent journalists as Eugenia Sheppard and Diana
Vreeland. As hats lost popularity, he branched out into informal ready-to-
wear before setting up his own couture house in 1968. He had a client list

that included Princess Grace, Babe Paley, Jackie Onassis, Lauren Bacall, and Liz Taylor as well as many society mavens. He also attracted a following from a more eccentric clientele, including drag queens, who met at his salon, which was seen as a sort of sartorial parallel to Warhol's Factory. Halston emerged as a glamorous personality through Studio 54. Always dressed in black and often wearing mirrored sunglasses, he became the 'personification of glamour', the 'king of New York nightlife'. According to journalist Steven Gaines, another Studio regular and author of the designer's biography, 'so tall and thin [was he] in his black cashmere turtleneck and sports jacket that he looked like a giant exclamation point, stern and final'.[72] A star of the social scene and the media, he was hailed as the designer of disco wear. He at once combined the snob appeal of a society couturier with the fashionable allure of a New York night owl. He was present at the famous Jagger party that won the club its reputation and then was there almost every night. The elegant casual wear for which he was known suited a time in which conventions and formality were giving way to more relaxed styles. Halston knew that American fashion was turning into a manufactured product to be sold through advertising and promotion. He opened several boutiques that connected him to a wider market, where he came to be seen as a master of US classics. The supple, unreconstructed style he was associated with was perfectly suited to mass production.[73] His perfume 'Halston' became a bestseller. More than any other designer, Halston reinvented himself through the nightclub. However, as cocaine addiction progressively dominated his life, he ceased to be a force in fashion.

Calvin Klein was also drawn to the flamboyant but ambivalent world of Studio 54, which he cruised with a loosely knit circle of celebrity cronies. In the club's atmosphere of feverish excitement he discovered his bisexuality and became a creature of the night, 'acquiring through gossip columns the status and glamour of a rock star'.[74] Like Halston, Klein first made his mark in the 1960s. However, he was never a couturier and had no high society clients. Fashion writer Alicia Drake's observation that 'fashion has always had a tradesman's fascination with nobility' did not seem to apply to him.[75] He got his first break thanks to the Bonwit Teller store in New York, for whom Warhol had dressed windows in the 1950s.[76] The store pioneered the idea of the designer boutique and sold the work of European and American designers. Bonwit's buyer, Mildred Custin, liked his detailed feminine blouses with delicate tucks and elegant well-cut trousers. The influence of early Chanel was evident in his collarless jackets and in the simplicity and wearability of his creations. Custin saw Klein as an 'American Yves Saint Laurent' and promoted his clothes in window displays and advertisements in the *New York Times*.[77] Klein adapted Saint Laurent's innovations to the American market, copying the latter's trenchcoats and pleated trousers and selling them much more cheaply. By 1973, Klein had defined a signature style of clean, sharp lines and a lack of frills. Like Giorgio Armani in Italy, who would present his first GFT-supported collection in 1975, his main colours were grey and camel, basic shades that advertising wrapped with images of old Hollywood.

In 1976, when he was still aged only 32, Klein's business had revenues of $40 million. These rose dramatically to $90 million in 1977.[78] The designer was young and good-looking, a sex symbol even, who had married his childhood sweetheart from the Bronx. But success changed him. As he became famous, he reinvented himself, dropping his Bronx accent and associations. He started going to fashionable restaurants and acquired new homes in more fashionable districts. A new world of glamour and style was opened to him that involved world travel and a new tenor of life. He soon became a polished PR version of his former self. From the start, Klein had been a salesman and communicator. He appointed an in-house publicist, realizing that a symbiotic relationship was developing between designers and the fashion press. He was also highly alert to trends and made it his business to be on the cutting edge of everything that was new and hot. In the night world he found the ecstasy of sex and drugs but also ideas that he would translate into lucrative innovations.

To develop the middle market, what was needed was not a prestige product stripped of quality and offered to the mass, or a run-of-the-mill item with a designer's name arbitrarily attached to it. Rather something entirely new was required to catalyse the passions of a market that was tending to connect personal happiness and fulfilment with the possession of prestigious material goods. While elite connotations were still marketable, these needed to be cleansed of snobbery and fused with modernity. While the customers for couture dwindled, the middle market showed a great desire for prestige products that carried a reputation for quality and exclusivity. Yet, to endow these with the right quotients of accessibility and rarity was not straightforward. The French designer Pierre Cardin had been the first to establish multiple licensing deals for clothes, allowing a French manufacturer to adapt his designs for sale at a lower price.[79] He had then licensed numerous other products including home-ware and furniture. However, Cardin failed to limit the number of deals or exercise control over his licensees, with the result that his name soon became linked with a variety of low-quality merchandise available in low-grade stores. In consequence, his label lost kudos at the crucial couture level and declined sharply in prestige. As a business model though it worked somehow, since his empire continued to be very profitable even without glamour.[80] But it only prospered at the low end. Halston too saw the potential of the mass market and even sold his own name to a corporation, Norton-Simon Industries. He also designed a line of clothes for the budget store chain J. C. Penney, which controversially brought his work to lower income brackets. However, as his drug addiction took hold, he was sacked from his own label in 1984 for poor deadline keeping.[81] The lesson of all this was that the aura of glamour that was so vital in driving the desires of consumers and that could induce them to pay high prices for a given brand could easily evaporate.

The winning formula was discovered when Warren Hirsh, the president of Mujani International, a Hong Kong-based manufacturer, invented the phenomenon of designer jeans. Up until the middle of the decade, such a notion would have been oxymoronic. Jeans were not high-style items but work-wear that had been taken up from the 1950s by youth. Even though some variations of shape and cut had been introduced to appeal to the youth market, they were still sold mainly as goods that were practical, tough, and egalitarian. Most makes did not do jeans for women and the most common motif of brands like Levi's, Wrangler, and Lee was the cowboy. Hirsh had wanted to make mass-market clothing with a designer's name on the label. After some rebuffs from leaders in the field, he embraced instead the idea of women's jeans bearing the endorsement of a social figure. When Jacqueline Onassis, not surprisingly, refused him, he turned to Gloria Vanderbilt. Vanderbilt was already a commercial figure who had recently launched her own line of home furnishings.

But she was also American royalty, the great-granddaughter of Cornelius Vanderbilt and niece of Consuelo. She not only agreed to the remunerative proposal but also modelled, which proved to be a vital factor in the product's astonishing success. Television commercials showed the smiling 40-something socialite wearing super-slim-fitting jeans that featured her elegant signature above a swan on every pair. Suddenly, well-dressed women started wearing jeans and the concept of designer denims was born. Vanderbilt's runaway success showed that socialites still exercised market appeal as examples of taste and style provided they positioned themselves in a way that could be conveyed as sexy and desirable through the mass media. The product, though, was not one that had trickled down from the top social echelon; on the contrary, crucially, it was a mass product glammed up. This success also showed that the marketing of leisurewear worked best through lifestyle ex- amples. These made fashion seem an essential component of modern life and turned it into a collective preoccupation.[82]

Although this success had the air of a fad, it set a precedent. Ever quick to spot a trend, Klein developed a line of own-name jeans that had more immediate sex appeal than any other brand.[83] Within a short time, his sales were second only to Gloria Vanderbilt's. Once the novelty of the latter had worn off, they moved into first place. Drawing inspiration from his experience of nightclubbing, he took conventional denims, accentuated the crotch, and gave more shape to the buttocks. Launched in 1978, they were sold only in select stores. Klein boldly used billboard advertising to promote them, engaging the young Brooke Shields as his model and having her photographed in black and white by Richard Avedon. An astute move was to label the garments 'Calvins' in advertisements, rather than jeans. Klein repeated this success several times in the years that followed, most notably with men's underwear, which was also given the designer treatment and sold with added sex appeal, and with fragrances including the first successful unisex product CKOne. With products like these, Klein touched something at the core of modern identity. To assert a sexy, modern identity that was utterly contemporary, the message seemed to run, there was no alternative but to wear Calvin Klein. Sex would remain a key inspiration for all fashion advertising and presentation but no label would use it more sensationally.

Klein's sexy buzz won many followers but it did not exhaust the range of suggestions available to the fashion business. Another designer found that the idea of the desirable wealthy lifestyle could be deployed in new ways to promote merchandise. Ralph Lauren (born Ralph Lifschitz—the family name was changed when he was 16) was no less a self-made man than Klein. Born like him to a Bronx Jewish family, he grew up without any connection to elite society or fashion, but soon developed a taste for expensive clothes. After working for the preppy outfitter Brooks Brothers, he founded a luxury necktie business called Polo. The name Polo evoked a sense of elegance and Europe, it mixed sport and lifestyle, it had cachet, and it was playboyish, international, and glamorous.[84] Classic rather than fashionable clothes followed, with womenswear being added from 1972. Lauren built an empire on the observation that certain basic and iconic items of clothing, like tweed jackets, Oxford shirts, Shetland sweaters, and chino pants, were no longer well made. A popular item like the polo knit shirt, that was closely associated with the French firm Lacoste and its crocodile symbol, was commonly made in poor artificial fibres and in a limited range of colours. What Lauren did was to take over these staple items, make them in a well-designed way, and ensure that they were available season after season in an impressive range of colours.

Compared to Klein, Lauren was a traditionalist. He was a family man who preferred home life to socializing. Despite their different temperaments, the two men had much in common. Although Klein came from a more conventional garment industry background, neither designer had a training in couture. Their role was closer to that of the *styliste* rather than the couturier. This was the term that had been used to describe any ready-to-wear designer who worked for a fashion company that was not his or her own.[85] However, even this label was not quite right, for Lauren and Klein were not employees but the founders and creative forces of their companies. Moreover, in addition to designing and selling ready-to-wear clothing,[86] they were purveyors of dreams, fabricators of lifestyles and themes.[87]

Lauren's main inspiration was classic Hollywood movies. Like Warhol, he adored the films of the 1930s and 1940s and in particular the smooth elegance of Grace Kelly, Audrey Hepburn, and Cary Grant. He was visibly star-struck when he met people like Hepburn or Grant. He dreamed of being a movie star and played up his associations with film-making. He also saw the utility of films in fashion promotion. When it was announced that a film version of F. Scott Fitzgerald's *The Great Gatsby* was to be made in 1974, he latched on to the project. Although the Academy Award for the film's costumes went to Theoni V. Aldredge, he made some suits for Robert Redford that featured on screen. He also claimed some credit for Woody Allen's film *Annie Hall* on the grounds that a few Lauren items had been used by Diane Keaton in assembling her character's look.[88]

Like the old studio-era moguls, Lauren conjured up an idealized America from a range of imagined sources. 'Everyone really liked the idea of Cary Grant,' observes one of the debonair star's biographers,[89] reflecting exactly the view that Lauren repeated to himself. The actor's classless and self-assured persona and his role as 'a democratic symbol of gentlemanly grace' were the premiss of the Lauren label's appeal to a mass market.[90] More than anyone else, Lauren understood that evocations of the wealth and glamour of the past, provided they were stripped of any precise connotations of class or place, were intensely appealing and very accessible.[91] The designer also developed western, American looks, drawing inspiration from Robert Redford and Steve Mc-Queen, to offer urban Americans a fantasy of a rugged casual lifestyle. Lauren had something of the Gatsby character about him. He was a self-invented persona who drew on a mix of Hollywood style and preppy insouciance, combined with a strong sports emphasis and some Old West touches. An inveterate role-player, he put himself in his own advertisements, in which he acted various parts such as the sports legend, the cowboy, 'Cary Grant', and so on.[92]

The advertising for Ralph Lauren and Calvin Klein took many different forms, as a variety of images were deployed to seduce the public into accepting the atmospheres that they wanted to create around their products. Despite the differences between them, their fundamental similarity of approach was demonstrated by the fact that they used the same photographer, Bruce Weber, to produce some of their best-known advertising campaigns. Weber was a master of the mythic photograph. His black-and-white images always featured clean-cut men and had a distinctively American feel. For Klein, he created homoerotic images of sculpted masculinity that suggested a raunchy, subversive sexuality, while for Lauren he produced more wistful and heritage-laden pictures that evoked scenarios of endeavour and leisure. He drew inspiration from the American photographers of interwar years and from the movies. Reduced to a formula, what he provided was heroic realism plus Hollywood glamour.[93] His images appeared at once to be classic and contemporary, out of time and in tune. Weber was able to use sex appeal in different ways, so that it was upfront and explicit for Klein and subtly woven into the context for Lauren. Aspirational themes were prominent in both cases and were crucial to the appeal that their advertising built up through a heavy magazine presence.

The designer of dreams with a special purchase on collective motivations and desires emerged as a figure at a crucial moment of transition in the economic, social, and cultural climate. Studio 54 was a vital experience that crystallized sixties' notions of freedom, openness, hope, sex, fun, and drugs. However, it did not connect these to any political project but rather to a commercial venture that encouraged individual expression and pleasure. Its heyday came at a time when Western economies were in the doldrums and older forms of leisure were in decline. The conjuncture produced a conservative backlash that won ground as the final radical impulses born in the late 1960s petered out. Studio 54 itself was raided and, after a system of double-accounting was discovered, Rubell and Schrager received a five-month jail sentence for tax evasion. Before going to prison, they held one last party entitled, in mock reference to the scandalized press coverage the club sometimes attracted, 'The End of Modern-Day Gomorra'. Following a closure and reopening, it steadily declined. While interest in disco music waned, the AIDS epidemic was a watershed. This cast a great shadow over the sexual excess that the club had celebrated and propagated. The philosophy of economic liberalism that won ground at this time complemented the ascendant social conservatism.

The election of Ronald Reagan in 1980 signalled a radical change in many areas of policy. It also heralded the first systematic use in a Western democracy of myths and images in the service of political power. Having a former Hollywood actor as president sanctioned the role of illusion and imagination in politics and culture. The particular combination of themes that was bound up with Reaganism was not taken up across the Western world, but the great power of the American economy and the international appeal of American music, films, and other cultural products ensured that it was influential well beyond the United States. The style that was associated with the era was not very distinctive. It had something in common with the ferocious eclecticism and exhibitionism of the Second Empire. Money was the cardinal value and its brashness was welcomed rather than disdained. In practical terms this was filtered through the opulence of old-style Hollywood glamour that provided the most recognizable template of the period. Whereas Jacqueline Kennedy had attempted to connect the past to the present through her careful restoration and tasteful entertaining, Nancy Reagan presided over a reckless appropriation of symbols of luxury and aristocracy. The former admired the style of the First Empire; the latter might have felt more affinity for the Second.

The opulence of the Reagan era was simultaneously elitist and populist. It mixed high and low themes, seduction and beauty, the classic as well as outright novelty. Diana Vreeland was one of the key tastemakers. By now a curator at New York's Metropolitan Museum, she chose ahistorical arrangements for a series of exhibitions on the material grandeur of the past. These promoted a deracinated cult of display and served to establish unabashed opulence as the cultural style of the period.[94] For example, the exhibition on 'La Belle Époque' was devoid of historical and contextual references and purely geared to visual pleasure and the celebration of pure style. Vreeland saw the *demi-monde* not as a specific social configuration but as a world of glamour 'full of laughter and fun, marked by lots of noise, lots of romance, and *great* style'.[95] Exhibitions like this were social events that were launched with the support and involvement of the city's elite and promoted as mass events not to be missed. They therefore had a significant impact on popular culture. Vreeland had been a great innovator in the 1960s and she championed the structural role of low culture in modern style. 'Vulgarity is a very important ingredient in life. I'm a great believer in vulgarity—if it's got vitality,' she declared. 'A little bad taste is like a nice splash of paprika. We all need a splash of bad taste—it's hearty, it's healthy, it's physical.'[96]

For the mass public, the maximum expression of glamour at this time was the television series *Dynasty*. Launched in the very week of the Reagan inauguration in January 1981 by the ABC network in response to CBS's success with the saga of a Texan oil family, *Dallas*, which had premiered three years earlier, it featured an oil family from Denver, Colorado. Although *Dallas* fielded a number of minor stars and sex symbols, it could not match the glamour quotient of *Dynasty*, which included in its cast a former matinee idol, John Forsythe as the patriarch Blake Carrington, and the film and television actress Linda Evans as his second wife Krystle. The latter show was also more woman-centred and glitzy. No one could say of *Dynasty* that its wealthy protagonists did not look rich or live opulently.[97] This was because its producer Aaron Spelling, who was also responsible for such hits of the period as *Charlie's Angels* and *Love Boat*, aimed to create a fantasy world of the rich and famous. The show entered its heyday when Joan Collins joined the cast in the role of Alexis, the businesswoman first wife of Blake, mother of his oldest children and rival of Krystle. A dark beauty who had been taught charm, posture, and elegance by the British Rank studio,[98] Collins had been groomed as England's answer to Ava Gardner in the 1950s. She knew the job of a star backwards and had no qualms about playing up to her role. The show's costume designer favoured power dressing and fitted her with Joan Crawford big shoulders that out did even those that were in vogue at the time. Scarcely an episode passed without the actress donning some hyperbolic retro-styled outfit that underlined her status as a femme fatale. However, Linda Evans's ostentatious evening gowns, which functioned as a badge of her husband's competitive success in business, were also symbolic. They were compared to outfits created for Nancy Reagan by New York designers like Bill Blass and Oscar de la Renta.[99] *Dynasty* has been described as an hour-long commercial for clothes in which the dominant style was 'a kind of out-of-date glamour with ornate clothing in bold colours and glitter'.[100]

The show captured the spirit of the times. Former President Gerald Ford and his wife Betty guested as themselves in scenes of lavish Carrington parties, as did former Secretary of State Henry Kissinger. Department stores offered *Dynasty* fashions, a fragrance, accessories, and lingerie, inviting consumers to 'share the luxury' and 'share the magic' of the show's wealthy clan by buying goods stamped with their imprint.[101] A popular show that complemented the fictions of the Carrington family was *Lifestyles of the Rich and*

Famous, which offered a voyeur's glimpse of the lives of the happy few. In such shows, the rich were humanized and shown to have personal and family problems like everybody else. Wealth was turned into spectacle and infused with entertainment values. Material objects, stylish living, and exotic travel were depicted not as privileges but as glamorous attributes which could enhance the life of anyone. This message contributed to the huge popularity of such shows across the world. The glamour of Collins/Alexis was powerful enough to make the return trip across the Atlantic. 'In so far as the public's appetite for glamour is satisfied today,' the British historian of the aristocracy David Cannadine affirmed, 'it is more likely to be by Joan Collins than the Duke of Westminster.'[102] The international rich and media stars had, he appeared to be saying, finally laid the ghost of the old aristocracy to rest.

In contrast to previous periods of major economic growth, there was no consolidated elite of taste and style to guide or contrast with newly emergent wealth in its customs and consumption. As at the time of the Empress Eugénie, a key role fell to fashion designers, as well as interior designers, architects, and other masters of style. Unlike the couturier Charles Frederick Worth, however, the new designers were not confined to the backstage. They formed a world with their clients and lived a superbly luxurious way of life, owning gargantuan apartments, entertaining regally, and travelling by private jet or yacht. They collected classic cars, old masters, and eighteenth-century furniture. They manufactured not just clothing but the contexts in which clothes were to be worn. Designers emerged as masters of style who showed people how to enjoy the finer things in life. 'Collectively, they [constituted] a society of material luxury' that was keen on going to the right places, seeing and being seen with the right people.[103] This was possible because designers became huge economic players in the 1980s. Ralph Lauren's personal fortune was estimated at $300 million in 1986.[104] He bought a Jamaican villa that had once been the home of William and Babe Paley, he owned a Colorado ranch, and a stone manor near Bedford, New York that he regarded as his 'family seat', and he collected vintage cars.[105] A little like Walter Scott at Abbotsford, he created a personal world in which he could live out dreams that he had grown rich on selling to a wide audience. In 1986, he opened his flagship Rheinlander store on Madison Avenue that was 'his glittering dream made concrete'.[106] It was a hymn to a charmed WASP lifestyle that Lauren himself had glamorized and made accessible even to ethnic minorities.[107] Sensing a shift of climate, even Klein once more reinvented himself. He married a former Ralph Lauren employee, Kelly Rector, in September 1986 in the Campidoglio, Rome. Showing that he was fascinated by the high life after all,[108] the couple moved to the Hamptons, on the south fork of Long Island, 100 miles from Manhattan, where they socialized with the wealthy bankers and stockbrokers that the economic boom of the mid-1980s spawned.

The lifestyles of the fashion designers were not private; rather they were endlessly publicized and exhibited. At the turn of the twentieth century, Thorstein Veblen had written that the new rich needed to advertise their wealth in such a way that even a running man could read its signature.[109] It seemed that little had changed, except that the motivation was no longer just vanity. The Americans and some continental Europeans understood that the way to sell basic items like casual shirts and lipstick was to connect them to a lifestyle so fabulous and alluring that everyone would want to buy into it.[110] The overt exhibition of lifestyle for commercial purposes had been used many times in the past but not on quite such a routine basis. Now it was favoured by the hegemony within the media system of television, which tended to normalize the thrusting of the private realm into the public arena.[111] The press slowly became beholden to the designer and adopted a sycophantic tone like the press that had covered Hollywood in the 1930s and 1940s. All the top designers had well-oiled publicity machines, vast advertising budgets, and were constantly in touch with fashion and women's magazine editors.[112] But the press was complicit. At a time when few Hollywood actors wanted to be glamorous, new heroes of consumption were needed. 'We were the ones to recognize designers as designers and "stars". We had started covering designers' every move—where they lived, what they ate, how they dressed, who they saw. Humanizing them was not difficult, because for the most part they are such lively subjects,' declared John Fairchild Jr., the editor of *Women's Wear Daily*.[113] Fashion designers acquired social power in a context in which a significant diversification of the sources of celebrity was occurring. 'The fashion for a schematic individuality that begins and ends with the image of one's material circumstances is the domestic aspect of what becomes on the grander and glossier public plane the cult of "celebrity",' Kennedy Fraser observed.[114]

Italian fashion was a significant new player in this conjuncture and its leading names quickly acquired mass recognition. The resurgence of a national industry that had once been a poor sister to Paris, known only for casual wear and accessories, owed much to the keen perception of the enormous potential of ready-to-wear. In contrast to Paris, where the couture tradition made innovation controversial, Italian fashion was dominated by textile industries that were powerful and ambitious. Also, it had acquired experience, during the period of American film-making in Italy in the 1950s, of contributing to American glamour. It had the advantage of having developed its own identity as a variant of this.[115] One of the most significant Italian designers had in fact been in business since the later period of Hollywood on the Tiber. Although he was frequently mentioned together with newly celebrated Italian colleagues, Valentino was not primarily a creator of ready-to-wear but a couturier, indeed the only prominent French-trained Italian couturier. He had founded his own fashion house in Rome in 1962 and had dressed many important international clients including Audrey Hepburn, Princess Grace, and Jacqueline Kennedy. For the foreign market, he represented the verve and style of the years of the *dolce vita*. His main interest was in designing ravishing gowns for the women of the international jet set.[116] Beauty for its own sake was Valentino's apparent motto and his best-known creations were evening gowns in his signature red, or scenic dresses for the rites of passage of the rich. However, thanks to the acumen of his business partner and partner in life, Giancarlo Giammetti, he branched out into the middle market, where the prestige of well-known couture clients brought kudos to the brand. Like Giorgio Armani and Gianni Versace, Valentino headed a fashion empire with ready-to-wear branches and diffusion lines, including jeans, as well as licensing deals. With the profits, he fashioned a fabulously luxurious lifestyle, surpassing all rivals in projecting himself as the epitome of all things luxurious, tasteful, and elegant. Not content with having a workplace situated in a Renaissance palazzo near the Spanish Steps in Rome, he acquired a villa on the historic Appian Way, a Fifth Avenue apartment in New York, a chateau near Paris, a London house, and residences on Capri and at Gstaad. He also owned a 152-foot yacht and maintained a personal staff of fifty, including a chauffeur and a butler. By comparison, other Roman couturiers, like the Fontana sisters, who had also catered to American visitors since the 1950s, lived like seamstresses.

A personal friend of queens, aristocrats, the wives of financiers, and film stars, Valentino created eye-catching garments that combined old glamour with taste and distinction. As always, the Americans were his best clients and most of them were concentrated in New York. Historically, the city's distinctive glamour, its sense of style, came from its high society. However, New York personalities of the 1980s were not generally well-born but rich trend-followers. Many socialites hired PR firms to package their image. Opulent couples like Ivana and Donald Trump, the larger-than-life real estate developer and entertainment magnate who put his own surname on every prestige property he built, lived and breathed brash big-money values. They belonged to what *Women's Wear Daily* editor John Fairchild Jr. cheekily dubbed 'Nouvelle Society', a category that was entirely based on the calculated ostentation of money and success. Many women in this category were quite happy with the local couturiers that Nancy Reagan patronized, Blass and della Renta. Others, usually those whose wealth was a little less recently acquired, were more European-oriented. But this does not mean that they were less exhibitionist. The leading hostess of the period Nan Kempner, who had been a socialite since the 1950s and was reputed to have the largest couture collection in New York, was anything but a wallflower. She had been a Studio 54 regular and was perennially at the centre of the fastest and richest social set. Stick-thin and chronically gregarious ('I feel terrible when I am alone,' she declared),[117] she adored the spotlight and was scarcely out of the public eye (among her bons mots: 'They say the camera loves me; the truth is I love the camera' and 'My theory is, whatever it is, if it's in print, it's gotta be good for you').[118]

The relation between contemporary New York high society and the media was complex. At one time, the social world would have found a mirror in Condé Nast's *Vogue*. However, the American edition of the magazine had broadened its appeal and now addressed the middle market. Its conventional role in representing the North-Eastern American elite to itself was taken over in part by *Women's Wear Daily* (*WWD*), a trade publication founded in 1890 that had evolved into a social gazette. The editor John Fairchild was as interested in personalities and gossip as he was in the facts and figures of the garment industry.[119] The periodical created a cast of fashionable New York women and recorded the social ostentation of the city. It determined who was in and who was out. It offered advice on where to go and who to talk about. The new rich had, Fairchild found, an insatiable desire for publicity. As he saw it, modern high society was not stable but subject to a constant game of snakes and ladders. With the multiplication of fortunes in the 1980s, ladders were plentiful and the jostling for position sharp. 'What the social world of New York really comes down to is that anyone—and I mean anyone—can become an overnight attraction of *W* or the gossip columns if he or she has enough money and stamina,' he declared.[120] The publication pioneered a type of social coverage that both provided a platform for the new rich and subjected them to ridicule; if they were too visible or too brash, then they would find themselves lampooned in *WWD*, or worse, subjected to a publicity blackout.

Valentino found many of his best clients in this milieu. He offered them the reassurance of prestige fused with the glamour of spectacle. He shared with them a common idea of glamour that was not complex or refined but which was rooted in popular culture and which drew from the cinema of the past. He happily acknowledged his debt to cinema, admitting that he had been obsessed with glamour from the time he was a teenager: 'I was a big dreamer, always a big dreamer. Vivien Leigh, Hedy Lamarr, Lana Turner, and Katherine Hepburn—I am a designer today because I would dream of those ladies in fox coats and lamé, coming down those grand staircases they had in the movies.'[121] 'When I was a boy, I used to steal film magazines from my sister,' he admitted; 'I dreamed of Lana Turner, Rita Hayworth, Elizabeth Taylor. . . . Even at that time, I was attracted by the shiny world of celluloid, I gorged on films.'[122] Yet, despite this, glamour for Valentino was never vulgar for it was filtered through Italian art cinema. 'It was the director Luchino Visconti who transmitted to me this limitless love for elegance that for me has the taste of an enchanting romanticism,' he claimed.[123]

Foreigners were often surprised by the Roman showiness of Valentino. Although his public declarations appeared to infuse glamour with taste in contrast to the cheerful populism of Vreeland and others, much about his lifestyle and work struck observers as flash and exhibitionist.[124] When a journalist asked him about the ostentation of his lifestyle, he responded tetchily, correcting the man's premiss by affirming, 'It's not opulence...it's elegant'.[125] The letter V is 'a worldwide symbol of luxury and not-so-discreet glamour,' remarked fashion journalist Georgina Howell.[126] For British Condé Nast editor Nicholas Coleridge, 'Some of the colours of his couture—the rich reds and blues—have a high Renaissance hue to them, but they are also the colours of Disneyland.'[127] The socialite Lily Safra recalled once being invited to dinner at the designer's villa on the Appian Way. 'After passing through tall, electronically controlled gates at the front entrance, we moved into Valentino's garden, something straight out of *Ben Hur*, with the grass dazzling emerald green and every plant bathed in light. There was a pool grand enough for an Esther Williams production number, and the palazzo, its already perfect lines enhanced by Italian Nouvelle Society decorator Mongiardino, would have made a Caesar smile. Yet across the road from Valentino's palazzo is a hamburger stand!'[128] Of this, Andy Warhol, who died in 1987, would certainly have approved.

Other Italian designers, including Giorgio Armani and Gianni Versace, were no less familiar with the heritage of old Hollywood than the Americans. They made much of the inspiration they drew from it. The champion of subdued hues, Armani won much success in the United States with his unstructured garments and flair for blurring the divide between casual and formal wear. In 1982, *Time* granted him the cover, which acclaimed 'Giorgio's Gorgeous Style'.[129] In interview after interview, Armani claimed that he drew inspiration from the costumes of American cinema and this was reflected in period-style advertisements for his label that evoked the Hollywood glamour of the 1930s.[130] The complex nature of modern mass society meant that all designers had to keep abreast of trends in popular culture, even if they were not interested in being at the cutting edge. The domination of a shared media-based culture meant that keeping in touch was paramount and all of them had staffs and muses to assist them with this.

For designers like these, Hollywood glamour was a very useful repertoire of proven persuasive efficacy that also had the advantage of being an international lingua franca.

Designers needed different, more contemporary appeals to communicate effectively with younger consumers. The mystique of Marlene Dietrich or the sensual allure of Rita Hayworth so beloved of middle-aged male designers were suggestive but remote and unrealistic. Modern glamour relied on fast-moving, dynamic lifestyles, on beautiful bodies, and on objects and environments that were not imbued with class connotations but rather with pleasure and escapism. These values were strongly present in some television series, the production quality of which improved significantly in the 1980s, rendering them more seductive and glamorous than ever before. For five years from 1984, NBC broadcast *Miami Vice*, a new-style police show about two undercover cops working in the South Florida city. Starring Don Johnson and Philip Michael Thomas, the show presented complex plots of corruption, drug-trafficking, and prostitution in the exotic, subtropical setting of Miami. As a cop show, it differed in many ways from the standard series (such as *Kojak*, *Cannon*, and so on) that featured eccentric personalities and neat plots. Its most striking innovations were in the field of visual imagery and style. Directed by Michael Mann, the show blended music, cinematography, fashion, and high-production values in a way that gave it a fast, upbeat, and materially opulent feel. The good-looking male protagonists demonstrated an acute sense of fashion, dressing informally in Italian labels and branded sunglasses. The producers made every effort to ensure that the show reflected the latest European styles with the intention of making it a model for menswear.[131] Macy's even opened a *Miami Vice* section in the young men's department of the store. Shows like this were vital in showing how fashion labels functioned as tools for glamorizing the self and how glamour could blend with everyday life both as entertainment and as imaginative projection. Their protagonists were eager consumers like their spectators, men who revelled in the way aspects of luxury lifted them out of the humdrum and the mundane.

Changes in the communications system in the 1980s, including the advent of the video cassette and the birth of the music video, radically changed the way people consumed media products and the impact they had on their lives. Sampling from high and low culture, and from past and present, became commonplace as choice widened. Designers including Versace and the Frenchmen Jean-Paul Gaultier and Thierry Mugler developed vibrant personal elaborations of glamorous themes that matched the demand for ever new eye-catching and dream-inducing visual experiences. They took advantage of the way the contemporary media tended to disassociate high social status from social prominence and wealth and instead bind it up with fame and with the fashion world itself. The master in this respect was Karl Lagerfeld, who single-handedly turned the Chanel label into a vibrant contemporary brand while also producing collections under his own name. He had always worked in ready-to-wear and was therefore a key player in its expansion. Constant renewal was his credo and 'vampirizing' trends and the ideas of young collaborators his method.[132]

Glamour became in the 1970s a paradigm of distinction that was more widely available than ever before. Rock performers and innovators like Warhol showed that dressing up and constructing a fabulous self with elements of media heritage, cosmetics, and coloured costumes was available to all, regardless of whether they lived in New York or Wolverhampton. Discotheques offered a stage for everyone to escape from everyday humdrum and present their glamorous persona at least once a week. The huge emphasis on physical beauty and sex appeal in the formula of contemporary glamour was testimony to this. Glamour has always had an appeal to the marginal and the oppressed, who have seen in its techniques of self-improvement and self-invention a way out of their situation, or a fuel to dreams of escape. At the same time, it has also been a fabulous platform for the new rich. It was the fashion designers who brilliantly bridged the gap between these two social strata and wove magical spells of seduction and self-transformation that enchanted the world.

CHAPTER 11

CONTEMPORARY GLAMOUR

When Lady Diana Spencer became engaged to Prince Charles in February 1981, she was a young woman from an aristocratic family whose modest education and limited experience of life were reflected in her demure appearance. A pretty and naïve 19-year-old, she seemed the archetypal English Rose. Thrust unknowingly into the media spotlight, she quickly became the nation's darling. Her wedding to Prince Charles in St Paul's Cathedral in July 1981 was given blanket press coverage and was watched by an estimated worldwide television audience of one billion people. The marriage was presented as a fairy-tale union of an eligible prince and a beautiful commoner, the aristocratic standing and royal ancestors of Diana's family receiving less emphasis than her more commonplace status as a young working woman. A decade later, Diana's public image was quite different. Her marriage to Charles bore two sons, but by the late 1980s it was on the rocks. The Prince and Princess of Wales formally separated in December 1992 and were divorced in 1996. Throughout this period, the press scrutinized every aspect of their body language and public appearances, separately and together, for indications of the state of their relationship. Both the prince and Diana briefed the press through friends and blamed each other for the breakdown of the marriage. Public sympathy was firmly with Diana and the affection for her was amply demonstrated in the emotional public reaction to her death following a car accident in Paris in August 1997. As she emerged from the shadow of her husband, Diana invested ever more energy in charitable works. Having herself suffered from the acrimonious divorce of her parents, and living the breakdown of her own marriage, she was in a position to offer comfort to others. Subsequently, she helped publicize the international campaign against landmines and to overcome discrimination against AIDS sufferers. Like a secular Mother Teresa of Calcutta, with whom she established a connection, she became identified with selfless devotion to the causes of the ill and suffering.

Diana was not originally associated with glamour. Mainly, she was presented within the framework of royalty. In the course of the twentieth century, the British royal family had had a complex relationship with glamour. It had flirted with the press, the movies, and publicity, but fundamentally it remained a thing apart, an institution that was theatrical, certainly, but respectable and not a little stodgy. Its capacity to enchant was founded on history and tradition, and was more ceremonial than personal. Thus Diana's spectacular wedding endowed her with a conventional aura, that of the fairy-tale princess. With its puffed sleeves, nipped waist, embroidered pearls and sequins, and 25-foot taffeta train, the bride's creamy silk dress contributed to the fantasy. The pomp of the wedding impressed not only the thousands who lined the streets leading to St Paul's, but the millions who watched the ceremony on television or read about it in the press. Over time, Diana's image evolved as she became more womanly and the press found that use of her image never failed to boost sales beyond measure. Designers competed to dress her and magazines ran features on her wardrobe, knowing that women regarded her as an inspiration. In subsequent years, as she acquired an independent profile and began to detach herself from the royal family, her conventional aura was displaced by glamour. She became a figure of beauty and style whose photogenic qualities turned her into the most photographed person of the age. Speculation about her love life in the final stages of her marriage and in the period prior to her death intensified interest in her to the point that almost her every move was tracked by paparazzi.[1]

Diana's beauty was central to the transition she made from demure and virginal princess to woman of glamour. Her girlish good looks at the time of her courtship and engagement drew some favourable comment but no one in those early days saw her as a great beauty. Rather, Diana grew into her body, which she turned by sheer dint of effort into one of her main tools of communication. A tall and well-proportioned woman, her appearance became splendid; she was toned, tanned, slim, blonde, and radiant and at no time more so than in the five years between her separation and her death. 'Providence gave her beauty, but it was she who contrived to project it until it radiated to every quarter of the globe,' noted the historian Paul Johnson in the days after her death.[2] The most important thing about her in this regard was that she was superbly photogenic. 'This was not merely beauty,' commented another senior male observer; 'this was beauty that lept through the lenses. She seemed chemically bonded to film and video.'[3]

The most remarkable series of photographic portraits appeared too late to shape responses to her, although they may have had some small influence on the reaction to her death. In 1997 *Vanity Fair* published in its July issue a series of pictures under the title 'Princess Di's New Look by Mario Testino'. The Peruvian photographer's work ensured that she exited the world at the height of her splendour. More than any of his colleagues, Testino had a gift for giving his subjects an electric charge of fabulousness. They positively glowed and glistened and always looked like euphoric, yet not unnatural, versions of themselves. In Testino's lens, Diana looked relaxed, rich (her rumoured £80,000 per annum grooming budget was evident in her beautiful skin, cropped and highlighted hair, and movie-star smile), and totally confident. The spectator could not but be mesmerized by her relaxed air and sleek surface.

It took Diana some time to understand how she could use fashion to establish a public identity and communicate messages but, once she did, she harnessed its power to maximum effect. Her glamour was inextricably bound up with her dazzling use of fashion. In 1994 one newspaper estimated that her wardrobe had a value of around one million pounds.[4] In fact, the charity auction of seventy-nine of her dresses in New York in June 1997 (for which the

Testino photographs were a promotional pitch) raised a total of $3.25 million. As the Prince of Wales's wife, her choice of designers was limited to the British or British-based, with exceptions being made only on royal visits for designers from the host countries. The London designers Catherine Walker and Bruce Oldfield were perhaps the first to see her glamour potential. They helped her forge a fashion identity that was varied but generally discreetly eye-catching during the day and fabulous for evening occasions. Diana dressed at first to please—to please above all her distracted husband by showing she could win the adoration of the gallery—but then increasingly for effect.[5] Demure dresses gave way to striking red and black gowns, chic pastel combinations, and toned-down looks for everyday charity work. By the mid-1990s, she had turned into a toned, tanned, and designer-clad blonde vision of incomparable allure. She wore international labels and showed a particular predilection for the creations of Gianni Versace, the Italian designer who was hailed after his murder in Miami Beach in July 1997 as the 'king of glitz'. Versace showered her with suits and dresses and she became a regular customer at the label's Bond Street store. She did not wear his starlet numbers but rather opted for the simple, sexy outfits that suited her fashion persona. One of the last memorable pictures of Diana is of her comforting a disconsolate Elton John at Versace's funeral in the Duomo in Milan.

Diana's glamour also derived from the spectacle of her personal trans-formation. At one level, this was composed of the narrative of her life, which dramatically shifted genre from fairy tale to soap opera. Diana's personal story and her great gift for empathy created a favourable predisposition towards her. But no less important were her obvious breaks with royal custom and determination to establish an original public presence in her own right. Her popularity destabilized the conventional relationship be-tween monarchy and the mass media. From being the icing sugar doll on the cake of monarchy, she turned into the sexy covergirl who found her peers in the worlds of fashion and celebrity. This transformation occurred quite literally before the eyes of everyone, as her body took on the glossy, honed appearance of the professional publicity-seeker. The more she suffered in private, the more she looked fabulous to those who met or saw pictures of her. The whole process was a visual phenomenon acted out largely as a mime show, without the benefit of words save for the confessional television interview she released to BBC reporter Martin Bashir in 1994.

Initially gauche and inexperienced, Diana learned to shape and manage her own image. At first, she studied her own press coverage and learned what sort of effects she could provoke by a choice of dress or gesture. Later, she enlisted the assistance of fashion advisers and designers, and grooming experts. These people provided her with a support system that was geared to maintaining and enhancing the value of her image. In this way, she created a world around her that maximized her ability to shine. She became the director and leading cast member of her own one-woman stage-show.[6] There was no shortage of people willing to testify to the effect that seeing or meeting her had on them. 'It's funny but when I met her I could swear I could tell she had come into the room even though my back was turned. The first thing that struck me was her glamour,' one charity lunch guest declared in the days after her death; adding, 'she had the most beautiful skin. The other thing was that she seemed genuinely interested.'[7] 'She had glamour in spades and, more than that, she reached out to the people in a way that none of the rest of the family did or could. Even the Queen Mother, who has had star quality (if not physical glamour) all her life, never received the same adulation as Diana,' observed biographer Sarah Bradford.[8] Testimonies like these suggest that Diana's glamour was a personal quality that was related to, but not entirely reducible to, her beauty. The references to her skin and physical being imply a bodily magnetism that amounted to an 'instant radiance' that lit up rooms and generated a rush of excitement.[9] Male observers often described this as sex appeal. In fact, such effects were the result of a predictable structure of relations between subject and audience.

Diana was not the first British royal to be fashionable or to be explicitly described as glamorous, since Edward, Prince of Wales had often been referred to in that way in the 1930s,[10] as had Princess Margaret in the 1960s. But since their time, both mass communications and the social scene had undergone major changes. Above all, entertainment had evolved into a lingua franca. Whereas she had at the outset been the perfect em-bodiment of virginal innocence, by the 1990s Diana had acquired a powerful allure that led her to be compared to stars like Grace Kelly and Marilyn

Monroe. Comparisons between Diana and other figures from the firmament of mass culture served to underline her iconic stature. The testimonies of her collaborators reveal that this was not accidental.[11] Movie stars provided her with a template for capturing public attention. She liked to camp it up like Marilyn Monroe in *Some Like It Hot*, and she carried over some of Marilyn's seductive demeanour into her public persona. Pictures of her imitating Audrey Hepburn in outfits taken from *Breakfast at Tiffany's* were kept on display in her private quarters at Kensington Palace.[12] Diana was an avid consumer of popular television and, it is said, never missed an episode of *Dallas* or *Dynasty*.[13] Joan Collins's strong femme fatale persona in the latter show appealed to her and taught her how to be strong and radiant in the face of personal adversity.

In the final years of her life, Diana became much more a figure of the celebrity realm. She found friends in show business, the fashion world, and among the international rich. Separation and divorce led to her being deprived of the prerogatives of royalty and she turned into a 'Jackie Onassis Diana who lolled sensuously on rich men's yachts',[14] a potential 'Diana Fayed of St Tropez and Knightsbridge'.[15] She was at once a princess, a celebrity, a clothes horse, a supermodel, a pin-up, a diva, a role model, a jet-setter, a super-consumer, and a movie star. Like all people for whom publicity is oxygen, she was as much a symbol and a signifier as a person. After the princess's death, these comparisons abounded. She became the rock'n'roll princess, the latter-day Eva Peron, the saintly supermodel who died at the same age as Monroe.

Diana's significance was by no means limited to glamour.[16] But it is around the theme of glamour that a significant number of the reflections on her life and meaning revolved. In her later years, she was either part of, or acted as a vehicle for, a series of phenomena that were concerned with image and appearance and with the effect of these on individuals, institutions, commercial practices, and communication. In the 1990s glamour became a social and cultural lubricant on an unprecedented scale. As a readily comprehensible visual repertoire that aroused responses of desire, envy, and emulation, it found more applications than ever before in a world in which people increasingly defined themselves by what they consumed. Its creation depended on a highly organized structure. Glossy images, sleek surfaces, and groomed exteriors were cultivated by swathes of professionals, including fashion producers, beauty consultants, hairdressers, stylists, photographers, and publicists, who were ready to turn every personality into a glistening object of desire, a walking cover shot.

The ubiquity of images of glamour was related to two things: the multiplication of media and the increasing interaction between them, and the huge development of fashion and luxury industries which these new media opportunities made possible. Synergies between cinema and television, popular music and television, the press and television combined to enhance the role of celebrity and image. Upbeat, consumer-oriented television shows featured good-looking, well-groomed people and ever more numerous magazines produced glossy, uncritical editorial content. When the Spanish magazine *!Hola!*, which had published in Spain since 1944 and also had a wide circulation in Latin America, launched a British edition in 1988 and named it *Hello*, the event was greeted with amusement. Fawning pictorial features on celebrities lavishly paid to open their luxurious pads to the prying eyes of the photographers or to have their wedding snaps taken exclusively by them did not seem like a recipe for success. In fact *Hello* was the precursor of a wave of what the journalist Tina Brown calls 'fabloids', that is magazines that 'combine the tabloid hunger for sensation with the requirement to always look fabulous'.[17] These extended the personality formula developed in the 1970s by weeklies like the American magazine *People* and were soon contaminating the mainstream press with their style of presentation. Magazines of this type worked on the assumption that famous people could be bought and that their acquisition would in turn sell magazines. They quickly bloomed and multiplied, even spawning raunchy and ironical competitors that offered a less enchanted view of celebrity lives.

The second development was the transformation of the consumer economy. In the 1970s, as we saw in Chapter 10, fashion designers emerged as lifestyle mediators and architects of glamour. In the course of the following two decades, they consolidated this position. They pursued a strategy of 'capture' towards public events and personalities in a concerted effort to gain publicity and establish their labels as indicators of status, style, and sex appeal. In this they were joined by producers of luxury goods of every type. On account of a trend towards corporate ownership of both fashion houses and producers of luxury goods, there was a general trend towards market expansion and the democratization of luxury. This term had first been used by department stores in the nineteenth century as industrialization made possible the production at low prices of goods that had once been reserved for the well-off. In the late twentieth century, consumers were, by contrast, given the impression that mass-produced goods were rare and desirable. Leather goods, jewellery, watches, and fashion were wrapped with the mystique of style and luxury and sold as superior indicators of taste and status. Companies that previously had been solely concerned with supplying elite customers sought to maximize profits by reaching the middle market.

Both these developments were facilitated and encouraged by a demand to accede to the higher realms of consumption on the part of middle-class and some working-class people in Western countries, as well as in the expanding economies of the far East and Asia. The far-reaching economic changes of the Reagan and Thatcher era saw a rise of the service sector and a historic decline of conventional primary activities like fishing and mining as well as manufacturing. Tax cuts fuelled consumer spending and produced a new demand for status symbols. Also important were cultural changes relating to the shift that occurred in the West towards secondary goals and aspirations once the satisfaction of primary needs of food, shelter, and clothing had been achieved. In addition, the loosening of social ties and of the institutions of civil society, as well as connections to place, through economic change, mobility, the diversification of family life, and the multiplication of the mass media broke old class and regional-specific cultural boundaries.[18] Social mobility in this context ceased to be a matter of moving between established classes and more a matter of moving away from them. An important consequence of this was an increased focus on consumption not only as a measure of success but as a vehicle of personal expression and of emotional satisfaction.[19] This produced pressure for the 'democratization of formerly exclusive types of consumption and styles of living'.[20] There was an established curiosity for wealthy or privileged lifestyles that dated back at least to the eighteenth century and which, more recently, had been institutionalized in the American TV show *Lifestyles of the Rich and Famous*, that broadcast from 1984 until 1995, and the British *Through the Keyhole*. Wealth, especially of the new variety, engendered not resentment but envy and admiration because it was given an appealing and accessible face by celebrities who seemed just like everyone else except that they were more successful.

Diana was a crucial factor in the development of a new buzz in a social scene that was stylish, fashionable, and money-oriented. Far more than any pop stars, models, or dashing entrepreneurs, it has been claimed, she single-handedly made Britain glamorous.[21] Like Jacqueline Kennedy in the 1960s, she did much to raise public interest in fashion. She was no mere local personality but something akin to a worldwide brand. Tina Brown, who was editor of the *Tatler* between 1979 and 1983, noted that a new synergy came into place between commerce, society, and philanthropy.[22] Companies that were seeking to take advantage of the booming economy of the mid-1980s were desperate to attract some of the stardust that was associated with Diana's glamorous presence. As the Princess of Wales, she could not get involved in anything nakedly commercial, but if a charitable veneer was added to a launch or a trade show, then she could attend and bring much-desired media attention. Her appeal was such that car and fragrance companies, jewellers, and luxury goods labels all rushed to sponsor events at which advertising would neatly combine with support for a worthy cause. *Tatler* itself hugely increased its circulation as the formerly stuffy society magazine experienced its own synergy with commerce and celebrity.[23] By the same token, virtually every cultural and sporting event, from pop concerts and football matches to polo tournaments, was sustained by sponsors who pumped in money and injected razzamatazz. Scarcely a single appointment in the once exclusive English social season, including Ascot, Henley Royal Regatta, Wimbledon, and Cowes week, was not branded and packaged by a producer of champagne, a chain of luxury hotels, or a travel company. The social pictures that once used to record the balls and dinners of high society, providing its members with a warm glow of superiority, were replaced by party pictures recording the presence of miscellaneous celebrity invitees and decorative aristos at a bash to mark the opening of a new

355

restaurant, fashion store, or the premiere of a film.[24] Their presence was a guarantee that the event would be covered by news organizations.[25]

The visual language of glamour had not significantly altered for several decades nor had the functions it performed. As in the past, it was flashy, eye-catching, sexy, and sometimes outrageous. Covered with the veil of glamour, people and places took on a special sparkle that dazzled and bewitched those who cast their eyes on it. What changed in the 1980s and 1990s was the *quantity* of glamorous images, the sheer number of people that to different degrees conveyed them and the wide variety of places, media, and media outlets that transmitted them. This meant that a new tension emerged between, on the one hand, a visual repertoire of glamour that was increasingly familiar, standardized, and quotidian, and an ever-wider desire to grasp the magical, exclusive, and exceptional qualities of glamour. Thus a distinct hierarchy emerged in which, on the one hand, certain individuals, categories, and contexts were seen to stand for relatively pure glamour, while others offered partial and temporary glamorous effects geared to given moments. In these circumstances three responses flourished: irony and pastiche; revival of the gestures and visual clichés of the Hollywood glamour of the past; invention and deployment of new vehicles of visual seduction by adapting old codes to contemporary conditions. All these strategies were employed by media, companies, and personalities who had a vested interest in manufacturing mass desire.

In Western Europe and North America, societies which had a high level of media development and media penetration of social relations, glamour's core appeal of magical transformation of the individual through the manufacture of a new self had the widest impact. It formed a collective discourse that did not merely complement social relations formed in primary contexts such as the family or the workplace. Rather it functioned in social settings that had been reorganized by the media and in which conventional ties such as the once strong relationship between physical place and social position had been weakened.[26] Glamour privileged fame, fashion, beauty, and feminine life narratives. These commanded widespread attention, but especially they touched those who found themselves on the margins of society on account of their economic position, ethnicity, or sexual orientation. This explains, to some extent at least, the public fixation with Diana. 'Diana's appeal as a postmodern icon resides solely in her ability to renew and transform herself—and by racing just slightly ahead of our imagination, to hold us in constant thrall,' wrote *Vanity Fair* one month before her death.[27] The princess's 'postmodernity' stemmed precisely from the changes that resulted in her role following the collapse of her 'fairy-tale' marriage and the efforts she made to establish and renew an identity in relation to the public sphere.

Diana's ascendancy occurred at precisely the time that ready-to-wear was being revolutionized and the public was showing signs of enthusiasm for designer labels. The attributes of a glamorous lifestyle were communicated widely by companies which promised that ownership of desirable goods would bring status and transform the consumer's life by making it enviable and exclusive. A key player in the field was Bernard Arnault, the French business-man who acquired Christian Dior in 1984 and went on to construct a major luxury group by creating the Christian Lacroix couture house, buying Céline, and aggressively taking over LVMH (Louis-Vuitton-Moët-Hennessy), which owned Louis Vuitton, Givenchy, and the Moët-Hennessy drink company. He consolidated his leading position by adding the smaller fashion houses of Michael Kors and Marc Jacobs. Other group players included Richemont, the Swiss-based firm that owned Cartier, Van Cleef & Arpels, Dunhill, Mont Blanc, and Chloe, and the Italian Gucci group, which warded off takeover by joining in 1999 with the French PPR (Pinault-Printemps-Redoute) company that also acquired Yves Saint Laurent ready-to-wear and cosmetics. PPR went on to acquire the historic label Balenciaga (originally founded by the Spanish couturier Cristobal Balenciaga in 1937), the Italian leather goods manufacturer Bottega Veneta, and the jeweller Boucheron, as well as launching the new labels of Stella McCartney and Alexander McQueen.[28]

Brand-building was the key strategy of luxury goods companies which first sought to consolidate their basic identity and then aimed to diffuse an image by advertising, sponsorship, and lifestyle endorsements.[29] All the luxury groups and many companies operating in the sector pursued a similar strategy. Old-established luxury companies had often existed for a century or more and had acquired over time reputations for excellence in craftsmanship and quality.

They advertised little or not at all and catered to a narrow clientele of wealthy people. More recently founded houses, like Dior and Givenchy, had similar reputations but had developed strategies to reach the middle market through licensed fragrances and other products. They seduced middle-class customers with atmospheres of refinement deriving from the cachet of couture. In the course of the 1980s, the enormous expansion of ready-to-wear clothing led established couture houses to follow the example of newcomers like Ralph Lauren and Giorgio Armani by producing diffusion lines and by expanding product ranges. The formation of conglomerates consolidated and rationalized this process along predictable business lines and heralded the end of old niche market practices.[30] Each individual company stressed its culture and heritage, its traditions and custom of excellence. It claimed its goods were manufactured to the highest standards of quality and it established a semblance of rarity by charging premium prices even for basic goods like jeans and T-shirts. Low quality licences were eliminated to preserve the image of exclusivity. Young designers were appointed to bring verve and controversy to once stuffy, if fine, products and to attract attention. Massive advertising campaigns were launched to arouse public awareness, that were consolidated through endorsements of events and associations with famous men and women. Finally, sales environments were carefully organized on a pyramid pattern. Flagship stores on key roads in major capitals were sumptuous, prestige outlets that were opened with much fanfare and publicity. Diffusion products were sold through branded second-level stores or prestigious department stores in large cities. Excess product was sold off through special outlet complexes.

One of the most striking developments was the expansion of luxury shopping in non-traditional locations. Companies backed up their desire to capture the global middle market by creating new sales outlets that lacked the intimidating atmosphere of the flagship stores or leading department stores. Carefully avoiding opening stores in unglamorous cities or shopping malls, they established outposts in second-tier large cities and high-profile tourist locations like Las Vegas and Miami Beach, as well as European airports. Las Vegas became a leading luxury resort and one of the principal shopping destinations in the United States. The one-time 'sin city' was a fabulous place of invention that lavished glitz and glamour on its visitors. The hotels and casinos on the famous strip were designed in the most eclectic and fantastic manner imaginable and they were continually being knocked down and rebuilt. From 1982, when the Mirage hotel opened, a shift occurred away from the emphasis on gambling towards entertainment and hospitality.[31] Fantasy and escape were always present—the Mirage featured a fake volcano while dolphins swam in a pool—but it was the total experience that counted. The gambler's paradise was the perfect location for designer brand stores because the entire city was founded on the dream of wealth and the possibility for self-transformation. Moreover, most of the 35 million people who visited each year only stayed a few days and, during that time, they were keen to pursue pleasure and move themselves temporarily upscale. Flashy and glitzy goods caught their eye in stores that were easy to enter and browse in and whose staff, unlike the notoriously ofhand salespeople in stores in capital cities, were relaxed and welcoming.[32]

Glamour was the motor of sales and it was carefully created and perpetuated by producers who knew that popular perceptions of a brand were what counted most. More important than the sheer quality of a garment or accessory in such a context was the recognition factor supplied by visible labels and logos, exterior signifiers of opulence in the form of gold or brillante touches, and the narrative forged by advertising and celebrity links. Unless genuine artisan work was involved, for example in the haute couture of Chanel or Saint Laurent or the luggage of Hermès, manufacturing methods were concealed to facilitate the creation of a neo-artisan mystique. It was not the products that were emphasised so much as what they *represented* in terms of cachet, status, fashionableness, novelty, and celebrity.[33]

While the brands in the Arnault stable sought to shake off staid images and win popular recognition by embracing sex appeal and celebrity, no designer more than Versace made these values his own. Versace was seen as the master of contemporary glamour. In contrast to most of his Italian contemporaries, who embraced bourgeois notions of taste and measure, he provided spectacle, luxury, colour, and sex appeal. He understood that to have an impact on the mass imagination, luxury could not be understated. A southerner from the city of Reggio Calabria, Versace launched his own label in Milan in 1978 and quickly opened a series of boutiques in prestigious locations around the world.[34] By the mid-1990s, these sumptuous emporia bore witness to the designer's trademark lavish, luxurious, and overtly sexual style. The explosion of colour, the sharply revealing cuts, and luxurious fabrics that characterized the Versace range were geared to those who wanted to be noticed, to assert their wealth and sexuality, to feel they were at the cutting edge of a rock'n'roll lifestyle. Versace offered customers the promise of standing-out, being noticed, and, almost, of wearing a price tag. His designs shouted wealth and status through a megaphone. This ostentation was enhanced by lavish advertising that ensured label recognition and public identification of the style. It was further charged by an insistent link with movie and rock stars in a reciprocal effect that added drama and value. His idea of glamour worked on the long-established combination of wealth and sex. Many noticed the sex first. Indeed he was often accused of dressing women like whores. In particular, his use of lurex and rubber, sometimes together with studs, safety pins, and rhinestones, recalled fetish wear. Versace, it was said, 'sold sex and glamour and he sold it with the gusto of the most garrulous second-hand car dealer'.[35] This did not undermine the appeal of the label. 'A strappy Versace evening dress which curves around the body before flaring out into a flirtatious kick, slashed to the thigh and with the deepest neckline in the business, is quite the most sensual garment any woman can hope to wear,' commented one woman journalist.[36] The designer always claimed that his supersexy clothes were inspired by the exaggerated finery of the prostitutes that came into his mother's dressmaker's shop in Reggio Calabria. He disliked modesty and promoted an 'if-you've-got-it-flaunt-it' outlook that cultivated a show-off attitude in his customers. Wealth took the form of eye-watering prices but also a photogenic lifestyle that was unashamedly materialistic.

Versace became a household name in Britain in 1994 when Hugh Grant's then little-known girlfriend Elizabeth Hurley wore one of his creations to the London premiere of the British comedy *Four Weddings and a Funeral*. The extraordinarily low-cut and revealing black gown was split down the side and held together with safety pins featuring the designer's Medusa's head logo. Front-page pictures in the tabloid and broadsheet press massively increased the curvaceous Hurley's profile and made Versace into a byword for show-stopping sexy clothes.[37] In the wake of this event, every publicity-hungry starlet in Britain aimed to grab the front page by turning up for a premiere or launch in a garment that showed off her figure to effect. Many of these were created by the London designer Julien Macdonald, who specialized in ultra-revealing evening wear.

Versace did not rely solely on show-business glitz. He liked to construct noble pedigrees and establish cultural kudos for his brand of glamour. In keeping with his eclecticism, themes, motifs, objects, and styles drawn from a wide variety of sources including ancient Greece and Rome, Byzantium, the Italian Renaissance, and the Baroque period marked Versace's home furnish-ings, fragrances, stores, advertising, and numerous coffee-table books. His books, including *Men Without Ties* and *Rock & Royalty*, were sumptuous productions. In his search for recognition, Versace sponsored exhibitions of his work in such august institutions as the Metropolitan Museum of Art in New York and the Victoria and Albert Museum in London. Like his rival Giorgio Armani, who also opened his archive for high profile exhibitions, he believed that such forays into the cultural sphere lifted his creations on to the plane of art and guaranteed them a place in posterity. However, it was the catwalk that was the scene of Versace's greatest innovations. Collections had once been presented in-house by fashion companies for clients and foreign buyers. The press was allowed in but publicity was carefully restricted to avoid pirating. Versace and his fellow Italians turned the catwalk into a stage and the show into pure theatre. They became large-scale productions, com-plete with music and lighting, that were aimed at gathering maximum coverage.[38] As such they were 'pseudo-events', to use the sociologist Daniel Boorstin's term for activities whose sole purpose was to garner publicity.[39] For seasoned fashion journalist Colin McDowell, catwalk shows were at the core of 'the deception which embroils the fashion industry in its attempts to keep us thinking "designer" and buying the clothes that bear the label'.[40] They were fashion's theatrical blockbusters that seduced commentators and critics 'into accepting anything and lauding it to the skies provided it is on a runway and the music is right'. In the high voltage setting of the Versace catwalk shows, models strutted their stuff with the confident sassiness of the dressed-up but none-too-respectable starlet. The shows were spectacular events with huge press appeal that were bathed in laser light and accompanied by pulsating beats; his front rows were stuffed with rock stars and actors whom he treated as friends and often hosted lavishly at his gorgeous homes, including the Casa Casuarina villa on Miami's South Beach where he would be killed.

Versace is often credited with having created the phenomenon of the 'supermodels'. While several models had individually and collectively achieved high exposure in the 1980s, and *Time* magazine devoted a cover to them in September 1991,[41] Versace enhanced their profile. He signed models exclusively for his shows and then used them collectively in his 1994–5 advertising campaign, shot by Richard Avedon.[42] Other fashion houses followed suit and soon no show was complete without them. Christy Turlington, Naomi Campbell, Linda Evangelista, Cindy Crawford, and Claudia Schiffer, plus a handful of variable others,[43] became as well known in the 1990s as the Hollywood stars of the golden age. They appeared on innumerable covers of the leading fashion magazines; they wowed the public through press coverage of spectacular catwalk shows; the top few became known by their first names only. In addition, they reached beyond fashion to undertake calendar, pin-up, and general magazine and advertising work. They became all-purpose celebrities who wrote books, made films, hosted television shows, made records and fitness videos, and whose lives were the stuff of dreams. Their rise was the product of three distinct trends: the globalization of the model industry, which occurred in the 1970s; the ready-to-wear revolution that took fashion to the masses; the absence of other figures capable of generating sufficient attention and interest to harness collective dreams. The supermodels were different from their predecessors in the sense that they were not drawn from a relatively narrow social environment; rather they were girls who had been spotted as teenagers in diverse local settings, mostly far-removed from conventional fashion strongholds. Schiffer was a lawyer's daughter discovered in a Düsseldorf discotheque; Turlington was noticed by a photographer at a local gymkhana in San Francisco; Campbell was spotted on the street in London's Covent Garden; Crawford was raised in the Illinois countryside and did not even seem physically suited to modelling; the Canadian Evangelista was the only one who admitted to always having wanted to be a model and was already on the books of an agency by the age of 12.[44] Each of them had a quality that distinguished her and rendered her iconic: Crawford's beauty spot, Evangelista's penchant for chameleon-like changes, and Turlington's pout were traits that were endlessly debated. Only the wholesome and strapping Schiffer was a conventional blonde, while Campbell was the first black model to reach the peak of the profession.

These women became the idols of an era.[45] More people were aware of them on a global level than any previous fashion models. The supermodels were the product of a period obsessed by image and glamour. They epitomized contemporary ideas of beauty and inhabited a world of dreams and fantasies. They began in the world of image as recruits of model agencies, who were packaged and shaped by photographers. In the 1970s and 1980s, a star-like approach to the grooming and presentation of models had emerged. According to fashion editor Polly Mellon, the founder of the Elite model agency—John Casablancas—was chiefly responsible for bringing sex appeal and sensuality to the business and making it much more profitable. 'He took a sleepy backwater business run by a dowager empress [i.e. Eileen Ford, who had founded the Ford agency in 1946] and turned it into Hollywood,' she declared.[46] Photographers including Patrick Demarchelier, Peter Lindbergh, and Steven Meisel shot the models for magazines and turned them into icons, while magazines across the globe clamoured for them. Even before they won general recognition, they were undertaking work outside the fashion field. They won lucrative contracts with cosmetics companies and undertook pin-up work for *Sports Illustrated*'s annual swimsuit issue and the Pirelli calendar. The shapely all-American Crawford even posed for *Playboy* magazine in 1988. Agencies were marketing them globally for ever-increasing fees and began insisting that they be given name credits by magazines. As their fame increased, *Vogue* and other publications began to appreciate the impact they had on sales and featured them heavily. In January 1990 British *Vogue* dedicated its cover to Turlington, Evangelista, Crawford, Campbell, and Tatiana Patitz, impressing pop singer George Michael so much that he cast them all in the video of his song 'Freedom'.[47] Paris-based agency boss Gérald Marie, who at the time was Evangelista's husband, persuaded Versace that it would work to his advantage to pay photographic models way over the usual rates and send them out on the catwalk in groups.[48]

Crawford, Schiffer, and company had glamour because of the special place they occupied in the dreams of society. They could persuade people to buy even at a time when spending was down by investing salesmanship with class and seductiveness. 'They have replaced the Hollywood stars in the hearts of a public starved for glamour,' proclaimed the first issue of a magazine from the *Elle* stable that was wholly devoted to them: 'They are real trend setters of our time; everything they do and say is talked about and imitated. They bring us beauty and the illusion of eternal youth. They are neither American nor Swedish nor Italian, but rather come from an imaginary land that knows no border. They speak without words, their faces and bodies spell the meaning of grace in a universal language that needs no translation.'[49] They were about selling. As novelist Jay McInerney expressed it in his *Model Behaviour*, they were women 'whose photographic image is expensively employed to arouse desire in conjunction with certain consumer goods'.[50] The supermodels were one-dimensional—no one heard them speak, but they none the less dazzled as protagonists of a world that had all the features of glamour. Their lives appeared to unfold between the catwalk, first-class cabins on planes, five-star hotels, photo shoots, millionaire or rockstar boyfriends, and extensive grooming. The distancing mechanisms that helped keep them remote were their silence, their cosmopolitanism, their physical beauty, and their belonging to a realm of dreams. Their accessibility derived from their visibility in the press, their ordinary origins, and their apparent lack of any real talent.

The supermodels were promoted because movie stars, once the prime bearers of glamour, were no longer able or willing to project the kind of enthusiasm and emotional involvement of their predecessors. Contemporary cinema had global reach but it allotted only a small place to glamour and stars like Meryl Streep, Jodie Foster, Sigourney Weaver, or Winona Ryder were unlike the goddesses of the past for whom it was a duty to look sensational at all times. Rejecting glamour in favour of an idea of acting as art, they did not mind being snapped looking less than bandbox perfect. At the same time, various industries needed dreams of allure and perfection to sustain business. The materialistic dream of beauty, success, luxury, fame, and sex was the lubricant of modern capitalism, a seductive magic that tied people to consumption by colonizing their aspirations and wowing them with visual effects. In the past, cosmetics, lingerie, fashion, photography, television, and popular spectacle had all based part of their appeal on the special allure of Hollywood. In consequence, the old glamour that, in its time, was seen as seductive and even vulgar in its desire to please, took on the air of the classic and the artistic.

The ready-to-wear designers all loved classic Hollywood cinema and often spoke of it. They knew that it was an unrivalled template and that its fabulous images were part of a repertoire of allure that was available for appropriation. Although no longer recent, the glamorous legacy of the major Hollywood studios of the past remained available to be imitated and reconfigured. Versace talked about drawing inspiration from ancient and early modern civilizations but what he served up was a 'raunchy and ersatz version of the ancient past'.[51] His 'Roman inspirations seem to stem from nothing more ancient than Fifties gladiator films starring Victor Mature and Gina Lollobrigida in the romanticised Technicolor world of Hollywood', observed Colin McDowell.[52] To convey the sort of women Versace might have dressed, one commentator suggested that Cleopatra, Jezebel, Delilah, Madame de Pompadour, Jean Harlow, Jane Russell, Lana Turner, Gina Lollobrigida, Marilyn Monroe, Brigitte Bardot, Claudia Cardinale, Cher were all 'Versace girls', 'glitter queens to a woman'.[53] Versace's models resembled fifties' film stars and they wore the make-up to match. Their faces were powdered pale and their lips pouted with brilliant, shiny red. Their appearance was exceptionally pliable. Schiffer and Crawford emerged because of their resemblance to films stars of the past—Brigitte Bardot and Marilyn Monroe respectively—while Evangelista was renowned for her chameleon-like changeability and Campbell reprised the looks of twenties' music-hall star Josephine Baker and other icons of colour. In 1996, French *Vogue* photographed leading models disguised as Marlene Dietrich and Ava Gardner. The supermodels were blank canvases of perfect but depersonalized femininity on which dream identities could be painted. Schiffer even posed as Barbie for more than one photo shoot.

The yearning for old-style glamour manifested itself throughout the cultural system. Volumes such as Len Prince's *About Glamour* or Serge Normant's *Femme Fatale*, that featured contemporary stars photographed in the manner of the old, covered their subjects in an aura of shadows, light, glistening surfaces, and seductive materials.[54] In this way, they recalled George Hurrell or Clarence Sinclair Bell's stills of Clark Gable, Joan Crawford, and Jean Harlow. At a time when celebrity was widely thought to have become irredeemably cheapened, the images of a handful of stars who enjoyed almost universal admiration in the 1930s and 1940s stood as a paradigm, or at least as a possible cloak, for the hundreds of television and film actors who sought to hold the attention of the public for more than the blink of an eye. The deaths of numerous old stars in the early 1990s projected their unrivalled allure once more into public consciousness. In 1990 the greatest star of the interwar years, Greta Garbo, died and so did Ava Gardner, one of the sultriest actresses of the 1940s and 1950s; in 1992 it was the turn of Garbo's one-time Paramount rival, Marlene Dietrich, in 1993 of Audrey Hepburn, and in 1996 of one of the most popular romantic heroines of the 1930s, Claudette Colbert. Each received fulsome obituaries and reverent evocations in the illustrated press.

In the heyday of Hollywood, stars were remote and fabulous beings who were none the less connected to the public by means of various devices dreamed up by the studios. Now the old idea of the star system was replaced by a wider category of celebrity whose members were omnipresent and produced by a variety of entertainment media. The 'blatant shallowness' of the celebrity arena was frequently deplored,[55] along with the personalities who inhabited it, but precisely this made it useful to cultural industries and to the sphere of consumption. It was a parallel world that was both superficial and alluring, amusing and enviably free of routine oppression. It appealed because it seemed accessible, especially to the young. Versace was well aware of the modern public's thirst for celebrity and often used references to it in advertising spreads. For example, in 1996 Bruce Weber shot for the Versace diffusion label Versus a series of black-and-white photographs that used the idea of young stars arriving somewhere, dressed up for an event and surrounded by paparazzi.[56] None of the faces in the photographs, however, was well known. Like Andy Warhol, from whom he occasionally drew inspiration (one gown featured a design based on Warhol's silk screen 'Marilyn'), Versace played with the language of fame. He was aware that it was detachable from famous people and could be fragmented into accessible parts. It could be appropriated, reproduced, and turned back on itself. It could be made to seem at once remote and magical and yet be made available to all.

Like film companies in the 1920s and 1930s, the leading model agencies organized worldwide competitions for new faces, while scouts of varying degrees of reputability were constantly on the lookout for the next Cindy or Claudia. The promise of model glamour was in fact that any girl could suddenly be propelled to the stratosphere. If a girl of West Indian origin from the backstreets of South London like Naomi Campbell could become a fashion superstar (working, in the process, 'on every inch of herself, from her accent to her taste in champagne'),[57] then in theory there was hope for everyone. Even those lacking height or classical features might appeal to a photographer or benefit from an unexpected turn towards the quirky. In a typical blurring of front- and backstage, magazines that specialized in revealing the 'real lives' of models ran features on the everyday lives of freshly recruited 'mini-tops' and promised readers the chance to join them.[58] The depiction of young models' lives in such publications was highly selective and focused mainly on its most attractive or commonplace aspects.

In his exploration of the world of modelling, *Model*, subtitled *The Ugly Business of Beautiful Women*, Michael Gross highlighted the risks that faced teenage models in the world's fashion cities. Although the old-established New York-based Ford agency was known for its chaperoning approach to young models, often they were unprotected and unguarded. In foreign cities—notably Milan, that was the leading forcing ground of models— they fell prey to local playboys offering them dinners, country weekends, parties, and drugs. It was not merely the sleazy milieu that formed around the girls that entrapped the weak and the guileless. Rather it was the agents themselves who often refused to promote models who declined to perform sexual favours. Some were quite simply 'glorified pimps' who realized that 'beautiful girls could be fucked in every way'.[59] In the case of one model agency boss, whose alleged weakness for teenage girls was legendary, naïve teenagers reportedly required sexual burnishing before they were ready to be promoted as the bearers of sexual fantasies. The boss in question had apparently 'long been a proponent of the theory that models were raw stones that needed work to become glittering diamonds'.[60] 'European men are important abrasives in the finishing process; they tend to be male chauvinists,' he had said; 'that attitude...gives the model an awareness of her femininity, which is an indispensable quality'.[61] Playboys or agents were ideally placed to perform the task.

Sex appeal in the fashion world may have been largely an artificial allure that was manufactured by designers, make-up artists, hairdressers, and photographers, but sexual exploitation was rife. The glamour of the model elite was dependent indirectly on the existence of a sub-world of debauchery and misery. Male models no less than female ones were liable to find themselves faced with demands for sexual favours in return for work. As in the nineteenth century, the world of prostitution was but a few rungs down the ladder from the glittering surface of famous men, fine restaurants, and elegant resorts.[62] Contrary to its dominant myths, the fashion industry was a dangerous game of snakes and ladders. In the dialectic of class and sleaze that is crucial to glamour, it positioned itself as a switching station, finding them both equally suggestive and remunerative. Consequently, it drew on them alternately. Versace was the leading designer to take inspiration explicitly from the worlds of prostitution and fetishwear in creating his more daring designs, but many others took cues from the brash flaunt-it and flog-it world of the street. Even Princess Diana's speech coach suggested that she could enhance her delivery by thinking of herself as a hooker.[63] The occasional model overdose and periodic revelations of sexual exploitation were scandals that the fashion world preferred to keep at arm's length, but they also endowed it with a frisson of danger that somehow made it more intriguing and desirable. Diana's sexed-up image was informed by the contact she had with this environment.

As with the courtesans of the nineteenth century, and the film stars of the middle decades of the twentieth, the models were bearers of the sexual fantasy of their age. Their notoriety rested on their desirability and their sexuality, their beauty being bound up with both. Just as a Parisian *viveur* might have courted a courtesan for the kudos it brought, so an ambitious late twentieth-century man-about-town like writer Toby Young could confess: 'Like most heterosexual men, I'd grown up fantasizing about sleeping with models. It wasn't the act of having sex with them I found so appealing...but the bragging rights afterwards. To be able to walk past a newsstand, point at the cover of a glossy magazine, and say, "been there, done that"—that was my idea of heaven.'[64] The magnetic allure that the models had for some men—who were infamously dubbed 'modelizers' by *Sex and the City* author Carrie Bradshaw—was the contemporary equivalent of the glamorous aura that golden age film stars had transmitted ('Men go to bed with Gilda and wake up with me,' forties' actress Rita Hayworth used to lament).

The allure of the models was shallower since they were not fully fledged public personalities and the narratives that were woven around them were flimsy. For teenage girls though, the dreams were powerful and they were fuelled by a para-literature sometimes sponsored by the agencies. Ford Models lent its imprimatur to a series of teenage novels published by an offshoot of Random House. With titles like *The New Me* and *Party Girl*, they appealed to the fantasies of pubescent readers keen to escape humdrum lives. *Party Girl* features a girl who fails to win the real model contest Supermodel of the World but is selected anyway by Ford. 'I was heading to New York, the modelling center of the world! I'd shop at fashionable boutiques, go to exciting parties, and entertain glamorous friends in my own chic little apartment. I had it all planned out,' she muses.[65] The sleazy underside of modelling was absent from such works, but it was highlighted in more adult novels set in the fashion milieu. Former model Judi James's *Supermodel* ('The looks of an angel, a heart of glass' warned the cover blurb) explored the secret hard-core past of a Russian model. A model who objects to nude work is bluntly told: 'It's porno darling, do you understand what I mean? Did we cover that term in our language education classes? Porn, porno, pornography. I fuck—you fuck—they fuck—we all fuck, get it? Every model's done it some time or other—it's part of the rites of passage.'[66]

The supermodel elite exploited its unique position and diversified into acting, singing, writing, photography, TV presenting, and even fast-food sponsorship (Fashion Café). They also became fodder for the gossip press. Cindy Crawford's engagement and marriage to Richard Gere, Stephanie Seymour's relationship with singer Axl Rose of Guns and Roses, Claudia Schiffer's curious pairing with magician David Copperfield, and Naomi Campbell's string of affairs with boxer Mike Tyson, musician Adam Clayton of U2, actor Robert De Niro, Formula One team boss Flavio Briatore, and others were as talked about as any movie star liaisons of the past. Having extended their reach from the world of fashion to the realm of pin-ups and men's magazines, the supermodels found that they were in demand from a wide range of manufacturers that wanted to reposition their products by adding some of their gloss. Although even some top models experienced drug addiction and other serious personal problems, the huge increase in their earnings in the 1980s was accompanied by a high degree of professionalism. They fulfilled fashion's need for a star system and contributed significantly to the rise of image and celebrity culture. But the models who followed the original five or six supermodels only in one or two instances achieved the same level of global recognition. Michael Gross believes that a backlash began after Linda Evangelista was quoted in *Vogue* magazine saying, 'We have this expression, Christy and I: we don't wake up for less than $10,000 a day.'[67] By putting a price tag on themselves, the models dissolved their own mystique. The comments were labelled greedy and tactless and the models denounced as over-priced packaged commodities. In fact, while some resentment was undoubtedly caused, the real problem was what underlay the remark, namely that they had become expensive and ubiquitous. Crawford was simultaneously advertising Pepsi, being the face of Revlon, and fronting her own fashion show on MTV, while also doing editorial work for magazines and catwalk shows. Schiffer became Chanel's favourite model while doing Citroën ads on television. By 1994, she had her own waxwork at the Musée Grévin in Paris, while all the supermodels had personalized Barbie-style dolls.

The derivative nature of the supermodel personae as they were forged and presented to the public may be explained in relation to the fact that contemporary glamour is itself derivative. It is not only an aspect of the particular drives of consumer society but of the sleek surfaces of an image culture that is often self-generating and self-referential. Up until the 1960s, magazines and photographers worked off real social environments or they imitated and elaborated on them. After the collapse of formal high society, and the demise of the well-bred or debutante model, it was the photographic styles and iconic images of the past that provided the most potent source of inspiration.[68] The globalization of fashion and its supporting structures in publishing, marketing, and advertising produced a certain standardization similar to that experienced by the Hollywood studios in the 1950s. Despite a wider ethnic and physical variety than at one time, the imagery surrounding models was repetitive. Photographers, in conjunction with editors and stylists, were the crucial players here. Contemporary fashion professionals are highly knowledgeable about the past of their profession and explicitly evoke the styles, iconic moments, and people that have defined the collective imagination. Indeed, the main role of photographers is to achieve this evocation in a contemporary way that dovetails with the requirements of advertisers and magazine editors.

The Canadian Steven Meisel, who became the most regular Italian *Vogue* photographer of the late 1980s and 1990s, was renowned for his postmodern appropriations and reworkings of the masters. He consciously mimicked the styles of every major photographer from the 1930s to the recent past, posing his models in the manner of the actresses and mannequins of earlier eras.[69] Lacking a distinctive style of his own, he was regarded by some as a 're-photographer' and dubbed 'Xerox' by one unimpressed gallery-owner.[70] Herb Ritts, who was responsible for some of the best-known group pictures of the supermodels also owed much to older photographers including Richard Avedon and Irving Penn. His fashion shots glorified gym-toned bodies while his mannered celebrity photographs relied heavily on masquer-ade and revival. Model-turned-photographer Ellen von Unwerth's fuzzy and aggressive black-and-white shots also had a strong retro aspect to them, although this was blended with upfront sexuality. Best-known for casting an unknown Claudia Schiffer in a campaign for the Californian denim company Guess, she specialized in assertive but provocatively sexualized pictures of women that replaced composure with immediacy. 'She deals with a 90s version of glamour: the shiny, neon-lit attractions of pretend sleaze,' commented one observer.[71] In this way, she remained within the idiom of male fantasy even if she supplied ironic twists on standard scenarios.[72] Surface visual effects—shiny plastic, glass, lipstick, and cosmetics—triumphed in her images.

In general, photographers did not object that their work was the subject of homage and appropriations on the part of younger colleagues.[73] Portrait photographers like George Hurrell and even *Vogue* master Horst had been out of favour for decades and the revival of interest in their work led to reappraisals, books, and exhibitions. A crucial supporting role here was played by John Kobal, who rescued many Hollywood studio stills from oblivion and placed them in his collection, from which several books were drawn.[74] When Hurrell and Horst died, respectively in 1992 and 1999, they received fulsome obituaries of a type that would have been unlikely two decades previously. Helmut Newton was less keen on the sort of tributes that he was paid by the fashion world's self-conscious revivalism. In their editorial work, Michael Roberts, Inez Van, and others created pastiche versions of Newton's trademark deluxe nudes that were sometimes indistinguishable from the real thing.[75] However, unlike the others, Newton was still at the height of his powers. He even created a new star to add to the supermodel firmament, the Teutonic Nadja Auermann, whose other-worldly appearance he connected to the classic canon of artificial sex appeal.

The fashion industry often works by proclaiming a seasonal 'look' to persuade customers of the need to renew their wardrobes. In autumn 1994 it launched 'glamour' as its seasonal watchword. 'Hard core glamour, high gloss and bright colour are back,' announced British *Vogue* in its October issue.[76] 'New glamour', another magazine declared, 'has evolved beyond the clichéd head-to-toe sequins of 50s Hollywood glitz. It has eased up from the 80s *Dynasty* suit with its galaxy of gilt buttons and flaunt-it jewellery.'[77] Instead, it was more 'pared-down, more self-assured and sexy'. This 'new glamour' took inspiration from various sources, including the sleek elegance of the 1930s and the sexy styles of the 1970s. All demanded poise, panache, and polish. The season's top lines consisted of sharply cut suits, classical evening wear, full accessories, high heels, and bold lipstick. It was striking that the interpretations of glamour that were offered at this time in women's magazines placed the emphasis squarely on polished, refined images of formal outfits. 'The story of glamour through the century is the history of women and their strengthening self-image,' wrote *She*.[78] It added, 'Glamour is make-believe, a veneer anyone can apply with the right clothes, strongly-defined make-up, coiffed hair and red lips.' Adult sex appeal with a sophisticated spin was the season's watchword. It was one that especially suited Versace, Valentino, Dior, Chanel, Alexander McQueen, and Helmut Lang. Another beneficiary was the Italian label Gucci that, under the creative direction of Tom Ford, sexed-up its ready-to-wear and embraced a widely praised and commercially successful, but fundamentally dull, corporate glamour reminiscent of the Yves Saint Laurent of the 1970s.

The launch of the look gave rise to reflections on the meaning of glamour and the range of its applications in fashion. 'Is glamour glitter—or a graceful line?', asked Brenda Polan in the *Financial Times*.[79] Was it in short the sort of flamboyant, eye-catching, colourful, and sexy look associated with Versace and his flashy clients, or the subtlety, harmony, and simplicity of the more restrained and classy creations of a designer like Giorgio Armani. This was matched by another tension, that between the lady and the tart, or between the dressed-up and the undressed. In this case the dichotomy was not within the world of fashion but between fashion as a whole and the sphere of male entertainment. Writing in *Vogue*, Sarah Mower powerfully asserted the female prerogative. 'For too many years glamour has been a joke—repudiated by feminists, used, tackily, by the pop industry from glam rock onwards, hijacked by the sleaze merchants of "glamour photography",' she argued, before lauding its reappropriation by models who were reconnecting it with 'a glorious, noble, stirring sense of womanhood'.[80] The history of glamour shows in fact that the unresolved dichotomy between class and sleaze lies at its core. Glamour is never so subtle that it is not eye-catching at some level, and the 'sex appeal of the inorganic' that Walter Benjamin identified as a core feature of modern fashion is always present. Even when there was a clearly defined high society, the language of glamour was defined by contributions from popular entertainment and the street. Ostensibly, there may be nothing in common between, say, Jacqueline Onassis and Madonna or between Princess Diana and Pamela Anderson. In fact all four women invested heavily in their physical appearance and were considered sex symbols. Their clothes and their bodies were key aspects of their public personae. All of them were part of the realm of the visual image and the magazine community. All of them, moreover, transgressed social and sexual norms and brushed with scandal. One of Princess Diana's defining moments came in 1994 when she confessed her infidelity on television.

Glamour was part of a complex and variegated media scene. The sampling of old Hollywood that became a trademark of fashion advertising and promotion gave rise to further derivations such as the 1993 success of drag artist Ru Paul's dance record 'Supermodel (You Better Work)'. He went on to score a top ten hit in a duet with Elton John. Paul became the first drag queen supermodel when MAC cosmetics signed him to a modelling contract. Proving that cosmetics really could transform their wearers, billboards of the 6-foot-plus African-American performer were adorned with the slogan 'I am the MAC girl'. His look, he claimed, was 'total glamour, total excess, total Vegas, total total'.[81]

The birth of the pop video and of MTV introduced a marked emphasis on the visual within popular music. Perhaps no one more than Madonna turned twentieth-century glamour into a repertoire to be harnessed and manipulated at will. After winning recognition as a New York City drifter in Susan Seidelman's *Desperately Seeking Susan* in 1985, she scored a worldwide hit with 'Like A Virgin' and went on to become the most successful female recording artist ever, selling an estimated 175 million albums and 75 million singles in a career lasting, to date, 28 years. She polarized public opinion by acting the part of the rebel and outsider, marginal and disruptive, above all by rejecting established female roles. Although Madonna's music was derivative, if catchy and often danceable, her visual style was an original concoction of virgin and whore, Catholic and pagan, high fashion and Hollywood parody. In a series of high-production music videos, she embraced a variety of gold-digger, showgirl, and bad girl personae and even cast herself as Marilyn and Marlene Dietrich, as well as Mexican painter Frida Kahlo.[82] In some respects, she used the strategies of a female impersonator by donning a series of guises. She received a high degree of attention not merely from the establishment and the press but also from academics fascinated by her impact on mainstream culture and subcultural domains.[83]

A barometer of cultural moods and conflicts, she attracted more publicity than most heads of state. Madonna was at one level a sex star. 'A certain sleaze factor was undoubtedly an important element of Madonna's initial rise to fame,' noted one keen observer of her career,[84] and in 1985 *Penthouse* and *Playboy* magazines published black-and-white nude photographs for which she had posed several years earlier.[85] She responded in 1992 by publishing her own coffee-table book of nudes by Steven Meisel, entitled *Sex*. This overt display of shiny, confectioned sexuality placed her in direct line from the soft-pornography of 1950s burlesque.[86]

Madonna's success has been traced to the high degree of personal auton-omy she exercised. In contrast to many pop stars, she was a powerful player who was defiantly independent of labels and media corporations. Moreover, she cheerfully engaged in self-commodification, transforming herself at will and pushing an inauthentic identity in contrast to rock's dominant, if often false, ideology of artistic integrity. She moulded her body with diet and exercise, turning it into a powerful tool of her various personae. Her tour titles, Blond Ambition, Girlie Show, and Re-Invention testified to her show-girl-inspired stage presentations. Curiously, for such a visually aware star, Madonna's numerous forays into the movies, including the big budget productions *Dick Tracy* and *Evita*, fell flat. Rather, it was still photographs and videos that best captured her allure. Meisel photographed her many times, while Helmut Newton revealed that, save for Elizabeth Taylor, she was the only subject to whom he had granted a right of veto.[87] Madonna's glamour was of a ruthlessly eclectic kind. She fashioned a persona across several media and bridged several glamorous contexts. She forged a collab-oration with designers including the Italian duo Dolce & Gabbana and appeared in a Versace advertising campaign. However, it was the idea of glamour that she derived from childhood memories of watching old movies that was her biggest influence. The video for her song 'Vogue' recreated the atmospheric style of the studio photographers and witnessed the singer disguise herself as the stars who inspired her, while the lyrics provided name checks to Dietrich, Monroe, Harlow, Grace Kelly, Katherine Hepburn, Bette Davis, Sophia Loren, Lana Turner, and Ginger Rogers as well as Brando, Dean, Astaire, and Gene Kelly.

The collaboration of Madonna with fashion designers inspired a whole series of developments in popular music and entertainment. New synergies occurred between different sectors. In pop, the showgirl-dance music pairing that Madonna pioneered was taken up by many artists, including Kylie Minogue, who exchanged her girl-next-door image for that of a feathers-and-sequins showgirl with a sexy image forged through relationships with INXS singer Michael Hutchence (who boasted that he had corrupted her) and French actor Olivier Martinez. First as singer of No Doubt and then as a solo performer, Gwen Stefani operated her own knowing blend of street style, movie glamour, and high fashion, while Christina Aguilera's overtly sexual image mixed old Hollywood and grunge with a mastery of soul, jazz, and blues music.

The appropriation of glamour by the music industry brought pressure to bear on Hollywood. This applied less to film production than to the public moments when the industry was on show. Many stars were no longer accustomed to dressing up as a matter of course and were clueless when required to do so. One of the most prestigious and valuable platforms in this sense was the Academy Awards ceremony in Hollywood every spring. Giorgio Armani established an office to lend dresses and outfits to the stars as early as 1983, while Valentino retained favour, especially but not only, with older stars. Fashion designers won a strategic place in the preparations for Oscar night because a successful and admired choice of gown could add glamour to a star as well as increasing the cachet of a designer. In the 1990s, just a handful of stars were willing to join veterans like Joan Collins and Sophia Loren in reminding the public of Hollywood's heritage of fabulous grooming and drop-dead queenly good looks. While Joan was happy ironically to dispense lessons in old-time big hair, big jewels, and big personality glamour, and join her sister Jackie in peddling pop literary doses of it in genre fiction,[88] only Kim Basinger, the star of *L.A. Confidential*, and an Oscar winner in 1997, and *Basic Instinct*'s and *Casino*'s Sharon Stone were willing to follow them. 'Sharon Stone is not in the Winona Ryder, Jodie Foster style. She's an old-fashioned star, the way they used to be,' noted one newspaper.[89]

This changed in the late 1990s and the early years of the new century. Luxury companies followed the fashion designers in targeting celebrities. The publicity to be derived from seeing a leading actor or personality wear a watch, jewellery, or shoes, was so valuable that goods were offered on loan or more often given as gifts. In the companies' strategies, celebrities took the place of models as they were deemed to be more effective at promoting goods. They were not shallow ciphers but realistic individuals whom consumers felt familiar with and could relate to.[90] This more than anything else brought ostentation and material goods squarely to public attention and popularized labels that had previously not been widely known. It complemented the strategy of establishing sales outposts in airports, second-tier large cities, and high-profile tourist locations like Las Vegas and Miami Beach.

Advertising, celebrity linkages, and visible logos made prestige goods desirable for all and brought the glamour of luxury within the purview of groups which had no previous contact with it. Such strategies turned them into aspects of popular culture. The appropriation of signature products by fast-money and downmarket celebrities, and even working-class subcultures, soon followed. This could not readily be prevented even though the potential damage for labels could be considerable.[91] The flamboyant styles popular in the Afro-American community in the 1970s created the precedent for 'bling' in the 1990s. Born within the urban musical community of hip hop, bling was all about the wearing of expensive gold and diamond jewellery and the ostentation of a highly materialistic lifestyle of cars, yachts, beautiful girls, designer clothes, and furs. Related to the 'ghetto fabulous' fashions of earlier decades,[92] it was a product of the ghetto rather than a denial of it. Rap artists vaunted gold and diamonds as rewards for success on a par with crime, that was itself often romanticized in hip hop lyrics. While Jay-Z and others launched fashion labels and spent fortunes making jet-set music videos, only producer and singer P. Diddy (Puff Daddy, aka Sean Combs) embraced every aspect of the movie-star lifestyle from the enormous entourage and summer encampment at St Tropez to Savile Row suits and outsize cigars. As with Beyoncé Knowles, the former member of the girl group Destiny's Child who established herself as a modern urban music performer in the showgirl tradition, his links to a predominantly poor black community withered over time. The glamour of bling was a powerful counter to the corporate control of luxury. But the new money of black entertainment inevitably found designers who were willing to cater to it and the sector also spawned artists who designed their own ranges of clothes and accessories. Far from being critical, bling was soon absorbed into a trash glamour aesthetic that celebrated the most brash, nouveau riche, and sleazy of styles and accessories. After the death of Versace, the Roman designer Roberto Cavalli emerged as the champion of the latter-day jet-set look. His beautifully made garments featured the boldest of animal prints and were covered with gold motifs.[93] Bling was even cautiously embraced by Armani's youth-oriented Emporio Armani line and especially by the Emporio fragrance Diamonds (which featured an image of Beyoncé on the presentation box).

Glamour at the turn of the century was a complex enchantment that was primarily connected to commercial milieux. The tight linkages between the press, television, merchandising, and fashion produced a striking glamorization of sectors once largely immune to its magic. A sport like Formula One had always attracted a high degree of glamour. Not only were races held around the world in alluring locations but the concentration of money, risk, speed, and possible death rendered the spectacle compelling. The racing community, moreover, was populated by young drivers who often enjoyed the fast life away from the track. In contrast to the interwar years, when there were a number of women drivers, Formula One drivers were uniformly male. The presence of models and beauty queens at races and on their arms confirmed a gender hierarchy and made ample use of ornamental femininity to enhance the sexual buzz of the occasion. However, the same could not be said of football which lacked the romantic appeal of individual sports and was strongly rooted to community and place. In the course of the 1990s, this changed as the sport's upper reaches became globalized and footballers' earnings spiralled. An elite of rich, stylish footballers made lucrative sponsorship deals, were recruited by fashion companies and were turned into all-round celebrities. David Beckham, the England captain from 2000 to 2006, was the most prominent of these. A certain feminization accompanied glamorization, provoking a rift with the unvarnished masculine values that in Britain had long dominated the game.[94] The glamorization of tennis followed conventional feminine lines. It produced a flurry of sponsorship deals and heavy coverage of a minor player, the blonde Russian Anna Kournikova, whose achievements on the court were outweighed by her good looks. Glamour was a distorting factor in the distribution of rewards that could not be entirely resisted because of the advantages it brought in terms of publicity and income to sport.

More than any other medium, it was the press that provided the key platform to make events and personalities glamorous. Glossy illustrated monthlies and weeklies possessed a unique capacity to distil lives and lifestyles into desirable capsules. They produced narratives of transformation that connected the ordinary and the extraordinary, the unlikely and the possible. As a heroine of the press, Princess Diana was a constant feature of readers' lives, her saga a meganarrative that provided a screen on to which dreams were projected. But it was not only personalities of her elevated status that received this treatment. Magazines existed at every level and in several varieties to cater for the specific needs of readers of different ages, interests, and income brackets. At the apex of the press pyramid were magazines belonging to the Condé Nast stable. Nearly one hundred years after the Midwesterner Nast had turned *Vogue* into the bible of the American rich, the magazine and its foreign editions occupied a different but not unrelated position in the creation and diffusion of desirable lifestyles. Never merely a fashion magazine, *Vogue* was always a style guide, trend-former, and cultural weathervane. The classic glossy magazine, under the Briton Anna Wintour's direction American *Vogue* maintained a sharp focus on high fashion while not disdaining popular culture. She applied the group editor-in-chief Alexander Liberman's injunction that what was needed was a glitzy mix of celebrity and sensation inspired by the supermarket tabloids.[95]

A similar mix characterized the content of another Condé Nast publication, *Vanity Fair*. With a title taken from Thackeray, *Vanity Fair* was edited in the interwar years by Nast's colleague Frank Crowinshield. It was revived in the 1980s under the editorship of another Briton, Tina Brown, who would later author a gossipy biography of Diana, Princess of Wales. Before ceding the editorship to Graydon Carter in 1992, Brown moulded it as a magazine dedicated to worship at the altar of celebrity, while championing quality writing, investigative journalism, and provocative photography. A typical issue at any time between the 1990s and the present might include a feature on a current celebrity, a reportage on a gruesome crime of the recent past, a picture sequence of groups of media industry professionals, a comment on politics, and an essay on some semi-forgotten glamour figure. In its pages, criminals, film stars, artists, politicians, heiresses, and tycoons all mingled without discrimination, while gossip took the place of reflection. By the early 1990s, it had become an upmarket version of the *National Inquirer*.[96] Even in its foreign editions, *Vanity Fair* breathed the high-pressure atmosphere of Manhattan, of which it became a social bible, and positioned itself as a guide to the zeitgeist. Although it retained editorial control of content, the magazine was utterly in thrall to show-business celebrity and the industries that sustained it. Its tie to Hollywood was demonstrated by its annual hosting of an exclusive after-Oscar party in Los Angeles. When he briefly worked for the magazine, British journalist Toby Young found that the shine and sparkle of Manhattan social life depended on a public realm in which notoriety had led to 'the disintegration of the self, or, at least, the transformation of the self into something less recognisably human'.[97]

Mario Testino, whose iconic portraits of Princess Diana graced *Vanity Fair* in 1997, was one of the preferred photographers of this age of celebratory celebrity. Like his professional colleagues, he had a keen awareness of heritage. However, only some of his work bore a resemblance to that of other photographers, such as his shots for the 2001 Pirelli calendar, which featured Newtonesque portraits of semi-naked supermodels in luxurious indoor and outdoor settings. In general, he did not explore the darker reaches of the imagination or resort to bizarre personal fantasies like Newton. Nor even did he use light and shade to create pure artistic effects. Rather he developed a sun-drenched style of celebratory photography and, in his many celebrity portraits, he always produced a result that flattered. Every one of them seemed to have been sprinkled with the distilled euphoria of a carnival in Rio. Not by chance, he discovered and (despite the initial scepticism of some fashion editors) launched the big-haired and moderately curvaceous Brazilian model, Gisele Bündchen. He created in his photographs a world that always looked glamorous, sexy, and fun and Gisele, with her expensive and unapproachable air, perfectly encapuslated this.

Testino was disdained by some photographers, such as Lord Snowdon, who snootily referred to 'that ghastly Peruvian'. 'All he does is: "Lovey, lovey, lovey, come on, smile,"' he grumbled.[98] His preoccupation with surfaces led to accusations that he 'sprinkled fairydust over eveything' and saw the world 'through a haze of Prozac'.[99] He belonged, it was said, to a tradition of sycophantic portraiture that went back to Sargent and to Gainsborough. When an exhibition of his work was held in London, the Communist *Morning Star* newspaper accused him of representing 'an unappealing and superficial world' and of providing 'an overly flattering and wholly dishonest view of what London is like for the majority of its inhabitants'.[100] Without doubt, his work was unmarked by the taint of harsh realism. Testino was a jet-setter who worked all over the globe and his world was one in which everyone was beautiful. One of his famous subjects once said that he brought out people's lightest side. His ostensibly natural pictures made their subjects look beautiful and happy, and situated them in a realm far removed from the mundane. Yet Testino was no simple snapper of beautiful people. To arrive at the euphoric results for which he was famous, he worked hard on his subjects, relaxing them with humour and creating an atmosphere of intimacy. They were made to feel safe and sexy through charm and flattery. Models were 'worked' at length, with a stylist, make-up artist, and hairdresser experimenting with numerous differ-ent looks to reach the clearest expression of their beauty.[101] On an assignment, an entire troupe would be present, including, other than the above, three assistants, a hair assistant, a prop stylist and his or her assistant, plus several production people and sometimes art directors and clients.[102]

No less than in the past, glamour was often a matter of men producing idealized or manipulated images of women. However, it would not be correct to conclude that female appearances were simply controlled and dictated by men. In an era in which sensibilities and attitudes had been shaped by feminism and the women's movement's message of empowerment and self-determination, things were more complex. In the so-called post-feminist era, women took over a range of female roles and images that had initially been produced for male pleasure and turned them to their own ends. Madonna was the pioneer here, a powerful entertainment innovator who selected roles from a wide repertoire thus highlighting her capacity for choice and her distance from each. But revivalism was complicated, par-ticularly in a culture in which the perfection not only of the visual image but also of the physical body was highly prized. While some women saw personal and professional potential in it, the manufacture and distribution of superbly glossed female images had complex implications. These had elements of irony but they were sometimes outweighed by the persistence of the conventional functions of female spectacle. One example was the reinvention of the pin-up, not as a marginal commercial form solely for male consumption, but as a crucial vehicle for the formation and diffusion of ideals of contemporary femininity. The focus on the female body that had always been the key feature of the pin-up was now complemented by a pronounced standardization that was shaped more by the work of 1940s' illustrators such as Varga and Gil Evgren than by creative contemporary photographers. The female flesh of the con- temporary pin-up was firm and pneumatic, her appearance perfected, and her curves improbably rounded. The most high-profile exponent of this modern take on retro glamour was Pamela Anderson. The Canadian model and actress first came to prominence in *Baywatch*, the popular television series about Los Angeles county lifeguards that ran from 1989 to 2001. With its slow-motion shots of Anderson, Yasmine Bleeth, and other female lifeguards running in swimsuits, the show won a reputation for its voyeuristic moving pin-ups ('Baywatch Babes'). Its male guards were tanned and muscular, while female ones were mostly slim-hipped and large-breasted. Anderson had appeared in *Playboy* prior to being cast in the series and her public personality would remain that of a centrefold. Hailed in the press as a 'living doll', she played cartoonish characters in several movies. Her surgically enhanced figure, bleached hair, and porn-star lips were admired and attacked in equal measure as signs of a femininity that was a pure projection of male dreams. She was an uncomplicated object of desire who had turned herself into a modern Ameri- can icon.[103] Other women found that moulding themselves into figures of male desire was remunerative and a sure way to attract publicity. But tragedies also ensued. The early deaths of the French porn star Lolo Ferrari, whose body had been transformed beyond all recognition to resemble an inflatable doll, and former Playmate and millionaire widow Anna Nicole Smith revealed that behind their Barbie-fied facades lay messy lives and serious personal problems.

Other forms of female spectacle flourished in the 1990s as retro entertain- ments which were embraced by their practitioners as forms of empower- ment. Burlesque was one of these. Retro-striptease began in upscale nightclubs in New York and Los Angeles and then spread more widely. The burlesque museum in Helendale, California also promoted it. The post-feminist mood witnessed a reflowering in new and old guises of a variety of entertainment forms that had been thought defunct. Pole-dancing, lap-dancing, and striptease were the tip of a recrudescent phenomenon of female spectacle that also saw the return not only of pin-ups, but of television hostesses and service industry beauties.[104] The allure of upscale settings was, as so often in the past, employed to disguise a direct or indirect commer-cialization of sex. The revival of burlesque was, however, an exception that was more or less single-handedly thrust into the mainstream by Dita von Teese, an artiste who aimed at an authentic reinvention of a show-business idiom that had died in the 1950s. Born Heather Sweet in Michigan, she reinvented herself as a persona with a unique retro allure. With her trade-mark acts, such as bathing in a Martini glass or emerging from a giant gold compact, she created a magical world of dreams and illusion. With her straight black hair, creamy white skin, blood-red lips, and shapely body, she was as much a photographic icon as a stage performer and in fact her fame derived largely from coverage in *Vanity Fair*, *Vogue*, *Playboy*, and other magazines as well as her picture book *Burlesque and the Art of the Teese*.[105] Always exquisitely attired, whether in a sheer evening gown, pretty lingerie, fetish wear, or feathers and sequins, her perfection was that of a plasticated mannequin. She was sex appeal without sex, an icy composition of material goods and dead dreams. Von Teese's mortuary sheen was programmatic. 'I live out my most glamorous fantasies by bringing nostalgic imagery to life,' she declared; adding that she advocated glamour 'Every day. Every minute'.[106] Precisely this lack of warmth and refusal to drop her stage mask gave her act a stunning artificiality. Whereas the theatrical excess of the original burlesque artists was demeaned by the harsh eye of photog-raphy, which revealed their physical imperfections, von Teese deployed the medium as a crucial prop to fantasy. She also revived the kinky style of pin-up art of the 1950s, posing as one of the leading models of that era, Bettie Page.[107]

Contemporary glamour is often a mix of ideas and themes drawn from the past and rendered contemporary by some skilful blending and fashioning.

Although men may sometimes enter the realm of glamour, it is still pre-dominantly feminine—and it is often assumed to be naturally so. The most contemporary forms of glamour are supplied by young starlets like Lindsay Lohan, Nicole Richie, Mischa Barton, and Jessica Simpson. For a whole generation, they are idols who have enviable, if sometimes turbulent, life-styles. In contrast to the studio-formed and studio-protected stars of the Hollywood golden age, they are continually forced to make choices about their own presentation. It is the task of publicists and other image-makers to 'gift wrap' such personalities and insert them in semi-fictional narratives comprised of simulated events and partially revealed lives.[108] Lohan and company are the sort of people whose wardrobes and red-carpet outfits are masterminded by the leading celebrity stylists. One of these, Rachel Zoe, developed a trademark style suited to younger female stars that was a clever mixture of street style and stage costume, with elements of early Bardot. Tousled hair, cropped jeans, little jackets, gold chains, and stilettos marked her signature day looks while designer wear and occasionally vintage wear was preferred for the evening.[109] Classic bags and jewellery were vital attention-grabbing extras (or 'excessories', as she termed them). She also addressed the issue of weight and was accused of encouraging the stick-thin 'size zero' look among her clients.[110] Like a handful of other stylists, Zoe became a public figure, who appeared on television, commented in magazines and authored a book entitled *Style A to Zoe: The Art of Fashion, Beauty and Everything Glamour.*[111] 'I've always been obsessed with style and glamour,' she told one interviewer,[112] while declaring in her book that 'My kind of glamour combines California ease with New York high life. It favors modern, even if it's vintage. It's browned to a deep Bain de Soleil tan and best served up with a crisp glass of champagne.'[113] She claimed that the key factor in achieving a glamorous identity was to create oneself: 'build, shape, construct, deconstruct, form—all terms conveying a work in process and one that's open to experiment'.[114] 'And it all begins with dreaming,' she added. Zoe saw herself as a fairy godmother, not just to her young stars, but to any woman who dreamed that she could 'create a better reality' for herself and who applied the lessons set out in her book.[115] Glamour was about trying harder and wanting a better life and then enjoying the rewards of designer clothes and a flashy car. 'There *is* something magical about glamour, but it doesn't just happen with a twitch of the nose or snap of the fingers,' she warned her readers.[116]

The marketed dream of a better life has always required role models, people who illustrated enviable lifestyles and gave them concrete form. In October 2005, *Vanity Fair* featured on its cover a young woman who was neither a movie star, nor a recording artist, nor even a model or a sportswoman, although she would have liked to have been most if not all of these things. Yet she was indisputably glamorous. By late 2005, the 24-year-old Paris Hilton had become 'The Inescapable Paris',[117] an ubiquitous presence on the American party circuit and the latest incarnation of the phenomenon of the heiress that had transfixed the United States from the middle decades of the nineteenth century.[118] Like Barbara Hutton and Doris Duke before her, Hilton was a product of an established commercial dynasty, in her case the Hilton hotel chain founded by her great-grandfather in 1919. Strictly speaking, Paris was not an heiress at all; with both parents living, she had no immediate prospect of inheriting a fortune. What is more, her father Rick was only the sixth child of the second son of Conrad Hilton. Nevertheless, with its base in Beverly Hills, the hotel chain was one of the largest in the world, with over 220 hotels in the United States and worldwide belonging to the group. Rick and his wife Kathy controlled a $70 million fortune and lived between a $6.5 million home in Bel Air, California, a $4 million house in The Hamptons, the Long Island summer playground of America's super-rich for over a century, and a permanent suite at New York's Waldorf-Astoria hotel. The family was rich and self-assured, almost American royalty.[119]

The Hilton family had always courted publicity and no one more than founder Conrad, who died in 1979 at the age of 92. He invited celebrities to hotel openings and mingled with the stars, marrying Zsa Zsa Gabor in 1946. His first son Nick, who died in 1969, was briefly married to Elizabeth Taylor. From an early age Paris featured in magazines, along with her younger sister Nicky. Her teenage years were spent not at any regular school but hopping between hotel suites. For a period, home was the Beverly Hills Hotel. She quickly learned that media interest could be turned to her advantage and she became a professional party girl, appearing in the tabloids at numerous events and learning that she could charge merely for turning up.

Her public personality is that of the carefree and not very bright girl having fun, trying her hand at whatever takes her fancy. Unlike heiresses of other eras, she does not appear to be the product of an inaccessible realm of privilege but rather to be imbued with pop culture. She has appeared in several movies, made a pop record, appeared on the catwalk, and authored a handful of books. 'I love junk food,' she proclaimed in her best-selling *Confessions of an Heiress*,[120] while simultaneously saying, 'I always try to travel first class or private' and turning up her nose at the New York subway ('It literally smells like pee').[121] She offers herself as an ideal for the lazy and unambitious, a young woman whose main interest is herself and her life-style. 'My life is a party,' she announced, while responding to those who had described her as 'Paris Barbie' by asserting that she regarded such a desig-nation as a compliment. 'My total fashion icon!' was how she described the celebrated doll.[122]

Paris Hilton's glamour is bound up with the image of Beverly Hills, that is of a residential district that is both impossibly rich and privileged but also brash and ostentatious.[123] Paris is the pink-clad, super-tanned spoilt child who has a customized Ferrari and a chihuahua named Tinkerbell. Like the Californian 'Valley girls' of the 1980s, whose self-obsession and materialism was satirized in the teen movie *Clueless*, she is vitally concerned with self-fashioning, regularly changing her hair colour and style to suit her mood. She is never very serious and is constantly photographed smiling. Like glamorous figures of the past, she is an astute merchandiser of herself. She has a profitable line of jewellery that bears her name, and also a line of fragrances. Her fame was boosted when she appeared in two series of a television reality show entitled *The Simple Life*, which saw her and her friend Nicole Richie abandon their golden lives for a period on a farm. Like Marie Antoinette at the Petit Trianon, Paris revelled in the artificial simplicity, sure in the knowledge that her real realm was the privileged one she knew best.

Hilton owes much of her fame to the internet and in this sense her glamour is mediated in a way that is original. She became a household name after a former lover released a sex tape on the net that was seen by millions. Indeed, thanks to this, 'Paris Hilton' became one of the most Googled terms. Far from damaging her reputation irretrievably, this scandal put her on the cover of tabloids and made her into a transgressive figure. As had previously occurred with revelations about Princess Diana's lovers, or the distribution of a similar sex-tape featuring Pamela Anderson and her then husband Tommy Lee, the brush of sleaze added spice to the cocktail of fame. She became a 'bad girl' in the eyes of the popular press, even if her boyfriend had betrayed her trust to release the film. It is noteworthy that her jewellery line is sold mainly through the internet. Hilton straddles celebrity and notoriety, switching between a lifestyle that is a fantasy for millions and real-life falls from grace. In 2007, her imprisonment following driving offences achieved front-page coverage around the world. She was described as 'oozing glamour' even in her jail pictures, while British tabloid the *Sun* described her transfer from a movie awards ceremony to a public penitentiary on the evening her sentence was to begin as a slide 'from glamour to slammer'.[124] After her release, she underwent a brief period of public repentance before resuming her party lifestyle as though nothing had happened.

Paris Hilton is the current embodiment of society's fascination with rich, beautiful, exhibitionist women. Her saleable self corresponds to a widespread desire for self-transformation and vicarious living that continues to fuel dreams of glamour. The modern media work to render everything immediately visible and blend the private with the public. This undercuts the distance usually held to be necessary to cultivate mystery and arouse envy. Yet, in a culture in which consumerism remains a central experience and in which media images are ubiquitous, glamour has not disappeared. The very plurality of enticing images, produced by magazines, the fashion industry, film and television producers, advertisers and public relations companies, fosters an idea of glamour as an accessible ideal, a touch of sparkle that can add something to every life. It is this idea that continues to work its magic even in the niche forums of new media.

CONCLUSION

F rom its origins, glamour has been associated with dreaming. The yearning for a better, richer, more exciting, and materially lavish life accompanied the development of modern consumerism and fuelled innumerable fantasies and fictions. Glamour took shape as an enticing image of the fabulous life that was lived before the eyes of everyone. Glamour provided the illusion that individual lives could be enhanced and improved by ostensibly magical means. The image was sustained and perpetuated by cultural products and commercial entertainments. It could also be approached through the practices of consumption, since goods carried ideas and suggestions that were as important as their practical uses. The power of transformation lay with anyone or anything that could persuade an audience that they or it possessed it.

Glamour was born and took shape in an age in which structured inequalities were in decline and were being replaced by ideas of formal equality combined with flexible economic inequalities. The industrial economy was producing consumer goods and the means of communication were providing new and powerful platforms for personalities and channels for information and entertainment. For most of the period covered in this book there was a gulf between the types of lifestyles associated with glamour and the modest and contained lives of the public. Glamour was experienced mainly in the press, novels, at the theatre, and though visual ephemera. Those living outside capital cities only occasionally might glimpse it with their own eyes. Its fascination depended on the glorious enviability of images that were far removed from the everyday experience of people whose possibilities for surplus spending, self-expression, travel, and sex were limited. Its appeal was most powerful to those who lay outside the realm of privilege and success.

As the consumption economy and the mass media developed, so the spectacle became more systematic: shop windows, posters, commercial publicity stunts, and professional performance gave the world of glamour a stable and predictable form. Cosmetics, fashion goods, accessories, and other goods that could be worn or carried fuelled the imagination. They were especially suggestive since they bore directly on personal identity and promised the immediate realization of a transformation of the self into something different and better.

The most glamorous figures of the past two hundred years have not been the hereditary rich or legitimate holders of power. They have been outsiders, up-starts, social climbers, and parvenus. Actors, socialites, politicians, and celebrities who have come up from the lower social reaches are always the most effective bearers of glamour. This is because they have a popular touch. They have a narrative that arouses not deference or resentment but admiration or envy. The rise from nothing is a powerful story that not only provokes sympathy and identification, it also reinforces the crucial promise of self-transformation. The pioneers of glamour were figures such as Napoleon and Byron, two men who profoundly upset the political and social order of their day and who shaped the mental horizons of the age. They were outsiders who dazzled their contemporaries with their achievements and who weaved myths around them-selves. They were eye-catching and fascinating figures who inhabited the realm of the imagination while also giving a solid rooting to the idea of personal transformation.

Glamour is always theatrical; it is a performance or parade that has no meaning unless it is widely viewed. Indeed, it is only through the perception and reception of visual effects that it comes into existence. For this reason, it is rarely subtle or complex. Glamour is an image that attracts attention and arouses envy by mobilizing desirable qualities including beauty, wealth, movement, leisure, fame, and sex. Bright colours, ostentatious signs of wealth, showy beauty, visible suggestions of sex are required to reach a mass public. There are, of course, differentiations internal to glamour. Certain qualities may be played down at times for reasons of variety or because of the particular nature of a target audience. A less overtly sexualized and ostentatious image may work better with urban middle-class audiences, for example, while working-class and rural publics may prefer a bolder approach. Further modulations cater to ethnic minorities and to gay and lesbian audiences. But, broadly speaking, glamour is always a fusion—if often a problematic one—of class and sleaze, of high style and lowly appeals. It is not conventional or, usually, institutional. Rather it works as a vaguely transgressive explosion of visual effects and publicity-seeking fireworks.

Mainly, it is the image of a category of big spenders and high consumers organized around these values that is the social bearer of glamour. Directly or indirectly, explicitly or implicitly, the attributes of this elite are made to appear imitable. This occurs in a number of ways. For example, its patterns of recruitment, in theory, are open. To have a chance of joining it, it is not necessary to be rich or well-born, since anyone of the right age and physical characteristics can be spotted by a model agency or signed up by a movie director. In addition, glamour is not a natural attribute but a manufactured one. Because image is so important in glamour, it has always required mediators. Painters, interior decorators, architects, fashion designers, novelists, photographers, film-makers, journalists, publicists, and stylists have been crucial in fashioning desirable images and glittering facades with which the rich, the famous, and the beautiful have seduced their fellow citizens. The many techniques that can contribute to the construction of a glamorous persona are publicized and their practitioners often well known. In more recent times, many have come from outside the elite and precisely this has helped them create images and effects for popular consumption. They understood what appealed, what was comprehensible, and what dazzled, and also what was best disguised or kept concealed. Some of them also exploited their talents commercially and marketed to the public the promise that glamour was within the reach of anyone.

Although numerous men over the last two hundred years have entered the realm of glamour, the vast majority of figures of glamour have been women. The language of glamour, moreover, has been configured largely in feminine terms. It speaks mainly to women, and it addresses preoccupations about appearance more or less exclusively that are most associated with them. Even today the power of glamour is still widely regarded as a resource available to women. In an advice book, seasoned journalist Lucia van der Post praised its usefulness. 'Never underestimate the power of glamour. It's life-enhancing and even the plainest woman can be glamorous,' she enthused, adding, 'It's quite different from beauty. It depends a lot on a sense of personal style and some inner confidence, which isn't easy to come by but can be cultivated.'[1] No matter what her age, she claimed, any woman could boost her self-esteem and wow her friends by means of a new haircut, jewellery, sexy clothes, or perfume. The emphasis on the feminine in glamour occurs because of the particular distribution of gender roles in bourgeois society, but it is related to the structure of the consumption economy. In the course of this book a whole range of female figures has been considered, from Marie Antoinette to Paris Hilton. Broadly speaking, the main figures of glamour have been identified as the socially prominent, entertainers, and what might be termed the professionally decorative. Some women, such as the nineteenth-century courtesans, bridged all three categories while others have been firmly confined to one. To be glamorous, the women in them had to mobilize qualities additional to simple membership. For example, many female members of the aristocracy and upper bourgeoisie were not glamorous even though they enjoyed membership of high society. Despite their wealth and status, they lacked visibility and the qualities of beauty and sex appeal that were required to arouse the interest and identification of the mass of the people.

Over the period of this book, one important female figure, closely tied to glamour, has risen and fallen. The femme fatale took shape in the nineteenth century as a powerful, exotic woman, irresistible, and a seductive enchantress. With roots in folklore and myth dating back to the ancient world, she was the personification of evil, a merciless destroyer of men. In decadent culture, this figure was tied to fashion and the arts. It inspired powerful roles for actresses and was later taken up by cinema, especially in film noir.

Although the cultural products in which they appeared in some cases live on, and the femme fatale still resonates, for example in neo-noir films and television melodrama, essentially this figure belongs to the past. This is not due solely to socio-economic change and to women's emancipation but also to the role of mass communications in merging—or partially confusing—once separate male and female spheres. This process, which has been linked especially to television,[2] undercut the mystery that each sex held for the other and heralded the demise of ideas of subversive sexual power. By the same token, the compelling Byronic hero, as an unsettling and romantic masculine ideal, also ceased to be contemporary.

This development could be interpreted as heralding the demise of glamour as we have known it. In reality, glamour is evolving rather than declining, on account of its close links to the development of consumption and the media. The connection between glamour and the cinema stems from factors concerning the medium itself and factors relating to its audience. First, cinema developed as a popular urban entertainment that took over the appeals of theatre and was closely related to the experience of consumption. It was the first medium whose products were consumed simultaneously by vast numbers of people. It also reached its heyday during the Depression, when its dreams provided consolation and escape to masses of impoverished people. This function was performed especially by American cinema, which emerged in the years after the First World War as the most powerful film industry in the world. The United States was a country in which the ideal of self-expression and self-transformation was culturally enshrined. Hollywood cinema contributed decisively to the development of consumerism, first in the United States and then in Western Europe. The American model of mass consumption provided images, techniques, and methods that shaped European consumption from the 1920s but most especially in the years after the Second World War. After the invention of sound recording, the stars of the American film industry became more realistic. No longer exotic and extreme, they became more commonplace ideals, perfect projections of everyman and everywoman. The wider availability of goods gave people the chance to introduce elements of glamour into their own lives. Later, television and other electronic media, combined with the press, further generalized these opportunities.

One of the themes of this book has been the dialectic between European and American ideas of glamour. The rise of the United States to the position of leading economy in the world from the 1880s onwards placed it at the forefront of innovations in technology, consumption, and communication. However, American glamour was never free-standing. It constantly relied on European inputs and supports, be it the past treasures appropriated by millionaires or the contribution of European actors, directors, technicians, and costume designers to Hollywood. What the US has offered has been a sense of the mass market and populism. But the persistence of European aspects is crucial. What Europe contributed was history, monarchy, aristocracy, and a repertoire of visual distinction and sexual allure. The simple fact of the spelling of the word is indicative. Glamour is the only English word ending '-our' which has not consistently been spelt in American English with an '-or' ending (like labor, harbor, and so on). Only in the middle decades of the twentieth century did Americans spell the word more frequently as 'glamor'. However, even then it was by no means universal, and the Condé Nast magazine *Glamour* (originally *Glamour of Hollywood*), founded in 1939, was always spelt the European way. Up to the 1930s both versions appeared, with 'glamour' probably being most common. 'Glamour' became once more standard American spelling in the 1990s.[3]

Glamour today is, as it always has been, a diffuse and seductive aura that envelops and enhances personalities, places, and objects. While it is widespread, only some of those in the public eye embrace this aura fully and endeavour to shape their public image through it. One figure who explicitly opted to define herself in relation to the classic appeals of glamour is Victoria Beckham. The former member of the Spice Girls pop group, whose footballer husband David captained the England football team for six years from 2000, turned herself in the early twenty-first century into one of the most visible and envied women in Britain. She pursued not only a musical career but a strategy of celebrity that was multifaceted. Although she was closely associated with fashion, she was not presented as a style innovator. She was, *Hello!* magazine affirmed, something more powerful and lucrative: 'the supreme role model for girls who like their fashion flash and their grooming full on. She represents the millions of women and girls who are interested in fashion, but only if it's body clinging, tan revealing, accessorised with giant sunglasses, three inch heels and a handbag that costs three figures—the ones that always want an extra half-an-inch, whether it's tighter or higher.'[4] Victoria Beckham moulded herself into an immaculate super-consumer and merchandiser of her own glossy image, positioning herself as an intermediary between designer style and the girl in the street. In this capacity, she not only turned her lifestyle into spectacle but also proposed herself as an example to others. When she moved to Los Angeles in July 2007, following her husband's decision to sign a record-breaking contract to play for LA Galaxy, the event was hailed as a new stage in the marketing of the couple. Victoria wrote a style book full of practical advice in which she was presented as living out a glamorous fantasy. She shared with readers the dreams she had cultivated as a girl and pointed to the inspiration she drew from 'the fashion icons of the last century: Grace Kelly, Jackie Onassis and my image-for-all-seasons, Audrey Hepburn'.[5] The key to her persona is the classic glamorous one of exclusivity combined with accessibility; through her, millions could imagine themselves leading a glamorous life, mingling with film stars, and married to a top footballer. In contrast to the model Kate Moss, who also acted as a style example for millions of teenage girls and young women in Britain, Beckham exhibited a consumption-driven personal life and never discarded the fantasy persona she had created. Unlike Moss, she did not step in and out of the world of fashion and publicity at will but blended her public and private personae.

Victoria Beckham first emerged from a synergy between the press, pop music, and fashion that was fast-moving and which continually produced young women with a similar profile. After the Spice Girls, girl bands flourished, propelling their members with almost assembly-line regularity from obscurity to widespread recognition. All of them paid great attention to grooming and image. 'Four years ago', OK magazine drooled in November 2006, 'Cheryl Tweedy was a wide-eyed wannabe from Newcastle, who could only dream of living a showbiz lifestyle and marrying a footballer. But now the ambitious glamourpuss will be spending her first ever Christmas as a wife and enjoying the spoils from the multi-platinum sales of Girls Aloud's greatest hits album.'[6] In these two sentences, the key to her rise was identified with three qualities: her ambition, her dreaming of a showbiz lifestyle, and her pleasing, glossy appearance.

The techniques for achieving glamour are widely propagated. Books like those by Victoria Beckham or stylist Rachel Zoe, discussed in Chapter 11, offer advice on how everyday normal lives can be glamorized, how red carpet moments can become part of the texture of ordinary lives. They point to discipline, grooming, self-presentation, ambition, and shopping. Similar qualities are exhibited by numerous women who act as role models for the young. A television presenter, actress, and model with the manner and figure of an old-time pin-up, Kelly Brook modelled in a number of lingerie and swimwear campaigns before launching her own line in 2006. Having made it into the movies and secured a Hollywood film star fiancé, she put her name to a lifestyle guide aimed at aiding young women to discover their 'inner pin-up'. In this, she claimed that her path to success began with dreaming. She recalled how, as a girl, she had dressed up in frilly pink or lilac items to act out her dreams. 'In those... numbers,' she revealed, 'I would be transported to another world: a place where women were glamorous creatures who wore pretty frocks with cherry-red lipstick and high heels. My fantasy world was a long, long way from the small town where I grew up in Kent, but I never let that deter me; I always aspired to live a more glamorous life.'[7] Like Beckham, she found inspiration in the past. In her book, she presented a selection of her own favourites that included Bettie Page, Ava Gardner, Gina Lollobrigida, Sophia Loren, Marilyn Monroe, and Brigitte Bardot.[8]

Glamour links the rare, the remote, and the desirable with the accessible. It connects the girl from Kent with the Olympus of Hollywood. Dreams are fuelled by examples, by fictions, by consumer goods, and by entertainments. It is a powerful sales tool that is mobilized by stores, clubs, advertisers, restaurants, and travel companies. As such, it has become a part of the texture of everyday life. Once, glamour was a remote fantasy that fuelled daydreams and aspirations. For most people, glamour today is an escape, less a remote fantasy than a temporary experience that can enrich the mundane. In autumn 2007 the British department store chain Debenhams launched the 'Star' range created by fashion designer Julien Macdonald. Among the items belonging to it were women's and girls' clothes, and home decorations including vases, candlesticks, cushions. Each item was black and shiny, sparkly and silver, or covered in an animal print. 'Julien Macdonald is renowned for his high glamour designer collections and has become synonymous with celebrity première dressing,' the store's advertising announced, before reminding customers of his period as creative director at the couture house of Givenchy and his regular awards at London fashion week. 'Star', it proclaimed, is 'a collection that reflects his ability as a maestro of glitz and glam.' By means of this designer touch, a simple object such as a vase, on sale in high street stores in provincial cities, was turned into a fragment of a larger world of celebrities, style, and sex appeal. By mentioning Macdonald's brief stint at Givenchy, a connection with Parisian haute couture was evoked, while the reference to 'glitz and glam' suggested a knowing irony. By buying into the 'Star' range, customers were not turning themselves into stars, just adding a touch of sparkle to their lives.

Goods for home decoration or personal embellishment do not have to be acquired ready-made. For those of a more creative bent, Ilene Branowitz's craft manual *Create Your Own Bling: Add Glamour to Your Favourite Accessories* took glamour out of the hands of the professionals and returned it to the dreaming public.[9] A similar work, *Crowns and Tiaras: Add a Little Sparkle, Glitter and Glamour to Every Day* by Kerry Judd and Danyel Montecinos, whose premiss was simply 'every woman is a queen', contained thirty-five handicraft projects 'to organise a proper coronation'.[10] The dream of a better, more fabulous life thus turned into a do-it-yourself project for a rainy afternoon. In a real sense, such books mark an end-point of an entire cycle of glamour that began with the fabulous fantasies of Scott and Byron.

In this book, we have seen how the fabulous world of the imagination first prospered at a particular moment in history when social, political, and economic relations were in flux. Later, the transformative power of glamour was harnessed by commercial enterprises and cultural industries. Over the whole of its history, it involved large numbers of people, for whom it was not a technique for reinforcing hierarchy but rather a supremely enviable demonstration of how life could be lived by those who were rich, beautiful, sexy, and mobile. Glamour fired the imagination and boosted aspirations, while also offering industries the opportunity to produce fragments of glamorous experience for those whose aspirations remained unfulfilled. Although glamour is ever less elusive, the insatiable desire for it sustains it and reinforces its driving role in modern consumption.

NOTES

INTRODUCTION

1. Sali Löbel, *Glamour and How to Achieve It* (London: Hutchinson, 1938), 11.

2. Andrea Stuart, *Showgirls* (London: Cape, 1996), 171.

3. *Interview* (Mar. 1997), page unnumbered.

4. Löbel, *Glamour*, 14.

5. This definition follows the ideas set out in Réka C. V. Buckley and Stephen Gundle, 'Flash Trash: Gianni Versace and the Theory and Practice of Glamour', in Stella Bruzzi and Pamela Church Gibson (eds.), *Fashion Cultures: Theories, Explorations and Analysis* (London: Routledge, 2000), 332–6, and Stephen Gundle and Clino T. Castelli, *The Glamour System* (Basingstoke: Palgrave, 2006), 8–9.

6. By contrast to ideas of glamour that situate it even in the remote past, Joseph Rosa locates its origins in Hollywood cinema and the industrial design of the 1930s. While, in a memorable phrase, he notes that, 'historically, glamour has figured as the ugly stepsister to elegance', he has little to say about its existence before 1945. See Rosa, 'Introduction: Fabricating Affluence', in Rosa (ed.) *Glamour: Fashion + Industrial Design + Architecture* (San Francisco: San Francisco Museum of Modern Art, and New Haven and London: Yale University Press, 2005), 16–17.

7. My view differs in this respect from those of Ross McKibbin, *Classes and Cultures: England, 1918–1951* (Oxford: Oxford University Press, 1998), 43 and Maureen E. Montgomery, *Displaying Women: Spectacles of Leisure in Edith Wharton's New York* (New York: Routledge, 1998), 122.

8. See Colin Campbell, *The Romantic Ethic and the Spirit of Modern Consumerism* (Oxford: Blackwell, 1987).

9. On the dangers and fears of anonymous urban social encounters, see Karen Halttunen, *Confidence Men and Painted Women: A Study of Middle-Class Culture in America, 1830–1870* (New Haven and London: Yale University Press, 1982).

10. Paolo Capuzzo, *Culture del consumo* (Bologna: Il Mulino, 2006), 188–95.

11. Jürgen Habermas, *The Structural Transformation of the Public Sphere* (1962; Cambridge, Mass.: MIT Press, 2001), 195.

12. See Sophie Gilmartin, *Ancestry and Narrative in Nineteenth Century British Literature: Blood Relations from Edgeworth to Hardy* (Cambridge: Cambridge University Press, 1998), 115–18.

13. See Lucy Riall, *Garibaldi: Invention of a Hero* (New Haven and London: Yale University Press, 2007), 194–203.

14. See Arthur Marwick, *Beauty in History: Society, Politics and Personal Appearance, c.1500 to the Present* (London: Thames and Hudson, 1988).

15. Abigail Solomon-Godeau, 'The Other Side of Venus: The Visual Economy of Feminine Display', in Victoria de Grazia and Ellen Furlough (eds.), *The Sex of Things: Gender and Consumption in Historical Perspective* (Berkeley and Los Angeles: University of California Press, 1996), 113.

16. On the general aspects of this, see Daniel J. Boorstin, *The Image* (London: Weidenfeld and Nicolson, 1962).

17. Marilyn Bender, *The Beautiful People* (New York: Coward-McCann, 1967), 54.

18. See Peter Bailey, 'Parasexuality and Glamour: The Victorian Barmaid as Cultural Prototype', *Gender and History*, 25 (1990), 148–72, at 152.

19. Clive Scott, *The Spoken Image: Photography and Language* (London: Reaktion, 1999), 156. See also Réka C. V. Buckley and Stephen Gundle, 'Fashion and Glamour', in Nicola White and Ian Griffiths (eds.), *The Fashion Business: Theory, Practice, Image* (Oxford: Berg, 2000), 37–54.

20. For a full analysis of the role of colours and particular visual effects in glamour, see part II of Gundle and Castelli, *Glamour System*. On account of the exhaustive account contained in that volume, little specific attention is given to these aspects of glamour in the present book.

21. Paul Staheli, 'The Making of a Glamour Queen', *Live Wire* (Aug.–Sept. 1996), 22.

CHAPTER 1

1. Edmund Burke, *A Philosophical Enquiry into the Origins of Our Ideas of the Sublime and the Beautiful*, ed. James T. Boulton (1958; Oxford: Blackwell, 1987), 78. The lesser but related phenomenon of splendour was held to be distinct in the Middle Ages. It marked the domestic riches of wealthy merchants and traders rather than the public exhibitions of princes. See Evelyn Welch, 'Public Magnificence and Private Display: Giovanni Pontano's *De Splendore* (1490) and the Domestic Arts', *Journal of Design History*, 15/4 (2002), 211–21.

2. See Paul Roberts, 'Sir Walter Scott's Contributions to the English Vocabulary', *PMLA* 68/1 (Mar. 1953), 189–210, at 204.

3. See Richard Wilkinson, *Louis XIV* (Abingdon: Routledge, 2007), 88–9.

4. John Adamson, 'The Making of the Ancien Régime Court, 1500–1700', in Adamson (ed.), *The Princely Courts of Europe: Rituals, Politics and Culture under the Ancien Régime, 1500–1750* (London: Weidenfeld & Nicolson, 1999), 11.

5. Jonathan Dewald, *The European Nobility, 1400–1800* (Cambridge: Cambridge University Press, 1996), 122–34, at 133.

6. Joan DeJean, *The Essence of Style: How the French Invented High Fashion, Fine Food, Chic Cafes, Style, Sophistication and Glamour* (New York: The Free Press, 2005), 2.

7. Adamson, 'Making of the Ancien Régime Court', 34–5. He notes that Louis XIV was himself probably inspired by the court of his uncle Philip IV of Spain.

8. Ibid. 34.

9. Marcello Fantoni, 'The Courts of the Medici, 1532–1737', in Adamson (ed.), *Princely Courts of Europe*, 272.

10. John Adamson, 'The Tudor and Stuart Courts, 1509–1714', in Adamson (ed.), *Princely Courts of Europe*, 101.

11. G. P. Gooch, *Louis XV: The Monarchy in Decline* (London: Longman, Green, 1956), pp. vii and ix.

12. For a discussion of this issue, see Antonia Fraser, *Marie Antoinette: The Journey* (2001; London: Phoenix, 2002), 160.

13. Evelyn Farr, *Before the Deluge: Parisian Society in the Reign of Louis XVI* (London: Peter Own, 1994), 45.

14. Stefan Zweig, *Marie Antoinette: The Portrait of an Average Woman* (1933; London: Atrium, 1988), p. xi.

15. See Nancy Mitford, *Madame de Pompadour* (1954; London; Reprint Society, 1955), 83–4, 117.

16. Philip Mansel, *The Court of France, 1789–1830* (Cambridge: Cambridge University Press, 1988), 6.

17. Émile Langlade, *Rose Bertin: The Creator of Fashion at the Court of Marie Antoinette* (adapted from the French by Angelo S. Rappoport) (London: John Lang, 1913), 36–7.

18. Fraser, *Marie Antoinette*, 143.

19. Ibid. 143–5.

20. Ibid. 145.

21. Ibid. 146.

22. Zweig, *Marie Antoinette*, 92.

23. Ibid.

24. Fraser, *Marie Antoinette*, 130–1.

25. Edmund Burke, *Reflections on the Revolution in France* (1790), ed. J. C. D. Clark (Stanford: Stanford University Press, 2001), 237–8.

26. See Amanda Foreman, *Georgiana: Duchess of Devonshire* (London: HarperCollins, 1998), 40–1; Paula Byrne, *Perdita: The Life of Mary Robinson* (London: Harper Perennial, 2005), 291.

27. Caroline Weber, *Queen of Fashion: What Marie Antoinette Wore to the Revolution* (London: Aurum, 2007), 6.

28. As queen, Marie Antoinette occupied an unusual position. In the past, royal mistresses had been the object of hostility on the part of those who resented heavy taxation. Their legendary extravagance and irregular position made them easy scapegoats. Because Louis XVI did not have a mistress, Marie Antoinette came to occupy in the public mind the position not only of queen consort but also of mistress. Not unlike Louis XV's Pompadour and Du Barry, she became the whipping boy of an impoverished and hungry population. In her day, Madame de Pompadour had been the object of vitriolic attacks on her spending and her morality. The same terms were used to hit at the foreign-born queen, who was widely characterized by her critics as spoilt and debauched.

29. Burke, *Reflections on the Revolution in France*, 239–40.

30. Alan Forest, 'Propaganda and Legitimation of Power in Napoleonic France', *French History*, 18/4 (2004), 426–45, at 436.

31. Olivier Bernier (ed.), *At the Court of Napoleon: Memoirs of the Duchesse d'Abrantès* (Gloucestershire: Windrush Press, 1991) (memoirs first published, 1895), 287.

32. Philip Mansel, *The Eagle in Splendour: Napoleon I and his Court* (London: George Philip, 1987), 10.

33. Mansel, *Court of France*, 49.

34. Luigi Salvatorelli, *Leggenda e realtà di Napoleone* (1945; Turin: UTET, 2007), 73.

35. Mansel, *Eagle in Splendour*, 11.

36. David O'Brien, 'Antonio Canova's *Napoleon as Mars the Peacemaker* and the Limits of Imperial Portraiture', *French History*, 18/4 (2004), 354–78, at 376.

37. Mansel, *Court of France*, 59 and 68.

38. Salvatorelli, *Leggenda e realtà di Napoleone*, 20.

39. Louis Madelin, 'La Cour de Napoléon', *Les Œuvres libres*, NS 14 (1949), 3–42, at 32.

40. Bernier (ed.), *At the Court of Napoleon*, 293.

41. Ibid. 26.

42. Quoted ibid. 11.

43. Carolly Erickson, *Josephine: A Life of the Empress* (1998; London: Robson, 2004), 119.

44. Ibid. 118–19, 136–7.

45. Ibid. 254–5.

46. On the French Revolutionaries' attitudes to women, see Joan Landes, *Visualizing the Nation: Gender, Representation, and Revolution in Eighteenth-Century France* (Ithaca, NY: Cornell University Press, 2001).

47. Burke, *Reflections on the Revolution in France*, 240.

48. See G. M. Treveleyan, *English Social History: A Survey of Six Centuries—Chaucer to Queen Victoria* (1944; London: Longman, 1973), 492–3. For a more recent discussion, see Linda Colley, *Britons: Forging the Nation, 1707–1837* (London: Pimlico, 1994).

49. See Simon Bainbridge, *Napoleon and English Romanticism* (Cambridge: Cambridge University Press, 1995), 1.

50. Ibid. 13.

51. See ibid. 125–7 for this and the following sentences.

52. Ibid. 111–12. On Hazlitt, see ibid. 203.

53. A. N. Wilson, *A Life of Walter Scott: The Laird of Abbotsford* (London: Mandarin, 1996), 4.

54. Ibid. 147. See also Donald Sassoon, *The Culture of the Europeans: From 1800 to the Present* (London: HarperCollins, 2006), 134–40.

55. On the development of the market for fiction, see Sassoon, *Culture of the Europeans* pt. I, esp. pp. 41–53.

56. Thomas Carlyle, *Critical and Miscellaneous Essays*, iii (1839; London: Chapman, 1894), 169.

57. See Sassoon, *Culture of the Europeans*, 147.

58. Roberts, 'Sir Walter Scott's Contributions', 204–5.

59. According to Walter Skeat, editor of the *Etymological Dictionary of the English Language* (Oxford: Clarendon Press, 1924).

60. *An Etymological Dictionary of the Scottish Language* (Paisley: Alexander Gardner, 1879–87).

61. For an overview of dictionary definitions of glamour, see Stephen Gundle and Clino T. Castelli, *The Glamour System* (Basingstoke: Palgrave, 2006), 2–4.

62. *The Lay of the Last Minstrel* sold 44,000 copies, a figure that was without precedent in the history of British poetry.

63. *The Lay of the Last Minstrel*, canto III, stanza 9, ll. 11–18.

64. Scott often included notes to explain the unusual terms he used and glamour was no exception. In a note to the text, he wrote: 'Glamour, in the legends of Scottish superstition, means the magic power of imposing on the eyesight of the spectator, so that the appearance of a subject should be totally different from the reality. The art of glamour, or other fascination, was anciently a principal part of the skill of the *jongleur*, or juggler, whose tricks formed part of the amusement of a Gothic castle.' See Scott, *The Lay of the Last Minstrel—With Ballads, Songs, and Miscellaneous* (New York: C. S. Francis & Co., 1845), 222–5.

65. Sir Walter Scott, *Life of Napoleon Bonaparte* (1827; Edinburgh: Black 1878, 2 vols.).

66. See Sudhir Hazareesingh, *The Legend of Napoleon* (London: Granta, 2004).

67. T. Carlyle, *On Heroes, Hero-Worship, and the Heroic in History* (1841; London: Ginn and Co., 1901), 277.

68. Salvatorelli, *Leggenda e realtà di Napoleone*, 8 and 119.

69. Canto XI. 55. See Bainbridge, *English Romanticism*, 2.

70. Canto III. 36. See Bainbridge, *English Romanticism*, 9.

71. Fiona MacCarthy, *Byron: Life and Legend* (2002; London: Faber and Faber, 2003), p. x.

72. Like his rival, Byron adopted an aloofly dismissive pose towards the book business. See Peter W. Graham, 'Byron and the Business of Publishing', in Drummond Bone (ed.), *The Cambridge Companion to Byron* (Cambridge: Cambridge University Press, 2004), 27.

73. MacCarthy, *Byron*, 158.

74. Ibid. 160.

75. Byron had little time for the age of chivalry and what he called 'monstrous medieval mummeries'. Quoted in Marc Girouard, *The Return to Camelot: Chivalry and the English Gentleman* (New Haven: Yale University Press, 1981), 33.

76. Peter Cochran, 'Introduction', in Cochran (ed.), *Byron and Orientalism* (Newcastle: Cambridge Scholars Press, 2006), 2–3.

77. Particularly informative on this is Paolo Capuzzo, *Culture del consumo* (Bologna: Il Mulino, 2006), pt. I.

78. Ibid. 8–9.

79. Frances Wilson, 'Introduction', in Wilson (ed.), *Byromania: Portraits of the Artist in Nineteenth and Twentieth-Century Culture* (Basingstoke: Macmillan, 1999), 5.

80. Ibid. 4.

81. Jerome Christensen, *Lord Byron's Strength: Romantic Writing and Commercial Society* (Baltimore: Johns Hopkins University Press, 1993), p. xvi.

82. Ibid. 13, 192.

83. MacCarthy, *Byron*, 290.

84. On this development, see G. M. Trevelyan's classic *English Social History: A Survey of Six Centuries* (1942; London: Book Club Associates, 1973), 487–8.

85. Christine Kenyon Jones, 'Fantasy and Transfiguration: Byron and His Portraits', in Wilson (ed.), *Byromania*, 109.

86. J.-G. Lockhart, *The Life of Sir Walter Scott, Bart.* (abridged from the larger work) (Edinburgh: Adam & Charles, 1871), 537 and 582.

87. Wilson, *Life of Walter Scott*, 150–4.

88. Sassoon also stresses the technique Scott had for making his readers identify with his heroes. See *Culture of the Europeans*, 149.

89. Sir Walter Scott, *Ivanhoe* (1819; Harmondsworth: Penguin, 1994), 32 and 41.

90. See Michel Pastoureau, *Une histoire symbolique du Moyen Age occidental* (Paris: Seuil, 2004), 332–3.

91. On the origins of the imaginative hedonism of the middle class, see Colin Campbell, *The Romantic Ethic and the Spirit of Modern Consumerism* (Oxford: Blackwell, 1987).

92. In an essay in which he compared Scott, Racine, and Shakespeare, Hazlitt found the Scottish author to be more of a compiler than an inventer. His talent, he claimed, consisted 'in bringing the materials together and leaving them to produce their own effect'. 'Sir Walter's forte', he added, 'is in the richness and variety of his materials, and Shakespeare's in the working them up.' Whereas the latter was dramatic, Scott was descriptive; his focus was not the soul but rather 'the external imagery or machinery of passion'. William Hazlitt, 'Scott, Racine, and Shakespeare', in Hazlitt, *The Plain Speaker* (London: George Bell, 1903), 478–9, 484, 487.

93. William Hazlitt, *The Spirit of the Age 1825* (Menston: Scolar Press, 1971), 147.

94. Andrew Elfenbein, 'Byron: Gender and Sexuality' in Bone (ed.), *Cambridge Companion*, 61.

95. Ibid.

96. Quoted in Lockhart, *The Life of Sir Walter Scott*, ii. 397. Quoted in Roberts, 'Sir Walter Scott's Contributions', 209.

97. Trevelyan, *English Social History*, 488.

98. W. M. Thackeray, *Rebecca and Rowena* (1850; London: Hesperus, 2002), 5. This view was echoed by Victor Hugo. See Pastoureau, *Une histoire symbolique*, 332.

99. Scott, *Ivanhoe*, 299.

100. The seductiveness of Rebecca was a product of a blend of her beauty and also her elaborate clothing and jewellery. 'Her form was exquisitely symmetrical, and was shown to advantage by a sort of Eastern dress, which she wore according to the fashion of the females of her nation,' Scott wrote. 'Her turban of yellow silk suited well with the darkness of her complexion. The brilliancy of her eyes, the superb arch of her eyebrows, her well-formed aquiline nose, her teeth as white as pearl, and the profusion of her sable tresses, which, each arranged in its own little spiral of twisted curls, fell down upon as much of a lovely neck and bosom as a simarre of the richest Persian silk, exhibiting flowers in their natural colours embossed upon a purple background, permitted to be visible.' The reader is told nothing of Rowena's physique but Rebecca's womanly curves are subtlely evoked. Sex is absent but the suggestion of sexual allure is not. 'Of the golden and pearl-studded clasps which closed her vest from the throat to the waist, the three uppermost were lest unfastened on account of the heat,' the novelist continued; and this 'enlarged the prospect to which we allude. A diamond necklace, with pendants of inestimable value, were by this means also made more conspicuous.' Rebecca is placed outside the conventional boundaries of good taste. 'The feather of an ostrich, fastened in her turban by an agraffe set with brilliants, was another distinction of the beautiful Jewess', Scott noted, that was 'scoffed and sneered at by the proud dames who sat above her.' However, the scoffing of these ladies conceals their secret envy. Scott, *Ivanhoe*, 82–3.

101. Daniel Defoe, *Roxana* (1724; Harmondsworth: Penguin, 1987). For the dance and Roxana's dress, see pp. 219–22. See Ros Ballanter, 'Performing *Roxana*: The Oriental Woman as the Sign of Luxury in Eighteenth-century Fictions', in Maxine Berg and Elizabeth Eger (eds.), *Luxury in the Eighteenth Century: Debates, Desires and Delectable Goods* (Basingstoke: Palgrave, 2003), 165–77.

102. Lockhart, *Life of Sir Walter Scott*, 786.

103. Captain Gronow, *His Reminiscences of Regency and Victorian Life 1810–1860*, ed. Christopher Hibbert (1862–6; London: Kyle Cathrie 1991), 21.

104. The gathering at St Peter's Field in Manchester in August 1819 was charged by the cavalry and resulted in eleven deaths and four hundred injured, among whom there were many women and children. This brutal action, which became known—in mock-ironic reference to the battle of Waterloo—as the Peterloo massacre, signalled the inability of the forces of order to come to terms with political reform and popular aspirations.

105. Gronow, *His Reminiscences*, 30.

106. Trevelyan, *English Social History*, 492.

107. Steven Parissien, *George IV: The Grand Entertainment* (London: John Murray, 2001).

108. Ibid. 304.

109. On the court of Elizabeth I, see R. Malcolm Smuts, 'Art and the Material Culture of Majesty in Early Stuart England', in Smuts (ed.), *The Stuart Court and Europe: Essays in Politics and Political Culture* (Cambridge: Cambridge University Press, 1996). *Kenilworth* was published in Jan. 1821 and the most magnificent segment of the novel recounts the visit of Queen Elizabeth to Kenilworth Castle. Scott evokes the celebrated splendour of the Elizabethan court in descriptions of the nobles and the pageantry that surround the visit. The queen herself is the central figure and is 'arrayed in the most splendid manner, and blazing with jewels'. Leicester, the host, 'glittered like a gold image with jewels and cloth of gold'. An equestrian cavalcade, music, torches, and floating pageants with an Arthurian theme provide a spectacle of unique beauty and suggestiveness. Together, these elements enact a 'work of enchantment' on all who witness it.

110. Of relevance here is David Cannadine, 'The Context, Performace and Meaning of Ritual: The British Monarchy and the "Invention of Tradition", c.1820–1977', in Eric Hobsbawm and Terence Ranger (eds.), *The Invention of Tradition* (Cambridge: Cambridge University Press, 1983).

111. Christopher Hibbert, *George IV: Regent and King 1811–1830* (London: Allen Lane, 1973), 191.

112. Ibid. 191–2.

113. For the development of this polemic in France, see Landes, *Visualizing the Nation*.

114. See Kenneth Baker, *George IV: A Life in Caricature* (London: Thames & Hudson, 1995).

115. See ibid. 366. Her dedication of *Emma* to him has been seen as a mark of approval. In fact it occurred at his own invitation. Saul David, *Prince of Pleasure: The Prince of Wales and the Making of the Regency* (London: Little Brown, 1998), 366.

116. William Makepeace Thackeray, *The Works*, x. *Roundabout Papers, The Four Georges: The English Humourists* (London; Smith, Elder, 1888), 353.

117. Ibid. 357.

118. Ibid. 361.

119. Ibid.

CHAPTER 2

1. Cited in G. M. Trevelyan, *English Social History: A Survey of Six Centuries—Chaucer to Queen Victoria* (1944; London: Longman, 1973), 473.

2. Ibid. 527.

3. Mary Robinson, 'Present State of the Manners, Society, etc. etc. of the Metropolis of England', *Monthly Magazine* (10 Aug. 1800), 35. The other instalments were published on 10 Sept., 10 Oct., and 10 Nov. 1800.

4. Ibid.

5. Robinson, 'Present State of the Manners', *Monthly Magazine* (10 Sept. 1800), 138.

6. Robinson, 'Present State of the Manners', *Monthly Magazine* (10 Oct. 1800), 228.

7. Sales increased steadily in the following years and by 1829 seven morning papers were selling an average of 28,000 copies while six evening papers had average sales of 11,000. Several Sunday newspapers that are still published were founded in this period, including the *Observer* in 1791, *The Sunday Times* in 1822, and the *News of the World* in 1843. See Judith Flanders, *Consuming Passions: Leisure and Pleasure in Victorian Britain* (London: Harper, 2006), ch. 4, esp. pp. 125 and 142.

8. Robinson, 'Present State of the Manners' (10 Nov. 1800), 305.

9. Ibid.

10. Flanders, *Consuming Passions*, 125.

11. William Hazlitt, 'On Londoners and Country People', *The Plain Speaker: Opinions on Men, Books and Things* (London: George Bell, 1903), 91–2.

12. Ibid. 104.

13. Maurice Guerrini, *Napoleon and Paris: Thirty Years of History* (1967; London: Cassell, 1970), 109.

14. Ibid. 119.

15. Alistair Horne, *Seven Ages of Paris* (London: Macmillan, 2002), 211–13.

16. Stella Margetson, *Regency London* (London: Cassell, 1971), 48.

17. Carolly Erickson, *Josephine: A Life of the Empress* (1998; London: Robson Books, 2004), 274.

18. Margetson, *Regency London*, 6.

19. Ibid. 127.

20. Captain Gronow, *His Reminiscences of Regency and Victorian Life 1810–1860*, ed. Christopher Hibbert (London: Kyle Cathie, 1991), 74–5.

21. Michael Levey, *Sir Thomas Lawrence* (London: Yale University Press, 2005), 52–3.

22. Sébastien Allard, 'Between the Novel and History: French Portraiture towards 1835', in Robert Rosenblum et al. *Citizens and Kings: Portraits in the Age of Revolution, 1760–1830* (London: Royal Academy, 2007), 37.

23. Gronow, *His Reminiscences*, 262.

24. T. H. White, *The Age of Scandal* (1950; Harmondsworth: Penguin, 1964), 18.

25. Robert Southey, *Letters from England* (1807; Gloucester: Sutton, 1984), 449.

26. See Alison Adburgham, *Silver Fork Society: Fashionable Life and Literature from 1814 to 1840* (London: Constable, 1983), 22–5. On p. 1 the author reports that the term was coined by Hazlitt in an essay in the *Examiner*.

27. Ibid. 1–2.

28. The most typical examples were authored by Hook; Catherine Gore; Marguerite, Countess of Blessington; and Benjamin Disraeli.

29. The novels were widely criticized for their supposed vulgarity and bad taste. 'The worst fault of such productions', comments Mr Vyvyan, a character in Catherine Gore's *Women As They Are*, 'is the distortion of their portraiture—the writers or painters generally move in so base a sphere, that their upturned and wandering eyes necessarily disfigure the object of their art' (Adburgham, *Silver Fork Society*, 171). The majority of readers probably never perceived such distortions and, if they did, they were not concerned with them. They derived in many cases similar pleasure from the novels as they gained from reading historical romances and exotic adventures.

30. 'Silver fork' novels owed something to Jane Austen. Indeed, Mrs Gore wrote in the preface to *Pin Money* that her aim was to 'attempt to transfer the familiar narrative of Miss Austen to a higher sphere of society', ibid. 211–12. While fashionable society is glimpsed in Austen and there are some striking caricatures of titled personages, provincial society and the country gentry provide most of her raw material.

31. Andrew Elfenbein, 'Silver Fork Byron and the Image of Regency England', in Frances Wilson (ed.), *Byromania: Portraits of the Artist in Nineteenth and Twentieth-Century Culture* (Basingstoke: Palgrave Macmillan, 1999), 79–80.

32. This hypothesis is advanced in Peter McNeil, ' "That Doubtful Gender": Macaroni Dress and Male Sexualities', *Fashion Theory*, 3/4 (1999), 411–48. See also, by the same author, 'Macaroni Masculinities', *Fashion Theory*, 4/4 (2000), 373–404.

33. Colin McDowell, *The Man of Fashion: Peacock Males and Perfect Gentlemen* (London: Thames & Hudson, 1997), 45.

34. Ian Kelly, *Beau Brummell: The Ultimate Dandy* (London: Hodder and Stoughton, 2005), 167.

35. Joan DeJean, *The Essence of Style: How the French Invented High Fashion, Fine Food, Chic Cafes, Style, Sophistication and Glamour* (New York: The Free Press, 2005), 161–3.

36. See Christopher Breward, *Fashion* (Oxford: Oxford University Press, 2003), 162.

37. Gronow, *His Reminiscences*, 469.

38. Richard Sennett, *The Fall of Public Man* (Cambridge: Cambridge University Press, 1977), 161.

39. Thomas Carlyle, *Sartor Resartus*, in *Works*, iii (London: Chapman and Hall, 1885), 184.

40. William Hazlitt, 'On Fashion', in *Sketches and Essays and Winterslow*, ed. W. Carew Hazlitt (London: Bell, 1912), 146.

41. Ibid. 147.

42. Trevelyan, *English Social History*, 474.

43. Robinson, 'Present State of the Manners' (10 Oct. 1800), 228.

44. Hazlitt, 'On Londoners and Country People', 89.

45. Ibid. 212. Gronow claims that the clubs were still almost exclusively restricted to the aristocratic world. See *His Reminiscences*, 76–7.

46. Gronow, *His Reminiscences*, 74.

47. Kelly, *Beau Brummell*, 268.

48. His aloofness may have been related to his sexuality, which remains a matter of speculation. Kelly suggests that he may have been homosexual and notes that he spent much time among courtesans.

49. Cited ibid. 206.

50. Southey, *Letters from England*, 291.

51. Horne, *Seven Ages of Paris*, 187.

52. Southey, *Letters from England*, 447–8.

53. This point is made by Andrew Elfenbein in 'Byron: Gender and Sexuality', in Drummond Bone (ed.), *The Cambridge Companion to Byron* (Cambridge: Cambridge University Press, 2004), 59.

54. See Venetia Murray, *High Society in the Regency Period, 1788–1830* (London: Viking, 1998), 30–1.

55. Ibid. 219–23.

56. Kelly, *Beau Brummell*, 264–5.

57. Robinson, 'Present State of the Manners' (1 Aug. 1800), 36; Hazlitt, 'On Londoners and Country People', 104.

58. Hazlitt, 'On Londoners and Country People', 104.

59. Elizabeth Burns, *Theatricality: A Study of Convention in the Theatre and in Social Life* (London: Longman, 1972), 10.

60. Fiona MacCarthy, *Byron: Life and Legend* (2002; London: Faber & Faber, 2003), 219, 256–7.

61. Flanders, *Consuming Passions*, 295.

62. Southey, *Letters from England*, 98.

63. F. W. J. Hemmings, *Theatre and State in France, 1760–1905* (Cambridge: Cambridge University Press, 1994), 123.

64. Ibid. 4.

65. Marie-Louise Biver, *Le Paris de Napoléon* (Paris: Plon, 1963), 132.

66. Charles Hindley, *The True History of Tom and Jerry* (London: Reeves and Turner, 1888), 2.

67. Ibid. 5.

68. Ibid. 11.

69. Adburgham, *Silver Fork Society*, 60–1.

70. Charles Dickens, *Sketches by Boz: Illustrative of Every-Day Life and Every-Day People* (1839; London: Oxford University Press, 1957), 55.

71. For full details of her varied career, including her rise and fall, see Paula Byrne, *Perdita: The Life of Mary Robinson* (2004; Harper Perennial, 2000).

72. Russell Jackson, *Victorian Theatre* (London: Black, 1989), 10.

73. Flanders, *Consuming Passions*, 313.

74. Jackson, *Victorian Theatre*, 2.

75. Percy Fitzgerald (1892), quoted ibid. 217–19.

76. Southey, *Letters from England*, 50.

77. Kelly, *Beau Brummell*, 190.

78. Evelyn Farr, *Before the Deluge: Parisian Society in the Reign of Louis XVI* (London: Owen, 1994), 74.

79. Flanders, *Consuming Passions*, 42.

80. Maxine Berg, 'New Commodities, Luxuries and their Consumers in Eighteenth-Century England', in Berg and Helen Clifford (eds.), *Consumers and Luxury: Consumer Culture in Europe 1650–1850* (Manchester: Manchester University Press, 1999), 63–85, at 65.

81. Maxine Berg, *Luxury and Pleasure in Eightenth-Century Britain* (Oxford: Oxford University Press, 2005), 9.

82. See Colin Campbell, *The Romantic Ethic and the Spirit of Modern Consumerism* (Oxford: Blackwell, 1987).

83. Maxine Berg, 'Asian Luxuries and the Making of the European Consumer Revolution', in Berg and Elizabeth Eger (eds.), *Luxury in the Eighteenth Century: Debates, Desires and Delectable Goods* (Basingstoke: Palgrave, 2003), 228–40, at 230.

84. Flanders, *Consuming Passions*, 62–74.

85. Richard Sennett, *The Fall of Public Man* (Cambridge: Cambridge University Press, 1977), 146.

86. Dickens, *Sketches by Boz*, 55.

87. Hazlitt, 'On Londoners and Country People', 89–90.

88. Ibid. 91.

89. Ibid. 92.

90. Rosalind H. Williams, *Dream Worlds: Mass Consumption in Late Nineteenth Century France* (Berkeley and Los Angeles: University of California Press, 1982), 9.

91. Walter Benjamin, *The Arcades Project* (Cambridge, Mass.: Harvard University Press, 1999), 63–74.

92. Ibid. 271.

93. Ibid. 272.

94. Williams, *Dream Worlds*, 34.

95. Ibid. 17.

96. Erika Diane Rappaport, *Shopping for Pleasure: Women in the Making of London's West End* (Princeton: Princeton University Press, 2000), 5.

97. Jackson Lears, *Fables of Abundance: A Cultural History of Advertising in America* (New York: Basic, 1994), 72.

98. Jackson Lears, 'Beyond Veblen: Rethinking Consumer Culture in America', in Simon J. Bronner, (ed.), *Consuming Visions: Accumulation and Display of Goods in America, 1880–1920* (New York: Norton, 1989), 77.

99. Williams, *Dream Worlds*, 61.

100. Quoted ibid.

101. Ibid. 63.

102. Ibid. 65.

103. Ibid. 69.

104. Ibid. 71.

105. Ibid. 71.

106. Michael Miller, *The Bon Marché: Bourgeois Culture and the Department Store 1869–1920* (Princeton: Princeton University Press, 1981), 165. See also Rappaport, *Shopping for Pleasure* and Bill Lancaster, *The Department Store: A Social History* (Leicester: Leicester University Press, 1995).

107. Miller, *Bon Marché*, 167.

108. William Leach, *Land of Desire: Merchants, Power and the Rise of a New American Culture* (New York: Pantheon, 1993), 9.

CHAPTER 3

1. Lesley Blanch (ed.) *The Game of Hearts: Harriet Wilson and Her Memoirs* (London: Gryphon, 1957) (memoirs first published 1828).

2. Lesley Blanch, 'Introduction', ibid. 32.

3. See Hallie Rubenhold (ed.), *Harris's List or Covent-Garden Ladies: Sex and the City in Georgian Britain* (London: Tempus, 2005), 22 and *passim*.

4. William Makepeace Thackeray, *Vanity Fair* (1848; London: Penguin, 1985), 738.

5. Fiona MacCarthy, *Byron: Life and Legend* (2002; London: Faber and Faber, 2003), 365.

6. Tracy C. Davis, *Actresses as Working Women: Their Social Identity in Victorian Culture* (London: Routledge, 1991), p. 82.

7. Frédérique Patureau, *Le Palais Garnier dans la société parisienne, 1875–1914* (Liège: Mardega, 1991), 362.

8. Mary Robinson, 'Present State of the Manners, Society, etc. etc. of the Metropolis of England', *Monthly Magazine* (10 Nov. 1800), 305.

9. Ibid. On Robinson as a fashion icon, see Paula Byrne, *Perdita: The Life of Mary Robinson* (2004; Harper Perennial, 2005), 27–8, 178–9, 203–9.

10. Philip Mansel, *The Court of France, 1789–1830* (Cambridge: Cambridge University Press, 1988), 191.

11. Quoted in Harold Kurtz, *The Empress Eugénie, 1826–1920* (London: Hamish Hamilton, 1964), 50.

12. Polly Binder, *The Truth about Cora Pearl* (London: Wiedenfeld & Nicolson, 1986), 40–1.

13. Michelle Sapori, *Rose Bertin: Ministre des modes de Marie-Antoinette* (Paris: Éditions de l'Institut français de la mode, 2003), 118.

14. Claire Wilcox, 'Introduction', in Wilcox (ed.), *The Golden Age of Couture: Paris and London 1947–1957* (London: V&A Publications, 2007), 12. On Worth, see Diana de Marly, *Worth: Father of Haute Couture* (London: Elm Tree, 1980).

15. Sapori, *Rose Bertin*, 119.

16. Quoted in Siegfried Kracauer, *Offenbach and the Paris of his Time* (London: Constable, 1937), 175.

17. John Bierman, *Napoleon III and his Carnival Empire* (London: John Murray, 1988).

18. Kracauer's study *Offenbach* remains the most illuminating study of the composer and his place in the culture of the age.

19. See Mansel, *Court of France*, 97–112.

20. T. J. Clark, *The Painting of Modern Life: Paris in the Art of Manet and his Followers* (London: Thames and Hudson, 1990), 35–6.

21. Ibid. 66.

22. Virginia Rounding, *Grandes Horizontales: The Lives and Legends of Four Nineteenth-Century Courtesans* (London: Bloomsbury, 2003), 3.

23. The contessa was received at court in 1856. See Kurtz, *Empress Eugénie*, 94.

24. Alain Decaux, *Amours Second Empire* (Paris: Hachette, 1958), 198.

25. Ibid. 170.

26. Simone de Beauvoir, *Le Deuxième Sexe*, ii. *L'Expérience vécue* (1949; Paris: Gallimard, 1976), 444.

27. Quoted in Patrice Higonnet, *Paris: Capital of the World* (Cambridge, Mass.: Harvard University Press, 2002), 301.

28. Alexandre Dumas *fils*, *La Dame aux camélias* (1852; Paris: Calmann-Lévy, 1965), 115.

29. De Beauvoir, *Le Deuxième Sexe*, ii. 451. On La Païva, see Rounding, *Grandes Horizontales*, ch. 4.

30. Émile Le Senne, *Madame de Païva: Étude de psychologie et d'histoire* (Paris: Daragon, 1910), 16–38.

31. Ibid. 71. On her residence, see Rounding, *Grandes Horizontales*, ch. 9.

32. Jean-Marie Moulin, 'The Second Empire; Art and Society', in Arnold Jolles et al., *The Second Empire: Art in France Under Napoleon III* (Philadelphia: Philadelphia Museum of Art, 1978), 12.

33. Ibid.

34. For Kurtz, the painting, 'flattered their mediocre sense of beauty, their modest aspirations to immortality in crimson and gold'. See *Empress Eugénie*, 63–4.

35. Joanna Richardson, *La Vie Parisienne 1852–1870* (London: Studio, 1971), 71.

36. Ibid. 72.

37. Joanna Richardson, *The Courtesans: The Demi-Monde in 19th Century France* (London: Weidenfeld and Nicolson, 1967) contains accounts of twelve of the most famous courtesans of the Second Empire.

38. Philippe Perrot, *Le Luxe: Une richesse entre faste et confort xviiie–xixe siècle* (Paris: Seuil, 1995), 184.

39. As Perrot expresses the appeal of the courtesan to the banker, industrialist, or speculator: 'for the aristocracy, appearance was its reality, its necessity and often its ruin; in the bourgeois world it is above all a shop window', ibid. 189.

40. Cited ibid. 183.

41. See Dumas, *La Dame aux camélias*, 150–1.

42. Colin Campbell, *The Romantic Ethic and the Spirit of Modern Consumerism* (Oxford: Blackwell, 1987), 60.

43. Alain Corbin, *Women for Hire: Prostitution and Sexuality in France after 1850* (Cambridge, Mass.: Harvard University Press, 1990), 133–4.

44. Ibid. 96.

45. Ibid. 55.

46. Ibid.

47. Quoted ibid. 62. See also Le Senne, *Madame de Païva*, 34–6.

48. Binder, *Truth about Cora Pearl*, 40, 66.

49. Many authors have tried to identify the principal source, Decaux opting for Anna Deslions—largely on the basis of her unredeemed vulgarity—while Jean Chalon prefers the statuesque beauty Valtesse de la Bigne. Richardson deploys several authorities including, indirectly, Zola himself, to support Blanche d'Antigny. See Decaux, *Amours Second Empire*, 139; Jean Chalon, *Liane de Pougy: Courtisane, princesse et sainte* (Paris: Flammarion, 1994), caption to illustration; Richardson, *Courtesans*, 9. The reigning queen of Offenbach's operettas, Hortense Schneider, has also been indicated as the main inspiration since she had in common with Nana a stage career and a liaison with the Prince of Wales (thinly disguised as 'the Prince of Scotland' in *Nana*). See Douglas Parme, 'Introduction' to Émile Zola, *Nana* (Oxford: Oxford University Press, 1992), p. xiv.

50. Zola, *Nana*, 274.

51. Ibid. 306.

52. Ibid. 360.

53. Ibid. 358.

54. Ibid. 353.

55. Ibid. 355–6.

56. Ibid. 274–5.

57. Ibid. 274–6.

58. Dumas, *La Dame aux camélias*, 231.

59. See Alan Krell, *Manet and the Painters of Contemporary Life* (London; Thames and Hudson, 1996) chs. 2 and 3.

60. Anon., 'Journal d'un fantasiste: Sur la galanterie', *Gil Blas*, 3 July 1895, p. 1.

61. See Noémi Hepp, 'La Galanterie', in Pierre Nora (ed.), *Les Lieux de mémoire*, iii (Paris: Gallimard, 1997), 3702.

62. Lucinda Jarrett, *Stripping in Time: A History of Erotic Dancing* (London: HarperCollins, 1997), 35.

63. Paul Derval, *The Folies Bergère* (London: Brown Watson, 1955), 14.

64. Javier Figuero and Marie-Hélène Carbonel, *La Véritable Biographie de La Belle Otero et de la Belle Époque* (Paris: Fayard, 2003), 106.

65. Quoted in Massimo Grillandi, *La bella Otero* (Milan: Rusconi, 1980), 142.

66. La Belle Otero, *Souvenirs et vie intime* (1926; Monaco: Sauret, 1993), 240.

67. Colette, *Mes apprentissages, La treille musicale, Colette, une vie une œuvre* (Paris: Club France Loisirs, 1997) (*Mes apprentissages* first published 1936), 16–18. See also Judith Thurman, *A Life of Colette* (London: Bloomsbury, 1999), 66–7.

68. See Albert Flament, *Le Bal du pré-Catalan* (Paris: Fayard, 1946), 107: 'Otero induces nostalgia for Seville, but, like a flower, Liane de Pougy fuels love for France.'

69. Jean Cocteau, *Reines de la France* (Paris: Grasset, 1952), 142.

70. Jean Cocteau, *Reines de la France* (Paris: Grasset, 1952), 30.

71. See Enrico Lucherini and Matteo Spinola, *C'era questo, c'era quello* (Milan: Mondadori, 1984), 27.

72. Jean Chalon, *de Pougy*, 85–100.

73. Jean-Yves Tadié, *Marcel Proust I* (Paris: Gallimard, 1996), 75.

74. Max Beerbohm, *Zuleika Dobson, or An Oxford Love Story* (1911; London: Folio Society, 1966).

75. La Belle Otero, *Souvenirs et vie intime*, 35.

76. Quoted in Charles Castle, *La Belle Otero: The Last Great Courtesan* (London: Michael Joseph, 1981), 113.

77. This anecdote first appeared in Hugo, *Vingt ans maître d'hôtel chez Maxim's* (Paris: Amiot Dumont, 1951), 32–3. Armand Lanoux quotes from this source in *Amours 1900* (Paris: Hachette, 1961), 167–8, and so does James Laver in *The Age of Optimism: Manners and Morals, 1848–1914*

(London: Weidenfeld & Nicolson, 1966), 238–9. In Chalon, *Liane de Pougy* the scene is not Maxim's but the Casino in Monte Carlo (pp. 73–4). The source is Albert Flament who, according to his own testimony, was an eyewitness of the scene, that took place on 6 Feb. 1897. Curiously, two biographers of Otero reverse the story and suggest that it was their subject who delivered the humiliation by appearing devoid of jewels. See esp. Grillandi, *La bella Otero*, 228. Castle, in *La Belle Otero*, 64, also has Otero as the winner, but her victim is not de Pougy but another lesser known courtesan, Diane de Chandel. It is impossible to separate fact from legend here but, given her reputation for excessive use of jewellery, it is reasonable to suppose that the victim of the prank was indeed Otero.

78. Chalon, *de Pougy*, 76.

79. De Beauvoir, *The Second Sex* (1949; London: Everyman's Library, 1993), 597.

80. Abigail Solomon-Godeau, 'The Other Side of Venus: The Visual Economy of Feminine Display', in Victoria de Grazia with Ellen Furlough (eds.), *The Sex of Things: Gender and Consumption in Historical Perspective* (Berkeley and Los Angeles: University of California Press, 1996), 131.

81. The quality of sexual 'awarishness' is examined in Maria-Elena Buszek, 'Representing "Awarishness": Burlesque, Feminist Transgression and the 19th-century Pin-up', *Drama Review*, 43/4 (1999), 141–62.

82. Umberto Notari, *Signore sole: Interviste e ritratti delle celebri artiste* (Milan: Edizioni del Giornale Verde e Azzurro, *c*.1903), 17–24.

83. Ibid. On Cavalieri, see Stephen Gundle, ' "Venus on Earth": Lina Cavalieri and the Professionalization of Italian Beauty between the Fin-de-Siècle and the Belle Époque', *Italian Studies*, 62/1 (2007), 45–60.

84. Michael Levey, *Sir Thomas Lawrence* (London: Yale University Press, 2005), 90.

85. See Stephen Gundle, 'Mapping the Origins of Glamour: Giovanni Boldini, Paris and the Belle Époque', *Journal of European Studies*, 29/3 (1999), 269–95.

86. The reference to de Mérode originally appeared in the section of de Beauvoir, *The Second Sex* dedicated to prostitutes and courtesans, pp. 595–604. De Mérode's name was struck from later editions of the book.

87. Liane de Pougy, *Les Sensations de Mlle de la Bringue* (Paris: Albin Michel, 1904), 123. Italics and capitals occur in the original text. For de Mérode's own account of this episode, see Cléo de Mérode, *La Ballet de ma vie* (1955; Paris: Pierre Horay, 1985), 147–57.

88. *Gil Blas* printed a satirical drawing of the statue looking very lifelike, complete with pubic hair. Five women and a man are shown studying it closely. Issue of 26 June 1896, p. 5.

89. Octave Uzanne, *Parisiennes de ce temps en leurs divers milieux, états et conditions* (Paris: Mercure de France, 1910), 442.

90. Chalon, *de Pougy*, 75.

91. See La Belle Otero, *Souvenirs*, 314 for the quotation and 179 on Ollstreder.

92. Mario Praz, *The Romantic Agony* (1933; London: Oxford University Press, 1970), 207.

93. Grillandi, *La bella Otero*, 16.

94. Lanoux, *Amours 1900*, 163.

95. Hugo, *Vingt ans maître d'hôtel*, 186–220.

96. Mary Blume, *Côte d'Azur: Inventing the French Riviera* (London: Thames and Hudson, 1992), 58.

97. Ibid. 63.

98. They are still referred to occasionally in this manner. See Claude Dufresne, *Trois Grâces de la Belle Époque* (Paris: Bartillat, 2003).

CHAPTER 4

1. See Eric Homberger, *Mrs Astor's New York: Money and Social Power in a Gilded Age* (New Haven and London: Yale University Press, 2002).

2. Amanda Mackenzie Stuart, *Consuelo and Alva Vanderbilt: The Story of a Mother and Daughter in the Gilded Age* (2005; London: Harper Perennial, 2006), 57–64.

3. Maureen E. Montgomery, *'Gilded Prostitution': Status, Money and Transatlantic Marriages, 1870–1914* (London: Routledge, 1989), 49.

4. Edith Wharton, *The Buccaneers* (1938; London: Fourth Estate, 1993), 155. His circle included wealthy plutocrats, members of the 'fast set', and others considered undesirable by many staid aristocrats. One royal mistress, the socialite Alice Keppel, who controlled access to the king, was privately dubbed a latter-day Pompadour by the American Nancy Astor (née Langthorne), who dismissed her as 'bejewelled and airified'. See James Fox, *The Langthorne Sisters* (1998; London: Granta, 1999), 115.

5. James Camplin, *The Rise of the Plutocrats: Wealth and Power in Edwardian England* (London, Constable, 1978), 103; F. M. L. Thompson, *English Landed Society in the Nineteenth Century* (London: Routledge & Kegan Paul, 1963), 302.

6. See Fox, *Langthorne Sisters*, 84–5.

7. Camplin, *Rise of the Plutocrats*, 103.

8. Keith Middlemas, *Pursuit of Pleasure: High Society in the 1900s* (London: Gordon and Cremonesi, 1977), 39.

9. Vita Sackville-West, *The Edwardians* (1952; London: Arrow, 1960), 95.

10. On the programmatic nature of luxury as aggressive, exhibitionist, and demanding of recognition, see Alberto Abruzzese, 'Il lusso', in Abruzzese, *Archeologie dell'immaginario: Segmenti dell'industria culturale tra '800 e '900* (Naples: Liguori, 1988), 54–81, esp. 54–7.

11. Middlemas, *Pursuit of Pleasure*, 56.

12. Ibid. 120.

13. Montgomery, *'Gilded Prostitution'*, 71.

14. Ibid. 153. See also Eric Hobsbawm, *The Age of Empire 1875–1914* (London: Weidenfeld and Nicolson, 1987), 184–6.

15. Many impoverished and displaced aristocrats found gainful employment in this and subsequent periods by instructing the new rich and the middle classes in matters of taste or in making or selling articles and services that carried by association an elitist connotation.

16. Montgomery, 'Gilded Prostitution', 46.

17. Molly W. Berger, 'The Rich Man's City: Hotels and Mansions of Gilded Age New York', *Journal of Decorative and Propaganda Arts*, 25 (2005), 46–71, at 48 and 68.

18. Ibid. 47.

19. Thorstein Veblen, *Theory of the Leisure Class* (1899; Boston: Houghton Mifflin, 1973), 64.

20. Ibid. 106–7.

21. See Fox, *Langthorne Sisters*, 8–9.

22. Montgomery, 'Gilded Prostitution', 150.

23. Veblen, *Theory of the Leisure Class*, 96–7.

24. See Mackenzie Stuart, *Consuelo and Alva*, ch. 4.

25. Montgomery, 'Gilded Prostitution', 140–1.

26. Consuelo Vanderbilt Balsan, *The Glitter and the Gold* (London: Heinneman, 1953), 41.

27. Ibid. 42.

28. David Cannadine, *The Decline and Fall of the British Aristocracy* (New Haven: Yale University Press, 1990), 350.

29. See Ross McKibbin, *Classes and Cultures: England 1918–1951* (Oxford: Oxford University Press, 1998), 23.

30. Walter Bagehot, *The English Constitution* (1867; Eastbourne: Sussex Academic Press, 1997), 146.

31. James Laver, *Taste and Fashion: From the French Revolution to the Present Day* (London: Harrap, 1937), 19.

32. Sackville-West, *Edwardians*, 12.

33. David Sinclair, *Dynasty: The Astors and Their Times* (New York: Beaufort Books, 1984), 5–6.

34. Fox, *Langthorne Sisters*, 11 and 30.

35. Quoted ibid. 122.

36. Maureen E. Montgomery, *Displaying Women: Spectacles of Leisure in Edith Wharton's New York* (New York: Routledge, 1998), 12–14.

37. Anon., 'Society; So Called', *Los Angeles Times*, 4 July 1897, p. 10.

38. Montgomery, *Displaying Women*, 147.

39. Ibid. 130.

40. Veblen, *Theory of the Leisure Class*, 72.

41. Edith Wharton, *The Custom of the Country* (1913; London: Virago, 1995), 15.

42. The hotel was demolished, amid considerable protest, in 1929. The short lives and brusque ends of the grand New York hotels of the 1890s is examined in Bernard L. Jim, '"Wrecking the Joint": The Razing of City Hotels in the First Half of the Twentieth Century', *Journal of Decorative and Propaganda Arts*, 25 (2005), 288–314.

43. Berger, 'Rich Man's City', 68.

44. Ibid. 63.

45. Caroline Seebohm, *The Man Who Was Vogue: The Life and Times of Condé Nast* (London: Weidenfeld and Nicolson, 1982), 102.

46. Ibid. 42.

47. Erika Diane Rappaport, *Shopping for Pleasure: Women and the Making of London's West End* (Princeton: Princeton University Press, 2000), 8–9.

48. Quoted ibid. 4.

49. Seebohm, *The Man Who Was Vogue*, 165.

50. Ibid. 166.

51. Diana Vreeland, *American Women of Style* (New York: The Costume Institute of the Metropolitan Museum of Art, 1975), page unnumbered.

52. Ibid. 182. See Veblen, *Theory of the Leisure Class*, 106–7.

53. Vreeland argued that there was 'a flash of mischief in her eyes and she was thought a trifle daring for her time'. *American Women of Style*, page unnumbered.

54. Fox, *Langthorne Sisters*, 49–50.

55. Veblen, *Theory of the Leisure Class*, 185.

56. Fox, *Langthorne Sisters*, 10.

57. Ibid. 165.

58. Lois W. Banner, *American Beauty* (New York: Knopf, 1983), 28–9.

59. Stanley Olson, *John Singer Sargent: His Portrait* (London: Barrie and Jenkins, 1986), 102.

60. For a full account of the episode, see Deborah Davis, *Strapless: John Singer Sargent and the Fall of Madame X* (Stroud: Sutton, 2004), chs. 11 and 12.

61. Dario Cecchi, *Giovanni Boldini* (Turin: UTET, 1962), 174. His portrait of Donna Franca Florio, the statuesque wife of Sicilian industrialist Ignazio Florio, was rejected by the latter on the grounds that, far from confirming his wife's position as 'Queen of Palermo', it portrayed 'a beautiful woman in the act of wiggling her hips, either before a mirror or worse: before the audience of a *caf'conc*'. Modifications were subsequently undertaken to tone down the general attitude and turn the glamorous portrait into a traditional depiction of a respectable woman.

62. Vanderbilt Balsan, *The Glitter and the Gold*, 61.

63. Alva Vanderbilt was probably ignorant of her reputation, and more especially of the fact that she enjoyed a liaison with Consuelo's father who, like other American millionaires, regularly crossed the Atlantic in his yacht *Valiant* to enjoy the pleasure of Paris. See Massimo Grillandi, *La bella Otero* (Milan: Rusconi, 1980), 167–8, 220.

64. Cecchi, *Giovanni Boldini*, 131.

65. Ibid. 274.

66. Ibid. 131.

67. See Rossana Bossaglia and Mario Quesada (eds.), *Gabriele d'Annunzio e la promozione delle Arti* (Milan: Mondadori/De Luca, 1988).

68. On d'Annunzio, see John Woodhouse, *Gabriele d'Annunzio: Defiant Archangel* (Oxford: Oxford University Press, 1998).

69. Rappaport, *Shopping for Pleasure*, 39.

70. Ibid. 184.

71. Judith Flanders, *Consuming Passions: Leisure and Pleasure in Victorian Britain* (London: Harper, 2006), 339.

72. Ibid. 122–3.

73. Quoted in Christopher Kent, 'Image and Reality: The Actress and Society', in Martha Vicinus (ed.), *A Widening Sphere: Changing Roles of Victorian Women* (Bloomington: Indiana University Press, 1977), 94.

74. Ibid. 164.

75. John Stokes, Michael R. Booth, and Susan Bassnett, 'Introduction', in *Bernhardt, Terry, Duse: The Actress in her Time* (Cambridge: Cambridge University Press, 1988), 5.

76. Ibid. 179.

77. Ibid. 183.

78. Bram Dijkstra, *Idols of Perversity: Fantasies of Feminine Evil in Fin-de-Siècle Culture* (New York: Oxford University Press, 1986).

79. Rita Felski, *Gender of Modernity* (Cambridge, Mass.: Harvard University Press, 1995), 139.

80. See Efrat Tseëlon, *The Masque of Femininity: The Presentation of Woman in Everyday Life* (London: Sage, 1995), ch. 1.

81. Camille Paglia, *The Birds* (London: BFI, 1998), 7.

82. See Joanna Richardson, *Sarah Bernhardt and her World* (London: Weidenfeld & Nicolson, 1977), 146.

83. Lucia Re, 'D'Annunzio, Duse, Wilde, Bernhardt: Author and Actress between Decadentism and Modernity', in Luca Somigli and Mario Moroni (eds.), *Italian Modernism: Italian Culture between Decadentism and the Avant-Garde* (Toronto: University of Toronto Press, 2004), 99.

84. Susan A. Glenn, *Female Spectacle: The Theatrical Roots of Modern Feminism* (Cambridge, Mass.: Harvard University Press, 2000), 12.

85. On one reception in New York, see Arthur Gold and Robert Fizdale, *The Divine Sarah: A Life of Sarah Bernhardt* (London; HarperCollins, 1992), 170.

86. See e.g. Corille Fraser, *Come to Dazzle: Sarah Bernhardt's Australian Tour* (Sydney: Currency, 1998).

87. Booth and Bassnett, 'Introduction', *Bernhardt, Terry, Duse*, 9.

88. See Fraser, *Come to Dazzle*, ch. 10.

89. Quoted in Anthony Glyn, *Elinor Glyn: A Biography* (London: Hutchinson, 1955), 49.

90. Edmund White, *Marcel Proust* (London: Penguin, 1999), 25 opts for the combination, broadly confirming the more nuanced account offered in Jean-Yves Tadié, *Marcel Proust I* (Paris: Gallimard, 1996). See esp. 206 and 656.

91. Marcel Proust, *Swann's Way*, in *Remembrance of Things Past I* (London: Penguin, 1983), 79.

92. Marcel Proust, *Within a Budding Grove*, ibid., 484–6.

93. See Laura Beatty, *Lillie Langtry: Manners, Masks and Morals* (London: Chatto & Windus, 1999), 234.

94. Abigail Solomon-Godeau, 'The Other Side of Venus: The Visual Economy of Feminine Display', in Victoria de Grazia with Ellen Furlogh (eds.), *The Sex of Things: Gender and Consumption in Historical Perspective* (Berkeley and Los Angeles: University of California Press, 1996).

95. Linda Nead, *Victorian Babylon: People, Streets and Images in Nineteenth Century London* (New Haven and London: Yale University Press, 2000), 188.

96. 'The last pleasure a working girl would deny herself, wrote one analyst, was the Sunday supplement, where she could find a fantasy retreat into a world of glamour, where actresses from working class backgrounds achieved fame and fortune, where chorus girls married millionaires and beauty contests gave hope to ordinary women that she, too, might be touched by glamour.' Banner, *American Beauty*, 200.

97. Peter Bailey has made a case for the Victorian barmaid as glamour icon. See his 'Parasexuality and Glamour: The Victorian Barmaid as Cultural Prototype', *Gender and History*, 2/5 (1990). For a critique of his argument see Stephen Gundle and Clino T. Castelli, *The Glamour System* (Basingstoke: Palgrave Macmillan, 2006), 12–13.

98. Anon., 'The Stage Craze', *Los Angeles Times*, 29 Mar. 1890, p. 3.

99. Ibid.

100. Pamela Horn, *High Society: The English Social Elite, 1880–1914* (London: Sutton, 1992), 90.

101. Anon., 'Money or Beauty?', *Los Angeles Times*, 28 June 1896, p. 8.

102. Alan Hyman, *The Gaiety Years* (London: Cassell, 1975), 100.

103. Anon., 'The Chorus Girl', *Los Angeles Times*, 2 Aug. 1887, p. 9.

104. Quoted in Cecchi, *Giovanni Boldini*, 45–6.

105. Maurice Talmeyr, 'L'età del manifesto', in Simona de Iulio (ed.), *L'età del manifesto: Sguardi sulla pubblicità francese del XIX secolo* (Milan: Franco Angeli, 1996, 113.

106. Lucinda Jarrett, *Stripping in Time: A History of Erotic Dancing* (London: HarperCollins, 1997), 47.

107. On La Goulue and the Moulin Rouge, see ibid., ch. 2.

108. Linda Mizejewski, *Ziegfeld Girl: Image and Icon in Culture and Cinema* (Durham, NC: Duke University Press, 1999), 66.

109. Jarrett, *Stripping in Time*, 25.

110. Mistinguett, *Mistinguett: Queen of the Paris Night* (London: Elek Books, 1954), 58.

111. John Hollingshead, *Gaiety Chronicles* (London: Constable, 1898), 30.

112. James Gardiner, *Gaby Deslys: A Fatal Attraction* (London: Sidgwick and Jackson, 1986), 190.

113. Jacques-Charles, *De Gaby Deslys à Mistinguett* (Paris: Gallimard, 1933), 21–2.

114. Quoted in Jean-Jacques Sirkis, *Les Années Deslys* (Paris: Jeanne Laffitte, 1990), 93.

115. The former *maître d'hôtel* of the Maxim's restaurant, Hugo, included her in his notebook of available women at the price of 1,000 francs per quarter hour, although he also included the annotation 'rien à faire'. See *Vingt ans maître d'hôtel chez Maxim's* (Paris: Amiot Dumont, 1951), 204.

116. Ibid. 200.

117. Cecil Beaton, *The Book of Beauty* (London: Duckworth, 1930), 22.

118. Ibid. 22.

119. Mistinguett, *Mistinguett*, 126.

120. Ibid. 32.

121. Ibid. 127.

122. Ibid. 128.

123. Ibid. 127.

124. Maurice Verne, *Les Usines du plaisir: La Vie secrète du music-hall* (Paris: Éditions des Portiques, 1929), 145, 211–12.

125. Ibid. 84–5.

126. See Anna Held, *Mémoires: Une étoile française au ciel de l'Amérique* (Paris: La Nef, 1954).

127. Banner, *American Beauty*, 186.

128. Mizejewski, *Ziegfeld Girl*, 38.

129. Anon., 'Woman and her Beauty', *Los Angeles Times*, 25 Nov. 1908, p. 114.

130. Paul Derval, *The Folies Bergère* (London: Brown Watson, 1955), 38.

131. Ibid.

132. Octave Uzanne, *Parisiennes de ce temps en leurs divers milieux, états et conditions* (Paris: Mercure de France, 1910), 18.

133. Ibid. 20.

134. Octave Uzanne, *Sottiser les mœurs* (Paris: Émile Paul, 1911), 169.

135. Dominique Kalifa, *La Culture de masse en France 1860–1930* (Paris: La Découverte, 2001), 42–3.

CHAPTER 5

1. Patrick Balfour, *Society Racket* (London; Lang, 1933), 73.

2. David Cannadine, *The Decline and Fall of the British Aristocracy* (New Haven and London: Yale University Press, 1990), 327.

3. Ibid.

4. Roger Wilkes, *Scandal: A Scurrilous History of Gossip* (London: Atlantic, 2003).

5. See D. J. Taylor, *Bright Young People: The Rise and Fall of a Generation, 1918–1940* (London: Chatto & Windus, 2007), 40; see also, more widely on the perception of high society, Ross McKibbin, *Classes and Cultures: England 1918–1951* (Oxford: Oxford University Press, 1998), 22–43.

6. Balfour, *Society Racket*, 89.

7. Ibid. 92.

8. Whigham's personal life was tumultuous. In 1930 her engagement to the Earl of Warwick was announced but the wedding was called off when she fell for Charles Sweeney, an American golfer. She married him in 1933 and had three children. They divorced in 1947. In 1951 she became the third wife of the Duke of Argyll. However, her serial infidelity led the duke to sue for divorce in 1963. In the course of the hearing, a list was presented of eighty-eight men with whom the duchess was alleged to have had sex. Photographs were also produced that showed her fellating a naked man, whose head was obscured. It was widely believed that the man in question was either Duncan Sandys, a Cabinet minister, or Douglas Fairbanks although the identity of the 'headless man' was never revealed.

9. Alan Jenkins, *The Thirties* (London: Heinemann, 1976), 24.

10. It was even implied by the romantic novelist Barbara Cartland, who was herself a deb in the 1920s, that she employed a press agent to handle her publicity, but she denied this: 'No-one promoted or paid for the publicity...it just growed [*sic*]'. Margaret, Duchess of Argyll, *'Forget Not'* (1975; London: Wyndham, 1977), 46.

11. 'The girls of 1930 not only had good looks; they knew how to dress; and they had far more self-confidence than their predecessors', Whigham later observed. Ibid.

12. Ibid. 47. On the freelance press activities of some young members of high society, see Taylor, *Bright Young People*, 184–5.

13. Gioia Diliberto, *Debutante: The Story of Brenda Frazier* (New York: Knopf, 1987), 99. On Frazier, see Karal Ann Marling, *Debutante: Rites and Regalia of American Debdom* (Lawrence, Kans.: University Press of Kansas, 2004), 91–4. She describes her as 'the ultimate glamor girl' and lists her advertising endorsements as well as the criticism she aroused.

14. See Cleveland Amory, *Who Killed Society?* (New York: Harper & Brothers, 1960), 178–81.

15. Ibid. 112.

16. Neal Gabler, *Walter Winchell: Gossip, Power and the Culture of Celebrity* (London: Picador, 1995), p. xiii.

17. Ibid., p. xii.

18. Margaret, Duchess of Argyll, '*Forget Not*', 35.

19. McKibbin, *Classes and Cultures*, 22–43; Taylor, *Bright Young People*, 41.

20. Cecil Beaton, 'Have You Glamour?', *Sunday Dispatch*, 11 May 1930, p. 12.

21. McKibbin, *Classes and Cultures*, 38–9.

22. See Ronald Marchand, *Advertising the American Dream: Making Way for Modernity, 1920–1940* (Berkeley and Los Angeles: University of California Press, 1985).

23. Quoted in Yvonne Brunhammer, *The Nineteen Twenties Style* (London: Hamlyn, 1966), 87.

24. McKibbin, *Classes and Cultures*, 23.

25. Barbara Cartland, *We Danced All Night* (London: Hutchinson, 1971), 150.

26. Gloria Swanson, *Swanson on Swanson* (London: Joseph, 1981), 508–9.

27. Kitty Kelley, *The Royals* (New York: Warner Books, 1997), 42.

28. Stella Margetson, *The Long Party: High Society in the Twenties and Thirties* (Farnborough: Saxon House, 1974), 230. See also Taylor, *Bright Young People*, 29–30.

29. Cannadine, *Decline and Fall*, 354.

30. HRH The Duke of Windsor, *A King's Story* (London: Cassell, 1951), 187–8.

31. See Matthew J. Bruccoli, *Some Kind of Grandeur: The Life of F. Scott Fitzgerald* (1981; London: Sphere 1991), 153–4. Fitzgerald first used the term Jazz Age in 1931.

32. In the early twentieth century, in New York, Mrs Stuyvesant Fish had enlivened dinner parties with stunts, practical jokes, entertainments, and send-ups of formal rituals, all of which provided amusement for readers of the press.

33. Taylor reflects on the difficulties of determining exactly who belonged to the group—if group it was—and finds it impossible, both because of the distancing of some of those involved and because of the press's role in applying the term to random phenomena. See *Bright Young People*, 6, 10, 15, 37.

34. For the details in this paragraph, see Philippa Pullar, *Gilded Butterflies: The Rise and Fall of the London Season* (London: Hamish Hamilton, 1978), 163.

35. Ibid. 195. Taylor questions in fact how much sex and drugs there in fact was. See *Bright Young People*, 110–12.

36. Harold Acton, *Memoirs of an Aesthete* (London: Hamish Hamilton, 1948), 223.

37. See Mordaunt J. Crook, *The Rise of the Nouveaux Riches: Style and Status in Victorian and Edwardian Architecture* (London: John Murray, 1999).

38. Arthur Vanderbilt II, *Fortune's Children: The Fall of the House of Vanderbilt* (London: Michael Joseph, 1990), 8.

39. Carol Kennedy, *Mayfair: A Social History* (London: Hutchinson, 1986), 212.

40. Amory, *Who Killed Society?*, 108.

41. Balfour, *Society Racket*, 111.

42. Richard Collier, *Rainbow People* (London: Weidenfeld and Nicolson, 1984), 36.

43. Ibid. 124.

44. F. Scott Fitzgerald, *The Great Gatsby* (1925; London: Abacus, 1991), 61.

45. One of Nast's editors, Edna Woolman Chase, who worked for *Vogue* for over fifty years, says that these parties were standardized and predictable. See her *Always in Vogue* (London, Gollancz, 1954), 171–2. But their routine quality was important in making intermingling the rule rather than the exception.

46. Ibid. 137.

47. Quoted in Caroline Seebohm, *The Man Who Was Vogue: The Life and Times of Condé Nast* (London: Weidenfeld and Nicolson, 1982), 195.

48. See Josephine Ross (ed.), *Society in Vogue: The International Set between the Wars* (London: Condé Nast, 1992). For a view of British *Vogue*, see H. W. Yoxall, *A Fashion of Life* (London: Heinemann, 1966).

49. Seebohm, *The Man Who Was Vogue*, 142.

50. Cartland, *We Danced All Night*, 55.

51. In Stella Margetson's view, 'Garbo killed the synthetic, tarted up image of the film star with platinum blonde wavy hair, red lips and a pink and white doll's complexion.' See Margetson, *Long Party*, 129.

52. She also wrote an autobiographical novel, *Save Me The Waltz*, in 1932.

53. Balfour, *Society Racket*, 57.

54. Billie Melman, *Women and the Popular Imagination in the Twenties: Flappers and Nymphs* (London: Macmillan, 1988), 75. Taylor suggests two possible real-life versions of the character of Iris Storm: Doris Delavigne and Brenda Dean Paul. See *Bright Young People*, 51 and 195.

55. Acton, *Memoirs of an Aesthete*, 223.

56. Margetson, *Long Party*, 124.

57. Cartland, *We Danced All Night*, 180. One of those who was entranced and profoundly influenced was the baronet's daughter Brenda Dean Paul. See Taylor, *Bright Young People*, 26, and her autobiography, published at age 28, *My First Life* (London: Long, 1935).

58. Charles Higham, *Wallis: Secret Lives of the Duchess of Windsor* (London: Sidgwick and Jackson, 1988), 92.

59. Philip Ziegler, *Diana Cooper* (1981; London: Penguin, 1983), 206. Mrs Simpson was a fashionable figure, but not an original dresser. She patronized Chanel and Schiaparelli, a Paris-based designer who drew inspiration from the surrealists. Later, she forged a distinctive, severe look with the help of the American-born designer Mainbocher.

60. For an account of Lindbergh's fame analysed in context, see Leo Braudy, *The Frenzy of Renown: Fame and its History* (Oxford: Oxford University Press, 1986), 19–25.

61. See Ronald Blythe, *The Age of Illusion* (Oxford: Oxford University Press, 1963), 94–102.

62. See Liz Conor, *The Spectacular Woman: Feminine Visibility in the 1920s* (Bloomington and Indianapolis: Indiana University Press, 2004), 69.

63. See Constance Babington Smith, *Amy Johnson* (London: Collins, 1967), 286–7.

64. See Miranda Seymour, *The Bugatti Queen* (London: Simon and Schuster, 2004).

65. Michael J. Arlen, *Exiles* (London: Penguin, 1971), 54–5.

66. See Sheridan Morley, *A Talent to Amuse: A Biography of Noel Coward* (London: Heinemann, 1969), 82–3.

67. Beaton, 'Have You Glamour?'

68. *The Sketch*, 29 Apr. 1925.

69. Philip Hoare, *Noel Coward: A Biography* (London: Sinclair-Stevenson, 1995), 114–15.

70. W. Macqueen-Pope, *Ivor: The Story of an Achievement* (London: Hutchinson, 1951), 170–1.

71. Ibid. 294.

72. For a testimony of this, see Acton, *Memoirs of an Aesthete*, 147. Novello could play the part of the fashionable gentleman and was a welcome guest at upper-class soirées and country house weekends. In *Gosford Park*, the 2001 film of interwar upstairs and downstairs living, he is played by Jeremy Northam. As he sits at the piano and makes his way through his repertoire of songs, the guests barely notice him while the servants sneak up behind doors and curtains to catch his popular motifs.

73. Hugo Vickers, *Cecil Beaton* (London: Weidenfeld, 1933), 36–8.

74. Hoare, *Noel Coward*, 201.

75. See Woodman Chase, *Always in Vogue*.

76. See Meredith Etherington-Smith, *Patou* (London: Hutchinson, 1983).

77. Hoare, *Noel Coward*, 162–3.

78. Elsa Maxwell, *The Celebrity Circus* (London: W. H. Allen, 1964), 11. See also her *I Married the World* (London: Heinemann, 1955).

CHAPTER 6

1. Barry Paris, *Garbo* (London: Pan, 1995), 74.

2. Ibid. 88.

3. Roland Barthes, *Mythologies* (London: Paladin, 1973), 56.

4. Paris, *Garbo*, 364.

5. For example, the Austrian designer Ernst Dryden worked for stores and advertising agencies in Berlin and Paris before placing his talent at the service of Paramount studios. See Anthony Lipman, *Divinely Elegant: The World of Ernst Dryden* (London: Pavilion, 1989).

6. Neal Gabler, *An Empire of their Own: How the Jews Invented Hollywood* (New York: Anchor, 1985); Jackson Lears, *Fables of Abundance: A Cultural History of American Advertising* (New York: Basic Books, 1994).

7. Richard Schickel, *Fairbanks: The First Celebrity* (London; Elm Tree, 1976), 12–13.

8. Anon., 'Metro-Goldwyn-Mayer', *Fortune* (Dec. 1932), reprod. in Tino Balio (ed.), *The American Film Industry* (Madison: University of Wisconsin Press, 1976).

9. Douglas Gomery, *The Hollywood Studio System* (London: BFI, 1986), chs. 2–5.

10. Quoted in Robert Sklar, *Movie-Made America* (New York: Random House, 1975), 191.

11. Anon., 'Metro-Goldwyn-Mayer', 269.

12. Gorham Kindem, 'Hollywood's Movie Star System', in Kindem (ed.), *The American Movie Industry: The Business of Motion Pictures* (Carbondale: Southern Illinois University Press, 1982), 86.

13. Anne Massey, *Hollywood beyond the Screen: Design and Material Culture* (Oxford: Berg, 2000), 21.

14. On the 1925 Paris exhibition, see Tag Gronenberg, *Designing Modernity: Exhibiting the City in 1920s Paris* (Manchester: Manchester University Press, 1998).

15. Lea Jacobs, *The Wages of Sin: Censorship and the Fallen Woman Film 1928–1942* (Madison: University of Wisconsin Press, 1991), 56.

16. Bevis Hillier, *The Style of the Century 1900–1980* (New York: Dutton, 1983), 81.

17. Anon., 'Metro-Goldwyn-Mayer', 269–70.

18. Quoted in Ronald Davis, *The Glamour Factory: Inside Hollywood's Big Studio System* (Dallas: Southern Methodist University Press, 1993), 225.

19. Quoted ibid. 83.

20. Ibid.

21. Edgar Morin, *Les Stars* (1957; Paris: Seuil, 1972), 43.

22. Gertrude Aretz, *The Elegant Woman: From the Roccoco Period to Modern Times* (London: Harrap, 1932), 294.

23. Ibid. 230.

24. The perplexity derived from the novelty of sexuality being displayed without sexual favours apparently being granted (notwithstanding the casting couch). For a discussion of this transition, see Arthur Marwick, *Beauty in History: Society, Politics and Personal Appearance c.1500 to the Present* (London: Thames and Hudson, 1988), 245–9.

25. Blaise Cendrars, *Hollywood: La mecca del cinema* (1937; Rome: Lucarini, 1989), 83–4.

26. Glyn's impact is chronicled in Gloria Swanson's memoirs, *Swanson on Swanson* (London: Joseph, 1981), 159–73.

27. W. Robert Lavine, *In a Glamorous Fashion: The Fabulous Years of Hollywood Costume Design* (London: Allen and Unwin, 1981), 38.

28. Alexander Walker, *Sex in the Movies* (Harmondsworth: Penguin, 1968), 36–43.

29. Marjorie Rosen, *Popcorn Venus: Women, Movies and the American Dream* (London: Owen, 1973), 118.

30. Ibid.

31. Richard Dyer, *White* (London: Routledge, 1997).

32. On Hollywood exoticism, see Sarah Berry, *Screen Style: Fashion and Femininity in 1930s Hollywood* (Minneapolis: University of Minnesota Press, 2000), 132–41.

33. See Gaylyn Studlar, 'Barrymore, the Body and Bliss: Issues in Male Representation and Female Spectatorship in the 1920s', in Leslie Devereaux and Roger Hillman (eds.), *Fields of Vision: Essays in Film Studies, Visual Anthropology and Photography* (Berkeley and Los Angeles: University of California Press, 1995), 160–80.

34. Sklar, *Movie-Made America*, 99.

35. See Richard Dyer, *Stars* (London: BFI, 1979); *Heavenly Bodies: Film Stars and Society* (London: Routledge, 1987).

36. Sklar, *Movie-Made America*, 77.

37. David Stenn, *Clara Bow: Runnin' Wild* (1988; London: Penguin 1990), 36.

38. Swanson, *Swanson on Swanson*, 177.

39. Anne Tapert and Diane Edkins, *The Power of Style* (London: Aurum, 1995).

40. See Amy Fine Collins, 'The Man Hollywood Trusted', *Vanity Fair* (Apr. 2001), 110–23.

41. See Lavine, *In a Glamorous Fashion*, 28–30.

42. Ibid. 33.

43. Elizabeth Wilson and Lou Taylor, *Through the Looking Glass: A History of Dress from 1860 to the Present Day* (London: BBC Books, 1989), 98–100.

44. See Catherine Herzog and Jane Gaines, 'Puffed Sleeves before Tea-Time: Joan Crawford, Adrian and Women Audiences', in Christine Gledhill (ed.), *Stardom: Industry of Desire* (London: Routledge, 1991), 74–91.

45. Bruno Rémaury, 'L'Illusion et l'Apparence', in Alain Masson (ed.), *Hollywood 1927–1941* (Paris: Éditions Autremont, 1991), 217.

46. Dyer, *Stars*, 42.

47. Quoted in Anne Tapert, *The Power of Glamour* (London: Aurum, 1999), 238.

48. Quoted in Patty Fox, *Star Style: Hollywood Legends as Fashion Icons* (Santa Monica: Angel City Press, 1995), 56–7.

49. Alexander Walker, *Sex in the Movies: The Celluloid Sacrifice* (Harmondsworth: Penguin, 1966), 102.

50. Sarah Berry, *Screen Style: Fashon and Femininity in 1930s Hollywood* (Minneapolis: University of Minnesota Press, 1999), 56–7.

51. Ibid., ch. 2.

52. Ibid. 83–4.

53. Letter from Clayton T. Lang, *New York Times*, 20 May 1934, p. E5.

54. James Robert Parish and Don E. Stanke, *The Glamour Girls* (New Rochelle, NY: Arlington House, 1975), 23.

425

55. John Kobal, *George Hurrell: Hollywood Glamour Portraits* (London: Schirmer, 1993), 15.

56. Ibid.

57. Anon., 'Ace Cameraman Sees Stars Sans Glamour', *Los Angeles Times*, 3 Mar. 1946, p. B1.

58. Marlene Dietrich, *My Life* (1987; London: Pan, 1989), 60.

59. John Engstead, *Star Shots: Fifty Years of Pictures and Stories by One of Hollywood's Greatest Photographers* (New York: Dutton, 1978), 72. Tapert, *Power of Glamour*, 230–1.

60. Dietrich, *My Life*, 72 and 85.

61. Quoted in Parish and Stanke, *Glamour Girls*, 17.

62. Dietrich, *My Life*, 105.

63. Josef von Sternberg, *Fun in a Chinese Laundry* (1965; London: Columbus Books 1987), 224–69. In her essay discussing the way spectators were turned into voyeurs who derived pleasure from the fetishization of the female star, Laura Mulvey singles out von Sternberg's use of Dietrich as the 'ultimate fetish'. In his meticulously composed and shot films the beauty of the woman as object and the screen space coalesce: 'she is no longer the bearer of guilt but a perfect product, whose body, stylised and fragmented by close-ups, is the content of the film and the direct recipient of the spectator's look'. Mulvey, 'Visual Pleasure and Narrative Cinema', in *Visual and Other Pleasures* (Bloomington: Indiana University Press, 1989), 22.

64. Dietrich, *My Life*, 116.

65. Ibid. 119.

66. Davis, *Glamour Factory*, 27.

67. Ibid. 139–44.

68. Ibid. 144.

69. Morin, *Les Stars*, 24.

70. Ibid.

71. Charles Eckert, 'The Carol Lombard in Macy's Window', in Gledhill (ed.), *Stardom*; Douglas Gomery, *Shared Pleasures: A History of Movie Presentation in the United States* (London: BFI, 1992).

72. See Patricia Bosworth, 'That Old Star Magic', *Vanity Fair* (Apr. 1998), p. 70.

73. Cited in Jeffrey Richards, *The Age of the Dream Palace: Cinema and Society in Britain 1930–1939* (London: Routledge, 1984), 157–8.

74. Anon., 'You, Too, Can Be a Glamour Girl', *Los Angeles Times*, 18 Feb. 1940, p. G4.

75. Berry, *Screen Style*, p. 93.

76. Ibid. 106.

77. Kathy Peiss, *Hope in a Jar: The Making of America's Beauty Culture* (New York: Metropolitan/Holt, 1998), 97.

78. Schickel, *Fairbanks*, 53.

79. Sylia Weaver, 'This Glamour Business', *Los Angeles Times*, 22 Jan. 1939, p. 5.

80. Ibid.

81. Sali Löbel, *Glamour and How to Achieve It* (London: Hutchinson, 1938), 11.

82. Ibid. 14.

83. Sally Alexander, 'Becoming a Woman in London in the 1920s and 1930s', in David Feldman and Gareth Stedman Jones (eds.), *Metropolis London: Histories and Representations since 1800* (London: Routledge, 1989), 263.

84. Ibid. 264.

85. See Jackie Stacey, *Star Gazing: Hollywood Cinema and Female Spectatorship* (London: Routledge, 1994), which explores British women's memories of watching American films before and after the war. The quotation appears on p. 115.

86. See Victoria de Grazia, *How Fascism Ruled Women: Italy 1922–1945* (Berkeley and Los Angeles: University of California Press, 1992), 201–33.

87. See Stephen Gundle, *Bellissima: Feminine Beauty and the Idea of Italy* (New Haven and London: Yale University Press, 2007), ch. 4.

88. W. E. Hill, 'Glamour Boys', *Los Angeles Times*, 11 Sept. 1938, p. G4.

89. Anon., 'Farmhands Must Have Glamour to Stick It; Otherwise We Go Hungry, Congress Is Told', *New York Times*, 17 Oct. 1942, p. 13.

90. Anon., 'Cow Glamour To Be Shown', *Los Angeles Times*, 22 July 1941, p. A1.

91. Marian Manners, 'Mushrooms Add Glamour to Carrots', *Los Angeles Times*, 23 June 1938, p. A7.

92. Parish and Stanke, *Glamour Girls*, cover flap.

93. B. R. Crisler, 'A Glance at that Awful Thing Called Glamour', *New York Times*, 12 Mar. 1939, p. 154.

94. Frank S. Nugent, 'A Universal Error About Glamour', *New York Times*, 26 Mar. 1939, p. 137.

95. Kenneth Crist, 'No Glamour Needed', *Los Angeles Times*, 23 July 1939, p. 15.

96. Edwin Schallert, ' "Glamour" Due for Discard, Says Goldwyn', *Los Angeles Times*, 13 May 1934, p. A1.

97. Anon., 'Glamour Girl Called Dead By Noted Photographer', *Los Angeles Times*, 3 Jan. 1938, p. 2.

CHAPTER 7

1. Quoted in Nigel Cawthorne, *The New Look: The Dior Revolution* (London: Reed International, 1996), 106.

2. Christian Dior, *Dior by Dior: The Autobiography of Christian Dior* (1957; London: V&A Publications, 2007), 27–8.

3. Harry Hopkins, *The New Look: A Social History of the Forties and Fifties in Britain* (London: Secker and Warburg, 1963), 96 and David Kynaston, *Austerity Britain, 1945–1951* (London: Bloomsbury, 2007), 257–8. Ridealgh was elected in the Labour landslide of 1945. She was a prominent figure in the Cooperative Women's Guild. This was not her only 'anti-glamour' statement as she also intervened on cosmetics and the influence of American film. See Robert Murphy, *Realism and Tinsel: Cinema and Society in Britain, 1939–1949* (London: Routledge, 1989), 104–5.

4. Antony Beevor and Artemis Cooper, *Paris After the Liberation: 1944–1949* (London: Penguin, 1995), 315.

5. See ibid. 305–7.

6. Dior, *Dior by Dior*, 28.

7. Paul Gallico, *Flowers for Mrs Harris* (London: Penguin, 1963) (first published in 1958 under the title *Mrs Harris Goes to Paris*).

8. Quoted in Beevor and Cooper, *Paris After the Liberation*, 137.

9. Cawthorne, *New Look*, 119. Dior denied having received any explicit encouragement in this sense. See Dior, *Dior by Dior*, 4–5, 22.

10. On the appropriation of the New Look by working-class British women, see Angela Partington, 'Popular Fashion and Working Class Affluence', in Juliet Ash and Elizabeth Wilson (eds.), *Chic Thrills: A Fashion Reader* (London: Pandora, 1992), 145–61.

11. Dior, *Dior by Dior*, 36.

12. See Nicholas Drake, *The Fifties in Vogue* (London: Conde Nast, 1987), 58.

13. Dior, *Dior by Dior*, 61. See also Claire Wilcox, 'Dior's Golden Age; The Renaissance of Couture', in Wilcox (ed.), *The Golden Age of Couture: London and Paris, 1947–1957* (London: V&A Publications, 2007), 42–4. Dior was awarded a Neiman Marcus Oscar in 1947 for his contribution to fashion and he went personally to Dallas to collect it, undertaking at the same time a full American tour. His commercial verve put paid to any idea that American designers might supplant Paris in the aftermath of the war.

14. Partington, 'Popular Fashion and Working Class Affluence', 151.

15. Marie-France Pochna, *Christian Dior: The Man Who Made the World Look New* (New York: Arcade 1996), 136. Dior claimed that the Americans were always his best customers, *Dior by Dior*, 34. He said that American women, from the top to the bottom of the social spectrum, were all perfectly turned out in 1947, and had 'all the shiny brilliance of a new penny', *Dior by Dior*, 51.

16. Nantas Salvalaggio, 'Linda e Tyrone acclamati dalla folla', *Il tempo*, 28 Jan. 1949, p. 3.

17. F.G., 'Finalmente sposi Tyrone e Linda', *Avantì*, 28 Jan. 1949, p. 3.

18. Salvalaggio, 'Linda e Tyrone', 3.

19. Linda Christian, *Linda: My Own Story* (New York: Dell, 1962), 101.

20. G.d.S., 'Linda e Tyrone hanno detto "si"', *Il messaggero*, 28 Jan. 1949, p. 3.

21. Ibid.

22. See Adrienne L. McLean, 'The Cinderella Princess and the Instrument of Evil: Surveying the Limits of Female Transgression in Two Postwar Hollywood Scandals', *Cinema Journal*, 34/3 (1995), 36–56.

23. Elsa Maxwell, *The Celebrity Circus* (London: W. H. Allen, 1964), 29.

24. Anne Edwards, *Throne of Gold: The Lives of the Aga Khans* (London: HarperCollins, 1995), 180.

25. Barbara Leaming, *If This Was Happiness: A Biography of Rita Hayworth* (London: Sphere, 1990), 209.

26. Edwards, *Throne of Gold*, 186.

27. Cited ibid. 186.

28. For a sketch of reactions to the couple, see Kynaston, *Austerity Britain*, 243–7.

29. *Time*, 5 Jan. 1953. Quoted in Robert Lacey, *Majesty* (1977; London: Sphere, 1978), 231.

30. Ibid.

31. On the emergence of one of these magazines and the development of its upbeat, celebrity-driven formula, see Nicholas Hewitt, 'The Birth of the Glossy Magazines: The Case of Paris-Match', in Brian Rigby and Nicholas Hewitt (eds.), *France and the Mass Media* (London: Macmillan, 1991), 111–28, esp. 124.

32. Roger Wilkes, *Scandal: A Scurrilous History of Gossip* (London: Atlantic, 2002), 198.

33. Hopkins, *New Look*, 300. Also cited in Wilkes, *Scandal*, 198.

34. Quoted in Andrew Duncan, *The Reality of Monarchy* (1970; London: Pan, 1971), 213.

35. Alexis Schwarzenbach, 'Royal Photographs: Emotions of the People', *Contemporary European History*, 13/3 (2004), 255–80.

36. Hardy Amies, *Still Here: An Autobiography* (London: Weidenfeld and Nicolson, 1984), 110.

37. Cited in Tom Nairn, *The Enchanted Glass: Britain and its Monarchy* (London: Radius, 1988), 77.

38. The historian of the culture of twentieth-century European royalty Alexis Schwarzenbach asserts that sex appeal is always absent from its image: 'In official royal representation—in contrast to anti-royal pamphlets or lurid press reports—I have never found any descriptions of real queens which comment on their sexual appeal to the general male audience. Of course the beauty of real queens was often publicly displayed. Yet the aim of this was to enhance her royal status. Her sex appeal remained exclusively reserved for her husband and was not commented on in any of the cases I have analysed so far.' 'Imagined Queens between Heaven and Hell: Representations of Grace Kelly and Romy Schneider', in Regina Schulte (ed.), *The Body of the Queen: Gender and Rule in the Courtly World, 1500–2000* (Oxford: Berghahn, 2006), 317.

39. Lacey, *Majesty*, 237.

40. Norman Hartnell, *Silver and Gold* (London: Evans, 1955), 133.

41. Ibid. 135.

42. *Roman Holiday* had the advantage of a Roman setting. But the film's storyline did have a precursor in *Princess O'Rourke*, an American-set comedy drama directed by Norman Kasna in 1943 and starring Olivia De Havilland as a European (probably British, but her country is unspecified) princess who falls for and marries a simple American soldier.

43. Peter Kramer, 'Faith in Relations between People: Audrey Hepburn, *Roman Holiday* and European Integration', paper presented to 'Entertaining' seminar, Keele University, 21 May 1997, p. 12.

44. Ibid.

45. The films were *Sissi* (1955), *Sissi—Die junge Kaiserin* (1956), and *Sissi—Schicksalsjahre einer Kaiserin* (1957). They were all directed by Ernst Marischka.

46. See Schwarzenbach, 'Imagined Queens between Heaven and Hell'.

47. See Ian Woodward, *Audrey Hepburn* (London: Virgin, 1983), 184–6; see also Stefania Ricci (ed.), *Audrey Hepburn: Una donna, lo stile—a woman, the style* (Milan: Leonardo Arte, 1999).

48. Gianluca Bauzano, 'Reasons for a Style' in Ricci (ed.), *Hepburn*, 58.

49. On Cary Grant's self-invention, see Graham McCann, *Cary Grant: A Class Apart* (London: Fourth Estate, 1996). Born into the Bristol working class, Grant (whose real name was Archie Leach) modelled himself on Douglas Fairbanks on his way to becoming the epitome of masculine glamour for generations of movie-goers.

50. Bettina, *Bettina* (London: Joseph, 1965), 54–5.

51. Jackie Stacey, *Star Gazing: Hollywood Cinema and Female Spectatorship* (London; Routledge, 1994), 153.

52. Simone de Beauvoir, *The Second Sex* (1949; London: Everyman's Library, 1993), 599.

53. Ibid.

54. Elsa Maxwell, *I Married the World* (London: Heinemann, 1955), 6.

55. David Cannadine, *The Decline and Fall of the British Aristocracy* (New Haven and London: Yale, 1990), 679.

56. Cleveland Amory, *Who Killed Society?* (New York: Harper, 1960), 135. On Britain, see Cannadine, *Decline and Fall of the British Aristocracy*, 691.

57. Amory, *Who Killed Society?*, 143–4.

58. Elsa Maxwell, *The Celebrity Circus* (London: W. H. Allen, 1964), 55–6.

59. Ibid. 52.

60. Sarah Bradford, *Princess Grace* (London: Weidenfeld and Nicolson, 1984), 76.

61. Ibid. 61.

62. Ibid. 128.

63. For a more detailed examination of these issues, see Stephen Gundle, 'Il divismo nel cinema europeo, 1945–1960', in Gian Piero Brunetta (ed.), *Storia del cinema mondiale*, i. *L'Europa*, bk. 1. *Miti, luoghi, divi* (Turin: Einaudi, 1999).

64. Bradford, *Princess Grace*, 139.

65. Mary Blume, *Cote d'Azur: Inventing the French Riviera* (London: Thames and Hudson, 1992), 144.

66. Amory, *Who Killed Society?*, 243.

67. Maxwell, *Celebrity Circus*, 31.

68. Marilyn Bender, *The Beautiful People* (New York: Coward-McCann, 1967), 89.

69. Ibid. 82.

70. Annette Tapert and Diana Edkins, *The Power of Style* (London: Aurum Press, 1995), 162.

71. Gerald Clarke, *Capote: A Biography* (1988; London: Abacus, 1993), 274.

72. Paul Fussell, *Caste Marks: Style and Status in the USA* (London: Heinneman, 1984), 27.

73. Tapert and Edkins, *The Power of Style*, 162–65.

74. Bender, *The Beautiful People*, 89.

75. Tapert and Edkins, *The Power of Style*, 166.

76. Alfred Allan Lewis and Constance Woodworth, *Miss Elizabeth Arden* (London: W. H. Allen, 1973), 87.

77. See Stephen Gundle and Clino T. Castelli, *The Glamour System* (London: Palgrave, 2006), 123–34.

78. Andrew Tobias, *Fire and Ice: The Story of Charles Revson—The Man Who Built the Revlon Empire* (New York: Morrow, 1976), 223.

79. The theme of self-invention and social climbing is recurrent in Lee Israel's unauthorized biography *Estée Lauder: Beyond the Magic* (London: Arlington, 1985).

80. Ibid. 114.

81. Estée Lauder, *Estée: A Success Story* (New York: Ballantine Books, 1986), 192–3.

82. See Christopher Sykes, *Evelyn Waugh: A Biography* (London: Penguin, 1977), 341–2 for the letter Waugh received from Pansy Lamb upbraiding him on this matter.

83. Erica Carter, *How German is She? Postwar West German Reconstruction and the Consuming Woman* (Ann Arbor: University of Michigan Press, 1997), 209–25.

84. The 1955 picture is reproduced on p. 58 of Wilcox (ed.), *Golden Age of Couture*.

85. David Seidner, 'Still Dance', in Seidner (ed.), *Lisa Fonssagrives: Three Decades of Classic Fashion Photography* (London: Thames and Hudson, 1997), 20.

86. Ibid.

87. Ginette Spanier, *It Isn't All Mink* (London: Collins, 1959), 207.

88. Praline, *Mannequin de Paris* (Paris: Seuil, 1951).

89. John Glatt, *The Ruling House of Monaco: The Story of a Tragic Dynasty* (London: Piatkus, 1998), 61.

90. Jeffrey Robinson, *Rainier and Grace* (London: Fontana, 1990), 163.

91. Blume, *Cote d'Azur*, 144.

92. Ibid. 166.

93. See Antonella Boralevi, *Capri* (Bologna: Il Mulino, 2001), ch. 4. On the Mediterranean style of this period, see Diane Berger, *Riviera Style: Lifestyle & Interiors of the Riviera, from St Tropez to Capri* (London: Scriptum, 1999).

94. Conrad Hilton, *Be My Guest* (Englewood Cliffs, NJ: Prentice-Hall, 1957), 112.

95. Ibid. 191.

96. Carla Stampa, 'Si è vestita come Tarzan per pronunciare il famoso "sì"', *Epoca*, 2 June 1956, p. 58.

97. Martin Heller, 'Glamour Pictures', in Edward Quinn, *A Cote d'Azur Album* (Zurich: Scalo, 1994), 189.

98. Edward Quinn, *Stars Stars Stars—Off the Screen* (Zurich: Scalo, 1997), 7–8.

99. Ginette Vincendeau, 'Brigitte Bardot', in John Hill and Pamela Church Gibson (eds.), *The Oxford Guide to Film Studies* (Oxford: Oxford University Press, 1998), 499.

100. Brigitte Bardot, *Mi chiamano BB—autobiografia* (Milan: Bompiani, 1996), 136–7.

101. Cari Beauchamp and Henri Béhar, *Hollywood on the Riviera* (New York: Morrow, 1992), 166.

102. Bardot, *Mi chiamano BB*, 156.

103. Pierre Cendrars, *Les Séducteurs du cinéma francais (1928 –1958)* (Paris: Henri Veyrier, 1978), 116.

104. For an illuminating portrait of one of these men, see Shawn Levy, *The Last Playboy: The High Life of Porfirio Rubirosa* (London: Fourth Estate, 2005).

105. See Alexander Walker, *Elizabeth* (1990; London; Fontana, 1992), 368. See chs. 27 and 28 for a full account of the scandal.

CHAPTER 8

1. David W. Ellwood, *Rebuilding Europe: Western Europe, America and Postwar Reconstruction* (London: Longman, 1992), 229.

2. Victoria de Grazia, *Irresistible Empire: America's Advance through Twentieth-Century Europe* (Cambridge, Mass.: Harvard University Press, 2005), 3.

3. Ibid. 5.

4. Stephen Bayley, *Harley Earl* (London: Grafton, 1992), 57.

5. Thomas Hine, *Populuxe* (London: Bloomsbury, 1987), 4.

6. Stephen Bayley, *Sex, Drink and Fast Cars* (New York: Pantheon, 1986), 13.

7. See Hine, *Populuxe*, 85.

8. Ibid. 101.

9. Ibid. 91.

10. See Hine, *Populuxe*, 106.

11. Marshall McLuhan, *Understanding Media: The Extensions of Man* (1964; London: Sphere, 1967), 232–6.

12. Dichter authored several books on motivational psychology, but his ideas gained wider currency thanks to the numerous references to them in Vance Packard's best-seller *The Hidden Persuaders* (New York: McKay, 1957).

13. Russell Lynes, *The Domesticated Americans* (New York: Harper & Row, 1962), 269.

14. For one not untypical Lancashire family, the car was treated 'like the Crown jewels' and brought out for a spin once a week, on Sunday, before being washed and put away again. Dominic Sandbrook, *Never Had It So Good: A History of Britain from Suez to The Beatles* (London: Little, Brown, 2005), 113–14.

15. Kristin Ross, *Fast Cars, Clean Bodies: Decolonization and the Reordering of French Culture* (Cambridge, Mass.: MIT Press, 1995), 27.

16. A. Bellucci, 'Trenta anni fa l'Italia si ritrovò per strada: Come la Fiat 600 cambiò la nostra vita', *La repubblica*, 12 Jan. 1985, p. 17.

17. For essays on the origins and impact of the Vespa, see Omar Calabrese (ed.), *Il mito di Vespa* (Milan: Lupetti, 2000).

18. For a wide selection of publicity material, see Jean Goyard and others, *Vespa: Les Années de charme* (Paris: Moto-Légende, 1992).

19. Roland Barthes, *Mythologies* (1957; London: Paladin: 1973), 88.

20. See Ross, *Fast Cars, Clean Bodies*, 27–54.

21. For an illuminating discussion of *Z Cars* including the production team's relationship with the Lancashire Police, see Sandbrook, *Never Had It So Good*, 377–81.

22. Barthes, *Mythologies*, 71–2.

23. Daniel Boorstin, *The Image* (1962; London: Pelican, 1963), 98.

24. Harold Mehring, *The Most of Everything: The Story of Miami Beach* (New York: Harcourt, Brace and Company, 1960), 34–45.

25. Ibid. 3; Polly Redford, *Billion Dollar Sandbar: A Biography of Miami Beach* (New York: Dutton, 1970), 240–3.

26. Joseph J. Corn, *The Winged Gospel: America's Romance with Aviation 1900–1960* (New York: Oxford University Press, 1983), 89.

27. See e.g. Joseph Kastner, 'Joan Waltermire: Air Stewardess', *Life*, 28 April 1941, pp. 102–12.

28. Ibid. 103.

29. The two sides of the stewardesses' role—glamour and servitude—are explored in Kathleen M. Barry, *Femininity in Flight: A History of Flight Attendants* (Durham, NC: Duke University Press, 2007).

30. Elizabeth Grey, *Air Hostess: The Story of Joyce Tait* (London: Robert Hale, 1957), 67.

31. Barry, *Femininity in Flight*, 2.

32. Grey, *Air Hostess*, 59–61.

33. Ibid. 12 and 100.

34. Aimée Bratt, *Glamour and Turbulence: I Remember Pan-Am 1966–1991* (New York: Vantage, 1996), 12.

35. Ibid.

36. This short film is discussed in detail in Stephen Gundle, *Bellissima: Feminine Beauty and the Idea of Italy* (New Haven and London: Yale University Press, 2007), 180–1.

37. Kastner, 'Joan Waltermire', 112.

38. Ibid. 35.

39. Barry, *Femininity in Flight*, 176–7.

40. Paula Kane with Christopher Chandler, *Sex Objects in the Sky* (Chicago: Follett, 1974), 12–13.

41. Ibid. 35.

42. Ibid. 12–13.

43. J. B. Priestley and Jacquetta Hawkes, *Journey Down a Rainbow* (1955; Harmondsworth: Penguin, 1969), 50.

44. McLuhan, *Understanding Media*, 238–9.

45. William H. Whyte, *The Organization Man* (1956; London: Pelican, 1963), 288.

46. David Riesman, *The Lonely Crowd: A Study of the Changing American Character* (New Haven: Yale University Press, 1950).

47. Ibid.

48. Ibid. 265.

49. Ibid. 147.

50. Ibid. 191.

51. Raymond Williams, *Television: Technology and Cultural Form* (London: Penguin, 1974), 26.

52. McLuhan, *Understanding Media*, 341–2.

53. Ibid. 339.

54. Susan J. Douglas, *Where the Girls Are: Growing Up Female with the Mass Media* (Harmondsworth: Penguin, 1994), 200.

55. Christine Becker, '"Glamor Girl Classed as TV Show Brain": The Body and Mind of Faye Emerson', *Journal of Popular Culture*, 38/2 (2004), 242–59.

56. See Stephen Gundle, '*Signorina buonasera*: Images of Women in Early Italian Television', in Penelope Morris (ed.), *Women in Italy, 1945–1960* (New York: Palgrave, 2007), 71.

57. Mary Margaret McBride, 'Much of Glamour Is the Unknown', *Los Angeles Times*, 25 Nov. 1953, p. B1.

58. Joe Hyams, 'Good by to the Glamour Girls', *Los Angeles Times*, 18 Sept. 1960, p. TW14.

59. McLuhan, *Understanding Media*, 342–3.

60. On this issue, see Lynn Spigel, *Make Room for TV: Television and the Family Ideal in Postwar America* (Chicago: University of Chicago Press, 1992); Denise Mann, 'The Spectacularization of Everyday Life', in Lynn Spigel and Denise Mann (eds.), *Private Screenings* (Minneapolis: University of Minnesota Press, 1992).

61. Gerold Frank, *Zsa Zsa Gabor: My Story* (1960; London: Pan, 1962), 251.

62. See Douglas, *Where the Girls Are*, 99–101.

63. Marina Coslovi, 'Il Glamour ci viene da Hollywood: L'Immagine dell' America in una rivista femminile del dopoguerra', unpublished paper, undated, p. 3.

64. See Malcolm Gladwell, 'True Colors: Hair Dye and the Hidden History of Postwar America', *New Yorker*, 22 Mar. 1999, pp. 70–81.

65. Stephen Fenichell, *Plastic: The Making of a Synthetic Century* (London: HarperBusiness, 1996), 112.

66. Ibid. 113. Helena Rubinstein offered her new face powder and rouge in a combination elegantly wrapped in cellophane. The lid of the rouge compact was held in place by a cellophane sheathing that was embossed with a 'personal' note in Helena's own hand.

67. Barthes, 'Striptease', in *Mythologies*, 85–6.

68. Barthes, 'Plastic', in *Mythologies*, 97.

69. Dea Birkett, 'I'm Barbie, Buy Me', *Guardian Weekend*, 28 Nov. 1998, pp. 13–21, at 15.

70. Ibid. 21.

71. Richard Horn, *Fifties Style: Then and Now* (London: Columbus, 1985), 118.

72. Penny Sparke, *As Long As It's Pink: The Sexual Politics of Taste* (London: Pandora, 1995), 201.

73. Barthes, 'Plastic', 99.

74. Fenichell, *Plastic*, 234.

75. Barthes, 'Plastic', 98.

76. Ibid. 197–8.

77. Joseph Rosa, 'Fabricating Affluence', in Rosa (ed.), *Glamour: Fashion + Industrial Design + Architecture* (New Haven and London: Yale University Press, 2004), 16.

78. Bill Davidson, *The Real and the Unreal* (New York: Harper, 1961), 4.

79. Ibid. 267.

80. See Richard Dyer, 'Monroe and Sexuality', in Janet Todd (ed.), *Women and Film* (New York: Holmes and Meier, 1988).

81. See Thomas Harris, 'The Building of Popular Images: Grace Kelly and Marilyn Monroe', in Christine Gledhill (ed.), *Stardom: Industry of Desire* (London: Routledge, 1991), 41.

82. One of her former charm school colleagues remembered her as follows: 'Diana Dors was fantastic—how she used to flaunt it. We used to call her Diamond Drawers. She'd arrive in low-cut gowns, with her hair piled up and all the make-up, great big high-heeled shoes and nylon stockings—which were ten shillings a pair on the black market. . . . I learned more from watching Diana than anything else. She could take a man into a corner and dazzle him.

She was as hard as nails but such a character: she'd tell us straight-faced that she didn't bleach her hair.' Patricia Dainton, 'Even at Charm School, Diana Dors Knew How to Dazzle a Man', *Daily Mail*, *Weekend* suppl., 19 Sept. 1998, p. 11.

83. Quoted in Sandbrook, *Never Had It So Good*, 126.

84. Elsa Maxwell, *The Celebrity Circus* (London: W. H. Allen, 1964), 11.

85. Edgar Morin, *Les Stars* (1957; Paris: Gallimard, 1972).

86. Ibid. 24.

87. Elissa Stein, *Beauty Queen* (San Francisco: Chronicle, 2006), 40.

88. Michele N. S. Bentata, 'The Beauty Contest in Women's History' (MA diss. Royal Hollo-way, University of London, 1993), 13.

89. On the 'Americanization' of beauty contest presentation in Britain, see Eric Morley, *Miss World Story* (London: Angley Books, 1967), 62–6.

90. Ibid. 105–6.

91. See Stein, *Beauty Queen*, 23.

92. Don Short, *Miss World: The Naked Truth* (London: Everest, 1976), 32.

93. Candace Savage, *Beauty Queens: A Pictorial History* (Vancouver and Toronto: Greystone, 1998), 9.

94. Bentata, 'Beauty Contest', 43.

95. Savage, *Beauty Queens*, p. ix.

96. Bentata, 'Beauty Contest', 41.

97. Ibid., app., questionnaire 7.

98. Ibid., app., questionnaire 10.

99. See Susan Dworkin, *Miss America, 1945: Bess Myerson's Own Story* (New York: Newmarket Press, 1987).

100. Betty Friedan, *The Feminine Mystique* (1963; Harmondsworth: Penguin, 1965), 198.

101. Riesman, *Lonely Crowd*, 146.

102. Ibid. 147.

103. Ibid. 116.

104. Friedan, *Feminine Mystique*, 231.

105. C. Wright Mills, *The Power Elite* (New York: Oxford University Press, 1959), 81.

106. Ibid. 236.

107. Rachel Shtier, *Striptease: The Untold History of the Girlie Show* (New York: Oxford University Press, 2004), 279. When Germaine Greer referred to 'the ebullient arabesques of the tit-queen', it may be assumed she had Tempest Storm and her colleagues in mind. See *The Female Eunuch* (London: MacGibbon and Kee, 1970), 45.

108. It has been reported that her lovers included Sammy Davis Jnr., Elvis Presley, and John F. Kennedy. See Steve Sullivan, *Va Va Voom! Bombshells, Pin-Ups, Sexpots and Glamour Girls* (Los Angeles: General Publishing Co., 1995), 267.

109. Quoted in John Kobal (ed.), *George Hurrell: Hollywood Glamour Portraits* (London: Schirmer, 1993), 13.

110. Susan Bernard (ed.), *Bernard of Hollywood's Marilyn* (London: Boxtree, 1993), 7.

111. Ibid. 8.

112. Cited in Jimmy McDonough, *Big Bosoms and Square Jaws: The Biography of Russ Meyer—King of the Sex Film* (London: Cape, 2005), 81.

113. Russ Meyer, *The Glamour Camera of Russ Meyer* (Louisville, Ky.: Whitestone, 195): 137–8.

114. Quoted in McDonough, *Big Bosoms and Square Jaws*, 61.

115. Bunny Yeager, *100 Girls: New Concepts in Glamour Photography* (London: Yose Ioll, 1965), 7.

116. Bill Osgerby, *Playboys in Paradise: Masculinity, Youth and Leisure-Style in Modern America* (Oxford; Berg, 2001), 146.

117. On Hefner's 'playmates', see Joan Acocella, 'The Girls Next Door', *New Yorker*, 20 Mar. 2006, pp. 144–8.

118. Osgerby, *Playboys in Paradise*, pp. 79–81.

119. Richard Hoggart, *The Uses of Literacy* (1957; Harmondsworth: Penguin, 1968), 232–3.

120. Priestley and Hawkes, *Journey Down a Rainbow*, 106–7.

121. Shtier, *Striptease*, 280.

122. Sandbrook, *Never Had It So Good*, 578.

123. For a historical analysis of the appeal of Bond, see ibid., ch. 16.

124. Graham McCann, *Cary Grant: A Class Apart* (London: Fourth Estate, 1996), 12, 122.

125. Ibid. 11.

CHAPTER 9

1. Camille Paglia, *Vamps and Tramps: New Essays* (London: Penguin, 1995), 191.

2. C. David Heymann, *A Woman Named Jackie* (1989; London: Mandarin, 1994), 254.

3. Her letter to him is reproduced in Oleg Cassini, *A Thousand Days of Magic: Dressing Jacqueline Kennedy for the White House* (New York: Rizzoli, 1995), 30.

4. Heymann, *A Woman Named Jackie*, 162.

5. Ibid. 184.

6. Quoted ibid. 220.

7. See Sarah Bradford, *Princess Grace* (London: Weidenfeld & Nicolson, 1984), 76–7.

8. See Arthur Marwick, *The Sixties: Cultural Revolution in Britain, France, Italy and the United States, c.1958–1974* (Oxford: Oxford University Press, 1998), 3.

9. Ibid. 13.

10. Guy Debord, *La Société du spectacle* (Paris: Buchet/Chastel, 1967).

11. Marwick, *The Sixties*, 18.

12. Stephen Birmingham, *Jacqueline Bouvier Kennedy Onassis* (London: Gollancz, 1979), 7–8.

13. Ibid. 178.

14. Heymann, *A Woman Named Jackie*, 138, 141.

15. The question of whether her patrician image was true or stylized was raised in Herbert Muschamp, 'Camelot's Once and Future Glamour', *New York Times*, 4 May 2001, p. E32.

16. In this sense they belonged to the most visible, lower stratum of the American upper class. See Paul Fussell, *Caste Marks: Style and Status in the USA* (London: Heinemann, 1984), 31.

17. Birmingham, *Jacqueline Bouvier*, 111.

18. Ibid. 112.

19. Wayne Koestenbaum, *Jackie under My Skin: Interpreting an Icon* (London: Fourth Estate, 1995), 70.

20. Ibid. 102.

21. Quoted ibid. 302.

22. 'She is . . . the most photogenic women in the world, infinitely more so than her infinitely more beautiful sister,' wrote Beaton in a diary entry. See Hugo Vickers (ed.), *Beaton in the Sixties* (London: Weidenfeld & Nicolson, 2003), 258. Her sister was Lee Radziwill.

23. Heymann, *A Woman Named Jackie*, 126.

24. Marilyn Bender, *The Beautiful People* (New York: Coward-McCann, 1967), 44.

25. Oleg Cassini, *In My Own Fashion: An Autobiography* (1987; New York: Pocket Books, 1990), 325.

26. Sarah Bradford, *America's Queen: The Life of Jacqueline Kennedy Onassis* (London: Viking, 2000), 506.

27. Ibid. 135.

28. Beaton did not like to think of himself as the royal photographer, yet he had been a royal favourite since before the war and was wary of pretenders to this role. At one time he feared Baron, a friend of Prince Philip's, and later Antony Armstrong-Jones. Hugo Vickers, *Cecil Beaton* (London: Weidenfeld, 1993), 367–78, 435.

29. Ibid. 499.

30. Kate de Castelbajac, *The Face of the Century* (London: Thames and Hudson, 1995), 129.

31. Bender, *Beautiful People*, 77.

32. Vickers, *Cecil Beaton*, 499.

33. Richard Martin and Harold Koda, *Diana Vreeland: Immoderate Style* (New York: Metropolitan Museum of Art, 1993), 8.

34. Ibid.

35. See Martin Harrison, *Parkinson Photographs 1935–1990* (London: Conran Octopus, 1998), pages unnumbered.

36. Anthony Haden-Guest, 'The Queen is Dead', *Observer Magazine*, 12 Feb. 2006, pp. 40–6.

37. Ibid. 95.

38. Vickers, *Cecil Beaton*, 436.

39. In his memoirs, the photographer dubbed *Queen* 'a truly revolutionary and fantastic magazine'. See Helmut Newton, *Autobiography* (London: Duckworth, 2003), 171.

40. Quoted in Haden-Guest, 'The Queen is Dead', 45. For a selection of features and photographs from the magazine, see Nicholas Coleridge and Stephen Quinn (eds.), *The Sixties in Queen* (London: Ebury, 1987).

41. For Vreeland's attitude, see Bender, *Beautiful People*, 109–10.

42. Patrick Lichfield, *Not the Whole Truth* (London: Headline 1987), 105–8.

43. Valerie Grove, 'Image Maker', *Cam*, 50 (Lent Term 2007), 11.

44. See his encounter with Prince Philip in 1960, described in Vickers, *Cecil Beaton*, 438–9.

45. Robert Glenton and Stella King, *Once Upon a Time: The Story of Antony Armstrong-Jones* (London: Anthony Blond, 1960), 13.

46. Lichfield made the point about the hairdresser in *Not the Whole Truth* (p. 90), while Aitken is quoted in Dominic Sandbrook, *White Heat: A History of Britain in the Swinging Sixties* (London: Little, Brown, 2006), 228.

47. See Jean-Noël Liaut, *Modèles et Mannequins 1945–1965* (Paris: Filipacchi, 1994).

48. Ginette Spanier, *It Isn't All Mink* (London: Collins, 1959), 198–9.

49. Bettina, *Bettina* (London: Michael Joseph, 1965), 57–8.

50. Ibid. 58.

51. See Nigel Cawthorne, *The New Look: The Dior Revolution* (London: Hamlyn, 1996), 88.

52. Ibid. 43.

53. Ibid. 42–3.

54. Jean Shrimpton, *An Autobiography* (London: Ebury, 1990), 38.

55. Ibid. 40.

56. Shawn Levy, *Ready, Steady, Go!: Swinging London and the Invention of Cool* (London: Fourth Estate, 2002), 30.

57. Ibid. 33.

58. Shrimpton, *An Autobiography*, 89.

59. Levy, *Ready, Steady, Go!*, 8–9.

60. See Coleridge and Quinn, *The Sixties in Queen*, 118–21.

61. See Anon., 'The New Class: A Postmortem', ibid. 142–5.

62. Ibid. 142.

63. David Bailey, *Box of Pin-Ups* (London: Weidenfeld & Nicolson, 1965).

64. Francis Wyndham, 'Introduction', ibid.

65. Cleveland Amory, *Who Killed Society?* (New York: Harper & Brothers, 1960), 143–4.

66. Philippa Pullar, *Gilded Butterflies: The Rise and Fall of the London Season* (London: Hamish Hamilton, 1978), 186.

67. On London nightlife in the mid-sixties, see Sandbrook, *White Heat*, 253–4.

68. The 'trickle-down' theory was formulated by Georg Simmel. See 'Fashion', *International Quarterly*, 10 (1904), 130–55.

69. For an exploration of the theme of movement and the single girl, see Hilary Radner, 'On the Move: Fashion Photography and the Single Girl in the 1960s', in Stella Bruzzi and Pamela Church Gibson (eds.), *Fashion Cultures: Theories, Explorations and Analysis* (London: Routledge, 2000), 128–42.

70. Sandbrook, *White Heat*, 232.

71. Quoted and discussed ibid. 244–6.

72. Michel Winock, *Chronique des années Soixante* (Paris:Seuil, 1987), 107.

73. Hedonism and fashion combined in sixties' New York to 'unlock the gilded cages in which some of the aristocrats had felt confined and gave the former outcasts a chance to have a whirl inside', according to Marilyn Bender in *Beautiful People*, 138–9.

74. On the culture of French youth in the 1960s, see Jean-François Sirinelli, *Les Baby Boomers: Une génération 1945–1969* (Paris: Fayard, 2003).

75. Linda Benn DeLibero compares Villeneuve to Epstein and Loog Oldham. See her essay 'This Year's Girl: A Personal/Critical History of Twiggy', in Shari Benstock and Suzanne Ferris (eds.), *On Fashion* (New Brunswick, NJ: Rutgers University Press, 1994), 41–58.

76. Twiggy, *An Autobiography* (1975; London: Granada 1976), 47.

77. Ibid. 27. On the Twiggy phenomenon, see Sandbrook, *White Heat*, ch. 15.

78. Quoted in Castelbajac, *Face of the Century*, 130.

79. See Sandbrook, *White Heat*, 224–7.

80. Twiggy, *Autobiography*, 44.

81. Clive Scott, *The Spoken Image: Photography and Language* (London: Reaktion, 1999), 145.

82. Twiggy, *Autobiography*, 74.

83. Ibid. 77.

84. Ibid. 101.

85. Mary Quant, *Quant by Quant* (London: Pan, 1966), 40.

86. Winock, *Chronique des années Soixante*, 119.

87. Alice Rawsthorn, *Yves Saint Laurent* (London: HarperCollins, 1996), 86.

88. Vickers, *Beaton in the Sixties*, 526.

89. Quoted in Vickers, *Cecil Beaton*, 511.

90. Quoted in Martin and Korda, *Diana Vreeland*, 18.

91. See Julie Kavanagh, *Rudolf Nureyev: The Life* (London: Fig Tree, 2007).

92. On the background to the film, see Levy, *Ready, Steady, Go!*, 181–6.

93. Sandbrook gives the film short shrift, claiming that it received a tepid critical and public reaction: *White Heat*, 382. In fact, it was hugely influential and more than any other single film was responsible for conveying the image of Swinging London to the world.

94. Susan Sontag, *On Photography* (1973; Harmondsworth: Penguin, 1979), 90.

95. Shrimpton, *Autobiography*, 77.

96. See Sandbrook, *White Heat*, 230.

97. Newton, *Autobiography*, 177.

98. Sontag, *On Photography*, 110.

99. Hoggart, *The Uses of Literacy*, 254.

100. Jacob Deschin, 'Glamour Across Decades', *New York Times*, 8 Aug. 1965, p. X8.

101. Corrado Morin, *Fotografia glamour* (Trieste: Edizioni Tec Foto, 1969).

102. Ibid. 28.

103. Rayment Kirby, *Glamour Photography* (London: Focal, 1983), 88.

104. Ibid.

105. Jon Stratton, *The Desirable Body: Cultural Fetishism and the Erotics of Consumption* (Manchester: Manchester University Press, 1996), 108.

106. Sandbrook, *White Heat*, 377–8.

107. Francis Wyndham, 'A Day With Elizabeth Taylor VIP', in Coleridge and Quinn, *The Sixties in Queen*, 96 and 101.

108. Winock, *Chronique des années Soixante*, 145–6.

109. Kathleen M. Barry, *Femininity in Flight: A History of Flight Attendants* (Durham, NC: Duke University Press, 2007), ch. 4.

110. Anita Colby, *Anita Colby's Beauty Book* (New York: Prentice-Hall, 1952), 2; Helen Hugh, *Glamour School* (London: Daily Mirror, undated *c*.1955), 5–6.

111. Princess Luciana Pignatelli, *The Beautiful People's Beauty Book* (New York: McCall, 1970), 16.

112. Ibid. 46 and 78.

113. Ibid. 81.

114. Birmingham, *Jacqueline Bouvier*, 167.

115. Bender, *Beautiful People*, 54

116. Ibid. 53.

117. Ibid. 44–6.

118. Ibid. 46.

119. Bradford, *America's Queen*, 439.

120. Ibid. 71.

121. Ron Galella, *Off-Guard: Beautiful People Unveiled before the Camera Lens* (New York: Greenwich House, 1987), 125.

122. Ibid. 124.

123. Sontag, *On Photography*, 67.

124. See Koestenbaum, *Jackie under My Skin*, 168–9.

125. Barbara Seaman, *Lovely Me: The Life of Jacqueline Susann* (London: Sidgwick & Jackson, 1988), 283.

126. Jacqueline Susann, *Jacqueline Susann's Dolores* (London: W. H. Allen, 1976), 27.

127. Jacqueline Susann, *Jacqueline Susann's Dolores* (London: W. H. Allen, 1976), 58.

128. Ibid. 55.

129. Koestenbaum, *Jackie under My Skin*, 248.

130. Ibid. 248.

131. See Scott, *Spoken Image*, 156–7.

CHAPTER 10

1. Mark Francis and Margery King (eds.), *The Warhol Look: Glamour, Style, Fashion* (Boston: Bullfinch Press, 1998), 36–7.

2. Interview in Patrick Smith (ed.), *Andy Warhol's Art and Films* (Ann Arbor: UMI Research Press, 1986), 458.

3. Ibid. 127.

4. For Juan A. Suárez, Warhol's superstars were 'a parodic simulacrum' in the void left by the decline of the star system. *Bike Boys, Drag Queens & Superstars* (Bloomington: Indiana University Press, 1996), 228.

5. Roger Baker, *Drag: A History of Feminine Impersonation in the Performing Arts* (1968; London: Cassell, 1994), 14–15.

6. Andy Warhol, *The Philosophy of Andy Warhol: From A to B and Back Again* (London: Cassell, 1975), 54.

7. Ibid. 54–5.

8. Ibid. 68.

9. Ibid. 54.

10. Richard Schickel argued that Warhol was 'a sort of demented Louis B. Mayer' who turned himself into 'the dumb blonde of Hollywood lore, displaced but distinctly reincarnated'. See *Intimate Strangers: The Culture of Celebrity* (Garden City, NY: Doubleday and Co., 1985), 237–8.

11. Fred Guiles, *Loner At The Ball: The Life of Andy Warhol* (London: Bantam, 1989), 53–4.

12. Schickel, *Intimate Strangers*, 157.

13. Ibid. 71.

14. See Jeffrey L. Meikle, *American Plastic: A Cultural History* (New Brunswick; Rutgers University Press, 1995). See also Peter Wollen, 'Plastics', in Francis and King, (eds.), *Warhol Look*, unnumbered page.

15. Warhol, *Philosophy of Andy Warhol*, 53.

16. Richard Schickel referred to Warhol's 'bland translucency' like 'frosted glass' and quoted him as once saying, 'If you want to know about Andy Warhol, just look at the surface of my paintings and films and me, and there I am. There is nothing behind it.' See *Intimate Strangers*, 236–7.

17. Warhol, *Philosophy of Andy Warhol*, 85.

18. See Justin Kaplan (ed.), *Barlett's Familiar Quotations* 18th edn. (New York: Little, Brown, 1992), 758.

19. Ibid. 56.

20. Ibid. 61.

21. Baker, *Drag*, 246–7.

22. Philip Auslander, *Performing Glam Rock: Gender and Theatricality in Popular Music* (Ann Arbor: University of Michigan Press, 2006), 122.

23. Ibid. 48. See also Baker, *Drag*, 241.

24. Baker, *Drag*, 206.

25. Barney Hoskyns, *Glam! Bowie, Bolan and the Glitter Rock Revolution* (New York: Pocket Books, 1998), 23.

26. Auslander suggests that some glam rockers also appropriated musical motifs from Elvis, Gene Vincent, and other 1950s rock and rollers. See *Performing Glam Rock*, 56–7.

27. Karal Ann Marling, *Graceland: Going Home with Elvis* (Cambridge, Mass.: Harvard University Press, 1996).

28. On the early years of Roxy Music, see Michael Bracewell, *Re-Make/Re-Model* (London: Faber, 2007) and his article 'Look Back in Languor', *Guardian Weekend*, 14 June 1997.

29. Bracewell, 'Look Back in Languor', 20.

30. Quoted ibid.

31. Ibid.

32. Ibid. 22.

33. 'I guess I have not been very good at timing in my career. In most cases I was a little early, but then I was too late for the glamorous Hollywood period. Maybe if I had woken up in Travis Banton's shoes, I would have done just fine, but there are not that many Marlenes around.' Antony Price, quoted in Iain R. Webb, 'Price of Perfection', *Independent Magazine*, 24 June 2006, p. 33.

34. Bracewell, 'Look Back in Languor', 25.

35. David Riesman, *The Lonely Crowd: A Study of the Changing American Character* (New Haven: Yale University Press, 1950).

36. Christopher Lasch, *The Culture of Narcissism* (1979; London: Abacus, 1980), 166.

37. Christopher Lasch, *The Culture of Narcissism* (1979; London: Abacus, 1980), 174.

38. See Tom Wolfe, 'The Me Decade and the Third Great Awakening', in Wolfe, *Mauve Gloves & Madmen, Clutter and Vine* (Tornot: Bantam, 1977). These positions coincided in general terms with the perspective developed a few years earlier by the French situationist Guy Debord, who wrote: 'Behind the glitter of the spectacle's distractions, modern society lies in thrall to the global domination of a banalizing trend that also dominates it at each point where the most advanced forms of commodity consumption have seemingly broadened the panoply of roles and objects available to choose from. The vestiges of religion and of the family... can now be seamlessly combined with the rhetorical advocacy of pleasure in *this life.*' See *The Society of Spectacle* (1967; New York: Zone Books, 1995), 38.

39. In a critique of Lasch's narcissism thesis, Russell Jacoby argued that narcissism harboured protest in the name of individual health and happiness against the ethic of sacrifice. See 'Narcissism and the Crisis of Capitalism', *Telos*, 44 (1980), 58–65. For his part, Stuart Ewen suggested that narcissism was not new; consumerism from the late nineteenth century had undermined traditional group bonds in favour of the satisfaction of needs. See 'Mass Culture, Narcissism and the Moral Economy of War', *Telos*, 44 (1980), 74–87. This process gradually made the individual more subject to the media, whose products, even if they were consumed collectively, were interiorized individually.

40. For a sustained reflection on surface and depth in fashion and appearance, see Alexandra Warwick and Dani Cavallaro, *Fashioning the Frame: Boundaries, Dress and the Body* (Oxford: Berg, 1998), ch. 4.

41. Gerald Clarke, *Capote: A Biography* (1988; London: Abacus, 1993), 541.

42. Bracewell, 'Look Back in Languor', 25.

43. See Michael Bracewell, 'The Return of the Glamour Boy', *ES Magazine*, 31 Mar. 2000, p. 20.

44. On early London discotheques, see Dominic Sandbrook, *White Heat: A History of Britain in the Swinging Sixties* (London: Little, Brown, 2006), 248–50.

45. Alicia Drake, *The Beautiful Fall: Fashion, Genius and Glorious Excess in 1970s Paris* (London: Bloomsbury, 2006), 119–20.

46. See Anthony Haden-Guest, *The Last Party: Studio 54, Disco and the Culture of the Night* (New York: Morrow, 1997).

47. Cited ibid. 50.

48. Ibid. 63.

49. Ibid. 52.

50. Truman Capote, *Unanswered Prayers: The Unfinished Novel* (London: Hamish Hamilton, 1988). Sections of the novel were published in *Esquire* in 1975 and 1976. The chapter entitled 'La Côte Basque', based on the personal life of CBS owner William Paley and his stylish wife Barbara 'Babe', one of Capote's confidantes, was seen as a betrayal. The author exposed

the glamorous life of the rich as a shark pool of confidence tricksters and sexual predators. In consequence, his one-time friends closed their doors to him.

51. Pat Hackett (ed.), *The Andy Warhol Diaries* (London: Simon and Schuster, 1989), 101.

52. Kennedy Fraser, *The Fashionable Mind: Reflections on Fashion 1970–1981* (New York: Knopf, 1981), 73.

53. Hackett (ed.), *The Andy Warhol Diaries*, 94.

54. Francis and King, *Warhol Look*, 248.

55. On the dawn of the style culture of the 1980s in Britain, see Dylan Jones, 'Hello Gorgeous', *The Sunday Times, News Review* suppl., 4 Apr. 1999, pp. 1–2.

56. The 15,000 clients that bought couture in the post-war years had shrunk, by the later 1960s, to just to 3,000. The number of couturiers in Paris was also shrinking, from around one hundred, they were down to forty by 1965. See Alice Rawsthorn, *Yves Saint Laurent* (London: HarperCollins, 1996), 84–5.

57. Ibid. 116–17.

58. The American model Pat Cleveland, who worked for the Paris house Chloe in the early 1970s, claimed to have introduced a new show-off element to modelling. Even though she was modelling in-house, in the time-honoured way, she discarded her usual poses: 'I started to smile, I started to move my legs. I was doing all sorts of poses on the stairs, I was doing every movie star I ever knew, Marilyn, Jane Russell, blowing kisses; I was touching my hair, touching my body and people were screaming and standing up, applauding and trying to touch me.' Her attitude was similar to that of Warhol's wannabe superstars: 'we had grown up with movies and movie star attitude and we were there to be stars, superstars. We wanted to shine day and night,' she recalled. Quoted in Drake, *Beautiful Fall*, 118–19.

59. Italian photographer Oliviero Toscani noted that Newton, who died at age 83 in Jan. 2004, had experienced a star's death, at the wheel of a Cadillac on Sunset Boulevard. Among the tributes offered by Newton's colleagues in French magazine *Photo*, he controversially observed that the late photographer's work was paradoxical. Despite his Jewish origins, 'it seems to me that the near totality of his photos bear the stigmata of the Third Reich', Toscani asserted. 'His models, his celebrated female nudes, seemed to me to be variants of a virtual Brunhilde, of an entirely Wagnerian Walkyrie. His imagination was concentrated on bodies that exhibit a sculptural immobility; he captured their potential cruelty and their inaccessible character. I am under the impression that in this he owed much to Leni Riefenstahl and to her Aryan models.' *Photo* (Spécial Helmut Newton) (Apr. 2004), 88–90. In his *Autobiography* (London: Duckworth, 2003), Newton confessed his great admiration for Riefenstahl (whom he met on several occasions) as a film-maker and photographer (p. 274).

60. See Karl Lagerfeld, 'Sa vie', *Photo* (Spécial Helmut Newton) (Apr. 2004), 28.

61. See Sean O'Hagan, 'The King of Kinky', *Observer Magazine*, 7 Aug. 2005, p. 20.

62. Newton, *Autobiography*, 189.

63. The photographer never bothered to counter criticism. Indeed, in his autobiography, he declared: 'I have always been very interested in prostitution, since I saw Red Erna at the age of seven. There is something about buying a woman that excites me. One of the things that used to excite me was the concept that the woman was like merchandise.' See ibid. 158.

64. He claimed never to consider what might excite the public: 'if I were to do that, I would never take a picture. No, I just please myself,' he stated (ibid. 241). However, when he took a picture of actress Hannah Schygulla as Lili Marlene for German *Vogue* in which her underarm hair was on view, he found that there were boundaries to his freedom. 'In the world of *Vogue*, there is no underarm hair, ever,' he was forced to acknowledge (ibid. 235).

65. Newton admitted that he had done some privately commissioned pornographic work. See ibid. 261.

66. See Natalia Aspesi, 'Lei, signora senza rimpianti', *La repubblica*, 14 Mar. 1999, p. 38.

67. On Deneuve and Chanel, see Judith Williamson, *Decoding Advertisements: Ideology and Meaning in Advertisements* (London; Marion Boyars, 1978), 27–30.

68. Lasch, *Culture of Narcissism*, 166.

69. See Riesman, *Lonely Crowd*. His analysis is referred to in ch. 8.

70. Boussac in fact failed to deal with the changes of the 1970s as well as he had those of the post-war world. He went bankrupt in 1978.

71. Drake, *Beautiful Fall*, 129.

72. Steven Gaines, *Simply Halston: The Untold Story* (New York: Putnam's, 1991), 8.

73. Fraser, *Fashionable Mind*, 114.

74. Georgina Howell, *Sultans of Style: Thirty Years of Fashion and Passion 1960–1990* (London: Ebury, 1990), 80.

75. Drake, *Beautiful Fall*, 163.

76. Steven Gaines and Sharon Churcher, *Obsession: The Lives and Times of Calvin Klein* (1994; New York: Avon 1995), 85–7.

77. Ibid. 93. See also Caroline Rennolds Milbank, *New York Fashion: The Evolution of American Style* (New York: Abrams, 1989), 242.

78. Ibid. 191.

79. Richard Morais, *Pierre Cardin: The Man Who Became a Label* (London: Bantam, 1991), 91.

80. Ibid. 150.

81. Gaines, *Simply Halston*, 239.

82. This process is analysed at length in Colin McDowell, *The Designer Scam* (London: Hutchinson, 1994).

83. Gaines and Churcher, *Obsession*, 235.

84. Ibid. 101.

85. Drake, *Beautiful Fall*, 66.

86. Ibid. 139–40.

87. Ibid. 130.

88. On these controversial episodes, see Michael Gross, *Genuine Authentic: The Real Life of Ralph Lauren* (New York: HarperCollins, 2003), 153–4, 176.

89. Graham McCann, *Cary Grant: A Class Apart* (London: Fourth Estate, 1996), 3.

90. Ibid.

91. See Colin McDowell, *Ralph Lauren: The Man, The Vision, The Style* (London: Cassell, 2002), 136–40.

92. See McDowell, *Designer Scam*, 176–80.

93. Ibid. 206.

94. Ibid. 11.

95. Ibid. 74.

96. Ibid. 122.

97. This difference was present in the mind of Esther Shapiro, one of the show's creators. See Jostein Gripsrud, *The Dynasty Years: Hollywood Television and Critical Media Studies* (London: Routledge, 1995), 34–5. In some ways Blake Carrington resembled the show's producer, Aaron Spelling.

98. Joan Collins, *Past Imperfect* (London: Coronet, 1978), 47.

99. Gripsrud, *Dynasty Years*, 152.

100. Patricia A. Cunningham, Heather Mangine, and Andrew Reilly, 'Television and Fashion in the 1980s', in Linda Welters and Patricia A. Cunningham (eds.), *Twentieth-Century American Fashion* (Oxford: Berg, 2005), 222.

101. Debora Silverman, *Selling Culture: Bloomingdale's, Diana Vreeland and the New Aristocracy of Taste in Reagan's America* (New York: Pantheon, 1986), 152.

102. David Cannadine, *The Decline and Fall of the British Aristocracy* (1990; New Haven and London: Yale University Press, 1996), 689.

103. John Fairchild, *Chic Savages* (New York: Simon and Schuster 1989), 88.

104. By 1996, the figure was $500 m. See Colin McDowell, 'Get a Life, Viv', *The Sunday Times, Style* suppl., 22 Sept. 1996, pp. 10–11.

105. Gross, *Genuine Authentic*, 227.

106. McDowell, *Ralph Lauren*, 136.

107. Ibid. 136–8.

108. Gaines and Churcher, *Obsession*, 389. Although drug addiction would shortly force him into re-hab, he returned to cultivate an image of a conventional lifestyle. On his drug addiction, see ibid. 217–19.

109. Thorstein Veblen, *Theory of the Leisure Class* (1899; Boston: Houghton Mifflin, 1973), 72.

110. See McDowell, 'Get a Life, Viv'. British designers, he argues, did not grasp this at all.

111. Joshua Meyrowitz, *No Sense of Place: The Impact of Electronic Media on Social Behaviour* (New York: Oxford University Press, 1986), 99.

112. See Rennolds Milbank, *New York Fashion*, 275.

113. Fairchild, *Chic Savages*, 78.

114. Fraser, *Fashionable Mind*, 154.

115. See Stephen Gundle, 'Hollywood Glamour and Mass Consumption in Postwar Italy', *Journal of Cold War Studies*, 4/3 (Fall 2002), 95–118.

116. See McDowell, *Designer Scam*, 54–6.

117. Quoted in Bob Colacello, 'Nan in Full', *Vanity Fair* (Apr. 2005), 183.

118. Ibid. 178.

119. See Fairchild, *Chic Savages*.

120. Ibid. 66.

121. Michael Specter, 'The Kingdom', *New Yorker*, 26 Sept. 2005, p. 126.

122. Quoted in Antonella Amapane, 'Valentino seduce con pizzi e drapeggi', *La stampa*, 10 July 2000, p. 14.

123. Quoted in Anon., 'Guardate questa meraviglia: È la ricca casa romana di Valentino, il sarto delle stelle', *Gente*, 25 Jan. 1993, p. 81.

124. William Middleton, 'Prince Val', *W* (Apr. 1997), 50.

125. Ibid. 135.

126. Howell, *Sultans of Style*, 27.

127. Nicholas Coleridge, *The Fashion Conspiracy* (London: Heinemann, 1988), 223.

128. The house was first displayed in the press in Anon., 'Guardate questa meraviglia', 80–3.

129. *Time*, 14 (1982). The cover read: 'Giorgio's Gorgeous Style', while the accompanying article praised his role in reshaping and restructuring the way people dress.

130. See, for example, Meredith Etherington-Smith, 'Smooth Operator', *Telegraph Magazine*, suppl. to *Daily Telegraph*, 23 Aug. 2003, p. 27.

131. See Cunningham, Mangine, and Reilly, 'Television and Fashion in the 1980s', 212.

132. Drake, *Beautiful Fall*, 129–30. See also John Colapinto, ' "You'll Think I'm a Madman" ', *Observer Magazine*, 27 May 2007, pp. 19–20.

CHAPTER 11

1. So insatiable was the thirst for pictures of her and so lucrative were the rewards for them that she became quite literally a prey for dozens of paparazzi photographers. Her death in Paris while seeking to evade their insistent attentions was, it was observed, like 'a ghoulish re-run of *La Dolce Vita*', the film in which these celebrity hunters first came to public attention and acquired their name. Simon Jenkins, 'No law could have shielded her', *The Times*, 1 Sept. 1997, p. 24.

2. Paul Johnson, 'The Two Sides of Diana', *Daily Mail*, 1 Sept. 1997, p. 4.

3. Bryan Appleyard, 'Diana, First Lady of the Global Village', *Sunday Times, News Review*, 7 Sept. 1997, p. 6. Compare his observation with Stuart Ewen's view that 'photogenic beauty rests its definition on a smooth, standardised and lifeless modernism, a machine

aesthetic in the guise of a human.' See *All Consuming Images: The Politics of Style in Contemporary Culture* (New York: Basic Books, 1988), 89.

4. Quoted in Georgina Howell, *Diana: Her Life in Fashion* (London: Pavilion, 1998), 151.

5. Ibid. 204.

6. Tina Brown, *The Diana Chronicles* (London: Century, 2007), 210.

7. Sarah Lincoln, untitled testimony, 'The day I met Diana', *Observer*, 7 Sept. 1997, p. 17.

8. Sarah Bradford, 'Princess of All Our hearts', *Mail on Sunday, Night & Day* suppl., 7 Sept. 1997, p. 6.

9. The most illuminating reflections on these aspects of Diana, which the author ties closely to her gender, are contained in Naomi Segal, 'The Common Touch', in Mandy Merck (ed.), *After Diana: Irreverent Elegies* (London: Verso, 1998), 131–45.

10. See the reflections on this point of the historian Ross McKibbin in 'Mass Observation in the Mall', in Merck (ed.), *After Diana*, 15–24.

11. The princess met and took some advice from Princess Grace and, when no one else in the royal family volunteered, she attended the latter's funeral in 1982. She compared herself to Jackie Kennedy and imitated the latter's crisp elegance and the simplicity of line of her evening gowns. She wore Versace's pastiche versions of Jackie's pastel suits and pillbox hats. Howell, *Diana*, 166–8.

12. Ibid. 165.

13. Ibid. 72. Brown, *Diana Chronicles*, 198–9.

14. Johnson, 'Two Sides of Diana', 4.

15. Lesley White, 'Only Dodi the outsider would do', *Sunday Times, New Review* suppl., 7 Sept. 1997, p. 5.

16. She was careful to adjust the glamour quotient of her appearance to circumstances—for example, pumping it up to full blast for charity fundraising bashes in the US and toning it down several degrees when visiting AIDS patients or pensioners—and was also seeking to add substance and depth to her involvement in campaigns and charity work.

17. Brown, *Diana Chronicles*, 337.

18. Sociologists referred to these currents as post-materialism and detraditionalization. The concept of post-materialism, meaning a shift from primary to secondary (or post-materialist, quality of life) goals, was developed by Ronald Inglehart in *The Silent Revolution: Changing Values and Political Styles among Western Publics* (Princeton: Princeton University Press, 1977). Detraditionalization is investigated in Paul Heelas, Scott Lash, and Paul Morris (eds.), *De-Traditionalization: Critical Reflections on Authority and Identity at a Time of Uncertainty* (Oxford: Blackwell, 1996). The important role of electronic media in weakening the relationship between physical place and social 'place' is explored in Joshua Meyrowitz, *No Sense of Place: The Impact of Electronic Media on Social Behaviour* (New York: Oxford university Press, 1986).

19. See Paul Ginsborg, *The Politics of Everyday Life* (New Haven and London: Yale University Press, 2004), sect. 2.

20. Ulrich Beck, *Risk Society: Towards a New Modernity* (London: Sage, 1992), 95.

21. 'Her worldwide fame made Britain shine more greatly. . . . I am no royalist, but even I can see it was her—not Oasis, Stella Tennant or Terence Conran—who made Britain glamorous,' Nigella Lawson, 'Why the nation is right to share family's grief', *The Times*, 1 Sept. 1997, p. 23.

22. Brown, *Diana Chronicles*, 245–6.

23. A typical feature in the new-style *Tatler* was 'Swankly, my dear, we don't give a damn' (July 1998) (pp. 106–52), which transformed Rhett Butler's famous retort to Scarlett O'Hara in *Gone With The Wind* into a suggested response of the rich to the rest. The feature endorsed material ostentation so long as it was tempered with style and sophistication.

24. The phenomenon was noted in *The Sunday Times*, *Style* suppl., 29 Sept. 1996, pp. 4–5. Three reporters covered its manifestations in London, New York, and Moscow.

25. Attending such events was described by the British columnist India Knight as deplorable 'ligging' (i.e. 'the act of turning up at some slightly embarrassing bash simply because you have been asked'). 'Here's Looking at Me', *The Sunday Times*, *News Review*, 18 Apr. 1999, p. 3. By contrast, Joshua Gamson sees it as an example of the industrial nature of celebrity work. Such events are part of the assembly line of the manufacture of fame. See *Claims to Fame: Celebrity in Contemporary America* (Berkeley and Los Angeles: University of California Press, 1994), 61.

26. See Meyrowitz, *No Sense of Place*, p. ix.

27. Cathy Horyn, 'Diana Reborn', *Vanity Fair* (July 1997), 84.

28. See Dana Thomas, *Deluxe: How Luxury Lost its Lustre* (London: Allen Lane, 2007), 44–9, 60–1.

29. Stefania Saviolo, 'Brand and Identity Management in Fashion Companies', Research Division, SDA BOCCONI, Working Paper 02–66 (Milan, 2002), 9. See also, on brands as a key example of American business practice, Victoria De Grazia, *Irresistible Empire: America's Advance through Twentieth Century Europe* (Cambridge, Mass.: Harvard University Press, 2005), 184–225.

30. The model illustrated in this paragraph is set out in C. M. Moore and G. Birtwistle, 'The Nature of Parenting Advantage in Luxury Fashion Retailing: The Case of Gucci', *International Journal of Retail and Distribution Management*, 33/4 (2005), 256–70.

31. According to Andrea Stuart, Las Vegas was the last home of the kitsch flamboyance of the showgirl. See *Showgirls* (London: Cape, 1996), 208.

32. Thomas, *Deluxe*, 235–45.

33. Ibid. 41, 221, 241.

34. See Réka C. V. Buckley and Stephen Gundle, 'Flash Trash: Gianni Versace and the Theory and Practice of Glamour', in Stella Bruzzi and Pamela Church Gibson (eds.), *Fashion Cultures: Theories, Explorations and Analysis* (London: Routledge, 2000).

35. *Sunday Telegraph*, 24 July 1994.

36. Denise Pardo, 'Filosofia della vistosità', *L'espresso*, 24 July 1997, p. 52.

37. For a discussion of the nature of Elizabeth Hurley's celebrity, see Lee Barrow, ' "Elizabeth Hurley is More than a Model": Stars and Career Diversification in Contemporary Media', *Journal of Popular Culture*, 39/4 (2006). On the dress itself, see Richard Martin, 'Gianni Versace's Anti-Bourgeois Little Black Dress (1994)', *Fashion Theory*, 2/1 (1998), 95–100.

38. On the history of the catwalk, see Caroline Evans, 'The Enchanted Spectacle', *Fashion Theory*, 5/3 (2001), 271–310. For an insider testimony, see Marie Helvin, *Catwalk: The Art of Model Style* (London; Pavilion, 1985), 87.

39. Daniel Boorstin, *The Image* (1962; London: Penguin, 1971), 21–3.

40. Colin McDowell, *The Designer Scam* (London: Hutchinson, 1994), 119.

41. The cover read 'Supermodels: Beauty and the Bucks'. However, only Naomi Campbell was pictured. *Time*, 16 Sept. 1991.

42. See Anon., 'Avedon and Versace's Top Show', *Elle Top Model*, 6 (1994), 14–21.

43. The number of 'supermodels' is not easy to estimate since the term was applied to many. One journalist estimated in 1995 that around thirty had joined 'the super club class'. See Peter Martin, 'Superpower', *Mail on Sunday, Night & Day* suppl., 13 Aug. 1995, p. 13.

44. See Anon., 'Linda Evangelista, Miss Sublimissima', *Elle Top Model*, 6 (1994), 33.

45. For Andrea Stuart, 'She, like the showgirl, is exaggerated and overblown, custom-built to meet our society's need for a glamorous icon whose desirability lies in her impossibility and inaccessibility,' *Showgirls*, 222.

46. Quoted in Michael Gross, *Model* (1995; London: 1996), 360.

47. Quoted in Michael Gross, *Model* (1995; London: 1996), 505.

48. Ibid.

49. Anon., 'Beauty Knows No Border', *Elle Top Model*, 1 (1994), 5.

50. Jay McInerney, *Model Behaviour* (1998; London: Bloomsbury, 1999), 1.

51. Colin McDowell, 'The Show Must Go On', *The Times Magazine*, 6 Dec. 1997, p. 42.

52. Ibid.

53. Brenda Polan, 'Is glamour glitter—or a graceful line?', *Financial Times*, 31 Dec.–1 Jan. 1995, *Weekend* suppl., p. vii.

54. Len Prince, *About Glamour* (New York: Simon and Schuster, 1997); Serge Normant, *Femme Fatale* (New York: Viking, 2001).

55. Gamson, *Claims to Fame*, 6. His work is an intelligent reflection on celebrity in general and on the debates that it has aroused.

56. 'The Limelight Club', *The Times Magazine*, 24 Aug. 1996.

57. Lesley-Ann Jones, *Naomi: The Rise of the Girl from Nowhere* (London: Vermillion, 1993), 19.

58. Anon., 'The Place the Mini-Tops Call Home', *Elle Top Model*, 4 (1994), 40–3.

59. Italian lawyer Auro Varani quoted in Gross, *Model*, 325. Sarah Doukas, founder of the Storm model agency, revealed that film stars would ring her requesting to meet the girl they had seen in this or that campaign. ' "It makes me giggle", she says, "when I get a call from a

household name. If the girl is under 16, I'd really think hard about passing the number on to her, but if she's older, I don't have much choice. And you know they are going to be impressed".' Quoted in Lydia Slater, '10 Years On: The Changing Face of the Model Agency', *Daily Telegraph*, 29 Aug. 1997, p. 20.

60. Gross, *Model*, 460.

61. Ibid.

62. See Michael Gross, 'Coming Apart at the Seams', *Tatler* (May 1995), 146–9.

63. The role of voice coach Peter Settelin is discussed in Sally Bedell Smith, Diana: The Life of a Troubled Princess (1999; London: Aurum, 2007), 246–7. He recalled his hooker suggestion in a television documentary.

64. Toby Young, *How to Lose Friends and Alienate People* (2001; London: Abacus, 2002), 290.

65. B. B. Calhoun, *Party Girl* (London: Red Fox, 1994), 5.

66. Judi James, *Supermodel* (London: HarperCollins, 1994), 163.

67. Gross, *Model*, 507.

68. See Gaia De Beaumont, 'Come…', *Vogue* (Italia) (Sept. 1994), 357–9.

69. Gross, *Model*, 485–6.

70. Ibid.

71. Anon., 'Glamour as it was and is', *Creative Review* (May 1996), 72–3.

72. In her introduction to a collection of Unwerth's photographs, Ingrid Sischy highlights the apparent spontaneity of her images. See 'WHOOPS, It's Ellen von Unwerth', in Ellen von Unwerth, *Snaps* (Santa Fe, N. Mex.: Twin Palms Publishers, 1995), page unnumbered.

73. However, Bert Stern threatened legal action when Meisel posed Madonna in the style of his late photographs of Marilyn Monroe.

74. See, among others, John Kobal (ed.), *Film Star Portraits of the Fifties* (New York: Dover, 1980) and *The Art of the Great Hollywood Portrait Photographers 1925–1940* (London: Allen Lane, 1980).

75. See Liz Jobey, 'Helmut's Second Coming', *Independent on Sunday*, 13 Nov. 1994, pp. 52–5.

76. Anon., 'Spy Beauty', *Vogue* (UK) (Oct. 1994), 241.

77. Liz Smith, 'Gotta Have Glam', *She* (Nov. 1994), 136.

78. Ibid. 137–8.

79. Polan, 'Is glamour glitter?', p. vii.

80. Sarah Mower, 'Now playing a major role in fashion and beauty, movie star glamour celebrates femininity', *Vogue* (UK) (Oct. 1994), 217.

81. Quoted in Roger Baker, *Drag: A History of Female Impersonation in the Performing Arts* (1988; London: Cassell, 2nd rev. edn. 1994), 258.

82. On Madonna's connections with the showgirl tradition, see Stuart, *Showgirls*, 211–13.

452

83. See e.g. Cathy Schwichtenberg (ed.), *The Madonna Connection: Representational Politics, Subcultural Identities and Cultural Theory* (Boulder, Colo.: Westview, 1993).

84. David Tetzaleff, 'Metatextual Girl >patriarchy>postmodernism>power>money> Madonna,' in ibid. 242.

85. Christopher Anderson, *Madonna Unauthorized* (London: Michael Joseph, 1991), 131.

86. Stuart, *Showgirls*, 218.

87. Photograph caption, *Photo* (French edn.) (Apr. 2005), 56.

88. See, for example, Vicki Woods, 'Forever Joan', *Vogue* (UK) (May 1996), 138–43. The article is illustrated with Mario Testino's photographs of the actress playing the glamour queen.

89. Sarah Gristwood, 'Whatever It Takes', *Guardian, Weekend* suppl., 5 Dec. 1998, p. 25. However, Stone was not always so and in fact turned up to one gala occasion wearing and old skirt and a turtleneck sweater from Gap. The implications of this are considered in Rebecca L. Epstein, 'Sharon Stone in a Gap Turtleneck', in David Desser and Garth S. Jowett (eds.), *Hollywood Goes Shopping* (Minneapolis: University of Minnesota Press, 2000), 179–204.

90. Curiously, in many beauty and fragrance advertisements the stars were airbrushed almost beyond recognition, with the result that it was necessary to print their names on the page to reassure potential customers that it was indeed Sharon Stone or Hilary Swank who was pictured.

91. Gucci's Tom Ford was allegedly appalled to see Victoria Beckham wearing his label, while Burberry suffered after troubled British television actress Daniella Westbrook was pictured dressed head-to-toe in its famous check. Bentley, Cristal champagne, and other prestige brands were also appropriated by footballers and pop stars in a process that came to be dubbed 'getting chavved' (after the youth subcultural group known as Chavs, whose members were distinguished by their use of selected prestige accessories, notably Burberry baseball caps). 'The beauty of watching bastions of privilege getting chavved is that it dispels the myth of entitlement surrounding essentially commercial transactions,' wrote Nick Curtis in 'You've Been Chavved', *Evening Standard* 26 July 2006, pp. 30–1.

92. For a discussion of the 'ghetto fabulous' style in film, see Stella Bruzzi, *Undressing Cinema: Clothing and Identity in the Movies* (London: Routledge, 1997), 103–7.

93. After Victoria Beckham was publicly disowned by Tom Ford, she was courted by Cavalli, who even recruited her for his catwalk shows. On Italian fashion and bling, see Stephen Gundle, 'Lo stile e la merce: La ricezione della moda italiana in Gran Bretagna e negli Stati Uniti', *Memoria e ricerca*, 23 (Sept.–Dec. 2006), 95–116.

94. On English football's encounter with Italian fashion, see Stella Bruzzi, 'The Italian Job: Football, Fashion and That Sarong', in Bruzzi and Church Gibson, *Fashion Cultures*, 286–97.

95. Jerry Oppenheimer, *Front Row: Anna Wintour—the Cool Life and Hot Times of Vogue's Editor in Chief* (New York: St Martin's Press, 2005), 204.

96. Ibid. 205.

97. Young, *How to Lose Friends*, 270.

98. Quoted in Pat Booth, 'A Man For All Seasons: Snowdon', *Photoicon*, 2/2 (2007), 51.

99. Andrew Billen, ' "A Lot of Me is Dirty and Seedy. I like Sex. I Don't Think I am a Goody-Goody Person" ', *Evening Standard*, 23 Jan. 2002, pp. 23–4.

100. Jared Schiller, 'An Unappealing Superficial World', *Morning Star*, 5 Feb. 2002, p. 9.

101. Marianne Macdonald, 'How I Made a Model of Diana', *Daily Mail*, *Night & Day* suppl., 22 Aug. 1999, p. 9.

102. Mario Testino, 'My Life in Pictures', *Independent*, *Extra* suppl., 3 Feb. 2006, p. iii.

103. See Sante D'Orazio, *Pamela Anderson: American Icon* (New York: Schirmer, 2005).

104. On striptease revivals in particular, see Rachel Shteir, *Striptease: The Untold History of the Girlie Show* (New York: Oxford University Press, 2004), 3.

105. Dita von Teese, *Burlesque and the Art of the Teese* (New York: Regan Books, 2006). In a magazine article, she declared, 'I wanted to be like Marlene Dietrich, Betty Grable and Rita Hayworth. But it struck me that you never saw those actresses shaving their head or going without makeup for a role. They were all perfectly made-up all the time. I was, like, "Wow"—any woman can create this glamour, it's not something you have to be born with.' See Camilla Kay, 'Glamour Goddess', *In Style*, Oct. 2007, p. 205. Von Teese, following Ru Paul, became a testimonial for MAC's Viva Glam range.

106. Von Teese, *Burlesque and the Art of the Teese*, cover flap and p. xi.

107. Dita von Teese, *Fetish and the Art of the Teese* (New York: Regan Books 2006), 29–41. It should be noted that this volume is the back half of *Burlesque and the Art of the Teese* turned upside down and endowed with its own title and cover.

108. Gamson, *Claims to Fame*, 74–96.

109. Thomas, *Deluxe*, 123–4.

110. Lina Das, 'The Stylist Who Shrank the Stars', *Mail on Sunday*, *You* magazine, 7 Oct. 2007, pp. 48–52.

111. Rachel Zoe with Rose Apodaca, *Style A to Zoe: The Art of Fashion, Beauty and Everything Glamour* (New York: Little, Brown, 2007).

112. Das, 'Stylist Who Shrank the Stars', 51.

113. Zoe, *Style A to Zoe*, 3.

114. Ibid. 11.

115. Ibid. 166.

116. Ibid.

117. Krista Smith, 'The Inescapable Paris', *Vanity Fair* (Oct. 2005), 149–233.

118. On the fascination of the heiress, see Cesare Cunaccia, 'The Glam and the Heiress', *Vogue* (Italia), *A Couture Dream* suppl. (Sept. 2006), pages unnumbered.

119. See Jerry Oppenheimer, *House of Hilton: From Conrad to Paris* (New York; Crown, 2006).

120. Paris Hilton, *Confessions of an Heiress*, with Merle Ginsberg (London: Pocket Books, 2004), 120.

121. Ibid. 93.

122. Ibid. 8.

123. See e.g. Judy Mazel, *The Beverly Hills Style* (New York: Stein & Day, 1985), which was translated into several languages, including Italian.

124. *Sun*, 5 June 2007, p. 4.

CONCLUSION

1. Lucia van der Post, *Things I Wish My Mother Had Told Me: Lessons In Grace and Elegance* (London: John Murray, 2007), 27.

2. Joshua Meyrowitz, *No Sense of Place: The Impact of Electronic Media on Social Behavior* (New York: Oxford University Press, 1986), 222–3.

3. At the start of the new century, Ralph Lauren even launched a fragrance named 'Glamour-ous,' a curious misspelling that was clearly intended to ensure that the adjective retained the European connotation of the '-our' ending.

4. Shane Watson, 'Britain's Most Photographed Woman Victoria Beckham Reveals Her Secrets', *Hello!*, 12 Sept. 2006, p. 76.

5. Victoria Beckham, *That Extra-Half Inch: Hair, Heels and Everything in Between* (London: Penguin, 2006), 6.

6. Anon., 'Cheryl Cole', *OK*, 17 Oct. 2006, p. 47.

7. Kelly Brook, *Life Style: How to Pin Down the Pin-up Within You* (London: Orion, 2007), 9.

8. Ibid. Victoria Beckham, Cheryl Cole, and Kelly Brook were not included in the list of seventy-three glamorous personalities featured in a special 'glamour issue' of British *Vogue* in Dec. 2007. For an explanation of the magazine's view of glamour, see Anon., 'Who's Glamorous Now?, *Vogue* (UK) (Dec. 2007), 71. Also relevant is Alexandra Shulman, 'Editor's Letter', *Vogue* (UK) (Dec. 2007), 17. The list of eighty included wealthy socialites, figures from the fashion world, actors, architects, a handful of other professionals, and a few young aristocrats who could have walked the length of Oxford Street without fear of being recognized, plus the Dowager Duchess of Devonshire and no less a figure than Queen Elizabeth II. The majority of nominees were experienced and worldly. The list contained just seven men, all of whom were deemed to be the supporting half of a glamorous couple. Nearly all those featured were British or British-based. Everyone mentioned enjoyed some reputation for dressing well, although not in a showy way for, the magazine affirmed, 'ostentation is a very different beast from glamour'. The magazine's list would have been considered backward and parochial even in the 1920s, by which time Hollywood stars, entertainers, sportsmen and -women, and pilots were all considered glamorous. It made the mistake of exchanging style for glamour and in so doing stressed exclusivity at the expense of accessibility. In consequence, glamour was stripped of all its accessible low cultural vivacity and presented as a feature of the social elite, widened for the occasion to include some selected creative talents. It was seen simply as a manifest-ation of that elite's superiority in matters of style, appearance, and taste. In this book a completely different and less elitist view of glamour has been set out.

9. Published by Krause Publications, Iola, Wisconsin, 2007.

10. Published by Lark Books, Asheville, North Carolina, 2007.

PHOTOGRAPHIC ACKNOWLEDGEMENTS

akg-images, London 16; Album/akg-images, London 18; author's collection 2, 4, 6; author's collection/© Reutlinger Studio 5, 7, 8; © Christie's Images Ltd. 9; © Bettmann/Corbis 10; © Gene Blevins/Corbis 24; © The Condé Nast Archives/Corbis 11; © Tim Graham/Corbis 23; © Hulton-Deutsch Collection/Corbis 20; © Underwood & Underwood/Corbis 14; RKO/The Kobal Collection 15; Riama-Pathé/The Kobal Collection 17; United Artists/The Kobal Collection 12; ARJ/Photos12.com 3; Collection Cinéma/Photos12.com 13; Paul Massey/Rex Features 22; Richard Young/Rex Features 21; © The Royal Pavilion, Libraries & Museums, Brighton & Hove 1; Courtesy of Southwest Airlines 19.

The publisher and the author apologize for any errors or omissions in the above list. If contacted they will be pleased to rectify these at the earliest opportunity.

INDEX

COLLECTED
STORIES

*

OSBERT SITWELL

GERALD DUCKWORTH & CO. LTD.
3 HENRIETTA STREET, LONDON, W.C.2

COLLECTED STORIES

LIST OF WORKS BY OSBERT SITWELL

Published by Macmillan & Co.

CONTENTS

PREFACE

HERE, at the beginning of my collected short stories, I propose for a little while to discuss with the reader how and why they were written — if I know how and why —, and then, ascending from the particular to the general, to proceed to survey the contemporary development of the short story and of the novel (for though very different in essence, one can never be divorced from the other), and so relieve my mind of various ideas I have formed. . . . To approach, then, the first theme : writers are accustomed, I think, to being asked silly questions, real conundrums which have in their own right no answer, but to which we are forced by politeness to invent glib replies; nevertheless, when, the other day, a woman fixed me with a glazed drawing-room stare, and demanded 'How do you write short stories? My son wants to know. He thinks of going in for it', I was really floored. I floundered. . . . How did I, I wondered, and why, and, in the first place, before approaching the short story, why does a man write at all, what impulse drives him to it?

One can only speak for oneself; I wrote, I think, rather as a child begins to build a sand castle, in an attempt to preserve certain things I had seen and felt from the encroaching tides of oblivion, racing in, one after another, or else to give an objective existence to some idea that had hitherto existed only in my mind. I wrote also, perhaps, out of vanity and ambition, and further because I retain a Victorian esteem for the triumphs of the human spirit and regard achievement in the arts as the highest form of human endeavour and reward, assessing Shakespeare — as I have written elsewhere — as a much greater victory for the English people than ever was Blenheim or Waterloo : (just as today the appearance of a great new English poet would, more than all its cups of tea and biscuits consumed in offices, prejudice me in favour of that political and economic deep-freeze, the Welfare State). That, I think, is why I began to write

vii

— why I began to write short stories is another matter.

Thirty years ago I started to write short stories, for these several reasons that follow : firstly because novels and short stories had always been my favourite reading; secondly, because I wanted to escape for a while from the orbit and range — I nearly wrote *rage* — of the poetry reviewers who had been the only critics concerned with my work so far; and thirdly, because I designed to save my stories for my own pen, since a friend of mine, a well-known author, a charming man, and a truly appreciative listener, had taken to writing the tales I could not resist relating to him, and to producing them either as his own short stories, or as episodes in the witty, rather bumpy novels he wrote. In this way I had seen — it was, of course, my own fault — several good things go out of my keeping, until finally, after I had told to an American friend, who knew the circumstances, the story that afterwards became *The Machine Breaks Down*, she said to me, 'Either you write that story tomorrow — or else I write it for you!' And so I began, sketching it out the next day in London, and elaborating it further at Renishaw. . . . The attributes I brought to my self-imposed task were mostly negative : no preconceived notions, no education (I can never recall having had a lesson in English grammar during the whole of my school career), and a hatred for dullness. Always, too, I set myself down before a blank page with a longing to write, and to tilt my pen at the appropriate angle. The epoch I began to write in was a fragmentary age, but still contained such masters of the short story as Rudyard Kipling, Somerset Maugham and D. H. Lawrence, as well as numerous experimentalists — perhaps more numerous than in any preceding period in England : and I was fortunate in coming of the last generation of writers — others, I hope, will emerge later — who belonged to a world, as opposed to a region. We did not seek in particular to be left-wing or right-wing, to be woldish with Yorkshire or wealdish with Kent, to be north-country, south-down or Welsh, but just to be writers, great writers if we could. And though the age *was* fragmentary, the ceiling had not yet come down (at first it seemed to be the ceiling, but it soon proved to be the sky) : the world had not yet split in half, nor with it the human heart. No curtains of iron on one side, or of cotton-wool on the other, cut off East from

West. It was as easy to journey to China as to Paris, it only took longer and was more expensive.

In this last respect, we certainly possessed advantages of which the younger generation has been deprived — though to counterbalance this loss, they have enjoyed, many of them, the advantage of being taught professionally, and professorially, how to use words. . . . But can, or does, even the most inspired and inspiring of professors ever impart it successfully to the young, or that most necessary secret of the craft — how to tell a story? Other abilities may derive from early reading, from the snubs and rewards of childhood, from the impressions of countless busy or lazy days: but this last is a gift that a man is either born with, or without; it can be found in the possession of minor writers, as much as in the works of Tolstoy or Balzac or Dickens. Cakes, moreover, are still cakes, a short story is a short story, and the same old rules apply. If you made a cake in King Alfred's time, Queen Victoria's or today, it burns as easily if untended. You should bring to the task of baking it instinct as well as experience or education; how far one can replace the other, I do not know — nor does anyone else as yet. In short, no recipe exists for writing short stories and each practitioner must find his own way.

To my self-appointed task as a short-story writer, I brought, I believe, two positive gifts, as opposed to negative: a love and understanding of human beings — a writer must from his earliest years have been an observer of people, interested as a painter must be in their physical aspect and their nervous tricks, no less than in the working of their minds and in the impulses of their hearts —, and that certain useful vanity I have mentioned.

It has sometimes been objected to one or two of my short stories, such as *Low Tide* and *Staggered Holiday*, that I have shown no sense of pity. This emotion is for the reader to feel and for the writer to make him feel; and the very complaint shows that the reader has felt it. As to the writer, it is difficult to write between sobs.

Never did it strike me that I might not be able to write a short story, for all art was one, and success, of however minor an order, in one field, portended, even ensured, success in at least a similar degree in another. Of three things I was certain: that I was going to become a writer of short stories and novels; that, as Somerset Maugham has succinctly stated, every story must have a beginning, a middle and an end; and that, in an age of rather misty half-statements and half-feelings, everything I wrote should be clearly visualised and strongly coloured. I did not want to write a Russian short story or one in the French mode: (when I began to write fiction, the Russians were in fashion in London intellectual circles, just as the French had been in the nineties: shades of feeling under fruit trees in bloom — see Katherine Mansfield — and faint Liberal regrets and aspirations lost in a cloud of ineffectuality and indecision set the pattern; to state anything outright was vulgar). Though I greatly admired the living masters in this medium, Kipling and Maugham and de la Mare, and several others, I proposed to myself no model, but held that each story should be conceived as a poem and fashioned in the style, couched in the language, that itself and its theme imposed — in fact, in the American slang phrase of today, that it should be 'dreamed-up'. Thus I sought to be eclectic, and was always surprised after reading a story of mine over, to find on it so clearly my own signature.

For the writer the short story — very short story — possesses its own most vivid technical interest. It is fascinating to be occupied with a medium that so stringently dictates its own terms and rules. In everything it must be the opposite of what a long book would be: every phrase must stand on its own, rather than be a modulation of, a reference to, another. Except in the long short story, the use of the long sentence — a device so often strangely neglected of latter years — must be avoided entirely. (Incidentally, I hope the publication of this collected volume may explode the popular critical fallacy that I write only in sentences of three or four pages, and at the same time employ these long sentences by mistake.) Even after it is apparently finished, a short story should be read by its author and re-read until its words smoulder in his mind, and in consequence every unnecessary word or action is able to be expelled.

It may be, indeed, that some happy writers begin their work with this condition fulfilled; but I belong, for better or worse, to that other category of those who cannot compose in the head, but only with the hand — with pen or dictaphone. I bring to my desk nothing but the essential plan or idea. . . .

On re-reading, however, I always want to rewrite; a temptation that today I fortunately find easy to withstand, since to attempt to reshape the hundred and fifty thousand words odd that this book contains would constitute no light task. The very reading of them takes the writer back to the beginnings at a stage when he might still be going forward, and since I keep — as Samuel Butler used to say — a cold larder of ideas in a notebook, equally with the desire to rewrite comes the urge to create something new. The germ of a short story and the plan for its execution may arise out of the sudden collision and explosion of two ideas in the mind, or through remembering some old experience, perhaps recalled to the writer by reading some passage in another author's book — the book need not be good, but the writer who has thus been enabled to recapture an event or a mood will always be grateful to the author of it. Some stories, again, may be born of a feeling for the times we live in — such is *Defeat*, a story that follows.

My first short story — which was, as I have mentioned, *The Machine Breaks Down* — I elaborated with some difficulty, because my father had somehow discovered — or surmised — on what I was working, and would repeatedly, and all in one movement, knock at the door, enter the room, and rush through it with his very rapid walk (which he claimed as an indication of the similar rapid action of his brain), saying with a note of injury and even of restrained agony in his voice, 'Two brains are better than one. . . . Such a mistake *not* to consult *me*!' The light, pattering footsteps would then depart, until another identical interruption would ensue in twenty minutes or so. (My father, though he mistrusted, and even hated, fiction, would always favour those staying at Renishaw with criticism of my work in this medium, and confided in Constant Lambert one day, when I was writing *Before the Bombardment*, that 'Osbert is writing a novel: it will be an odd sort of book, with no hero or heroine, and no love interest!') . . . My second story, written at Amalfi, where I pen this preface, was of a very different kind, on a different level; *Low Tide* (which the typist in New York who recently copied out my List of Contents, renamed *Low Tick*, so that it nearly made its appearance here under this new guise) had been travelling round the inside of my head for a number of years — ever since, in fact, I had begun to observe people and things, and to comprehend to what a spiritual extent material objects and habits could be an expression of men and women, as well as noting for myself the tricks played by the implacable Fates, the sequences of riches and poverty, and the stern revenges of nature, and — such as the plagues of the Middle Ages — of the poor upon the rich : beliefs which I have always in my writings tried to emphasise. It was full, this story, so far as I could make it, of little things I had seen for myself, no less than of the huge unpredictability of mankind, its fears and fevers and loves and hatreds and superstitions, all liable to sudden and treacherous changes, because such emotions are founded solely on the personality of him who feels them — emotions that rack the elderly, rich and respectable, no less than the young and inexperienced ; full, too (again, as far as I could make it), of the ape-like excesses, shallow or outrageous, and the angelic heights and diabolic depths to which Man, 'that paragon of animals', will stride or sink.

When the story appeared in print, I was successful in eluding the reviewers of poetry, and was more fortunate with the new band of critics I encountered — though I remember the late James Agate, who liked my books, pronounced of *Low Tide* that its first page contained every mistake it was possible for a writer to make. . . . With these two, and the stories that followed, I tried, then, to force the reader to see and realise utterly the persons, places or objects as I had seen them ; for the achievement of this purpose I had to materialise them very vividly, and it happened, sometimes, for example, that in working at a description of a flower, I so successfully re-created it, at least for myself, that it would seem to scent the whole room, and, forgetting, I would turn round to see where the fragrance came from, and whether there were not a rose, or whatever the blossom might be, near me. . . . What I hope is that in some of my stories I may have been able to communicate to the reader a comparably vibrant sense of this world, and that in others I may have been similarly able for a moment to transmit 'overtones from worlds unknown', intimate, slight, to be heard like music in the mind. The short story is, in addition, perhaps the form to which local colour, the ruin of so many books, is the most appropriate. It should be, too — though I doubt whether it is — as perfect and brilliant a vehicle for the national genius as the water-colour, that English invention, has proved to be in the realm of art : since a power of conciseness and an eye for essentials (as well as for quirks, customs and eccentricities) have always distinguished the masters in our tongue. The writer of short stories must also know how to translate into his own medium and approach Blake's dictum that the senses are the gateways to the soul. Thus only is it possible for him to surmount the barriers of age, race, sex and class, and to recognise mankind as one and indivisible.

If, as I have suggested, short stories can be very near in their conception to poems, they may also be akin to them in the way in which they rise in the mind of the writer — rise in the mind, I have written, for that seems to me precisely to describe the process — sometimes singly, sometimes in batches. For instance, I made full notes for six or seven while in bed one afternoon with an attack of gout — a disease which is said at first to sharpen the mind, and then at times to cloud it, as with a drug. This occurrence of stories in groups affords to a writer of any versatility a great chance in their treatment, as well as exhibiting its own peculiar fascination in that it enables him to identify and trace the veins of ore that he possesses running through the mass of his mind. If they are many, he may only reach the same vein once in the space of twenty years. For example, I tapped one in 1922 when I wrote *Triple Fugue*, but I did not again find it until 1945, for it cannot be reached at will or deliberately. On the other hand he may discover it more often, and *Before the Bombardment*, part of *Those Were the Days*, and in this volume *Low Tide* and *Staggered Holiday*, all manifest a similar run of feeling and expression : just as clearly as *Death of a God* belongs in essence to the vein which underlies the five volumes of my autobiography, *Left Hand, Right Hand!*

The majority of the later stories were written at Renishaw during the last war, but the earlier volumes were composed wherever I happened to be, so that to me reading through them brings back many far and strange lands — for as I have declared earlier, we were not, the writers of my generation, fettered by regionalism — Guatemala and China, Italy, Spain, Greece, Portugal and Morocco, islands in the Mediterranean and the Atlantic, France and Switzerland. I was compelled to write almost anywhere I found myself, for financial stringency, due to natural extravagance, forced me to work, even if I did not want to, and thus widened the natural aptitude. I had to make money and — contrary to the lament of publishers — I found short stories easy to sell, as well as interesting to write. Moreover, in the sort of life I led, where I was obliged — or, by the stupidity of my conduct, obliged myself — to write articles on every sort of subject several times a week, short stories were less difficult to write on the days off than were novels; which require an immense stretch of time without worry, to start them, let alone bring them to completion. To write at all with any continuity, I had to go abroad where my father could not contrive by any parental claim to kidnap me and perpetually to divert my attention. So I wrote the earlier of these stories in bitter cold or in great heat, in a disused kitchen in Antigua, Guatemala, where a vulture had been placed on guard outside the window by his aerial unit to signal if necessary the latest news of my health to his circling brothers in the blue dome above, or in a room of a house in the Tartar city in Peking, where the wind would often deliver on my desk a sample of dust from the Gobi Desert, or in a square box of a room, its outside walls covered with the waxen orange trumpets of *Bignonia grandiflora*, on the roof of a small villa in Madeira, in my whitewashed monk's cell at Amalfi, or on a terrace at Marrakesh, and in many ordinary hotel bedrooms, cabins on boats, and in the special ivory towers I can temporarily but most successfully erect for myself in railway carriages. Much as I love the anonymous conversation in trains, I like still more than to talk, to write in them. Thus, *The Man Who Drove Strindberg Mad*, the first draft of it, was written in the train going down to Brighton on a Sunday in the notorious frozen February of 1940. Certainly I was given more hours in which to work than I had bargained for : because the train which started on its normal run at eleven, and should have arrived at noon, was delayed by the intense cold freezing the damp on the electrified line and therefore did not put in its expected appearance at Brighton Station until nearly four o'clock — at which hour it was time to return, without luncheon, to London. After hours of dragon's breath on the air, red noses and half-tipsy community singing, I eventually reached Victoria at ten at night, too late to get dinner. The downward journey had been quiet, if slow,

however, and time had passed as quickly for me as I wanted
it to pass for the reader. At any rate, I returned cold but safe,
and clutching a note-book that contained a story thus chiselled
out of chaos.

I do not know when the first short story came into being,
or how; I do not know when the last will be read, or what
direction it is taking at present. But I recall, and must in turn
remind the reader that during the whole of my lifetime the
Decay of Fiction has been almost continuously announced in
the literary journals. Yet looking back through the years
fiction can now be seen to have remained almost the one solid
fact in a dissolving universe. Those who have perpetually
foretold its approaching demise have slid downhill with a
bump, but, while fact ceases to be fact, and matter itself
ceases to be matter, fiction remains fiction. Kings and kingdoms
have come and gone, great empires have ceased to exist, but
still the output of the novel and short story, though it may be
uninspiring for the most part except in its sheer torrential
spate, floods the countries of the world. Scientific barbarism
encroaches on every side, the living — as opposed to dead —
arts have become unpopular : only the novel and the short
story flourish on the dunghill that men have made of the
world. So that, after all, fiction may have a future (the
Future of Fiction is another well-known theme in the newspapers) : though the future of fiction must depend on the
future of those who write and read it ; and the prospect for
them both seems rather dubious at present. If a third, and
in every sense final, War to End Wars, descends upon us
within the space of a few years, let us say seven, then a very
limited period of development lies before it — and us. Or,
again, we may be about to pass under the portcullis of Ant-
land, and ants do not make good heroes or heroines. Moreover
they have no time to write novels — or to read them : (they
are only permitted to read instructive treatises on how one ant
may learn to do the work of seven — or, better still, of seventy).
But for the purpose of our diagnosis and prognostication, it is
necessary to postulate a long period of time in which works
of art and commerce can be born and prosper, as well as
decay and die. If such a stretch should lie before us, it is
possible to foresee an enormous enriching and widening and
deepening of fiction, and its progress along many new lines,

scientific or psycho-analytical, in a world of leisure, a society freed from the cramping effects of class, though shorn equally of its fascinating shibboleths. In such an atmosphere, fiction should flower again, or continue to flower. The truth is that novelists die, but not the novel. And the reason, I suspect, is because the novel is not an art form.

Of course it can be made into an art form by anyone who happens to be an artist — and I for one am biased, because I am an author who, for better or worse, cannot write without making of what he is writing a work of art. . . . No, fiction is not by its very essence (unless it is written by an artist) an art form, as, for example, must be any poem. It is merely a convenience. Thus, in reality, to talk about the Future of Fiction is comparable to talking about the Future of the Suitcase or Grip (ex-portmanteau). It depends on who packs it, what it contains, and on where the traveller is going and whether his journey is necessary — albeit the journey can be in any direction. And protean as the novel continually proves to be, in this respect the short story surpasses it. In the course even of the past two decades an immense advance in the scope and technique of the short story has been effected, and in the splintering of life which it represents.

It is necessary always to bear in mind that fiction has, withal, obtained a great hold upon the affections of the public. This, I apprehend, is due to Man's conceit, and in its quiddity resembles the compelling attraction that a piece of looking-glass exercises upon an ape. Man dominates fiction. It is entirely concerned with him — and therefore to him fiction is good. But alas ! — and this militates against future development —, the ape has of late years grown hysterical; to the point that he is now more hysterical than inquisitive. The reality of his own reflection is no longer what he is after. Now he must be shown himself as he *wishes* to see himself : a noble, but not an intelligent, ape — nobility consisting in the form in which he likes to see it — a patriotic ape to the patriotic ape, or let us say, a socialist, fair-shares-for-all ape to the socialist, fair-shares-for-all ape. But the general tendency in fiction, though each community of readers is catered for by writers of like mind, has been for the tramp, the down-and-out, in the course of a century to usurp completely the place of the old Byronic hero, just as the hobo's feminine counterpart has ousted from her throne the exquisitely civilised hostess of Henry James's novels, and has come to be regarded as the ideal after which mankind should strive. Mademoiselle de Maupin, the heroine of the romantics, to a new generation now yields in interest to the really awfully plucky charwoman who stood her ground in the air-raids and is known to everyone as 'Ma'. During the war, and the few years immediately following it, the public, drunk with its own heroism, demanded only stories of war fortitude, revelled in tales of bombs, well or ill directed, of the happy community life of bomb-shelters, of overcrowded trains, running late, of queues and the noble, tenpenny hardships of rationing. (Even painting came to be occupied with the same themes.) Yet the artist — in the widest sense — must, even to deal with such incongruities, be allowed to get his nose off reality for a little : he must be permitted to remain for a while aloof, and for a few moments, but only for a few, to pop into an ivory tower, even if it is only a railway carriage. . . . But after the war ends — an eventuality no one ever expects, because to think of an end to it during the course of a modern, democratic war, which is by its nature so terrible that, in order to endure it, the feelings of the public have continually to be whipped up to the pitch of hysteria by those in charge, constitutes treason — after the war ends, I was saying, and when its foggy aftermath of feeling has dispersed, no one will read any more of bombs and bomb-shelters, and even the idolised down-and-out may too have to be shifted back to the rubbish-dump, a most unfair and unfriendly proceeding.

Fortunately, the reporters of events — those Mercuries whose names I forget, but whose works, *Muscling in on the Fal of Paris*, or *Tiddlywinks in Berlin*, are to be seen on every railway bookstall — have rescued fiction from the tyranny of unwanted contemporary fact, in the same way that the invention of the camera rescued painting. Fiction must now find its own educated public, and then its future will lie in all directions. . . . I wrote just now that much depended on who packed the suitcase, where the traveller was going, and whether his journey was necessary ; Wells, for example, was always on his way to a Socialist rally or a Scientific Study Group, Arnold Bennett to a directors' meeting at the Grand Babylon Hotel ; Henry James, armed prominently with a first-class ticket, *en route* to spend Saturday to Monday with a cosy but scintillating company in a famous country-house; Aldous Huxley on a journey with many changes, starting from Garsington, via the villas of Florence, to a cœnobitic enclave in Hollywood; D. H. Lawrence from the Sunday suits and prosaic smoke-stacks of Nottinghamshire to the dark and hidden gods of Mexico and Etruria; myself from — but no, my own journey can be traced through the stories that follow, and the reader who has accompanied me thus far is now at liberty to turn to them, and epitomise for himself my voyage. He will find, no doubt, that in each story I have contradicted in practice several of the theories I have promulgated in the foregoing pages.

OSBERT SITWELL

AMALFI
March 16, 1952

DEFEAT

Battle alters the face of the world, but defeat and collapse may at first leave it intact, just as a gutted house often shows no change, except for its dead, blank windows. . . . So it was with the little town of Château-Vignal, formerly so prosperous. Ruin and chaos were implicit in it, but, at first sight, did not show themselves. Its structure was bony and enduring, and its grey-white streets ran from either side of the Loire like ribs from the backbone of a carcase. The trams still creaked down narrow alleys under the overhanging sculpture of gothic churches; in the one broad boulevard the shops still boasted displays of goods at high prices; fruits and vegetables lay heaped up in baskets, level with the knees of the old peasant women who sold them, under the hot and radiant sunshine of the open market, and, though meat, sugar, spices were unprocurable, other, younger peasant women carried hens under their arms and cackled to each other across the struggling, feathered bodies. Beneath the tall, glossy-leaved trees on which magnolias, large and white as the soup-bowls of the alms-houses near by, were flowering sweetly, the local idiot still sat slobbering in the empty public garden. The only change noticeable was that the tramps, who usually slept here at night, were now seeking this escape during the day-time and formed those almost inconjecturable mounds of rags — lifeless save for a slight, nearly imperceptible, heaving — which could be seen lying in several directions upon the yellowing grass. The fishermen still lined the banks of the river, with its high and, as it seemed at this season, unnecessary stone walls, and one or two, more intrepid, stood in the water up to their knees. (Indeed, owing to the scarcity of provisions, there were, perhaps, more of them, and they were even more patient.) The cafés were still open, too, though the regular clients were ruffled at being unable to obtain their favourite drinks, and in the chief café the band of four ancient men in dinner-jackets still played 'Selections from *Carmen*', the 'Barcarolle', and various waltzes, and a woman singer, in a pink evening dress, and carrying with her the invisible prestige attaching to many diplomas from many provincial *conservatoires*, still sang the Jewel Song from *Faust* and various well-known airs from the operas of Puccini.

Little change manifested itself: nevertheless the poison of defeat ran through the corpus of the people in the same manner in which a poison circulates through the body with its blood, by the aid of its own blood. And the outward form that the poison took during this stage, which resembled the unconsciousness of a patient, broken by fits of delirium, was a chaotic, meaningless placidity, relief at the coming of a peace that did not exist, varied by sudden spasms of virulently anti-foreign, and especially anti-British, sentiment. But this xenophobia did not extend towards the conquerors. The German officers, the German soldiers were even regarded momentarily with a certain admiration, a certain wonder at their hard, mechanical bearing and efficiency, and the women of the town looked at them more curiously, and longer, than at their own men, yet covered, many of them, with dust, slouching past impassively in twos and threes, unshaven, silent, vacant-eyed, puffing at cigarettes that never left their lips even when they exchanged a few words.

It was a Sunday afternoon. On the terrace of the public gardens, under the delicate fluttering of acacia leaves, the usual Sunday family groups, the usual Sunday combinations — like a family tree in reverse — of grandfathers, grandmothers, uncles, aunts, parents, all in dark clothes, with, as their culmination, a single, small, pale child, wandered and stared without purpose, and from the interior of the Café de l'Univers came the familiar dull crack of billiard balls and shuttered laughter. Vanished were the Algerian, Moroccan and Tunisian troops who usually lent colour to the scene, but at a few tables some French soldiers were playing cards, and at another sat a Captain in the French army, the young girl to whom he was engaged, and her mother. . . . Not far away, near the entrance to the public gardens and divided from it by the usual line of green boxes containing nameless evergreen shrubs, a German officer, with a creased neck, ox-eyes, a monocle and a tunic that appeared to contain a wooden body, was consuming a *bock*.

The Captain did not look at him. He had only returned home yesterday. His eyes were entirely reserved for his younger companion, the daughter of Doctor Dorien; in a way she was pretty, but her essential correctness — the result in conjunction of a convent upbringing and the inherited burgess virtues of her home —, her clothes, with the typical dowdy *chic* of the French provincial town, and her carefully coiffured hair, all combined to impart to her an air of insipidity, of primly decorated nullity, as though she had long been prepared, and was still waiting, for the vital forces to descend and give her life. Her smile, on the other hand, was quick and alert, and her eyes soon warmed, soon lost their emptiness and gained fire.

The face of the Captain, sensitive and, in spite of the several ribbons he was wearing, almost feminine in fineness of cut and expression, was drawn and exhausted, for he had only stopped fighting three days before, and within him his soul was dead. Notwithstanding, the bond that united him to Estelle, that mutual but indefinable flow of sympathy which seemed to pour into every cell of each body from the other, comforted him. They had been friends from childhood, and their marriage had been arranged since their earliest infancy. . . . Perhaps theirs was not love in the romantic sense, but, from the Latin approach, it constituted love. On his side composed of tenderness, affection and physical desire, on hers it rose out of her respect for his qualities of command and valour, and from a need for mental and physical subservience. He fully appreciated the nature of it, that Estelle looked up to him, and he was relieved to find that this feeling of hers still persisted after what had happened. . . . But he knew it was deserved, because he was no coward and, where many brave men had been routed, he had stood his ground.

He realised — and she had been able to make him realise — that this respect for his valour, like his valour itself, had suffered no diminution from defeat — 'defeat'. . . . He supposed it must be because he was so tired, but through the tinkling phrases of the Delibes ballet music now being played, the words 'defeat', 'defeat', 'defeat' drummed in his ears, and with his inner eye he still watched — and, he thought, would watch eternally — the armoured columns advancing, those immense and senseless machines, trundling and thundering along at a rate no Frenchman could have anticipated, could still see them, hear them, crushing the heads of men like nuts ground under the heel, could still see the cowering, surging waves of humanity upon the roads, the household goods, upon barrows and carts, the clocks and trunks and vases, for better protection covered beneath the best mattress, could still see the old women and the ill left behind, fallen in the ditches beneath the grey and suffocating hedges, could still hear the nearing remorseless thunder, and rattling machine-gun fire from the dive-bombers, swarming above the civilian crowds, scattering them and rounding them up as they ran hither and thither, all wearing, as though in self-protection, the sheep-coloured, shameful livery of the dust. Such sights and sounds were as yet more real to him than the silvery perspective of tall, shivering poplars and flowing river, its cool islands of willow and tamarisk lying like full baskets of feathers upon the water, upon which his glance now rested, and were not far from him even when he gazed into the calm and limpid brown depths of Estelle's eyes.

He must pretend to be the same or it might shock her. . . . But he knew that he had changed, and the world with him, and he wished the band would not continually play the old gay melodies of a dead life; it was like seeing the ghost of someone you had loved. . . . 'Defeat.' . . . And yet there were in it certain pleasant prospects, though tinged with the year's shame. The war, a bad war, badly begun, had stopped. His men would no longer be slaughtered. Above all, his marriage, hitherto delayed first by the previous economic collapse and then by the war, could take place almost immediately, their parents agreed. And their old affection remained steadfast. . . . But sometimes he almost wished that the kind of affection he read in her eyes, that respect for a man who was brave and could command, had ceased to exist, replaced by some other kindred but more reasonable sentiment; for of what use was courage, individual courage, now, against this armoured mass; how could flesh pit itself against iron?

Meanwhile their conversation, albeit desultory, was, on the surface, gay enough. They avoided all mention of the war, but teased one another and preened themselves like any other young couple in ordinary times. They discussed how they would live after their marriage, and seemed to forget for a while the presence of her mother, and then, all at once, to remember it and try to make amends. All three of them made

4

their cakes and *tisane* — for there was no coffee — last as long a time as possible.

'Remember, I shall have to find a trade now,' the Captain said, 'I shall no longer be in the army. I shall have to get up every morning to go to the office, and probably my temper will be very bad, for I am not used to it. . . . And you will have to prepare for my home-coming, and walk back with me so that I get air, or otherwise I shall take the tram to be with you the sooner, and so shall soon grow old and fat.' (Her face fell, he noticed, when he told her that he would leave the army; evidently she had not fully grasped that the French army was in dissolution.) 'And I shall dine every night with you and Maman,' he continued, taking the older woman into the conversation, 'but I shall be very cross unless you both give me the food I like.' (But inside his head, the words 'defeat', 'defeat', sounded like advancing columns.)

'And what about *me*?' Estelle answered; 'you will have to study me now, and come home early so as to be with me. If you leave the regiment, there will be no talk of being "on duty", or of "having to dine in the Officers' Mess". . . . No excuses will exist any more.'

But all this talk, he felt, meant so little. Like the scene itself, it was curiously on the surface, with no shades or under-tones. The sun glowed down now through the acacia leaves, seeming to consume them, and rested full on the faces round them. The woman in the pink evening dress had, amid much applause, stopped singing, and conversation and laughter swelled up from the tables.

Then the band struck up again, a waltz, the 'Wiener Wald' by Johann Strauss. . . . Hardly a place empty. . . . A party of four or five gaping soldiers came in, near the entrance by which the German officer was sitting. They passed him, and came towards the Captain; they dragged their feet, were dishevelled and untidy, talked loudly and smoked cigarettes. He re-cognised them; they were men who for long had served under him, but they stared at him idly, without saluting, and slouched past him to a table beyond. They were noisy, but possessed the very look of men who have lost all spirit, except a new will to insolence. ('*Defeat*': this was defeat.) He looked away and did not glance at Estelle, fixing his eyes upon the distance, where the water rippled by the edge of rushes and flowering clumps of yellow iris. . . . But suddenly a guttural sound obtruded and made him take notice. (The conversation stopped at the neighbouring tables, though the aproned waiters continued to perform their clever acts of equilibrium, with arms poised and trays uplifted above the heads of their customers, in the manner of jugglers.) It was the German officer, summoning and beckoning to the men ; the Captain's men. Now they pulled themselves together. Their false aggressiveness ebbed away and they filed back solemnly and saluted the foreigner, as he bade them.

'Now go back and salute your Captain,' the enemy continued in his thick, distorted French.

The men sheepishly did as they were told. . . . The Captain acknowledged their salute in the customary manner, nonchalantly and as though at his ease, and his soldiers returned to their table. . . . *Defeat*. Defeat. This was Defeat. And the world lay broken round him. He felt, perceived immediately, that nothing in his own life would ever be the same again. This incident had transformed Estelle's view of him, and her new attitude towards him was defined and without the possibility of retrieval : it was final ; he knew it, deep in his bones. The bond had snapped. Never now would they be married. It was as though for her the virtue had gone out of him. His manhood lay shattered for both of them, wrecked by the clumsy courtesy, or (who could tell ?) the cruel courtesy of a victor. . . . But he was tired, so tired that he scarcely suffered. It was over.

THAT FLESH IS HEIR TO . . .

OR

THE HISTORY OF A BACILLUS

'. . . Disease, then, represents this struggle for life, and it is in this sense an advantage: for without " diseases " man would quickly fall victim to the injurious agents which surround him. Man is essentially a potential invalid, since he is a potential battleground in his struggle for existence. Disease is the chance of victory.'—ALAN MONCRIEFF, in an article entitled ' The Nature of Disease ', in the *Nation and Athenæum*, March 16, 1929.

'. . . Man may be a potential invalid, but he is not an invalid by choice.'—*Ibid.*

I

WHEREAS a man can only die and be born once, the race of microbes suffers a thousand grievous deaths in each human recovery and is born anew, a million times triumphing, in each corpse for which it has hungered, and as I hope to show, planned. But this very wealth, this plethora of energy, makes it hard to compress the birth, the upbringing, the career of a germ within the space of a short story: more difficult, indeed, than to force into the same compass the span and achievements of a human life. There are other reasons, too, that force me to regard the task as a piece of work not lightly to be undertaken. This story is essentially one of adventure, and it is not easy, for example, even with the aid of a map, to concentrate so much picturesque geography, so much tragic social-history as it demands, into a few pages. Nevertheless it seemed, in spite of all obstacles, that the experiment was worth attempting, if only because I would fain place my little offering of personal observation as a tribute upon the altar of science.

Yet, being no professor, I am not compelled to take up with this subject a whole volume, however well it might be filled. All that duty imposes on me is to state the story, and to indicate, for the benefit of those who specialise in such things — but who, not having the imaginative writer's outfit, cannot detect for themselves the connection between these footprints in the sand — its subsequent and certain developments. If one were to write a life of that Count of the Empire under Charlemagne who was the founder of the Este family, it would be well, as throwing light upon his destiny, to indicate that he was the common ancestor of the royal houses of England, Saxony and Ferrara : but it would be obligatory on one neither to prove their descent, nor to write the history of every later member of the family. So, too, I shall not essay to correlate the microbe, which is the invisible but most potent hero of my story, with his obvious descendants, interesting as such a digression would be, nor to dwell upon the more crucial and public stages of that career of conquest which found its culmination in the dengue-fever epidemic that devastated Greece in the autumn of 1928 and in the influenza outbreak of the winter of 1928-9 : a wave which swept across the whole world. That is the business of those who come after, and whose calling lies in such research.

A microbe, I have said, is the hero of the tale which follows : and this necessitates that, when it so suits the author, the hero should be regarded as both singular and plural, as an individual and a tribe, as a great general and a mighty army in one : nor is this all that one is forced to demand of the gentle reader, for, since microbes neither marry nor are given in marriage, the hero is also heroine, is masculine and feminine as well as singular and plural : for such licence I must crave the reader's indulgence, asking him to consider and weigh the difficulties of my task.

So enormous, then, is the subject to be imprisoned within these limits, that one is forced to be ruthless, to prune the Mediterranean cities of their tingling life, their hoarse shouts and shuddering glamour, the desert of its beauty born of solitude, the blue, transparent sea of its dolphins leaping up and down through the waters in segments of circles as though they were swift wheels, revolving partly above and partly below the surface, and of its strange fish that at night carry their own illuminations through the glassy depths. Moreover, apart from the protagonists, who will, whether one wishes it or not, most surely demonstrate their characters, the minor figures — our companions on this odyssey, or the royal victims, the attendant train of diplomats and consuls, the crews of ships and staffs of hotels, who are the dramatis personae — should as far as possible be puppets, ninepins to be knocked over at very rhythmic but ever shorter intervals by the overwhelmingly simple, yet accurate and terrible, machinery invented by our super-germ.

To the working of this engine I now hold the secret. And as, with, it must be confessed, no little pride, I reflect upon this discovery of mine, my mind goes back once more to that dark winter night of two years ago, and to how little then I expected the curious developments that were so near me.

II

I hurried away from the paraphernalia of polite leave-taking, from the clustered top-hats and walking-sticks, down the steps gilded by the light of the open door, into the dead November square. Each lamp-post bore aloft a wavering halo of golden drizzle, and the tall, contorted red-brick houses had assumed a tone of purple, until, beneath the uncertain and swinging illumination of this windy month, they seemed but a faint discoloration, an opaque deepening of the night itself. What a charming, rather mysterious woman Mrs. Chitty was, with that indefinable and enigmatic smile and the glowing intensity of her brown eyes ! (Fitful and anonymous farewells still pursued me from the gaping mouth of her mansion : cars began to purr, and keen patches of light sped over the muddy wastes of the road.) I hurried, hurried on, for I was not feeling well — rather shivery — and hoped the walk would warm me. . . . Charming woman, but a little mysterious . . . unusual. How peculiar, for instance, was the composition of her dinner-parties : the human ingredients never varied. Why should a woman, whose interests in life were mainly musical, artistic and literary, thus live almost entirely in the company of diplomats, Foreign Office officials and scientists ? Even though it might be that this choice imparted to her house an atmosphere distinctive and rather cosmopolitan, what was there in her mind to make her thus yoke the scientist with the diplomat ? Yet I enjoyed these gatherings, for the diplomats lisped to one another in undertones or babbled in foreign languages, and thus I was left to listen to the scientists,

9

whose theories one needs must love for their wealth of fantasy, intense but serious.

That night, for some reason, the conversation had mainly turned upon the influenza epidemic of 1918 : a scourge that, it will be remembered, helped to enwrap the final phases of the 'Great' War in a blaze of glory — for glory is ever strictly in proportion to the number of dead bodies upon which it is fed, and this particular wave of illness had made the war-casualties appear almost minute. Seven million people, it was roughly calculated, had perished of it in six months. By christening it *Spanish Influenza*, however, instead of bestowing upon it some picturesque, gothic title such as the *Black Death*, the doctors reduced for us both its terror and romance, even if it cannot be pretended that this castanetted euphemism in any way diminished the death-rate or revealed the cause of the pestilence. And, though nine years had now passed since the outbreak, little more light could be thrown upon its origin. Climatic conditions could not much enter into the matter, for in India, glowing under the tropical heat like an ember, entire communities had been wiped out in a few hours. Mrs. Chitty, who was fond of travelling, had been there when it started, and told us that often by the time the nearest medical aid could be rushed up to some distant village, the cruel, dusty red sunlight glared down on houses in which there was no human movement, no sound, not even a cry.

I had, at the time of this plague, formed about it my own opinion : which was that Nature — who often must be regarded as the Goddess of Reason, a divinity, that is to say, indulging in anthropopathic flights of logic, and only differing in kind from man because of her greater power — had, as she watched the war, very justifiably concluded that since men were so plainly bent on their own extermination, herself had better have her fling and join in the fun. After all, killing people had always been her divine monopoly as well as her chief hobby (thorough good sportsman, Nature !). In England, before a cygnet is killed and eaten, the Royal sanction must be obtained : so, too, Nature expected that before any human being died, before even a doctor was allowed to slaughter a patient, her aid and permission should be invoked. It might only be a formality nowadays ; but why, she asked herself, should she sit there quietly — especially considering all the new, untried microbes in her possession — and see her prerogative usurped by man, an animal she had never much cared for? Of the many beasts she had created, he was the only one that had become discontented, then mutinous; had attacked her rights and privileges, attempting to curb her supreme power and to degrade her rank from that of Goddess-Autocrat down to a mere constitutional monarch. Indeed in every direction this pitiable creature had challenged her authority. She had given him a skin of his own for his covering, and he had chosen to wear that of others (often murdering a fellow-beast to get it): she had provided him with plain, simple food to eat, and he had chosen to warm it and burn out of it its virtue; with caves in which to live, and he had built huts and houses; she had given him rain to wash him, and he had collected the water, cooked it and taken unto himself soap! But her little influenza-germ would soon put things to rights, for this latest-evolved pet was house-trained, most flourished exactly in those circumstances man had rebelliously contrived for himself.

Thus, I imagined, had Nature argued and plotted in her own mind. But, since 1918, influenza had periodically returned, and one had been forced to abandon such a theory. Now, in the winter of 1927, a season singularly exempt from this particular evil, as I walked home — feeling rather odd and cold — I was just as much in the dark about its origin as any of our scientists could be. (How icy it was, and my eyes were beginning to ache; a curious sensation as though the eyeballs did not belong to their sockets, square eyeballs in round holes. However, one should never encourage pains by thinking of them, and resolutely I focused my thoughts back again on to the conversation at dinner.) We had been informed that, ever since the close of the great epidemic, the medical and scientific authorities had kept constant watch for this criminal bacillus, who even now might be moving unidentified among us: for influenza was peculiarly difficult to cope with, in that, upon each new and considerable outbreak, it assumed a fresh disguise. Like Charley Peace, it was able after every crime entirely to alter its outward appearance, while leaving invariably some novel and obscure disease in its wake. Thus the name 'influenza' was merely a courtesy-title conferred by popular consent upon an anonymous and dangerous microbe (here Mrs. Chitty had smiled her curious, enigmatic smile), just as the author of the terrible Whitechapel murders had been known far and wide as 'Jack the Ripper'. Attempts had been made to fix the responsibility for these recent outrages in many quarters, but so far without success. A million germs had been caught and kept under observation for long periods, only, in the end, to demonstrate unmistakably their innocence.

The stories that Professor Chilcott and Dr. Bidham had told us only served to confirm my impression that science had lately grown a little wild, somewhat apt to overlook and overleap the obvious. They admitted that, in their nervous eagerness to solve the problems of this illness, they had kidnapped an enormous quantity of the free field-mice of Great Britain, and were keeping them captive all the winter in order to observe the various infections which they might breed. This, I had thought, was surely going too far (the dark, furry and whiskered tribe, thus, to its surprise, comfortably installed in winter-quarters, had, as a matter of fact, never since ailed, but had thrived and increased like the seed of Abraham) . . . and, even if it has now been established that bubonic plague is engendered by starving squirrels in Central Asia, which, in dying of famine, pass on the fleas that live upon them to the black rat; and that, when the black rat, travelling all over the world, dies of the pestilence, the flea then attacks human beings and infects them, yet why attempt to lay the blame for influenza upon the poor little English mouse, a harmless and quite different creature? I had thought myself bound, in fair play, to protest. A suspect tribe, the rodents : and for a little I had tried to arouse pity and interest on their behalf among these icy, calculating hearts by drawing attention to the extraordinary and romantic vicissitudes of fortune which had lately been their lot. Think on the piebald and downy guinea-pig, I had urged, hailing originally from the suffocating forests of South America, brought across all those leagues of ocean to become a pampered pet. I had seen its image lolling or frolicking among roses or exotic flowers, set over the elaborately carved doors of Prince Eugène's winter palace in Vienna. Then subsequently it had become the playmate of wealthy children, its ears flopping freely upon the honest English breeze. But, suddenly sinking into poverty and obscurity once more, it now only exists here as a subject for medical experiments, a beast upon which to practise operations not yet made perfect, upon which to test numberless germs, to be infected, whenever possible, with every disease not yet fully understood, as well as to be inoculated with all the more authentic and recognised microbes of typhoid, malaria, anthrax, paralysis, diphtheria and the like. On the other hand, the common household rat, long one of the chief enemies of mankind, the Ishmael of the animal world, outcast and driven from door to door, a creature to whom no law of charity applied, to be killed in any manner possible, poisoned, shot or burned alive, now found itself enjoying in scientific circles an unexpected popularity. Once on the operating table, and nothing was too good for it. Gland operations and graftings were performed, the only object of which was to prolong its valuable life, and one of biology's chief boasts up to the present was that it had succeeded in extending the lifetime of a male rat to three times the normal span. But my scientist friends had sternly refused to be moved to compassion by any such eloquent expositions of these strange reversals of fortune. Mrs. Chitty had again smiled mysteriously, as though in the possession of some secret happiness or cause for amusement. Perhaps, I was to think in after years, it was because to her, too, it seemed as though the scientists, while indulging in countless fantasies, extravagant as those they played upon mice, rats and guinea-pigs, were inclined to overlook the obvious — had, in fact, overlooked Mrs. Chitty.

They would continually dine in her house, give her all the latest expert information in their possession as to the progress of new crusades against disease. Never did they entertain the slightest suspicion. . . . It certainly was a very bad attack of influenza from which they were recovering, they would decide, ten or twelve days later — no doubt they had caught the germ in a bus or in the Tube — or, perhaps, from one of those horrid, hypocritical little field-mice (that would be a matter worth going into, when they were better, in another week or two) — and then there had been that cold night air — so damp — after Mrs. Chitty's dinner-party. They remembered quite well how chilly they had felt going home after it. Mrs. Chitty! There was a brave woman — nice of her to come and see them like that, with grapes and calves'-foot jelly, in the middle of the infection, and to take such an interest in the children, to play with them in her charming way (poor little mites, what a shame that they should now have influenza, too : and after so many precautions had been taken) — a remarkable, as well as brave, woman. Think of how she had nursed the troops through that really terrible epidemic of 1918 ! As though guided by some special instinct she had always gone straight to the spot where the death-roll was to be worst — and yet she had never caught it herself, albeit she was a nervous delicate woman upon whom any effort was a strain. -Though never well, she had not broken down, but had stuck to her post. And then, straight to India after that — in the epidemic there, too, where it was ever so much worse.

And when, a few days after the dinner-party, Mrs. Chitty called on me, though my temperature was very high and I was in no mood for seeing most people, similar emotions of gratitude and respect beset me. She had heard I was ill, she said, and had come to see for herself 'how I was getting on'. She was really extremely kind, visiting me several times during my convalescence. For a long while I had been growing to like her, and now I more than ever appreciated her character, for I had learnt to estimate at their true worth her many admirable qualities, while, indeed, no one could fail to come under the sway of her charm.

Muriel Chitty was, in fact, all that had been said of her, and much more. She inspired any company, however dull, in which she found herself, with a curious, usually agreeable, feeling of nervous tension, as though something were about to happen. Her beautiful, rather haggard face had the sallow asceticism, her dark, large, slanting eyes, where lingered many an unshed tear, had the fire, her spare figure, the taut and gaunt expressiveness, that distinguishes the saints evoked against bare grey and purple rocks by El Greco. Her clothes, too, were in keeping with this conception : sombre and severe, with an occasional Spanish accent of deep, rich colour. There had gone to her making, one felt, something of the religious bigot, something of the musician, much of the actress. She possessed a subtle but keen sense of humour, and was, when the mood for such frivolity descended upon her, an exceptionally acute mimic. Nevertheless, as one watched her, observed her vehement gestures and flashing eyes, or listened to the earnest and hollow notes of her voice, a voice that was yet altogether

persuasive, it was less of Sarah Bernhardt than of Savonarola
that one was reminded, although mimicry was the last, and
most genial, vice which one would have imputed to that
cavernous-eyed and dreary burn-book. It seemed as though
in everything she did there was concealed a religious, if unfathomable, intention. Yet not for a moment was she priggish,
redeemed from it by many unexpectedly human frailties. She
was, for instance, feminine in an almost extinct, Victorian way.
Passionately devoted to all other animals, she hated mice and
cried if she saw one. Then she had developed a special technique of dropping and forgetting things, so that they must be
picked up or fetched for her by her men friends thus enslaved
— for this mechanism was calculated, I apprehend, to deal out
either reward or punishment according to the manner in which
the request for help was made — and was always a little late
for everything. These superficially clinging characteristics,
however, cloaked a will that was Napoleonic in strength and
purpose : indeed the dropping and forgetting of things was,
perhaps, but one of the means she had devised for getting her
own way. It showed her men friends how helpless, how
dependent on them she was, and that, in consequence, it was
cruel to oppose her. Yet all her failings, all her devices, quite
genuinely and without her being aware of it, only helped to
throw into relief her essential mystery and attraction.

She was, one understood, a rare, very sensitive, and in
many ways delightful character. And much there was about
her that charmed while it eluded one. Even her worship of
diplomats was intriguing — not, of course, that I am suggesting
that there is anything peculiarly bizarre in choosing them as
companions, but that she seemed to bear toward them a
devotion that was almost fanatical. A party at the Foreign
Office, to be received at the top of those marble stairs under the
allegorical, monster-patriotic paintings of Mr. Goetze, would
be her translation into a temporary, but none the less heavenly,
heaven. She was aware of the exact position of every member
of His Majesty's Diplomatic Service abroad at any given
moment of any day, for her life's supreme interest was in the
news of the latest swops, the promotions or occasional degrada-
tions. These she followed with the same passionate attention
that a schoolboy devotes to the cricket averages of the paladins
of his chosen county, or with which a retired official of the

Indian Civil Service, now living in England, regards the vagaries of the barometer in his draughty hall. Yes, she was a remarkable and curious woman, I decided. Under her manner, which displayed the identical combination of flaring pride and meek submission that in the animal world distinguishes the camel from other beasts, there was something really interesting, something that matched her obscure and haunting beauty. Further, there was nothing that she did not — or rather could not — comprehend, and, when it pleased her, she was both witty and subtle.

It was with definite pleasure, therefore, that in the spring of 1928 I heard that Mrs. Chitty was to be of the same party as ourselves. Seven of us had already decided to travel together and visit various Mediterranean towns. We were to start on a liner which was setting out for a pleasure cruise : and it had been arranged that where we wished to stay longer than the other passengers, we could wait behind and catch the next boat. The tour we had planned was rather an extensive one and would occupy some two to three months. Our proposed itinerary was Genoa, Palermo, Athens, Constantinople, Rhodes, Cyprus and Beirut. There we were to disembark and visit Damascus and Jerusalem : after which, returning to Beirut, we hoped to catch a boat for Alexandria. We were determined to spend some time in Egypt, seeing everything that it was possible to see. We were to ride on camels out into the desert, and to sail up the Nile on a dahabiya. From Egypt we were to go by car to Libya, that enormous and fascinating country which has only so recently been opened up, thence return to Italy, visiting the various places of interest that lay on our road back to England. (See map.)

The party in all was to consist of Mrs. Rammond, Frank Lancing, Mrs. Jocelyn, Ruth Marlow, Julian Thackwray, Mrs. Chitty, my brother and myself. This, as it afterwards turned out, was to be the human material for Mrs. Chitty's experiments : but in our innocence at the time it was about Muriel Chitty, rather than the others, that we felt anxious, for though we all knew that she was an expert traveller, she was rather delicate, and we feared that so strenuous and prolonged a tour might fatigue her.

A letter from her that reached me a few days before we

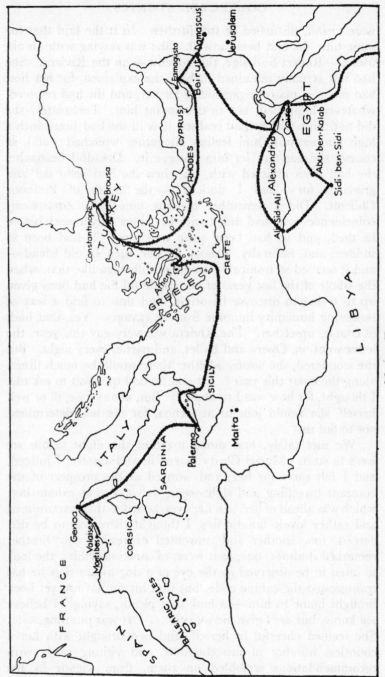

MAP OF TOUR

were to sail, disturbed us still further. In it she said that for some time she had been unwell. She was staying with an old friend — Robert Sutledge, the novelist — on the Riviera. She had not actually remained in bed, she explained, for her host had made so many engagements for her, and she had resolved, whatever happened, not to disappoint him. Fortunately she did not think that he had realised how ill she had been, with a high temperature, and feeling altogether wretched; and, of course, she had not let him observe it. Dreadful headaches she had been afflicted with, but then she had been sad and grieving, for — had I noticed? — the death of Professor Chilcott. Did I remember meeting him? An *extraordinary* coincidence — he had dined with her alone only a week before he died, and he had been quite well then. It had been so sudden, and, naturally, a shock for her, such an old friend — and it seemed so ironical — to die of influenza like that, when the whole of the last years of his wonderful life had been given up to trying to discover its origin, and thus to find a way of rendering humanity immune from its ravages. Yes, that had, of course, upset her. The Riviera was very gay this year, the letter went on, Opera and Ballet, and parties every night. But she wondered, she wrote, whether there would be much illness along the coast this year? (It was an odd question to ask me, I thought, for how was I to know?) But, in any case, ill or well herself, she would join us at Genoa, for she was determined not to fail us.

We met safely, and dined together the night before we were to start. Muriel Chitty looked ill and austere, I judged, and I felt sorry for her, and worried at the prospect of the constant travelling and sight-seeing (always most exhausting) which was ahead of her. In her eyes, added to their accustomed and rather lovely fanatic fire, I thought there was to be discerned, too, another and unwonted expression (my brother remarked it also) : one, as it were, of conscious guilt; the look so often to be observed in the eye of a dog aware that he has transgressed the canine code, but that his sin has not yet been brought home to him — a look that pleads, saying, 'I believe *you* know, but *don't* give me away'. . . . It was puzzling. . . . She seemed cheerful in herself, and had brought with her a countless number of introductions, and visiting cards with recommendations scribbled on them, from friends in the

Foreign Office. Indeed it seemed as though there were at least
one or two letters apiece for every Ambassador, Minister,
Consul-General and Consul in the Near East, Syria and North
Africa ; not altogether, the rest of our group secretly agreed, a
blessing, for our days were limited in number considering how
much there was for us to do in them, and the mere personal
delivery of this script must occupy, one would hazard, a solid
month of time.

The whole journey, despite its adventures, seems in retrospect
to have passed very quickly and in a succession of cinema-like
flashes. The next morning we embarked. Genoa, frost-bitten
in the early February wind, piled itself up dustily behind us
on its terraces, amid the clanking of trams and hooting of
trains and liners, and we were soon heading for the undulating
serpents of the sea, that here and there lifted a white-crested,
venomous head. Nòtwithstanding how rough it was, and that
the remainder of our party stayed below until we reached
Sicily, Mrs. Chitty sat on deck and talked to me. She made
of her deck-chair a little nest of her own and everybody else's
fur coats, and in this remained snug and warm — like one of
those mice, I thought, for whom the scientists had prepared
such comfortable winter-quarters. But our conversation was
not in the least monotonous, for she would banish any chance
of this by indulging in occasional frantic pantomime. Here
all her latent powers of acting found an outlet. She carried
with her — and they must always be near her — a great
number of large, brightly coloured, leather hand-trunks, each
filled with a different species of railway-ticket and foreign
money, for she never believed, she said, in putting all her eggs
into one basket. Thus, if by any mischance she lost the
miniature portmanteau which contained her ticket to Damascus,
she might still have that which held her ticket to Cairo, or if
she lost her Greek money, she would still have Syrian or
Egyptian.

First, and as prelude to the play, she would strike an
attitude which at once and most expressively conveyed to all
in her neighbourhood the idea that she thought she had lost
one of these 'little bags'. There would be a moment's dramatic,
tragic pause : and then a wild scene would ensue. Rugs and
rainbow-lined fur coats would execute mad furlanas and jotas
in the air as they were feverishly searched in turn. All the

men on deck would soon be bent double or would be crawling on all fours to examine obscure crannies between the wet and slippery boards, until it looked as if a game of 'animal-dumb-crambo' was in progress, or again, taking Mrs. Chitty and one of these figures as a separate group, the detached spectator, if mortal so hardened could exist, was reminded of that moment in the bull-fight when the matador, drawing himself up tautly, waves a flaming scarlet banner, behind which he shelters long, agonising darts, or his sword ready for the blow, in the very face of the charging bull. But now, it might be, there would be a triumphant gesture of discovery, and the miming would cease, for, as suddenly as it had vanished, the 'little bag' had materialised once more. She had been sitting on it, it appeared, or it had perhaps been in her hand the whole time, or even inside another 'little bag'. But this was by no means all her repertory, albeit it was the piece in which she most frequently presented herself. Sometimes, for instance, when in really high spirits, Mrs. Chitty would explode, as though it were a gigantic bomb, a special 'little bag', full of letters of introduction and visiting-cards. A miniature snow-storm of whirling white envelopes and oblongs of cardboard would zigzag up above us on an eddy of salt wind, and for several minutes the whole ship's company, and all the passengers well enough to be out, led by Mrs. Chitty herself, would be running along the deck together, with a frequent rhythmic halting and leaping high up into the air, until, in example of her art, this time they resembled a well-drilled corps-de-ballet under the guidance of its prima ballerina.

Indeed, so practised did all on board become at both these games, that the deck appeared to have become the sports-ground on which a number of celebrated athletes were re-hearsing for some great occasion. Mrs. Chitty would make the initiatory gesture, equivalent to the revolver-shot that opens such mysteries. Before that, and quite automatically, all the men had crouched down, their bodies thrown forward, ready to start. One . . . Two . . . Three . . . Go! and now they were off! There would be a sound of rushing, a tremendous scuffling and scrambling, as they sped past. But soon the referee would make another familiar gesture and we would await the next event. Whenever, during the course of this story, we are on board ship, the reader must conjure up for himself these constantly recurring pantomimes. They were a feature of our tour.

In the interval of such games as these, Mrs. Chitty would talk to me . . . talk with her face rather close to mine, otherwise, no doubt, the words would have been lost on the disinfectant wind. She dwelt much on her illness at the Villa Sutledge (I wondered, for her eyes glowed as she spoke of it, whether she might not still boast a slight fever?). She had, she said, in spite of that queer attack, enjoyed the visit enormously, though the Riviera did not usually appeal to her. But the garden was delightful, and Robert Sutledge was such a wonderful host. Her chief difficulty, really, had been that he was so kind, far *too* kind. She had not taken many frocks with her, for she knew that we would not want her to bring too much luggage on her travels, and, besides, dressmakers were so expensive now, and one had to be careful in these days about money. (At this point a 'little bag' broke open with the tinkling sound of a musical box, and a torrent of Greek drachmas, Turkish piastres or Syrian silver coins bounced, rolled and spun about the deck. Eventually, and by the united efforts of all in the vicinity, this particular currency was stabilised again, and Mrs. Chitty was able to continue.) About money, careful about money — Oh, yes! she remembered now. She had been going to say — but Robert would insist on carrying her off to royal dinner-parties : and it was so awkward having to attend them without the proper clothes. She was surprised that a genius like Robert cared for that sort of entertainment. Personally, she would much have preferred to sit quietly in the garden — though, of course, it became cold at night — talking to him, or playing the piano — a little Beethoven. . . . Now she *had* enjoyed seeing the Russian dancers at Montibes — but, after all, it was not as though it amused her to meet the Grand Duke Gabriel, the ex-King of Milesia (who couldn't talk in any language, but instead barked like a dog), or the old Duchess of Chester, that guttural Guelph Amazon, however wonderful she might be for her age. . . .

Yet, as she mentioned these royal names, her whole face was illumined . . . and this, again, what could this mean, I wondered. For assuredly she was no snob. What, then, did this light of pleasure signify? I tried to trace it, by analogy. It might, it seemed to me, have glowed in the face of a burglar after some unprecedentedly large haul, or have played round the stern, ascetic features of a missionary, who one day to his overwhelming surprise discovers that he has converted an entire tribe of natives, led by the Princes of the Blood — a tribe of which for many years now he had despaired.

We arrived at Palermo in the lime-green early morning. Then the sun came up, first gilding the two horns of the Conca d'Oro. Trucks of oranges and lemons stood near the docks, and the gaudily painted carts, drawn by straining mules, were jingling over the cobbles. We dawdled about; and after luncheon, Mrs. Chitty elaborately organised herself for a call on the Consul, while the remainder of us went up to Monreale. On the way I bought a continental edition of the *Daily Tribune*, and opened it as the tram slowly screamed up a sharp hill through a tunnel of giant red geraniums. At once my eye was caught by a heading:

SERIOUS ILLNESS OF WORLD-FAMED NOVELIST!

CRITICAL CONDITION OF ROBERT SUTLEDGE IN RIVIERA HOME

As, an hour or so later, we were still staring up at the vast gold mosaics, subtle and mysterious as Mrs. Chitty, and not unlike her in their personal style, we heard a dramatic, hollow voice, and turned round to find that she had driven up to join us. I broke to her the sad news about her friend, but she showed less surprise and dismay than I had feared. He had looked ill for some time, she said: and she imagined that his constitution was a very strong one. He did not catch things easily, she knew . . . yes, she was sure of that. Incidentally, she added, the Consul was charming. She wished we had come with her: we should have liked him. . . . He was rather a delicate-looking man (she had taken quite a fancy to him), but he had told her that Palermo was a very healthy place — practically no illness there ever.

For the next few mornings I neglected to buy a paper, and did not indeed see one for several days, since we soon set out on that wonderful journey to the Piraeus. The sun set and rose in Homeric splendour, and the purple shadows of the Greek islands fell down upon us. Mrs. Chitty was very cheerful, appeared to be enjoying herself, I thought. From the Piraeus we drove straight to our hotel in Athens. The city lay white and dusty beneath its primrose-coloured sunshine, even the bare bones up on the hill almost glittered, so strong and pulsing was the light. I tried to persuade her to come with us to the Acropolis, but she declined. She *must* call both on the British Minister and the Consul-General, she said, or Gerry Flitmouse, who had given her the letters, might be offended. He was always rather easily hurt, and snuffled terribly for months if one annoyed him. A dear boy, but delicate.

We walked up the steps that lead to the Acropolis, hot and dazed with the beauty of the light that seemed actually to glow through the tawny marble, and lingered among the huge, broken drums of the overthrown columns that litter the ground about the Parthenon. But, as we approached the great temple, our attention was drawn away from it by the sound of scampering feet, and we looked round to find a strange procession, a ribald frieze from a Greek vase come to life. It was, in fact, merely the arrival of the 'Friends of Greece' off their steamer, the *Dionysus*.

Twice a year these tours are arranged, at very high prices. The boat sets out from London, with a select list of passengers, and its own staff of attendant lecturers on board, for a course of intensive culture. They anchor for a day or two at all the places of Hellenic interest, Sicily, Corfu, the islands, on their way to Athens, and then on to Constantinople and Asia Minor. Never a morning, afternoon or evening passes without at least one instructive lecture. Most of the passengers are rich and ignorant, while others are enthusiasts who have saved up toward this trip for half a lifetime.

As they drew nearer us, the noise increased. First came a running battery of cameras, held by eager, whistling schoolboys under wide grey felt hats; then followed a succession of hatless schoolmasters — some of whom I remembered from Eton — tripping swiftly across the boulders with a curious lurching, lumbering gait as though still dribbling across the football fields: then a famous dean, with two sprained ankles, supported on the arms of numberless admirers; then an esthetic duchess caught in a cloud of gauze; now again, several deaf clergymen, a rather dingy lecturer, and finally a bevy of rich ladies, while two men wearing sun-helmets, in unspoken opposition to the schoolmasters, wound up the whole thing with an exotic flourish. To my surprise, Mrs. Chitty, looking very beautiful, with, as it seemed, an expression of religious ecstasy, only softened by her charming smile, stepped out suddenly from the middle of them. It was unlike her, for she detested crowds. . . . But she explained that she could not resist it — there were old friends of hers among them, and soon they would be leaving Athens, moving off toward numberless islands. No doubt the ship was comfortable. But it must be a rough life. . . . There was no doctor on the *Dionysus*, she was told, and not a medical man, not a single one in all those lonely isles which they were about to visit. . . .

Then she took me up to introduce me to Lady Richborough, who exuded a pale, esthetic, clipped muddle-headedness. 'Love Athens,' she was saying, 'delightful place. Like it even more than what's-the-name, you know, Muriel, that place we stopped at — but of course you weren't with us — with the large old buildings on it. And then there was that lovely island too. . . . I shall never forget it — and the Greek exchange is so good — I never can remember quite how much you get — but such a lot for a pound — better than the French exchange. . . . Do you suppose our own exchange will *ever* be so good?' After which, still pondering the possibilities disclosed by this question, we turned away.

As we left what is perhaps the most venerated skeleton in the world, I heard a delightfully modern sound. A Greek child of about seven, but with, already, an enormous scimitar of a nose, and black eyes that sparkled like new boot-buttons, was shouting, '*Dily Mile* an *Dily Tribeune* on sile — *Dily Mile* an *Dily Tribeune*'. I bought a paper. On the first page was the photograph of a familiar royal face, an iconic and dignified countenance.

SERIOUS ILLNESS OF GRAND DUKE

I read; and again:

The Grand Duke Gabriel's countless friends in England, and indeed all over the globe, will hear with full measure of sorrow that he is the victim of a new and obscure disease, which is causing the doctors grave anxiety. In its simpler aspects, it somewhat resembles influenza. Several people in the neighbourhood have recently been attacked by it, but so far there have been few fatal cases, though the illness is not one to be treated lightly.

The Grand Duchess, four nurses and His Imperial Highness's

six physicians-in-ordinary are in constant attendance, day and night. Letters and telegrams of inquiry, many of them from Great Britain, and requests for the latest bulletin on the distinguished patient, arrive without intermission at the door of Nishkynashdom, his palatial Riviera residence. The Grand Duchess, who has been a tower of strength in the sick-room, has helped the doctors in countless ways, though it is not as yet generally known that Her Royal Highness has adopted the uniform of a nurse and has abandoned her proposed exhibition of water-colours.

His Imperial Highness, who has been a well-known and popular figure on the Côte d'Azur for half a century, is seventy-eight years of age, and married in 1871 a Princess of Mannheim-Düsseldorf. He is also President of the Mont-Ferrat Golf Club and the Société Anonyme des Agronomes de Nice, the corporation responsible for running the New Casino outside the town.

Further down, in a chat-column, I read :

Hopes are still entertained, Delilah writes me from the Riviera, that Robert Sutledge, England's most famous novelist, will be well enough to come home in two or three weeks' time. It would be little less than a tragedy for his friends were he obliged to abandon his famous annual visit, for which an immense amount of entertaining takes place : but it is, alas, no secret to them that, for the past ten days, he has been very seriously ill.

I drew Mrs. Chitty's attention to the illness of the Grand Duke Gabriel.

'How very odd,' she said to me, with a bayonet-like glint in her usually warm eye. 'So soon after poor Robert, too. It looks almost as if they must have caught the same germ, doesn't it ? Perhaps I had it also. I felt very ill at the time, but wouldn't give up. I've always said, "If you want people to be ill, go with them to the Riviera." By the way, I think I must have had a slight temperature again last night.'

The next few days in Athens passed very swiftly and without event, except that Muriel Chitty, who insisted, apparently, on sleeping without a mosquito-net, was, in consequence, very badly bitten. It was curious, for usually she was so careful, even fussy about herself; and we had advised her to be on her guard . . . yet she was the only one of us to suffer in this way.

The passage to Constantinople was ideal. We arrived safely, and were duly astonished at the number of bowler-hats :

but even that could not destroy our excitement, or the beauty of the setting: the water on every side, and the silhouette of numberless, grey, spider-like domes, very squat under their needle-shaped minarets, that crept over every hill, and crowned the lower ones.

Mrs. Chitty decided that she felt too tired to visit Santa Sofia, and that, instead, she would rest a little and then leave letters for, and call on, the British Representatives. She might, perhaps, meet us afterwards — somewhere in the town — perhaps near the Delphic Serpent. . . . And indeed as, later, we looked at it, lost in wonder at its long and marvellous history, a hollow, oracular voice, with all the ecstasy of divination in its tones, woke us from our reveries by exclaiming just behind us:

'Well, here I am. . . . But you none of you look very well . . . I hope you're all right?'

It was Mrs. Chitty, fresh from consular triumphs.

While I was waiting in the hotel before dinner I saw, lying on a table, a new copy of the *Daily Tribune*, just arrived. I opened it.

SUDDEN ILLNESS OF EX-KING BORIS OF MILESIA

was the caption that met my eye.

ALL ENGAGEMENTS CANCELLED

His Ex-Majesty was suddenly seized with illness after attending, as is his wont, the Friday 'Dîner Fleuri' at the Hôtel de Bordeaux. His companion, Mlle Donescu, immediately summoned a doctor.

On the next page I read:

SEVERANCE OF LAST LINK WITH GEORGE III
DEATH OF H.R.H. THE DUCHESS OF CHESTER

We regret to announce the death of H.R.H. the Duchess of Chester, who passed away peacefully in the presence of her family during the early hours of this morning. The sad event took place at her marine residence, the Villa Britannique. Her Royal Highness, who was in her 92nd year, was the last surviving granddaughter of George III, and with her passing a notable link with the past is for ever severed. The Duchess, always one of the most beloved of English princesses, was a wonderful specimen of English grit of the

26

Old School. During the war, though then in her 81st year, she spent several days in the trenches, distributing chocolates to the men, and even in the tightest corners contrived to keep a stiff upper lip. Deservedly popular with all classes, it was Her Royal Highness who popularised the word 'Schweinhunds' for the German troops during the war.

It is worth recording, as an instance of this wonderful old lady's undiminished activity and interest in all that pertained to literature up to the last, that only three weeks ago she attended a dinner-party in her honour given by Mr. Robert Sutledge, the novelist (now, unfortunately, himself an invalid). During the evening, Her Royal Highness, who loved everything modern, gave an exhibition of her skill on the saxophone. Accompanied, on the piano, by her Lady-in-Waiting, she played Liszt's 'Liebestraum', Mendelssohn's 'Spring Song', and ended up, amid great applause, with 'You're the Whitest White I know', and her own rendering of the 'Black Bottom'. Two days later Her Royal Highness was suddenly taken ill, and the doctors, seeing that the end could not long be delayed, summoned the family.

I showed these three paragraphs to Mrs. Chitty when she came down.

'Quite a coincidence,' she observed bitterly. . . .

And these words, it seemed to me, were addressed to myself rather than to my companions; were spoken, moreover, as though she thought they might convey to me an inner significance hidden from others.

'No wonder you were ill, Muriel darling,' I heard Mrs. Rammond say to her. 'I've always maintained that the Riviera was unhealthy: a perfect death-trap. Think of the microbes there must be hanging about those hotels and villas, not to mention casinos! It's extraordinary, though, this year. Absolutely everybody there seems to be ill.'

But at this, though it did not very much differ from the sentiment herself had expressed at Athens only a few days before, Mrs. Chitty suddenly became cross. (Perhaps, one thought, the mosquito-bites were still irritating her, making her sleepless.) She dropped two bags, half an earring and a diamond pendant, and so, for a time, her conversation was lost to me. As, however, we emerged from under our various tables, she was saying very decisively, and in a tone of voice which suggested that she considered herself slighted: 'Well, all I can tell you is, there was no one ill there before I arrived : no one. I was the first — and probably most of them aren't ill even now. They are a regular pack of old *malades imaginaires* : that's what *they* are. If they were to become really ill, goodness knows what would happen to them!'

Our time at Constantinople fled past us, with little personal to record except that it seemed to me that every day, as she was further removed in hours and miles from home, Mrs. Chitty became ever more feminine — but in a distinctly Victorian, rather than modern, way. It was there, too, and more specially in Brousa, that she first began to parade her ardent love for animals. There were several vociferous and vituperative differences between herself and the drivers of donkeys. The Turkish language won, for its throaty sounds suggested, even to those who could not understand them, a wealth of obloquy not to be attempted in English or French. But Mrs. Chitty was left with that comforting, unimpeachable serenity which comes to all those who defend dumb brutes.

Borne on by blue phanariot breezes, that yet hardly ruffled the surface, we visited in turn Rhodes and Cyprus. Here, again, there was little to record. At Rhodes, an island that rises from a sea paved with medieval stone cannon-balls, we found great activity among the restorers and strippers of ancient buildings, while huge white peonies, like water-lilies, were in bloom under the darkest shade of cedars. Furthermore, as we approached this much-conquered island, we heard an American lady summing up the confusion of our epoch by inquiring of her companion in a plaintive voice, 'Tell me, dear, where *used* this to be?'

At Cyprus, on the contrary, we discovered a British island, full of discontented, undersized Levantines, gorged on honest British beef and suet. No building had been restored, but there were hill-stations and topees, and the ponderous red shadow of India brooded over the western hills and streams.

But the journey seemed to suit our health. We all felt peculiarly well — generally a bad omen — and even Mrs. Chitty's mosquito-bites were healing. She liked the place, and while calling on various officials, had met the Anglican Bishop and made great friends with him, she said.

Sailing from Famagusta to Beirut, however, the sea suddenly began to grow rough again : and soon Mrs. Chitty, my brother and myself were once more the only members of our party to venture on deck. But on this occasion she was not so communicative ; seemed lost in her own thoughts. Yet we could not help being impressed, and rather intimidated, by a new and singular manner of looking at one which at this time she developed. It was a steady, unfaltering brown gaze that united the watchfulness of a doctor expectant of symptoms with the frigid, measuring, detached glance of an undertaker : a gaze that one could never afterwards forget.

When, though rarely, she talked, she would tell us of the south of France. Perpetually she reverted to it : to the kindness and subsequent illness of Mr. Sutledge, to the dinner-parties she had attended, the Royal Personages she had met. It was unlike her. César Franck or changes in the Foreign Office would have been more usual, more in style. . . . But no ! Back we would go to the Riviera. Really, I said to myself, it was as though she had committed some murder there, among the planted-out and varnished palm-trees, the carefully manicured carnations (each one was stated to be given its own hot-water bottle at night), and must ever return in spirit to haunt the scene of it. She resembled those poisoners who, though their guilt has passed quite unsuspected at the time, inevitably attract attention and are in the end caught because they insist on revisiting of their own free will the spot where their evil deed was perpetrated, to inquire, too innocently, of the police whether anyone had died in the neighbourhood ? Or again, one said, she behaved as if, with some atrocious crime on her conscience, she thought that I had guessed her share in it : and so, partly out of bravado, partly because it was a subject that quite genuinely she could never banish from her mind for an instant, and partly moreover to test how much I knew, and to try to trap me into some speech, look or action which would betray that knowledge, she would, and with a show of indifference, continually persist in talking of the lonely village where it had taken place, boasting how often she had been there and how well she knew it.

At Beirut we had intended only to spend an hour or two, just long enough for Mrs. Chitty to call on the Consul (how *could* it amuse her, I wondered, for she was very tired ?) and then to drive on at once to Damascus. Nevertheless, we were delayed a little, for since she was determined to see him personally, in the end we were all invited to tea. The conversation was rather formal: but I heard her ask him in anxious tones whether there was much illness in Syria at this season? None at all, he replied.

In Damascus, on arrival, I bought a copy of the *Daily Tribune*, despatched by air from Paris. There was nothing very new in it. The body of H.R.H. the Duchess of Chester had been carried on board an English battleship, with the customary honours, and was to be conveyed to a final resting-place in her native land. Another column informed us that ex-King Boris of Milesia was making a plucky fight against an insidious and treacherous foe. He had now been ill for many days. His pulse was feeble, his temperature high. Robert Sutledge was, it appeared, still in bed: in fact, had experienced a slight relapse, and his friends continued to suffer much anxiety for him. About the condition of H.I.H. the Grand Duke Gabriel there was an ominous silence.

Mrs. Chitty had been somewhat dejected, and had complained of feeling ill in Damascus (though I think she enjoyed seeing the ruins which mark the French occupation of that city): so I did not show her the paper until we were on board the steamer bound for Alexandria. I had feared the news in it would depress her still further, but she took it well, and became quite cheerful.

One morning, while we were on the boat, she turned to me, and with an intensity of emphatic meaning in her voice, asked, 'Do you know Valaise?' I replied, no, I didn't. 'Well, that's a pity, a great pity,' she rejoined. 'It's such a lovely little place, on the hills just above Beaulieu. I drove there several times with Robert Sutledge. An old Saracen village; just a cluster of white houses with flattened domes. You'd adore it. . . . But I shouldn't say it was healthy . . . a lot of illness there, I'm sure.' And suddenly she laughed, looking at me as though she expected me to join in her cryptic mirth.

It was this significant confidence, as a matter of fact, which finally gave me the clue. We disembarked at Alexandria and, as soon as Mrs. Chitty had left her letters of introduction, proceeded to Cairo. The next morning I remembered to buy a copy of the *Daily Tribune*. I opened it and read — right across the top of the paper:

RIVIERA VILLAGE DECIMATED
Outbreak of Mystery Disease at Valaise

For a moment all the things that in bad novels are said to happen at such a crisis happened to me together. I was struck speechless; the print danced before my eyes; my teeth chattered; my hair stood on end; I felt I had an iron band round my forehead; there were icy shivers down my spine; and the very blood in my veins ran cold — for at last I understood. Everything explained itself; I understood only too well. Mrs. Chitty was no longer a woman, but merely the living vessel that contained a microbe, a versatile master-microbe who never repeated himself. She was the fully disciplined, loyal slave of this ferocious and tyrannical germ; the medium for a single-purposed and evil control. She was a person possessed, not, as in the old sense, by a demon, but instead by a bacillus — albeit one of very phenomenal power and completeness. It was thus a physical, not a spiritual possession. The only aim of the governing organism within, and of its innumerable progeny, was to procreate and spread still further. Toward this one purpose, every cough, every movement, every decision that Mrs. Chitty made was calculated: but though to every act she imparted the appearance of free-will, all she did depended, in reality, on the secret wishes and plans of this inner and invisible dictator. Why, her very resolve to join us on this journey, what was that but another scheme for propagation? For this tour was no ordinary one, but the brave missionary voyage of a militant and proselytising microbe; a journey equivalent to the first Mediterranean mission of St. Paul.

And of course . . . I realised it now: she was, from this point of view, at once the ideal means of transit, the best possible laboratory for experiment, and a model breeding-ground and nursery for young germs. Delicate enough always to harbour them, she was yet too weak, too thin and nervous, her blood too impoverished, to afford continual sustenance for so mighty and immeasurable a tribe. An imperialist bacillus, ambitious for the future of his race, could find no land that would offer so perfect an upbringing and training-place for the young as did Mrs. Chitty. Just as the sparse diet, hard work and meagre earnings which Nature enforces there, compel the

Japanese nation, heaped up on its rocky, barren and picturesque isles, to seek fresh lands for its surplus but very hardy population, so Mrs. Chitty's spare and bony frame, though unable to support the countless progeny of microbes it had raised so frugally, taught them to be all the more self-reliant and courageous. They were forced to find a new outlet for their energy, and became adventurous, crusading, piratical as our forefathers of Queen Elizabeth's reign, would execute with gusto the most daring raids on stronger and more active people, would seize colonies, found an empire. But here all parallels stop short, and the microbes clearly have the advantage of men. For Mrs. Chitty was their magic carpet as well as Motherland. While the English and the Japanese are forced to emigrate from their emerald isles set in the sapphire sea, are forced to go long journeys by boat, the microbes are conveyed to the very portals of each promised land, not by a ship, but by their own country itself. Think of what that must mean. How little compared with us will they feel the severance of home-ties! Imagine the interest and change implied for the entire population, if England could travel each year to Canada and India! Mrs. Chitty was truly the land in which to raise a breed of heroes, an imperial race.

Nor need this moving, living Motherland ever fear revolution, be afraid lest her children should turn against or seek to harm her. Even if they attempted it, they could not kill her, for she was not full-blooded enough to kill. Moreover, brought up within her, they cherished a true sentiment of loyalty toward their home and must be aware, withal, that her every thought was for the furtherance of their cause since she still placed herself at the entire disposal of the governing germ.

And how every idiosyncrasy in her character, every action of hers, notwithstanding that it may have seemed erratic and without purpose at the moment — became clear and rational under this sudden apocalyptic illumination, declared itself beyond doubt as part of the wily and Machiavellian scheming from which the hidden control never ceased, for it worked remorselessly day and night. In the same way that the painted ceilings of certain Italian eighteenth-century churches — such as San Pantaleone in Venice or Sant' Ignacio in Rome — at first appear to the stranger as a meaningless muddle of distorted architecture, puffy clouds and inflated goddesses, until he is led to one small circle in the centre of the marble floor, and looking up, is now able to behold the roof opening up like a flower, blossoming into a strange, miraculous, but yet quite logical and lovely world of its own, so, once one had gained the clue to its perspective, the planning and arrangement of Mrs. Chitty's life became quite simple and easily comprehended. For example, if you were a modern-minded, rather hustling germ (a real 'go-getter' as the American phrase is) who wanted to get about the world a bit, and quicker than Mrs. Chitty could take you, what better instrument could you find for this constant voyaging than a member of His Majesty's Diplomatic or Consular Services? No wonder that Mrs. Chitty loved those that dwell in Foreign Offices and took so lively an interest in every swop and promotion: no wonder that she called on every Minister and every Consul in each town abroad she visited, and, in addition, left on them letters, the envelopes of which she had fastened, sticking down the flap, and thus personally infecting them, with her own tongue! Then, too, I recalled the talk at her dinner-parties — conversations that so often turned on the newest mode of combating, and, if possible, extirpating, the influenza and kindred microbes. And all the time, these methods, and the experiments that led up to them, things on which science had concentrated so much toil and hope, were being explained to one who was not only Mother, home and country to these actual microbes, but, as well, an immense and living testing-ground for their researches, a laboratory in which they were continually engaged in the most lively counter-experiments.

III

The position was in all truth serious enough. For several days two members of our party had been ill, though their symptoms differed. Ruth Marlow had a temperature that raced up and down continually, and was forced to live entirely on orange juice. Julian Thackwray complained that he had a headache that nearly blinded him, that he could only see half of the palm-trees and pyramids, that his right arm was quite numb and that he had lost the use of the index finger of his left hand. Obviously, then, the germs were in active and experimental mood, and who could tell what novel and acute diseases they would not leave in their wake after the first alarm had subsided? The doctor, called in, pronounced it to be 'only influenza'. 'Only', indeed!

I took precautions, bought cinnamon, bottles and bottles of it, eucalyptus oil, gargles of every description, quinine and a thousand disinfectants. And thenceforth it seemed to me that Mrs. Chitty's Theotocopulos-like and lachrymose eye reflected very clearly the new consciousness of her protean master-microbe within that myself was his chief enemy, and that, in so far as I was concerned, he was in for the battle of a lifetime, a fight to a finish. I cannot think that this was conceit, or that I was in any way exaggerating my own importance. No, he was a good sportsman, and recognised that by nature, as much as now of intention, I was going to be a particularly rare and difficult bag . . . indeed, he had foreseen it long before I had discovered Mrs. Chitty's mission . . . and that was, no doubt, why she had so often sat on deck with me and talked: for to be heard above the winds that, born from its speed, leap and play like dolphins round any ship, it is necessary for those who converse to bring their heads near together; a splendid opportunity for infection.

Meanwhile one must not despair. The news in the paper the day after my revelation a little allayed concern. The account of the progress of the Grand Duke Gabriel was reassuring. I read:

H.I.H. THE GRAND DUKE GABRIEL

His Imperial Highness's many friends will be relieved to hear that his medical advisers are confident that, should no new complications arise (and, of course, it must be remembered that even now it is impossible to rule out such possibilities; that to estimate the likelihood of such developments, the length of time during which the Royal patient has been ill must always be borne in mind), His Imperial Highness should be out of danger in another two months' time. A week ago he recognised the Grand Duchess for the first time (she was in nurse's uniform), and though still suffering from shock, he was well enough yesterday to be propped up in bed, and to enjoy the broadcasting of his favourite song, Tosti's 'Good-bye'. He also received the latest shipping-signals from Rio de Janeiro and Vladivostok. His Imperial Highness is now encouraged to take proper nourishment, and was yesterday ordered half a glass of hot milk with a dash of the national beverage, vodka, in it.

One was glad to see, too, that Robert Sutledge had survived his relapse and was now really 'making headway'. It was hoped that in another week or two, if he continued to recuperate with the same speed as heretofore, and if the present fine weather held, he might be allowed to sit out in the garden for half an hour.

On the other hand the mystery epidemic at Valaise showed no sign of abating, and the Rockefeller Institute had despatched scientists to study the outbreak on the spot and draw up a report upon it. The remains of H.R.H. the Duchess of Chester, borne on a battleship, escorted by four cruisers, had arrived at Southampton, and there was a description of the Municipal Brass Band playing the 'Last Post' as the Death Ship drew in to the harbour of a city hung with funebrial purple.

What was to be done? There was no time to be lost. . . . I determined to confide in Mrs. Rammond and my brother. They were the ones I most wished to save from the holocaust. At first they did not take my discovery very seriously, terming it 'ridiculous' and 'fantastic'. Ruth and Julian were soon able to move about again, and it was now supposed that they had caught a 'mere chill'. But both of them protested that they were still desperately ill, and almost paralysed. Mrs. Chitty herself had not been idle. She, too, had achieved a racing temperature but, though she owned that she felt desperate, was determined to see everything, and not to '*give in*': quite a new development on her part, for hitherto she had absented herself from any sight-seeing expeditions and had harboured all her strength for calling on Consuls. But now she tramped tirelessly through the heat, while, in addition, continuing to visit every possible British Representative, diplomatic, consular, military, or naval.

Ruth and Julian seemed well enough to accompany us, and we were just about to start our trip up the Nile on the dahabiya, when Mrs. Jocelyn and Frank Lancing collapsed, and were taken to the British Hospital. But as soon as we had seen the new invalids comfortably established there and had been assured that they were at present in no actual danger, we thought it best to proceed with our original plan. However, the fate of our two friends depressed the party considerably, and Mrs. Rammond and my brother began to treat more seriously the theory I had advanced to them.

On the dahabiya the situation became acute. Since Mrs. Chitty now fully recognised in me her microbe's chief antagonist, she sat by me whenever possible . . . and still there were no signs of my ailing. Obviously the new offensive, to the preparation of which her germ had devoted so many anxious months of careful experiment and audacious imagination, was failing, was breaking down. (So it must have seemed to her.) The microbe was not, after all, invincible : and a bitter sense of disappointment must have swept down on her. Certain it is that under the charm, of which she could not divest herself, fear and hatred could be seen mingling in her poignant glance, and that the prolonged and cheerful sound of gargling which ostentatiously issued from my cabin constituted to her ears a most melancholy and distressing music. Perhaps the best thing she could do, she must have thought, was to turn her attention to my brother. But, here again, she was checked and, apparently, crushed. There we sat, under brown awnings that never stirred, and watched each sunset unroll its panorama of coloured-picture-postcard tints ; palm-trees, springing lithely, several stalks from one root, camels silhouetting themselves vulgarly against an oily red-yellow sunset — a sunset that had never progressed since the oriental paintings popular during the Second Empire — or else narrow-waisted figures moving through a fertile field in short white tunics and with long, shaven heads, performing against it their second-rate hieroglyphs and bas-reliefs, while the alligators thawed to movement in the sticky yellow water beneath us. . . . But as each sunset died away in cheap flames, and then remained for an instant a stain upon the luminous canopy, faded away, as it were, with the last self-conscious if well-practised bow, of a famous prima donna acknowledging her applause, Mrs. Chitty, though not yet giving up hope, became sadder and ever more sad. . . . But, since fortune is so fickle, one who does not admit defeat is never defeated. Now a change occurred, and Fate unmistakably declared itself for her. The crew suddenly fell ill, and, because they were natives, unused to any such northern infection, with them it took a much more severe form.

At one moment it looked as if we might have to work the ship back to Cairo ourselves. The invalid members of the crew now lay on the deck, under canopies, with Mrs. Chitty looking after them, while we sweated in the miniature engine-room and were instructed by a survivor or two in their hot and oily trade. We began to grow nervous. Cut off from the outside world as we were, and overwhelmed by the microbe's unexpected and very decisive victory, we could not help wondering what new developments might not be taking place, might not greet us on our somewhat problematic return? But, in sweet content, Mrs. Chitty sat on deck, gently tending the sick, and smiling. It was, indeed, a smile altogether beautiful to behold, a smile of pure, kindly joy, of a spirit uplifted, such, one would have said, as might have lighted up the austere features of Florence Nightingale when, rustling through the wards at night, shading the lamp with her hand, she looked down on all those whom she had saved. And near the surface of the thick yellow water, the alligators, too, bared their sharp teeth in a subtle but appreciative grin, and played and tumbled quite lustily.

The crew behaved, as it turned out, very well, and contrived to get us back to Cairo. There we found the two patients out of hospital. It was true that they were so weak they could scarcely drag themselves along, so tired that they could see and understand nothing, so poisoned after their illness that even cigarettes were no solace to them, but they were alive : that was the important thing. And as — for it was, naturally enough, at that moment the only thing that interested them — they discussed how possibly, and where, they could have contracted this infection and, without any suspicion of the identity of the link that connected the two things, happened to observe that they had read in the newspapers at the hospital that there was a good deal of this same sort of odd illness on the Riviera, once again I saw a smile, but of a different kind from that we have just described, play quietly round Mrs. Chitty's ascetic and thoughtful countenance. It was the smile that had so often perplexed me in the past ; an enigmatic and beautiful curling of the mouth, which seemed as though, after the manner of the Gioconda's, it had been summoned up by the sound of hidden and distant flutes.

For many days I had seen no newspaper, and it was evident,

directly I bought one, that in the meantime the situation had developed. For the first item that caught my eye was

MEMORIAL SERVICE AT NICE FOR EX-KING BORIS OF MILESIA

A memorial service was held yesterday afternoon at the Orthodox Church at Nice for His Majesty ex-King Boris of Milesia. Nearly every European Royal House was personally represented. Among the congregation were the ex-King and ex-Queen of Ruritania, with ex-Crown Prince Danilo, the ex-King and ex-Queen of Carolia with ex-Crown Prince Paul, the ex-King of. . . .

So another one was gone, I reflected sadly . . . and then looking at the next page I noticed that the four principal Russian dancers of the Opera at Montibes had been taken seriously ill, and that, in consequence, all future performances had been abandoned. Further, the Rockefeller Institute had sent four more specialists to Valaise, the first two having fallen ill, forty-eight hours after their arrival, of the same mysterious disease that was mowing down the villagers. All fountains and streams in the neighbourhood had been sprayed with paraffin on their advice, and the force of the epidemic had a little abated, although isolated cases of this illness had been identified in seven other widely removed mountain villages. H.I.H. the Grand Duke Gabriel was said to be progressing steadily.

We spent a few more days in Cairo—but now the party began to break up. Julian and Ruth fell ill again (she had a slight temperature), and Frank and Mrs. Jocelyn maintained that they were too weak to take any risks. The remaining four of us, therefore, set out into the desert alone.

Mrs. Chitty, though we had urged that the fatigue might prove too much for her, had insisted on accompanying us. But, once in the sandy wastes, she began to complain of feeling unwell. Nestling in furs again, she went to bed very early each night, while Mrs. Rammond, my brother and myself wildly caroused on cinnamon beneath stars crystal-bright in their blue firmament; caroused, as it were, with something of the defiant and boisterous recklessness that inspired those rakish Restoration nobles who remained in London during the Great Plague: for such a scourge, it is said, always affects profoundly the moral outlook. 'Eat, drink, and be merry, for tomorrow we die', was the motto engraved on our, as on their, hearts. There, then, we sat on, recklessly quaffing the flowing bowl of quinine, and wantonly sprinkling our cubes of sugar with camphor and eucalyptus, until the early hours of the morning — notwithstanding that the feathers of the palm-trees which lay motionless on the air above us were the only plumes, and the sound of the heavy and inexorable snoring that issued from Mrs. Chitty's tent was the sole and rather menacing music afforded us for our feasting. Indeed this rhythmic rising and falling announced all too plainly that the germ was still on the march; almost amounted to a solemn declaration of new hostilities.

The days passed and still we held on. Mrs. Chitty perhaps now felt genuinely ill, for she was again becoming desperate. As we advanced further into the desert, her Victorian helplessness was manifested more and more often. It was no easy matter to find the English or Libyan coins that she scattered in such thoughtless profusion among the golden grains which lay spread round us for hundreds of miles : and many an hour we passed, hot and tired, scratching and grubbing in the sand like so many animals burrowing, until a miniature sandstorm was raised about us, while Muriel Chitty sat a little way off, continually repining. . . .

The weather, she said, was cold. She had always expected the desert to be hot. She wished she had brought another fur coat with her (just a little one, like the one I was holding) : except that she thought the desert must be full of moths, for, she added with a slightly malicious smile, she continually smelt camphor — she supposed it must be against moths, for it was entirely useless against anything else. . . . The palm-trees were ugly, the sunsets monotonous, the camels lazy — they were always lying down — and greedy ; though she had always felt sorry for them hitherto, because they looked so long-legged, round-backed and awkward ; and she was sure they were badly treated. She didn't like the faces of the camel-drivers, wouldn't trust them, wouldn't trust them an inch, herself. Perhaps it was as well that one did not understand what they were talking about. For what did all the natives eat? One couldn't eat dates for ever. And then the water — she was sure that the drinking water in the oases was not *reliable* : but she could not drink mineral water because it contained no vitamins. If the Arabs wouldn't mind — and, after all, they couldn't, could they? — she would like to pour a whole lot of disinfectants down the spring. Oh, but she forgot, she hadn't brought any with her. Might she have ours — they would do just as well — ? (And only just in time we stopped her : for, with extraordinary skill, agility and presence of mind, she here made a dash for our row of bottles, gargles and the like — our only safeguard and refuge — intending to empty them down the well.) All right, she wouldn't, then. But she was sure that there would be an epidemic one day — still, of course, if *we* didn't worry about that, it didn't matter. . . . The Arabs couldn't care for music, or they wouldn't make those extraordinary noises at the camels. . . . She was *certain*, now, that they treated the camels brutally. It was terrible to see them, they looked so bony and emaciated. Although they were not animals she cared for, she really would like to buy one, if only to get it away from those awful men (terrible faces). The camels looked as if a good graze on green English grass would do them all the good in the world : but, then, if she bought one, where could she put it ? . . . And, besides, perhaps she oughtn't to buy one, really. It would be, after all, an extravagance. She knew the trustees would say that. Carriage was so expensive, too — and taxation was going up all the time (at least she supposed it was, but one couldn't tell, for there were never any letters or newspapers in a place like this). Where could she put it ? Of course, she might keep it somewhere here, and have grass sent out to it — but, then, that wouldn't be the same thing, not at all the same. And even that would cost money. And then the desert was so big that, if one did put one somewhere here, one might not be able to find it when it was wanted, for when one had discovered places here, places in which to put things, often one could never find them again. Oh, dear ! she believed that, after all, she had lost her 'little bag' — the one with her Libyan money in it. Where did she think she had left it ? Oh, but she was certain — she knew quite well — she was sure she had put it down, just for a moment — somewhere in the desert. . . .

But now Fortune, turning once more, smiled on Mrs. Chitty, and she smiled back. The tragedy was mounting to its inevitable climax. My brother, in spite of all our carefully thought-out methods of prevention, in spite of cinnamon, camphor and quinine, began to fail for a day or two — and then fell victim. Like a hero he stuck to his post. Even when finally overwhelmed, he refused to acknowledge defeat. Mrs. Chitty was, naturally, the first of us to notice the symptoms. To her it was like watching a race with the prospect of an exciting finish. Her colours were ahead now. Daily she became more worked up. It was certain, too, she must have supposed, that Mrs. Rammond and I would catch it. . . . The desert: the *wonderful, wonderful* desert. There was, she reflected, something incredibly beautiful and romantic about it — what glamour ! Doughty, and all those slow, eternal camels, and the Arabs, such dignity, and palm-trees and Colonel Lawrence and all that. . . . Wonderful. . . . But Mrs. Rammond and I were without hope and drank cinnamon without end.

In the few, recurrent, lucid moments which his illness granted him every day, my brother explained to us the precise nature of the microbe's ravages. The sensation, he told us, was comparable to being knocked on the head and drowned simultaneously. Only for about five minutes a day, just long enough to realise how sweet life could have been, was he permitted to come up to the surface, take a few breaths, and then, once more, he was sent spinning down again into the depths. He could walk, even talk a little — but automatically, as though he were in a trance. For the rest, there was an intense aching in the roots of his hair, shooting pains in the eyes, slight deafness, acute anguish between the vertebrae, pains in the toes, a perfect agony in the lobe of each ear and a sense of partial paralysis in the left hand. This journey was something to which for a whole decade he had eagerly looked forward, as to something transcendent and unattainable, and here he was being whirled through the desert (for at Sidi-ben-Sidi we had met our car) in a state of unconsciousness, or, at best, of semi-consciousness.

Her horse, Mrs. Chitty must have thought, was just rounding Tattenham Corner ; but on the contrary, the invalid came to, suddenly after a week, to find himself in the large native city of Abu-ben-Kalab. We were staying in a little white hotel, owned by a Greek. It was very clean, and had a quite pretty garden which, by an extraordinary stroke of luck, was planted with such trees and shrubs as eucalyptus, camphor and castor-oil. Moreover, in one corner of it there even flourished a cinnamon-bush. Out of this shady and restful grey-greenness, aromatic and health-giving breaths were wafted on every slightest fluttering breeze. From the first moment Mrs. Chitty evinced a particular aversion to this spot, declaring that when she was in a garden, she liked to *feel* she was in one, and not in a chemist's shop.

The town itself was fascinating, I thought. For hours you could wander round the *souks* — the light falling through the branches that roofed them to dapple and splash the bearded, bartering figures beside the stalls — without feeling a moment's fatigue, so new and alive was the scene. In the public places one could listen to poetry being declaimed, with an accompaniment of gourds and gongs, to an entranced circle of yellow-faced, squatting figures. And sometimes, too, one could hear tall, lank Senegalese minstrels, the colour of black-lead and wearing necklaces of cowrie shells, singing their high-pitched songs, see dancers, belonging to the unknown tribes that inhabit the interior of the continent, whirling round feverishly in a cloud of white dust, or watch the dark mountebanks from distant Marrakesh performing their grotesque and epicene antics. Such was the fascination of the city, strange and varied. But Mrs. Chitty liked it no better than the garden. There was not a Minister in the place — not even a consul; no European shops, no papers (so that it was impossible, she said, to tell what was going on. Everyone in England might have the plague itself, and one would not know about it.)

It was a complete transformation. This subtle lady, who at home was intensely cosmopolitan, eschewing English phrases wherever possible, and substituting for them Foreign Office *clichés* in French, German and Italian, was each day becoming more English, more Victorian. As though in an effort to sum up her own tendencies, she asked me one day to go into the town and find her a bottle of Rowlands' Macassar Oil — the very sound of which conjured up in my imagination ottomans, crinolines, double-jointed little parasols edged with black lace, beaded flowers, plush chairs, draped table-legs, soft, sentimental whiskers and curling, pomaded locks. . . . Assuredly this was not the place to choose for such a whimsy. Nor, perhaps, ought one to have encouraged a caprice so exotic in this place and century, unless one was certain (and this was improbable) that it was comparable to the longing for a 'dish of apricocks' entertained by Webster's Duchess of Malfi. However, Mrs. Chitty's eagerness was so pathetic that, though fully aware of the futility of my errand, I tramped up and down the *souks* for hours, searching for this strange and ancient elixir. And hereafter at every village, however small, and even if entirely composed of wattle-huts, I was asked to get out and look for it.

At Abu-ben-Kalab, it was, withal, that the ever-increasing feeling of fondness for animals that she paraded reached a point that was unpleasant and even dangerous in its consequences, as much for them as for ourselves.

It cannot, I am afraid, be disputed that the natives of these regions ill-treat their animals, though I do know to what extent this neglect or brutality can be palliated by the fact that there live, not so far away, great numbers of dangerous and dis-agreeable beasts — lions, leopards, apes and crocodiles — and that the men themselves, or their not-far-distant ancestors, have suffered cruelly at their paws and teeth. Meanwhile, in the interior of the continent the dusky brothers of these men — and the brothers of these animals — still wage against one another a grim and endless warfare. This must, if one comes to think of it, alter the human attitude toward other creatures. In England, it is the animal which has to be afraid : all the ferocious creatures of our country, fox, stag and otter, hares, pheasants, rabbits, ordinary field-mice and guinea-pigs, must by now have learnt their lesson. But to ignorant Africans an animal, even a domestic animal living among them, is regarded much as an interned German was regarded in England during the war. Not a word it says is understood, and its every action ought to be regarded with suspicion, as part of a plot : nor would it seem fair, they might urge in conversation with us, to be too kind, too generous with food to these brutes, whose brothers and cousins are killing our relatives and co-religionists the other side of the Atlas.

Mrs. Chitty naturally did not share or indeed comprehend these feelings, so different from our own. Apart from mice, she had no enemies or rivals in the animal world, and was horrified at the African outlook on brute beasts. She therefore secretly resolved to buy a few of the worst-treated animals, and under-took a self-appointed pilgrimage of pity round the town, guided and advised by a black and evil interpreter. Un-fortunately, as we learnt afterward, whereas she never made an offer for a whole, unmaimed, unscarred and well-fed animal, she was willing to offer comparatively fabulous sums for any halt, maimed, starved, wounded, scarred or diseased mule or donkey. This was disastrous. Even those Arabs who had hitherto been kind to their animals, had been governed in this rather by financial than moral principles. A healthy, well-fed brute had been, up till Mrs. Chitty's advent, a paying proposition. But now it was so no longer. Her motives eluded them, and they very logically concluded that here was a mad-millionaire-white-woman with an unhealthy passion for seeing animals suffer. And since their faith taught them that, while both women and animals have no souls, Allah inspires the insane, and because life had taught them that gold was necessary to men, it seemed only right — and certainly good business — to gratify her curious desires. Thus, it appears, all night they would sit up, ill-treating their unfortunate beasts, kicking and beating them, inflicting hellish and ingenious tortures upon them, in order to be able in the morning to extort a good price from her. A suffering mule was now worth ten, twenty times even, a healthy, happy one. Acute speculation in sick animals set in : there were, of course, fluctuations, but, on the whole, it was a steady, rising market. The results were lamentable and heart-rending.

Ignorant of that which had been in progress, we returned to the hotel one day, after an expedition, to find it besieged by a mob of eager, shouting natives, determined to sell Mrs. Chitty their tortured beasts ; for it had somehow become known that we were leaving the next morning. Flocks and flocks of suffering and ill-tempered creatures, including a number of gigantic, knock-kneed and macerated camels, and crowds of jostling, bargaining, jabbering, quarrelling natives, all wrapped in a suffocating cloud of thick, white dust, surrounded the building. The proprietor was at the same time both furious and in a panic. He protested that all the guests were leaving, his business was ruined, and the authorities accused him of attempting to stir up sedition among the natives. Mrs. Chitty began, in her turn, to grow equally angry. (That Rowlands' Macassar Oil was unattainable only made matters worse.) Moreover we were forced to speak to her, however gently, about the suffering to dumb animals that her kindness was causing. And personally, though I did not permit myself to tell her so, when I considered how little she allowed the ills of human beings to count with her as against the welfare of her microbe, when I reflected on her indiscriminate massacres in the south of France, her attitude genuinely shocked me.

Nothing we could say would melt that heart. She only grew more resolute, more obstinate. And even if, on this occasion, the very abundance of the sick beasts defeated her, she never subsequently lost a chance of repeating her conduct. Only their price limited her opportunities of well-doing: for each day their cost increased. It is surprising how swiftly news travels in these dark, intuitive lands, and all round Africa spread the legend, ever more exaggerated, of the immensely rich, mad, white woman, with her strange *penchant*: until in Guinea and the Gold Coast, Dahomey, Ashanti, Benin and the Congo it was rumoured that she was on her way, and the naked, grinning figures dancing round the fire spared the last missionary, abandoned their cannibal feasts, in order that they might rush to their kraals and prepare their animals for her coming. It might be, even, that she would give them a string of glass beads, a bottle of whisky or a pocket-knife in exchange! And they set to work with a will. Thus, perhaps, some may consider that in the end she did good: for in the excitement many human beings were saved, though the animals suffered.

As my brother grew stronger, and Mrs. Rammond and myself remained immune, Mrs. Chitty began visibly to pine. Her respect for us had, I think, increased. She would now take the greatest trouble to prevent one from discovering what plans she was maturing, what manœuvres she had already carried out. Her craving for Macassar continued unabated, but she found out how to make a use of it. Let us assume that, without my knowledge, she had effected some tremendous bargain — a donkey, perhaps, so ill that it had died in the night — and that, in her anxiety to dispose of the body, she had reached the conclusion that the best thing for her to do was to have it tied on with the luggage at the back of the car. Before we started, then, she would lament the Macassar famine, and would be so charming (and her charm was ever irresistible), would allow such a wealth of pathos to creep into the hollow but musical tones of her voice, and such a deep well of tears unshed to shine in her eyes, that of my own accord, and without the slightest suspicion of what was on hand, I would volunteer to search the village for the magic Macassar. Tired, hot and footsore, I would limp back to find the car ready, Mrs. Chitty, swathed in veils and rugs, comfortably enshrined there, and behind it, neatly rolled and folded up on the top of the luggage, a grey and furry carcase.

'I thought we might leave it somewhere on the way', she would urge. 'Perhaps, if we could find a pretty spot, you wouldn't mind digging a grave for it? Nothing elaborate, just a plain grave. It's very good exercise, and you don't look too well. They have no proper animal cemeteries here. It's a disgrace!'

We passed a night or two on the way and then arrived — truly it was one of the chief attractions of the whole of our long journey — at Ali-Sid-Ali, that great native city only recently opened up to tourists. Capital, shrine and trading centre in one, it is a place of pilgrimage for all Mohammedan Africa, yet this sanctity is not allowed to interfere with the ever-growing volume of business transacted with Europe. The hotel, too, is a fine and new one, and after so much rough travelling it was most agreeable to be in such comfortable quarters. But, alas, worry returned with civilisation, for we found a telegram waiting for us to announce that our four friends in Cairo were back in hospital, seriously ill.

Though she had brought with her a letter of introduction to the British Consul-General, Mrs. Chitty, to our surprise, for once failed to deliver it in person. She, or rather her microbe, was evidently engaged in devising a different system of tactics. . . . Mrs. Rammond and myself were still in good health, my brother was fully recovered. Such a state of things could not be allowed to go on. Something *must* be done. Accordingly, she went to bed, immediately evolved one of her racing temperatures, and during several days made brave endeavours to consume our whole stock of medicines. This, doubtless she felt, would put her in a better position for developing her new offensive. But I had a hidden reserve of cinnamon and quinine, and thus she found herself unable to exhaust our supplies. Indeed, I think that so great was the quantity of these drugs which her new scheme of tactics forced her to swallow, that in all truth she began to feel ill. Certainly her temperature touched unprecedented heights. Meanwhile, she had posted her letter of introduction to the Consul-General and had explained in a letter of her own, enclosing it, that she was unwell, most unwell.

The atmosphere of Ali-Sid-Ali at this season was most fanatic. It was the fast of Ramadan, and the Mussulmans could be heard, in every direction, knocking their muffled heads against the marble floors of the mosques, while the holy dancers gyrated wildly round the street corners. The muezzin singers were in most formidable, if beautiful, voice : and at night, all night, a sonorous music, a deep bass chanting that was ominous and extremely impressive, conveyed continually the glory of Allah to every nook of the city, and floated above the flat roofs up in a stream towards his sacred garden.

Mrs. Chitty seemed to gather unto herself some of this surrounding fanaticism. As she sat in her large, airy room, decorated with Saracenic icicles, painted bright red and blue, it was easy to detect in her eye the kindling of a new religious fire. More than ever did she resemble Savonarola, but there was, too, now more than a touch of the dancing dervish, a suggestion, even, of the Mad Mullah himself. Her voice sounded a note of doom that was menacing and unmistakable.

Her bedroom faced a Mussulman cemetery, and tethered in this was a little white kid which frisked and gambolled so prettily that the children used to come and play with it. But Mrs. Chitty, seeing them hugging it, maintained that they were ill-treating the poor creature, and after much bargaining, succeeded, behind our backs, in buying it.

There was an uproar in the hotel. Every manager and director came and shouted at us, until eventually we understood one of them, who said that only yesterday he had been obliged to ask an English lady to send away her pet Pekinese, and that, therefore, he was very sorry, but he must quite definitely refuse to have a goat brought to live in the hotel. No doubt it was usual in Europe, but here people did not understand that sort of thing, he added.

Mrs. Chitty, securely established in bed, refused to give way, and the kid was tethered in the corridor outside. The authorities became yet more frantic. They had heard about the lady before : a guide from Abu-ben-Kalab had told them about her behaviour there. The hotel proprietor in that town, they understood, was in consequence of it a ruined man. Well, she could not repeat that sort of thing in Ali-Sid-Ali. It wouldn't do here, and they weren't going to stand it. . . . Perhaps the police could arrange matters. . . .

It was an *impasse*, a deadlock. We began to fear race-riots, so intense was the feeling. But, by the greatest good fortune, at this very moment a note was brought round to Mrs. Chitty from Lady McAlister, the wife of the Consul-General. In it she invited the invalid to stay at her house, saying that she and her husband would be only too pleased to nurse and look after any friend of Gerry Flitmouse. Mrs. Chitty at once accepted, scenting new victims for her germ. And then, too, there would be Foreign Office talks and every sort of delight.

When she went to pay her bill, she took the kid down to the desk with her, and, still accompanied by it, walked through the hall with great dignity. She then bore it off in triumph to the McAlisters. Lady McAlister, we heard afterward, was sympathetic : but Sir William, an old gentleman with white corkscrew moustaches, a Vandyke beard and an eye-glass, drew the line at such a guest, and made his wife explain that it would be difficult to find suitable food for it. Mrs. Chitty now (I thought rather brutally) abandoned the little thing, and sent it back to the cemetery whence it had come. And there, since it was now ownerless, it would quickly have starved to death had we not been informed by the vindictive hotel-manager of its plight and decided to make it a small allowance in perpetuity.

Mrs. Chitty remained in bed for several days, 'having a rest', and being waited on and made much of. Soon, however, her interest was aroused by the news that Forling, the explorer, was coming to stay, and she decided to get up to meet him. Lady McAlister kindly asked us to luncheon the same day, and I thought I had never seen Mrs. Chitty look more beautiful, nor ever had her charm impressed me more.

One of Forling's chief assets, the thing which had perhaps aided this great man in his wonderful career more than anything else, was his remarkable constitution. Moreover, he was, like so many persons of immense achievement, extremely modest : and his only boast was that, though now seventy-three years of age, he could walk as far and do as much as a boy of twenty, and, above all, that he had never spent a single day of his life in bed. Very foolishly (but then, how was he to know?) he mentioned this at luncheon . . . and once more I saw Mrs.

Chitty smile her dark, enigmatic smile. At tea-time she had a relapse, and was forced to go to bed again.

Mrs. Rammond, my brother and myself felt that we must return to Cairo in order to look after our four invalids there. We went to Muriel Chitty's bedroom to talk with her. She did not feel well enough to travel, she said, and decided to stay on with the McAlisters. They were very kind, so hospitable, and, besides, she would like to see more of Forling : an exceptional man, that. . . .

We said good-bye to Muriel, but with real regret. It was impossible not to admire, not to be fascinated by her ; indeed her faults only accentuated her strange charm and beauty, and the subtle wit and understanding that, though they were not always with her, often came to surprise and please one. . . .

But forty-eight hours afterwards the explorer began to feel unwell. The following morning, just as we were leaving Ali-Sid-Ali, we were told that he was very seriously ill, and the Consul-General had felt himself compelled to wire to Cairo for a specialist. He was expected to arrive that night by air. Alas, the rest of the story is known. The specialist arrived, but it was too late. Forling had spent his first, and last, day in bed, and the microbe had won a notable victory. . . .

In Cairo, a few days later, I bought a copy of the *Daily Tribune.*

Mr. Robert Sutledge, I read, had been ordered a sea-voyage for three months. One of the Russian dancers was dead. His Imperial Highness the Grand Duke Gabriel had been allowed out in the garden of Nishkynashdom for the first time since his illness. He was said to be looking very frail, and was supported on each side by a hospital nurse. A memorial plaque had been erected to the memory of ex-King Boris of Milesia in the foyer of the Folies Bergère at Monte Carlo, and a bronze statue, life-size, of H.R.H. the Duchess of Chester had been unveiled on the sea-front at Montibes. . . . The summer was coming on, and the epidemic at Valaise was dying down. . . . That was all. . . . But was it ? . . . I read on.

There was, I noticed, a curious outbreak of illness at Palermo and Constantinople. . . . The French General in Command at Damascus had retired, pleading ill-health. The Governor of Rhodes was indisposed. The Anglican Bishop of Cyprus was on his way home after several weeks of illness. At

Alexandria our Representative had been granted sick-leave: the Sultan of Libya had abandoned his first levee . . . Stop press: 'Liner *Dionysus* with Friends of Greece on board in quarantine Gibraltar, owing to mystery outbreak. Notable invalids on board include Lady Richborough and Dean Squirrel.'

The future, too, held its sequels. In Greece, dengue fever, which had doubtless been gathering strength for months, broke out as an epidemic in August. It was stated, at the end of September, that there had been 300,000 cases in Athens alone —Athens, where, it will be remembered, Mrs. Chitty had been so badly bitten by mosquitoes. During the winter months of the year a great wave of influenza spread over Europe. But Mrs. Chitty had gone again to the East . . . the unknown East, which is the cradle of the human race, the birthplace of every religion, every mystery, every disease. . . . Who knows what may not again come out of the East, the unchanging East, or what the year may bring? . . .

. . . . .

And even as I have sat writing this story, a ghostly influenza, conjured up out of its pages, has attended me, and I have not the strength to pick up my pen. *Absit omen*: let me pray that the reader of it will not be similarly afflicted.

STAGGERED HOLIDAY

Miss Lumsford always put her aunt away upstairs before she came down to dinner, even in the summer. It was so draughty in the lounge. Usually she played patience by herself afterwards until bedtime, or sometimes bridge with three other ladies of her own age, who were also looking after relatives. But tonight she must begin her packing, for they were going down to the country on Monday — the first time since the war began — with dear old Miss Flittock and her companion, Miss Brimbleby, and it would not do to leave everything till the last. Country air for a month would do them all good — you could see Aunt Fanny needed it. Aunt Fanny was not rich, and so, in addition, it would be a comfort to be able to share the expense, as well as have someone to talk to. All the same, Miss Brimbleby was . . . well, rather worldly and mercenary in her outlook : but then a paid companion was *never* like a niece, could not give the same affection : how could she ? It was different.

It seemed quite like old times having a holiday — though later in the year, September; perhaps that was what was meant by 'staggered holidays', of which she had read in the papers (the papers were so puzzling now, and difficult to follow, not like what they used to be). They were taking two Daimler hire cars, and Miss Flittock's Bedlington — dear dog — and her maid would go down with them. It was quite a short run, and the motors were big enough to put a bed in. . . . And when they came back, they were going to move into the Fairlawne Hotel so as to be *together*. It would make a lot of difference to the old ladies — much *nicer*, that way. Of course it was really too expensive, but as Miss Flittock was rich and took a lot of extras, and was a valuable client, and because Miss Brimbleby had told them how *quiet* Aunt Fanny was, and that she ate so little and gave so little trouble, the management had agreed to make special terms for her.

It was really wonderful the way — with all her disabilities — Aunt Fanny made friends. People would often come up to

51

look at her and say, 'Well, I hope when I'm her age, I shall
be like that'. . . . Not that she was really old, only seventy-
six — whereas Miss Pandlecross, who lived in the room next
door and still did her own hair, was ninety-two, but with all her
faculties about her — except for those silly fits of hers, when
she thought she was somebody else. . . . Somebody more
important; who was it? . . . Miss Lumsford couldn't remember.

'You're very *distrait* to-night, aren't you?' her bridge
partner inquired towards the end of the rubber, and after Miss
Lumsford had lost, and had gone upstairs to bed, this acquaintance had confided in the porter that she thought Miss Lumsford was 'getting queer'.

. . . . .

A broad road and several sets of railings still divided Hyde
Park from Kensington Gardens, the statue of Peter Pan,
Watts's Horse and the groups of shouting, playing children.
By the Round Pond their cries filled the air under the elm
trees. But below, towards Kensington Gore, there is a corner,
running from the Albert Memorial to the beginning of
Gloucester Road, that seems devoted to old people. Deeply
sheltered on each side by banks loaded with flowers and
flowering shrubs, is an asphalt path, in fine weather lined
with seats and chairs. From here you see nothing of the town,
only the golden dagoba that forms the top of Albert the Good's
mosaic shrine. The rich, closely cropped grass, with the
undulating line of its herbaceous border, the beds that fitted
so cleverly into its shape; all this is varied with semi-exotic
trees and shrubs, each bearing its own zinc identity disc.
And the flower-beds themselves are full of new varieties of old
favourites, or of flowers that have been trained to come out
at the wrong time and are now all ablaze in their perverted
season. . . . Nature is tame and easy here, and the roses smell
particularly delicious as their freshness mingles with the acrid
scent of tar from somewhere hidden but near by.

The sun usually seems to be out in this corner, even when
it is late autumn, and it is here that the inhabitants of those
yellow-stuccoed hotels of South Kensington, whose tribes form
a city, almost a nation, by themselves, gather together to sit
and talk and knit. It was always crowded and everybody
appeared to know everybody else — or, at least, certain sets to

know certain other sets — and this inspired an air of seeming gaiety, of perpetual, superannuated garden party. Passing by, you would hear women say, while they gave a violent dig with a long stiletto-like needle at a piece of knitting as in other ages they would have lunged at a lover's glowing heart, 'Really, you would never think you were in London!' so that, obviously, it was the resort of those who would rather be in the country or at a spa. You never — or hardly ever — saw children here, but dogs, lots of dogs. A border of steel hoops, and leashes and cries of peremptory affection, kept these off the flowers.

If a child strayed hither with a nurse, he would feel uncomfortable, and his supplanters and substitutes would set up an intolerable barking. There were fox-terriers, fussy and inquisitive, and rough-haired terriers, with square-cut noses, Pomeranians, one or two Dalmatians, dogs shaggy and dogs smooth-coated; some dogs were clipped and some wore jackets; there were Airedales and Scotties and Sealyhams and pugs, and one or two proud but slinky Bedlingtons, with mauve fringes, curled like Parma violets. . . . These last looked out of place here, where Queen Victoria and her son still ruled. They seemed too modern among these quilted forms and trailing draperies, grey waistcoats and grey bowler hats, as well as every variety of soft hat.

Nevertheless, fashion occupied only the middle of the path, and formed a self-provided pageant for the watchers, the knitters, solitary or clustered. Sometimes, it was plain, those who loved trees and nature resented the display; they would fix their gaze on the leaves, green or golden, and pretend not to see the procession of presumptive colonels and their wives, though hardly able to resist giving a smile and a pat to the accompanying dogs. They would say nothing, but keep their lips as straight as parallel straight lines — though, after they had passed, they would bestow a glance of shrewd estimation upon their backs, or, if grouped, would whisper together. An unwilling backward flicker of the eye on the part of the victims who had run the gauntlet would show that they were conscious of their ordeal: but this awareness never prevented them from walking past again in the opposite direction.

But I have kept the chief feature of this walk until the last. If you stood at either end and looked up and down the gay and flowery aisle, umbrageous yet dappled with hot sun, looked at the silks and laces still here extant, and the hats that were like the good things you used to see exposed for sale in peace-time in the windows of the Maison Lyons, the impression was of a series of courts being held, round thrones on which the kings and queens reclined rather than sat : for the place was so *nice* and countrified, yet never dull, and so the elder daughter, or the niece or the companion, or sometimes the two daughters, would wheel hither their mothers or aunts or protectors in their various chairs or on their various trays. . . . It meant just a quick bolt across Kensington High Street at the broad part. The policeman by the island was always kind and held up the traffic for them to pass, and even the bus drivers, though brought to so abrupt a halt, would be kind too, and try to look bored and yawn and so not rivet their gaze upon the phenomena being shot past underneath them ; creations by Breughel and Bosch, but adapted to a mechanical age subject to wheels and levers and a hundred ingenious devices to enliven and give speed. It was *extraordinary* how kind people were. No trouble seemed too much. And when they had crossed over, the attendants at the new brick public lavatories just outside the garden by the railings would be sure to be there in the doorway, and would come out with a smile and a nice word for the invalid. Miss Lumsford often said you felt that they would go through fire and water for Aunt Fanny.

'And how is Mrs. Hampton-Ditchcote this morning, Miss ?'

'Well . . . don't you think she *looks* better today, Mrs. Dingle, now that she's got that nice new hat ? . . . We're quite smart today, aren't we, dear ? . . . All right, you old dear, don't try to answer if it's difficult. You mustn't worry yourself. We know you like it. Yes, *like* it. Do you hear her, Mrs. Dingle, she's telling you she likes it. Yes, li' it. Isn't she *splendid*? And Dr. Mactavish was so pleased with her yesterday. . . . We're going for a holiday, too, on Monday — the day after tomorrow.'

'That will bring the roses back to her cheeks, won't it, Miss ? I don't wonder you're proud of her !'

They always had a little talk like that, and then they would turn up a path and soon be in the strip of paradise that I have described. . . . The ritual was the same every week-day ; but on Sundays it was different. Then the crocodiles that joined together from the various hotels came out later that day, for, before leaving their rooms, the daughters, nieces or companions read prayers to their captives, bound hand and foot by infirmity, and decked out in special Sunday finery, with ribbons and bows. When at last they issued forth, there was less traffic and in consequence it was easier to cross the road; and the lavatory attendants were wearing their best clothes too. And Mrs. Dingle would be sure to say, 'And have we been to church today? . . . You look as if you had, Miss. I always love the way you dress Mrs. Hampton-Ditchcote on Sundays — so many of the ladies are just alike. It's not easy to be original.'

'I thought it better not to take her *today*,' Miss Lumsford would reply. . . . 'Perhaps next Sunday. But it is dreadfully hot in church, and my aunt was always so keen on fresh air, and it is not easy to get out.'

That was life on Sunday; but today is Saturday, and now we can view with a full knowledge the whole scene as it was on a summer day in early September. The trees, the sunlight mixing with the leaves, the gay, feathery shadows, the flowers, in broad bands and splashes, all preparing a sort of *fête-champêtre* atmosphere, and then the little animated knots of people, each surrounding a chair or a tray that jutted out into the path, and, in the middle, the promenade of red-faced men with jutting chins and arthritic hips, whom we have classified as colonels and civil servants, hobbling along with their wives, pale from too long a sojourn in southern climes, and dressed in flowery fantasies that are the ghosts of garden-parties given a quarter of a century ago, while, over all, there spread the noble anthem of free, English dogs, barking like drawn string, on and on and on, to their hearts' content. Dear Little Dogs.

Dear Little Dogs! . . . On their ledges and various supports, the invalids watched them fondly: there were old ladies who sat up with an effort and talked; there were old ladies who reclined at full length, so that all you could see was the front of a baby-cap and two gleaming eyes; there were old ladies, red and rotund, who seemed to be roasting before an eternal fire, and old ladies who trembled and shivered as if fixed and remote in an arctic world of their own creation. Some faces were mottled, some purple, some jaundiced, some bore on their surface large brown patches, and one, well known, was of a pale and silvery blue. The worse the condition of the invalids, the more cheerful their attendants had to appear; their faces wreathed in smiles, it seemed as though an insane gaiety inspired them. There was constant movement, flow and chatter, from one court to another, though those that reigned were static. And it was to be noticed that the gallant old gentlemen who passed from time to time and stopped to talk to invalids, never addressed them in the conventional second-person plural, but all of them adopting the same jocose formula, asked, 'And how are *we* this morning?' or 'Did we have a good night?' But it was not easy to hear the replies, for those dear little square-cut Scotties or Airedales were bouncing up and down on their straight, squat legs, barking as though they contained rattles within them.

Very strong was the scent of roses this morning, for the gardeners seemed to take a special pride in this walk and spent endless hours cherishing each blossom and sprinkling it with water, and seeing that the zinc labels were clean and could be easily read. The war had made no difference to this yet, nor much to the general tone of the place. If men in uniform passed through, they hurried. This was no haunt for them. One or two soldiers from far away, Canada or Australia, sometimes strayed here and sat for half an hour or so, musing and mute. Miss Lumsford had been surprised, only the other day, at the bold manner in which Miss Necker, that horrid old Mrs. Lamberton-Jenkins's niece, had accosted them, going up to talk to them and offer them cigarettes! But that was exceptional, as a rule people behaved beautifully. The old ladies seemed scarcely to see them. Most of those on trays moved their heads with difficulty, so they were obliged to take a special interest in the groups opposite them.

And here, in friendship, as so often in love, the law of natural selection, which ever favours the average, manifested itself. Just as people not seldom select mates because of the opposite qualities they possess, so here, an old lady, rubicund and with weak eyes, would prefer the shade, while the old lady opposite, with mauve or yellow skin and a terrible internal shiver, would prefer the sun to warm her bones. Since their favourite stands were immediately recognised as theirs by the laws prevailing here, no one would dream of usurping another's pitch. In consequence these two would be opposite each other every fine day for years; for death comes to this sort of invalid by instalments, and there was only one more lot to pay. Thus confined to staring at each other across the path, warm friend-ships would grow up, often without speaking, and each old lady would from time to time flutter a finger or even the end of a mittened hand — or perhaps her companion might have to take it and wave it for her — at her opposite number.

It had been in this precise fashion that Mrs. Hampton-Ditchcote and Miss Flittock had met — if met it can be called. Mrs. Hampton-Ditchcote spent the morning under a weeping acacia that looked as if it had been created to shelter a nymph, while Miss Flittock lived in the brave sunshine.

'Look, Aunt Fanny!' Miss Lumsford would say, 'there's Miss Flittock! Wave at her, she's smiling at you. Shall I run over and tell her how much you're looking forward to going to stay with her at Horsham on Monday? (How happy you two will be, seeing such a lot of each other!) Look, again: Miss Brimbleby's helping her to wave!'

Certainly, Miss Lumsford reflected, as she sat down to talk to Miss Brimbleby, it was a pretty place and convenient. It seemed so safe and nice. People were so kind. That dear Mrs. Dingle — they had made friends the day Aunt Fanny had fainted. The doctor had told Miss Lumsford that she could expect this symptom, and to look out for it — but it wasn't always easy to *tell* when the old lady had fainted; for she wasn't very mobile or animated. Suddenly, sitting here just as they were this morning, she realised it had happened and had run to Mrs. Dingle in the lavatory. Kind soul, she had at once brought out lavender-water and eau-de-cologne, and even a thimbleful of brandy, and these cross-Channel restora-tives had soon pulled the old lady round. It was a relief to feel there was someone like that *near*; for Miss Brimbleby, though no doubt a charming woman — lots of people found her charming — was not so practical, not so quick or resource-ful in a tight corner.

Tranquil times, you would have thought, lay ahead for these old ladies on whom so much care was lavished. But suddenly, that very day, things altered. They had gone back there again at four in the afternoon, it was so warm and sunny, and, just as the last invalids were being wheeled away, a battle took place high above London. The sirens sounded but no one took much notice. Nothing had happened up till now. And the noise only made people feel pleasantly that they were '*in* things'.

Miss Lumsford stopped wheeling Aunt Fanny, and *made* her take an interest. It was good for her.

'Look there, darling,' she cried, 'more aeroplanes. Look, you can hardly see them. Up there! and the pretty white puffs. They're chasing one another, do you see, over there? Puff! Puff! Puff!'

Aunt Fanny stirred uneasily on her tray.

A fire began that evening, and the first real bombing of London occurred. Once or twice, the enormous noises of the night approached very close to the city of yellow hotels that seemed always to exist within their own protecting fog; very near. It seemed, indeed, at one moment as though some vast extinct beast or reptile had been woken from millennium-old sleep in the Natural History Museum near by and had begun to bray at the strange orange glow that suffused the eastern sky. Yet that first night was not so bad. People were alert and amiable and talkative — and there was something to talk about — and dinner was nearly over before the noise became overwhelming. Miss Lumsford went upstairs then and sat with her aunt, and tried to explain about what was going on.

'It's *fireworks*, darling,' she insisted kindly, 'only fireworks. You used to love them, do you remember, at Cheltenham? Listen, there's another — such a fine one!'

It was difficult to know how much Aunt Fanny took in, Miss Lumsford thought. What a blessing it was that, though high up, they were so near the lift. But it would be difficult to dress her aunt and take her down to the air-raid shelter. It had looked so damp and draughty, and the old lady would be sure to catch cold, so, as they were going away so soon, it was wise to get on with the packing. The noise could not continue like this for long. As she wrapped things up in tissue-paper, she tried not to hear it. But she wished Aunt Fanny had got a dog. What a comfort an Airedale would be now! The noise seemed to be getting worse instead of better! All the same, she managed to go to sleep.

The next morning, Sunday, everything was calm and fine

and quiet, and at half-past eleven they set out as usual. Nothing between the hotel and the gardens seemed to have been destroyed.

After they had crossed the road, Mrs. Dingle came out to talk. She looked pale and untidy this morning, quite unlike herself. But she did not complain, but said:

'And did Mrs. Hampton-Ditchcote, dear old lady, mind that dreadful bombing?'

She oughtn't to speak like that: Aunt Fanny didn't know! But the Lumsfords had always prided themselves on showing nothing, so Miss Lumsford restrained her anger, and merely replied:

'Not at all!' and then added, 'It's the sirens my aunt does not like. They make her so nervous; I thought she was going to speak when she heard them. But she doesn't mind the bombing; not a bit.' ('We don't mind the bombing, do we, dear?' she asked the old lady, tidying her hair, and tugging at a muslin collar.) 'You see, she's used to that sort of thing. Why, my mother told me that Aunt Fanny, before her illness, often used to go out shooting with the men.'

When they reached the path, embowered in blossom, it was peculiarly empty, except for a few invalids, whose incomes were so close cut to the *pension* terms in their hotels that they could make no preparations for going away. Hardly any courts were being held, and the usual promenade of Anglo-Indians did not take place. Some women still sat knitting, but even they were talking in a lower voice than usual, as if afraid that some German aeroplane might overhear them. . . . Still, it was quite pleasant there, in the sun — except that Aunt Fanny lay there in the fronded shade, with no complement opposite. One could not help missing dear old Miss Flittock, and Miss Brimbleby. No doubt they had decided to stay at home at Fairlawne today and do the packing: Miss Brimbleby was rather the kind of person who liked to leave things till the last. Never mind, the two old ladies would see a lot of one another in the next month, so it did not matter. There was a new catalpa in bloom today, she noticed; creamy blossom, yellow and pink-tongued, clustered among broad leaves that, unlike other green trees at this season, seemed always to hold the green of the spring within them. She pointed it out to Aunt Fanny.

'Look there, darling,' she said. 'Even the Huns can't keep the catalpa from flowering.'

She spoke in a rather loud and ostentatious voice, and the knitters lowered their tones still further in contradiction. Or were they talking about her? she wondered. But they couldn't be. 'Odd,' she heard one of them say, 'odd in her manner.'

About 12.30, just as they were starting home for luncheon, the alert sounded again. If it had not been for kind Mrs. Dingle, they would *never* have got home in time. But Mrs. Dingle had hurriedly put on her hat and coat, locked the lavatory door, and helped push Mrs. Hampton-Ditchcote home on her wheeled tray.

'Well, we must say good-bye nicely to Mrs. Dingle, mustn't we?' Miss Lumsford had said to her aunt, as they reached the hotel. 'We're going away tomorrow for a month, for a lovely holiday with Miss Flittock and Miss Brimbleby — you know, Mrs. Dingle, the two ladies opposite — an hotel in Horsham. Oh, we're looking forward to it *so* much. It's a lovely country place, they say, with two converted oast-houses in the garden. Say good-bye, dear! Good-bye! Do you see, she's saying good-bye! Thank you, thank you!'

It was really extremely kind of her — especially as she was worrying the whole time in case she might have locked someone in. Still no message from Miss Brimbleby about the motor. It was strange — still, she was always a bit unpunctual, casual as it were. She was sure to telephone tonight. Not until after dinner about half-past eight did she receive the explanation, when the other guests came up to talk to her and told her that Fairlawne had been blown up last night, with everyone in it. The bodies were still being looked for.

She didn't know *what* to do — and it would be a great shock to Aunt Fanny: what *could* she tell her? For Aunt Fanny knew all about the holiday, she was sure about that. And they couldn't go by themselves, it would be much too expensive for two people alone: on the other hand, if she started unpacking, Aunt Fanny would notice that at once — she was so sharp — and begin that funny noise, like someone humming, that she made sometimes. . . . She decided to say that Miss Flittock had got a slight cold, and the holiday was 'put off'. But just as she was telling the old lady this, the bombing began again — and without the sirens sounding first.

Really one could hardly hear oneself speak! Suddenly she felt annoyed, overwrought. Something in the way her aunt lay there and said nothing annoyed her. Miss Lumsford began to shout.

'They're bombs you hear! *Bombs*! The same things that killed Miss Flittock and Miss Brimbleby. Can't you hear, can't you answer? Do speak; I'm tired of always doing the talking' — and she gave her aunt a slight shake. 'There it is again! Bang! It's a *bomb*!'

Afterwards she regretted having spoken like that: but the old lady naturally hadn't taken it in. She said nothing more about the holiday, and decided to leave the unpacking until the next day.

.   .   .   .   .

All that night her aunt had been very restless. It had been impossible to sleep. And then, about six, she had seemed to be quieter. Miss Lumsford woke at nine (how late they were!) and opened up. At first she hardly remembered — and then it came back to her. But really now she didn't bother much about the night and its happenings; had forgotten the way she had spoken to her aunt, could not worry over Miss Flittock and Miss Brimbleby — that was past. What could you do about it? She ordered her aunt's breakfast and took in the tray herself. She propped up a pillow or two and began to feed the old lady. But Aunt Fanny was still in one of her difficult moods, and would not co-operate, but kept her mouth open. Well, you can't *make* people eat. If they won't, they won't. And one meal more or less, the doctors say, makes no difference. But it was trying of her, when everyone was tired.

Miss Lumsford had difficulty too, later, in dressing the old lady. She began to feel angry with her again. Of course, partly it was her illness, but all the same she made no effort, none at all. Indeed, today she seemed, if anything, to be resisting the clothes that her niece was putting on her. (It reminded Miss Lumsford of how she used to dress her doll, oh, so long ago now!) No, she ought to *try* more. If she didn't make more effort soon, Miss Lumsford decided she would give her another shaking. But no, she mustn't: after all, her aunt depended on her.

Eventually she finished dressing her. It was a hot day again, by the look of it, so she put a nice wide, lacy hat on the old lady's head, with a transparent brim that shaded the eyes. And then she got her somehow into her chair without having to call Elsie, the housemaid, to help. (Somehow or other, she wanted to do things by herself this morning, didn't feel inclined to have a lot of people running in and out of the room.) She went into the passage, rang for the lift, wheeled her aunt into it, took it down, and wheeled her out of it, through the hall, into the open air. Yes, it was a lovely morning again.

After they had reached Kensington Gore and crossed the road in the usual manner, Mrs. Dingle came out again to speak to her.

'Oh, Miss Lumsford,' she said, 'what a *dreadful* night! . . . I don't think you should have brought the poor old lady out again this morning. You said you were going away. It would be much better for her. There'll be another attack soon, I expect.'

Miss Lumsford kept her temper and did not explain, though she would have liked to argue. (She felt like that this morning.) She merely said to the figure on the tray-chair :

'We can't wait in all day, can we, Aunt Fanny ?'

The particular immobility which the invalid showed this morning attracted Mrs. Dingle's attention.

'I know Mr. Fowler, next door, wants to say good-morning, Miss,' she said, and fetched him to have a look. They both gazed curiously at the old lady, who was staring in a fixed way beneath her lace hat.

As Miss Lumsford passed on, wheeling her charge in front of her, the two attendants looked at each other.

'Well, whatever do you think of that, Alfred ?' Mrs. Dingle asked.

'Scarecrow's a bit potty, I should say,' he replied. 'There's something wrong there ! Better tell the constable.'

Miss Lumsford settled herself and her aunt in the usual place, under the acacia. Everything seemed so quiet. Even the day seemed depressed. The little paradise was empty except for the few invalids who were so poor they still could not manage to go away. Down the broad road on to which the street of hotels converged could be seen the strangest procession, all the morning long, of huge old-fashioned motors pounding away to the country, carrying their precious freight. Some had beds in them, with figures lying at full length ; others contained sitting figures, but shaking, quaking, so that they had to be strapped into place, shivering over their reins like a baby strapped into his chair; others, again, bore figures stiff, yellow and richly dressed as the images held high at religious festivals.

Miss Lumsford sat with her back to them as they passed, and between was the barrier of shrubs and flowers, a wide stretch of grass, and the line of railings, like spears. But she could hear the sound of the traffic, and no doubt it brought back to her the idea of their lost holiday. She talked a little to her aunt.

'Look, dear! The catalpa has come on wonderfully,' she said.

But it was no use. Her aunt seemed to take no notice of anything today. She could not help feeling annoyed again; it was better to employ herself somehow, good for the nerves. So she was just settling down to knit when a sergeant of police and a constable passed by. . . . They looked at the old lady rather intently, she thought.

Then they turned and came back to her.

'She oughtn't to be 'ere, Miss,' the sergeant said to her. 'She's *dead*. Look at her eyes, poor old lady!'

Miss Lumsford began to argue.

'Is it likely I should wheel about a corpse?' she asked haughtily — and then suddenly began to laugh. Peals of laughter sounded in the green shade under the acacia, until the pounding of the huge motors along the road obliterated this other sound. But she was still laughing.

THE LOVE-BIRD

'. . . The paragon of animals! And yet, to me, what is this
quintessence of dust?'

It was impossible not to wonder what Robert Mainwroth
would be like as an old man, or even as a middle-aged one, for
elusive, witty and individual as he was, one yet could not fail
to assign him to these especial years of which I write. And it is,
actually, so much more difficult to be purposely amusing at
seventy-five years of age than at thirty-five, so much easier to
be so without the intention. His little eccentricities might by
that time have sunk into absurdities. But old age was to be
spared him. We shall never know now what manner of
development or deterioration would have ensued, for he died,
a few years ago, in his early forties.

He left me his journals and writings, but these served to
reveal little of his character. One simple entry, however, I
thought was an exception: though this may have interested
me so much more than his ambitious pieces of writing only
because I had witnessed the beginnings of, or at any rate the
prelude to, the episode described. Yet it certainly seemed to
me that this slight, obviously true, story contained more
poignance than all his efforts at literature. It implied, one
felt, a curious and sad allegory, which, though he may have
been unconscious of this, summed up a side of his life, and
filled him, even if he did not interpret it, with a deep sense of
melancholy. I know, from the diary, that a sense of dejection
out of all proportion to the trivial event itself did actually
attend it in his mind.

The facts, then, slight as they are, were jotted down quite
plainly, with no attempt to throw them into any form. I had
always intended to sort them out, but time passed, my memory
betrayed me and I might never have done so if I had not
happened, a week or two ago, to look in at the window of a
large antique-dealer's shop in King Street, St. James's. There
in front of me, behind its sheet of ice, stood a very magnificent

64

bird-cage, containing a stuffed or made-up bird that would doubtless chirrup when a spring was pressed. This rich and artificial prison seemed about to waken in my mind a very definite string of associations, for I was sure I had seen it before, though at first I could not remember where. I wasted a little time, therefore, in staring at it, and suddenly the scene of our first acquaintance materialised for me, summoning up round it a number of varied and scintillating objects. Convinced that it was the identical cage itself, and recalling very vividly the part it had once played in the life of my friend, the minute drama it had once housed, I went back to the forgotten diaries, determined to try to draw together the fine threads of which this story is composed.

.   .   .   .   .

To those who did not care for him, Robert Mainwroth gave an impression of being a scoffer, one who was rather eccentric and outside life. To those, on the other hand, who liked him — and, as his sensitiveness gradually evolved round itself the defensive armour of a perfect but laughing worldliness, they formed a steadily increasing band — he was a pivot of very modern, if mocking, activity. He was so intensely aware of all that was going on in the many different worlds round him, albeit so much of this action and effort appeared to him in itself to be ridiculous. In any case his character, under its out-ward suavity, whether assumed or innate, was definite enough to drive even those who met him for the first time into either one or the other pen, and matched the strongly drawn, rather Habsburg cast of his features, his natural air of quiet, ugly distinction.

His chief interests had always lain in art, music and litera-ture. But as a young man he had passed a year or two in the Civil Service, and had, during that time, quickly obtained a reputation, deserved if not difficult of achievement, as a wit. Indeed, in the decorous deserts of our public offices, amid the glue, the ink, the roll-top desks, he must have seemed an oasis of pure fun. In those days he had been penniless except for his salary, but a sudden heritage both removed him from his office and provided a much wider circle of appreciation for his wit.

Most people take the extreme strokes of Fortune, whether good or bad, in much the same manner : there is little variety in their reception of them. But Robert, it must be admitted by enemy as much as friend, regarded his good luck from a personal angle and treated it in his own particular fashion. Finding himself encumbered with houses and estates that lay scattered over half England, the new Sir Robert Mainwroth, in spite of a certain family pride which stiffened him at moments, proceeded at once, and with characteristic energy and enjoyment, to divest himself of everything that did not appeal to him personally, either esthetically or through his humour — and his senses of esthetics and humour were perilously akin. By so doing, he defeated in many different parts of the land rustic proverbs, such as

> Come may, come what, much ill will fall
> When Mainwroth parts with Mainwroth Hall,

and, I apprehend, was rather pleased at the storm of tumbling superstitions he had provoked, thereby sharing that particular modern sensation originated by the famous lady who first carried a pig up in an aeroplane, and thus killed a proverb stone-dead. It was so simple, he said, to build up for one short generation your own part of an antiquated family machine, but so hard to smash it deliberately and inaugurate in its stead a new instrument tuned to the times.

Consequently, estates, which had belonged to the Mainwroths since first they had begun to bully their male and marry their female neighbours, were sold, without apparently causing their vendor a pang of any sort — but then they were very well sold. This was not all. The portraits of his ancestors in armour, as much as the armour itself, the pictures of later Mainwroths in long coats and periwigs, in tie-wigs, in powdered wigs of short, natural hair, the loose-lipped ugly beauties of Charles II's court, caressing the most innocent and beribboned of white sheep, then the family beauties, eighteenth-century sisters as a rule, swaying outward from, as it appeared, one slender-waisted stem, miniatures of Elizabethan and Jacobean members of the family, in ruffs and with their coats spattered with the spring flowers of English history, miniatures again, of the later epoch, mincing, rose-coloured but wistful — all, all were disposed of in dusty auction rooms, together with two vast libraries, one of which had been formed for an ancestor by Gibbon, and a whole corps de ballet of Meissen and Chelsea figures, pirouetting with their fragile, too pink-and-white legs over the greenest of green grass, sprinkled with the little blossoms of innocence, or blowing their minute, soundless pipes under the shade of never-fading trees. He also caused to move in the direction of the sale-room a jingling mountain of plate, Charles II and Queen Anne silver, the second of which, especially, by its utter simplicity and want of imagination, sent a thrill of excitement through every silver-bore in London (and the silver-bore, to be seen top-hatted and at work each Sunday afternoon in the marble halls of the Victoria and Albert Museum, constitutes a sub-species sans-pareil of his tribe). Still the work of breaking up the centuries continued. Now oak settees of elaborate and embossing design, tall, gilded chairs and tortoise-shell cabinets, ivory dressing-tables from Mogul India, painted chests from Italy, leather screens from Spain and lacquer ones from China, French clocks of green enamel, tapestries that re-created the tents of the Middle Ages, were all torn apart, snatched out of the entity they had helped to form, and went to find a living death in the petrified perfection of some millionaire period-room.

Such smaller, in the sense of less valuable, objects as the moth-eaten heads of stag and buffalo, eagles with fly-blown plumage, rare albino rabbits, the varnished masks of ferocious fish, their glass eyes glaring wildly, and fossils that resembled small Catherine-wheels, which must, at some time or other, have caught Medusa's eye, Robert divided among his numerous relatives. More especially did he distribute among them the multitudinous triumphs of the chase, furry or feathered mementoes. And a very long chase it had been : for, ever since the dawn of English history, the Mainwroth family had carried on a ceaseless but victorious feud against stags, otters, hares, badgers, rabbits and any bigger non-domestic animal of which they were able to get within reach, every kind of fish, and pheasants, grouse, snipe, woodcock, partridges and a quantity of other birds, and thus, during the passing of the centuries, had collected innumerable, but rather frayed, bits of them. All these Robert now, as we have said, presented to the Mainwroths, and felt a great joy both in the giving of them and in their reception. But of the large, valuable things he kept practically none and certainly gave none away. And the disposing of all this accumulated matter was no light business, occupied him for many months : nor do I regard it as inspired by selfish motives, though there is little doubt in my mind that he was pleased at having created this false impression of brutal lack of sentiment.

Actually and in fact, he had been thoughtful and practical, had adapted his situation to his time. It was pointless and hopeless, he felt, in these days to own vast, draughty, machicolated mansions, ugly in their conglomerated selves, even if full of beautiful objects, all over one small land. The modern world dictated its terms to the rich, and the moneyed nomad, with a few tents pitched ready for his use in various parts of the world, in, let us say, Paris, London, New York, Seville and Budapest, and with very easy means both of reaching them and leaving them, was the fortunate man of today. His heirs, as much as himself, ought to be gratified at the firmness and foresight he had evinced, for many a man would have been intimidated by the mere weight of such possessions into keeping them. Now they, too, would be equipped as modern men out of the increased income into which all these belongings had been transmuted, and would have no desire, and certainly no room in their small houses and large motor-cars, either for monumental pictures and pieces of furniture or for loads of clustering, clattering little things. No! Housemaids, those cross, shrill and superannuated vacuum-cleaners, were the only ones who must incur an inevitable loss. (Moreover, he used to add, he had been forced to these actions by the horde of indigent uncles and cousins inherited with the estates.)

Far from the ruthlessness of this prodigious sale being founded on a want of proper feeling, he maintained, on the contrary, that it had been to a great extent inspired by sentiment. Consider, for example, the family pictures. To display a preference for one ancestor over another constituted a species of favouritism : he hated favouritism — and in any case, what principle was to guide you in it ? If you decided to retain one picture, because it was a fine one, excellently painted, you both made a considerable financial sacrifice and slighted the other dead members of your family, who were doubtless just as estimable in life : probably more so, for, alas, the wicked man, no one will ever know why, is inevitably recorded by a better artist than the righteous man. Perhaps, Robert sug-

gested, this might be because the profligate never considers
expense or his heirs, and therefore pays the best artist of his
time to paint his portrait : whereas the good man, ever mindful
of future generations, at the time saves money on their behalf
by commissioning a fifth-rate artist, recommended by a
country neighbour, instead of a first-rate one, to execute his
likeness, and through this act of thrift fines them an enormous
fortune in subsequent years. It could not be too much stressed
that in buying or ordering contemporary works there is nothing
that pays in the end like 'wanton extravagance'.

Similarly, how could you be guided in your selection by
the interest attaching to the persons represented ? For the rake
and wastrel notoriously absorb more of the attention of later
generations than the prudent, diligent or prudish — Rochester
and Pepys are remembered where so many more worthy are
nameless and forgotten — and, indeed, the excesses of an
ancestor tend in time, he thought, to become a source of real
pride to his descendants.

Out of the very substantial wreckage of his inheritance,
then, all that Sir Robert Mainwroth elected to keep was such
light flotsam as a musical-box, on the top of which, when you
turned a handle, a few white-wigged figures in minute, ever so
dusty, brocaded dresses danced a very staccato minuet; a
French *singerie* panel of playful indecency, which was rescued
from a gutted panelled room ; a photograph, in a red plush
frame, of two of his great-aunts, now very much of the old
régime, and proving it by their constant abuse of Robert and
his behaviour, but here depicted riding on a tandem bicycle,
dressed in bloomers and straw hats ; some humming-birds in
a glass case ; some birds of paradise mounted in the same way ;
a silver snuff-box which played a tune by Mozart ; an illustrated
contemporary edition of Mrs. Hemans's poems ; an 1820 razor,
with a carved ivory handle and a hunting scene engraved on
the blade ; a tablecloth in blue and pink sateen, with a lace
fringe, bought at the 1851 Exhibition ; a signed photograph of
Lord Tennyson, wearing a Scotch cape ; a group (1848) of
the Royal Family in Derby Biscuit ; some water-colours representing the arrival of King Louis Philippe in England, on a
state visit, with all the details of the decoration of the dining-
car and saloon of his train, and culminating in a meeting,
bright with uniforms, of the English and French Royal Houses ;

a French eighteenth-century watch of ingenious mechanism and impropriety; a copy of the first of Bradshaw's Railway Guides; a water-colour by one of his aunts of a lonely light-house and a sunset; and two rare Victorian ornaments, again under glass covers, wrought in pinchbeck that comprised three shades of gold. Since these require a more elaborate descrip-tion than the items catalogued above, but are most difficult to sum up in words, it may be best to state plainly that they represent little dolphins, holding bunches of grapes in their mouths, and climbing or wriggling up rose bushes, of which the actual blossoms are fashioned in pink-and-white and blue-and-white porcelain, and to ask the reader to construct them boldly for himself in his own imagination. These last, airy if substantial, mixed metaphors were a source of keen pleasure to their new owner, as was one other object we have not men-tioned in the list: a really magnificent bird-cage made of tortoise-shell and nacre, in which a bird, feathered but in-animate, sang very sweetly when a spring was pressed. If one were to seek the derivation of this lovely toy, one would evoke Turkey, the eighteenth-century turbaned Turkey of Blue-beard's Palace and a thousand irrigated gardens of rose and myrtle, as its natural home. The materials of which it was made were much esteemed, though in quite ordinary use, there. It might well have been the solace in long, idle hours of some Sultana in a harem; for the secluded life, the lack of education and outside interest, induced in its victims a great passion for all mechanical toys, and, more especially, for such other artificial beings, singing in their ornate and costly prisons. Robert, however, used to say that he liked it because the sham bird sang just as well as any real one, needed much the same care and affection and differed only from the living creature in that it was cleaner, never sang save when you wished it, and did not impose upon its proprietor the necessity of ever peering about in fields and gardens for a tuft of groundsel.

Robert, now that he had successfully disengaged himself from his inherited effects, bought a small house in London, a flat in Paris, an apartment in Venice, a cottage in Bavaria, a little wooden palace on the shores of the Bosphorus, and two motor-cars, all of which resembled one another in their comfort and gaiety. Thus fitted out, he turned away from any pro-fession toward his own enjoyment.

He was, in fact, a dilettante, but one in the best sense : for he aspired to be nothing but what he was. He talked well and amusingly; painted and wrote fluently, even with talent of an order. He often asked me to read what he had written, and occasionally, very occasionally, I thought I could distinguish another quality ruffling the surface of it, something sad and understanding that, it might be, he was at great pains to hide. So it seemed to me. Yet when others averred that he was artificial, cynical and heartless, these were accusations difficult to rebut, for such sayings and tastes of his as we have detailed lent some colour to them. People wondered if he had ever loved, loved anybody or anything, had ever really cared? And what could one say, for as he sat in his drawing-room, smoking a cigarette, laughing — his usual mood — and surrounded by his, it must be admitted delightful, toys and musical-boxes, it could but appear to the casual onlooker rather as though he was engaged in keeping life at arm's-length.

Yet if this was so, there must — and this his enemies could not comprehend — be some very good reason for it. It is easy, of course, to credit people with too much feeling, but had not something, I wondered, wounded him very deeply in early life? Might it not be that this Puck at the end of a long line, who mocked us all with his practical modernity, hid far down, but very far down, an unusual sensitiveness; that perhaps he had so much felt the fear, love, excitement, terror and beauty of existence, had been so early singed by these things, that he would rather avoid life if he could, while yet, in attempting this, he had understood that by so doing he was forfeiting many things of inestimable value, and ran the risk of losing among them the very thing which might have tamed and humanised life for him? Or again, had these emotions existed formerly, and were they now, under the mask of fun and witty observance with which he had overlaid them, atrophied through long disuse? Creative talent might have cured him, I thought, but he had, and by so little, missed it. As it was, the refuge of the romantic lay, as ever, in illusion. Just as Pirandello's Enrico Quarto found his happiness and his reality in a false and distant epoch from which he refused to emerge, so perhaps did Robert Mainwroth discover his reality and his happiness, which in this case signified calm, among all the paraphernalia of his carefully planned months, full of little, beautiful surprises, birds that jumped out of boxes and sang, or photograph-albums that played the Wedding March.

However, whether he loved or did not love, whether he felt so deeply or did not feel at all, there was no doubt that he was a delightful companion and a very good friend. Numberless people genuinely liked him. His nature was interesting, too: because in spite of its mocking quietude, there were obscure lapses of hot temper, and one was able to obtain out of him suddenly, when it was least expected, some angry response. At the time of which I am writing he was in his early or middle thirties, yet in some ways, in manner for example, gave an impression of being older. Underneath his calmness, moreover, he could fret about small things after the fashion of the elderly: and, though he knew many people and entertained many, when he was alone he seemed more alone than anybody I knew. Not that he was often bored, for he was in his own way energetic, and made a continual use of his continual leisure: in addition to writing and painting, he read an enormous amount. Or again he was perfectly happy engaged for hours in some entirely futile and pointless occupation, such as himself inventing a small, silly toy or executing drawings and caricatures from old photographs. At such things, he evinced considerable skill: and the more futile they were the better he was amused. Yet it looked as though every year there would be less room, less use, for singing birds, real or artificial: even less for artificial than for real ones. (Perhaps this was why he loved his toys; some predilection for lost causes?) And he was, I believed, too wise behind his frivolous mask not to be aware of this.

. . . . . .

Though, as we have suggested, Robert was usually too busy, too much engaged in weaving his silken web of life, to be bored, he was nevertheless occasionally liable to moods of apparently reasonless depression: but are any moods of depression in fact unjustified? In his case, the origin of them may have been that he was conscious of possessing everything that, according to his own theory of life, was necessary to his happiness . . . and therefore, if temporarily he knew himself to be unhappy, his misery was by that much further aggravated.

In the full dead heat of one chattering July in London he

was virulently attacked by such a feeling of heaviness at heart. It was, perhaps, because he was tired ; so he comforted himself, but for some days it had seemed to him that nothing he did was worth doing, nothing he said worth saying, nothing he bought worth buying. He had, in fact, bought a model of a small piano, in ivory, which played Chopin waltzes when wound up : for he had attempted to use money in this way as a drug, to make him forget. And the antique-shops were so many caves of oblivion and hallucination. But it was not a success : the melancholy, nostalgic, minute tinkling that ensued served merely to emphasise his state of mind. Naturally his gloom deepened as Saturday night set in, with its misleading, noisy promise of incipient Sunday. And he had made no plans for warding it off.

On Sunday morning, he thought of a thousand pleasant things to combat the calendar — motor down to Bath for the day, visit some friends in the country, spend the afternoon at Millbank examining the modern pictures, or go to sea or river to bathe — but no sooner did one of these ideas occur to him than it at once lost its attraction.

Outside it was brilliantly warm and fine. The Boy Scouts, or some kindred black-hand association, were making a great noise of marching milk-cans and mad motor-horns not far away. Further, there was a group of sweating Salvationists not far off, howling in joyous unison to the tinny accompaniment of their tambourines, while two maimed soldiers in the distance were playing 'The Rosary' on a clarinet and phonofiddle. (And then, Robert reflected, people insist that we are a musical nation : as though any other people in the world would tolerate such musical dementia in public places !) For the rest, top-hats and prayer-books and feather boas could be seen returning from church, and the smell of warm tar came in heavy gusts of acrid scent through the open windows. It was, in fact, a typical Sunday noon, and he felt that he did not want to go out. Yet he could settle to nothing. He sat down at the piano, and played for a few minutes, then shut it, and got up. He turned on every musical-box in his rooms in rotation, pressed all the buttons on his various trick clocks, so that little figures shot out at him unexpectedly, while an eighteenth-century tune lifted its sweet but feeble rings of sound into the air. He tried the wireless, but found himself listening to the

sermon which was rounding off a children's service in Edinburgh. The clergyman was just explaining to 'his little ones',
as he called them, that every flower was a love-letter from God
(Robert decided not to go to Kew that afternoon, after all,
and switched it off). He went back to the piano : then looked
through some caricatures he had done, and an old album of
valentines. Now he rapped out a newly invented spelling-
game on the dial of his automatic telephone. Then he played
for a little with those strange Victorian pictures, in cut-paper
frames, of sailing-ships which, when a tag at the bottom is
pulled, turn into mid-Victorian beauties, with ringlets, holding
a bouquet, next into a cornfield sprinkled with red poppies, and
in the end into a bleeding heart bordered with pansies and
forget-me-nots. Alas ! nothing really amused him. He could
not read, but began to examine each sentence critically. Now
everything outside was quiet : but suddenly a hymn-tune,
called up by the Sunday quality of the day outside, and borne
to him on a wave of ennui issuing from the countless dead
hours spent in school-chapel, buzzed round inside his head like
a sleepy bluebottle. For a moment, its inevitable, wheezy
circlings amused him. But there was no means of ridding
himself of it. Finally, he went to the piano and played a few
bars of 'God Save the King', hoping in this manner to impress
mechanically upon the stranger within, who was responsible
for the melancholy outburst, that he had endured enough of it.
Even this did not suffice. He now, therefore, deliberately
summoned up in his memory the most vapid refrains to combat
it. Eventually the tune left him, but still he could settle to
nothing, was more than ever depressed. It was ridiculous, a
confession of failure, he felt, to be surrounded here by everything one wanted and yet to suffer this vague discomfort, this
sense of something lacking or amiss. . . .

At last, just before luncheon, an excellent meal to which
he sat down alone, a new plan entered his head. He knew
what he must do. It was best to struggle no longer, but instead
submit, yield utterly to Sunday. (Why had he not gone to
church ? It would for him have been an experience.) Was
there anything, he asked himself, that was more typical of a
London Sunday afternoon than a visit to the Zoological
Gardens ? Alas, he was not a member of the Society and so
would not be able to obtain the necessary ticket of admission

— and then remembering that I was in London, he rang me up and asked if I could take him there. It was arranged : and he would send his car round for me first.

I came into the house for a few minutes before we started. When I entered, he was finishing luncheon, and on the sideboard were little mounds of fruit, peaches and grapes. Real this time, not artificial, and I recall asking him whether he fed his clockwork birds on them ? Then he took me up to the drawing-room. I decided that the house was charming. There was about it an enchanted absurdity, of which beauty was born. And how refreshing, I thought to myself, to see a rich man in possession of a house which he has made for himself, that has not been foisted on him by some firm of exotic but willowy decorators, or taken out of cold-storage on his behalf by immensely learned period-mongers. How happy he ought to be here, in his own world ! The sunlight struck glittering reflections out of countless glass-cases, each one of which held in its convexity the dissolving mirage of another until the entire room seemed full of variously shaped, transparent bubbles, and played within them upon the lyre-shaped tail of a bird of paradise, crystal flowers or a miniature ship, of which the hull, sails and rigging were all wrought of glass, or drew flights of colour from the flashing throats and wings of humming-birds as you walked. Each footstep made little jewelled nightingales, in their glass cages, quiver among their enamelled, blossoming trees, of which the branches were made of watch-springs, so that bird and flower ever moved as though upon an invisible breeze, and the room was soon filled with trills of bell-like music that resembled the smallest jets of fountains. Everything — flowers, carpets, chair-covers, the modern pictures which hung on the walls — praised life, as it were, against the living death that every period-room hymns. Many of the objects were beautiful in themselves, and all seemed so here, linked together as they were by the elusive personality of their owner. I remember particularly admiring the magnificent cage that has been already described, and the very tuneful singing of its mechanical prisoner, as, at a touch of the spring he fluttered into life, opening and shutting his beak and wings. Once more I thought, as I looked round, how happy Robert ought to be here, in his own world. But today I could see he was restless, unsettled, and longing to escape out of his artificial paradise : and we hurried down into the car and off to the Zoo.

Samuel Butler has said somewhere, I suppose in his Note Books, that there is no cure for nerves or unhappiness so complete and effective as to watch the quiet antics of the larger animals ; it is possible to lose oneself entirely in observing these moving hills of natural energy. Certainly the healing effect of it upon Robert was remarkable. His mood was changed abruptly. First we went to see the elephants, plodding heavily, swinging their trunks lithely from side to side, and regarding the world of men with an infinite wisdom, a great experience of good and evil, from those narrow little eyes set in the enormous, grey, wrinkled bulk of their heads. Then there were the polar-bears, with their little heads set upon cruel, thick necks and clumsy shoulders, beckoning with abrupt and coaxing gestures to their keepers for more, many more, still-living fish. The terrible, beautiful whiteness of these animals imparted a spectral quality to their movements, and made one think of the men done to death by these quietly padding, shuffling ghosts in the frozen silence of a Polar night. Nothing, one knew, could stand up against the machinery of their strong and stealthy muscles. Meanwhile, near by, little brown bears were rattling at the bars of their dens, screaming with rage like spoiled children, at the sight of jars of honey or golden syrup being carried past them to other animals. Then there were lions and tigers, panthers and black pumas, all of them executing within their dens, for they expected to be fed soon and were restless in consequence, the superb *chassés* of their lithe and ferocious tangos ; and hippopotamuses and rhinoceroses, deep in their armoured dreams of Africa and its hot and turbid rivers, or, it may be, lost in some far more ancestral, prehistoric vision of a quilted world dominance, when the steaming swamps of the world were their playground, and they could wallow in the conquered mud of the five continents. Well, those days were over ; and here they were, limited to small cement baths within a den, and, temper to be deduced in each gouty, swollen limb, they grunted loudly, after the fashion of old men in clubs. Other dreamers, too, we visited : giraffes lost in their high-minded visions of the young green shoots of palm-trees — palm-trees that were ever trying to starve them, for the higher up grew these tender morsels and the barer grew their long and plaited trunks, so much the farther up had their necks to stretch through the generations. We watched, too, the tribes of deer and antelope, leaping, spitting and butting on their terraces; the supercilious, self-indulgent camel, carrying the burden of its seven stomachs; and that paragon of virtuous motherhood, the kangaroo. We ignored the turtles, peering cautiously out of their armoured umbrellas, the crocodiles smiling within their heated, stinking pools, and the monkeys leaping and chattering on their hill, swinging and hanging head-downwards from the branches of their trees. The seals and sea-lions, combining all the charm and cleverness of both land and water animals, engaged our interest for a little by their evident enjoyment of their own obviously highly perfected technique in games and tricks. But now we passed on to lesser things, to the blue-crested pigeons of Australia, and, from them, to a venomous little rock-garden sprinkled with delicate flowers. Indeed, this small plot of ground offered a rational explanation for the horror of rock-gardens which every person possessed of an esthetic sense must feel. It had always seemed a strange phobia, without foundation: but here, under every demure Alpine or sub-arctic blossom was coiled a very malignant little serpent, or stretched in pretended death like a dead twig, lay a virulent lizard. At first you did not notice them. Only a running movement along the coil, a glimmer down the scales, would give warning of the viper, only a wicked occasional flickering of the tongue would betray the presence of all these dwarf dragons. New ones quivered into squamous life each instant, as one gazed at rocks and flowers. Robert, I remember, pointed out to me the similarity between this sensation and the one which seizes on him who looks for a minute or two at 'The Convent Garden', that masterpiece of pre-Raphaelite art, in the Ashmolean at Oxford. The Nun, in her grey clothes, stands in a garden. The grass at her feet is powdered with the innocent faces of spring flowers; in the foreground lies a pool, with a tadpole floating through it . . . apparently a solitary tadpole. But if you regard the painted water with sufficient care, tadpole after tadpole wriggles itself into your consciousness, and where before you saw only this one, now you see half a hundred. Counting them, seeing who could spot the greatest number, was at one time a recognised sport. So it was here, in this garden, where gradually, if you watched long enough, every pansy and rock-pink revealed a minute, spotted and poisonous monster. All the same, I reflected, this little flowery enclosure displayed rather the same brightness, the same counterfeit innocence and cheerfulness as Robert's home. But then, as for that, so did the parrot-house — into which he insisted on going, for he was very much attached to the conjunction of their brilliant colours and inconsequent chatter — albeit the squawking and screaming there was very different from the clear but stifled music that issued out of his every room.

We spent a considerable time in watching the birds; blush-coral, stately cockatoos like palest-pink dowagers, that mumbled gently for a few minutes and then suddenly emitted an ear-splitting screech, their crests rising on their heads as though we had pressed the spring of one of Robert's toys; the macaws, like lackeys in their gorgeous liveries of blue and scarlet, chained to their perches, and pecking at the world with cruel, sneering beaks; and then the little love-birds, nestling close to each other in couples — all, that is to say, except a solitary, green-feathered one who sat quietly on a perch of its own. It could not have mated yet, we surmised, for they say that when a love-bird dies its mate dies too.

Sometimes an animal or bird shows an immediate response to a human being, and this little bird showed signs of approval as we approached him, coquetting with head on one side, and advancing along the perch to meet us. Perhaps he thought we brought him food; he remained extremely amiable, but on closer acquaintance evinced a quite unmistakable preference for Robert Mainwroth. This was a love, too, that was returned, for Robert could not tear himself away, stayed there for nearly half an hour, stroking its green, downy head and talking to it. Moreover, as he turned away, he confessed how much he wished that he was the owner of this fascinating little creature — or one resembling it. But probably, even if he could contrive to get possession of it, there would be no room for it in his house, he added.

He drove me home. We parted, and the rest of the episode, or shall one say the sequel to this episode, is extracted from his diary. No sooner had he returned to a solitary, very solitary tea, in his drawing-room, when in at the wide-open window, from this typical Sunday afternoon of chirping sparrows and

distant, rasping-voiced dogs, there flew a green love-bird —
to all appearances the same one he had so recently left. It
fluttered round the pink-painted ceiling, but without any of
the bumping of fear or surprise : nor did it for an instant, as
might so easily have happened, knock into any of his clustered
fragilities.

Robert was startled at the coincidence, for though it could
scarcely be the actual bird from the Zoological Gardens, this,
too, was an Indian love-bird, identical to look at, so that only
another love-bird could have presumed to tell the difference.
He had expressed a wish. Here, and in so short a time, it had
been answered. That, in itself, constituted an occurrence of
such rarity that it was sufficient both to please enormously and
rather to frighten one. And, after all, the love-bird was not a
common feature of the English landscape or townscape. No,
it was a surprising, extraordinary event, which one would never
forget. And, as the bird fluttered round about him, there
seemed to him something symbolic and incomprehensible in its
flight, in its arrival. It must have escaped from somewhere, he
supposed. He had heard it said by the superstitious that it
brought bad luck to the owner of a house if a bird flew into it ;
but that, he comforted himself, applied more to choleric, red
bullfinches and homely starlings than to a jade-green parakeet
from distant Asia. Meanwhile the bird was shortening the
circles of its flight. Suddenly it settled near him, showing no
terror, but remaining there quite contentedly. He grasped
it firmly, and placed it on his other hand. It balanced itself
on an outstretched finger, and allowed him to promenade
with it round the room. He rang for the footman, and told
him to bring some fruit for it up from the dining-room. It
was brought, and the bird accepted a freckled strawberry from
his fingers with grace and promptitude.

And now a quite irrational joy seized on Sir Robert Mainwroth for his good fortune. He was more pleased, excited,
than he had ever been at his large and unexpected inheritance.
A deep, inner joy welled up in him and he was in a different
world from that of the morning, when the gloom of this
particular Sunday had for him summed up and crowned the
depression of a hot and tiring week ; a tiring, pointless week
that had seemed the epitome of a lifetime. A different world
— and yet the same, save that his whole house looked as he

D

had wished it to look, and that every object, every toy was fresh in its appeal. But now a fear swept down on his heart, a new fear — lest he should lose this lovely, living green toy, which appeared to know that it belonged to him : a terror that it might fly away again, be caught by cats, or singed by the lights in the room even. It was necessary to be practical. But there was no bird-cage in the house. It was Sunday, and impossible to buy one.

And then he remembered his cage. The only thing to be done was to place the newcomer in the grand mother-of-pearl and tortoise-shell affair that contained the stuffed bird. The living thing could not injure the dead one. But the parakeet would not enter, and Robert was afraid of hurting it. They resorted to stratagem. The small gate in the vast cage was left open, and grapes, strawberries, and bits of peaches were pressed enticingly between the precious bars of the further side, opposite the door. At last the love-bird responded, entered the trap, consented to be shut into this transparent, harem-like magnificence and solitude. Alone again, perhaps it thought. Alas, not so alone, after all ; for now, of a sudden, its round, twinkling eyes espied the brightly coloured, though somewhat moulting, bird-effigy that, with a certain stiff pride, occupied the centre of the golden perch. Its staring, unquivering beads of glass mocked the whole parrot-tribe. The love-bird was first struck motionless, and then made a high, shrill sound of anger. For a moment it hovered, a green flame in the air, round this stuffed image in a minute but quite comprehensible dance of rage ; after which it fluttered at it with sharp claws and tearing little beak in full battle-array of ruffled plumage. In the beginning it must have thought the creature alive, but this hard, inanimate dummy of an enemy that it proved to be was even more unendurable : and it pecked at it long and viciously, loosening one or two feathers. The scene was in its way so comic that Robert was almost tempted to wind up the machine and make the effigy pipe out its song. But this would be unkind, he felt. Already the little bird was disheartened, spurned the cornucopia of honeyed, jewel-like fruits with which it had been provided, and that matched so well the richness of its prison. Retreating now to the far end of the perch, it swivelled its green head right round behind, after the manner of all parakeets, and burying it in the green, soft feathers under the back of its neck, appeared to sleep. In any case it remained completely irresponsive to the coaxing of its new master, paid no heed at all to him. But after about an hour's rest, it roused itself again, sidled gently toward its hated rival, and proceeded to peck it once more, but this time slowly, deliberately and with no sign of anger, as though to discover to what lengths one could go, to what extent attack it without provoking an onslaught in return from this larger and most unusual bird. Then, having carried out this scouting expedition, it retired again to the farther end of its golden perch, and slept, or pretended to sleep. So it remained that evening, until a cloth was put over the cage for the night.

But none of these happenings altered Robert's new mood. They only made him love this toy the more. At any rate, it was safe in the cage for the night : nothing could attack it. And he went to bed in this new happiness and easiness of spirit, his only fear that in the morning the owners might trace and attempt to reclaim it.

The next morning Robert found his love-bird still cross and sulky. The fruit was untouched. But this did not worry him, for soon it would have a cage to itself; and he left the house at once to buy it one.

When, within half an hour, he returned with his new purchase, the drama was over. The artificial bird had been torn feather from feather, its remains spread all over the splendid cage ; even the glue, with which the plumage had been stuck on, was revealed upon this now hideous, bare mockery. But the little love-bird lay dead, too, in a corner.

There seemed to have been no reason for its death : though it might, the housekeeper suggested, have died, poisoned by some preservative in the feathers of the sham bird it had fought, or perhaps the sparrows had chased it and pecked it the evening before. But it had seemed well enough on its arrival in the house. . . . So the real bird, then, had been killed by the artificial one it had fought, had died from jealousy of it.

.   .   .   .   .   .

An intense sadness, it appears from Robert's journal, fell down upon him : a sadness quite out of all proportion, sensible people would have said, to the actual loss. Here he possessed everything he wanted, could possibly want, and yet was moping over a bird — and one he had only known for a few hours. If he had not minded selling all the furniture and pictures of his own family, why should he mind a small thing like this, they would have asked? Perhaps it was only because a perfect and beautiful little incident had ended so pitifully. Or was it that some meaning he could not fathom was concealed in it?

He never found out to whom the bird belonged or where it had come from. The cage he had bought for it was hidden and put away: but he could not bear to see the other, beautiful cage either. The effigy was never repaired, nor a new one constructed. And now Robert, too, is dead — has been dead three or four years. The bric-a-brac he loved, the mechanical nightingales, the clocks and musical-boxes, are broken or in dusty shops for sale, since nobody wants them. Little is left of him save this story — and this itself was dependent on the chance which led me to look in at the window of the antique-shop in King Street. But certainly I recognised the large bird-cage of tortoise-shell and nacre: and I thought that the renovated, stuffed bird within looked younger and more modern than when I last heard him sing in Sir Robert Mainwroth's house.

PRIMAVERA

By his entire nature the Italian is both simple and subtle. Vincenzo, though he came from Sicily, was no exception to this generalisation. His remarkable good looks, his delightful, tumbling English, spoken with an Italian lisp, accompanied by a smiling and innocent character (innocent in the sense that a young animal is innocent), but with, in contradiction, a certain almost Chinese wiliness over matters of buying and selling, had served him well. In the space of twenty years he had risen from being a waiter, with no friends, no money and little education, to owning two fine businesses — he dealt in antiques — which necessitated knowledge and judgment, numerous clients and a fair amount of capital.

He had spent his first year as a waiter in London, and had then taken a job in an hotel in Oxford. During his spare time there he had attended lectures in order to educate himself, in a cap and gown given him as a tip by an undergraduate who was leaving. Then in about 1908, in that brief glory of Edwardian days, he had returned to work in London, and had lived somewhere near the Crystal Palace (*Il Palazzo di Cristallo*: that figure of speech so compelling to all of Italian race who know the rock-crystal cups and jewelled crystal dragons of Benvenuto Cellini and his followers, and who see in the phrase some towering, overwhelming, superlative creation of the same kind).

He had lodged with Miss Miranda Starbottle, the granddaughter of a Sicilian refugee from oppression. Her grandfather had served Garibaldi and had been obliged, with his daughter, to seek sanctuary in England during the forties of the last century (his wife had died on the journey). In those days refugees had glamour, were not the broken, pitiful creatures that they are today, and this girl, who was beautiful, had soon married an Englishman, a merchant, who had fallen passionately in love with her. Materially, it was a better match than she could have hoped for at home. But Miss Starbottle certainly proved a queer offspring of so romantic a marriage. Her mother had died when she was three, and she had never been to Italy, could speak no Italian, and, except in her dark hair and now faded yellow complexion, showed little sign of southern descent. Indeed, she had always appeared somewhat ashamed of even this element of nonconformity to English Victorian standards.

When Vincenzo first met her, her father, too, had long been dead and she must have been about sixty years old, or perhaps more; equally, she might have been seventy. She seemed never to alter, a typical late-Victorian spinster, frozen into whalebone stays and layers of thick clothes covered with meaningless, fussy ornament, with lace and embroidery and filigree, and with a fringe that crept in black, Medusa-like curls over her forehead; a style which she made no attempt to modify or soften. If she went out — which was seldom — she carried on her head a large black creation, crowned with purple and white ostrich feathers, and in her gloved hands a mauve-silk sunshade with a filigree silver handle. Over her left temple and the upper part of the cheek spread a large birthmark: but her face, apart from this livid continent, was sallow and lined, for she possessed the Victorian horror of face cream and rouge, of lipstick and 'enamel'. She still occupied her father's substantial house in Penge, but she had come down in the world, money was scarce, and she now took in a few lodgers — a few, I say, but no doubt as many as the house would hold. Under her vague superintendence and direction two or three servants attended to their wants. She, as a rule, did little herself for them.

All Sicilians, whether nobles, bureaucrats or officials, are related, and Vincenzo, being in some manner a connection of hers, had been recommended to her care. At first her frigid manner of living — to an Italian so empty and desolate — her severe abstainer's outlook, her horror of wine and good food, of comfort and of warmth, had repelled him: but gradually he had grown to like her and respect her admirable characteristics, her hidden kindness, her shrewdness — except in business matters — and, above all, her reliability. And perhaps the Italian sun, so strong in his blood and skin and bones, called out some response in her. . . . At any rate she thawed, became his chief confidante and adviser, a very kind and devoted friend, willing to forgive in him various trifling and impulsive faults which in others she would with severity have condemned.

Thus his occasional excesses of various kinds were over-looked. Perhaps she reflected, in a heart now hidden away, that he was a foreigner and knew no better, or perhaps, even, some similar but repressed strain in her own nature made her exult secretly in his southern conduct. While Vincenzo lived in her house, his parents died in Sicily, and the sense of his loneliness gave her a new and motherly affection for him. 'Poor boy', she used to repeat to herself, 'poor boy!' And, though formerly she had, because of the same taint in herself, despised foreigners, she now encouraged him to bring his Italian friends to see her. Moreover, Vincenzo dramatised and presented her, until, to a whole circle of Italians living in England, 'Miss Miranda', as they called her — for their tongues could not form the alien, syllabic music of Miss Starbottle —, became for them, like the Crystal Palace, a symbol of England. And though, indeed, they laughed at her, they respected her, revelled, even, in her thoughts and sayings, as being those of an unfailing representative of her nation and period. And no doubt their coming and going made her blossom a little, softened the hard edges of that drying heart.

Meanwhile, Vincenzo had started his antique shop in Oxford Street, and was making money.

.   .   .   .   .

When he returned to London in 1919, after the war, Vincenzo decided to open a branch establishment in Naples, and to have a flat there as well, for he was longing for Italian life once more. But, though his shop had prospered, owing to the boom in old furniture during the war years, Miss Miranda and her affairs had, on the other hand, gone very much further downhill. All her small investments had collapsed, and she could no longer afford to keep on her old servants : yet without them she was lost. She could not do the housework herself and her general inefficiency aggravated the situation. . . . She must, by now, have been seventy or over (some people said seventy-six), but outwardly she remained just the same, with no diminishing of the settled richness of curled fringe or lace or jewellery. Her large hat still sported the ostrich feathers ; no paint or powder disfigured her face and only the birth-mark seemed to have become emphasised in its wrinkled pallor.

Just the same; except that she cried a little when she saw Vincenzo, and that he had never seen her cry before.

Directly he observed the state of the house, he realised what had occurred. Something must be done to help her, and his warm, impetuous nature decided him at once what to do. With her permission an English friend of his, a lawyer, examined her affairs. It transpired that if she sold her house, she would be left with about eighty or ninety pounds a year upon which to live. In those days the pound was beginning to buy many lire and so that income would suffice her in Italy.

Vincenzo arranged, therefore, that Miss Miranda should dispose of her belongings and come to live with him in his flat in Naples. In order to overcome her possible objection he told her that it would aid him financially if she were to pay him a small sum every week and 'look after the flat' (though, since it was plain that she could not look after her own house, and could speak no Italian, this aid was problematic). . . . Indeed, she must have been lonely while he was away, have craved his company and that of his friends, because though her character always led her to oppose any plan, even when she secretly wished for it, she soon acquiesced, after a few protestations that she would 'only be in the way', and that before long he would want to marry and be rid of her. . . . Previously she had shown little enthusiasm for Italy, but now, at the age of over seventy, she faced the total change of climate and living that awaited her with complete equanimity.

. . . . .

By the spring of 1920 they were settled in Naples. Their flat, the top storey of an eighteenth-century palace, faced the Castel dell' Ovo (the fortress that grew, so the Neapolitans say, out of a magic egg placed there by the sorcerer Virgil), against the classic Neapolitan view of sea, island and mountain. Furnished with part of the stock from the shop, the magnificence of its big and lofty rooms, its gilded beds and chairs and painted hangings and later Empire furniture, might have proved somewhat overpowering to one fresh from Penge. Further, though Miss Miranda's self-respect was propped up on a small weekly contribution to Vincenzo for food and rent, she exercised from the beginning only the empty shell of house-keeping prerogatives. A woman, Maria, came in to cook and do the work, and Pancrazio — a relation of Vincenzo, a boy of sixteen who aided him in the shop — slept in the other spare bedroom and occasionally condescended to help with odd jobs in the house.

Pancrazio was lazy, everyone saw that at once. He was also untrustworthy and a liar: but the sleepy warmth that broods on the ruined Greek temples of Sicily, where flowers grow from stones and snakes lie baking under them, glowed in his eyes, in his smile, in the movements of his limbs, and this birthright brought him with ease many friends, persuading them to condone the execrable qualities of his nature. His voice, his hands even, had this warm, animal glow that pleaded so eloquently for him. Moreover, in the shop, he was quite useful, a born salesman (people liked to buy things from him), and in the house he was quiet. . . . Something of the old apprentice attitude to life still lingered in Italy, and so Pancrazio — or Pancras, as Miss Miranda uncompromisingly called him — being, as it were, both friend and servant, would always accompany Vincenzo and Miss Miranda on their excursions and picnics.

His duty it was to unpack and arrange the luncheon and pour out — and help to drink — the wine. . . . Yes, *wine*; for Naples was helping to thaw Miss Miranda's disposition still further, and already she drank a little wine. And perhaps — for it could not surely be the beginning of vanity? — perhaps the heat of this spring, when summer had for once started in April, was responsible for other changes. Certainly she had modified her clothes. Her hats had ceased being architectural, were now flimsy, quite gay affairs, suited at any rate to the climate, and she must have steeled herself to throw away several petticoats and tight stomachers, with the result that she had become — though no younger — by several degrees more human and less like an African idol in the process. Even her fringe she had discarded, and Vincenzo had persuaded her to consult a former London friend, a hairdresser, now chief of his trade in Naples, who was enchanted to advise her concerning the best fashion for her to assume. In fact, Vincenzo was obliged to confess to himself that she had come out of her shell nicely, and reflected credit, and not ridicule, as subconsciously he may have feared, on her rescuer, her Perseus.

Nor did she appear to feel homesick or ill at ease in this strange city, though there was nothing for her to do but to sit on the little arboured terrace, dawdle round the flower-pots, fetch the London papers or occasionally call at the English Tea-rooms for a chat. . . . No, she was not bored : for her, she was cheerful and jaunty. She loved particularly their excursions : for once or twice a week he would run them out to lunch at Sorrento, La Cava, Castellamare or Pompeii in his little motor.

How much they had all three enjoyed Pompeii ! How often and how long they had laughed during the meal ! They continued frequently to refer to this with pride (because simple minds seem to consider laughter as a virtue in itself) : how much they had laughed ! . . . They had not been able to have a picnic within the walls, but had been obliged instead to go to a Swiss restaurant, just outside them. This place, created for tourists, might almost have been built by Bulwer Lytton himself, so full of ancient Roman colour was it : but the food proved to be good. They had eaten *lasagne*, had drunk *gragnano* — that purple, sparkling wine of the district, with its faint, sweet taste of sulphur and strong, deep taste of iron — had listened to an over-ripe warbling of 'Sole Mio' by a fat Neapolitan determined to resemble Caruso, had heard blind men clawing at mandolins and singing with a horrible false gaiety 'Funiculì, Funiculà !' and had, further, watched the antics and grimaces of an old man and woman, dressed in exaggerated peasant costumes of a hundred years before, who had danced the tarantella with a scrawny exaggeration of youth and grace — all for the price of a rather expensive luncheon. They had drunk a lot of wine which had flushed their faces and given fire to their laughter, and Pancrazio had sprung to life : his words, usually few, had now torrented over one another. He was transformed. All his sleepy grace became active and vigorous. But Miss Miranda, though she looked at him often, could not, of course, comprehend what he said, though she must have understood his mood. . . . They stayed there, drinking coffee and *strega*, until long after the other luncheon guests had departed on their earnest task of sightseeing.

When at last they entered the dead city, the heat of the sun, beating down upon them and reverberating up from the tufa pavements, seemed to bring with it a life of its own, so that instead of the individual existence of man or beast, brick and stone formed an entity, lived and quivered. The droves of visitors had passed on, and the three of them were able to laugh and joke by themselves, alone, except for the custodians of the ruins. The animation, derived equally from sea, sky, air and landscape, of which formerly this extinct pleasure-town had been the scene, seemed to inspire them, so that they laughed on through the streets of broken houses, feeling no fatigue.

It had been, in fact, an unforgettable day; one of those few occasions that happen to come flawlessly right, so Vincenzo thought; a day with a memorable quality of both satire and perfection. Even the phalluses carved on pavements and walls, and always so carefully indicated by the guides, albeit explained vaguely away as 'fecundity symbols', appeared in no way to shock Miss Miranda. (Notwithstanding, Vincenzo, with the curiosity of all Italians in these matters, could not help wondering what the old lady made of them and of their frequency in this buried past.) She had seemed positively anxious to enter certain houses, forbidden to her sex by the authorities, in order to examine the erotic paintings therein. But the custodian obliged her to sulk impatiently in the atrium, while he showed her instead articles of feminine vanity, scent-bottles from which the perfume had evaporated two millenniums ago, and pots of rouge cracked and riven by two thousand years of cinders. . . . But soon the others joined her, and they were outside again, laughing and talking, or sat on a roof watching the faintly glowing plume of smoke that blew just above the baked, purple cone of the volcano.

Naples and the long, viridian spring appeared altogether to soften and humanise Miss Miranda. . . . But in the month of May the atmosphere began to change. At that season the country invades this great city with a magic unknown elsewhere. It turns stones and pilasters, pedestals and broken columns to life. Flowering weeds flamed down in festoons from every cornice and every roof. Age-old and fecund, every scrap of ground, even in the centre of the city, is covered with innumerable and diverse flowers; purple and blue and pink and yellow, they grow from the feet and shoulders of statues and under the trampling hooves of bronze horses. The air itself blossoms with an indefinable life and scent, and a peculiar excitement and heightening of human senses pervades the square and street and room — a sense of expectancy. A subtle uneasiness seems to spread circumambient to every object and every person, and as thus day followed day, Miss Miranda appeared, equally, to become increasingly different, increasingly more human ; a touch of coquetry, even, started to manifest itself now in the style of her dresses and her hats.

Presently, indeed, Vincenzo thought that he had noticed that she had begun to use a little rouge and powder. But the idea was untenable. It just could not be, knowing her prejudices. . . . Certainly, though, it looked as if the birth-mark had begun to fade out beneath a coat of some thick paint. That was different : probably the consciousness of it had long haunted her, and now, in her new independence, she wanted to be rid of it. Then, too, her hair surely had become fairer ? . . . He would try and allude to it some time, in a non-committal, inoffensive way. . . . But before long, there could be no doubt that she *was* using scent — and a good, French scent. Vincenzo was pleased : he felt it a tribute to his powers of civilisation.

The whole time that these gradual yet comparatively sudden changes were in progress, the full Neapolitan spring was entering into the darkened rooms. The sun, reflected from a thousand walls painted pink and scarlet and tawny red, crept through the shutters and played quiveringly upon the objects within. On the terrace outside, the massive foliage of orange and lemon was sprinkled with white stars, gold-dusted, and the heavy, obsessing fragrance swept through the apartments on every puff of warm air. The vine of the arbour, too, had released tight golden coils, like the hair of the Parian statues of Antinous and Ganymede which still littered the bed of the sea that now, day after day, exhibited a hundred different suffusions of blue and lilac and green and silver. The Greek frieze of mountain and island that lay above the water on the horizon, every moment adopted in this golden month new aspects, legendary and fantastic in their beauty. Sometimes Capri opposite looked hazy and remote as the Hesperides, sometimes so near that those who gazed at it felt they could clasp its white houses in their hands.

Within the apartment, shuttered in order to obtain cool air, the atmosphere became darkly oppressive. It was often too hot to talk, and things unformulated in speech, and almost in thought, lay behind the lips of these three people, as they sat staring at the sea, waiting for its cool evening breath, or moved with a sullen dream-like quality through the ponderously ornate rooms. Their silence, masked with an unreasoning irritability, held in it no contentment of mind or body.

Even Vincenzo, in spite of his happy and easy-going disposition, must have shown his feelings. He often longed to be alone, and wished with fervour that Miss Miranda would not smother herself in scent and — there could be no secret about it now — thus daub herself with rouge. She looked, he admitted to himself at this moment, grotesque, with her hair turning golden (alleged to be its natural colour revived by camomile shampoos), and with her old, wrinkled face smeared so badly with paint that the spot of high colour on each cheek flared up in contrast against the dead white powder of the rest. Her birth-mark, shaped like South America, showed, too, through its camouflage. Why, she was like a Goya; exactly like! All she needed was a bridal veil and a wreath of orange blossom to make her into one of his *Caprichos*. She was old enough in all conscience, and, as every Italian knows, dignity and reserve belong to old age. This fantastic mask, and these short dresses and short sleeves, accorded but ill with the corrugated, tortoise-like neck! It would cause any man a passing shudder.

By June, everyone agreed that it must be an unusually hot year. . . . Yet Miss Miranda, who had never hitherto set foot abroad, remained unaffected, scarcely seemed to feel it, except that the dark substance she spread in the hollows under and over her eyes began to run, tingeing the pink and white. But she was never ill for a day, was always there. And Pancrazio, too; silent, furtive, brooding no doubt over some unpleasant secret of adolescence. . . . Well, by the look of him, Vincenzo thought, he would have adventures. But there it was; the boy was probably bad, he admitted, yet, in spite of his lies, he liked him for his young and sulky grace.

Toward the end of June sleep became impossible. All night long the crowds from the slums of the old city sought cool air on the promenade below, laughing, talking, singing. Odd fragments of unconnected song — silly Neapolitan songs — floated in at the wide-open windows until four or five o'clock in the morning. (What could these revellers be doing, Vincenzo wondered.) During the long nights, as he lay there, he began to question whether the flat was not perhaps haunted. Or was it merely that he was so exhausted by the heat and by trying to sleep? . . . Certainly on several occasions he had imagined that he heard sounds and movements and whisperings in the darkness. Stealthy steps crept along the passage, boards creaked, or there was a secretive shutting of a door; *shutting* was scarcely the right word, it was too muffled and padded and gentle a sound for that. The hushed sibilance of voices, the suppressed and distant echo of a laugh, seemed to lie under the noise from outside, and to come from within the large old flat itself. Yet, it may be because he was tired, he did not wish to investigate. Something, though he had little belief in ghosts, held him back. The sounds must be, he told himself, of his own imagining. But he did not mention them to the others, did not wish to give his companions any information, or they might start a scare, and begin talking and talking and talking about it in the heat of the day.

Then one night — it was just before three — he heard something. . . . Unable to bear the mystery any longer, he sprang out of bed and flashed on the light in the passage outside. . . . There, dazzled and blinking, creeping and sidling along from the direction of Miss Miranda's room, was Pancrazio. He wore an old pair of trousers, but was naked above the waist. Even in these strange circumstances, a certain grace and beauty surrounded him, Vincenzo saw, but something was wrong — he could see that too — and shouting 'What are you doing there?' Vincenzo seized him, dragged him into his room, shook him until his bones rattled. A silly smile stretched over the boy's face, but he made no effort to struggle or escape. In his hand, Vincenzo found a hundred-lire note. '*Ladro!*' he shouted, striking him, 'Thief!' But Pancrazio, though he cowered, seemed stupefied. 'She gave it to me, Vincenzo,' he said. 'I am not trying to deceive you. She gave it me. I have spent the night with her — many nights, *la vecchia putana!* You never told me I was not to. . . . But it was no pleasure to me, so why should she not give me money? . . . But it *is* true, I'll prove it. You can tell for yourself. You know English. She taught me to say these words, though I don't know what they mean.' And then out of his mouth issued, pronounced with extreme care, a repetition of words and phrases of the most obscene and erotic significance. He articulated syllable after syllable, but without emphasis, like a child who has learned a lesson. Word after word blossomed lewdly, evilly from his lips in the surrounding and culminating silence — for at the moment there came no other sound.

SHADOW PLAY

You must imagine three young girls, each an only child, all beautiful and all rich, immensely rich. They were not related, but among their parents prevailed that particular sentimental feeling, stronger than friendship, composed of intimacy, good-fellowship and complete interdependence, that exists only among the cosmopolitan-millionaire class. . . . Well, these three children had been brought up together, had played together, had spent each Christmas together, shared the same governesses, the same instructors in riding and dancing. Together they had learnt French, Italian and German (which, unlike the members of their mothers' generation, they could speak with fluency and correctness). They had been trained, too, to be 'simple' and 'unspoilt' and slightly infantile, as the super-rich like their children to be, but they had been taught nothing about how to manage their fortunes, how these had been amassed or why they would one day inherit them. Finally, they had been sent to the same fashionable finishing-off schools in Florence and Paris. Now they were eighteen, and the waiting earth lay at their feet.

With the hard, brilliant prettiness of a diamond, Zoë carried prettiness to an extreme. Her hands and feet were exquisite, and her voice, though in no way ugly, was so distinct it would have cut glass. Pauline was like crystal, a little larger in her loveliness, so clear but by no means soft, with the body and carriage of a young goddess walking over hills in the dawn, and a deep, throaty laugh. Her hands, too, were small and beautiful. Both of them looked outwards on the world: but they fastened their bright gaze upon it with such eagerness that they saw nothing.

The third friend, Lorinda, was different. Slim and tall and dark and restless, she had large mournful eyes that looked inwards on herself, and so sometimes saw the world. Perhaps because of a latent softness of heart in that long, slender body, others, not of her sort, and living in the wild places beyond the gold bars, interested her: her blood beat in common with the

94

blood of all human beings. In consequence, she seemed to herself among her own friends always a little unpopular, a little upon the edge of life. Being very young, moreover, though occasionally she made her own observations, she had not found out how to deduce from them.

Zoë, Pauline and Lorinda, in that dawn of the world as it was for them, spent much time together. It was as though this had been ordained. No one had ever suggested to them that they would be happier apart, and so they met continually, went expeditions, visited shops and art-galleries together. Their mothers, as they played bridge of an afternoon in their drawing-rooms, so full of light, among the French furniture — signed pieces, and formal photographs of plumed and helmeted personages — signed pieces, and Ritz and Fabergé *bibelots*, said to each of them, in their tired voices, 'All right, darling, you can go, so long as the other two girls are going. Don't stay out too late. And you'd better take your fur coat, and arrange not to be called too early. . . . And don't forget to come and say good-night to Mummy before you leave the house.'

That kind of life was only just starting. It was in the twenties, and the young and rich, if they would promise to remain content with the gold bars behind which they were fastened, would find their pleasures in plenty and brimming over. They would have, as their mothers said, 'a glorious time'. In the spring, of this, their first year, the families of Zoë, Pauline and Lorinda went to stay in Paris; they took up their quarters, two in their own houses, one in the Ritz. In May, they would return to London; after that, in the autumn, they would go to New York.

During this visit to Paris, then, there was to be one afternoon a sale of stuffs, silks and velvets and brocades, and the three girls decided to attend it. They had been there for about ten minutes, in an enormous, crowded, hot room, and Lorinda had been looking inside herself, not paying much attention to the frenetic yet dawdling tumult around her, when suddenly she saw Zoë and Pauline as though for the first time. Schooled in the arts of elegance though they were, they had for the moment shed these accomplishments. Their hands, always so cool and pretty, had become claws, like those of an Egyptian Hawk-God, and all the possessiveness and greed of those ancestors, generation after generation, robber barons, Dutch from New York, railway kings and market-riggers, and New England farmers squeezing the last ear of wheat out of the soil, who had built up these vast fortunes now tottering under their own weight, manifested themselves in their furious, grabbing fingers, swollen by the excitement of possible bargains. Their eyes remained fresh and glittering as usual, their features cameo-clear, but their hands grasped and wrenched and plucked and clutched and tugged at the stuffs on the counters.

And this appeared to be the point, too, at which the touching *camaraderie* of the super-rich broke down, for neither of the girls seemed, during this delirium of shopping, to be conscious of the other's presence — let alone of that of a third, and non-possessive, party. When they saw her, they elbowed her out of the way; she was nothing, thistledown. They, Pauline and Zoë, were worthy to fight between themselves for a prize, or bid in competition at an auction, where the race and reward is to the richest, but, for all her wealth, Lorinda, so their grappling, despoiling hands and knife-sharp elbows told her, must just keep herself out of the way!

Directly they left the shop, they were themselves again, with a well-defined sweetness and steely distinction, their hands pretty as flowers. But for Lorinda, the scene she had witnessed retained an extraordinary, almost apocalyptic quality. These two other young creatures had become amazons, beings to be feared. Sometimes in nightmares she saw their hands once more turning the stuffs on the counters, pulling and grabbing them, feeling their web and the texture. The hands then held some fulfilment in them, a hint of menace that eluded her when she awoke, became vast raven-hued clouds overshadowing her whole future.

Lorinda was young, and the lines of her life were as yet vague, unset. When she gazed within herself the vista was indistinct; while outside herself things seemed almost as she had been told they were; *almost*, for she was one of those who develop late, and already she noticed that they did not tally absolutely. How was it that she saw in some directions differently from her mother and her mother's friends? Why did the idea of staying in nearly every afternoon to play cards so much appal her? And what was the world, for example, to which the work of the great musicians carried her; a world wherein her closest friends, Pauline and Zoë, appeared to have no part, nor her family, neither her father nor her mother?

But she only attained to the kingdom of art long afterwards. . . . Now she was eighteen. Every night she attended dances, so as to meet the young men with one of whom it was supposed that, after a few months, or even a year or two, in which to decide her preference, she must spend the rest of her life. A semblance of gaiety masked the seriousness which underlay these occasions. Huge awnings flowered in red and white outside the great yellow-stucco houses, and the rhythm of dance music, a beating and tattooing without tune, drifted out from them into the squares and gardens, and down to the hot pavements where always stood a few lonely watchers, silent, hungry, curious, their ragged poverty consuming with straining eyes these riches. On the balconies the young couples would look at them and say, 'What a funny old man down there!' and from top to bottom, rooms, staircases and halls were full of happy, meaningless chatter.

This kind of life seemed to continue for a long time, she could hardly tell, so confused did the delicious, long slumber of late hours render her, how long. . . . And gradually she found that she had fallen in love — or thought that she had fallen in love — with Ivor Harley, a young man who was shortly sailing for India with his regiment. It was understood between them that they should marry. He was young and gay and good-looking, and his eyes were full of truth.

He was leaving England in August, and so, some time soon, she must tell her mother, and then, next year, she would join him in Delhi, and they would be married. . . . She did not think that her mother would welcome the idea, for though he was rich, he did not belong to the super-rich; in whom alone virtue resided. It would be, she expected to be told, throwing her fortune away, — two fortunes, for one was to come to her from her father and one from her mother. She foresaw difficulties, but she knew she could obtain her parents' consent in the end, since it was a match to which no reasonable person of their world could object, and, in her own way, Lorinda could assert her dark, mute will, if her mind was made up. Besides, her mother, she knew, would like Ivor, for his good looks, his manners, his quickness. . . . She would tell them in August, before he left for India, but at present she did not want any awkward discussions to mar the happiness of their meetings.

However, in the early part of July a dreadful thing happened. Her mother died suddenly from heart-failure. The event convulsed Lorinda's whole life and outlook. To the young, death is so remote as not to exist at all and, in spite of the difference between their temperaments, she had always been very close to her mother. In the days that followed she had gone down to their country place with her father. She felt so sorry for him that she almost forgot about Ivor, though they exchanged letters; at first, every two or three days. As if the yawning of the grave had for the time chilled his emotions, the warmth in them had a little died down. She could understand that. No doubt he did not wish to intrude his own sentiments, did not quite know what to say, except to offer sympathy and continue to offer sympathy. She could hardly ask him here at present, so she would be compelled to go up to London to see him, and arrange matters before he left. It would be quite easy, because the house was near London.

Under the grey and sulphurous skies that herald thunder the early August heat brooded, lying heavy upon the gardens and the old trees, and in the large, hot, dark rooms, padded with brocade and full of expensive objects, china, bronze, furniture, pictures, the loneliness of their lives became more apparent to Lorinda and her father. . . . The only thing that comforted her was the splendid way in which Zoë and Pauline behaved; kindness itself. She had written to Zoë, soon after leaving London, confiding in her about Ivor, and asking her to look after him, in case, without her presence there, his last few weeks in London should prove dull. And Zoë — it was evident from Ivor's letters — could not have taken more trouble to be helpful. While Pauline, in order to cheer her friend up, came to live with them for the summer and, with her practical nature, took off Lorinda's shoulders the domestic burdens of seeing the servants and ordering the food. (How much she hated these things! And her life would be full of them now, for, by her mother's will, she was already a rich woman.) In consequence, Lorinda was able more fully to give way to her grief.

It was silly in a way, she knew, to grieve continually as she was doing. Everyone told her it would do no good and could not bring her mother back to life; but she could not help it. (Pauline was sensible and left her a great deal to herself: she appreciated that.) Her days were poisoned by the shock and by the sense of her loss, although they possessed a trance-like quality, unreal in the extreme. And she could not sleep. Uneasy slumber came to her for a few hours, but even then, full of dreams, sinister dreams, with grasping, dominating hands. . . . But perhaps they would stop when she went up to London to see Ivor. Her father, now that Pauline was here, could surely spare her for two or three nights! And she could stay with Zoë. She could not at present face her own home, after what had happened there. It really was kind of Zoë to stay on in London, right into August, when all the gaieties were over, in order to look after poor Ivor. . . . Lorinda thought of Ivor, and it calmed her. In her mind, she looked into the candid depths of those blue eyes, in which all truth and frankness dwelt, and presently she fell asleep.

The next morning she wrote to Zoë, explaining that she was obliged to come up to London for a few days the following week to see Ivor, and asking if she might stay with her. The reply came by telegram, 'Certainly darling and may I motor to lunch with you to-morrow Zoë'. Lorinda was enchanted. She longed to see her old friend again, and they could talk of Ivor. (He had not written, she remembered, for some days.) . . . It was curious, though, Pauline did not seem to be at all pleased when she heard that Zoë was coming down, and said something about how reluctant she herself would have been to push her way in like that! . . . Rather silly of her, Lorinda thought, as she was there already. But that was only Pauline; she got into these moods sometimes. They meant nothing, so Lorinda let it pass.

When Zoë arrived, driving her own motor and looking enchantingly pretty and competent, they kissed, and then Lorinda took her into the garden. . . . The leaves lay flat as cardboard on the air in the curious hush of full summer, no sound to be heard except the heavy droning of insects, which seemed, from the surrounding silence, to obtain a new and menacing tone. The enormous trees towered up, leaf upon leaf above them, towards the sullen, dove-coloured sky. It was very beautiful; a sort of peace descended on her at last, and as she walked between the huge green masts of the avenue, she felt a presentiment that all her life she would remember walking here with Zoë. . . . At first they did not talk much. How silent it was! Lorinda, looking at the leaves of the horse-chestnuts which composed the avenue, noticed how they extended towards her, motionless; (like swollen, stretching hands, she thought to herself). They made their way to a pillared temple by Kent at the end of the avenue, so that they could sit and talk undisturbed.

Zoë looked lovely today, prettier than she had ever seen her, Lorinda decided. Zoë took off her gloves and placed them beside her on the old carved and painted garden seat. And Lorinda, who seemed to find herself nearer the surface, as it were, today, perhaps from the pleasure and surprise of her friend's visit, thought to herself, as she examined Zoë's hands, how silly — and jealous, too, she supposed — she had been before to imagine that, even for a moment, they had not been pretty. They were beautifully formed, slender, with almond-shaped nails. . . . Zoë was holding up her left hand at arm's length, staring at it in an absent-minded manner. What a lovely ring she was wearing! It must be new. Lorinda had never seen it before. It was not the *sort* of stone she liked but it *was* a beautiful stone: her mother would have admired it, she thought with a pang; the pang of one who had forgotten for a moment the newly dead. . . . And so for a while she pursued her own sorrow, her own thoughts, not attending to what Zoë was saying. Zoë had put on her gloves again, and was laughing and talking almost too much. . . . Lorinda began to listen.

'So I shall sail for Bombay on the 7th of next month,' she was saying.

'I had no idea you were going there,' Lorinda interrupted, 'but isn't it rather early? Won't it still be frightfully hot? . . . I wish you'd stay here. I shall miss you dreadfully, darling.'

'But I've got to go. I can't help myself. . . . I was telling you: Ivor and I are to be married in October.'

. . . .

Pauline was horrified when Lorinda told her of it after Zoë had left. Lorinda had related it quietly, without comment. She was becoming trained to life.

'I should have thought her family would have stopped Zoë from making such a fool of herself,' the other said; 'after all, they're both very young. And he isn't such a rich man as all that. . . . I think you are well out of it, Lindy, if you ask me,' Pauline continued, 'but then young men bore me. *I* like people of experience,' and she flourished a hand, a pretty hand.

At the time, Lorinda thought she was merely trying to be kind. But, some considerable time afterwards, she saw her friend had meant what she said. For it was not until a full year after her mother's death that Pauline and her father announced their engagement.

THE MACHINE BREAKS DOWN

HUGH DEARBORN was already middle-aged when I first remember him some ten years ago, but middle-aged with an unparalleled elegance, an unimpeachable style. His greying hair, his mask-like face, through which peered those witty, rather wicked eyes, his hands of carved ivory, were all made with an exquisite but rather snuff-box-like finish. This well-groomed and tailored figure, this Voltairean mask, rather too developed for the slender frame and covered with small, delicately chiselled wrinkles, formed but the very gentlemanly shell for an intense vitality out of all proportion to it — formed, in fact, the beautifully finished cabinet-gramophone case, from which sounded a wonderful but intolerable music. Not that his voice was musical, in the sense that our grandmothers used that term. It was not. His laugh never resembled a peal of church bells sounding at eventide, or a rather carelessly played xylophone, as did the elegant tremolos of various old Victorian ladies. On the contrary, his voice, touching every emotion for the necessary moment, never sank into cloying sweetness, having, rather, that enchanting trick of putting a note in the wrong, unexpected place, and then recovering, which you find in the best modern music — find originally in Rossini's *Can-Can*, that first clear gem of modern music, and then in Debussy, Ravel and Stravinsky.

The actual manner of his conversation was perhaps less modern than its content. Artists of the spoken word vary in their methods. One, whose manner I admire most of all, talks, argues, sinks beneath the logical waters, is on the point of drowning, but as he touches the ocean bottom, finds some new pearl, and swiftly brings it to the surface : his is an absolute reliance on his own brain and tongue, never afraid to risk all on an absurd argument, never fearing to sink, knowing always that he will find a new treasure. But Hugh's system is different, formal ; it is as the Garden of Versailles compared with that of Hampton Court — stiff, mathematic, well ordered ; his voice a terrible instrument, his art one that dies but never surrenders.

From the first Hugh Dearborn possessed a peculiar interest for me — an interest aroused by some apparent contradictions in his character. Here was this exquisite shell, the fruit of fifty or sixty years of toil, but an instrument for an hour's conversation — conversation that like a flower blossoms and then dies — a mule-like art without hope of progeny. Usually the artist is led on by a desire for immortality or perhaps fired by a craving for money, but here was a real case of 'Art for Art's sake'. The best Hugh could hope for was an invitation to dinner, but the very perfection of his conversational technique, the very insistence and monopoly of his great art, often tended to prevent his humble end.

And this art itself, unpremeditated and yet such a technical achievement, surely could not flower on the barren air without any but purely physical preparation? Then again, after Hugh's performance of the new Symphony at the luncheon table, I once heard a rather unkind friend say to him : 'Really, Hugh, you ought to put it in a book!' And this made me wonder why he had never employed these gifts in some other, more permanent, form. And how much longer, in any case, could this delicate, ageing instrument stand the ceaseless wear and tear of such a vitality?

Thus, from the first, Dearborn interested me and I collected information about him. It was certainly a mysterious life. A friend of mine, I found out, had met him originally in the garden of Walter Pater. I pictured the scene. To us children of sadder and wiser days the eighties of the last century seem a halcyon but ever-so-distant age ; Alfred Lord Tennyson ever so much more distant than King Alfred burning the cakes ; the young manhood of Mr. Arthur Balfour ever so much more remote, more legendary, than the youth of King Arthur or the Quest of the Holy Grail. A halcyon time indeed, with spring always in the warm crystal-clear air ; with the laburnums, the lilacs, the lobelias and copper beeches in a perpetual riot of unsubdued and unbridled colour. There was a continual movement and sparkle in the lives of the well-to-do. Poet Laureates still wrote quite successful odes to members of the reigning family, who were then of greater interest to their subjects than professional cricketers or the doped death of Miss Flossie Highfly. The county families were yet safely out of the way, secure in their distant tea-bound mansions, busy killing the beasts of the field, the birds of the air. Riches were still respectable, the rise of a millionaire was yet a romance. On the other hand, you could be poor without being thought insane, and the silver epergne was gradually retiring into the lodging-houses of Bloomsbury. Shepheard's Hotel would soon be open in Cairo (or was it already?), and we were on the verge of an optimistic young Imperialism that would grow to a climax with Kipling and Lady Butler. And, to those who liked it, there was a pleasant stir in the world of art. Painting and prose were both stretching themselves after a long sleep that had been broken only by the short Pre-Raphaelite nightmare. This was the time of the neo-Greek: white marble mantelpieces, Alma Tadema, the prose of John Addington Symonds, the drawings of Du Maurier and Frank Miles — all were supposed, rather vaguely, to recall, to equal even, the art of Phidias. Bustles, bonnets, straight profiles and diamond myrtle-leaves were the order of the day. For the more precious there were water-lilies, almond-blossom and flowing draperies; for the very knowing, chatter about Whistler and Walter Pater.

Thus, in the garden of that old-world city, through Parnassian groves, over smooth classical lawns that glowed, as they would have said, like sad green velvet, under weeping willows which wept more gracefully than they do now, and through which there always rattled a slight fresh wind from the East, suggestive of the clattering of willow-pattern plates, wandered our young hero, in ever so clean white-flannel trousers, talented and exquisite. The old esthete, who seldom committed himself to prophecy, leant over to my friend and said: 'That young man will go far!' . . .

From those days, alas, until the early nineteen-tens I know little of Dearborn's career. He went everywhere, knew everyone — poets, painters, the first lady who wore 'bloomers', boxers, philosophers, and Channel swimmers, wasting the perfect blossom of his art on the worthy and unworthy alike. His art developed continually. His talk became something outside himself, a disembodied spirit. From a fine art it became a devouring growth, that in the end swallowed up the author of its being. He was Frankenstein, his conversation the monster . . . but a monster with charm.

To meet him was always a pleasure, to part with him the subtle torture of a thousand farewells. Perhaps Hugh himself wished to leave you, but his art forbade him. It made him linger, led you to the longed-for terminus with a hundred little anecdotes that crucified your spirit; though regarded objectively they were round, full, delicate and smooth as a ripe peach. But his conversation, monstrous ectoplasm that he materialised, wound round you like a serpent, bound you with a thousand octopus-like tentacles, released you for a moment, like a cat with a mouse, and then grabbed you again, draining your blood like a vampire.

Dull people used to think it funny to say: 'I wonder what he does when he is alone'. Others suggested (and this was to me an interesting hypothesis) that he only existed in relation to his friends and acquaintances — his conversation but the magic rope up which clambered this fabulous spinner of words, like an Indian juggler, till, ceasing to climb it, he dissolved into the void. This perhaps might account for that lingering farewell; for when it was said, Hugh too would cease to exist for a while. But he was too personal, too positive for that; and, like all people of talent, as opposed to genius, he was too dated. He had little tricks, and these tricks belied his mask and proved him to be real. That manner, for instance, of wiping his eye, on entering a room, with the corner of a beautifully-folded, slightly scented pocket-handkerchief, as one who was still laughing at some witty conversation that he had just left, did not that betray him? Was not that conversation one that he had held with Whistler, Pater or some other already legendary figure? — was it not perhaps only a forty-year-old memory? On the other hand, it may have been a signal, like a bugle call, for focusing the attention; for Hugh, a true artist, liked to have the attention of his audience, and, if slighted, if interrupted, a strange fury gleamed from those wicked little eyes.

Like all beautiful objects, Hugh never aged, only becoming a little more worn — worn with the thin wrinkled elegance of a Chinese grotesque; but his talk became always fuller and richer. He was never silly, never dull; and again, like all *objets d'art*, though mannered, he was never really affected. Yet there was about him a quality that was sometimes a little sinister, sometimes a little sad; a mystery, certainly. But from the first, being an artist myself, I guessed that his art was a hard mistress. I have said that Hugh Dearborn knew everyone —

the world, the flesh, the devil, the ass and the artist. Among his greatest friends (for his art was bilingual and surmounted all obstacles) was Henri Schmidt, the famous Parisian portrait-painter, himself a master of conversation, in an age of which he and Hugh were perhaps the only two high exponents of that art. Schmidt painted his portrait, and it is a masterpiece. Dearborn is presented to us sitting in an armchair with his beautifully crinkled grey hair, his mask wrinkled and wicked, and rather over life-size, looking straight out of the picture. All his attributes are here — ring, cigarette-case, tie-pin, cane and, so to speak, the rest of the artist's equipment. This, then, was Mr. Dearborn when silence took him . . . when he was — alone! On the exquisite mask was a smile, like that Leonardo portrayed on the face of the Gioconda, the smile which, we are told, was caused and maintained by the music of hidden flutes — and this wonderful smile of Hugh is as surely caused by hidden music, by the dead music of his own young voice, by remembered passages from talks with Whistler, Pater, and Oscar Wilde. This picture ranks high as a work of art, but its sadness is unbearable.

Hugh was, however, grateful to the painter for it, and many of his preambles ran : 'As I was saying to an old friend of mine, who I know would interest you, especially with your real interest in, and love of, modern Art (but I expect you know him already?) — a man who really is, I think, one of the most interesting and (though perhaps I ought not to say it, for he is one of my greatest friends) amusing, but I·mean really one of the most (*crescendo*) brilliant men, the painter, Henri Schmidt.' . . .

The war came and went, rolling me over, submerging me as it did most of the younger generation, filling our souls with anger, rancour and hatred, with pity and love. Mr. Dearborn, unsubmerged, began to work at other things than talk for the first time in his life. He worked hard and usefully translating various papers for the Government, being a master of languages as well as of language. The war did not break his indomitable spirit ; he never grumbled, nor did he envy the younger men in the trenches, as did so many of our over-age patriots. He behaved, in fact, like what he was — a gentleman. Though there may have been little cracks in the foundation of his spirit, he appeared more elegant and gay than ever, and even took to dancing once more. After working ten arduous hours, with very little actual conversation, in a horribly improvised office, he would dine and then dance till five o'clock in the morning. His vitality was more amazing than ever. High above the coon-born music, above the vulgar, savage and sentimental strains, one could hear the floating 'dying fall' of his voice. Never was anyone so gay, so young, for his age as Hugh Dearborn, but it must have been a strain even on that giant energy. He would go to bed at three o'clock, at four o'clock, at five o'clock each morning, in the highest spirits; but who can bear to think of him, as he slept alone and old, in his charming flat? But the next day at ten o'clock he would walk to his office, gay and beautifully dressed as ever, and alas (as journalists write about royal visits), with a word for everyone.

Soon after the war I paid a visit, in search of health, to the plaster shores of the French Riviera; and at Monte Carlo we met. Every morning at twelve o'clock, to the droning snort of a brass band, Mr. Dearborn, in white flannel trousers (oh, how long ago was that day in the garden of Walter Pater! . . .), would descend the steps on to the pink-sugar terrace. The war had altered him, and although looking no older, he was beginning to show signs of eternal youth. But under the blue skies, in this hard, trembling light, enhanced by cacti and tropic flowers, and by this sugar-icing world, his appearance took on a new quality, his voice a new tone. He became more real, his warning voice took wing, soared out to sea like the albatross in the *Ancient Mariner*, borne in, as it were, on the crest of a returning toy wave. His essentially aristocratic finish, and even the rather tired rasp, felt more than heard, of his voice, put the population of international profiteers to shame. It would be many years before these beaked harpies could produce an article with such a finish. . . . I saw and heard a good deal of Mr. Dearborn that spring, and grew to love his conversation. My mind would wander in it, as in a forest; I would lose my path, led away by strains of unfamiliar music, and then be pulled up suddenly by some well-known landmark — the name of Henri Schmidt, or of Durant the boxer — and in that forest I found many homely things that I little expected, and, though on the whole exotic, it was decidedly less so than the war, which at the time we conspired to consider a natural life — and much more restful.

In May I left Monte Carlo, and for nearly two years lost sight and sound of Mr. Dearborn.

Two years afterward I was wandering about Italy with young William Erasmus, the writer. It was his first visit to the peninsula, and he was very much on the look-out for copy, though his calm, languid air, as of one dwelling on Olympian heights, was calculated to disguise the fact. But he was always watching, listening, and peering. He had, I suspect, written several Italian travel-sketches before leaving England. He was, however, a charming companion — a companion only too appreciative and receptive, his appreciation of anything amusing or interesting that was said being made even more obvious later, and in print, than at the time. Truly we must have livened up the landscape with the necessary grotesque touch, I with my fleshy Hanoverian face and big body, William, tall and thin as a young giraffe, with the small head of some extinct animal, some kind vegetarian creature that subsisted on the nibbled tops of young palm-trees in the oases — the Giant Sloth, for example! And how often, when I saw silly little jokes of mine appearing under the guise of musical or scientific articles in the weekly papers, did I wish that his character had been true to his appearance, that he had indeed resembled more nearly the Giant Sloth instead of possessing that vast and terrible assimilative and possessive energy.

After leaving South Italy we visited Rome and Florence, from there exploring some of the smaller Tuscan towns. The country was in the full efflorescence of early May, only the vines were a little backward, the leaves and tendrils still looking like golden coils about to spring out and release their stored-up energy. Little hills vibrated into the distance like rings of smoke, and the foreground was full of blossom — not the impressionist drifts of colour that you find in northern Europe, but flowers of every colour, each one separate, stiff and geometrical in design, as those in an Italian primitive, or in one of the landscapes of the Douanier Rousseau. The days grew even hotter, and any sudden little blue wind that rose among the distant hills, and played for a moment in the flowering fields, bore an unimaginable load of scent.

One morning we reached the delightful small town of Lucca, finding our rooms in the chief hotel, which had been the palace of one of the noble families in the eighteenth century, when Lucca had been a rich and independent State. The hotel was full of large, lofty rooms with golden curls and network, the prevailing tones of the old paint being light blue or pink, the whole effect being more that of the French than the Italian eighteenth century. The rickety bedstead, shabby German tablecloth and dingy modern furniture looked very remote in these chambers built as a background for gilded beds, rich brocades and powdered wigs. The sounds of the street — shouting, snarling song and shrilling bird-chatter of the market-place — were very faint at these patrician windows, lapping at them softly like small waves. Everything in the room was bright and quiet as in a coloured glass slide. In fact, the whole hotel had an indefinable atmosphere.

The town itself is a lovely one, with gardens and avenues of chestnuts, whose heavy leaves support their glowing, torch-like flowers on the thick battlemented walls that girdle it. We examined the churches, mostly Romanesque buildings of black and white marble, exotic as zebras, of a fabulous sculptural beauty, but seemingly less connected with the present town or its inhabitants than any pagoda whose blossom-like bells drip down their honey on the Chinese gardens. Yet none of the inhabitants seemed to feel the contradiction between their lives and their back-cloth. There the cathedral stood, like a zebra in the market-place, or like an elephant supporting a howdah — they paid no attention to it. In England these things are different. Any stranger stranded under the wide arches of York station for five minutes would guess instinctively the nature of the Minster, the Bishop's Palace, and even of the Archbishop himself. There is no need to explore. Anything queer will soon be tidied up, and, as they say, 'put to rights'. But in Italy civilisations crowd together: marble churches of the twelfth century, brick-built Gothic palaces, gilded rooms with bellying balconies, and finally the iron bedstead and newspaper, universal symbols of modern culture, cling to each other, each the concrete form of a different view of life.

Thus we explored the town, talking. Then followed an early luncheon, after which Erasmus, who during his four and a half weeks in Italy had already become more Italian than the Italians, even talking the language with such an exquisite *bocca Romana* that the Romans were unable to grasp his meaning, retired for that siesta which was to him the crowning proof of belonging to a cosmopolitan *intelligentsia*. He had, however, already peered into the visitors' book for copy, but found none — not even a resident or casual Englishman in the hotel, which was, as he remarked, none the worse for that; and no doubt comforting himself with thoughts of how unspoilt was this really very sophisticated small town, he retired to rest.

The afternoon passed quickly, and the day dwindled into the dinner-hour.

For a time we walked about the brightly lit town, but the cinemas were full, and we had seen *Lucia di Lammermoor* the previous evening, so that we returned through the humming streets to our hotel. William went to bed at ten o'clock. Half an hour afterwards he called me excitedly into his room, high, gilded and full of dead air that magnified each sound. His lanky pyjama-clad figure and receptive ear were pressed ecstatically against a door — one which led into the next bedroom. 'Who can it be? Who is it? Who is it?' he whispered. And then, quite clearly, each word taking on a greater significance in this room that seemed like a gilded tomb, I heard . . . 'As I was saying only a few days ago to a man, a great friend of mine, who has, I think, really one of the most amusing and interesting personalities — a man who, I know, would delight you, with your knowledge and genuine appreciation of modern Art — a really witty, but, I mean to say, brilliant and delightful man, Henri Schmidt.' . . .

Thus the poor tired voice dragged on, trailing away into the huge silence of the palace. Hour after hour the monologue continued; sometimes the voice stumbled and there was a weak repetition. Often the stories belonged to an earlier date, the references to those long in their coffins, and through the weak tones of an old man you could catch the fresher notes of an art whose technique had not then been perfected to such a metallic pitch. His smiling, trembling voice conjured up the applauding laughter of other days, when he had possessed a more appreciative audience than latterly. This, then, was how Hugh had talked to Whistler, to Pater; this was how . . . But now at three o'clock in the morning the voice sank down to a slight moan. It haunted me, the stillness of the room. What was the mystery of that beautifully finished being, lying in that vast apartment that belonged to another age of perfected technique? Whose voices answered him in his mind? Whose laughter?

Morning came to find Erasmus charmed and inquisitive, myself uneasy, not daring to break into the darkened silence of that room. No name was in the visitors' book; no one was to be seen, no voice sounded. Luncheon came, and we watched with mute inquiry.

But at about two-thirty Mr. Dearborn came downstairs, elegant and gay; his mask was rather heavy, tired and ill at ease, though the detail of his appearance was as fresh as ever. But there was a curious thick dragging of his speech, an occasional twitching in the muscles of his mouth. He gave me a hearty but uncertain welcome, avoiding my name. He told me he had been rather ill, and had come here to be alone until he was better able to face the world — his world.

Then it was that I understood — realised the full tragedy of that vocal practice in the small hours. He had been pleading with his art, his Muse, his cruel mistress, to return to him, but the string was broken; she had spread her wings and left the tired old mask: the shell, though still perfect, was empty. The cabinet-gramophone case was complete and beautifully finished; but it was made for only one purpose, and there came no sound of the old music. Art is a hard mistress, mysterious in her intentions. As I left him, never, alas, to see him again, there was a slight return of his powers, and, looking at me, he said: 'One spring afternoon I was in the garden of Walter Pater, walking over the lawn.' . . . And then I remembered the Parnassian groves, the weeping willow-pattern trees, the exquisite and talented youth in white-flannel trousers, and the words of the old esthete: 'That young man will go far!' . . .

DUMB-ANIMAL

(For Francis)

Railway carriages provide a perfect, neutral ground for conversation. There is enough grinding and rumbling to enforce the voice being a little uplifted, and this in itself gives confidence, sureness of aim. If, for example, a public speaker begins his exordium in too quiet and diffident a key, his speech will hold no ear, brings no conviction; is doomed to failure. A competitive noise, however, will remedy such a weakness. As a rule, too, the Englishman only talks of impersonal things that neither interest him nor the person to whom he is speaking: for we are a shy, silent and especially a polite race, wherefore it is our convention that the talk must be adapted to the intelligence of the stupidest person present, and, if we are unaware of the mental calibre of anyone in the room, we must, out of good manners, presume that he is fatuous. But the anonymity of the railway carriage, once conversation is started, gives us release, makes confession, personal confession, quite easy. It is the under-the-rose intercourse of disembodied, nameless spirits floating swiftly through the air, inspired by the same ear-behind-the-grating anonymity that makes the confessing of their sins possible to Catholics. And subjects which require both thought and feeling are there approached as continental nations approach them, without embarrassment.

From York onwards the train was certainly a slow one, and the afternoon dark, for all the shimmering reflections into which the planes of the countryside had been transmuted. There had been a heavy fall of snow, and trees and telegraph-poles were hung with festoons and cobwebs in white and silver. But the windows were frosted with our breathing, and if you wiped them to look out, left a track of dribbling dirt on glove or newspaper: and all this, combined with such details as the heavy tin foot-warmers, resembling milk-cans that angry porters had hammered flat, the cigarette-smoke, the faint but nauseating smell of tunnels that never quite cleared away, the rattling of windows and doors, tended to focus the attention on the human elements rather than their surroundings. Up in the roof a star of yellow gaslight blossomed like a cherished plant beneath an inverted and sweating bell-glass. To this star our eyes now and again rolled upwards in despair. In every station the red-nosed porters shouted to keep themselves warm, threw their loads heavily, and then, still cold, threshed their arms together.

After a time, however, a pleasant conversation sprang up. The cheerful young doctor at my elbow took off his pince-nez, rattled a paper by his side, lit a cigarette and began to talk. Soon we were all of us exchanging intimate memories of childhood. The direction veered from time to time towards a semi-scientific discussion of the dawn of memory or the difference between the animal-mind and the child-mind. The glum, yellow-faced man, with the trembling red fingers, opposite me, turned out to be a famous, now fever-stricken big-game hunter, though I have by this time forgotten his name. He told us of the pygmy-race he had discovered, and of its primitive beliefs. Perhaps the need to worship differentiated man from the other animals. Once, he told us, he had lived for several years in Central Africa, inhabiting a two-storeyed house of whitened mud, built round a large central courtyard. All the little iron-barred windows, high up in the walls, gave on to this enclosure, for it was not safe to have them facing outward. One evening a huge and ferocious man-ape was captured and brought in from the great forest many miles away. The span of its hideous, hairy arms was something that even he had not been prepared for, accustomed as he was to these forest-giants. It was, I do not remember why, impracticable to kill the creature that night, and accordingly it was let loose in the courtyard, for there it could do no harm. At first it grimaced horribly, and drummed in a martial way upon its chest; vain summons to its distant wives — though when darkness fell it became quiet. But in the middle of the night the hunter was woken up. He did not know what had wakened him, but he experienced a sensation that something was happening, something curious and a little disturbing. He had been dreaming of an enormous cathedral, where people were praying for salvation under vast arches, sprinkled over with little lights, and had woken suddenly. He looked round his room. Green, tropical moonlight was splashing the floor, lay on it in pools, like water. He crept to the window, for an odd, low monotonous sound — did it remind him of chanting, he wondered? — was wafted therefrom.

He looked through the thick bars. The moon was round and high in the heavens, and just under him, in the brilliant, jade-green arena of the moonlit courtyard, was the gigantic, shaggy, heavy-shouldered form of the ape, engaged in a sad, most moving ritual, bowing low to the moon, walking backward before it, prostrating himself on hands and feet, and making the deep but quiet, never-ending rhythmic mumble that had woken him. . . . And so this dull, shaking little man opposite, one realised, had witnessed a unique spectacle, the very dawn of religion.

.   .   .   .   .

Skating lightly over that quicksand for conversation, the wisdom and long-memoried gratitude of elephants, once more we reverted to children. At what age, we wondered, does the child begin to surround the central fact of being, of existing, with little clusters of things felt and seen, pleasant and unpleasant? At what age does the memory, once a temporary affair of days and weeks, apply itself to years, and remain unimpaired through decades? The nose, of course, rather than eye or ear, is guide to the past. Memories of each long summer and winter come back borne on a stream of smell, of flowers in a garden, warm scents of box and rosemary, stocks, carnations or wallflowers, of bread being baked or jams being made, of bonfires blazing in the dull late autumn air, of paint and varnish and a thousand other things. My first memory, I thought, was of my nurse and sister under a tree covered with golden apricots — but where it was has always baffled me. But at what age do emotions first remain within our consciousness, somebody inquired? I certainly remember, I said, the inability to express my thoughts in words, a very early memory that must be: yet there are those who maintain that no thought is possible without the appropriate words to clothe it, that no colour is seen by us for which we have not a name! There had been some paltry, infantile crime of which I had been accused falsely, and could not, for want of words, make clear my innocence. Only the blind faith of children in their elders made me feel secure. Of course they would under-

stand : and their failure to do so overturned my whole childish
world, shook my being to its foundation. God had tumbled
out of the star-spangled heaven in which I had placed him.

The young doctor snapped his pince-nez into a case, and
said he would tell us a very youthful experience of his own.
He was getting on now, he was thankful to say, quite well,
had a satisfactory practice ('This kind of weather,' he added,
laughing, 'helps us a lot, you know'), but in the past his dislike
— no, his horror — of animals, especially dogs, had hindered
him. There were a great many old ladies, bath-chair and
armchair old ladies, in the seaside town from which he was
travelling (indeed, they were the chief source of local medical
income there), and they all owned two or more dogs. Naturally,
if they saw him wince at the advances of their pets, they
classified him at once as an 'odd sort of man'. It did not
matter so much with cats, but every man should love dogs.
Well, latterly he had contrived to simulate a liking for them,
and he hoped his lapses had been forgotten. But the horror,
actually, still remained. It had been during his whole life a
source of pain and injury to him, and was founded on a
particular incident that had occurred in childhood.

It was impossible to be sure at what age it had taken place
— three or four, though, he supposed : between the ages of
three and four. He knew that he looked strong enough now,
but we must imagine a delicate little boy, left in charge of a
nurse in a small seaside village, a collection of a few square,
red-brick houses with blue-slate roofs, on the East Coast. His
parents had bought a cottage there, in which to spend the
summer months ; had bought it, probably, for his sake, since
he was weakly and an only child, and they were nervous about
his health. Yet this, of course, he was too young at the time
to understand. During the winter, then, he was left alone :
quite alone there with his Nurse, who, though of rustic origin,
was a very reliable, highly trained young woman. She cooked
all his food herself, so frightened was she of its possible con-
tamination, and had a real hospital horror — quite rightly —
of dirt and germs. In consequence she would never allow him
to play with the other children of the village, who were rather
squalid and unkempt. He supposed really that his Nurse had
been very fond of him, but she was a thoroughly sensible
woman, and believed in her modern, educated way that it was

wrong to show sentiment, dangerous to show affection, to children. Moreover, his parents, in their kindness and concern for him, exercised a similar control. It is likely that it pained them very much to leave him, and not to be able to see him more often. But this again was beyond his comprehension. To beings as young as he was then, life appears in its most simplified form: if people wanted you to be with them, you were with them. And they never allowed themselves to show any sorrow at parting from him, for the Nurse said that one ought to be very careful not to upset children, and as a child he had been very easily upset.

His first impression, thus, was one of loneliness, and, much worse, of being unwanted; a feeling that undermines existence, and, with the feeble, in the very old or very young, can make for death. The background against which these sensations were to be placed was eroded, grey, high, gloomy cliffs and a winter sea. The cliffs were not high enough to be imposing, but only to be forbidding, and their erosion was a matter of feeling. You knew instinctively that they were stricken and retiring bulwarks. The sea, on the other hand, imparted an overwhelming and savage sense of power, as the long grey battering-rams rolled on towards you, breaking on the nearer rocks into explosions of white, dying wings.

We must picture, too, a stretch of tawny sand, along which two figures promenade: the pale, nervous little boy; the Nurse, straight, tall and unsentimental as a young tree. And, to finish off the scene, we must conjure up the image of a few stray dogs, their barks and howlings lost in the muffled thunder of the sea, and the feel of an intensely cold wind that tears the flesh of face and neck with its numbing iron beak. Sea air was good for him.

Here was the dawning of his memory, the first certain thing he could draw out of the universal darkness that had preceded him. He could not be absolutely certain of his age . . . but he could see the dogs now. They seemed an Ishmael race, ownerless and outcast. And among them, especially, he remembered his first friend. He had loved it; but, regarded from an unprejudiced angle, doubtless it would have appeared a horrible, cringing, mangy little cur of a dog, very dirty and uncared-for. He could see it now though, spinning round after its tail like a whiting, curled up. Searching its tail, he imagined now, for fleas. A toffee-coloured dog, with long, sharp ears and deep yellow-brown eyes. Its stomach was fawn-coloured, and it rather resembled an ill-bred fox-hound. In spite of its ugliness, however, it had the alluring grace of all young animals.

Actually, he had not taken to this dog in the first place. But it had been so patient in its show of affection for him, had so obviously adopted him, that he had grown to love it. It waited for him every morning on the sands, jumped up and kissed his face, played with him, and, in fact, was a companion. Indeed this daily meeting with the mongrel became, secretly, the event of his day, and if by any chance it was too wet for him to be taken out, he was most unhappy, as he thought of the dog, soaked through, waiting by the seashore. But this he kept to himself, for grown-up people, he had already discovered, were intent on killing every pleasure.

This state of affairs lasted some time, and the Nurse paid little attention. But one day, quite suddenly, she realised how dirty, how filthily dirty, the dog was. Perhaps she had not noticed it attentively before, for she would often stand gazing at the sea, while her ward ran and played near at hand behind her on the beach. Of what use, she must have demanded of herself, were all her care and cleanliness, her sterilisings and boilings and washings, if the child behaved in this way behind her back? A strange, mangy cur of course harboured innumerable germs, was no fit companion for a delicate child. Having driven the dog off with the threat of a stick, she seized the boy by the hand, shook him, and dragged him home.

'Master Humphrey,' she cried, 'you ought to be ashamed of yourself in your nice clean suit, playing with that little wretch, so dirty and unhealthy-like. If you lets him jump up at you like that tomorrow, I'll kill the little beast, I will.'

He wondered how his Nurse, whom he knew to be fond of animals, could be so suddenly cruel. And yet he knew that she was direct, a woman of her word. He believed her. What was he to do? . . . If the dog came near him, she would kill it, then.

A deep sense of gloom and tragedy enveloped the small boy. If only it would rain tomorrow, so that he might put off his decision. . . . For at any cost he must save his friend from this fate, steel himself to be brutal if necessary. All night long in his dreams, the dreadful situation presented itself: and his courage failed him.

The next morning dawned, a clear winter morning, with a thin, false blue canopy spread over all this bareness. In the clean, very ordinary light, he was confident that so terrible a thing could not be true; this vast cloud of sorrow which had blown up over him. He dreaded the beach, cried a little as he approached it. The Nurse wondered to herself whether he was not well — he had seemed restless all night — and promised aloud to give him a dose that evening.

There, sure enough, was the dog, waiting for him, very alert and joyful, for it was sufficiently inured to rebuffs not to have taken the Nurse's threat with her stick very seriously the previous morning. Now, the boy realised, before his Nurse saw him, was his chance to save his loved comrade: and taking up pebble after pebble, he threw it with all his strength at the dog.

At first the mongrel thought this was only in play, and skipped and leapt gaily to one side: at the third or fourth stone, it stopped, cringed away, making itself small. Then it gave a howl of pain, and was sure: slunk away into pariahdom, its tail between its legs, ever and again looking round, the orange-brown eyes full of a mute but immeasurable reproach, at this friend who had encouraged and then denied it. The pebbles still followed the cur, as it crept and cringed away, pleading: for the boy stood there, intent on saving this only friend, throwing stone after stone, while tears streamed down his face.

The Nurse, who had been watching the fierce play of the waves, had completely forgotten about the dog of yesterday. All at once, she looked round and saw what was happening. 'Oh, you horrid little boy, you,' she exclaimed, smacking his hand very hard. 'Oh, you horrid little cruel monkey, torturing dumb animals,' and took him home.

He had been afraid of animals ever since. He was sure that was what it was.

·   ·   ·   ·   ·

The train roared through a tunnel, gave a bump. We collected our coats and papers, called for porters and were lost, disembodied again under the vast arches of foggy darkness, lit up, as it seemed, by the tinsel splinters of huge circus lamps.

THE GLOW-WORM

(For L. D.)

When the war broke out in 1939, Sebastian Corble — *of course* you know the name — was nearly forty. At first sight he still kept a look of youth, almost of being boyish; except that he seemed too large, just as a child-impersonator on the stage often succeeds in giving an impression of being childish, but in an over-life-size manner. His hair, though a little thinner than in Oxford days, still retained a thick golden gloss as, in rather tattered array, aureole-like, it encircled his round cranium. Each individual hair, each tooth, each pore, seemed to claim more value in the whole presentation of his appearance than formerly; that was all. He was pale, and this lack of colour imparted to him, if the light came strong enough and from the right direction, a certain aspect of nobility, an air almost of that holy illumination to be found in the transparent countenances of the boyish saints depicted in late nineteenth-century church windows: but from this lack of humanity, his charm — his all-pervading, rather rancid charm — rescued him.

In every succeeding generation, a journalist makes a substantial fortune out of certain subjects: gardens, fashionable chit-chat, spiritualism; but who would ever have imagined that in a wicked age — for, to the good people of today, it seems as though any age in which the world was not dedicated to the high mission of destruction and massacre must have been a wicked age, lacking in democratic ideals — a fortune could have been made by the skilful exploitation of mere goodness and domesticity? This, then, had been Sebastian's discovery. To him it had been left to find out and explain that religion could be 'fun', and eternity, 'cosy'. He could make his million readers feel at home in Heaven. A more masculine Mrs. Beeton, he would sometimes begin an article by describing the 'divine' new curtains in his bedroom, and end with an account of his child, Little Tessa, talking to him of God. But he did not belong to the Mrs. Winniver School, he could be strong as well as good. Strength, rather than sour whimsy, tempered so much sweetness, and he was adept at scenting-out and denouncing moral dangers. Such authors as D. H. Lawrence and James Joyce he had flogged through his daily, and flayed in his weekly, columns. The peroration of his famous Sunday article denouncing Joyce's *Ulysses* is still remembered by many who have never read the book: 'And after that I had climbed a little hill to gaze into the eyes of God's Primroses, I rested, but still the foul miasma of that book pursued me, until I cried aloud, "Pshah! Who will sweeten my nostrils with an ounce of civet?" . . . And a small sweet voice behind me said, "I will, Daddy!" . . . And there behind me, in the sunshine of that spring day, stood Little Tessa. Rather would I that she quaffed the hemlock cup than that one day she should read another such book if another such book there should be!'

Yet sweetness always followed such outbursts of strength, and, on Sundays especially, a great army of admirers turned to him for comfort; and oh, the comfort, pressed down and of full measure, which they received! Round them he distilled the sweetness of his own home. Of difficult domestic material, even, — of his wife's telling him not to be silly or of Tessa having German measles — he was able to make some of his most appealing articles. He was never ashamed of sentimentality, and when a reader read one word, he knew what the next would be. To give a single instance, in no way remarkable, I recall a 'splash' headline of 'Wot's Wong? by Sebastian Corble'; a description of how Little Tessa tottered up to him on her 'baby feet', and, 'gazing up into his eyes', 'hissed out' — no, I am not giving you the right counter, I mean 'lisped pleadingly' — '"Daddy, wot's wong?"', while a linnet flew in at the window, and trilled its way backwards and forwards over their heads as if in an effort to comfort them.

And something *was* wrong: for, good in the main as Sebastian found both this world and the next, a sense of discouragement, an inevitable feeling of disappointment, would sometimes assail him. For example, his fellow-writers were often unappreciative, seemed to perceive the beauty of his writing no more than the peculiar virtue of his life. Again, Margaret, his wife, whom he really adored, was too retiring, even threatened to leave him if he brought her into an article.

She would not play any of the parts he would have liked to assign to her, while Little Tessa — to be frank — trod the boards too heavily. . . . But then Tessa, everybody said, was 'just like her father'.

Thus both father and daughter lived, you might almost say battled, for publicity. She had become nearly as popular as he was, yet he dared not stop it, for in a sense they were complementary and, also, there were the funds she brought in to be considered. Her vogue was, all the same, fantastic. Every autumn, a calendar, specially illustrated, was on sale for the New Year; reluctantly, no doubt, edited and selected by her father, it contained a gem, in the form of a question, for every day in the week: Jan. 1 : '*Why is the snow white, Daddy?*' Jan. 2 : '*Why did God choose white, Daddy?*' Jan. 3 : '*Is it because white is good, Daddy?*', and so on, seasonally, until the end of the year. . . . Admiration grew, sales mounted. Her adherents founded 'The Tiny Tessa Tub' (she could not say 'Club', her father had written) and thousands of children who modelled themselves on her wore a special button, with a photograph of her enamelled upon it, in the buttonholes of their coats.

Soon she would be six. . . . 'Nasty little publicity-hound!' her father reflected to himself in an access of irritation. It really was time for her to give up all that baby-business, and be content to merge decorously into his background. But such, plainly, was not her intention. . . . And she was as clever as she was good. Often she sent for representatives of the Press on her own initiative (already she could use the telephone as well as if she were twenty!); and if he were to become too repressive, she was quite capable of summoning interviewers, and with those great, welling eyes of hers of blurting out to them, 'You don't think my Daddy's jealous! It's a wicked "fought".' (That would be a nice sentiment to have to record on the calendar for 1939.) . . . Of course, he was devoted to the little thing (he must be, he knew): but sometimes he wondered in his heart whether he really cared much for children. His wife would say, 'Don't be irritable with her, Basty; she's too much *like you*, that's all it is.' And then, in her turn, she would warn the little girl, 'Now, Tessa! I've told you. Don't irritate Daddy on purpose. . . . And I've said before, you're too young to be photographed for the *Daily Mirror*! And don't whine!'

He knew that, for all his goodness, he *was* irritable. The strain of writing, the strain of money-making, the strain of always being good, had in time caused him to be afflicted with insomnia. His own goodness, as it were, kept him awake at night. He found it difficult to endure the ridicule of the music-halls, as well as that of the comic papers — for, in addition to being a very popular writer, his renowned virtue had made him a very popular joke (a combination that could only exist in this country). But he did not allow such mockery to deflect him from the straight and narrow path. Virtue still offered him a very glittering reward. Think of those articles, those great articles that rolled away into infinity! The very titles of some of them come back to me: 'I Believe in the Old Stories', 'Saints Have Haloes', 'Don't Insure Your Life, Insure Your After-Life!', 'Cleanse the Stables!', 'Who's Who in Heaven?' Politicians praised him and sought his advice: but somehow, his popularity survived their fleeting shadows. The immense esteem in which he was held extended its bounds to the United States, the citizens of which adopted with fury the new cult. Tessa, too, remained more than a good second. . . . It was gratifying. . . . Yet, as he would have phrased it, the maggot bitterness still dwelt in the heart of the rose. For some people — some poor, lost, unregenerate and ungenerous souls — laughed at him in a disagreeable way: he knew it. In a news-film, for example, he had been shown making a speech at the opening of 'The Tiny Tessa Garden of Friendship' on the roof of one of the great London stores, and the public had laughed till the words were inaudible.

Then war came — and with it that great advance of moral values everywhere in Great Britain that war is always said to bring us. The values of peace-time were precisely reversed. The Common Man, recognised as arbiter, now in his generosity did not denounce the political leaders and incompetent club-room soldiers who had betrayed the men and women of two generations, but instead turned fiercely on the artists and writers of the last twenty years who had given that period its chief claim to distinction. Anything that helped us to kill was good, and Sebastian's goodness helped the killing, and so was better. His former popularity became an all-devouring rage. And many writers in the Press openly gave expression to an opinion that countless readers echoed: 'If only we could have Sebastian

Corble or Our Gracie as Prime Minister, the War would soon be over!'

He worked day and night. The Government, observing his vast influence with public opinion, allowed him special facilities for directing it. . . . Scarcely ever was he at home in Hampstead now. One night he would spend in the Maginot Line ('impregnable as the front line of Heaven', he wrote), the second flying over the lines, the third on board a submarine, the fourth in a tank, the fifth on a destroyer in the North Sea, the sixth in the 'Clipper' *en route* for a week's lecturing in the United States. He was sent on picnics with soldiers and sailors and airmen and munition workers, he was allowed to attend Divine Service in the Desert during the Libyan War, he flew to Malta and back to collect money for Spitfires. He and War Publicity illumined each other equally. But though the aid he rendered was invaluable, he wore himself to a shadow, spent himself utterly in the cause. Fortunately, the good, the real good, he was doing gave him new strength (and think of the money he was earning, even if half of it went to the making of the war which was making him!). 'You're a Saint', people used to say to him, and he was able to feel that there was a grain of truth in their praise.

There *was* something saintly about him now, and the look of a saint, which he had always a little possessed, had greatly developed. And he was much less irritable and nervous, though he missed dreadfully his home. . . . At last, tired out but happy, in September 1940 — just a few days before the first intensive bombing of London began —, he went home for a week of rest, a week of utter peace.

. . . . .

Tessa looked forward to his home-coming even more than did Margaret, for, with the outbreak of war, she had swung a little into the background. She was nearly eight now, and had been very excited ever since she had heard the news. She smelt publicity again, her mother thought. It was so bad for her — and she prevented the child from telephoning to editors, to tell them that 'Daddy was on his way home', or, as she put it to her mother, 'to give the Boss the low-down'. . . . She was allowed to stay up for dinner, an unusual treat, the night he arrived.

Everyone had always noticed how very observant Tessa

was. 'So wonderful of a little thing like that to see everything', her parents' friends used to remark, with a secret sense of unease, and would then add, with a conscious and shameful lack of frankness, 'But for all that, she's a thorough child; dear Little Tessa!' . . . After being fairly quiet throughout the meal until she had finally consumed the sweet, an ice-cream of which she was over-fond, she then proceeded to bounce up and down on her chair, on a new method she had discovered, until the room shook. Sebastian expelled all feelings of irritation and radiated love towards her; also on a new method he had discovered. He comforted himself, moreover, with the reflection that, if *he* were to dance about like that immediately after dinner, he would feel sick, very sick — but that was being uncharitable, he must be ever on the watch. '*Tes-sa, dar-ling!*' he called lovingly to her, dwelling on each syllable. . . . For a few moments she sat in silence, motionless, watching him — with suspicion, you might have thought, as if she imagined he was trying to gain some advantage over her —, and then her restraint broke down, and suddenly, angrily, she burst out with:

'Daddy, what's that funny light round your forehead?'

For a moment her father's mood changed. 'Silly little beast!' he reflected uncharitably, in a spasm of annoyance, 'indulging in stupid fancies!' He said nothing, however: but, as the words passed through his mind, Tessa added, in a voice that showed traces of relief:

'It's gone now, Daddy!'

Margaret regarded her daughter with curiosity. It was evident to her that she *had* seen something, which herself had missed.

'I didn't see anything, Tessa,' she said. 'What do you mean?'

But Tessa jumped down from her chair and ran up to the nursery without answering. When her mother later went to say good-night, she found the child looking earnestly at her own head in the mirror.

.   .   .   .   .

The next day, Sebastian was busy. It was a Thursday, and he had to work on an article for the *Sunday Debacle*. It was one of the best, literally the *best*, he had ever written. But all the time, even while he was composing it, Tessa's strange remark had hovered in his consciousness, behind every word and every thought. Probably the child had meant nothing; but it was odd. . . . And an unusual sense of contentment, of being at one with Nature and the Universe, seized upon him; a feeling of inner peace and satisfaction, as though he had been engaged in utter fulfilment, physical as well as spiritual, not so much after the manner of a great painter executing a great picture, as of a peacock expanding its scintillant and jewelled tail, or a swan exchanging the ruffled beige of cygnetcy for its adult and undying white.

After tea, Tessa continued to eye him at intervals with a singular persistence: until her mother, misinterpreting the effect upon Sebastian (for this evening her intent gaze in no way troubled him), sent her to bed. She protested, but it was long past bed-time already, and she had only been allowed down to dinner last night on her solemn promise not to expect such a treat again. So she was led upstairs, moaning, 'But I want to see Daddy when it's dark'.

Margaret and Sebastian went to bed early too that night, and in his prayers he made a special recommendation for notice and mercy on behalf of his 'darling child, Little Tessa'.

· · · · ·

When they were called the following morning, the sunshine seemed to fall with peculiar strength upon the pillows. Before long, Margaret had to ask Sebastian to pull the blind down, so that the light did not catch her full in the eyes. Then they had breakfast in bed, and though himself did not so much notice the brightness of which she several times complained, somehow he could not succeed in arranging the blind to suit her. As soon as he had jumped out of bed, she would — almost before he had reached the window — cry, 'That's better!' but the moment he got back into bed she would declare that the light was dazzling her again. . . . A year ago, all this jumping in and out of bed at a woman's caprice would have irritated him: but not so now. He was master of himself. . . . He openèd a letter. It proved to be from an admirer, and began, 'You're a Saint, a *real* Saint!' . . . At this moment a suspicion, bordering upon a certainty, of the immense and impossible truth entered his brain.

It grew dark about eight o'clock that evening and, before dinner, he had a bath and changed. And it was while he was brushing his hair, in the dusk, in front of a looking-glass, that he first noticed the faint, bluish-white radiance spreading after the fashion of a diadem or crown about his forehead. . . . He recognised it at once : a halo, it *was* a halo, plain, without the red bars to it one sometimes sees in church windows. (He was glad of that, he did not wish to be ostentatious.) His spontaneous feelings were those of gratification rather than of surprise, together — and this was odd — with a wish to hide his new spiritual distinction from his wife. . . . No, he had to admit it, he did *not* want her to see it — at any rate, not yet ! So he had better avoid Tessa, who would be sure to spot it at once. . . . Otherwise, he was pleased. After all, it constituted an award from the highest authority. And it would aid his popularity and circulation. (In his mind's eye, he could see the enormous placards round the tops of the buses, 'Corble, The Man With Halo, Writes For The Daily Dustbin Only'.)

At dinner he turned up all the lights in the room so that his new nimbus should not be observed. Tessa was upstairs — he felt too tired, he said, to climb to say good-night to her — and Margaret noticed nothing unusual about him. The evening passed quietly and pleasantly enough, and they went to bed early. . . . Almost before Margaret's head touched the pillow she fell asleep. But Sebastian, on the other hand, found it unusually difficult to relax. The light from his head kept getting into his eyes. Even if he shut them, he could still perceive the glow. Really, it was blinding now ! . . . And the more patient he grew, the more careful not to become flustered or angry at this unnecessary waste of candle-power, and of the time he so urgently needed for repose, the stronger grew his aureole in intensity, a positive dazzle. . . . What a blessing, he reflected, that Margaret could not see it — and then, all at once, as he experienced a contradictory spasm of annoyance because she had not beheld, or *would not* behold, it (a wilful manifestation of a sort of spiritual blindness that afflicted her), the light faded a little of itself, and slumber, in consequence, engulfed him.

.   .   .   .   .

Though he was on holiday he devoted the next morning, Saturday, to seeing his editor and to good works. He lunched at his club, and then visited old friends in the East End, insisting on reading to them his favourite extracts from *The*

Stones of Venice, and from a new book by the head of the Foreign Office, entitled *The Trail of the Hun.* He wound up with 'a few little things of my own'. He did not return home until after dark (they were going to have supper late that night). And as he walked back from the Tube station, once or twice he heard an angry, brusque voice calling from the darkness, 'Keep that light down, man, can't you?' or 'Don't flash it about like that, or you'll find yourself somewhere you don't expect. Didn't you hear the sirens?'

Tessa was already in bed, and her father again alleged that he was too tired to go upstairs and say good-night to her. She was anxious to see him, it appeared. And Margaret pleaded for her:

'After all, Basty,' she said, 'the child is devoted to you. You know she is, and you oughtn't to neglect her.'

But he would not give way. The doctors had told him not to exert himself or do anything that was against his inclinations.

Still Margaret noticed no change in him, and they enjoyed a quiet evening until they had just finished supper, when the bombs of the first great night attack began to rain down on London. He must write about it at once for the New York paper. ('Hot News from Sebastian Corble', he could already picture the caption, splashed across the page.) What did danger matter, after all, he asked himself, and slipped into the garden, alone, for Margaret preferred to stop indoors. He repressed his annoyance as he tumbled over a stone toadstool with a tin gnome sitting on it, and had soon reached the little terrace at the end. Once there, he forgot everything else in the interest and horror of the scene below.

About a quarter of an hour later, the telephone bell rang in the house. Margaret answered it. A voice said:

'Is that you, Mrs. Corble? This is North Hampstead Police Station. We are informed that someone is signalling from your garden, but we know you too well to suppose that you would permit any foreigners about the place. You don't think, perhaps, as Miss Tessa 'as got hout and is being mischievous with a light?'

Margaret promised to make inquiries, and then to speak to them again in a few minutes' time. But no sooner had she put the receiver down than she heard an urgent knocking at the door. She opened it, and a very angry and officious air-raid warden informed her that he had seen lights floating in the garden.

'There's too much of that sort of thing going on,' he added. 'Shooting's too good for 'em.'

She contrived to calm the new-comer by telling him that she had already promised to investigate the matter for the police, and that her husband, Sebastian Corble, was there, and together they would search the place thoroughly.

'Oh, I didn't know it was Mrs. *Sebastian* Corble to whom I have the honour of speaking,' the warden answered. 'I'm a great admirer of your husband's. There's real *goodness* for you, and *guts* too' : and he left, mollified.

Sebastian's virtue had its uses, his wife thought, as she shut the door, but, all the same, life was growing insupportable with all these silly scares. Was it likely that anyone could get into the garden and signal? . . . But she had better tell Sebastian, so she went out to join him. . . . It was certainly mysterious that *two* complaints should have been received. What *could* be the explanation; just hysteria, she wondered? . . . Then, as her eyes grew accustomed to the darkness, she understood! Sebastian's halo was visible, its pale yet scintillant radiation coming and going like that of a firefly.

But the effect of it upon her was indeed unexpected. Perhaps the noise of the bombing had unnerved her tonight, though she had not been aware of it, for she laughed out loud, and could not stop, laughed all the more as, when this ribald sound asserted itself beneath all the banging from earth and sky, she watched the aureole of her husband's sainthood and suffering glow yet more brightly.

Weakly, nearly crying, she said to him, 'Basty, *please* go inside, or you'll be fined!' . . . With a gentle air of reproach and dignity, he asked her why she laughed, and she told him that the police and the A.R.P. authorities thought they had caught a foreign spy signalling from the garden. 'And now,' she added, 'I must go into the house too, and tell them what I've found. "It's only my husband's new halo, Inspector."'

· · · · ·

Neither of them slept well that night. In the morning he said to her apologetically :

'Darling, I'm afraid all that dreadful bombing kept you awake last night?'

'No, Sebastian,' she answered, 'I didn't mind the noise, but your halo kept getting in.my eyes. I can't share my bed with a Saint; that's all there is to it!'

They had a quarrel about this — both of them were feeling rather on edge no doubt — and his radiance temporarily faded.

He looked in the glass before leaving the house, and decided that in the day-time it only slightly accentuated his usual pallor, and a certain air of distinction which he hoped he had always possessed. Of course, if he put his head back on a cushion, for instance, the light played upon it, but that merely resembled the 'shaft of sunlight' which, in a romantic novel, always falls upon the hero's face as he is saying good-bye. . . . No, it was in the evenings that it was a nuisance.

He did not talk much to Margaret, for he wrote all day in his room, and only saw her at luncheon, when she was engaged in keeping Tessa's mind occupied. At seven he had to address a meeting of the Golders Green Branch of the Tiny Tessa Tub. . . . Usually he walked about bare-headed, but tonight, without Margaret seeing him do it — for he did not wish to provoke another of those very trying hysterical scenes, they must be so bad for her — he encircled his head with the two regulation thicknesses of tissue-paper. That should prevent his being stopped, or threatened with a summons: people would just imagine that his cap was too big for him and he was trying to make it fit. . . . In the brightly lighted hall nothing would show. . . . So he could take the whole thing off in the cloak-room and leave it there until after the meeting.

Alas, on the return journey, after the meeting, he found that his attempts to comply with the regulations had been of no avail. Men could not understand. For them, a halo was merely a reprehensible light, to be treated with hard words and fury. The old complaints sounded from the darkness. 'Switch it out, man, can't you?' 'I'll summon yer for this, young feller, if yer don't alter yer wise. I'll tike yer nime and address.' 'Wot yer think yer doing? A blarsted light'ouse, are yer?' . . . And, which made the scene the more distressing, at each undeserved rebuke, the light of its own accord grew stronger.

No peace anywhere! But one must be good and meek and gentle. He took off his coat in the darkness and covered his head with it. Thus he managed to reach home without being arrested.

He could not, when he arrived, avoid going to say good-night to Tessa, for, as well as its being Sunday, they were sending her away tomorrow to avoid the bombing. . . . She had been unusually reserved the whole day, but now she threw her arms round her father and said simply, sleepily:

'Good-night, Daddy, I'm a glow-worm too!'

Her father looked at her, but she must have fancied herself into the statement. It would be most unfair if the daughter — even of such a father — were to receive the same award. He could see no sign of it, not a ray.

.   .   .   .   .

That night, alone in the spare bedroom, he thought things out. . . . A Saint has no place for earthly ties, he decided. Like Saints of Old — was it St. Andrew, in the hymn? — he must leave home and kindred. He made no charges, no allegations of want of faith, never even reproached Margaret, but the next morning he left to join the Fleet and gather material for a new and stirring article. He arrived just in time for the famous Battle of the Bombs, as the Press called it — the only journalist present. It was the first scoop of a Saint. But the Admiral never discovered that it was the trail of a halo that, by indicating the position of the ships, was responsible for so much damage. In whatever direction Sebastian moved, he was sure to be followed by an explosion and a cry, 'By Jove, that was a narrow squeak!'

Always, he was in the thick of things. Even if he went on a lecture tour, every town at which he stopped the night would be raided, and this, in turn, would provide him with the material for a splendid and heartening article the next day. (To protect himself against the police, he had now adopted a steel helmet with a special lining of cotton-wool. It appeared to be impervious. But often, when he was sure of being alone, its weight would induce him to take it off for a moment.) His rhetoric was unmatched, and he became the highest-paid journalist in the country. Little Tessa was hopelessly out-classed.

'He can't always escape like that,' people used to say as they read of his adventures. 'One day the enemy will bag him!' But they never did. For, in the end, peace came, and with it the great deterioration of moral values which is always said to manifest itself in a period when killing again becomes a sin. In time — in a very, very short time — the public changed its allegiance and went whoring after new gods. The Common Man — still, of course, arbiter of taste — no longer read Sebastian Corble's strong stuff on the evils of peace, but threw him, together with Shakespeare, on the scrap-heap, and turned with relief to the life-stories of the new Hollywood favourites. Before long, a bitter note crept into Sebastian's denunciations: they grew still more strong, and, in these degenerate days of which I write, as they grew stronger the readers became fewer. And, as the note of bitterness deepened, so did the radiance fade, until Sebastian Corble was mere man again.

HIS SHIP COMES HOME

ARTHUR BERTRAM, or not to deprive his personality of its full efflorescence we should perhaps record in their entirety the names Arthur Otho Augustus, had for many years enjoyed that distinction implied in being what is sometimes referred to in the obituary notices of fashionable journals as 'a familiar figure about London'; and, for his proper appreciation, it is necessary to consider what this to him so particularly appropriate journalistic phrase is intended to convey. Surely not merely that he spent his life wandering through the various streets, metropolitan or suburban, of our island-capital? Nor, to the initiate, would it suggest for a moment that his demeanour was marked by any peculiarity that would make him the centre of a vulgar attention, prompting children to cry out or point a finger, as, to give an instance, was noticeable in the behaviour of that retired General whose wont it was for many years to stroll down Piccadilly neighing like a horse. Idiosyncrasies of this kind are apt to make their owners too conspicuous, and the rather unconventional conduct of this latter gentleman did focus a part of the public attention upon him — so much, in fact, that when finally he attacked a hay-cart passing down the street in front of his military club, in order, as he said, to find forage for himself, he was, as we think, erroneously deprived of his personal liberty. Injustice is sometimes more visible to children than to those better able to express their feelings, and, even at that early age, it seemed to us that the poor General, as a soldier, a cavalryman even, who had mixed more with horses than with men, and indeed always made a point of neighing himself rather than speaking, had in reality some claim to that distinction which he boasted; while, for the rest, there can be no doubt that he set a fine example to his fellow-clubmen, on whose part a gradual awakening to the fact that they, too, had practically become horses, could but add to the amenities of our social life. But no obsession, such as this, separated Arthur Bertram from his kind. He was much more human than horse-like. His behaviour, on the contrary, was noticeable for its extreme correctness; so that the phrase we are discussing must be taken not to mean that he paraded any of the many streets in the town, but as indicative of the fact that he knew in what streets to walk, there to be observed by fellow-readers of the fashionable journals. Summed up, then, it implies the possession of enough leisure to display in the correctly chosen place characteristics sufficiently, but not too, personal to be noticed by others of equal leisure but less individuality. Thus a seemingly hollow little phrase can, like a cipher, convey an exterior, an outlook, a way of life almost, to those for whom it is intended.

Yet it was only as a middle-aged man that Bertram's ugliness, enhanced by a highly stylised manner of dressing, became so intense as to shed upon him a certain lustre. When he was young, it was his companion whose smile crowned him with a reflected glory, like the Aurora Borealis that plays round the Northern skies, giving him more interest even than that possessed by the original. From the beginning of his life as a man of fashion, he made it his rule always to be seen in the company of the Woman-of-the-Moment, and, if possible, to be in love with her. He had one remarkable gift in that he could foretell the advent of fame six months before it blazed up. This gave him time to make friends. His instinct in this matter was really unusual. He was seen, first with the leading professional beauty of Marlborough House days, then with the wife of the rising playwright, the most famous actress of the year, or the sister of an artist whose renown had at this moment reached its zenith. The discrimination he showed in, so to speak, 'spotting the winner', gave a flattering quality to his attentions, which no doubt helped him to other conquests. His affection became the equivalent of a bestowal of a public laurel-wreath upon the lady, or upon her brother, or husband — a halo of which Arthur kept just a chip, sufficient to illumine himself, as commission. It helped him, too, with other women to be seen in the company of some famous person: to those who did not know him he seemed a distinguished, almost a brilliant, figure.

But the world hinted that Bertram occasionally reaped other, baser, more material rewards than the acquisition of fame, or requited love, from those connections — or should one write transactions? — that the laurels turned to gold within

the hands of this alchemist; that he was not above writing to
the 'Woman-of-the-Moment', informing her, rather needlessly,
of his poverty, in letters which she would be unwilling for her
relatives to read, hinting, as they did, at some association
between them which had, in fact, never really existed; and
if his hints, his demands, were not satisfied, would always refer
to her in public with a tender leer of implication. Combined
with these tastes and recreations Arthur was a fervent Catholic,
and an arbiter of good form, though, as the public suspicion of
him gained ground, he cleverly cultivated the style and manner
of a successful brigand.

Scandalous rumours, such as these we have mentioned, are
often the fruit of the imagination, the invention of enemies;
yet if, as was apparently the case, Mr. Bertram had no fortune
of his own, it must be admitted that he enjoyed an unexampled
run for other people's money. A younger son of a younger
son, his natural advantages were limited to a magnificent air,
an amount of self-possession, certain aristocratic relatives, and
an ugliness that in its ultimate blossoming was to attain a real
significance. To these was added a talent for dress, into which
he threw all the energy usually absorbed in, and the imaginative
qualities often killed by, the practice of cricket or golf. Also he
was generous, undoubtedly generous. The bouquets which
he was in the habit of presenting to his favourites would have
filled the Crystal Palace, the fruit would have won first-prize
at any show; however poor he was, however short of money
the recipient of these soft tributes, he never failed in their
offering. But, afterwards, would come a day of reckoning.

Arthur must have first assumed his rôle as a very young
man in the early 'seventies of the last century, a period that
offered to any adventurer of aristocratic connection an unrivalled opportunity for polite plunder. 'Society' — the word
was one of bounded application never then used to indicate
any community including brain or manual worker — was
undergoing those changes that would, in the space of another
thirty years, put an end to it in this sense. It was, though
seemingly stagnant, already in a state of corruption that would
make it a perfect Golconda for any adventurer with the right
attributes. For, being a world much talked of, but unknown
except to a few who never spoke of it, it possessed a certain
glamour, like that appertaining to some superlatively secret

form of freemasonry — a glamour which, with its gradual expansion, it was to lose for ever. As in those days large hotels and restaurants were nearly unknown, it follows that the habit of eating in public was not much indulged in by any class. It was not even easy, therefore, to see the world unless you were of it. This cloak of invisibility was very valuable, giving to it the attraction of the unseen, as well as of the unknown : here was some influence in the midst of us, some veiled mysterious power, the respect for which was like that felt for the Dalai Lama — a feeling which, were he to show himself, would swiftly diminish. Yet the process of visibility had already begun, so that at this particular stage 'society' was like a partially materialised spirit at a séance, something that might appear in your own house if you encouraged it sufficiently with baked meats or human sacrifice, employed the right medium, had enough superstitious belief in its existence, and would swear not to turn the light on suddenly or ask an unexpected question. Mr. Bertram might, if suitably rewarded, attempt to materialise it for you in your own rooms, though possibly he promised more than he could achieve.

Arthur Bertram was related to more than one peer ; and all through the first three-quarters of the nineteenth century members of the English nobility were regarded with the reverence due to an almost supernatural order of beings. Illustrative of this is the following quotation from the second volume of a trilogy which we found recently :

' "Oh, Lady Arvon," said Hester, in a scared kind of voice, "will Mr. Brown, I mean Martin, ever become a peer ? I did not think of that." . . .

' "Certainly he will, little Hester, if IN THE NATURAL COURSE of things HE should outlive HIS FATHER," answered Lady Arvon, as she lovingly kissed the flushed cheeks.' . . .

One would diagnose the years 1860 to 1870 from the descriptive passages in the book ; for in its sentimental pages the ladies recline on circular settees — ottomans, as they were called — from which their skirts billow out in front at the angle of falling water, while the gentlemen, with dark whiskers still clinging to their cheeks, lean over them in positions of polite but easy elegance. But, actually, this book, perhaps the last of a long tradition, was written in the year 1888 and dedicated to William Ewart Gladstone !

This respect, this reverence, for the invisible world of which the peerage formed a sacred inner core, deepened with the wealth of the person who felt it. To bathe in this radiance, to share this true light, was the ambition of many. Thus, though 'society' was still dominated by the great territorial magnates, and yet enjoyed a certain political power which was the legacy of the eighteenth century, the great outcrop of rich people created automatically by the diversion of trade to this country from France and Germany during the war of 1870 was already knocking at the door with a golden nugget. Their method was at the same time to propitiate and outbid the world, by the magnificence of their entertainment; and Arthur Bertram, trading on his advantages, was often a guest at the intensely respectable but otherwise rather Trimalchio-like banquets of Sir Gorgious Midas.

Though his ugliness was yet in its raw stage, Arthur had already shown the sureness of his instinct, not by any attempt to improve those qualities of heart or head in which he may have been slightly deficient, but, on the other hand, by a resolute insistence on his bad ones. This gave him what was taken by many for an easy, aristocratic air. Through these gilded saloons, full of tall palm-trees, that soared up into the hard gas-light of mid-Victorian nights like so many giraffes, their glazed and withered leaves spreading out bone-like structures till they seemed like the skeletons of some extinct monster, through smaller rooms full of roses, orchids and carnations, the exquisite colours of which threw into a more hideous contrast the suffocating draperies of that dusty age, through corridors full of huge plants, their leaves blotched with corrupt colours like those of decaying flesh, he would strut to the bobbing tune of some now obsolete polka, talking in a loud insolent voice about the rarity in these places of 'really well-bred people'. He would stare long and impertinently at those not fulfilling his standard in this respect; nor would he spare his host or hostess, for, whereas others laughed at them fitfully and behind doors, Bertram had the courage to do it constantly and in the open. His calculated drawl, a dry creaking sound as of some box with rusty hinges slowly opening, alternated with slow important clearings of the throat, and was accompanied by a complete set of facial grimaces, regular as Swedish exercises. There would be that fascinating twitch of the mouth, or that. lifting of the skin from the forehead; an enchanting shutting of one eye, opening of the other, such as were introduced as the symbols of Upper and Lower Egypt into the ceremonial mummification of dead Pharaohs. All these little touches were added to his appearance in order to combine a quality of dignity with natural fascination. The open eye, however, was alert and twinkling, the skin, sallow and rather lined, had about it something of the texture of crocodile-skin. If any woman, particularly one of his famous companions, was mentioned, he would smile in, as he thought, a pleasing way; the rusty hinges would creak open and eject some phrase such as 'poor little woman', or 'divine little creature', by which you were intended to assume that the lady referred to had loved and lost; for he based his policy as a professional on the axiom that nothing succeeds like success; and it was his arrangement with the world, an understood thing, that in his rôle of Don Juan he was irresistible.

Thus, past those same circular settees that we have mentioned, now burdened with no crinolines, where men, moustached and not whiskered, talked, with perhaps less easy elegance, to ladies with bunchy little skirts, sitting demurely upright under palms mangy as tropical beasts in an English climate, by plants that seemed to harbour cruel insects of the burning forests, Arthur Bertram would lounge, strut and swagger. While, from the near distance, the sound of a string band, like the humming drone that comes up from jungles, would reach you with warm gusts of air. Against this background his dry voice would be heard, alternately insulting the rich and deploring his own poverty; but always he hinted, in his own phraseology, that one day his Ship would Come Home. But in what that frail barque consisted, — Corsair, Indian treasure ship or the floating barge of Elaine — was never to be discovered.

Thus his life passed easily enough, except for periodic financial crises, which always seemed to be the worst of troubles. He lived in two small rooms, dark as Caliban's cave, in Ebury Street. But one could not think of him in that setting; for out of his dingy retreat, dirty and uncomfortable, he would appear resplendent, bearing his daily tribute of flowers, a gardenia in his own buttonhole, glorious as any peacock leaving its nest, and mouthing such phrases as 'well-bred', 'distinguished-looking', 'Soi-disant, of Our Class'.

For a brief interval of three years the regular course of his life was interrupted by marriage. It soon resumed its normal trend when, true to his reputation as a gallant man, he allowed himself to be divorced. Much sympathy was felt for Arthur. On the one side was to be considered a certain financial gain, on the other his reputation as a man of the world, a modern censor of morals (for such he had now become), his profession of the true faith, which does not allow of divorce, and his rôle of gentleman. It was a struggle for him; but in the end Arthur was relieved of his religious scruples, and Mrs. Bertram of a share of her small fortune and her husband's bullying manner. Let it be understood, however, that his wife regarded it as a bargain.

She had, in any case, been too poor for her husband. A pretty, rather silly woman of provincial upbringing, she had been caught by his amazing manner, by the reflected glory of his friends, the distinction of his relatives. He was so well-bred too. While Arthur, for his part, imagining her to be richer than she was, felt a longing for a quieter, less transient way of living. Perhaps, too, owing to difficulties, he had been forced to realise his assets rather suddenly. Then, though Ina was of bourgeois origin on her father's side, her mother came of Russian princely stock. This gave Arthur a new opening. He would meet you in the street, and roar like an angry lion about those pretenders to Russian princely rank whose names were not even mentioned in the *Almanach de Gotha* . . . 'while my wife's mother tells me' . . .

Poor Mrs. Bertram sank back into a welcome obscurity, and Arthur resumed a life based on the broad foundations of his small, though slightly augmented, capital and his renown as a Don Juan. In this third phase, which was but a continuation of the first, Arthur wore a double tiara: the aureole of success in affairs of the heart, of failure in those of the world; the latter, by its interest and appeal, helped him to fresh conquests. And his appearance, too, was more developed. By now he possessed a really magnificent ugliness, and one of which he made every use. It may have been due either to some form of esthetic perception, or to quite unconscious artistry, but having always had a slim, rather elegant figure, he appeared early in life to have realised the great artistic truth that elegance of form and distinction of dress enhance the quality, whatever it may be, of the face above; that a slim figure and well-made, well-thought out clothes can make an ugly face more hideous a thousandfold. How much more effective would Caliban be in what is known as 'faultless evening-dress', than in those conventional clothes of the cave-man which he usually affects! Thus Arthur used his figure, his dress, his manner even, to enhance the awfulness of the face that crowned them, set like a grotesque jewel. And, indeed, in contrasts such as these, lies the whole art of the grotesque. The gargoyle aids the leaping spiritual beauty of flying buttress, Gothic arch and spire, while the cathedral in return lends its loveliness to display each individual gargoyle. A dragon makes plain the ideal and peaceful beauty of a Chinese landscape. The sad ugliness, the useless effort of a dwarf, enhance the richness of seventeenth-century costume. Thus, Arthur pressed his youthful slim figure and stylised clothes into the service of the sallow muzzle-like face that surmounted them. No woman could pay a greater attention to her toilet than did Bertram. He achieved distinctly the personal note. In London he wore an idealised version of the usual dress that belongs to the familiar figure about London: striped or check trousers, beautifully creased, a black tail-coat — what used to be known as a 'fancy waistcoat' — a stock-tie with a pearl pin, the gift of his unfortunate wife, and, finally, balanced above that head as by a conjuring trick, a grey top-hat. A Malacca cane of unusual height completed the effect, while his walk was so calculated as best to display each elegance.

The background of the early 'nineties against which Arthur now found himself, after the rapine and triumphs of nigh twenty years, had a certain amount of character. Our hero would explain 'that things change so fast nowadays' — for the Opopanax and White Rose of his early youth had now given way to the odours of 'Chypre' and 'New Mown Hay'; odours which were actually allowed to mingle in the drawing-rooms with the fragrant smoke of Egyptian cigarettes! What is more, certain young men did not hesitate to wear in public, in London even, shoes of brown leather, a recent discovery.

But the London background of this period had more character than the present one, was more essentially different from that of other cities ; and Arthur, in his small way, had become one feature of a familiar prospect, since sadly altered. The narrow streets, full of shops engaged in a more dignified competition to attract the senses, were fresher, brighter than they are now. There was then about Bond Street and Piccadilly an almost patent-leather finish. Everything shone with paint and sparkled with varnish. Through the large sheets of glass, shelves and rows of bottles gleamed like coloured crystal. The frayed edges of Northern sunlight rehabilitated themselves in the depth of these green, silver and crimson waters, even recovering and giving out a little warmth, bringing the perfume out of the bottles as they would draw the secret breath out of country flowers, or press it out of tropical blossoms that live but a day, until a surge of scent, stronger than that of any garden or forest, poured in overwhelming torrent from the shop into the street that lay cold and hard as a canal outside. Passing on farther, behind yet more glass, we see sparkling silver, crystal and scaly leather mirror-like with varnish — those ugly useless ornaments for which the English are still justly famous. Everything is neat and well ordered, everything is well made. Here the smells of leather, of lion and crocodile skin, of sweating African jungle and slimy Indian river bed, were strong enough to frighten the horses — arranged in pairs like those animals you see advancing into a diminutive ark in early tapestries — were they aware of anything but attentive grooms in comfortable stables, or, perhaps, of being given apples and carrots on Sunday mornings after church. Flowers, arranged skilfully yet with an unbelievable want of art, pressed their hot faces against the crystal walls that imprisoned them — the open pleasant faces of roses, orchids like battle-scarred generals, flowers of fever and blood, and carnations, looking as if they were cut from stiff, frilly paper, while little india-rubber bands held up their chins from an elderly sagging, giving a forced, fresh look of youth. Among this well-organised, rather tired, riot, a love-bird pecks at steel bars with hard metallic clatter. Then there were windows full of baskets of fruit, of the full, healthy scent of mould and autumn orchards, though in the same place were queer toys, fruit scaled like reptiles, so that no man would willingly eat of them, and oranges, round and warm as the sun. Then follow open marble shelves of cold, shiny fish that look as if they came from the Dead Sea, displaying damply white tones or circles of rainbow colour, while near by hangs a whole world of birds, hams and meat, that would please equally a housekeeper or the denizen of a jungle.

In the centre of this narrow street stands, like a granite rock, a broad figure in a large square blue coat, with boots like ships and a hat that is a blue dome. This is the guardian of 'lor-an'-awder', straight out of the last Drury Lane panto-mime harlequinade, a gruff, burly, blue figure with one white-gloved paw held up in warning. This uplifted hand holds in check, as if by magic, a line of vehicles more frail, more fantastic, than any in the world. Stranger and more unreal than any gondola that cuts the Venetian waters with knife-like prow are these angular, black scallop-shells on high, round wheels, scallop-shells like those from which Botticelli lets his golden Venus be borne in upon the foaming tides. High up above the shell, so that his weight must surely overbalance his frail equipage, sits, like a monkey, a red-faced figure with shiny top-hat, whip and red buttonhole. Fabulous, indeed, is the speed of them, as they roll along, jolting slightly in the fashion of a man walking a tight-rope. And, straight out of this queer, narrow perspective of houses, shops and carriages, two figures impinge on our sight. A tall good-looking lady, in leg-of-mutton sleeves and a little hat, and — with her — a well-dressed, elegant figure, mouthing and twisting its great muzzle like some Red Indian chief in war paint. It is Arthur Bertram with the Woman-of-the-Moment; and how this background displays our hero! About him is the same ugly element, the same hideous smartness. The shape of his top-hat fits in with the perspective of the chimneys, the glaze of it echoes the paint and varnish of the shops. His patent-leather boots reflect, as in a black mirror, the huge slabs of glass in the windows, the trivial objects behind them, while they in their turn send back a watery reflection of Arthur and those glittering ornaments that distinguish him. Even the well-marked brick of the houses helps to show off the texture of his face.

But, alas! this townscape dissolves as we look at it: the strange vehicles have been dashed up like shells by the raging tides, shattered on the beach of time. Here and there are survivors, in the museums, beside a family coach. Perhaps one may lurk in the back alleys of those streets of which for so long it was the ornament, sought out and made much of, but now an outcast. The Woman-of-the-Moment is thirty years older, and Arthur — well, Arthur is just his own dear self!

In the country, or still more at foreign watering-places, Arthur could give freer rein to his personal taste. There, quite frankly, and, we think, from his point of view, wisely, he based the harmony of his clothes upon the brigand-theme: flowing blue cloak, romantic hat, long gauntlet-gloves and a cane, higher than his London one, persuaded the inhabitants that here was someone of immense renown. Used as they were to the ways of the English, yet here was something odder still. No one, surely, but a Personage Incognito would dare to attract to himself so much attention; surely that face, too, was the property of one of the European Royal Houses, a Prince in Exile, the King of . . . ?

The years went by, ever more swiftly, as is their way, but Our Familiar Figure would still be seen walking down the customary streets at the correct hour, though he was more often alone than formerly. His nimbus was now his own. With head erect, balancing that grey top-hat apparently without an effort, he would straddle down the street, snuffling like a bull-dog, grimacing horribly to himself and making wry faces. The innumerable little leathery lines in his countenance were led up to by the single immaculate crease in each trouser, or thrown into bold relief by the sober patterning of his cravat. A friendly but rather unprepossessing leer would greet his friends. There would be a roar, the angry roar of an old man, rather inarticulate but ending in the well-known phrase, 'Soi-disant, of Our Class'. Then he would remain silent for a moment, and, drawing a folded handkerchief out of his pocket by its angle, would brush away invisible specks of dust from his sleeve. The friend would now be treated to a fixed stare of some duration, followed by a writhing of the facial muscles, and then, swivelling one bright-gleaming eye round the corner, he would remark with the usual drawl, the usual loud, dry-throated rasp in his voice: 'Ah! there goes that divine creature; such a well-bred woman, too, which is none too common in these days. We used to be great friends.' Or, 'Do you know who that is? If you'd known her, my boy, as I did (poor little woman) twenty years ago.' . . . Then would come variations based on the same theme, and the climax would be a short sermon on the morals of the day, followed by the customary dissertation upon his own poverty, which was indeed becoming a problem for him.

By now between the ages of sixty and seventy years, Arthur may fairly be said to have reached the Awkward Age. Women with famous husbands or brothers now preferred the company of these relatives to the tiresome attentions of, as they put it all too frankly, this old bore. No more loans of fifty pounds from ladies, following upon a written account of Arthur's romantic dramatisation of their friendship, came his way. But he never lost faith, firm in the belief that one day his ship would come home — a supposition that had sustained him through many difficulties and for many years. Though the impoverishment of the whole world, as a result of the war, made existence more difficult for him, though he was now forced to spend a great part of the year in being looked up to by the English colony in cheap foreign watering-places, yet he was still always to be seen in London at the correct time, in the correct place. His manner, his air, were more in the Grand Style than ever. He let it be seen and understood that he was a relic of a past epoch, a grand old English gentleman, damn it, such as could not flourish in this degenerate age! Still there were, undoubtedly, moments in the night when Arthur asked himself what the future held for him. It might not be a long one, but it might be extremely unpleasant. His bills became to him a maze, which he walked blindfold, and with no hope, while through the thick hedges peered the evil gleaming eyes of his enemies. And when he woke again to the still blackness of the middle night, it must have seemed as if the banquets of Sir Gorgious Midas were, too, but delightful, fantastic dreams. He would sigh, reflecting how his world had changed out of all recognition, but unaware of the minute part himself had played in this dissolution of the old order, as is the ant of the overthrow of a garden-bed, or the coral insect unconscious of his destructive yet creative mission.

The Midas family, though they, too, had changed with the times, were still on very good terms with Bertram, whose insolence in the house of the old merchant was transformed into obsequious praise in the grandson's ancestral hall. No one could play the old family-friend better than he could, and a long-standing connection like this was felt to be part of the Midas feudal make-up. Bertram used to tell his friends that it made him blush, absolutely blush, to think how the country had treated Lord de Normanville, old Sir Gorgious's grandson. No one had been more 'keen-on-the-war', no one had lent more motor-cars, believed more spy-stories or given more vegetables to the wounded than had this peer! No one had so swiftly observed — immediately before the Armistice, indeed — the danger of our falling into the enemy's trap by accepting their complete submission — by, in fact, allowing a premature end to the war; no one had denounced this folly of unheeding statesmen more energetically than had Lord de Normanville from his seat as hereditary legislator; and, finally, no one was more surprised when asked to contribute towards the cost of our glorious battles!

The family of old Sir Gorgious were now fast selling the great bulk of their inherited acres, and were content with two motor-cars, where formerly they had been forced to employ seven. In fact Lord de Normanville could cry poverty with the richest in the land. But though the stately homes were going one by one, there were consolations; and on the top of all his other sacrifices he still managed to entertain a few friends from time to time, though, of course, in a very simple manner. It was at one of these pleasant gatherings that Arthur met his second destiny, whose rôle was filled by the ample fortune and generous figure of Mrs. Fullard: this lady, a fascinating widow, was possessed of much wealth and sprightliness.

These parties always had something very original about them, quite different from other people's. Lady de Normanville always liked to *mix* her guests; that was the secret of it, she confessed — though at first sight the personnel appeared to be much the same as at other 'simple gatherings' of the kind. In a curious way the talk always showed a tendency to return to finance, by which was meant the iniquities of taxation — though, of course, other subjects would be touched on. Dinner, on the first night, was most amusing. Arthur sat next to Mrs. Fullard, while the eruptions of green and purple brocade and the numerous ancestral portraits on the wall threw into rich relief every detail of their appearance. Old Sir Hankey Twadham, the former Minister at Sofia, was

there, too, with a new — or at any rate new to him — rather
risqué story, the worst of which was that, as he confided to all
the guests in turn, you had to be careful to whom you told it.
His eye wandered round the table mournfully, in search of a
possible victim. Then that round disc of glass behind which
his eye was displayed like some precious object in a crystal
vitrine would twinkle gleefully, and he would say : 'I shall try
it on Mrs. Fullard. She's all right ! It will make her roar.
It makes me laugh every time I think of it.' Dear old General
McKinnan was also one of the party, and could be seen heavily
crunching his red, swollen mandibles, or moving a hand like a
lobster's claw in occasional explanatory gesture of some killing
anecdote in connection with the Irish Rebellion. 'The curious
part of it, too, was that the leaders were all clever men.
But they don't go far, do they ?' he asked with a first suggestion
of passion. 'Look at Curzon ! I remember him at Eton.
Could anyone call *him* a *clever* man ? and look where he is
now !' This peroration of the General's made an immediate
appeal to the audience, who took it up and worried it in
couples, carefully, in their various corners. Again he focused
attention by another of his *killing* stories about the rebellion.
'What an extraordinary thing !' everybody screamed. But the
conversation did not remain long at this frivolous level. The
Prince of Wales's tour of the Empire was discussed. It was
marvellous how the Boy had Smiled. The General expressed
it as his opinion that once he had got over those blackguardly
hurdles, or hurtals, or whatever they are called, the Royal
Tour would do more good than a thousand machine-guns.
Meanwhile, at the other end, Lord de Normanville held the
field with some interesting reminiscences of his more recent
disputes with the Inland Revenue and Super-Tax Authorities.
He felt it his duty, though always unwilling to make himself
conspicuous, and, indeed, always trying to pass as an ordinary
citizen, to write to them pointing out that after deducting
Income Tax, Super-Tax and his annual expenditure, he was
left with an income of six hundred a year. An answer had
been returned to him, couched in the most insolent terms,
suggesting that he should cut down his expenditure. He had
replied, with dignity but without loss of temper, making it
clear that any curtailment of his expenditure would increase
unemployment, already sufficiently prevalent, and that he was

unwilling at this juncture to do anything that might in any way injure the Commonwealth. Followed a short but very interesting discussion on Bolshevism; Sir Hankey, who plunged into this discussion off the deep end, forgot the point of his story in the middle, and, instead, gave minute details of what he had heard in Sofia before the war. If, he added, he told them only half what he *knew* now . . . and the pearls encircling billowing necks became a shade paler in their radiance. Several people, indeed, felt positively faint. Lady de Normanville rallied the talk by appealing to General McKinnan. 'General, if you had to have your portrait painted, whom would you choose?' The gallant old soldier, who considered portrait-painting as quite a different thing from any other form of painting, and always attended the opening days of the exhibitions in Bond Street, was immensely flattered by this question — much more so than if his opinion had been asked on tactics or horses. 'Why not Oswald Birley? There was a man who could paint what *he* saw, what *you* saw!' Mrs. Fullard, who was very artistic, suggested McEvoy, but Arthur thought McEvoy's work was rather *too* weird, wasn't it? Lady de Normanville pointed out that he never seemed to finish his portraits; besides he made everyone look alike. Whereas Glyn Philpot finished them all, absolutely, and made everyone look different. 'A clever man, that!' said the General suspiciously.

Conversation split up again, drifting into sets of twos and threes, and it was now that Evelyn Fullard completely captivated Arthur Bertram by confessing, with that pretty trilling little laugh of hers, that if she had her way she would *make* the miners go down the mines and work. While people with fifteen thousand a year were paying nearly half their income in taxation, the colliers — who had nothing to keep up — were earning five pounds a week and paying no taxes at all. As for herself, she had been obliged to borrow money from the bank this year to pay her Super-Tax! It was this adorable mixture of wit, charm and common-sense, that fascinated Arthur. He proposed after three days; and they were married within three weeks of their first meeting. It was a real romance!

The honeymoon was spent on the shores of Lake Maggiore, in the Pucciniesque setting of soft air, palm-trees and lapping waters; a neighbouring casino added interest to the natural beauty of the landscape. While there Arthur managed quite quickly to solve that Super-Tax trouble. Wherever they went, the romantic couple attracted great interest. They were an interesting pair. Arthur was triumphant; he appeared, bathed in that tender, rosy glory in which the later Venetian painters depict, on wall and ceiling of patrician palaces, the apotheosis of Procurator or Doge. And, on his return to London, he became a more familiar figure than ever. He had entered the third phase; he had conquered the Awkward Age.

It looked, in fact, as if his ship had come home at last. Alas! it was merely the Hundred Days over again, the ship but that *Bellerophon* which was to make him an exile in a foreign land. For now Mrs. Bertram made manifest the devil within her; her pretty little golden laugh showed itself to be the key to a temper infinite and terrible in its variety. The plebeian origin of his wife, to which Arthur had willingly and, as he now said, foolishly blinded himself, peeped out from behind the enamel. She made it clear that she had no intention of allowing Arthur to relieve her of the necessity for borrowing from the bank to pay her Super-Tax; she even refused him a small allowance. She irritated his susceptible nerves at every turn with vulgar little tricks, and displayed a revengeful, unforgiving spirit. How, he asked himself aloud, could he introduce such a woman to his friends? It was impossible . . . Mrs. Bertram, in a fury, the varnish cracking in every direction, shouted out that he had no friends now, if he'd ever had any! Finally, in an almost apoplectic temper, the fair one had him turned out of the house. An intense domestic warfare of manœuvre and counter-manœuvre, attack and counter-attack ensued. Arthur fled to Atterly, her 'place' in the country, and succeeded in enlisting the sympathy of the agent, who particularly disliked Mrs. Bertram. But the agent received orders — which he could not disobey — to cut off the water and the electric light, and was thus prevented from following the dictates of his heart. Then Mrs. Bertram came down in person to superintend the siege. Arthur was ejected — but with great skill commandeered his wife's motor-car, and before she could arrive back in London by train had already seized her house there. Finally, both of them felt that the position was an undignified one. The lawyers now swooped down, and by their various proposals netted in a good haul. Arthur's old religious scruples returned to him with redoubled force. His fervour was extraordinary. He became a Savonarola. Would he consider ten thousand pounds down for the selling of his soul? Certainly not! Twenty thousand? But even this did not tempt him. He became too obstinate in his desire to outwit his wife; and Mrs. Bertram became thoroughly out of temper again. She made up her mind to be rid of him without any payment at all, and — being a woman used to getting her own way — by sheer brutality, ill-temper and insult succeeded eventually in dislodging him from her home. Arthur was goaded into such a fury that he left of his own accord, to spend the remainder of a broken life declaiming against the former object of his affections, or, as he now called her, 'that scheming old woman'.

His clothes remained glorious as ever, his manner as magnificent; he still talked of his ship coming home; but gradually poverty forced him into a bitter exile. One heard of him taking his aristocratic relatives out from their camphored chests, and airing them, before old ladies, in those *pensions* of France, Germany and Italy that had become for him a series of more comfortable but even more desolate St. Helenas. The tale of his wrongs, one heard, was ever fresh in his memory. Bravely as ever, no doubt, he pursued his allotted path; but silence sank down on him, and the London that had known Arthur Bertram for so long, knew him no more.

.   .   .   .   .

The sea was smooth as a watered-silk banner, and no wind lifted the white edges. Hot and calm was the water on that summer day. The growing detail of the harbour approached us swiftly, veering in its position from time to time. Lighthouses, piers, quays, trolleys and cranes, dividing up the horizon with angular but rhythmic precision, were imprisoned in the tawdry blue, in the transparent ball, of sky and sea, as in crystal. Every sound seemed struggling to escape from the hard, material globe that contained it. Porters cried nasally, old women hawked oranges and chocolates, while small boys cried ecstatically the French versions of the names of English newspapers. All round us was the usual disorderly bustle that masks the deadly efficiency of the French people. We were discharged over small bridges into this throng and out of it —

and beyond, almost automatically, into a motor-car. The streets were dull, the coast-line flat; nothing to do in all this weary waste except, we supposed, to watch the ship come home each morning from England.

And just then our attention was suddenly riveted by a familiar figure bearing toward us. Magnificent in flowing blue cloak, his long gauntlet-glove made a majestic movement with a very high walking-stick, as this straddling, snorting personage, grimacing and making wry faces, went on his way towards his ship that had already come home. He was rather late that day, and in his hurry did not notice us.

CHARLES AND CHARLEMAGNE

'What has not fired her bosom or her brain?
Caesar and Tall-boy, Charles and Charlemagne?'

About a month ago it must be now, I was sitting in the glassed-in cage at the top of a motor omnibus which had settled down amid an inanimate fleet of similar conveyances. It had sidled itself along and was anchored, apparently for all eternity, against the pavement in Park Lane. Only the gentle purring that pervaded the whole vast machine communicated any hope, announced to the passengers a mechanic conviction that sooner or later this stagnation would thaw, and it would be able again to roar its way along the streets like a red, armoured lion. The present passive state in which we found ourselves was rendered the more irritating because the other side of the road, by the Park railings, was completely unencumbered, and large, gondola-like cars were gliding, vans and omnibuses thundering, along its smooth water-coloured surface. Beyond, over the railings that divided up the green grass into rectangular, coffin-like compartments, I watched the listless afternoon life of the Park. The trees looked metallic as the green tin trees of a toyshop, and under them a few weary individuals rested on green tin seats. One or two crouching, whiskered horsemen, crowned with grey bowler-hats, and conscious enough of their obsoleteness to assume an air of defiant importance, trotted slowly along: and I reflected that in all probability the whole of this traffic block, in which we found ourselves thus frozen, was due to one solitary horse with a van, happily lumbering its way along somewhere in the heart of the City. Now there was a slight jolt: we moved on for a few yards, and then, tantalisingly enough, stopped again. My eye turned from the Park to the buildings which overshadowed it. Huge edifices were being improvised . . . buildings that resembled impregnable cliffs, full of luxurious caves in which the rich middle classes were encouraged to hide themselves before the coming of that Day of Judgment, so often invoked by communist orators near by at Hyde Park Corner, when with a loud-mouthed bellow of trumpets and running of blood the virtue of the workers would be recognised and rewarded. Sprinkled among these rocks, however, are still a few old-fashioned, bow-fronted houses : and suddenly I found myself looking down into one . . . staring down into the familiar, but now derelict, dining-room of Lady de Montfort's house. Above the window, standing on a gibbet-like framework, two large black-and-white placards, that resembled in their angles the jutting-out prow of a ship, announced the sale of a 999-years' lease.

The room was, as I had last seen it, decorated as a grotto ; but now that it was empty of furniture, now that dust had formed the thickest possible carpet and the windows were already dim from Time's hands, it was more realistic, seemed a cavern, crumbling and forgotten, from which the sea had receded and withdrawn its life. And I wondered whether her impersonal, lacquered but vivacious ghost — a ghost that would never, one felt certain, be clad in any of the multitudinous styles that had pertained to its lifetime, but would always be robed in the latest creation of the moment in which it materialised — did not sometimes roam among these artificial ruins of her earthly past ? And then I thought of a cage built of steel and crystal, borne on the deep currents of a tropic sea, bumping and turning over and over, with a rattling of dry bones midway between air and ocean-bottom, an anonymous yet unique end from an anonymous beginning . . . and meditated how strange it was that a life which belonged essentially to its own day, which was responsible for some of the stir and gaiety, and much of the gossip of those hours, should, soonest of all, sink into oblivion : for that which is the most typical is often the most transitory. Herself, I felt, albeit she had cared little enough for public interest, would have been surprised at so evident a lack of it in so short a space. How strange, again I reflected. The travellers on each omnibus will look down into this empty room, and will consider it a grotesque and useless piece of decoration, nothing more ; will entirely miss its significance, its very actual foundation in life. And I recalled the time, not so many months ago, when one glance from a passing omnibus at the decoration of Lady de Montfort's dining-room (the easiest room in the house to overlook) would reveal to the initiated a whole section of her life and the progress of a passionate and inquiring physical love.

.   .   .   .   .

Almost the first thing I can remember is one of my parents remarking to the other how astonishingly young Lady de Montfort looked. And if it was astonishing in 1896, it must have been very much more so in 1930. For though the art of looking young has in the meantime become a vocation like conjuring, and by that degree less rare, nevertheless when I saw her for the last time, it was clear that she remained at the top of a difficult, and even upon occasion dangerous, profession. In a sense, however, it still remains in the hands of the amateur, for though every suburb now has its beauty-parlour, yet only the rich can afford to indulge in the very real physical torture that beauty-worship imposes on its devotees.

Lady de Montfort, then, had been one of the pioneers of the Peter Pan movement; for that play, I fancy, popularised the notion that there was something glorious in never growing up. Peter Pan in fact was the child-father of face-lifting. The ethical side of the wish to remain young out of season is not easy to grasp, any more than is the practical. Alas, life must end in the same way for all. The full stop closes every sentence whatever the joy or agony of its meaning. The anonymous death, the death of the rich, well-preserved nomad in a richly appointed hotel, for example, has the same pathos as that of a wrinkled old woman of the same age in some pauper institution, and more, it seems to me, than the death of an old, rheumatic crone in a cottage. Much better is it to pass through the seven allotted stages, much better even to be cut off, as the phrase is, 'in the flower of her youth' than in the artificial flower of a deceptive youth. Yet the sums of money spent on this pitiful aim are prodigious, while hints on the subject (combined with details of free-insurance schemes and lists of the sums paid out, which point to a very regrettable mortality among the registered readers of daily newspapers; a mortality, indeed, so remarkable that it seems almost perilous to subscribe to these journals) compose much of the Press today, so there must be an appeal in it to our natures.

But if Beauty is Truth (which, incidentally, it is not), certainly the results of beauty culture are a lie, and should therefore be recognised as ugly. To all those who can afford the best advice, false youth, when attained, imparts an identical appearance: the same corn-gold hair, the same angular, fashion-plate eyes, raised upward at the corner, the same straight nose and lips carved into a double curve, the same strained mouth — slightly open like the mouth of a Roman Mask of Tragedy — that the knife of the plastic surgeon dictates. They have the same figures, the same hands and finger-nails, more or less the same dresses, and the same impersonal, cosmopolitan accent, with, rising and falling smoothly within it, the concealed sound of an American elevator. They do not look young, except by convention, but, instead, they all look the same age: almost, indeed, the same person. And of these Adèle de Montfort was not the least.

But let not the reader conclude that Lady de Montfort's character was after a similar standardised pattern. It was not. For notwithstanding that most of the Regiment who adopt the uniform and faith we have described, do so from a quite genuine desire to resemble one another, Lady de Montfort elected it as a deliberate disguise for a very natural, if rather varied, character. We must, then, lift up the mask, and peer for a little underneath, if only to understand the mask's significance.

.   .   .   .   .

Originally, it must be assumed, she had been small and pretty and golden-haired, with a fair, almost pallid skin, behind which roses blushed from time to time, and the tiny hands and feet that are the birthright of every American woman. 'Fresh' was the epithet often used to describe her, for in those days a naïve lack of artifice was much admired, and she was without any of the elegance which she ultimately evolved round herself. Somewhere in the early 'eighties this girl had materialised herself out of what was then the misty void of the great American Republic. She did not belong to any of the few families who at that time floated garishly on this dull, nebulous surface: but she was distantly related to various American women, well married in England, and her fortune, which was adequate to the game she meant to play, was all the more respectable for not being unwieldy. But of her parentage and upbringing, people in England knew nothing, while she speedily contrived to forget more about herself than others had ever known. Outwardly she bore no labels except a slight accent, which only manifested itself in moments of anger or excitement, when suddenly, too, she would fall back into the use of transatlantic idiom; inwardly none except a secret, and, in those days, most rare, lack of them, combined with an adventurous spirit. Indeed her own mind was so free of conventional prejudices that in others they positively attracted her. Thus she set out, like a female Dick Whittington, to seek her destiny : thus, like Venus fair and pale, she had risen from the billows. In fact, if it had not been for the anchor of her independent fortune, she might have passed as that free spirit of the air, an adventuress : and so by nature, and at heart, she was. For all adventuresses are not bold-looking and hard-mouthed. And a quiet adventuress is the one whom the world should fear.

Arrived in London, she sought the protection of her American relatives (who were then much older than she was, though forty years later all of them looked more or less the same age), and under their tutelage made an appearance in the world. They formed at once the guarantee of her character and the guardians of her secret : the almost sordid respectability of her origin. For, though each of these ladies allowed it to be known that in the land of her birth her own 'social standing' had been exceptional, there was yet between them all a tacit, undefined agreement that no home secrets should be revealed. Adèle served her apprenticeship to this guild and learnt much that was of use to her : that, for example, although before marriage it was wise to dress as simply as possible, and look exactly like an English girl, after marriage she could reap the advantage of being an American. For while English women, with a singular obstinacy, persisted in buying their clothes in London, or even in the provinces, she, being of a less insular outlook, could obtain them from any of the great dressmaking houses in Paris : nor would she look *odd* in them. Paris clothes were in the American blood. At the worst, people would say she looked 'rather foreign'. And the men liked it.

Adèle proved clever and adaptable. She was presented at Court, danced, hunted, played tennis, did all the right things and triumphantly concealed her possession of a sensuous intelligence, modern and acute, if rather apt to swing at random. This was a secret, too, which her preceptors respected. Apart, however, from a quiet but continual attendance at concerts, and a constant but hidden reading of poetry and novels — habits which, in her native country, she would have been forced to parade — her general behaviour undoubtedly entitled her to an honorary place among the English ruling class of that epoch. Yet she did not marry for several years : and when she did, though it was a sound marriage, it was scarcely as brilliant a one as her chaperons had hoped. Like her fortune, it was nevertheless all the more respectable for not being of a sensational order. A title was a title, even if it were only a baronetcy : and it attracted her by its strangeness, would add to life the zest and romance (until she became used to it) of a perpetual masquerade.

The name of Sir Simon de Montfort sounds almost too good to be true, and, in fact, was so. Old Solomon Mondfeldt, grandfather of the present baronet, had crept out of a German ghetto about ten years before the Battle of Waterloo, and, looking round, had very wisely decided to settle in the city of London. There he had established himself as a merchant and banker : more, he helped to found the whole edifice of inter-national finance. For he, and a few friends in other countries, maintained at their own expense a reliable news-service, and whenever they heard of a victory for any country in which they were operating, they first announced a defeat, and then bought up all the shares that would be affected. Subsequently the news of the victory would be made public, the shares would rise, and they would sell out. Peace consolidated their efforts, and now he adhered to the more strictly legitimate side of his business, in which, as his obituary notice proclaimed many years later, 'his native shrewdness and foresight swiftly won him recognition'. (It was, perhaps, easier to have foresight then, when there were no possible dangers to foresee.) He was, in fact, a clever, vulgar, grasping, kindly old ruffian, very religious withal; a pillar of the Synagogue, always willing to help his co-religionists — even with large sums of money.

Despite a certain pride in his race — or, at any rate, a loud insistence on it — it was not long before the rough Saxon syllables of Solomon Mondfeldt had melted into the chivalric enchantment of Simon de Montfort. Moreover, his eldest son, another Simon, was smuggled somehow or other into Eton without protest; though at that time it was a difficult school for a boy to enter if he did not conform to the nationality or religion of his comrades. Once installed at Eton, he was popular, for, since he was the only little Jew there, his schoolfellows did not recognise the genus, but appreciated that in the understanding of life in some aspects he was their superior. He bought more and better strawberries than they did, and paid less for them: and on them he forcibly fed his friends. How intelligent in reality he was, who can tell? But it is certain that he very quickly seized on the principles of English public-school education, for he openly refused to learn anything, became maniac about cricket, exulted in the correct shibboleths of dress, speech and deportment and adopted ostentatiously the public-schoolboy-code-of-honour; which, summed up, encourages bullying, but forbids 'sneaking' — thereby assuring the bully of an absolute impunity. And a jolly good code it is, too, if you mean to be a bully.

By this time the family were in possession of a castle in Scotland, and a fine old 'place' in the 'Shires', with all its furniture, portraits, silver and tapestries intact, and its own chapel. A baronetcy followed. He had married at an advanced age, but even before the old man died the Christmas parties, when the house abounded with bounding young de Montforts, solidly eating their way through the week, were models of what such gatherings should be. And after his death the young baronet quietly slipped into the Christian faith. He put up several new armorial windows in the chapel, and it made one almost cry to hear him read the lessons every Sunday. Soon he married into an impoverished aristocratic family, so that his children were well-connected. And, indeed, by the third generation, the conventional, unquestioning stupidity of the children was as genuine as formerly it had been assumed: one symptom of which was that themselves were entirely taken in by their own faked pedigree, and were even apt, when they talked about a cousin, to say of him, 'Oh, of course he has the de Montfort eyes', or, worse, 'he has the de Montfort nose'. Entire books, connecting them with the ancient de Montforts, were written under the supervision of the elder members of the family, by specialist authors who found in it their living. Innocent outsiders, withal, were beginning to believe. Thus in two generations was built up a feudal house.

When the third Sir Simon, Adèle's husband, succeeded, the

elder branch of the family had become, like so many great families, convincingly impoverished. The business had been allowed to pass into the hands of cadets, because they were more interested in it, and so that the Sir Simon of the day should always be free for country pursuits, engaged as he was, would and should be, in shootin', huntin' and fishin'. Our Sir Simon, therefore, spent the greater part of his young bachelordom either in these sports or in sitting, as befitted an English sportsman, in the smallest, ugliest room of a large, rather beautiful but very cold house, surrounded by stags' heads, an imported bison or two, fish in glass cases, fossils, pipes and cigar-boxes : and, in order to keep warm, even in this den, he had to drink a great quantity of port, which gradually undermined his constitution.

Brought into this, for her exotic, environment, Adèle was an undoubted success. Her husband was devoted to her, while her fortune, too, was most welcome : since the prize-pigs and potatoes, the model dairies and cattle-breeding that were incumbent on the head of a historic family, combined with an iniquitous income-tax of a shilling or so in the pound, had made dreadful inroads into the estate. For Sir Simon, Lady de Montfort completed life : and for her, brought up as she had been, it must have been an experience that transcended reality. Nor was it, in any case at first, monotonous : for there were two sides to it. One was a miniature Royal-Family existence, spent in opening bazaars, sales of work and jumble-sales, mouthing at unknown and indistinguishable babies, and in giving or receiving prizes (it seemed to her afterwards that a large part of her early married life had been spent in giving or receiving prizes) for fruit, flowers, potatoes, onions, shorthorns and agriculture generally : while the other unfolded the whole pageant of a barbarous society. There were family parties and shooting parties ; there were the 'bloodings' and the 'rattings' ('No fun like rattin'', Sir Simon used to say), and innumerable other forms of well-meant cruelty to animals, which must have satisfied some primordial female instinct in her ; and, best of all, there were the hunt-balls. Even now, reading over the lists of 'those present', in some newspaper of the day, one can comprehend a little the ecstasy into which these festivities threw her. For far more than the Roll of Domesday do they sum up, by the very sound and rhythm of

the names, the life of that time, and, even, the queer results
of the Norman Conquest : moreover, apart from the odd juxtaposition of names essentially matter-of-fact with others so
unusual as to be romantic, the lilt and rhythm is in itself
fascinating, there are unexpected trills, and the vagaries of
fortune are reflected in the inexplicable runs on names beginning with the same letter, the long and the short runs, comparable to those unexpected runs on one number or colour that
are encountered on the gaming-tables. For example, on January
18th, 1888, we read in one of the leading London papers :

About 350 guests attended the Hunminster Hunt ball, held at
the Queen's Hotel, Hunminster, last night. Godefroy's Pink
Hungarian Band, of Hunminster, supplied the music.

In addition to the Master and Lady de Montfort, those present
included the Earl and Countess of Hunminster, Viscount Humble,
Miss Mowker, Miss Marcia Mowker, F.M. Lord Cummerbund
and the Honble. Cycely Cuddle, Miss Moocombe, Miss Malcolm,
Miss Mink, Miss Denyse Malpigian, Miss Myrtle Malpigian,
Major McCorquodale, Lady Cundle, Miss Coote, Mr. Hartopp
Hayter, Miss Hunt, Miss Handle, Mr. Handcock, Mrs. Haviour
and Miss B. Haviour, Mrs. Bullamy, Miss Heather Hellebore,
Major Colin Coldharbour and Lady Isabel Hamilton-Hootar.

The Earl of Dunbobbin, the Honble. Doughty Dullwater, Miss
Daphne Diddle, Colonel Haggas, Lady Hootman, Dr. Prettygole,
Mr. Palmer, Mr. Plummer, Miss Plummer, Mr. Plymsoll, Captain
Pymm, Miss Penelope Pitt-Pitts, Mr. Percy Pitman, Miss Frolick,
Mr. Fumble, Miss Rowena Rowbotham, Miss Donkyn, Miss
Dunderhead, Mr. Roger Randcock, Major Minney, Miss Dingle,
Mr. Malcolm de Montmorency, Mrs. Slinkworthy, Captain
Hercules Slowcoach, Lady Slaunder, Miss Slowcombe, Mr. Sleek,
Miss Eager, Mrs. Stanley Stobart, Miss Serpent, Colonel Cooper-
Copeland, Sir Joseph Slump, Miss Eileen Shrivel, Major Spiridion
and Lady Muriel Portal-Pooter.

And then the rollicking aspect of the festivities captivated
Adèle. She loved to watch the huge, thumping dowagers
romping round in their bustles, covered from head to foot with
jewels like Hindu idols and whirling round in the figures of the
Lancers until they seemed to have as many vast, red arms as
those deities. She liked to talk, or be silent, with these long-
legged and languid men, with their drawling yet clipped talk
and military moustaches. Certainly, then, she enjoyed herself

at first. And all these people liked her, though, of course, to begin with they had thought the Parisian clothes, which she had now adopted, 'quaint'. But soon they became accustomed to her, and would remark enthusiastically, 'Nobody would ever take her for an American'.

So the first years passed . . . and then there were her children, three of them, born within the first seven years of their marriage. In her later period, one was astonished that anything as elemental as child-bearing should ever have formed part of Lady de Montfort's life : but so it was. And there were short visits to London. She had never renounced her Guild, and corresponded regularly with her early preceptors, though seldom asking them to visit her. But she saw them in London, and this made the atmosphere different for her. She seemed contented enough, they thought : but she never really talked to them, never said anything except what the world expected of her. But in about 1890 a change came.

As she was clever as well as pretty, her ascendancy over her husband became complete. Now, suddenly, she insisted on spending half the year in London. He was in no position to object : she had taken an infinity of trouble with his friends and relatives, while much of the money was her own. But for him the reality was to be worse than the anticipation. His wife for the first time revealed an intense, American interest in the arts notwithstanding that Sir Simon had a wholly British prejudice against artists. The species positively invaded his London house at this period ; but it never actually descended to blows. As he said about the matter to his friends, 'After all, one must live and let live . . .' and so, when it became too much for him, he would instinctively go back to the country and kill a fish or a bird instead. . . . Alas, there was worse to come. He could not be away from her always. And now there were — musicians in the house ! She had always been musical ; he had been forced in secret to recognize this — musical in a passive sense. But this was different, this was monstrous ; amounted almost, he said, to deception, so little had he suspected it. . . . For all at once she produced a certain, if limited, executant ability ; that is to say she installed two pianos, side by side, in the drawing-room, and upon them she loved to play duets with eminent musicians. This she did well and gracefully. On one piano, however, and, as it were, by herself, she floundered hopelessly and was lost; a dangerous symptom — if her husband had identified it — the symptom of a temperament that, in spite of its native American independence, demanded, and relied on, continual masculine assistance. Notwithstanding, at present her behaviour grew no less conventional, her conversation not a whit more individual.

Sir Simon's troubles, if he had known it, were but beginning. Now was the first time she indulged a repressed desire for house-decoration; one which later, as we shall see, became unconsciously entangled with sex-expression, and almost developed into a mania. And innocent as it seems from this distance, her initial attempt annoyed Sir Simon quite as much as any of her subsequent ones. The Louis Quinze *salons* of the de Montfort mansion in Park Lane were scrapped from top to bottom; and, instead, oak beams squared white ceilings, Morris chintzes enwrapped the chairs and sofas, and a gothic wallpaper supplied a background of dim, golden nebulosity. The two pianos were draped in faded Japanese kimonos, but this could not muffle the thousand minute, clear-throated songs called out from countless blue-and-white china bowls and plates when any note was struck: for the whole room was a-clatter with willow-pattern porcelain. On the top of the wainscoting, even, fragile objects were perilously balanced. Then there were drawings by Simeon Solomon, and, in the place of honour, two large portraits of the master and mistress of the house, by Godwyn. (Poor de Montfort had particularly objected to sitting for his portrait, but had been forced into it by Adèle.) Lacquer was there too, of the Oriental, not the European variety, and many Oriental screens crept like angular, gigantic caterpillars across the floors. Oscar Wilde sometimes attended the musical parties which Lady de Montfort had now inaugurated, and these screens were the subject of a famous telegram. She had written to him, saying that she had received from the East a consignment of lacquer screens, and hoped he would give her the benefit of his advice as to their arrangement. In answer, she received a telegram: 'Do not arrange them. Let them occur.—Oscar.'*

* Great letter-writers have been plentiful, but, as far as one can judge, Wilde was the only great telegram-writer that the world has seen as yet. A volume of his collected telegrams would make very good reading. And who, one may wonder, is the master of the long-distance spoken-word, the telephone — short, concise, witty?

Yet, though her parties became celebrated, the character of the hostess still seemed vague and diaphanous. At what precise age her appearance of youth first called for comment, I am unaware; but at these entertainments, I apprehend, guests were already saying to one another, 'How wonderfully young our hostess looks tonight'. After a few years, however, these gatherings came to an abrupt end. Sir Simon did not enjoy them, though he talked loudly, and without a moment's pause for breath, throughout every evening of music. But even when there was no music, he felt out of it, and as if they did not want to listen to him. The Wilde scandal occurred, and Sir Simon, who, furthermore, was aware of having sat, as it were, for one of that author's most applauded jokes,* insisted on having the decorations torn down. The house, as he said, must be 'decently furnished again'.

The change that took place was just as startling in its way as any of those subsequently organised by Adèle. The Godwyn portraits were removed, but preserved in a lumber-room in case they might some day become valuable, and hastily improvised likenesses by Herkomer were substituted. Armchairs in flowery chintzes, little gilded chairs, eighteenth-century footstools which tripped up every visitor who walked into the room, and Dutch brass chandeliers soon restored the house to its accustomed worthiness; while to add a special touch of incontrovertible respectability, Sir Simon transported from the country several stags' heads and pike and salmon in long, glass-fronted cases, and personally superintended the sprinkling of these about the house. In all this, he was successful. Yet it was the cause of the first quarrel between Lady de Montfort and himself, and it is to be doubted whether she ever forgave him.

At the time, though, he scored a point. Visits to London were few, and Adèle relapsed from a metropolitan into a provincial life. In England, of course, this last is more exclusive, more difficult to enter, more the 'right thing': but now it had lost for her its fascination. It must be remembered that by type she was an adventuress. And, having established one method

* One day Sir Simon had led the esthete up to his portrait by Godwyn, and had said to him, 'I don't like that: my wife made me sit for it. But you're supposed to know about that sort of thing. What do you think of it?' — And the author had replied, 'Sir Simon, it is a speaking likeness . . . but there are occasions when silence is more welcome'.

of life so thoroughly and completely, the adventure was over, should be disposed of.

In the few years that were to pass before she was free, something happened to Lady de Montfort. Books no longer lent her their support, and though music retained its purely sensual attraction for her, she lost now the magic key which had enabled her in a moment to enter other worlds. Novels and poetry no longer disclosed enchanted avenues along which she might wander, and, instead, she welcomed romance on a more material plane. Presently, and for the first time in their married life of nearly fifteen years, Sir Simon had cause for jealousy. She was always to be seen in the company of a neighbouring, notoriously unfaithful peer. Sir Simon, with a touching ancestral belief in the word of a Gentile, made his wife sign a paper in which she undertook never to see Lord Dunbobbin again. Why she signed it, I do not know : but she did. Alas, she broke her promise.

Bicycling was now the rage, and strange as it may seem, though there were no motor-cars, people contrived to have serious accidents. Clad, therefore, in those peculiar clothes immortalised by the painter Seurat, those clothes which seem specially designed to bring out the miracle of the bicycle's spider-like feats of balance, for, regarded from the back, the whole line, from shoulder to wheel, forms an inverted pyramid, Lady de Montfort and her lover would speed down lanes that have never since been so leafy; propel themselves down the centre of these green tunnels at such a prodigious rate, as it seemed that the little nuzzling winds of the spring would attack the mesh of her green pointillist veil, and even push her round straw hat to the back of her formalised fringed head. Such happiness could not endure. A governess-car was the machine planned by the gods for its destruction. The physical damage was not severe, but a lawsuit was threatened. The case would be reported, and Sir Simon must be told. He lost his temper, created a scene : tactics which, for the last year or two, had ever crowned him with success. But this time Lady de Montfort joined battle. At every point, he was defeated. He shouted 'Divorce' at her. She replied that he had no evidence, but should her own action, based on his prolonged cruelty, fail, she would be delighted to supply it. But neither of them wished it in reality, for divorce was then, even so short a time ago, a step down into obscurity rather than up into fame. 'For the sake of the children,' they decided, 'it must not be.' So, for a year or two longer, the children were forced to know them together and quarrelsome rather than amiable and apart. During these months, though she lived in his house, Adèle behaved as she wished.

With King Edward on the throne the whole atmosphere had changed, and now the relaxation began to be felt even in these fastnesses of an almost palaeolithic Society. In about 1906 a separation was arranged, and she took over the Park Lane mansion, while he continued to live in the country. From time to time, after this, they would meet pleasantly and without reproach, each delighted to be independent : nor did either strive to prevent the children from seeing the other parent, but, with good sense, encouraged it. And here, having mentioned the children, we can dispose of them. They grew up, as they should, into rich but deserving men and women. When with their mother in London, they spent as much time as they could out of it, on golf-course or tennis-court — in the evenings attended the right sort of musical comedy or revue, and could soon whistle every tune out of every 'show', as they called it, with the ease and accuracy of an errand-boy. More-over they could banter one another with a thousand memorable clichés culled from the repertory of their favourite comedians, enjoyed 'fizz' and 'bubbly', and believed, generally, in 'having a good time'.

Meanwhile their mother's life was assuming a new texture. This was a second, but transitional, period for her. The last adventure was over and complete. The next one must be to smash it and conquer a new world. Her pioneer blood was still in the ascendant. Edwardian days were in full, overfull, bloom : now she could avow her artistic proclivities, consort with people of her own type. Many of them, like herself, were American. She became a mote in new sunshine, whirled in a gilded, pointless activity, organised balls or tableaux in aid of any charity that asked her help, displayed real ability in selling the tickets. Her appearance in one of these enterprises, as Penelope spinning, will long be remembered. She dressed now in the exuberance of fashion, and created a stir — unrivalled by any horse — in the Royal Enclosure at Ascot. Sheathed in a mauve Directoire dress, with a large silver bangle on one ankle, where the split in the dress revealed it, and balancing a vast picture-hat on her head, she attracted the Royal attention, as much by her clothes as by the well-enamelled spring of her complexion.

She prospered, achieved a reputation for beauty as much as for youth, and became sufficiently friendly with King Edward to ask for that signed photograph which afterwards remained the one fixed star in an ever-changing sky: for, whatever the wild revolutions of her house which I shall describe later, this royal, bearded geniality continued to authorise her indiscretions. She gave musical parties, played duets with all the leading pianists. From having been un-labelled, a person, indeed, to whom it was impossible to attach a label, she now manufactured for herself a very recognisable one: so that it was easy for her many new friends to foretell exactly what she would say in any given circumstances. Thus they were enabled to mimic and, by so doing, to advertise her. She became, and remained for many years, a familiar, and therefore popular, landmark of London life. And the fox-hunting squires, as they looked at the weekly illustrated papers, would gulp their port, gape and roar with surprise as they gazed upon the likeness of this very young-looking, elegant spectre of the world of fashion, who, even then celebrated for her youth, had once moved so unostentatiously through their midst.

But her triumph was so quick, so easy in the more cosmo-politan life of the city, that for Lady de Montfort it lost its savour. Her next adventure must be to break this too; break it, if she could. But her popularity was almost too strong.

King Edward died, and there were many who would have liked, many more than one would have imagined, to move back the hands of the clock. People began to look forward with pleasure to a renewal of the Victorian era. But Adèle was not among them. Her heart had never accepted the Victorian fog of morality. Indeed had she been able to diagnose her misfortune, she would have known that she had been born thirty or forty years too early. She was a post-European-War type. Moreover, the predilection for mono-gamy, so strong a trait of many characters, was lacking in hers. To be true to one man was against her nature: but this very deprivation, which for so long she had undergone in order to play her part, full of the lure of the unknown, in the primitive society of the Shires, had, in fact, communicated to her for a time a rather perverse sensual enjoyment. But those days were finished.

Perhaps her attitude to love was rooted in her blood. The Americans run to extremes, oscillate violently, for instance, between Total Prohibition and Total Inebriation (and each makes the other an inevitable reaction). The Pilgrim Fathers, when they left England, were most surely essaying to run away from themselves, to elude the strength of their own passions, that, pent up, had distilled them into so gloomily bitter and cantankerous a minority, quite as much as to escape a problematic religious persecution. As well attempt to avoid your own shadow.

And when they reached the Land of Promise and had set up their rigid little gods, planted the altars firmly in this alien soil, perhaps they found it already possessed. It was almost as though the native gods of this continent, hidden far away under vast, dreary plains and huge, rocky mountains, had laid on this race that was to come a peculiar curse, had decreed that the descendants of these seekers after an iron-bound truth, these people who sought so hardly the things of the spirit, and despised the flesh and the fleshpots, should be endowed with every material blessing, every comfort that wealth and prosperity could give, and yet should always be restless, unable to achieve a spiritual consolation or any balance between the body and the spirit. The fruits have been twofold; one exemplified by Purity Leagues and book-bannings, the other by the enormous quantity of divorces in America, and the very free codes of behaviour that characterise life in the American (Bohemian) quarter of Paris. And it may be that Adèle was now unconsciously bent on exacting in one lifetime — rather late in it, too — an adequate compensation for all the repressions of her ancestors.

She began then — at first, quietly — to indulge in affairs of the heart. But, however discreet, she always loved with fervour. Meanwhile her mind, small, free, erratic and original within the compass of its power, roamed at ease in the upper air, released from those dungeons of despair guarded by the twin Freudian ogres of Inhibition and Complex.

Soon she paraded her lovers a little more openly: and it

was now that a second passion, to become inextricably entangled with the first, definitely manifested itself.

In the days of her tableaux, her home had been comfortable, exotic, full of incense, cushions, orchids and tuberoses. One room alone in all the house had been permeated by a gentle, phthisic pre-Raphaelitism: monochrome cartoons by Burne-Jones and a large painted cupboard by the same wistful hand figured in it. But the rest of the house had been conceived purely as an impersonal background, adjunct of scents, dresses, flowers. Little tables swarmed with the precious inutilities of Fabergé: miniature trees in gold and silver; flowers made of the wings of butterflies with emerald calyxes; jade toads, with ruby eyes, holding a lapis ash-tray; pink quartz rabbits, nibbling green blades of chrysoprase, that proved to be bells; crystal owls that were inkpots.

But now decoration obsessed her, though at first she exhibited no symptom of the virtuosity — for virtuosity, however ludicrous, it was — that she later displayed. Perhaps she did not personally supervise, left it to others in this first instance. Indeed it lacked the charm, even, of the house as she had dramatised it twenty years previously; seemed a pitiful example of that period-furnishing which was already laying waste her native land. A Mermaid Tavern ensued. There was much expensive German-oak panelling, while upon every ceiling, very obviously put up in squares, mermaids played their lutes, and the plaster roses of secrecy bloomed in the least expected places. Old oak settees, cupboards, dressers filled every room with a creaking, numskull woodenness, and there were oak armchairs, built up entirely of a sequence of hard, wooden protuberances, electric, unflickering candles, iron bolts of a truly lockjaw rustiness upon oak doors, wooden latches with strings attached and many other of the cruel, catch-finger devices of the Tudors: last, but not least, there was an Elizabethan lover. He was a pioneer of the waste places (or is it spaces?), a man as much given to climbing mountains as any schoolmaster during his summer vacation, an explorer, a poet; but, like all his type, alas, his exploring was better than his poetry. The Elizabethan phase lasted for a year or so. But one day the lover left — or was dismissed; the house was dismantled, refurnished, and a Roman Prince reigned in his stead.

Far from wishing to drop her because of this indiscretion, people now gave her an instance of how staunch friends can be (for there is only one unforgivable sin in the eyes of such loyal, worldly friends, and that is loss of money). They flocked round her, eager to see every detail of the palace that had been born within this bellying, yellow-fronted Regency house. And they admired the Ispahan carpets and Genoese velvets, the tall, gilded chairs, the Venetian brocades, the hooded mantel-pieces and *torcieri*, the bronzes on tables of Italian walnut, painted balustrades from churches, and fine pictures. It was effectively scenic. From a decorative, as probably from an amorous point of view, this was a successful moment in her life. The house looked well, had developed airy vistas, seemed bigger : the Prince was large, handsome, cultivated and attentive. Then, after many months, there was a sudden reversal. The Prince went back to Rome, and, as if by magic, an over-elegant young German, like a too-willowy, canary-coloured bulldog, was found in his place. Within a week or two, the de Montfort house had turned München, 1914. Its shiny black walls were now splashed with rich orange and pale yellow, there were divans of red and purple, black-glass bath-rooms with sunk baths of malachite, and the whole place was filled with very excitable Munich glass and groups of Nymphen-burg china ; for the Germans are a patriotic race, and German trade followed German love. Her friends had noticed, too, that the food varied with each régime, in accordance with style and lover. Plain Elizabethan fare of an overwhelming abund-ance, pies and puddings and oyster-and-lark patties, had given way to more elaborate and Machiavellian dishes, to ducks, for example, that were assassinated, torn limb from limb before your eyes, then pounded and boiled in brandy, and now yielded again to over-rich, German dishes. It seemed as if everything was stuffed with lobster and truffles, and served up with cream.

The young German stayed, month after month. But now the two processes, which were starting to work together, though not yet at an excessive rate, were arrested by the 'Great' War. Upon the outbreak of it, Lady de Montfort was, I think, glad to intern her lover. At any rate, she 'did up' her house as a hospital at great personal expense. She had forgotten, however, to consult the War Office before putting the work in hand, and

when, now that it was completed, she offered it to them, coupled
with an intimation that she did not desire rent for the premises,
technical difficulties ensued. Various War Office departments
played battledore and shuttlecock with the question for several
years, but since the war ended before they were ready for its
beginning, nothing was ever decided. And so Lady de Montfort had to be content with living there herself (as she said, it
brought the war home to one) and with doing her own modest
bit, by 'giving the boys on leave a good time': though for this
she was unrewarded, and received no recognition from an un-
grateful country. The war stopped at last — and the next time
I saw the house, the white paint, the white enamel furniture,
the iron-rations laid by the place of each guest, as graceful,
picturesque adjunct to a rationed diet, and, as remembrancer of
mortality, the smell of chloroform with which during those years
she had so modishly invested it, were gone, gone for ever: and
the sober Park Lane shell now contained a Petit Trianon.

$$\cdot \qquad \cdot \qquad \cdot \qquad \cdot \qquad \cdot$$

It was with this Petit Trianon period, I consider, that Lady
de Montfort entered on her grand period of beauty, youth
and fame, and that the processes, which we have watched at
work, grew together like two trees and culminated in monstrous
blossom after monstrous blossom. From now onwards, until
she disappears out of this story — and it ends — the mask is
the same, even though the clothes vary: the manifestations are,
to all purposes, identical, and the flowering is mechanical. We
have lifted up the mask a little, in order to understand how
human features have grown into it. Just as in Soviet Russia
it has recently been discovered that under the varnished ikons,
which are so alike as to be indistinguishable, an original art
and form lie hidden; and that to see them the restorer is
forced, so thick and deep are the later coatings of paint with
which the personal delineation of a true artist has been covered
up year after year, to attack the outer surface with a chisel, so
here we have attempted some such rather rough operation. But
now it is finished. We must accept the appearance — and
replace the mask.

Let the reader at this very moment picture Adèle for himself, but do not let him place this lacquered apparition in the
dress of any one period: rather let him, instead, animate for
himself a fashion-plate, the most fashionable fashion-plate he

can find, from the illustrated papers of whatever week in whatever month of whatever year it may be in which he reads this story. Thus will he see for himself our heroine, as she looked, wished to look, would look — if she were alive. For, however different, the heights of fashion in a way resemble one another. It is the intensity of it that matters. We realise that this is the 'latest thing'. Even though she be dead, we must take her embalmed corpse and clothe it in the dress of the actual moment. In this manner she will most assuredly come to life . . . only the reader, for his part, must always remember to make her look 'astonishingly young'.

. . . . .

Whether I was the first, the only one at the moment, to watch the development of these strange traits, to comprehend the unfolding of these curious and perverse flowers, I do not know. Certainly myself discovered, quite by chance, how it was possible by riding past the front of Lady de Montfort's house on the top of a motor-omnibus to deduce the main outlines of the drama that was taking place within it. Just a glance from above through the dining-room window, as one was whirled along, and I could divine with tolerable precision, if not the name, at least the nature, of the favourite of the minute : notwithstanding, of course, there were moments of bewilderment, as the kaleidoscope revolved with ever-increasing swiftness. Still, as a rule, a single glance would be enough. 'Hullo,' one would exclaim, 'the Spanish attaché has been dismissed, and by the look of the walls, it must be a Russian refugee now.' Or, again, 'So the Austrian dramatist has gone — I thought so. I imagine that macaw in the cage must mean a South American of some sort.' And I found, even in these most transient attempts at decoration, a quality that was a little touching ; the revolving of a primitive machinery, very unexpected in one so modern and removed from nature, which love alone can set into action . . . the instinct of a bird to build a nest. And this perpetual building and rebuilding of a nest that served no purpose was to me rather pitiful.

And now, lest it should be thought that this was the interfering, salacious curiosity of a stranger, let me try to explain the peculiar nature of the link that subsisted between Lady de Montfort and myself. It must be clearly understood that, while never familiar with her in the sense of an intimate exchange of sentiments, I was yet a certain amount in her company: that albeit rather seldom bidden to her house, except for large parties to which all the world was asked, yet from time to time I was, though not one of her very definite 'set', so invited. Perhaps she felt obliged thus silently to enable me to watch her, thus tacitly to let me into her secrets, since doubtless she was aware, as I was, of an indissoluble tie. — Everybody is somebody's bore. (Nor need this for an instant be taken as a reflection on anybody's particular bore, for the boredom is contained, not in him, but in the relationship between him and the person he bores. In fact, with very few exceptions, it takes two to make a bore.) Moreover this relationship is a thing preordained by an inscrutable Providence. I, then, was Lady de Montfort's bore; recognised it, made the most of it — nay! gloried in it. To be, after this manner, a specially appointed bore by divine warrant, carries with it its duties as much as its privileges. In this story we are not dealing with her voyages. They pertain to one that is yet to be written. But she belonged to the floating pleasure-seekers of Europe. I travelled too. So that, whether I saw her in a London ballroom, in a Berlin concert-hall, at the Opera in Vienna, at the 'Ritz' in Paris, bathing at Antibes or whatever the fashionable beach of the moment might be, sitting at a table in the Piazza at Venice, at a dance in New York, or in Fez, Cairo, Leningrad or Seville, I made a point of talking to her . . . or, if not talking, of remaining a little by her side. For what God hath joined together, let no man tear asunder: and we were, as it seemed through all eternity, bound helplessly together in the coils of an intolerable, though on my part interested and admiring, ennui.

I observed Lady de Montfort with care, but there was no longer any actual need for it. The world now knew everything about her, except her age and the means by which she kept it secret. At first her friends, again, were startled by the quite brazen parade of her lovers which she affected, for she would never lunch or dine with them unless she were allowed to bring with her the man of the moment. (She always had a delightfully inappropriate phrase to explain the appeal he made to her.) And sometimes, as though by a feat of prestidigitation, a new man would appear without warning in place of the one who had been expected, and a new phrase would surely be found ready to describe him. For, since her war experiences, another strongly racial quality had grown to inspire her passions: an insatiable demand for novelty. But she loved with an equal ferocity, with her body and her soul, whether it was for a year or a night. And her love affairs were very defined: the next began where, and when, the last had ended.

Yet, notwithstanding their infinite variety, there was at the same time now visible in her lovers — with one or two notable exceptions to which we shall revert — a quite evident line of descent. Heretofore they had not resembled one another; but now, of whatever shade, colour, creed or disposition, it was possible to reduce the majority of them to a common denominator, so that they ought perhaps to be considered, either as manifold expressions of some ideal lover, or as the persistent, identical expression which she called out from any miscellaneous sequence of men. Her lovers must amuse, as well as love her: they must learn to laugh, act and 'do stunts' in much the same manner, they must be able to mimic her friends. Above all, they must take as much interest in decoration as herself, and, finally, must play the piano sufficiently well for them to form a rock to which the delicate tendrils of her duets could cling: for now she had discarded the eminent musicians, and only desired to play duets with her lovers. But however much approximation to type there was in these men, yet, as one succeeded another, the spiritual differences remained so marked that her friends never lost their curiosity about them.

As for herself, Lady de Montfort had become a more amusing character than one would, twenty years before, have deemed possible. It would, perhaps, be incorrect to describe her mind as being fashioned on unconventional lines, since this would impute to it too much importance. But if on the whole conventional, there were yet ominous gaps that could never be filled, depths that it was impossible to plumb, unexpected corners of knowledge, and hidden trap-doors from which the most personal, puck-like of harlequins would leap out on a sudden and rap you with his baton.

She had, of course, long ago given up reading novels or poetry, things which had once supplied an element of beauty in her life: consequently, her thoughts were more original, in the sense that they were less borrowed, while at the same time the discovery that many years ago she had read this or that book, and that it had left this or that impress on her memory, brought into her conversation all the elements of surprise, pleasant surprise. And just as she had speeded up the tempo of her life, so had she allowed the engine of her mind to race. She had, in fact, torn off her label. Far from being able to predict, as in her middle period, exactly what she would say, now her friends never knew what she would say next: or, again, it would be more accurate to state that they knew now that they never knew what she would say next, so that after all, and despite herself, this very absence of labels amounted to a new one. She had wanted to smash her former mode of life, but all these things meant that her friends remained as much her friends as ever. She could not shock, she could only amuse them.

And then she was so energetic that, however much she had longed to destroy her creation, she did not want to give up her activities, being content to outrage the conventions without forgoing the pleasures they sheltered. She lived always in a whirl of activity. Even the ease, one suspected, with which she looked 'astonishingly young' must have consumed an ever-increasing portion of those years left to her. For she who wishes to remain young out of season must now submit her body to an iron discipline, must be ready when least disposed for it — when, for example, still sleeping after the ball of a few hours before — to contort herself into the most unusual and ungraceful of postures, to be flung round and round her trainer's head like a lasso, to roll, undulate and writhe on the floor, to forfeit for ever the solace of good food and good drink, to go for days with nothing but half a cup of *consommé* to support the flesh, to sit through long and exquisite meals, eat nothing, and show no symptom of torture, to stand up for hours against a wall daily, while an attendant turns on her naked body a hose of battering, pommelling water, alternately ice-cold and boiling-hot, and finally at intervals to be carved about like a fowl, and without complaint or any reception of sympathy : because she must never admit how her days are engrossed, and least of all may she confess to the brutal knife of the 'plastic surgeon'. Suttee would teach these ladies nothing. But then women are more single-minded than men, and, though uncontrolled and uncontrollable, it was extraordinary to observe how serenely Adèle had disciplined herself in some directions, how, furthermore, she was willing to subordinate everything to one purpose, use everything she possessed toward an intensification of love.

And in addition to love, there was the rival passion, decoration; which, as we have said, now even extended to the food. She was at heart eclectic, I fancy, with no particular sympathy in her own mind for any one period. Out of each one she adopted, she brought very easily, very cleverly, its particular characteristics, and also added to it, perhaps, something of her own. And with the full flowering of this talent, however absurd, it was as though she furnished a house with such skilful understanding that it actually materialised for her some ghost of the time she aimed at, or conjured up for her some daemon of the element or machine, or whatever it might be, that at the moment she was attempting to paraphrase. For now she was no longer content with period-furnishing, but essayed things more difficult, elusive. And, incidentally, she showed real genius in the continual, recurrent disposal of the furniture. Expensive as the habit sounds, she often made, rather than lost, considerable sums of money over each unfurnishing. But then, she attended to it personally, bought the things herself. And often I would meet her in auction-rooms, bidding feverishly for her fetish of the hour, or would see her returning home, her smart, lacquered car loaded very inappropriately with all this new fuel for a new fire.

It is, indeed, impossible to say where love began and decoration ended. Did the man dictate the style, or the style the man? For ever could this point be argued, since it is comparable to the old question, not nearly so silly as it sounds, as to whether the hen lays the egg, or the egg the hen. Did the man keep pace with the house, or the house with the man: or did they keep pace together? It is a sequel impossible to drag apart. Sometimes there would be a lull of a few months, and then change would succeed change with an inconceivable, a stupefying, rapidity. Some of the men and houses, it may be, promised well, but were, in one way or another, in practice disappointing: or, again, it might be merely that she was in a fickle, uncertain mood. Then the Park Lane mansion would break into short, syncopated fits of decoration, that would serve to put anyone save a great detective on the wrong track.

One day it would begin to assume a grand, *settecento* Italian air, on the second a prudent Biedemeyer, the third an elegant Chippendale, the fourth a fiery Magyar, the fifth a frigid Norwegian, full of painted furniture and Viking designs, the sixth it would be School of Fontainebleau, the seventh a solid Queen Anne. The alteration wrought within each of the earth's short transits would seem almost a miracle in its abrupt completeness.

During those frenetic hours of preparing, in which the work gathered momentum like a boulder rolling down a hill, Lady de Montfort would be present, in order personally to cheer the workmen on, or would occasionally herself mount a ladder and join in with a paint-brush : for the house must be finished before she wearied of the man . . . was that it? And I wondered if the honest British workmen to whom she gave such constant and diversified employment had formed any just idea as to the nature of the intrigues which they were thus called upon to assist? But Adèle herself had developed such a truly amazing technique of arranging her house, that it was quite possible that soon she would be able to dispense with their services altogether. One touch from her long fingers enabled even the most cumbrous objects to move as though affected by some occult process of levitation. Huge pianos, enormous cupboards, vast tables, all slid, ran or leapt upstairs with scarcely any assistance.

.   .   .   .   .

It is, of course, impossible to remember all the changes. The Petit-Trianon period endured for some little time. The cause of it was a young French diplomat of good but boring family, who was a skilful, rather skittish writer upon the gallantries of the period. He told amusing little stories, and played the piano well. Panels of old *toile-de-Jouy* lined the walls, the chairs and sofas were exquisite with their slight, gilded frames and *petit-point*, while tall specially designed *vitrines* exhibited arrangements of pastoral skirts, shoes, shepherds' crooks and flat, ribboned hats of straw, and in smaller glass cases stood painted fans and snuff-boxes. The food was delicious, simple French food. But now there intervened a rather bad, late-Léon-Bakst fortnight of Oriental lampshades, cushions covered with tassels, poppy-heads treated with gold paint, and arranged in wide glass bowls, luxurious divans, incense of an Oriental, unecclesiastical variety, while kebabs, yaghourt and Turkish Delight were the only refreshments supplied. Sherbet was served with the coffee after dinner. This proved to be the necessary dramatisation for a young Jewish musician. Then, suddenly, all such trumpery was swept away by a breeze from the great open spaces of Empire. A rough lover from New Zealand (though he, too, adhered to type, played the piano and sang a little) succeeded, during which the high plaster ceilings were hidden by wattle roofs, supported on carved totem-poles, and guests at luncheon and dinner openly complained that their salmon was tinned, their mutton frozen : but this fortunately for them proved as mutable an affair as the decoration indicated. A relapse into a Queen Anne style followed. This was occasioned by a young literary critic who enjoyed excavating that period. Together Adèle and he played the composers of the time, and she offered to her guests good, plain, substantial English fare. But a surprise was in store. Without any warning the house in Park Lane broke out into the most complete and fantastic *chinoiserie*; old Chinese papers, lacquer furniture, dragon tables and gold temple flowers. Adèle's old friends were really alarmed, for a rich young Chinese Prince had just arrived in London to be educated. Nevertheless, their fears proved groundless, and (did they feel rather disappointed?) the man who had inspired the decoration turned out to be a young German writer on art, a specialist in this style : but the chop-suey, the pickled sharks' fins, bamboo shoots, lily-of-the-valley and narcissus bulbs soaked in white wine, the hundred-year-old eggs, so beautiful to look at when cut in slices, with their malachite-green yolks and polished, deep black, outer rings, and with their curious taste of all things buried in the earth, of truffles, mushrooms and their like, did not tend to make him popular with those who frequented the de Montfort house. This lover lapsed, and a young Frenchman succeeded to the position : a Frenchman whose family had sprung up under the shielding wings of the Imperial eagles. An airy Empire style, therefore, with plenty of gilded caryatids supporting branched candelabras, ensued. The walls were painted in bright colours and the beautifully made furniture of simple line suited the proportions of the rooms. A French chef was encouraged to do his best, and was not restricted by any fantastic rules. But there followed a reversion to Charles II, though on this occasion without any Italian influence: a dignified, gilded Charles II.

The daemon of this transformation was a writer, again: a writer, moreover, upon gallantries, but of course upon those of the Stuart period. Nevertheless, he used for his work the same 'devil' formerly employed by the Petit-Trianon lover; a poor, half-starved, religious, mild, grey-haired, Church-of-England, spectacled little woman, named Miss Teresa Tibbits, who was the last surviving descendant of a thousand curates, and who now, rigged out with a green shade over her eyes, like a pirate with a bandaged forehead, was forced by her poverty thus for ever to grub away among the most intimate possible details of the love-affairs of dead duchesses in the Reading Room of the British Museum. And since she must be acquainted with the most scabrous minutiae, she was continually forced to blush for herself by having to ask the attendants for the most daring and unexpected books; the most lurid of which, she was informed by them, with a look of intense disapprobation, could only be seen by someone duly armed with a certificate, which guaranteed moral rectitude and the fact that the bearer was a responsible person, autographed by the Archbishop of Canterbury and witnessed by all the Trustees of the Museum. Miss Tibbits occasionally visited the house in Park Lane on business; and I wondered whether her trained eye observed the living material that waited for some unborn Miss Tibbits of the future.

The luxury, the gilding, the soft carpets of this Charles II epoch suddenly went — as the hair of someone struck with an appalling sorrow is said to turn — white in one night. Everything was painted white. The furniture was stripped; beautiful old gilding and old paint were torn remorselessly from the objects to which they belonged; and ash-colour and mouse-colour were the only tints, however faint; grilled bones and peeled oranges the only food, however monotonous, that were permitted. This, again, was mysterious; seemed to her friends to indicate some fresh aberration. Lady de Montfort's phrase, to explain this favourite, too, was embarrassing. She would say, 'Why, he's wonderful. One glance from him strips you bare.' But, in the end, it was discovered that this denudation portended nothing more exciting than the fact that the new favourite was a psycho-analyst, who boasted that he could unravel and strip the soul.

Life never stops still, and soon colour came back to the house — rich, abundant colour. It was transformed into a Spanish palace. The 18th Duque de Bobadilla, 10th Grandee of the First Class, the 17th Duque de Miraflores y Mirador, the 15th Duque de Salamandar, the 12th Duque de los Nuevos Mundos, the 10th Duque de Alcama Alcarbareo, the 20th Marques de Carabas Viejo, the 19th Marques de Guadalajara, the 18th Marques de Rosina Media, the 28th Visconde de Nuestro Salvador and 42nd Conde de la Estramadura Este, reigned over it in perfect unity, for they were one person. There were Sevillian, white-flashing *patios* with white flower-pots and the inevitable jasmine and orange-blossom, and out of them led the saloons furnished with Spanish rugs and tapestries, Mudejar plates of a strange, gold bronze and cream intricacy, lovely cabinets of tortoise-shell, ivory and gilded wood, and deep sombre velvets. Pictures by Goya and Velasquez hung on the walls. And the food was tinged, too, with the prevailing fashion : there were such stuffed and pungent dishes as Huevos à la Flamenco, Arroz Valenciano, Olla Podrida, Tortillas, Pollo Cubano, such soft melting sweets as Turron and Membrilla. And it was in this period that there took place an unfortunate incident which occasioned a lot of talk at the time, and even found its way into the Press : for example, 'Dragoman' of the *Daily Express* reported it in full.

It is, of course, impossible for us to be certain whether the face-lifting operation of that summer — it would be about August 1924 — was the first that she had undergone, but, at any rate, if not the first, it was the most noticeable, tightening, as it did, all the lines of the face, and imparting to the mouth a strained pursing of the lips that prevented her from closing her mouth. The healing occupied some weeks, and she was ordered to go abroad in order to recuperate. Filled with enthusiasm for all things Spanish, she set out in September to visit Spain with Lady Robert Chickmuster, daughter of Mr. Silas Minkin, Third. This fascinating woman had recently suffered the same treatment at the hands of her plastic-surgeon. Conversation cannot have been easy, for the actual muscular movement of the lips, which talking induces, still occasioned both of them great anguish, and, in addition, each was aware of, but must not mention, the fact of this identical agony. They motored to many places, including Seville, where they stayed with the Duque de Bobadilla. One morning the two ladies wanted to see the Cathedral, and while standing in the Capella Mayor, a verger approached them. This unfortunate man was afflicted with deafness and, looking at their faces, very naturally concluded from the shape of the sewn-up mouths that they were whistling. Explanation was impossible, and they were turned out of the Cathedral for sacrilege. . . . A most painful scene ensued. Tension mounted for weeks. The British Embassy made representations to the Spanish Government and the Vatican : but the deaf verger stuck to his guns, and no apology to the two ladies was ever forthcoming.

Nor was this all the harm that so small an unpleasantness engendered. The Andalusian peace of the Casa de Bobadilla was shattered by a most bitter quarrel which broke out between Lady de Montfort and Lady Robert; a quarrel which rent London for more than six months. It must be remembered that both of them were doubtless much tired after several weeks of arduous sight-seeing, a very fruitful begetter of trouble, and that Lady Robert had in the near past been exacerbated by various matrimonial difficulties which had culminated in an annulment.

But such sudden tempests always arise out of a trifle. Lady de Montfort had said, 'I think, dear, you should be more careful. Of course, knowing you as I do, the old man's suggestion is absurd. But since that last little illness of yours, before you came abroad, you do shape your mouth in a peculiar way, as though you were whistling.'

'Is it *likely* I should whistle, Adèle? *I* can get all the attention I need without that sort of thing, thank you. *I* don't have to whistle, I assure you. I'm not as old as all that.'

'I don't quite see, dear, what "being old" has got to do with it? We're all as old as we look, they say.'

'Well, I don't think what *you* did made *you* look any younger. You mustn't mind. Of course everybody knows you look "astonishingly young", Adèle. The papers are always telling us so.'

'Well, I thought by the way you were talking to me you must be older than me. I don't know, I'm sure.'

'But I wasn't whistling, and I saw no one.'

'And if you had been whistling, nobody would have looked. . . . But I wish you'd stop lecturing.'

'Well, dear, then that's all right, but . . . How do you mean, "looked"?'

'Anyhow, Boo-boo, if you didn't whistle *then*, you needn't shout at me *now*.'

'Shouting at you would be no use. It would be like shouting at an *image*. I don't know what's the matter with you. Your expression never changes.'

'Well, yours is quite different, Boo-boo, to what it used to be. You used to look so smiling and good-tempered. All I meant was that it seemed kind of silly to whistle at that foolish verger.'

'Verger yourself, Adèle. What d'you mean, "verger"? I'd like to know. And if I am, is there anything wrong in it?'

'No, my dear, I didn't say that — you know I didn't. It's a misunderstanding. I said "verger" — you know . . . the man in the Cathedral.'

'Oh, then there *was* a man in the Cathedral, was there? I didn't see him, but I'm not a bit surprised. . . . I suppose now you'll have that house of yours done up as a Cathedral, won't you? . . . I can just see the gargoyles.'

'Well, if I do, dear, I shall ask you to come and whistle in it.'

At this moment, fortunately, the Duque de Bobadilla, his attention attracted by the noise, entered, and the ladies melted into tears.

Possibly this unpleasantness embittered Lady de Montfort against all things Spanish. In any case, on her return to England the Spanish background was swept away, and there ensued, for a time, a quick, rattling succession of styles, culminating in an African house of little wooden stools and ricebowls. 'Queer . . .', people said, and personally I received a shock, for one day I visited an auction-room, and was much perturbed to see Lady de Montfort, obviously in high spirits, herself openly bidding for negro fetishes, for ivory masks from Nigeria and wooden ones from Dahomey, for tusks of carved ivory and bronzes from Benin: while the fact which lent colour, if one may use the expression, to these black innuendoes was that the man of the moment now never appeared at luncheon or dinner, though everyone knew that a man there must be and was, and even as they wondered, the sound of a gurgling, jungle-like song would be heard from an upper storey.

Relief, therefore, was general when before six weeks had elapsed Lady de Montfort fell in love with a hunting-man. This was a break-away from her usual type, for, unlike even the last invisible and anonymous ghost, he was unmusical: no jungle-song rolled deeply from under the roof-tops, and only very occasionally a fragment of 'D'ye ken John Peel' would break what seemed almost the dumb silence of the animal world. But the foundations of this new affection must have been well and truly laid, for it endured six months. And though he seldom spoke, he had side-whiskers and a handsome face, and was quite happy for hours sucking a straw. Moreover, if he was not altogether at home in the world of men and women, Adèle found the means whereby he might feel less strange. Promptly she had her bedroom done up as a stable. All the chairs, even the bed itself, were re-stuffed — with horsehair. The curtains, too, were of box-cloth. The dining-room became an ostler's room, with bits and harness, and such other things, hanging from wooden pegs. Roast mutton, toasted cheese and ale were the order of the day for guests.

Next, as far as I can remember, came a famous Russian singer. Now she reverted to type. But, nevertheless, Lady de Montfort suffered a great shock. There is no doubt, I think, that they loved with passion. Moreover, each of these two, who in spite of certain tastes in common appeared to be so different, idealised the other. In Lady de Montfort he saw the perfect English liberty-loving aristocrat: when she looked into his eyes, it seemed to her as though she were gazing down into the dark depths of the Slav soul. He was, for her, the Slav soul personified. And when by chance they found that in reality they both hailed from the same home-town in the Middle West, on each side the disillusionment was utter, the upbraiding acrimonious. Each felt as though caught in the revolving, circular movement of maelstrom or whirlwind. However far we travel, we come back to our starting-point, whether we wish it or not.

Next morning the blood-red domes of the Kremlin faded out from every wall, and Park Lane went Mexican. High plumes, jade masks, crystal skulls, silver ornaments of a later period, and a young Mexican oil magnate of musical and artistic tastes, completed the effect. Followed soon a Charles X period; romantic, redolent of Balzac and Chopin. Fans once more littered the tables, and there were small walnuts, with white kid gloves folded up in them, to show how tiny the dead hand had been. Miss Tibbits reappeared from her lair in the British Museum, for, again, it was a young French writer who had evoked this change.

So the days passed. Take, for example, the chart for just a month or two from one of the later years. Where facts are uncertain, the space is left blank: where one must deduce one's own conclusions, a question mark is substituted.

STYLE OF DECORATION AT PARK LANE
(and, where details are remembered, of food offered to guests)

1928		*Description of Man*
Jan. 1–22	German Baroque—silvered tables and chairs. Wiener Schnitzel and Moselle.	German Baroque Baron with grey hair.
Jan. 22–25	Rumanian. Painted boxes and painted clothes. Caviare and Rumanian sweets with every meal.	Rumanian Pianist.
Jan. 25 to March 3	Ceilings painted light blue or dark blue, with appropriate sun or stars. Furniture made of broken propellers, curtains of grey balloon silk.	Musical young Airman.
March 3–13	Moghul. Curries served with 'Bombay duck'.	?
March 13–26	Portuguese 18th-century.	Dwarf Diplomat.
March 26 to April 28	Cinquecento Italian.	Italian Count.
April 28–30	Gipsy Caravan. Hedgehogs baked in clay.	?
May 1–10	Czechoslovak.	
May 10 to June 2	Toucan and parrots' feathers.	Peruvian Diplomat.
June 2–18	Dutch pictures and furniture. Tulips in bowls.	Dutch Novelist.
June 18–19	Norwegian painted furniture installed. Smoked salmon.	?
June 19–23	Mid-Victorian. Very long meals. 'Roasts' of every description.	Young Photographer, English.
June 23–29	Persian 18th century. Tiles, carpets and silks. Two cypress trees in tubs outside the front door. Lamb, served with almonds and roots of lily-of-the-valley.	Young Persian Prince.

It was in 1932 that Adèle branched off very sensationally from the type she generally cultivated. She fell in love, desperately in love, with Thomas Cruikshank McFlecker, the famous deep-sea fisher; a man who for his own pleasure moved through the dangerous, undulating vegetation of tropic waters. Sometimes he would descend just for a few hours, in the outfit of a diver — that rare, armoured robot of the seas, attached by so slender an umbilical cord to his mother, Earth; or, perhaps, he would instead be lowered down into the depths in a device of his own invention, a large steel and glass cradle, and would there remain for days or weeks, dangling in front of the tantalised but ogling sharks and giant cuttle-fish, until they gradually lost their appetites and wilted. Actually McFlecker had come to England on business, for he had placed the contract for one of these new and improved cradles (this one was to be as big as a small room) with a firm of shipbuilders, and was waiting until it was finished, and he could return to his work. Meanwhile he needed recreation.

Adèle let herself go thoroughly in every direction. She bought eight new ropes of pearls (for now, since the war, she was a very rich woman), and filled the house with dolphins, mermaids and seaweed; that is to say, chair and table assumed marine shapes, being supported by silver dolphins or mermaids, or a bearded Italian Neptune. with a rakish crown and a trident like a gigantic toasting-fork. The armchairs were all of them restuffed for the second time — on this occasion with seaweed, which, she said, was much more healthy, she was certain, than feathers, wool or horsehair. The mattress of her bed, of course, was filled with seaweed and enclosed in a gigantic shell — a real, not artificial one, from the South Seas. In all these rooms there were flat glass bowls in which were arranged shells, pearls and sharks' teeth under shallow, flickering surfaces of water. Chinese goldfish, with three tails, goggled and performed their crinolined tangos up and down the length of their narrow, oblong tanks. The dining-room was now a grotto, a beautiful imaginative grotto, in which the chairs were modelled after open scallop-shells, and the table itself was made of nacre, while above it, over the heads of the guests, was suspended a vast sunfish which concealed a light. Here, during the whole of the season, she gave a series of fish-lunches and fish-dinners, which she would preface, when she sat down, with one of her explanatory phrases. Pointing at the deep-sea fisher, she would say in her voice with its slightly rising inflection : 'That is a very remarkable man. He teaches one all that there is to know about the ocean bed.' In the drawing-room she had installed a sizzling machine that shot out sparks at unwary guests and filled the house with ozone, until, in consequence, it smelt like a night-club or Tube station (the only places in which ozone is ever consciously encountered). Furthermore, her face had again been lifted that spring, and the fresh tightening of the mouth had made it assume a very piscine expression.

.   .   .   .   .   .

The end was drawing near. . . . He must return to the islands. New and interesting studies awaited him there. The steel and crystal cradle was ready. She determined, which was unlike her, to accompany him. So, early in October, they set out, sailing first to the West Indies.

I met her the day before she left England, and never had she looked younger or more radiant. She was now a famous beauty, whose photograph, taken upside down from an airplane or from below by the photographer — who must lie flat on the floor while she was suspended head downwards, like the sunfish, from the ceiling — appeared in every week's illustrated papers ; a renowned forcible-feeder whose food no one was enduring enough to refuse ; a figure in the land, in spite of every mitigating circumstance ; and one felt that her absence, even for a time, would make a gap, would sadden, not only her friends, but every gossip-writer in this country — of which gossip, gramophones and biscuits at the time seemed the only flourishing industries.

My readers know the rest. Arrived at the ocean-gardens of the Southern Seas, the cradle, which, like a submarine, manufactured its own air, was let down by steel cables. A terrible storm, unexpected by the Weather Bureau, and of an unequalled severity, blew up without warning. Something, we know not what, occurred to break the metal ropes. And so, deep-down, turning over and over, bumping on every current, the steel and crystal cage, devoid of any decoration, essentially stark in outline, now floats along with its two skeletons. She is still dressed in the fashions of 1932, and wears eight rows of pearls ; a grotesque exhibit for the fishes that

peer and point their cruel sneering or sworded beaks at it, or
lash at it in fury with their tails. Or, again, as though in
mockery of an idyll that is over and yet is thus forced for ever
to parade its continuance, the cradle settles for a while in
some leafy, spring-like glade of the ocean bed, some watery
glade that resembles a grove in England, with little flowers
blowing from the rocks, and small highly coloured fishes
moving through the foliage, as birds move through the branches
of the trees on land, and over all the refracted light plays in an
illusional splendour of sunrise, patches falling here and there :
and sometimes the light hits the glass of the cabin, and reveals
within it the terrible white-fingered figures, knocked together
by the rolling, until, as it were embracing, their mouths meet
in a double, lipless grin. Then the swell comes, and the figures
fall apart : and so for countless ages, these figures, in their
barnacled hut, moving and tumbling on every tide, will dwell
in a semi-eternity of endless green water, alone, and now
forgotten. For though, at the time of their deaths, people
could, as the phrase goes, talk of nothing else ; though the
memorial service was very largely attended, and letters and
telegrams of condolence reached Sir Simon from all quarters
and from every class, yet now, and after so long, there has
come a generation that knew her not. The gossip-writers have
passed to other and newer topics, and the house in Park Lane
— that seems with its grottoes, though emptied of its painted
fish and oceanic effects, to mock her end — is dusty. And
even at this very moment the vans may be calling to remove
the furniture from the piled-up lumber-rooms . . . as they
called so often in her lifetime.

PLAGUE-CART BEFORE HORSE

Now the flights of pigeons that executed their strange symphonies far above us — for each bird had tied to its body a wooden whistle — had stopped their music. The sky had become an immense blue dome, deepening in colour, and no wings seemed to be beating in it, or against it. . . . The evening belonged to the first spring heats, and the air was scented with the lilac, which in this climate had sprung to blossom in a day. We sat out in the courtyard, five of us, talking and drinking cool drinks, and to us, through the immediate and outlying silence, reached the cries and sounds of a great Chinese city: cries and sounds which were to continue without ceasing, drums and gongs and bells and wooden clappers (no one who has not visited China can imagine the variety of sounds that wood striking wood can produce), each one denoting a trade — peddler or juggler or mountebank or fortune-teller — until the morning, when the terrible anthem of the pigs being killed, thousands of them having their throats cut at the same moment, would complete the concert.

The talk, like one of the kites that could, in the day-time, be seen zigzagging up into the sky, veered hither and thither — first touching on people in general, thence to criminals, to crime, and then on to what part, as it were, the scenery might play in a drama. . . . I had seen, I said, in a far, dead island in the western Mediterranean, a house which had the reputation of being cursed: in every generation some terrible, irremediable event occurred within its precincts. This miniature palace lay nestling only a little way above the tideless blue waters that lapped the very foot of the garden; a beautiful, pink marble, eighteenth-century house, surrounded by giant olive trees and by palms. On its scented terraces, broken and crumbling, brooded the doomed Latin decadence of D'Annunzio's novels; here mother killed son in one generation, and brother killed brother in the next. And the criminals whom this little sea-palace bred were handsome and noble, terrible in their crimes. Through the hot days and nights the house smouldered in that dark wood by the sea. There was nothing gloomy about it, only something infinitely passionate and beautiful, but indefinably wicked, so that it was impossible not to wonder whether, at least in this instance, the house had not in reality influenced its inhabitants towards their various cruel deeds and inexorable fates, rather than that the inhabitants had influenced their shell. . . . This delicate, pale rose-coloured dwelling, so elegant, so lovely in proportion and design, was yet an expression of the dark and ancient soil out of which it had grown; its strength — one had almost written 'virtue' — rested in the earth in which it was rooted — and what strange histories haunt that luxuriant, desolate shore! . . . Thus it may be that, if a modern palace were built at Mycenae, on that tremendous and terrible hill, the Furies would come to life again and rush full tilt through the ravine below, till the air would sweep shuddering up to its halls for a moment, as now the tops of the trees, after the aeroplanes have passed, cower down and tremble under the very icy breath of doom. . . . So, too, the peace that pervades many monastic dwellings — even though, long ago secularised, they have sunk to being hotels — may be due more to their structure and site than to the monks who laboured. Why, for example, had they chosen this position? — because it was, to their minds, blessed. What spirit inspired the humble, whitewashed yet aspiring beauty of the design, fitting as closely to the rock, and belonging to it as much as a barnacle to a ship's bottom, and why, before that, had a temple stood here? Similarly, think of the now domesticated temples near us in the Western Hills, with their sweet wistarias, their apple trees in flower, their pools and slanting eaves; the Buddhist priests had surely chosen them because the outlook from them influenced the mind towards peace and virtue?

Christopher Standish took on the argument in a different, more material vein, telling us, from his medical experience at Liverpool and in industrial Lancashire, how typhus can haunt the soil, so that the ground may never be cleared of infection. Thus a slum could be destroyed and a new palace erected instead; yet, however many times the buildings on this site were burnt or pulled down, the typhus would inevitably return. . . . But then, this disease is carried by vermin, and

vermin can survive fire, and sword, and even sanitation:
(think of the gaol-fever that used to make English prisons such
haunted and horrible places of incarceration, attacking even
at times the judges and the juries, so that it seemed as though
this fever, born of criminals, were seeking to enact a revenge
for them upon society!). . . . Such fevers are intelligible;
nevertheless, it would perhaps be true, he thought, to say that
typhus *haunted* the site of such a building. . . . Standish
became silent, and again the cries and various metallic musical
sounds of the night reached us. A fortune-teller was tapping his
way down the lane outside, and one could hear the creaking
wheels of the carts; (so, in England, centuries ago, must have
sounded the plague-carts as they creaked through the streets
of the city at midnight, their husky drivers crying, 'Bring out
your dead!').

Now Angus Rockingham struck up for the first time. 'I
suppose you will think that it is putting the cart before the
horse,' he said, 'but somehow it seems to fit what you are
saying. . . . You know that before I came out here, I was
in Cyprus. I lived there for five years — in that outpost of
empire where every day in the broiling heat the Briton takes
off his topee, and eats roast beef and steak-and-kidney pudding,
roly-poly, and then, as an offering to local colour, devours a
viscous, melting square of Turkish Delight, to the accompaniment of sticky sweet wines. It is the only Greek island with
no Greek statues, no Greek temples, no shape to its landscape;
nothing except its one incomparable Bel Paese — a French
Gothic building, flowering in a beautiful but inapposite position
— and a few, as they seem, whitewashed English parish-
churches masquerading as mosques. The natives, too — you
must call them *natives* — are for the most part not Greek, but
descended from the slave races of Roman times: dirty, stupid,
cringing and for ever unfortunate. . . . However, you won't
want to hear my views about Cyprus, for whenever an English
paper reaches us, you always read that it is the Jewel of the
Empire. Further, I lived, admittedly, in the most beautiful
part of the island; in an ancient Turkish city some three miles
from the sea. There, at least, as one walked by the tideless,
deep-blue waters, something of Greece lingered. Although
there were no temples, not even a pillar of them surviving, the
shore was lined with fragments of marble wall and pavement,

and with shells that seemed, equally, to be the work of some great, long-dead architect. Acanthus and asphodel grew from the broken, shapeless masonry, and anemones turned their fluttering eyes to the sun from any bank where there was soil : and any bank where there was soil indicated foundations lying buried beneath it. . . . On the surface there were neither ancient nor any modern buildings : at least, only one, a large, unused, melancholy looking low structure with the damp-stained plaster peeling from its walls. . . . It had been built as a smallpox hospital some twenty years before, I found out : and then, since smallpox here had been eradicated and extinguished — that much, at least, is to our credit — had, for some reason or other, never been adapted to any other purpose, but had remained virgin and desolate — though, as for that, had it been used, the desolation would, I thought, have been of the very same kind. In this climate — for so far as I could see, no attention had been paid to the fabric — it had remained marvellously whole. Flowering weeds grew on the roof, but the roof itself was still perfect.

'I have said that the building was desolate, but this does not mean that I want you to think that it was ugly : it was not ugly. On the contrary, it was spacious and well-constructed, standing upon an exquisite site ; a poem, as it were, a *fleur du mal* in brick and plaster. The government official who had designed it must surely have been a genius, for, with the little money at his disposal, he had symbolised the idea of illness in general and smallpox in particular. Just as Vanbrugh piled up Blenheim Palace into a triumphal ode for the Great Captain's victories, so this obscure, perhaps unconscious, artist had made out of his rather pitiful materials an absolute expression, a personification, of smallpox, that horrible and disfiguring disease. . . . Not for a moment could you have mistaken it for a prison, nor even for an ordinary isolation hospital. No : smallpox was expressed in its every aspect. It seemed dedicated, in some way, to the development and flowering of this particular plague. Long before I knew its history, I had formed a correct conclusion — as it turned out — concerning its original purpose.

'After I had been there for a year or two, a retired merchant from Bombay came to settle in the town with his wife and children. It was cheap and warm, and after a long sojourn in the East he could not support the English climate. . . . But even here life was difficult; he was never well, he could not find a house, and he did not like the only hotel in the town. (Indeed this was not surprising, for the Cyprus hotel combines the worst points of the English inn and the Turkish caravanserai. . . .) The arrival of the Verskills was a great comfort to me, for I was growing more and more tired of the place, and the family afforded me pleasant companionship. I quickly formed a friendship with Clare, the daughter: a lovely girl and worthy of better things. Her charm, like that of her brothers, was obvious, and consisted in her vitality and health and good spirits. . . . But all the same she was charming, and charged with an energy delightful in this environment. I don't think any of them had much imagination, but they possessed the good-nature of all things that are young and healthy.

'Certainly the father was not imaginative, yet he allowed the town to get on his nerves. He could not bear the system of life he found in the hotel there, for he was used to being master of a house. . . . And then one day, walking among the deserted foundations of temples, down paths lined with asphodel and acanthus that had once been great roads, he saw this low building I have described, and in his dismal discontented fashion fell in love with it. He liked its air of space. Perhaps he even liked its air of loneliness — in any case, with his family about him, he could never be lonely. Servants were easy to secure in Cyprus, though difficult, perhaps, to drill; and he could run it. It would give him something to do. He, rather than his wife — that placid, silent woman — would assume the organisation of the house, inside and out; he would draw up charts for the servants, so that they should know when to get up, and what to do. As for the outside, he would decorate this terrace with geraniums (they grew here as easily as wild flowers), and there he would plant a grove of fruit trees, so that 'the missus' could make her jams again, as she had done, long years ago, in England. . . . I tried — I hardly know why, except that I liked Clare — to dissuade him, invented reasons for not taking the house, said it was damp, and that the provincial government would not sell it. It was silly of me, for after all there was nothing against it — there had never been a case of illness there. However, my arguments were of no avail; the authorities responded more quickly than usual, and, in spite of my pleading, Mr. Verskill acquired his bargain, and was delighted with it. . . . Here it is only fair to say that, to my surprise, he made his new dwelling in its own way charming and agreeable. It became much less depressing, seemed to have come into its own. The colours were cool and gay, the furniture quiet and very English. Even the fruit trees didn't look out of place, and I much enjoyed sitting out in the garden of an evening with the family. . . . I dined there, I remember, the last night before my leave.

'When I returned', he continued, 'they were dead, all dead of smallpox; the first cases in the island for twenty years. . . . And do you know, such a massacre, a family of five, and eight servants, lacks the poignance of an individual tragedy; leaves little but horrified surprise behind it. . . . This is not to say that I did not miss them; I could never bear to pass that way. But sometimes I had to. . . . The house, I suppose, had been fumigated; the windows were shut and barred, the eyes closed again; no air ever blew in. Poor Clare!'

His voice trailed away, to be lost in the sounds of the Chinese night, drums and gongs and bells and wooden clappers, sounds that would continue until the morning; when the terrible anthem of the pigs being killed, thousands of them having their throats cut simultaneously, would complete the concert.

POMPEY AND SOME PEACHES

A STEREOSCOPIC STORY IN TWO PARTS

(For Lorna Andrade)

I

OLD Mulready Maure had been at one time the leading English art critic. He had known every great figure of his period. But when he retired to the gaunt country house near York whence he had originally emerged, his neighbours complained that this lean, angular, quixotic man was a bore. Stories of Rossetti and Whistler, of Swinburne and Morris, meant nothing to these faces that looked permanently 'blooded', indelibly tainted with the smear from the fox's brush. Though my nature prompts me to dislike critics, seeing in them members of the opposite team in the game of Gentlemen *v.* Players or Foxes *v.* Birds of Paradise, I liked listening to the old man's talk, and it was he who first told me, one day when I went to see him, the story about the peaches.

'Even towards the end of Dubosque's life, you could have bought a picture of his, not for a song, but for the mere trouble of crying "Rags and Bones" out in the street. Whereas now that he's dead (where the dealers wanted to get him), only a millionaire can afford to *look* at his work, let alone buy it.

'And what an extraordinary man he was, what an extraordinary painter, more particularly for an Englishman!

'Some great artists construct, like Rubens or Titian or Tiepolo or Delacroix, their own gigantic and overwhelming lands of fantasy, new Indies of the imagination upon whose shores men have never yet set foot: others, like Rembrandt or Chardin or Cézanne, reveal a world equally new, whether dark or glittering with light, within the most familiar objects. And it was to this latter, perhaps almost rarer, division that Richard Dubosque belonged.

'In appearance, as well as in the way in which he approached the art of painting, he resembled much more a

Frenchman than an Englishman, and, as his name showed, he was of French blood; I believe, Huguenot. Even before he came to live up here, the life he led was extremely ascetic. By that, I don't mean that as a young man he had not had his fling, for he was full of temperament, but that his life was dedicated: his desire to paint ousted every other passion, and he would rather look at a glass of Margaux, let us say, and study it, than drink it. But the austerity of his life compared strangely with the greed — if you see what I mean — of his painting, in which I always felt a sense of consuming appetite. No French master, not even Cézanne, possessed a more complete understanding of material objects, a greater feeling for their texture, their volume and the unseeable — if I may phrase it like that — organisation of the interior as expressed by their contour and surface. With his painting of an apple, for instance, he seemed to tell us everything that was known, not only of this particular apple, but of every other apple in the world, and by the voluptuousness of its presentation it was plain that Eve had confided to him the secret hissed into her ear by the serpent. That is what gave him his unique place in English art; he painted objects, material objects, as only a lover could paint them.

'He did not really like seeing *people*, his life was too much occupied by his painting, and he had no wish for distraction. And so his cottage up here on the wolds suited him perfectly. It was a dear little rough, white-walled house, with a garden divided into four compartments by box hedges, and with a wall of loose stones enclosing it, an oasis in the vast prospect. This was his part of the country too, and he loved it and understood it, and the fact that the nearest village to his home was five or six miles away appealed to him as a positive advantage. Of course, various admirers — for he always had a little circle of fervent lovers of his art — used from time to time to stay in the district, so as to be near him. . . . Then, too, he and I were old friends, and now that I was living in the vicinity as well, I used to see a good deal of him. Indeed I believe my chief claim to renown after I have gone, will be that my articles on Dubosque's paintings helped to place him as a great modern master: but I don't think he liked me any more for that. He could have done without any of us. Even if he had made money in his lifetime it would have meant nothing to him — but, as you know, it is his widow who reaps the benefit of the vast sums his pictures fetch today.

'He had married this woman a few years before he settled in the neighbourhood. Perhaps he had not known much about her (for in matters of life, as opposed to those of painting, he always showed the vagueness of the disinterested) except that she had been his mistress, could cook and liked looking after men and things. She did not, of course, he must have realised, understand his pictures, or care for them : but after all, how few people did. And if they married, she could superintend the house, and so he could have more hours in which to paint. . . . There was always so little time, it seemed to him.

'Deborah was tall, large-framed, a handsome creature; about forty then, some fifteen years younger than her husband. And she could be pleasant, in a natural sort of way. But soon after their marriage she began to change. . . . Of course, in spite of the general neglect of him, he was always the centre of interest to a chosen — or rather, choosing — few, a prince of a territory composed of princes. And, now that she met his friends as equals, she became aware of it. . . . What it was all about she could not comprehend, but of one thing she was certain : he *could* make money if he wanted. But he did *not want* to, he was obstinate — pig-headed, she called it. And then, as he was poor — at any rate poor compared with many of his friends — he should not be so wasteful. Beautiful plates of apricots and peaches in the summer, just left to rot so that he could paint them ! "Mustn't touch this" and "Mustn't touch that" ! Never even asked if she'd like to eat one. And often he wouldn't even paint them, he would just sit there staring at the fruit in a way that irritated her beyond bearing, gazing at them as though he were consuming them in a sort of silent, mystic passion of the eyes. (I have often seen him do it.) Well, why didn't he eat them ? He always seemed to keep the best fruit for painting, and when once in the morning, just before he woke, she had stolen into the studio and eaten two of the peaches on the plate, he had made a row ; an awful, vulgar row, to her way of thinking.

'But she'd given him as good as she got : that was one good thing. He'd never had the rough side of her tongue before, she had always treated him different from other people.

But now he was her husband, and she meant to show him, just like she had shown Jack and Andy in the old days. . . . After all, if she stayed there, hour after hour, staring at the slops or the unmade bed instead of doing the chores, how would he get on, she would like to know! . . . Of course, she was fond of him, she admitted to herself (let anyone else venture to criticise him to her!), but he was silly, soft, let anyone treat him anyhow, so long as he could go on painting or staring. . . . And he hardly ever looked at *her*. She was just a fixture. If only she had been an old turnip or an apple or something, he would have sat gazing at her for hours with those love-sick eyes, she supposed. No, all he cared for was his painting; and what came of it? Never even a picture in the Academy: (they might think she knew nothing about Art, but she knew that painters ought to have pictures in the Academy). And no money. She was surprised his friends weren't ashamed of him, instead of crying and fawning round, with their "Yes, Dubosque" and "No, Dubosque" and "Do you really think so, Dubosque?"

'As for Dubosque himself, I imagine, from what I saw, that, as he grew ever more used to her, he became more steadily attached to her. . . . I don't know, but I think, all the same, that he hated her change of voice; for, as his wife, and so the equal of his friends, she had adopted a new voice, like theirs, she thought — a new "*accent*", as she would have said. The old rustic burr, that had been one of her chief attractions for him, had vanished, except when she was angry and momentarily reverted. I used to notice, when I was with them, how her new voice continually surprised him, in the same way as the new attitude of superiority she had developed in order to match it; the jump he gave, for instance, at her "Gharstley Creatchah!" . . . He had a pet tortoise in the garden, a wise tortoise that loved him, and, silently and slowly plodding, never interrupted him during his painting, though it entered the studio whenever it liked. "Pompey", he used to call it. "Pompey, armoured proudly as the greatest of Roman warriors." And in the autumn, Dubosque said, Pompey would go, just like a Roman General, into winter quarters, embedding himself till the spring in a mound of dry grass and sweet herbs specially prepared for him every year in the garden.

'Dubosque loved to paint Pompey. He would gaze at the

tortoise for hours, enraptured, unravelling the design of its
armour, the marking and corrugation of its shell. . . . You
would have thought, Deborah used to say to herself, that he
was in love with it, ghastly creature! And, whenever Pompey
was mentioned — and Dubosque's friends always made a point
of inquiring after the tortoise —, she would scream out
"Gharstley Creatchah!" in her new, affected voice. . . .
Waste of time, she thought, looking after it; in the same way
that it was waste of money to send her to buy those roses in
York, in the middle of the winter, just because he "wanted to
paint roses", and waste of good peaches, to leave them there,
rotting on the dish!

'As her husband grew older, he seemed to her to grow
more obstinate. She saw in him no longer that ardent,
romantic youth of thirty years before, as she had first known
him, and in whom she had in some dim, groping way divined
the genius, but a tired elderly man whom it was her duty to
look after, but who always tried to escape and to raise difficulties. . . . As a matter of fact, in a kind of way, perhaps
she was right: as often occurs with a genius, with the passing
years the fire had left him, and entered exclusively into his
work. It flamed through his canvases, but no longer showed
in word or look or action. He was gentle now, still without
guile, and he did not want to talk much even to those who
could understand what he said. He seemed to enjoy, chiefly,
the company of my two daughters, who were then little girls;
he loved the society of children. As for Deborah, he always
treated her kindly, and with respect in front of his friends,
however trying she might be. But he was determined not to
encourage her to chatter in private about the high cost of
housekeeping in this part of the country, or to complain about
the tortoise, when he could be alone in his studio, either
painting that old bottle he had found, and a glass and some
oranges, or looking at them. . . . And why did she bother
about money? — she had never enjoyed *any* before she married
him, even if they did not have much now.

'His health gave way before such a collapse was due or
could have been foretold. The fire had burnt him up. He
cannot have been more than sixty. I know that, because we were
about the same age, and that was eighteen years ago. . . . I
suppose to you it sounds a great age: but I can assure you,

as one gets on, it seems nothing at all. . . . But to continue.
. . . It was that final winter on the wolds that finished him.
In the autumn, when the last flowers, belated white roses and
scarlet snapdragon, still nodded in the particular misty, golden
sunshine of its early mornings and late evenings, we warned
him. Already he had begun to cough. His friends, my wife
and myself among them, implored him to go abroad, to Italy
or the South of France, for the winter. But he would not listen
to us. Though the hours during which he could paint at this
season were so few and fitful, this was his chosen light, the
light by which he saw, in which he lived and all objects lived
for him.

'Just as the painters of Italy and the Netherlands have
recorded for ever the quality and texture of the days in their
countries, so it has been left, it seems to me, to two English
painters alone — to Constable first, and then to Dubosque — to
sum up and present the look and feeling of the light of their
native land. This peach or this jug could have been painted
nowhere else in the world : and an apple or an egg, which to
the ordinary eye has so little individuality, was to him, in this
clear, pure light, more beautiful, more worthy of being looked
at, examined, searched, as it were, than were the most sumptuous objects elsewhere : the great mosaics of Constantinople or
the jewelled enamels of medieval France.

'It was this light which "sang" to him. . . . But, alas, in
the winter, his beloved light failed him. It was not that his
eyesight had begun to go, but that the light itself suffered a
change, for the snow, when it first fell, did not melt in a day
or two, as usual, but rolled over the abrupt and breath-taking
perspective of these parts its thick ugly carpet. It was impossible for him to indulge, even, in that laziest and most
agreeable winter pastime of the painter, to look at the pictures
he had painted in the summer and criticise them. He could
not "see them", he complained. (Grumbling again, Deborah
said to herself, as if no one had ever seen snow before ! . . .
Why couldn't he set to work, hard, and make money ? . . .
Portraits, for example. . . . Why, they'd easily be in time for
the Academy, if he started them now. She saw it in her mind's
eye, "Study in Scarlet and Silver : the Artist's Wife". . . .
And everyone stopping before it in admiration.)

'Day after day the snow lay there, or it snowed again :

day after day, in consequence, lost interest for him. There
was nothing to do. Wise Pompey slept in his mound: there
was no fruit to look at, and even if there had been, it would
have signified nothing. Every morning the same white light
entered when he pulled the curtains, a hard, pitiless whiteness
that glared up through the windows of the cottage from the
ground, reached the white ceiling, to fall back with a redoubled
white numbness on to the objects in the room or studio. He
could see nothing, look at nothing. He wandered about continually, in and out of the house, wondering when the sky
would alter, and the whole world with it. Surely it could not
go on, day after day? Within himself, he asked which of his
peers in painting would have derived inspiration from these
scenes. Manet, perhaps, would have intoxicated his senses
with this new light, and its effect on familiar things: the
swooping lines of the wolds and the movement of the thick,
foreshortened figures on the frozen mere below would have
brought ecstasy to the heart and hand of Breughel the Elder;
but to him, Dubosque, this world in which the ground in the
distance was paler and more perceptible, and stretched further,
than the sky above, held a terrible quality of sterilisation, as
though the whole country had been transformed into a hospital
ward.

'So he fidgeted, and grew to look more and more miserable.
Deborah, who usually attacked him for working too hard, and
thinking of nothing but his work, now reversed the engine, as
it were, and, in the old language of her unregenerate days,
"ticked him off proper" for being lazy. Why didn't he go to
sleep for the winter, and bury himself in a heap of leaves, like
Pompey, "Gharstley Creatchah"? But, even if *he* could, she
couldn't afford to stand about talking all day: any more than
she could afford to leave peaches about like his Lordship. (Oh
no, she didn't forget those things!) *She* had work to do. She
must, somehow or other, and it wasn't easy in this weather,
get to the village for shopping — otherwise he'd have nothing
to eat, and how would he like that? And also to see the new
boy, who was coming in twice a week, as soon as the weather
altered, to help keep the garden tidy. (She didn't like his
friends to go away and say she didn't know how to keep the
place decent for him, even if *he* didn't mind!) . . . But there
it was, if he went on mooning about like that, he'd catch

another cold, and then she'd have to nurse him, into the bargain, she supposed.

'And catch cold, sure enough, he did. . . . By then it was February, and the cold settled on his lungs. I saw him. In the morning, Deborah said, he had been quite clear in his mind, but in the afternoon he was both listless and feverish. Deborah did not seem to think much of it: it would pass. But I was disturbed about his condition. And though I didn't like the two children to see anyone seriously ill, for they were only about fifteen and sixteen then, I told them to ride over and call on him one day soon. I knew he was particularly attached to them — and they to him — and I thought their visit would cheer him up. When they went, they took with them — dear girls, it was their own idea — a basket of South African peaches, which they had bought specially for him in York out of their own money.

'It was, apparently, a lovely afternoon that they chose for their visit, mild and full of a serene light, for at last the weather had changed, and the snow had melted. Deborah took them in to see him. "Look, Rich, what lovely peaches they've brought you", she said, as they entered the room. . . . But he had seemed very odd, that afternoon, hardly noticed the children, they thought, and they returned home very distressed about him. From what they said, I don't believe he recognised them at all. He mumbled something when they came in, and then his eyes followed the basket of peaches, that swam that afternoon in a perfect painter's light. His eyes devoured them, he appeared to see nothing else. . . . And then suddenly, as he remained in this rapt staring at the fruit, large tears began to roll down his finely sculptured cheeks; rolled down them. But he did not speak. . . . The children thought it better to go home: it was too painful. As they left, they heard Deborah, behind them, reproving her patient for his manners. "That's a nice way to say 'Thank you' for a present. . . . Such lovely peaches, too. I shouldn't think they'd bring you anything another time."

'When the children told me, it sounded to me like his farewell to the visual world he had loved and served so faithfully. . . . After that, during the next three days I can only piece together what happened, from things Deborah and the doctor told me: I did not like to go over and interfere myself, and, indeed, now that pneumonia had set in, there was nothing one could do. I am sure Deborah looked after him well in her own way. But a year or two before, when they had the quarrel (about which I told you) over the peaches, he had said to me, laughing — for he told me about it at the time, making a joke of it — "If ever I see her eating another of my peaches, I'm afraid it will kill me!" And that, I believe, is, in a sense, exactly what occurred.

'He was only allowed orange juice, nothing to eat, the doctor said, when I telephoned to ask if there was any food I could send over for him. He had been told he could have a peach. But he would not; he just lay there, Deborah complained, staring at the basket, looking at the peaches with gooseberry eyes. Just the same he was, well or ill. She priced them up in her mind. They must have cost from 1s. 6d. to 1s. 9d. each, at least. And they'd been there three days, wouldn't last another twelve hours, and if there was one thing she hated, it was waste! . . . Now that it was growing too dark to go on staring at the peaches, he had shut his eyes. He must be asleep, she thought, so she snatched a peach. He wouldn't notice, was feverish all the time.

'Delicious, it was, but difficult to eat, there was so much juice in it. It ran down the corners of her chin, and she had to gobble it to prevent the juice from spoiling her dress. (There, that was better.) But just as she was finishing it, a glow shone in through the window. Something must be alight in the garden; a bonfire. It showed her face very clearly and outlined her figure against the darkness. The dying painter opened his eyes and saw her, huge and dominating to his sick brain, against the darkness, her face, very clear, as she munched, with the little rivulets of juice wetting her chin. For a moment he sat up and watched with intensity. "Richard, Richard!" she cried, but he had fallen back, and his panting for breath had ended.

'Outside in the garden, the bonfire began to die down. Near its still incandescent heart, Pompey, that "Gharstley Creatchah", "armoured proudly as the greatest of Roman warriors", had been sleeping. . . . The new garden boy had forgotten, had thought the mound in which Pompey passed his royal winter sleep was rubbish to be burned.

'Later, his gutted shell was found in the ruins of his funeral pyre. For a long time Deborah would not throw it away. After all, she said to herself, it was tortoise-shell now, and might be worth something to the right person, to someone who was looking for such a thing. I believe when she left, she took it up with her to London. . . . That was eighteen years ago, or so. But it was only two years ago that she parted, for eight thousand pounds, with the famous "Pompey and Some Peaches", which used to hang over the chimney-piece of her house in South Audley Street.'

POMPEY AND SOME PEACHES

II

'EVERYTHING is the same,' Miss Gertrude Stein says somewhere, 'and everything is different.' When the doctor told me the same story, it sounded different.

'If I were an artist feller, I wouldn't mind painting that view myself', he said to me one day, looking out of the window of the bedroom in which I lay ill. 'But I'm surprised *you* never have a shot at it! I should have thought painting was in your line. — Besides, a man ought to have hobbies. You'd find your health much better if you took to one.

'You're so artistic and all that, you ought some time when you're in London to go and call on Mrs. Dubosque. I've often wondered why you don't. She'd be pleased to see you, I know. And I'm sure the pictures would interest you : a wonderful collection. . . . Oh, my God, no! *Real* pictures; not by her husband. She got rid of most of those ages back. The last went two years ago — fetched eight thousand pounds, if you please !

'Never could make out how they brought those prices. Extraordinary thing. . . . Of course, I'm only a country doctor, so I know nothing about it. I don't pretend to be a judge. But to my mind they were just daubs, anybody could have done them. (The other day, the wife showed me a drawing in coloured chalks, what they call crayons, by Elise, our little girl, and I can tell you it was a masterpiece compared to many of his things.) He just didn't know how to put the paint on. I've never seen any other painter put it on like that. Never could understand how he got it across — and yet some of the critics thought the world of him. It's my belief you or I could hoodwink them, if we wanted to. . . . Anyhow, as I was telling you, with the money she made out of the sale of his pictures, she bought a house in South Audley Street and some magnificent paintings, new as well as old. After her husband died, she used to go round the Academy every year and pick out the best, didn't mind what she paid for 'em. Real high-class things, with no nonsense about them.

'Oh, Deborah's got taste! You can see it directly you enter the house. You'd be surprised at the dining-room, a huge great room, painted like that green stuff from Russia, with black marble pillars, and over the mantelpiece a magnificent portrait of her by László. It's a stunner: real good style, in a silver dress with a tiara and white fox fur, and her pearls. (Lovely pearls, she's got.) It might be she herself — and opposite, another one, nearly as good, by Simon Elwes.

'Of course her hair is white now (by Jove, didn't László know how to paint white hair well!), but she's still a fine-looking woman. You know, one of those figures, like that', and the doctor stuck out his chest, and drew Mrs. Dubosque for me on the empty air. 'Very striking, with wonderful eyes.

'I first came up to this mouldy part of the country just after I'd qualified. Knew nobody. Of course, I've got used to it, but it seemed funny then, after always living at the governor's tidy little place at Wimbledon. One was at the heart of things there, and could always run up to town for a show and supper afterwards, and get back easily. . . . So it seemed very cut-off and uncivilised here. No tennis. And I missed my people and the girls (three sisters, I had then). No one to talk to. . . . So I suppose I was rather taken by Deborah — Mrs. Dubosque —, and I often used to walk up there and talk to her. In time we became very good friends, for we "spoke the same language", as they say.

'People used to have it that she'd been a bit gay in her time, but I never saw a sign of it. She was handsome then, very handsome, but what I liked most about her was the way she spoke. A lovely voice: you know, *refined*. Quite different to all the people round here. And much too good for *him*, in my opinion. Always thought he was a fake, with nothing to him. And *funny*, too. Often I've seen him sit for hours without speaking, just staring at something. *She* was the real thing, worth a hundred of him. . . . And if, after his death, his pictures fetched those ridiculous prices, it must have been her doing. A clever woman, with her head screwed on the right way, and always very careful, keen on her money's worth and hating waste. . . . He was a lucky man, if only he'd had

the brains to realise it. You don't find many women like that
nowadays.

'It used to make my blood boil, the way he treated her. . . .
Of course, looking back — I suppose one gets more tolerant as
one gets older — I can see that, though different from other
people, he wasn't *all* bad. But, by Jove, he *was* a queer chap.
Couldn't paint at all — that was obvious — and yet you'd
have thought that nothing but painting interested him. I
wonder it didn't get more on her nerves, the way he behaved.
. . . You know, all sorts of little things. . . . Often when I
went to see them, he'd fasten his eyes on one particular thing,
a basket of fruit it might be, or a bunch of flowers, or that
beastly, smelly tortoise he always had about the place in the
summer, and just stare and stare, as if hypnotised. When she
spoke to him, he'd often make no reply, but just go on staring.
And the same with me — would hardly speak to me, didn't
seem to see me. (I tell you, I've attended cases no worse
than his — dementia praecox, they call it — in the County
Asylum before now.) Wouldn't answer when I tried to be
polite: but then, I'm a man, and it didn't matter. But you
can't treat a woman like that. (The governor was always
pretty strong about that sort of thing with me, when I was a
youngster, I can tell you. If any man had dared to treat the
Mater in that way, he'd have knocked him down.) Yet, when
some of his friends came to see him from London — their gross
flattery of him used to make me feel sick —, he'd fairly talk his
head off. All rot, of course, but still, it showed he *could* make
himself pleasant, if he wanted. And his friends would repeat
what he'd said, and even go on repeating things he'd said
years before, as if they were wonderful.

'Dubosque was always painting that tortoise and making
a fuss of it. I can understand a chap making a friend of a fox-
terrier or an airedale — after all, they're very *like us* — much
more intelligent, I often say, than any human I know. . . .
You know my dog "Spot"? Well, often he'll bark at me for
half an hour at a time, and I'll answer him. Each of us understands every word the other says. . . . But a tortoise! I
wouldn't touch one with a pair of tongs. *A tortoise!* And I'm
sure Deborah can't have liked the way he used to stroke it,
and talk to it and stare at it, while paying no attention to her.
But she never said much, not even to me. . . . Sometimes,

she'd just look at it and say, in a voice that showed how much above that sort of thing she was, "Ghastly Creature!" Just like that, "Ghastly Creature!" Withering!

'And then he was so mean. I suppose he wasn't rich, but he didn't seem to *want* to make money. (It was as though it didn't interest him, extraordinary chap.) Still, he had a little put by : she'd seen to that. But he seemed to grudge her every single thing, even the fruit he was painting. Often I've seen him forbid her to eat a peach, or even an apple, just because he happened to be painting it. ("The poet of still life", indeed!) No, it had to be treated like something sacred, not dusted, not touched. Sometimes — there weren't any people up there for her to talk to — she'd confide in me. And I remember her telling me that once she'd taken two peaches off a plate in the studio, because she saw they'd be bad by the next day, and had eaten them herself, so as not to feel that they'd all been wasted. But, when he noticed, he made a fearful rumpus, went right off the deep end. . . . Well, you know, it's not nice, that sort of thing. It isn't playing the game with a woman. It wasn't straight. . . . And another thing. In those days — though you wouldn't think it to look at her now — she used to do most of the housework herself, and liked sometimes to sing as she worked. But he wouldn't let her. Said it distracted him from his painting! Imagine it! . . . At the same time, nothing was good enough for that beastly tortoise. "Pompey", as his friends used to call it, could have anything he damned well liked. Milk in saucers all over the place at all hours of the day, lettuces and fresh fruit and rose petals in the summer, and in the winter a special mound of grass and stuff for him to sleep in, piled up for him in the garden.

'As for Dubosque, summer or winter you could hardly get him out of the house. I'm surprised the muscles of his legs didn't atrophy! Never took any exercise, and I spoke to him about it — he was my patient (we doctors can't pick and choose our patients, unfortunately ; have to place our scientific knowledge at the disposal of anyone who needs it), and it was my duty to look after him, whatever I thought of his "art". When I told him, straight out, that he must walk more and take more fresh air, what do you think he replied ? . . . That he "hadn't time"! That'll show you the sort of feller he was. Lazy as they're made. And did nothing but paint — and paint badly at that, to my mind ! . . . After all, it's not a matter of argument, but of fact. What would happen to me if I diagnosed measles, and it proved to be gallstones or appendicitis ? In the same way, a peach is a delicate thing, no one can pretend it isn't, so it's obviously bad art to paint it with great, heavy clumsy strokes. All thumbs, as you might say. (Next time you come up to see me, when you're better, I'll show you a little gem of a water-colour of some peaches and a bit of mimosa that the wife did on our holiday at Cannes last spring. . . . I appreciate good work when I see it.) So it used to make me cross to hear his silly friends discussing his way of painting in their mincing, arty jargon : "Richard's brushwork is superb !" or "Just look at the broad treatment of those roses !" or "I feel I've never seen a tortoise before, till I looked at that picture !" Affected set of beggars, if ever there was one !

'He didn't show it much to me, but he had a *nasty* temper. Sulked about things that wouldn't affect you and me. So, one year, when the snow came down nearly every day for two months, it happened not to suit him, and he fell ill and developed "pneumo". After all, it's never exactly the Riviera touch in this neighbourhood during the winter ; he ought to have known that, being born up here. Besides, you'd think that any real artist would have *liked* the snow. Lovely, it was. But I think he'd begun to go a bit balmy as well ; and "pneumo" always attacks mentals. No resistance, you see. . . . Well, for weeks beforehand, he'd been skulking about the house and garden, sulking, and now, when he fell ill, he'd hardly speak ; hardly even speak to me, though I was his medical adviser. Deborah behaved like an angel, the way she nursed her husband : and all the pipes bursting from the frost, all over the place ; worked her fingers to the bone for him. He never so much as said "Thank you", just lay there, in bed, and even when the weather changed and became mild, he didn't get any better. Made no effort. And no doctor can cure a patient unless he tries to cure himself.

'Then one afternoon, some friends of his — the daughters of "Old Maure", as they call him here, affected old blighter — brought him a basket of peaches. Very kind of the children, really, don't you know. Had paid for them themselves. But when he saw the fruit, he paid no attention to anyone or anything else, but began to blubber, without even speaking to the little things who'd brought it; there he lay for hours, tears running down his face, and staring at the peaches — which, I must say, looked very good — in a way that made one's blood curdle. . . . Perhaps he knew he wouldn't see any fruit where he was going. But he should have been more considerate to his wife, and not shown his feelings. Besides, they'd been got for him to eat. (I allowed him fruit and things like that and orange juice: one day when we've got more time, I'll give you my views on orange juice.) But he wouldn't touch them. Just left them there in the basket, and stared and stared, perverse devil that he was.

'There the peaches stayed, on a table by his bed for two or three days. I went back to visit him one day in the evening; when I entered the room, it was difficult to see at first, it was dark, but there was a sort of glow coming through the window. The patient was lying back, asleep, — a good sign, for he'd been very restless — and Deborah was standing in the middle of the room. I'd walked up the stairs quietly, and she didn't see me, and, I don't know why, but I stood still in the doorway. There seemed something important — perhaps *dramatic* is the right word — about it. There she stood, you know, a great, big woman, outlined by that funny sort of light. "Eerie", I suppose, people would call it. I remember thinking how fine she looked, monumental. The windows were opposite, and this queer red glow wavered round her body, and shone full on her face. She was eating one of the peaches, because he wouldn't eat them, and they'd have gone bad by the next day. But what struck me was, I'd never seen anyone enjoy anything so much as she enjoyed that peach. It did one good to watch her (that's what I admired about her, the way she made you feel she'd enjoy things), and you could see it was a lovely, juicy peach. . . . At that very moment he sat up in bed, suddenly, without warning. And there was just enough light to see him staring and staring at Deborah, without saying a word. When she saw him, for at first she was intent on the peach, I could see it gave her a fright, and she uttered a cry. Then he fell back, still without saying a word.

'I had to sign the death certificate. I very nearly entered "Temper" as the cause of death: for that is what it was, in my humble opinion. Sheer rage, because she was eating one of his peaches. Real dog-in-the-manger: wouldn't eat it himself, and wouldn't let anyone else eat it. Much rather it went bad. . . . Now can you imagine a man's mind working like that? Extraordinary. Just Temper! . . . But, of course, he'd undermined his constitution, too, by never going out and by working at all sorts of hours.

'And, do you know, that tortoise died at the same time? A new garden lad mistook the creature's mound for a rubbish-heap, and had set a light to it. And that's what the glow came from, in the room. . . . Of course, Dubosque didn't know that, or he'd have died twice over from rage. . . . Funny thing,' he added, rising unexpectedly to a point of imagination, 'the way those two died together, like a witch and what they used to call . . . what was it? . . . a familiar spirit.

'Then, after he was dead, the dealers and critics set to at their games and, between them, rushed the prices up. . . . And Deborah, I must say, got out while the going was good, though — the most odd thing of all — the prices, I'm told, are higher than ever. . . . But I always say, it can't last. After all, it's people like you and me who are the final judges. . . . And I wouldn't pay a penny, not for one of them. . . . Anyhow, she's made good; she's a rich woman. *And* charitable! Always doing her bit at those balls and supper parties and things you read about in the papers. . . . Sometimes I wish I'd had more time for painting, myself.'

TRIPLE FUGUE

FOREWORD

Unfortunately a story so far removed from the usual human experience demands some preliminary explanation of the scientific, political and social facts with which it is connected.

During the course of the last twenty years much has been written, in police-court news as well as in fiction, of the occurrence of triple or quadruple personality. Instances have emerged of an individual possessing three or four distinct egos, souls, personalities or whichever of the three terms is at the moment most in favour. Each of these entities, while unconscious of the proximity, the existence even, of the others, is yet liable, through we know not what operating cause, at any instant and without warning, to yield place to one of them. It is possible, therefore, that this rarer, more unusual narrative of three separate bodies with but one animating force between them, and each normally ignorant of the intimate tie which binds him to the other two, may be found to possess a certain psychological interest.

A theory has long been formulated as to the 'group-soul' belonging to various of the lower forms of life. Several eminent scientists and philosophers have suggested that, for example, blackbeetles — though each is physically an entity, a smaller or larger insect of dark colouring — exist spiritually (if the use of this adverb in such a connection is pardonable) solely as a group, or, perhaps, as a small number of groups. Each individual beetle forms a single link in the spiritual chain that binds them and is called the group-soul; each is a component part in a composite personality. And this supposition, too, may explain the phenomenon of enchantment. For these repulsive little insects can, like rats or snakes, be charmed, enticed, by one who has the gift or secret, out of the house. The professional usually claims to have inherited this faculty; it is difficult to get from him any explanation of it. But probably his secret is that he can practise a form of mass-hypnotism — he can hypnotise the group-soul of these creatures and lead them out into the wilderness. Thus is revealed to us the secret of the Pied Piper.

Similarly it should not surprise us to learn that one individuality is shared by several human beings; we have only to look round for it to be suggested to us that this form of economy is one that commended itself to the Creator. Indeed the possession by one person of more than one ego is increasingly, enviably rare. In genuine instances of this sort some method, surely, should be discovered of isolating the surplus ones; they should be treated as unearned increment, distributed among the many thousands in need of them — even if this filling of empty places should entail for their owners a fate like that which overwhelmed the Gadarene herd. Each individual, or perhaps one should say each unit or numeral, should possess under a democracy,* as adjunct to three acres and a cow, one personality — neither more nor less. But, alas, the influence of democracy, as we know it, appears to have been not so much to give each man a soul as to make the absence of one not so unusual as to be noticeable. Its trend has been, increasingly, to banish eccentricity and encourage its reverse; to make man alike in the possession of useless but pretentious knowledge, ill taught and ill digested, alike in their lack of simplicity, intelligence and personality. All that is now needed to make the tyrannical triumph of this system complete, is some form of eugenic control, which will finally banish both genius and imbecility, ill-health and unbounded vitality. And the reverse of eccentricity is, undoubtedly, that simian quality of mimicry which, inherent in man, now makes all men alike. Mimicry, indeed, is man's original sin, for when the first individualist monkey had decided to stand up for his rights and be a man (an eccentric monkey that, if ever there was one!) his fellows proceeded to mimic — or some say 'ape' — him, thus building on an insecure foundation, since, in the very act of declaring themselves to be men, they were in reality making a proclamation of essentially monkey characteristics.

The old dynastic and aristocratic systems of government encouraged, subsidised almost, eccentricity worthy and unworthy alike; and no eccentric, not even the least estimable,

---

* *N.B.*—When we refer in these pages to 'democracy' we are not considering it as an idea, but *practically*, as it has been known for the last fifty years in Europe and America.

would deign, except in the spirit of satire, to mimic his fellows. But with the coming of industrialised, commercialised and capitalised democracy, every man and woman too had, under pain of ostracism, to dress, talk and behave alike — or rather as they imagined their 'betters' would dress, talk and behave. Previously there had been no 'betters' — only richer or poorer, stupider or cleverer, only those better or less good-looking, less or more powerful; facts were acknowledged without envy; but now, with envy, came the assumption of 'betters'. A vicious circle was established. Everyone pretended feverishly to be something or someone he was not. The workman pretended to be a small shopkeeper, the small shopkeeper to be a large one, the large shopkeeper to be that mysterious thing a 'professional man', the professional man to be a country squire, the rich manufacturer to be a nobleman of long pedigree, dukes to be workmen, kings to be democrats and hereditary presidents. Each, by his own act, laid claim to some distinction which could never be his, and by this very claim admitted an inferiority. For if I shout in your face that I am as good as you are, at once I prove myself inferior in manners. Except for those whose struggle for life was so hard as to leave them no time or desire for self-deception, the world became a matter of acting and make-believe, giving such falsity to every value, such crooked perspective to every event, that when the greatest tragedy in human history came, every nation was equally surprised and unprepared, though each had, in reality, done nothing else except prepare for it, consciously or unconsciously, during the previous half-century. The war, certainly, was the final triumph of the system. Every man, the world over, was forced to fight to make the world Safe for Democracy, whether he believed in it or not — though the war itself was undoubtedly due to the very form of government for which he was now urged to fight, and one, in any case, peculiarly unsuited for the prosecution of a successful war. Emperors and kings, manufacturers of armaments, wealthy noblemen, humble profiteers, none of whom had previously shown much affection for his darling ideal, now advanced into the market-place to demand, to insist, that the world be made Safe for Democracy. And the Democrats of a lifetime were taken in once more. The people of every country allowed only the most brutalised or hypocritical of their countrymen to come to the top and rule them, thereby proving how much they had gained by education and the other blessings which they owed to the system they were now called upon to defend. The few democrats who really believed in the people, and saw how disastrous a war would be for them, were either hounded out of public life or thrown into jail.

Just as one man had for a century past been taught to regard himself as the equal of another, so had each nation been taught to consider itself the equal of its neighbour. Each country must have a bigger navy, bigger army, be a greater power, than those that bordered it. The result of this healthy competitive and democratic spirit was a war disastrous for all who entered it: and once the war started, since each man must be as his fellow, each country had to join in. It became 'the thing to do' — 'good form'. Every nation — except Spain, which had never been democratic, and the Scandinavian countries which were genuinely so — had to enter the arena on one side or the other. Even Oriental, lazy countries like Turkey lost their heads, or were driven into it. Each land must show that it was as great a power, that it could spend as many million pounds a day, as many million lives a year, as its neighbour. The general attitude towards a non-belligerent country was 'Yah-boo! You're not a great power. You can't afford a great war. Yah!'

The ultimate consequence for democracy of this orgy of killing and spending, was the utter revolt against it of Russia and Italy, two of the more intelligent European peoples, who seem to prefer, in the rage of the moment, any tyranny however awful as long as it is not the peculiarly smug one from which others are suffering. For years democracy had been talked of as if it were the ultimate aim of humanity, an end in itself; instead of being merely one more experiment in government, at the best one of many other methods of governing, and one obviously unsuited to certain races. But the war has broken down the tyranny of this idea in several lands.

In the meantime the same old system continues in most of Europe; for how long, no one can tell. Every man and every woman still insists on the acquisition of new rights and the abnegation of old ones. And in the middle of this whirlpool of aggressive action and abject renunciation, is still stranded, on a level surface of peaceful but quite pointless life, a society which insists on no rights and admits no duties except that of self-enjoyment — a worthy though humble aim, which it nevertheless seldom has the intelligence to maintain.

Even thirty years ago this world must have displayed character, a stupid, horsey, sporting character. But the bankruptcy of the aristocratic principle, the advent of industrialism and, above all, the arrival of rich Jews and Jewesses, entirely altered the scene. Mimicry became more general, for of all races the Semitic is most imitative, original as are many descendants of this remarkable stock. In order to mingle with the people among whom they must live, it has been necessary for them greatly to increase their natural gift for protective colouring. Even physically they alter their characteristics, becoming paler and fairer as they move north, darker as they move south, darker yet towards Africa, yellower and more almond-eyed as they move eastward once more. Theirs is essentially a cuckoo-civilisation. As artists they prove themselves executants more than originators. They excel in dramatic art, they play the tunes that others have written better than the composers themselves. They it is who have, perhaps, infused into the world of pleasure a new love of millionaire-art and respect for it, a love of the theatre, of dressing-up, and creature comforts. But there is a bad side to these activities; for the Jew who cannot pass as one of a crowd has to design a rôle for himself, and many of these are engaged in a febrile but fruitless attempt to be something other than they are — Irish patriots or Spanish gipsies, French barons and Austrian noblemen, viceroys or Pre-Raphaelite painters, Celtic mythologists and American citizens, Armenian poets and Persian princes. At the same time, without being eccentric, they are apt to run to extremes — to be poorer or richer than all others, greater capitalists or greater Bolsheviks, more 'modern' or more conventional in their taste for art.

The world they have influenced for the last quarter of a century is, then, perhaps a little more intelligent, but one with far less character, than before the corruption began; more cosmopolitan, more like the world of pleasure in every other capital — in New York and Paris, Berlin and Rome. But it has become the 'right thing' again to manifest a faint interest in music, poetry, portrait-painting, above all in house-decoration; and books, even if their pages are still uncut, lie about once more on the drawing-room tables.

In this world the prevailing and unexciting vice is that of mimicry. Each man has become the shadow of his neighbour, each woman the reflection of another. A few people, a very few who have personality, who are prominent for beauty, wit, impertinence or even for that attractive capacity for enjoyment which among these attenuated phantoms has become uncommon, are reflected a million times in their friends. A woman will see reflections of herself as many and varied as those contrived in the mirrors at a dressmaker's. Gesture, smile, colouring, clothing, even the tone of the voice, are aped by hundreds and passed on, like the sacred lamp, from one to another. In someone met casually a whole portrait gallery of friends can be discovered; while these, in their turn, will dissolve, to reveal the further, paler spectres of their ancestors. Depth after depth they stretch; a continual deepening of dimensions that becomes like the discovery and exploration of secret caverns, an exploration attended always by a quality of horror, for you may find the gigantic skeleton of an extinct animal, the remains of a dead friend; and places unlived in are apt to be haunted. To meet one of these shadows is not unlike pulling out section after section of a telescope — only, at each prolongation of it, to be greeted by a familiar yet unexpected and indistinct feature — which had previously escaped you — of the landscape. Another section is extended and focused, in order that you may concentrate on this new landmark and see it more clearly, but in the very act a further familiar object is disclosed to the eye, always slightly distorted by the lens, until the whole process becomes a nightmare.

For at each handing on of it, the imitation, though very recognisable, becomes a little different, as if the colourless soul of the person through whom it has passed had yet contrived to alter the image ever so minutely. One line is slightly firmer, coarser, in its drawing; another more blurred. Each image has behind it other ones, the family features, its portion of the group-soul. Each image is like one of those old-fashioned Christmas cards with a view on it, which, when a tag of paper is pulled, dissolves slowly into other landscapes; and at times the two melt into a muddled whole.

Apart, then, from the few genuine persons who move

among the shadows, each new arrival at party, theatre or restaurant exhibits a soul that is like one of those rooms of distorting mirrors that were to be met with formerly at Earl's Court, the White City, and Luna Park. Someone is reflected, reflected for ever in a thousand distorted variations, while the number of the reflections helps to disguise the emptiness and small dimensions of the place itself. In the relation of one mirroring to another, fresh designs are formed constantly, other shadows suggested, as in a kaleidoscope the same small pieces of coloured glass move ever towards fresh arrangements. Pondering every movement of these exquisitely lacquered but composite figures, new distant views are conjured up. At the end of one gesture you will see, as in a garden, a perspective of gracious but silent deities; and these again are reflected in the water that hurls them downward, head first, into the blue void of the sky. Each distant-sounding voice has an echo of other utterances; some even are echoes of voices, genuine voices, now for ever silent. The dead speak for a time as clearly as the living in these empty houses; yet are as bare and desolate, a vacuum into which no great wind will ever sweep.

It is, in fact, possible to unpack many people as if they were so many portmanteaux of stolen personal belongings; to take out of them a gesture, an expression, a tone, the palpable and familiar property of another. Let us illustrate this. Once we sat in a restaurant, at the next table to a polished and elegant lady, unknown to us, but whose every movement was recognisable; in whom, as she talked, a whole ancestry of shadows could be unravelled. That lifting of one finger like a shepherd's crook declared itself as a reflection of an early copy of Mme de Blank's rendering of a mannerism in her friend, Lady Carabas. To watch the wistful smile unfolding on those lips was equivalent to peeping through the keyhole of the garden of the Knights of Malta at Rome, where far away can be distinguished the solid, very personal dome of St. Peter's; for far away, behind this delicate echo, lies the caressing but bulky smile of Lady de Bludyer. The little dry laugh, too, lacquered as the west wind on a Chinese screen, is but a transposition in key of Mrs. Kinfoot's serving-up of Ethel Misborough's laughter; while that innocent, round-eyed sucking-of-the-thumb is merely an unauthorised version of

Lady Ethel Cressey's almost unconscious imitation of her cousin, Lady Septuagesima Goodley, a woman of genuine, if difficult, character, who, now in late middle age, employs this trick as proof of her lamb-like and misunderstood disposition — a proof which has finally convinced her easily gullible friends.

Thus in these varnished hollows could we isolate for the moment a hundred reflections of a few genuine personalities. Nor, altogether, do these mirrorings make the world unpleasant. The student of social life can play a detective game for his own amusement; while to the mirrors and mirrored, the constant vibration and echo, the innumerable variations on the same key, give a certain brilliancy and cold sparkle to gatherings, filling empty rooms with a scintillation of light thrown back as through crystal and deep waters. One or two colours are vibrated in every tone and shade; a note is struck out that is responded to by every shallow object, every translucent substance, in the room. Who knows but that if every shade became a person, every echo a genuine voice, there would be a riot of colour, a storm of sound too strong for us? . . .

.   .   .   .   .

In order to write it, the story that follows compelled us to advance along various tracks, already noticeable, until these converged, and we found ourselves in the year 1948. This future already looming over us is more difficult to grasp than any other, just as the equidistant past is the hardest to recall. Both are so little divided from the present, so fantastically alike, so grotesquely different.

If we take a compass and, fixing the leg that is to remain steady in the present year, begin to circumscribe, as it were, a circle, the diameter of which is twenty-five years, we shall notice that the people and background of the year 1898 through which it passes seem slightly contorted, are invested with a certain air of improbability which is termed 'quaintness' — rather ugly quaintness still, for it is too near to have become focused and 'picturesque'. Similarly, if we continue the circle into the future, the people and background near that circumference have the same quality — one which would be lacking in a more remote age, so strange would it seem.

Among a myriad possibilities the immediate future holds always two highly probable alternatives. One, ever the most likely and at this moment seeming almost a certainty, is of a complete break, a tremendous reaction against the immediate past and all that it represented; the other, an exaggeration of present tendencies. From these two it has been necessary to choose the latter, to make the future age like our own, so that as if comparing two similar profiles, we notice the likeness by the slight differences, and gain a more complete knowledge of one by gazing on the other.

We move, then, in the same world of rather hysterical shadows, the same state that somehow moves on by its own impetus. We are greeted with the familiar echoes and reflections that we have been discussing. Many of those prominent in the arts, in literature, in the State, are the same persons we know, only older and no wiser, while all are seen through the glass of time as men are seen through the medium of water. The water is unruffled and deep, so deep; and the bodies of the swimmers are near the surface; yet all are elongated and drawn out, or broadened and foreshortened, their colour subdued òr accentuated by this seemingly transparent element.

PART I

The first scene of our strange drama unfolds itself in the respective bedrooms of Mr. Valentine Leviathan, Lord Richard Cressey, and Mr. Freddie Parkinson at the hour of 7.55 one Friday evening in the early May of 1948. In this way we are enabled to make the acquaintance of our three protagonists while they are still dressing for their parts.

Mr. Valentine Leviathan, impoverished but hopeful — from his own point of view — member of the great Anglo-American mercantile house of Leviathan, is discovered, hurried, harried and out of humour in front of a diminutive looking-glass in a hired flat off Belgrave Square. The apartment is fussily decorated, over-upholstered, yet uncomfortable in a hotel fashion. The softness and depth of the armchairs, the thick carpet and other properties would produce in one unused to them a feeling of asthma, hay-fever and croup. Too proud to work much, too poor to be idle, Valentine writes articles on French politics for *The Morning Star* — a newspaper, the venerable owner of which is a friend of the family. He knows no French and little politics, but by dint of a certain facility

for skating over ice that no longer exists — which he was forced
to acquire during several years at a large public school, where
it was understood that though you need not learn anything
you ought to pass the examinations — just manages to impress
his readers with what he leaves unsaid.

'Clever chap, that! You can read a lot between the lines',
the old gentlemen used to say, puffing whale-like in their club
windows, which seem the glass walls of some gigantic aquarium.
And, indeed, reading between the lines you could distinguish
almost anything which suited your mood. Regarded strictly,
however, as to what they said and how they said it, Valentine's
articles were sympathetic yet impressive, having the character
of essays written by a sick schoolgirl and subsequently corrected
by a prim but kindly nursery-governess. They were full of
suggestions, suppressed enough to be convincing, of being-
very-much-in-the-know, and of what-fun-we-are-all-having.
Occasionally these would be varied with distinguished compliments and authoritative warnings to our Allies. At other
times this one of our three heroes turns a more honest, congenial, but secret penny by revealing the movements of friends,
and interesting facts about them, to the readers of the illustrated
daily papers.

While, with little corners of white lather still on his face
from shaving, he hurries from one room to another looking for
a towel, we are privileged to read the latest of these ramblings.
'Hats off to President Trotsky' we shall read tomorrow glancing
through the pages, 'Salute Denmark', and then, sandwiched
between these commands, come to Valentine's gossipy page,
typical development of his time. At present these social jottings
are lying in a scrawling handwriting on an untidy desk, while
near to them is their envelope, ready, and addressed to the
editor.

'A friend tells me', they run:

The Pecksniff Prize

'Pamela tells me that Lord Richard Cressey has been asked
to present this year's Pecksniff Prize for English Literature;
an event which will take place in late July at the Skimpole
Hall. Lord Richard is, of course, the third son of the fourth
Duke of Kirkcudbright and brother of the present Duke. He

is also known as a promising diplomat (he is said to have been responsible for that *thrilling* Yugo-Slovak Jingo-Slav crisis last year) and is already quite a figure in literary and artistic circles. His novel of Balkan life, *In a Yashmak Garden*, created quite a stir, and, it is rumoured, was mentioned in private conversation by Professor Criscross to the venerable Earl of Chiswick, that last of the Great Victorians. He has also published latterly a slim volume of powerful nature-poems, under the title of *The Buzzard's Bastard*, in which he makes a strong plea for the feeding of young cuckoos. This, too, has been very favourably received by the critics, and has already gone into a fifth edition. Lord Richard's many friends hope that as well as being asked to present the prize, he will also be allowed to receive it.' . . .

A Notable Wedding

'Dearest, the Cressey wedding was quite the event of the 1946 season, wasn't it? How strange it seems that it is already two years ago! Both the bride and bridegroom, who are very artistic, were related to numerous important families, and such lovely clothes! The six bridesmaids were all dressed in sheath-gowns of ruby tinsel, and a note of originality was struck by the bride's wreath, which was made of silver paper and worn upside down. The orange flowers were made of mother-of-pearl, with gilded-tin stalks, and sewn on to the bandeau. So chic! Lady Richard — or Goo-Goo as she is known to her friends — is petite, piquante, and pimpante, and was, of course, niece to Baroness d'Arenheimer, the well-known French philanthropist, and daughter of Mrs. Silas B. Guggerty, a popular and charming transatlantic visitor who often has the honour of entertaining both Princess Marie-Antoinette of Metro-Schinkenberg and Princess Antoinette-Marie of Metroberg-Schinken in her fascinating London home. All six of them, Lord Richard, Lady Richard (Goo-Goo), Mrs. Guggerty, Baroness d'Arenheimer, Princess Marie-Antoinette and Princess Antoinette-Marie, are, of course, exceptionally artistic. I met Mrs. Guggerty in Bond Street yesterday and thought her looking quite a picture, with her mass of snow-white hair, in a short bolero of blue coney-skin, with a hussar-collar of Trotsky-lapin. Such a becoming toque, too, dark blue, trimmed at one side with little bunches of coque's feathers.'

TRIPLE FUGUE

An Original Hostess

'Dinky writes to me today that she immensely enjoyed the interesting party of artistic people that Lady Richard entertained last week at her country home, Little Titterham, Old Twits, near Cinderbury. Situated on the barest parts of the Sussex Downs, Little Titterham was just a small two-roomed cottage, with the dearest old barn, till Lady Richard — who, like her husband, is, of course, immensely artistic — turned out the family who lived there and converted it into an ideal country residence. It is unnecessary to say that she is extremely popular in the neighbourhood. Each guest is given a bathroom, swimming bath, tennis court and croquet lawn of his own, and a delightful note of simplicity is struck throughout. One of a number of charmingly modern touches that mark this unique home is the placing in each bedroom of a little homespun sack full of lavender, on which are depicted scenes from the Soviet-Art Cabaret; these are executed by Lady Richard herself, and are signed "Goo-Goo" in diminutive letters. These little touches, needless to say, are immensely appreciated by Lady Richard's friends.'

An Interesting House-Party

'The artistic party of interesting people at Little Titterham last week included Baroness d'Arenheimer and her two pretty debutante daughters, Angel and Desirée (doesn't she seem young, darling? to have grown-up daughters!); Sir Booster Babboon, the Picturesque Persian Philanthropist (who is taking such an *interest* in the bazaar that the Baroness is getting up in aid of the "Superannuated-Moneylenders'-Children-Benefit-Fund". He can always be depended on to help forward any worthy charity); Mrs. Guggerty; Mr. Matthew Dean; Mr. Valentine Leviathan, the clever and popular young writer on international topics; Mrs. Kinfoot, the well-known hostess, who has just returned from her first lion-hunt in Africa; Lady Selina Moonbury; Adèle Lady Fortcarrick (who is supposed to have gone round in four); Mr. Edward Tush; Mr. Charles Rotumjhy, the famous Hungarian portrait-painter; Mr. Freddie Parkinson, and others equally well known. Lady Richard, who, besides being *exceptionally* artistic, *adores* music, delighted her friends by a rendering of the "Jewel Song" from

219

Faust on the water-whistle and has now left for Aix-les-Bains. It is hoped that she will be back in Little Titterham, where she will be much missed, by the middle of next month.'

Valentine has re-entered the room, and is wildly opening and shutting various drawers, and ringing wireless-electric bells, which he knows quite well will not be answered : a form of neurasthenia resulting from a long period of underwork, for he does not really in the least mind how late he is for an engagement. As he moves about, very swiftly, half-dressed, it is difficult to grasp the salient features of his appearance. He is youngish, perhaps about twenty-seven, and taller than the average. Though still somewhat flushed from the bath, his skin is yet rather yellow and very smooth, his eye of that vacant blue which clearly demands a monocle ; but in this case the demand is unsatisfied. His toneless fair hair is brushed back, sleek and shining, and he boasts a moustache, short, fair, rather more bristling, drooping, and untidy than one would expect from the rest of his aspect ; for, as his dress grows more complete, a certain rather insect-like elegance evolves round him. Clothed, brushed, polished, he has a suave yet overblown quality, like the scent of syringa or the glossy, rounded and enamelled form of certain beetles. The rather shabby moustache, therefore, detracts from this, making it more bearable, like a flaw in a precious stone, though, at the same time, it imparts an air of premature age.

The rooms, usually noisy, are very quiet at this instant. Obviously, then as now, the taxicabs are in hiding, the drivers playing piquet in a thousand obscure shelters, happy in the knowledge that this should be their busiest hour. Hastily snatching coat, top-hat and cane, Valentine dashes out to retrieve one.

. . . . . .

Half a mile away Lord Richard Cressey is presented to us in an upper bedroom of Kirkcudbright House, the family mansion in London. He has arrived back, rather late, from the Foreign Office, and is tired. The swelling waves of the treetops, now in their full green spray, stand frozen below, as if some wizard had thrown a spell over them just as they were about to flood the wide-open windows of this gaunt, severe mansion. Led by one of those small grey puffs of wind that are a feature of the London parks in summer, they advance once more; this time, surely, they will invade the house, for the leaves are tilted up by the breeze, overturned for a moment with a flash of silver till they become the white-horses of this green sea, or the outriders of such an army as marched against Macbeth. Beyond the Park, above the droning, groaning clamour, broken by shuddering hoots, of the distant traffic, beneath the softer dragon-fly note of the hovering aeroplanes that pass every second, Lord Richard's wandering blue eye is rested by the stiff cubist arrangement of slate roofs, gables, spires, huge flat square warehouses, looking like magnified Roman tombs, and angular towers, that constitutes the London horizon. In among these, contrasting with the great width, heaviness and solidity of these buildings, rise the giant but slender wireless-masts, which, growing thus in clumps, look like cuttings of bamboo waiting for the spring to touch them into leaf. The prevailing colour of the outlook at this hour is soft grey, softer blue and a little gold, while over these pastel tones is superimposed the patine of light and shade that London has breathed on them, blurring and silvering them gently, as the breath of man lingers for a moment on a mirror or pane of glass. The three square windows that allow these tall buildings to lift their heads above the trees into the room are set in a large square chamber that has a steady air, like that of an old-fashioned butler. There is much solid mahogany furniture and a singularly respectable wallpaper. The air is pervaded with the familiar smell of ancient polished wood, and in this evening light the walls are enveloped in a rather thick golden glow, like the varnish on one of those screens composed of scraps, prints and Christmas cards, which, made in the early decades of the nineteenth century, still show boldly in the mess-rooms of old regiments, or lurk abashed in the lumber-rooms of decaying country-houses. No sign is here of Lord Richard's modern taste in decoration; but then this is not his house, for Lady Richard is away at Aix: his house is shut up, and he is staying here for a few weeks with his brother.

Under the shadow of a large mahogany four-poster, placed on a thick white counterpane, white as a winding-sheet, lie the folded corpses that will soon be quickened; black clothes that, as they lie there in the strong light, seem green, rather mouldy with age, but, when once more in contact with human vitality, will become fresh again, almost smart; for clothes are essentially vampiric, taking part of our life, though in return they give us something back. There lie, too, a white shirt, rigid and shiny, and a white collar like the section of a drain-pipe, stiff with death. On the dressing-table are a black tie, folded and looking like a large frayed moth, a square folded white handkerchief and a little mound of copper coins. These latter suggest, by their presence, that in due course a professional is coming in to lay out all these corpses in the proper manner, weighting down their empty eyes with these coins. And, indeed, the professional (Barnacle, Lord Richard's valet) is waiting outside even now for a summons.

Above the dressing-table, supported by two pillars, is balanced at an angle the reflection of what is apparently some sea-creature, some light-blue and deep-pink sea-monster, but is in reality merely a rare edition of Lord Richard — Lord Richard as he appears each day to his valet but not to the world, blue as to underclothes, coral-pink from his bath, while little sequins of steam glitter like sea-water on pink face, feet, arms and calves. This deepening of colour, accentuation of light and shadow, rather obscures the face, so that at one moment he looks in the later twenties, at another in the late forties, and is probably somewhere between the two. We notice a rather bristly downward moustache, fairish, rumpled hair and blue, blue eyes. The mirror reflects hurried movements : in it we see Lord Richard plunging head foremost into his white shirt. There is a rattle of white spray, and he comes up to the surface, his head showing again at the crest of this foaming, flashing wave, like the moustached countenance of a seal revealed from some breaker. As if he had really just returned from the salty depths rewarded with precious trophies of his skill in that other element, the reflection presents to us a pearl, round, fair and velvet-soft, being secured by red fingers, like crustacean pincers, in the centre of a flat surface of white foam.

Piece by piece the corpses assume vitality : the warm, magnetic flow of life courses through the fibre of shirt, collar, socks, trousers, waistcoat; and even the frayed moth takes the air again with a certain jauntiness. Lord Richard looks, on the whole, rather well dressed, but in contrast to our first hero, as if he did not care very much about such things. He glances anxiously at his watch, dashes with short, very quick steps downstairs, where he is helped into a large overcoat, his own quickness of movement being in such contrast to the leisurely actions of his valet that he is nearly strangled in the process. He runs into the waiting taxicab, shouting to the valet : 'Don't wait up for me, Barnacle. If anyone radios me, tell them to ring up 9234 Holborn, Mr. Dean's. And you might let them know at Mecklenburg Square that Her Ladyship won't be back until the middle of next month. Good night!' And, heralded by a startling series of rattling alarms, is borne out of the large sombre backwater into the choked streams of traffic beyond.

Westwards, Freddie Parkinson is nearly dressed, but in no great hurry. Valentine is sure to be late. The small, demure house always smells as if it had just been painted. The walls are nearly always grey, the carpets invariably green and self-coloured. There are, placed about in the rooms downstairs, several subtly ugly and completely undecorative little pieces of early Chinese pottery, which have either been snatched out of the sacred earth by tomb-plunderers and handed on through dealers at a price completely out of proportion to their value, or have, perhaps, just been made at that new factory outside Peking, where they will busy themselves with such things. Freddie is devoted to these 'pots' — pronounced 'pahts' — and is constantly caressing them with rather insensitive, blunt finger-tips, imagining that he can determine their age by the feel of their glaze, or get some esthetic pleasure out of the handling of them. These things are now everywhere inheriting the place of willow-pattern plates and long-ladies. Very few pictures hang on the walls, but there are a few etchings and woodcuts, simple and at the same time very fussy. It is curious that Freddie should collect both these 'pahts' and these etchings ; it is a curious combination, for though he takes both seriously, one completely denies and cancels-out the artistic principles of the other. But above all Freddie collects the scandals of the day ; on these he is a recognised authority, a connoisseur who is consulted upon scabrous discoveries, just as a great authority on early Italian pictures would be asked to pronounce his opinion upon some new and precious find. Upstairs, on the second landing, the door is open, and

Freddie is fastening his collar. In appearance he is taller than either Lord Richard or Mr. Leviathan, and older, about ten years older. His face is more furrowed, and is becoming somewhat leathery. His hair — for he shows no trace of baldness — is more stubborn, his eye of a more faded, and therefore a more piercing, blue. Eyebrows and moustache are very definite and stubborn. He carries his head rather forward, peering a little, as if scenting some new scandal, and already well on its track. He comes out of his room to shout to the maidservant that he wants a taxicab; and it is noticeable that as she comes nearer, he shouts louder. Freddie looks rather tired; for, in this respect totally unlike Valentine, he works hard in an office all day for money that he does not need. He is well known in the social world — in fact everybody knows him because he knows someone else. Two gaunt sisters, tall as grenadiers, are his companions in the house, sisters who adore yet despise him. He is very fond of them, but is not attached to his numerous other relatives, of whom he is really rather ashamed, apt to avoid, however willing are they to see more of him. His voice getting ever louder as he goes downstairs, he bears off an old opera hat, which he opens with a snap, until, like himself, it is tubular in form. It elongates him, as if a snake had added to its stature — completes his appearance. He is seen sitting in an open taxicab, its wheels grinding slow, like the mills of God, until it has disappeared round the corner.

.　　.　　.　　.　　.

At this moment Mr. Matthew Dean, R.D.O. (Royal Dodonian Order, 2nd Class, Grand Cross), is waiting rather agitatedly in his house near Queen Anne's Gate. There is little reason for agitation, but Mattie cannot bear being kept waiting; it is bad for his nerves. He walks from room to room, gazing vaguely, without seeing anything, at the pictures old and modern which are so numerous as almost to blot out the gaily painted panelling. The blinds are drawn, though a faint, cold light still penetrates them, and the rooms are lit by old-fashioned electric lamps, well shaded, that throw down rather ruddy circles of light (so much softer and prettier, his guests invariably say, than the hard false daylight of wireless lighting) on the tables where they stand. There are several of these tables in each room: on them, framed in tortoise-shell, stand signed photographs of many social and stage celebrities, reputed beauties, and a few popular, but not *too* popular, poets and writers. Lying about carefully arranged, but with an appearance of freedom, as if they had just been put down for a moment, are various books, political or literary, collections of rather rare modern first editions, novels or the last word in poetry or the drama. Among these, taken at random, we read such titles as *Down Sussex Way*, by Jacques Rosenheimer; *My Part in the Third Great War*, by the Rt. Hon. Winston Churchill; *Limpet, and Other Poems*, by Ego Aneurism Jones; *Scribblings*: a book of Literary Criticism, by H. Mollycod Moiré; Vol. II of the 'Bloomsbury Painters Series', *From Giotto to Gertler*; and several rare Squireana, consisting of *Baudelaire Flowers*, by Jack Collings Squire — suppressed by the author; a book of Early Essays by 'Solomon Eagle'; *Collected Parodies* (very rare), by Jack Squire; *Songs of the Slaughterhouse* (early and rare), by Jack C. Squire; *The Lily of Malud* (rare and curious), by J. C. Squire; *Australian Poems*, by J. Collings Squire; *The Soccer Match, and Other Poems*, by Sir Collings Squire; *Lesser Lyrics of the First Half of the Last Decade but One of the Seventeenth Century*, compiled by Ego Aneurism Jones, with a prefatory note by Lord Squire of Chiswick; *Simple Lyrics of the Countryside, with Glossary*, by Raoul Gelding, prefaced by a brief explanatory note by Lord Squire of Chiswick, O.M., and 'A Catalogue of a Portion of the Library of Viscount Squire of Chiswick, O.M., compiled by Professor James Criscross and Ernest Lympe, with a new portrait of His Lordship by Solomon Gluckstein, and an original poem by Mr. Edward Shanks'. On another table we see piled up, *From a Library Stool*, by James Criscross; *Drivellings*, by K. Mimicky Murrain; *Heather o' Moors*, a volume of Verse by Vincent O'Coddell; *How I won the Third World War*, by the Rt. Hon. David Lloyd George; *Myself and Trotsky*, uniform with *A History of my Fourth Campaign in the Dardanelles*, by the Rt. Hon. Winston Churchill; the last six volumes of Verse by Mr. Edward Shanks; the last dozen by Mr. W. J. Turner, and the last dozen and a half volumes of Collected Essays by Sir Robert Lynd. On a larger table are several bulky and fantastically bound scrap-books, in which during his leisure moments Mr. Dean, with one or two chosen allies, pastes photographs, and newspaper cuttings, or induces his numerous friends among present-day poets to write a favourite set of verses. There are also several vases of flowers.

It must be admitted from the first that Mr. Matthew Dean — or poor Mattie as he is to his friends — is essentially himself and, in spite of a rather feeble character, is reflected by many, while never reproducing the ways or tricks of others. Coming out of a solemn background at once scholarly and ecclesiastic, he has reacted away from it, towards, as he thinks, the worlds of fashion, gaiety and wit. These he has frequented for over thirty years; so, though his appearance does not suggest it, he must be between fifty and sixty years of age. But, since a man is judged by his friends, he must be counted as an honorary young man — young enough, in fact, to know better. His body, though not stunted, is punily, uneasily built; the shoulders are too broad, both for the head and body, more especially for the neck, giving from a distance an impression of strength that is immediately contradicted by the rest of his physique, and by the face. This latter is sallow in colour, nearly circular in shape except for a slight squaring of the forehead, and a dent, like a nick clipped out of a coin, that marks the chin. The black eyes are alive and kindly; the eyebrows, thick and dark, grow up at an angle, ending in a Mandarin-like tuft. These eyebrows, tilted up like the eaves of a Japanese temple, are really the natural feature of the face: but art has helped Nature, for beneath one of them is a round monocle that echoes in miniature the larger circle of the face, seeming to be a young one budding out of it. The hair follows the line of the eyebrow, turning up slightly at the temple, and is brownish-grey. The neck, as we noted, is peculiarly long, thin and out of proportion to the shoulders, so that when Mattie lifts up his head, with the nervous wriggling waggle that is his way, to talk, it is as if a ventriloquist's dummy is speaking — so thin is the wooden stalk of the neck moving in the too-wide socket of the collar-bone. The voice itself, when with great effort it sounds out, is extraordinarily high, lisping, innocent and irritating as the twittering of a fluffy young bird that lifts up head and gaping mouth from its nest, expecting to be fed. Like such a fledgeling, too, is the manner in which he raises his head, and moves his neck — or perhaps like a newly hatched chicken looking up out of its broken shell! — while the bright nervous eye, which seems to twitter also behind its glass section, has something of the bird-effect as well. On the other hand,

when in a very good mood, his face and shoulders remind one
a little of a smiling, purring cat. At this moment, however,
he is more bird-like than cat-like; he is obviously waiting for
someone, and as obviously dislikes the process. He is now
dressed in a black dinner-jacket, black tie and white shirt: his
clothes are always well made, almost too appropriate for the
occasion, and must require an amount of attention.

Mattie, as we have noticed from the furnishing of his
house, is a great patron of the arts, ancient and modern; a
patron of advanced art even — as long as it has not advanced
too far to make safe its retreat. In the social world he is one
of the acknowledged arbiters of taste, especially of things new,
and is being constantly implored in the drawing-rooms for help
and advice on matters concerning art and literature, what
pictures to invest in, what books to borrow. 'I'll ask Mattie;
he'll tell me what to get', is to be heard on all sides. He is on
every board and committee that exists for the acquisition of
modern works-of-art, or for the reward of virtue in literature,
and is one of the permanent judges who each year assign to
some suitable neophyte the Pecksniff Prize. This consists of
a cheque for £200, awarded to the writer of what is, in the
opinion of the judges, the year's best piece of imaginative
writing, whether in poetry or prose. Mattie therefore is
essentially for Safety First in literature and the arts, for though
he must startle his friends occasionally, and can afford to be
a little daring every now and then, he does not want to risk
the reputation for sound judgment which he has acquired
among those friends who know less about such things than
himself. His own personal inclination is toward an affected
simplicity in art, just as the dyspeptic finds more enjoyment in
plain food than in complicated dishes. But his own natural
impulse has somewhat broken down. For, in spite of a genuine
instinct and love for art and literature, he was originally a prig;
an artistic prig, no doubt of it. But now success has made him
a snob instead. He appears terrified that his past will be
revealed, that his smart friends will know him for a prig!
Thus he is battling always against an unspoken accusation,
anxious to prove it false. This process has made his taste
muddled and flaccid, for he has been forced to talk of musical
comedies as if they were as important as the greatest operas, of
music-hall comedians as if they were the greatest executants

in the world; and in a voice so high that like a bat's note it is scarcely audible to the human ear, he is for ever singing inane little jigs and jingles to prove how up to date he is, and how much he enjoys these entertainments. And, as a matter of fact, he has really grown to like them. He attends every theatrical first night, of whatever kind, which gives him an opportunity to show his tact, for his clothes must ever be appropriate to the occasion, and yet he must differentiate according to the status of the theatre. A Lyceum melodrama demands from him quite a different turn-out from that which is necessary for a musical comedy, or Covent Garden. But if two first-performances at the theatres occur on the same evening, then his grief and perturbation know no bounds! He becomes a baby claimed by two mothers and awaiting the judgment of a wiser, more merciful, Solomon. Altogether, in order to prove that he is no prig, Mattie has had to cultivate that odious, authority-sapping theory of relativity in the arts that is so much in evidence. The chief symptom of this softening of the mental fibre is the series of tremendous attacks on such men as Dante, Shakespeare, Virgil and Titian, delivered by such 'high-brow' journalists as write every week for 'low-brow' readers. I am as good as you, Tchekhoff as great as Dante, Lord Squire as Shakespeare, McEvoy as Mantegna, Grock as Greco. This trait of Mattie, this equal devotion to God, Demigod and Beast, is the most modern thing about him, since, though he would never admit it, he actually belongs to the period of the first Great War — of Illustrated Society Papers and 'Jazz Bands'.

His position as a man behind the scenes in politics helps his prestige as a connoisseur of art, and is of use to him generally. He is of the type that, like certain Orientals, enjoys obscure power, loves power without the public appearance of it. Not for a moment does he wish for any more prominent position than that which he now occupies. Politically he has had much experience, has acquired much knowledge. His career had begun, as a matter of fact, many years before the violent disruption of the old Party System by the Press Barons, as they are called. Those of my readers who are old enough, remarked for themselves, doubtless, that steady increase of power which accrued to the Newspaper Proprietors over a period of some thirty years — a steady development only set back occasionally, or even tragically, by some such incident as that which befell Bottomley-The-Martyr. The first sure sign of the new power was the substitution of Newspaper, for National, Insurance. It was not until that momentous meeting in the spring of 1934 that the Press Barons openly claimed the right of the Journal with the Largest Daily (Net) Circulation to govern the country. They pointed out that the time had come for a more modern, more democratic, form of government, and that they were the fully developed heirs of the old system. For the old Party System had over a period of a century rightly attached supreme importance to universal education; it had taught every man and every woman to read — and what they read were these journals. Thus the power of the Press was proved to be the offspring of compulsory education.

And the politicians, or Elder Statesmen, as they are now officially designated, welcomed the change; before the *coup d'état* they had been the targets at which had been constantly fired the most poisonous darts of the Press. The latter would insist simultaneously on such things as Retrenchment and the most expensive Social Reforms, a great increase in armaments together with a reduction of 5s. in the £ on the Income Tax, Peace and a policy which would inevitably lead to War, thereby pleasing, by one proposal or another, every possible reader of their papers. As for the politicians, they had neither the strength nor the desire to struggle against these contradictory demands. At the same time, in order to keep up, or to increase, its circulation, the interest of every newspaper was really in the direction of greater excitements — more frequent and more brutal murders, vast explosions, huge conflagrations, gigantic battles on land and sea. Even Nature itself seemed anxious to please the omnipotent Barons, presenting them with tidal waves of unusual size, thrilling earthquakes, devastating eruptions.

Before the new system was declared, each succeeding Government was in turn exposed by the Press: Government succeeded Government with a bewildering rapidity — a rapidity made more bewildering, indeed, by the fact that, though differently labelled, the personnel of each Government was nearly identical with that of the one which it had replaced. The combinations of politician and politician were infinite and kaleidoscopic. At one moment they would be abusing each other like fish-wives in the market, at the next they would

'Achieve Unity' and embrace: within a month they would together form a new Government. This, in its turn, would fall within a few weeks, to be succeeded by a new arrangement of the dear old faces. Elderly ponderous peers would tread weightily from one party to the other and back again; but at each change the country would be put to the expense of a General Election.

Thus, when toward the end of the Third Great War (the Chinese one) the Barons seized the executive and proclaimed themselves the Trustees of the Nation, the politicians welcomed it, actually, as a release, for they were still to carry on the actual work of Government; but now the Press assumed openly the responsibility, and there would be no need for sudden changes of policy and, better still, no possibility of an election. The same old faces, under the Guy Fawkes-like masks of the Press Barons, still make our laws; and owing to the prolongation of human life made possible by the great advance in biological and surgical knowledge, it seems as if we shall be able to benefit indefinitely by the ever-increasing wisdom and experience of these Elder Statesmen.

The latter, it was arranged, were to be paid large salaries by the Press Barons, though liable to instant dismissal if they failed to please their masters; heavy penalties also were incurred by any attempt at insubordination. Till the new system was in proper working order, the two proprietors of the two journals with the Largest Daily (Net) Circulation formed a coalition in order to draw up the New Charter. We owe much to these two patriots, who sank their differences for a common purpose, Lord FitzBison and the old Duke of Badgery St. Lawrence. How typical it is of that admirable British spirit of compromise which has always influenced, for the good, our Rough Island Story, that these two men should have chosen to govern on their behalf those very same politicians for whose impeachment they had been clamouring but the night before!

The New Charter was drawn up with great moderation. No change was made — or even contemplated — in the Constitutional Monarchy, for, apart from any question of the relative merits and demerits of the monarchic and republican systems, the Sovereign grows, if possible, ever more popular as the years pass. Measures enacted have still, before they become the law, to receive the Royal Assent. But the Press Baron of the moment is, like the Sovereign, advised by his ministers, and can now do no wrong. Let it not be supposed for a moment, though, that by this I am suggesting the possibility of a newspaper peer doing wrong before his infallibility was thus legally established.

The old House of Commons was closed and converted into a Museum of Progress — showing the invention of the printing press, and its subsequent developments. The House of Lords, which had, some years before the *coup*, been reformed, was allowed to continue its deliberations and to a degree, to increase its power. Since 'the backwoodsmen', as they used to be termed, had been removed, no rancour was felt in the country at the influence of this august assembly, for the latter had taken care to make it obvious that not one among them could be accused of being a gentleman. It had become, in fact, under the final Labour Governments, a more democratic institution than the House of Commons.

Financially the Charter established important reforms. The National Debt now amounted to £1,000,000,000,000,000,000, 000,000,000,000,000,000,000,000,000,000,000,000,000, 000,000 : it was necessary, therefore, to increase the taxation on small incomes. Tax-payers with incomes of £50 per annum had, of course, to pay £25 a year in taxes. Though this at first seemed hard, the Press Barons felt it to be a necessary measure, and were not afraid to govern justly. Alleviations were made in other directions. The tax on incomes of over £100,000 was halved, the Super-Tax abolished, and taxation on incomes of over £200,000 done away with altogether, in order, as the Charter phrased it, 'to encourage thrift by a sane measure of economic democracy'. On the other hand, it was made compulsory for every citizen with an income of under £5000 per annum to buy a newspaper every morning and every evening (after this measure had been passed, it came as a surprise to find how many men there were in the country who admitted to an income of over £5000) and, on leaving his home for the day's work, to stand still in the street, at attention, and doff his hat three times to that foreign power to which, on this particular day, the governing newspaper had decreed the compliment. This — as we are all aware — one ascertains by opening the day's paper, which will have in large letters, at the top of its principal page, such captivating captions as

'Salute Denmark' or 'Hats off to Holland'. The enactment of these daily greetings, too, has done much to improve our relations with the Continent. Sometimes individuals are substituted for countries or the actual compliment is varied. A Two-Minutes' Silence may be proclaimed in honour of some more than usually public-spirited millionaire, Sir Booster Babboon for instance; while a silence of Ten Minutes is imposed each year in memory of Bottomley-The-Martyr. Indeed, one of the decrees to which the Coalition attached the greatest importance was the setting up of a statue of heroic size to Bottomley on Parliament Green. Of gilded bronze and nearly fifty feet in height, it was erected as a tribute to the memory of that pioneer who had first both divined the power of the Press and exploited its financial possibilities. Alas, since public opinion had been in his lifetime so backward and ill educated, Bottomley had suffered for the cause, had paid the price for his initiative, as had many a martyr before him! But there were many glad faces in London when the Bottomley Shrine was publicly unveiled four years ago, by the venerable Duke of Badgery St. Lawrence himself.

The three most important clauses in the new Constitution we have left to the last. Firstly, a ban was placed on the development of loud-speakers for news-giving, since it was thought that these might interfere with the legitimate power of the Press. The use of the radio was thus confined to purposes of business and communication, and was made, for political ends, dumb as the old telegraph wire. Secondly, it was made illegal for any British subject, or any foreigner domiciled in Britain, to start a new journal without the permission, signed and sealed, of the Governing Baron. Any infringement of this law was punishable with imprisonment for life — a more serious sentence now that the length of life has been so much increased. For though, as we shall see, the lengthening process has not been made compulsory outside the prison wall, yet it is felt that to allow a prisoner to die at his natural age would be to defeat the ends of justice — equivalent, indeed, to the encouragement of suicide.

Thirdly, it was decreed that no mention of public affairs was henceforward to be tolerated in the Press: these mentions, it was felt, would only serve to inflame public feeling, to stir up discontent, since, in order to conquer the Largest Circula-

tion, and thereby the Government of Great Britain, the rival
newspapers would have to make politics too thrilling to be
truthful or healthy. This, the chief rivals agreed, was in the
present circumstances undesirable. Royal speeches, accounts
of the Royal Tours of the Empire, the epigrams of the various
guests at the Mansion House Banquet — these can still be
reported in full — will kindle the flame of loyalty, tend to keep
public opinion patriotic. But such matters as Social Reform,
National Finance, or Armaments, were, it was decreed, never
again to be mentioned in the Public Press. This wise law has
been of inestimable benefit to the nation in the increase of
stability it has given, and could have been enacted under no
other form of government. Yet, to those of us who are old-
fashioned, and remember the reign of Queen Victoria, there is
perhaps something a little dreadful in the thought that, since
the Government of Britain goes to the journal with the Largest
Daily (Net) Circulation and since no matters of public importance may be mentioned in the Press, the ruling and administration of the country actually fall to the owner of that paper which
for the moment reports the most divorces, gives the fullest
details of them, gets the first news of some really first-rate hold-
up, enthralling murder, extraordinary villa-mystery, entrancing
poison-case, curious suicide, or holds the most successful beauty
competition of the year.

The Government, on behalf of the Barons, were still to
speak and act as if they possessed the executive power. The
old Civil Service, the Permanent Officials, still served the
country as before; and Mattie, in his capacity of private
secretary, still serves a minister; and being a kindly, timid
little man, it has invariably been his fate to be the slave of
the most filibustering, bellicose and braggadocio minister of
whatever Government, or whatever form of government, was
in power. These several swashbucklers he has served with the
reverence and loyalty born of mingled love and fear, and with a
surprising competence. They teased him, bullied him, made
a butt of him, yet it was he, in every case, who composed their
most fervent, characteristic and effective speeches (for though
the Barons dictated policy, they encouraged the oratory of
their ministers so long as it was understood that it must not be
reported in the Home Press); his piping falsetto it was that
first rehearsed and recited their most baying and leonine

utterances. For example, that famous fanfaronade that once roused a weak-kneed Britain was, in reality, poor Mattie's: out of this sweetness came forth strength:

'Ladies and Gentlemen (thump), let me put it to you (crash and cheers): ARE WE to Meet the Menace of Armed Might (shame!), yes, Armed and Hostile Might, with a weak, and what seems to One here to-night (gesture) at any rate UNBRITISH, shrugging of the shoulders (long and painful silence)? . . . Or shall we look our foes Undaunted in the face, relying on the Strength of that Great Fleet whose ships crouch low (shudders) in the water, their iron prows curved like the Backs of Giants bent in prayer, ever on the Watch (frantic cheering and even more effective gesture)? Shall we, for fear of risking a few hundred thousand lives — a fear which I think, Ladies and Gentlemen, has never yet swayed a British Government Worthy of the Name — discard that National Honour which has been built up through so many centuries? Shall we, I say (I say it and I REPEAT it again), shall we lightly throw that away? England, look to your laurels! (Fine bulldog grimace by watchful and expectant orator. Transcendental cheering, whistling, cat-calls and unfortunate cry of "Good Old Bottomley!" from rather muddled old gentleman in corner who remembers better days.)'

Yes, it was Mattie's! and this political connection gives the panelled rooms, in which we are waiting, a character and fame of their own. There would be, continually, little political, social and artistic parties, for it was Mr. Matthew Dean's pleasure to present the writers of nature-poems to politicians, to mix together several minor musicians, a duchess, musical-comedy heroines and young revue writers, to introduce obscure and penniless painters-with-a-future to prominent and penniless ladies-with-a-past. Little parties, not too big. There must always be a nucleus of young genius — pudding-basin hair, straight fringe and all the familiar apparatus of unprejudiced voice and vague, wide-open eye. Elegantly dressed shadows would engage in intellectual converse with rather untidy geniuses, would experience a thrill of excitement as if they had been talking to a bandit; though the bandit is of an origin as bourgeois and respectable as their own. Occasionally a real Whitechapeller would be called in, and oh! what flutterings would follow. *Such* an extraordinary-*looking* man, and what an interesting life! And the shadows would shudder and tremble with delight. People would come in after the theatre or opera; exotically dressed young men would be seen talking to tweed-clad, bearded critics; musical-comedy heroines would giggle artistically to earnest-eyed writers; our bull-dog politician would discuss Modern Art with Lady Carabas and Professor Criscross; Lord FitzBison, the reigning Baron, would ponder on the more obscure problems of literature with Bébé Milson, the leading lady in *Whatever Are We Coming To?* — while their host would sit there, smiling and feline, his eyeglass apparently budding from the outer circle of his face, his eyebrows uplifted as by a Chinese wind, wriggling his head and neck, laughing or talking in a twittering bat-like voice.

It was supposed that these gaieties were of use to the mop- or bobbed-haired, the earnest-eyed and tweed-clad; but their effect was more to benefit Mattie, bestowing upon him an importance in the eyes of both sides. The Ghibellines would welcome this whiff, as they thought, of the East End; for, while it made their flesh creep, and reminded them of the French and Russian revolutions, they yet experienced a feeling of pleasurable excitement. And really how clever Mattie was, so-modern-and-all-that, and such interesting people, always! The Blacks, for their part, would be overwhelmed with the lacquer and varnish of these elegant shadows and exquisite reflections, though sometimes surprised by a frankness of speech to which they were unaccustomed in their own almost Victorian homes; slightly intimidated, perhaps, but happy in the feeling that they were seeing life, and for this they would thank Mattie in their hearts. Then there was always a hope — always an unfulfilled hope — that one of the shadows would commission a portrait or buy a landscape, would give a concert for that new string-quartet, or buy the latest volume of verse. But the shadows preferred speech to action. They enjoyed talking about these things.

At this moment, however, the room is empty even of shadows, and Mattie is pacing irritably up and down, stopping every now and then to touch a book, to open and shut it swiftly. The lamp is brighter, or perhaps it is merely that the cold squares of light behind the blinds have faded out.

Suddenly, with no murmur leading up to it, sounds out the tinny rattling of several taxicabs, and, as if arriving down

the three crowsfoot-alleys of the old conventional stage, three
of these vehicles converge from three different directions on
to the doorway below. They arrive there at the same moment,
as though a careful stage-entrance had been contrived. Three
taxi-doors are slammed simultaneously. Mr. Dean remarks to
himself expressively, if not grammatically, 'This must be them',
as an immense booming, roaring, and daft, cackling laughter
floods the house. The sea, surely, must have burst in, and be
whirling and swirling down in the basement. The flood mounts
higher, sweeps relentlessly up the stairs, for a second dies
down as the door is flung open, and a loud voice with no trace
of comment in it, the voice of a machine, announces sonorously :

LORD RICHARD CRESSEY
MR. PARKINSON
MR. VALENTINE LEVIATHAN

When the three guests are in the room, the wave of sound
leaps up into the air again, punctuated by little jets and spurts
of talk from Mattie. In this confusion only a few sentences
can be isolated. 'Mattie, I am so sorry, but it is this beastly
Daylight Saving Bill. When it was one hour, I could manage
it, but now that it's three—' '. . . They kept me so late at
the F.O. One never gets away now till about eight.' . . .
'. . . Had to write an account of the reception of President
Trotsky at the Élysée for *The Morning Star*, and only got back
at seven.' Mattie seems rather overwhelmed by the sheer
volume of sound. His voice seems less now to spurt up, than to
come down from above, as if a bat were bumping blindly
against the ceiling, as if the invisible ventriloquist had just
made up his mind to speak from an angle of the cornice.

The guests are still standing near together, side by side
almost ; and out of this juxtaposition gradually the fact of an
extraordinary resemblance between them emerges. In opposition to the generality of persons encountered, among whom,
as we have remarked, but one or two out of a large gathering
are definite individuals while the remainder imitate them, copy
others who are not present, or are even content to reflect these
mimickings, we have here in front of us three persons who,
though when apart from one another they present little
personality, yet together, and in combination, seem to possess
a collective character. Not so much that they are exactly

alike, these three, as that out of their present proximity to each other it can be seen that through them runs a common denominator: three flowers from the same stalk or three separate stages of the same disease.

Here, then, in these three friends, we have what may be termed a 'short-circuiting' of reflections. Each member of this little group presents countless mirrorings of the other two, innumerable reflections of these two unconsciously mimicking each other; these are echoed on, *ad infinitum*, among the three, but going no further, not getting out of the group, are always thrown back upon themselves. Yet so used are we to the encountering of shadows, to the feeling that it is impolite to detect them as such, so accustomed to an endless repetition and reflection, that the similarity between them passed unnoticed until Fate itself drew attention to it: and even then, as we shall see, little was said about it, for fear that man should be undeceived about his soul, for fear of lowering him in his own eyes. At present the few who detected any resemblance were only pleasantly reminded of dear Valentine, dear Freddie or dear Richard.

Observed thus, seen together, they are somewhat like the various phases of development of some insect — caterpillar into chrysalis, chrysalis into butterfly: but the order of this evolution is reversed, as it would be if time were a mirror in which we could see these gradual changes reflected. Valentine is twenty-seven, Richard thirty-seven, Freddie forty-seven years old. Ten years separate Valentine from Richard, Richard from Freddie. But Valentine, not Freddie, is the most perfect expression of the slow transition from caterpillar to butterfly; his is the winged metamorphosis. With the over-full lines of his still-young body, with his rather full yellow skin, sleek yellow hair, small, fair moustache and general false air of prosperity, he yet has about him a certain overblown, insect-like elegance. But soon he, too, will have passed beyond this into that chrysalis stage in which we find Lord Richard. The latter is thinner, his body a little baggy, but sagging, his skin more lined, his moustache more stubbly, his hair less smooth, the aquiline tracing of his features more pronounced, his eye more vague, his clothes less elaborate; obviously his is the chrysalis, the torpid, stage. While Freddie, with heavier eyebrows and moustache, coarsened skin and a long thin body that wanders uneasily down the length of his shabby clothes, is plainly the caterpillar of this trio. Yet looking at them was like reading a palindrome — the same words, the same meaning, though perhaps not very much of it, manifested through them from whichever end you start. For all of them had the same dusty fair hair and eyebrows, the same dim, blue, vacant eye with an uneasy look, more often found in the eyes of older men. Each has, when talking, the same method of avoiding the eyes of others, without seeming to wish it, of behaving as if this was but a mannerism, the result of intense mental effort. The eye then assumes a sideways and upward glance, as if searching for something within, as if looking up and away from the drooping yet rather bristly moustache, which, in its turn, seems to be looking sideways and down, as it were, in the other direction. Each has the same loud yet hollow voice, as though perpetually engaged in an effort to communicate some item of news into the very impersonal black-frilled nautilus of an ear-trumpet, which, like a real shell, can never hold any sound with sense in it, but only a distant rushing of waters in buried caverns, an ominous roaring, a perpetual rolling-round of pebbles on the ocean-bed; and the latter is an accurate summary of their conversation — a continual grinding, rolling and polishing of pebbles — fashionable pebbles, though!

Yet each of them, as far as any one of them can be said to exist apart from his comrades, is a little more intelligent than the average — who, luckily for the rest of mankind, never exists at all! All the small stories that circulate in the London drawing-rooms, stories that revolve round and round until a feeling of nausea is induced, pass through them, are sifted, sorted, separated, boomed abroad, roared back again and distributed, finally, for general use, to be echoed, lisped and twittered-at in a thousand homes. In this respect they are like the sorting-machines in the Post Office, or the engines that beat out the chaff from the grain. They never originate a story, not even the most minute of this pygmy race, never initiate a thought; but, again, they never reject a thing of value to them as gossip, never choose anything unsuitable, and launch them, when tested, in the best possible manner. All three friends have the artistic and literary catchwords of the moment — which they are the first to jeer at when uncertain of their success, the first to grasp when successful, the first to discard when worn out — perpetually blowing off their tongues, lightly as bubbles. All three are absolutely saturated in the scandals of the moment. They are the possessors, too, of an endless curiosity, and will return to peck at the same subject day after day, pecking, mimicking and screaming like so many dull-plumaged parrots. Though they do not indulge in unconscious imitation, they have developed a fashionable talent for intentional mimicry which fits in well with their little stories: these imitations are not very realistic, but must pass as hieratic likenesses. With this mimicry, unlike yet recognisable, they usually invoke the memory of very distinguished persons. To those who are acquainted with the victims, and know whom the impersonations are intended to represent, the performance is a quite diverting one: while to those ignorant both of the victim and the intention it is a subtle tribute of flattery, suggesting, as it does, that the audience are themselves very important, very-much-in-the-know.

The actual volume of sound that they make, the sheer loud boisterous thunder of it, has helped to create for them a reputation for being 'so amusing'. And what courage they possess! Not one of them would hesitate to attack, when meeting a man or woman for the first time, the subject most dear and sacred to his or her heart; the topic most unapproachable, and by others the most feared. There are parrots in New Zealand which, though once vegetarian, and that not so long ago, have, since the introduction of sheep into their country, learnt to swoop down from a great height, tear open with their huge, hard beaks the woolly back of that animal, rip open the flesh, and remove the kidneys (their favourite food) all in a moment. The sheep has not time to resist. At one moment it is in a large green field, happy and stupid; the sky is blue and clear, the grass green and sweet; and the next it is doomed, writhing in mortal agony. This too, was their method. They would strike suddenly out of a clear sky; while even if detected in their preliminary swoop, surprise would paralyse their prey. And, though our three friends did not meet their victim again over a space of ten years, yet, when they did meet him, they would at once recall the position and nature of the wound and would proceed immediately to probe and deepen it. No matter how many thousands had fallen victims to them in the interval, they would remember. To

I

watch the proficiency, adroitness, science, yet frank brutality with which they first attacked, veering down swiftly out of the void, was also, in a sense, like watching an operation performed, without the use of an anaesthetic, by some great surgeon. So violently, remorselessly, swiftly, was it done that the patient, overcome by shock, would at first feel nothing. But if ever one of them bungled an operation of this sort, his latest indiscretion, which he would attribute to a childlike innocence of disposition, would add to the volume of fashionable chattering and twittering. Without any respect for the feelings of others, themselves were somewhat pompous, easily offended, easily vulnerable.

By this time Mattie had managed to get his three guests anchored safely in front of their dinner. The dim golden light smoothed out the differences in age, distributed part of Valentine's over-glossiness among the two elder members of his spiritual family, making the likeness between all three of them more remarkable. It is obvious to a stranger, and probably to the host, that they appreciate to the full every peculiarity, physical, mental, and vocal, of Mattie's personal style, and are eagerly awaiting more material for little stories and little imitations. They respect, however, his position both as a source and object of gossip, as a man behind several scenes. The talk, though loud, was not without effort. 'Mattie,' boomed Freddie, as if trying to make his voice heard through a storm, from a vast distance, 'what has happened to that queer, interesting little man I met here last time? A poet, I think he was, or a painter or something?'

'Do you mean Jacques — Jacques Rosenheimer?' Mattie replied in a voice so high that it had an impact on the air like a diamond cutting glass. 'Wonderful little man . . . exceptional promise . . . such heavenly lyrics, full of real June . . . real English countryside.' . . . The sentences were thrown up into the air, staccato, abruptly, for only with effort could he make even these dying sounds! While to emphasise his feelings, he would let his monocle drop down on its string, clashing against his stiff shirt-front like a cymbal; and then he would go again through the ritual of fixing it in his eye, like a schoolboy trying to hold a penny there. '. . . Understands the birds and natural history.'

Lord Richard intervened. 'I believe he's going to be at

Old Septua's tomorrow. I've promised to take Valentine and Freddie down to Dodderingham tomorrow in my new plane. (Oh yes, I've got a new one : haven't you seen it ?) I thought she'd amuse them. She's hardly ever in London now and has the most extraordinary people there.' (Mattie produced an angry spurt of sound. 'Well, you won't . . . find Jacques at all extraordinary . . . I'm afraid.' . . .) 'She goes in for farming. I think it's a great mistake. They neither of them understand it ; the sheep have got something wrong with them this year, and walk about all over the place on their knees. One Sunday the Bishop came over and asked if he might hold an open-air service in the park — one prayer and a sermon ; there wasn't a large congregation, but when he had prayed he looked round, and there were all the sheep on their knees ! As he got up, they got up too. Septua was furious, and blamed poor Tootsie for it.'

'I can quite believe it !' Freddie roared, 'because I remember that in my grandmother's lifetime we used to have family prayers. When she said "Let us pray", all the servants got up from their chairs, arranged in line, and revolving silently, as if performing some well-practised exercise in Swedish Drill, went down on their knees ; and an old parrot, standing in a cage in the corner, would invariably revolve through its hoop and then fold one claw over its eyes as if joining in the worship.'

'. . . Wonderful thing, birds' intelligence,' lisped Mattie ; but his friends intended to escape romanticised natural history for the moment and essayed to trail a red herring. 'Isn't it true, Richard,' Valentine asked, 'that there has been a serious outbreak of Hand-to-Mouth disease at Dodderingham ? I heard that Lady Septuagesima, wandering in the lanes, met a sow that was shortly going to suffer an accouchement. Being awfully kind and generous, she asked it to stay, and took it in at once. The bailiff warned her that the disease was very prevalent, and extremely infectious, but she wouldn't turn it away. Not, of course, that it mixed much with other people. She gave it a separate bedroom and all that sort of thing, but directly afterwards there was a fearful outbreak.'

'Poor Septua,' Richard murmured, 'I'm afraid she'll lose a lot. But she will do these things.'

'Talking about grandmothers,' Freddie prepared to embroider his theme, 'it appears that poor old Hetty Wardeburgh

has developed a passion for death-beds — a regular complex!
They say she positively breaks into the bedrooms of the dying.
She got in . . .' But Mattie had got his voice under way and
meant to be heard this time.

'. . . Wonderful thing, birds' intelligence,' he lisped again,
'and Jacques is the only man who understands them. In confidence, as you have promised to give the prize, Richard, I'll
tell you, though I oughtn't to really, that we've decided to give
the Pecksniff to Jacques. Don't forget, Richard, the 12th of
July . . . I rely on you to whip people up for it . . . so
important that the prize should be a success. Naturally Goo-
Goo will be there, but we must make other people come.
Goo-Goo must be made to bring all her friends. Can't you
persuade Lady Septuagesima to come up for it? I don't
mind even if she brings some of those people with her —
though (and he winced) I must admit they are a little too
advanced for me — but I suppose I'm getting an old fogy',
and he tittered in expectation of a friendly denial. Since none
came, he continued, 'And Jacques really deserves support, . . .
such lovely poetry, . . . simply steeped in beauty . . . steeped
in beauty; do you know that last poem, *Denial*? It decided
us . . . lovely . . . I think . . . I'll try to remember it.'

The guests exchanged looks of self-compassion; and Mattie,
throwing his head back and up, produced those high little jets
of sound that bumped against the ceiling like a bat flying into
a sudden light, and at other times was the cry of the bat, the
fluffy twittering of young birds:

'I would not, if I could, be called a poet,
(Oh, tweet-tweet, feathered friends, how you do go it!)
But rather would I cricket in the sun,
Share in the genial crowd's warm-hearted bun
And ginger beer — go into politics and play
A man's stout part; let no man say me nay.
(Oh, dear, how does it go? Say nay, me nay, say me nay.
I've got it.) Let no man say me nay.
Build empires, or in some rough country place,
Throw silken flies, or tickle silver dace,
Watch happy pigs a-waffle in the weir,
The mornings come, the evenings disappear.
                                        Like grains of sand!
                                        Come, friend, your hand!'

PART II

No more perfect morning for a flight could be imagined —
blue sky, with little cool bunches of white cloud knotted
together above the horizon, waiting as if afraid to advance
alone into the emptiness. They seemed, these white clouds,
like ballerinas against an over-painted back-cloth of blues and
violets, a cloth painted so brilliantly that the colours have
split into refracting and scintillating fragments, a haze of
diamond dust, while the dancers themselves are for once
nervous, loath to respond to the music's invitation, fearing the
huge empty stage in front of them, with its circle after circle of
eyes, dull or mocking. Occasionally a grand cloud, a giant,
flaunts across like an iceberg seen from under the transparent
depths of water beneath it, so that its full thickness of ice-greens,
ice-blues and faint rose colourings is visible to us, and it
becomes a matter of wonder that the weight of this floating
mountain does not overturn it. The air is warm, yet so coldly
white is this giant that if it were only nearer, the polar animals,
bears whiter than snow, and all the other creatures that have
fashioned for themselves skins out of their native element,
would show on it, horrified at its breaking away thus from
their home in the frozen seas, looking down with wonder and
resentment. The trees are very still. In the open space in
Hyde Park where stretches the public landing-stage, the plane
is waiting for them. The vast cement quay glares out,
painted crudely with signs and symbols, placarded with gay if
somewhat hideous advertisements. A great droning rises round
it, as a thousand planes are launched on one side or come to
anchor on the other, coming and going like a horde of dragon-
flies, a swarm of bees, round some tropical plant. Lord
Richard's machine was at the near end, looking in the morning
light as if it were a swallow-tail that had fallen into a tub of
liquid silver. The pilot, whom they were not taking with
them, got out, and Lord Richard sat down at the wheel with
Valentine and Freddie behind him. Suddenly the pilot,
standing on the quay to see them off, grew smaller and smaller,
as though performing the Indian vanishing-trick, but climbing
down, instead of up, his long rope, and the earth swung away
from them. The whole width of London swung beneath them,

revolving round St. Paul's, the dome of which stood out as the hub of the wheeling city. A myriad grey ribbons, grey ribbon after grey ribbon fluttered and swerved beneath them, and over these crawled and hurried minute ant-like creatures, ever diminishing in size, fetching and carrying, dragging or propelling great loads. So much did the ribbons flutter and wave, that it seemed a miracle that those tiny creatures could keep their balance at all. Now the wheel of London trundles itself away into the distance, and they hang apparently motionless, over the open country, which slides beneath them, pushing them on, like a moving staircase. This prospect changes in the space of a few minutes from a landscape into a realistic but metallic-coloured map. Occasionally the atlas would be hidden from them, as they traversed white seas which, though floating in air, looked so solid that a man, willing to face the coldness of their breakers, would surely be able to wander among the hillocks of these waves, snapping off, here and there, a sprig of frozen spray, pure and flower-like : for the waves had been crystallised, seemingly, in the very rhythm, the very tilt of their life, the foam still leaping upward from their rush caught in attitudes as true yet conventional as the uplifted springing claw of a wave that leaps at you from a screen by Korin. And these seas were but what appeared from the city as timid little clouds ! Now, again, the air below grew clear, and the ocean, the real ocean, revealed itself below ; the whole line of east coast and Thames estuary showed there, as far as you could see, and the geography that had been to them as children so improbable, assumed for a space a reality of its own. Exhilaration seized Freddie and Valentine, and they roared and boomed loudly at each other, forgetting for a moment that no sound is audible up here, until each wondered at the other's mute grimaces.

Deep down under them grow tufts of grass that are really trees, spreading and noble, ant-heaps that are hills. The diminutive pediment, the prim dovetailing of grey slates would mark a Georgian mansion ; and little figures would walk under the grass-blades or move over open spaces of green baize. And, as the plane passed over, it cast down on them a blue or mauve winged shadow, a small shadow that skimmed like a dragon-fly just brushing the still greenery with a breath of coolness. And within that flying speck, high up among the drifting white clouds, cheerfully roaring to themselves, Lord Richard Cressey, Mr. Freddie Parkinson and Mr. Valentine Leviathan are in the clutches of those Demons of the Upper Air, who, unappeased by any sacrifice, can still be heard howling, far away above us, on a dark winter night.

. . . . .

Dodderingham Old Hall, their intended destination, lies beside the Cam : a simple Queen Anne house, like a pavilion of red velvet, with a long and wide staircase leading up to it, and down from it, on to stretching green lawns. It seems to have been improvised for some pageant that has passed long ago, lies embedded in all this intense verdure, sinking slowly into the flat country which is as rustic now as before the house was built. Only the avenue of wireless masts at intervals of five miles, rising to fifty times the height of the huge old trees, shows that the age of the Virgin Queen is over — for so Elizabethan is the countryside that Dodderingham Old Hall seems as much of an anachronism as the masts that join it to London. The present régime in the house appears to have something Gothic still lingering about it, strange and fantastic. For Lady Septuagesima patronises the advanced guard of art and literature. The large panels of the walls that had before shone dully, grey or brown, full of low lights and mouse-like colour, now blush under bedizenments of purple, scarlet and apricot, are blazoned with stripes, are chequered, or have gathered constellations of gold and silver. The pictures that liven, or sober, these walls are either frighteningly old or terrifyingly new ; illustrating the theory of the most modern painters that their wagon is hitched on to such stars as Giotto and Duccio. On the other hand, Raphael, who had enjoyed a temporary popularity with the vanguard, now bows the knee to Guido Reni and to Carlo Dolci, once again the last word in esthetic thrills. A small picture by Sassetta would hang side by side with the work of the youngest self-taught genius ; Guido would pair with Renoir ; a huge early Matisse faces a chiaroscuro altar-piece from Bologna ; yet all the pictures, all the furniture, are arranged with a dramatic sense that has enabled Lady Septuagesima to mount herself superbly.

This remarkable lady came, as can be deduced from her name, of a peculiarly religious family. Her father, the late Lord Fortcarrick, one of the richest land and mineral owners in Lancashire, had harnessed his portion of a notorious family eccentricity, and turned it into religious energy. This, though trying to his relatives, was in the end perhaps to their advantage. 'An odious bore,' old Lady Fortcarrick used to characterise it, 'but better than gamblin'.' To an extent she even encouraged this fervour, while, at the same time, keeping it in bounds. In her lifetime he was merely aggressively Low Church; but after his wife's death he became more imaginative. He would spend his time now, with enormous notebooks in front of him, reckoning out the precise date of the Second Coming; a calculation based, even more elaborately, upon such foundations as Joanna Southcott's unopened box, and statistics of the growing Catholicism in England, and inextricably intertwined with the fact that the Kaiser Wilhelm II of Germany was the Beast-in-the-Revelation. As time went on, as he became older (for this was before the prolongation of life had become such a simple affair), his mind became ever more original in its working. He would invariably invest his income (he was a very rich man) as it came in, and then, forgetting what he had done, would declare, would insist, that he had no money to live on unless he raided his capital. The necessary sums for his support he would borrow from his children. Finally, in a fit of prophecy verging on apoplexy, he identified poor Lady Septuagesima, to her face, with the Scarlet Woman of Babylon, and, shortly afterwards, passed peacefully away.

His daughter had started life by being as religious as her father. Devotion was bred in her; and many farmers and miners, who owe their conversion to her, would be surprised if they could see her now — which is improbable, since, whereas the late earl accused his daughter of being the Scarlet Woman, the present one, her brother, has proved her to his own satisfaction a Bolshevik; and the latter, however popular politically in London, is still a word of reproach in ancestral halls.

But in the early days of which we are writing, not even her brother could have brought against her such an accusation. She affected, then, an almost Salvationist simplicity of dress, demeanour, and speech. This continued until she was about thirty-five, and then a change came. The scene of her charitable activities had gradually shifted from the country village to the poorer districts of London. Another transformation,

and she began to do her slumming in the studios of Fitzroy
Street and Chelsea. It was a miracle. At once her religious
zeal was converted into an artistic one, but equally Protestant,
equally unyielding and fanatic in its new direction. At this
time she would surely, without scruple, have started a crusade,
a holy war, against the Royal Academy. To her they were
now what the Church of Rome had been previously. Even the
ever-present, farcical spectacle of these poor old men, in their
greed for money, rushing out after Modern Art like a fat man
after a passing omnibus, and always failing to catch it, could
not soften her. Yet at the same moment that this miraculous
conversion took place, herself became transfigured. The former
possession of ordinary, simple good looks she now bartered for
a grotesque yet actual beauty ; while from her previous austerity
of dress she blossomed into a garish glory of clothes, such as
was never seen in this world before. Her language, her conversation, too, now threw off their swaddling clothes and came
of age in a day.

Of impressive height — a height that was over life-size for
a woman, so that without looking a giantess she might yet
seem an animated public monument — Lady Septuagesima
had an almost masculine face, deep-set flower-like eyes with a
golden calyx, a long, definite nose and cut-out chin ; strong,
large animal-like teeth, which showed when she laughed, and
a mass of red-brown hair, cut short but not cropped. Many of
these features do not sound attractive, but it is certain that there
was about her a quality of crazy, ludicrous, abstract beauty
that few, happily, possess. Her voice, personal to herself as
her looks, was equally absurd, and in it mingled the peaceful
lowing of cattle and the barbed drone of wasp and hornet. As
she moved (never afraid of attracting attention — indeed
apparently oblivious of it) through the London streets in her
gaudy clothes, large hooped skirt and vast hat loaded with
feathers as that of any coster's wife, many who stopped to stare
supposed that she was staggering by under the weight of odd-
lots that, now past their use, had been bestowed upon her by a
charitable theatrical costumier. Every year her appearance
became more eccentric, more grim and yet more decorative,
having the desolate yet rather extravagant beauty of a ruin-
picture by Pannini ; of severe classical remains decked out
with bunting ; of the Colosseum seen alternately under soft

moonlight and by the fire and fizzling glitter of fireworks. In vain the crowd of dirty wide-eyed children, who would accompany her when she walked in London, raised their shrill anthem in the air :

> 'I see no reason
> Why gunpowder treason
> Should ever be forgot.'

For Lady Septuagesima these words contained no hidden implication. She liked children and, alas, had none of her own. She would merely remark, casually, on arriving home, that the children in London were so friendly and would walk with her all the way, singing.

At Dodderingham Old Hall the individual note in her clothes was accentuated still further. She would walk down the deeply hedged lanes, the flat roads, accompanied by her noble-looking, rather horse-like husband, and by a perfect menagerie of young artists and intellectuals. In winter or summer she would be supported, apparently, by the same court. But though identical in voice and look, those strolling companies were, with the exception of her husband, never the same in their composition for more than one quarter of the year : she quarrelled with them regularly every three months, and then no abuse was too bad for those for whom, only two months previously, no praise had been good enough. 'Never in my life have I been treated like that before', was invariably the burden of her song to the next assembly. The latter, this permanent though shifting circus, cultivated always the look of its part. One inevitable ingredient in it was a group of undergraduates from Cambridge, which, in its turn, could invariably be divided into two portions : one division consisting of youths painfully well-clothed, too precious in manner, with eyes too liquid ; while the other was made up of callow young men, intolerably dirty, whose friendship was valued because of their simplicity. Then there were mop-haired, moist-handed individuals with greenish faces, grotesque and damply chilly as deep-sea monsters ; art-critics, like sea anemones, with circular floating fringes of red hair, or with matted beards that seemed tentacular as the arms of an octopus ; a superannuated bishop who believed in seeing life and making the best of things ; one or two stray individuals from London, with no particular point; and several young women with golden hair and strawberry-and-cream complexions, who had, therefore, to insist on intellect by the cropping of their hair, by wearing breeches and by speaking about peculiar subjects in a peculiarly frank way, in voices whose even tones displayed no trace of emotion. Then there were oldish women with short grey hair, tweed skirts and green-leather football boots; middle-aged ones decked out with pince-nez and crowned with plumes — synthetic ones, though — of victory, like the goddess Bellona. This perambulating group was further augmented by a few stray 'studio-sweepings'. As they walked, one could see that some of them were tall . . . much too tall — others short . . . far too short: but all, as they marched through the rustic landscape beside their hostess, assumed an air of bourgeois respectability, of utter commonplaceness. And though in London the children followed her, here they were respectful and subdued. As she swept along, her clothes lent colour, an unusual quantity of colour indeed, to the insinuation of her enemies that in order to find such garments she must attend secret rummage-and-jumble-sales at the Local Asylum. But there was something splendid about her appearance; no snowball greeted her even on the coldest winter day, nor, as she sailed past, was any cry of 'Aunt Sally!' wafted to her ear by the spring breezes.

And the course of her previous progress through the countryside was afterwards easily to be traced by strangers; for, as she went, the most extraordinary, the most extravagant, objects fell from her and were lost. These, if left for future generations to discover, will greatly puzzle posterity. What strange race, it will wonder, what extinct civilisation had its centre, as testified by this accumulation of grotesque objects, in this flat, green, peaceful land? Even now the passing pedestrian is filled with awe and surprise. Tall trees rise up, covered with leaves from head to foot, every tiny twig of every branch flooded with leaves, the very trunks and arms green with moss, gold with lichen, as if they had just risen, dripping, cool and watery-green, from the ocean bed. Under them are whitewashed cottages, very white and crumbling, with windows, like wide-open eyes and thatched roofs that jut out over them, hair, brow and eyebrow combined in one slanting, moss-covered greenness. The whole area is calm, sleepy. Cottage gardens, raised above the road, are bulging with stocks and sweet-blowing flowers of many colours, are full as cornucopias. Even the windows of these cottages are full of flowers, whose faces, red and hot, are flattened against the windows, as ever tightly shut; the blossom in each pane seems the iris of an eye, alive and vibrant. Against this background, pasted on the boles of trees so ancient that they are antlered like king stags, or pendent in the boldly curving bow-windows of a village post office, among open boxes and glass jars of sweets like small overripe fruits, among barley-sugar gold as corn and twisted like the pillars of the Temple, among bundles of brown and black bootlaces hanging up like hairy scalps, among pyramids of snow-white sugar or mounds of honeyed Demerara, rods of coloured sealing-wax, rusty steel pens and all the other familiar properties of village life, he reads some such notice as this that follows:

LOST

LOST between here and Dodderingham Old Hall on the afternoon of May 2nd, 1948:
Seven herons' plumes set in brilliants.
A green ostrich-feather fan with tortoise-shell mount.
An Elizabethan whale-bone hoop.
One crimson shoe-heel with cairngorm inset.
A tartan shawl.
A Japanese embroidered bag, with panels of flying storks worked in salmon-pink and rose silks, containing:
> A stick of orange-coloured lip-salve, with black onyx mounting and
> A purse with platinum fastening, in which were:
>> A card of permanent invitation to the Trafalgar Gallery of Modern Art, London.
>> £3 12s. 6d. in silver, and
>> A paper bag full of bull's-eye peppermints.

ALSO

LOST between Skipton and Dodderingham Old Hall:
A blue-silk cushion of native workmanship.
A Congo Fetish in ivory.
A first edition of Milton's *Paradise Lost* (Simmons, in 10 books, 1667).
A volume of Jules Laforgue's poems.
The second volume of the Bloomsbury Painters Series — *From Giotto to Gertler*.

A photographic miniature of Cézanne, presented by the painters of
the Black-Friday Group, set in half-pearls.
A green amber amulet.
A New Zealand Totem Pole, converted into a walking-stick, and
A wisdom tooth, mounted in turquoises, and inscribed 'To Septua
from Tootsie, 1943'.
 The Finder, on returning these items to their owner, Lady
 SEPTUAGESIMA GOODLEY, Dodderingham Old Hall, will be
 SUITABLY rewarded.

Tootsie, it must be confessed, was Thomas Goodley, her
husband. Thus, in her progress round the countryside, would
Lady Septuagesima distribute regal, if involuntary, largess.

On this fine Sunday morning, however, she indulged in no
ambulatory adventures, preferring to stay in the garden surrounded by her court of the instant. Seen from a little distance,
it was quite a spectacle. The entire assembly was broken up
into knots of two or three persons; but all these groups were
yet near together, as if each one feared to be out of earshot of
any other; each listening to the conversation of the one
farthest removed from it, while, at the same time, carrying
on a conversation amongst itself. Some members of these
various court factions were sitting on garden seats painted in
sugar-stick stripes of red and white, some were lying curled up,
or were crouching uncomfortably, hands clasped round knees
in the manner of those rigid mummies of pre-dynastic Egypt,
while others were sitting easily on the ground, as if never
accustomed to any more comfortable posture. Under them
were square rugs decorated with large square patterns, and
over each knot spread a large striped umbrella. The light
dripping through these, and cast up again by the rugs and
flat stretches of green grass, spattered them with vivid patches
of scarlet, purple, blue and sea-green, till they seemed hotly
coloured insects nestling under the shade of a clump of iridescent,
rather deleterious toadstools. A cloud floating overhead reduces
the colouring, lowering it a tone or two for an instant as if a
tinted glass had been interposed between the groups and the
onlooker. The cloud would pass and the tones would jump
up again to their normal violence. From under the fungi rose
a continual droning, shrilling, hoarse cackling and shooting-
out of the tongue, as the chameleon-coloured groups conversed.
Little spirals of smoke rose, coloured, too, by their surroundings.

Nearly the whole day was spent here, and in this manner, for Lady Septuagesima was expecting three guests down from London. They should have been here by twelve o'clock or in time for luncheon at the latest; but there came no sign of their arrival. In the garden it was very restful; the lowing, whinnying laughter of the hostess fitted in with the prospect disclosed between the high green trees, pillars that framed-in the view, with its foreground of sun-baked, red-brick walls, seeming already to breathe out the honey-sweet scent of ripe fruit, though at present the flattened forms of espaliers, that clung to them like green cobwebs, bore only small constellations of delicate blossom, apple and peach, pear and plum.

The conversation was woven equally of high art and low scandal. An enormous man, with a blue shirt, an open coat, no waistcoat and a belt, a costume singularly courageous for so large a person, was, though he had an air of easy well-being combined with little intellectual effort, taking a severe line about esthetics. The cropped-haired young women were voluble too; their voices, calm and even, indicated clearly a conscious superiority which enraged the large gentleman; for as the Quakers are confident of the spiritual revelation within them, so were all these combatants sure of their essential rightness. The undergraduates were present as usual; the untidy spoke seldom but loudly, and when they spoke would not be silenced; the ones elaborately groomed and dreamy-eyed gazed on mutely, lost in some adolescent stupor. Jacques Rosenheimer interrupted occasionally, with abrupt, authoritative and rather snapping utterance; short, dark and thick-set, he was curly haired and curly nostrilled. Then, distributed among the groups, there were some cosmopolitans: a Danish dancer, a Spanish gipsy, a Russian artist, swelling out of his clothes, full of compliments, ever so gallant; and all the usual court, except the bishop, who was resting within. Tootsie, monumental, like one of the togaed statues outside the old House of Commons, remained immersed in his own nobility of mien and character.

All day the conversation wove its arabesque design, a design barely traceable, seldom leading to any very definite pattern; but the threads, drawn up above the several umbrellas by one hand, would have a certain vague significance.

The fat man's voice, loud and distinct, sounded out his

bass theme. 'Give me Giotto, give me Giotto,' he reiterated solemnly. 'I don't see how you can compare Guggenheimer with him. . . .'

'It isn't that' (and a feminine hand was waved descriptively), 'it's the solidity, the *pure* painting, if you know what I mean, the actual *pure* painting . . . like Defoe or Sterne,' and her voice drooped back into the general shrilling.

The threads are drawn closer, so that the fabric can be regarded.

'. . . Well, of course, if you're going to talk in that way, the argument simply can't be continued . . . must compare one painter with another. . . . But why? There is a likeness, don't you think, the same definite hardness, you know . . .' (Fresh theme announces itself.) 'Well, all I can tell you is, *he* told me so himself. I know she didn't. She didn't want it talked about, naturally . . . but he happened to tell me himself . . . After all, it had been going on for years, hadn't it, Septua? You know as well as I do . . . Oh! Breughel's not to be compared with Giotto . . . not in it simply. Besides, I don't like Ingres's drawings, I only like the *drawing* in his *paintings*. . . . Well, I'm glad he left her: came down here for two nights three years ago, stayed ten days; poor Tootsie was nearly driven off his head and played the electric organ for seven hours without stopping. So exhausted that the doctor . . . immensely improved . . . fine thing that, at the Black-Friday Club . . . Impressive design . . . I shall be out if she comes again — such a bore . . . She always was one, and quite crazy into the bargain, now. Why should one be lumbered up with people like that? . . . all I can tell you is this. Giotto and Tolstoy, they've made the difference to my life . . . don't see that Blake's a bit like Cézanne . . . and when she'd got into Italy, they had to come back again . . . very queer and interesting . . . and in Petrograd we (how you say it in English?) sledged down the Neva . . . what I wonder is will Mingler become a SUBJECTIVE or an OBJECTIVE writer? That is what I ask myself . . . judging by the last one, sub-jective and objectionable, I should say . . . that's merely silly. Of course, I like him, but he is pompous, isn't he? Goo-Goo is charming . . . pretty, and personally I like her accent. Of course no talent, either of them . . . Aix-les-Bains . . . no, I haven't seen the ones in Vienna, but in any case Breughel had no sense of form . . . Mattie . . . ridiculous but kindly. (Giotto and Tolstoy, Giotto and Tolstoy, Giotto and Tolstoy . . .) The minister had to disarm him. It simply wasn't safe to let him shoot. But he was allowed to carry a white sunshade; and the very next day he was charged by the only white rogue-elephant in Africa . . . never been the same . . . and the minister only laughed and said (Giotto and Tolstoy) that Mattie had got a white elephant in his sun helmet . . . well, you may not agree with me; but there it is, Giotto and . . . I can't bear that barn. It would drive me mad if I had to live in it (Giotto, and give me the Primitives). Doesn't look lived in somehow . . . for his children, but now they've had to abolish death-duties altogether . . . not quite so pleased . . . solidity, that's what I mean — pure painting . . . like Mozart. . . .'

But the fabric was torn suddenly by a maid, who hurried out of the house to tell her ladyship that she was wanted on the radiophone.

'The Superintendent, Cambridge, speaking . . . speaking . . . yes, yes. Is that you? Three miles away . . . like a lump of lead? Terrible . . . terrible! Yes, radio at once. Are you ready? Lady Richard Cressey, Hotel Splendide, Aix-les-Bains. Return at once Richard unwell will meet you Cambridge Septua. And one more, please; yes, Superintendent. Sir Vincent McNabb, 142 Wimpole Street, Inner London. Please engage Express Flyer Cambridge at once grafting operation Lord Richard Cressey most important on no account fail me. Stay night here Lady Septuagesima Goodley, Dodderingham Old Hall.'

. . . . .

One of the most pleasing features of the progress of civilisation during the last quarter of a century has been the immense advance in the art of surgery, as well as in healing, mental and physical. If the dominating features of the nineteenth century were concerned with mechanics — with machines and mechanical inventions — this one surely will be remembered always as the Biological Century. Biology has disclosed to us miracle after miracle, and has not yet bestowed upon humanity the last of its gifts. To those who were children during the course of the First or Small 'Great War' (that one which, beginning in 1914, lasted until 1918) — still more to those born since that event — the extent to which the old pre-war world of 'statesmen', 'newspaper proprietors' (as they were then called), millionaires and philanthropists, was dominated by death, and by the idea of death, can hardly be credible. However accustomed the new generation may be to the prospect of that triple span which life holds for them, to us older men it must remain a continual cause for wonder, making us rub our eyes to see if we are awake. Nor are the full implications of the life-lengthening operation fully grasped even now. Because, since the first operations were performed barely twenty-five years ago, there are still with us but few men who have achieved over eleven decades, whereas in the future there will be many, mentally and physically in the prime of life, at the age of one hundred and eighty. To remind us that we are not dreaming (if one may still, without impropriety, mention that word . . .) there are, luckily, certain concrete facts constantly before us. When I first began to read the newspapers as a child of seven — for in those distant days the reading of newspapers, far from being compulsory for children, as it is now, was discouraged or actually forbidden — it was noticeable that hardly a day passed without the death of A Last Great Victorian having to be recorded. It was very depressing reading, that list of obituaries, which became like the accounts of the-positively-final-farewell-performance of some great stage favourite. Suddenly the torrent was checked, and, as we know, many of the last really great ones have been declared 'public monuments', and are with us yet.

Another proof that the miracle has actually been achieved is to be found in the abolition of death duties. Curiously enough, it was the iniquitous and vindictive incidence of this taxation — aimed solely at one small class rich enough to pay it — as much as any single fact, that in the end, perhaps, was responsible for the lengthening of life. An inevitable evolution it was, comparable to that neck which the giraffe has developed in its continual search for food at a considerable altitude. Each rich man was determined for the sake of his family, nay, of his country, to live as long as lay within his power. Each wealthy pioneer of longevity — for, as in so many other charitable causes, it was the millionaires who took the lead — made a public declaration that it was not the fear of death (on the contrary, such were his responsibilities that he would welcome a release from them) that made him wish to postpone the end, but the fact that if he surrendered to care, illness and old age, a disgraceful and punitive impost would fall upon his children. Nor, he would add, was this bad for the family alone, since the Family is but the Unit of the State! What, therefore, is injurious to the family, damages the State; what impoverishes the family, though it may at first appear to enrich, yet surely in the end impoverishes the Motherland. I remember what an effect a certain simile made on me in this connection: it has often been noticed that powerful and original minds work in much the same manner; and several of these grand old men said to me, oddly enough, the same thing in almost the same words. As they pronounced their faith, with a fervour that was convincing, there was about them something, perhaps a little ponderous, yet noble and statesmanlike. 'You cannot,' they would say, 'you cannot both have your cake and eat it!' And one felt, somehow, from the fact that they had thought out and pinned down the same phrase, that deeply, deeply, must these pioneers feel the truth of it. Great was their courage and resolution. No matter how their sons gave way to their own feelings, crying and imploring their fathers not to sacrifice themselves, not to pass this stern self-denying ordinance, urging them to release themselves from this bondage of family feeling which required such inverted immolation of father to son, the old gentlemen remained firm in their resolve. Patriotic, as well as family, scruples had entered into their decision; they could not, therefore, look back. Nor even did the threats of the Church intimidate for an instant these patriots. The Church, as ever behind the times, began by denouncing the surgical prolongation of life as a sin against God's ordering of the world, and one that would entail damnation eternal, the complete conquest by Satan of the soul of each man operated upon. A breath of humour was brought into this controversy by the declaration of old Lord Badgery St. Otter (as he then was), now the Duke of Badgery St. Lawrence, who, being eighty years of age, and about to submit to the operation, said: 'If the devil waants me, 'e can coome an' fetch me, an' a devilish touff job 'e'll 'ave!'

Such was the spirit of these men, willing to risk a presumable certainty of eternal happiness for the sake of another span of worldly care and sorrow in which to help their fellows.

Undaunted, these fine old Die-hards damned the consequences, flinging themselves down on the operating table in the same spirit in which Abraham had sought to sacrifice his dearly beloved son. And the sacrifice has not been made in vain, for the substitution by the Press Barons of the 'Re-marriage' — or, as they are popularly called, 'divorce duties' — for Death Duties, has been to many a great relief. The Death Duties had, as a matter of fact, long ceased to bring in much revenue; and the new ones are both less heavy and less easily avoided — for a man can, after all, avoid death more easily than marriage. But if the tax should become too heavy, it is not to be doubted that — ever at the call of patriotism and the family — the same grand old pioneers will no more hesitate to give up making a fresh start in their new life, than, on behalf of the same ideals, they feared to give up making a fresh start in death.

The Press Barons were among the first to undergo what was at the time a dangerous experiment; and while we owe our good government to them, and to the increasing wisdom and generosity with which the passing years have endowed them, it is right, surely, to admire that very British spirit of freedom which has actuated them throughout. Never, for an instant, have they sought to force these discoveries on others, to thrust them, for example, upon the poor! From the first they understood that the world was over-populated, and for the sake of those same ideals, for faith, family and Fatherland, the workers should be permitted to die at that age at which they had formed the habit of so doing — or, if they wish it, at one yet earlier. For, in effect, they are too old at forty. Thus it can never be said that the men with responsibilities sought to shift their burden on to the shoulders of those free of them; and it remains one of the consolations, the compensations, of poverty that a double — or even a full — span of life is not obligatory.

These political and social benefits are all due, in the first place, to the marvellous science of human grafting, the effect of which has been increasingly toward national stability. The workers must realise by now, one would imagine, that the holding of wealth, with its privileges and responsibilities, in the hands of a few permanent, indeed almost eternal, individuals, is a guarantee that while the former will not be abused, the latter will be respected. Apart from this self-obvious con-

clusion, it is one of the blessings of our present form of government that every day, in every way, in every paper, this thought
is enunciated, this lesson taught. Again, it had long been
noticed in every country where hereditary monarchy survived,
that there was never a revolution against any king who had
reigned for over fifty years — however good a ruler he may
have been. And since 'O King, live for ever!' is now hardly
an exaggerated expression of good-will, since reigns of two
centuries will automatically become quite normal, the fear of
revolution becomes continually more remote.

The first operation that proved the value, and advertised
the miracle, of grafting was that performed upon Prince
Absalom, son of the Emperor Dodon of Aquitania. It is not
yet twenty years, though it may seem more, since that well-
beloved prince, the darling rival of every cinema star, and
scion of an ancient and august house, which had in an amazingly short period consolidated one of the greatest empires —
and by making no use of it had managed for an amazingly
long time to keep it — met with a terrible, an appalling,
accident. Though possessed of immense charm, he was of a
puny, frail physique, that contrasted forcibly with his marked
mental powers and attainments. While seeking recreation one
evening, in those few moments of leisure spared him from
Empire's Call, by performing in what was then called a 'Jazz'
band (a fashion that had spread to Aquitania from America
via England), he fell into one of the noise-contrivances, his
right leg being terribly lacerated. At the news, a thrill of
horror passed, not only through his own people, but through
the whole of the civilised world. At first the contraption
refused to let go of his leg, but eventually its jaws were broken,
and followed the tragic announcement that the surgeon had
found it necessary to amputate the injured limb. Day after
day enormous crowds, some of them sobbing or weeping
hysterically, would gather outside the Emperor's palace in
Atlantis to read the latest bulletins.

Then, one day, with a burst of joy, with such startling
demonstrations of loyalty, such outbursts of shouting, dancing
and singing as usually only mark the periodic declarations of a
war to end war, it became known that one of the duskier
players (or coons, as they were called) in the orchestra had
come forward to give his leg in the Cause of Empire! And

that operation, first of its kind, was successful.

In those inspiring days I happened to be in Aquitania, and through the generosity of Lord FitzBison, who had just at that moment appointed himself English Ambassador at the Emperor Dodon's court, was enabled to be present at the Solemn Service of National Thanksgiving at St. Andrew's which celebrated Prince Absalom's recovery. The discourse of the Archbishop of Atlantis was particularly impressive, full of original thinking, and I translated some portions of it.

'We are gathered together today, brethren,' he said, 'to celebrate the recovery of one beloved beyond all princes — by the people of this mighty League of Free Peoples, Nations and Commonwealths which we call Empire. And in him, for whose recovery we thank our God today — for whose recovery humble couples in their forest homes, in log-cabins and cottages, men gathered in the Service of Industry, and the darker peoples who kneel in their tents of grass and wattle, thank God too — we have more than ever, in his own person, what he has so long been called, "The Ambassador of Empire". In his own body blends he now the fair people of Atlantis and the northern states, with the dusty — dusky, I should say — dwellers in the jungle. One foot is set in Africa, the other in the Northern Isles. In his own body he binds together every class, every colour, nay, every creed; and the Thin Red Line of Empire cements the union. And, brethren,' and his voice sank dramatically, 'it is only right that' (crescendo), 'in this hour of triumph, our thoughts should go out to another son of Empire, to one of lowly condition and perhaps of but modest pretensions, yet one who, in his humble way, has done much to make possible this Union of Peoples. Hath a man greater love than this . . . that he lays down his foot for a friend ? . . . can we not put it like that, brethren ?' (Hissing slightly.) 'In that dusky and obscure player, too, was found the heart of Saint and hero; and there may be many of us amongst this great congregation who, though we have not appreciated the music of jazz bands in the past, will never be able to hear the sweet tones of the Swanee Whistle or the deep, melodious notes of the saxophone without heartfelt sympathy and emotion, roused by the memory of a great and gracious deed.'

But, though the happy recovery of the prince was everywhere acclaimed, yet from that moment, in spite of the Archbishop's prophecy, syncopated music began to lose its grip on the people of the world. Jazz it was that died.

This same accident was responsible for a curious fashion among royal princes, and one which is still prevalent, though it may seem strange to the Victorians who survive — that fashion of having the limbs variegated in accordance with the people of the dominions over which they rule. Thus they have now become, in their own bodies, walking examples of Representative Government.

In spite of the fact that the most important of these grafting operations is still known as the 'monkey gland', it ought now to be needless to point out that the use of these simian cells has long been abandoned. For the introduction of any element foreign to it into the human body, inevitably sets up an irritation, which is sure to develop into some serious, and possibly fatal, trouble. • Whereas the same operation, with human material substituted, is without any possibility of danger. In view of this, special laws were passed, many years ago, to ensure an adequate supply of human material and a proper use of it.

As we know, every young man killed by chance, in street accident or sudden explosion in a factory, is sent at once to the Royal Analysing Institute, whence, if his remains are found to be satisfactory, they are passed on, for the necessary treatment, to the nearest Young Man's Dissecting and Cold Storage Association (Y.M.D.A.C.S.A.). Here, if his relatives so desire, a funeral service can be held by Royal Licence; and many relatives have found a funeral without any corpse — and with no actual expense, save that of the service — most comforting; preferable, indeed, to the ordinary arrangement. In the building of the association, each limb, each cell, waits till the time comes for it to serve its purpose with Elder Statesman, millionaire philanthropist, or famous general. Wars, even, have ceased to hold for the civilian population their former terror. For the essential horror of war was its utter waste and uselessness; but now, after each battle, there is a short armistice, and the slain are swiftly collected and laid by, that we may benefit — and our enemies as well — by the ever-increasing wisdom and ripe experience of those who have guided us through, and themselves survived, so many crusades to end war. Surgeons, as well as statesmen, may now declare:

'We will not lightly sheathe the sword. . . .'

In spite of these well-thought-out preparations, it has been found that freshly dissected limbs are more effective, safer to use, more swift in their results, than preserved ones. So, when Sir Vincent McNabb was warned of the accident that had befallen Lord Richard Cressey, he determined to patch the patient together — if it should prove possible — without the use of any but his own limbs, glands and other material. This might mean that the actual reconstruction would be a more lengthy affair, but in the end it would be of the greatest benefit to the patient, aiding his speedy recovery. In order, however, to be ready for any eventuality, the great surgeon brought down with him from London a complete regulation set of anatomical sections.

Within a half-hour of his urgent summons, Sir Vincent had arrived at Cambridge. There he was met by the Goodleys' agent; for Lady Septuagesima and her husband had been forced to stay at Dodderingham to make arrangements for the nursing of Lord Richard and the reception of his wife. The menagerie had been hurriedly dispersed, the striped umbrellas had been struck, the raggle-taggle gipsies were on the move once more. The wolves and jackals were already howling in the outer wilderness of London, the hyenas were laughing more hysterically than ever in their own homes, and the few lions that there had been were back in their dens, roaring sardonically. Everything had been tidied up, under the supervision of two trained nurses; and, as soon as the preparations were complete, Lady Septuagesima would join Sir Vincent. Meanwhile, the agent conducted him to where, among torn brambles, smashed hawthorn bushes, and earth thrown up as by a miniature volcano, lay the wrecked flyer, guarded by police. Several nurses were on the scene, in readiness. It was now getting dark; but with that rapidity and sureness of judgment which, in surgery as in other professions, is the very stamp of genius, Sir Vincent was soon able to decide that it was possible, as he had hoped it would be, to operate with the material on the spot. The mutilations and injuries were terrible: but a reconstruction was undoubtedly feasible, however formidable the difficulties. A theatre, fitted with the new wireless lighting, was hastily improvised. Everything, now, depended on swift, on determined, action.

During four hours the remains were under an anaesthetic, while the great surgeon grappled with the problem of their reconstitution. But, in the end, the problem was solved, and Lord Richard Cressey was given a chance of a remodelled but adequate survival.

So immersed had Sir Vincent been in the pathetic and perplexing work before him, that it was not until the long process of his art was completed that he observed, with considerable surprise, the presence among the wreckage of what were apparently, in his technical language, spare-parts. This astonished him; for not even the most thoughtful — or morbid — of airmen would prepare for eventualities in this way. Superstition, alone, would forbid it; nor, in any case, is flying sufficiently dangerous to warrant such an outlay. And, strangest thing of all, the texture of the skin, the tint of hair, the structure of bones, the composition of the flesh — all at once confirmed the first supposition of the trained eye that they, too, must belong to that body that was still lying, unconscious but reconstructed, upon the operating table. The great surgeon was puzzled . . . distinctly puzzled. In the whole course of a long professional career he had never . . . no never . . . met with a case like it! Was he, then, to conclude, in the face of those very laws of nature by which he was permitted to practise his art, that Lord Richard, like some Hindu divinity, had been the possessor of six arms, had, like Diana of the Ephesians, boasted more than the normal pectoral development . . . or, like Janus, with his two faces, like Cerberus, with his three heads, had rejoiced in the distinction bestowed upon him by an unusual plurality? Puzzled was Sir Vincent, distinctly puzzled. . . .

The timely arrival of Lady Septuagesima helped to clear up what was apparently inexplicable. Lowing and neighing at him, charmingly, she explained. It was so stupid of her, so careless, she whinnied — but in the sudden shock of evil tidings, in her sorrow for her cousin, her bewilderment as to how to break the bad news to Goo-Goo, she had completely overlooked the existence, and ignored the fate, of the unfortunate Messrs. Leviathan and Parkinson. The very fact of there being two such persons had left her. In the same manner in which she was accustomed to shed those fantastic articles we have described about the countryside, so, in that moment,

had the lives of that ill-fated pair fallen from her, unnoticed —
'lost between here and Dodderingham Old Hall'. . . . Oh,
how tiresome and unfortunate! And really too bad of Tootsie,
who had never reminded her! He was getting so very careless
and remiss. He knew quite well how forgetful she was! And
now it was too late, was it, Sir Vincent, for anything to be
done? She lowed entreatingly at him. Alas! it was now no
longer possible for him to treat the other two passengers. The
police had better warn the relatives by radio. Sir Vincent
came forward heavily, and informed the police that, in any
case, the fragments were so much injured as to defeat any
attempt at reconstruction.

Lady Septuagesima, in order to pacify the two families,
who might think she had been careless or inhospitable toward
her guests, undertook to use her influence with the old Duke
of Badgery St. Lawrence, and the Home Office, to secure for
the two victims a special Burial-Permit under Clause 2 of the
'Only Children to Widows Relief from Compulsory Anatomical
Service Act of 1936'. She obtained the further favour for them
of interment. They were laid to rest in one grave in the
cemetery of the Parish Church at Cambridge — in which
latter place, too, the funeral service was held — though usually
in such cases it had to be celebrated on the premises of the
local Y.M.D.A.C.S.A.

The return to consciousness of Lord Richard took a more
than average time. For ten days he lay in the darkened room
at Dodderingham, not speaking, hardly breathing. Goo-Goo
watched by his side. His pale face, with its closed eyes, seemed
to her, in the twilight of that sick-room, to be remote and
strange. Some indefinable alteration had, surely, taken place
in him? . . . Did he look older or younger — ten years older,
or ten years younger? Yet though he remained lying there
senseless all these long days, Sir Vincent appeared pleased with
the patient's progress. There were no signs of a relapse; the
grafting had been completely successful, a triumph such as
could only have been achieved by the skilful use of the patient's
own limbs and material, the surgeon said. The scars were
healing, were disappearing. But Goo-Goo was puzzled by the
presence of two birth-marks, one on the neck, and one on the
right wrist, which, though they were familiar to her, had been

absent, she was certain, in her husband formerly. At any rate, compared with his recovery, the presence of these two blemishes was unimportant.

In the house reigned a great stillness : no rolling-round of tongues sounded from the lawn, and a ban had been placed on the electric organ. Day after day Goo-Goo sat there, dressed as a nurse; for even in her blackest hour she could never resist the lure of an appropriate costume. However admirably a widow's weeds would have suited her — and it must be confessed that in idle and impersonal hours the image of herself floating ethereally in a cloud of black chiffon with those large eyes and a small black cap, had visited her — yet she was willing to forgo them for her husband's sake. But who knows (her mind took wings, without her wishing it) that she might not marry again ? White chiffon suited her better than black; and another image would float through her imagination; large black eyes looking through a white veil, a cloud of white — rather as a mosquito tries to get through a mosquito-net. But the latter comparison did not suggest itself, and in any case she was willing to forgo all these things for her husband's sake. Yet as she sat there, waiting, waiting, everything seemed unreal, and she could not help wondering . . . was that really Richard, lying there, white and drawn, upon the bed ?

Then one day, about four o'clock in the afternoon, he began to speak a little; he looked round, recognising pieces of furniture and pictures — but ones that were not in the room ! Indeed, as far as Goo-Goo could remember, the things her husband saw and described had never been in any room he had occupied; in his talk, rather broken and rambling talk, he recalled incidents from the past — but was it the past of Lord Richard Cressey ? As he grew stronger, he would tell the nurses of things that had happened to him at school . . . but when they told Goo-Goo of them, she was surprised to hear the name of the school, which was not the one at which he had been educated ! Then, one day, the truth (or at any rate a very agitating inkling of it) began to dawn on her mind : for he asked her to fetch his mother and sister (the Duchess had been for many years in her coffin, and Lady Ethel was in South Africa), and added, as if each man was born into the world with several mothers and a variety of species of sisters, 'You know, either Mrs. Leviathan or Miss Isabel Parkinson'. Then, again, his mood would alter, and he would talk to Goo-Goo about herself, himself and their home, very rationally, very sensibly. When she mentioned these inconsistencies to Sir Vincent, the great doctor pronounced that they were nothing, and would pass away with the patient's gaining strength. — 'Growing pains, dear lady, growing pains! That's all. Don't worry yourself. Leave it all in my hands!'

But the periods of insensibility continued, and when he roused himself from them, it took a little time, apparently, for him to focus his mind. He looked up at his wife one morning and said, 'Goo-Goo, when is your husband coming to see us? . . . It's very kind of you looking after us, but I can't say that I think *he* behaved very well!' and then once more lapsed into oblivion, as his voice trailed off. What could it mean? In any case there could be little doubt that, as Barnacle put it, 'His Lordship didn't seem quite-himself-like'.

Convalescence was, to those by his side, an eternity. The fortnight was magnified into a hundred years. As the invalid's strength increased, his mind grew more logical; but, at the same time, his aberrations, though they occurred less often, were more concrete and tended to last over a longer period. For days he would be perfectly sure of himself, would talk to Goo-Goo about Little Titterham and how he longed to get back there. He seemed, even, to want to get back to his work at the Foreign Office. Then his wife would leave him, hoping he would sleep a little; but, when she returned, would find him quite different, wild-eyed, as if possessed, his bed littered with papers. His counterpane was so completely covered with these white drifts, that at the slightest movement there was a rattling and crinkling and falling as of autumn leaves. He had, evidently, got up (which he was forbidden to do), and had found these sheets, and a pencil as well! These various papers, none of them completed, were all addressed to the editor of *The Morning Echo*, and contained such matter as this that follows:

Lord Richard — Cuckoo writes to-day from Dodderingham Old Hall — is making a splendid recovery after his recent serious accident. Lady Richard — or Goo-Goo as she is to her friends — has borne the tragic events of the past three weeks with stoical fortitude, and looks sweetly pretty and piquante in the nurse's uniform which she has adopted for the occasion. With it she wears no jewellery except a large ruby and diamond swastika, once the property of the ill-fated Czarina of Russia, which was given her by her mother, Mrs. Guggerty — which reminds me, darlingest, how beautiful we all looked in nurses' uniforms in the last Great War! I sometimes wonder . . .

But the documents differed. One, at least, had an almost sinister tone:

From Dodderingham Old Hall, where she is the guest of Lady Septuagesima Goodley, or 'Mad Septua' as she is known universally to her friends — Grannie writes to me by today's post. Apparently Lady Richard — or Goo-Goo as she was to those who were her friends before she took to the water-whistle — has been pretending to nurse her unfortunate husband. It is to be supposed that she likes dressing-up, or perhaps she thinks that a nurse's uniform suits her. One can never tell these things oneself, can one, dearest? Her husband, naturally, is not progressing very fast; and his action in absorbing the two friends who were with him at the time of that fatal flight has, of course, created considerable and rather hostile comment. Lady Richard's common old mother . . .

And here, again, the manuscript, which did not even appear to be in her husband's writing, broke off. But poor Goo-Goo, on reading this brutal reference to herself, and still more, to her mother, fainted away.

Another document was yet harder to explain; it ran:

The funeral took place last Friday fortnight, at the Old Parish Church, Cambridge, of the mortal remains — or rather of such as had not been appropriated by Lord Richard Cressey — of Mr. Valentine Leviathan and Mr. Frederick Parkinson. These two brilliant men — now, alas! no more — were deservedly popular wherever they went, but among . . .

The queer thing was that, though Richard must have written this, he had never been informed either of the fate of his two friends, or the date and place of their burial!

Then there were also lying about several importantly written disquisitions, of unmistakable style, on the subject of the Détente Cordiale between France and England, and several letters to dim dwellers in the country, people of whom Goo-Goo had never heard. The letters appeared to be in two different hands, while the persons to whom these strange com-

munications were directed were addressed in them as relatives :
'Dear Cousin Toto', 'Dear Uncle Harry' or 'Dearest Aunt
Violet'. The signature on most of them was 'Your affectionate
nephew' (or cousin) 'Freddie', though some were signed
'Valentine'.

As his vitality grew day by day, the patient's voice became
more resonant. And in the middle hours of the night, when
so fragile is the dark crystal bowl of silence that any vibration,
scratching it ever so faintly, smashes it utterly, making an
overwhelming din and clatter, the nurses would sometimes be
woken by a roaring of empty, vacuous laughter. They would
find Lord Richard sitting up in bed, telling himself fashionable
little jokes or stories, or performing one of those hieratic
mimickings which we have mentioned. There were questions
and answering voices; it was as if a conversation were being
carried on between two or three people. But the next morning
he would remember nothing about it, and the doctor thought
it better not to disturb the patient's equilibrium by asking him
about it, or recalling it to his mind in any way.

Ignorant of his night's doings, he would be charming to
Goo-Goo when she went in to see him, talking to her affectionately, discussing with her the many subjects that had interested
them before his accident. Yet within a few seconds of her
leaving him he would begin to act strangely again. He would
examine his own looks and character with the nurses, acknowledging things about himself quite needlessly, things which it
had not previously been his habit to confess — in fact, he
would say such things about himself as were, in his world,
usually a privilege confined to intimate friends. He would
criticise and laugh at his personal appearance, he would deride
his manner very frankly, and neutrally. And, more embarrassing still, he would make remarks about his wife that were as
unnecessary as they were untrue.

Poor Goo-Goo, her mind almost unhinged by suffering, had
retired to seek a temporary consolation by indulging her
artistic and musical gifts (the latter ever so quietly), while
upstairs, unbeknown to her, Lord Richard was denying her
water-colours and anathematising the water-whistle.

On another night the nurses, hearing a sound coming from
His Lordship's room, peeped through the door, having opened
it soundlessly, and caught him examining the bedroom china,

fingering the glaze, and murmuring soft 'Sung's, 'Ming's, 'Han's or 'Pu's to himself — almost, had they known it, in the manner of the late Mr. Frederick Parkinson.

The serious thing about these outbreaks was the fact that they were gradually beginning to impinge upon Lord Richard's consciousness. From being unconscious impulses, they were becoming conscious; and the effort to repress them was a constant strain upon the patient. He underwent, now, trials such as he had never known; he experienced the uncanny sensation that while being one ego, he was yet three people, the three separate branches of the same tree; worse than this, he was often affected with harassing doubts as to his own physical identity, or with even more puzzling convictions of it. In fact our three poor heroes, now surviving in one body, were soon unable to make up their minds which they were — or rather which he was. Richard, though he never openly confessed these uncertainties, became painfully, tragically depressed, or unnaturally hilarious. One day Goo-Goo caught him before a mirror, gazing into its watery depths. 'Funny thing,' he said, pointing to the birth-mark that she had noticed when he had been lying unconscious, 'curious, but I've got a birth-mark here ! I'm sure it wasn't there before the accident, but I remember that Valentine had one like it !'

This was the nearest approach to the subject that he ever made. Nor did his realisation of these outbreaks, and of the need to repress them, prevent their recurrence, though he tried to control himself.

A very unfortunate incident took place on the occasion of Lady Septuagesima's first visit to him since his accident. She had been goodness itself; the whole house had been turned upside down on his behalf, and he was always telling Goo-Goo how grateful he was to his hostess, how he felt that such kindness could never be repaid. She swept into the room, neighing sweetly, a very tall and gracious presence, her red-gold mane floating, her large yellow skirt, like a crinoline, swaying a little, as she walked. Lord Richard at first thanked his cousin in the most heartfelt manner for saving his life, and talked to her rationally and intimately — for he was one of the few relatives with whom she had never quarrelled, had always been on terms of affection. Then, suddenly, she noticed an alteration in the expression of his eye, which seemed to become vaguer, bluer, yet more faded : the voice lost its warm tone and became, though the same voice, that of a stranger ; he burst into rude, shuddering hoots of laughter, and said, talking obviously to himself, yet as if to a second person : 'Richard always liked her, I know. He used to say to me, "Poor old Septua's not a bad old thing really ; she'd amuse you and she's very picturesque to look at !" But she looks to me just like a mad chestnut mare that's got entangled in one of Queen Elizabeth's old dresses !'

In a moment he was again transformed into himself, and Lady Septuagesima — though Tootsie remarked that she seemed rather 'upset' for the remainder of the day — maintained a discreet silence.

Soon Richard asked if he might be allowed to see other visitors. The doctor thought it would be a valuable discipline for him — as well as for his friends ! Goo-Goo decided that Mattie was the best subject for a first experiment — bright but sympathetic, dependable and even-tempered. It was, therefore, arranged that he should come down. But he was only granted a half-hour's interview with the invalid, since it was still most important that the latter should not be fatigued. Richard remembered quite well dining with Mattie the night before his accident. He was full of questions about — and seemed to look forward to — the Pecksniff Prize, which would be the occasion of his first public appearance. They discussed books for a while : Mattie brought him down several new ones — a novel by Edward Shanks — the first that writer had published for six months — and a reprint of the earlier poems by the Earl of Chiswick. Richard was delighted with them. Then they reverted again to the dinner-party at Mattie's, and, this time with no change of expression, the invalid observed : 'I thought Richard so very pompous that evening. Of course I'm devoted to them both — though I know they're pretentious — but I think Goo-Goo's the better of the two as long as she doesn't let herself go on that sanguinary water-whistle. But what a pity it is that they neither of them know anything !' Poor Mattie wriggled, winced, wavered and twittered, and by the time he had managed to produce his voice, Richard had gone back to the more usual incarnation of himself, appearing, luckily for Mattie's peace of mind, to be quite unaware of his words a few seconds before. As Mattie left the room Richard was leaning back ; his vague eyes were looking upward and away from his moustache, which was drooping down and under. It was curious how alike those three had been, but till now Mattie had never noticed it!

Goo-Goo talked to her guest, and to a certain extent confided in him. As far as she knew, Richard had not displayed any symptoms of aberration for a fortnight; while Mattie, for his part, was still far too taken aback to recount his recent experience. He urged her, nevertheless, to let Richard fulfil his engagement at the Skimpole Hall in a month's time. It would dispose of rumours. He need not be on the platform long enough to tire himself. The others could make the speeches, while he could just give the prize away. And what a wonderful reception he'd get! Incidentally, from the prize-winner's point of view, it would be an excellent thing; Richard's first appearance since his accident would lend an added interest to the proceedings and ensure a full hall, since, besides all his friends who would wish to be there to welcome him, many people who would not otherwise go to such a function would come to this one out of curiosity — for a man who has met with an accident will always receive both more attention and more sympathy than a poet! One has only to notice the relative density of the crowd that collects round an overturned hand-barrow, and the one that surrounds a poet declaiming his verse in public, to observe that! Besides, Richard was much looking forward to giving away the prize, while both Sir Vincent McNabb and his own doctor admitted that there could be no harm in it.

As Mattie went back to Cambridge he reflected how strange it was that he had never remarked the likeness before . . . Valentine . . . Richard . . . Freddie . . . He supposed that there had always, yes, he was sure that there had always, been a look . . .

PART III

The hall seemed to be filling quite satisfactorily. Not that there was as yet anyone in it, but peeping out from a little punch-and-judy window at the far side of the darkened stage, Mattie could distinguish, beyond the open doors, the shifting white lights (for outside it was a fine summer day) that fell between the flower-like shadows of the assembling audience.

These shadows on the floor were agitated as if by some wind, while an insect-like chirping, chattering and chirruping was borne into the sombre hall, as though this were a Southern night, where the cicadas were so insistent in their crinkling, castanetted music that the lolling stalk of every sun-weary flower, the cool glazed leaves of every cone-shaped magnolia-tree, rattled and sang together. Out of this general seething and murmur it would be difficult to disentangle a particular tune ; yet occasionally an individual insect voice shrilled loud enough to be heard above its comrades. Thus, too, out of the voices beyond the door, from this distance alike as grains of sand rolled round by an eddy of wind, a particular tone, however infrequently, was sometimes recognisable. For instance Mattie was able to identify that plaintive yet playful neighing as Septua's property.

A few single figures were now making their appearance in the hall — men, nearly all of them, and each obviously a lonely, mocking genius, betraying the stigmata of the consciously inspired and persecuted — overcoats on this hot day, mop, bobbed or pudding-basin hair, pince-nez that made the eyes prominent as those of prawns, or owl-like tortoise-shell circles, open collars and vague distinguished looks, a few beards and solitary misunderstood voices. In fact they were all remarkably alike — more especially in the persistence with which each protested his dissimilarity from his neighbour. After glowering furiously, but wonderingly, at each other, they sat down in a very determined manner, as if once more publishing their resolution to Make No Compromise with the Public Taste. Then opening their eyes rounder and wider, they gazed through, right through, poor Mattie, as if, by reason of some inner revelation, they were able to use him as a telescopic lens through which to examine some bewilderingly interesting object beyond.

Poor Mattie was already beginning to feel very ill at ease, when the timely arrival of his Chairman, Professor James Criscross, completed his discomfiture. The Professor's face was feline — more feline than Mattie's — but his heavy, greying, downtrodden-looking moustache showed, as well, a certain canine sympathy. A very old dog, he seemed, with a cat's soul, and a cat's stealthy gait and claws. His smile of exquisite malevolence, as he came forward, was an index of his intention, which was, now as always, to throw down, by a form of mental and verbal ju-jitsu of which he alone held the secret, anybody with whom he shook hands. In this drawing-room-sport he displayed an ingenuity and agility completely out of keeping with his years. Mattie went down at his first clutch.

As the beloved author of *From a Library Stool* and a million critical articles advanced across the stage, he looked round constantly, as if both expecting a welcome and fearing an ambush. Next, he allowed the smile to fade out of his face, as though the hall were a large railway station at which he had just arrived, where he was to have been met by some dear friends, but, on looking round, had this moment discovered the long draughty platform to be bare and desolate, with only a plaintive clanging of milk-tins for his comfort. Finally, he arrived in front of Mattie, looked at him fixedly for some seconds, without the faintest glint of recognition in his cat-green eye, then gave an almost too realistic jump, and treated him to an affectionate pat on the shoulder.

These paraphernalia were but the stage-properties which the Professor had, through a long course of years, constructed for himself, without which he never ventured out of his own house — stage-properties at once the disguise and weapon, the cloak and sword, of a curious and intricate terrorism. The method of it was very personal. Certainly he was old, aged indeed, but not so old as he pretended. His vagueness, and the senility which excused it, were in reality part of that armour he had evolved for himself, while from under its protective shelter he aimed his cruellest and most deadly shafts. Thus he made it his rule at first not to recognise his friends, and then, when recognised, to call them by some unfamiliar and unwelcome variant or, if possible, variants of their name. This subdued their spirits at the start; and he would follow up his preliminary advantage by inquiring, in a voice that was painfully sympathetic, after some ailment which was altogether confined to his imagination, some illness from which they had never suffered or even claimed to suffer, talking about it as if it were a permanent disability with which they were well known to be afflicted. This should, if the victim were an instrument sufficiently sensitive, worthy of the Professor's virtuosity, crush resistance and make the rest easy. For example, Mattie was called Mattie. Anyone who knew him

well enough to call him by name at all, called him Mattie —
and nothing else. Further, he was very timid; while the
only peculiarity about him, of which naturally any mention
would make him additionally nervous, was that high, jumpy
little voice. Professor Criscross began, therefore, by saying to
him :

'I'm so sorry, Mark, that I did not at first recognize you;
but being so short-sighted and old (too old, too old, my dear
Matt*hew*) I mistook you, until I saw your face more clearly,
for one of your own geniuses — not one of whom, I may say,
is familiar to *me*!' And then, beaming over his gold spectacles,
added, before Mattie had time to answer: 'And, poor Mat,
how is that tiresome sore throat of yours that gives you so much
trouble?'

It was hopeless for Mattie to attempt battle. The only
gap in the Professor's armour was an intense snobbery; but,
at the moment, there was no title available with which to hit
him over the head and temporarily stun him.

The gloomy geniuses, in their seats apart from one another,
had watched the encounter with intense relish, and it was all
very annoying. The Professor was just about to start a new
skirmish, when the other chief speaker of the afternoon, Mr.
Ernest Lympe, the well-known critic and man-of-letters,
arrived on the stage. The long thin body, shaped like a capital
S reflected in a mirror, was surmounted by a small head and a
face that was brave, and consciously noble in the extreme. A
grey kiss-curl floated down over the upright forehead; and he
had a smile, grave yet excruciatingly sweet, that at the same
time understood and pardoned everything. In fact he looked
like a missionary who had taken the wrong turning and become
a writer — which is exactly what had happened. His father
was a little-known but decorative clergyman of the Church of
England, and enemies cite the son's continually appearing
volumes of bright leading-articles — which on their appearance
in book-form are immediately converted by the other critic
of the very paper in which they had been served up daily into
'Mr. Lympe's brilliant book of essays' (a miracle as great as
that other transmutation of water into wine) — as the final,
undeniable argument in favour of priestly celibacy. Poor Mr.
Lympe was terrified of only one man in the world — and that
man was Professor Criscross! He dared not try to oust him

for, in this era of grafting, the Professor would have a century in which to revenge himself — which, noticing what he could do in this way during a few seconds, was a formidable thought. Besides, Mr. Lympe's façade of knowledge was an eighteenth-century library door on which are presented in counterfeit the bindings of many rare books. And the Professor, who had at any rate read very many more books than he could understand, had detected, but not yet published, this fraud. Hence poor Mr. Lympe's abject terror.

Leaving the latter gentleman with no straw to catch at, Mattie walked away to meet Lord Richard Cressey, who looked quite well now, in spite of that air of distinction so often bestowed by the winnowing fire of a long illness. On seeing him, the Professor stopped his little games, and became, this time genuinely, solicitous about his health. Mattie thought — and the other two agreed with him — that it would be better for Lord Richard to wait in the small room at the back of the stage until it was time for him to make the presentation. It wouldn't fatigue him to the same extent; while, too, it would be a very dramatic appearance, just giving that necessary touch to the whole proceedings. As they came on to the stage, Lady Richard's voice could be heard outside the door, coming nearer; and then the insect-like chirruping and drone invaded the room all at once, pouring in at the door, giving the room a life of its own, till the lifeless void that it had been began to throb and stir. The light, giving a radiance to the hall without being visible, was turned on, and the drone increased its volume, as if the sun had risen and drawn out the winged creatures from their hiding-places. After infinite hoverings, whisperings, and rustlings, the audience settled; only a few remained standing. Heads would nod together and sigh in rippling waves, as if the wind were breathing down a cornfield, tossing the golden heads together. There would be a silence, and then a sudden movement in one patch of the audience, as though some animal, that had been sleeping among the golden stalks, had stirred and woken. There was, for such a gathering, an unusual air of excitement. These things are hard to explain, and the reason may have been merely that the fine day of early summer outside was sufficient to stir the blood, however wooden, of any audience. Mattie could recognise a great many of his friends, but from where he was seated it was

difficult to see 'who everybody was'.   Whether it was the light,
or this year's fashions, he couldn't make out; but somehow or
other from this distance everybody looked the same, shadowy
and indistinct.   It was very good of so many of his friends to
support him, for Mattie could not help regarding it — except
when he caught the gold-rimmed eye of Professor Criscross —
as rather 'his show'.   Over in one corner he observed the
familiar grimace, bull-dog and triumphant, of one of his
favourite bellicose filibusterers and 'Shall We, I say, yield to
the Menace of Armed Might?' rang in his head like the
latest successful musical-comedy number.   Beyond, in an
almost royal seclusion, sat those two rival Trustees of the
Nation — Lord FitzBison and the Duke of Badgery St.
Lawrence.   Wonderful old man, that!   So small, and yet so
dignified with his aquiline, rather curling profile, and little
bunches of yellowy-white ringlets beneath each ear.   Poor
Goo-Goo, he thought, looked rather worried.   She must have
spent a very trying two months: still, *he* looked much better
today.   With her was Baroness d'Arenheimer, with Angel and
Desirée, looking very Spanish, he thought — gipsy-like, almost!
Sir Booster's voice was also to be heard in the land: how odd
it was, that habit of his of speaking so loudly; but then, like
many other remarkable men, he was completely unself-con-
scious!   As he spoke you could almost hear the rolling 'r's'
gathering moss as they rolled; the guttural, agglutinous sound
of his voice, like the speech of the ghost for ever imprisoned
within an American soda-fountain, could be heard all over
the hall; and his genial smile was spotted on everyone in
turn, like a limelight, with an orange-slide over it, at a theatre.
Able and philanthropic, as he was, Nature, Mattie reflected,
had yet hardly treated him as he deserved; and surely it was a
mistake on the part of the Press Barons always to put up
Sir Booster to lead the attack on Socialism, the defence of
Capitalism, when, to anyone ignorant of the sterling qualities
of this Persian Philanthropist, his personal appearance must
seem ultimately the complete refutation of the very arguments
he was advancing.   Lady Babboon was with him, looking very
young, rather wan and blanched — a little bleached, even,
Mattie thought.   The strabismal glance of her eyes, when she
smiled, was so attractive — a slight cast often helps a face.
Behind her he noticed Eddy Tush with Selly Moonbury, and

Ned, looking rather like a seal out of water, with a large party of overfed, under-bred friends, youthful revue-writers and elderly stage beauties; the latter looking, under this artificial light, very young and exactly like both each other and everyone else. Many of the shadows were so animated that Mattie could not see who they were. And all those mirrors at the back of the hall helped to muddle one, making a stage-army, reflecting the same people, giving the reflections a certain life. Rustlings and whisperings still ran through the audience as the shadows of leaves move on the ground when a slight wind plays above. Meanwhile Mattie, up on the platform, was communicating with his friends in his own way, shaping sentences at them with his mouth, letting his eye-glass fall or loop-the-loop on its black string, or making daft little beckonings and esoteric signals. Twined in among his gaily coloured friends, like a dead branch in a rosebush, he noticed two strings of black. One in the fourth row, one at the back of the hall. Gazing intently through his monocle, he recognised the nearest string. It was the Leviathan family! He jumped down at once to speak to Mrs. Pulborough, Valentine's aunt. Yes, she said, they had come to welcome poor Lord Richard, who had been in that terrible accident with her nephew. Oh, yes, a dreadful affair! Besides, though she had little time for it, she had always been very much interested in poetry — it was that lovely line . . . for the instant she couldn't remember who'd written it, 'A thing of thingamajig is a what-d'you-call-it for ever' — lovely. Oh, yes, Keats, wasn't it? And then, what she really liked was originality; and she was told that Mr. Rosenheimer was so original, wasn't he? Perhaps dear Mr. Dean would bring him up to her afterwards, and introduce him . . . but Mattie had at this moment to get back on to the platform, as the Professor was beginning to get restive. Gripping his monocle with Chinese eyebrow, Mattie peered over the heads of his friends at the other black line. That tall ebony regiment of women seemed familiar . . . of whom did they remind him? Richard? . . . there was a look, too, of Valentine. . . . No, no, of course, it was Freddie Parkinson! They must be poor Freddie's relatives, but how many there were of them, and how few of them had he ever mentioned! Obviously, then, they had come up to London for the same reason as Mrs. Pulborough and the others. It was really very nice of them.

The ceremony began. It was Mattie's duty to make a small preliminary speech of introduction. Coming forward, Mattie spurted his jets of sound up into the air in such a manner that only a few truncated sentences were audible. '. . . and gentlemen . . . not going to speak . . . only to tell you . . . that Professor Criscross (hear, hear) . . . in the chair, I need say no more to introduce . . . so deservedly beloved . . . in literary circles . . . Lympe . . . later.' . . . Then, following a few remarks, quite impossible to hear, about literature in general, Mr. Dean sat down.

The Professor, with a really intimidating glance of dislike and disgust toward the audience — a glance much enhanced by an evidently false look of nervousness — then formally took the chair. The audience, quite unafraid, fluttered and preened itself to silence, like a bird alighting on a branch. This stillness, gradually making itself felt, welling up from them, was only broken by the voice of a gloomy genius at the front of the gallery, who was blowing his sentiments up into the air, like a whale spouting water. After rising some distance in the air, they fell back on the audience and the platform. 'Simply doesn't count, you know', he was saying in a painfully level voice. 'Afraid Leonardo doesn't interest me at all : just l'Art Pompier : has nothing to tell me . . .' The Professor looked up over his gold rims, as if ready to spring at this intrepid sparrow — and the consequential voice died suddenly in a violent spasm.

This afternoon the cat had the upper hand of the dog. The Professor looked the sublimation of smiling felinity — as much at home in the Chair as the Cheshire Cat in his tree, purring already, as if stroked by the public applause. Mattie had twisted into the seat on his left, and was trying to look as if he wasn't on a platform at all. Mr. Lympe had, like a serpent, coiled himself into the seat on the right. The prize-winner, looking prosperous and curly, sat at the corner of the gangway below, ready to scramble up the side and receive his cheque. If he climbed up, instead of walking round, it would look more boyish and unconventional. Besides, they must all know that he was an athlete. Still, Jacques Rosenheimer could not help feeling that he was not quite the hero he had expected to be on this occasion. The Professor looked down at him for a moment, as if intimating that he would settle him after he had finished with the rest of them. As the speeches proceeded poor Jacques felt, indeed, less and less as if he were there at all. For whereas the prize-giver, the judges, the speakers, the person who presented the prize, were all made much of, the name of the prize-winner scarcely occurred. Mattie had lisped the learning of Professor Criscross, and piped the virtues of Mr. Lympe. The Professor, after his own fashion, paid a few cat-and-mouse compliments to Mattie, dealt a few more to Mr. Lympe, spoke of the prize, the history of it, dwelt a little on his own life, and wound up with a warm tribute to Lord Richard Cressey. The amiable and brave Mr. Lympe, next, sang loudly the attainments, virtues and popularity of Professor Criscross, presented a verbal bouquet to poor Mattie, a verbal palm-leaf to Lord Richard. He then very nobly denied his own merits. But not one of the speakers appeared to be aware of the existence, even, of the prize-winner, Mr. Jacques Rosenheimer.

'Ladies and Gentlemen,' the Chairman began with a literary clearing of the throat, 'I had come here with a few suitable platitudes prepared; but, sure enough, Mr. Dean has already delivered most of them to you, and the rest of them I shall leave for Mr. Lympe. I must, therefore, confine myself to a few historical remarks. It is but thirty years since the first award of the Pecksniff Prize took place at this hall. And I think that, if we examine the Roll of Winners, we shall feel that it is one that reflects credit on the judges, and on the late Sir Champion Pecksniff, who instituted this annual award. We do not, perhaps, find on it any names famous in poetry; yet we do undoubtedly find the names of many distinguished critics and men of letters. Mr. Lympe (with a bow) was one of the earliest prize-winners, with that charming if slender little volume of poetry which first established him in the hearts of all book-lovers, and endeared him to all those whose soul is with the birds, out in the fields — I refer to *Crowsfeet*.' (Applause.) The Professor's expression had relaxed, for his intention was to charm and captivate. But now his face assumed a more stern expression as he said: 'The Pecksniff has never, I think, stood for mere eccentricity or contortion. It has never — and I think you will agree with me, Ladies and Gentlemen, that it has *rightly* never — been associated with the names of those young men and, I regret to say, young

278

women as well, who believe that to stand on their heads is the only duty of the modern poet. On the contrary, from its inception it has been connected with those poets of good heart and upright living, who sing, dulcetly as ever, of English countryside and of those wild creatures that move through it — those poets, modern in the best sense, who are inspired by the sweet English sentiment so well summed up by a predecessor in that exquisite line, 'Llewdly sing Cuccu'. (Rustlings, cheers and cries of 'Oh, how sweet!' 'Oh, how pretty!' and 'Isn't it like him?' from those admirers in the audience who are under the impression that the Professor himself has written the line.)

'It is, perhaps, not yet the moment for me to disclose the name of the winner of the prize, for we are concerned' (with a look of mingled hatred and contempt at poor Jacques Rosenheimer) 'not with the man, but with those principles which, *however unworthily*, he represents. Nor need we discuss my two fellow-judges — or should I say *conspirators?*' (mischievous glance through gold rims, and delighted cooings from audience) '— Mr. Dean and Mr. Lympe! — they are too well known to you for any word of mine to help them — but we shall, I am sure, all of us, be particularly delighted to welcome in a few minutes' time on this platform, the Prize-Giver — Lord Richard Cressey!' (Here the Professor's too genuine, sincere and perhaps not un-English affections — one for a title, the other for an amateur — the force of which is quadrupled by the combination of the two — nearly overcame him. He sips the names, turning them on his tongue as if he were going to pronounce upon the merits of some rare vintage wine — 'generous, fruity, full-bodied'. Tears appear about to spout from his eyes, as from the eyes of those lachrymose loyalists who, when a military band passes, rush from bar-parlour into the street. 'Not only shall we greet him warmly this afternoon because it is his first public appearance since the terrible and painful ordeal through which he has passed; we shall welcome him, also, as one who has already made for himself a name in those worlds of diplomacy and literature to which it has pleased God to call him.' (The Professor's voice took on the lyric note.) 'We owe to Lord Richard — I say it with no fear of contradiction — the solution of that recent crisis between the Yugo-Slovaks and the Jingo-Slavs, which, because Englishmen still believe that right is stronger than might, he had himself done so much to create and foment. But the strong know when to give way; and by a graceful diplomatic gesture, which consisted in losing all the papers concerned with the matter, he was able to solve the very difficulties which he had himself designed. But we have in him also an author and poet of considerable distinction. Those of us, and I hope we are many, who had enjoyed reading *The Buzzard's Bastard*, have found in it an unaffected simplicity, moral purpose and genuine strength, for which we have to search in vain through the pages of even the strongest lady-novelist — while to many of us, and to me amongst others, *From a Yashmak Garden* brought a new revelation of beauty.' . . . After this the speech trailed off into a series of compliments, interspersed with a great many pin-pricks, for Mattie and Mr. Lympe. As each bouquet was handed to them, a pin, hidden among the stalks of the flowers, drew blood.

The Chairman sat down, amid considerable applause, and soprano but muffled cries of '*Isn't* Mr. Criscross wonderful?' then stood up again, and, as if looking for something he had lost, called on Mr. Ernest Lympe to address the gathering.

The latter gentleman uncoiled himself from his chair, and, tossing the careless kiss-curl back from his forehead, proceeded to say a few words about Professor Criscross, who watched him as if willing to play cat-and-mouse again for a minute or two. But, at the lightest sound of insubordination! . . . Mr. Lympe, however, was far too frightened to make any attempt at retaliation.

'It is a great pleasure to mey', he said, 'to be on the same platform this afternoon with one who may well be termed the Grand Old Man of Literature. Eminent as is our friend in the Chair, busy as he is, he yet still finds time to come down here among us and encourage the young. Ai will not speak to you about the praize-winner; but Ai should like to be allowed to speak a few words about Professor Criscross. A famous poet, distinguished as a Munofletters even above his contemporaries, one whose learning and whose delicate malice has long endeared him to us' (Professor looks pleased, loud applause and stifled cries of 'Isn't he delicious?') 'in the pages . . .' And the speech rambled on for another five minutes.

The Chairman stood up again and gazed, almost benignantly

for him, at the audience, now thoroughly settled in their stalls, and with a tone of rapture in his voice, called on *Lord* . . . Richard Cressey . . . to come forward and present the prize.

Little eddies of curiosity and interest passed through the audience, rustlings of heads like branches swept by the wind, as the tall, spare form of Lord Richard stepped forward across the stage. Applause started with an unexpectedly loud smacking rattle of hands clapped together — surprisingly loud ; yet, while continually increasing in volume, the character of the welcome appeared gradually to change. It seemed as if little sighs, sobs, cries and exclamations were mixed up with, and covered by, the volume of sound. The Chairman looked startled and, standing up, gazed toward the back of the hall. Perhaps someone was unwell. The noise was swelling, rising crescendo like the solemn roar of an organ when first its spray breaks against the stone walls. The noise was swelling, increasing in volume ; a clamour, as when some sudden hit at a cricket match, sudden goal at a cup-tie, or sudden dagger at a bull-fight, rips open the chests of those watching and lays bare their pulsing hearts. The Chairman looked taken aback, this time really old and vague. The applause, ever louder, had yet altered its kind. The change was gradual in a sense, yet very swift. The cries were rising, coming to the top. People stood up on their chairs to see they knew not what, and the very action of standing, peering, increased the expectation and excitement. The cries were rising in it, but feet as well as cries sounded in the tumult and there was movement. The clamorous confusion increased : like a cuttle-fish it seemed both to discharge a cloud of blackness under which it could hide, and then, octopus-like, to stretch long tentacles toward the stage. A tall black line, noticeable among the colourful, fluttering audience, surged from the back of the hall, and rushed up the gangway, waving hands and black parasols, shouting 'Freddie ! . . . Freddie ! . . . it is Freddie !' . . . Louder and indescribable grew the commotion, fiercer the excitement. The audience were all standing, moving, waving, watching. The Professor's dog-like reproofs could scarce be heard through the uproar, though occasionally an angry barking sound would be audible through the other noises from the platform. Goo-Goo's convulsive calf-sobbing sounded in the air like the gurgling of a fountain. But little attention was paid to these minor manifestations, for another, nearer, black line advanced, waving and shouting, 'Valentine! . . . Valentine! . . . It is Valentine!' . . . and closed round the platform which was attacked, stormed, lost in a dark, dancing, whirling cloud of revolving black arms and parasols. Out of it came the far-carrying suctional clucking of kisses, as a hundred unknown relatives embraced Lord Richard and claimed him as their own. Excitement had spread to the gallery, where could be heard, winging up above, the tired, fluttering, bumping cries — like a bird bumping against the ceiling — of poor Mattie lost and bewildered; cries like those of a bird that is trying to escape from a room into which it has flown blindly. Lord Richard's head could still be seen, as he stood encircled by his smaller relatives, the point of the swarming, the centre round which the whirlwind spun its course, distracted, almost hypnotised by the sudden roarings; distracted, pulled, tugged; his clothes hanging in shreds and blown up, as if by winds, with all this fury of sound and movement. A machine working on three gears, slipping back from one to another continually . . . Richard . . . Freddie . . . Valentine . . . Freddie . . . Richard . . . Valentine . . . Valentine . . . Freddie . . . Richard . . . Three tunes that were continually being broken and resumed . . . forty-seven . . . thirty-seven . . . twenty-seven . . . thirty-seven . . . forty-seven . . . twenty-seven . . . ten years older . . . ten years younger . . . Yes, he was Valentine . . . he was Freddie . . . he was Richard. Yes, yes, he was, he confessed. He was. Rival parties of relatives were appealing to the audience to bear witness to this birth-mark and to that, through the gaps torn in his clothing . . . Yes. He was. . . . The audience began to take sides; and, at the same time, the hysteria was mounting. The confession of his triple yet single identity completed the work. Everyone in the hall was laughing, crying and sobbing. No one remembered why he was there, why she was there, or what had happened — for the great truth had dawned on them! The hysteria passed in waves through the assembled shadows. A few minutes before they had been quiet and peaceful, cultivating this smile, that gesture, this voice, that look of the eyes, forming fresh reflections of the same thing, revealing endless vistas and avenues of repetition. But the truth had now dawned on them, and was animating them with a false vitality; like a current

of electricity it made these corpses twitch and caper, shudder
and jig. With this scene of riotous confusion can only be
compared one of those outbreaks of epidemic dancing-mania
that seized on Greece and southern Italy in the Middle Ages,
when those infected danced on, whirling and shrieking, in the
market-place, till they died. Everyone was shouting, waving,
gesticulating, dancing, even. Some saw the tall ghost of
Freddie, others the spectre of Valentine, standing, like the angels
of Mons, beside their spiritual brother on the stage. The mob
surged round the platform, hats lay like trampled flowers,
crushed under the triumphant progress of a Bacchanalian rout.
Veils were torn, clothes were ripped and dragged, faces were
like large poppies, red and angry, or excited and pleased. A
few held out, a few isolated towers, like the towers of the nobles
in the Middle Ages. Lady Septuagesima could be heard telling
the wife of a bishop that she was not her, and never had been.
What is more, she did not intend to be! For the confession of
identity was spreading, as the figure on the platform confessed
he was Freddie, he was Freddie . . . he was Richard . . . he
was Valentine. Yes, he was. He was Valentine. He was
Freddie. He was Richard. As if the atom had been exploded,
and all the atoms had broken with it, confessions were hurled
up into the air, shouted and boasted. The whole miniature
world of the hall confessed too. He confessed, and the world
with him. At last they realised that they belonged, one to
another. The tumult was now indescribable. Handkerchiefs
and hands were waving through the air of the hall with one
movement, as at an arena during a bull-fight. This one was
the same as that; I am as the same as you : only shadows are
real in this world of shadows.

      .   .   .

The starched exterior of Bond Street quieted them. What
had happened? It had been enjoyable, very enjoyable, but
what had taken place?

'All the same,' said the venerable Duke of Badgery St.
Lawrence, as he tried to bang out with his fist a dent acquired
somehow in his top-hat, 'all the same' — this to Lord FitzBison,
his powerful and formidable political rival — 'I don't believe
there's much difference between us !'

IDYLL THROUGH THE LOOKING-GLASS

'THE service in this hotel is shocking, very bad indeed', the Count pronounced. . . . At this point, as though the remark were in some way connected with what he was doing or, further, had served to evoke his action, he rose from his chair to regard his image in the mirror opposite, first examining minutely eyes and mouth and nose, the innumerable connecting lines incised by laughter or anxiety, and then, sprucing himself, fingered his tie and touched the grey hair on his temples.

Startled at such an irrational outburst — as it appeared — of personal vanity, I, too, considered the features and the rather small figure reflected in the tall glass. . . . At any rate, he should be easy to recognise, I decided; except, of course, that he must have presented a very different aspect as a young man.

But then, somehow or other I had never thought of Count Dragone di Dragora as a young man. . . . Ever since I could remember him — and that was now for some thirty and more years — he had looked the same, as though he had triumphantly defeated time by outliving it. . . . Not that he was old, any more than that — so it had seemed to us as children — he could ever have been young: he must have been born thus, found inside a cabbage, dressed in a frock-coat and high collar, and top-hat. And in my mind this diplomat, with, despite a rather tropical air, his Edwardian suavity and gloss, had been posed, always, against the contemporary London background of Grosvenor Square, hansom cabs — those equipages as frail and delicately balanced as the shell of Venus — and rooms full of palm trees and royal photographs in silver frames; so that it was with difficulty that I had accustomed myself to the idea that his proper setting had been one of prickly pears striking their attitudes from tufa rocks, or orange trees and lemon groves, and the smoke-tufted summit of a volcano. (Indeed, it must have been inside a cactus, rather than a cabbage, that he would have been found as a baby, according to the innocent deceptions of his period.)

All this had naturally lain beyond my vision, as a child of seven, but, nevertheless, in his English surroundings he had been able to exercise upon my mind a very special fascination, an exotic charm such as would have attached to a Zulu chieftain or Red Indian brave; and, since Italians are invariably fond of children, we soon became most intimate friends. . . . How clearly I can see him, as he was then, when he came to stay with my parents in the country; moving among the croquet hoops in the summer, in white flannels with a thin black stripe, and a panama hat; in the winter, for shooting parties, dressed in the most elaborate check creations — English 'sporting' clothes dramatised by a rich southern imagination, so that, on him, these garments were in no way ostentatious, matched his style, in the same manner that the mandolin-like twang of his accent in French and English — both of which languages he talked fluently and well — suited his speech. However, to one of my years he had seemed vastly, immensely old, and, because we were such good friends, I have little doubt that I must often have told him so.

Of course, as I now rather covertly considered his reflection, I could see that he did look, after all, a little older; the lines were still more numerous than I remembered, and the frizzled hair, grown grey, made his skin of an even darker tint than formerly. . . . His whole appearance proved his descent as plainly as did his choice of clothes and personal adjuncts: for he was head of a famous Neapolitan family and possessed his share of Spanish and Sicilian, and so of Arab or Saracen, blood. The whites of his eyes betrayed a curious dark, shadowy glitter, and his skin was very thick and yellow, like that of tough-hided, tropical fruit. Moreover, a southern love of jewellery showed itself in rings and tie-pins which would have pleased the Gabriele D'Annunzio of pre-1914 days. . . . Never before had I tried to picture him as a young man, and it had been a surprise to me to be told, a year or so previously, when the conversation had turned on the Dragon, as we affectionately called him, that, as a boy, he had been very good-looking, in the flowery, volcanic fashion of his neighbourhood. Nor had I realised, until I learnt it at the same time — for he always seemed, when I knew him, to have been destined for a bachelor existence, and the love-affairs in which he had been engaged (and to which, as I grew older, he made frequent allusion), had been those, plainly, of a very matter-of-fact, Edwardian order — that as a young man he had been of an intensely passionate and romantic nature, suffering deeply, continually threatening to emigrate, or to shoot or drown himself. It was as though, in his soul, the tender and amorous airs of the Italian seventeenth- and eighteenth-century composers had yielded to the rather sodden harmonies and tunes of Puccini, as though the scents of bath salts and pomade had replaced the odours of jasmine and orange blossoms in which he had spent his youth. Of his sufferings and passions, nothing was left but an immense tolerance for the weaknesses of others, and an intelligence which was intuitive rather than intellectual. But intelligent he certainly was, well read in several languages, and with a fine taste in many directions : but all this he subordinated to life ; his sole aim, perhaps, being to curb his sensitiveness, and so his powers of suffering, and only to make use of it sufficiently to enable him to obtain the most enjoyment out of existence.

Even after the Count had left the Embassy, he had always spent part of the year in London, as well as a month or two in Paris, Vienna and Rome. Friends welcomed him in every capital, for he was cosmopolitan in the mode of the day ; European, more than purely Italian. And the reason for this, it may be, was principally that as a young man he had developed (if we may suppose a thing, so common today, to have, equally, existed then) an 'inferiority complex' ; because, if in those times an Italian hailed from any part of the country south of Rome, he experienced certain disadvantages, even apart from the main one, that, in addition, he would certainly be poorer than someone from the north of similar origin and situation. Moreover Count Dragone could remember better times, could just recall the old kingdom of the Two Sicilies and its decaying court, the disintegrating splendours of Caserta and of the capital itself : for he had been six or seven years of age when the insurgent troops had invaded Naples, and had finally driven the King and Queen to Gaeta, where they had endured a long siege, and then to exile ; an exile which the Count's father, as Chamberlain of the Court, had shared until his death a year or so later.

A fate similar to that which overtook the rich families of the Southern States of America after the Civil War had now fallen to the lot of many of the noble houses of Naples, and specially of Sicily. Some became destitute and disappeared entirely, while the palaces, even of those who survived, lay empty. The long vistas of rooms, with their pillared, marble-panelled walls and mirrored ceilings, their periwigged busts of ancestors, the gardens, with their parterres and gesticulating statues, stood deserted through the long, burning summer days ; while the cactuses and circles of prickly pears grew more thickly and violently round them, as though to hide their present void of humanity with an African pullulation of green life. . . . But the Dragone family had been more fortunate than many of their friends and relatives, and the Count seemed rich in a modest fashion, though — or, perhaps, because — he had never yet inhabited, since he came of age, any of his ten palaces that, now largely unfurnished, were scattered over the country from Naples to Syracuse, far across the Straits.

As a boy, he had lived with his mother, the old Contessa, in the smallest of his houses, situated at Sorrento : a little rococo pavilion, very elegant and old-fashioned, full of mirrors and tortoise-shell cabinets, with twisted tortoise-shell pillars crowned by little golden capitals, and of gilded chairs and Neapolitan pictures of the same epoch, displaying chiaroscuro processions of camels and turbaned drivers winding under palm trees, and many Madonnas melting into clouds. But, since I had known him, he had never until now visited any of his ancestral estates, had never ventured farther south than Rome, as though, indeed, he had feared that, were he to do so, the past would steal back upon him to his disadvantage. . . . When the 1914 war had come, however, he had returned to Italy, to make it his home. We heard that he had been working in some capacity for the Italian Government, and had settled in the capital, but otherwise we had, during that period, lost touch with him completely ; as, indeed, with all our other Continental friends.

It was not, then, until a year or two after the war that I saw our dear 'Dragon' again, meeting him thus by chance one afternoon at Sorrento. . . . I supposed he was about sixty : the mirror did not really, to my mind, register much change in him, apart from the details I have noted. He had seemed pleased to see me, if only, it may be, because of many visits, many years spent in England in younger and happier days, and overwhelmed me with questions concerning his friends. In return, he told me that he had been living here, in this hotel, for a whole year ; during which time (for he was a sybarite by nature — as, indeed, he should be, since the site of Sybaris itself was in his possession and had for centuries belonged to his family) his own little palace was being prepared for him. Bathrooms and heating and electric light were being installed, carpets were being introduced upon the bare *terrazza* floors, and the furniture was being thinned out, and rearranged in a more modern mode. (I thought these last improvements sounded a mistake, but I was careful not to say so.) The workmen had taken six months longer than they had estimated already, and the alterations, apparently, were by no means as yet completed. . . . But he loved his house, he said, and would be quite happy there, would never want to go abroad again, even if he had been able to afford it . . . but think of the exchange !

'I never thought to return to Sorrento,' the Count explained (how often have I wished that I could reproduce his voice, how much I long now to be able to treat his Italian accent phonetically, but these are tasks too complicated and beyond my powers), 'but I am getting an old man — yes, I am, my dear boy, you know I am : I saw you examining me just now in the mirror. . . . Don't make excuses : it's quite natural when we haven't met for years — and in the end something drew me home. Do you know, it was over forty years since I had been here ? I was nineteen when I left, and very different from what I now am. . . . Sorrento, too, how different it was ! a joy to visit, for there was nothing like it in all Italy. You should have seen the lovely English carriages driving down the little Corso here, every bit as good as Naples itself, with smart English coachmen in capes and with cockades in their top-hats, and horses and equipages all shining and varnished. . . . And even this hotel, in which we are talking (though I seem to be doing most of it !), was, though smaller, infinitely more agreeable, always full — and full of people the like of whom you do not see here now ; people from England and France and Austria and Russia — and from America. . . . For those were the days when American girls were beginning to take Europe by storm, and they were lovely, *lovely*, with their beautiful neat hands and wrists and feet, and their odd little voices and use of words. . . . There was something very strange about them to us Europeans : they showed such an unusual combination of boldness and prudery, of sophistication and naïveté. And such beautiful clothes; for they bought them in Paris, when English and Russian and Italian girls had to be content to buy them from the nearest town in their own countries. . . . (Ah, you young men laugh at such antiquated fashions, but then, you can have no idea of the *allure* of the dress of those times, the bustle, the small waist, no bigger than my neck, the fringe, the bonnet, trimmed with flowers or cherries, all full of style : and the rustle of the skirts as they walked.) . . . And life here was such fun (I love that English word, for which there is no translation) : for many of us Neapolitans then still lived in our villas, and, you know, we are not the Tuscans or Venetians, who will seldom ask a friend, if he is a foreigner, inside their homes : but we, even when we are poor, give dinner-parties and dances and enjoy ourselves. So, though my mother, being a widow, entertained little, there was my cousin, Leo Casteleone, who received a lot, and Giuseppe di Bandanera and the Nestore di Noceras. Then there were the Ouraveffskys, who had a villa here and were very generous and hospitable, like all their countrymen, and the Mellins, an American family, who lived up there on the hill, and three English families, all cousins, the Cleghornes, who were the great wine people and owned the whole valley and mountain side towards Positano; there was always a great deal going on. All this, perhaps, may bore you, but just the same, I must tell you, even the climate seemed better. It was never like today, with a cold wind — hotter, though not too hot (but we none of us ever felt the need of central heating, as we do now) — and the flowers sweeter. In the evenings, from the terrace, which then only reached as far as that black rock down there — you could watch the little feather of a cloud, which always lay on the very summit of the volcano's cone, glow with an inner radiance shot with flame : (whereas now Vesuvius, like Europe itself, seems always either dead or in eruption). A thousand boats would gleam, in front here, on the softly rippling water, each with a bright lantern (such as our ancestors used to say the mermaids carried) to attract their prey, and every now and then the fishermen would beat the boards of the ship with their oars, for that sound, too, entices those poor silly fish. The lights would seem a thousand glowing stars reflected in the water, the sea broke in the lightest foam upon the pebbles, as though in accompaniment to the serenade of the nightingales (how they sang then, day and night!), and over every wall was carried the heavy scent of orange blossom when a sudden little warm breeze played among the glossy leaves. . . . Whereas now, when you stand out there in the evening, all you can smell is petrol!

'And the hotel, though there were only two bathrooms in it (quite enough, people considered: think of it!), was so well managed. Never, as now, did a guest have to ask for anything twice. . . . Of course, I lived in our little *palazzo* with my mother, but I often came here to lunch and dine, though my mother — she was very old-fashioned and thought I should only know the people she knew — kept a strict watch on me; as strict a watch as she was able. I suppose "our misfortunes", as she always called them, the loss of her King and Queen, and the whole system of life — to which she had belonged — that had revolved round them, had made her proud: she was not what you would call a "snob", but she did not like the rich and the modern. According to her code, and to that of her ancestors, I must marry a girl whose parents she had always known, and whose grandparents had, equally, known mine throughout their lifetimes: that was the least upon which she must insist. . . . And so, in the end, I never married at all.

'It was here that I fell in love (and though you never tell me your love-affairs, I tell you mine, for I am from the south), fell in love, you cannot imagine how deeply, how violently, with an American girl, Ethel Burkefield-Stoddard; to me, this was a beautiful name then, making my heart beat, my eyes flash. She was rich, an only child, and so beautiful: but we were never allowed to marry, for I was only nineteen, and my mother became very angry (she brought in those wretched priests to talk to me by the hour, and I, though my heart was breaking with love, had to listen to them with respect and attention). Nor did Ethel's father like the idea, for I was too young, he said, and he would not let the millions he had made be wasted. I told him I did not want any money from him, but I think he disliked and distrusted all foreigners, especially if they possessed an old name. . . . But at any rate my darling loved me, though I say it myself, and though she was a little older than I was, would have married me, if only her parents had consented. Nor did she have any distrust of me — but then, she was not *like* an American girl, for she had a romantic and passionate nature, similar to my own in those days. . . . And, of course, I did not look then as I look now: by no means. . . . I would bring her every day enormous bouquets of flowers, and I believe her people laughed at me, saying they were taller than I was — for to present flowers was a southern custom, not Anglo-Saxon: many hours, too, I spent under her window, for the whole world seemed full of music, and I could not sleep. Or sometimes I would hire bands of Neapolitan singers (and in those days, again, they were not merely hoarse beggars, trying to earn money by blackmailing our ears, but had lovely voices, soft and full) to serenade her. . . . And though to me, thinking over it all, thinking back, the whole thing is sad, it was at the time beautiful and wonderful and, besides, as I have said, "fun". . . . And then came a great quarrel between our parents; her father took her away. . . . And though we had so often pledged our faith, our love, for all eternity, yet, as a matter of fact, I never heard from her, never heard of her, again. . . . Nor ever, after that, did I fall in love in the same way. . . .

'As you see, then, from what I have been telling you, I often came here. The entire place spells my youth to me. I know every inch of every path up the mountains, of every rock in the bay, where I so often used to swim. . . . But now, I never bathe: the water is too chilly . . . or perhaps it is my blood . . . I do not know. In youth, blood is hot, and one is strong.' And the Count, after this typically Italian generalisation, threw out and squared his shoulders, as if about to box.

'No, everything is different,' he continued. 'In those days you asked for something, and it was brought before you had time to say — who is it, I forget, Jack Robinson? But now, as I started to tell you, the service is very bad. You are left to ring the bell for ever; no one answers it. I have talked to you, *car' amico*, already far too long: but let me tell you, at least, about that.

'When I returned to Sorrento a year ago, I came straight to this hotel, and, though it seemed different and is, of course, double the size, at first there did not seem to have been such a big change — except that today everyone is so independent.

. . . But it was just the same weather as it had been when I left, over forty years before, and at times I had almost the illusion that I had never gone away. (Such weather now is rare, but I did not know this.) As I walked in the town, many of the shopkeepers, and of the peasants, standing in groups by the market, recognised me and saluted me, and my tenants hurried to kiss my hand, so that I became proud, and thought, after all, it seems a very little time ago, and it may be I have not changed so much. . . . The hotel was rather empty : and, though the waiters seemed more numerous than the guests, none of them ever answered a bell : but they would rush about, in opposite directions, with napkins in their hands, looking eager and occupied. . . . Well, one day I saw an old lady, very fat and lame, get up with difficulty from her chair, and waddle over to the mantelpiece to ring the bell. . . . No one answered. . . . So then I rang the bell for her, a second time. It was, as I have said, a very hot day, and she wanted a glass of iced water. But even when she had ordered it, no one brought it. So at last I became very angry, and I rang the bell again, and said : "Unless that glass of water is brought immediately, I shall leave the hotel. It is a scandal !" And then, since they knew me, they were frightened, and brought it at once. . . . Well, that started an acquaintance with this poor old lady, for whom I felt so sorry, because she was so lame and looked so ill : and I think she was grateful to me, and liked me. . . . And I wondered, once or twice, how she had appeared when she was young, for if you stripped the fat from her face, and imagined a different colouring, she might have been handsome in her way. I asked her name of the concierge (she was a Mrs. Clacton-Biddle). Every day at luncheon she would bow and smile, and perhaps, afterwards, we would exchange a few words in the hall, about the weather, or politics. . . . Then, one day, I said to her : "So this is your first visit to our beautiful Sorrento ?"

'"No," she answered, "I stayed here once before, long ago. . . . I should hardly like to tell you how long. Twenty-five years ; a quarter of a century. . . . Just such days as these."

'This interested me, and I said : "Did you know any of the people in the villas here ?'

'And she replied : "Yes, I knew many of them : but they

are all gone now, Nestore di Nocera, and the Cleghornes and the Mellins."

' "They were all friends of mine too," I said. "Though you must excuse me for saying so, it is a longer time than you think, for it is over forty years since Nestore was drowned in this very bay. . . . I wonder if we ever met, for I lived here too then?"

'But she was thinking to herself, and paid no heed to my remarks. There was a smile of reminiscence on her face, which lit it and made it momentarily assume a certain familiar beauty, and yet one which I could not identify in my own mind: though now I saw that she must, indeed, have been beautiful in days gone by.

'"They were all friends of mine," I repeated.

'"And then," she continued, "there were the Ouraveffskys and the Bandaneras; so many friends: and my particular friend, Count Dragone di Dragora: but he is dead, too, they tell me."

'"Madame," I cried, "everything you tell me is true except that. Count Dragone di Dragora is not dead: he stands before you!" . . . And then I saw who she was, this fat, lame old lady. . . . It was Ethel Burkefield-Stoddard: and, as her eyes rested on mine, just for that one instant I heard all the nightingales singing again in the glossy darkness of the orange trees. . . .'

.   .   .   .   .

'But do you know, the queerest part of it: afterwards, now that she knew who I was, it seemed as though she wanted to put a barrier between us. . . . She became more distant in her manner, grew unwelcoming, and spoke to me little. . . . I do not know why. . . . Perhaps — who knows? — she regretted our intimacy; perhaps — indeed, surely — I disappointed her, and she bore me a grudge for it; perhaps she felt a different person herself, and thought I knew too much about her; or, again, she may have wished that, as she now was, I had never recognised her, and thus been forced inevitably to match against her present appearance the image of her which I must retain from past years. . . . Or perhaps it was merely that she had been married — and widowed — in the interval . . . I do not know. . . . But, after a time — shorter, I believe, than she had intended — she left, and sailed home from Naples. . . . And, since then, I have received only two letters from her:

the first to ask me to obtain for her one of those red lacquer boxes — you know, the kind that they make here — in which to keep her handkerchiefs: and the other, remote and bleak and impersonal, to thank me for having sent it. . . . It was all such a long time ago, I suppose.'

The Count stopped talking, and looked in the glass again. And for a moment I, too, caught a glimpse of a person lost long ago; a different dragon, warm and with a soft shell. And then again, it hardened into everyday armour.

CHAMPAGNE FOR THE OLD LADY

One of the most peculiar qualities of gambling is the power it possesses to make even the laziest man work hard, if only for a limited period; the period being, of course, limited by the money he has — or can borrow — to lose. Any gambler will toil through long, exhausting hours until daylight creeps cruelly through the curtains to reveal columns and shafts of cigarette-smoke and a suffocating atmosphere in which only germs could thrive; toil, at that, only in order to squander as much money as he could gain elsewhere by honest work in an infinitely shorter time. . . . Certainly I laboured far harder in the Casino — or 'the Studio', as, for that reason, I preferred to call it — than I do now in writing this story.

Roulette was the game. We were both of us far too poor to afford to gamble, and we both liked to lose our money in different ways. John Treguze had invented a real system for it, and whenever he had lost at the tables the whole of the money he had taken in with him, would comfort himself with the same vague sentiment: 'It's no good breaking off now. I ought to give my system a fair trial'. As for myself, I relied for my efforts upon intuition — a gift which can prove quite as expensive as any more intellectual method, for he who is endowed with it just scatters the counters over all the numbers that catch his eye or take his fancy. On the other hand, should he win, the laurels that crown prophecy are added to those of triumph.

We often argued the faults of our various ways of play. To begin with, I would point out to John, his methods were too complicated: for, if you were determined to experiment with a system, this necessitated taking with you to the table an immense quantity of counters of every sort, from ten-thousand and five-thousand francs down to hundreds and tens — far more than you could afford to lose; but the possibilities of a system, a thing so high above mere chance, justified in your mind the slight risk, as you saw it, of losing them. Indeed, it became a duty. (If you had lost heavily before, it was not because your system had betrayed you, but because you had not played it long enough.) And then, always just as the end to which you had so long been progressing was at last beginning to come in sight, human frailty entered too; either you forgot for a single throw to back one of the essential numbers, or the ball might be started over-soon (so that you were not given the time in which to complete your usual lay-out of counters), or you found that you had already, without noticing it, lost all the money you had brought in, and so were obliged to miss the very spin that would have made your fortune. Whereas my lack of system — which, in itself, almost amounted to one — was simplicity itself, easy to manage: you took as many counters as you wanted, placed them where you liked, and when you had forfeited them all, you either left the building or obtained some more — and lost them in addition. No fuss or brain-fag. . , . Nevertheless, at times when I scanned John's face, looked at his dark, luxuriant hair, his regular and determined features, his eyes that, though short-sighted, were so far-seeing, or regarded his large frame, his system seemed to me so well to match and express his physique that I wondered whether he might not win with it after all.

That night at dinner, on the terrace in front of the hotel, we discussed these problems again. Dinner lightened the sense of our losses: it was a warm night of early summer, and the grass, of so vivid a green, and growing singly from the soil like the tenderly nurtured hairs on the head of a bald man, the flowers and palm trees and kiosks and cupolas of this holy city of chance, presented the enchanting vistas of a mid-Victorian stage-setting. And all this beauty had been created out of the money lost by gamblers! We began to feel that we, too, had 'done our bit' towards it, for this evening we had been victims. . . . But soon, over our brandy, we began to talk of other things, until it was nearly time to go, to start again. . . . John chose a cigar — to smoke later, he said, when he was winning, for it helped him to keep his head cool; and then we spoke of cigars, how expensive in France and England, how cheap and good they were in Holland and Germany — and in Austria; where, he informed me — for he had at one time lived there — even women, and especially those of the former, aristocratic régime, smoked them in preference to cigarettes. . . . I wondered if I had ever seen a woman smoke a cigar in England. . . . But I was sure I had not, for it would have looked so odd that one would remember it.

We walked across to the Casino and found its marbled saloons, smelling so strongly of post-offices and old scent, unusually crowded, airless to the point of suffocation. A pleasure-cruise had touched here this afternoon, and the pleasure-crusaders were standing round the tables in staring groups, ox-eyed with Swiss or Scandinavian wonder, and getting very much in the way of the habitual, as it were resident, gamblers : those old ladies with delicate complexions enamelled over thousands of cobweb-like wrinkles, with many veils and bags, and a slight, harassing twitch, who, harmless old flotsam of Edwardian days, compose the steady population of such places. Little processions of black-clothed croupiers, with down-turned eyes, like the mutes at a funeral, marched through the rooms, guarding a coffinful of counters.

The public rooms were too thronged tonight for John to be able to obtain the share of the croupier's attention which his system demanded ; besides, it was far too hot and one felt penned-in at the table, as though one were waiting to be sheared, so we entered the *Salle Privée*, usually to a certain degree free of tourists. It was now about a quarter to eleven, and the gambling was in full swing ; it seemed much cooler, though we found that the cruising parties had even penetrated here in their urge to gape. In addition, there was, of course, the usual *Salle Privée* circle of old witches, with tousled white hair, sitting round the table, staring at the wheel, mumbling spells and curses through nut-cracker jaws. They themselves never played now, all their losses were in the past, but they paid money still to enter, in order to inconvenience as much as they could the real players by taking all the chairs so that the others had to stand up, thus too far from the table to be able properly to place their stakes.

John, however, found a good seat, next the croupier, and began sorting out and arranging his columns of counters as a preliminary. I stood for a moment to watch. The old lady who had at the same time taken the empty chair next him attracted — and held — my attention. She differed so greatly from those all round her who so plainly lived in the town and made this their headquarters. Unused as she must obviously be to the Casino, she appeared too good — too *morally* good, I mean — for her environment. Well over seventy, I should say, she was slight in figure, her complexion was that of a girl of seventeen, and her eyes still had a youthful, meaningless caress in them when she looked at you. She was dressed quietly in black velvet. A sort of black lace mantilla framed her head and flowed over her soft white hair, being tied in a wimple under the chin, thus emphasising a profile that was, even now, of a du Maurier-like calm and purity; and she carried, as her only impedimenta, two fans, one painted, the other of black lace : these she put down on the table by her. Regarding her, one saw that she was, in fact, one of those rare creatures, an old lady who, besides retaining her beauty, had retained her prettiness — a far more difficult achievement.

I reflected how lucky John was to find her as a neighbour instead of one of the usual clawing harpies of the Casino, and then left him, in order to have a drink in the bar. There people were swallowing coffee and cocktails and brandy and every sort of drink for every hour. For a while I listened to their desultory fragments of talk. An elderly, voguish American gigolo with very smooth black hair, and hands flapping like a seal's flippers, was heard remarking to a much older American woman, dressed in a low evening dress of white lace sprinkled with pink roses, 'My dear, it's *chic*, and it's *soignée* (swánee), but it gets you nowhere!'

When I returned to the table John was immersed in his system and had lit his large cigar. Smoking was, of course, allowed, but I noticed (as he did not, for he was too busily occupied) that the pretty old lady next him, with her soft white hair and large soft blue eyes, had begun to show symptoms of distress, to cough and fan herself gently. John's great frame, posed next to hers, served to make her look still smaller and more shrinking. The coven of Casino witches round the table, with their gnarled, veined, grabbing hands that might have been carved from the root of a box tree, their hard faces and circular parrot's eyes, seemed by no means impressed by this display of sensitiveness, and glared cynically at the victim (this, no doubt, would have been their attitude to any show of natural feeling), but the strangers near by, and the barricade behind her of Scandinavian and Swiss tourists, soon became interested and sympathetic, solicitous on her behalf. What a shame for a great big man to smoke a huge cigar like that, next to her, their plain faces said plainly! Probably in the old French *manoir* whence she must have sprung, she had never even seen a cigar, far less smelt it. (How curious, indeed, to see a lady of that kind in the Casino : she was not at all of the type they had expected to discover ; must, somehow, have wandered in here by mistake.) But that was the rich all over, trampling on the feelings of the poor and refined. Why, though she was sitting down, if you looked, she was not even playing! Too poor to afford it, that must be the explanation. *There* was self-restraint for you! But you did not see people of that stamp nowadays ; too gentle and good for this gas-mask, weakest-against-the-wall world.

The old lady was by this time fanning herself vigorously, first with one fan, then with the other. She would take one up, use it, and then lay it down again on the table, near John's counters. Her manipulation of these instruments was wonder-fully expressive. Like that of a geisha, or a great Chinese actor, every movement bore its burden of significance. She turned her exquisite profile away from her neighbour, and his vile habits, as though to obtain air. By now both the cigar and the system were well under way, and I do not think that, until this minute, John had been at all aware of the growing interest and disturbance round him. But suddenly the old lady became vocal, began to complain audibly, partly to herself, partly to the crowd, in beautiful old-world French ; and the crowd started to take her side, to murmur in their various doric tongues. (As she spoke, I wondered was there not, after all, a hint of foreign intonation in that telling, vibrating voice ; was not the use of idiom a little too perfect for a woman speaking her own language?) The croupiers alone remained unmoved, their eyes glazed with fatigue and boredom, or with a slight furtive and reminiscent smile hovering round their colourless lips, according to their types. Now she fanned herself, almost truculently for one of so gracious a personality, grimaced, showed her distaste in many evident ways, and finally made an open protest to the croupiers and the world in general. The croupiers remained silent, indifferent, but the world in general responded. Once more she appealed to the nearest croupier, who, waking himself from a despondent trance, in which, obviously, he despaired of humanity and its greed, declared that he could do nothing ; smoking was allowed.

She demanded to see the *chef du parti*, and plied the fans incessantly, taking them up, putting them down, holding them at angles, in order to protect herself, and using them to attract the crowd's attention and to point out to them the delinquent. Meanwhile, John had grown conscious of the tension in the air, and had become thoroughly annoyed, for his neighbour had created and worked up this scene without ever addressing a single request to him personally : so he continued to smoke, and endeavoured, against increasing odds, to maintain outward calm and to concentrate successfully on his complicated system of gambling. Eventually, however, the muttering, and the general carefully cultivated feeling of antipathy towards him, affected his nerves, and, accosting the pretty old lady, he offered to put out his cigar, adding that he would have been delighted to do so at any previous moment, had she seen fit to ask him. She did not even reply. It was too late : she was offended beyond repair. Elegantly, with conspicuous grace of carriage and dignity, she collected her fans, rose from the table, and glided out of the room in a rustle of resentful black velvet. The onlookers glared furiously at John, who, in return, blew out defiantly a small cloud of smoke. Poor old lady, they said, to treat her like that ! What a shame ! A great big brute, with no respect for age or delicacy. But how truly she had shown her breeding ! How beautifully she had walked out, without a word ! Why, she could not have done it better if she had practised it for years ! There was a *real* lady for you ! You didn't see that sort nowadays.

John certainly felt uncomfortable at her ostentatiously quiet departure (moreover, he had been losing again for some time, though he had begun well this evening, when he first arrived. Because gambling has an element of exhibitionism in it : the player, to win, must compel the wonder and admiration, even the envy, of the spectators ; but their disapproval and dislike will ruin his game). The whole affair had depressed him and spoilt his evening — but it was not until ten minutes or so after she had left that he realised that all his high counters had gone with her. The better system had won.

The pretty old lady, I was told afterwards, was an Austrian, in spite of the elegant and lovely French she spoke. And it was her custom always to select an evening when the rooms were crowded with Swiss and Scandinavian naïfs for the testing of her system. The smoke-screen was a regular trick, and one that usually worked well, since large cigars and quantities of counters seemed to go together in the Casino : like the chatter of a conjurer at the moment of counterfeiting his magic, her protests were designed to distract the attention, both of her audience and of her chosen dupe, from the sleight-of-hand which was in progress before them. The opaque film from the cigar resembled, too, the cracking of the magician's pistol, while the smoke itself afforded some disguise, comparable to the cloud of ink thrown off by an octopus when engaged in combat, in order to mask its manœuvres — except that, in this instance, it was the octopus, still more wily, who compelled her prey to emit the concealing veil. But, had she been ejected by the authorities, doubtless aware of her game, a riot would most surely have ensued, so firmly did she always establish herself in the hearts of the onlookers.

I did not stay in the Casino long enough that evening to see the end of John's system. (We were leaving the next day.) The rooms were far too hot, and I strolled out towards my hotel. The night was delicious. The feathery palm leaves lay motionless on the air, laden with the scent of orange blossom and strong-smelling night flowers. On my way back I passed a large café, like an illuminated conservatory, with a uniformed Tsigane band stationed near the entrance, playing waltzes. The chairs set outside looked so inviting that I took one and ordered a drink. In the opposite corner sat the pretty old lady, nodding her head in time to the waltz the band was playing; she had evidently just finished her supper; an empty half-bottle of champagne stood in a silver pail of ice by her side. And, as I got up to go, I noticed that in the manner of many compatriots of her sex in the old days, she was just lighting a cigar.

LOVERS' MEETING

It was the ideal afternoon of a May day. Down below, ants moved along their tracks, and we flew over a model of Petworth, over miniature bare slopes, over towns and then across a marbled sea. The plane was crowded. A few 'good-timers' were still there, faithful to an ideal that grew increasingly difficult to follow, loyal to their favourite beat: Paris for Whitsun.

'I may as well have a holiday,' my neighbour remarked, a smooth-faced, rather handsome Jew of the Stock Exchanges. 'I shall never have another. I join up next month.'

In the enormous omnibus, dashing up from Le Bourget, several fat women, rolling luxuriously at each turn of the road against their neighbours, made friends with them in this way. The men rolled back at them, hip to hip, with a *can-can*-like audacity: (the local atmosphere must have affected them). Though so near, the noise forced them to shout to one another.

'I always say there's no place like Paris!' they yelled. 'You feel different directly you get here. . . . Especially now, with all the chestnuts in flower. It ought to be lovely. . . . And Josephine Baker is back at the old Casino! I *love* her, don't you?'

'*Shan't* we look silly if the Germans invade Holland and Belgium, and we can't get back? . . . But they won't: they can't: of course they won't, or our people wouldn't have let us come. . . . Yes, it was quite easy. I was surprised. But I felt I wanted a change; growing stale in Brighton all those months. . . . Look, there's *Le Lapin Vert*! It's still open then? Someone said it was shut.'

The next morning, Friday, I was woken at five by wailing sirens, and again at eight by the voice of the speaker on the French Radio, his calm and politeness exaggerated a thousand-fold by the impersonality of the instrument. Moreover, the very loudness of its amplification made it sound as though the announcer were glad and the news were good. No one would

302

dare to give bad tidings in such a tone. . . . The German armies had invaded Holland, Belgium and Luxembourg during the night, and had launched their great attack on the West.

It was difficult for me to know whether to continue my journey to Italy. I had been told not to go 'if the situation deteriorated'. At moments I thought that the dissolution of three further independent states marked such a stage. Besides, I knew that Italy was planning to enter the war, was convinced of it. Accordingly I cabled to the authorities, 'Shall I still proceed Italy'. . . . After three days of suspense, and of mingling with crowds walking up and down in the holiday sunshine, the reply came, on the very afternoon on which my train was due to leave.

'Think you had better continue but must be on your own responsibility.'

I cabled back, 'Proceeding Italy this afternoon but consider Tennysons celebrated lines theirs not to reason why theirs but to do or die would have lost in vigour had poet added further line on their own responsibility Sitwell', and drove to the Gare de Lyon.

The train happened to be the last permitted to reach Italy by the Simplon route. When we left, there was still some doubt as to whether the Swiss Government would allow it to enter Switzerland. But the conductors, who, looking in their hats and uniforms like overgrown telegraph-boys, stood poising pencils above charts, remained sanguine. It was impossible to divine their race, they belonged to the blue-chinned international tribes of the European *wagons-lits*, super-gipsies with a languid *chic* all their own. They showed no animus. Nothing would happen : why should it ? The Italians would not enter the war. . . . But Sanctions, those Sanctions !

As usual I reached the station too early; so, having secured my compartment, I walked up and down the platform, watching fellow-passengers arrive : Balkan diplomats, with sleeked hair and high, giggling voices, returning home, French business men, Americans *en route* for their ships at Naples; and an enlarged — you could not have said *fat* — middle-aged French-woman, much painted, with very golden hair and dark eye-brows and with several extensions of personality outside herself; jingling bangles provided, for example, music for every gesture, and there were cigarette cases and holders, bags in which to lose things and, finally, a minute, high-stepping griffon which, with a collar of bells, also contributed its own music for each step it took. A coat was strapped to its middle to keep it warm. (It was so small, the creature, that it made me think of Jean Cocteau's story of the woman who bought from a Paris dealer a little angel of a dog, in a coat, with little shoes even, on its feet. Naturally she was obliged to give a large sum for such a treasure, but none the less delighted with her purchase, brought it home. Once safely there, she left it for a few minutes alone in the drawing-room while she found it some food. . . . When she returned the little creature had run up the curtain; it was a rat, disguised.)

The owner of bangles and griffon was certainly very conspicuous. . . . Nevertheless the least conspicuous person on the platform was at the same time the most noticeable to myself, as she walked slowly up and down it. She was a woman of between sixty and seventy, bulky, dressed in black, with a puffy, emotional face, its flush emphasised, as is so often the case, by the whiteness of her hair. It was a kindly, silly face, and of a type often encountered. She was, no doubt, a person who obeyed the conventions and who, while good in the sense of being generous and amiable, was also greedy and, to some mild extent, pleasure-loving, indulgent to herself as to others. She might have been the original of Frances Cornford's

> O why do you walk in the fields in gloves,
> Missing so much and so much?
> O fat white woman whom nobody loves . . .

Yes, somewhat self-indulgent. And she had the air of one who was used invariably to kindness, had always been protected. Yet her face held the attention, for there was more in it than that; something mad and tragic, the dignity of Lear in his appalling abnegation and abandonment. Her blue-grey eyes, unimaginative and rather protruding, were strained, and straining, full of emotion, did not see, but nevertheless saw, surely, beyond the objects at which she looked. Her mouth, which many years ago must have been so pretty — though its pouting had now, at her age, grown ridiculous — worked the whole time as if she were talking. . . . One could not help wondering about her, because of the contrast between her appearance of being so ordinary, her mobile, puffy face, and the attitude and the mask of classic grief which her pose and countenance sometimes assumed. . . . But the passengers were getting in, the train was starting.

Next morning I sat in my *wagon-lit*, watching the touchingly beautiful Italian landscape roll by, under the tender early light. This country of mountain and lake pulled at the heart-strings, even if this were the first time you saw it; still more if you were familiar with trees and flowers, and loved the people as I did. But under the lightness and sweetness of the air could be detected the stench of the treachery infecting it. Now we were passing Baveno, and Stresa, and Isola Bella with its marble decks and pinnacles, and old trees in shrillest green leaf, lay like a full-rigged ship above the calm, mirror-like water. . . . How often had I seen it, how often had I done this journey! It seemed just the same. . . . Suddenly I heard a voice, hesitating and sad, speaking behind me, from the doorway, in broken English.

There stood the old woman in black, her eyes seeming fuller and more brimming as the light from the windows fell direct on her puffy, discoloured face. Her whole attitude, even through the jolting of the train, seemed inspired by some unbearable dignity, forced upon her in rigid, unwelcome mould, as if a great sculptor had chosen for once to shape a conception out of a medium so unsuitable as to make the effect of it all the more astonishing.

'Do you speak English?' she asked. 'Forgive me, but I must talk to someone. I cannot stop talking. I am a bit crazy, I know. But I do not know what to do or what I should have done. I come from Belgium; you cannot believe what I have seen; my only child, my son, home on leave, seized out of my own house before my eyes by German soldiers, before I knew we were at war. I could not follow him. I do not know whether he is alive or dead. Perhaps I should have stayed there, but I did not know what to do, and all my friends were leaving. . . . And the roads, the refugees, the poor refugees; two days to go a few miles that in peace-time would take an hour. No pity, no pity anywhere. I saw Louvain burning for the second time. . . . I do not know; what could I do? Oh, what could I have done? I could not follow my son, they would not let me. My friends made me go to Paris, and from there, from the Embassy, I telephoned to my husband in Venice, where I am joining him — he is our Consul-General. All my life I have loved him, but now he is old, and when, at last, we were able to get him on the telephone, he could not hear well. He could not understand about our son. He thought I should not have left him — but what could I do? They caught him and took him away. And I never stop thinking of him, saying to myself, what could I do or have done? . . . The poor refugees, struggling, running down the roads, all of them the colour of dust, and some lying where they fell in the ditch, not troubling to get up. . . . You don't mind my talking. I must talk to someone, or I shall go mad. (But I am a little mad already, I know.) . . . I could not have believed what I have seen. All my life I have been *dévote*, but now I ask *le bon Dieu* how He could have permitted it. The fires, the people, the poor people, running. . . .'

There was a pause. The sweet, calm Italian country sped past the windows. In the corridor, just outside, the fussy, spindle-legged, *petit-maître* griffon danced and pranced and sneezed and thrilled with pleasure, his bells jingling at each movement and curvet, while his mistress sounded her bangles, giggled in the manner she had for more than a generation found successfully attractive, and shouted, slapping the front of her thigh with a fat hand, '*Ninon, Ninon chéri, viens voir Maman*'. The dog danced more than ever, its eyes bulging with pleasure.

The monologue in the doorway started again. 'All in three days! The roads choked, and I saw the faces of the German airmen as they dived and machine-gunned us, saw them laughing. . . . No pity anywhere in the world. . . . And my son! . . . What am I to say to my husband? He will be at the station. He is perhaps angry and I do not know how to explain, do not know what to say . . .'

THE WOMAN WHO HATED FLOWERS

My parents had sent me into a nursing-home. The hours were of the usual grey monotony, and the day-nurses seemed to spend their periods of duty in whisking flowers in and out of the room, pouring more water into the vases or spilling a little out of them, in offering me glasses of a thick, viscous barley-water, very tainted in its taste, and in talking interminably — it was spring — about 'daffies'.

The night-nurse, though, in spite of her plainness, was not ordinary; in her quietness she was unusual. Her voice was a human voice, containing no special inflections for the 'cheering up' of patients. She brought into the room a certain air of humanity, a quality of comfort. Reserved, placid, her lashless eyes — the irises, not the whites — shone sometimes with a glow of their own, as she sat gazing absorbedly into the embers, while her tall, spare body rocked a little, and by this movement rescued itself from the immobility of sculptured stone.

One night, I believe she told me her story. . . . But I could never be quite sure, for every evening I became feverish, and she never referred to the incident afterwards.

When she came in, the day-nurse had only just left me and had omitted to turn down the lights. I saw the new-comer breathe heavily as she entered, her nostrils dilating. Then, their scent attracting her attention, she noticed a vase of flowers — wallflowers, they were — which her predecessor had forgotten to remove, and at once carried it away into the passage.

This action I thought out of keeping with her usual dignity and slow-moving restraint, just like that of any other nurse. . . . On her return, she stood watching me for several minutes without speaking, then said, suddenly, with great force, 'I *hate* flowers!', switched off the lights and went out.

I woke up later, and could distinguish her figure by the fire. She was rocking a little, as though her body were still seeking that marvellous balance which her soul at such cost, and with so little reason, had long found. Sleepily I asked

her, speaking partly to myself, 'Why do you hate flowers?'
And perhaps the fact that I was then very young, or perhaps
merely the anonymity of darkness, made her tell me. But alas,
from this distance I can no longer offer you her precise words;
can only tell you what I remember. And some of the details
will be inaccurate, for it is long ago; but I can give you the
general impression of what I believe she told me.

Aurelia Graybourne had come out of a comfortable home
in the suburbs of Dublin, but it nevertheless contained a spiritual
suffering that outweighed material circumstances. Her father
had long been dead, her three sisters were married, and her
mother drank with ardour and endurance, devoting her life
to this almost touching appetite. For its sake, she would brook
any discomfort, mental, physical or of the soul. Even the
priests proved unable to restrain her in her pursuit of it.

The outward respectability of Aurelia's middle-class home,
the chintzes, the bureaux, the fringed cushions, the calendars,
the 'easy-chairs', the 'occasional tables', the Victorian knick-
knacks in silver, all threw into a greater relief the grotesque
horror of life within its walls. Hogarth's 'Gin Lane' would
have supplied a far more apposite background for the squalor
of dozens of empty whisky bottles, ingeniously but often inadequately concealed, and for the snoring torpor or crazy
gaiety that resulted from them. The working-up of scenes, the
horrid, dull satisfaction of the drunkard in the pain which her
inspired words could give, and the subsequent maudlin scenes
of reconciliation, poisoned equally the whole existence of this
young girl.

Even when drunk, Mrs. Graybourne, as the daughter of one
officer and the widow of another, felt obliged to keep up appearances, so she sought no convivial cronies but vented all the
technique of her recurring bouts upon her youngest daughter.
In the morning, when well enough, she went out shopping
alone, a sort of martyred, mystical sweetness, together with a
very red nose, being the only visible tokens of those hectic
afternoons and evenings which she spent in the torture, conscious
and unconscious, of the being most dear to her in the world.

Eventually, after a very bad outbreak, the doctors and
priests intervened and insisted on the eldest daughter, now a
widow herself, coming to look after Mrs. Graybourne. They
said she needed someone of experience with her. . . . During

this interlude, Aurelia declared her intention of entering a convent. Ada, her sister, who, though perfectly aware of what had been going on, had, until the priests sent for her, never offered to help in any manner, now took sides openly against her. But Aurelia was just of age, and could do what she liked : she possessed a hundred and fifty pounds a year of her own. No one could move her, hitherto so gentle.

Mrs. Graybourne, too ill to argue, wept a great deal, but could not succeed in persuading Aurelia to remain at home. At last, though, she relented sufficiently to promise that for the first two or three years she would work as a lay sister, thus giving herself time to see whether she was fitted for the novitiate. But this affectation of lowliness, as she chose to consider it, yet further embittered the convalescent.

When Aurelia left, Mrs. Graybourne was still confined to her bed. Sweetness and resignation, with a dash of menace and a hint of prophecy, were her specialities at the moment. 'To think that you should leave a loving mother and a comfortable home, all because of your own unnatural selfishness,' she had begun, when the cab was at the door. But sobs choked her at this point, and she had been obliged to pause. 'I've nothing to say against convents,' she had continued, in her wily brogue. 'I'm a religious woman, I hope. But I warned Father Clement . . . "That girl will bring disgrace on St. Ursula's, just as she has on her poor mother".'

.   .   .   .   .   .

Aurelia had driven up to the convent in an old cab, through pouring rain, but in spite of the clouds that lay low upon the mountains, her heart was at rest. From the first moment when the Abbess received her, she felt she had done the only thing that could give her peace. The rain, the calm, the routine, soothed her nerves and made her happy. Through serving so humbly, she regarded herself already as dedicated to God's service. Perhaps Mrs. Graybourne's reproaches had touched her, and underneath her extreme devoutness may have existed the apprehension that only by an entire surrender of herself could she atone for abandoning the earthly ties of duty, however degrading and destructive. Henceforth no task could be too menial for her.

The severity of the life suited her. Her eyes took on reflections of sea and lake and cloud and mountain, and her skin attained the delicate suffusions of colour that tinge Irish cheeks alone, nourished by generations of soft, continual rain. Notwithstanding her desire for self-suppression, a sort of animal radiance, derived from a new contentment with her surroundings, became manifest in her, showed through the movements of her limbs, encumbered by their heavy, medieval garment, and, with the conviction it carried of youth and innocence, appealed to every heart.

The seasons were quickened in their passing by the regular tenor of her existence. Twice she had seen the winter disappear. Soon she would become a novice, and sever the last tie with her old self. Meanwhile a thousand tasks employed her time, cleaning the rooms and passages, gentle gardening, picking fruit. Since she had soon won the trust and affection of the nuns, she would often be left alone at such pursuits. Or it would be her duty to sweep out and adorn the chapel; that Irish-Gothic edifice of the nineteenth century, vast and ill-proportioned, every pillar and arch too narrow and too poor, but built, nevertheless, with a sense of the theatre, full of bright light and deep shadow and incense through which the realistically painted saints trailed flaring and tawdry dresses, their shrines decorated with arrangements of tinsel and imitation flowers.

Outside now, the days of spring were thick and heavy with a pagan, impermanent joy. The sunlight issued in spears and shafts from behind fat, lolling clouds. It lay like cream upon clustered blossom of apple and pear tree, and gilded with a warm effulgence the grass at their roots, throwing into vivid individual relief the flowers among it. The wallflowers, with their turrets of crumpled tawny velvet, growing by the base of the chapel walls, hummed with drowsy insect life, and their sweetness, which appeared to be less a scent than the very perfume of the golden day itself, hung above the paths and entered a little way into the chapel, there to be defeated by the Christian smell of incense. Often, the glittering lances of the showers in their sudden charges similarly dispersed it for a time in the garden itself. . . . But directly the sun came through, those sweet odours mounted once more into the air. Vague, luxurious longings of the flesh assailed her, and she would return to the chapel for the seeming permanence of its meagre arch and pillar, cold stone and hard benches, to allay them.

These by now familiar objects offered their own assurance; here things were as they always were, had been, would be, unaltered and inalterable as the love of God. The life in the garden, though temporarily disturbing to the senses, was fitful, seasonal. . . . But how sinful, she reflected, that the flesh of men and women should be subject to these earthy and godless permutations.

Nevertheless, as she swept clear of dust the ugly ecclesiastical patterns of the tessellated floor with her medieval broom — composed, like a gardener's, of twigs bound together — she was conscious that the joy from outside had invaded the most sacred places. The welling up of life in her body, as much as in every tree and flower, now tinctured for her every inanimate object, so that the paper flowers appeared to blossom more bravely, the patterned floor to assume harder, brighter colours, the incense, even, to become less spiritual in its appeal.

One day, when she was sweeping the chapel, she thought she would look into the street, and, just as she opened the door, it happened that a man she had known in Dublin passed by. About ten years older than herself, he was a musician (indeed, many thought that he possessed great talent as a composer), and her mother disapproved of him, which had added to his already considerable charm. In spite of the change in her attire, he recognised her at once. (She supposed, afterwards, that when he called her name she ought not to have answered. But how could she have refused? It would have been rude and unkind.) She stood there in the warm shadow, and he in full sunlight, so that it beat down on his dark, handsome face and bold jutting features, and showed her a flattering admiration, surprise and pleasure in his large, dark eyes, usually nonchalant and melancholy. As he spoke to her, her whole body came to life beneath the heavy, stone-like folds of her dress, as though a statue were starting to breathe.

After that, she did not so clearly remember the course of events. Some intoxication of the senses appeared to have affected her, leaving behind it a state bordering on oblivion. For about two months, however, she struggled for her beliefs; then she began to meet Terence Marlowe by appointment on many occasions. After all, she would argue with herself, she was free, she had as yet taken no vows.

Chance favoured their love for each other; almost miraculously, they were never seen together. The months passed. But though gay and happy when in his company, at other times a consciousness of the wickedness of what he had asked her — and what she intended — to do, weighed her down. For he pleaded with her continually to abandon the idea of the cloister and run away to London; where, later, he would come to marry her. . . . Not at once, or the Abbess and the nuns would talk, and would no doubt find a way of injuring him in the eyes of members of his family. And that neither he nor Aurelia could afford, because by copying out parts and by playing the organ, he was earning little enough money: but he possessed expectations of a moderate sort from his relatives.

Many were the nights when desolation of the spirit kept her awake, and by day in the garden, as she swept the paths and inhaled the perfume of the wallflowers, her face often burned with shame. But at other moments, when she recalled that Terence loved her, just as she loved him, a certain feeling of joy and pride comforted her. . . . It was indeed fortunate, she would then reflect, that she had allowed her family to persuade her to wait, before making any irrevocable decision. She could still escape. The life of the convent would soon be behind her, just as was the life of her old home. . . . Almost she had forgotten the existence of her mother and sister, the protests and uproar that would arise when they heard that she was taking their advice. . . . Meanwhile, she could not bring herself to tell the Abbess or consult the nuns, though, but for her fear, there was nothing to prevent her. No obstacles would have been placed in her way, whatever she had decided to do. . . . But in her own mind she still regarded herself as dedicated to the service of God, not of man. . . . She loved the sisters, so she must run away without saying good-bye to them.

When she ran away, leaving behind her a letter to the Abbess, worded in a business-like, brisk manner, she hardly experienced the remorse she had anticipated. It seemed no more than the changing of her old-fashioned livery for the dress of the times. In the same style, her old life was folded up, hidden out of sight. She stood on deck now — so she felt — a modern figure, finished with restraints, welcoming the life of the day. And though numbered among those in whose hearts, however much they may transgress its teachings, religion had taken root, and would never die, of this she was unconscious, and she rejoiced as the sea and air sang the word 'freedom' in her ears.

She was to wait a month in London for her lover. At first time sped by, but as day followed day and six weeks and more had elapsed, it began to drag. His early letters, long and affectionate, had been frequent as even she could wish, but they were now few. And, although she was living cheaply in a boarding-house in Bloomsbury, her money showed signs of becoming exhausted. She began to lose interest in this city, so new to her. . . . And still he did not arrive to claim her. . . . Not even now, however, not for a moment, did she doubt him. If she did, the world would fall in ruins round her.

Letters started to arrive from her mother and sisters, who had succeeded at last in tracing her. These contained dull reproaches, coarse taunts and much talk of the suffering she had brought upon them. 'You have', Mrs. Graybourne wrote, 'cast a slur upon your own father's good name.' . . . *Who* was the *man*? the chorus demanded and reiterated. . . . Aurelia did not answer. . . . Then Ada came to see her, and talked of their mother as a martyr, never even allowed herself to admit that Mrs. Graybourne drank. *Who was the man?*

All right, if she would not say, they would find out. But, whoever he might be, he was after her fortune. (To many men, it might seem a lot.) Of that, both Ada and Mrs. Graybourne were sure.

. . . .

At last a letter arrived. It could not have been an easy letter to write. . . . She opened it in her room. He was afraid, he said, that she might think he had been silly, but he was sure that if they had gone on, they would only have regretted it. He had just married; an old friend of his. He hoped Aurelia would be sensible and would not write to him, as Naomi might see the letter and it would upset her, since she knew nothing about their friendship. . . .

So they were wrong! He was not after her money; nor after herself. It had been merely a matter of play. . . . He had waited two months — until the spring had come again — and then had married this woman of whom she had never heard.

'Nothing', that was the word that haunted Aurelia.

Nothing. It had meant nothing; nothing. She was not even to be given the crown of a great betrayal. It was all paltry, insignificant. She felt sick, suddenly, as though she were going to die. (She could not bear that scent of wallflowers: on her dressing-table stood a small bunch she had bought yesterday. She got up, took it from the vase, went to the window, and threw it out into the yard.) Nothing. . . . For days she stayed in her room, shunning the light, sitting dully in her chair in her sordid, damp-stained attic, for she feared the repercussion, even from a distance in a great city, of the humming ecstasy of apple trees in blossom and the indefinable, pervading sweetness of wallflowers. She feared the air itself.

.   .   .   .

At any rate this intolerable misery had been real. Soon — after the passage of these first few days, and then of a month or two — she was real no longer, even to herself; nothing. Now she could go out again, buy newspapers, walk in parks, reply to letters; reply to them, moreover, hit by hit, kick below the belt by answering kick. But she was nothing.

Her religion, dormant in her, proved of no avail, for she had betrayed it, as Terence had betrayed her. She could not face a confessor. . . . To what could she turn, so as to escape the misery of the senses, to avoid trees and music, sunlight and moonlight and, above all, flowers?

She found the answer. Hospitals resembled convents in their routine; only the religious core was absent. She was intelligent and soon learnt her profession. And in this world of order, devoted to healing the body, she found an anodyne for her wounded soul. Its matter-of-factness, its strict rules, its divisions of light and darkness, were helpful to her, and the antiseptic smell of ward and corridor drove out the scent of the day and season, triumphed over the perfume of the flowers in the wards, sterilised them.

It was, she thought, as though her heart had been cauterised. She altered in her aspect, became part of the hospital and its routine. Her body now seemed rhythmless and without purpose, except for giving medicines and smoothing pillows. Her efficiency transcended kindness, a loveless, sublimated love. And, if she felt no pleasure, she felt no pain. . . . Night-duty she enjoyed, for then she saw no daylight, slept through it, and the flowers had been put away by the time she arrived in the evening.

For many years (endless years, they appeared to her) this kind of existence continued; until you would have thought that Fate had forgotten her, had thrown her life aside, intending to make no pattern out of it. . . . And then, one night, a case was brought into her ward, a drunken man who had been knocked down and crushed by a motor-car. . . . She recognised him at once. He had become poor and old, his talent for music had come to nothing. His wife had left him. He had no children. . . . There was no one to look after him except Nurse Aurelia.

She used to sit with him in the day-time, as well as nurse him at night. The great bare windows were flooded with the golden light of unforgettable spring days, and the scent of the flowers that had been brought to the patients by relatives and friends, apple blossom and cherry, tulips, narcissus and wall-flower, was often overpowering under the strong sun. . . . Day by day the old man grew worse, and after ten days he died. He had never been fully conscious, so she was not sure how much he knew or whether he recognised her. . . . But somehow or other, through looking after him, she had regained her faith.

After it was all over, she had left the hospital and taken a post in a nursing-home. She had felt she needed a change, she said.

.   .   .   .

Nurse Aurelia was silent for a while, staring into the embers, and then she turned to me, the irises of her eyes glowing with that strange fire of the animal world, and added, 'But I still hate flowers'.

LOW TIDE

It was an entrance that, however unconscious, never failed of its effect, and one to which the eye could never become accustomed. The two little figures at the top of the steps, though put-in on a large and crowded canvas, inevitably and entirely dominated the scene at this precise moment of the day. Behind them under the pale blue canopy of the sky rose the intricate perspective of steep cliffs, trim but wind-cut trees, and dells of a cultivated wildness; while the sharp cries of the children, as they raced round these, falling down, laughing, and dropping wooden spade or metallic pail, gave a certain poignancy to the otherwise flat blur of the band wafted up from below. The staircase was the culmination of the garden. On to it led every dell, dingle, and asphalt path. With heavy stone balustrades, crushed down beneath rows of weighty, clumsily carved, stone vases overflowing with purple petunias and a new, very municipal variety of dwarf sweet-pea — salmon-pink in tone — it held its own with any other feature of the town. It competed successfully for the attention with funicular-trams, which by their movement continually caught the eye as they performed their geometrical operations up and down the cliff with the precision of a drill-sergeant; it outshone the flashing eyes of the bandstand, encased in panes of glass, and even outvied in interest the lion-coloured sands flecked with moving, gaily dressed people, and spotted with trestles, centres of little groups, on which white-clad figures gesticulated, or opened and shut soundless mouths. On each side of this imposing structure, set in wide sloping surfaces of grass, smooth and green as baize, two enormous five-pointed stars — frilled out at the edges with variegated leaves of iodine-brown, ochre, green-white and lemon-yellow, lined again within by lobelias of a copper-sulphate blue that in their turn enclosed a round pupil of coral-pink begonias and red and purple fuchsias — glowered out to sea like two bloodshot eyes; one Cyclops guarding each side of the steps.

When the first terrace, overlooked by all this glory, was

reached, the blur of the music sharpened into focus, settling
into so many familiar and machine-made moulds, for its
broad platform was level with the gilt knob of the circular
cage from which rose all this sound. Under cover of that
cage — or glass case — alternately scorched on warm days and
frozen on cool ones, the band discoursed the whiskered,
military joviality of Waldteufel or in a sudden frenzied
modernity hurled itself with ineffable vigour into the country
dances of Edward German. Then, though the majority of
residents were content with such a programme, the orchestra
must also propitiate that select few who took pride in knowing
'what was going on' in London almost before Londoners
themselves had found out. This section of Newborough was,
apparently, satisfied that the only important happening in the
capital was the advent, and subsequent failure or success, of
the latest musical comedy. Nothing else counted. For the
Winter Garden band to be a fortnight late in their first reproduction of the strains which accompanied it — if it had proved
a 'hit' in London — would be, one understood, a local disaster
of the first magnitude. Thus, for the benefit and edification
of the select, the orchestra must rehearse feverishly, and perform quite soon, such forgotten favourites as *The Belle of New
York*, *The Geisha*, *San Toy*, *The Country Girl*, *The Messenger Boy*,
and innumerable other and equally popular variants of these
masterpieces.

Distributed round the centre of music was a mathematical
arrangement of seats ; while beyond, on the deaf side of the
bandstand — for it was glazed toward the sea — stretched a
long terrace, its farther wall dropping, according to the tides,
straight down on to sand or sea, rising out of them, shaded
toward the bottom with dark, tough seaweed and well
plastered with limpets and barnacles. This final and most
important promenade, from the whole length of which the
steps above are visible, was crowded with young women of a
provincial smartness, wearing dresses in such a height of
fashion that they would have been unrecognised in Paris or
London ; light-coloured young women from Leeds or Halifax,
with turquoise or false-pearl ear-rings jangling down hardly
on diminutive gold chains or screwed tight into the unpierced
ear. With them would stroll laughing young men in white-
flannel trousers, crowned with straw hats, or, more imposingly,

with panamas. The latter were a sign of grace and distinction but recently come into favour, entering hand in hand with ping-pong and the Boer War on a short but strenuous conquest of England. Cecil Rhodes had patronised them; and a good one, it was murmured, cost £100! Then there were the residents. Old military gentlemen, rather red and puffing, with long white mustachios, and heavy walking-sticks, are pacing up and down, their elbows out-turned, the two joints of the arm forming a right angle; they are continually pulling at their cuffs — stiff, white cuffs with coloured lines on them — as if on the point of conjuring, the verge of exhibiting, an alive but miraculous white rabbit. All the summer days they spend here, in-the-open-air-damn-it, and all the winter on the cliff above, with eyes fixed to the end of a gigantic telescope, pointed like a gun at the sea, in the bow-window of the commodious Gentlemen's Club, the exterior of which is painted a thick but appropriate magenta. Then, but sitting down more often than walking, there are groups of two or three old ladies, grey-haired, broad-based, who, if they move, sway a little from side to side like ducks on their way to the pond. There are always a few curates, thin, eager, and raven-coated, who have come down from the Ecclesiastical Rest Home on the West Cliff; while several bath-chairs are wheeled up and down or remain stationary — bath-chairs that, so near the sea, look like the gigantic shells of ocean snails, deposited and overturned by some fierce wave, their tenacious inhabitants, sadly out-of-element, stretching out wandering tentacles and adhesive surfaces. Finally, Newborough being a health resort, there is spread among the rest a whole cohort of infirm, elfin, and imbecile. As if in some nightmare drama, these men, women and children loll and lollop about, with curious uncouth gait, blind or deaf or dumb, hunchbacked or idiot, or armless from birth. But none of these, as they move among the throng, attract much attention. It must, therefore, be taken as a tribute to the personality of the Misses Cantrell-Cooksey that they should invariably claim such a measure of public notice on their arrival.

Perhaps the best place from which to witness their triumph was from one of the seats on the upper terrace, though the spectacle was visible, actually, from nearly every chair in the gardens. The flight of steps, like all monuments of its period both mean and magnificent, looked theatrical as well, as if set for some very material but ridiculous ballet of the Second Empire, some startling and quite pointless convolution of blue muslin, yellow hair, and arms and legs of full muscular development. In place, though, of this ordered and golden whirlwind came down the steps, treading very gingerly, yet unable in their good-natured weakness to resist keeping time to the domineering rhythm of the Waldteufel that greeted them, these two little elderly ladies of the same height and dressed alike. Sisters obviously; indeed, such was the resemblance between them that they might have been taken for twins. Mild and timid in bearing, they yet boasted a singular bravery of apparel, in which, though the nineteen-hundred note was dominant, there were many recollections of past fashions. They were bedizened and a-jingle with little crinkling ornaments, ruby bars, gold bangles, slave bracelets, small watches set with half-pearls hanging from enamelled brooches shaped like true-lovers' knots; they were decked out with little pieces of lace, numerous ribbons and a thousand other joyous trifles. Regarded more as objects of virtu than as the covering or decoration of human beings, their dress had a certain beauty, a very intricate quality of design — design that, while outwardly unconnected, had in it a strange rhythm and logic of its own. It was as full of *motifs* as Burmese art, and as complicated. If the band stopped playing, if every voice in the garden sank down for an instant, the dress of the Misses Cantrell-Cooksey would, one felt, play its own accompaniment, announce the entrance of its wearers. All these small, shining ornaments, apparently meaningless, would tinkle, trill, and jingle sweetly, giving out a sound peaceful and silly as any cow-bell heard in the Alps. But, alas! Waldteufel offered no such opportunity.

If their dresses were individual, so were their faces; for though the Age of Cosmetics had not yet returned to us, the cheeks of the two sisters, both of whom had surely seen sixty summers, were a blaze of Babylonish colour. The lips were of a cherry richness, and the hair, showing under the fashionable toque, was not so much golden or primrose as succulent scarlet. All this flaunting splendour was in rather quaint contrast to the gingerly tripping walk, the hair and cheek in direct contradiction to the pale but kindly timidity of their eyes — and, indeed, in the latter difference lay hidden the clue to their entire appearance. Determined to look young, they refused to wear glasses : and to insist on youth after it has passed requires sound eyesight as well as sound judgment. Resultantly, they looked like a pair of music-hall sisters, some popular variety turn of the late 'seventies, left over from that age but defiant of time — looked as though they had made up for their entertainment by the green, value-changing gaslight of mid-Victorian times, and after a Rip Van Winkle slumber, had woken to find themselves here, alone on the staircase, under the sunshine of the East Coast, in the hard dawn of a new, rather sinister, century.

Their appearance, in fact, as they descended the steps, was distinctly open to ridicule, yet so painfully lonely that it was with a feeling of relief that one saw them gain the upper terrace in safety, for the descent of these *opéra-bouffe* steps had taken a considerable time.

The numerous youths who were always to be found loitering on this platform, staring down at the people below, now turned round slowly, drew the knobs of their walking-sticks out of their mouths with a loud pop, as if a cork were being drawn, planted their backs firmly against the railings, and thus outlined against the sea, transferred the extreme vacancy of their gaze upon the two sisters, staring at them fixedly, and, after a time, smiling. The small boy selling programmes, and frilly-edged carnations of an ice-cream pink, made a ribald joke. But then, as the Misses Cantrell-Cooksey rounded the farther corner on to the steps that led below, the sensation on the first terrace began to die down. The youths once more pivoted round listlessly, their eyes following the bands of giggling young girls who strolled beneath them, staring in awe at the smartly dressed visitors, or resting quietly beyond on the similar blue vacancy of the sea.

When the two sisters arrived on the lower terrace, where the band played, there was again a distinct sensation. As they progressed down the middle of the audience, glancing from side to side in the hope of securing adjacent chairs, with a loftiness of manner that was the disguise both for bad eyesight and an intense shyness, a small, rustling, tittering wind moved the heads of the flower-bright rows of people, and even the groups walking up and down the promenade beyond stopped to watch. On the other hand, a few elder members of the feminine section of the audience — residents, probably — far from being amused, appeared to disapprove, quite definitely to disapprove.

Pretty Mrs. Sibmarsh, the wife of Dr. Sibmarsh, was sitting with her back to the sea talking to her friend, Mrs. Merryweather. As the two sisters went by, her face was contracted with a spasm of absolute fury. 'I don't know how they dare come down like that; I don't really!' she said in hard, even tones. 'Perfect sights I call them! Twenty-eight, indeed! more like sixty-eight! If you'd seen them, Mabel, at the Hospital Ball at the Royal the other night, dressed like débutantes, with white feathers in their hair. I'm surprised they were let in. They've been here about fifteen years now, and know no one; and I always say that if people have no friends, it is their own fault. And odd, odd to a degree! I can't bear people who aren't like anybody else . . . a little too odd for my taste!' And Mrs. Sibmarsh looked severely at the band and tiers of greenery above, for it was before she had become artistic and psychic, before she had begun to cultivate originality, before the coralline stethoscope of Dr. Sibmarsh, which, like a conjurer, he produced out of his top-hat, had reaped its asthmatic harvest, and her house had become, as her friends said, 'a perfect museum'— a wilderness of old oak and Staffordshire pottery. No, that story belongs to the subsequent development of Newborough, which one day we hope to relate. At present, then, oddity offended Mrs. Sibmarsh, and looking at them once more with an intense disgust she completed her verdict: 'Odd to a degree — and rich — very rich; and mean into the bargain! And to look at them, it wouldn't surprise me if they drugged! They've got a very queer look in their eyes.' And she sent up a shrill spiral of hard laughter into the blue air.

Owing to a fortunate concatenation of circumstances, it was some time before the Misses Cantrell-Cooksey discovered the disfavour with which they were regarded in the town. Indeed, at this period they were happy — more happy than they had ever been in their lives. Even their loneliness was not felt by them, so devoted was Miss Frederica to Miss Fanny, so devoted Miss Fanny to Miss Frederica. If they were both rather 'odd', as Mrs. Sibmarsh stated, yet the accusation of being unlike everybody else was unjust. On the contrary, they were all too human. Nor did they drug, as was suggested, but found their release from a reality which at any rate was not too hard upon them in material matters, in the roseate view of life inherent in those gifted with the Romantic Temperament. In fact they still believed in the Age of Miracles. They felt young, to each other looked young, and when, however seldom, a doubt assailed them as to whether they appeared as youthful to others as to themselves, they found a refuge in cosmetics. The rouge and dye-pot they affected were only the methods through which a laudable, very respectable desire to keep up appearances found its vent. But, while growing ever more devoted, while hardly noticing their lack of friends, themselves accentuated their isolation by the extreme vividness of their exterior. Otherwise, loneliness was no such uncommon thing in Newborough as to have attracted all this attention. Through their own fault, alas! they had made themselves targets for ridicule; and the vision of the town, a vision sharp and narrow, could not pierce through this extraordinary outward aspect to the essential goodness and kindness within.

Apart from the childish vanity that prompted the extravagance of their appearance, and the simplicity which led them to believe that Newborough would accept their own conservative estimate of their age, not much oddity was evident in them. These facts would lead one to suppose that they had always led rather secluded lives. This, then, would account for their being unaware of their loneliness, for their rather painful gaiety, and the resolution with which they participated in every local function. Thus were they making up for a youth that had lacked diversions by extreme merry-making in their latter years.

The daughters of a country clergyman, whom they had worshipped, and on whose behalf both of them in their young days had made certain sacrifices — suffered certain disappointments, one understood — they had found themselves, some fifteen years before the time of which we are speaking, possessed of a considerable fortune and alone in the world. For, unlike most of his calling, old Mr. Cantrell-Cooksey had been a rich man. Furthermore, the sisters were undoubtedly 'well-connected' — a fact which, owing to their disposition, afforded them a more constant and considerable pleasure than the inheritance of wealth, since, in its milder forms, snobbery is but a symptom of the Romantic Temperament.

They had been pretty, with a surface prettiness of skin and eye, golden hair and round, pale blue eye. The Rector would never, of course, for a moment have condoned the use of cosmetics, so that it was only when at his death they emerged from some forty-five years of seclusion, that they adopted such methods of beautifying themselves — methods not meant so much to attract others as to calm themselves. And one consequence of the pavonine glory into which they then blossomed was to make those valuable connections of theirs seem rather frigid in manner. The more rosy grew their skins, the more golden their hair, to that extent the less friendly grew their relatives. One season, the second summer after their father's death, they spent in London, but the neglect of their numerous cousins, the barren coldness of a great city in which they had no friends, were more than their sensitive hearts could bear for long: and sensitive their hearts undoubtedly were! It was a curious trait in their characters, pointing to some latent eccentricity in them, that while thus responsive, they should have still done nothing to tone down the intensity of their clothes and colouring. Surely they must have felt that there was some little connection between these and the coldness with which they were treated. Either their weak eyes must have prevented them from realising the full oddity of their appearance, or else their romantic disposition must have already and for ever warped their judgment.

They were well pleased to settle in the large red-brick house overhanging the cliffs at Newborough. Their dear father had been fond of the town, and though they had not visited it for many years, they had often been taken there as children and, as a place to live in, it suited them exactly. The Red House, appropriately named, was large, and besides what was described by the agents who disposed of it as its 'unique situation' — which consisted in the dangerous angle of the cliffs beneath — had the additional advantage of raking, enfilading indeed, the Promenade with its east-facing windows. In this new house the sisters began a life of peaceful happiness, and at the same time, contrasted with their former existence at the Rectory, of feverish excitement. They loved the house, and each one of the fifteen years they had spent in it had made it more dear to them. They liked the town — like is but a moderate term for the affection they felt for it — and were superbly unconscious of unfriendly eyes or cruel laughter. 'We like Newborough', Misses Frederica and Fanny would say together, as if with one voice, 'because there's always something going on — and then it's so pretty! We can never look out of our windows without being reminded of the Bay of Naples. In the summer there is always the band; and London is so *noisy* nowadays.' And they loved the house. Yes, they *loved* it. It wasn't quite like anyone else's. Oh, no! Not, of course, that it was 'queer' in any way — for the sisters, curiously enough, shared Mrs. Sibmarsh's horror of oddity. It was such a comfortable house, and had such a 'nice' garden, too, on the other side — quite like being in the country. It was difficult to imagine, when one was in it, that one was in a town. The garden, edged with split-oak palings, was full of speckled laurel bushes and dirty evergreens, graced in the spring by the spidery, thin mauve flowers of a few Indian lilacs, the dying fireworks of a laburnum tree with a hollow in its centre which had at some time been filled with cement, and later by a few perfectly correct but rather scentless roses. And in the autumn, chrysanthemums ('they do so well here') — beds and beds of chrysanthemums! The garden acted as clock for the seasons. Laburnum pointed to full spring, roses to full summer, chrysanthemums to rich autumn. Though Newborough was situated so far to the north, the climate seemed to them so mild — but very bracing, of course. The east winds were, perhaps, a little trying. Then everything had its disadvantages, hadn't it? And it was a source of the greatest pride to them that in the depths of winter, between Christmas and the New Year, it was usually possible to find one unfolded and frost-bitten rosebud, brown as if it had passed through the ordeal by fire, dank and dark as a drowned man — but a rose none the less — lurking in the garden. In fact this square space was a continual delight, so admirably suited for garden party or church bazaar, just big enough but not too big, and so convenient! But no function of any sort ever took place there.

Nevertheless, the sisters were always remarking to each other that it was 'so nice for entertaining one's friends'.

In anything they did or proposed to do, this phrase was for ever on their tongues. Whatever they contemplated was considered only in the light of aid or hindrance to the entertainment of this imaginary horde; an evidence of a need for friendship and of a hospitable disposition.

Beyond the garden, as far as the eye could see, rolled what in our childhood we were taught to regard as the 'German Ocean', displaying its various shrill and strident moods, lapping, singing, shouting, roaring or moaning. And this music, so romantic and strange, was always the pleasantest of sounds to the two sisters.

In the summer, as we have seen, Miss Frederica and Miss Fanny Cantrell-Cooksey would, on each fine day, walk down by the carefully preserved cliffs, through the trim woods, on to the terrace by the sea where the band played. They were due to arrive there between 11.15 and 11.30. In the afternoon — after lunch (at 1.15) — they would walk a little or sit in the garden. There were, of course, frequent rests, for one got so tired doing all these things, and lying-down freshens one up so. Tea at 4.30 with a large silver kettle, with a flame under it, silver teapot and silver sugar-basin. Ceylon, *not* Indian tea. The milk must, naturally, be poured *first* into the teacup. So many people fail to do this. And one must make the tea *oneself*: servants never learn to do it properly, do they? Emily, for instance, though she had been there many years, had never learnt to use boiling water. It must be *boiling* water. Miss Fanny, in person, would pour the water from the kettle into the teapot; and, in due time, Miss Frederica, the elder sister, would pour out the tea.

Tea, regarded not as a beverage but as a social function, was one of their extravagances — for though few people came, unless Archdeacon Haddocriss looked in to tell them about one of his new funds, it was always prepared for ten people. Lots of little cakes; and scones, supported on a bowl filled with hot water. There were certain days, however, when, if the ladies felt the need for some unusual excitement, they would inform Emily that they would be out for tea, and would walk to one of those artistic and half-timbered cafés which were becoming such a feature of the town, where, beneath Gothic canopies of fumed German oak, and by simple dressers of peasant and cottage crockery, in a stifling atmosphere of English coffee and strong tea, they would partake of a cup of chocolate — very dainty — with the white of an egg frothed on top of it to represent cream. This would appeal to their feelings, reminding them, as it did, of that visit to Germany, in company with their Dear Old Father, some fifteen — or was it fourteen? — years before he passed away. Thus stimulated, they would return home.

Dinner, the crown of the day for every respectable inhabitant of Newborough, was at 7.30 P.M. The Misses Cantrell-Cooksey had always been used to dinner at this hour, so for them it was nothing unusual. But for most of the well-to-do in the town, dinner was a shibboleth, its hour dividing mankind — not so much a meal as a Declaration of the Rights of Man. A whole revolution was fixed between those who enjoyed their dinner at midday, and those who dined in the evening. Between those addicted to late dinner and those who still revelled in the primitive simplicity of high-tea was fixed such a gap in the social ranks as could never be bridged. And for the former, two things were of the utmost importance. One of these was never, in any evil hour or by any unfortunate accident, to refer to the midday meal under any other title than 'luncheon' — or perhaps the more familiar, more vulgar, 'lunch'. Dr. Sibmarsh had, for instance, once referred to it in public as 'dinner' — and it took him long to live down. The other, and even more vital, thing to keep in mind, was the absolute necessity of 'dressing' for dinner. Invariably, inevitably, one must 'dress' for dinner — otherwise the nature of the meal might be mistaken! Once 'dressed' one was secure, since no man 'dresses' for high tea.

Thus in every red-brick villa in Newborough at 7.30 on a summer evening the dining-room would be illuminated; the electric light would show splendidly in its mounting of chased or wrought copper through shades, bell-like shades, of opalescent glass; and, though it was still daylight without, if one were lucky enough to walk down Prince of Wales's Avenue or Albemarle Road at this hour, one would see row after row of these glowing interiors, the very pageant of late Victorian and early Edwardian prosperity. Beneath the golden lustre of four lights that hung from the ceiling, seated before a white table, in the centre of which was usually a large doily composed of lace over a ground of dead-orange silk, upon which would stand four little trumpet-shaped silver vases, with frilled edges like sharks' teeth, each displaying at this season three or four

yellow poppies, four or five sweet-peas, and misty bunches of
that nameless though universal white blossom that is more like
white muslin than a flower, the diners would be sitting, carefully dressed. The hostess, in a pretty gown of pink satin,
low at the bosom and with puffy sleeves, wearing an amethyst
or aquamarine brooch, would be talking amiably and sweetly
— wearing that charming smile that made such a difference
to her face, 'lit it up', as the phrase was — to the gentleman
on her right, while at the same time directing a glance of such
flaming contempt at her maid-servant for falling into those
very mistakes of service about which she had warned her all
day — and as for that, just a moment before dinner — striking
her dead with a look of such awful, such diabolical hatred
that any other mortal, except this girl accustomed to it, would
on the spot have perished and sunk down. The earth itself
might well open beneath such vehement passion — so well
disguised.

The rules-of-the-game, too, were very strict. It was not,
even, an easy affair to get into the dining-room; for again in
this it was necessary to disprove the possible if unspoken
allegation of transcendentalised high tea. If there were more
than four or five guests, a regular and courtly procession
would walk across the small space from drawing-room to
dining-room: arm-in-arm: lady on right, gentleman on left:
polite, but easy, conversation. If, however, there were but a
few people, three or four, the same effect could be produced
by saying in a careless Bohemian way: 'Oh, don't let's bother.
Can't we go in as we are?'

Fortunately Emily was seldom forgetful, and unfortunately,
it was seldom that Miss Frederica or Miss Fanny Cantrell-
Cooksey was able to sweep in to dinner on the arm of a cavalier.
If, though, one was alone for dinner — and had not got a
headache — one could go down to hear the band again.
When the evenings were cool, the orchestra, escaped from
their glass case, were sure to be playing 'inside'. 'Inside'
indicated an enormous hall near the bandstand, built to look
as if it were part of the Louvre — Newborough architecture
was both informed and cosmopolitan — and tastefully decorated
within, in a Second Empire scheme of chocolate, turquoise-
blue and gold — all by now very faded and dry-looking, like
an old sugared biscuit. Round the frieze, high up, were

inscribed on scrolls the names of composers at the height of their fame when this hall was constructed. A queer medley it was, and one that would be an interesting footnote to that *History of Taste* which is now waiting to be written — for these names, considered then of equal value, represented the judgment of a generation . . . MENDELSSOHN . . . HANDEL . . . SPOHR . . . BEETHOVEN . . . GOUNOD . . . VERDI . . . SCHUMANN . . . WEBER . . . DONIZETTI . . . BERLIOZ . . . LISZT.

The hall had been specially built for music, but unfortunately the acoustic properties were such that not a note could be heard properly, except from the roof, where the sound was as nearly perfect as possible, but there were no chairs! The concerts were nevertheless much appreciated. Every evening the bandsmen became suddenly transformed into individuals, escaping from a sober uniform into evening dress; became definitely recognisable as persons. This, again, affected their playing, making it more individual, less a composite whole. The two ladies had in some mysterious way conceived a great passion for the music of Wagner; and since in the evening performances the conductor, who prided himself on being catholic and modern, was allowed more to please himself than in the mornings, they were often able to gratify this passion. Perhaps this Wagner-worship was one of the oddities to which Mrs. Sibmarsh had alluded: it was a curious phenomenon certainly, for otherwise they were devoid of any musical appreciation. But there is no doubt that, as much as anything in Newborough, they enjoyed sitting here in the evenings, and wallowing in the sensual melodies of that master, as in a hot bath.

In addition to these concerts there were, in the season, other entertainments. Touring companies would come down for six nights to the two theatres, the 'Royal' and the 'Ghoolingham'. Our two heroines did not often visit these, except during the annual appearance of the D'Oyly Carte Gilbert and Sullivan Opera Company. For this event, to which all the year they looked forward, it was their habit to book a box on the opening night and a stall for each subsequent performance. Such pretty music, and oh! how witty and amusing. And nothing in bad taste, nothing that anybody need be offended at! Even the Rector, who had not much cared for festivities, had thoroughly enjoyed *The Gondoliers*. Otherwise they did not go much to the theatre unless it was something special. Then, out of curiosity, they would book seats. Once, for instance, they had been to hear Sousa's Band, which paid a flying visit to the Ghoolingham. What an extraordinary man! how extraordinary it all was, so noisy and vulgar! Still, the marches were most inspiring, one must say, and so patriotic! He had, had he not, a true gift of melody?

Then there were the occasional appearances at a special performance of famous but ageing actresses — Lady Bancroft and Mrs. Kendal — or of indomitable but ageless beauties such as Mrs. Langtry. It would be a pity to miss such a treat. Thus there was always something going on.

This continual round of diversion was broken every seventh day by church-going, the event of the week. Now that the Rector was no longer with them they went to church only *once* on a Sunday (churches are so badly ventilated); in the morning. After church ensued church-parade. This took place on the promenade overlooked by the Red House, and lasted until the luncheon hour.

Clasping a black-bound Prayer Book, divided by a vivid blue or purple watered-silk marker, in a well-gloved hand, and gorgeous as the Queen of Sheba, Miss Frederica and Miss Fanny Cantrell-Cooksey would walk — though 'walk' hardly describes such stately progress . . . march . . . saunter . . . up and down, as would all the other respectable inhabitants and worthy visitors. It was, consciously, one of the 'prettiest' sights of the town, and, what was of more importance, an observance that helped to keep up appearances.

Innumerable people walked up and down, up and down — individuals for a moment, then dovetailing into the crowd. Most of them were elderly — though there were a few children — and looked incongruous in clothes of such elaboration, as must all people of over middle-age who adopt a minutely decorated style. For a surfeit of decoration is no more suitable to the elderly than a surfeit of food. Up and down they paced, under the hard northern sunlight, anthropoids that having massacred a diverse regiment of beasts-of-the-field now masquerade in their pitiable skins; to the latter they have added the feathers raped from the osprey, and now look as though decorated for some primitive, some awful, rite. Up and down they progress, past cream-painted houses, roofed

with damp-blue slates; on each sill is a box of red geraniums,
before each house a stretch of green, prim grass. Far below,
constant companion to their march, rolls the steely northern
sea : the prospect on the other side varies. The cream-painted
houses give way to golden lawns, the colour of which is enhanced by an artistic green-painted cab-shelter covered in by
red tiles, a recent inspiration of the municipal architect : then,
again, follow Gothic stone drinking troughs for beasts, and
portentous stone houses for men. Not all the people walk. A
few drive in large open cabs, that rumble slowly; while
others, ladies of fabulous age, with trembling blue lips and
palely purple faces, with hairy growths on the chin, and black
bonnets nodding on the top of their helpless heads, are being
drawn along in bath-chairs that are so many black insects.
As they are rolled past, in a flutter of bugles, heliotrope-velvet
ribbons and black kid gloves, there is a trilling of jet-like
petrified laughter. Each venerable image, thus trundled,
would be accompanied by a niece or daughter, pale, flat-
looking women with vague but crucified expressions, like the
female saints whose tortures are depicted by German Primitives.
The aunts and mothers in their bath-chairs look happy though
grim ('poor old things', the Misses Cantrell-Cooksey would
say, rather nervously) as they clasp a Prayer Book tightly in
their gloved hands, as if it were a passport for that equally
tedious Heaven which they had prepared for themselves.
Already there sounded from them the characteristic music of
their Heaven, asthmatic and wheezy; so old were they that
when through blue lips they murmured, their voices sounded
like harmoniums played at a distance; and when their faces
were in repose, the bones would show under the sagging parch-
ment, for the skull was already asserting its lordship over
the flesh.

In this setting our heroines showed almost to advantage.
Yet as they went by, while other promenaders would be
continually stopped by friends, and would stand talking
together in little groups, they would never be greeted. The
old ladies would stretch out tentacles from their shells in
welcome to others; but our two friends would never be
hailed by them. Indeed, the old ladies would be galvanised
into life by the sight of them, looking at them as sourly as
any younger members of the community. The burden of

their complaint was the same as that uttered by Mrs. Sibmarsh. 'Perfect sights! How they can get themselves up like
that I can't think! And they were properly brought up too.
Twenty-eight, indeed! they'll never see sixty-eight again, I
should say! Real Aunt Sallies!' And after some such
declamatory effort their voices would ooze back to a whisper.

In among the promenaders and listening groups Mrs. Sibmarsh herself was continually imparting information. 'Have
you heard the latest, Mrs. Spirechurch? What do you
think those two old bundles have done now?' And many a
macabre march was halted for an instant in order to hear a
recital of the latest Cantrell-Cooksey folly. About three years
before, the two ladies had undoubtedly given their age in the
census return as twenty-eight and twenty-six respectively. By
7.30 the next night every dining-room in the town was discussing this lamentably absurd lapse from verity. It became,
this topic, another thing that divided dinner from high tea.
It lightened the life of Newborough; and, ever since, each
movement or saying of the sisters had become an object of
mingled interest and contempt.

On wet Sundays — which were almost as enjoyable as fine
ones — Miss Frederica and Miss Fanny would drive to and
from church in their heraldic 'Lonsdale Wagonette'. This
vehicle, of which they were intensely proud, was regarded by
others almost as the symbol of original sin. It was, in
truth, an odd conveyance: a large, long, polished, black,
roomy affair, lined with railway-carriage-blue material; indeed
the interior was not unlike a railway carriage, except that the
windows were above the seats, one narrow end turned toward
the horses. Whichever seat one occupied, one's back shut out
the view, while the view opposite was likewise obscured by some
person. When the door shut, the step shut with it; when the
door opened, the step precipitated one upon the pavement.
How either of the two ladies ever got in or out of their conveyance, with their weak eyes and faltering footsteps, remains
one of the mysteries of the past! The coachman, smartly
dressed in a buff coat, sat — immense — on the box, while
the door had emblazoned on it the very rampant arms of
Cantrell-Cooksey. The wagonette was, really, an extraordinary
creation; one of the last, most imbecile inventions of equine
traffic, originally intended to aid the more rapid and complete

incarceration of guests in various country houses. Its owners, however, were very content, regarding it as the supreme achievement of civilisation. It was neater and more unusual-looking than a brougham or victoria; not so 'fast' — in any sense — as a tandem; and how much nicer than those horrible, snorting motor-cars that were coming in! Not that they would ever be seen in one of those things; so trippery. And then the 'Lonsdale', most important quality, was so hospitable. There was room in it for one's friends. It would hold at least eight people, where a brougham would hold three, and it would be so useful for picnics in the Sherbourn Woods. In fact this lumbering conveyance made a special appeal to the Romantic Temperament.

Sunday afternoons in the season were also very pleasant, for there were concerts in the Winter Gardens at 3.30. The band, discarding its uniform, would adopt frock-coats, while the conductor would walk round the corner into his glass case, curling a waxed military moustache and sporting a top-hat. When securely within the shelter, the bandsmen would stand up to greet him; he would take off his hat, turn round, and bow. *God Save the King* — for it was Sunday — would then be played. Usually a *vocalist* would come down from London for these concerts (a vocalist is a very different thing from a singer — more sabbatical). The vocalist, running to extremes, was generally a very young girl or very old man. The pro-grammes of these concerts were, of course, composed of sacred music, and were regarded by the town as being 'very classical'. Some, even, took objection to them on this score, for not all Newborough enjoyed 'classical' music. The adjective had a special significance. For the town divided all sounds made by piano, orchestra, or human voice into two categories: 'classical' music and — just music! Music meant *The Country Girl*, *The Belle of New York*, Offenbach, Waldteufel and, generally, anything that had 'a tune in it'; Sullivan — except for *The Lost Chord*, acknowledged as sacred — was an exception, belonging to both worlds, pagan and 'classical', but universally popular. Then came the 'classical' division, com-prising any composers who had comprehended and used the rules of counterpoint, the laws of harmony, and at the same time any mid-Victorian composer, who, neglecting both, had written anthems or oratorios. For sacred music was the inner and spiritual core of 'classical' music. Furthermore, it was understood that any music played on an organ became transmuted in some mysterious fashion into sacred music. And, by virtue of this, Wagner had crept into the Sunday Afternoon Concerts, as a sort of Honorary Sacred Composer; for it was well known that the organist at Holy Trinity — the best organist in all Newborough — played Wagner at his recitals. Thus our two ladies were privileged to bathe in those luscious strains each Sunday.

After music came tea again, at five o'clock, half an hour later than usual. It was always nice to have a cup of tea.

This routine continued through their fifteen years of prosperity, from about May 24th till September 27th. About this latter date, every year, it would occur simultaneously to many that the evenings were drawing in. Chrysanthemums would strike a rich note of gloom and warning in many gardens, and through the windows of the Red House, especially, would be borne-in their peculiarly muffled and musty smell, mildewed and damp as the air of the tomb. Poor old Miss Waddington — whom they saw from time to time — would inaugurate the winter season with one of those cyclone colds that were her unique gift. Bath-chairs would disappear from the Promenade and Winter Gardens. The band would be dispersed, its members drifting away to London or to various theatre-orchestras elsewhere, and soon the whole town would be echoing with the more wintry music of howling gale, roaring sea, and their domestic equivalents, wheezing, sneezing, snoring and coughing. Blinds would be drawn down for tea. There would be comfortable fires; the yellow wallpaper of the drawing-room would take on a warmer tone, the large oil-picture of 'Sunset, Egypt' of which old Mr. Cantrell-Cooksey had been so fond, a richer glow; and all would burn more brightly again in the various items of the silver equipment on the tea-table. Christmas, it would be felt — in the Red House, and universally — will soon be here again. Already the shops would be getting ready for it, with an ever-increasing number of imbecile 'novelties' and a great display of red flannel and cotton-wool snow.

The winter festivities would start in mid-November. Every five weeks there would be a hospital ball, a hunt ball even — so picturesque with all the red coats and bits of foxes and things — or perhaps a concert in aid of the local lifeboat, or the performance of the Newborough Philharmonic Society which took place every six months; these concerts were also very picturesque — quite a sight indeed — with all the girls in white dresses and all the men in black and white evening clothes. In every one of these gaieties Miss Frederica and Miss Fanny Cantrell-Cooksey would, for a varying payment, participate. Yet at the most spirited and exhilarating of these functions it may be surmised that though clad in a low-cut glory unequalled by any other ladies present, though boasting diamond constellations fixed in their hair like those stars that twinkle so brightly above the head of the Queen of the Fairies in a pantomime, the two ladies were more lonely even than in their unfrequented house. Not, one imagines, that they realised quite what it was they felt; for as the only form of human companionship to which they were accustomed was to be together but otherwise alone, or else to be together in a crowd but equally alone, since few spoke to them or acknowledged their presence, they were not so much aware of the separation from their kind as to let it altogether spoil their pleasure. In order fully to appreciate the honour of being sent to Coventry, it is necessary to have experience of other countrysides and towns. Such had never been the lot of our heroines. Nevertheless, as they left concert or ball, as wrapped in filmy, feathery cloaks they waited outside on the doorstep for the arrival of their Lonsdale — which, in spite of their constant generosity to the commissionaire, was always the last to be ushered up to the door — an inexplicable and terrible feeling of depression would assail them. Perhaps, they thought, it was only the reaction that follows on intense enjoyment. It was curious, though, for in the Rectory they had experienced no such feelings. But then life at the Rectory had not been so full of pleasure and excitement, had it, dear?

When the Carnival Ball (Costumes Voluntary) took place in February, in aid of the Children's Convalescent Home, a riot was very nearly provoked in fashionable circles by the two sisters. Few people wore fancy dress. The arrival, therefore, of Miss Frederica as a Dresden Shepherdess and Miss Fanny as Carmen was all the more noticeable. Miss Frederica wore a white-powdered wig, a sprigged-muslin dress, carried a crook, and had one very captivating black patch near the chin; while Miss Fanny, particularly alluring in a bright red gown in which sequins glittered like a rainbow, and with an orange Spanish shawl flung jauntily round her shoulders, cast sparkling glances over her fan from those weak, pale eyes. It was rather an appalling spectacle, this *danse macabre*, though they enjoyed it thoroughly, quite unaware of the sensation caused. They stood among the waiting groups of young girls at the ballroom door, or sat together by one of the walls. But Newborough never forgot: it ranked as an event, as a topic, with that census return.

In the winter, too, there were countless bazaars in aid of various charities — not so important as the ones that took place in the summer, but more of them, and, in a sense, more exciting, more personal. The great lady of the district, Lady Ghoolingham, let it be understood that though willing to open an infinity of bazaars and sales of work in July or August, nothing and no one would, or ever should, induce her to face the harsh winter winds of Newborough, the cold of the railway carriage that would take her there from London, or the over-heated atmosphere of the restaurant car, full of that mysterious and emetic scent of cabbage that haunts it always in the winter. It became necessary, then, for the organisers of good works to find continual substitutes for Lady Ghoolingham. And the Misses Cantrell-Cooksey would often remark to each other that they could not — no, they could not — think what they would do if Archdeacon Haddocriss should ask them to perform some such ceremony on his behalf. You see, it must be quite twenty years since Miss Frederica had opened that one for her father at Hubbard Stanton, and that was only a jumble sale! But Miss Fanny had seen the Archdeacon out that morning, and thought he had looked rather as if he wanted to ask something. No, she wouldn't be at all surprised; and if Frederica was asked, it would hardly be graceful to refuse. . . . Alas! the venerable gentleman knew that if out of respect for their wealth and generosity he invited one of 'those two gaudy old scare-crows' — as he had heard them termed in his presence — to open any function, or even so much as to appear on the platform, the parish would be rent in twain. There would be civil war. If he wanted trouble of that sort, he might just as well introduce ritualism at once.

We have noticed, in passing, some of the minor eccentricities

335   M

of the two sisters, which might possibly justify the charge brought against them of 'oddness', but now we come to other, more marked, peculiarities. Every fine morning or afternoon in the winter they would, like most other respectable inhabitants of the town, call at the lending library to exchange their novels. There was nothing very unusual in this, except that little Mr. Garrett, behind the counter, founder of the establishment, had become almost a friend. He was more friendly to them than were most of the townsfolk. Like other habituals of the library, they would demand a new novel every day — something 'amusing' and 'light' — an E. F. Benson, for example — and, unlike them, would actually get it. Mr. Garrett was such a nice polite little man. A pity he was so untidy! They would then leave the library, exchanging its warm smell of cloves, sealing-wax and thumbed volumes, for the salt air outside. Coming out into the air was, indeed, like being hit in the face, at this time of year. And now they would turn their steps towards the sea-front! This was considered an extraordinary thing to do. Of all the wealthier members of the community, they were the only two who did not conspire to regard the sea as non-existent except in the summer months. All the rest of them forgot the ocean till the first spring day, and preferred to walk in the streets, among the shops, away from the fierce white wings of spray that fluttered and flapped up over the stout stone walls below. Every day in the winter, when it was not actually raining, our heroines, with that love of extremes — great light and great shadow, sun and black cloud — which is the portion of those afflicted with the Romantic Temperament, would walk by the cold, tumbling brown cliffs along the tawny sands, away, even, from the humanised sea-front. Especially after a storm would they enjoy walking along the lonely white sands. Their scarlet hair, their faces so badly made-up that the expression of each side would vary as if one half of the mask were tragic, the other comic, their absurd and complicated dresses, looked all the more fantastic for this submarine setting; and such it seemed after a storm, some strange undersea view. The sloping, pebbly border of sand and sea would be littered with a wild disarray of broken glass, worn down to round gleaming jewels by the constant fret and foaming of the breakers, of starfish, sea-urchins and queer-shaped monstrosities, heaped up with seaweed like small brown palm-trees or the long black matted hair of mermaids. There were so few people about, and the few there were would haunt the sands each day. There was always a tramp, keeping in to the shelter of the rocks, a little bent man with a thin red beard, a battered bowler hat and a torn frock-coat, a queer parody of prosperity. Then there were the gatherers of limpets and winkles, who would pile up their salt harvest in scaly baskets. One of these men, especially, they noticed — a broad bacchanalian character, with huge northern physique, who ought to have found work harder and more remunerative than this. Him they would see bent nearly double over the flat rocks that were covered by the sea at high tide, as with a knife he removed the molluscs and threw them into the deep basket at his side.

And, most interesting of all, after a storm there would gather together those men who make a living by combing the golden sands. What profession they followed in between the gales, or where they came from, it was impossible to find out. The bacchanalian character would join them, deserting his limpets and winkles for this more profitable and entertaining employment. They would rake over the slope of pebbles and the sands beneath, just at the point where the high tide deposited its hostages. It was a gentle but fascinating exercise, and one requiring very competent eyesight and a certain agility of mind. The sisters would stand there for many minutes watching the alternately romantic and prosaic treasury which the storm had precipitated on these bleak sands. As the men combed, they would find silver pennies of the Plantagenets, old biscuit tins full of sea-biscuits, gold coins from Spain, a piece of rusty armour that had been gnawed by the waves for centuries, coppers that had been thrown to the pierrots in the summer, a glass bottle with a faded message in it — the family to which this agonised scrawl was addressed had been dead these ten years! — a bit of a weighing-machine that had stood on the sands in the summer, a Dutch cheese still round and fresh and cherry-coloured, a long clasp-knife with a curious tortoise-shell handle — all the trifles that time and the cruel tides had left over. Really Miss Frederica and Miss Fanny felt that they could stand here for hours watching, if it was not for the cold. Even when they had walked away a little, they would return for a last glimpse. Gradually a bond grew up between them and these strange diggers for treasure. To the latter there was such a break in the surface of the world between themselves and the dwellers on the West Cliff, that these two queerly caparisoned elderly women, with their dyed hair and painted faces, seemed no further removed from everyday experience than any others of their class. They were a funny lot, ladies and gentlemen! But these two, though they asked constantly to which parish the treasure-seekers belonged, also distributed shillings. Suspicion was allayed. 'It was meant kindly', the men thought, and in the presence of Miss Fanny and Miss Frederica the very living language of the fish-market was stifled by unexpected better feelings.

In short, to watch these men at their work was, to the two sisters, like looking-on at gambling. And here we have the second secret. This was the spark of passion that burned in them. In spite of the quiet orderliness of home and upbringing, these two ladies were, by nature, born gamblers. But for many years timidity, not of the possible consequences — for these held no terrors for them — but of the means and methods by which gambling could respectably be effected, had deterred them from rash action. They must not do anything 'fast'. Horse-racing was out of the question, since their father would never have countenanced the smallest bet. It must be very absorbing, though, they thought. Monte Carlo, too, was a dreadful place, full of *queer* people : never a morning went by — the Rector had told them — except a revolver shot rang out a life. One did not always see these tragedies reported in the Press, because the Casino authorities hushed them up. It was disgraceful — a blot on Europe ; but then, of course, queer people *would* do queer things. And foreigners were so queer, what with Monte Carlo and bull-fighting and things like that!

Their own method of gambling would not be gambling, so much as speculation ; quite a different matter. And for them an unfortunate sequel to their actions was incredible. Security had ever stood by them. Their world was not subject to these chances, these accidents, but was a solid affair of Law-and-Order, Church-and-State, governed for sixty years by Queen Victoria and now inherited by her worthy and popular son ('God Save the Queen' . . . somehow they felt they would never get used to 'God Save the King' . . . it sounded so funny, didn't it? . . .). Investments were not like gambling at Monte Carlo, but part of an ordered and stately society. 'The very life-blood of commerce' they had read in a *Times* leading article, not long ago. No ill would befall them, for they, too, were part of an ordering of the world. It had pleased God to call them to their position. And things were going on as well as could be expected, considering that the Queen was dead. The Income Tax, though deprecated by all Newborough, was negligible; and the pale spectres of disaster and revolution were still stalking the outer confines of the world, to which they had been banished by the general prosperity, unable as yet to make a sufficiently imposing reappearance on the modern stage after such long exile. The Boer War was dreadful, but apart from the revelation of human brutality and degradation offered by the obstinate desire to fight on behalf of their country shown by those brutal, bearded farmers, there had never been really much reason for worry. After all, we were an island, and brute force had never won yet! And we had the Navy, and our generals too. Of course it was true that there were 'cranks' at large in London, 'Fabians' who wished to overturn the whole system of civilised society. But one did not hear much of them now at Newborough. And since the ordering of the world had been ordained by God, it could hardly be upset except by the Devil himself; and even he would not prevail for long.

If they gambled, being part of the ordering of this world, they would win. Of course they would win! Their temperament assured them of success, and urged them to find the means. Ever since the death of their father they had been able to gratify every desire within a limited circle — that wagonette, for example! If they could find some method of gambling which — since success was inevitable—meant that they could double or treble their income, two birds would be killed with one stone. For, while it would satisfy their need for excitement, the extra wealth accruing to them would thus enable them to buy more 'Lonsdales' — taking 'Lonsdales' as the symbol of worldly ambition. It never occurred to them that there was a penalty attached to possible failure. They had not the nervousness of the very rich. Yet the absence to them of danger did not make the game any less exciting.

Some years before the time of which we are writing, Miss

Frederica had, after a period of study, found the way. Her conclusion was that herself and her sister should sell out of Consols, which now only brought in 2½ per cent, part with their other gilt-edged securities, and invest in one of her own discoveries. Miss Fanny, implicit believer in Frederica's genius, at once concurred.

The elder lady, like many of her generation, had been greatly impressed by the towering genius of Cecil Rhodes — a millionaire was then regarded as a being of high romance, a Napoleon of Finance, a Caesar of Commerce — and by his roseate views of the future in store for South Africa. With utter faith in his views and in the solidity of wealth, Miss Frederica invested most of their joint fortunes in South African Mines and other speculative concerns. Their trustees, in this case powerless to forbid, implored them not to alter their old investments. But Miss Frederica knew better. She knew — for the newspapers had told her — that one must Think Imperially. What were those lines of Kipling's?

She wrote a severe, identical letter to trustees and lawyer, in which she pointed out that one must cease 'thinking in a *narrow* little way', adjured them to put away notions inherited from the past, and to realise that we were, all of us, treading (and how true were her words) on the path that would lead us to an Imperial Tomorrow.

Not one single word of these unusual developments reached Newborough, and for some time the ladies prospered almost as much as they had anticipated. Soon, though, the first cracks appeared in the ice upon which they were skating; but warnings held no meaning for them, and were not heeded. Another year passed. Nothing exceptional transpired. The summer passed, and they were a little behindhand with their accounts. The winter began, and the storms raged.

One afternoon they had been down to the sands, as was their custom, to watch the disentangling of that irrelevant treasure accumulated by the northern waves. As they walked along the Promenade they noticed that the storm was dying down. The lamp-lighter was pursuing his magic calling, and as he touched the lamps with his tall wand there was no flicker of wind and light. The blinds were already down at home. But a rich glow showed through them. It looked so comfortable. The postman had been, too. And a letter was waiting for them. Their tomorrow had come, and they were ruined.

. . . . .

So rooted were they in material prosperity, so protected had been every thought in all their lives from any frosty breath of reality, that at first they were not so much worried as excited. But then, suddenly, the world began to take on the most unexpected and unpleasant contours. Action, for the first time, came into touch with them. Their loss unlocked the gate, and all the aversion and contempt in which they were held came pouring out, overwhelming them in a filthy, muddy torrent. Little pity showed in any face. Even those who had greatly prospered by the worldly possessions of the Misses Cantrell-Cooksey, tradesmen and their like, could not now see any further reason to disguise their feelings, however carefully they had concealed them before. People became offhand, and so rude. Some had always disliked them for their 'oddness' (they had never been like other ladies), while the rest were jealous, feeling that to be ruined was a luxury of the rich. Miss Frederica and Miss Fanny felt that they could stand anything but rudeness, for even yet our two heroines could not envisage the full consequences. Their instinct was to keep up appearances; and this was their courage. Not one word of reproach passed between them, not by one syllable would either admit that the world had changed. Everything now depended on keeping up appearances, on seeming not to mind. The fear was there, buried and smothered, but the material pinch was as yet absent.

They were perhaps a little more excitable now in their manner — on the verge of a breakdown, I thought. Miss Fanny, the injured one, had nothing but soothing and heartfelt compassion for her sister, who, though she would not discuss their calamities, would sit alone, silent, and trembling. Before Miss Fanny she was different, more talkative, more uneasy, for in truth she felt too ashamed and remorseful in front of her handiwork to utter, but she must keep up appearances.

In every shuttered red-brick villa, in every avenue and terrace in the town, the Cantrell-Cooksey affair was discussed at 7.30 each night. Folly of this sort was felt, generally, to be equal to villainy. It was, Mrs. Sibmarsh opined, more than a personal disgrace on the two painted old hags; it was a blot on the fair name of the town. What would tradesmen think that Newborough was coming to? Running up bills with no intention of paying them. An absolute disgrace! But then one only had to look at their eyes . . .

Other people were kind but rather inquisitive. Old Miss Waddington, who happened to be laid up with a bronchial cold that was bad enough to prevent her leaving the house, even on such a visit of commiseration as this one would be, sent her niece across to them at once. The latter returned to her aunt in a marvellously short time with a full budget of information, and Miss Waddington seemed really to be 'more herself' that evening, and had a glass of port after dinner, which she seldom did — invalid port, of course. The Archdeacon, too, was kind, very kind. Directly he heard of the affair he came round to the Red House (the sisters were still in it) and offered to say a prayer with them. Afterwards he addressed a few solemn words to them on secret vices, and, arising out of this, on the particular iniquity of avarice and gambling. But his words served no purpose, because, even if the Misses Cantrell-Cooksey had wished to continue such a career, they had now nothing with which to feed their passion. Avarice would be henceforth a difficult vice for them to practise.

The house was sold. The horses were sold. Everything went, and was lost to them beneath the ghastly sound of the hammer. The Lonsdale fetched but seven pounds. Even the silver teapot, kettle and equipment were taken from them. Nothing remained except a few of their old clothes — which did not prove very attractive items at the sale — and some photographs. The servants had left, two by two, as if leaving the ark on an excursion, laughing, happy and without leave-taking, a few days before the Public Examination.

This event was the wonder of all Newborough, and the charge of 'oddnesss', so often brought against the sisters, was fully borne out by their demeanour in court. The suggestion that they drugged — for drink was too trite an explanation of such behaviour — was widely accepted by that more temporal section of the community which, although it existed in a seaside town, was alive to all that was going on in London, knew every musical-comedy success, had visited all the large hotels there for dinner on Sunday night, and had thus acquired a thorough knowledge of the greater and more wicked world. No secret vice could for long be hidden from them.

Rouged, dyed and a-rattle with little ornaments, Miss Frederica and Miss Fanny arrived in court. Their answers were mostly inaudible, except that when Miss Frederica was asked where she was born, she replied that she did not know, and, in answer to the next question, gave her age as twenty-eight; and then broke down.

The total outcome of the affair was that the Misses Cantrell-Cooksey of the Red House were now left homeless, with twenty-six pounds a year between them. With unexpected generosity a few distant but notable relatives, to whom the Archdeacon sent a written appeal, came forward and made up the sum to fifty-two pounds a year — on the condition that the extra twenty-six pounds per annum should be divided into a fortnightly allowance of one pound, and given to them personally, every other Saturday, by a responsible individual. For the relatives were determined that there should be no more extravagance, no more gambling. Finally, dear old Miss Waddington, in spite of growing infirmity and advancing age, volunteered for the office of bursar. She was fond of good works.

The relatives considered that the two sisters should now find some work to do, and perhaps in time relinquish their allowance. They ought to make an EFFORT, they ought to DO SOMETHING. People must learn to support themselves. However, even Archdeacon Haddocriss, sensible man as he was, had to admit to himself that it was difficult to know for what exact profession the two ladies were fitted.

Now, indeed, the pinch had come and the excitement had gone. But the two sisters kept up appearances to each other — for no one else was taken in! 'The worst of it is', they would say, 'that we shall never be able to entertain our friends again.' Though the physical deprivations, to which they were condemned from this time forward, became gradually manifest, and must, after such a comfortable life, have seemed more cruel, neither of them ever mentioned these. Even less than mental torture can cold and hunger be acknowledged by respectable members of society. Once their presence was admitted, even tacitly admitted, self-respect would go out of the window.

At any rate it looked very clean. That was a comfort! Their room was right at the top.

The tall boarding-house, fronted with that particular white brick which is only to be encountered at seaside resorts, rose like a tower of ice, with blue shadows, from beside a suspension-bridge. The Gothic doorway, carved with cast-iron ivy leaves, had a crooked notice, 'Apartments', stuck against the glass above the door, like a rakish patch over a very Wesleyan eye. The white side of the house, fronting the street which was a continuation of the bridge, was only five storeys high; but the back of the house went down another two storeys: here the brown brick of which it was built showed undisguised, and rising among tall green trees and slopes of grass — for the back looked out on the Dale — a public pleasure-ground — it lost some of its horror, becoming merely a high brown tower. The Misses Cantrell-Cookseys' room was the top one on the street side, under the tall gable covered with rain-blue slates. The window, from the street, looked like a sinister eye. Inside, the bottom of the window was on a level with the floor, while the top of it was so low down that it was necessary to bend in order to get the view from it. The vista it disclosed was made up of a large asphalt playground flanked by a red school-building, with lines of cinder-coloured brick inset in the façade. Away on the right rose the stone clock-tower of the railway station, modelled on eighteenth-century Dresden architecture, for the architect of the railway company had been a man of wide knowledge and appreciation. On the left was the bridge, with a few tree-tops showing above it. In the day-time, especially in the summer, it was quite lively. The sound of traffic, the vibration of the bridge, the clanging of trams, cawing of rooks, and cries of the children as they tumbled round their playground, came in at the high window. For some reason or other Miss Frederica and Miss Fanny found the noise made by the children very irritating — upsetting indeed. In the winter the days were quieter; but the evenings were so long — and the nights!

It had been March when they had moved in: very cold, but the warmer weather would come soon. At first the change was so abrupt, the contrast to their past life so fantastic, as to be equally unreal. It was like playing a game, a childish game of house-keeping or Red Indians. It must, surely, be

only make-believe, and at any moment they would find themselves back in the Red House, able to resume their old life.
The last few days there had been — though they would never
admit it — very bitter. Everyone on the West Cliff knew them ;
and if they moved out of their home, people stared so. Here
they had not been so well known in the days of their prosperity.

They missed their bedroom more than anything else. In
this house they occupied just one room, sleeping in one hard
bed. There were a few rickety pieces of yellow furniture, an
empty fireplace, a tin basin to wash in. Of course, in the
summer, the house was full of visitors, and it was not dark till
nine. But the winter evenings were very long. They had no
novels to read, and it was very cold — no fire, and nothing
to do except go to bed — not even a hot-water bottle. They
thought they could not be very well — so chilly and stiff, with
a funny sinking feeling inside. It might, Miss Fanny thought,
it might be the food. It was not quite what they were used to.
Meat, for instance, only twice a week. Still, some people
thought meat-eating bad for one, and in the end one might
feel all the better for the absence of it . . . when one had got
used to it. And no dinner at all seemed strange, didn't it ?
And then, that horrid Indian tea. She was sure she would
never get to like that !

Yes, the nights were long, especially the winter nights, and
so cold, but they had never before moved in a real world ;
and if now it had become painfully real, it should yet be
kept at a distance ! Never would they admit to each other
their fear of the winter. They might complain themselves of
small things — of the tea, for instance — but they must never
voice to each other any mortal dread. Yet though they never
mentioned it, each knew that the other did not sleep for long
through those interminable winter nights. It was too cold, so
near the roof. Outside the bare branches would be swaying
and creaking in the wind. The bridge would surely be blown
away one night. At about ten a cab would rumble over it in a
leisurely manner. And then for hours there would be no
sound except that of the striking clocks — it would be too
quiet, except for that icy sound. The sound was so cold, it
was like touching iron rails in a frost. It almost froze the
ears, and the brain within. Certainly it gave them a headache.
The station clock would start first : the four quarters, and

then the hour; but a fairly cheerful, business-like sound. Then would toll out the others in a sequence, each following at an interval of a few seconds. Each one would strike the four quarters and then the hour; and for all the clocks audible in the town to strike midnight took up a full quarter of an hour. St. Catherine's would knell eastward with its deep bell; Christchurch would sound near by, scolding and shrewish. St. Thomas would be angry and foreboding, Holy Trinity surprised. The hour was tolled out as if in sorrow: perhaps a worse one was coming in. Sleep was at an infinite distance, beyond the sound of bells and the touch of cold iron bars. Their minds were waking. They were living, and it was cold.

Then the winter days, though actually so short, seemed both long and cold; and the landlady was not at all a nice woman, very impolite. In time they grew to avoid Mrs. Snaggs whenever it was possible. When they passed by they would hear her laughing and giggling. She was not respectful. 'Goodness, what sights!' they would hear her say.

No longer could they go to concerts or bazaars, nor were they ever asked to knit anything for the Christchurch sale-of-work. It was too tiring to go out for a long walk, and too cold to stay in. They had been forced to give up the lending-library: thus that stroll, which would have given them something to do, was barred to them; and if they stayed at home, they had no books to read. Except that Mrs. Snaggs had once lent them a copy of *The Family Herald*. And Mr. Garrett was very kind and had offered to continue their subscription until better times came. But they could not accept his offer; it would not be the right thing to do. And then Mr. Garrett was altering; his waxed moustache was very untidy, his hair dishevelled, he had a vacant eye. Things were going badly with him, too. Newborough was altering. The new big chemist's at the corner had started a lending-library; and things were not prospering with the smaller shops. Drink was a dreadful thing, but they could understand it. Poor little man! He had always been so kind and respectful. No, it was no good staying in unless the weather forced them to do so. A little walk in the streets, but not in the main streets. People stared so.

Alas! there was some excuse for the staring. Now that

there was no one to look after their clothes, hats and boots, the two sisters presented a more than ever extraordinary spectacle. The dresses, getting daily more antiquated in their design, were yet as gorgeous in colour, and were still fluttering with torn ribbons and cobweb-like lace, but draggled, torn and untidy. Their hats had acquired shapes that could only be described as grotesque; their bronze buttoned-boots were dirty and worn down; but cheek and hair still burnt with an unnatural and unsteady flame.

One day two little boys followed them right up to Miss Waddington's door, making fun of them. It was too bad! Every fortnight they paid this, their only visit in the town, to old Miss Waddington. They would arrive in time for tea. At first, going so near their old house was very painful to them. They would ring the bell, and the maid, Elsie, would open the door, leave them waiting in the small hall between the two doors for some little time, and then usher them into the drawing-room. In the winter, when the blinds were drawn, it reminded them so much of the drawing-room at the Red House. A fire burnt brightly under a solid white-marble mantelpiece, on which were several photographs in rococo silver frames and a solid white-marble clock. On each side of this were a Dresden shepherd and shepherdess. But the old lady was 'artistic', and there were several ferns, especially little ones, in art pots, green merging into yellow-ochre. There was usually, in the winter, a silver vase, shaped like a small trumpet with a crinkled edge, full of jonquils, so pretty and bright, like the spring; nice comfortable armchairs, and a sofa, full of dark green silk cushions, with large frills.

Sometimes Miss Waddington would not be well enough to come down herself, and her niece would give them tea instead — such good Ceylon tea. The niece was not exactly pretty, but bright-looking: yes, that was the word, bright-looking: people said she was 'clever'. 'Aunt Hester is not so well today', she would say as she came in, 'and has asked me to entertain you for her'; and then, before they answered, as if entering a preliminary defence, she would add quickly: 'How well you both look. I am sure they must make you very comfortable in your lodgings. I saw Mrs. Snaggs the other day, such a clean, sensible, respectable-looking woman!' Tea would be brought in, many small cakes and scones. And finally, after a visit lasting from half an hour to three-quarters, they would get up to go, and would be handed an envelope containing a cheque for one pound. No other visitors ever disturbed these tea-parties.

As a rule, though, Miss Waddington would make a special effort to be there herself to talk to them. She thought that she really must be getting quite fond of the two Misses Cantrell-Cooksey; at any rate she enjoyed their visits. Perhaps they were nicer since their misfortunes — but they were certainly rather odd. She was, therefore, not 'at-home' to other friends. No, Elsie.

There would be a preliminary coughing and wheezing upstairs and in the hall. The door would open, and the dear old lady, with a white shawl round her shoulders, would totter in, shivering as if it were very cold. Miss Frederica and Miss Fanny found it rather difficult to talk to her. Indeed, the former lady seldom spoke now, even to her younger sister. Besides, what was there to talk about? They had seen so little and done so little. There remained in the summer the weather and the visitors, in the winter the weather. Or Miss Waddington would try to impart a little religious consolation to them, endeavour to make them go to church again, for latterly they had given up going to Christchurch. Certainly, Miss Waddington reflected, as they left the house with their envelope, they were getting very odd, very odd indeed. But after they left she felt better than she had done all day. Kindly and charitable; and at the same time the room had grown brighter, the fire warmer. It was a terrible thing, to gamble!

And the two Misses Cantrell-Cooksey would be walking, under cover of the winter darkness, back across the suspension-bridge to their high back window in the tall white house.

Apart from their fortnightly call, the chief thing they looked forward to in the winter was their walk on the sands, away from the town. They grew to look forward to this event of the day with more and more pleasure. Even when the north-east wind blew straight from the top of Norway, they would sit on a rock, impervious to any chill, and converse with their friends, who would, if there had not been a storm, be gathering their winkles and limpets. If there had been a gale, on the other hand, they would be engaged in the more exciting task of combing the gold sands. Excitement would flare up again in the eyes of the two old ladies as they watched the sea-hoard being uncovered. And, though they were now no longer able to distribute shillings, the men who lived by this strange employment were, even when a little the worse for drink, so kind and respectful. They treated these two poor old bundles of bones, decked out in their torn fine feathers, as if they still lived on the West Cliff. They even appeared to regard them as human beings. And, to the men's great credit, they never allowed their pity to obtrude itself.

The summer was not so difficult. The town was full of visitors and cheerful sounds; while, at low tide, they could walk under the wall of the terrace where the band played, and hear it quite well. And if they kept close to the wall they could not be recognised from above by people leaning over — though once Mrs. Sibmarsh caught a glimpse of them from one of the gaps — like the intervals between battlements — in the wall. It gave her quite a turn. Still pretending to be young — and to be rich, she supposed — dressed up like that. They didn't behave like poor people; so stuck up; and one ought to cut one's coat . . . oughtn't one? Their eyes were worse than ever. There could be no doubt about it. They must drug . . . morphia . . . cocaine . . . though how they could get it without money, she didn't know. It was positively disgraceful.

The sands themselves were so crowded with mothers and children, nurses and children, donkeys and pierrots and ice-cream carts, so vibrating under the reflected lights of sea and pool and sky, that the presence of the two sisters attracted but little attention there, except once; when, advancing near a group waiting round an empty platform, they were asked what time the performance began. After that they began to avoid the sands, until the winter brought loneliness back to them. Yet, curiously enough, they made no effort to quieten their clothes, or to subdue the colouring of hair and cheek. Though cosmetics were costly, they clung to them. For, once they let these pretences die, with them would perish the last vestige of self-respect. Their eccentricity had turned into this extreme patience, and into the final agonising pretence that all was as it should be.

They had almost lost count of time. How many years was it? The most definite fact in their lives was a continual dread

of the coming winter, the cold, the cold! The long winter
nights closed round them. And there was nothing to do but
lie awake, for they had no books, and they must save the cost
of lighting.

And this November Miss Fanny began, suddenly, to
notice a change in Frederica, something vague in her manner.
All one night she muttered to herself, and the next day, coming
up from downstairs, Miss Fanny found her crying. She did
not feel very well, that was all. Appearances were a heavy
burden, a difficult load. How was she to keep it up?

It was an extravagance, she knew, but would Fanny mind
fetching her a small bottle of sal volatile from the chemist?
Yes, it was only a headache, but a rather severe one. It would
be gone by dinner. Miss Fanny walked out with the money
to Hoare & Blunt, the chemists. Mrs. Snaggs, downstairs in
the empty house — for in the winter there were no guests —
heard Miss Frederica calling her. It was really too bad! One
might be a slave, running up and down stairs with nothing to
do except look after those two. Miss Fanny, indeed! For
Miss Cantrell-Cooksey had asked Mrs. Snaggs to tell Miss
Fanny, when she returned, not to worry. She was just going
out for a walk, and might not be back for a little time. She
was fully decorated, a-jingle with ribbons and ornaments,
while a hat, gorgeous but flattened and out of shape, crowned
it all. Under her arm was a brown-paper parcel. Mrs. Snaggs
looked at her in amazement, and then went back to the kitchen.
She did not actually hear her go out, but, though angry, gave
Miss Fanny the message when the latter came in, muttering
and making the most of the two flights of stairs she had been
forced to come up by panting in a hollow, owl-like way. Miss
Fanny stood with her back to the door, talking to Mrs. Snaggs
for a few seconds. Just then there was the sound of a gathering
crowd outside on the bridge, and looking back out of the door
Miss Fanny saw a murmuring circle of black-coated men and
a few women backing away toward the other side of the road,
with white, mask-like faces. Within the circle Miss Frederica's
clothes were lying in a heap. She had gone out for her last
walk. She had stepped, fully-dressed, with a brown-paper
parcel under her arm, straight out of that high window on to
the stone pavement below. She must have had to bend down
to get out of it. In the parcel were a black-bound Prayer Book

and the few old photographs that belonged to her. But she had kept up appearances.

Miss Fanny did not really feel it much. There was the inquest, and then the funeral; a great deal of activity! Mrs. Snaggs had given her the message. And she often sits up quite late expecting Frederica to return, till the light in her eyes equals the flame of cheek and hair.

I last saw her at low tide, one winter morning, dressed in a white-flannel costume (a new departure for her) and very much made-up. She must really be old by now. There had been a storm, and she was sitting on a rock talking to the men who were raking over the pebbly edges of the sands and watching them capture their strange treasure. They found that morning a William-and-Mary gold piece; a small chest covered with rusty iron nails and green with age, with nothing in it; a small box, hermetically sealed, of China tea; a straw ship in a glass bottle, and two George IV four-shilling pieces.

THE MAN WHO DROVE STRINDBERG MAD

Sitting in this large old house, in this freezing winter, in this winter of the world, with icicles clustering their stalactites round every old lead pipe, transforming the implements of utility into shapes of glittering fantasy, much as the mind of the poet changes all that he sees, or the magic of time touches the forest in which lies buried the palace of the Sleeping Beauty, transforming every dull material object into something brilliant and crystal-clear, I thought of lands across the grey and swirling waters where every year these processes take place. I thought of the north — but my mind recoiled from the horrors of Finland and Russia. Sweden, whatever the immediate future may hold in store for it, is still (as I write) itself, and so I thought of the snowy slopes and bare trees of Uppsala, so like a Hoxton print in their clear blue-and-white tinsel precision, and of the life, on skate and sleigh and ski, so suited to its conditions, which prevailed there. . . . Here the snow drifted in long, upward curves towards the tall eighteenth-century windows, and we watched for the thaw : but all the pipes were solid, and even the telephone wires had in some fashion given way to the spite of winter. . . . And now, as I thought of Sweden and Uppsala, of Uppsala always more than of Stockholm, all the electric bells in the house began to ring without stopping — the frost and snow working on them in some manner unknown to me, I suppose : but I do not understand the ways of machines or of currents, can form no conception of the tricks by which inanimate objects pursue their careers.

．　　　．　　　．　　　．　　　．

For an hour or more the bells continued, and, thinking of Sweden, my mind reverted to Strindberg, the greatest artist Sweden ever produced, and I wondered how he would have treated this incident, from what cocoon of fiery and unbalanced poetry the episode would have emerged. Because, as you, Gentle Reader, will remember, he was ever assailed by the spite of inanimate objects, trying to plague him, trying to drive him

352

mad. In many books, but especially in *The Inferno*, he tells us of their dull but deadly machinations, the sponge that threw itself into his bath from the wrong and ominous corner, the picture-frame that fell as he passed, and, above all, the bells, the bell. The front-door bell, especially, was rung at intervals, day by day, and only stopped when he went to answer it and found no human being waiting there . . . above all, the bells; and as I thought of him, pursued by these innumerable in-animate materialisations of fate, suddenly I recalled an incident which I had forgotten, and longed to record it. Not only did it in itself appeal to my way of thinking, but, in addition, it carried me to a distant equatorial land where the heat broods all the year over mirror-like lagoons and where, at dawn and dusk, the thousand little winged inhabitants of the jungle open and close their day with such a shriek of pride and possession as can only be imagined by those who have heard it; so loud and victorious a paean that listening to it throbbing through the ground, through ear and throat and limb, one was obliged to doubt its very existence, it was too loud and insistent to *be*, just as the heat was too hot to appear genuine.

I suppose it was because I have so great a reverence for Strindberg and understand so well how his mind worked, and why in its particular directions, and because I think, although I usually do not care to admit it, that his theory of life contains more truth than would seem possible to the dull disciples of everyday (indeed this war is the culmination of his theories, the fulfilment of them upon the *world*, instead of upon the *individual*), that this incident occurred to me. But however that may be, when I was seventeen or eighteen and attached to a cavalry regiment, I discovered two stars for myself, the dire radiance of Strindberg — a light, indeed, from another planet — and the middle-class comforting doctrines of that lesser luminary, Samuel Butler. With Strindberg, I, too, watched the conspiracies of little objects, the way they pre-cipitate the imaginative into disaster, and it seemed to me then — as it seems to me still — that in his work was a beauty that, also, lay beyond the world of reason. His heroines could live for years in cupboards, then half-way through the play turn into parrots, and yet they existed in their own burning world of unreason, quite as surely as you or I in ours. . . . In any case I have a special and personal feeling for this sad and tortured author; even though I suppose — I do not know — that I have little in common with him, for fun comes easily to me and I was — I hope the reader will excuse my boasting — born with wit in the tips of my fingers as much as on the tip of my tongue. I have a natural vitality, born of centuries of riding and not-thinking (as opposed to not being able to think); a vitality which it has taken two world wars to destroy. . . . But all the same, in spite of my own innate attitude toward life, I reverence Strindberg as a great writer with, for me, a personal illumination.

.   .   .   .   .

The rains were coming in San Salvador : the bootblacks kneeled listlessly at their work and the dark-skinned singers were silent. All day long, grey clouds drifted over the top of the palm trees and a hot wind ruffled and scurried their plumes. An emanation of former massacres seemed to invest the city, the fires of the Inquisition seemed still to smoulder just below the ground, and the rain of bullets that, only a few months before, had been responsible for the deaths of ten thousand Communists, shot *à la russe* in droves of fifty by machine-guns, seemed hardly to have spent itself in the air. At the windows, relentless parrots clacked their iron tongues like castanets and gave way to bouts of Delphic prophecy in Spanish. Old gentlemen were eating enormous ices in the windows of the clubs, and marimbas sounded their haunting, icy music down the lost alleys of the city. . . . The world was waiting — it, for the rains, and I, for a boat — and so I, too, sat in the club, reading the newly arrived European papers and hearing in them the six-weeks-old rumble of impending tragedy. . . . Every day, as it came, seemed to contain a number of siestas, but of such a kind as to be free of peace, invaded by poisonous thoughts; every night brought the glamour of southern nights, their sounds and scents and relaxations; and to these last I added my private gambler's joy.

At ten-thirty every night I would sit, in that tremendous heat, in a large over-illuminated room, helping, for once, the dull spite of inanimate objects as an ally, or being, in turn, its victim. I love even the sound of the roulette wheel, and often it has seemed to me that some special link connects its spirit temporarily with those of some of its devotees. For hours at a stretch, without a hint of boredom, I could play this game in which only good — or usually bad — fortune exists, where there is no such thing as skill or intellect : only swift action and luck, and an ability to be for an instant in league with the spirit of the inanimate, the blind, the thing without thought — yet as you watch its revolutions, it seems very surely to possess an individuality, to have its own inexplicable preferences.

Sometimes I can win — though even then the quickness and alertness which, in order to gain, must accompany good fortune, soon desert me, rapidly worn down, like every other gambler, by worry, excitement, fatigue and heat : generally, like all gamblers, I lost. Even then, in this climate, I would find it impossible to go to bed. The heat was too great, the excitement too recent. . . . I would stand for a time on the balcony, watching how the very fireflies in their curves were trying to outline the numbers that lie between zero and thirty-six, watching their scintillating implications, trying to gather their meaning. Then, for a moment, forgetting that I had lost all my money, I would return to the table ; only to find myself obliged to assume a passive rôle. Fortunately I had exhausted every shilling that was on me and so I would sit in a sullen sweat and observe the intricate design in numbers woven by the wheel spinning.

Every night the man of whom I am going to tell you came in very late and by himself, with a pile of chips, and played with an enviable — and yet in a sense, it seemed to me, un-enviable — good fortune. At first I thought he was English. He was still young-looking, and rather handsome. He was certainly well dressed and dressed with a touch of vanity, but his appearance exhibited also a touch of over-sleekness, while his eyes, hard and yet pleading, seemed to belong to some other body than his own. Their blue and rather cruel, if cringing, inconsistency did not seem to match the physique of the athlete, the rhythmic body, the fair hair and fair skin. For the eyes were cold, very cold for all their strange and inconjecturable pleading. He played with courage, conviction and an almost diabolic luck. I had never seen a man who, at certain times, seemed more sure of what was coming. His long, well-shaped fingers — one, with a sapphire and platinum ring on it — knew exactly where to place his stakes : never, for a moment, did he show indecision, although his system was founded, so far as I could see, on nothing but a belief in his own good fortune. There was about him, as he played, something immensely attractive and repellent, an air of mystery. He never spoke: but I could see now that he was not English: nor German, I was sure, he was too like an Englishman for that, so he must belong to Denmark or Sweden or Norway. . . . Yet he seemed at home here. He suited, for all his northerliness, the tropics, as a snake suits the burning ground over which it darts. He seemed very much at home, too, without speaking; and to be on good terms with the world, with people and with things; above all, with *things* — hence his diabolic fortune at roulette. . . . But there was nothing mysterious about him. I made inquiries, and was told that he was a prosperous Swedish merchant. He possessed an interest in the railways here, and he also exported coffee and spices to Sweden. . . . It was true that he won great sums. He would not bring his wife to the Casino, for people distracted him: hence, too, he always entered late, when the majority of gamblers had met their destiny, and his icy judgment came fresh to a community of soiled and broken players and of tired, despising croupiers. In this disruptive world he could hold his own. If he lost, he left: if he began to win, he seized with a cold imaginative power upon his good fortune, and left as soon as it began to desert him. . . . But in the phrase of the gamblers there, 'the table liked him'. He was its favourite. The dull, inanimate creation beamed upon him as upon one of its own.

Then I met him at luncheon in a pavilion under a tree. The vultures alighted ponderously on their observation posts and watched us with the heavy, hooded eyes of armament kings. Occasionally they staggered, as though from sleep, and turned reflective profiles to the sky. In the darkness of the scrub beyond, many other birds yelled out. The clouds, day by day, hour by hour, were drifting down. There were only present my host and hostess — American friends — myself, and the gambler and his wife. After luncheon our hostess, together with that other plain and resonant-voiced woman, left the table and I sat next to him and we talked. He spoke excellent English, but with a typical northern inflexion. I told him with how great an interest I watched his play, and we discussed many things and places; drifting towards Sweden and then to

Strindberg. He did not seem to be proud of the greatest poet his country had produced, though he had lived for a long while in the same small town in which Strindberg had lived while he was writing, among other books, *The Inferno*. I told him how deeply I admired the great writer, but he did not seem interested in such a subject, and wanted to talk of other things or, perhaps, not to talk at all. And then presently, as I insisted, as I continued to dwell on Strindberg (for I felt he must know something of him), I noticed for the first time a light, other than that cold light I had observed in the Casino, illumine his eyes; they flickered with the memory, you would have said, of some past joy, became alive, animated in a pleasurable way. Presently he said in his soft, low voice: 'As a boy I used to make fun of him. . . . Often I would run into his garden, ring the front-door bell, and then hide until he had opened the door and had gone away again, finding no one there. . . . And then, ever so many times, I would creep out, dart up the stairs and ring again. . . . And how puzzled he would look! . . . One never has fun like that nowadays; too sophisticated, I suppose.' But I was silent, overcome by horror at this being in league with the inanimate in its dull, cold vendetta against a man of genius. . . . 'Childish pleasures are the greatest of all,' he continued in his mechanical, meaningless, sing-song voice.

DEATH OF A GOD

(For Alice)

THE chief difficulty under which, at the moment of writing this story, the creative artist, more especially the novelist, labours is this: that the violent agitation, from end to end, and from top to bottom, of the background against which his figures are placed, renders the movements of these characters meaningless and unimportant. As well try to concentrate upon a game of chess in an earthquake! The act of writing (if you think of it — which fortunately the born writer seldom does) is comparable to the action of the band which played a hymn as the great ship *Titanic* was sinking. . . . Well, the loss of the *Titanic*, 'the luxury liner on her maiden voyage', as the papers of that day loved to describe her, was symbolic of things to come, but not more than the disappearance from this earthly scene of Mr. Snowberry. . . . With him, for many others as well as for me, went the whole of the nineteenth-century panorama, and especially the works of Henry James and George Meredith. Even more than the novelists of convention, Mr. Snowberry belonged to a dying age.

Ever since I could remember, my life — and long before that, the lives of my parents and their neighbours — had been regulated and set in motion every week by Mr. Snowberry. Without him we should have been lost. He was our god, controlling the life of each week. Lacking his aid, the vague, Meredithian life of childhood in a country house would have come to nothing. Dressed in a faded livery of dark suit, bowler hat, heavy gold chain, which divided his little body into two halves, his face adorned with moustache and whiskers, he drove over the moors to us every eighth day from Bakewell to wind the clocks. The chain I have mentioned supported a heavy gold hunter watch: and by this watch he set the clocks.

These machines were numerous in all the houses he visited. At home there was the stable clock (the pendulum of which subsequently proved, appropriately enough, to be the seventeenth-

century sundial from the old formal garden, removed to make
way for a landscape in the mode of Capability Brown); the
lacquered Queen Anne clock, on the stairs, with flamboyant
flamingoes blown in gold upon the surface of its case; the Louis
Quatorze *buhl* clock in the Cocked Hat Room; the tall walnut
clock with a silver dial, surrounded by patterns of fruit, in the
Ballroom; in the Boudoir, the *Directoire* clock, which played a
minuet by Mozart at the end of every hour; the tortoise-shell
clock, with a gold figure of Father Time and his Scythe, in the
Great Parlour; and the inlaid and domed clock which my
father had brought back some years before from Sicily. This
stood in the dining-room, and with an extreme display of
individuality, indulged at odd hours in almost any form of dis-
sonance that it chose. . . . (And all these instruments of time
were still ticking, perhaps, in the age appropriate to them,
controlling on some other plane of vision the movement of
their coeval puppets: Dutch figures with periwigs and large
feathered hats were walking hand in hand in a tulip garden to
the ticking of the walnut clock, and, already coming up the
other side of the Revolution, the *Merveilleuses* were conducting
their exaggerated lives to the beating heart of the little gold
clock; while my parents and their friends, in the bowler hats,
tight trousers and coats, the tailor-made skirts and leg-of-
mutton-sleeved coats of the 'nineties, were still playing croquet
to the rhythm of that little clock in a leather case which my
mother told me had been given to her as a wedding present.)
Thus everything we did or said, our every function and thought
and dream, was instigated by Mr. Snowberry. We could
hardly have eaten without him.

Moreover, the same thing was true of daily life in all the
country houses round; that existence which has now so completely disappeared. On Monday he drove, let us say, to
Chatsworth — a full day's work there! — on Tuesday to
Hardwick; on Wednesday — I remember it was always
Wednesday — to Barlborough and Renishaw; on Thursday
to Clumber; on Friday to Welbeck; on Saturday, perhaps,
to Wentworth Woodhouse. On Sunday I imagine he must
have wound his own clock (but of that I have something to
say later). He was the local god of time: albeit sometimes
a breakdown in it caused him to be summoned earlier, so
that he became the healer of time, as well as its overlord. At

his nod innumerable clocks sounded their silver tinkling, or echoing, rhythmic or cracked notes over the little corner where the counties of Derbyshire, Nottinghamshire, Yorkshire and Lincolnshire meet. Week after week for nearly fifty years this amiable, good little deity had progressed from temple to temple — this prince, from palace to palace.

Round Mr. Snowberry, then, the whole invisible mechanism of many great estates revolved. The woodman in the shrill green light of summer mornings, when the call to action from the ground seemed to sound clear as a hunting-horn on a frosty morning, rose to his chimes. Later, when the sun had rolled above the horizon, and its rays glowed among the feathery tree-tops of the avenue, the horses would begin to neigh in the stables, but the grooms did not get up until Mr. Snowberry's clock sounded the correct hour. In the spring, when, after the hard winter of the north, the bulbs could almost be seen growing, whole russet choirs of birds sang uninterruptedly from the earliest dawn, but even they seemed to cease from their carolling when one of Mr. Snowberry's clocks struck the hour. In the brittle, icy winter, when trees as tall as a ship's masts were roped with frost, and every blade of grass became a crackling spire, it was Mr. Snowberry who roused the sullen housemaids from warm slumber.

On the other hand, while Mr. Snowberry made time advance for others, it seemed, equally, to stand still for him. I had grown from childhood to man's estate without being able to observe the slightest change in him — none at all; not by the greying of a hair, nor by any variation or loss of strength in his voice (which so often betrays the ageing of those who do not show it in other ways), had he altered.

What life did the god of time lead at home, I wondered, between these ceremonial visits to great and lesser houses; between the greetings of grooms and footmen: 'Good morning, Mr. Snowberry!' 'Good morning, John!' 'Pony going well, Mr. Snowberry?' 'Yes, thank you, John. . . .' 'Lovely morning for the time of year, Mr. Kembley.' 'Yes, Mr. Snowberry, what we want is three munths o' this, and then tak' oop.' How did he spend the crisp October evenings, or the lazy summer twilight up there on the moor near the site of the Roman camp, so close under the sky, where heather and bilberries supplied the only vegetation? Just as an emperor is always said to live so simply, to lie on a camp-bed in preference to a state four-poster, and to prefer a glass of fresh milk and a rusk to meals prepared by a most skilled French chef, so, too, doubtless this Mexican Prince-Priest, this Maya Time-God preferred, when he considered the riches and extent of his kingdom, to live on goat's cheese, and on bilberries which stain the inside of the mouth to the blue-black of a chow's tongue.

As a child his trade fascinated me and I used to conjecture what his own clock, by which he set his gold watch, could be like; the clock that governed this god, though equally governed by him; the central clock, as it were, of the whole universe. . . . And, finally, I found out, when I went to tea with him and was thus able, on the same Saturday afternoon, to satisfy my curiosity concerning his house. It was a very small house, not a cottage, with mullion windows, and the stone between them quilted with little pink roses. In the porch stood an enormous very clean-looking wooden spade, which showed very distinctly its grain, and which was for shovelling away the snow, so it should not even in the winter prevent him from reaching the various temples so dependent upon him. The sitting-room was full of feathers, feather-flowers and stuffed birds and patchwork cushions. . . . But when he showed me his bedroom, I was dismayed to find that the all-important clock upon which he, and, in consequence, our whole world, depended was an alarm clock, a common machine of base metal, the tintinnabulations of which awoke him every morning. . . . I must have shown my surprise and disappointment, for he added, 'Well, my dear young man, you see I'm alone here now. Mrs. Snowberry and Esther have been dead these last ten years.'

Somehow, I had not previously connected him, so highly did he stand above mortals in my regard, with earthly ties, and it was only then that I realised that the monster over which he reigned had dared to devour those dearest to him; so that his own life was an insecure tenure, his seat on the throne shaky in the extreme. But even when I grew up, I still continued to feel that he should be immune from time's laws. . . . It did not surprise me, therefore, that he showed no signs of growing old. And, in consequence, I was in no way prepared either for his own final disappearance, or that of the system of which he seemed the mainspring.

Right up to that moment the machine was ticking away without a sign of any internal corrosion. There had been changes, of course : one or two mansions had passed to newer and richer owners (Mr. Snowberry disapproved of such usurpers) : no grooms now saluted him, but though the chauffeurs were more independent and wished him 'Good morning' in colder, less rural and rather condescending voices, nevertheless, the fact that the motor had replaced the horse seemed only to emphasise the beneficent influence of Mr. Snowberry's activities.

The whole world seemed to be working up, like a magnificent and ingenious clock, to strike, under Mr. Snowberry's governing, its comfortable, full, rich, traditional chimes. . . . Towards the end of June, however, something went wrong. An Austrian Archduke, who had often been entertained in one of Mr. Snowberry's palaces, now, while driving in an open motor-car through a distant Mohammedan town, fell victim to a bullet from the hand of Gavril Princip. . . . I was with my regiment in Wellington Barracks at the time, and my sister wrote to me from my home to tell me how upset Mr. Snowberry had been at this regrettable occurrence. Just as if a person under his protection had been injured, some sense of responsibility seemed to haunt him, she said.

In July I came home on leave for a month or two, and in the peculiarly golden summer of that year, under the old trees or in the cool interior of the darkened rooms, rumours from the outside world drifted in sleepily. It seemed as if the whole earth were waiting, waiting for bells to sound or a clock to strike. . . . And, being of a superstitious turn of mind, I was unhappy when on the 1st of August (for by then the outside world had already invaded us with clouds of flying, scurrying reports) I counted the lacquered clock on the stairs outside my bedroom strike thirteen at midnight. . . . It had never done this before, so it must have been my reckoning, I supposed, that was at fault. . . . All the same, two veins of uneasiness now ran through the substance of my mind : one concerning Mr. Snowberry, and the other for the whole world : (and as it happens, I have never in my life, so far, heard a clock strike thirteen again).

I went to London on the night of the 2nd. On the night of the 3rd, I was among those who saw the Lord Mayor's gilded coach roll trundling up the Mall, moving, unless my memory misleads me, along the narrower side-path strewn with peat moss for riders, to Buckingham Palace; a sure sign of the imminence of the catastrophe that was coming. On the 4th, war was declared, and on the morning of the same day Mr. Snowberry met with his accident. . . . Pan and Mars had broken loose together and had set out to conquer the newer god, Mr. Snowberry.

In spite of the general progress, himself had never approved of motor-cars, and he was driving his pony-cart in the neighbourhood of Renishaw when this event occurred. I know the place well. The cinder pyramid of a small mine heaped an ugly screen against a wide expanse in which huge chimneys, plumed with smoke, and stout furnaces raised their bulk. Behind the slag-heap crouched an Elizabethan house, lost and desolate, and then came a rustic prospect in which industrialism did not exist. First, there was a lane between deep hedges, and the other side of it stood a small stone farm, while beyond, an abrupt perspective of stone walls and meadows that leapt and fell at improbable levels stretched towards the moors and the far horizon.

Mr. Snowberry was coming down this lane. For all that the coal-mines were so close, it was a lovely place in summer, the old stone farm, the near meadows with two spoilt donkeys stretching their furry muzzles across loose stone walls in hope of sugar, the pigs grunting from their sties, or hurrying with their clumsy, fairy-story bodies inflated above short, thin legs, across the green grass — the mountain grass, like the green hair of mermaids, of the high places in this district. Bracken grew tall along the sides of the lane, making intricate, lacy patterns. The air coming from the moors smelt pure and mossy, and you could hear the trout-stream purling below. The whole of this vista exhaled a primitive, Noah's-ark charm and offered a feeling of comfort; the green meadow and stone wall, pigs and chickens, donkeys and orchards and stone trough, had always been there and, even in spite of changes for the worse elsewhere, would prevail, and with them a certain rough kindliness. It was this impression of comfort and kindliness that perhaps made the shock which Mr. Snowberry was to receive all the worse.

He was driving quietly along, when suddenly he saw before

him a white billy-goat tethered tight, but wildly running round a post, rearing up in pain and then jumping down again on its four cloven feet; a pure white goat that was like a flame in its proud, white maleness against the dark green of trees and grass. In front of the animal were two girls, fourteen or fifteen, with the flaxen and tow-coloured hair of the countryside, rolling with lewd, brutish laughter, and aiming as hard as they could at the most vital part of the goat's body. Something in the masculinity of the goat maddened them beyond bearing, for they were at that queer stage of adolescence when young girls are no longer themselves, no longer individuals, their consciousness joining that of all young female things, so that they are able, as we see from time to time in the cases of haunting by poltergeists, to produce psychic phenomena mysteriously and with an inexplicable ease. They were laughing under the influence of some horrible kind of intoxication or control — perhaps at other moments they were good children, perhaps they would grow up to be reasonable human beings, but now they were possessed. The god Pan was loose in them, and they were in reality crucifying that which was within themselves.

Mr. Snowberry, a lover of animals, who was filled with a loving-kindness towards all the created world, made no allowance in his mind for such fury. Anger beat up in him at the sight of this cruelty; he pulled up, shouted, and was just going to jump out of the pony-cart to stop them torturing the poor beast, when all at once they saw him and, in their fright, hurled a stone at him, which hit the pony. The pony ran away, and Mr. Snowberry was thrown out and killed instantly. The watch he carried with him stopped at the hour of his death.

Beyond the sea, as here, the primeval, brutish world was breaking out, and it was several days before the little universe of which he was god discovered what had happened to Mr. Snowberry. Everywhere in Elizabethan long-galleries, with their stucco figures in green and pink hose hunting through dark forests, in panelled drawing-rooms, Palladian stables and Adam dining-rooms, the machinery of the clocks ran down and no chimes sounded the hour. It seemed, my sister wrote to me, as if the figures, too, had run down with the being that regulated their lives. No one now knew what was going on in the world beyond: no one in these houses knew the correct time to take a walk, to eat, or to sleep. Everything was running down. And in that priest's cell high up on the moors, the metal, clacking tongue of the alarm clock, the central clock of the universe as it were, set by Greenwich, itself remained silent and unwound.

LONG JOURNEY

In the Tuscan towns the sound of trams creaking, their bells ringing, and of the open exhausts of motors blares through the narrow streets at sundown; streets, tawny as a lion, but in which it is nevertheless impossible to observe the full drama of the autumn, so intense on the outskirts and in the country behind, where it drags a hem of purple over the dusty hills and into the woods of ilex, the leaves of which glisten like the glossy night forests in the canvases of Uccello. Through the middle of each town flows desultorily a dwindled yellow river. The palaces, balanced and proportioned as a mathematical formula or a problem in Euclid, hang above streets too narrow, again, for the passer-by to be able to judge of their pure, incredible beauty, now for the most part remote and dead as that of the Parthenon or of the clustered, broken towers of San Gimignano. The streets, for all their bustle, are similarly dead; it is the activity of the devouring worm more than of life itself. The palaces, except for the cobblers and fruit shops on the ground floor, are dead too; but the cobbler hammers all day long at his last, and the old women, who gossip or haggle over *soldi*, peering from behind their autumnal mounds of green figs and purple figs, of grapes and of orange persimmons, fit into these elegant, slightly rusticated arches so well that they seem as much part of them as a snail of its shell. . . . Up above on the *piano nobile*, either a dressmaker, as if engaged in black magic, stabs a silken bust with pins, her mouth still full of them, or a lawyer interviews his sullen peasant client, so unable to explain himself, or an American is giving a cocktail party. For the most part, the former owners, the renown of whose ancestors has echoed down the centuries from the time of Dante — just as a footstep now echoes through the mirror-like view of door after door, ceiling after ceiling, room after room —, have disappeared, have sunk like stones to the bottom of these clear pools, leaving only the enlarging circles of their proud names to float upon the darkening surface.

The Palazzo Corineo, however, is an exception. Built by

Alberti, it lingers with reproachful perfection in a crowded by-street: where its fragile arcaded façade, one of the surviving wonders of the world, hangs almost out of sight, so that the lover of beauty who wishes to examine it will very soon be hooted out of his survey by a motor-car or belled out of it by a cycle. Herein, however, the descendants of those who caused it to be built still live, far down their endless pillared vistas; there are footmen in livery, and a vague air of the eighteenth century still attends upon the public goings and comings of the old Prince and Princess. Yet even for them the view here is one that diminishes year by year, uncertain to the point of certainty; for they are childless and have few relatives. The last palace will soon be uninhabited.

The Prince, a quiet, bearded scholar of the mandarin type, sadly floating above the life of the day, possesses manners as formal and beautiful as the rooms in which he lives: but the Princess, on the contrary, opposes to them a different and ebullient system of life, a different upbringing, a different set of manners. A Russian Princess in her own right, a Cossack by blood and inclination, she was born during a Court Ball in the Winter Palace in St. Petersburg, and was, so she says, baptised in a golden ice-bucket filled with the pink champagne reserved for the use of the Imperial Family. This indomitable old lady remains unaware that she appears as much a stranger to the present day as would a Princess of Byzantium. The double-headed eagle still flutters its wings about her: her hoarse, interminable chuckle fills the dead rooms with life. Many of them she has reduced to the level of an Oriental bazaar; Russian silver and ikons, jewelled watches and boxes, tinsel brocades, swinging censers and the endless junk of that lost civilisation, litter and clutter-up the delicate, finely counter-pointed perspectives. . . .

The Princess's day is a full one. Every morning she rolls for half an hour on the floor, to keep her back straight and preserve her suppleness. Then she skips. Then she has to dress, a complicated process, arrange her wig and eyebrows, and colour her complexion. Her morning is divided between prayer and the samovar. About twelve, the ravages of time repaired as far as she can repair them, she comes downstairs in full splendour. But by this time the Prince is working, dis-entangling the pedigrees of noblemen long perished, restoring order down these other perspectives of time — arches which have collapsed beneath their own weight and have become overgrown. (Italian culture resides in these finely balanced vistas which it has invented, vistas of rooms, vistas of music — each note echoing under a vault —, vistas of the theatre, fading and illusory.)

Luncheon is at twelve-thirty, and they eat often alone, one at each end of an immense table. All through the day the table-cloth, very large and very white and clean, is left on the table and is thickly encrusted with glittering, bulbous Russian silver, with silver roses and silver flowers (the dowry of the Princess); even Nanina, her fringed and fussy dog, eats off a silver plate in its own corner.

For the Princess, the day begins with the afternoon, when she goes out driving with Nanina and Count Ranucci, her *cicisbeo* (for she is one of the last to preserve this Italian habit). Barricaded against the wind behind a cockaded and cloaked coachman and footman, wearing Russian capes of fur, they drive interminably through the public gardens, round and round that delta between the two yellow rivers, arguing, laughing, quarrelling at the top of their voices, while Nanina snarls and motors whizz and hoot past them. Then come interludes of tea-parties and cocktail-parties, or else the Princess receives until seven — when, unless there is a ball, which happens very rarely, the day ends for her and the night swallows her up. She dines alone with Nanina and the Prince, or with Count Ranucci. When the Count is there, the Prince goes to bed, where he dreams of climbing family trees and swinging from heraldic branches. With the Count, her loved Pepino, the Princess plays bezique in her boudoir until two or three in the morning.

Even in warm weather the room is very hot from a porcelain stove, and the chuckles and laughter, and the angry interludes, are wheezy as the asthmatic breathing of Nanina in her tight-laced coat; that odious, corseted dog, with her false voice continually rapping out commands and saying things which she does not mean. And Nanina is always hiding, always having to be called, replying with a horrible yapping, the direction of which she yet contrives to disguise, so that both her mistress and her friend have perpetually to rise from their game and hunt all through the long, dark vistas. Ever, with one exception, since the Princess married and came to live here nearly sixty years ago, there has been a Nanina: and it has always looked like this, twelve years old, with a pointed, dancing-master nose and a corseted bust, an air of busy, fussy command, wheezy but inconsequent.

I could never make out to what breed Nanina and her four or five predecessors belonged, but it appertained obviously to the sixties of the last century; a breed imported into the cushioned, silken boudoirs of Russia from the Paris of the French Second Empire, a living symbol of western culture and emancipation. When she was not carried, the feet of this dog seemed to rap out, like a step-dance, the mid-nineteenth-century French airs of Delibes or Offenbach upon the hard, polished *terrazza* floors of these unending vistas. . . . Sometimes I thought that Nanina, the apparently eternal, was, despite her western origin and affinities, — in this comparable with the mounds of Russian silver and jewelled dolls —, but another symptom of the emphatic opposition the Princess offers to the classical and orderly life under the arches and coffered ceilings of her palace: for the Princess's blood must ache at moments for the gipsy wailings and the songs from barges, for the immoderate and unmodulated landscape of Russia — so large as to have no perspectives —, for the glitter and illusion of the Old Régime, for the bulbs and spires and crowns of the Kremlin and the amethyst-quartz grottoes in the frozen gardens of Tsarskoe Selo.

One evening I sat with her, drinking honey-tasting tea and eating complicated sandwiches (for the Princess loved people to be with her, was especially kind to those younger than herself and liked to examine them about their love-affairs). But for my presence, indeed, she would have been alone this evening, for there were no parties in the town and she had indulged earlier in the afternoon in one of her violent, recurrent quarrels with Pepino, that large, big-featured punchinello. Through the door of her little sitting-room, crowded with ill-assorted objects (a room which in its essence — though not, perhaps, in its profusion — so much resembled the dressing-room of a great theatrical star), I could perceive the darkening vista of the grand halls, room after room, *sala* after *sala*, empty, sad and echoing, yet full of beauty and courage and vision. Usually their extraordinary quality vanquished the human interest of the people who had lived in them: you did not wonder concerning them, did not muse about the men and women of succeeding generations — in armour, in striped hose and doublets, in wigs and velvet, in crinolines and panniers —, who through a lifetime had walked down these perspectives until finally they reached the past: you did not try to catch the dying sound of their voices, their accents echoing down through their descendants, in the same way that, in their own day, they had echoed up into nothingness under these high ceilings.

It was a warm evening as we drank our tea. Our room alone blazed with light, and from those beyond were wafted darkness, coolness, and, it seemed, a feeling of expectancy. . . . Someone out there, one might have imagined, was waiting for us — or were we waiting for someone? There was a crackling outside, and Nanina creaked her bones about her and barked. . . . A ghost, I wondered: and I recalled that the palace bore the reputation of being haunted. . . . So few Italian palaces possess ghosts that you would have thought the story easy to remember. As I talked, I tried to recollect what it was, and to what age the haunter belonged. . . . Not later than the time of Napoleon; because this whole system of life had died with him and Stendhal. Now the owners possessed no souls to leave behind them, were only animated shells, for all the Princess's energy. And certainly upon this evening the past seemed nearer than the present.

After a time I gave it up, and asked the Princess openly about the ghost, and if she had ever seen it. . . .

It had belonged, apparently, to the age of Romeo and Juliet, a fifteenth-century apparition, a girl who had died for love of a man whom circumstances forbade her ever to see, for he was a Guelph and she was a Ghibelline, or vice versa (indeed, I *ought* to have remembered, for she had been famous for her beauty, and her name was a household word here). It had been a romantic love, of swords and flowers and cloaks and serenades; a fifteen-year-old girl, with golden hair braided round her forehead, and with the dark, golden skin, slanting blue eyes and softly moulded aquiline nose of the Tuscans. There had been a portrait of her in the palace, but it had been sold and carried off to America more than thirty years ago. . . . Only the house itself remained, and its shadows, living and dead.

Even as we talked, it seemed to me, at any rate for the moment, that the air began to alter, to inspissate, to become colder; every teaspoon taken up or put down redoubled its tinkle; every plate was moved with a thud. The house seemed, more than ever, to be waiting. It was that hour of silence before the innumerable sounds of the Italian evening begin.

'No, I have never seen the ghost, the poor thing,' said the Princess, 'but once, long ago, I heard her voice. It must have been soon after I married, and long before we sold the Botticelli portrait of her in order to install the electric light. (Now, you see how comfortable it is!) It was an evening like this, and in those days, after Petersburg, it seemed quiet here, and I was restless. I remember what a beautiful disturbing day it had been, like this one; I could not sit still as I do now; I suppose it was my nomad, Tartar blood. The Prince had gone out, and my dog, my first dog, who was named Tita (though my husband didn't like my calling her that, because it had been the name of his ancestress, the ghost, the famous Tita), had disappeared, just as Nanina does — Nanina, darling, where are you? — and I could not find her anywhere. (She is always so naughty, my beautiful angel! Although my Tita has long been dead, she was just the same to look at, though not so lovely — no, darling, not so lovely!) The sun had not long hidden itself behind Santa Croce opposite, but it became very dark in this house and I walked through room after room calling "Tita! Tita! Tita!"; but there was no sound of my dog, not a bark from that angelic, furry throat. My voice echoed strangely under those high ceilings that were now so black, and little breaths of cold air swept over the bare floors. Even my footsteps echoed, and if I had not already come to know the rooms so well, and how they were disposed in a square round the court, I would have been afraid of losing my way. . . . Still I went on calling, calling, until the whole air seemed full of the cries: "Tita! Tita! Tita!" . . . You know, I am a Cossack, and I am not nervous. At the age of seven I saw the peasants riot and try to burn our house and did not flinch when they were beaten and mown down. I have — how do you say it? — no *fancies*. . . . And yet the number and size of the rooms, room after room, their coldness and darkness, began to weary me. In the furthest *sala* one window was open, and the blue dusk came in at it. I wondered for a moment, as I entered, if I saw a figure standing by the balcony. . . . There was nothing . . . I called again, "Tita! Tita! Tita!" . . . And, suddenly, a voice — a lovely, golden, warm Italian voice, sounding, though, as if, in spite of being in the room, it came from a great distance, down a vista of centuries — answered me: "Here I am, here I am! *Eccomi!*" and then seemed to diminish — *diminuendo* — and die away back into those endless years down which it had travelled. After that, the silence gathered round again, with no sound except the thudding of my heart. It had seemed cold, very cold, during those moments, the cold of the tomb or of an infinite distance. It was a lovely voice, though — poor thing, poor thing! But I never saw her, saw nothing, only the blackness which gathers to itself all shadows. . . . And I never again named a dog Tita: my husband had been right for once. Now, if Nanina is lost, I can turn on the electric light and call boldly — I never miss that picture. . . . Later, I found the dog in the street outside.'

Beyond the windows the animation of the evening was beginning. I heard the trams clanking and ringing, and the resonant strong voices of workmen returning home; and in the room, too, the sounds had regained their proportions. Nanina began to bark comfortably. No one was waiting: the story had expelled all shadows.

TRUE LOVERS' KNOT

Even when I first knew him — and it must be many years ago — Carey Totnell appeared to be an old man, with the bearded face of Socrates, only in appearance a more elegant philosopher, tinged, in the passage of time, by the epicurean. He seemed to survive as a type, the perfect bachelor of the eighties of the last century, suave in manner, cultivated in mind, leading a life both ordered and orderly. He might — except that his mind was more emancipated — have stepped straight out of the first act of one of Pinero's plays, set in Albany. Well read, in a fashion now almost extinct, a lover of the classics, so that he would often read Greek and Latin poetry for his own enjoyment, he displayed in his choice a natural taste for all good things, and he showed, too, a great respect for food and wine. I much appreciated his taste and intelligence and culture, his tired wisdom and kindliness; but sometimes I wondered at the garnished emptiness of his existence.

Only once, I think, did I hear him enunciate, in a deliberate, very individual voice which gave point to every word he said, sentiments that sounded as though in some way bound up with his life. And the theory that he had then propounded, fantastic as it seemed that evening, returned to my mind later when I heard of his death.

I had been dining with him — in Albany, of course — and he was talking to Robert Hovingford — then a young poet — and to myself in a corner of the library, while the others played bridge. Both Robert and I were in our twenties at the time, and he was rallying us on a supposed desire to avoid family responsibilities and ties. 'My dear boys,' I remember his concluding, 'it's no use your ever trying to escape. You are provided with only a few people among whom to play during your life. Some enter at birth, others drift in later. You can hate or love them as the threads that are their lives touch and knot yours, inextricably or loosely, as it may prove: but that doesn't matter; there they will be at every turn in your life, whereas

373

others, whom you may like better, appear only once, for a month or two, and it will be no use your trying ever to see them again. . . . Better at once to accept defeat and try to like those with whom Destiny has thrown you. It saves trouble; for there they'll be, sure enough, at the end! And so it is, too, with places. In normal times — not, of course, during wars or revolutions — only a few scenes are provided as background to the action of your whole life: to these you seem chained throughout your career on earth, and even when Death himself arrives for you.'

. . . . .

All those who had ever stayed in Miss Pomfret's house liked to return at least once a week to see her, because it was easy to look in at St. James's Place and they were sure of welcome and amusement. Moreover, she could boast that strange gift, given to so few, of making all her friends their friends. Originally, I had found my way thither by chance, her lodgings having been recommended by the porter of my club. But I had soon — in company, indeed, with all her guests — taken a great liking to her. She was a personage altogether uncommon, surviving from the age of Shakespeare, audacious and robust as Juliet's nurse, and with a natural gift for original observation and trenchant phrase. By nature Elizabethan, it had been her earthly lot to live through more than half of the Victorian reign, and so she had learned that people could now be shocked, and that a great many of them deserved the sensation.

However, to tow this warm-blooded, vigorously reacting human being, built on so magnificent a scale, both morally and physically, with her keen, peasant understanding of men and women (rare, because reached entirely through her individual eyes, in an age when the whole population has been taught to read and write), to attempt to tow her, then, and anchor her within the limited space of a short story, is a little like trying to introduce a whale within the confines of a swimming-pool. We will only, therefore, take a single glance at her large frame, its many rotund contours encased in black silk, on which were disposed several gold ornaments, and at the high black collar round her neck, surmounted by a little white ruff, which imparted to her smiling and rather creased face the shining geniality of a Frans Hals; so that, most of all, her visitors liked to see her — as sometimes, but not often, they did — holding up a wine-glass under the light, drinking to the health of a friend.

One evening, I found, as usual, a good many people in her sitting-room on the ground floor; and among others, Carey. . . . I had not realised before that Miss Pomfret and he were friends. I remember the occasion well, because she gave us a lively description of her new lodger, above, in the best suite. She had taken a great fancy to him — though he was a spiritualist, a faith of which she could not altogether approve — for he sent her enormous bunches of flowers from time to time, and she admired, too, the way in which he had done up his sitting-room, with, as she said, 'Hindian 'angings and Hegyptian bronzes on marble pedestrians', cats, bulls and hawks. 'Five thousand years old, some of 'em are,' she said confidently. But now came the sound of a bump overhead, followed by intoning, and Miss Pomfret broke off to remark, 'That's 'im. Pr'ying to that blooming 'awk agine, I suppouse.'

She liked to stay up talking as late as she could, till two or three in the morning if possible — perhaps because this to her was a symbol of being her own mistress at last, with no need to get up early. So, to gratify her propensity in this matter, I stayed behind after the others had gone, and it was then that she told me she had been nurse and personal maid to old Mrs. Totnell, Carey's mother, from about 1882 till her death in 1900, and had known intimately her numerous — there were seven sons and daughters — offspring. Their father, a famous counsel, had long been dead, and Carey was the eldest son, the cleverest, the pride and despair of his family. . . . I obtained from her, little by little, a picture of my old friend as a young man; a full-length portrait in the pointillist manner, acquired by placing a blob of paint here, a blob there.

In spite of those same responsibilities, about which he liked continually to harangue me, the inhabitant of that elegant, empty shell of today had been, it appeared, fierce, wild and untrammelled, a source of anxiety, instead — as now — of quiet comfort to his relatives. And in any particular difficulty that arose — or, more generally, that himself had created — it had been his very sensible habit to consult Miss Pomfret, since she could understand anything, however unglossed, that

belonged to human nature, to ask her advice, and to request
her to act as intermediary between himself and his family.
Moreover, whatever he did, or whatever she may have pretended to the contrary, she was, in reality, fonder of the gay,
exquisite, audacious 'Mr. Carey' than of all his brothers and
sisters, with their better regulated lives — of everyone, indeed,
except his mother, to whom she was devoted.

I gathered that by far the greatest imbroglio (one could
not say *scandal*, but difficulty is altogether too mild a word for
it) in which Carey had been involved, was a tremendous love-
affair with an Italian *prima donna* of international fame. For
two years he had lived with Forelli in a house in Welbeck Street,
and during that comparatively brief period there had arisen a
succession of tempests and hurricanes, born of the hot suns of
her native Neapolitan country, and often culminating in
episodes of intense strangeness and absurdity.

Always bounded by the conventions of the Italian operatic
form, limited to weeping, storming and threats of suicide, even
to the pretence of madness, they were followed by scenes
excruciatingly sweet, for all that their airs were yet unformulated, but nevertheless peculiarly unsuited to the social
life of the English capital and the quiet of the London clubs.
(I mention clubs advisedly because on several occasions Forelli
invaded the upholstered seclusion of the Mausoleum in quest
of Carey, and had to be barred from a search of its cloistral
apartments by an unspeakably shocked, if comprehending,
hall-porter.)

The effect of this upon his relatives can be imagined. They
had accused him of bringing scandal on the family, and of
neglecting his affairs in the City. Accordingly, Miss Pomfret
had often been designated to approach him with suggestions of
reform. But, as it happened, Miss Pomfret was, rather surprisingly, a devotee of grand opera; which, together with
racing, constituted the twin lights of her life. Moreover,
Forelli had taken a great liking to her, and this flattered such
an amateur. . . . Indeed, in only two matters had Miss
Pomfret stood against the lovers : she blamed him for causing
continual worry to his mother, and she did not want them to
marry. ('It wouldn't do.') But in any case, nothing would
have persuaded Forelli to marry him, and this had been, in
fact — though his relatives were too proud to believe it — the

most frequent cause of the quarrels between them.

Opera has fallen low in man's esteem, and no one now, I am aware, ever falls in love with a *prima donna*, but in those halcyon days of waists and bustles and bonnets, of hansom cabs and top-hats and frock-coats, when life was serene and unruffled except for the disturbances that you, as an individual, chose to make for your own diversion, nightingales were lovely of feather, as of voice. Into the brief space of their singing lives they crammed whole careers of artistic and amorous experience. When, for an immense fee, paid in gold sovereigns, such a diva consented to sing at a private house, at the mere opening of her lips talk would die away as though the archangel of music himself had entered the room and clapped his wings for silence. And the crowds that applauded her singing would be interested, equally, in the events of her private existence, would be in possession of a great many true, as well as false details, and would discuss them eagerly. Every night elegant, ardent young amateurs waited outside the stage door to see Forelli emerge and drive off with Carey in his private hansom, and nearly every day, too, he could be seen attending her in the Park or escorting her through a restaurant with something of the pride of a drumming peacock. Bouquets and messages, lyres and harps and wreaths of roses and carnations, arrived for her at all hours. And these tributes helped to charge the atmosphere suitably for scenes of passion in real life.

In spite of their reasonless and perpetual differences, in spite of incongruity, in spite of her willingness to live with, and yet steadfast refusal to marry him, each had been in reality devoted to the other. Carey was in love with her voice as much as her person, and for him she would sing as for no one else. Notwithstanding frequent ludicrous and painful situations, there had existed in their relationship a quality not only genuine, but tragic and unforgettable, and this Miss Pomfret had seen for herself and somehow managed to convey to me, even after the passing of many years. Here, then, in the drawing-room of his house in Welbeck Street, the turmoil of both their lives had spent itself (for, being a born *prima donna*, Forelli preferred scenes set in the drawing-room to, as it were, bedroom scenes), and they had loved and quarrelled with a vehemence and ebullition unsuited to this city and its sur-roundings, had often parted for ever, only to return, dove-like, within a few hours. Here, with her back to the huge piano smothered up in a Chinese shawl, with many objects standing upon it, she had practised her parts, and trilled her joys and griefs in coloratura.

Miss Pomfret described the room well, could even remember the identity of some of the silver-framed, enthusiastically autographed portraits of tenors with whom Forelli had sung; for she had often been sent there with messages from anxious relatives, or had been summoned by one or other of the lovers themselves. Evidently Carey had furnished it for his mistress with an ostentation born of the recent romances of Ouida and of the influence of Sarah Bernhardt; had filled it with arabesque hangings, with Persian rugs and flowers and palm-trees, with bronzes and fine pictures, ancient and modern; and Forelli, for her part, had added operatic trophies, crowns and sheaves of flowers, photographs of elephantine tenors in armour, or with lace collars and hats crowned with flowing feathers. Certainly for him the place had been charged with vital vibrations such as he was never to give out, or receive, again. The battery, the dynamo of his soul, had been, for those two short years, working at its highest pressure. After that, he became the shell I knew.

Eventually the lovers had quarrelled and really parted for good, much to the satisfaction of all concerned, except themselves. And not long after, Forelli had died in Paris, still in the height of her powers and her celebrity, so that only the echo of that golden voice lingered in the minds of men.

. . . . .

It was Miss Pomfret who told me first of Carey's death. He had been nearly seventy — a good span, I suppose: but somehow, all his qualities, physical and mental, had appeared to be specifically calculated to support him into extreme old age, so that the news came as a shock to his friends. Though, as I perceived, she deeply felt his loss, and his sufferings, yet, reverting again to her Elizabethan character, she could not help manifesting something of Webster's fascinated delight in death. She showed herself determined, in spite — or, perhaps, because — of my affection for him, to spare me no detail of Carey's final distress and dissolution. One could almost hear in her voice, as she talked, the rhythm of the poet's lines:

Of what is't fools make such vain keeping?
Sin their conception, their birth weeping,
Their life a general mist of error,
Their death a hideous storm of terror.

When he sent for her, she had found him in a typically
fashionable nursing-home, made up of several old houses,
superficially altered. The lift, she had noticed, was hardly
wide enough to hold her, but possessed a curious, long rectangular shape, just able to receive a coffin when it came down.

'Oh yes, he's getting on nicely,' the sister had said in a
'pleasant' voice, cool and clear, 'and much more "comfy"
than he would be at home. . . . There's always a nurse with
him, even at night, to cheer him up. And he's less grumpy:
quite affable to everyone now.'

Carey Totnell lay, propped up on pillows, in a large front
room on the first floor; rather dark, and to Miss Pomfret's
way of thinking, 'too cold-looking', with its sanitary surfaces
and enamelling. It contained, also, a litter of pseudo-scientific
apparatus, lamps and cylinders and bed-tables, and of spindly
fittings in aluminium and steel, the uses of which remain
fortunately unknown to the lay mind. 'Why, the very bed
'e l'y hin 'ad more the look to me of a dentist's chair than a
Christian bed,' Miss Pomfret remarked to me. . . . Nevertheless, she had rather liked the room; it had seemed in some
way familiar and, in consequence, comfortable and not to be
feared.

But she was shocked at the change she saw in the invalid,
for he had paid her one of his usual visits, apparently in his
normal health, only a few evenings previously. Carey had
betrayed from the first, it seems, 'that nasty blue look', his voice
had come from far away when he spoke, his nails ''ad no life
in them', and his hands kept plucking at the sheets; all these
symptoms being well-known harbingers of death in the system
of divining which she had projected for herself. ' "You'll never
come hout of 'ere, except a corpse, laid hout flat in that lift,
my man," Hi said to myself,' she added, 'but, of course, I
didn't let 'im see anything. Hi couldn't 'elp crying a little,
and jest said, "Oh, Mr. Carey, dear, to think of seeing you
like this!"'

The sister had first turned the nurse out of the room, then,
after indulging in a miniature power-dive, patting and tugging

at the pillows which he had managed at last,to make comfortable for himself, and pulling cords for windows and ventilators, she had squared her chin, saying, 'Now I'll go. I know I can trust you not to tire the patient or stay too long', and had left them.

At once Carey had turned his face to Miss Pomfret and said (he seemed to have to make an effort, she had thought, even to speak), 'Mary, my old friend, I'm a dying man. I know. It is only a matter of hours, not of days. . . . So I wanted to see you once again, to thank you for everything you've done for me, always . . . and to ask you one question. . . . You've seen so much of the course of my life : do you recognise this room?' . . . And then, as she looked round, she had understood ; the enamelled cornices and doors, the distempered walls, the metal furniture, had taken on other colours, other lines. A gold-lacquered paper flowered again over the walls, a Chinese screen stood in front of the door, a Symphony in White, by Whistler, hung over the mantel. (The fireplace was now filled in, to hold an electric heater.) In the far corner, on the muffled piano, stood rows of silver-framed photographs of Forelli in the rôles of Carmen, La Sonnambula, Lucia and a hundred other operatic heroines, or of mellifluous male singers decked for their parts, and on the tables the vases of sick-room flowers had been ousted for the instant by vast, formal trophies of roses, orchids and lilies. . . . He lay now dying in the very room of the very house in which his life had been crowned and consumed.

.   .   .   .   .

He told her that he had fought — as she had been certain he would — against the idea of leaving Albany at all. But the doctor had ordered him to be taken at once in a motor-ambulance to his favourite nursing-home. Carey had not even known where it was situated, and had felt too ill to ask questions. On arrival, when the old atmosphere had begun to distil itself round him in the room, he had felt sure that this was the result of his fever : but during the night, as he lay awake there, he had become convinced, on the contrary, of its reality. And a curious mingled sense of comfort and inquietude had assailed him. . . . However, the slight effort of describing his feelings evidently tired him out, and as he seemed to be growing sleepy, Miss Pomfret had soon left him.

Next morning she had returned again to see him. But this time he did not know her. . . . He was apparently talking Italian to someone on the other side of the bed. She tried to make out what he was saying, but it was no use: she only knew a few words of Italian. Then he fell silent again, intent, as though listening. . . . And was it her imagination, she wondered, or did she really distinguish, just for a moment, a coloratura trill, high up and far away, almost out of hearing? . . . She wished her ears had been sharper, for it sounded, oh, beautiful; heavenly, you might say.

Probably it was a gramophone or radio somewhere near by. You couldn't get away from them nowadays. But she was never sure.

THE MESSENGER

It was in the afternoon, for there were no evening performances. We had both of us seen *Les Sylphides* a hundred times,
and much better danced, so we left the theatre and waited in
the empty *foyer* until the next ballet began.

Painters are apt to talk well, writers badly; for by the end
of the day they are tired of words. (The members of no other
profession are obliged to express themselves solely by means of
their wares.) Robert Hovingford, though an excellent writer
— no less original and celebrated as an author than his wife
is as a painter —, stands out, an exception to this rule. I love
to listen to him, however preposterous may be the theories
which he continually expounds, for underneath the queer
brand of decorative nonsense in which invariably he indulges,
gleams a vein of truth; a vein strange and at first unconvincing,
because so unlike the truth of other people.

A man passed, without seeing us, and Robert smiled and
called out to him, 'Good luck!'

'That's my mascot,' he remarked to me. 'And he knows
it. I feel elated, for whenever good fortune is in the wind for
me, I see him — though I have never got to know him very
well. But he understands that, too. It's part of his contract,
so to speak.'

'If you both like the Ballet, it's inevitable that you should
see him,' I began to argue. 'I don't think much of your
reasoning, Robert.'

'"Inevitable", *inevitable*,' he repeated, 'don't use that word,
please. . . . Did I tell you about The Messenger? . . . No?
Then I must tell you now. . . . "Inevitable" is the word I
dread. All my life I have been able to hear the Juggernaut
creaking down the immutable course of its steel rails towards its
destiny. I cannot explain the reason *why* things happen as
they do; I can only humbly note fragments of the design, the
vast scale of its conception, here and there the minute working-
out of the details attached to it. . . . You know that I have
long held that, if you are frightened of something happening,

that event is brought so much the nearer to you by your fear : or you may even be treated to a counterfeit semblance of it, or a rehearsal for it, in order further to terrify you. The sort of thing I mean is that, if you have a peculiar dread of, shall we say, smallpox, and think you have been exposed to infection, then, the very day on which you expect to develop the disease, your body will come out in a rash : but, instead of smallpox, it will prove to be some lesser, children's illness. . . . But I mustn't wander away from the question of inevitability.

'Do you remember old Carey Totnell and his theories ?·* I used to make fun of them, but events have since converted me to them. I believe, too, now, that we are born into the world with certain people for our companions ; these alone we may see, play with, quarrel with : we cannot avoid them. We are confined with them, as it were, in a compartment of eternity of which the walls are invisible, so as to give us the illusion of the whole earth at our choice. It is futile to try to escape the reiterant impacts of these people on our lives. They may bore us, they may enchant us, but there, sure enough, they will stand at our life's end as at our life's beginning. . . . And this story — an episode more than a story — which I want to tell you, shows at least how superb is the timing of Destiny, and proves that it is of no use attempting to delay the effects she wishes to obtain.

'First of all, let us for a moment examine the nature of the playmates provided for us. I hope I am not over-superstitious. but I observe coincidences. . . . There is the man who passed by just now, for instance : my mascot. Obversely, there are those whose presence darkens the air for me, the harbingers of evil. This whole genus, an important one, can be divided, I think, into two species : the first, harmless chatterers who, as the whole world reels for you though you must not show it, rush up to worry you about things that do not matter. They seem to emerge suddenly, from nowhere, with a certainty of technique that belongs only to the virtuoso — for their mere appearance discloses whole avenues leading back into the past, down which Disaster stalks towards you. They like to ask questions : "How is your dear Aunt Emily ; have you heard from her lately?" or "Did you ever get the address of that shop I

* See 'True Lovers' Knot' (p. 373).

wanted you to go to? You never let me know", or "I thought of going down to Dorset in April to stay with your cousins; will you be there?" or "Have you seen Dicky lately?" (a man you have been avoiding for years). Indeed, this branch of the tribe never fails to collect the friends you have shed in the course of a lifetime. (And, let us be frank, the friends we possessed at eighteen are not, if we develop normally, those we should choose, or choose to see, at forty.) They are like retrievers, producing corpses for you, with an air of pride, just at the moment you least expect it. They specialise also in knowing, never the celebrated man himself, but always his duller connections; had they then been alive, they would have concentrated their attention upon Leonardo da Vinci's maiden aunt or Michelangelo's cousin ("So much more original, yet simple", they would have, no doubt, explained), though occasionally, of course, they would have materialised in some moment of agony, to ask the Master after the tedious relatives whom he had for so long striven to forget.

'The second species, however, is more incisive in action. Retrievers, too, to a man, they are also essentially the bearers of tidings. If there is something it would be better for you *not* to know at a particular moment, they spring out of the earth, like a *jinnee* out of his bottle, to tell you, with a grisly savouring of their pleasure, rolling the words round in their mouths in the same way that a connoisseur allows the flavour of good wine to linger upon the palate. They belong to a race apart, the witless avengers of forgotten injuries; their whole bearing, inspired by their subconscious minds, testifies to it. The countless indignities inflicted unaware upon the dwarf by the man of ordinary stature, upon the ugly by the beautiful, the stupid by the clever, boil up suddenly within their brooding blood.

'You may think I exaggerate; but let me tell you. . . . Do you know Ralph Mudey-Mulhall? Well, he has the attributes of both the species I have described. Please don't mistake me. He is kind — more than kind, tender-hearted. He possesses many invaluable qualities that in someone else we should all of us estimate at their true worth. He works hard, supports several idle relatives, is a faithful friend, and does good in many directions. I could never dislike him, never be rude to him. I wish him well, infinitely well, but

384

from a distance — it must be from a distance. . . . To begin
with, when I meet him he always talks to me, immediately, of
those friends of my parents whom I most dislike. They speak
of me, he tells me, continually, and he repeats some of "the
nice things they say". Thus his conversation, always bringing
with it the memory of distant but unhappy days, lowers the
temperature of mind and heart and body. "You cannot
escape us", the voices of the Gorgon sisters moan in your ear.

'Both Frida and I have known Ralph since we were
children — before we had ever met each other. He had
attended all the same children's parties to which we went.
And then, when we had grown up and frequented ballrooms,
there, too, he would be; now a very tall, stooping, lanky
figure, dark, with a bumpy forehead, a small, clipped moustache, and brown eyes, intent but curiously empty, and a
voice, deep and deliberate, summoned up like the voice of a
ventriloquist rather than seeming a natural mode of expression.
On these occasions he would appear always to be rather lonely,
would dance seldom, so that one wondered why he came. But
to us he was very friendly, and, at the time that Frida and I
became engaged, just before and just after, he would invariably
suggest joining us for supper. It was difficult to refuse, but
you know, when you are in love, you want to be alone and
don't relish extraneous company; so that, though we still
liked him, we tended to try and escape his presence, but that
only added, you would have thought from the result, to the
fascination we exercised upon him. He was willing — and
able — to ferret us out anywhere.

'The years went by then, and we saw less of him, because,
as he grew older, his utter contentment, the fact that he was
so happy with the collection of old silver and of our old-style-
calendar friends that he was forming — for this, too, had
become really a *collection* — irked us. He was quite rich; so,
feeling the necessity of perpetuating his likeness, he sat, of
course, to Laszló, and it was very trying to be invited to see
that painter's flashy misrepresentation of him as a dashing
Magyar magnate rather than a mild English business man.
We grew tired of hearing of his garden, the new kind of sweet
peas he was growing, and the perfection altogether of his way of
life. In fact, he was so enchanted with himself — in a lesser
degree, often a delightful characteristic — that it became a bore,

as did his quirks and quips, his little jokes and sallies and imitations. Much more full of talk than formerly, he liked to tell you all about himself, what he ate every day, what he felt, at what time he was called and when he went to bed : these things were all of intense concern to him and so he thought they would equally interest his listeners. And he would give us, too, the opinions of his friends on many matters ; he seemed to live in a perpetual house-party of those who had been dead to us since we had reached years of discretion. While, therefore, he has no spite in his whole composition, not a grain of it, he is himself its blind and unavowed instrument, the Mercury of the forces that govern the lower regions.

'You can understand how bad things have been for us lately, because you know the circumstances ; cruel for Frida and bad enough for me. John is our only child, and it would have been dreadful to see any child, even if he had not been our own, suffering like that, so ill and helpless and unable to understand what was the matter or tell us what he felt. And, in order to be near the right doctors, we had to stay in London through the bombing, exposing him to dangers of that kind as well.

'As a mother, Frida is sometimes a bit vague. She has always adored John, but, all the same, her whole life goes usually into her painting. (And, what's curious, I believe the little chap comprehends it and isn't jealous.) But, when he fell ill, the full strength and resilience of her character came out. She gave up her work entirely, and nursed the boy night and day. I don't know how she did it, for she wasn't used to that kind of fatigue : but I think that was what pulled him round ; because it's a rare illness, and the doctors cannot help much as yet, though they do their best. For a whole fourteen days, she never had a thought for anyone but John. I was completely forgotten. She would hardly even allow her sister, Isabelle, to help her. The strain must have been — and anybody could see it was — immense. . . . At last, one morning, about a fortnight ago, the specialist pronounced, "If the child gets through the next twenty-four hours, his temperature will drop. He will live, and the illness will leave no mark on him. . . . It is a terrible thing to have to say to his father and mother, but I must warn you ; it all depends on the next twenty-four hours."

'Isabelle had been splendid. Her kindness and tirelessness, her support of Frida, and the consideration she showed for her in everything, great or small, won my affection more than ever. (And I've always said that I would have married her, if I hadn't married Frida.) On the morning that the crisis of John's illness began, she came to me and said :

'"Robert, what are we to do? . . . Natasha Danbury is dead. She has died of pneumonia following on influenza. We *can't* tell Frida at a time like this. And if we don't, she is sure to find out."

'Natasha — I don't believe you ever met her — had been an old neighbour of Frida's parents in the country, and Frida and she had soon become great friends. As her Christian name tells you, she was Russian by origin, and she had married a delightful old man, much older than herself, Bill Danbury. He was rather an extraordinary character in his way, a squire, devoted to country pursuits, but loving books and music as much as hunting. Really, very exceptional. Natasha was beautiful, like a greyhound, and, while Bill was alive, passed for an intelligent woman. Alas, when she became a widow, the full extent of the influence her husband had exercised upon her became apparent. She had absorbed his taste. But now she showed that she had no opinions of her own, though she produced every *cliché* with an impressive manner. She needed someone like Bill to grow round, and to take her out of herself. Now that he was no longer there, she brooded in a mystical way upon the intricacies of her own uninteresting nature, and expatiated upon them incessantly to her friends, in a special voice she reserved for this subject, slow and emphatic. The high points she marked, sometimes by affected spirals of laughter, sometimes by a trick she thought attractive, of putting out her tongue at right angles, and in the opposite direction from that in which she rolled her eyes. (A very difficult feat of facial acrobatics; you try it in front of the mirror when you get home!) . . . Poor Natasha! She expected her friends to give the whole of their time up to her. In the end, a year or two ago, Frida, who has all the hardness, as well as all the softness, of the artist, came to me and said :

'"Robert, I've got to choose between Natasha and my painting. I've chosen my painting. I am fond of her, but she's inflated herself into a whole-time job, and I can't take it on. . . . Besides, she has plenty of other more suitable friends. I know she'll *pretend* to mind my neglect of her. I feel a brute, myself. But she won't *really* mind, though she will enjoy being huffy and mysterious when my name is mentioned. She won't *really* mind, because she knows how interesting her character is, how important to the world, and she knows, too, that we don't know it.''

'I don't blame Frida. Her first duty was to her painting. All the same, since she is genuinely kind, I thought I saw, from time to time, signs that Natasha weighed on her conscience. And so now the news of this sudden death — Natasha who was so healthy and had never been known to be ill for a day — was bound, especially in the circumstances in which we found ourselves, to upset Frida beyond reason.

'Her sister and I talked it over. We settled to keep *The Times* away from her — Natasha's death wasn't in the other papers —, at least until our own crisis was over. If the boy took a turn for the better, she would be more fitted to hear the news ; if he grew worse, nothing would matter any more. . . . The hours dragged on, the strain increasing all the time. How we got through that day and night I shall never know. They seemed interminable. . . . Then, all at once, about eleven o'clock the next morning, the danger was over, — John's temperature had fallen, and he breathed without difficulty and slept, for the first time for a fortnight, the easy, unstirring sleep of childhood. . . . The change was incredible at first.

'It was only, though, in this moment of utter relief, that the full fatigue of what we had been through settled upon Frida, Isabelle and myself. You can't imagine how tired we felt.

'None of us had left the house for many days, none of us had eaten a proper meal, or felt that we could eat one, and now, in spite of our exhaustion, there suddenly welled up in us a sense of gaiety, a need for relaxation. It was as though we had been on a long and very rough ocean voyage and had at last reached land. There was no reason to stay at home any longer ; John could be safely left to the nurse's care. So we decided to dine out, tired or not ; but, since we did not feel inclined as yet to face people who had not shared our experience, we selected Le Perroquet Vert ; because it's amusing, the food is excellent and you never see anyone you know there. . . .

And since Frida still had not looked at the paper, and was in this mood, we determined again to put off telling her about Natasha, to leave it till the next day; otherwise, it would only spoil her evening.

'We had ordered a table, but when we arrived we found the *maître d'hôtel* had made a mistake, and that it had been set for four persons; a nice table with a wall-sofa and two chairs. . . . It really was enjoyable to be out of the house again, to be able to order a dinner, to be able to eat it. And there were no sirens tonight, none of those wailings which are the signature-tune of the twentieth century. . . . We might as well have a cocktail, we thought; it was an occasion.

'Indeed, we were feeling care-free in spite of the war — and I believe both Isabelle and I had, for the time being, completely forgotten about the death of Natasha, which had been haunting us all day, because of its possible effect upon Frida.

'"How lovely," Isabelle said, "to be by ourselves, but to have the whole evening before us without anything on our minds . . . I long to hear you talk again about other things than medicines."

'Almost as she said the words, we saw Ralph Mudey-Mulhall, sitting there, alone, in the middle of the restaurant, reading a book.

'"It's all right, he doesn't see us," Frida reassured us. "And it's a good thing. I'm happy, but I'm too tired to deal with people — especially Ralph. I only want to see you two."

'"Oh, he sees us; never you fear," I replied. "He is preparing something, an eclectic joke of some kind or other, I should say." I could deduce it from the manner in which his head never moved from behind his book.

'Isabelle urged, "Have the fourth place removed at once! Or he'll come and sit through dinner, this heavenly sense of being at peace will be broken and we shall none of us be able to talk at all. . . . And I have masses to say; I don't know if you have? *Please* call the waiter and have it taken away."

'"We can't," I said. "It will take too long and look too rude."

'Now a waiter hurried up to us, with a note written in pencil: "Herr Hitler would like to look at you". The waiter pointed out the table (we pretended not to know it), and we gazed across. Suddenly Ralph dropped his book. Then he pulled — for imitations of Hitler were fashionable at the moment, and Charlie Chaplin's "Great Dictator" was the popular film of the hour — a lock of hair over his bumpy forehead and treated us to an impersonation of the Nazi Leader. I must say, with the hair and his little moustache, he succeeded in looking — though one would never have expected it — terrifyingly like him, or, at any rate, like other imitations of him one had seen. . . . We smiled and laughed, in what we hoped was a convincing manner, although the astonished expression on the faces of the people sitting at tables between us and him made us feel a little self-conscious.

'Ralph then reassembled his features, laughed a good deal at the joke, as he considered it, that he had played on us, and got up and stalked towards us, rather like, I thought, a walking lighthouse, with his lanky form and projecting eyes, shallow but burning. He still laughed and chuckled as he approached us. Once near enough to speak, however, his expression changed to one of sympathy and commiseration. . . . For an instant, I thought he had heard, somehow or other, about John's illness. Then I realised.

'"Frida, dear Frida," he was saying. "I was *so* grieved to hear of Natasha Danbury's death. I know what friends you two were. Though I never knew her very well, I had seen more of her lately, and had grown to appreciate her, and her wonderful powers of introspection and self-analysis. Introspective people *are* so interesting, don't you think? I can quite see why you two got on so well."

'Two spots of colour leapt suddenly into Frida's pale, tired face, and she said:

'"*Natasha? Natasha dead?* . . . Surely not? We should have heard," and she gazed at her sister and myself with a sort of shocked inquiry and reproach in her eyes.

'There was no help for it. We had to explain.

'"Isabelle and I decided it was better not to tell you, darling, at present: you've had so much worry lately. We were going to break it to you tomorrow. . . . She died two days ago." And to Ralph I said, "You see, Ralph, I didn't let her know, because she has been nursing our little boy — and it's been a great strain. He has been very ill for the last fortnight. But the crisis is over now. . . . This is the first

time we've been out since his illness began : and I didn't think we should see anyone who would be likely to tell her."
. . . Meanwhile, Frida was mastering her surprise and shock.

'Ralph is kind, really very kind. An agonised look came over his face. "Oh, how dreadful ! I am so sorry. You *didn't know*? How stupid of me ! I wouldn't have done such a thing for the world."

'Then he stopped apologising. I saw the thought go through his head, "I must help them", and he said, in his ordinary, deliberate way :

'"Well, as it's your first evening out, you'll want cheering up, so let *me* sit down here and talk to you."

'All through our dinner — for he had finished his — he sat in the fourth place at the table, thereby in his own mind atoning for his lapse by charity — I never saw a man work so hard, either, to be kind. . . . At first, to distract Frida's attention, he talked of friends, old friends, friends of her parents, all of them longing to see us, he said, and often wondering how it was they never ran across either of us. Of course, they didn't approve of my wife's painting, he added, or of her marrying a man who wrote for his living : but they were fond of her, oh, so fond, and anxious to *help*. And they liked me, too, it appeared, would like to get to know me better ; they thought there was probably a lot of good in me, *when* they got to know me. Similarly, he said, he had seen many old friends of *my* parents, and they were eager to get to know Frida better, were sure they would perceive things in her that they had not hitherto noticed, if only they saw more of her. And they were quite sensible, and stated openly that they did not expect even to understand — or like — her paintings. It was so much better to be frank, like that, and not to pretend, wasn t it ?

'I am afraid he saw this line was not proving a success, so he imitated Hitler again, in order to give himself time to think. We all three laughed a lot. Then he told us about the last few bits of silver he had bought before the war, and where he had sent them for safety. From that subject he passed on to his life in the country, to his evacuees, and how it had turned out — you'd never guess, he said ! — that my old tutor and Frida's governess were among them. They were always talking of us, telling stories of our childhood, and of what *absurd* children we had been. "Mind you," he said, "they're fond of you ; don't think they're not." Now he veered towards more congenial subjects.

'He confided in us what he ate, and what he drank. Sometimes, owing to the organising genius of his cook, he had meat three times a week, sometimes four. Good meat, too. The cooking was good *bourgeois* cooking, and there was nothing better ! On the whole, perhaps, he ate less than in peace-time, but he felt none the worse for it — if anything, better. (He had got into his stride by now, and at times stopped the flow, copious but deliberate, to regard us, most severely, to make sure we were paying attention. The slightest failure in this respect, the flicker of a single eyelash in another direction, he seemed in almost psychic fashion immediately to divine.) Often he drank cider now, he avowed, or ginger-beer, even. After all, it was war-time. And coffee, lots of coffee. He was called at 7.30, or, it might be, on one or two days a week, at 8. . . . We seemed almost to be watching the hours going round.

'We did not speak : there was no necessity, he did not expect it. We did not dare, even, to catch one another's eye. We gave — had to give — our whole attention, concentrated on the vast vista he was unfolding. . . . Suddenly he broke off, looked at his watch, and said :

'"*What* a time you've kept me here ! . . . Why, it's ten, long past ten, and I see the waiters are trying to clear away. We mustn't delay them. I always say it's unfair on them to sit on and on. So I shall leave you now. I ought to have gone an hour ago, for I'd promised to go in, Robert, and see your Aunt Muriel for a few minutes on my way home. We often talk of you, she seems so lonely and loves to talk of past days. . . . Now you've made me late."

'He went to get his coat and hat and then, just as we thought him gone, returned to say, "I forgot to tell you, Frida, how I stuck up for you the other day. . . . No, I won't tell you who they were, or what they said, but I always stick up for you with everyone. You can depend on that."

'*He* had forgotten all about Natasha Danbury, I think, and went home quite happy.'

Robert stopped speaking, and we got up to go into the theatre, for the next ballet, *Petrouchka*, had already begun, and the puppets were moving their feet and arms within the open booths, while the old magician watched them.

ALIVE — ALIVE OH!

It has long been apparent to the discerning that in this country to be a poet — or, at any rate, a good one — is a rash, a hazardous, activity. It may be that there are critics who will object to this doctrine, who will urge that, for example, Byron, Keats and Shelley were not driven from their native land, but quitted it of their own accord, gladly even. Nevertheless it cannot be disputed that these three most remarkable Englishmen of their day preferred to spend their last years, or months, in a foreign country. Whether hounded out to die or themselves eager to go, they went: that is sufficient. Nor will it be disputed, one imagines, that since their passing weak health has come to be demanded as first token, an early death as final guarantee, of poetic genius.

Historically, the death of the three poets I have mentioned was divided by no very great interval of years from that of Nelson, who had first framed in burning words the national conception: 'England expects that every man will do his duty'. Once this doctrine had been formulated, the part oı the poet in the community immediately became defined and acknowledged: it was to die young. Surely, too, he must be, not only willing, but anxious to aid those critics who spend so much of their time in helping him? A post-mortem is always more certain than diagnosis (vivisection, though it would be a more complete solving of the difficulty, is at present forbidden on human beings, even on artists), and it is inevitably easier to spot a dead poet than one alive and kicking. Moreover, once the man is removed, the critics, like so many calamaries, can surround the body of his work with such a cloud of ink that it soon becomes impossible to distinguish its essential features. Thus it must be admitted that more has been written about Shakespeare since his death than ever in his lifetime, albeit his plays are more seldom performed: and that the mass of critical footnotes that, much as parasites cling to an animal, encrust the text of every classic does not make it any the easier to read.

Yet when all these arguments have been stated, there are still to be found those willing — or, if not willing, obliged — to pay the penalty of genius. Perhaps, just as the great whales have, during the last century, transformed their tactics with the object of making the hunting of them the more perilous, so the poet may have become better, if more difficult, sport. I know not. But surely some facts of this kind can be deduced from the story of Joseph Bundle, the Georgian poet, and of his untimely death; that true though tragic narrative, which, never before told in full, I now propose to relate.

There must, of course, be others who have survived these long years : there must be others who recall, as I do, the aureole of fame which once emanated from those four inspiring syllables — Joseph Bundle. It was some fifty years ago, toward the end of the First European War, and in the lustrum following its conclusion, that they reached their fullest effulgence. Yet even before that splendid culmination to diplomacy — one, of course, to which no Englishman can ever look back without experiencing a physical tingle of pride at the magnitude of the national effort and its resultant losses — had been reached, the name Bundle was one of a growing celebrity, a sound seldom off the lisping lips of the more cultured. Nor was it difficult to comprehend why such a coruscation issued from the very music of these syllables. Everything about Bundle, everything that concerned him, was romantic, mysterious. Apart from his altogether exceptional knowledge of bird-life (the only other qualification, besides ill-health and its latent promise of an early decease, that is demanded by the public as essential in an English poet), it was understood from the very beginning that in some peculiar, almost mystic, way he was not only connected, but positively identified with the soil of Sussex, whether chalk or clay : that, like Venus arising from her shell, borne in by the racing, foam-flecked horses of the tides, so had Bundle been discovered by Mattie Dean * and other *literati* — though, of course, fully dressed and more conventionally educated — cradled in some half-hidden juniper-bush on the Downs.

And this impression of secret contact with Mother Earth that he induced was not misleading, for he was in reality —

* For a full description of Mattie, though when he is some years older, see 'Triple Fugue', p. 224.

and he kept it skilfully concealed — the son of a prosperous doctor in Shoreham, and though he had been, as it were, born with a silver thermometer in his mouth, this was indeed due to the united action of the Sussex soil, and its faithful ally, Winter, upon the tubes, livers and lungs of wealthy old ladies in the neighbourhood. This same rich hibernal harvest it was that had supported the expense of his excellent education, and that had finally enabled him to study for a year at that Dramatic Academy where he had acquired the pleasant, rustic burr of his speech — a burr which never deserted him and much enhanced his popularity with those crowds of nature-lovers immured in cities — though I have heard a cavilling native purist denounce it as more Somerset than Sussex.

His appearance, too, fitted him admirably for the part he had so judiciously chosen. Its chief attribute, and that most responsible for his early success, was a perhaps deceptive effect of extreme physical delicacy. And then, hollow-cheeked and hollow-chested though he was, yet with the deep-set brightness of his eyes, the curve of nose and chin, the long body and rather anomalous legs, he suggested — and what could be more appropriate? — a bird — the Bird of Wisdom, the Athenian Owl. At this period the old-fashioned poetic preciosity he exhibited was comparatively little. He to a greater degree cultivated, on the other hand, a you-don't-mind-if-I-slap-you-on-the-back-though-I've-just-been-cleaning-my-Ford-car heartiness of manner that must have been somewhat disconcerting at first to those esthetes accustomed to a more lilied artificiality. But this soon earned him a reputation for being simple, and unaffected. He encouraged his intimates, too, to call him 'Joe' rather than Joseph, Joe Bundle, so that his name might link up with those of Will Shakespeare, Ben Jonson and Kit Marlowe, and was wont to drink ale in almost too Mermaidenly a manner. In all he said or did there was a smack of the soil — a smack so pronounced as almost to constitute a 'knock-out'. Yet though at the beginning of his career he valiantly upheld what he conceived to be the Elizabethan ideals of beer, sweet and rich, full-mouthed, full-blooded, English — a girl, for example, was always to him a wench — yet he was capable of modifying his affectation to his environment. Thus, were one to inquire of those who remember him, one would be given many varying and apparently contradictory accounts of him. For the Mermaid Tavern rôle was only the chief of the several he could play: indeed, his appearance of ill-health tugged in an exactly contrary direction, never allowed him entirely to forget Keats, or Shelley either as for that: and often even in those days, working as it might be on a sort of spiritual second gear, he would open his collar romantically for a day or two and dart liquid fire out of his eyes: while in after years, when clamorous critics had so obviously given him his cue, and when he had at last come to realise the full significance of his destiny, he was seldom seen except in this other part.

Bundle's first volume of verse, which was published some time in the year preceding the war, had won for him a swift and gratifying recognition, for the poems combined many familiar and therefore delightful ingredients: a sound bottom of Cowper and Wordsworth (Clare was to come later), a little Marlowe, a hint of Shelley, a dash of Marvell, with Keats's beaded bubbles winking at the brim, all shaken together by the local village idiot and served up very cold with a plate of bird-seed to accompany it. The slight foaming which resulted was Bundle's own contribution. Yet in all this there was nothing to startle or affright, everything was soothing and of the kind to which one was accustomed. Indeed, the most sensational feature of the first book was its success. 'The critics', quoted the publishers, 'are unanimous in hailing an English poet not unworthy of his forebears.' And Mattie Dean, who, since he did their reading for them by some process of substituted service, had long been the arbiter of things poetic in a thousand drawing-rooms, became so excited and over-wrought by the book that he read two poems from it aloud after dinner to three Cabinet Ministers (two of whom had never heard a poem before); their wives, whose quarrelling was so suddenly stilled by this shrill, sweet piping that they even forgot, for a moment, how the score of the evening stood; a young priest singular for his journalistic wit — one, that is to say, the existence of which only journalists could perceive; an old lady who in her young days had been painted by Burne-Jones and had never since allowed anyone to forget it; a middle-aged woman who had sat to Sargent for her portrait thirteen times and had since been able to remember nothing else; two celebrated, serious-minded but dreadfully bad

actresses of musical comedy, who said 'sweet-sweet' and 'I call
that clever' throughout the recitation; an esthetic general
with very white antennae; a mad, canary-coloured hostess
from Paris, the only possible explanation of whose appearance
must have been that she had, by some obvious mistake, been
interned in a home for lunatic children and had escaped with
one of their dresses as her only wear; the literary editor of a
literary weekly, very mousy, with the furtive eyes of the
school-sneak and hair which had just greyed in time to impart
an almost distinguished expression to his rather mean
features; the actual editor, who more resembled another
public-school type, the fat-boy-bully; two young artists, naïve
and surprised; and the Burne-Jones lady's athletic granddaughter, rather large and 'out-of-it-all', and whose only
interest was in breeding dachshunds. 'Eckthquithite,' pronounced Mattie, 'thuch marvellouth underthtanding of birdth.'
And, indeed, his delicious twittering of the two poems had
been so soft and feeling that it had sounded like a flight
of young starlings. Everyone was glad to accept Mattie's
judgment.

The heralds went forth, and Bundle's name was securely
established in nature-loving Mayfair. For Mattie, as we have
had occasion to point out before, when genuinely enthusiastic
would spare himself — and others — no pains.

.   .   .   .   .

Then the War came, and to the recipe which he had
already invented, Bundle now added a very personal brand
of pseudo-maternity — as if there were not in the world at
that moment already enough suffering mothers. He seemed to
have appointed himself as a sort of literary *Marraine*, a synthetic
Mother, not only to the men under him (he was a lieutenant
now) but to all the troops everywhere. Oh, the hidden, the
haunting, sob of Motherhood which convulses every line in
these new poems! A few simple onomatopoeic devices were
introduced, in addition, to produce an impression of the 'real
thing'. The old gentlemen of literature — and all the old
ladies too — went wild about his work. He became the Head
Boy of the Younger School. Old women read his poems aloud
to one another at sock-knitting parties, young ladies edited
anthologies solely so as to have an excuse for writing to him,
in various schools the masters made their pupils learn them

by heart, and all of them were set to music, and sung whenever possible at every charity concert. And each time they were read, sung or recited there was a glow at the heart. For Bundle was at the front. There was something glorious, wasn't there, in giving of our best?

It can be imagined, then, that it was not without apprehension that the elders received tidings that their new favourite had been invalided back to England. There was almost a slump — but soon a firmer tone established itself. For he was in a bad way, it was said, a really bad way. Not only was he suffering from shell-shock, but he had broken his leg for the cause. Well — well — well! It was an inspiring example. 'Always knew the boy would do us credit.' But there was a certain vagueness as to the particulars of the valiant act responsible for this physical and mental damage.

Quite by chance, however, I was to learn the details. And here I should like to confess that from the very beginning I always felt about everything connected with the poet a singular curiosity, as though his career was in some way very specially my own affair. It was as if some prophetic instinct had warned me that alone of his contemporaries I should see this life, and see it whole. And as though he in his turn felt some responding chord he would, when I was present, often address to myself his remarks on life and literature.

One day, then, I was standing up at the bar, drinking a cocktail, when I noticed next to me an officer leaning with an air of negligent elegance across it, occasionally emitting a loud laugh, and jerking back his out-turned, angular arms with a marked effect of dalliance, as he flashed his eye-glass over the polished wood barrier that divided them at the rotund and purple lady, much powdered so that she seemed built in layers of white and purple Turkish delight, who served the drinks. She, in her turn, was heliographing back her pleasure at his sallies with a flashing, golden tooth. In spite of the no doubt numerous years she had spent behind the bar, heavy curls of farmyard laughter hung about her in the smoke-stained air, and struck answering notes out of the thousand bottles (each one stuck with an Allied flag) behind her, while from above the fat golden cupids of the 'nineties peered curiously down. 'Well, you are a one,' she was pronouncing, 'but still I always say that all you boys are like that naow. It's the war 'as done

it.' Watching them, as he began to speak I recognised in the
jaunty figure at my side an officer whom I had known slightly
in France, and who had belonged to that very unit to which
Bundle had been attached as artillery-observer. Thus it was
very resolutely that I broke in on this gallant conversation,
and after a few preliminary greetings, inquired about the poet.
Those were heroic days, in which men had forged for themselves a language in keeping with their deeds. I therefore
transcribe in his own words this eye-witness's narrative, otherwise it may seem as though a certain savour had been allowed
to evaporate from it. Moreover, though, looked back on, it
seems a queer, stern, concentrated tongue, it yet gives the
atmosphere of reality more than can any words of mine. 'I
hear Bundle's got shell-shock,' I said. 'I'm so sorry.' 'Doncher
believe it, old bean,' my friend replied. 'If he ever had, it
must have been before the war — must have brought it with
him. But I don't mind telling you how he broke that damned
lower-limb of his. We were billeted in an old farmhouse, a
mile or two behind the lines. It was just before luncheon on
Christmas Eve, about one pip-emma ; Bundle was on the roof
observing. All the rest of us were having sherry inside. The
Colonel, not a bad old bird, had been having one or two
lately : but that day he was quite cheery. He was just saying :
"Well, boys, there'll be no Father Christmas down the chimney
this year to fill our stockings," when there was a blasted crash
down the bloody chimney, and out of a blinking cloud of soot
came that mingy blighter Bundle. My word, the Old Man
was upset ! Thought he'd got 'em again, he did. Knocked
the blooming glass straight out of his funny old hand. My
word, that was Tootaloo for Bundle — a fair tinkety-tonk, I
assure you. What had happened was that the poor boy had
seen one of those ruddy birds he pretends to be so fond of, and
had stepped back suddenly and down the chimney without
looking. We did have a Christmas-and-a-half, I can tell you.
Well, chin-chin, cheerio, so long, old boy' — and delicately
selecting a clove, he continued his interrupted conversation
across the bar.

After this adventure, Bundle's war-poems became more
tenderly bloodthirsty than ever. A new volume soon made its
appearance, for which it was claimed by the publishers in their
advertisements — and rightly : 'This little book of poems has

swept the critics clean off their critical feet'. Nor were eye and brain for a moment allowed to enter in. They had been eagerly scanning the bloodshot horizon for a Great War Poet (only he must be after a certain model) and now they had found him. Just as, though Generals are always prepared for war, it is never the next, but always, alas! the last, one for which they are ready, so are critics invariably prepared for the reception of a great poet. In the days of Keats they had looked earnestly out from their high watch-towers, anxious to acclaim another Dryden: similarly, in 1917, they were determined not to allow Keats or Shelley to escape them. And now they had captured him. The sensitive feet grew weaker and weaker from enthusiasm. A week before they had proclaimed Bundle only as an embryonic Milton: today he was a full-fledged Keats.

Yet even now the young poet was as far as ever from seeing whither the path he trod, so blithely yet yearningly, would lead him. Milton, it is true, had lived out his span before the rule that immortal singers must die young had been established. Blindness was all that had been required of him. But when, amid the universal acclamations, Joe Bundle was compared to Keats, he ought to have searched diligently for the cause of such exceptional popularity: he ought, then, surely, to have understood the fate immanent in it. Had he read *The Golden Bough* all would have been plain to him. For in those pages we read much of a custom, a common custom more usual among the primitive races, but which was to be studied in its most extravagant development in the ancient civilisation of Mexico. In that world of remote and fantastic beauty, where the great cities stood on lakes in the craters of the high mountains, and the white-clothed walkers in the streets, instead of leading dogs behind them on a chain, are said to have been accompanied by brilliantly plumaged song-birds that fluttered and leapt and sang above, attached to the outstretched hand by a coloured ribbon; where the flowering was so intense that one blossom when it opened exploded with such violence that it even shattered the houses that gave it shelter; in that civilisation so strange yet so pronounced, there were many features which strike us as revoltingly barbaric because we cannot at first find for them any parallel. Thus it is with a feeling of horror that we discover that one man, picked for his type of looks and for his talent, was chosen by the priests and elders each year for the purpose of human sacrifice : but first, for twelve long, golden months, he was Emperor and Dictator, was invested with powers of life and death, not merely over the nobles and the people, but also over the priests, those very persons who had appointed him to his fate. Unimaginable wealth, countless wives, were at his disposal, every whim of his must be obeyed, every wish gratified. But always underlying the beauty and power was the ineluctable condition — Death. Every morning that 'he rode out with falcons and a retinue to the chase, while the snowy summits of the mountain towered above to temper for him with their ice the heat of the crystal-clear days, every night that, wearing a golden or jade crown from which whirled the dyed plumes of Mexico, he feasted among the flowers, brought his terrible end so many hours the nearer. The gods were inexorable : and soon his young red blood would spout into the blue air, stain the vast and garlanded stone altar, and drip down to the terraces below, while the crowds who now cheered his progress, would shout their joy to the heaven and struggle to dip a corner of their garments in his blood. So, too, it was to be for Joseph Bundle.

The priests of literature had selected him and now with varying degrees of patience awaited the end. Yet not for a moment did he feel the thorns clasping his brow under the very mutable roses with which he appeared to be crowned. He sometimes, it is true, had a queer lurking impression that something was expected of him : but what was it ? He reached no conclusion. Meanwhile he still existed in the full glory of his brief reign, the full tide of his temporary infallibility.

Yet it would not be correct to think that the priests were entirely displeased at his return. Theirs was a far, far higher standard of culture and kindliness than that of their prototypes in ancient Mexico. From their point of view an early death from tuberculosis ranked higher than a mere name in the Roll of Honour (for that was a very common fate just then) : while, if peace were not too long delayed, a peace-time death would be more effective, and much more creditable to those who had sponsored him. Certainly if he could not die then he should have sought his end at the War. But luck favoured him : his appearance of frailty had accentuated itself, and now won for him a job in the Ministry of Propaganda. And here, too, the results were very satisfactory. As a casualty, he could, after all, only have been one in a million: but now his name was worked-up into that mysterious thing, a 'clarion-call', and through his hysterical advocacy thousands of boys of eighteen were induced to look on a war as a virtue and thus to meet their deaths happily.

His most famous poem (which was not only recited on every possible occasion in England, but was even read aloud to neutrals, whenever they could be induced to listen, in Sweden, Holland and Denmark, as propaganda to impress them with our genius, to show them 'what England is doing') was that one — is it forgotten now? — in which a fortunately imaginary mother carries on a quiet, imaginary conversation with her dying son.

> MOTHER:
> Even such gentle things as birds and mice
> Must pay the fair, the final sacrifice,
> And, though the way be hard, you'll see it through
> Remembering that Mother follows you.
>
> SON:
> But did I love you, Mother, had I love
> Ever but that for brothers now above?
> I have forgotten — ooh — ah — It is done.
> (Rat-tat-tat of rifles — A bullet spun.
> Rattery-tat-rattety-tat-tat of machine gun.)
> Oh, Captain Donkyns — good-bye, Sir — the sun
> Declines . . . I must away — is that a swallow
> That blithely (chirrup) leaps and I must follow?

Such poems further endeared him to the great-big-baby-heart of the public. They sold by the thousand. He, though still ambitious, was content: while the literary hierarchs had what seemed the certainty of his death to look forward to at no very distant date. (Then, what junketings beside the tomb, what jubilant trumpetings through the Press, what perfumed bouquets to those who had discovered him!)

.   .   .   .   .

The War ended, and it was now that Bundle really proved his cleverness. Within a month or two of its conclusion, he had converted the large munition works over which his Muse had so long presided to peace-time service. He succeeded, as it were, in beating his literary sword back into a rusty plough-share. Sussex came into its own again. He offered a special line in birds, fresh-water fish, and saying good-bye to bull-dogs. Now that he was by circumstance compelled to abandon that maternal note towards the troops which he had adopted, his innate humanity directed itself instead towards the old people in alehouse and workhouse. In fact, he skipped a generation, and became a spiritual and synthetic grandmother. At times, too, the *vox humana* of sexual frenzy dying down to a deep roll of Byronic disappointment was allowed to make itself heard, but never *too* often or *too* obtrusively. The factory must have been working all hands and twenty-four hours a day. It issued continually new books of poems, received everywhere with the usual ecstasy. Then was announced the news that Mr. Joseph Bundle was at work on his FIRST PROSE BOOK. 'For that England which cares for literature', the paragraph added, 'it is an event for which to wait with bated breath.' Critical feet must have been in a state of presumably almost painful sus-pended animation. The day came, the book appeared and was, just as I had expected, extremely, beautifully simple, though full of whimsy and rising, indeed, at the end to a climax of tragedy.

The story concerned Shelley. In it he was represented not, as in reality, drowning at sea (that was merely a ruse of his to escape from the world), but, instead, as going home to Sussex to become a shepherd on the downs. He lived, it appeared, to a ripe old age, but eventually was made to lose his teeth. Anxious to preserve his looks, and not altogether to lose his power of conversation (he was always talking with the other shepherds, and had, as time passed, instinctively adopted the Sussex dialect), yet nervous, naturally enough, at having to face a local dentist after shunning the world for so long, he decided to contrive a false set for himself: thus, after killing a sheep, he took its jaws and adapted them to his own. But since sheep have some forty odd teeth to the human thirty-two, they were an ugly failure. Here the book ended.

As to the merits of this novel, the priests of literature were divided. Some critics were so enraged at the nasty idea of Shelley evading his fate — it was really tactless of Bundle — that, quite unmoved by poetic fantasy, they hinted that, judging by his conversations with his fellow-shepherds, the mind of the great poet had scarcely been improved by the new, free, open-air life of the downs. Some, again, accused him of plagiarising a story by Miss Sheila Kaye-Smith, while others found the discussions entrancing, and voted the book 'a classic and a gem'. Yet it certainly did not achieve the success, measured by sales, that had been expected of it.

The hierarchs in private were much more disquieted at his behaviour, though they could not afford to let him down yet a while. . . . It was nearly a year after the War — but, if anything, he looked stronger. But Bundle, though he noticed in their eyes an increased brightness of querying expectancy, still had no notion of what it was they awaited from him. Not for a moment did he notice the earnest examination of his features to which the literary elders subjected him, nor the quiet prods, even, with which they sought to gauge the date of his impending doom. He had blundered through instinct, and with none of that intention of revolt which they imputed to him.

Fortunately, and again without intention, he followed up *Nameless Shepherd* with a book entitled *Dialogues on Parnassus*, which consisted of a series of discussions on life and literature between himself and the soul of Keats. In it the spirit continually dwells on the beauty and advantages of an early death for a poet. And in a moment Bundle had recovered his lost prestige and was once more Head Boy.

'It is', wrote one of the high priests, 'a singularly happy coincidence which has inspired Bundle to write a book of conversation with one with whom he has so much in common, both in mind, and, as many think — and have not been afraid to say —, in outward appearance. A book crammed with insight and teeming with beauty, it is a book for which we have long been waiting.' *

---

* This passage, subsequently quoted on the jacket of the second edition by the publisher, earned for poor Bundle his only bad review. So quickly had the first edition been sold out that this sentence caught the eye of Mr. Shins (another Georgian poet) before that gentle young man had finished his review of the book for a leading morning paper. For some years Mr. Shins had made a practice of sitting directly under the portrait of Keats — at the Poetry Bookshop, in his own room, or in any other place where he could find one — with his profile at a similar angle to emphasise what he believed to be a quite extraordinary resemblance: when, therefore, he saw the pretensions of his rival so boldly stated, he tore up his favourable review on which he had been at work, and made of it the full, furious use which the opportunity afforded him.

It was soon after the publication of his dialogues, when the halo of success blazed once again, and more radiantly, round his pale features, that I met Bundle for the first time since the War. The occasion was one of those artistic yet 'chic' little parties given by Mr. and Mrs. St. Maur Murry in their charming small house in Chelsea. Anne Murry particularly cultivated those artists, poets and musicians who were very advanced — so advanced, indeed, as to be out of sight altogether. By certain painters of this school she was much admired, and often served as their model: and, indeed, with her little whitened face, smoothed-back hair, lashless green eyes peering out from above her trim figure, rather as a snail from its shell, she had something essentially of the age about her. With these friends she would giggle feverishly at the dull ordinary lives of those other artists who occasionally do a little work: 'Too queer and absurd', she would titter attractively, and the loose, grey lip and chin, the batik kerchief that half-strangled a stringy neck, would ripple with delicious laughter. Yet the tracks were there for one to examine, and if her inclination appeared to be toward advanced artists, she yet could never resist the famous ones. But this must not for a moment be known, so when successful in kidnapping them to her parties, it was always to be assumed by her intimates that she had no idea of the identity of such guests (how like Anne, so unworldly, so artistic), but had taken a fancy to them for some obscure, capricious reason — a mole near the eye or a way of walking.

Meanwhile her method worked in smoothly with that of her husband: for St. Maur Murry, a wizened little man, always convulsed with a boisterous laughter which in itself passed for wit, aimed at fashion. Thus a party organised by his wife had all the mystery and attraction of a first-rate circus for *his* friends — who were, therefore, for the evening, civil to *hers* — while *her* friends in their turn regarded the 'beau monde', as Anne called it, with a charming affectation of eighteenth-century *cliché*, in precisely the same light. 'Simply too extraordinary', they would murmur in corners to one another. Meanwhile each menagerie, completely unconscious of its own tricks and mannerisms, stared with that blinking which is born of intelligence, or with the perfect assurance that lurks under plucked eyebrows, at the other, while the two trainers bravely cracked their whips.

This gave to the parties an atmosphere, at once stilted and over-familiar, that was all their own. As we have said, Bundle's celebrity was at this time at its height, and it was now that Anne, who had known him for many years, of a sudden took a fancy to his 'funny little smile'. She had contrived, withal, to make him feel that his own and her notion of his importance coincided.

She led me up to him. Bundle, I soon decided, had some-what modified his style. The eighteen-twenties had gained at the expense of the Mermaid Tavern. He was in the highest degree affable, but his voice had taken on that bitter, broken cackle so widely recognised as one of the stigmata of greatness, while each time he looked at you, he now slightly opened his eyes, thereby just for a second revealing a flashing white under and above the iris, as though attempting some subtle species of hypnotism or one of the snake-with-rabbit tricks developed by Rasputin.

This new grimace served with most people to enhance the original impression of genius. He also limped a good deal. Yet the distant, almost tragic look of the eyes, when not thus in action, made me wonder afterwards whether he was not already beginning to guess that which lay ahead of him. In any case it must be admitted that he made full use of the plenary powers which the irrevocability of his fate for so short a time bestowed on him. For the party was 'going' beautifully, the preliminary surprised snigger of introduction had swelled into successful fits of tittering and giggling, when, without any invitation, Joe Bundle suddenly advanced into the centre of the room, and announced that he would read his poems aloud.

This, first heralding it with a little address on the principles of true poetry and what the War had taught him, he proceeded to do with immense effect until two o'clock. The two circuses, even the two trainers, were disgusted, resenting this rival one-man-show that had usurped their place ; but nothing could be done, and no one even dared move, such was the compelling force of that poetic eye.

The only diversions were a maid, who obtained a sudden but violent popularity by upsetting a tray of plates outside just at the most effective passage in a poem, and an old lady who woke up with a start and began crying like a baby.

If the months that ensued were the greatest in his career, it is true that tragedy now ever mingled with his triumph.

Even if Keats and Shelley found themselves every day more
and more attached to the name of Bundle, on platforms, at
prize-givings, in every literary column and above all in the
woolly pages of the *London Hermes*, bound captive, as it were,
to the progress of his chariot; even if I heard, as I did, Professor Criscross say, as Bundle left the room, to Mr. Lympe:
'There, Lympe, goes, perhaps, the most remarkable and gifted
young man since the death of Keats', yet into the volume of
this praise had crept so general, so unmistakable a note of
macabresque but pretended apprehension, that Bundle could
no longer misunderstand, pretend to misunderstand, or in any
way resist the decrees of those who had made him. At last he
comprehended fully the brutal determination that lay buried
everywhere under the sweetness of the bedside manner, at long
last he perceived the empty, the waiting coffin, under the piles
of laurels, bays and roses. And since he had delayed, sales were
falling. Now he understood the anxious looks with which the
elder *literati* scanned his face — not, as he had thought, to reassure themselves as to his health — but eagerly, to welcome
the first sign of ailing lung or heart. (Sales were falling.)

The priests were impatient for their sacrifice, began to feel
that his fame had been obtained on false pretences. Even
Mattie, dear, mild Mattie Dean — he noticed — allowed his
bird-like eye, incubated behind its monocle, to wander over
him cruelly in search of symptoms. (Would he never be able
to publish all those letters? Mattie was thinking.) Nor was it a
happy time for the priests. After all, they reflected, he was
nearly twenty-eight. But, and herein it seemed to the hierarchs
lay the essential unfairness of their situation, it was difficult
for them now to rend him. The trumps of praise must blare
on, though the hollow, owl-like hooting of expectancy might
be more emphasised.

Yet they possessed one mighty ally on whom they had not
enough counted. Sales were falling, falling: and Joe Bundle
knew it. For if the English public is thwarted of its rightful
poetic prey by a strong constitution it soon turns nasty, demands
its pound of flesh, endeavours to starve him in a garret. Nevertheless this great-big-baby-hearted public is a treacherous one,
for if too long disappointed and kept waiting, it will turn even
on those who feed it, the priests themselves, and devour them,
just because they have misled it as to its feeding-time.

The elders were in danger, and therefore would soon be dangerous. Bundle saw it (and sales were falling, falling!).

It was true that he still had the good luck to look fairly delicate (this a little appeased them). But it was all very well for the high priests to say continually within his hearing that he was too good, too clever, too sensitive, to live. Himself was not so sure of it. The nature of his quandary, enough to crush a lesser man, was only too clear to him now. Something must be done, he knew. But to die is not necessarily an easy matter. Suicide was, as it were, a breach of rules. It made winning too easy. Even the death of Shelley, for example, was hardly playing fair (Keats's end was, from the critical point of view, the perfect score). Moreover, Bundle was young: possessed, despite his appearance, of much natural health. What was he to do? (Sales were falling.) And as he pondered, fretted and worried, fortune favoured him again; for so intense was his genuine love of life, that the prospect of the early death demanded of him nearly brought it about. Visibly he began to wilt and wither. No sooner had this process become notice-able than a glad shout arose from the watching priests. Every day the trumpets trumpeted more bravely, and jubilant whispers puffed out the grey moustaches of the hierarchs in their literary clubs. Bundle was all right; Bundle was 'doing his bit'. Once more they had backed a winner for the Parnassus Stakes. Always put your money on 'Skull and Crossbones'. In the smoking-room of the Lumley Club, old Sir Wardle Diddlum, Joe's publisher, dispensed a veritable fountain of port wine. A winner again. (Sales were mounting, mounting!)

Alas, Bundle could not bring himself to it. Again he held on a little too long. (Sales were falling, falling!) Through the notices of his last book of poems crept a horrid, malicious, menacing note. A chill wind enwrapped him, who so long had been tenderly treated in the literary nursery. When he showed himself at 'the Lumley', where of old he had been eagerly welcomed, the hierarchs would hide behind their news-papers, or even put on a pair of black spectacles, presumably as a hint of that mourning which it was now their due to wear. This they would follow up by coughing in a death-like way, in intimation of what England expected from him. 'How is your health, Bundle? We hear very favourable reports of it', they would say in the most mordacious manner. (Sales were

falling.) One or two early turncoats began openly to announce
in paragraphs that Mr. Bundle's later works had disappointed
his many admirers, and poor old Sir Wardle, who was made to
feel that the whole thing was his fault, had to adopt, by doctor's
orders, a special diet to reduce his blood-pressure.

But now Bundle executed a really amazing piece of strategy,
not unworthy of Fabius Cunctator, and by it succeeded in
delaying his enemy. He realised undoubtedly, I think, at this
point, that which was expected of him. He was aware, too,
that the conditions of his past success were irrevocable, that he
could not repudiate his bargain without bringing disaster on
himself. But for a little while longer he was able, by his own
cleverness, to remain dallying in the world he loved, his fame
and repute ever increasing. For, all this time, he had been
preparing in secret a new book of poems. This was the moment
to publish it. It was called *Farewell to Poesy*; each line was
permeated with a wistful note of unmistakable self-elegy. The
sob had deepened into a death-rattle. Pegasus had donned
bat-like wings and was flying through these pages, decked out
in considerable funereal pomp, for the last time. In this book
Bundle boldly proclaimed who were his equals, for at this
solemn moment who was to say him nay?

And how warmly Bundle was now taken back to the fold!
Songs of sad, glad rapture echoed and re-echoed through the
Press. The undertakers of literature dusted their top-hats,
cleared their throats, allowed a tear to fall on their black-
bordered handkerchiefs, while they measured the body with a
practised eye and prepared for it their articles of obsequy. In
the offices of every newspaper the obituarists nonchalantly
whetted their nibs. (Sales were soaring, soaring!) It was the
climax of Bundle's career. The chorus of praise never faltered,
except that the mousy little literary-editor described in an
earlier page wrote, probably with unintentional ambiguity:
'This book is one which you will want to give away', a phrase
rather unfortunately quoted at once in every advertisement by
Diddlum & Co. Nevertheless it obtained the greatest sale that
any book of poems had achieved since the early days of Alfred
Austin.

Yet, he realised it only too well, either himself or his sales
must sink — they could no longer, soaring together, keep
company, and herein, as Bundle must have reflected, lay the

most cruel part of the poet's lot. For, should he die, his triumph would be more than ever broadcast through the Press : those who had first detected his talent would see to that. Money would, consequently, pour in — but he would not be there to receive it ; indeed in this instance, unless he made a will, old Dr. Bundle, who had never for years been anything but unpleasant to him, who was already rich and whose very existence he had managed to disguise, would reap the benefit.

It was after the publication of *Farewell to Poesy*, after his ill-health had become more accentuated, that I met Bundle for the last time *before* his death. The occasion was a memorable one. And it seems to me that, for my young readers apparently eager to collect anecdotes that belong to the period as much as its paintings and furniture, a description of this party may convey a sense of the advanced scene of those days as vividly as would any picture of the old *London Group*, or the finding of a forgotten poem by some such author as Mr. Conrad Aiken or Mr. Maxwell Bodenheim delved for in the pages of a now dusty but then very up-to-date American journal ; but to appreciate it, it must be remembered that at the time of which I write the great religious revival of the early thirties was as yet undreamed of, and that, for the intelligentsia, psycho-analysis had usurped the place of religion, and was treated with an awe and deference accorded to nothing else in this world or any other.

The setting was for Bundle in any case a new one, and, as a habitat, rather unsuitable. Spiritually, it was many thousands of miles removed from Sussex ; in its style nearer to the jungles of Africa, with their zebra-striped flashes of light and darkness ; nearer to the hot, moist, scented and voluptuous airs of the Brazilian forests, resonant with the xylophone-tongued cries of tropical birds — forests where even the sleek, snarling pumas that glide and sway stealthily through the undergrowth are too languorous to be of very much danger to mankind — than to his beloved downs, for ever swept by the steel-billed breezes of the northern seas.

But then this constant, though always unexpected, mingling of sects that proceeded in the London of my youth must be regarded as one of the chief delights the age afforded, for it imparted to life a great variety. Just as it was the first epoch in which it was possible to be comfortably nomadic, ever in luxurious flight from Cairo to Rio, from Rio to New York, from New York to Morocco, from Morocco to London, each journey taking up the space of but a few days, so in any great city was it possible mentally to traverse whole continents and centuries, to move from this to that civilisation in as many seconds.

But in this perpetual migration Bundle took little part: he was one the boundaries of whose temporary kingdom were so defined by the tastes of his subjects that it made his appearance here a singularly gracious act. It is true that he would have told you — as would every other person in the room — that his predilections in art were all for the primitive: but lovers of the primitive, since they are apt to pride themselves on their sincerity, are thus wont to quarrel among themselves more than any other tribe, and between the rival lovers of the African kraal and of the Sussex cottage (however alike in their simplicity these may seem to outsiders) is fixed a deep chasm over which no rope-bridge may be thrown. In art it was not so much that Bundle knew what he liked, as that he liked what he knew. After the manner of all English-village-life-enthusiasts, he was as ignorant of everything outside his own county as he was misinformed about the village itself. Every architectural system devised seemed to him a decadence from the high art of thatching a cottage — of which he had read, though he had never seen it. Oast-houses, like comfortable red brewers sporting an incongruous witch's hat, and the flinty tower of any local village church, were also agreeable to him. In painting there were Cotman and Crome, but even these were a little beyond his taste in their range; in music, an old folk-tune, scratched out on what he would be careful to term a 'fiddle', to which accompaniment a few whiskered and toothless octogenarian gaffers, first carefully excavated and coached in their steps by horn-rimmed-spectacled young Jews from Oxford and Cambridge, would gaily foot a measure.

One did not, therefore, expect to encounter him among people who worshipped strange gods: gods among whom he was not numbered. The party was given by an acquaintance of mine, in conjunction with three or four other men, in a large room up in Hampstead. I had never been to the house before, and found it crammed with guests, their arms pinned to their sides, unable, perhaps fortunately, even to reach the little cup of dark green, searing coffee that was so hospitably provided for each of them. Gazing over the sea of heads, a whole new world was exhibited to me. Alas! myself in evening clothes, I felt rather uncomfortable, for most of the men present were dressed in the loose, floppy esthetic manner of the time, corduroys and bandanas, tweeds and pipes, while the only people attired in the conventional men's evening clothes of the period, black coat and starched white shirt, were a few heavily shod, self-conscious but determined-looking middle-aged women, most of them with an eyeglass clinking against the buttons of their white waistcoats. It was obvious that, except for them, anyone in evening dress was regarded as an unpleasant anachronism. Luckily, the packing of our bodies was so close that what I now began to regard as my shameful nudity might pass almost unnoticed. Wedged in as I was, my face only a few inches from other and unknown faces, I began to feel lonely, except that from time to time a shaggy head would drift up and — with some difficulty, for it was like trying to maintain one's place and balance in the middle of a football scrum — inquire, politely yet intimidatingly, if I had visited Dash's or Blank's last exhibition. Rather priding myself on my acquaintance with modern art, I could not but be profoundly chagrined at my ignorance in being unaware of the names they mentioned — or, rather, for the noise was great, roared — with such reverence. After confessing, then, one was left to stare this close-up of curious heads directly in the eye, always a rather confusing experience. My gaze wandered in search of rescue, over the jostling waves of faces. Who was there? Not far from me, rising up out of them like a jaunty if rather angular boulder, I observed a well-known lady novelist, the ends of her long ear-rings swinging down in the crowd. Who else was there? Did I see a glossy white shirt flashing its kindred signal to mine? Was it — it was — Bundle!

At first, then, I was astonished to find him in a room painted with yellow, scarlet and purple stripes, and further embellished with such innocent, unsophisticated ornaments as totem-poles from New Zealand, fetishes from Dahomey and the Congo, blood-bowls from the South Seas, and two or three wizened, black and dried human heads, hung up on the wall and swinging above us from their nails by a few remaining locks of coarse, lank hair. The explanation of his presence in these surroundings was to be found, I take it, more in the fact that he realised only too acutely how numbered were the weeks that now stretched in front of him, in which to play his kingly part, than it lay rooted in the essential eclecticism of the age. It was bold of him, too, one reflected, to venture thus far afield, for the immunity and infallibility bestowed upon him by his approaching fate was not, as a rule, recognised here among the grinning ogre-masks and phallic symbols of a different and alien superstition. Doubtless, though, he had been inducted hither by Mrs. St. Maur Murry, whom I now saw smiling subtly in a corner to a few very civilised devotees. The subtle smile was intensified soon into a shrill, frenetic giggle. He could here have found no more influential sponsor.

At this moment and as I thus studied the scene, a sudden, a very positive and ominous silence — all the more menacing in this tropical room — fell down upon it. It resembled that instant of dreadful calm that precedes an equatorial hurricane. The only person who did not immediately respond to this magic and infectious cessation of effort was the lady novelist, whose barking, busy, inquisitive voice hung dramatically in the air. Resolutely she finished her sentence to the little group of heads clustered round her shoulders. 'I know it's *true*,' she was saying, 'for *he* told me *in confidence*.' After this little effort, she, too, became mute. And now the threat inherent in this silence materialised itself. The floor was cleared. 'Something must be going to happen', everyone said as they scurried away to the sides of the room, where those who could find them sprawled on cushions. Some went out, while others leant upon the mantelpiece, draped themselves limply round the doorway, or sat, even, in a bowl from the South Seas. Chatter subsided again. Somebody, wisely hidden behind it, struck up on a piano, and into the centre of the floor minced a very young but tousled and dishevelled zany of a young girl, with a tangled mop of flaxen hair hanging over a freckled, earnest, though at the minute smiling and rather damp, face. Her feet were bare, and she was dressed in a classical, night-gown-like toga. Obviously, if only on account of her pretended timidity, she must be a favourite, one felt. Sure enough, after a preliminary rattle of starched cuffs, as the women in men's evening dress adjusted their monocles to see and applaud, there was a regular burst of enthusiasm. Now the piano broke into a regular rhythm, and the dancer began to caper, peer and prance round the room to the immense, if solemn and scientific, appreciation of the audience. Rather puzzled by the significance of some of her gestures, I turned to my shaggy, long-haired-terrier type of neighbour, and asked: 'Could you tell me exactly what she is dancing?' and he replied lightly: 'Oh, just two rather jolly little things out of Krafft-Ebing.'* From these she passed on to interpret one of Freud's instances of the 'Œdipus Complex', which was generally held to be her finest achievement, both in conception and execution.

These dances were much encored. The artiste slunk out deprecatingly amid cheers and calls. Then, again, there seeped into the room the silence of expectation. One of our hosts came in with a reading-desk and announced that Mr. Joseph Bundle had kindly consented (alas! a euphemism, I fancied, for 'insisted') to read some of his new poems, if his health would permit him to do so, from *Farewell to Poesy*. The guests at once began talking and looking angrily round. However, Bundle was not to be thwarted. He began by asking his audience to forgive and understand, should he be forced to break off during a poem. He was not, he said, very strong (as they might have heard) just now. And after this he put up such a good act of coughing, finding the place, and clearing his throat, that even this gathering of modernists was in spite of itself impressed. Anne Murry could be heard in a corner, saying hopefully: 'Now, didn't I tell you? — there is something in his odd little smile — it's like Blake.'

He read on. It was the first time I had heard these poems, and one detected the invention of several new and poignant devices. In several of the verses Keats and Shelley are addressed personally, directly by name, as though they were boys in the sixth form and Bundle was the popular master in charge ('an awfully decent chap, and talks to the Pater about Footer'). The tone was one of 'Smith Major, it's your turn now. What do you say?' I remember a couplet or two:

> Shelley and Keats! By your example borne
> I quaff the potion from the bitter horn.

> My heaven will be where the sheep still bleats
> Of Sussex: there I'll meet you, Shelley, Keats!

* Author of *Psychopathia Sexualis*.

In others he would direct the boys, knowing his influence over them. This sentiment, for example, was beautifully contained in the little poem he wrote to his friend, and contemporary poet, Mr. Edward Shanks. It ran:

> And when you go to brighten Heaven, Shanks,
> Shelley and Keats will offer you their thanks.

However, to return to our party, his health permitted him to read to the end, though the lilt and dying fall, alternating with the bitter, broken cackle, of his voice took on a note that was a little wearied.

In spite of the original prejudice of his audience, Bundle achieved almost a triumph. At the end there was loud applause, and my neighbour said to me: 'I must own I'm agreeably surprised. There's something positively Polynesian in their starkness.'

After he had finished, Bundle came up to me, bringing a friend with him, and suggested that he should take us in his car to 'the Lumley' for a drink. Much flattered, I consented. We sat in a large, empty room, red, with vast chandeliers. I examined the poet carefully. Though still sure of himself, he was certainly much changed. There were distressing signs of the internal conflict through which he must have been passing. In his eye there shone, too, the light of an heroic resolution. Looking back upon that night, I can see now that to him we were posterity. Much time he spent, almost as though he wished us to hand on his banner, in telling of his work and its aims, of early life on the downs and of the message, of which he was, all too unworthily, as he said, the medium. Birds, birds, and again birds, he conveyed to us authoritatively, was the Message of Life. And after them, bulldogs, and again bulldogs. And, of course, sheep. He spoke to us, too, of the names of poets: of how the very sound of them 'smacked of the earth'. 'Let the words loll on the tongue, so that you get the full flavour of them', he advised us. 'Drinkwater, Keats, Shanks, Noyes (pronounced, I then discovered for the first time, in no equivocal, facing-both-ways manner, but, boldly, to rhyme with "cloys") and a hundred more.' . . . '(Think, too, on the names of the great double-barrelled women of fiction . . . Sackville-West . . . Kaye-Smith . . . Kean-Seymour.)' . . . 'Even my own name, Joe Bundle,' he said, 'has something, perhaps, of Sussex in it.' Now, again, the talk veered in its direction, and the Christian names of famous figures — though sometimes in an unusual and abbreviated style, which served both to cause you to ask whom it was he meant and to prove his intimacy with them — would trip easily off his lips. We were made the repository, perhaps owing to our appearance of health, of many little stories of the great, of which, years afterward, we were doubtless to inform the young: 'I remember Bundle telling me in '23'. A sigh of wonder, a new light in young eyes, and an awed voice, trembling out: 'Do you mean to say that *you* knew Bundle?'

Now we had to leave him. He accompanied us to the door of the Club. Love, he confided on the way, had treated him as it always treats a poet. 'It's the penalty we poets pay', he announced with amiable condescension. He coughed once or twice, a hollow, dramatic cough, put out his hand and shook mine in a marked and morbid fashion, looked into my eyes, blinked his eyelids several times very widely, as though this was the last occasion on which the snake would fascinate the rabbit. The door swung to, and he was swallowed up in its blaze of light.

. . . .

Rumour spread, evil rumour, that Bundle was ill, very ill indeed. The literary world was intent, waiting. Then came the news. Bundle was a dying man. He had been ordered to Italy under the care of a nurse — gone thither, like those with whom he had so often been compared — gone there to die. The eyes of the elders glistened fondly as they thought of that other corpse so soon to rest under the wistaria in the little English Cemetery at Rome — stretched out there by the side of his peers. The obituarists even went so far as to get ready their captions and to turn down the corner of the page of Rupert Brooke's 'There's some corner of a foreign field', for they must not be behindhand with appropriate quotation.

The dark horses could be heard taking a preliminary canter through the Press. The mutes chattered shrilly while they might.

'Lovers of English poetry', we read in *Gleanings*, 'will hear with regret mingled with anxiety that Mr. Joseph Bundle, perhaps better known as "Bundle of Sussex", and assuredly the leader of that striving young England that found itself in the War, has suffered a complete breakdown in health. Always of a rather frail physique that was the counterpart of a fiery spirit and a rare poetic intelligence, he never spared himself in Beauty's cause. It has long been an open secret that our leading critics and literary men, who had hailed him as heir and successor to Keats, were fearful of the strain that his genius — for such they deem it — might place upon his health, which must, indeed, in these days be regarded as a national asset.' Or, again, the paragraph might be couched in language yet more grave : 'There is always something singularly tragic', it would run, 'in the delicacy of men of genius, and were it to force Bundle to relinquish his work at an early age, our literature would undergo a loss only comparable to that it sustained by the deaths of Marlowe, Keats, Shelley, Byron, and Rupert Brooke. . . . Bundle comes, of course, of Sussex stock, and is peculiarly identified in the minds of all lovers of poetry with the soil of London's favourite county. Nor is he the only Bundle to have attained national fame — for many will be interested to discover that he is a cousin of P. T. Bundle — "P. T. B." as he is affectionately known to thousands in the football world — England's foremost dribbler. Some readers may infer that the relationship between poet and athlete is no casual one. Both of them stand rooted in English earth. The famous poet is now far from the country he loves, for the doctors have ordered him to Italy — where in earlier days other English poets have sought solace — and many will be the good wishes he will take on his way with him.' The paragraph ended 'God speed!' though it did not enter into details of what, exactly, the writer wished sped.

These little notices — who knows but that perhaps they may have been breathed into the ears of the paragraphists by a confiding publisher ? — ran round the Press, and inspired, indeed, one regrettable error. The literary editor of the *Sunday Depress* had latterly been very much overworked. The owner of the paper had told him to praise, the editor to abuse, the same book. In addition, while reviewing a novel, he had mistaken a rather unfortunate passage quoted in it from the Bible for the work of the writer before him, and had called loudly on the Home Secretary for its suppression, and for the prosecution of the author. The Home Secretary had eagerly responded, but had inadvertently omitted to read the book:

the publishers had kept their secret; and consequently, when it leaked out in court that the author of the passage in question was no less or younger a person than Moses, the prosecution had broken down. After it was over, the proprietor, himself a particular authority on the Holy Book, had sent for the literary editor and had reprimanded him. This had much shaken his nerve, and, soon after, since things never go wrong singly, he, owing to some slight confusion, published an article on Bundle, in which he treated Bundle as though he were already dead. After the inevitable comparison to Keats and Shelley, and congratulations to him on what was captioned as his 'Sane Sex Viewpoint', he had hailed him as 'Lord of Lyric Verse', and had proceeded to demand his interment in Westminster Abbey, 'the National Valhalla'. Moreover, he insisted violently that the Peers and Peeresses should be made to attend the service in their robes, for, he added, with one of his most picturesque touches, 'only with passionate purple and screaming ermine can they do justice to the immortal singer now no more'. This article had induced his chief to purchase a story by Bundle, to be run as a serial, under the idea that, now he was dead, people would stand it, however good it might be. It can be imagined, therefore, what were the feelings of proprietor and editor, when they discovered that Bundle still survived. They relapsed once more into insurance talk, their trump card. But meanwhile the rival journals were immensely enjoying themselves with talk of 'a lamentable error of taste', and 'ill-informed and wicked gossip'.

Yet the impression was rife that the end could not be long delayed. All the old gentlemen of literature joined in the death-bed revels. The consequent rush on Bundle was immense. First editions soared to a price which only ghouls could afford to pay. So it was with the familiar waving of flags, beating of drums and blare of trumpets that Bundle faded out into the azure horizon of Italy.

. . . . .

What was the precise nature of the drama enacted there, I know not. But it was a year or more before the awaited obituary notice actually materialised. Few details of the end were given. It ran, as he would have liked it, simply: 'On October 27th, 1924, in Italy, Joseph Bundle, of Sussex, Poet, in his twenty-ninth year. Nursed through a long illness by his devoted wife.' It was obvious, then, that Bundle had married his nurse; and this was all that could be deduced until the next day, when the more fully inspired, appreciatory notices began to appear.

Now even the most august papers thundered England's loss. We were treated to charming little stories of the death-bed ceremony, when Bundle was married to his nurse. Not one romantic detail was spared us. The literary editor of the *Sunday Depress*, spying an opportunity for rehabilitation, repeated his former obituary, clamoured for a burial in the Abbey, so that All should Take a Part. Other critics even went so far in their enthusiasm, and perhaps in the need they felt for a day's outing in good country air, as to demand that Bundle's ashes should be brought home and scattered over the Sussex Downs by the Prime Minister. But the inconsolable widow intimated that such junketings were not at all what her husband would have desired for himself. She communicated to one or two papers an intimate, but no doubt highly paid, account of his wishes. One day, she had left him for a few minutes it appeared, and when she returned he sat up suddenly in bed, and with the utmost clarity of diction, so that there could be no mistake of his meaning or of his being fully conscious at the time, had said : 'I remembered England in Her Need. She will remember me. Let no one meddle with my bones. Let me be laid down by the Man Keats. I shall be content. Where I am, there shall a smaller Sussex be.' And though he had never reverted to the topic again in the few days which he had still to live, it was generally felt that in this touching idea there was much that was appropriate.

. . . . . .

Many critics have pointed out how in *Frankenstein* it seems as if Shelley had been able to transfer some of his sombre genius to his wife's pen. It is as though, while he was with her, he had been able to infuse into her at least a little of his overwhelming power : yet even he had not been able to bestow enough genius for her to continue writing at this level after his death. But with Mrs. Bundle it was otherwise : it was as though some portion of her husband's magic mantle had descended on to the shoulders of his forlorn widow. In the numerous articles about him which she now contributed to every paper, there were whole phrases and turns of speech that, it seemed to me, bore his imprint. Yet though the stories of him, the diminutive tales and touches, were typical of the man, the mystery which had ever surrounded all he did still attended on him, even in death : for little was told us of its actual circumstances. Yet that description of him in his last moments, how true it rang, and how the actual writing of it reminded me of the deep, compassionate instinct of motherhood manifested, for example, in his war-poems !

'There he lay,' Mrs. Bundle wrote, 'ashen and listless under the ilexes, with the rich Italian sunlight drifting down to him through the branches and a wistful smile ever touching the pallor of his features. How poignant was the sight of that white bed upon the burnt-up grass ! But never for a moment did he repine : never, never for an instant, did he allow himself in his suffering to forget or upbraid Nature. Always, racked and tormented though he might be, did he gladly suffer little birds to come unto him.

'There are some moments in life so peculiarly tender, so mystical, that they cannot be revealed. It may be, even, that there are those who will consider that it is not strictly the duty of a wife to reveal them. But Bundle belonged to England, and I shall tell, for only England (and, of course, the United States of America) could appreciate such a memory. Right up to the last, then, right up to the final, bitter hours, he would commune with the birds. It was pretty to see them together, for they, too, seemed to understand. Well, one day I heard a sound of twittering, and stealing up on tiptoe, so as not to disturb Joseph, found that he had, without telling me, sprinkled his moustache with hemp-seed, and that the tiny feathered things were chirping and tweet-tweeting at his mouth. It was a sacred moment : one of such a kind that nobody who has experienced it would ever be able to forget.

'After this, it became a regular practice with him. And, one day, as thus he fed them, the end approached. Came a time when he was delirious, racing again over those downs from which he had sprung, his boots, his clothes, all covered with the good earth of Sussex. He called the birds that still fluttered round him, addressed them by name, under the impression that they were his favourites of fifteen years before. His speech became once more the musical speech of the countryside. Again, again he was running merrily over the downs, or climbing a juniper bush to help some little bird in travail. Now came the great events of his life: once more he was performing that valiant deed that won him honour in the War; once more he was batting for the *London Hermes* Eleven; and then, turning over on his side like a child in bed, gently sighing, he was at rest. . . .'

Bundle, I reflected on reading this account of him, had been very fortunate in finding birds in Italy, where they are more often to be found on a plate in front of you than singing in the bushes. The only bird one ever sees there is, in the mountains, an occasional eagle, and that, from the angle of the English bird-lover, scarcely counts as a bird at all.

Mrs. Bundle, of course, inherited all the dead poet's property and effects, and was also found to be his sole literary executor. In most ways she was, however, very easy to deal with. She appointed Mattie Dean to edit his letters and write his biography, only retaining a final veto as to what was or was not to be included. The letters had a great sale. The reviews transcended even expectation. The only critical exception came from Lady Richard Cressey, who in a letter to one paper stated that Mattie had cut out, in the letters from Bundle she had lent him for publication, several passages in which her poems had been warmly approved and commended and had substituted for them instead paragraphs, presumably written by himself, in praise of his own critical insight. In one of these, indeed, Bundle was made to hail him as first patron and discoverer. This allegation on the part of Lady Richard was never definitely either proved or disproved. But a certain amount of unpleasant bickering broke out in the Press from the hierarchy, each of whom was now publicly claiming to have singled out Bundle originally. All this, however, only served to heighten interest in all that pertained to him.

Mrs. Bundle continued to live in Italy. She was, it appeared, so overcome by the tragedy, of which she had been so close and intimate a witness, that only once after the death of her husband was she able to summon up the courage necessary to meet his friends. (Memories of him were both too dear and too painful.) It was for the opening of the 'Bundle Bird Fountain', erected in Kensington Gardens to the

memory of the dead poet some eighteen months or two years
after his decease, that she made her sole, brief, public appearance in England. Even then she was, it seemed, nervous and
ill at ease, anxious to return, to be alone, to bear the burden
of her recollections by herself: a phenomenon very sad in one
still young.

The ceremony of inauguration was singularly simple, and
gained much in interest from the presence of the widow. The
elders had thought it advisable to capture a lay-figure for the
chair, and had successfully contrived to entice old General Sir
Blundell Bullough-Bloodworthy to occupy it for the occasion.
As a speaker, he was effective and thoroughly in keeping with
the proceedings, while he possessed in addition an undoubted
talent for anecdote. First of all he blew out his red cheeks
and white moustache as though inflating an invisible air-
balloon, and then suddenly addressed his audience of bishops,
old ladies, venerable critics, publishers and esthetes, as though
he had them before him on the parade-ground. 'Not much
of a poet-chap myself,' he roared at us, 'but I do know a bit
about birds. Love 'em, I do. Know more about birds than
poets. Positively love 'em. Never so happy as when shootin'
'em. (Birds, I mean, doncherno, what, what!) Shot thousands
of 'em myself in my time. But getting old now, ha-ha' (and
here he was convulsed with laughter for a minute or two).
'Spent a great part of my life in India. Not many birds there
— Vultures, of course, and plenty of 'em. After one of my
victories, battlefield used to be a perfect sight. Bird-lovers
would come for miles to see it, so my aide-de-camp told me.
Tell you an extraordinary thing. Forget if I tolger: Lady
Bloodworthy, doncherno, decided to give a tea-party at
Government House. I was always against it — ha-ha! Well,
there we were, all sitting in the garden in our topees — might
have been in an English garden. Tea with silver kettles and
scones and all that, when (would you believe it?) crash in the
middle of it all fell a human leg and arm, ha-ha! What it
was was a vulture was flying over from where a Tower of
Silence was, doncherno, where a poor devil of a Parsee was,
donchersee. Devilish clever bird, what! Wonderful thing,
birds' intelligence. Extraordinary, I said at the time, extraordinary, quite extraordinary it was. But nothing in India
except vultures — and parrots: and minahs, cunning little

devils they are, too, I tell you! Had a minah that imitated the Missus so as you simply couldn't tell. Used to answer it myself. Why, that minah can make a fool of *me*, I used to say to my aide-de-camp: remember it quite well, doncherno. Still, nothing comes up, in my opinion, to a good English bird. And I'll tell you another thing about birds. Some of 'em sing beautifully, by gad, what, what! Wouldn't have believed it till I heard 'em, ha-ha! Well, what I mean to say is, donchersee, is that poor fellow — Mumble — Trumble — Stumble (Thankee, Sir, thankee) — Bundle, knew about birds, too, I should say.' And the General sat down amid prolonged cheering. After strength came sweetness. Mr. Mattie Dean was called upon, rose, adjusted his monocle, inquiringly, and, mildly beaming, said : 'All thothe, I think, who love Thuthekth, all thothe who love poemth, will realithe only too thurely, that in Jotheph Bundle — "Joe", ath thome of uth were privileged to call him — we have lotht a mathter. The thoughtth of thome, it may be, will, like my own, turn to Keatth and Thelley : two other gentle poetth lotht to uth.' The speech continued for some time. The old lady who had been painted by Burne-Jones fainted from excitement and had to be helped out of the crowd ; while her rival with the vacant eyes, who had sat thirteen times to Sargent, could be heard saying in a loud voice : 'How true — So true ! Just what Mr. Sargent used to tell me.' At the end of it, an old gentleman like a foolish verger stood up and said : 'La—dies and Gentle—men, I have now a lee—tle treat for you — Mrs. Bundle.'

Amid tremendous applause the widow of the great man stood up. She was nice-looking, dressed in very fashionable black, but to my mind, rather inappropriately covered with every possible assortment of dried fin, dead fur and dyed feather. She was a perfect riot of shark-skin bags and shagreen purses, sealskin coats and ermine trimmings, osprey feathers, tortoise-shell umbrella handles and animal-skin gloves. Owing to nervousness, her speech was quite inaudible, but the gestures with her hands, her playing with a rope of false pearls, were all that could be desired. The silent opening and shutting of her mouth, as by a goldfish, the whole galaxy of tricks she displayed, was singularly moving : so much so, indeed, that at the close of the proceedings, the Committee of the Pecksniff Prize for English Literature, anxious not to omit so novel a turn from their platform, waited on her to inquire whether she would not present it for them at the Æolian Hall in a few days' time. It was always difficult to find something new, they said : though whether they referred to the book which would incur their prize, or to the stage début of Mrs. Bundle, remained uncertain. But she refused, and left for Italy the next morning.

A few days later it was announced that Mrs. Bundle had been awarded, on account of the services of her dead husband to literature, a Civil List Pension of three times the customary amount. This served to mark definitely the apotheosis of Bundle. The Prime Minister of the day referred to him at a Guildhall banquet as one of the Future Glories of the English Heritage. Sir Wardle Diddlum was advanced from a knighthood to a baronetcy. Mattie was given a 'K.C.B.' It was rumoured that a Great Personage had bought 2000 copies of *Farewell to Poesy* (Sir Wardle said that he had made a wonderful bargain, too) for distribution to his friends next winter in place of a Christmas card. The Archbishop quoted two touching lines about a robin in one of his sermons. A Bundle Society was formed, the members of which were to dine together twice a year — and once every summer must meet for a picnic luncheon on the downs. Now the boom spread to America : a branch of the Bundle Society was formed there, and it was arranged that the American section should entertain the English one the following year. Yet there now entered into the cult that touch of exaggeration which many of our fellow-countrymen are apt to associate with the States : for example, several enterprising journalists started a 'story' that the great poet was not dead at all, had been seen walking, apparently under the spell of some unbearable sorrow, by lonely stretches of the Italian coast. Soon, the English papers retorted, the American Press would announce that Bundle's poems had been written by Bacon ! Such discussions, however, served but further to increase the enormous sales of his works : for the dead man's books now sold by their tens of thousands. Money poured in, and he no longer there to receive it ! Such always is the way of the world. Still, it was a comfort to think that poor Mrs. Bundle would not now be entirely dependent on her pension. But gradually, very gradually, the interest died down. Even his widow's essays and articles on his work became less frequent, and then ceased altogether. As a topic at lunch or dinner Bundle was dead.

Little, I think, has been heard of Bundle for the past forty years. Yet during a recent visit — alas! it will probably prove to have been my last — to Rome, my thoughts wandered back to early days. I thought of Bundle as an old man thinks of those he has met in his youth. It seemed to me sad and pitiful that one who had been so sure of immortality, and indeed so famous in his day, should now be held, even by students of poetry, in so little esteem, and be by the world forgotten. Would it not be kind, I wondered, to visit his tomb in the English Cemetery? There, hemmed in by the dark blades of the cypresses, under those small bushes of pagan roses — not the big-headed darlings of the horticulturist, but loose-petalled pink roses with that faint and ancient smell which no visitor to Rome in May can ever forget — under the mauve rain of the wistaria (the only rain which, it seemed that spring, ever fell to cool the dry earth), while high up above them the bare branches of the paulovnias held their mauve torches toward the blue sky — lay those whom he had definitely adjudged his august compeers. But where, I wondered, was the grave of poor Joe Bundle? The sacristan disclaimed all knowledge. I could not find a tablet. To me this seemed to make his fate all the more tragic. A man famous in his generation; and now no stone, even, to mark his grave. And was Mrs. Bundle still alive? I could not remember.

Some weeks later I visited a little town on the southern coast of Calabria. Even now its exceptional beauty attracts no tourists. In these days of flying, people like, I suppose, to go farther away, to India, China, Africa; and though the great aeroplanes continually hum like a horde of wasps over this walled rock, clustered with white houses and set in so transparent a sea, not one stops here for its passengers to admire such miniature and intimate loveliness. It seemed to have been overlooked by the world since the time that, a thriving fortified town, it had defied first the enemies of the Hohenstaufens, and then the Turkish slave-raiders, or even since, many centuries before, it had been one of the great cities of Magna Graecia.

I had been here as a boy, and really it seemed to have changed not at all. The crumbling walls were yet as they had been in my youth, further guarded by an outer fortification of Indian fig-trees, some of the stalks thick as an olive-trunk, such as one might see growing round an African kraal. The golden, slender towers still rose like minarets above a town of dazzling whiteness — so white that the sun glowing down on it threw up dancing lights like those given back by a mirror to play on the walls opposite. The kilted giant of a Roman Emperor still smiled cynically in the piazza, which rested heavily above the Roman theatre, while the harbour had yet lingering in its shelter one or two large sailing-boats. Out of the enormous cellars, natural caves deep in the rock, issued the heavy, acrid smell of southern wine. Over the cliffs still fell in formal swags the trailing, fleshy, green leaves of the mesembryanthemum (that flower the name of which has the sound of an extinct animal), sprinkled with magenta tinsel stars. The olive groves seemed no older — some of the trees were, it was said, above a thousand years of age — and the drifts of spring flowers still surged over the edges of the roads. Only one new feature did I notice in the landscape, a very large, white villa : modern, though it had been probably built within ten years of my previous visit. It looked well-kept, comfortable and incongruous. Though created in a muddled southern style (Spanish-Italian-American), it lacked the flimsiness and squalor of modern construction in this neighbourhood. All round the garden, a large one, was a very high, solidly built wall. It seemed, I thought, an odd place to choose for building. Though the town was enchanting enough to make anyone wish to live in it, the country outside was flat, and, in spite of the beauty of its groves, dull to live in, one would have supposed. There was, I reflected, a great deal to be said, after all, for English landscape (think of the Hog's Back, or the rolling Sussex Downs, with their delicious air). Probably, though, it was some emigrant to South America, at last returned to his native place, to which he was devoted as only an Italian can be, who had built this rather palatial dwelling, thereby also ridding himself of the inferiority complex which early poverty begets. However, the whole matter intrigued me, challenged my curiosity to a degree that is rare when concerned with a matter so essentially unimportant and unconnected with oneself. It was very singular how interested I felt in it.

I decided, therefore, to make inquiries from the *padrone* of the inn in which I was staying. In spite of his numerous activities, talking, cooking, taking orders, bustling from one room to another with a plate of succulent soup in which little octopuses floated all too realistically, waving the napkin held in his other hand imperiously at the knock-kneed waiter who assisted him, and moving his vast bulk about with surprising ease considering the limited space, he had yet found time to pile up an amazing store of knowledge relating to local life.

Yes, he said, the villa had been built some thirty or forty years ago. The man who lived in it was a great English milord. Enormously rich. Lived in great style, with clean sheets every week, they said, and everything he wanted to eat. A great English milord, in disgrace, it was supposed. People knew very little about him — he was just known as 'Il Milord Inglese', though his letters were addressed 'Smithson'. But there were very few of them. Nobody ever came to stay with him, and he never went outside the grounds. What the scandal could be, he did not know. Milord was respectably married. His wife was a very nice lady, and sometimes came into the town. But neither of them ever stayed a night away. He was, of course, eccentric, like all Englishmen. Not a soul was admitted into the house, and the servants were forbidden to answer any questions. (Still they must like him, or they would not have stayed so long.) Very eccentric. For example, he had a curious dislike, more than dislike, a horror, of birds. And while all round in the countryside they were now trying to preserve them, prevent their extermination, any bird on his property was shot at sight — and he employed several men specially to guard him from them. And it was not that he liked to eat them. Never a thrush was put on his table, not one. No, it must be connected with this story — with the scandal. They reminded him of something he wished to forget, or else it was his wife, perhaps, who thought them bad companions for him. What it was, the *padrone* had never been able to make out.

How odd it was, I thought, this continual tradition of the eccentric Englishman living in some small Italian town, and how well justified one always found it to be. (I remembered the English hermit I had once seen living in a cave near Ancona.) But what kind of sad story was it which had been responsible for making these two people, now old, and obviously, by their surroundings, very prosperous, stay here all these long thirty summers or more, never to go away, never to see anyone of their own kind? Even in that comfortable villa, the summer heats must have been very severe and trying to the health (think of this flat countryside under the blazing sun of July or August). Perhaps they had lived a long time in India. But, surely, then they would have been more frightened of snakes than of birds! Indeed, the bird-phobia was the most unusual, the most individual, feature of the entire story. How, I wondered, did it link up with the reasons which had forced them to come here to live? The whole thing was inexplicable, and the only answer possible to the queries one framed to oneself was to be found in the simple reply that he was just an 'eccentric Englishman'. That was probably all there was in it.

However, my interest did not in the least fade during the few remaining days I stayed there. Involuntarily, my mind would play about the facts, and try to find some solution. Several times, many times even, my feet led me past the smartly painted and handsome iron gates, with their high spikes, past the stout, tall walls, their tops glittering with the varying angles of the broken glass that crowned them. And one evening, the last evening, my curiosity was rewarded. As I walked, screened from view by the shelter of the walls, towards the gates, I heard voices — English voices — speaking. Somehow, I knew the tone (unconnected as I was with the whole affair, my heart was yet beating with excitement). — Surely I knew it — a hollow, rather impressive, but now very irate voice. I heard it ejaculate: 'There, there! another beastly bullfinch! Why hasn't it been shot? What can the men be thinking of?' And the answering female cry: 'Don't worry yourself, dear. Don't let it upset you. After all, the poor little thing can't do you any harm now.' Carefully, soundlessly approaching, I looked round the corner at the gate. There, pressed close up against the bars, stood an old lady, with white hair, an old man, very carefully dressed, with a trim beard trained to mask rather cavernous cheeks. He saw me. A terrified glance of recognition darted out at me from his rather inspired eyes, that, as they gazed into mine, mechanically opened wider, and then narrowed, to give an effect of radiance. Hurriedly he turned away and shuffled behind the wall; but not before I had, in my turn, been able to identify the body of the dead poet, Joseph Bundle.

A PLACE OF ONE'S OWN

(For Sybil Cholmondeley)

THE facts which follow have long been known to me and I have always intended to put them together; but, remember, I do not pretend to offer any explanation, can only record them as they were told to me.

The Dale, a green, residential valley enclosed between steep hills, leads down to the sea and forms, as it were, the backbone of Newborough, dividing the body of the town into two parts. Behind the tall trees which line the broad grey road that flows through it, taking the place, surely, of a stream now buried, stand houses and gardens and, just as the trees have been drawn up from the darkness of the valley, so, too, these houses seem, long ago, while they were being constructed — 'long ago', I say, but they are ageless — to have outgrown their strength. Built of brick, either in a dark colourless red, with, over it, an insect-like blue sheen, or the dirty grey-white, intensely spectral yet matter-of-fact, in which seaside resorts love to indulge, they had upper windows level with the rooks' nests that sway all the year through with the northern winter's bellow or on the thin, restless wind of summer. From above, from the lofty iron bridge, which in a gale shudders also a little, you look down on a maze of tree-tops and slate gables, the very colour of rain; and a perpetual cawing, mingled with the striking of innumerable clocks and, very often, with peals from bells of countless frosty, mock-gothic churches, serves as an orchestration for all the happenings there below; where, in the centre, a long pool with an island and, on it, a summer-house of thatch and contorted woodwork, to which fragments of the original sheath still adhere, lend interest to a wilderness of asphalt paths, spotted with black and white after the fashion of a Dalmatian dog.

Down these, steep and slippery, in the long-eyed months when dawn and dusk were almost one, droves of trippers used always to stamp happily from the station towards a day of freedom on the beach, where the roar of the summer sea and the summer crowds, the cries of hokey-pokey men and of the sellers of bananas — an exotic novelty — and of chocolates, nougat and Newborough Rock, the clamour of several packs of stray dogs, manœuvring over the sands to the waves' edge for a piece of wood, about to be thrown for them by a bark-lover, and the singing of rival pierrot-shows, nigger minstrels and German bands, blended into an unforgettable and intolerable whole.

With these gay months, then, during the golden Edwardian reign, and not with today or with those dark hours of winter when the town rocks with the northern blast or wears a shroud spun of its own spume, my story deals. For, so far as I can recollect, it must have been in 1902 or 1903 that Mr. and Mrs. Smedhurst, after four decades of successful shopkeeping in Leeds, and anxious now to pass some lotus-eating, if declining, years in an agreeable neighbourhood, came to Newborough to find a house, a place of their own in which to settle. And, though admittedly they had been in a good way of business and had always lived well in a frugal Yorkshire fashion, their acquaintances were a little surprised at their purchase of Bellingham House, one of the largest, though outwardly most plain and yet imposing, of these mid-Victorian mansions in The Dale.

Solidity and respectability were Mr. Smedhurst's outstanding physical qualities. A stranger seeing him for the first time felt immediately that the cloth he wore and the leather of his boots might not be the most splendid or attractive, but were the most substantial and enduring, the least pretentious in their composition. Even his white moustache and the wart at the side of his rosy nose would, it was obvious, stand as long as flesh and blood could bear it. Further, everything was his own, and its very lack of compromise with any standard of beauty proclaimed it to be so. And, in consequence, for a man of between sixty and seventy years of age, he remained unusually well preserved. Mrs. Smedhurst, however, was of a lighter and more impermanent mould and, with her clear skin, soft brown eyes and a 'transformation', made of her own hair,

P

was still pretty. Resolution, kindness and a certain natural gaiety were the qualities which showed most in her regular-featured face, but, in a conventional way, she was not unimaginative.

Husband and wife were mutually devoted, and Newborough had been connected always with the story of their lives. They had, for example, they often used to remind each other, spent their honeymoon here (in those days, Mr. Smedhurst had been a shop-assistant; think of it!), and since that time, with one or two unfortunate exceptions, had passed all their holidays in the same place. In addition, Mr. Smedhurst had always tried to attend the Newborough Cricket Festivals, early in September, if only for one match, because, after the manner of so many people of his sort, this game constituted the sole link he possessed with the open air and with the careless life of boyhood, and, in consequence, it infatuated him and he read the cricket averages and scores in the papers every day during the summer months. Moreover, it reinforced his other love, already great; they had, both of them, long loved Newborough and had long determined hither to retire when the moment came; *loved* it.

Any house, therefore, here, where they had enjoyed so many happy times, would have pleased them, but in Bellingham House they had plainly secured a bargain. . . . Of course, they acknowledged, their new home was too big for them, not *quite* what they had intended; for, being a childless couple, they had, with their northern sense of thrift, made up their minds, even though they could well afford it, not to keep more than one servant. On the other hand, it was situated in the most aristocratic part of the town, where all the best people in Newborough lived, and the air, siphoning through the valley from the sea, seemed always at its freshest, most invigorating. And, though it had stood empty for several years, it was so well fitted up; *you know*, really *good* fittings.

The house must have been almost the first in Newborough to be equipped with electric light. The converted gas-brackets and chandeliers of former days displayed a chiselled, decorative richness which later objects, created solely for their own purpose, would have lacked. If they were a *little* 'old-fashioned', still, as Mrs. Smedhurst said, they were handsome, undeniably handsome; all their friends would marvel at them. And, what was most uncommon, nearly every room, certainly every principal room, was provided with a *speaking-tube*, rearing its head up at the side of a heavy, white-marble chimney-piece. (Except in the best bedroom on the second floor. There it was fixed to the wall, by the door — near the place, evidently, where the bed had stood.) First of all, to use this contrivance, now nearly extinct, you seized it by the supple, undulating neck, unhooked it from its brass support, removed its crest-like stopper, and lifting the vulcanite cup to your lips, receiving in the process a suffocating mouthful of dust, blew down the tube to make it give a vibrant whistle in the room to which you wanted to speak. You then gave your instructions.

Actually, neither Mr. nor Mrs. Smedhurst had noticed the speaking-tubes at first — no doubt because they had not been expecting them. (They were not mentioned in the printed description.) . . . This is how it was. Mr. Tidcroft, the young house agent, who bore the reputation of being the most enter-prising in the whole town, himself conducted them to Belling-ham House; partly because he was most anxious to dispose of the property, which had been on his books for a long time, and partly because he believed that what counted most in business deals was 'the personal touch'. He had made himself most affable, talking all the way there; such a well-spoken gentleman. When they had arrived, he said to them:

'It's better for you to look round the place by yourselves, Mrs. Smedhurst; you can talk so much more freely. I'll stay down here in the hall.'

It was a lovely October morning, and Bellingham House wore none of the forlorn aspect that most houses untenanted for a long period manifest. Of course, as Mr. Smedhurst said, it was a little dusty, but that would soon clean up. And, as the crisp autumn sunshine poured in at the windows, it seemed, though empty of furniture, to have quite a 'lived-in' look. That was what most attracted Mrs. Smedhurst about it, a kind of living brightness. . . . But both husband and wife had taken a fancy to the place from the very opening of the front door. The dining-room was splendid — too good, really, for what they wanted, and a very nice room behind it. Then they went up to the former drawing-room, on the first floor (a lovely room, too, though less original, and oddly cold today, colder than the other rooms — because of the large windows, no doubt), and it was there that a sudden piercing whistle drew Mr. and Mrs. Smedhurst's attention to the existence of the speaking-tube. For a moment, since she had not been expecting it, it had given Mrs. Smedhurst quite a turn. . . . She answered, but there came no reply. . . . And then she guessed the explanation : it must be that nice young Mr. Tidcroft, afraid that she might overlook these instruments because he had omitted to point them out.

Well, it showed how useful they were in a house, even without talking down them — and must have cost a lot of money. Though the place appeared to be so large, communication would be easy — especially convenient for a small number of people — and would save the servant so much trouble. You could just whistle, and then inform her of your wishes. Thus you would avoid all bells and stairs ; so Mrs. Smedhurst, urging him on to the purchase of the house, explained to her husband as, after a satisfactory tour of the whole premises, they descended to rejoin Mr. Tidcroft.

'You gave me quite a fright, Mr. Tidcroft, I declare,' she said to the young man, 'whistling down the speaking-tube like that. I wasn't expecting it. Old people like us don't have the nerves of you youngsters !'

'Oh, you weren't expecting it, weren't you ?' he had replied, giving her rather a queer sort of look, and laughing nervously.

From his manner, Mrs. Smedhurst deduced that he must have felt that she was accusing him of being over-familiar, so she tried to convey in return that she entertained no grudge. But she did not make progress. He continued to be unlike himself, diffident and absent-minded.

The work at Bellingham House had been finely executed all through ; no expense had been spared, you could see that. The one monumental bath, which was on the second floor, had mahogany casing and high brass taps, really magnificent. Even the wallpapers were still in good condition ; rather dark papers with incised patterns, they looked costly and impressive, the sort of thing you could not obtain now that the Queen was dead and everything was cheaply made. Though the nails, from which some former owner's pictures had been hung, remained in certain instances, this did not seem to matter. . . . Better not to remove them and so leave the surface of the wall pitted with little holes. After all, they were scarcely noticeable, and the papers had hardly faded at all, showed no darker oblongs and squares where the frames had been.

There was no need, as Mrs. Smedhurst pointed out, to go to a lot of expense where it was not necessary. Their own pictures and ornaments would, admittedly, look very small here, but the rooms were beautiful, that was the main thing. Every house had its drawbacks, and, though a lot of dusting would be needed — oh no, she did not attempt to disguise that — well, Ellen, you could see, was a strong girl. In her last place, they had said she was good at her work and took a pride in it. Elbow-grease could do a lot. . . . Besides, where was the necessity to fuss with all the bedrooms? Just shut them up, and only worry with the rooms they were using — for they had not left many friends behind them in Leeds who would want to come and stay with them here. On the contrary, they had settled here in order to make nice new friends.

In fact, the size and grandeur of the interior appealed to a streak of romanticism present, albeit they were unaware of its existence, in both their natures. . . . And it was true : Bellingham House *was* unlike the ordinary house, exhaled a character of its own ; further, it had been *remarkably* cheap — perhaps because the place had stood vacant for so long. And, as things happened, no one related to them the history attaching to it, for they were newly arrived, and, up to the present, had been too fully occupied in house-hunting to have had the time to meet many people, and such new acquaintances as they had made were so far mostly recruited from the same stratum as themselves, rich, retired tradesmen and their wives, hailing from the industrial cities and not long settled in Newborough. A few said, 'Oh, you've taken *that* house, have you?' in a rather ominous tone of voice, but this reference to it was made from jealousy and not because they knew the story.

. . . . .

It was something about a rich old lady — no doubt the house had been so well fitted up for her use. . . . Let me try and recollect. . . . Yes, an old Miss Bezyre, an uncommon name. I say 'old', because she was old when as a child I first remember her, but she had come to live here some time in the sixties. Newborough, in addition to being in the two following decades a centre of northern fashion, was, as it still is, the very metropolis of the halt and maimed, yet you could not say that she was mad, or that those people, Mr. and Mrs. Pont, whom I recall as looking after her latterly, were her keepers. Nor could it be alleged against her, as against that blessed band of glandular idiots (creatures so permanent in their type as to seem both eternal and eternally youthful, who, in charge of a serenely smiling grey-haired woman of determined mien, continually paraded the newly washed expanse of gleaming sands, straining at their leashes, picking up, as it appeared, after the manner of a pack, some invisible trail, understanding nothing, intent only on the scent, their little eyes peeping in brutish fashion from highly coloured cherubic folds of flesh, their foreheads and cheeks and chins distorted and ill-proportioned as though seen through the wrong end of a telescope) that she was 'odd-looking' or 'a little dull'. With her slim, tall figure, fresh colouring and finely shaped oval face, Miss Bezyre remained, in spite of her grey hair, extremely young for her age. Perhaps one physical trait alone afforded a clue to her inner lack of balance, and that was her voice, which seemed not to tally with the rest of her ; a curious, childish, half-strangled voice rather like that of a male impersonator or as though another voice, not her own, spoke from her body. Otherwise, she was all of a piece, well bred, even her hands and feet showing a natural distinction.

Sometimes for months together she would appear to be quite ordinary, only rather delicate, sensitive, full of an elusive charm and an indefinable personal dignity ; a little singular, whimsical, perhaps ; that was all. . . . And then suddenly her condition would change and, for a few days at a time, she would become a lunatic of an exceptional, peculiar kind, a being composed entirely, not necessarily of malice, but of mischief, exulting in pranks and tricks, supernormally active and strong, able to plan surprises and delighting in outbreaks of meaningless temper, breakings and grabbings like those of an ungovernable child, or, still more, it may be, of a pet monkey, and demonstrating in these expressions of her new and temporary self a curiously sub-human cunning, very irritating to those who looked after her. She would, for example, now find pleasure in smashing to fragments her own fine china vases, generally so prized by her, and, giving the prolonged and high-pitched cackle of laughter that was a habitual warning and symptom of this state of mind, would sweep them off the mantelpiece or throw them down into the road. Or she would barricade herself in one of the rooms in which there was a speaking-tube, and blow down it until Mr. and Mrs. Pont's ears nearly split their drums, and, when they came up to try to persuade her to stop and to open the door, she would laugh again or say something stupid and incomprehensible, until, in the end, her behaviour would oblige them to force the lock and enter. Or at other times, she might hide behind a curtain and jump out at you, shrieking, or contrive any of a whole repertory of sad, zany devices, thereto impelled at these moments by the inexhaustible ingenuity of her ailing brain. It was very difficult to defeat such surprises.

These manifestations — of which, after they were over and she had relapsed into her usual dignified self, she remembered nothing — ill suited the appearance I have tried to describe, which, indeed, prepossessed strangers in her favour. If they did not see her 'in one of her moods', as the Ponts euphemistically termed it, everyone liked her and was charmed by her; for there was something very lovable about her, a kind of unexpected, gay elegance that infused her whole being. Moreover, the whole town gloried in her as an exhibit; the last of a family that had gathered distinction in many fields, though always its members had tended toward eccentricity; had, in addition to their attainments, been 'beaux' and 'macaronis' and 'dandies', fashionable, self-willed and vicious, their actions not to be conjectured by ordinary laws. She was rich, too, and, it was said, 'could have married the Prince of Wales himself in her time'. But she had refused to look at any of the men in love with her, because she had been so proud, so erratic — or perhaps because she had been aware of the doom lurking in her own blood. . . . And so, at the age of forty, she had fallen a victim to it, and had come here to live in retirement, to escape unnoticed. For she was not certifiable — or, if at moments she were, people of her position, it was felt, should not suffer such an indignity. In any case, she was not certified.

At the time of which I write, Miss Bezyre had resided here thirty years and more — indeed, though I cannot vouch for it, Bellingham House may have been built for her and thus from the beginning have owed its individuality to this strange woman. The old lady's-maid, who had looked after her for so long, had died and Mr. and Mrs. Pont now served her, or guarded her, and had been here, already, eleven years. Apparently, she now possessed no relations, only trustees, who seldom troubled themselves to come down from London to visit her. When they did, however, they invariably found everything in perfect order, the house well run. Indeed, Mr. and Mrs. Pont bore all the semblance of an exemplary couple, perfect custodians for an old lady of this type, very calm and respectful, very fond of her, even if she did on occasion give them trouble and oblige them to be firm with her. . . . It might be that, having been constrained through her own wilful behaviour to use force, to break open the doors of the rooms in which she had barricaded herself, they had found that a little violence paid in their dealings with her and that, as, when she returned to her right mind, she remembered so little of what had occurred, they resorted to its use more frequently as time went by. . . . But the winter months in Newborough made people turn in upon themselves for news, and they were therefore wont to exaggerate. It was wiser to believe nothing.

Certainly in the town, though, the legend grew, — no doubt from servants' talk, for a great many were employed at Bellingham House and they were always either new servants or just on the point of leaving and, further, the supremacy of the Ponts in the house would be sure to render them unpopular with jealous subordinates. It was even said, then, that during her periodic outbursts Mr. and Mrs. Pont ill-treated old Miss Bezyre, tied her up and gagged her to keep her quiet, beat her without mercy and inflicted many cruel little tortures upon her in the tradition of the eighteenth-century code for the treatment of lunatics. Occasionally, late at night, issuing from her bedroom on the second floor, at one place level with the road that ran zigzagging up the hill behind it to the Promenade, passers-by affirmed that they had heard a curious, loud, childish voice, sometimes laughing, but not seldom whining, or was it moaning? — and that this whimpering had risen now and again to a high scream.

Probably, others maintained, it was all talk, and if there were sounds at all, it was only the perpetual wind whistling and howling round the corners of the tall, angular house. And there was the roar of the sea; always, the roar of the sea. Her old doctor was dead, it was true, but that nice, dapper young

Dr. Favelle attended her — though he seldom had to be called in except during one of her bouts, for her physical health was excellent. All his patients loved him. He would never allow such a thing. Further, when she returned to her normal state Miss Bezyre never complained of the Ponts' conduct towards her, nor did she at any time appear to be timid of them. And if, during 'her moods', she indulged in wild assertions and injurious allegations against them, why, it could only be a symptom of her malady. . . . Besides, she must have liked and trusted the Ponts, as much as she did Dr. Favelle, because, when her old trustees had died, she nominated, first the doctor, in place of one, and then Mr. Pont, in place of the other.

Nevertheless, the legion of invalid old ladies in the squares and crescents above, with servants, nieces and companions subdued for a lifetime to their tyrannical powers of will, of one kind or another, liked to believe these rumours and, in consequence, ignoring the total lack of evidence, continued to do so. . . . And, one winter day, faith enjoyed its reward.

'Have you heard', the watchers at the bedsides would inquire of the indomitable mummies, embalmed in shawls and propped upon pillows, 'Have you heard' — and then would pause again, conscious of being about to spring a pleasant surprise and, also, of being obliged to speak even more loudly and distinctly than usual, for the north-east wind, which had roared all the night through, was still blowing a gale, — 'did the doctor tell you, when he called, that old Miss Bezyre has *gone*? Committed suicide, so they say.'

And the aunts and mistresses, melted by the news to an unusual geniality, would reply either, 'Stuff and nonsense. Suicide, indeed! It's stiff, stark, cold-blooded murder! I've been waiting to hear it for a long while'; or, 'I don't call *that* old; she ought to have been good for another twenty years'; or else, 'I've no patience with that sort of thing; if one suffers, one must learn to bear — "grin and bear it", as my poor old aunt used to say'. . . . But each, whatever her view, added in the end, 'But tell me about it, all the same, my dear'.

It appeared that the old woman had been found hanging, and, to execute this design, must have jumped off the chair. . . . At the inquest, a few days later, it transpired that her body was covered with bruises. But though various statements and questions in court, concerning Miss Bezyre's testamentary

439

dispositions, caused a certain amount of prejudice in the minds of those present, the evidence of Mr. and Mrs. Pont, and of Dr. Favelle, served to dispel it to a considerable extent. (There are, of course, some people who persist in believing evil report.) The old lady, having no relations, had bequeathed a large part of her substantial fortune to charity (that, dissentients maintained to be the cleverest touch in the whole affair!) and small legacies to servants still in her employ : for the rest, Dr. Favelle came into thirty thousand pounds, the London solicitor into five thousand, while the bulk, some eighty-five thousand pounds, together with Bellingham House and its contents, went, in the phrase of the testator, 'to my friends Jeremiah and Mary Pont, in some slight token of my gratitude to them for their devoted service to me for so many years'. . . . Incidentally, the document was in perfect order, had been drawn up a year or two previously and had been witnessed by two servants who were still with her at the time of her death.

Mrs. Pont, a rosy-faced woman of middle age, with frankness written upon her round, voluminous pink cheeks, with dragged-back hair, deep-set brown eyes, blinking honestly behind very powerful spectacles, slightly protruding teeth and a very pronounced dint in her resolute cloven chin, had been especially good in the part. Her grating matter-of-fact voice carried conviction. Miss Bezyre, she told the Coroner, had seemed perfectly all right that evening. There was no question of her being 'in one of her moods', and, that being so, and knowing that when normal she was safely to be trusted and liked to be left alone, Mrs. Pont had not slept in her room, as was her wont when Miss Bezyre was 'bad'. If the old lady wanted her during the night, she had only to use the speaking-tube — a great convenience in sick-rooms — which was beside the bed. . . . Well, Mrs. Pont had gone in, at about ten o'clock, to see that she was comfortable and to say good-night to her. Yes. That was the last time she had seen her alive. Everything had been in order, and she had seemed happy and sleepy, really 'comfy'. The night had passed without event, she had heard nothing . . . but, in the morning, entering, she had found (here Mrs. Pont took off her spectacles, with their strong, distorting lenses that, by magnifying her eyes and, as it were, floating them to the surface, so greatly emphasised their appearance of ox-like frankness and good-humour, and

applied a handkerchief. The Coroner ordered an attendant
to give her a chair and smelling-salts. 'Thank you, sir, I'm
very sorry to have broken down. I'm all right now again'),
had found her dead in this dreadful fashion. . . . Naturally,
it had been a great shock after eleven — no, nearly twelve —
years of waiting upon the dear old lady, anticipating her every
wish and guarding her against her own erratic impulses.

Then Dr. Favelle took his stand and certified that death
had taken place at about 2.30 on the morning of the twenty-
first, and that the bruises and abrasions on the body of the
deceased had been due to a fall she had suffered a few days
previously. Next, the servants — the Ponts thought them the
nicest staff of servants they had ever had, so willing and obliging
— came forward and declared on oath that there had been no
call from the speaking-tube in any of the upstairs bedrooms,
and that they had heard no sound at all during the night. It
was true, they added, that the clamour of the sea had been very
great, and the wind had howled round the house so loudly
that other noises were more difficult to catch than usual, but
they had heard nothing; no, nothing but the screaming of the
wind — there was always the wind — round the corners of
the house. . . . It must have been the wind.

The jury brought in a unanimous verdict, approved by the
Coroner, of '*Suicide while temporarily of unsound mind*'. Nevertheless the Ponts soon decided, after all that had occurred, to
leave Newborough. They felt they needed a change. They
missed the dear old lady so greatly, they explained to their
friends, and they were reminded of her nearly every day in the
dear old house. Besides, it was too large for their simple
requirements; what would they want with all those servants?
And Newborough itself had changed so much, was not half so
refined as it had been when they had first come here. . . .
And the Doctor, too, chose to retire, though comparatively
young, and went to reside in Sussex. (I never heard what
happened to him after that, but it was a long time ago, and
he can hardly still be living.) As a matter of fact, however,
Mr. and Mrs. Pont did not continue to enjoy good fortune.
It had been some time before they had seemed able to settle
down — after a wrench like that, it was not to be wondered at!
And they were discovered one morning, about two years after
Miss Bezyre's death, gassed, in the charming small house they

had recently bought in Bournemouth. They had not lived in it for more than two months. They appeared to have had no worries to account for their suicide — unless, of course, it had been an accident.

Meanwhile, after the passing of a few months in New-borough, the talk there had subsided. The behaviour of rich strangers or of poor trippers offered other and equally appetising subjects for conversation. The strange death of Miss Bezyre was forgotten. Someone, I forget who, had bought Bellingham House. But the new-comers did not stay, and the same autumn let it to a rich draper and his wife. Certainly there was no idea of there being anything *wrong* with the place until *after* the death of the Ponts. No doubt, the report of their suicide in the newspapers started it off. At any rate, the occupants now declared that they were always being disturbed at night, and gave notice. Since then, no one had seemed to remain in the house for longer than a few months, or. even weeks. Indeed, it let more easily at first than later on, for, after six or seven brief leases, it stood vacant for as many years — until, in fact, Mr. and Mrs. Smedhurst bought it.

．　　．　　．　　．　　．

The new owners moved into Bellingham House at the end of November, so as to avoid spending another winter in Leeds. Of course, it had been a sad moving, leaving the old house at Leeds; such a comfortable, roomy home, even if it were rather black. But the excitement of their new dwelling had quickly put it out of their minds, and the past few weeks had been a turmoil of measuring, choosing and matching with the aid of their friends — or, rather, of fellow-guests from the Eglantine Hydro, who seemed almost as interested in the new house, and proud of it, as the principals themselves. (Really, they were very kind, if scarcely 'the sort' that Mr. and Mrs. Smedhurst had migrated to Newborough to make friends with.) But then, after all, as Mrs. Smedhurst recognised when at night she communed with her own soul, it *was* interesting, because it formed a culmination to all the worldly strivings of two lives. On the day itself, she tried to take the matter calmly, not to show anything as she said good-bye. It was bad to get over-excited, especially for Mr. Smedhurst. All the same, as she paid off the cab at the door of their new home, where Ellen stood in her new uniform to greet them, she was surprised to find that, in spite of the many happy holidays spent there, it was a relief to have left the Eglantine and to be in a place of one's own again.

Soon, after their own fashion, they had made themselves very comfortable. The rooms had, of course, been thoroughly washed, every inch of them, and it was wonderful how they had cleaned up; really wonderful. And since Mr. and Mrs. Smedhurst had not been obliged to spend anything upon re-decorating, they could afford to lay out a little bit extra upon the furnishing. 'You know, nice "homey" things', as Mrs. Smedhurst explained, chintz covers and plenty of those new, round cushions in bright-hued, pleated and embroidered covers. She had draped the massive, white-marble chimney-pieces, square and uncompromising, with pretty fringed materials, with loops and borders and tassels, very stylish, and had filled the sitting-room and Mr. Smedhurst's 'den' with that delicate-looking wicker furniture in cream and pale green, that had just come in as the fashion, and with wicker stands, too, for plants, so that the rooms should not-look 'cold' or 'stiff'.

The dining-room, done up in the Moorish style (it must have cost hundreds to make!), they preserved as it was, and bought for it a Spanish suite of ebony and ivory — they had been lucky enough to find it at a sale; the very thing. . . . Perhaps the room, with its horse-shoe arched recesses and high, honeycombed ceiling, was a little dark, but it was a wonderful room really, just the sort of room, Mrs. Smedhurst thought, that an Italian Cardinal might have built in order to give dinner-parties (a dinner-party, with little silver trays of almonds, and of chocolates, wearing glittering crystallised rose and violet petals like tiaras, was something she had hitherto seldom glimpsed; as opposed to high tea, it still constituted both an ideal and a symbol. . . . And it would mean hiring a waiter and, too, that Mr. Smedhurst could not slop about in his slippers). They made their sitting-room next the dining-room, and there was, behind it, another small room; the perfect den for Mr. Smedhurst, in which to smoke his pipe, read his papers and keep his letters. They took the whole of the first floor for themselves; the back part for Mr. Smedhurst's dressing-room, and the large apartment in front — the former drawing-room — as their joint bedroom. (Perhaps it was rather *too* big, after their bedroom at Holmdene, Mrs. Smedhurst admitted this to herself, but they would soon grow accustomed to it.) And so Ellen was particularly fortunate and got that lovely big room on the second floor — it had been the best bedroom — for her use. It was bigger even than their own, for it went right from the front to the back, and had windows both sides!

'You ought to think yourself a lucky girl, Ellen,' Mrs. Smedhurst said kindly. 'I don't know another maid who has such a lovely airy room.'

'Yismoom.'

'Any girl ought to be pleased to be in service in New-borough. . . . Look at that view! Why, you can see the ducks on the mere, and, if you lean out, like this, there's the sea with all the fishing smacks on it!'

By this time, intoxicated with her own generosity, Mrs. Smedhurst had given the girl the whole of the North Sea and the herring fleet; but alas, as in life so often, bounty met with little response.

'Yismoom.'

'Look at those tints, too! . . . It's just like the country! Listen to the rooks and all the dogs barking down there. . . . I only hope you'll show your gratitude to Mr. Smedhurst and myself by working hard and being pleasant-spoken. . . . But all you girls are the same today; all spoilt.'

Ellen made no reply this time. . . . Still, Mrs. Smedhurst was pleased with her, a new acquisition, about twenty-six or twenty-seven years of age; a good, healthy, pleasant girl from the wolds, reliable and well disposed, who plainly understood, and enjoyed, her work, even if she was somewhat solid, heavy of foot and hand; but that was better than being hysterical, like most of the creatures you were recommended nowadays. One did not want a maid to chatter and behave in a fast way.

. . . . .

The winter months passed quietly and agreeably, and it was not until one Sunday morning at the beginning of April that the trouble started. It was a lovely morning and Mr. Smedhurst and Ellen had gone to church — not together, of course. (Indeed Mr. Smedhurst felt much annoyed with her; she had done a very stupid thing that morning. Perhaps church would cheer him up.) Mrs. Smedhurst had 'a cold and was obliged to remain in the house, reading her chapter. It was a pity, because she had been looking forward all the week to the austere elegance of Church Parade, and people said that the tulips in the beds at the side of the Promenade had never been so gorgeous as they were this year, nor the lilac, that lay like mauve rain-clouds poised on the terrace gardens which rose, tier upon tier, from the gull-winged sea. . . . Still, it could not be helped.

Nevertheless, though the chapter, the twenty-eighth of the first book of Samuel, usually interested her, she found it hard to concentrate this morning, was always coming back to the printed page with the realisation that for several minutes it had meant little to her, albeit her lips had shaped the sounds. She did not know what it could be, but she felt, well, 'fidgety', as though waiting for something. She must make an effort. . . . Her eyes returned to the book, and she had just reached the words 'Then said Saul unto his servants, Seek me a woman that hath a familiar spirit . . .', when suddenly a prolonged whistle issued from the speaking-tube.

'So the girl can't have gone out after all! How queer; something must have happened!' Mrs. Smedhurst exclaimed to herself. . . . What could it be? Well-trained servant that she was, Ellen would normally never dare to use the speaking-tube to her mistress unless — as occasionally during the past few weeks — to announce visitors. But nobody would be calling at this hour.

In the instant before she answered, while getting up from her chair and proceeding to cross in front of the fireplace, Mrs. Smedhurst felt, somehow, uneasy; the room appeared to have increased in size, to be very large, lonely and cold; curiously cold, as though an instantaneous but marked drop in the temperature had occurred. (The whistle sounded again. Surely it was not necessary, whoever it was, to *go on* whistling in that way!) She looked at the 'daffies' (she had lately caught the habit of calling daffodils 'daffies' from Mrs. Beazley-Boggarde, the wife of the Canon) that were standing near by in a little three-lipped vase of iridescent glass — five or six blossoms only — in order to reassure herself. (How silly to get into this condition because of an ordinary, material thing such as a whistle on a speaking-tube!) They looked so yellow and transparent in the bright spring sunshine; very comforting. . . . And then, while she looked, a single flower suddenly broke into a violent oscillation, as sometimes you may see one leaf quiver upon a tree, its leaves otherwise without motion, upon a still summer evening. But the flower stopped this warning as swiftly as it had begun. . . . Well, it *could* only be due to a draught — no wonder the room was cold, though all the windows and doors seemed to fit so well. . . . Oh, that noise !

By this time, she had reached the speaking-tube. She unhooked the instrument, and held it close to her ear, listening. . . . But nobody spoke. She replaced it on the hook. At once the strident insistence of the whistle began again. The process was twice repeated. The third time she took it down, however, a high childish voice, with a sort of insane and querulous gaiety in it, cried, 'Come and find me ! I'm hiding !' . . . Mrs. Smedhurst of course saw the explanation at once. With Mr. Smedhurst and Ellen both out, one of those naughty children from next door must have crept in, unobserved, and be hiding somewhere in the rooms above. (Mrs. Smedhurst, though she had none of her own, loved children, encouraged them to come and see her, and spoilt them with barley sugar and chocolate — the delicious new 'Swiss Milk Chocolate' that had just made its appearance.)

'Is that you, Hilary ?' she demanded loudly ; but she received no reply. So she went upstairs. . . . In her own room, she had the impression — it was difficult to define — that somebody was there, quite near her, and in the passage outside she could have sworn for a moment that she had been touched, softly, on the face. But she could find no one, though she made a thorough search, everywhere, including in Ellen's room. (The upper rooms were locked, so she did not bother about them.) Directly, however, she had shut the door, and was going downstairs, she heard the shrilling of the whistle in the room behind her. Patiently she climbed up again, although she was a woman of spirit who disliked to be made to look foolish : some instinct warned her that she must not get angry or in any direction let go of herself. She took up the tube. The same voice as before (it must have been Hilary's, but in spite of its childish timbre it did not altogether resemble hers — no doubt the tube distorted it a little) said :

'You've been hot, very hot. . . . Once I touched you, but you couldn't see me !'

Full of mischief, the child sounded, Mrs. Smedhurst said to

herself, glossing over, for her own solace, the alien quality she had noted. (It must be Hilary!) At that moment, a door slammed. . . . Of course, Hilary escaping! . . . But though Mrs. Smedhurst walked as fast as she could to the window, she could see no one passing through the garden.

She decided not to tell her husband. He disliked children — or said so —, and it would only make him worse if he knew that she had been treated with such a lack of consideration. Instead, to relieve her feelings, she wrote a pleasant little note to Hilary's mother, telling her what had taken place and confessing that she was growing old and did not like to have tricks played upon her, though she always looked forward to visits from the dear child.

She tried to show nothing of her feelings at dinner, but that same afternoon she received an answer from Mrs. Thatcher, in which the injured mother protested that both she and Hilary had been in church at the time mentioned. . . . Mrs. Smedhurst now almost wished that she had told Mr. Smedhurst, since, what with her cold, the strange episode of the morning, and then this letter, she felt quite 'queer'. She decided to rest. It *must* be her imagination. If she could be quiet for a little, she would soon forget all about it.

Everything was very still, for it was Ellen's afternoon off, and Mr. Smedhurst had gone out for his Sunday walk. (She had explained that her cold was still very heavy and prevented her from accompanying him.) Certainly she was tired. She lay down on the sofa in her bedroom; such a nice comfortable sofa that she had bought at a sale. It was curious how cold it was in the house today; Mr. Smedhurst had said it was quite hot out. Perhaps she only *felt* cold because she was not well. . . . So she pulled a blanket over herself and was asleep before many minutes had passed. . . . But she was woken, about a quarter of an hour later, by that whistle — at least she thought so, but she could not be sure, as there was no answer this time. . . . Perhaps she had dreamt it. All the same, she said to herself, she hoped her imagination would calm down, or she would begin to feel uncomfortable in the house. (She shivered suddenly. At the back of her mind, I believe, were two ideas: that unconventional things should not happen to people who led conventional lives, and — though this was still more undefined — that a man-made convenience, planned for the use of human beings, such as a speaking-tube, rendered the opportunity it here offered as a medium for haunting all the more horrible, in somewhat the same manner as, to some minds, the application of electricity to the old, barbarous habit of putting a criminal to death, always invests that kind of execution with a greater sense of horror, even, than attaches to hanging, which itself is primitive and savage as the sentence it consummates. But these thoughts nevertheless remained very much in the background, unformulated, for she dismissed such reflections from the surface of her mind as 'morbid'. Nor would she allow herself to use, even to herself, the word 'haunted' in connection with Bellingham House, of which she was so proud. . . . Once that word were admitted, it would be irremediable.)

Somehow or other, she could not settle down again for two or three days, and the persistent cawing of the rooks, as they flew backwards and forwards, laden with huge twigs, much too big for them, in their spring fever of house-building and house-warming, for the first time annoyed her. . . . And Mr. Smedhurst seemed so irritable.

As a matter of fact, if only she had realised it, Mr. Smedhurst had been given cause for irritation, though he had said little about it. . . . Things had begun to go wrong on Saturday night, when he had been reading in his den. He had tried to concentrate : but it had been impossible, he found. First, the two wicker armchairs had begun to creak, for all the world as if two people were sitting in them or had just got up, and then, at that very moment when his book was beginning to grip him — and it was a book everyone was reading, *The Garden of Allah* —, the light had been snapped off at the door ; snapped itself off, he supposed, as he blundered through the darkness to turn it on. . . . Well, that was enough for one evening. . . . The next day, when he had gone up from his bedroom to the floor above for his hot Sunday morning bath, something still more annoying had occurred ; he had un-suspectingly swung right into it, unable to stop himself, only to find it was stone cold ! (And he had been feeling oddly cold before that, so that in consequence he felt chilly all the morning, even in church : but the walk home had put him right.) Yet Ellen, who had prepared it a quarter of an hour before, maintained that she had, according to her custom, felt it with her finger, and that it had been the temperature he liked. If she was telling the truth, there had not been time for it to grow cold. A bit of a mystery there! All the same, though she did not usually lie, it *must* have been her fault; these modern girls were so careless. And the next day — or was it the day after? — she must have begun to talk to herself, for he had distinctly heard voices; low voices; a man and a woman, he would have said, if he had not been aware that Ellen was the only person upstairs. . . . And he wished, too, that she would not giggle in that funny, high voice: it did not seem to 'go' with her. But he had heard it on several occasions lately in the passage downstairs. He would have to speak to her about it.

Then, all at once, everything became quiet again for a spell. Mrs. Smedhurst immediately sensed the change in the atmosphere. In spite of the delicious spring weather and the fires that had been kept in, past April the fifteenth, the house had been cold for a full fortnight; frigid, with a leaden quality of cavernous chill. But now, though the days were colder and overcast outside, the rooms were warmer. Her cough, too, was better, and she soon expelled a faint, lingering sense of uneasiness, that lurked somewhere among the shadows of an infancy long past. Indeed, only for a moment did it revive; when she came to look through the list of things, to see what had been broken during the last fortnight, and discovered that, instead of the single plate or saucer which she would have expected, Ellen had smashed more than a dozen of each! When Mrs. Smedhurst had drawn her attention to it, the girl had burst out crying, insisting that she had not done it, but that, a few evenings before, she had heard, just behind her, a singular, cackling laugh (she imitated it — and for a dreadful instant Mrs. Smedhurst recognised it); when she had turned round to see who was there, all the china on the third shelf of the dresser had been suddenly swept off it, as though by an invisible hand, for there was nobody there. . . . Of course, it was an impossible tale; it must be an excuse. . . . Yet it was not *like* Ellen, Mrs. Smedhurst recognised, to invent a story, nor did she seem to be lying now. Nor was it like her to cry in that way; *hysterical*, that must be it.

However, since she was a useful, willing girl and a good cook, all Mrs. Smedhurst said to her was:

'I'm surprised at you, Ellen! You must be careful another time. . . . *Now*, I don't want to hear any more.'

.　　.　　.　　.　　.

With the approach of midsummer, the days were lengthening rapidly to their climax. In spite of the noisy trippers — who, as Mrs. Smedhurst said, appeared to think they had bought the whole town for the price of an excursion ticket (there was no such thing as Respect nowadays), life was exceedingly pleasant. Peonies and flags offered their large faces to the sun in the gardens of square and crescent, and the bushes of syringa were starred with blossom, too fragrant and languorous for northern air. And joys, other than those of Nature tamed for residential consumption, were also at their height. Church Parade, for example, had become really exciting.

For many years past, Mrs. Smedhurst had been looking forward to being able to study it every Sunday instead of for only a few hours torn from a normally humdrum existence. Between morning and dusk it was — except at mealtimes — full of beautifully dressed men and women ; just like Paris, she conjectured, but without the horrid foreign flavour. Nor was it in the least 'spoilt'. The trippers, for all their vulgar audacity, just did not *dare*, she supposed, to frequent it, but confined themselves to the roar and clamour of the moth-coloured sands below. Of a Sunday, the battalions of old gentlemen with a nearing eternity on their hands, so smart, in an almost military manner, with their curled white moustaches, blue chins and nicely flushed faces — Mrs. Smedhurst liked a man to have colour in his face — exchanged their brown or grey billycocks for brown or grey top-hats. (Mr. Smedhurst himself now sometimes wore a grey tail-coat and a brown bowler, though he had taken much persuasion ; he had rather the air of a major, she thought, if only he would brush the ends of his moustache *up* a little more.) Fashionable family parties, with low-waisted women in toques and feather-boas, and elaborate gowns of lace and embroidery, holding their moon-faced children to them, drove in carriages or smart open cabs along the road at the side, against a background of pillared, primly painted Regency houses, with stout, round bow-windows, or delicate balconies of iron trellis supporting Chinese canopies.

The Winter Garden running down between the Promenade

and the sea, stood also at its zenith. The flower-beds were beautiful, in their intricate, involved designs, and the groves of stunted trees were carrying their fullest summer sail in the cool, refreshing wind, laden with salt. All the shops were now open along the stone deck that, strongly fortified, rose from the sea itself when the tide swept in; sweet-shops and leather-shops and shops full of attractive new 'transformations' and — for fancy-dress balls, of course — of white Pompadour wigs displayed above waxy faces frozen into dimpled smiles. And, right in the middle of the terrace, there was a pavilion of elaborate and gaily painted iron-work, filled with trim button-holes, roses with a florist's false dew lying upon them and picotees striped like summer dresses, all mounted on a shield of green plush. (Even the holy band of cretins and mentally defectives, those hopping, lolloping, loose-eyed cherubs, now paraded here to lend an undeniable interest to the scene, were brought to the kiosk in twos and threes, so that a woman, with her mouth bristling with pins, could select one from her lips in order to fasten a neat flower on to each of these distended coats in turn. It made the wearers look 'jollier', their grey-haired guardians proclaimed.) And, on week-days, the celebrated Winter Garden Orchestra played selections from Waldteufel and Johann Strauss or, better still, from *modern* pieces like *Florodora* or *San Toy*; three programmes a day, morning, afternoon and, most enjoyable of all, in the long gloaming when the lights shone yellow against the prevailing blue, dark but luminous, and the glow of their cigars replaced the colour that dusk removed from the faces of the old gentlemen.

With this atmosphere prevailing throughout Newborough, there were other things to do besides sit moping at home and wait for mysterious incidents! Nerves, all nerves! How silly it seemed, Mrs. Smedhurst said, when you looked back on it! In this delicious sunny weather, not too hot and not too cold, even The Dale, formal and sober as it was, had grown animated. The idle, summer repartee of tennis-balls here and there replaced the prevalent cawing, the gardens were full of roses — rather chlorotic and drawn up, it is true, because of the tall trees overhead — and flotillas of ducks proudly sailed on the waters of the pool that seemed to catch all the more light because of the surrounding shade, and fussily trimmed their chequered and streaked wings or waddled up on to the island, where now the rustic summer-house was embowered in pink cushions of Dorothy Perkins roses.

How enchanting Newborough could be, and Bellingham House, too! Mrs. Smedhurst once more congratulated Mr. Smedhurst and herself on their joint choice of a residence, and of the town in which to find it. There was no doubt of it, in spite of its size, Bellingham House was comfortable; though that, of course, was largely their own doing. And they were making such nice new friends, *very refined*. A whole world of social activity had opened itself to them and they were thoroughly enjoying themselves, though sometimes things became a little difficult, sometimes conversation was not easy, because Mr. and Mrs. Smedhurst had, as it were, been born, elderly and fully dressed, on the arrival platform of New-borough Station. The commercial past it would be bad form to mention or admit, for it would taint their new friends as much as themselves. Nothing had existed before they had arrived here; nothing. . . . Among their acquaintances now were a few Army people, and though they undoubtedly gave tone to any gathering, at Bellingham House or elsewhere, they were over-given to inquisitiveness: both men and women shot questions at you, as though they were bullets from a quick-firing machine-gun: 'Where did you live before you came here?', 'Do you know Lord Ghoolingham?', 'Have you ever been to India?', and many other such inquiries. Yet they certainly lent an air, and added an excitement of their own. But life here was full of pleasure and excitement. . . . And then, abruptly, after weeks of peace, about the middle of July, everything changed again.

This time they were both present, sitting in the 'drawing-room' (Mrs. Manning-Tutthorne, the wife of the Major, and almost the nicest of their new friends, had gently but firmly insinuated the *drawing-room*) after dinner — or *luncheon*, as they were now obliged, with a certain lack of sureness and con-tinuity, to call their midday meal —, when a strident whistle announced a summons to the speaking-tube. (Somehow, though it was so convenient, Mr. and Mrs. Smedhurst had not used it much for the last month or two.) Mrs. Smedhurst was nearest to the instrument, and waited a moment, until the shrill, childish voice she had heard before said:

'You weren't expecting me today: I can see that. I know when I'm not wanted.'

Then there was a laugh, and nothing else — except that, though it seemed a quiet enough summer afternoon outside, the French windows rattled with a singular hammering tremor, and finally, with a crash, blew wide open. And a lovely little vase, to which Mrs. Smedhurst was much attached — she had bought it at the Wedgwood factory while on a holiday in the Potteries many years before — fell off the mantelpiece and was smashed. (It could be riveted, she decided, examining the damage.) Mr. Smedhurst said nothing, he did not ask who was speaking. . . . For the first time she understood why earlier in the year her husband had been so irritable; they shared an unspoken secret.

Practically every day for a week or more — and such lovely weather, which made this inner fear seem so much worse — one odd incident or another had occurred. Mr. Smedhurst now usually answered the whistle and, every time, heard a voice; it must be the same that she heard. But neither of them showed by a flicker of a muscle in their faces that anything might be amiss with their house. After all, it might suddenly stop. . . . So, by a serviceable compromise, each pretended to the other to think it was Hilary. 'Really, Hilary is very naughty today,' one of them would remark. 'I must speak to her mother.' But this brave simulation deceived neither of them. It was only a shield, a small, pasteboard shield contrived against the immensity of the universe.

In general, but not invariably, events were heralded by the speaking-tube. Once, for example, without any warning, Mr. Smedhurst, while going into supper, received a blow on the temple. He supposed he must have bumped himself — after all it could not be the voice, could it? . . . But it was strange: he could not remember how he had done it, and he did not feel inclined to go back and look, for it had made him quite giddy and cold — so cold. He could not get warm again the whole night, not even with the help of the cup of hot Van Houten cocoa he always drank last thing. . . . Then, another time, Mrs. Smedhurst had been watching Hilary's younger sister, Marbelle, who was five years old, laughing and playing by herself in the garden — she was allowed to come into the garden of Bellingham House and play, for Mrs. Thatcher knew

she could come to no harm there. But really, when you came
to think of it, the child was behaving in a very odd sort of
way, talking and laughing as though there were someone else
there! Mrs. Smedhurst called to her rather sharply, 'Marbelle!
What are you doing? Don't be silly, child!' But Marbelle
only looked at her, surprised, and answered, 'I'm not being
silly. I'm playing with funny lady who lives with you.' . . .
It had been disconcerting.

.   .   .   .   .

At the end of ten days or so, Ellen asked leave to speak to
them, and said she must give notice, could not stand it any
longer. At first she would state no reason, except that she was
frightened in her room and could not sleep; she would rather
say no more. . . . When pressed, she pleaded the difficulty of
describing her experiences; she did not know how to put it,
but lately she had begun to wake at one or two in the morning,
disturbed by the sound of voices, and though it had been dark,
it had seemed as though she could see shadows struggling in
the darkness, could feel the movement of these figures in the
air by her. Several times after long, violent dreams in which
she had been struggling and fighting, she had woken up to
find herself standing in the dark, close against one of the walls
of her bedroom; the same place, always, because she could
tell it by a nail on the wall. And one night she had been
attacked. She had been woken up — she was sure she had not
still been dreaming — by violent blows, a rain of them, on her
body from each side of the bed. Besides, she still bore the
marks, and she lifted up the sleeve of her dress to show a bruise
on her arm. Nor even did these happenings stop by day, for
the other morning, when she had got up, tired out by not
sleeping, somebody had been hiding behind the door of the
housemaid's pantry and had sprung out at her with a horrid
screech of laughter; only Ellen had seen no one, had merely
felt an ice-cold wind sweep past her.

'The place must be 'aunted, moom, it mus',' she ended up
stoutly.

Haunted: the two syllables fell on the air with an astonishing impact, as though Mr. and Mrs. Smedhurst had been
waiting for it. Neither of them looked at the other, but they
knew that, now that the word had been mentioned, Bellingham
House would never be the same to them. (In her own mind,

Mrs. Smedhurst admitted it; yes, *haunted*. . . . But it seemed so silly, such a lovely house, and so cheap too. In her imagination she saw Ellen's room. There was *something* she did not like about it; she knew she would never have felt comfortable in it herself. . . . Perhaps it was only just the size, much bigger than her own room.)

'You mustn't imagine things, Ellen,' Mr. Smedhurst said. 'Ghosts don't exist — if they do, it's our own wicked consciences.'

Mrs. Smedhurst added, kindly, 'You're a little overdone, Ellen, that is all. Your room is bigger than you are used to, and it's the strong sea air. . . . But we don't want to lose your services, so you had better take a month's holiday.'

A month was a long time. . . . Ellen was so pleased at the idea of immediate release from the house, as well as of a holiday, that she at once withdrew her notice and started that very evening for the wolds, returning to her native existence of placid farmhouse life, of processions of geese to a pool, waddling unsteadily on their clumsy webbed feet, of chickens and ducks and pigs and cows in chorus at feeding-time, and fritillary-speckled guinea-fowls, of loose stone walls and of tufts of mountain grass like the flowing hair of the Nereids, and of apricots and peaches ripening upon their lichened trees through the long golden silence of the long afternoons.

.   .   .   .   .

During her absence they managed without a regular servant, going for their meals to one of those nice half-timbered cafés that had lately sprung up in the town, or eating cold things at home. But Mrs. Kimber, the widow of Kimber, the former captain of the Lifeboat, came in every day 'to do the rooms': for Mrs. Smedhurst had retired, as it were, at the same time as her husband and, whatever might happen, did not intend to demean herself or to bring discredit upon her new friends by making the beds or dusting in person. Things went round the town so quickly, even without a servant in the house! People seemed to know exactly what was going on.

For about a fortnight after Ellen had gone home, everything appeared to be normal again. But this improvement was not long maintained. Though Mr. and Mrs. Smedhurst still continued to share their secret, heavy and interminable as it seemed, in silence, never, even now that their maid had brought it into the open, mentioning it to one another, yet both of them had obviously grown more nervous and, on days when the atmosphere was serene and plainly there was nothing to fear, would sit waiting, listening in a strained sort of way. Mr. Smedhurst, indeed, now gave a jump at any little thing that occurred. (His wife decided that soon she must take him away for a little holiday — only they could not very well leave Ellen alone in the house directly she came back. . . . The best thing they could do at present, in this lovely weather, was to go out a lot, benefit by the Newborough air.)

It was true: Mr. Smedhurst's nerves were very bad indeed. For so steady a man, he had become full of fancies. . . . For instance, though he could never prove it, he was sure that someone was moving his things and hiding his letters. Every single object on his desk seemed to be in a different place, or would vanish for a whole day and then turn up again as unexpectedly. On the lowest plane, if Mrs. Kimber were responsible — and it was wiser *not* to ask her —, this proved extremely annoying. Then, in the last few days, the creaking of the wicker chairs in his den had grown beyond bearing. Sometimes he could have sworn that he had not only heard, but almost *seen* people getting up out of them; the hazy, blurred outline, filled in, as it were, clumsily, with tobacco smoke, of two squat and dumpy figures. . . . Of course, though it had seldom troubled him before, it must be his imagination. It *must* be, because there were no such things as ghosts. They did not exist. . . . And yet, uncomfortable ideas shaped themselves in his head; for example, if chairs could for so long hold the impression of the living body that had sat in them — his own wicker chair was still creaking from the release of his weight — why should not a room, or a whole house, hold something of its former occupants, long after they had gone? (Who had they been? he wondered; though he would rather not have known, would never ask for fear of hearing.) But all that whispering — the summer wind among the leaves, Mrs. Smedhurst had assured him —, all that stealthy coming and going, would make any man nervous; even without the whistling.

For the whistling had begun once more, and had, further, grown so frequent that Mrs. Smedhurst, who had fallen a victim to the great Bridge epidemic which was sweeping the leisured classes of the country, scarcely dared to ask her friends in to make a four. (And she would lose ground if she failed to do so. . . . After all, what was the use of having a place of one's own — 'one's own', a mocking, high voice seemed to echo — if you could not entertain your friends in it?) And what she had feared would happen had now happened on several occasions. People *must* notice that something was wrong. They knew Ellen to be away, and of course they observed the trembling of Mr. Smedhurst's hand as he unhooked the mouthpiece, and the sort of false cheery manner he adopted when he replied — such non-committal answers, too, — though his face lost temporarily its accustomed colour. (He *had* to answer, he realised, *had* to pretend to reply, even to carry on a conversation, or it would look odder still.) Sometimes, when outsiders were present, the voice would not talk at all, there was just the whistle, and then only that high, meaningless laugh. It was very difficult, when that occurred, to make the conversation sound natural.

Or, again, the voice might be quite loquacious in an inconsequential way. Once, for instance, it had said a lot about people called *Pont*. ('The Ponts can't get *me* now,' it had remarked distinctly, and another time, 'Turn them out of your room; the Ponts are sitting in your room. Tell them to go.') More than once Mrs. Manning-Tutthorne had asked, point-blank, who was at the other end, speaking to Mr. Smedhurst, and Mrs. Smedhurst had found herself obliged to invent a lie, so as to disguise the disreputable truth.

'It's a friend of ours upstairs, dear,' she had said; 'she's an invalid. You've never met her. She's spending a little time with us, so as to get the Newborough air.' Another time, when the Major had demanded who it might be, she had pretended it was a temporary servant asking for instructions.

'By Gad, madam,' he had replied, 'I wouldn't let a servant of mine, temporary or not, whistle for Mrs. Manning-Tutthorne in that way! Downright impudence, I call it!'

The Catterwicks, too, were observant. One really hot day Mrs. Catterwick shivered in the drawing-room and had said how singular it was that this house should be so cold in hot weather. She had harped on it with curious insistence, as if she suspected something. . . . But what could you do? Mrs. Smedhurst asked herself. You could not sit by yourself all day — or be out the whole time, for that made you nervous of returning. You began to dread the moment of arriving at the gate.

The fact was that they had come to hate the tubes which had once — and how long ago it seemed ! — appeared to them as such a delightful convenience. When alone in the house, they would no longer answer — at least, they would try not to answer — the instrument. But it exercised upon them a kind of fascination. Moreover, often if they failed to reply, a little vase, or some object they valued, would fall down and be smashed, or Mrs. Smedhurst's thimble, even, be swept off the table by her side, as she sat mending, or embroidering the centre for a cushion cover. . . . Perhaps it was best to give way to the thing, to humour it —, and yet this method was not always successful either, since if they did not respond the very moment that the instrument sounded, it would often refuse to speak and just go on whistling whenever it was replaced.

Then the manifestations began to alter their character. Mrs. Smedhurst, though she had not been conscious of it before, grew to dislike sitting in the drawing-room, because of the incessant creaking of those wicker chairs of which she had been so proud. Probably, she said to herself for her own comfort, they had always done it, or it might be due to the weather; a fall in the temperature, perhaps. But her own arguments did not convince her. Often, too, she heard whisperings outside in the large, cold passage, and when at last, in desperation, she would tiptoe to the door and fling it open, nobody would be there. The hall was empty, as she had known it would be, though the whispers had only stopped at the very moment she had opened the door and had started again as soon as she had shut it. . . . What could they be saying so secretively ? what could they be plotting, or have been plotting in the past ? was it something fresh or something that had taken place long ago ? . . . Her heart told her they were plotting.

So far, her husband and she had slept well, but now, two nights running, they were woken up by the sound of thuds and moans, as if someone were being attacked upstairs in Ellen's room, and then by a loud screaming. . . . Nothing there, either, for Mr. Smedhurst went up to look. . . . It must be rats — though Mrs. Smedhurst had never seen a sign of them —,

they told each other ; rats made such strange scuffling sounds.
It must be the wind howling. It *must* be. (But how suddenly
the wind had swept down on this soundless summer night.)

After that, the darkness of the long, long nights became less
active, more stealthy. It was silly to be nervous like that, but
sleep was impossible, there was an inexplicable sense of expectation and tautness in the air ; no blows or moans, only all night
the padding of too quiet feet, the clink or crack of little objects
that had been moved, often in the room itself, the restrained,
unbearable stir of voices hushed for some purpose, the feeling
that something — something appalling — was in preparation
behind the velvety unfathomable silence. And if you turned
on the light, it was as though you had stopped a play that was
in progress by blundering on to the stage.

Then, just as the misery of this life at Bellingham House
had overwhelmed them altogether, and they had made up
their minds, each of them, that they must face the mystery,
discuss it together, and take the decision to leave and find
another home, the disturbances stopped. The atmosphere in
the house cleared, became ordinary, so that it could no longer
be recognised as the same place. During the hours of August
sunshine, when a honey-coloured haze lay on sea and land, the
whole of the experiences through which they had passed
appeared to be remote, silly, impossible, though on certain
nights their fears returned, for a short while and in a diminished
form. But they were able once more to sleep, and thus, in
comparative peace, the days passed quickly.

.   .   .   .   .

Mrs. Kimber had been so careless, letting things slip out
of her hand, that Mr. and Mrs. Smedhurst were quite glad
she was leaving the next day. You could say what you liked
about Ellen, but she was a well-trained servant. It would be a
treat to see her about the place again. . . . Mrs. Smedhurst
felt so tired herself that she was sure that she and Mr. Smedhurst ought to go away soon. In spite of her thriftiness, she
decided to try and find another good servant temporarily to
keep Ellen company, and then Mr. Smedhurst and herself
could take a holiday. You see, it was important to get their
nerves right, for if it leaked out that they could not sleep there
and had become 'nervy', people might guess there was something wrong with the house and, if they were even obliged to

sell it, they might then lose on the transaction; a shame it would be, such a fine, well-built residence; (that was the word, *residence*). Or their friends might even think them mad. 'Ghosts, indeed!' she could imagine, could almost hear, how Major Manning-Tutthorne would pronounce the words. The very curl of his white moustache by itself would announce that, to his way of thinking, well-bred people did not behave in such a manner, running away like little children from a dark corner! It was not done.

On the other hand, going away for a holiday was, most emphatically, 'done'. She might not know much of fashionable ways, but she knew that. Indeed 'a change of air' would add to, rather than diminish, local prestige; say, first ten days at Hindhead, with walks over the moors and excursions to that extraordinary 'Devil's Punch-Bowl' — she would never forget it —, and then a few good shows in London. . . . The train service from Newborough was wonderful; one ought to make more use of it. A change, that was what they needed to put an end to such fancies. But they had better not go away before the Newborough Cricket Festival, which was due to open now in a few days. Mr. Smedhurst always looked forward to it so much and, besides, there was going to be a great Cricket Ball in the Hotel Superb. They said it would be a lovely sight and she had persuaded her husband, in spite of the expense, to take tickets, so that they could watch it for an hour or two and have supper. (One must have a little amusement; it took one out of oneself.) Meanwhile, it was necessary to make the best of things, go out a great deal and enjoy the air, and the sense, too, of mounting excitement which always accompanied the coming of the Cricket Festival. In this perfect weather, with a healthy crispness in the air and the golden clouds of sunshine lying over the world, altering every distance and every prospect, lengthening or foreshortening it, there was a charm which Mrs. Smedhurst could not define. And the town was 'filling up', not with those horrid trippers — their August orgy was nearly over, and on the sands a certain flaccidity, a failure of the communal effort to enjoy, already manifested itself — but with nice, substantial persons in flannel suits and panamas and the esoteric striped ties of the cricket world, and with women neatly dressed in tweeds, who sat all day long waiting for the approaching carnival round the

canopied doorways of the chief hotels. And Major Manning-
Tutthorne said it was difficult to recognise the Club as the
same place, full as full now, and always at least one member
with his eye clapped to the telescope in the bow window.

So, husband and wife clung to the exterior world, hoping
that its glare would blind them to other vibrations. Yet they
were not cowardly. Moreover, Mr. Smedhurst, in spite of his
ordinary and unimaginative outlook, and Mrs. Smedhurst, in
spite of her respect for public opinion, were, both of them, by
nature kind and conscientious. When, therefore, her husband
announced that he proposed to pass the night in Ellen's room
upstairs, in order to be able, if necessary, to assure her, when
she returned the next day, that he had slept there and found
nothing wrong with it, Mrs. Smedhurst made no objection,
though she did not much relish the idea of being alone in their
big room for the whole night. . . . Still, things had been quiet
for the last ten days or so, the house seemed all right at present.
And in fact, nothing occurred to disturb her and she slept
better than of late.

Mr. Smedhurst's night began well too. He went upstairs
about eleven, said good-night to Mrs. Smedhurst, undressed,
and fell asleep almost immediately. He remembered nothing
more until he woke to find himself upon his feet, standing
somewhere in the uncharted darkness of a strange room. . . .
For a moment he could not, try as he might, recollect where he
was. . . . Then it came back to him. So unusual was the
experience that, though startled and alarmed, too, by the
curious atmosphere prevailing around him, he did not have
much time for fear. Consciousness of danger — which, afterwards, he could not explain to himself — overwhelmed every
other sensation. He must reach the switch at once and turn
on the light. Groping, he stretched out his arm, and discovered that he was quite near, almost touching, a wall.
Moving his hand along, he scraped the edge of a finger against
something. He felt it; a large nail, he perceived. But it
was no helping guide to him through the blackness, for he
could not remember ever having seen it in the day-time,
though it seemed now — as everything does in the darkness —
large enough to have attracted anyone's attention. Presently,
however, he touched the edge of a frame, and since there was
only one picture hanging in the room, he now knew where he

was and — albeit the process appeared, in the suspense he was enduring, to occupy a full hour or more — soon attained the door and turned on the light.

Yet at first the flooding illumination from the naked bulb did not help him, afforded no greater sense of security. He recoiled from the brilliance of it as much as formerly he had wanted to escape from the darkness. It exposed him, he felt, like an animal out of its burrow, to eyes he could not see. He hated this room; something was wrong with it, something mad and something cruel. Nevertheless, it was empty, superficially in order. He could not tell the right time, for his watch, he now noticed, had stopped just before two o'clock — though he was sure he had wound it up before going to bed. (It could not, he thought, have stopped long, however.) But, notwithstanding that everything was so normal outwardly, the more he looked back on what had occurred, the more uneasy Mr. Smedhurst became. After all, he had never been a sleepwalker. And at the back of his mind, something remained; he tried to summon it up, to drag it up forward from the troubled recession of his dreams — a dim, confused memory of being hauled out of his bed and propelled towards the wall.

Howbeit, as the minutes drew out, and the sleep he had left in so peculiar a manner became further away, his fears began to be allayed. Now that his eyes had grown accustomed to the light, everything was ordinary again with no undercurrent to it. Almost, he was ashamed of himself. It just showed what nerves would do, for he supposed he must have been — well, nervous, all the previous evening, and his effort not to show it had only made matters worse. (He went back to examine the nail on which he had caught his hand; a nail stouter than usual and driven well into the wall, about a foot above his head. . . . It was strange that he had not noticed it before, it was so prominent.) No, he did not feel nervous any longer, only relieved for some reason or other to be awake, to be alive. He smoked a cigarette — how delightful to be *able* to smoke a cigarette! —, then returned to bed and read a magazine and dozed, with the light on, until dawn; when he fell into a profound and delicious sleep until Mrs. Kimber called him.

The next morning his emotions of the night before and its incidents seemed merely foolish. Why spoil such a lovely day

— it was the first of September and one of the best days he ever remembered — by thinking about things; why spoil it for Mrs. Smedhurst by confiding in her the long rigmarole of his adventures? After all, they amounted to nothing. So let Mrs. Smedhurst and himself enjoy, instead, the sparkle of the golden air, the indescribable cleanliness of air and light which this northern town manifested on such days as this — though, indeed, a day such as this was rare, even here, in dear old Newborough. Mr. Smedhurst's heart warmed to the place. He loved it, and was looking forward with the utmost eagerness to the Cricket Festival, which would open the day after to-morrow. Already, in his mind's ear, he could perceive the dull wooden response of the bat to the ball, the eager hum of interest from the deck-chairs, the roars and cries of delight or rage from the crowded tiers of seats at the back; could see, in his mind's eye, the enormous tents of the President and of the various cricketing clubs, the confetti-like gaiety of the onlookers, and the shifting score on the blackboards, let, like eyes, into the contorted scarlet pavilion. In the face of real things, such as cricket, how fantastic the events of last night seemed! Besides, reaction had set in; now being at peace with the world, he could not bear to upset anyone. He could see that Mrs. Smedhurst had been worrying lately, so why disturb her further? How could he, for instance, tell her of anything so ridiculous as the incident of the nail? He could not; he resolved, therefore, not to say anything. And, having made this decision, he saw it was impossible, when he had not told his own wife, to say anything about it to Ellen either.

Thus when, after Mr. and Mrs. Smedhurst returned from an excellent dinner — no, luncheon — at a café on the West Cliff to find that Ellen had made her appearance, Mr. Smedhurst felt still more sure of the correctness of the line he was taking, and contented himself with telling Ellen, in front of Mrs. Smedhurst, that he had slept the previous night in her room and had found it quite all right. (Subsequently, he blamed himself bitterly for this 'deception'; he ought to have told his wife and sought her advice; he ought, further, to have possessed the courage of his own instincts, and to have ordered Ellen not to sleep in that particular room again.)

For her part, Ellen had been restored by her holiday and was glad to be back in Bellingham House. The pay, nineteen shillings a week, was good, and she liked Mr. and Mrs. Smedhurst. In rather a shamefaced manner she admitted that she had quite overcome her silly fancies. She must have been tired, she supposed, what with getting the house ready, and one thing and another. But it should not happen again, she promised them that. . . .

'And you look tired, too, moom,' she added. 'It must be the air, like what you said.' (Mrs. Smedhurst was glad the girl had proved so sensible; that was just it. Mr. Smedhurst and herself would be all the better, too, for a change of air.)

. . . . .

That night, as she foretold, Ellen was not in the least nervous. She got out of bed to turn out the light, and returned through the darkness to its shelter without qualm. . . . And Mr. and Mrs. Smedhurst also felt the safer because she was in the house.

All the same, Mrs. Smedhurst did not like the 'feel' of the place that evening, and was glad Mr. Smedhurst was sleeping in her room. There was something odd about it. For example, though it was so late in the summer, and the air, in spite of its Newborough freshness, was warm, warmed through by an uncommonly hot season, she found it so chilly in her bedroom that she was obliged to ask Mr. Smedhurst to take an extra blanket out of the cupboard and put it on the bed. . . . She must not 'let herself go', she reflected, as she lay there waiting for Mr. Smedhurst to rejoin her. It would never do. So, in order to avoid this process of disintegration, she concentrated upon pleasant things, thought how glad she was that Mr. Smedhurst was looking forward so enthusiastically to the Newborough Cricket Festival — it would keep him occupied — and meditated upon the perfection of Church Parade two mornings before. . . . It had been lovely. . . . Then she dwelt on how comfortable they would be, now that they had seen the last of Mrs. Kimber. . . . It was a blessing, too, to have a third person in the house again.

But that took her back; why, she asked herself, should it be such a relief? In itself that was an admission that something was wrong, must be *wrong*. . . . The lurking sense of uneasiness returned; she fixed her attention, therefore, upon the details, so satisfactory in their outer aspect, of her big bedroom. (Material objects, she must have felt, were of help in tethering her to the ordinary world of which she was an inhabitant.) She appraised the comfort, beauty, solidity of the various fixtures and pieces of furniture. . . . And then, how bright the room was, how airy! (A little *too* airy, perhaps, too large; in front of the windows the curtains stirred in a cold strange breeze that they alone caught in this stillness. . . . How quiet Mr. Smedhurst was, next door!) Such a fine, bright room. The brass bedstead looked splendid, she said to herself, desperately clinging to the supports she knew. (She must keep a hold on herself.) It presented such a dainty appearance with its cover — over the central rails — of quilted, tinned-salmon pink, embroidered with mauve chrysanthemums, and with the brass knobs catching the light. (There was no need to be frightened: Mr. Smedhurst would be here in a moment.) And the big, ivory-painted, crescent-shaped dressing-table, with the glass top and electricity attached to the mirror, was just what she had always longed for. It was so — well, so convenient, like much else in the house; 'Like those speaking-tubes, for instance', another voice, it seemed almost, said to her. (Why *must* her mind revert to such things? How stupid of her to think of them! Would Mr. Smedhurst *never* come in? She called him but he did not hear.) Yes, that dressing-table was ideal! How she had longed for one, nearly every day during the last ten years. . . . What happy years those last, just before Mr. Smedhurst's retirement, had been, with the vision gradually turning into reality before their eyes.

As she drew further back into those days, things became better, more reassuring. And now, at last, Mr. Smedhurst entered, in a pair of new pyjamas (he had always worn a night-shirt until he came to live in Newborough).

'I thought you'd never finish undressing, Ernest,' she reproached him.

'Why, it's only just eleven,' he said. 'I wasn't more than ten minutes.'

Mr. Smedhurst turned out the light, and before long they were both snoring in quiet, contented counterpoint.

.   .   .   .   .   .

Suddenly — it was difficult to tell how long they had been asleep — something woke them. . . . What was it? . . A heavy silence ensued of a few seconds' duration, and then a whistle. The speaking-tube!

Mr. Smedhurst lumbered out of bed and switched on the light as quickly as possible. They looked at each other. . . . This was new. Hitherto, the whistle had not been blown during the night. Neither spoke, but both of them understood that it would be better to answer, to try and find out what was wanted or what was amiss. Mr. Smedhurst approached the coiled instrument carefully, as though it were a serpent, unhooked it. . . . The loud and prolonged scream that reached him down it was almost a word; it seemed to be trying to form the word 'Help!' An exclamation, at any rate, with an immense urgency implicit in it. So loud was it, that it jarred the air of the whole room, and Mrs. Smedhurst, still in bed, plainly heard it. . . . Then nothing more . . . nothing.

'What is it, what is it?' Mr. Smedhurst demanded, but there was nothing now except this seemingly interminable and agonising silence. . . . 'What is it, what is it?' he implored.

Then, at last, a voice spoke a few words; that high-pitched and childish voice he had come so much to dread. But its bitter, senseless tones had now acquired a curious and despairing quietness.

'. . . Mad . . . mad and useless . . . unwanted. . . . But now it's someone else. Come up! Come up!'

'I think I'd better go upstairs, dear,' Mr. Smedhurst said timidly.

'Not without me, Ernest,' Mrs. Smedhurst answered, putting on her dressing-gown. And he did not try to dissuade her.

He looked at his watch. It was just two o'clock. . . . Then, seizing the poker — though everything seemed very quiet in the house, not a sound overhead — they advanced into the passage, Mr. Smedhurst going first, and crept upstairs by the light from their bedroom door, which they left open behind them. They did not turn on the switch at the top of the stairs, outside Ellen's room, because they could tell by the golden chinks between the door and its frame that the light was on in her room. . . . Still not a sound. . . . Mr. Smedhurst turned the handle softly. . . . The bed was empty; that was the first thing they noticed, no sign of anyone. . . . Then by the brilliant illumination of the one naked bulb, they saw Ellen, looking very lonely in this enormous room. She was sitting upon the floor, against the wall by the door, and with her back to it, in a curiously listless attitude. Her legs were stretched in front of her, her arms lay limp at her side. Her round, bucolic eyes were wide open in a fixed and glassy stare, and her neck was creased into bulges of flesh by the cord of her dressing-gown, wound about it and secured tightly to a nail on the wall.

.   .   .   .   .

Medical evidence at the inquest proved, however, that the cause of death was not suffocation, due to hanging, but heart-failure from shock. The noose was not tight enough to have killed her. If, as was plain, she had just been about to hang herself, death had intervened in another manner, and she must have collapsed in the posture in which Mr. and Mrs. Smedhurst had found her. There was no indication of the nature of the shock she had received, but her body showed bruises on it, inflicted apparently very shortly before her death. . . . The Coroner, commenting on the facts, found them rather difficult to reconcile, but said two things stood out : that Ellen Pycroft was a very highly strung, nervous girl, and that death had been due to natural causes, as the jury had found. No blame, he added, attached to Mr. and Mrs. Smedhurst.

Soon Bellingham House stood empty again, to be let or sold — and perhaps stands empty to this day —, the windows dead, like the eyes of a corpse, even though it may be that a mysterious life, or reflection of life, still proceeded behind them. And sometimes, when I was a boy and obliged to go through The Dale on a winter day, when the grey clouds scudded only just over the house-tops and the rooks' nests swayed wildly in the north wind, which whistled at every angle of every building, I would notice how the passers-by seemed to hurry on the faster in the wind's teeth for the sight of its cold and derelict desolation. And at night, it was said, the wind howled and screamed and whistled round the corners of the house with a particular vehemence. There always seemed to be wind there, even on fine days. . . . There was always the wind.

FRIENDSHIP'S DUE

(To Muriel Draper)

Some have for wits, and then for poets passed,
Turned critics next, and proved plain fools at last.
—ALEXANDER POPE

IT was on a particularly crystalline morning in the early
spring, after street and square had been cleansed for a while
of their flowing smoke-draperies by the splashing and tin-
tinnabulation of a hundred country-scented showers, that I
was first enabled — compelled even — to observe the hero of
this story. The omnibus, empty save for myself, glided
smoothly on its way, and from the level of the middle branches
flung out by the fine old trees that still linger in the lower
part of King's Road, Chelsea — old trees, though edged now
with fresh green lacings, on which the distilled moisture
glistened like so many fragments of crystal, echoing back the
various hard lights refracted by the wall-topping of broken
glass — I could watch the antics of my kind.

Suddenly there sounded a muddled hurricane of hurrying,
rather clumsy, feet; but to my surprise only one person, to
whom, as to Jove, these thunderbolts must have belonged,
was precipitated on to the seat opposite as the omnibus sailed,
red and proud as a turkey-cock, round the corner. Thus
were we isolated on our noisy moving trestle, set half-way
between the tree-tops and the ant-like world below. My
fellow-passenger enjoyed the fresh air, obviously; yet it seemed
somehow as if he regretted the absence of the larger, more
appreciative audience which, at this time of the morning, he
had the right to expect. Was he, then, with his obvious love
of public notice, an actor? In any case he did not look like a
prosperous one, but undoubtedly there lurked in his eyes the
expectation that he would be recognised. In a sense he
resembled an old-fashioned player. He possessed, superlatively,
that air of dominion by which it is possible to single out the
stage favourite — and even more, perhaps, the stage failure.

468

Yet though his appearance was highly accentuated, it was hardly sufficiently so for an actor; he was like an old 'But-me-no-buts' ranter, seen through the minimising glass of a *Punch* drawing. Still, if he belonged to the stage, he was a ranter, and not a naturalistic-whimsical-charm-schooler.

His face was heavy; not fat, but heavily boned. Yellowish in colour, it seemed to be supported on the two sharp points of a high white collar — higher in front than at the back — round which was twice wound a large black tie. This apparatus helped to define the prominent nose and protuberant mouth which, when open, displayed strong bony teeth that suggested a Scottish origin. His hair, black and lank, flowed a little over the back of his worn fur collar, while in the buttonhole of the stylised but anciently cut blue-cloth coat he affected sprouted that small bunch of faded violets that was, in truth, the freshest thing about him. A dandified cane was held in one hand, and with the ochreous black-tipped fingers of the other he was continually rattling and scratching the dull-gilt interior of a large silver cigarette-case, which lay open on his knees, taking out a cigarette, lighting it, and then throwing it away. These convolutions, obviously, were intended either to draw attention to himself, or by their familiarity to secure his recognition from others better informed than myself as to the genius of the day. Could it be, he hoped I was thinking, could it be the famous man-of-letters — the poet? . . . But, unfortunately, my mind had wandered along the wrong track, and I was busily scanning my memory for the faces of actors in the old Lyceum dramas.

How, in any case, could he have expected me to think of him, in these days and without a knowledge of his identity, as a poet? It would have been a survival almost too interesting and absorbing . . . for though I have known many poets (and already wish that such had not been my privilege) I have never encountered one by whose face could be distinguished his calling. Well-shaven, clean, and short-haired, the poet of today resembles a prosperous business man; but, and I ought to have recognised it, here was that unique Victorian survival, 'the poet's brow'! Under the grey felt hat, black-banded, bony ridges and angular wrinkles dwindled down from beneath the greasy locks to an almost horse-like nose. Perhaps, if my mind had not been otherwise occupied, I might, on the

strength of nose, teeth and hair, have diagnosed a critic —
but never should I have dared to hope for a poet — for I
have seen many decorative critics with curly hair, pince-nez
and an earnest look. But, as I afterwards discovered, this was
Ferdinand H. McCulloch, a former writer of verse, and a critic
who is still allowed to thunder denunciations of modern poetry
in various twopenny-weekly or halfpenny-daily papers.

Now because the hero of this tragi-comedy is a critic (but
remember that he is a poet as well), and even though I have
been so old-fashioned as to head my sermon with a text (an
instinct dormant in the right hand of every author of our
Puritan race), it must not be concluded that I am so antiquated
as to indulge in any attempt at throwing the slightest shadow
of ridicule upon the critical calling. That I leave to the poets
who have gone before me ; for such an attempt at it on my
part would be ungenteel, unnecessary and injudicious, insomuch as I am here on my trial, and to throw a boot at the
jury, however unbiased they may wish to appear, would be an
act little calculated to prejudice them in my favour. Nor,
perhaps, is the quotation that precedes this story altogether
apposite, for in this serious age of co-ordination and psycho-
analysis no wit would ever be taken for a poet, while the link
between humour and criticism appears to be even more frail —
only to be found, in fact, in the eye of the watching poet. For,
as our text shows, and this is my excuse for embroidering such
a theme, it has long been the custom of poets to watch with
interest the critical hoop-revolving of their span — a span
which this hoop-revolving has so often helped to shorten.

When an epigram becomes a platitude (the Hell to which
all epigrams are eventually condemned) the truth is no longer
in it ; and that critics are but disappointed poets has long
been a platitude. In these days, on the contrary, they are the
only satisfied ones, able both to confer the cake and then,
subsequently, eat it themselves. Curiously enough, too, though
the critic is popularly supposed to have a more logical mind, to
wield a more consistent pen than the poet's, it is a fact that
while critical opinion is still divided as to the comparative
merits of our more famous English bards, the judgment of the
latter as to the critical opinion of their day appears to have
been nearly identical. Could a written testimonial be obtained
from the shades of, let us say, Dryden, Pope, Coleridge, Gray,

Keats, Wordsworth, Shelley, Byron, Swinburne, and from their heirs, the worst-sellers of today, it is probable that though the words would differ with the individual, the purport which this varying language would serve to illumine, or perhaps for the sake of decency to obscure, would be found on examination to be remarkably alike in every case. Some poets have even gone so far as to pretend that there must be more than a casual connection between the decay of poetry, which criticism has from its birth detected, and that rise of the professional critic which was apparently coincident with this disintegration. But, for myself, I prefer to think that this gradual falling-away of the English Muse is due to the fact that the better, nobler, more serious minds among us are tempted from the profession of poetry alone towards the higher, more lucrative one of journalism; for, as many critics have themselves informed us lately and in print, their contribution to literature is, in reality, one of more importance than that of the creative mind, whether poet's or prose-writer's — the shadow more lasting than the substance, the parasite more interesting and enduring than the victim on which it thrives! Then, too, one has to live. . . . Reviewing, compared with the profession of poetry, is a well-paid one; and, as for that, the wielding of a critical pen need not prevent an occasional 'banging of the tins' (i.e. TREES — BREEZE; WOOD — GOOD — GOD; LARK — HARK; WIND — SPIN'D — BLIND), provided that it is a simple one, and may, indeed, procure for that music a more favourable reception than it would otherwise be awarded.

No one then, it is established, has a greater respect for the professional critic than the writer of this homily — because for a man to surrender the unravelling of his own mind and soul (unless these be tedious ones) in order to tear off the draperies concealing those of other people must be an act of noble altruism and Christian abnegation. And, to make a personal confession, let it be recorded that it is impossible to admire more than I do the weekly pursuit of Dostoieffsky and Tchekhoff through the Fourth Dimension conducted by the Ariel-like mind of Mr. Muddleton Moral; while after Mr. Jack Daw's revelation of the dormant beauties in the verse of Mrs. Hemans, I, too, can only cry 'Excelsior!' and am the more prepared for the perception of these same qualities in his own — at first sight — strangely different subject-poems, *Soccer* and *The Slaughter-*

House. Excelsior, indeed! For when these distinguished critics, very busy men, find time to use the antiquated medium of verse, yet never fail in a twice-weekly-and-once-on-Sunday donative of buns and ginger-beer to their protégés, or even an occasional laurel for the fallen (from whom no rivalry need be feared), my admiration knows no bounds.

If, then, this story is headed with a text, it is because that unpleasant and needlessly spiteful couplet, though no doubt useless as a generalisation, helps to explain something in this particular instance. For though the suicide of a minor poet would, as being an example of cause-and-effect, excite little interest, to poets the suicide of a critic — even his attempted self-destruction — would be a matter for wonder. The critic, in the exercise of his calling, commits a thousand attempts, successful or unsuccessful, at literary murder, and goes unpunished; yet if he were to attempt his own death — and fail — he would be tried, and possibly punished, for endeavouring to take his own life. And how curious is the law's accusation of a man for attempting suicide, when obviously his crime (except in cases of incurable disease) must be, not his failure to die but the confession of his failure to live, which is what attempted suicide amounts to! But of this a man is never accused, for this never punished.

. . . . .

Even as late as the year 1907 the name of Ferdinand H. McCulloch was one to conjure with in the more serious salons of West Hampstead. His reign had then lasted about ten years. For it was in the late nineties, only a few years before the armed might of the Great Transvaal Republic threw down its gauntlet to the people of these little islands, that our hero, already and always his own impresario, made his bow to the London public. He was then about thirty years of age, and but recently escaped from — though this was a secret hidden even from his appointed biographer — Ulster! There he had received a very Orange upbringing at the hands of three gaunt, rigorous maiden aunts, for his father, a clergyman, had died before Ferdinand could remember him, and his mother had married again. For this sin against the Victorian moral code the Misses McCulloch had never forgiven her; and devoted to the memory of their late brother, they succeeded in wresting the infant from her (she did not, in reality, seem very unwilling to part with him), and then brought him up in the same stern family tradition that had made themselves and their brother what they were. But Ferdinand, and this was in his favour, proved a difficult child. Nothing could be done with him. The Church, even, was out of the question. But he must earn his own living; so, as a very young man, a boy even, he scraped together a few pounds by writing what, we believe, are technically known as 'fashionable pars' for the Belfast papers. It cannot be said that the Misses McCulloch approved of this; but it brought in a little money and kept him out of mischief. Ferdinand, for his part, was thoroughly frightened of his aunts, and would have welcomed anything that took him out of their clutches. Soon the glamour of London and of the escape it meant cast its spell on him, and he began to dream of the city he had never seen. Latterly he had been reading the lives of great men — an interesting study, no doubt, but one perilous for youth, and still more fraught with danger for the elders of the house. The life of Michelangelo, for example, is responsible for more trouble between budding artist and — if such a person still exists — art patron than is imaginable. In that school it is that the Slade student learns with surprising ease the importance, not of being an artist, which is, after all, the fact that really matters about Michelangelo, but of being disagreeable, grasping and rude. Similarly, lives of Napoleon and Lord Byron have unforeseen and deplorable consequences; while we are told that every dirty and uncouth versifier at the universities, should he occasionally get a little drunk, excuses it by announcing that he is the reincarnation of Verlaine — or (even at this date!) of Dowson! Luckily Ferdinand had got no further than the Borgias, Michelangelo, Napoleon and Byron. Still, he was determined to be a great man, perhaps more of a Byron than a Bonaparte; and for the accomplishment of this design he must be daring and a little wicked. How, then, was he to do it? For though it is easy to be unpleasant anywhere, it is difficult to be a Borgia in Belfast. What is more, the gaunt and triple-headed spectre of the Misses McCulloch guarded, like Cerberus, the mouth of any possible Hell, ferociously barking. There was, of course, only one thing to be done — to escape to London as soon as he found a chance of doing so. After that it would be easy. Only one obstacle would then interpose between Ferdinand and Lord Byron — the writing of verse, and this was an impediment he was determined to overcome.

It must be five years before we meet Ferdinand again; five years must elapse between his escape and his transfiguration.

In those days two traditions strove and clashed together in the drawing-rooms of artistic ladies, for the shadow of the Celtic twilight, destined later to attain the density of a London fog, already lay heavy on the suburbs, and the Voice of Cuchulain was uplifted in Liberty's Drapery Department, or wailed through Soho; while older, but competing with it, although perhaps already a little losing ground, was the influence of Ernest Dowson. In many gatherings of 'modern young people' the mist wafted from the Land of Heart's Desire would be rent in twain, as an even then slightly old-fashioned 'advanced' young woman would rise to thunder 'Cynara', or a romantic-looking young undergraduate from Oxford would proclaim, and reiterate, that he had been faithful to the lady in his own fashion. Alas! these things are altered: the daughter of the 'advanced' young woman, her hair cut short like a pony's mane, now plays the more intricate game of complex-and-inhibition with the romantic young man's son (who, like all the young men of today, has a post on the League of Nations), and the leaden weight of *The London Mercury* now rests on those slender tables upon which had once been laid the grotesque beauty of Beardsley's drawings.

In this mingled atmosphere of a wet-Sunday-afternoon on the Irish Lakes and Greek Passion, which we have attempted to outline, out of the harder, more material light that beats upon the city-ways of Belfast, stepped Mr. Ferdinand McCulloch. But it was a Ferdinand transfigured, for like a chameleon he had absorbed both the colour and tone of his new surroundings — and had already composed numerous sets of verses! The clean, callow, tweed-clad, large-boned, Ulster-mouthed boy had flowered into what in those days was known as a 'Real Bohemian', a dashing yet dreamy-eyed figure, full of psychic qualities and the charm of the Southern-Irish people. He sported now, for the first time, that bunch of violets to which he still clings; his black hair became lank and matted, his finger-nails were allowed to grow longer, while his formerly harsh voice became almost too soft and dove-like, for he had

474

developed what he yet considers to be a very attractive brogue. Ulster, with its business habits, worldly outlook, and stern Puritanism, he placed behind him, becoming — or rather pretending that he had always been — Catholic, Celtic, and sometimes, we regret to say, a little Twilight. For in the very advanced taverns, like caves, which he frequented, it was necessary occasionally, for the sake of his reputation, to plunge through the purple mists of wine. After midnight he could sometimes be seen stumbling out of his cave, like Caliban, his hair tousled, his feet a little uncertain. Once too (and it made him a memorable figure) McCulloch met Dowson in a cab-shelter. It is true that the latter poet did not pay much attention to him, hardly, indeed, appeared to see him; but it gave our hero an aura, created a legend that clung, so that years afterwards, as with head held up, and a winsome smile hung across the protuberant cavity of his mouth, he entered a room, there would be a rustling whisper, 'You know . . . the friend of Dowson's!'

Though McCulloch was not a clever man — in the sense that few ideas visited him — yet his hold on one, when once he had grasped it, was singularly tenacious. Quite early in his career he managed to pin down one principle of success — that lesson about which we heard so much, twenty years later, from the weekly preachers in Sunday papers — the VALUE of CO-OPERATION and UNITY. It will be remembered by those who succeeded in living through the 'Great War', that our Best Minds, in the course of 'giving one furiously to think', founding bond-clubs, or 'exploring avenues', announced constantly that the war had not been fought in vain if we learnt the 'Value of Co-operation' — a lesson, it appeared, well worth the losing of a few hundred thousand lives. There would be no more strikes or disturbances; the workman, in the sacred cause of unity, would always give way; and a maypole and morris dance would flourish once more in the congenial atmosphere of Sheffield, Birmingham, and Manchester. Well, McCulloch realised the value of co-operation and unity at an early date; and it was his own discovery. In fact, he formed what would now be known — according to whether you liked or disliked its members — as 'an interesting little group of thinkers', or a 'clique'. There is, by the way, I believe, supposed to be something peculiarly disgraceful about a 'clique' — and if a book by someone you dislike happens to be well received, you should invariably describe its success as being the work of a 'little clique'. Ferdinand's 'clique' was a small one, consisting, as it did, of three members. For the other two he chose, wisely, Arthur Savage Beardsall, an amiable minor poet, of rather bad health, a little real talent, and a certain slapdash facility combined with an admirable aptitude for posing, and T. W. Frendly, a poor but intensely energetic little Cockney journalist. In appearance Beardsall was slight, short and bearded — the dark beard disguising his want of chin and look of ill-health — and Frendly, with his beady little eyes, was dapper, small and sharp as a sparrow, while his voice would trail off unexpectedly into a high Cockney accent. His simple mind was intensely impressed with the genius of his two companions, and he reserved all his energy for the preaching of their gospel. In this association of three friends his was the humble part; he would listen admiringly, collect their epigrams and sayings, repeat them on every occasion, learn their poems by heart, recite them, and generally do an immense amount of clique and claque work. He might be described, indeed, as their boom-companion.

Beardsall, McCulloch and Frendly became inseparable; they would lunch together, dine together, and toward the end of an evening get a little drunk together. They would write, even when seeing each other every day, 'Posterity-letters'* to the other members of their clique — or rather Beardsall or McCulloch would write them to Frendly, whom they had tacitly appointed as their biographer.

Each of the three would quote, praise, imitate, caricature the two others, and finally write articles about their work, though to get either the former or the latter writings printed, it was first necessary for a review — expensive but short-lived — to be started by the richer members of their as yet limited circle of admirers. For gradually there formed round this nucleus an outer circle of Admirers of the Misunderstood. The

---

* Letters written by minor poets for posthumous publication to friends whom they can trust to print them. For this purpose should be chosen a rather old, distinguished critic, who will at once understand what is wanted and whose position guarantees that after his death (which, with any luck, cannot be far distant) all the letters he has put away will be published by a literary executor, or a still younger minor poet, who can be depended upon to treasure the letters, and publish them subsequently for the sake of his own importance.

leaders of it, who lent a little feminine grace to the gatherings, were Mrs. Stilpepper and Miss Ellen Durban. Juliet Stilpepper, small, dark and rather pretty, known among her friends for the charm of her speaking voice and laughter, was the wife of that well-known artist whose problem picture at the Academy in 1897, depicting a woman in leg-of-mutton sleeves and a straw hat, kneeling down on a sandy beach, her face wet with tears, with one hand pointing to an enormous orang-outang, the other to a whale spouting water — the whole composition entitled *The Mother of the Gracchi* — caused such a sensation. Her *salon* was famous throughout Hampstead. Within the hospitable red-brick house one would meet prominent exponents of Woman's Rights (not yet become notorious as Suffragettes), a few Fabians, many Irish and neo-Greek poets, a few lesser stage celebrities, and, later on, numerous hysterical admirers of Mr. Stephen Phillips. Between the latter and McCulloch's group there was an incessant, deadly warfare. But in these battles their hostess always gave her valuable aid to the three friends; for if they prospered, how much the greater would be her credit for discovering them. It was a gamble — an outside chance; but she meant to win. This, then, was the chief platform upon which our three characters disported themselves before an appreciative audience of young ladies shod in sandals, and crowned with dusty golden hair, whose curving necks still showed a trace of the gradually disappearing Pre-Raphaelite goitre. To this latter class belonged their other chief supporter, Ellen Durban, whose sandals betrayed her as one of the first, last — and, alas, least successful — of classical dancers.

Juliet Stilpepper and Ellen Durban, the earliest and most fervent disciples of the three friends, soon began to feel that their faith had been justified; for the clique began to arrive at a certain importance. Beardsall's small, easy, meretricious talent was winning him a wider recognition — shedding even on the other two a certain lustre, which at the time could not be distinguished as a borrowed radiance, but appeared to emanate from themselves. This recognition was just enough to make the clique a matter of wonder, but not sufficient to deprive its members of their prerogative of feeling ill-used, neglected and misunderstood; while it seldom occurred to them that, had they really been good poets, they would be

objects, not of interest, but of ridicule. Their lives, and carefully prepared little eccentricities, helped them, too, with their
special public. From the taverns and clubs where they spent
their evenings the rumour of their Tiberian but really very
innocent orgies would spread excitement through Hampstead,
or flicker like marsh-fire through Chelsea. By this time they
had all bought brown velvet jackets, with a sash round the
waist, and large romantic black hats. Beardsall had in his
room a skull out of which he pretended to drink (this must
have been a recollection of some life of Byron which he, too,
had read as a boy), while McCulloch had, hung round one of
the brass knobs of his bed, a long necklace, made of vertebrae
torn from the skeleton of a man, stained purple and looking in
reality rather like the chain of a bicycle after an accident.
Much of their time, when not occupied in praising one
another or laughing in a hollow Homeric manner, was
spent in contemplation of suicide. Only after death — they
felt — would their genius be fully recognised, while the more
sudden and violent their end, the more effective for their
posthumous glory. Cups of poison, a fall to the crowd below
from the Nelson Monument, the lily-green death-look of
Chatterton, the decline of Keats, a cloaked figure found
floating on the Thames, a revolver shot in Piccadilly followed
by a dramatic collapse, or the quieter, less sensational, but
sudden 'Strange Death of a Literary Recluse' — all these
passed through their minds, were mentioned in low tones or
lay hidden, for all to read, in the intentionally gloomy fire of
their eyes. But the chorus of sandal-footed and golden-
crowned young ladies implored them constantly to remember
their families — not to do anything rash — though perhaps
these same young women found that the thought of it gave
them, too, no less than the three protagonists, a little tremor
of wonder, excitement and importance. In their less exalted
moments, however, the chance of getting this thrill in real life
seemed ever so remote — merely a dream of fair women.

But, to return to our hero, Ferdinand was by now turning
out stanza after stanza, poem after poem, and in these masterpieces very cleverly backed both popular favourites at the same
time, for while in feeling they were fervently pagan, full of
wine and roses, full of the free life of the Greeks as seen through
the dusty spectacles of the nineties, they were yet addressed

to a dreamy deity, implored by the poet as 'Dark Rosaleen' —
or when it became necessary to find a rhyme for 'Thee', as
'Rosalee'; later, he was even clever enough to mingle with
these other ingredients, neo-classic or Irish, a little of the epic
touch conveyed by Mr. Stephen Phillips. Very poignant were
these odes, and the Belfast accent made manifest in them was
audible only to Hibernian ears. 'Oh, Mr. McCulloch,' they
would importune in the *salons* set on the hills, 'do recite that
one . . . you know . . .' At first he would refuse, gracefully
refuse, offering instead to read them a short lyric by Beardsall,
but in the end he would always yield and recite to them his
favourite poems, which, as with many other poets, luckily
happened to be his own. Sometimes he would refuse to
declaim without a harp accompaniment from Mrs. Stilpepper.
'It reminds me of Erin', he would say, and while Juliet's
slender fingers would draw out the syrupy music from the
strings, he would wail scarcely recognisable words in a gloomy,
pathetic, almost frightening way, or sing on one note in a
winsome, tenderly caressing manner. 'Doesn't it make you
understand *them*?' the earnest, enthusiastic band of young
women would remark rather vaguely.

As he stood in the centre of the room, with eyes half closed,
his face, framed in by its dark hair, and balanced over the
two points of his high white — still white — collar, seemed to
have little connection with the short, thick-set body below.
Hanging there, among faded green velvet curtains and the
spreading host of little pieces of pseudo-Oriental china, that
surged in blue-and-white foam over the walls, tables and piano,
it seemed but a large mask for his voice. Through the mouth,
with its too prominent lips and teeth, came the warm high
tones and winning pronunciation — tricks which, as he intended them to do, prejudiced many women in his favour,
and secured him a few lifelong friends: friends who would
have remained faithful to the end — if only there had been
one! Thus Ferdinand, his boots planted uneasily in the Celtic
twilight, his head bathed in the sunshine of the growing garden
cities, spent many pleasurable years, passing through the long
level plateau of early manhood with his two friends beside him.

.   .   .   .   .   .

When the suicide of one of these three did occur, it came
with the greatest shock of all, the shock of the long-discussed

and half-expected; for when something long talked-about, and even long prepared, happens — as was the case with the European War — then surprise overwhelms one. Beardsall, on a short holiday from his journalistic duties, and possibly from his friends, was found shot dead in the bedroom of a small, shabby hotel in Paris. Ferdinand, Frendly and his group of admirers were overwhelmed with sorrowing astonishment. His death was, perhaps, a greater tragedy than any of them imagined, since the end of this poor, tired, ill, little man may have been due, not so much to poverty, weariness or ill-health, *or* to the feeling that he was an unappreciated genius, as to his recognition of the fact that he possessed very little real talent, and that his reputation was already out of proportion to it. For a long time he must have felt the strain of being forced to carry more than he could bear. It was in August that his death took place, and one hardly likes to think of him wandering about in the city with its holiday air. To the English, accustomed to London, there must be always something heartless and too logical about Paris, a quality that must make even death more hard to bear. The streets, set out for the pageant of a vulgar imperialism that has long been swept away, are like a plutocratic feast prepared years ago for some swindling financier, a feast that still remains dusty and untouched. The architecture, always hard, logical and equal, is nowhere as good as London's best, nowhere as bad as London's worst. The large stony gardens, set with hundreds of statues that lack the wistful, unconscious humour of our togaed senators, or Achilles Monument, are emptier than usual, and the sun beats fiercely down upon them, while the idyllic, rich tranquillity and falling green shadows of the Bois only mock the lives of the needy, reminding them of the hateful contrast between farmhouse and city slum, garden and tenement, rich and poor. In this smooth-faced, very luxurious city, the sad little poet's fate overcame him; he was in his room for some two hours before he died. We know nothing of his thoughts during those two long hours that preceded him into eternity, as he walked about in that small, hot, gloomy bedroom.

After the first shock had passed for the two survivors of the clique and their friends, a period of intense activity set in. First of all there were obituary notices to be penned, articles on Beardsall's life, accounts of his death to be written, then his literary remains to be edited and many poems and letters to be published. How well, and with what kindness, the dead man had played his part, for in all the letters, and even in most of the poems, were affectionate references or glorious tributes to Ferdinand and Frendly. Finally came the great work, *The Life and Letters of Arthur Savage Beardsall*, by T. W. Frendly and Ferdinand H. McCulloch, profusely illustrated, and issued by a famous publishing house at a guinea net.

This book was a masterpiece of judicious booming. Frendly did the hard work, McCulloch embellished it; and as far as the latter was concerned it was a truer form of autobiography than many to which we have lately been treated. Affectionate references to him appeared in nearly every letter, while not only did our hero-editor include in the volume poems, letters, jokes, epigrams and denunciations of his own, but there were almost as many photographs of him as of Beardsall, and whenever the latter appeared in group or caricature, there, at his side, was the very easily recognisable face of Ferdinand! After the publication of this *Life*, the dead poet's work received a wider recognition than he had ever hoped or deserved, so that in country-houses, when conversation had ebbed, the artistic member of the house-party would say, 'I suppose you knew Arthur Beardsall?' and point to a book lying uncut on the table. But, oddly enough, Ferdinand McCulloch's fame did not appear to grow similarly, or to the extent expected of it.

During the two or three years taken up by this juggling of life, letters and poems, there were, of course, many meetings between the two survivors of the group and their old friends. At first our hero was seen — if anything more often than formerly — in Juliet Stilpepper's drawing-room, or in the *salons* of the other artistic ladies; though, whereas at one time he had always been asked to recite his own poems, he was now invariably requested, instead, to declaim those of his dead friend. Even Ellen Durban, formerly the most fervent admirer of his Muse, now only asked him to recite Beardsall's work. The truth of the matter was that their friendship with a temporarily rather famous poet — and still more with one who had perished by his own hand — shed an unearthly radiance not only on Ferdinand (which halo cancelled out his own) but on all the friends, and especially on Mrs. Stilpepper and Miss Durban.

This was not at all what our hero had expected. Gradually he began to shun these parties, and would more frequently meet the ladies at some club or restaurant, pleading as excuse a growing absorption in literary criticism and journalism. But the truth is that he did not care much for gatherings at which he was no longer the chief personage, ousted always by the spectre of his dead friend. Frendly, or 'T. W.' as he called him, was still in constant attendance, doing as much propaganda as ever. Ferdinand's verses were yet to be met with in the pages of journals, but his signature seemed an omen of little prosperity, insomuch as his name printed — if only in the list of possible contributors — was a sure indication that this new review would live for one number only. By this time the world of the late nineties had passed with the Boer War, and we soon find ourselves in Mid-Edwardian days. The neo-classic form of verse, though still surviving — like everything else — at the universities, was dead elsewhere; the Irish twilight was beginning to deepen into night; and signs began to appear of a modern movement in English poetry, similar to that which had blossomed in France through the last few decades of the old century. And this new poetry attracted to itself all those who liked — or liked to like — things modern, so that many of our hero's former admirers forsook him, and even neglected to read Beardsall. Ferdinand's verses appeared less and less often, and, instead, he wrote critical articles devoted to the iniquity of the new verse, and signed, impressively, 'Ferdinand H. McCulloch'. And what thunder of the Gods against modern decadence was contained in these prophetic messages, though he always attacked the less well-received, and therefore probably better, poets. For he would never attack popular idols, hoping always to obtain their favour. His abuse of those he dared to abuse only equalled his fulsome praise of those he dared not attack, whom he would describe as 'Standard-bearers' or 'Knights-of-the-Grail'! But what roused his ire especially was that quality described as 'obscurity' (the latter being anything he could not understand), and one could only conclude that to be an 'obscure' poet was somehow worse than to be an obscure journalist.

It must be admitted that, with the passage of time, Ferdinand's manner lost none of its jauntiness. On the contrary, he developed more and more that air of dominion we have noted, remaining faithful to all the developments of his personality. His long finger-nails, the fingers stained orange with nicotine, still feverishly scratched the inside of his cigarette-case as he drew out a cigarette, lit it, threw it away. His long hair, bunch of violets, Irish brogue, high collar and serpent-like tie were all in their pristine splendour. Constant he remained, as well, to his *lares* and *penates*; however often he changed his apartments, there you would find that necklace of purple-stained vertebrae, which had been hung round the end of how many lodging-house beds, and the skull-loving-cup which he had inherited from Arthur Beardsall. Only two alterations, apart from those which Time made for him, could be detected in his appearance. The collar was less white — had now more the tone and texture of vellum — while the velvet jacket and large black hat had been discarded for more sober garments, better befitting a critic and solid man-of-letters! The rest of his detail sufficiently proclaimed him a poet. Whatever the development of his personality or circumstances, our hero could be trusted to dramatise them for his friends.

Lately Frendly appeared to have been doing more propaganda for himself than for Ferdinand, and was in consequence prospering, for he was a sharp, active little man. This unexpected turn of events — or of the worm — annoyed McCulloch considerably, and, consequently, he saw less and less of 'T. W.' Other admirers, such as Juliet Stilpepper and Ellen Durban, clung to him; for now that the boom in Beardsall was beginning to decline, they remembered the second string to their bow. They cherished him, still expected something of him. . . . But what was it? — what could it be?

Ferdinand would never enter the *salon* now. He was determined never more to risk being asked to recite the poetry of another, and Mrs. Stilpepper's harp lay there dim and golden as Ellen Durban's hair, its strings silent and untouched. Instead, then, of his going to these gatherings, the two ladies would meet him each week for luncheon in a little restaurant at the side of a narrow alley off Fleet Street. The meal was fixed, always, for the unusual, almost exciting, hour of 2.15. Ferdinand's office was round the corner, and though he occupied a rather subordinate position there, at each step away from it his importance grew visibly.

In the midsummer of which we are writing the sunlight falling through the leaves of the few scraggy trees in the court outside made a pattern of wavering golden disks, flat and round, on floor and pavement. It played, too, with rather terrifying effect on the faces of those eating, bringing out again the more dusty, less golden, tone of Ellen's hair, exaggerating her high cheek-bones, revealing her large bony feet shod in sandals, and contrived a whole set of tricks for poor Mrs. Stilpepper's too sweet countenance. It magnified the pores and wrinkles, intensified the romantic lines, of Ferdinand's head, till one was reminded of Gulliver's horror when, lifted up to the level of the Brobdingnagian faces, he observed the pits, hollows and furrows that graced them. In the room, too, the sunlight seemed to draw out the smell of stale food, to unmuffle the incessant noise. But not one of those present talked louder or more often than Ferdinand, though it was, in reality, quite unnecessary, as this little table of three people was in any case very noticeable; even Juliet, the most ordinary of the group, won public attention by her speaking voice, which, noted among her friends for its dulcet tones, was now almost too musical in its utterance. As for Ellen, her appearance could be trusted to gain attention anywhere, since with her large sandalled feet, big bones, general untidiness and that cloudy crown of golden hair which had been — and still was — her pride, she now more resembled an animated haystack than a human being.

At the end of luncheon, when our hero leant back to light a cigarette, taking one with difficulty from that voluminous and dented silver case, drinking a cup of coffee — which, like the coffee in most English establishments, tasted alternately of meat-extract and iron dumb-bells — it was an experience to see his manner, as of a conqueror, at whose slightest word the journalistic world, here assembled, would quake. The ingratiating brogue slid on its oiled passage round the room, winging its easy way from table to table, so that all could hear; while invariably, at the end of the meal, would come the familiar menace of suicide. Year by year, month by month, these threats increased. But it almost seemed, as he continued to talk in this way, as if the expression on the faces of the two ladies brightened a little, for an instant became animated, as though instead of threatening them he had promised them

something . . . Ferdinand was too immersed in his own
grievances, in the perpetual recitation of his troubles and ill-
treatment, to notice any of these subtle, very slight, changes of
expression. Perhaps it may have been due to some alteration
in the falling lights and shadows dripping through the small
branches of the trees outside. Yes, he was sick of it! he said
. . . absolutely sick of it! . . . (and he would laugh in that
hollow way) . . . sick of it! Ellen and Juliet were, naturally,
very upset. It would be too, too dreadful — appalling —
after all that had happened . . . Still, of course, he was right
in a way, in what he said, and they agreed with him that he
would probably never be properly appreciated in his lifetime.
After his death, undoubtedly, his reputation would stand
higher, much higher. One couldn't doubt it. Look, for
instance, at the posthumous appreciation of Beardsall, a friend
of all of us, a good poet, certainly, Ferdinand, but no better
than you are! But McCulloch, though looking rather pleased
at this declaration of faith, would point out that such was the
deterioration of the public taste that even Beardsall's fame
stood less high than it did ten years ago, just after his death.
'I'm sick of it!' he would reiterate; 'I've nearly made up
my mind to do it — sick of it all.' . . .

But, 'Oh, no,' they cried, he couldn't, he mustn't do it!
He must think, not only of himself, but of his friends . . .
think how they would miss him, reminded at every turn by
letters, poems, photographs . . . might even be blamed. . . .
(As they talked the colour came back a little to their faces.)
After all, they might say it, mightn't they? Wasn't there
something . . . something due to friendship? Something?
And as they continued to plead they experienced again that
little thrill of wonder, expectation and importance which had
visited them after Beardsall's death. 'But promise us, swear
to us, that you will never DO IT!' they cried.

'I won't promise now,' Ferdinand answered, 'but I will
give you m' definite decision on Monday at this table, after
luncheon. But in your turn y' must promise NOT to mention
the subject to me till after the meal is over, for if it must be
m' last, at least let it be a jolly one'; and soon after this the
two ladies fluttered out into the open air, while Ferdinand, a
grim look on his face, his chin upheld by the apparatus of tie
and collar, slowly swaggered out after them.

Now it happened that on the Monday I witnessed the final scene of the drama ; but, alas ! the final scene was laid not at the end but in the middle of the tragedy, which may continue for another three decades after it should have finished.

Rather later than the usual luncheon-hour I went to the restaurant to meet a friend. The room was very full and noisy ; there, at a table set for three persons, were seated two rather queer-looking middle-aged women. They were very quiet, hardly speaking to each other at all, but on their faces could be detected a slight flush of expectation, while in their eyes gleamed a fire which I had seen before in other eyes, but when ? Then I recalled the faces of the older women-gamblers at Monte Carlo.

Presently there was borne in on us the sound of important footsteps outside, and a little man entered, with a large bony face and a high, not necessarily white, collar, round which was coiled twice a large black tie, like the Delphic serpent. In the buttonhole of his coat was a bunch of violets — or rather violas, for the former could not be obtained at this season ; and I remembered, suddenly, my earlier meeting with him on the top of a motor-bus a year or two previously.

He wished his two friends, whose excitement had, in the meantime, obviously increased, a good-morning in his succulent Irish voice, ordered luncheon, and sat down with the air of a monarch, who sits down so that others need not stand. But, in spite of his importance, he seemed depressed. His two companions said little and ate less, but fever shone in eye and cheek. It was a rather gloomy affair, the luncheon, though it lasted long. The conversation was confined to politics and a certain amount of heartfelt condemnation of modern poetry. Only once, too, sounded out that hollow laugh. But it seemed to me, watching, that the excitement of his two companions was steadily increasing.

And, after the coffee, the little dark woman said, in a voice musical as a xylophone or a set of musical glasses : 'Well, have you decided . . . Ferdinand ? Tell us as quickly as you can ; remember Our Suspense.' And, with a solemn expression, came the answer, in that rich tone, 'I have' (and after a long pause) 'I have decided . . . NOT TO . . . ! I give you m' word.'

The light faded out of their faces as they thanked him ;

and for the first time in all these long years of association they found they had to hurry away quickly, after paying the bill. Ellen Durban had to take her class in classical dancing earlier than usual that afternoon ; Mrs. Stilpepper had her family (and all that) to look after. . . . So he wasn't going to, after all . . . and the two women stepped into the bright sunshine outside and quickly parted.

In the dining-room I was asking my friend, 'Who is that little man just going out?' and he replied : 'Oh! that's an Irish journalist ; McCulloch. I believe he used to write verse ; he's always here with those two women . . . he was a great friend of that poet, the fellow who committed suicide . . . what was his name?'

Many times in the years that followed we saw him there lunching alone, for the other actors in the small drama would no longer play their parts.

TOUCHING WOOD

I DO not yet know how this story ends : for what I am going to tell you happened only yesterday morning, before I left the boat at Suez.

With a pile of books and an empty soup-cup beside me, I sat in a deck-chair, staring out into mist-edged nothingness, where not even a dolphin or a flying-fish leapt for the diversion of the passengers. Everything seemed to be warm and damp, very damp. The edge of the sky was hung with ragged banners of cloud, and the edge of the sea melted into it. My neighbour, also with several books by his side, and one lying open upon his knee, stared, with a similar fixity, into the watery, empty perspective. The vast melancholy of the sea — only supportable because of the laziness it engenders, and of the manner in which it causes one day to telescope into another, inducing in many persons the subsequent conviction that they must have enjoyed the voyage for the time to have passed so quickly — hung over both of us : that much was clear. Tall, thin and with rather fine hands, my neighbour displayed in his physique an unusual sensitiveness, and I wondered, idly, who he was. . . . The books afforded no clue, for they were of several sorts ; a translation of the Greek Anthology, a novel by P. G. Wodehouse, Dunne's *Experiment with Time*, a new biography of some dead diplomat by Mr. Harold Nicolson, a volume of short stories by the late D. H. Lawrence, and — I noticed now — one of my own books, *The Man Who Lost Himself*. Suddenly he turned his eyes from the water and addressed me.

'Do you *like* the sea ?' he asked.

'Yes, I love it, in a way,' I answered, 'in spite of the boredom — and, with me, alas, of the terror. For I'm quite a good sailor : but when other people are lying in their bunks, wishing they could drown, I'm lying, fully dressed, on mine, praying that I shan't, and thinking of the wastes of water on which a man's head would be almost imperceptible. That's why I prefer the Mediterranean, where you can usually see land. . . .

488

But it seems to have disappeared altogether today. . . . Or, better still, give me the Suez Canal; I look forward to an enjoyable afternoon.'

'Oh, I know: I'm a bit like that myself,' he said. 'In fact, as you're a writer, I'll tell you a story about it. But I hope you're not superstitious?

'Perhaps you can hardly call it a story, really,' he added; 'it's an illustration, more than a story, or the proof of a theory. . . . And in this instance the theory or the moral is the old, obvious one, which D. H. Lawrence was so fond of emphasising, that what you *feel* is — and must always be — more true than what you merely think: judge by touch, as it were, rather than sight. But people don't have the courage nowadays to act on what they feel: they act by reason, and then try to invent rational explanations afterwards, of the singular things that happen to them. But it's no use: no use at all.

'The ship, bound for South America, left Tilbury on a wet December afternoon: but the next day and for two days afterwards the sea, even when we crossed the Bay of Biscay, resembled a blue summer lake. In spite of the calm, though, we were late in arriving at Lisbon, while, once there, the interminable arguments of the harbour authorities seemed specially calculated to make us later still in leaving it. I stood watching the departing passengers, and listening to a fierce Portuguese quarrel that spluttered like a damp firework, between the ship's agent and an official of the custom-house. . . . There were only two new arrivals of whom to take notice, an Englishwoman and her husband. She was certainly beautiful in a curious way, like one of the Fates. Her eyes, wide open, had the blue depths of an oracle, in which many meanings, one true and many false, could be read. There was something classical, or pre-classical, about that startled and stony visage, something of Cassandra, something of the doom of the House of Atreus. . . . Something, too, I thought — or should I say, I felt? — at the time, of a mermaid: for her eyes belonged to the sea. . . . And yet it was at Mycenae, in the broken palace above the deep ravine; on that hill which seems to be alone for ever with the sea and the sky, as though they were washing it free of that doom, and the taint that caused it, that she would have been, I think, most at home. . . . Beside her, her husband looked pleasantly matter-of-fact: but it was only her appearance which was unusual; her clothes seemed specially designed to destroy the particular kind of beauty she possessed, to degrade it and make it ordinary.

'The following morning, sitting on deck, as we are now, I found myself next to them, and, after playing for a while with our books in the listless manner which the movement and vibration of all ships — for there is a very strong link between sea-sickness and print — enforce, we began to talk a little. . . . They gave an ordinary enough impression, too, when they spoke, and her voice — quiet, busy, comfortable, though rather empty — had no element in it of either prophecy or tragedy. . . . And yet I knew, I felt, I was *aware* — informed, I suppose, by the exploring of those antennae which so much excel the faculties of the mind — that, somehow or other, she was inextricably associated with these qualities. . . . We talked in a desultory manner for two hours or more, and during the whole of that time the sea, which had been up till now so unruffled — even in those latitudes where you would have expected it to be at its most swelling and boisterous — began indubitably to show increasing symptoms of a change of mood. It felt as though it were trying out its powers, though only, as yet, with some future occasion in view. Little winds whistled in the corners, and there was a roll on the boat that caused the usual jokes and laughter among the younger passengers, tramping noisily round the deck, and instilled in the players of quoits and other games a desire to be more hearty and jolly than ever, in order to cover up a certain incipient queasiness. . . . You ask what we'd been talking about? . . . Well, I forget, but all sorts of things, politics and books — safe, dull books — and travel.

'With every minute, though, conversation became more difficult, for there were sounds of things crashing from time to time, and the wind howled ever more loudly, though ours was a comparatively sheltered corner. . . . They were going, she told me, to Buenos Aires — or "B-A", as she called it, with her affectation of ordinariness — for the voyage; weren't even going on shore for a day or two at Rio. No, a week at "B-A", and then straight back home; "that's the place for us", she said. Mr. Ruevinny — for that was their name — had been ill, it appeared, and had been ordered this voyage by the doctor. "I tried to persuade my wife not to come," he explained, "but she insisted. I didn't persuade you to come, did I, darling?" he added, turning to her. "I did everything I could to stop you."

'No, I don't recall the whole conversation with any distinctness: only one or two things like that. I remember Mrs. Ruevinny saying, in her practical, putting-up-with-no-nonsense and yet singularly empty voice — a voice which said things as though it did not mean them — "Well, I'm a fatalist: you can't escape what's coming to you — so there you are! You must make the best of it. No fox can escape for long, if the pack is out after him." . . . I recollect that very well, for at the moment this remark — so ordinary, and of a kind to which we have all had to listen against our wills so often — irritated me almost beyond endurance. It accorded so ill, I thought, with that curious beauty, with that face which seemed waiting for one of the great emotions — and it was *fear*, I felt sure — to make it a supreme vehicle of expression. . . . But in that way, people so often disappoint one by enunciating sentiments which do not suit them. . . . Then she went on to talk of bazaars in the home counties, and gave way to little bursts of self-importance, equally inappropriate.

'And yet were they, I wondered at the time, in reality bursts of self-importance? She brought them into the conversation, I felt, not so much to impress a stranger as to comfort herself. Because such functions belonged to everyday life, as a rule lacking in both heroism and disaster, just as the opinions she voiced were the opinions of everyday life: and she clung hard to them because she was desperately anxious to impress upon herself that life was really of this pattern for her, and that some dim, huge existence of antique catastrophe, to which she belonged, and from which she had once fled, possessed no actuality. Every opinion she uttered, every occasion to which she referred, was as though she pinched herself to be sure that she was awake, and that the nightmare had passed. . . . So, I felt, might one of the Atridae, Clytemnestra or Elektra, in the intervals of those catastrophic events to which their names are, for us, indissolubly attached, have told acquaintances of the Sale of Work she was getting up in order to aid the honest poor of Mycenae.

'Rougher and rougher it grew; and I did not see them again that day. Certainly it had grown too stormy now for

491

one to take any sort of pleasure in the voyage. It was not even possible to sleep: though storms, as a rule, make me feel sleepy; and at night, if for a single moment you dozed off, you were sure to be woken at once by the flying open, flapping and slamming of cupboard doors, or by the sensation that the soul itself, the *psyche* round which the body is built up, had slightly shifted its habitation. . . . "Why," all the passengers, as so often during a voyage, were asking themselves, "*why* did I do it?" . . . But my own chief emotion, and one that I nearly always experience on the Atlantic, though it has been my lot to travel a good deal upon it, was of fright: I did not feel sick, I felt frightened of those cold valleys beneath, endless and undulating, as deep, we are told, as the island mountains are high. . . . Incidentally (forgive me for interrupting my own story), hasn't it grown much rougher since we began talking, or is it my imagination?'

I had to admit that the weather had changed. The boat had begun to pitch about in an unexpected way.

'I thought so,' he said, and paused a moment. 'Still, it will at least be smooth in the Canal. . . . But let me proceed,' he continued. 'Fortunately I was leaving the boat at Madeira, and that was only two days ahead. But how sincerely during those hours I longed for it, that nest of purple bougainvillea and peroxide blondes, poised in mid-ocean under its cosy of Atlantic cloud.

'The next day was of too unpleasant a character for one to be able to take an interest in anything, in food or drink or sleep or passengers: but I noticed, all the same, that Mr. Ruevinny was alone at luncheon. . . . The following morning the storm appeared to have abated a little, though not much, and, while walking up and down the deck, I met him.

'"Good morning!" I cried, with false sea-heartiness. "And how are *you* this morning? . . . I'm sorry to see you're alone."

'"Yes, it's a nuisance," he replied. "I had so much hoped it would be fine. . . . After all, we're getting near Madeira now, and it ought *not* to be like this. . . . I tell you, it worries me. . . . You see, it isn't so much that my wife's a bad sailor — she doesn't really feel ill now; the truth is, she's frightened in a ship!"

'"That's nothing to be ashamed of," I said. "I am, too.

. . . I believe a good many people are, if only they'd allow themselves to admit it."

'"I dare say. . . . But you see, it's different for her: the last time she was on a proper voyage was in the *Titanic*: her twin brother went down with it, and she was only rescued herself by a miracle. . . . Why, for years she wouldn't go abroad at all, even refused to take on the hour's journey across the Channel; though, before that, she used to love Paris. . . . And I'll tell you a peculiar thing: the sea can be as smooth as anything, and the moment she sets her foot on board, sure enough, it begins to get stormy. I've seen it happen in the Channel, scores of times, so that often I wished I hadn't persuaded her to change her mind and come with me, even for that short distance. . . . I ought never to have let her come on this journey; never; I ought to have forbidden it absolutely, from the start. . . . But she had been worrying about me — I'd been ill a long time, and those damned medicos said a long sea voyage was the only thing to put me right — and she insisted. I couldn't stop her: it seemed as though she *must* come, although she dreaded it, if you can get my meaning." . . . So that was it! . . . no wonder she was frightened, even at the surface level. I thought of the magnificent ship on her maiden voyage, of the two bands playing, and of that sudden ice-cold crash, and silence, as the breath of destruction reached it; and then of the watery confusion, of the strange, voiceless last meetings in green, deep alleys between the waves, where those who could swim bobbed up and down; or were knocked together like corks, but, their voices being lost already beneath the sound of the ocean, could not communicate in any way, and thus, it must have seemed, had become hostile to each other. . . . So that was it! . . . That was the meaning in those wide-open eyes, like the eyes of a statue in bright sunlight: that was the meaning, perhaps subconscious, under her casual, silly yet intent words, "No fox can escape for long, if the pack is out after him". . . . No, nor a human being, if the whole pack of Furies attend his coming and his going.

'That afternoon we arrived at Madeira, and I said goodbye. The Ruevinnys — beset though they were on deck by the islanders, who were trying to sell them embroideries, flowers, sandals, boxes of palm-wood, models of bullock-carts, native dresses and budgerigars — waved to me as I left for the shore in a motor-boat: and I noticed, again, the singular lack of expression in her face, which yet showed, when once you comprehended, so much more terror than terror itself. She gave a look, too, I thought, of longing towards the land: but I was too far away to see clearly. . . . At any rate, they should be all right now. The rest of the journey, especially at this time of year, should be one of tropical calm, of deep, blue phosphorescent gardens beneath the waters, and of flying-fishes leaping over them as birds skim a lawn.

'It was not until a fortnight later, not until a fortnight after it had happened, that I saw the newspaper: "*Hurricane in South Atlantic Seas. Coastline Towns Swept by Tidal Wave*", I read. "*British Liner Sinks Off Rio. All Lives Lost.*" I thought at once of Mrs. Ruevinny. . . . So it was over now. . . . She belonged in some way to the sea, and it must reclaim her: she had always known that, I reflected; even though she could not always rationally believe it. At any rate, it was over, whatever it might mean: the end of some long pursuit, of which one could not tell the beginning; or perhaps — who knows? — it was only the middle act of a drama laid over several centuries, or epochs. . . . I wondered how that lovely face had looked at the end, and, knowing what was in store for her, how much more matter-of-fact she had contrived to make her voice, when she talked to her husband for the last time. . . . And yet, as so often happens, actuality and its foretelling had been a little at odds. . . . I turned over to the stop-press news. "*Survivor Rescued*", I read. "*Strange Coincidence.* . . . Mrs. Ruevinny, who was rescued yesterday afternoon in a state of exhaustion, proves to be one of the survivors of the *Titanic*: her twin brother perished with that ship. It is feared that Mr. Ruevinny, well known in the sporting world, and all the other passengers and hands are lost." . . . So it had not got her after all: the fox was free once more. The last act, poor woman, had not been played.

'. . . I suppose you'd call it superstitious of me to feel like that? But life sometimes seems easier to understand, if one is superstitious. . . . Well, that was thirteen years ago. . . . And, touching wood, she's on this ship, bound for Ceylon to see her son. (I spoke to her this morning: doesn't look a day older.) But what ought one to do, act on superstitious belief or defy it? . . . Somehow I lack the courage to do anything so silly as leave the boat at Suez.'

He stopped talking, and became silent, pondering — while I, though obliged to hold on to every object I saw in order to preserve my balance, managed to get downstairs to send a cable.

DEAD HEAT

Looking back, the story of the friendship between the old Duchess of Martenburg and Princess Mouratinzky, the actual length of it, and the opposing points of view upon which it thrived, seems to me to possess all the fascination of a nursery rhyme, such as 'Jack Sprat', or of a fairy-tale similar to the 'Three Bears', exhaling in its essence a numerical, repetitive beauty implicit and continuous throughout its unfolding. . . . And for this reason I want to tell it to you.

I knew them both for what to me was a very lengthy period, but no doubt to them, out of their great age, merely represented the time occupied by the flashing of an angel's wings. . . . When I was a child, I first knew the Duchess of Martenburg. By birth a Princess of Southern Germany she had, with her wrinkled skin and brown eyes, rather bulbous now, albeit full of fire, all the charm of a well-educated and cultured toad, but a toad that was talkative, warm-blooded and loved dancing. (Indeed, she danced well, when I first remember her, though even then she was much over sixty.) With all the good-humour and high spirits of the Southern Germany of former uncontaminated days, she was witty in a straightforward way, and courageous: very downright and sure of her own mind: further, she was religious, intensely devoted to her Church — rather unexpectedly, the Protestant Church of the North. According to the ritual of the seasons, she moved with considerable pomp from one palace to another, from one set of Italian rooms decked out with plaster cupids, red brocade and pillared cabinets showing false perspectives of tortoise-shell, coral and lapis, from one grouping of plumed fountains and cut trees, to another. . . . And every autumn, for a fortnight — the equivalent perhaps of a Catholic retreat — she came to England to stay with a bearded bishop, with whom, to the pride and pleasure of his wife and eleven moustached daughters, she was carrying on one of those mild flirtations so often manifested among the devout. . . . How well I remember her then, the Parma-violet-coloured velvet

496

toque and dress which she always at that time affected, and the way she had of wrinkling her already wrinkled nose when she laughed.

But the 1914 war — still more perhaps the coming of Nazidom — had obliged her to alter completely her manner of life. . . . So that when I saw her again, after a lapse of twenty years, she had become a dignified refugee, banished from Germany because of her too great love for her Church, and because of her alleged consequent anti-Nazi activities. In the interval she had grown (and one could have expected nothing else) immensely old and very poor — for her, very poor. Nevertheless, she could still indulge in a certain style of living, for she dwelt now in a small *pension* on the very shore of the Lake of Geneva, and against this economical background, could still afford a maid (who, in any case, after fifty years would have refused to leave her), a footman and a sitting-room. But though her exile was easy, she resented her place of refuge. After the pleasant Bavarian Alps, these mountains seemed to her exaggerated and melodramatic. Despite her Lutheran affinities, she missed the graces of old Catholic Germany, the Madonnas at the corners of buildings high above the junctions of streets, the bunches of flowers upon the ledges of rustic shrines, the deep purple petunias hanging from the window-box of every window; things for which not all the blue and yellow tinsel stars of the Swiss spring sweeping over meadows and dark, damp earth, spread with scented pine-needles, could compensate her. . . . She was old, far too old for exile, she would say (indeed, she was over ninety), and what harm could a poor old woman like herself have accomplished, she asked, even if she had been wicked enough to wish to injure her own country?

Still, one must make the best of it. The fish was good (those nice pink trout); that was one thing. . . . And there were — yes, there were — a few nice people here. She admitted it; that was why she was at-home every evening from four until seven. For at that early hour she retired for the night, being called at six the next day and breakfasting on fine mornings at seven under a glossy-leaved magnolia by the side of the Lake.

Indeed, she possessed a fanatical love of fresh air, lived in it the whole spring, summer and autumn. Even during the winter in this climate, her windows were always wide open. Sometimes I used to try to soften her feelings concerning her place of exile, by saying to her how good the air was. 'Look at the way you can sit out here under the magnolia all day long!' I used to urge, but nothing would mollify her. 'I know,' she would reply; 'that is why I chose it — that, and to be near my dear old friend Princess Mouratinzky (I fear she is getting *very* old and infirm now, though she makes out that she is a few years younger than I am). But I do not like it: no, I do not.'

A different hurricane had blown hither the Princess. In her youth a great and famous beauty, still, at her present vast age (for she was a contemporary of the Duchess, though, as we shall see, the vanity of former years prohibited her from boasting of this), she retained the manner and bearing of one; even a certain worldly wit, which sometimes goes with this kind of appearance and renown. Coquettish, alluring, full of *brio*, she talked continually, laughing and fanning herself the while — she was always opening and shutting a fan. And into the quality of her attraction yet entered a great deal of feminine hard work, none the less arduous because it was unconscious. Apart from her animation, apart from her beauty, she might have seemed at first sight a more usual character than the Duchess; just a very pretty old lady with round blue eyes, beautiful and undimmed. But such a conclusion would have been false. . . . So far as her history was concerned, this fascinating old woman had become an orphan at an early age. Brought up at the Smolny Institute, she had, through the influence of the Tzarina of the day, been married on her seventeenth birthday to a great Russian nobleman and land-owner, and had become one of the leaders of fashionable life in Petersburg. Subsequently for thirty years she had been lady-in-waiting to the Grand Duchess Vladimir Constantine, and had been driving with her mistress in the second carriage at the moment when that clever, gigantic monster, the Grand Duke, with his courage, his immense stature, his brutality and fatalistic wit, had been blown up by Nihilists as he was returning from a review of the Imperial troops. For a further twenty-five years, until the Revolution, it had been her lot to comfort the beautiful and saintly Grand Duchess in her widowhood.

But the assassination of Russian royalties had now ceased

to be an individual martyrdom, and had become degraded to mass-murder, a holocaust : (a dead man may trail a shadow behind him as a memory, but a dead army has none ; wars and revolutions leave no ghosts). The Grand Duchess herself, who had formerly been so beloved and respected, had now been murdered these many years, her body robbed and thrown into the Black Sea. . . . But fortunately her lady-in-waiting, the Princess, had been staying with a married daughter in the south of France when the war had broken out in 1914. Unable to return to Russia, she had so escaped sharing this fate, though the death of her mistress in such a manner was something from which she could never recover. It had been, in fact, more of a grief to her than the loss of her own fortune — for now she was penniless, living here, in the middle of a little Swiss town, in a boarding-house.

This establishment, however, was less. unfriendly and impersonal than it sounds. Her daughter and son-in-law managed it, and they looked after her as well as they could. Her room, at the top of the house, was excessively small, and (though I think the Princess herself remained unaware of this) it had been in this same attic in which she was now dwelling, then cold and bare, that Lenin, a bitter fugitive, had existed for two years, working all day and all night, turning letters into cypher to send to Russia, writing endless pamphlets and books, eating nothing except when forced to do so by Kroupskaya, talking seldom — though when he talked a faint line of foam flickered from his sneering lips. Now, however, it was no longer a Swiss garret, for the Princess belonged so completely to her dead world of sleighs and furs and jewels and musical-boxes, that everything round her still proclaimed her adherence to it. No trace of Lenin here now, only endless photographs, signed, of murdered Russian royalties : the Tzar and Tzarina ; the unfortunate young Tzarevitch and his four lovely sisters ; Grand Dukes and Grand Duchesses and their children ; photographs of their palaces and the gardens ; photographs of them sleighing and skating and, for the rest, many brightly coloured ikons and bits of fur and lace — all that was left ! But there was also a large stove, out of all proportion to the size of the room, and some small vases of flowers. . . . And these, for the momentary comfort they gave her (and all through that long life, after the manner of most Russians, she had lived from

moment to moment), enabled her to bear her age and misfortunes more lightly.

For seventy years she had been the Duchess of Martenburg's
most intimate friend. Neither of them had allowed so big a
thing as being on different sides in the bitterest, so far, of all
wars to make a difference to their friendship. There existed,
nevertheless, *little* hindrances. Though they lived so near to
each other — in order, they said, to be together — it was not
easy for them to meet at all, and, further, proved still more
difficult for them, despite their mutual affection, to meet
without quarrelling; because the Princess for her part rose
at five every evening and retired to rest at five every morning.
(You may ask how, in a neighbourhood not famed for the
gaiety of its night life, she spent the small hours. . . . Well,
there was always tea and cigarettes; and often there were
parties, for the boarding-house was full of Russian relatives and
connections, all engaged in trades which apparently obliged
them to come in, from time to time, during the night — and,
of course, to reach their work late. And so they clustered round
the tall china stove, in the communal sitting-room, talking to
the old lady; otherwise she would have died of ennui long
ago. . . .)

It was only, then, during that single hour between 6 and
7 P.M. — before dinner for the Duchess, and after breakfast for
the Princess — that the two old ladies could meet. Nor was
this the sole obstacle to their companionship even during that
short space of time, all too brief, one would have said. For in
the summer the Princess would not sit out in the garden with
her friend; it was too draughty, very treacherous, she would
protest. Still less would she remain out of doors in the yet hot
but shortening evenings of the early autumn when the mist
rose from the Lake, like the wraiths of the murdered (certainly
the Duchess's mind would never have entertained such fancies),
and filled her bones with a chill depression. Sometimes at this
season the Duchess would insist on remaining out of doors,
and so reaching a compromise they would face each other
angrily across the window-sill for nearly the full hour, handing
cakes and tea sullenly across this bar which divided the Teuton
from the Slav. In the winter, the Princess, fitted out in the
remnants of a fur coat which, though tattered, still possessed a
certain air, could only bear to sit in a room with the windows

fast shut, and an enormous stove burning in it; while the Duchess, dressed as though for a heat-wave, felt it essential for her health to have all the windows wide open. It was an especial offence to her, as well, that the Princess should live in an attic in the town, in the very heart of noise and heat and dust, when she might dwell in this glorious, cool air by the side of the Lake.

It was not easy, then, this friendship. To each of them, their years had now become a source of pride. They had grown — though originally the contrast between their natures and outward appearance had been the foundation of the feeling between them — into rivals, competitors for the palm of old age, and, in consequence, the two old friends allowed themselves in this hour of frost for one, and fire for the other, to quarrel a good deal. . . . For, years ago, many long years ago, when the Princess had been forty, the, as it seemed now, needless fear of growing old, combined with a certain vanity, had driven her to underestimate her age, so that even today, when she was in reality over ninety, her former deceit debarred her from any hope of ever catching up in the race. The Duchess, of course, knew her friend's age quite well, for it was the same as her own, but she intended to see that the Princess never staked a full claim, or that if she did, she would be convicted in no uncertain terms, and possibly before other people, of lying and self-pride. So she must remain a poor eighty-seven to the Duchess's self-avowed ninety-two; a sad eighty-eight to her ninety-three. Of course, even the eighty-eight to which she could admit was creditable, but ninety-three, ninety-three, ninety-three! . . . How deeply, how frequently, the Princess regretted that now so distant moment of coquetry! . . . Moreover, though she knew that the Duchess was well aware of her real age, she must never allude to it. On the other hand, the Duchess could, when it suited her, taunt her with it in a veiled way. . . . Sometimes their conversation would be in English, a neutral tongue, for the Princess refused to talk German and the Duchess to talk French.

'Anastasie, I can't believe you are cold in that fur coat, and with such a fire! . . . But if you are so, why fan yourself continually? Even *I* should feel cold if I fanned myself the whole time! I'm sure that house of yours is unhealthy. . . . Perhaps you have a fever like one gets in one's youth.'

'No, I can't help it, Rita, I always fan myself. It's like you, how you do all that embroidery, so pretty, with your good German taste! . . . Besides, if you suddenly feel hot, *you* can ask your maid to open the window for you; but I can't. . . . I have to do everything myself.'

'But work is useful, Anastasie: fanning oneself is *not*. . . . Why, you fan yourself enough to turn a windmill: and at your age, it is not good! . . . But I forget, I was back in years long ago. You are younger, much younger than I am now, are you not? . . . You must look after your old friend. . . . How I wish you would come to live here in this glorious air, where you can hear the birds!'

'But I do not wish to hear the birds, Rita. I ha-a-te them! They are so cruel, with their beaks! . . .'

Nor were these the sole seeds of discord. The Duchess thoroughly disapproved of the Orthodox Church and all its ways, and though a service was only held in the minute Russian Church here, with its mad, painted domes and bulbs, once a month, and though, even then, the Princess did not attend it, since she was in bed and asleep in the mornings, the Duchess would often make pointed references to 'mummery' and to 'gingerbread places of worship', while the Princess would in turn feel herself called upon to defend the cause, and to attack in return the undecorative Lutheranism of Germany. Further, the Duchess would very seldom visit the Princess, would always insist on her coming to the *pension* to see her. This was because she pretended not to like Anastasie's daughter; it was a fiction, long kept up. . . . Really, I think, they had long grown fond of each other; but pride prevented them from publicly admitting by a reconciliation that their misfortunes had to this extent softened their natures. Nevertheless, on the rare occasions of their meeting, they got on well, seemed pleased to see each other. When the Princess was unwell, however, the Duchess would continue always to say 'That stupid girl of hers' (she was sixty-seven), 'she does not look after her mother properly'.

Then, too, though originally the Duchess and the Princess had thought — or should one write, felt? — alike, of late years the direction of politics in their countries had tended to separate them. . . . The Duchess possessed a radio, with which, from time to time, she fiddled, producing the sounds of whole covens of witches riding through the air on broomsticks over snow-covered peaks, shrieking, singing, screaming; she seemed, even, to like these noises. But, occasionally, she would during that hour, and always by mistake for some concert or entertainment, tune in to one of the speeches of the dictators, and the Princess could, in those days (for it was before the Hitler-Stalin pact), no more help applauding the words of Hitler, who then saw 'the Bolshevik demon' as the chief opponent of civilisation, than the Duchess could prevent herself from showing enthusiasm at the utterances of the Paladin of Bolshevism when he so piously acclaimed democracy and denounced Hitler and persecution. Thus from six o'clock to seven would often grow poignant enough.

In spite of their differences of view, in spite of their dis-agreements, however, if either of them ailed or was unhappy, the other felt it as though it had happened to herself. Through the long days spent without her, though she was so near by, the Duchess would continually refer to Anastasie, her friend, just as during those long nights round the stove, drinking tea and smoking cigarettes through long paper holders, the Princess would talk of Rita, her energetic and lively compeer. In addition to the warm feeling that existed between them, it became clear to those round them that the continued existence of one supported that of the other; they resembled the balanced scales of a machine finding an equilibrium, the equilibrium of truth. If one fell, the other would rise unduly.

Both, on the contrary, continued to prosper. The sensibilities of those who have lost profoundly become hardened except in small things, and the perpetual tragic developments of the thirties seemed now to worry them but little. They lost no faculties. The Duchess, in her charming way — in, even, her beautiful way — with her skin infinitely wrinkled and yet soft, her glowing brown eyes and uptilted nose, humorous and contemptuous and proud, grew still more ugly, her manners more typical, more imperative and abrupt: the Princess more vivacious, her blue eyes, still so large and full of light, more rounded, her white hair, that had formerly been golden, now still more white and soft — she seemed to smoke yet more cigarettes, as she sat in the corner by the stove, fanning herself, while through her head ran the nostalgic, circular melodies of Tchaikowsky, so that once more there came back to her the swinging movement of the Court Balls, the uniforms and crinolines and scents and sloping shoulders, the pink champagne, the whiskers, and the dying hum of talk at the rattle and drumming of the tall golden maces on the floor when the Imperial Family entered the room. As though the exile which cut them off from the circumstances and places that had formed their characters had yet still further defined their respective traits, made each of them more typical, the Princess could now detect a draught at one hundred yards, the Duchess feel faint in the frostiest winter room if a jonquil scented it. The Princess would sit almost at the side of the stove, like a cat warming itself, while the Duchess would complain, even, of the heat of her unheated church. They altered little, very little : though the Princess would, from time to time, shuddering in her furs, allow herself the indulgence of a cold, while eau-de-cologne and smelling-salts would aid the Duchess's headache, caused — after one of her rare visits to the boarding-house — by Anastasie's stove. . . . For the rest the two old ladies were sound in wind, hair, eye, ear and tooth.

And so they lived on through the changing seasons by the side of the Lake, watching the glacial shadows of green deepen to summer blue, watching the magnolias extend white cups that later turned to tawny vellum on the glossy trees, the mauve chalices of the autumn crocus starring the lawns, until even the Princess could admit to ninety-two and the Duchess was undeniably within sight of her century. Both ladies grew more and more revered each year ; for death is the chief — if last — dishonour to the living (and one which most of us will go a long distance out of our way to avoid), and so, in consequence, great age is everywhere honoured, because the overdue survival of any individual proves that in the long run humanity in the mass can lengthen, albeit only by ever so little, the normal span of its days.

Nevertheless the end was, naturally enough, drawing near. . . . This particular year had been, as usual, an unusual one. In March, it had been August ; in May all the flowers of the vines had been destroyed by a hail-storm ; in July there had been such a drought that the Lake had evaporated far enough down to show the lake-dwellings of paleolithic times, still fixed in primeval mud ; September had exhibited the borders of the Lake again with all its luxuriant gardens flooded and drowned; and now, at Christmas (admittedly for once at the right season), came the Great Frost. The whole Lake was frozen over, a thing that had not occurred for a century, and people accepted the event with joy.

For a full week the entire population skated day and night, with a strangely anti-Calvinistic fervour. Flares could be seen after dark, in every direction, gilding the flanks of the mountains, and bandsmen, with faces and hands blue from cold, blared out Waldteufel waltzes, leaving a dragon's-tail of breath behind them on the air, while dumpy, Breughel-like figures, in their warm, padded clothes, danced and glided in ecstatic time to them. Huge fires were lighted on the ice, and oxen were roasted whole.

Frigid as was the air, the Princess could not resist this gaiety. And so, when it was at its height, she persuaded the Duchess to walk down with her to the edge of the Lake to watch the carnival. The Princess moved a little tremblingly with the aid of a very delicate, tortoise-shell-topped cane; the Duchess walked boldly, supporting herself with a stout country stick. The Princess wore her fur coat; the Duchess, a thick woollen outfit of some sort. It had not been long dusk; the fires were blazing, the torches flickering in a light breeze flecked with particles of ice. Both of them stood there in their snow-shoes in this icy world on the border of the Lake — on, as it were, the very edge of eternity — watching and listening. What a delightful scene!

'Do you remember the first time you came to stay with us in Petersburg, Rita, and all the bells ringing as we tore through the night on sleighs . . . and how we thought those times would never end?' . . .

'And that winter in Munich, Anastasie, the skating and the supper-party in the Pavilion?' . . .

The Duchess looked at her watch. 'But that was all long ago — and now it is my bed-time.' . . . Indeed it was ten minutes past seven, very late for her, and they both returned to their homes, one plodding her way along, the other swaying a little on her feet.

It proved to be their last appearance together. The next day the Duchess developed a fever which she attributed to the heat of the fires, that had flamed, waving their golden wings, high above the ice; whilst the Princess was attacked by ague, due, she said, to the intense cold of the previous evening. Within forty-eight hours they were both dead.

Their illnesses were not painful, and merely seemed the ailments of two children. . . . It was nothing, the Duchess said, and would soon yield to fresh air. Through wide-open windows she had listened to the music on the ice and had enjoyed it. When darkness came, she would not have the curtains drawn, but watched the fires — which she considered responsible for her present state — being rekindled. At seven in the evening, the hour, originally, of her retirement, she sat up in bed and with great vigour asked her maid to push up the windows still further. Elsa, the woman who had for so long attended the Duchess, did as she was bidden, and to her surprise, heard the old lady croak a few notes, harsh but gay : then the voice stopped. And, when she turned round, it was to find that her mistress was dead.

The Princess had not slept. All day long in her room, so high up, with panes of glass misty from the heat, she had bent across the vases of anemones and narcissus to peer at the flying figures on the ice. From time to time she would retire to bed again, but always the distant sound of the music drew her back tremblingly to the window. The curtains were drawn as soon as it was dusk ; the music only reached her faintly and she lay still. When she looked at her watch it was about six o'clock — she was late ! It was past the time for her to begin getting up, she said. . . . But she was tired. She shivered, and fumbled with the things by her side, boxes, bottles, ikons. She pressed a button, and up out of a box sprang a little enamelled nightingale, moving from side to side with fluttering wings, and for a moment sang. She smiled and listened, and then, as it fell back into the darkness of its box, her heart, too, fell suddenly, and all her memories went with it. . . . Even from the neighbouring houses her relations could be heard crying the whole night long, and the whole of the next day.

'YOU CAN CARRY IT, MRS. PARKIN'

OR

MONOLOGUE WITH A CLOTHES-BRUSH

(From A Century of the Common Man)

'You can carry it, Mrs. Parkin. . . .' She could see Madame Rosalie — now as she had knelt on the floor, and then suddenly looked up and said, so nicely, with a smile full of pins, 'You can carry it, Mrs. Parkin'.

Mrs. Parkin gave the coat a despairing, angry shake, and then a hit, and disconsolate threads, hairs and pieces of mud and fluff floated down from it. Her face must for many years have been that of such a pretty baby, but now it was only a round disc with a stubby nose thrown upon it — fortunately in the centre. When she grew angry it puckered and pouted, the lines hardened beneath the surface of fat, the lips became two violin strings, parallel, in a hot mould of anger.

Six weeks the coat had been used, if not seven ! . . . She gave it another shake and a large piece of trimming fell from the sleeve — fur trimming. 'Never be fit to put on again, never . . . must have been wearing it day and night, by the look of it, and it isn't even as if it *could* have suited her. It wanted a woman, not just a girl, flat all over, someone with what you call *presence*.' And, oh, it had been a fine thing, a lovely thing. . . . Mr. Parkin always believed in getting the best. 'Best in the beginning is best in the end,' he used to say, 'and then it lasts.' So Mrs. Parkin had ordered the coat to be made for her specially. . . . Arthur was doing nicely now and she could afford it, could easily have a car and two maids, dressed differently in mauve and brown, with caps to match — if only there were cars and maids to find. As it was, just as she had been expecting to sit back and have a little comfort at her age, here she was, obliged to work harder than ever. And that was what made it so much worse about the coat. 'I wouldn't have minded,' she said to herself, 'if the girl couldn't

507

have afforded it. Neither I nor Mr. Parkin are the sort to be mean and miserly — but after all I've known Doreen — to me she'll *never* be *Dolores* — since a child, and Mrs. Ridder, her mother, had always been a friend of mine. In all the twenty years — or is it twenty-one? — I think it's twenty, but I won't be sure — we've never had a wrong word, except once, nor has Mr. Parkin with Mr. Ridder — and then to return the coat in that condition! Not that I'm saying anything against *Mrs. Ridder*. I speak as I find.'

Mrs. Parkin could see the scene now, as if it had been yesterday, how the coat had been chosen; how she had worn it. . . . It must have been three years before the war, when things were already going better, that she had decided on it. 'But just look at it now! The buttons gone as well — and you can't find buttons!' she said aloud in a tone of anguish. 'Can't get 'em — at any rate to match. . . . All the airs and all the graces, and to look at it you wouldn't think she kept good company. . . . *Ugh! It smells awful, too!*' she said, holding part of the coat close against her nose, 'awful. I can't think where she has been, all creased and greasy, worn here and there. You might think she'd been sleeping on the Embankment. You wouldn't know it for the same thing.'

Mirrors, dusty and fly-blown mirrors, black-framed mirrors that seemed freckled and wrinkled with time, had stared each other in the eye, with Mrs. Parkin pressed between them, when she had tried it on. Oh, Madame Rosalie knew how to make a good thing and was not expensive. 'Not that I'm saying,' Mrs. Parkin would say, 'that it is cheap. It *isn't* cheap, but that you can't expect, and Mr. Parkin wouldn't wish it. He often says to me, "Mother, I am not a rich man," he says, "I've had my ups and downs, as one might say, but you must have the best, always the best. The best is only good enough for Mrs. Parkin."'

Madame Rosalie had crouched there like a black dwarf. Sometimes she knelt and sometimes stood on tiptoe. She could not speak, except in a muffled voice, because of the pins — and even that required concentration. Every now and then she took a pin, miraculously saliva-free, from rouged lips, looked at Mrs. Parkin attentively, and stabbed the bust, drew in the cloth, just where it was needed. It was extraordinary the way she *built* that coat — that is where the art comes in.

'And I should have the fur edge a little lower here,' she had said, 'or it might be a little higher there. It wants what I call a sweep. Anything smaller would look skimpy on you. It isn't that you're stout. Of course you're not. But you've a figure, and it's a pity not to show it, only we must be careful — a little carelessness, a little negligence, and we lose the whole effect.' . . . The dressmaker now revolved the image of Mrs. Parkin in the fly-blown mirror, as if her customer had been a bit of meat — hung not in good cloth, but in muslin to protect her, in a cool and stony larder, the mirrors being the gratings for the air. 'It wouldn't do. It's no good pinching, pulling in and lacing you, Mrs. Parkin. *You* don't want lots of fussy little ornaments, *you* want something bold and with a line. . . . You see what I mean, a sweep towards the hip, and just a simple pleat below the bust. The stripe *is* broad. I admit it. The fur *is* highly coloured, I confess. It would not suit everyone. But you can take it, madam; *you* can carry it, Mrs. Parkin.'

When finished, it did not cling to her, the coat; it swept round her like a battleship pursuing its own course upon the sea; a rich sepia brown with a suggestion of every sort of varnish chequered by a musty, botulistic stripe of purple, and edged with lilac fur that looked the *real* thing. . . . The first time she had worn it was at Newborough and, as she had advanced down the steps from the Italian Pergola into the Rosarium, as they called it, the coat had caused a sensation; that she could feel; *where* had she got it, the shouting crowd of holiday-makers was asking, where had she got it, the musing crowd of rose-lovers demanded. And yet it was not that the people looked at it because it had a bit of this and a bit of that, it was the *line* and the *colour*. ('You can carry it, Mrs. Parkin.') She had worn a hat to match, a fur-trimmed hat with a purple flower, but of course, coming down the flight of steps, with the blue peace-time sea below and sands lying, where the sea had receded, like acres of washed-out linen, and the bands playing swing, and Sandy Macpherson sounding out from the cafeteria at the corner, she could see it *would* look its best, wouldn't it? . . . She felt she walked differently, too, when she was wearing it, sailed as you might say, for though it swept quite low towards the skirt's hem, it was loose, fell as though draped, and in no way impeded movement.

People admired it equally at home when she got back. She did not put it on every Sunday, not by any means, and more in spangled summer than in spring. It seemed to suit that time of year when all the flower-beds groaned with bees and blue-bottles. If she went to church with Mr. Parkin and Sonia, she would wear it sometimes, and everybody liked it, and she'd worn it at the Confirmation. 'Three years ago, already. . . . Dreadful how time flies! It seems it was only yesterday that Sonia was christened!' . . . She remembered well the first time she had worn the coat at church and Mr. Pilcher, by the lych-gate, had stopped her, and stood there talking, and had said, 'It's a lovely coat, Mrs. Parkin, the sort of thing you would expect a Bride's Mother to wear at a fashionable wedding, with lots of big people there. And who knows, Mrs. Parkin,' he had added, 'that you won't soon be a Bride's Mother, Sonia as pretty as she is, and like her mother?' And then Mr. Pilcher had pinched the child in a way that Mr. Parkin had not liked at all. (You never could tell, Mr. Parkin used to say. 'Stranger things have happened, mother. You don't read the Sunday papers like I do. *Pretty as she is!* . . .') 'And who knows,' Mrs. Parkin asked herself in a fury, 'that Mr. Pilcher mayn't be right? After all, there *are* coupons now, and things *are* difficult, and if Sonia and Basil do get on together — I know it sounds silly when they're so young — but *if* they *do*, then where, I ask you, can I get another coat like this? I might well have chosen to wear it. . . . Look at it now — and all, as usual, because of kindness.' Her face set firmer. 'But I must say one thing, Mr. Parkin always warned me. Time after time, he said, "Mother," he said, "you're too kind. That's what it is. You let them all make a fool of you, but I see through them! You may *think* they like you. They don't mean a nice word they say. *It's all put on.* You're too kind, far too kind. You *ought* to give them the rough side of your tongue, Mother, like I do. I wish you'd heard how I ticked off Mr. Pilcher afterwards, Mother." (There's something mean and sly, I don't know what, about him. . . . Sonia! Sonia! Where is Sonia? Her father thinks the world of that girl: I don't know what he'd do if anything went wrong.) "And I ticked him off like that, too, when he asked me to lend him the ladder again. 'Ladder,' I said, 'ladder? Not on your soul,' I said, 'and if you ask me again, you won't want anything any more, you dirty, sneaking hound, always coming round for this, that and the other. I'd be ashamed in your place,' I said, 'I'd be ashamed.' But you are too kind, Mother. No, I won't say kind; I call it soft. You *won't* give them the ticking off they need. You let your name be dirt, you do. Don't stand for it. Don't let them ride rough-shod over your body, Mother." And he was right. . . . Look at the coat now!'

Last summer the girl had come down to see Mr. Ridder. And since Doreen — I can't and won't call her Dolores — has been on the films, Sonia had sort of taken a fancy to her (and I don't like the child to see no one. I'm not that kind. To my mind, it was what led to Pamela going odd like that. Her mother never let her see boys and girls of her own age.) . . . Well, Mr. Parkin and me are not like that. Live and let live, we say — of course, if we like them — and Sonia *is* a funny girl : very artistic, they said, at the school, sings now quite a lot as well as plays, for I was determined to have her taught the piano. "She must have a chance," I said. "*I* never had it." "Chance of what?" Mr. Parkin asked. "I think you're silly, Mother, spoiling her and wanting to buy a fumed-oak-harpsichord-piano for all that money, and things what things are now." But I had made up my mind, because my cousin Betty — the one that married Mr. Barber — could play anything she heard by heart, straight out of her head, and only with two fingers, though it sounded so natural that strangers often thought she must be using ten. So it's in the family, you see, and I want her to have a chance. *I* never had it, and if she don't take her chance, then she doesn't deserve it, and I'll sell the piano. It's always worth the money. . . . But everyone now says that I was right. Sometimes she'll play with all the wireless going, and still you'll hear her. . . . Well, she took a sort of fancy to Doreen. I said to her, "Sonia, you *are* silly. Don't cheapen yourself. People will say you are running after her, just because she has made a hit, and *I* think she gives herself airs. If I were you I'd tell her off. I'd tick her off, I'd tell her straight, I would ; I wouldn't put up with it, and you know what your father says, 'As it is, you're too easy, Mother.'" . . . Well, Doreen came down, and I'm not saying that she wasn't nice spoken. It was June and hot, and she had a swanky fur rug and no coat. Of course she had been accepted, and passed the tests, and *had* walked on in the films, that one can't deny, and she was nice to Sonia and made her play the piano to her. "I think you are too wonderful, you little darling," she said to her, very old-like, "and it's just what the Public adores." Well, after that, when it turned cold and I found she hadn't got a coat, I said to her, "Doreen — you won't mind *me* calling you *Doreen*, I know — *I* could lend you a coat to go home in, but send it back to me directly — not that it's the only coat I've got, but I value it because Mr. Parkin likes it, so you will return it, won't you? You'll be sure to send it back to me tomorrow or Tuesday at the latest? Send it back to me, won't you, Doreen?" And she said, "Of course, darling Mrs. Parkin. How angelic of you!" — like that. And seven weeks, nearly eight, passed by — and then returned to me — just look at it — with a note I wouldn't have written to a chimney-sweep!

' DEAR ALL,
            Thanks awfully. Here goes to return the coat in case you still need it.
    All the best.   DOLORES

'Eight weeks, it was, and nearly nine, and I'll tell her straight, I will, I'll tick her off if ever I see her, and so will Mr. Parkin. "So will your dad, Sonia," I said. "And it isn't even as if she'd looked well in it. She's got a skimpy, niggling figure."' . . . Then Mrs. Parkin fell silent and hit the coat again with the brush, and was quiet, for high in the air, sweet but melancholy angel voices sang for her, 'You can take it, madam. You can carry it, Mrs. Parkin.'

THE GREETING

From outside the long, large windows fires could be seen flickering in many wide grates, while the comforting sense, more than smell, of warm food oozed out of the whole house, subduing the sharper scent of frosty air. The dining-room table, she noticed as she passed by, was laid for three persons, and decorated with four small silver vases, from which a few very rigid flowers drew themselves up into the light of the windows. The sideboard showed beyond, bearing various drab meats and some pieces of plate, its cold glitter tempered by the flames with patches of warm orange.

As soon as Nurse Gooch was shown into the drawing-room, almost, indeed, before she had shaken hands or remarked how nice it was to see a fire, they went in to luncheon. But seated before this white expanse, these three people could not succeed in materialising any conversation that, as talk should, drawing its strength from the group but stronger than any individual member of it, would continue almost automatically, reproducing itself or taking on a fresh form from time to time. In the same way in which spiritualists claim that the presence of one sceptic at a séance is sufficient to prevent any manifestation, however hoped for and credited by the majority, here it was difficult for the talk to glow or prosper, when one of this small party was continually exerting her will to the utmost in order to produce a lasting and uncomfortable silence. The stagnant quiet of the room was seldom broken, then, except by the rather horse-like stepping of the footmen, or by the thin, stringy voice of the invalid projected through the mute air in querulous inquiry. And, in the very act of speaking herself, both by the purpose and calculated tone of her question, she enforced a silence on the others. Colonel Tonge tried to make conversation to the new-comer, placed between him and his sick wife, but his abrupt, pompous little sentences soon withered, frozen on the air by his wife's disapproval. Mrs. Tonge, however, as we have said, permitted herself to ask a question occasionally — a question which, though it appeared innocent, was designed to convey to her new nurse the impression that she was an injured, ill-used woman. 'When, Humphrey,' she would ask, 'do you intend to put electric light into the house? I have asked you to do it for so many years now. I am sure I should sleep better, and should not be such a worry to you or to Nurse', or 'What about that summer-house, Humphrey? Will it be ready for me in the spring? If I am still with you, I intend going there every day when the weather is warmer. Perhaps I shall find a little peace there in the woods. But I fear it hasn't been touched yet.' To these questions the Colonel returned smooth, soothing answers, but ones which did not commit him in any way; but these, rather than conciliating the invalid, seemed only to vex her the more. But at this early period, before she understood her nurse, before she knew that anything she said would soon be pardoned, she did not actually as yet accuse her husband of doing all in his power to make and to keep her ill, but was content to let this accusation remain implicit in her questions, and in the sound of her voice. Still, Nurse Gooch felt instinctively that Mrs. Tonge did not want to hurt her, that she was not in reality ill-natured, but that this calculated putting-out of the social fire was the outcome of a thousand little injuries inflicted by an imagination warped by constant illness and want of sleep. But whether it was due to the atmosphere created by this friction between husband and wife, or to something in the surroundings — in the house itself — she did most certainly, at this first moment of her arrival, experience an uneasy feeling, a slight repulsion from the Grove, which passed as soon as she became better acquainted with it.

Tonge's Grove, a square house, lies like a box thrown down among hanging woods and open commons — a charming residence in many ways. Like a doll's house it seems, each room giving the correct proportion to the rather under-life-size figures it displays. A curiously inappropriate setting, certainly, for any drama, the protagonists of which must find themselves cramped in their action by the wealth of detail imposed. The very comfort and well-being of the place would give a grotesque air to any but an accustomed or trivial event. For here, long habit appears so much more important than the occasion or fact it originally enshrined, inanimate objects so much more actual, more active, than human beings, that it is upon the house, and not upon its owners, that our attention is first focused. It is this superfluity of things, combined with a rigorous pruning of reality, that gives a certain significance to any fact of life should it be strong enough to enter these gates, yet remain quick. For reality, which is usually unpleasant, seldom touches lives such as these except at birth, of which, fortunately, we are all ignorant, or at death, a latent, lurking fear (an ogre at the end of every passage), but one which it is our very human convention to ignore.

The Grove is not really a small house; the rooms in it are large and numerous; but, like a square toy thrown in among garden beds and stables, crinoline-shaped lime-trees and red-walled angular orchards, among, in fact, all the long-settled paraphernalia annexed to a prosperous, well-ordered way-of-life, it was endowed with a perfection such as at first to make it seem miniature, like some exquisite model seen through a glass case.

Certainly there is beauty about an estate of this kind: that tamed country sentiment, so English in quality, clings to it, till even the bird-song that trickles down through the dripping blue shadows thrown by tall trees seems arranged, punctual, and correct as the mechanical chirping of one of those clockwork birds that lift enamelled wings out of a square black box; and even the cuckoo, who makes so ominous a sound from the cool green fortifications of wood or hedgerow, here changes his note till it rings hollow and pure as a church bell. No sense of mystery broods in the green and open spaces bathed in yellow summer sunlight; here are no caves, grottoes, tumbling torrents: everything is neat, shallow as the clear, slightly running streams that border the wood; yet surely such beauty is, in a way, more fantastic than any of Leonardo's piled-up rocks or those worlds of ogres and giants to which we are carried off by some of the primitive painters.

In the winter it is that all these country places are seen in their best, their most typical, phase. Stout built for cold weather, these houses take on a new quality, upstanding among hoar-frost, glowing warmly through the crisp, grey air. The first impression of the Grove would be, we think, a childlike memory of potting-shed smells, full of the scents of hidden growth; an odour of bulbs, stoves, rich fibrous mould and bass, mingles with the sharp aromatic smell of the bonfire that crackles outside. On the walls of the shed the bass is hung up like so many beards of old men — ritual beards, like those of Pharaoh or Egyptian priest, which, perhaps, the gardener will don for the great occasions of his year. This one he would put on for the opening of the first spring flower, coming up glazed and shrill, its petals folded as if in prayer, out of the cold brown earth, beneath the laced shadows woven by the bare branches of the trees; this he will wear for the brazen trumpet-like blowing of the tulip-tree; while that one he reserves for the virginal unfolding of the magnolia, or the gathering-up of petals let drop by the last rose. But the gardener himself soon dispels these tender imaginings, as you see his burly form bent over various cruel tasks — the trapping of the soft mole, or in aiming at the fawn-coloured fluffy arcs of the rabbits, as they crouch in their green cradles, their ears well back, nibbling the tender white shoots that he has so carefully nurtured.

Outside the shed in many glass frames large violets, ranging in tone from a deep purple through magenta to an almost brick-red, their petals scintillating damply, glisten like crystallised fruit seen through a glass window, sweet but unapproachable. The ground of the kitchen garden is hard and shiny, starched with frost; trees, shrubs, and the very grass are stiff and brittle, sweeping down under the slight wind with a shrill, steely sound. But the orchard walls still glow as if stained with the juice of the ripe fruits that press against them in summer and autumn, red, purple and bloomy, while the house beyond shows warmly through the tree whose topmost twigs pattern themselves about it, like cobwebs against the sky; soft it is, as if cut from red velvet. Out of its doors and windows sounds the monotonous, dry-throated rattle of pet dogs setting up a comfortable yet irritating competition with the noises of stable and farmyard, where rosy-faced men bustle about, lumbering in heavy boots; or, leaning to one side, the right arm lifted and at an angle, blow loudly and whistle, as they polish still more the varnished horses, their breathing lingering on after them in the sharp air like dragon's-breath. Through the windows of the house each fireplace shows up, while the red flowers blaze in it, or die down to a yellow flicker, fighting ineffectually against the thin silver rapiers of the winter sun.

But more than all these things would you notice here the bitter cackle of a green parrot, falling through the drawn-out air with a horrid clatter, tumbling all lesser sounds down like a pack of cards. Certainly that menacing silly sound of a parrot's laughter would be your most abiding memory.

On such a noon as this it was that Nurse Gooch had first driven up to the Grove; so that, even if her first impression was a rather uneasy one, she had at any rate seen it wearing its most pleasant, most comfortable, aspect; for at night the character of every house changes — and this one alters more than most. The smiling comfort of the surroundings is lost, fades out into utter blackness, and a curious sub-flavour, unnoticed in the day, manifests itself. There are places and moments when the assumptions, the lean conventions on which our lives are based, become transparent, while, for an instant, the world we have made rocks with them. It is, for example, usually assumed that there are no such creatures as sea-serpents, yet there are certain places in Europe, on our own placid coasts even, of such marvellous formation that we feel, suddenly, that the existence of these monsters is a certainty — that it would surprise us less to see a vast beast, such as those painted by Piero di Cosimo, with flame-forked tongue, gigantic head and long writhing body, coming up out of the fathomless green depths, than to see a passing country cart, a clergyman or anything to which our experience has accustomed us. There are moments, too, when death, which, as we have said, it is usually our custom to hide away in a dusty corner of our minds, peeps round at us, grimacing — and we realise it as one of the universal and most awful conditions upon which we are permitted to take up life. So it was with the Grove, when darkness coffined it round. The dwarf perfection, which we have attempted to describe, would gradually disappear; for the very dimensions of the house seemed to alter as the rooms became swollen with darkness, full of inexplicable sound. Dead people walk here with more certain step than the living, their existence seems more substantial, their breathing more audible. The boarding of the floor yields under an invisible step, as if some strange memory stirs in it, and the panelling of the walls, the very furniture, make themselves heard with a hard, wooden creaking, which is magnified in these rooms now grown to the new proportions with which night endows them. And, in the darkness outside, everything moves, stirs, rustles.

It was therefore not to be wondered at that the Grove should have acquired the reputation of being haunted, though, really, the unhappy restless air that pervaded it at night may have been due more to its long association with a family of sad, unfortunate temperament — amounting in certain cases to something worse — than to the actual walking presence of any ghost. For ever since the present house was built, late in the seventeenth century, it had been in the possession of the Tonges and, until recently, until in fact the present owner had inherited the estate, there had been a long history connected with it of brooding melancholy, that must have been nearly allied to madness.

But Colonel Tonge, as we have seen, presented an ordinary enough character, with nerves unaffected, betraying no sign of hereditary disorder. Among the properties we have described — house, lawn, garden, farm and stable — this not altogether unattractive figure emerges, strutting like a bantam. A proud little man, with a fairly distinguished military career, fond of hunting and shooting, he was much engaged in the business of an estate, the extent and importance of which he was apt to magnify in his own mind. In addition to these interests, he was involved in the affairs of every district committee, and, as became him in his dual capacity of squire and military man, was much to the fore in all those local philanthropic schemes which had for their object the welfare of the ex-soldier, or the helping of widow and children.

Yet in spite of this inherited make-up of country gentleman and the acquired one of soldier, there was about the Colonel on closer acquaintance some quality that removed him ever so little from the usual specimen of his class, just as there was something about the Grove that differentiated it from the run of English country-houses. In what, then, did this difference consist? Partly, perhaps, in the stress that he laid upon the importance of his belongings, and therefore of himself; but more, surely, in the extraordinary calm that marked his demeanour — a quiet unruffled calm, not quite in accord with his bristling appearance and apparent character. One never saw him lose his temper, never even about trivialities, such as is the way of most military commanders; yet his restraint did not seem to arise so much from good nature as from the fear of losing his self-control even for a moment — suggesting that he was suppressing some instinct or emotion which must be very strong within him, if it was necessary continually to exert such an iron self-discipline. This contrast between nature and manner showed itself, too, in the difference between his uneasy, wandering eyes and the tightly drawn mouth. But if Nurse Gooch had, with more than her normal sensitiveness, felt at first that there was a rather queer atmosphere about the house, she had at any rate detected nothing unusual in the look or manner of this amiable, rather pompous, little man, and, indeed, the only person who appreciated thoroughly these various subtle distinctions was Mrs. Tonge. This poor lady had married her first cousin, and appeared to have inherited or acquired his, as well as her own, share of the peculiarly nervous temperament of this family. Thin, tall, and of that ash-grey colour which betokens constant sleeplessness, her rather sweet expression, while it was in direct contradiction to her restless, irritable soul, was the only remnant of a former prettiness. For, when first she married, she had been a good-looking, high-spirited girl, but had suddenly, swiftly, sunk into this state of perpetual and somewhat nagging melancholy. She was in reality a stupid woman, but her frayed nerves bestowed upon her an understanding of, and insight into, the unpleasant side of life that were alarming in the sureness of their judgment, and must have made of her a trying companion. She added to these heightened perceptions a sense of grievance aggravated by an absolute lack of any interest or occupation, and by the fact that she was childless. She complained constantly, her chief lament being that there were only three creatures in the world that cared for her, two dogs — a Pomeranian and a Pekinese — and her beloved green parrot! Often she would add a remark to the effect that her husband would like — was, in fact, only waiting for — Polly to die. His triumph would then, apparently, be complete. And it must truthfully be said that the only thing which ever seemed to disturb the Colonel's calm was the idiot-laughter which the parrot would let fall through the darkened air of the sick woman's room. But though the slightest noise at any other time would strain Mrs. Tonge's taut nerves almost to breaking-point, she appeared actually to enjoy her bird's head-splitting mirth; while the parrot, in return, seemed to acknowledge some bond of affection between his mistress and himself, for, were she more than usually ill, he would be ever so quiet, not venturing to exercise his marked mimetic gifts, even repressing his habitual laughter.

This love for her parrot and her pet dogs, together with a certain trust in, more than affection for, her young nurse — a trust which developed as the months passed — were all the assets of which Mrs. Tonge was conscious in this life. For the rest she was lonely and frightened . . . very frightened. Her whole existence was spent in a continual state of fear — one of the worst symptoms, though quite a common one, of neurasthenia; she was afraid of her neighbours, her husband, her house, terrified by everything and everybody alike. But, while frightened of everything, she was as consistently opposed to any plan for the alleviation of these imagined terrors.

Afraid, though seemingly without reason, of her husband, she was yet never able to refrain from making the fullest use of any opportunity to irritate, hurt or annoy him. But he was very patient with her. She would taunt him with things big and little; she would attack him about his self-importance, or goad him before the nurse about his fondness for giving good advice to others, in a manner that must have made him feel the sting of truth. She would even accuse him of wishing to be rid of her — a poor invalid and one who was in his way — an accusation which, however, she could never really have believed for a moment. She would tell him that he had a cruel soul, and in her sick mind seemed to have fashioned a grotesque, caricatured little image of her husband, which, to her, had at last come to be the reality — an image, unlike yet in a way recognisable, of a queer, patient, cruel, rather wolf-like creature, hiding his true self beneath the usual qualities attached to the various very ordinary interests and pursuits in which his life was spent.

In spite of this extraordinary conception of him, Mrs. Tonge was always calling for her husband. Her plaintive voice echoing through the square, lofty rooms would be answered by his gruff, military tones so often that one of the parrot's most ingenious tricks was a perfect rendering of 'Humphrey, come here a minute!' and the answering call

'Yes, Mary, I'm coming', followed by the sound of hurrying footsteps. Thus, though frightened of him, though almost hating him, the invalid would hardly allow her husband to leave her, if only for a day.

Still more was Mrs. Tonge frightened of her house — that home which she knew so intimately. But, in the same perverse manner, she would never quit it, even for a night. While suffering terribly from insomnia, and from that fear of darkness which, though it usually leaves us when our childhood is past, had never wholly left her, she was steadfast in her refusal to allow Nurse Gooch to sleep in the same room, thus lessening these nocturnal terrors by human companionship. On the contrary, the sick woman not only insisted on being alone, but was resolute in locking both the doors of her room, one of which led into her husband's bedroom, the other into the passage outside, so that had she been seized with sudden illness, which was not altogether unlikely, no help could have reached her. Thus, bolted securely within those four walls, she would indulge her broken spirit in an orgy of sleepless terror. The dogs slept downstairs : her only companion was Polly, noiseless now, but faithful as ever, sitting hunched up on his perch, his dome-like cage enveloped in a pall of grey felt ; and, even had he sounded his bitter, head-splitting laughter, it would have seemed more sweet than the music of any southern nightingales to the poor invalid, tossing about on her bed. For the parrot, alone of the animal world, could give his mistress some feeling of momentary security.

Day would come at last, to bring with it an hour or two of grey, unrefreshing sleep. The afternoon she would spend knitting, seated in a large arm-chair in front of the fire, in her overheated boudoir, crowded with strong-smelling flowers. Photographs of friends — friends whom she had not seen for years and had perhaps never really cared for — littered all the furniture, and clambered up the walls, over the fireplace, in an endless formation, imbuing the room with that peculiar morbid tone of old photographs, yellow and glazed as death itself. Bustles, bonnets, then straw hats and leg-of-mutton sleeves, showed grotesquely in these little squares of faded, polished cardboard, set off by a palm-tree in an art-pot, a balustraded terrace, a mountainous yet flat background, or one of those other queer properties of the old photographic world. The wistful smiles on these pretty faces were now gone like her own, the smoothness of the skin was now replaced by hundreds of ever so small wrinkles, the fruit of care, sorrow or some seed of ill-nature or bad temper that, undreamt-of then, had now blossomed. The rest of open space on table, piano or writing-desk was taken up by diminutive unconnected vases of violets, freesias or jonquils, their heavy breath weighing on the air like a cloud, seeming among these photographs so many floral tributes to dead friendship, each one marking the grave of some pretended or genuine affection. The room was overloaded with these vases; the flowers lent no grace to the room, no sweetness to the over-burdened air. The Pomeranian yapped at Mrs. Tonge's feet, the Pekinese lay curled up in a basket, while at her elbow the parrot picked at a large white grape, the stale odour of the bird's cage mingling with the already stifling atmosphere of the room, till it became almost intolerable. Here the invalid would sit for hours enjoying one of the thousand little grievances from which she was able to choose, turning it over and pecking at it like the parrot at his grape; or, perhaps, she would be gripped by one of the manifold terrors of her life. Then that supreme horror, the fear of death (which, as she grew older, claimed an ever greater part of her attention), grimaced at her from the scented shadows, till it seemed to her as if she sat there knitting endlessly her own shroud, and the vases of flowers transformed their shapes, rearranging themselves till they became wreaths and crosses, and the hot smell they exhaled became the very odour of death. Then she would ring again, calling for Nurse Gooch, but even that familiar footfall would make her shudder for an instant.

Her only pleasure now consisted in the tormenting of her even-tempered husband, or, in a lesser degree, of the poor young nurse — to whom she had now become attached in the same sense that a dog is attached to any object, such as a doll or an indiarubber ball, which it can worry. But Gooch, good and amiable, clean-looking rather than pretty, her face fully expressing that patience and kindness which were her two great qualities, won the affections not only of the invalid but of Colonel Tonge, and even of the servants — this latter no mean conquest when it is remembered that there is a traditional feud between servants and trained nurse, almost rivalling the other hereditary vendetta between nursery and schoolroom. Nurse Gooch was really fond of her patient, in spite of the maddening irritation of her ways : nor had she been unhappy during these eighteen months that had followed her luncheon at the Grove on that first winter day. For after the hardships of her own childhood, she appreciated this solid, very comfortable, home, while it presented to her a full scope for the exercise of those protective instincts which were particularly deep-rooted in her nature. Often, in a way, she envied Mrs. Tonge her kind husband and charming house, thinking how happy the invalid might have been had only her disposition been a different one. For in Colonel Tonge the young nurse could see nothing but consideration for his ill wife, and kindness indeed to everyone, till, slowly, she formed in her own mind an image of him very different from that fashioned by his wife. To Nurse Gooch he was a model of suffering chivalry ; to her his stature and heart seemed great, his importance equal to his own estimate of it. In fact, he became that very appealing combination — one which always fascinates the English people — a hero in public, a martyr in private life. And it was a source of great comfort for her to reflect that by keeping Mrs. Tonge in as good a mood as possible, or, to borrow a military phrase, by intentionally drawing the fire on to herself, she was able to some small extent to alleviate the trials of the husband. Then she could feel, too, in some mysterious manner, that he was grateful for it, that he began to take a pleasure in her society, in the knowledge that she understood his difficulties, applauded his moderation. Often they used to sit together, consulting with Dr. Maynard, a clever doctor, but one who lacked courage, and was in the habit of giving way to his patients. Gradually, therefore, if any new symptom showed itself, if any new problem arose regarding the invalid, it was with the nurse and not with the doctor that Colonel Tonge would first come to talk it over.

Existence at the Grove, though each day appeared to her encompassed in the span of an hour, so that she was continually finding herself landed, as if by some magic carpet of the fourth dimension, at the corresponding time of the next day, yet seemed eternal ; even the state of the sick woman, though her nerves became ever more affected, appeared to be stationary. Outside there was the fat, placid life of the countryside to be watched, the punctual revolution of the seasons. First came the ice-green glitter of the snowdrops, frosting the grass of the park with their crystal constellations; then these faded, withered, turned yellow, deepened to the butter-colour of the daffodils that ousted them, flowers swaying their large heads under the spring winds, transparent, full of the very colour of the sun; and, almost before you had time to observe it, they would flush to a deep purple, would be transformed into anemones, the centre of their dusky blossoms powdered with pollen, black like charcoal dust, or would adopt the velvet softness of texture which distinguishes the rose from other flowers: and summer would be in its full flame. Then, inside the Grove, you found good food, punctual hours, a calm routine broken only by the outbursts of Mrs. Tonge, or by the bitter cackle of the parrot, its feathers green with the depth of a tropical forest, its eyes wary and knowing. It looked cunning, as if in possession of some queer secret — some secret such as that of the parrot encountered in Mexico by the traveller Humboldt — a bird which alone in all the world possessed a tongue of its own, since it spoke a language now extinct. For the tribe who talked it had been killed to a man in the course of America becoming a Christian continent, while the bird had lived on for a century.

The summer was a particularly hot one, and as it burnt to its climax, Mrs. Tonge's irritable nerves inflicted an increasing punishment on those around her. The Colonel, who was drawn away on various long-promised visits to old friends and taken to London several times on the business of his estate, left the Grove more than usual this July, so that the full brunt of any trouble in the house fell upon Nurse Gooch, who would often have to shut herself up in her room, and, strong-minded, well-trained woman though she was, cry like a hurt child, so intolerable was the strain imposed upon her by the invalid. The latter soon realised when she had made the tactical error of being too disagreeable — or, perhaps, one should say of concentrating a day's temper in one short hour, instead of spreading it thinly, evenly, over the whole of the sun's passage, so that, looked back upon, it should tinge the day with some unpleasant colour in the minds of her companions or servants. And being possessed of a certain charm or a false kindliness, which she could exert whenever it was necessary to her, she was soon able again to engage the nurse's pity and affection.

'Poor thing', Gooch would think to herself. 'One can't blame her for it. Look how she suffers.' But however true was this reflection, it was the sick woman who was still the chief opponent of any plan for the mitigation of her sufferings. Though her sleeplessness became worse, though the prospect of those long, dark hours threw a shadow blacker than the night itself over each day, yet she still refused to allow Nurse Gooch to rest in the room with her; while Dr. Maynard, who should have insisted on it, was, as usual, completely overborne by his patient.

It is difficult to describe, though, how much Mrs. Tonge suffered, locked in her room during those sultry nights, for their darkness appeared to cover a period easily surpassing the length of any winter night. As she lay there, her limbs twitching, memories dormant in her mind for forty years would rise up to torment her. Her parents, her old nurse (all dead how many summers past!) would return to her here in the silence. All the disappointments of her life would revive their former aching. Once more she would see the gas-lit ballrooms in which she had danced as a girl, and the faces of men she had forgotten half a lifetime ago. Then, again, she would see her wedding. All these memories would link up, and coalesce in feverish waking dreams of but a moment's duration, but which would yet seem to hold all eternity in their contorted perspectives. Wide awake now, she would recall her longing for children, or ponder upon one of her thousand little grievances, which took on new and greater dimensions in these hours. Here she was . . . with a parrot as her only friend . . . in this everlasting blackness. The thought of death would return to her, death that was at the end of each turning, making every life into a blind hopeless cul-de-sac. Long and hard she would fight this spectre of finality, against which no religion had the power to fortify her spirit. Then, after midnight, new terrors began, as the Grove woke up to its strange nocturnal life. Footsteps would sound outside, treading stealthily, stealthily on the black, hollow air; the furniture in the room, cumbersome old cupboards and chests of drawers, would suddenly tattoo a series of little but very definite hard sounds upon the silence, as if rapping out some unknown code. But when everything was swathed in quiet once more, this new absence of noise would be worse, more frightening than were the sounds themselves. It would smother everything with its blackness; everything would be still . . . waiting . . . listening! The silence, from having been merely a form of muffled sound, or perhaps a negation of it, became itself positive, active — could be felt and tested by the senses. There it was again, that creaking — as if someone was listening . . . someone certainly . . . someone standing on a loose board, crouching down in the darkness outside, afraid to tread for fear of waking one. Then would follow a distraction. A new code would be rapped out as something tapped on the window-pane . . . tap — tap — tap, like a mad thing. Only the wind with that branch of ivy, she supposed. There it was again . . . tap — tap . . . like a mad thing trying to get into her room . . . tap — tap . . . into her very head, it seemed! Outside the house a dog would bark once, menacingly, and then its rough voice would die suddenly, as if silenced. Footsteps would tread again down the long passages, footsteps more distinct than ever this time. And once or twice they lingered stealthily at the bolted door; the handle would creak, grasped very carefully, turned by an invisible hand; and was there not the sound of a smothered, animal-like breathing? The wolf-at-the-door, the wolf-at-the-door, she says to herself in that fevered mind, where it seems as if two people, two strangers, were carrying on a whispered conversation of interminable length. Then silence comes once more; an unequalled stillness pours into the room, and into the corridors outside, so that the tapping, when it returns, takes on a new quality, rippling this quiet blackness with enlarging circles of sound, as when a stone is cast into a small pool. Tap — tap — tap . . . again tap. Perhaps she is only dead, being fastened into her coffin. Tap — tap . . . they are nailing it down, tap — tap; and she lies dead in the silence for ever. Then far away the taps sound again and the coffin is unnailed. But this time it is the parrot rapping upon the bars of his dome-like cage with his hard beak; and she is reassured. Grey light clutches again at the swathed windows, and the furniture of the room grows slowly into its accustomed shape; the things round her fall back again into their familiar contours, and are recognisable as themselves, for in the night they had assumed new positions, new shapes, strange attitudes . . . and the poor nervous creature lying on the rumpled bed falls asleep for an hour or two.

But as the light drips stealthily in, filling the black hollows of room and corridor, the housemaids, warned by Nurse Gooch to be more than usually quiet, scratch gently in the passage outside like so many mice, scratch with a gentle feeble sound that must inevitably rouse anyone — even a person who sleeps well by habit and is at that moment deep-rooted in slumber. For this timid, rodent-like noise is more irritating to the strongest nerves, will awaken more surely, than any of that loud, sudden music to which we are accustomed — that music of blows rained accidentally but with great force upon the fragile legs and corners of old furniture or brittle carving of ancient gilded frames — blows delivered with the back of an ever so light feathery brush. Thus Mrs. Tonge would open her eyes upon one more hot and calm morning.

As she lay there, in the semi-darkness, she could hear faint voices sounding in the passage. Soon after she has rung her bell, Nurse Gooch comes in with the letters, as clean and kind as is possible for a human being to be, bright as are all trained nurses in the early morning; too bright, perhaps, too wide awake, and already making the best of it. Her hair has a dark golden colour in it under the light, and gleams very brightly under the cap she is wearing, while she talks in an even, soothing voice. As she goes down the corridor toward the invalid's room the housemaids take her passing presence for a signal that they may resume that noisy bustle of cleanliness with which they salute each day. Suddenly motes of dust whirl up into the air beneath their brushes, turning under the already searching rays of the sun to columns and twisted pillars of sparkling glass that support this heavy firmament, pillars prism-like in the radiant array of their colour. As the housemaids, bent nearly double in their long white print dresses, move slowly over the carpet, brush in one hand, dust-pan in the other, their movements break up these columns, so that the atoms that compose them fall through the air like so many sequins, and are violently agitated; then these take on new shapes, and from pillars are converted into obelisks, pyramids, rectangles and all the variety of glittering forms that, bound by the angles of straight lines, can be imposed upon this dull air and earth by the lance-like rays of the morning sun.

In the room she still lies in bed, turning over the unopened envelopes of her letters. Gooch goes to the window and talks to the parrot. As she uncovers the cage the bird breaks into its metallic laughter, that rattles down through the open window into the shrubbery, like so many brassy rings thrown down by a juggler, for they curve in again at the pantry-window, where John the footman is standing in an apron, cleaning the silver with a dirty-looking piece of old yellow leather and some gritty rose-pink paste. As he polishes the convex mirror formed by the flanks of the silver bowl, while his face reflected in one side assumes a grotesque appearance, the contorted trees and twisted perspective of lawn and garden show in the other. The second housemaid peeps in. 'Oh, you do look a sight!' she cries, bridling with laughter, pointing to the bowl in his hand. 'I may be a sight,' he says, 'or I may not, but I'm not a blarsted slave, am I?' 'Well, you needn't answer so nasty', she said. 'It's not that, it's that parrot— 'ark at it now. I shall be glad when 'e comes back; one can't do no right in this place. Everything is wrong. First it's one damn thing, then another. Nurse sticks it like a soldier,' he says, 'but I stand up for my rights! I'm not a slave, I'm not, that I should stand there letting that blarsted parrot screech at me like a sergeant-major on a parade ground, and her talking a lot of nonsense. I'd like to wring its bloody neck, I would — they're a pair of them, they are!'

And certainly — Nurse Gooch herself had to admit it — the invalid was this summer more than ever exacting. For many months past she had worried her husband about a summer-house, for which she had formed one of those queer, urgent longings that sick people consider themselves free to indulge. The hut had stood there in the woods, year after year, unnoticed, falling to damp decay, when, as if given new eyes, Mrs. Tonge saw it for the first time, and determined to make it her own. Here, she felt, it would be possible to sit quietly, rest peacefully, in an atmosphere different from that of the Grove, and perhaps find that sleep denied her in any other place. As the summer-house was in a very dilapidated condition, she asked her husband to have it repaired for her, but met with a very unexpected opposition. The Colonel, used as he was to furthering every plan of his sick wife, absolutely ignored this new entreaty. Which fact, unfortunately, only strengthened her determination, and made her persist in her caprice.

There was, in reality, some danger in letting Mrs. Tonge remain alone for a long period in a spot so remote from the house — she refused, again, to allow anyone to wait with her in this solitude — for though, as is the habit of permanent invalids, she might live for many years, yet she was a nervous, delicate woman, very liable to a sudden attack of illness, and here no help could reach her. But Dr. Maynard, with his customary inability to say 'No' to a patient — or, perhaps, because he felt that the rest she hoped to obtain here would be more valuable to her than any unexpected attack of illness would be dangerous — gave his sanction to the new scheme. Colonel Tonge, however, still urged the doctor to forbid it, making a strong protest against what he considered this folly, and himself steadfastly refused to have the place touched up in any way, or even swept out. The invalid changed her tactics : from anger she passed to a mood of plaintive injury. 'I know, Humphrey,' she moaned at him, 'that you only go on like that because you hate to think that I am having a peaceful moment. What harm *can* there be in going to the summer-house ? It doesn't hurt you, does it ?'

The Colonel, patient as ever, would show no sign of ill-temper, putting the case as reasonably as he could. 'Mary, my dear, it is really very unwise and foolish of you. I know how much unemployment there is, how unsettled is the countryside. You should see some of the tramps that are brought up before me on the Bench. That summer-house may seem deep in the woods, but it is very near the high-road. You can never tell who will come into the park. Anyone can get in. There's no lodge near that gate. I tell you, my dear, it isn't safe. I can't think how you can be so silly. It's folly, sheer folly !'

Mrs. Tonge cried a little : 'I'm not afraid of tramps or motor-cars, or of anything on a road. But I know you'd do anything to prevent my getting any rest, Humphrey. I believe you'd like me to go without any sleep at all, as long as it didn't worry you. I know you're only waiting for me to die.' . . . And the poor little man, discomfited, walked away. He was always so patient . . . like that . . . and kind, it made Nurse Gooch feel a great pity for him. But she thought he was wrong in this particular instance — wrong ever to oppose the invalid's wishes, however seldom he did so ; and knowing her influence with him, she persuaded the Colonel to say no more about it, though he still seemed a little uneasy. Yet so great had become his reliance on the young nurse's judgment, that she easily induced him to pretend to his wife that he now thought his opposition had been mistaken.

But Mrs. Tonge could not be deceived. She knew perfectly well that he did not really approve, and it therefore gave her an increased pleasure to rest in the summer-house. Getting up later than ever in these hot months of the year, she would go there every afternoon. She forbade her two pets to be with her, so that a piteous, plaintive yapping filled the Grove each day after luncheon ; only Polly, devoted Polly, was privileged to share this new solitude. Curiously enough, she did not feel frightened here. The rather ominous silence of the woods held no menace for her ; she was happier among these dank shadows than in her own bedroom or placid flowering garden ; and, whether from perversity or from some form of auto-suggestion, it was a fact that when the nurse walked out to the hut to bring the sick woman back to the house for tea, she often found her in a slumber more peaceful than any she had enjoyed for years.

Between two and three o'clock each fine afternoon a queer procession could be seen walking over the lawn between the beds of flowers that lay like embossed embroidery among the sleek grass. First of all came Mrs. Tonge, never glancing aside at flower or tree, her upright carriage and slow-moving walk bestowing an almost ritual air on the proceedings ; then followed the uniform-clad figure of the nurse, holding news-papers and a small cluster of three or four grapes for the parrot in one hand, while from the other dangled the sacred dome. The grapes, transparent, jewel-like, catching the prevailing colour, which was that of the penetrating glow of sunlight through green leaves, focused the eye as they moved along, till they seemed like some mystic regalia, even drawing the eye away from the more metallic colouring of the parrot, who, as he was borne along, shrieked continually, taking an obvious pleasure in scaring the poor timid birds of the English countryside by a display of flaming plumage and alien, rather acrid, laughter. Slowly they passed over the shrill, water-smooth lawns, where single high trees stood up fleecy against the sky, or, over-burdened by the full weight of summer, trailed their branches right down upon the fragrant ground, into the dark woods cloudy with foliage and rank with the smell of tall nettles, elder-trees, bracken, and all those things that grow in unkept places. No bird-song sounded now in this ultimate unfolding of the seasons, and the little path that led winding through this wilderness lay like a curling green ribbon, of a brighter hue than the surrounding shrubs and velvety with moss, from which weeds sprouted up at the corners like small tufts of feathers. This untidy ribbon, lying without purpose across the woodland ground, led to the rustic hut which the caprice of some former mistress of the Grove had caused to be built here, rather pointlessly, some ninety years ago. Under a round roof, sloping down from its centre, and covered with the rough bark of trees, it lay mouldering beneath the structure of branches which hung motionless, as if cut from cardboard, on the heavy air. Sponge-like, it seemed, in its dampness, like some fungus lying about at the foot of a tree. Great knots of ivy clung to the upper part of the door, while, where the peeling bark had fallen away, were revealed arrangements of rusty nails, geometrical, but growing like thorns out of the wood. No view was framed in the pointed spaces of the two windows, except the light which trellised itself with the shadow of green leaves along the ground, or, flooding a stretch of bracken, played first on one leaf, then on another, bringing out unexpected patterns, making each bent-back leaf, as it was touched, the centre of some shifting arabesque design such as is woven in Eastern carpets.

The parrot would be placed on the dingy, bark-covered table; a grape would be half-peeled, and pressed, like a melting jewel, between the bars of the cage. The wire dome would then be draped ceremoniously with grey felt; the invalid would lie back in her long chair, a rug over her knees, the countless newspapers which it was her habit to read placed at her side; and Nurse Gooch would walk back briskly through the dark stillness of the wood out again into the droning odorous languor of the garden.

As Mrs. Tonge rested in her long chair, she found, certainly, a peace otherwise denied to her in the grim world of a sick woman's fancy. No argument, she determined, should ever persuade her to give up this siesta. Day followed day, each warm and bright-coloured as the other; only the leaves became a little ranker in their scent, the woods yet more silent. But sometimes, as she was on the border of sleep, already seeing the queer avenues of that land which she could so seldom reach, while through its landscape she could still distinguish the more rational, familiar features of her real surroundings, a sound like a rushing wind or as if gigantic wings were beating on the taut drum-like fabric of the air, would startle her for a moment, and, looking round, she would see the tall stiff trees lift up their canvas branches, caught by a false breeze, as a motor-car passed between the two high hedges that concealed the road. Above this hidden white scar a high whirling column of dust would dance for a few seconds, as if it were some jinnee of the air made visible for the moment; or, again, she would be lulled by the kindly, cooing voices of the country people, which floated over to her, for, as her husband had pointed out, the road was in reality very near the summer-house. But these things did not appear unpleasant to her; and, in any case, how much better were these explicable sounds than that state of suspended animation, alternating with a sudden show of life, which she had grown to dread so much at night in her own room!

The hot weather continued, and with it the life of the Grove. Colonel Tonge, as we have remarked, was away this summer more than was his wont, but the routine of the invalid, the nurse, and the servants repeated itself almost automatically. Every afternoon Nurse Gooch would walk out with the patient to the hut and would leave her there, only returning in time to fetch her back to the house for tea. One afternoon, when the Colonel was expected home from a short visit to Major Morley, an old friend and brother-officer whom, though a near neighbour, he saw very seldom, Mrs. Tonge suddenly made up her mind to stay out in the summer-house for tea, telling the nurse to bring it out to her at five o'clock. Now, though there was nothing very original or startling in this idea, Gooch, who in matters relating to an invalid did not lack a certain subtlety, at once expostulated — not, indeed, from any feeling of disapproval, but because she well knew that the sick woman would in reality be deeply disappointed if her nurse seemed pleased, or even satisfied, with this new break away from the normal programme. The nurse, therefore, succeeded in putting up a show of anxiety, saying such things as that the patient ought not to be too long alone, or that the Colonel would be hurt and annoyed at finding his wife absent on his return. Finally, pretending to be persuaded against her better judgment, she agreed to bring tea out to the summer-house at five o'clock; then, placing the parrot's cage on the table, she covered it up, completed her ritual, and walked back to the house through the hot, strangely sultry, afternoon.

Mrs. Tonge felt an unaccustomed luxurious ease steal over her as she lay stretched out on her couch reading her papers, though perhaps perusing them less carefully today than was her custom. As a rule, she read them from cover to cover — births, deaths, marriages, sales, advertisements of all kinds; and, while these journals represented every shade of political opinion, she was quite unmoved by their varying propaganda. She regarded them, in fact, as her one form of relaxation. This afternoon, however, she could not fix her attention on them. She peeled an amber, honey-scented grape for Polly, who mumbled back lovingly but softly. What a difference even an hour's sleep makes! She wondered when Humphrey was coming back, feeling that she had been rather hard with him lately — in fact, for some time past. With a sudden impulse of affection the image she had formed of him in her own mind was broken, and he became to her again the young man whom she had loved. She determined that she would be nicer to him; and certainly she felt a little better today. The afternoon in the summer-house seemed just warm enough . . . and quiet . . . nicely quiet, she thought. Slowly, almost contentedly, and for the first time for many years without any fear, any nervous feeling, she stretched her limbs until every nerve in her body became quiet, and sighing gently, let sleep wash over her tired limbs, her worn-out mind, in soft delicious little waves.

But, though the dampness of the hut may have tempered that afternoon heat for Mrs. Tonge, it seemed very breathless outside. Even Nurse Gooch, as she sat sewing in her usually cool room, felt rather overcome. Oh, how hot it was! And the house was very still. As a rule you heard the servants chattering, moving through the passages; the jingling of silver or the rattling of plates would reach you from pantry or kitchen. But today there was no noise — not a sound, except the hot insect-like droning of the sewing-machine, as she bent over it, running the needle along the white edge of the new linen, which filled the room with a rather stifling scent. But directly she stopped, even for an instant, silence flooded the room. Well, one can't look after a case like this for eighteen months without feeling odd oneself sometimes, she supposed! Yet there was something queer about the stillness. There must be going to be a storm, she thought.

No sound came in from farm or stable at this high-up, open window, on a level with the motionless green cradles of the birds; but down below on the lawn a single leaf would suddenly burst out into a mad fluttering, as if trying to indicate the secret of this general alarm, and then be still, too still, as if it feared to be caught in an act of rebellion. . . . In the flower-beds, then, a single violent-coloured blossom would wave out wildly, flicker for an instant like a tongue of flame, then float once more stiffly upon the glazed heat. She was quite glad to finish her sewing, get the tea ready and leave the house. But the air outside was even hotter than within — suffocating — so that one could not breathe, and as she passed out into the furtive silence of the woods she seemed separated from the world she knew. If I go on like this, she said to herself, I shall soon be the next invalid! Yet the walk seemed longer than it ought to be, so that she was continually being confronted with little twistings in it which she did not remember, though she had trodden this path at least four times a day for several months past. Still she knew, of course, that it must be the right one. But somehow or other, she was startled this afternoon by things that usually she would not notice — the ordinary, rather in-explicable rustlings of the woodlands, for instance. Doubtless these were audible yesterday as today, but as a rule she did not heed them; and once or twice, certainly, it seemed to her that she heard a peculiar scampering, as of a hurrying through thickets, or the dragging crackle of twigs and brambles as they released their clinging hold on invisible garments. It was with a distinct feeling of relief, then, that after what seemed quite a long walk, she caught sight of the summer-house round the next turning. It had a very human, friendly look to her this afternoon ; yet it belonged so much to these woods, this soil, that it was like a large mushroom growing out of a taller green tangle. The invalid did not call out to her, even the parrot was silent — an indication, usually, that its mistress was asleep. (How queer it is the way she can sleep here, and nowhere else !) Nurse Gooch cried out cheerfully, 'Wake up, wake up ! I've brought you your tea !' Still there was no answer, and, skirting the blind corner of the hut, carrying the tray in front of her, she was already standing in the low doorway before she had even cast a glance at its dark interior. Thrown suddenly into the quiet smallness of the summer-house, where she was at such close quarters with everything, almost within an arm's span of each wall, she was unable to breathe for a moment. An overwhelming sensation of nausea took possession of her, so that she felt that she, too, would fall upon that terrible floor. Yet, though the whole universe swung round, her trained eye observed the slaughter-house details. There lay the murdered woman, her head on one side, her skull crushed by some ferocious blow, her face twisted to a mask of terror — that queer unreasoning terror which had never left her. Dumb, blinking in its overturned cage, the parrot was hunched up, its feathers clotted together with blood. Clutching the bird's cage as if to save it from some fresh disaster, Nurse Gooch rushed wildly out of the summer-house into the motionless woods.

．　　　．　　　．　　　．　　　．

As she approached the Grove, her own sense of discipline asserted itself, forcing her to slow down her pace, to set her mind a little more in order. But now it was, actually, that the full shock came to her, for in that sudden blind moment of fear, when her limbs had melted one into the other, when her heart had bounded to her very lips, she had been unable to think, had experienced no feeling except an endless surprise, pity, and disgust. Afterwards curiosity, as well, intervened, and she began to wonder who had done this thing, and why such a brutal fate had engulfed the poor, timid, elderly woman. And then she was forced to steel her soul for the next ordeal : she would have need of every particle of strength in mind and body, since it devolved upon her to break the news. Through the library window she could see Colonel Tonge standing by the empty fireplace, and even while she was still labouring under

535

the blow that had befallen her, she dreaded telling him of it as the not least awful incident in this terrible adventure — nearly as overwhelming, indeed, as had been the actual moment of discovery. Her respect, and fondness, even, for him, her knowledge that his had not been a happy marriage, only made the task a more difficult one to face and endure.

With an unexpected nervous susceptibility the Colonel seemed to feel the burning, panting breath of tragedy almost before she had spoken. Perhaps something out of her control manifested itself in her face, in her air; but as she entered, he looked at her with eyes as fearful as her own, and it seemed as if he, too, were mastering his emotions to confront something that he dreaded. 'Go on, go on,' he said, 'what is it?'

.   .   .   .   .

Month followed month, and he still shut himself up in his room, till he became so changed in looks, in manner, as hardly to appear the same man. All pride, all self-importance had left him. The spring had gone out of his walk, the jauntiness out of dress and carriage. Every hour of the day he loaded himself with reproaches — for not having been firmer, for not having absolutely refused to allow his wife to stay out there alone — for having been away at the time of the tragedy. Gooch would hear him, unable to sleep at night, walking about the passages, pacing up and down, up and down, till the first grey light crept in at the corners of blind and curtain. It was as if the spirit of sleepless terror that had haunted his wife had now transferred its temple to his body. Incapable of attending to the business of his estate, to which formerly he had devoted so much consideration, he now seldom left the house in the day-time, and, if he did, in whatever direction he might set out, his feet always led him sooner or later to the same place, and he would be startled, aghast, to find himself in the woods again.

Anything that reminded him of his dead wife had to be hidden away. The two poor little dogs were removed by his married sister when she went home, after a quite unsuccessful attempt to cheer her brother and give him comfort. The parrot, now never laughing, never speaking, languished in an attic, attended only by Emily, the housemaid. The other servants, too, were kind to the bird, since it had for them a fatal attraction: not only was it connected with death, having about it the very odour of the cemetery, but it was in itself the witness and only relic of a brutal crime, so that it possessed the charm popularly associated with a portion of hangman's rope, and, in addition, was a living thing possessed of a dreadful secret. But the parrot would never utter, and downstairs — where the conversation, however wide the circle of its origin, always in the end drew in on to one topic — they had to admit that Polly had never been the-same-like-since. Occasionally Emily would leave the door of the cage open, hoping that he would walk out or fly round as he used to do. But nothing could tempt him out of his battered dome. As for Colonel Tonge, he had never liked the bird, hating its harsh laughter, and this solitary, now silent, witness of his wife's end filled him at present with an unconquerable aversion.

Great sympathy was evinced everywhere for the poor widower, crushed under a catastrophe so unexpected and mysterious. But the public sympathy could do little to help him; and though some solution of the mystery might temporarily have distracted his mind, even if it could not have rallied his spirits, none was forthcoming. He went through all the sordid business associated with murder — inquest and interview; the crime remained odd as ever in its total absence of warning, intention or clue. Who, indeed, could have plotted to murder this invalid lady, possessed of few friends and no enemies? And what purpose was served by this intolerable brutality? It is true that, after a time, the police found a stained, blunt-headed club, obviously the weapon with which the fatal wound had been inflicted, buried deep in the bracken; but, in a sense, this discovery only removed the murder further from the public experience, in that the possible motive of theft was at the same time disposed of — for with this weapon were found the few rings, the gold watch and small amount of money that the dead woman had about her, as she had lain asleep in the summer-house on that sultry August afternoon. The police, thinking it possible that these articles had been hidden from an impulse of fear, that the original motive had indeed been the ordinary one, arrested a tramp found wandering in the district, hiding himself at night under hedges and in the shelter of empty barns; but though he could not give a very detailed or convincing account of his doings on the day of the 'Hut Murder' — as it was called —

the evidence that connected him with the crime was not enough to secure his conviction. It remained, however, the impression of many people, among them of both Dr. Maynard and Nurse Gooch, that he was in reality guilty of the foul act of which he had been suspected. Colonel Tonge, though he followed every detail of the trial with a painful interest, could never be induced to discuss the possible guilt of the tramp, but it was noticeable that after the man's release his nervous condition became more than ever marked, which led them to conclude that, in his opinion too, the person accused should never have been acquitted.

The bereaved husband's insomnia troubled him sorely; he had no peace, no rest by day or night. The only person able to bring him relief, to lighten his burden even for a moment, was Nurse Gooch; so that Dr. Maynard felt it his duty, for once, to insist on her remaining at the Grove until the Colonel should display some sign of returning health and a reviving spirit. The nurse, for her part, had always liked, pitied, and admired him, while, by one of those curious human instincts, all the compassion, all the affection even, which she had given so freely to the dead woman, was now made over to her new patient. And then she, too, felt remorse; had things on her mind with which to reproach herself. How well she could understand and sympathise with his self-accusation! Why, conscious as she had been of her influence over him, had she not supported the Colonel's wise protest against his wife's use of the summer-house, instead of urging, as she had done, that it was a reasonable plan, and finally persuading him to withdraw his objection to it? Terribly she felt now the responsibility so foolishly incurred, that perhaps she was in part to blame for the tragedy, even in the matter of allowing the invalid to wait out in the summer-house for tea on that dreadful afternoon; and in the months that followed the murder it was one of the few pleasant things in her life to reflect that she could, by her presence and sympathetic understanding, lessen his misery ever so little, giving him for a little while a passing sense of comfort.

When, after many long, lonely months, he made her an offer of marriage, saying that life without her support would be to him an intolerable burden, she accepted his proposal, realising that the interest she felt in him, the overwhelming

538

pity that sometimes clutched at her heart, was but a disguise
for love. Regardless of any difference in age or outlook, she
hoped, by becoming his wife, to help and ease the remainder of
a life, the unhappy tenor of which had now deepened into a
more dreadful tone.

．　　　．　　　．　　　．　　　．

The honeymoon was spent in France, in order to make
for them both a complete break from the background of their
lives. But even among the lush meadows and rich trees of
Normandy, away from any sting of association, Humphrey did
not recover at once, as she had hoped, his old buoyancy.
Listless, uneasy, restless, he would for hours be silent, wrapped
in a melancholy that did not ordinarily belong to his temperament, while, in his broken slumber and sudden awakenings,
his wife could detect the existence of a great well of sorrow
that even her anxious affection could not plumb, a grief her
love could not solace. The discovery of the extent of his
affliction caused her further worry, made her dread their
return to the scene of his past life. But as time passed it was
obvious that his spirits were returning; and when he told her
that during their absence the Grove had been entirely repainted
and redecorated, she began to feel happier, hoping that it
would seem to him like the beginning of a new life.

Almost two years to a day after the crime, they returned
from their honeymoon, but Colonel Tonge did not seem
conscious of any sense of anniversary, while she, naturally,
would not mention it to him. But it made her feel a little
uneasy.

As they drove back from the station, the new chauffeur
quite by chance, by one of those dreadful inspirations which
are only given to stupid people, drove the newly married
couple down the concealed road near the summer-house,
instead of taking them in by the near lodge. Colonel Tonge
obviously experienced no emotion, but his wife felt for the
moment as if she would be stifled between these two high
hedges. How like was this afternoon to that other one! No
leaf moved on any tree, no bird let its song trickle through the
cloudy, too-dark leafage; the air was hot, motionless and
still, though through it ran those same secret tremors, inexplicable tremblings. For the new Mrs. Tonge the whole
atmosphere was stained with memories.

Yet she soon forgot the uneasy promptings of her heart and mind in the pleasure she felt at the reception which awaited them. She had always been a favourite with the servants, and the latter could never forget the poor Colonel's sufferings, so that they had taken an especial care to give the newly wedded pair an inspiriting welcome. The Colonel stopped to talk to them, while Mrs. Tonge, eager to see what alterations had been made, stepped into the house alone. It looked charming, she thought, with the new smooth paint on the old walls ; and, unable to repress a slight thrill of pleasure, which she felt to be wrong, though she could not quite exorcise it, at being for the first time mistress of a house — and such a lovely house — she walked on through the empty, gleaming rooms that led one into the other. The last room was the boudoir. She entered it softly, closing the door behind her, wishing to explore its impression to the full, for she wondered whether it would make her feel a usurper, a stranger in someone else's place. But no ! it was a new room to her : gone was the feverish atmosphere of the sick-room, with its dead air, over-heated and scented with innumerable flowers : gone was that dead look imparted by the yellow glaze of countless old photographs and by the spreading litter of trivial little objects. And while she bore towards the dead woman no feelings but those of pity and affection, yet, being of a practical nature, she was glad that nothing remained of the old mistress — nothing that could call up painful memories. The room was quiet and restful ; the long windows stood wide open on to the pleasant water-cool spaces of the lawn, that unfolded up to the borders of the wood where stood tall fleecy green trees, while under their blue shadows ran the murmur of shallow streams. The healthy scents of tree and grass, the peaceful watery sounds, and honey-gathering, contented drone of the bees as they hung over the flowers, drifted into the house, diffusing an air of ease and comfort. This was *her* house, *her* garden, *her* home, and she now had a husband to whom she was devoted. Why, then, should she ever allow her mind to dwell on the tragedies of the past ? Was it not better to forget utterly, to obliterate the memory in her husband, by offering him all her love, till gradually these possessions to which he had been so attached became dear to him again ? . . . but just then, behind her, she heard the thin voice of the dead woman crying out — a voice grey with fear and breaking. 'Humphrey,' it sighed, 'what is it? Oh, my God!' . . . And then the sound of a heavy dumb blow and low moaning, followed by burst after burst of idiot laughter, as with a fluttering whirl of flaming green feathers the parrot flew up again to its empty attic.

THE END